corporate finance
CORE PRINCIPLES & APPLICATIONS

THE MCGRAW-HILL SERIES IN FINANCE, INSURANCE, AND REAL ESTATE

SIXTH EDITION

corporate finance
CORE PRINCIPLES & APPLICATIONS

Stephen A. Ross

Randolph W. Westerfield
University of Southern California, Emeritus

Jeffrey F. Jaffe
Wharton School of Business
University of Pennsylvania

Bradford D. Jordan
Gatton College of Business and Economics
University of Kentucky

CORPORATE FINANCE

Published by McGraw-Hill Education, 2 Penn Plaza, New York, NY 10121. Copyright © 2021 by McGraw-Hill Education. All rights reserved. Printed in the United States of America. No part of this publication may be reproduced or distributed in any form or by any means, or stored in a database or retrieval system, without the prior written consent of McGraw-Hill Education, including, but not limited to, in any network or other electronic storage or transmission, or broadcast for distance learning.

Some ancillaries, including electronic and print components, may not be available to customers outside the United States.

This book is printed on acid-free paper.

1 2 3 4 5 6 7 8 9 LWI 24 23 22 21 20

ISBN 978-1-260-57112-7
MHID 1-260-57112-2

Cover Image: *Chatrawee Wiratgasem/Shutterstock*

mheducation.com/highered

ABOUT THE AUTHORS

Stephen A. Ross

SLOAN SCHOOL OF MANAGEMENT, MASSACHUSETTS INSTITUTE OF TECHNOLOGY

Stephen A. Ross was the Franco Modigliani Professor of Financial Economics at the Sloan School of Management, Massachusetts Institute of Technology. One of the most widely published authors in finance and economics, Professor Ross was recognized for his work in developing the arbitrage pricing theory, as well as for having made substantial contributions to the discipline through his research in signaling, agency theory, option pricing, and the theory of the term structure of interest rates, among other topics. A past president of the American Finance Association, he also served as an associate editor of several academic and practitioner journals, and was a trustee of CalTech. He died suddenly in March of 2017.

Randolph W. Westerfield

MARSHALL SCHOOL OF BUSINESS, UNIVERSITY OF SOUTHERN CALIFORNIA

Randolph W. Westerfield is Dean Emeritus of the University of Southern California's Marshall School of Business and is the Charles B. Thornton Professor of Finance Emeritus. Professor Westerfield came to USC from the Wharton School, University of Pennsylvania, where he was the chairman of the finance department and member of the finance faculty for 20 years. He is a member of the Board of Trustees of Oaktree Capital Mutual Funds. His areas of expertise include corporate financial policy, investment management, and stock market price behavior.

To Stephen A. Ross and family

Our great friend, colleague, and coauthor Steve Ross passed away on March 3, 2017. Steve's influence on our textbook is seminal, deep, and enduring, and we will miss him greatly. We are confident that on the foundation of Steve's lasting and invaluable contributions, our textbook will continue to reach the highest level of excellence that we all aspire to.

— R.W.W. J.F.J. B.D.J.

Jeffrey F. Jaffe

WHARTON SCHOOL OF BUSINESS, UNIVERSITY OF PENNSYLVANIA

Jeffrey F. Jaffe has been a frequent contributor to finance and economic literatures in such journals as the *Quarterly Economic Journal, The Journal of Finance, The Journal of Financial and Quantitative Analysis, The Journal of Financial Economics,* and *The Financial Analysts Journal.* His best-known work concerns insider trading, where he showed both that corporate insiders earn abnormal profits from their trades and that regulation has little effect on these profits. He has also made contributions concerning initial public offerings, the regulation of utilities, the behavior of market makers, the fluctuation of gold prices, the theoretical effect of inflation on interest rates, the empirical effect of inflation on capital asset prices, the relationship between small-capitalization stocks and the January effect, and the capital structure decision.

Bradford D. Jordan

GATTON COLLEGE OF BUSINESS AND ECONOMICS, UNIVERSITY OF KENTUCKY

Bradford D. Jordan is professor of finance and holder of the duPont Endowed Chair in Banking and Financial Services at the University of Kentucky. He has a long-standing interest in both applied and theoretical issues in corporate finance and has extensive experience teaching all levels of corporate finance and financial management policy. Professor Jordan has published numerous articles on issues such as cost of capital, capital structure, and the behavior of security prices. He is a past president of the Southern Finance Association, and he is coauthor of *Fundamentals of Investments: Valuation and Management,* 9th edition, a leading investments text, also published by McGraw-Hill.

FROM THE AUTHORS

IN THE BEGINNING . . .

It was probably inevitable that the four of us would collaborate on this project. Over the last 20 or so years, we have been working as two separate "RWJ" teams. In that time, we managed (much to our own amazement) to coauthor two widely adopted undergraduate texts and an equally successful graduate text, all in the corporate finance area. These three books have collectively totaled more than 35 editions (and counting), plus a variety of country-specific editions and international editions, and they have been translated into at least a dozen foreign languages.

Even so, we knew that there was a hole in our lineup at the graduate (MBA) level. We've continued to see a need for a concise, up-to-date, and to-the-point product, the majority of which can be realistically covered in a typical single term or course. As we began to develop this book, we realized (with wry chuckles all around) that, between the four of us, we had been teaching and researching finance principles for well over a century. From our own very extensive experience with this material, we recognized that corporate finance introductory classes often have students with extremely diverse educational and professional backgrounds. We also recognized that this course is increasingly being delivered in alternative formats ranging from traditional semester-long classes to highly compressed modules, to purely online courses, taught both synchronously and asynchronously.

OUR APPROACH

To achieve our objective of reaching out to the many different types of students and the varying course environments, we worked to distill the subject of corporate finance down to its core, while maintaining a decidedly modern approach. We have always maintained that corporate finance can be viewed as the working of a few very powerful intuitions. We also know that understanding the "why" is just as important, if not more so, than understanding the "how." Throughout the development of this book, we continued to take a hard look at what is truly relevant and useful. In doing so, we have worked to downplay purely theoretical issues and minimize the use of extensive and elaborate calculations to illustrate points that are either intuitively obvious or of limited practical use.

Perhaps more than anything, this book gave us the chance to pool all that we have learned about what really works in a corporate finance text. We have received an enormous amount of feedback over the years. Based on that feedback, the two key ingredients that we worked to blend together here are the careful attention to pedagogy and readability that we have developed in our undergraduate books and the strong emphasis on current thinking and research that we have always stressed in our graduate book.

From the start, we knew we didn't want this text to be encyclopedic. Our goal instead was to focus on what students really need to carry away from a principles course. After much debate and consultation with colleagues who regularly teach this material, we settled on a total of 21 chapters. Chapter length is typically 30 pages, so most of the book (and, thus, most of the key concepts and applications) can be realistically covered in a single term or module. Writing a book that strictly focuses on core concepts and applications necessarily involves some picking and choosing with regard to both topics and depth of coverage. Throughout, we strike a balance by introducing and covering the essentials, while leaving more specialized topics to follow-up courses.

As in our other books, we treat net present value (NPV) as the underlying and unifying concept in corporate finance. Many texts stop well short of consistently integrating this basic principle. The simple, intuitive, and very powerful notion that NPV represents the excess of market value over cost often is lost in an overly mechanical approach that emphasizes computation at the expense of comprehension. In contrast, every subject we cover is firmly rooted in valuation, and care is taken throughout to explain how particular decisions have valuation effects.

Also, students shouldn't lose sight of the fact that financial management is about management. We emphasize the role of the financial manager as decision maker, and we stress the need for managerial input and judgment. We consciously avoid "black box" approaches to decisions, and where appropriate, the approximate, pragmatic nature of financial analysis is made explicit, possible pitfalls are described, and limitations are discussed.

NEW AND NOTEWORTHY TO THE SIXTH EDITION

All chapter openers and examples have been updated to reflect the financial trends and turbulence of the last several years. In addition, we have updated the end-of-chapter problems in every chapter. We have tried to incorporate the many exciting new research findings in corporate finance.

- The Tax Cuts and Jobs Act of 2017 is incorporated throughout. This major legislation covers many aspects of corporate finance, including (but not limited to):
  - Corporate tax. The new, flat-rate 21 percent corporate rate is discussed and compared to the old progressive system. Entities other than C corporations still face progressive taxation, so the discussion of marginal versus average tax rates remains relevant and is retained.

- Bonus depreciation. For a limited time, businesses can take a 100 percent depreciation charge the first year for most non-real estate, MACRS-qualified investments.

- Limitations on interest deductions. The amount of interest that may be deducted for tax purposes is limited. Interest that cannot be deducted can be carried forward to future tax years (but not carried back; see next).

- Carrybacks. Net operating loss (NOL) carrybacks have been eliminated and NOL carryforward deductions are limited in any one tax year.

- Dividends-received tax break. The tax break on dividends received by a corporation has been reduced, meaning that the portion subject to taxation has increased.

- Repatriation. The distinction between U.S. and non-U.S. profits essentially has been eliminated. All "overseas" assets, both liquid and illiquid, are subject to a one-time "deemed" tax.

- In the 12 years since the "financial crisis" or "great recession," we see that the world's financial markets are more integrated than ever before. The theory and practice of corporate finance has been moving forward at a fast pace and we endeavor to bring the theory and practice to life with completely updated chapter openers, many new modern examples, and completely updated end-of-chapter problems and questions.

- In recent years we have seen unprecedented high stock and bond values and returns as well as historically low interest rates and inflation.

- Chapter 10 Risk and Return: Lessons from Market History updates and internationalizes our discussion of historical risk and return. With updated historical data, our estimates of the equity risk premium are on stronger footing and our understanding of the capital market environment is heightened.

- Given the importance of debt in most firms' capital structure, it is a mystery that many firms use no debt. There is new and exciting research of this "no debt" behavior that sheds new light on how firms make actual capital structure decisions.

- Chapter 15 Capital Structure: Limits to the Use of Debt explores this new research and incorporates it into our discussion of capital structure.

- Chapter 16 Dividends and Other Payouts updates the record of earnings, dividends, and repurchases for large U.S. firms. The recent trends show repurchases far outpacing dividends in firm payout policy. Because firms may use dividends or repurchases to pay out cash to equity investors, the recent importance of repurchases suggests a changing financial landscape.

- There are several twists and turns to the calculation of the firm's weighted average cost of capital. Because the weighted average cost of capital is the most important benchmark we use for capital budgeting and represents a firm's "opportunity cost," its calculation is critical. We update our estimates of Eastman Chemical's cost of capital using readily available data from the internet to distinguish the nuances of this calculation.

Our attention to updating and improving also extended to the extensive collection of support and enrichment materials that accompany the text. Working with many dedicated and talented colleagues and professionals, we continue to provide supplements that are unrivaled at the graduate level (a complete description appears in the following pages). Whether you use just the textbook, or the book in conjunction with other products, we believe you will be able to find a combination that meets your current, as well as changing, needs.

—**Randolph W. Westerfield**
—**Jeffrey F. Jaffe**
—**Bradford D. Jordan**

Corporate Finance: Core Principles & Applications is rich in valuable learning tools and support to help students succeed in learning the fundamentals of financial management.

Chapter Opening Case

Each chapter begins with a recent real-world event to introduce students to chapter concepts.

Finance Matters

By exploring information found in recent publications and building upon concepts learned in each chapter, these boxes work through real-world issues relevant to the surrounding text.

OPENING CASE

Making Capital Investment Decisions

8

Everyone knows that computer chips evolve quickly, getting smaller, faster, and cheaper. In fact, the famous Moore's Law (named after Intel cofounder Gordon Moore) predicts that the number of transistors placed on a chip will double every two years (and this prediction has held up very well since it was published in 1965). This growth often means that companies need to build new fabrication facilities. For example, in 2018, Samsung announced that it would start producing 7 nanometer (nm) chips at its $6 billion extreme ultraviolet lithography (EUV) line at the company's plant in Hwaseong. The 7 nm chips are faster and more energy efficient than previous chips. And although Moore's Law might be in jeopardy as the doubling has slowed down for many manufacturers, Samsung stated that it planned to build 4 nm chips beginning in 2020 and 3 nm chips in 2021.

This chapter follows up on our previous one by delving more deeply into capital budgeting and the evaluation of projects such as these chip manufacturing facilities. We identify the relevant cash flows of a project, including initial investment outlays, requirements for net working capital, and operating cash flows. Further, we look at the effects of depreciation and taxes. We also examine the impact of inflation and show how to consistently evaluate the NPV of a project.

Please visit us at corecorporatefinance.blogspot.com for the latest developments in the world of corporate finance.

FINANCE MATTERS

BEAUTY IS IN THE EYE OF THE BONDHOLDER

Many bonds have unusual or exotic features. One of the most common types is an asset-backed, or Mortgage-backed securities were big news in 2007. For several years, there had been rapid growth prime mortgage loans, which are mortgages made to individuals with less than top-quality credit. Ho tion of cooling (and in some places dropping) housing prices and rising interest rates caused mortga and foreclosures to rise. This increase in problem mortgages caused a significant number of mortgage to drop sharply in value and created huge losses for investors. Bondholders of a securitized bond re principal payments from a specific asset (or pool of assets) rather than a specific company. For exan rock legend David Bowie sold $55 million in bonds backed by future royalties from his albums and s serious ch-ch-ch-change!). Owners of these "Bowie" bonds received the royalty payments, so if Bowie' there was a possibility the bonds could have defaulted. Other artists have sold bonds backed by futur ing James Brown, Iron Maiden, and the estate of the legendary Marvin Gaye.

Mortgage-backs are the best-known type of asset-backed security. With a mortgage-backed bo chases mortgages from banks and merges them into a pool. Bonds are then issued, and the bondho ments derived from payments on the underlying mortgages. One unusual twist with mortgage bonds rates decline, the bonds can actually decrease in value. This can occur because homeowners are like the lower rates, paying off their mortgages in the process. Securitized bonds are usually backed by ass

SPREADSHEET TECHNIQUES

Most spreadsheets have fairly elaborate routines available for calculating bond values and yields; many of these routines involve details that we have not discussed. However, setting up a simple spreadsheet to calculate prices or yields is straightforward, as our next two spreadsheets show:

	A	B	C	D	E	F	G	H
1								
2		Using a spreadsheet to calculate bond values						
3								
4	Suppose we have a bond with 22 years to maturity, a coupon rate of 8 percent, and a yield to							
5	maturity of 9 percent. If the bond makes semiannual payments, what is its price today?							
6								
7	Settlement date:	1/1/00						
8	Maturity date:	1/1/22						
9	Annual coupon rate:	.08						
10	Yield to maturity:	.09						
11	Face value (% of par):	100						
12	Coupons per year:	2						
13	Bond price (% of par):	90.49						
14								
15	The formula entered in cell B13 is =PRICE(B7,B8,B9,B10,B11,B12); notice that face value and bond							
16	price are given as a percentage of face value.							

Spreadsheet Techniques

This feature helps students to improve their Excel spreadsheet skills, particularly as they relate to corporate finance. This feature appears in self-contained sections and shows students how to set up spreadsheets to analyze common financial problems—a vital part of every business student's education. For even more help using Excel, students have access to Excel Master, an in-depth online tutorial.

$20, which is $18.18 (= $20/1.10).

Now that we know how to determine both the delta and the amount of borrowing, we can write the value of the call as:

$$\text{Value of call} = \text{Stock price} \times \text{Delta} - \text{Amount borrowed} \qquad [17.2]$$

$$\$6.82 \;=\; \$50 \;\times\; \frac{1}{2} \;-\; \$18.18$$

We will find this intuition very useful in explaining the Black-Scholes model.

RISK-NEUTRAL VALUATION Before leaving this example, we should comment on a remarkable feature. We found the exact value of the option without even knowing the probability that the stock would go up or down! If an optimist thought the probability of an up move was very high and a pessimist thought it was very low, they would still agree on the option value. How could that be? The answer is that the current $50 stock price already balances the views of the optimist and the pessimist. The option reflects that balance because its value depends on the stock price.

This insight provides us with another approach to valuing the call. If we don't need the probabilities of the two states to value the call, perhaps we can select any probabilities we want and still come up with the right answer. Suppose we selected probabilities such that the return on the stock is equal to the risk-free rate of 10 percent. We know that the stock return given a rise is 20 percent (= $60/$50 − 1) and the stock return given a fall is −20 percent (= $40/$50 − 1). Thus, we can solve for the probability of a rise necessary to achieve an expected return of 10 percent as:

Numbered Equations

Key equations are numbered within the text and listed in Appendix D for easy reference.

END-OF-CHAPTER MATERIAL

The end-of-chapter material reflects and builds on the concepts learned from the chapter and study features.

QUESTIONS AND PROBLEMS

1. **Building a Balance Sheet** Och, Inc., has current assets of $6,400, net fixed assets of $29,300, current liabilities of $5,100, and long-term debt of $11,800. What is the value of the shareholders' equity account for this firm? How much is net working capital?

2. **Building an Income Statement** Higgins, Inc., has sales of $517,400, costs of $296,300, depreciation expense of $42,300, interest expense of $20,400, and a tax rate of 21 percent. What is the net income for the firm? Suppose the company paid out $27,000 in cash dividends. What is the addition to retained earnings?

3. **Market Values and Book Values** Klingon Cruisers, Inc., purchased new cloaking machinery three years ago for $7.5 million. The machinery can be sold to the Romulans today for $5.6 million. Klingon's current balance sheet shows net fixed assets of $3.9 million, current liabilities of $1.125 million, and net working capital of $340,000. If all the current accounts were liquidated today, the company would receive $380,000 cash. What is the book value of Klingon's total assets today? What is the sum of the market value of NWC and market value of assets?

4. **Calculating Taxes** Timmy Tappan is single and had $189,000 in taxable income. Using the rates from Table 2.3 in the chapter, calculate his income taxes. What is the average tax rate? What is the marginal tax rate?

5. **Calculating OCF** Masters, Inc., has sales of $32,400, costs of $14,300, depreciation expense of $2,200, and interest expense of $1,160. If the tax rate is 23 percent, what is the operating cash flow, or OCF?

6. **Calculating Net Capital Spending** Bantam Egg's 2019 balance sheet showed net fixed assets of $3.82 million, and the 2020 balance sheet showed net fixed assets of $4.63 million. The company's 2020 income statement showed a depreciation expense of $405,000. What was the company's net capital spending for 2020?

Questions and Problems

Because solving problems is so critical to students' learning, we provide extensive end-of-chapter questions and problems. The questions and problems are segregated into three learning levels: Basic, Intermediate, and Challenge. All problems are fully annotated so that students and instructors can readily identify particular types. Also, most of the problems are available in McGraw-Hill's Connect.

What's on the Web?

These end-of-chapter activities show students how to use and learn from the vast amount of financial resources available on the internet.

WHAT'S ON THE WEB?

1. **Expected Return** You want to find the expected return for Honeywell using the CAPM. First yo need the market risk premium. Go to money.cnn.com and find the current interest rate for three Treasury bills. Use the historic market risk premium from Chapter 10 as the market risk premium go to finance.yahoo.com, enter the ticker symbol HON for Honeywell, and find the beta for Hone What is the expected return for Honeywell using the CAPM? What assumptions have you made t at this number?

2. **Portfolio Beta** You have decided to invest in an equally weighted portfolio consisting of America Express, Procter & Gamble, Home Depot, and DowDuPont and need to find the beta of your portfo to finance.yahoo.com and find the beta for each of the companies. What is the beta for your portfo

3. **Beta** Which companies currently have the highest and lowest betas? Go to finance.yahoo.com find the "Screeners" link. Enter 0 as the maximum beta and search. How many stocks currently beta less than or equal to 0? What is the lowest beta? Go back to the stock screener and enter 3 minimum. How many stocks have a beta above 3? What stock has the highest beta?

4. **Security Market Line** Go to finance.yahoo.com and enter the ticker symbol IP for Internationa Follow the "Statistics" link to get the beta for the company. Next, find the estimated (or "target") in 12 months according to market analysts. Using the current share price and the mean target p compute the expected return for this stock. Don't forget to include the expected dividend payme over the next year. Now go to money.cnn.com and find the current interest rate for three-month Treasury bills. Using this information, calculate the expected return on the market using the reward-to-risk ratio. Does this number make sense? Why or why not?

9.2 percent, 11.8 percent, and 14.3 percent, respectively. What is the expected return on the portfolio?

 4. **Portfolio Expected Return** You have $10,000 to invest in a stock portfolio. Your choices are Stock X with an expected return of 11.9 percent and Stock Y with an expected return of 9.7 percent. If your goal is to create a portfolio with an expected return of 10.3 percent, how much money will you invest in Stock X? In Stock Y?

5. **Calculating Expected Return** Based on the following information, calculate the expected return.

State of Economy	Probability of State of Economy	Rate of Return If State Occurs
Recession	.35	−.14
Normal	.50	.16
Boom	.15	.43

 6. **Calculating Returns and Standard Deviations** Based on the following information, calculate the expected return and standard deviation for the two stocks.

State of Economy	Probability of State of Economy	Rate of Return If State Occurs	
		Stock A	Stock B
Recession	.10	.01	−.19
Normal	.60	.09	.11

Excel Problems

Expanded for this edition! Indicated by the Excel icon in the margin, these problems are integrated in the Questions and Problems section of almost all chapters. RWJJ offers students more practice using the Excel functions they will use throughout their futures in finance.

EXCEL MASTER IT! PROBLEM

ExcelMaster
coverage online
www.mhhe.com/RossCore6e

Companies often buy bonds to meet a future liability or cash outlay. Such an investment ~~portfolio~~ because the proceeds of the portfolio are dedicated to the future liability. In ~~~~ folio is subject to reinvestment risk. Reinvestment risk occurs because the company w~~~~ coupon payments it receives. If the YTM on similar bonds falls, these coupon payments ~~~~ a lower interest rate, which will result in a portfolio value that is lower than desired at ~~~~ interest rates increase, the portfolio value at maturity will be higher than needed.

Suppose Ice Cubes, Inc., has the following liability due in five years. The company is ~~~~ bonds today to meet the future obligation. The liability and current YTM are below:

Amount of liability:	$100,000,000
Current YTM:	8%

a. At the current YTM, what is the face value of the bonds the company has to purc~~~~ its future obligation? Assume that the bonds in the relevant range will have the s~~~~ the current YTM and these bonds make semiannual coupon payments.

b. Assume the interest rates remain constant for the next five years. Thus, when the~~~~ the coupon payments, it will reinvest at the current YTM. What is the value of the ~~~~

c. Assume that immediately after the company purchases the bonds, interest rates ~~~~ 1 percent. What is the value of the portfolio in five years under these circumstan~~~~

One way to eliminate reinvestment risk is called *immunization*. Rather than buying bonds wit~~~~ the liability, the company instead buys bonds with the same duration as the liability. If you thi~~~~ portfolio, if the interest rate falls, the future value of the reinvested coupon payments decrea~~~~ est rates fall, the price of bonds increases. These effects offset each other in an immunized ~~~~

Another advantage of using duration to immunize a portfolio is that the duration~~~~ weighted average of the duration of the assets in the portfolio. In other words, to find t~~~~ folio, you take the weight of each asset multiplied by its duration and then sum the resu~~~~

CLOSING CASE

THE COST OF CAPITAL FOR SWAN MOTORS

You have recently been hired by Swan Motors, Inc. (SMI), in its relatively new treasury management department. SMI was founded eight years ago by Joe Swan. Joe found a method to manufacture a cheaper battery with much greater energy density than was previously possible, giving a car powered by the battery a range of 700 miles before requiring a charge. The cars manufactured by SMI are midsized and carry a price that allows the company to compete with other mainstream auto manufacturers. The company is privately owned by Joe and his family, and it had sales of $97 million last year.

SMI primarily sells to customers who buy the cars online, although it does have a limited number of company-owned dealerships. The customer selects any customization and makes a deposit of 20 percent of the purchase price. After the order is taken, the car is made to order, typically within 45 days. SMI's growth to date has come from its profits. When the company had sufficient capital, it would expand production. Relatively little formal analysis has been used in its capital budgeting process. Joe has just read about capital budgeting techniques and has come to you for help. For starters, the company has never attempted to determine its cost of capital, and Joe would like you to perform the analysis. Because the company is privately owned, it is difficult to determine the cost of equity for the company. Joe wants you to use the pure play approach to estimate the cost of capital for SMI, and he has chosen Tesla Motors as a representative company. The following questions will lead you through the steps to calculate this estimate.

1. Most publicly traded corporations are required to submit 10-Q (quarterly) and 10-K (annual) reports to the SEC detailing their financial operations over the previous quarter or year, respectively. These corporate filings are available on the SEC website at www.sec.gov. Go to the SEC website and enter "TSLA" for Tesla in the "Search for Company Filings" link. Find the most recent 10-Q or 10-K and download the form. Look on the balance sheet to find the book value of debt and the book value of equity. If you look further down the report, you should find a section titled either "Long-Term Debt" or "Long-Term Debt and Interest Rate Risk Management" that will list a breakdown of Tesla's long-term debt.

2. To estimate the cost of equity for Tesla, go to finance.yahoo.com and enter the ticker symbol "TSLA." Follow the various links to find answers to the following questions: What is the most recent stock price listed for Tesla? What is the market value of equity, or market capitalization? How many shares of stock does Tesla have outstanding? What is the beta for Tesla? Now go back to finance.yahoo.com and ~~follow the "Bonds" link. What is the yield on three-month Treasury bills? Using a 7 percent market risk~~

Excel Master It! Problems

These more in-depth mini-case studies highlight higher-level Excel skills. Students are encouraged to use Excel to solve real-life financial problems using the concepts they have learned in the chapter and the Excel skills they have acquired thus far.

End-of-Chapter Cases

Located at the end of each chapter, these mini-cases focus on common company situations that embody important corporate finance topics. Each case presents a new scenario, data, and a dilemma. Several questions at the end of each case require students to analyze and focus on all of the material they learned in that chapter.

COMPREHENSIVE TEACHING

INSTRUCTOR SUPPORT

- **Instructor's Manual**

  prepared by Bruce Costa, University of Montana

  A great place to find new lecture ideas. The IM has three main sections. The first section contains a chapter outline and other lecture materials. The annotated outline for each chapter includes lecture tips, real-world tips, ethics notes, suggested PowerPoint slides, and, when appropriate, a video synopsis. Detailed solutions for all end-of-chapter problems appear in Section 3.

- **Test Bank**

  prepared by Heidi Toprac, University of Texas

  A great format for a better testing process. The Test Bank has 75–100 questions per chapter that closely link with the text material and provide a variety of question formats (multiple-choice questions/problems and essay questions) and levels of difficulty (basic, intermediate, and challenge) to meet every instructor's testing needs. Problems are detailed enough to make them intuitive for students, and solutions are provided for the instructor.

- **Test Builder in Connect**

  Available within Connect, Test Builder is a cloud-based tool that enables instructors to format tests that can be printed or administered within an LMS. Test Builder offers a modern, streamlined interface for easy content configuration that matches course needs, without requiring a download.

  Test Builder allows you to:

  - access all test bank content from a particular title.
  - easily pinpoint the most relevant content through robust filtering options.
  - manipulate the order of questions or scramble questions and/or answers.
  - pin questions to a specific location within a test.
  - determine your preferred treatment of algorithmic questions.
  - choose the layout and spacing.
  - add instructions and configure default settings.

  Test Builder provides a secure interface for better protection of content and allows for just-in-time updates to flow directly into assessments.

- **PowerPoint Presentation System**

  prepared by Bruce Costa, University of Montana

  Customize our content for your course. This presentation has been thoroughly revised to include more lecture-oriented slides, as well as exhibits and examples both from the book and from outside sources. This customizable format gives you the ability to edit, print, or rearrange the complete presentation to meet your specific needs.

- **Excel Simulations**

  Expanded for this edition! With 180 Excel simulation questions now included in Connect, RWJJ is the unparalleled leader in offering students the opportunity to practice using the Excel functions they will use throughout their careers in finance.

- **Corporate Finance Videos**
  New for this edition! Brief and engaging conceptual videos (and accompanying questions) help students to master the building blocks of the Corporate Finance course.
- **Finance Interactives**
  New for this edition! These unique, interactive applets give students the chance to manipulate and interpret the data points that define key concepts in Corporate Finance. With accompanying questions, these can be found in Connect.

STUDENT SUPPORT

- **Excel Master**
  Created by the authors, this extensive Excel tutorial is fully integrated with the text. Learn Excel and corporate finance at the same time.
- **Excel Templates**
  Corresponding to most end-of-chapter problems, each template allows the student to walk through the problem using Excel.
- **Narrated Presentations**
  Each chapter's slides follow the chapter topics and provide steps and explanations showing how to solve key problems. Because each student learns differently, a quick click on each slide will "talk through" its contents with you!

PACKAGE OPTIONS AVAILABLE FOR PURCHASE & PACKAGING

You may also package either version of the text with a variety of additional learning tools that are available for your students.

FinGame Online 5.0

by LeRoy Brooks, John Carroll University
(ISBN 10: 0077219880/ISBN 13: 9780077219888)
Just $15.00 when packaged with this text. In this comprehensive simulation game, students control a hypothetical company over numerous periods of operation. As students make major financial and operating decisions for their company, they will develop and enhance their skills in financial management and financial accounting statement analysis.

MCGRAW-HILL CUSTOMER CARE CONTACT INFORMATION

At McGraw-Hill, we understand that getting the most from new technology can be challenging. That's why our services don't stop after you purchase our products. You can e-mail our Product Specialists 24 hours a day to get product training online, or you can search our knowledge bank of Frequently Asked Questions on our support website. For Customer Support, call **800-331-5094,** or visit mpss.mhhe.com. One of our Technical Support Analysts will be able to assist you in a timely fashion.

ASSURANCE OF LEARNING READY

Assurance of Learning is an important element of many accreditation standards. *Corporate Finance: Core Principles and Applications,* 6e, is designed specifically to support your Assurance of Learning initiatives. Every test bank question is labeled with level of difficulty, topic area, Bloom's Taxonomy level, and AACSB skill area. Connect, McGraw-Hill's online homework solution, and TestGen, McGraw-Hill's easy-to-use test bank software, can search the test bank by these and other categories, providing an engine for targeted Assurance of Learning analysis and assessment.

AACSB STATEMENT

McGraw-Hill is a proud corporate member of AACSB International. Understanding the importance and value of AACSB accreditation, *Corporate Finance: Core Principles and Applications,* 6e, has sought to recognize the curricula guidelines detailed in the AACSB standards for business accreditation by connecting selected questions in the test bank to the general knowledge and skill guidelines found in the AACSB standards.

The statements contained in *Corporate Finance: Core Principles and Applications,* 6e, are provided only as a guide for the users of this text. The AACSB leaves content coverage and assessment within the purview of individual schools, the mission of the school, and the faculty. While *Corporate Finance: Core Principles and Applications,* 6e, and the teaching package make no claim of any specific AACSB qualification or evaluation, we have, within the test bank, labeled selected questions according to the six general knowledge and skills areas.

You're in the driver's seat.

Want to build your own course? No problem. Prefer to use our turnkey, prebuilt course? Easy. Want to make changes throughout the semester? Sure. And you'll save time with Connect's auto-grading too.

65%

Less Time Grading

They'll thank you for it.

Adaptive study resources like SmartBook® 2.0 help your students be better prepared in less time. You can transform your class time from dull definitions to dynamic debates. Find out more about the powerful personalized learning experience available in SmartBook 2.0 at **www.mheducation.com/highered/ connect/smartbook**

Laptop: McGraw-Hill; Woman/dog: George Doyle/Getty Images

Make it simple, make it affordable.

Connect makes it easy with seamless integration using any of the major Learning Management Systems— Blackboard®, Canvas, and D2L, among others—to let you organize your course in one convenient location. Give your students access to digital materials at a discount with our inclusive access program. Ask your McGraw-Hill representative for more information.

Padlock: Jobalou/Getty Images

Solutions for your challenges.

A product isn't a solution. Real solutions are affordable, reliable, and come with training and ongoing support when you need it and how you want it. Our Customer Experience Group can also help you troubleshoot tech problems— although Connect's 99% uptime means you might not need to call them. See for yourself at **status. mheducation.com**

Checkmark: Jobalou/Getty Images

Effective, efficient studying.

Connect helps you be more productive with your study time and get better grades using tools like SmartBook 2.0, which highlights key concepts and creates a personalized study plan. Connect sets you up for success, so you walk into class with confidence and walk out with better grades.

Study anytime, anywhere.

Download the free ReadAnywhere app and access your online eBook or SmartBook 2.0 assignments when it's convenient, even if you're offline. And since the app automatically syncs with your eBook and SmartBook 2.0 assignments in Connect, all of your work is available every time you open it. Find out more at **www.mheducation.com/readanywhere**

> *"I really liked this app—it made it easy to study when you don't have your text-book in front of you."*
>
> - Jordan Cunningham,
> Eastern Washington University

Calendar: owattaphotos/Getty Images

No surprises.

The Connect Calendar and Reports tools keep you on track with the work you need to get done and your assignment scores. Life gets busy; Connect tools help you keep learning through it all.

Learning for everyone.

McGraw-Hill works directly with Accessibility Services Departments and faculty to meet the learning needs of all students. Please contact your Accessibility Services office and ask them to email accessibility@mheducation.com, or visit **www.mheducation.com/about/accessibility** for more information.

ACKNOWLEDGMENTS

To borrow a phrase, writing a finance textbook is easy—all you do is sit down at a word processor and open a vein. We never would have completed this book without the incredible amount of help and support we received from our colleagues, students, editors, family members, and friends. We would like to thank, without implicating, all of you.

Clearly, our greatest debt is to our many colleagues (and their students). Needless to say, without this support and feedback we would not be publishing this text.

We owe a special thanks to Joseph Smolira of Belmont University for his work on this book. Joe worked closely with us to develop portions of the Instructor's Manual, along with the many vignettes and real-world examples. In addition, we would like to thank Bruce Costa for his work on the PowerPoint and Instructor's Manual. We would also like to thank Heidi Toprac for her terrific work and attention to detail in updating our test bank.

Steve Hailey and Emily Bello did outstanding work on this edition. To them fell the unenviable task of technical proofreading, and, in particular, careful checking of each calculation throughout the text and Instructor's Manual.

Finally, in every phase of this project, we have been privileged to have had the complete and unwavering support of a great organization, McGraw-Hill. We especially thank the McGraw-Hill sales organization. The suggestions they provide, their professionalism in assisting potential adopters, and the service they provide have been a major factor in our success.

We are deeply grateful to the select group of professionals who served as our development team on this edition: Chuck Synovec, director; Jennifer Upton, senior product developer; Trina Maurer, senior marketing manager; Jill Eccher, core content project manager; Jamie Koch, assessment project manager; and Matt Diamond, senior designer. Others at McGraw-Hill Education, too numerous to list here, have improved the book in countless ways.

Finally, we wish to thank our families, Suh-Pyng, Mark, Lynne, and Susan, for their forbearance and help.

Throughout the development of this edition, we have taken great care to discover and eliminate errors. Our goal is to provide the best textbook available on the subject. To ensure that future editions are error-free, we gladly offer $10 per arithmetic error to the first individual reporting it as a modest token of our appreciation. More than this, we would like to hear from instructors and students alike. Please write and tell us how to make this a better text. Forward your comments to: Dr. Brad Jordan, c/o Editorial-Finance, McGraw-Hill, 120 S. Riverside, Suite 1200, Chicago, IL 60606.

—Randolph W. Westerfield
—Jeffrey F. Jaffe
—Bradford D. Jordan

CHAPTER TWENTY

International Corporate Finance 620

CHAPTER TWENTY-ONE

Mergers and Acquisitions (web only)

APPENDIX A

Mathematical Tables 647

APPENDIX B

Solutions to Selected End-of-Chapter Problems 657

APPENDIX C

Using the HP 10B and TI BA II Plus Financial Calculators 663

APPENDIX D

Key Equations 667

LIST OF BOXES

Introduction to Corporate Finance

In 2009, Travis Kalanick and Garrett Camp started the ride-sharing app Uber. Uber shot out of the gate, completing more than five billion rides by the middle of 2017. Even though Uber was losing more than $100 million per quarter, its market value reached $70 billion, with Kalanick's personal wealth exceeding $6 billion. Unfortunately, Kalanick was accused of knowing about sexual harassment in the company and doing nothing to resolve the problem. Then, he was videotaped berating an Uber driver. As a result, he was forced to step down as CEO of the company in June 2017, although he remained on the company's board of directors. In 2018, Kalanick became the CEO of start-up City Storage Systems, which focuses on turning distressed real estate, such as parking lots and abandoned malls, into spaces for new industries.

Understanding Kalanick's rapid, bumpy ride from co-founder of a start-up worth $70 billion to ex-CEO takes us into issues involving the corporate form of organization, corporate goals, and corporate control—all of which we discuss in this chapter. And if you are willing to share the ride with us, you'll learn an uber-lot as you read.

Please visit us at corecorporatefinance.blogspot.com for the latest developments in the world of corporate finance.

1.1 WHAT IS CORPORATE FINANCE?

Suppose you decide to start a firm to make tennis balls. To do this you hire managers to buy raw materials, and you assemble a workforce that will produce and sell finished tennis balls. In the language of finance, you make an investment in assets such as inventory, machinery, land, and labor. The amount of cash you invest in assets must be matched by an equal amount of cash raised by financing. When you begin to sell tennis balls, your firm will generate cash. This is the basis of value creation. The purpose of the firm is to create value for you, the owner. The value is reflected in the framework of the simple balance sheet model of the firm.

The Balance Sheet Model of the Firm

Suppose we take a financial snapshot of the firm and its activities at a single point in time. Figure 1.1 shows a graphic conceptualization of the balance sheet, and it will help introduce you to corporate finance.

The assets of the firm are on the left side of the balance sheet. These assets can be thought of as current and fixed. *Fixed assets* are those that will last a long time, such as buildings. Some fixed assets are tangible, such as machinery and equipment. Other fixed assets are intangible, such as patents and trademarks. The other category of assets, *current assets,* comprises those that have short lives, such as inventory. The tennis balls that your firm has made, but has not yet sold, are part of its inventory. Unless you have overproduced, they will leave the firm shortly.

Before a company can invest in an asset, it must obtain financing, which means that it must raise the money to pay for the investment. The forms of financing are represented on

FIGURE 1.1

The Balance Sheet Model of the Firm

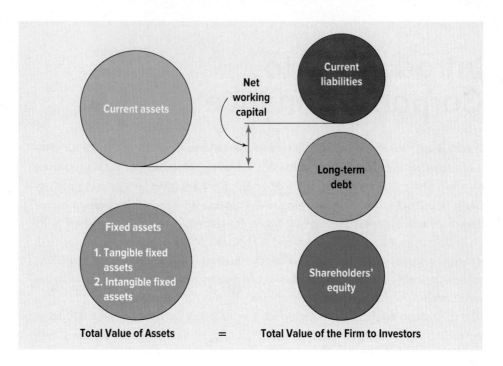

the right side of the balance sheet. A firm will issue (sell) pieces of paper called *debt* (loan agreements) or *equity shares* (stock certificates). Just as assets are classified as long-lived or short-lived, so too are liabilities. A short-term debt is called a *current liability.* Short-term debt represents loans and other obligations that must be repaid within one year. Long-term debt is debt that does not have to be repaid within one year. Shareholders' equity represents the difference between the value of the assets and the debt of the firm. In this sense, it is a residual claim on the firm's assets.

From the balance sheet model of the firm, it is easy to see why finance can be thought of as the study of the following three questions:

1. In what long-lived assets should the firm invest? This question concerns the left side of the balance sheet. Of course the types and proportions of assets the firm needs tend to be set by the nature of the business. We use the term capital budgeting to describe the process of making and managing expenditures on long-lived assets.

2. How can the firm raise cash for required capital expenditures? This question concerns the right side of the balance sheet. The answer to this question involves the firm's capital structure, which represents the proportions of the firm's financing from current liabilities, long-term debt, and equity.

3. How should short-term operating cash flows be managed? This question concerns the upper portion of the balance sheet. There is often a mismatch between the timing of cash inflows and cash outflows during operating activities.

Furthermore, the amount and timing of operating cash flows are not known with certainty. Financial managers must attempt to manage the gaps in cash flow.

From a balance sheet perspective, short-term management of cash flow is associated with a firm's net working capital. Net working capital is defined as current assets minus current liabilities. From a financial perspective, short-term cash flow problems come from the mismatching of cash inflows and outflows. This is the subject of short-term finance.

FIGURE 1.2

Hypothetical Organization Chart

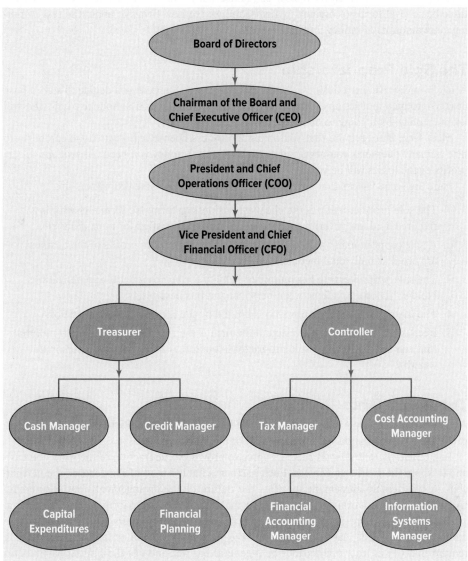

The Financial Manager

In large firms, the finance activity is usually associated with a top officer of the firm, such as the vice president and chief financial officer, and some lesser officers. Figure 1.2 depicts a general organizational structure emphasizing the finance activity within the firm. Reporting to the chief financial officer are the treasurer and the controller. The treasurer is responsible for handling cash flows, managing capital expenditure decisions, and making financial plans. The controller handles the accounting function, which includes taxes, cost and financial accounting, and information systems.

For current issues facing CFOs, see www.cfo.com.

1.2 THE CORPORATE FIRM

The firm is a way of organizing the economic activity of many individuals. A basic problem of the firm is how to raise cash. The corporate form of business—that is, organizing the firm as a corporation—is the standard method for solving problems encountered in raising large amounts of cash. However, businesses can take other forms. In this section we consider the three basic legal forms of organizing firms, and we see how firms go about the task of raising large amounts of money under each form.

The Sole Proprietorship

A sole proprietorship is a business owned by one person. Suppose you decide to start a business to produce mousetraps. Going into business is simple: You announce to all who will listen, "Today, I am going to build a better mousetrap."

Most large cities require that you obtain a business license. Afterward, you can begin to hire as many people as you need and borrow whatever money you need. At year-end all the profits or the losses will be yours.

Here are some factors that are important in considering a sole proprietorship:

1. The sole proprietorship is the cheapest business to form. No formal charter is required, and few government regulations must be satisfied for most industries.
2. A sole proprietorship pays no corporate income taxes. All profits of the business are taxed as individual income.
3. The sole proprietorship has unlimited liability for business debts and obligations. No distinction is made between personal and business assets.
4. The life of the sole proprietorship is limited by the life of the sole proprietor.
5. Because the only money invested in the firm is the proprietor's, the equity money that can be raised by the sole proprietor is limited to the proprietor's personal wealth.

The Partnership

Any two or more people can get together and form a partnership. Partnerships fall into two categories: (1) general partnerships and (2) limited partnerships.

In a *general partnership,* all partners agree to provide some fraction of the work and cash and to share the profits and losses. Each partner is liable for all of the debts of the partnership. A partnership agreement specifies the nature of the arrangement. The partnership agreement may be an oral agreement or a formal document setting forth the understanding.

Limited partnerships permit the liability of some of the partners to be limited to the amount of cash each has contributed to the partnership. Limited partnerships usually require that (1) at least one partner be a general partner and (2) the limited partners do not participate in managing the business. Here are some things that are important when considering a partnership:

1. Partnerships are usually inexpensive and easy to form. Written documents are required in complicated arrangements. Business licenses and filing fees may be necessary.
2. General partners have unlimited liability for all debts. The liability of limited partners is usually limited to the contribution each has made to the partnership. If one general partner is unable to meet his or her commitment, the shortfall must be made up by the other general partners.
3. The general partnership is terminated when a general partner dies or withdraws (but this is not so for a limited partner). It is difficult for a partnership to transfer ownership without dissolving. Usually all general partners must agree. However, limited partners may sell their interest in a business.
4. It is difficult for a partnership to raise large amounts of cash. Equity contributions are usually limited to a partner's ability and desire to contribute to the partnership. Many companies, such as Apple Computer, start life as a proprietorship or partnership, but at some point they choose to convert to corporate form.

5. Income from a partnership is taxed as personal income to the partners.

6. Management control resides with the general partners. Usually, a majority vote is required on important matters, such as the amount of profit to be retained in the business.

It is difficult for large business organizations to exist as sole proprietorships or partnerships. The main advantage to a sole proprietorship or partnership is the cost of getting started. Afterward, the disadvantages, which may become severe, are (1) unlimited liability, (2) limited life of the enterprise, and (3) difficulty of transferring ownership. These three disadvantages lead to (4) difficulty in raising cash.

The Corporation

Of the forms of business enterprises, the corporation is by far the most important. It is a distinct legal entity. As such, a corporation can have a name and enjoy many of the legal powers of natural persons. For example, corporations can acquire and exchange property. Corporations can enter contracts and may sue and be sued. For jurisdictional purposes, the corporation is a citizen of its state of incorporation (it cannot vote, however).

Starting a corporation is more complicated than starting a proprietorship or partnership. The incorporators must prepare articles of incorporation and a set of bylaws. The articles of incorporation must include the following:

1. Name of the corporation.
2. Intended life of the corporation (it may be forever).
3. Business purpose.
4. Number of shares of stock that the corporation is authorized to issue, with a statement of limitations and rights of different classes of shares.
5. Nature of the rights granted to shareholders.
6. Number of members of the initial board of directors.

The bylaws are the rules to be used by the corporation to regulate its own existence, and they concern its shareholders, directors, and officers. Bylaws range from the briefest possible statement of rules for the corporation's management to hundreds of pages of text.

In its simplest form, the corporation comprises three sets of distinct interests: the shareholders (the owners), the directors, and the corporation officers (the top management). Traditionally, the shareholders control the corporation's direction, policies, and activities. The shareholders elect a board of directors, who in turn select top management. Members of top management serve as corporate officers and manage the operations of the corporation in the best interest of the shareholders. In closely held corporations with few shareholders, there may be a large overlap among the shareholders, the directors, and the top management. However, in larger corporations, the shareholders, directors, and the top management are likely to be distinct groups.

The potential separation of ownership from management gives the corporation several advantages over proprietorships and partnerships:

1. Because ownership in a corporation is represented by shares of stock, ownership can be readily transferred to new owners. Because the corporation exists independently of those who own its shares, there is no limit to the transferability of shares as there is in partnerships.

2. The corporation has unlimited life. Because the corporation is separate from its owners, the death or withdrawal of an owner does not affect the corporation's legal existence. The corporation can continue on after the original owners have withdrawn.

3. The shareholders' liability is limited to the amount invested in the ownership shares. For example, if a shareholder purchased $1,000 in shares of a corporation,

the potential loss would be $1,000. In a partnership, a general partner with a $1,000 contribution could lose the $1,000 plus any other indebtedness of the partnership.

Limited liability, ease of ownership transfer, and perpetual succession are the major advantages of the corporate form of business organization. These give the corporation an enhanced ability to raise cash.

There is, however, one great disadvantage to incorporation. The federal government taxes corporate income (the states do as well). This tax is in addition to the personal income tax that shareholders pay on dividend income they receive. This is double taxation for shareholders when compared to taxation on proprietorships and partnerships. Table 1.1 summarizes our discussion of partnerships and corporations.

To find out more about LLCs, visit www.incorporate.com.

Today, all 50 states have enacted laws allowing for the creation of a limited liability company (LLC). The goal of this entity is to operate and be taxed like a partnership but retain limited liability for owners, so an LLC is essentially a hybrid of partnership and corporation. Although states have differing definitions for LLCs, the more important scorekeeper is the Internal Revenue Service (IRS). The IRS will consider an LLC a corporation, thereby subjecting it to double taxation, unless it meets certain specific criteria. In essence, an LLC cannot be too corporation-like, or it will be treated as one by the IRS. LLCs have become common. For example, Goldman, Sachs and Co., one of Wall Street's last remaining partnerships, decided to convert from a private partnership to an LLC (it later "went public," becoming a publicly held corporation). Large accounting firms and law firms by the score have converted to LLCs.

A Corporation by Another Name . . .

The corporate form of organization has many variations around the world. The exact laws and regulations differ from country to country, of course, but the essential features of public ownership and limited liability remain. These firms are often called *joint stock companies, public limited companies,* or *limited liability companies,* depending on the specific nature of the firm and the country of origin.

Table 1.2 gives the names of a few well-known international corporations, their countries of origin, and a translation of the abbreviation that follows each company name.

TABLE 1.1   A Comparison of Partnerships and Corporations

	Corporation	Partnership
Liquidity and marketability	Shares can be exchanged without termination of the corporation. Common stock can be listed on a stock exchange.	Units are subject to substantial restrictions on transferability. There is usually no established trading market for partnership units.
Voting rights	Usually each share of common stock entitles the holder to one vote per share on matters requiring a vote and on the election of the directors. Directors determine top management.	Some voting rights by limited partners. However, general partners have exclusive control and management of operations.
Taxation	Corporations have double taxation: Corporate income is taxable and dividends to shareholders are also taxable.	Partnerships are not taxable. Partners pay personal taxes on partnership profits.
Reinvestment and dividend payout	Corporations have broad latitude on dividend payout decisions.	Partnerships are generally prohibited from reinvesting partnership profits. All profits are distributed to partners.
Liability	Shareholders are not personally liable for obligations of the corporation.	Limited partners are not liable for obligations of partnerships. General partners may have unlimited liability.
Continuity of existence	Corporations may have a perpetual life.	Partnerships have limited life.

TABLE 1.2 International Corporations

Company	Country of Origin	Type of Company	
		In Original Language	Interpretation
Bayerische Motoren Werke (BMW) AG	Germany	Aktiengesellschaft	Corporation
Rolls-Royce PLC	United Kingdom	Public limited company	Public limited company
Shell UK Ltd.	United Kingdom	Limited	Corporation
Unilever NV	Netherlands	Naamloze Vennootschap	Joint stock company
Fiat SpA	Italy	Società per Azioni	Joint stock company
Volvo AB	Sweden	Aktiebolag	Joint stock company
Peugeot SA	France	Société Anonyme	Joint stock company

1.3 THE IMPORTANCE OF CASH FLOWS

The most important job of a financial manager is to create value from the firm's capital budgeting, financing, and net working capital activities. How do financial managers create value? The answer is that the firm should create more cash flow than it uses.

The cash flows paid to bondholders and stockholders of the firm should be greater than the cash flows put into the firm by the bondholders and stockholders. To see how this is done, we can trace the cash flows from the firm to the financial markets and back again.

The interplay of the firm's activities with the financial markets is illustrated in Figure 1.3. The arrows in Figure 1.3 trace cash flow from the firm to the financial markets and back again. Suppose we begin with the firm's financing activities. To raise money, the firm sells debt and equity shares to investors in the financial markets. This results in cash flows from the financial markets to the firm (A). This cash is invested in the investment activities (assets) of the firm (B) by the firm's management. The cash generated by the firm (C) is

FIGURE 1.3 Cash Flows between the Firm and the Financial Markets

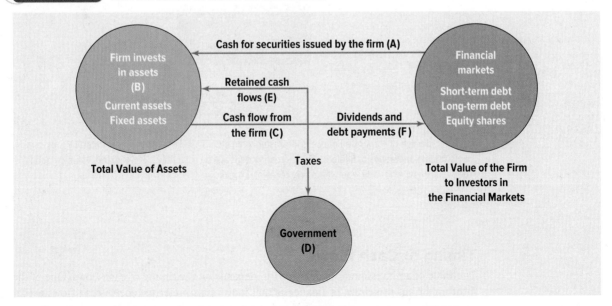

paid to shareholders and bondholders (F). The shareholders receive cash in the form of dividends; the bondholders who lent funds to the firm receive interest and, when the initial loan is repaid, principal. Not all of the firm's cash is paid out. Some is retained (E), and some is paid to the government as taxes (D).

Over time, if the cash paid to shareholders and bondholders (F) is greater than the cash raised in the financial markets (A), value will be created.

Identification of Cash Flows

Unfortunately, it is sometimes not easy to observe cash flows directly. Much of the information we obtain is in the form of accounting statements, and much of the work of financial analysis is to extract cash flow information from accounting statements. The following example illustrates how this is done.

Accounting Profit versus Cash Flows

The Midland Company refines and trades gold. At the end of the year, it sold 2,500 ounces of gold for $1 million. The company had acquired the gold for $900,000 at the beginning of the year. The company paid cash for the gold when it was purchased. Unfortunately, it has yet to collect from the customer to whom the gold was sold. The following is a standard accounting of Midland's financial circumstances at year-end:

THE MIDLAND COMPANY
Accounting View
Income Statement
Year Ended December 31

Sales	$1,000,000
Costs	900,000
Profit	$ 100,000

By generally accepted accounting principles (GAAP), the sale is recorded even though the customer has yet to pay. It is assumed that the customer will pay soon. From the accounting perspective, Midland seems to be profitable. However, the perspective of corporate finance is different. It focuses on cash flows:

THE MIDLAND COMPANY
Financial View
Income Statement
Year Ended December 31

Cash inflow	$ 0
Cash outflow	−900,000
	$−900,000

The perspective of corporate finance is interested in whether cash flows are being created by the gold trading operations of Midland. Value creation depends on cash flows. For Midland, value creation depends on whether and when it actually receives $1 million.

Timing of Cash Flows

The value of an investment made by a firm depends on the timing of cash flows. One of the most important principles of finance is that individuals prefer to receive cash flows earlier rather than later. One dollar received today is worth more than one dollar received next year.

Cash Flow Timing

The Midland Company is attempting to choose between two proposals for new products. Both proposals will provide additional cash flows over a four-year period and will initially cost $10,000. The cash flows from the proposals are as follows:

Year	New Product A	New Product B
1	$ 0	$ 4,000
2	0	4,000
3	0	4,000
4	20,000	4,000
Total	$20,000	$16,000

At first it appears that new Product A would be best. However, the cash flows from Product B come earlier than those of A. Without more information, we cannot decide which set of cash flows would create the most value for the bondholders and shareholders. It depends on whether the value of getting cash from B up front outweighs the extra total cash from A. Bond and stock prices reflect this preference for earlier cash, and we will see how to use them to decide between A and B.

Risk of Cash Flows

The firm must consider risk. The amount and timing of cash flows are not usually known with certainty. Most investors have an aversion to risk.

Risk

The Midland Company is considering expanding operations overseas. It is evaluating Europe and Japan as possible sites. Europe is considered to be relatively safe, whereas operating in Japan is seen as very risky. In both cases the company would close down operations after one year.

After doing a complete financial analysis, Midland has come up with the following cash flows of the alternative plans for expansion under three scenarios—pessimistic, most likely, and optimistic:

	Pessimistic	Most Likely	Optimistic
Europe	$75,000	$100,000	$125,000
Japan	0	150,000	200,000

If we ignore the pessimistic scenario, perhaps Japan is the best alternative. When we take the pessimistic scenario into account, the choice is unclear. Japan appears to be riskier, but it also offers a higher expected level of cash flow. What is risk and how can it be defined? We must try to answer this important question. Corporate finance cannot avoid coping with risky alternatives, and much of our book is devoted to developing methods for evaluating risky opportunities.

1.4 THE GOAL OF FINANCIAL MANAGEMENT

Assuming that we restrict our discussion to for-profit businesses, the goal of financial management is to make money or add value for the owners. This goal is a little vague, of course, so we examine some different ways of formulating it to come up with a more precise definition. Such a definition is important because it leads to an objective basis for making and evaluating financial decisions.

Possible Goals

If we were to consider possible financial goals, we might come up with some ideas like the following:

- Survive.
- Avoid financial distress and bankruptcy.
- Beat the competition.
- Maximize sales or market share.
- Minimize costs.
- Maximize profits.
- Maintain steady earnings growth.

These are only a few of the goals we could list. Furthermore, each of these possibilities presents problems as a goal for the financial manager.

For example, it's easy to increase market share or unit sales: All we have to do is lower our prices or relax our credit terms. Similarly, we can always cut costs by doing away with things such as research and development. We can avoid bankruptcy by never borrowing any money or never taking any risks, and so on. It's not clear that any of these actions are in the stockholders' best interests.

Profit maximization would probably be the most commonly cited goal, but even this is not a precise objective. Do we mean profits this year? If so, then we should note that actions such as deferring maintenance, letting inventories run down, and taking other short-run cost-cutting measures will tend to increase profits now, but these activities aren't necessarily desirable.

The goal of maximizing profits may refer to some sort of "long-run" or "average" profits, but it's still unclear exactly what this means. First, do we mean something like accounting net income or earnings per share? As we will see in more detail in the next chapter, these accounting numbers may have little to do with what is good or bad for the firm. We are actually more interested in cash flows. Second, what do we mean by the long run? As a famous economist once remarked, in the long run, we're all dead! More to the point, this goal doesn't tell us what the appropriate trade-off is between current and future profits.

The goals we've listed here are all different, but they tend to fall into two classes. The first of these relates to profitability. The goals involving sales, market share, and cost control all relate, at least potentially, to different ways of earning or increasing profits. The goals in the second group, involving bankruptcy avoidance, stability, and safety, relate in some way to controlling risk. Unfortunately, these two types of goals are somewhat contradictory. The pursuit of profit normally involves some element of risk, so it isn't really possible to maximize both safety and profit. What we need, therefore, is a goal that encompasses both factors.

The Goal of Financial Management

The financial manager in a corporation makes decisions for the stockholders of the firm. So, instead of listing possible goals for the financial manager, we really need to answer a more fundamental question: From the stockholders' point of view, what is a good financial management decision?

If we assume that stockholders buy stock because they seek to gain financially, then the answer is obvious: Good decisions increase the value of the stock, and poor decisions decrease the value of the stock.

From our observations, it follows that the financial manager acts in the shareholders' best interests by making decisions that increase the value of the stock. The appropriate goal for the financial manager can thus be stated quite easily:

The goal of financial management is to maximize the current value per share of the existing stock.

The goal of maximizing the value of the stock avoids the problems associated with the different goals we listed earlier. There is no ambiguity in the criterion, and there is no short-run versus long-run issue. We explicitly mean that our goal is to maximize the *current* stock value.

If this goal seems a little strong or one-dimensional to you, keep in mind that the stockholders in a firm are residual owners. By this we mean that they are entitled only to what is left after employees, suppliers, and creditors (and everyone else with legitimate claims) are paid their due. If any of these groups go unpaid, the stockholders get nothing. So if the stockholders are winning in the sense that the leftover, residual portion is growing, it must be true that everyone else is winning also. In other words, managers should make decisions that they believe will achieve the highest firm value because by doing so shareholders will benefit the most.

Because the goal of financial management is to maximize the value of the stock, we need to learn how to identify investments and financing arrangements that favorably impact the value of the stock. This is precisely what we will be studying. In the previous section we emphasized the importance of cash flows in value creation. In fact, we could have defined *corporate finance* as the study of the relationship between business decisions, cash flows, and the value of the stock in the business.

A More General Goal

If our goal is to maximize the value of the stock, as stated in the preceding section, an obvious question comes up: What is the appropriate goal when the firm has no traded stock? Corporations are certainly not the only type of business; and the stock in many corporations rarely changes hands, so it's difficult to say what the value per share is at any particular time.

As long as we are considering for-profit businesses, only a slight modification is needed. The total value of the stock in a corporation is equal to the value of the owners' equity. Therefore, a more general way of stating our goal is:

> **Maximize the value of the existing owners' equity.**

With this in mind, we don't care whether the business is a proprietorship, a partnership, or a corporation. For each of these, good financial decisions increase the value of the owners' equity, and poor financial decisions decrease it. In fact, although we choose to focus on corporations in the chapters ahead, the principles we develop apply to all forms of business. Many of them even apply to the not-for-profit sector.

Business ethics are considered at business-ethics.com.

Finally, our goal does not imply that the financial manager should take illegal or unethical actions in the hope of increasing the value of the equity in the firm. What we mean is that the financial manager best serves the owners of the business by identifying goods and services that add value to the firm because they are desired and valued in the free marketplace.

1.5 THE AGENCY PROBLEM AND CONTROL OF THE CORPORATION

The processes, policies, laws, and institutions that direct a company's actions are all included under the broad category of corporate governance. Corporate governance can also include the relationships among various stakeholders including shareholders, management, employees, the board of directors, suppliers, and the community at large, among others. As such, corporate governance is a wide-ranging topic.

We've seen that the financial manager acts in the best interests of the stockholders by taking actions that increase the value of the firm and thus the stock. However, in large corporations, ownership can be spread over a huge number of stockholders. This dispersion of ownership arguably means that stockholders cannot directly control the firm and that management effectively controls the firm. In this case, will management necessarily act in the best interests of the stockholders? Put another way, might not management pursue its own goals at the stockholders' expense?

Corporate governance varies quite a bit around the world. For example, in most countries other than the U.S. and the U.K., publicly traded companies are usually controlled by one or more large shareholders. Moreover, in countries with limited shareholder protection, when compared to countries with strong shareholder protection like the U.S. and the U.K., large shareholders may have a greater opportunity to take advantage of minority shareholders. Research shows that a country's investor protection framework is important to understanding a firm's cash holdings and dividend payouts. For example, studies find that shareholders do not highly value cash holdings in firms in countries with low investor protection when compared to firms in the U.S., where investor protection is high.[1]

In the basic corporate governance setup, the shareholders elect the board of directors, who in turn appoint the top corporate managers, such as the CEO. The CEO is usually a member of the board of directors. One aspect of corporate governance that has received attention recently concerns the chair of a firm's board of directors. In a large number of U.S. corporations, the CEO and the board chair are the same person. An argument can be made that combining the CEO and board chair positions can contribute to poor corporate governance. When comparing corporate governance in the U.S. and the U.K., an edge is often given to the U.K., partly because over 90 percent of U.K. companies are chaired by outside directors rather than the CEO.[2] This is a contentious issue confronting many U.S. corporations. For example, in 2018, 31 percent of the S&P 500 companies had named an independent outsider as board chair, up from only 10 percent 11 years earlier.

You can find the changing composition of boards for S&P 500 companies at www.spencerstuart.com.

Agency Relationships

The relationship between stockholders and management is called an *agency relationship*. Such a relationship exists whenever someone (the principal) hires another (the agent) to represent his or her interests. For example, you might hire someone (an agent) to sell a car that you own while you are away at school. In all such relationships, there is a possibility of a conflict of interest between the principal and the agent. Such a conflict is called an agency problem.

Suppose you hire someone to sell your car and you agree to pay that person a flat fee when he or she sells the car. The agent's incentive in this case is to make the sale, not necessarily to get you the best price. If you offer a commission of, say, 10 percent of the sales price instead of a flat fee, then this problem might not exist. This example illustrates that the way in which an agent is compensated is one factor that affects agency problems.

Management Goals

To see how management and stockholder interests might differ, imagine that a firm is considering a new investment. The new investment is expected to favorably impact the share value, but it is also a relatively risky venture. The owners of the firm will wish to take the investment (because the stock value will rise), but management may not because there is the possibility that things will turn out badly and management jobs will be lost. If management does not take the investment, then the stockholders may lose a valuable opportunity. This is one example of an *agency cost*.

More generally, the term *agency costs* refers to the costs of the conflict of interest between stockholders and management. These costs can be indirect or direct. An indirect agency cost is a lost opportunity, such as the one we have just described.

[1] See, for example, Rafael La Porta, Florencio Lopez-de-Silanes, Andrei Shleifer, and Robert Vishny, "Investor Protection and Corporate Valuation," *Journal of Finance* 57, no. 3 (2002), pp. 1147–70; Lee Pinkowitz, René M. Stulz, and Rohan Williamson, "Cash Holdings, Dividend Policy, and Corporate Governance: A Cross-Country Analysis," *Journal of Applied Corporate Finance* 19, no. 1 (2007), pp. 81–87.

[2] Ralph Walking (moderator), "U.S. Corporate Governance: Accomplishments and Failings, a Discussion with Michael Jensen and Robert Monks," *Journal of Applied Corporate Finance* 20, no. 1 (Winter 2008), pp. 28–46.

Direct agency costs come in two forms. The first type is a corporate expenditure that benefits management but costs the stockholders. Perhaps the purchase of a luxurious and unneeded corporate jet would fall under this heading. The second type of direct agency cost is an expense that arises from the need to monitor management actions. Paying outside auditors to assess the accuracy of financial statement information could be one example.

It is sometimes argued that, left to themselves, managers would tend to maximize the amount of resources over which they have control or, more generally, corporate power or wealth. This goal could lead to an overemphasis on corporate size or growth. For example, cases in which management is accused of overpaying to buy up another company just to increase the size of the business, or to demonstrate corporate power, are not uncommon. Obviously, if overpayment does take place, such a purchase does not benefit the stockholders of the purchasing company.

Our discussion indicates that management may tend to overemphasize organizational survival to protect job security. Also, management may dislike outside interference, so independence and corporate self-sufficiency may be important goals.

Do Managers Act in the Stockholders' Interests?

Whether managers will, in fact, act in the best interests of stockholders depends on two factors. First, how closely are management goals aligned with stockholder goals? This question relates, at least in part, to the way managers are compensated. Second, can managers be replaced if they do not pursue stockholder goals? This issue relates to control of the firm. As we will discuss, there are a number of reasons to think that, even in the largest firms, management has a significant incentive to act in the interests of stockholders.

MANAGERIAL COMPENSATION   Management will frequently have a significant economic incentive to increase share value for two reasons. First, managerial compensation, particularly at the top, is usually tied to financial performance in general and often to share value in particular. For example, managers are frequently given the option to buy stock at a bargain price. The more the stock is worth, the more valuable is this option. In fact, options are often used to motivate employees of all types, not just top management. In 2018, the total compensation of Hock Tan, CEO of Broadcomm, was $103.2 million. His base salary and cash bonus was $4.8 million, with stock and options of $98.3 million. Although there are many critics of the high level of CEO compensation, from the stockholders' point of view, sensitivity of compensation to firm performance is usually more important.[3] By way of comparison, also in 2018, Floyd Mayweather made $285 million and George Clooney made about $239 million.

The second incentive managers have relates to job prospects. Better performers within the firm will tend to get promoted. More generally, managers who are successful in pursuing stockholder goals will be in greater demand in the labor market and thus command higher salaries.

CONTROL OF THE FIRM   Control of the firm ultimately rests with stockholders. They elect the board of directors, who, in turn, hire and fire management.

An important mechanism by which unhappy stockholders can replace existing management is called a *proxy fight*. A proxy is the authority to vote someone else's stock. A proxy fight develops when a group solicits proxies in order to replace the existing board and thereby replace existing management. In 2002, the proposed merger between HP and Compaq triggered one of the most widely followed, bitterly contested, and expensive proxy fights in history, with an estimated price tag of well over $100 million.

---

[3] This raises the issue of the level of top management pay and its relationship to other employees. According to recent research by the Economic Policy Institute, the average CEO compensation was 20 times greater than that of the average employee in 1965, 58 times greater in 1989, and 312 times greater in 2017. However, there is no precise formula that governs the gap between top management compensation and that of other employees.

Another way that management can be replaced is by takeover. Firms that are poorly managed are more attractive as acquisitions than well-managed firms because a greater profit potential exists. Thus, avoiding a takeover by another firm gives management another incentive to act in the stockholders' interests. Unhappy, prominent shareholders can suggest different business strategies to a firm's top management. This was the case in November 2018, when famed soup company Campbell's settled a proxy fight with hedge fund Third Point, which won two seats on the board of directors. Third Point agreed to withdraw its lawsuit against Campbell's and withdrew its bid for an additional three board seats.

Historically, proxy fights have been relatively rare. One reason is that the expenses in a proxy fight can become quite large. Further, outsiders waging a proxy fight must cover their own expenses, while the current directors use company finances to back their bid to retain board seats. Proxy fights appear to have become more civil. In recent years, about 50 percent of proxy fights went the distance, meaning they ultimately resulted in a shareholder vote. Before that, it was not uncommon for 70 percent or more of proxy fights to result in shareholder votes. Companies today appear to be more willing to work with activist shareholders, perhaps because both parties have become more concerned with the potential high costs of a long, bitter proxy fight.

CONCLUSION   The available theory and evidence are consistent with the view that stockholders control the firm and that stockholder wealth maximization is the relevant goal of the corporation. Even so, there will undoubtedly be times when management goals are pursued at the expense of the stockholders, at least temporarily.

Stakeholders

Our discussion thus far implies that management and stockholders are the only parties with an interest in the firm's decisions. This is an oversimplification, of course. Employees, customers, suppliers, and even the government all have a financial interest in the firm.

Taken together, these various groups are called stakeholders in the firm. In general, a stakeholder is someone other than a stockholder or creditor who potentially has a claim on the cash flows of the firm. Such groups will also attempt to exert control over the firm, perhaps to the detriment of the owners.

1.6 REGULATION

Until now, we have talked mostly about the actions that shareholders and boards of directors can take to reduce the conflicts of interest between themselves and management. We have not talked about regulation.[4] Until recently the main thrust of federal regulation has been to require that companies disclose all relevant information to investors and potential investors.[5] Disclosure of relevant information by corporations is intended to put all investors on a level information playing field and, thereby, to reduce conflicts of interest. More recent regulation has been aimed at corporate governance. Of course, regulation imposes costs on corporations, and any analysis of regulation must include both benefits and costs. Our nearby *Finance Matters* box discusses some of the costs exchange-listed companies face arising from corporate governance requirements.

---

[4] At this stage in our book, we focus on the regulation of disclosure of relevant information and corporate governance. We do not talk about many other regulators in financial markets such as the Federal Reserve Board. In Chapter 5, we discuss the nationally recognized statistical rating organizations (NRSROs) in the U.S., such as Fitch Ratings, Moody's, and Standard & Poor's. Their ratings are used by market participants to help value securities such as corporate bonds. Many critics of the rating agencies blame the 2007–2009 subprime credit crisis on weak regulatory oversight of these agencies.

[5] Here, we are speaking mostly of public companies and not private companies. You will learn more about this distinction in Chapter 19. If you can't wait, go to investopedia.com and search "public vs. private companies."

SARBANES-OXLEY

In response to corporate scandals at companies such as Enron, WorldCom, Tyco, and Adelphia, Congress enacted the Sarbanes-Oxley Act in 2002. The act, better known as "Sarbox," is intended to protect investors from corporate abuses. For example, one section of Sarbox prohibits personal loans from a company to its officers, such as the ones that were received by WorldCom CEO Bernie Ebbers.

One of the key sections of Sarbox took effect on November 15, 2004. Section 404 requires, among other things, that each company's annual report must have an assessment of the company's internal control structure and financial reporting. The auditor must then evaluate and attest to management's assessment of these issues.

Sarbox contains other key requirements. For example, the officers of the corporation must review and sign the annual reports. They must explicitly declare that the annual report does not contain any false statements or material omissions; that the financial statements fairly represent the financial results; and that they are responsible for all internal controls. Finally, the annual report must list any deficiencies in internal controls. In essence, Sarbox makes company management responsible for the accuracy of the company's financial statements.

Of course, as with any law, there are costs. Sarbox has increased the expense of corporate audits, sometimes dramatically. In 2004, the average compliance cost was $4.51 million. By 2007, however, the average compliance cost had fallen to $1.7 million. More recent numbers show that Sarbox costs are becoming more manageable. In 2012, 10 years after Sarbox was passed, it was reported that most small companies spent less than $100,000 on compliance annually, and a third of midsized companies spent $100,000 to $500,000. And there appear to be economies in Sarbox costs. By the fourth year of Sarbox compliance, a company is expected to spend between $100,000 and $500,000, regardless of size.

However, the added expense of Sarbox compliance has led to several unintended results. Over the seven-year period from 1998 to 2004, 484 firms delisted their shares from exchanges, or "went dark." Within the first two years alone of Sarbox, 370 companies delisted. Many of the companies that delisted stated the reason was to avoid the cost of compliance with Sarbox. And small companies are not the only ones to delist because of Sarbox. For example, German insurer Allianz applied to delist its shares from the New York Stock Exchange. The company estimated that canceling its listings outside of its home exchange of Frankfurt could save 5 million euros (about $6 million) per year.

A company that goes dark does not have to file quarterly or annual reports. Annual audits by independent auditors are not required, and executives do not have to certify the accuracy of the financial statements, so the savings can be huge. Of course, there are costs. Stock prices typically fall when a company announces it is going dark. Further, such companies will typically have limited access to capital markets and usually will have a higher interest cost on bank loans.

Sarbox has also probably affected the number of companies choosing to go public in the United States. For example, when Peach Holdings, based in Boynton Beach, Florida, decided to go public, it shunned the U.S. stock markets, instead choosing the London Stock Exchange's Alternative Investment Market (AIM). To go public in the United States, the firm would have paid a $100,000 fee, plus about $2 million to comply with Sarbox. Instead, the company spent only $500,000 on its AIM stock offering.

The Securities Act of 1933 and the Securities Exchange Act of 1934

The Securities Act of 1933 (the 1933 Act) and the Securities Exchange Act of 1934 (the 1934 Act) provide the basic regulatory framework in the United States for the public trading of securities.

The 1933 Act focuses on the issuing of new securities. Basically, the 1933 Act requires a corporation to file a registration statement with the Securities and Exchange Commission (SEC) that must be made available to every buyer of a new security. The intent of the registration statement is to provide potential stockholders with all the necessary information to make a reasonable decision. The 1934 Act extends the disclosure requirements of the 1933 Act to securities trading in markets after they have been issued. The 1934 Act establishes the SEC and covers a large number of issues including corporate reporting, tender offers, and insider trading. The 1934 Act requires corporations to file reports to the SEC on an annual basis (Form 10K), on a quarterly basis (Form 10Q), and on a monthly basis (Form 8K).

As mentioned, the 1934 Act deals with the important issue of insider trading. Illegal insider trading occurs when any person who has acquired nonpublic, special information (i.e., inside information) buys or sells securities based upon that information. One section of the 1934 Act deals with insiders such as directors, officers, and large shareholders, while another deals with any person who has acquired inside information. The intent of these sections of the 1934 Act is to prevent insiders or persons with inside information from taking unfair advantage of this information when trading with outsiders.

To illustrate, suppose you learned that the ABC firm was about to publicly announce that it had agreed to be acquired by another firm at a price significantly greater than its current price. This is an example of inside information. The 1934 Act prohibits you from buying ABC stock from shareholders who do not have this information. This prohibition would be especially strong if you were the CEO of the ABC firm. Other kinds of inside information could be knowledge of an initial dividend about to be paid, the discovery of a drug to cure cancer, or the default of a debt obligation.

A recent example of insider trading involved New York Congressman Christopher Collins, who was arrested on insider trading charges in August 2018. Collins was accused of tipping off his son and friends of a failed clinical trial for a drug. Collins was a member of the company's board and received the information before it was released to the public. His son and others sold the stock before the news was made public and the stock price subsequently crashed.

SUMMARY AND CONCLUSIONS

This chapter introduced you to some of the basic ideas in corporate finance:

1. Corporate finance has three main areas of concern:
   a. *Capital budgeting:* What long-term investments should the firm take?
   b. *Capital structure:* Where will the firm get the short-term and long-term financing to pay for its investments? Also, what mixture of debt and equity should it use to fund operations?
   c. *Working capital management:* How should the firm manage its everyday financial activities?

2. The goal of financial management in a for-profit business is to make decisions that increase the value of the stock, or, more generally, increase the value of the equity.

3. The corporate form of organization is superior to other forms when it comes to raising money and transferring ownership interests, but it has the significant disadvantage of double taxation.

4. There is the possibility of conflicts between stockholders and management in a large corporation. We called these conflicts *agency problems* and discussed how they might be controlled and reduced.

5. To create value, companies must generate more cash than they use.

6. Until recently, the main thrust of federal regulation has been to require companies to disclose all relevant information to investors and potential investors. More recent regulation has been aimed at corporate governance.

Of the topics we've discussed thus far, the most important is the goal of financial management: maximizing the value of the stock. Throughout the text we will be analyzing many different financial decisions, but we will always ask the same question: How does the decision under consideration affect the value of the stock?

CONCEPT QUESTIONS

1. **Forms of Business**   What are the three basic legal forms of organizing a business? What are the advantages and disadvantages of each? What business form do most start-up companies take? Why?

2. **Goal of Financial Management**   What goal should always motivate the actions of the firm's financial manager?

3. **Agency Problems**   Who owns a corporation? Describe the process whereby the owners control the firm's management. What is the main reason that an agency relationship exists in the corporate form of organization? In this context, what kinds of problems can arise?

4. **Not-for-Profit Firm Goals**   Suppose you were the financial manager of a not-for-profit business (a not-for-profit hospital, perhaps). What kinds of goals do you think would be appropriate?

5. **Goal of the Firm**   Evaluate the following statement: Managers should not focus on the current stock value because doing so will lead to an overemphasis on short-term profits at the expense of long-term profits.

6. **Ethics and Firm Goals**   Can our goal of maximizing the value of the stock conflict with other goals, such as avoiding unethical or illegal behavior? In particular, do you think subjects like customer and employee safety, the environment, and the general good of society fit in this framework, or are they essentially ignored? Try to think of some specific scenarios to illustrate your answer.

7. **International Firm Goal**   Would our goal of maximizing the value of the stock be different if we were thinking about financial management in a foreign country? Why or why not?

8. **Agency Problems**   Suppose you own stock in a company. The current price per share is $25. Another company has just announced that it wants to buy your company and will pay $35 per share to acquire all the outstanding stock. Your company's management immediately begins fighting off this hostile bid. Is management acting in the shareholders' best interests? Why or why not?

9. **Agency Problems and Corporate Ownership**   Corporate ownership varies around the world. Historically, individuals have owned the majority of shares in public corporations in the United States. In Germany and Japan, however, banks, other large financial institutions, and other companies own most of the stock in public corporations. Do you think agency problems are likely to be more or less severe in Germany and Japan than in the United States? Why? In recent years, large financial institutions such as mutual funds and pension funds have been becoming the dominant owners of stock in the United States, and these institutions are becoming more active in corporate affairs. What are the implications of this trend for agency problems and corporate control?

10. **Executive Compensation**   Critics have charged that compensation to top management in the United States is too high and should be cut back. For example, focusing on large corporations, Frank Bisignano, CEO of First Data, was one of the best-compensated CEOs in the United States in 2018, earning about $102 million. Are such amounts excessive? In answering, it might be helpful to recognize that superstar athletes such as LeBron James, top people in entertainment such as Dwayne "The Rock" Johnson and Kylie Jenner, and many others at the peak of their respective fields can earn at least as much, if not a great deal more.

WHAT'S ON THE WEB?

1. **Listing Requirements**   In order for a company's stock to be listed on an exchange, it must meet certain requirements. Find the complete listing requirements for the NYSE at www.nyse.com and NASDAQ at www.nasdaq.com. Which exchange has more stringent listing requirements? Why don't the exchanges have the same listing requirements?

2. **Business Formation**   As you may (or may not) know, many companies incorporate in Delaware for a variety of reasons. Visit BizFilings at www.bizfilings.com to find out why. Which state has the highest fee for incorporation? For an LLC? While at the site, look at the FAQ section regarding corporations and LLCs.

CLOSING CASE

EAST COAST YACHTS

In 1969, Tom Warren founded East Coast Yachts. The company's operations are located near Hilton Head Island, South Carolina, and the company is structured as a sole proprietorship. The company has manufactured custom midsize, high-performance yachts for clients, and its products have received high reviews for safety and reliability. The company's yachts have also recently received the highest award for customer satisfaction. The yachts are primarily purchased by wealthy individuals for pleasure use. Occasionally, a yacht is manufactured for purchase by a company for business purposes.

The custom yacht industry is fragmented, with a number of manufacturers. As with any industry, there are market leaders, but the diverse nature of the industry ensures that no manufacturer dominates the market. The competition in the market, as well as the product cost, ensures that attention to detail is a necessity. For instance, East Coast Yachts will spend 80 to 100 hours on hand-buffing the stainless steel stem-iron, which is the metal cap on the yacht's bow that conceivably could collide with a dock or another boat.

Several years ago, Tom retired from the day-to-day operations of the company and turned the operations of the company over to his daughter, Larissa. Because of the dramatic changes in the company, Larissa has approached you to help manage and direct the company's growth. Specifically, she has asked you to answer the following questions.

1. What are the advantages and disadvantages of changing the company organization from a sole proprietorship to an LLC?

2. What are the advantages and disadvantages of changing the company organization from a sole proprietorship to a corporation?

3. Ultimately, what action would you recommend the company undertake? Why?

Financial Statements and Cash Flow

In December 2017, the Tax Cuts and Jobs Act was enacted into law. The new law was a sweeping change to corporate taxes in the United States. For example, rather than depreciating an asset over time for tax purposes, companies are allowed to depreciate the entire purchase price in the first year. Another change was a limit to the tax deductibility of interest expense. However, possibly the biggest change was the switch from a graduated corporate income tax structure, with rates ranging from 15 percent to 39 percent, to a flat 21 percent corporate tax rate.

While the change in the corporate tax rate affects net income, there is a more important impact. Because taxes are a key consideration in making investment decisions, the change in the tax rate could lead to a significant change in corporate investment and financing decisions. Understanding why ultimately leads us to the main subject of this chapter, that all-important substance known as *cash flow*.

Please visit us at corecorporatefinance.blogspot.com for the latest developments in the world of corporate finance.

2.1 THE BALANCE SHEET

The balance sheet is an accountant's snapshot of the firm's accounting value on a particular date, as though the firm stood momentarily still. The balance sheet has two sides: On the left are the *assets* and on the right are the *liabilities* and *stockholders' equity.* The balance sheet states what the firm owns and how it is financed. The accounting definition that underlies the balance sheet and describes the balance is:

ExcelMaster
coverage online
www.mhhe.com/RossCore6e

Assets ≡ Liabilities + Stockholders' equity [2.1]

We have put a three-line equality in the balance equation to indicate that it must always hold, by definition. In fact, the stockholders' equity is *defined* to be the difference between the assets and the liabilities of the firm. In principle, equity is what the stockholders would have remaining after the firm discharged its obligations.

Table 2.1 gives the 2019 and 2020 balance sheets for the fictitious U.S. Composite Corporation. The assets in the balance sheet are listed in order by the length of time it normally would take an ongoing firm to convert them to cash. The asset side depends on the nature of the business and how management chooses to conduct it. Management must make decisions about cash versus marketable securities, credit versus cash sales, whether to make or buy commodities, whether to lease or purchase items, the types of business in which to engage, and so on.

The liabilities and stockholders' equity side reflects the types and proportions of financing, which depend on management's choice of capital structure, as between debt and equity

Two excellent sources for company financial information are finance.yahoo.com and money.cnn.com.

TABLE 2.1   The Balance Sheet of the U.S. Composite Corporation

U.S. COMPOSITE CORPORATION
Balance Sheet
2019 and 2020
(in $ millions)

Assets	2019	2020	Liabilities (Debt) and Stockholders' Equity	2019	2020
Current assets:			Current liabilities:		
Cash and equivalents	$ 157	$ 198	Accounts payable	$ 455	$ 490
Accounts receivable	270	294	Total current liabilities	$ 455	$ 490
Inventory	280	269	Long-term liabilities:		
Total current assets	$ 707	$ 761	Deferred taxes	$ 104	$ 113
Fixed assets:			Long-term debt*	458	471
Property, plant, and equipment	$1,274	$1,423	Total long-term liabilities	$ 562	$ 584
Less accumulated depreciation	460	550	Stockholders' equity:		
Net property, plant, and equipment	$ 814	$ 873	Preferred stock	$ 39	$ 39
Intangible assets and others	221	245	Common stock ($1 par value)	32	55
Total fixed assets	$1,035	$1,118	Capital surplus	327	347
			Accumulated retained earnings	347	390
			Less treasury stock†	20	26
			Total equity	$ 725	$ 805
Total assets	$1,742	$1,879	Total liabilities and stockholders' equity‡	$1,742	$1,879

* Long-term debt rose by $471 million − 458 million = $13 million. This is the difference between $86 million new debt and $73 million in retirement of old debt.

† Treasury stock rose by $6 million. This reflects the repurchase of $6 million of U.S. Composite's company stock.

‡ U.S. Composite reports $43 million in new equity. The company issued 23 million shares at a price of $1.87. The par value of common stock increased by $23 million, and capital surplus increased by $20 million.

and between current debt and long-term debt. The liabilities and the stockholders' equity are listed in the order in which they would typically be paid over time.

When analyzing a balance sheet, the financial manager should be aware of three concerns: accounting liquidity, debt versus equity, and value versus cost.

Accounting Liquidity

Accounting liquidity refers to the ease and quickness with which assets can be converted to cash. *Current assets* are the most liquid and include cash and those assets that will be turned into cash within a year from the date of the balance sheet. *Accounts receivable* are amounts not yet collected from customers for goods or services sold to them (after adjustment for potential bad debts). *Inventory* is composed of raw materials to be used in production, work in process, and finished goods. *Fixed assets* are the least liquid kind of assets. Tangible fixed assets include property, plant, and equipment. These assets do not convert to cash from normal business activity, and they are not usually used to pay expenses such as payroll.

Some fixed assets are not tangible. Intangible assets have no physical existence but can be very valuable. Examples of intangible assets are the value of a trademark or the value of a patent. The more liquid a firm's assets, the less likely the firm is to experience problems meeting short-term obligations. Thus, the probability that a firm will avoid financial distress

Annual and quarterly financial statements for most public U.S. corporations can be found in the EDGAR database at www.sec.gov.

can be linked to the firm's liquidity. Unfortunately, liquid assets frequently have lower rates of return than fixed assets; for example, cash generates no investment income. To the extent a firm invests in liquid assets, it sacrifices an opportunity to invest in more profitable investment vehicles.

Debt versus Equity

Liabilities are obligations of the firm that require a payout of cash within a stipulated time period. Many liabilities involve contractual obligations to repay a stated amount at some point, along with interest over a period. Thus, liabilities are debts and are frequently associated with nominally fixed cash burdens, called *debt service,* that put the firm in default of a contract if they are not paid. *Stockholders' equity* is a claim against the firm's assets that is residual and not fixed. In general terms, when the firm borrows, it gives the bondholders first claim on the firm's cash flow.[1] Bondholders can sue the firm if the firm defaults on its bond contracts. This may lead the firm to declare itself bankrupt. Stockholders' equity is the residual difference between assets and liabilities:

Assets − Liabilities ≡ Stockholders' equity	[2.2]

This is the stockholders' share in the firm stated in accounting terms. The accounting value of stockholders' equity increases when retained earnings are added. This occurs when the firm retains part of its earnings instead of paying them out as dividends.

Value versus Cost

The accounting value of a firm's assets is frequently referred to as the *carrying value* or the *book value* of the assets.[2] Under generally accepted accounting principles (GAAP), audited financial statements of firms in the United States carry the assets at cost.[3] Thus, the terms *carrying value* and *book value* are unfortunate. They specifically say "value," when in fact the accounting numbers are based on cost. This misleads many readers of financial statements to think that the firm's assets are recorded at true market values. *Market value* is the price at which willing buyers and sellers would trade the assets. It would be only a coincidence if accounting value and market value were the same. In fact, management's job is to create value for the firm that exceeds its cost.

Many people use the balance sheet, but the information each may wish to extract is not the same. A banker may look at a balance sheet for evidence of accounting liquidity and working capital. A supplier may also note the size of accounts payable and therefore the general promptness of payments. Many users of financial statements, including managers and investors, want to know the value of the firm, not its cost. This information is not found on the balance sheet. In fact, many of the true resources of the firm do not appear on the balance sheet: good management, proprietary assets, favorable economic conditions, and so on. Henceforth, whenever we speak of the value of an asset or the value of the firm, we will normally mean its market value. So, for example, when we say the goal of the financial manager is to increase the value of the stock, we mean the market value of the stock.

The home page for the Financial Accounting Standards Board (FASB) is www.fasb.org.

---

[1] Bondholders are investors in the firm's debt. They are creditors of the firm. In this discussion, the term *bondholder* means the same thing as *creditor.*

[2] Confusion often arises because many financial accounting terms have the same meaning. This presents a problem with jargon for the reader of financial statements. For example, the following terms usually refer to the same thing: assets minus liabilities, net worth, stockholders' equity, owners' equity, book equity, and equity capitalization.

[3] Generally, GAAP requires assets to be carried at the lower of cost or market value. In most instances, cost is lower than market value. However, in some cases when a fair market value can be readily determined, the assets have their value adjusted to the fair market value.

Market Value versus Book Value

The Cooney Corporation has fixed assets with a book value of $700 and an appraised market value of about $1,000. Net working capital is $400 on the books, but approximately $600 would be realized if all the current accounts were liquidated. Cooney has $500 in long-term debt, in terms of both book value and market value. What is the book value of the equity? What is the market value?

We can construct two simplified balance sheets, one in accounting (book value) terms and one in economic (market value) terms:

COONEY CORPORATION
Balance Sheets
Market Value versus Book Value

Assets			Liabilities and Shareholders' Equity		
	BOOK	**MARKET**		**BOOK**	**MARKET**
Net working capital	$ 400	$ 600	Long-term debt	$ 500	$ 500
Net fixed assets	700	1,000	Shareholders' equity	600	1,100
	$1,100	$1,600		$1,100	$1,600

In this example, shareholders' equity is actually worth almost twice as much as what is shown on the books. The distinction between book and market values is important precisely because book values can be so different from true economic value.

ExcelMaster
coverage online

www.mhhe.com/RossCore6e

2.2 THE INCOME STATEMENT

The **income statement** measures performance over a specific period of time, say, a year. The accounting definition of income is:

$$\text{Revenue} - \text{Expenses} \equiv \text{Income} \tag{2.3}$$

If the balance sheet is like a snapshot, the income statement is like a video recording of what the firm did between two snapshots. Table 2.2 gives the income statement for the U.S. Composite Corporation for 2020.

The income statement usually includes several sections. The operations section reports the firm's revenues and expenses from principal operations. One number of particular importance is earnings before interest and taxes (EBIT), which summarizes earnings before taxes and financing costs. Among other things, the nonoperating section of the income statement includes all financing costs, such as interest expense. Usually a second section reports as a separate item the amount of taxes levied on income. The last item on the income statement is the bottom line, or net income. Net income is frequently expressed per share of common stock, that is, earnings per share.

When analyzing an income statement, the financial manager should keep in mind GAAP, noncash items, time, and costs.

Generally Accepted Accounting Principles

Revenue is recognized on an income statement when the earnings process is virtually completed and an exchange of goods or services has occurred. Therefore, the unrealized appreciation from owning property will not be recognized as income. This provides a device for smoothing income by selling appreciated property at convenient times. For example, if the firm owns a tree farm that has doubled in value, then, in a year when its earnings from

TABLE 2.2   The Income Statement of the U.S. Composite Corporation

U. S. COMPOSITE CORPORATION Income Statement 2020 (in $ millions)	
Total operating revenues	$2,262
Cost of goods sold	1,715
Selling, general, and administrative expenses	327
Depreciation	90
Operating income	$ 130
Other income	29
Earnings before interest and taxes (EBIT)	$ 159
Interest expense	49
Pretax income	$ 110
Taxes	24
Current: $15	
Deferred: $9	
Net income	$ 86
Addition to retained earnings	$ 43
Dividends	43

Note: There are 29 million shares outstanding. Earnings per share and dividends per share can be calculated as follows:

$$\text{Earnings per share} = \frac{\text{Net income}}{\text{Total shares outstanding}}$$

$$= \frac{\$86}{29}$$

$$= \$2.97 \text{ per share}$$

$$\text{Dividends per share} = \frac{\text{Dividends}}{\text{Total shares outstanding}}$$

$$= \frac{\$43}{29}$$

$$= \$1.48 \text{ per share}$$

other businesses are down, it can raise overall earnings by selling some trees. The matching principle of GAAP dictates that revenues be matched with expenses. Thus, income is reported when it is earned, or accrued, even though no cash flow has necessarily occurred (for example, when goods are sold for credit, sales and profits are reported).

Noncash Items

The economic value of assets is intimately connected to their future incremental cash flows. However, cash flow does not appear on an income statement. There are several noncash items that are expenses against revenues but do not affect cash flow. The most important of these is *depreciation*. Depreciation reflects the accountant's estimate of the cost of equipment used up in the production process. Suppose an asset with a five-year life and no resale value is purchased for $1,000. According to accountants, the $1,000 cost must be expensed over the useful life of the asset. If straight-line depreciation is used, there will be five equal installments and $200 of depreciation expense will be incurred each year. From a finance perspective, the cost of the asset is the actual negative cash flow incurred when the asset is acquired (that is, $1,000, not the accountant's smoothed $200-per-year depreciation expense).

Another noncash expense is *deferred taxes.* Deferred taxes result from differences between accounting income and true taxable income.[4] Notice that the accounting tax

---

[4] One situation in which taxable income may be lower than accounting income is when the firm uses accelerated depreciation expense procedures for the IRS but uses straight-line procedures allowed by GAAP for reporting purposes.

shown on the income statement for the U.S. Composite Corporation is $24 million. It can be broken down as current taxes and deferred taxes. The current tax portion is actually sent to the tax authorities (for example, the Internal Revenue Service). The deferred tax portion is not. However, the theory is that if taxable income is less than accounting income in the current year, it will be more than accounting income later on. Consequently, the taxes that are not paid today will have to be paid in the future, and they represent a liability of the firm. This shows up on the balance sheet as deferred tax liability. From the cash flow perspective, though, deferred tax is not a cash outflow.

In practice, the difference between cash flows and accounting income can be quite dramatic, so it is important to understand the difference. For example, in February 2018, Spotify reported a loss of $461 million for the previous year. That sounds bad, but Spotify reported a *positive* cash flow of $133 million for the year!

Time and Costs

It is often useful to think of all of future time as having two distinct parts, the *short run* and the *long run*. The short run is that period of time in which certain equipment, resources, and commitments of the firm are fixed; but the time is long enough for the firm to vary its output by using more labor and raw materials. The short run is not a precise period of time that will be the same for all industries. However, all firms making decisions in the short run have some fixed costs, that is, costs that will not change because of fixed commitments. In real business activity, examples of fixed costs are bond interest, overhead, and property taxes. Costs that are not fixed are variable. Variable costs change as the output of the firm changes; some examples are raw materials and wages for laborers on the production line.

In the long run, all costs are variable. Financial accountants do not distinguish between variable costs and fixed costs. Instead, accounting costs usually fit into a classification that distinguishes product costs from period costs. Product costs are the total production costs incurred during a period—raw materials, direct labor, and manufacturing overhead—and are reported on the income statement as cost of goods sold. Both variable and fixed costs are included in product costs. Period costs are costs that are allocated to a time period; they are called *selling, general, and administrative expenses.* One period cost would be the company president's salary.

2.3 TAXES

ExcelMaster
coverage online

www.mhhe.com/RossCore6e

Taxes can be one of the largest cash outflows that a firm experiences. For example, for the fiscal year 2018, ExxonMobil's earnings before taxes were about $30.95 billion. Its tax bill, including all taxes paid worldwide, was a whopping $9.53 billion, or about 30.2 percent of its pretax earnings. The size of the tax bill is determined through the tax code, an often-amended set of rules. In this section, we examine corporate tax rates and how taxes are calculated.

If the various rules of taxation seem a little bizarre or convoluted to you, keep in mind that the tax code is the result of political, not economic, forces. As a result, there is no reason why it has to make economic sense.

Corporate Tax Rates

As we discussed in our chapter introduction, after the passage of the Tax Cuts and Jobs Act of 2017, the federal corporate tax rate in the United States became a flat 21 percent. However, tax rates on other forms of business such as proprietorships, partnerships, and LLCs did not become flat. To illustrate some important points about taxes for such entities, we take a look at personal tax rates in Table 2.3. As shown, in 2019, there are seven tax brackets, ranging from 10 percent to a high of 37 percent, down from 39.6 percent in 2017.

TABLE 2.3   Personal Tax Rates for 2019 (Unmarried Individuals)

Taxable Income	Tax Rate
$ 0–9,700	10%
9,700–39,475	12
39,475–84,200	22
84,200–160,725	24
160,725–204,100	32
204,100–510,300	35
510,300+	37

Average versus Marginal Tax Rates

In making financial decisions, it is frequently important to distinguish between average and marginal tax rates. Your average tax rate is your tax bill divided by your taxable income, in other words, the percentage of your income that goes to pay taxes. Your marginal tax rate is the tax you would pay (in percent) if you earned one more dollar. The percentage tax rates shown in Table 2.3 are all marginal rates. Put another way, the tax rates apply to the part of income in the indicated range only, not all income.

The difference between average and marginal tax rates can best be illustrated with a simple example. Suppose you are single and your personal taxable income is $100,000. What is your tax bill? Using Table 2.3, we can figure your tax bill as:

.10($ 9,700)	= $	970.00
.12($39,475 – 9,700)	=	3,573.00
.22($84,200 – 39,475)	=	9,839.50
.24($100,000 – 84,200)	=	3,792.00
		$18,174.50

Your total tax is thus $18,174.50.

In our example, what is the average tax rate? You had a taxable income of $100,000 and a tax bill of $18,174.50, so the average tax rate is $18,174.50/$100,000 = .1817, or 18.17%. What is the marginal tax rate? If you made one more dollar, the tax on that dollar would be 24 cents, so your marginal rate is 24 percent.

The IRS has a great website! (www.irs.gov)

EXAMPLE 2.2

Deep in the Heart of Taxes

Algernon, a small proprietorship owned by an unmarried individual, has a taxable income of $80,000. What is its tax bill? What is its average tax rate? Its marginal tax rate?

From Table 2.3, we see that the tax rate applied to the first $9,700 is 10 percent; the rate applied over that up to $39,475 is 12 percent, and the rate applied after that up to $80,000 is 22 percent. So Algernon must pay .10 × $9,700 + .12 × ($39,475 − 9,700) + .22 × ($80,000 − 39,475) = $13,458.50. The average tax rate is thus $13,458.50/$80,000 = .1682, or 16.82%. The marginal rate is 22 percent because Algernon's taxes would rise by 22 cents if it had another dollar in taxable income.

With a flat-rate tax, such as the U.S. federal corporate tax (as of 2019), there is only one tax rate, so the rate is the same for all income levels. With such a tax system, the marginal tax rate is always the same as the average tax rate.

WHAT IS WARREN BUFFETT'S TAX RATE?

In 2011, famed investor Warren Buffett, one of the wealthiest individuals in the world, created a stir when he publicly stated that his tax rate was lower than the tax rate paid by his secretary. The previous year, Buffett's gross income was about $63 million, on which he paid only a 15 percent tax rate. (Remember, this was before the Tax Cuts and Jobs Act of 2017.) His secretary (with a substantially lower income) had a 31 percent marginal tax rate. Also in 2011, when Republican presidential contender Mitt Romney released his income taxes, it was revealed that he, too, only paid an income tax rate of 15 percent on his $21 million annual income.

Why do Buffett's and Romney's tax rates appear so low? In 2011, under the U.S. tax system, wage income was taxed at a much higher rate than dividends and long-term capital gains. In fact, in 2011, in the highest tax bracket, wage income was taxed at 35 percent, while dividends and long-term capital gains were taxed at 15 percent. Most of Buffett's and Romney's annual income came from their investments, not wages, hence the 15 percent rates.

So do rich guys get all the (tax) breaks? Former U.S. President Barack Obama seemed to think so. In his 2012 State of the Union address, with Buffett's secretary Debbie Bosanek joining First Lady Michelle Obama in her box as a special guest, he called for the creation of a "Buffett tax." As he described it, such a tax would be an extra tax paid by very high-income individuals. Maybe President Obama was angry about the fact that he and the First Lady paid $1.7 million in federal taxes on their joint income of $5.5 million in 2009, implying an average tax rate of 31 percent.

Of course, you know that income received from dividends is already taxed. Dividends are paid from corporate income, which was taxed at 35 percent for larger dividend-paying companies. Effectively, any tax on dividends is double taxation on that money. The tax code realizes this. The lower tax rate on dividends lowers the double tax rate. The same thing is true for capital gains; taxes are paid on the money before the investment is made.

In Buffett's case, most of his wealth stems from his approximately 30 percent ownership of Berkshire Hathaway Corporation. Based on its 23,000 (no typo!) page tax return, Berkshire's 2014 corporate tax bill was $7.9 billion on income of $28.1 billion, a 28 percent average rate. Buffett's share of Berkshire's tax bill therefore amounts to something on the order of $2.37 billion! If we include Berkshire's corporate taxes, Buffett's average tax rate is more like $28 + 15 = 43$ percent.

To give another example, consider the situation described by N. Gregory Mankiw, the well-known economist and textbook author. Mankiw considers taking a writing job for $1,000. He figures that if he earns an 8 percent return and there are no taxes, he would be able to leave his children about $10,000 in 30 years when he passes on. However, because of federal, state, and Medicare taxes, he would only receive about $523 after taxes today. And because of corporate taxes and personal income taxes, his return on the same investment would only be about 4 percent, which will result in a balance of $1,700 in 30 years. When he dies, his account will be taxed using the marginal estate tax rate, which is as high as 55 percent. As a result, his children will receive only about $1,000, implying a tax rate of 90 percent!

It will normally be the marginal tax rate that is relevant for financial decision making. The reason is that any new cash flows will be taxed at that marginal rate. Because financial decisions usually involve new cash flows or changes in existing ones, this rate will tell us the marginal effect of a decision on our tax bill.

Before moving on, we should note that the tax rates we have discussed in this section relate to federal taxes only. Overall tax rates can be higher if state, local, and any other taxes are considered. Of course, income taxes can be more complex than we have discussed. For a discussion of some of the complexities of the tax code, see the nearby *Finance Matters* box.

For information about IFRS, check out the website www.ifrs.org.

2.4 NET WORKING CAPITAL

Net working capital is current assets minus current liabilities. Net working capital is positive when current assets are greater than current liabilities. This means the cash that will become available over the next 12 months will be greater than the cash that must be paid out. The net working capital of the U.S. Composite Corporation is $271 million in 2020 and $252 million in 2019:

ExcelMaster
coverage online
www.mhhe.com/RossCore6e

	Current assets ($ millions)	−	Current liabilities ($ millions)	=	Net working capital ($ millions)
2020	$761	−	$490	=	$271
2019	707	−	455	=	252

In addition to investing in fixed assets (i.e., capital spending), a firm can invest in net working capital. This is called the change in net working capital. The change in net working capital in 2020 is the difference between the net working capital in 2020 and 2019; that is, $271 million − 252 million = $19 million. The change in net working capital is usually positive in a growing firm.[5]

2.5 CASH FLOW OF THE FIRM

Perhaps the most important item that can be extracted from financial statements is the actual cash flow of the firm. There is an official accounting statement called the *statement of cash flows*. This statement helps to explain the change in accounting cash and equivalents, which for U.S. Composite is $41 million in 2020. (See Section 2.6.) Notice in Table 2.1 that cash and equivalents increase from $157 million in 2019 to $198 million in 2020. However, we will look at cash flow from a different perspective, the perspective of finance. In finance, the value of the firm is its ability to generate cash flow. (We will talk more about cash flow in Chapter 8.)

ExcelMaster
coverage online
www.mhhe.com/RossCore6e

The first point we should mention is that cash flow is not the same as net working capital. For example, increasing inventory requires using cash. Because both inventories and cash are current assets, this does not affect net working capital. In this case, an increase in a particular net working capital account, such as inventory, is associated with decreasing cash flow.

Just as we established that the value of a firm's assets is always equal to the sum of the value of the liabilities and the value of the equity, the cash flows generated from the firm's assets (that is, its operating activities), CF(A), must equal the cash flows it can distribute to the firm's creditors, CF(B), and equity investors, CF(S):

$$CF(A) = CF(B) + CF(S) \qquad [2.4]$$

The first step in determining the cash flow of the firm is to figure out the *operating cash flow*. As can be seen in Table 2.4, operating cash flow is the cash flow generated by business activities, including sales of goods and services. Operating cash flow reflects tax payments, but not financing, capital spending, or changes in net working capital.

---

[5] A firm's current liabilities sometimes include short-term interest-bearing debt, usually referred to as *notes payable*. However, financial analysts often distinguish between interest-bearing short-term debt and non-interest-bearing short-term debt (such as accounts payable). When this distinction is made, only non-interest-bearing short-term debt is usually included in the calculation of net working capital. This version of net working capital is called "operating" net working capital. The interest-bearing short-term debt is not forgotten but instead is included in cash flow from financing activities, and the interest is considered a return on capital.

TABLE 2.4

Cash Flow of the U.S.
Composite Corporation

U.S. COMPOSITE CORPORATION Cash Flow 2020 (in $ millions)	
Distributable Cash Flow of the Firm	
Operating cash flow	$234
(Earnings before interest and taxes plus depreciation minus taxes)	
Capital spending	−173
(Acquisitions of fixed assets minus sales of fixed assets)	
Additions to net working capital	− 19
Total	$ 42
Cash Flow to Investors in the Firm	
Debt	$ 36
(Interest plus retirement of debt minus long-term debt financing)	
Equity	6
(Dividends plus repurchase of equity minus new equity financing)	
Total	$ 42

	In $ Millions
Earnings before interest and taxes	$159
Depreciation	90
Current taxes	− 15
Operating cash flow	$234

Another important component of cash flow involves *changes in fixed assets.* For example, when U.S. Composite sold its power systems subsidiary in 2020, it generated $25 million in cash flow. The net change in fixed assets equals the acquisition of fixed assets minus sales of fixed assets. The result is the cash flow used for capital spending:

Acquisition of fixed assets	$198	
Sales of fixed assets	− 25	
Capital spending	$173	($149 + 24 = Increase in property, plant, and equipment + Increase in intangible assets)

We can also calculate capital spending as:

Capital spending = Ending net fixed assets − Beginning net fixed assets   [2.5]
+ Depreciation
= $1,118 − 1,035 + 90
= $173

Cash flows are also used for making investments in net working capital. In U.S. Composite Corporation in 2020, *additions to net working capital* are:

Additions to net working capital	$19

Note that this $19 is the change in net working capital we previously calculated.

Total cash flows generated by the firm's assets are the sum of:

Operating cash flow	$ 234
Capital spending	−173
Additions to net working capital	− 19
Total distributable cash flow of the firm	$ 42

The total outgoing cash flow of the firm can be separated into cash flow distributed to creditors and cash flow distributed to stockholders. The cash flow distributed to creditors represents a regrouping of the data in Table 2.4 and an explicit recording of interest expense. Creditors are paid an amount generally referred to as *debt service*. Debt service is interest payments plus repayments of principal (that is, retirement of debt).

An important source of cash flow is the sale of new debt. U.S. Composite's long-term debt increased by $13 million (the difference between $86 million in new debt and $73 million in retirement of old debt).[6] Thus, an increase in long-term debt is the net effect of new borrowing and repayment of maturing obligations plus interest expense.

Cash Flow to Creditors (in $ millions)	
Interest	$ 49
Retirement of debt	73
Debt service	122
Proceeds from long-term debt sales	−86
Total	$ 36

Cash flow distributed to creditors can also be calculated as:

$$\textbf{Cash flow paid to creditors} = \textbf{Interest paid} - \textbf{Net new borrowing} \qquad [\textbf{2.6}]$$
$$= \textbf{Interest paid} - (\textbf{Ending long-term debt}$$
$$- \textbf{Beginning long-term debt})$$
$$= \$49 - (471 - 458)$$
$$= \$36$$

Cash flow of the firm also is distributed to the stockholders. It is the net effect of paying dividends plus repurchasing outstanding shares of stock and issuing new shares of stock.

Cash Flow To Stockholders (in $ millions)	
Dividends	$ 43
Repurchase of stock	6
Cash to stockholders	49
Proceeds from new stock issue	−43
Total	$ 6

In general, cash flow to stockholders can be determined as:

$$\textbf{Cash flow to stockholders} = \textbf{Dividends paid} - \textbf{Net new equity raised} \qquad [\textbf{2.7}]$$
$$= \textbf{Dividends paid} - (\textbf{Stock sold}$$
$$- \textbf{Stock repurchased})$$

---

[6] New debt and the retirement of old debt are usually found in the "notes" to the balance sheet.

To determine stock sold, notice that the common stock and capital surplus accounts went up by a combined $23 + 20 = $43, which implies that the company sold $43 million worth of stock. Second, treasury stock went up by $6, indicating that the company bought back $6 million worth of stock. Net new equity is thus $43 − 6 = $37. Dividends paid were $43, so the cash flow to stockholders was:

$$\text{Cash flow to stockholders} = \$43 - (43 - 6) = \$6$$

which is what we previously calculated.

Some important observations can be drawn from our discussion of cash flow:

1. Several types of cash flow are relevant to understanding the financial situation of the firm. Operating cash flow, defined as earnings before interest and depreciation minus taxes, measures the cash generated from operations not counting capital spending or working capital requirements. It is usually positive; a firm is in trouble if operating cash flow is negative for a long time because the firm is not generating enough cash to pay operating costs. Total distributable cash flow of the firm includes adjustments for capital spending and additions to net working capital. It will frequently be negative. When a firm is growing at a rapid rate, the spending on inventory and fixed assets can be higher than cash flow from sales.

2. Net income is not cash flow. The net income of the U.S. Composite Corporation in 2020 was $86 million, whereas cash flow was $42 million. The two numbers are not usually the same. In determining the economic and financial condition of a firm, cash flow is more revealing.

A firm's total cash flow sometimes goes by a different name, free cash flow. Of course, there is no such thing as "free" cash (we wish!). Instead, the name refers to cash that the firm is free to distribute to creditors and stockholders because it is not needed for working capital or fixed asset investments. We will stick with "total distributable cash flow of the firm" as our label for this important concept because, in practice, there is some variation in exactly how free cash flow is computed; different users calculate it in different ways. Nonetheless, whenever you hear the phrase "free cash flow," you should understand that what is being discussed is cash flow from assets after adjusting for capital spending and changes in net working capital or something quite similar.

2.6 THE ACCOUNTING STATEMENT OF CASH FLOWS

ExcelMaster
coverage online
www.mhhe.com/RossCore6e

As previously mentioned, there is an official accounting statement called the statement of cash flows. This statement helps explain the change in accounting cash, which for U.S. Composite is $41 million in 2020. It is very useful in understanding financial cash flow.

The first step in determining the change in cash is to figure out cash flow from operating activities. This is the cash flow that results from the firm's normal activities producing and selling goods and services. The second step is to make an adjustment for cash flow from investing activities. The final step is to make an adjustment for cash flow from financing activities. Financing activities are the net payments to creditors and owners (excluding interest expense) made during the year.

The three components of the statement of cash flows are determined below.

Cash Flow from Operating Activities

To calculate cash flow from operating activities, we start with net income. Net income can be found on the income statement and is equal to $86 million. We now need to add back noncash expenses and adjust for changes in current assets and liabilities (other than cash and notes payable). The result is cash flow from operating activities.

U.S. COMPOSITE CORPORATION Cash Flow from Operating Activities 2020 (in $ millions)	
Net income	$ 86
Depreciation	90
Deferred taxes	9
Change in current assets and liabilities	
Accounts receivable	− 24
Inventories	11
Accounts payable	35
Cash flow from operating activities	**$207**

Cash Flow from Investing Activities

Cash flow from investing activities involves changes in capital assets: acquisition of fixed assets and sales of fixed assets (i.e., net capital expenditures). The result for U.S. Composite is below:

U.S. COMPOSITE CORPORATION Cash Flow from Investing Activities 2020 (in $ millions)	
Acquisition of fixed assets	−$198
Sales of fixed assets	25
Cash flow from investing activities	**−$173**

Cash Flow from Financing Activities

Cash flows to and from creditors and owners include changes in equity and debt.

U.S. COMPOSITE CORPORATION Cash Flow from Financing Activities 2020 (in $ millions)	
Retirement of long-term debt	−$73
Proceeds from long-term debt sales	86
Dividends	− 43
Repurchase of stock	− 6
Proceeds from new stock issue	43
Cash flow from financing activities	**$ 7**

The statement of cash flows is the addition of cash flows from operations, cash flows from investing activities, and cash flows from financing activities, and is produced in Table 2.5. When we add all the cash flows together, we get the change in cash on the balance sheet of $41 million.

There is a close relationship between the official accounting statement called the statement of cash flows and the total distributable cash flow of the firm used in finance. Going back to the previous section, you should note a slight conceptual problem here. Interest paid should really go under financing activities, but unfortunately that is not how the accounting is handled. The reason is that interest is deducted as an expense when net income is computed. As a consequence, a primary difference between the accounting cash flow and the cash flow of the firm (see Table 2.4) is interest expense.

U.S. COMPOSITE CORPORATION Statement of Cash Flows 2020 (in $ millions)	
Operations	
Net income	$ 86
Depreciation	90
Deferred taxes	9
Changes in current assets and liabilities	
Accounts receivable	− 24
Inventories	11
Accounts payable	35
Total cash flow from operations	$207
Investing activities	
Acquisition of fixed assets	−$198
Sales of fixed assets	25
Total cash flow from investing activities	−$173
Financing activities	
Retirement of long-term debt	−$ 73
Proceeds from long-term debt sales	86
Dividends	− 43
Repurchase of stock	− 6
Proceeds from new stock issue	43
Total cash flow from financing activities	$ 7
Change in cash (on the balance sheet)	$ 41

SUMMARY AND CONCLUSIONS

Besides introducing you to corporate accounting, the purpose of this chapter has been to teach you how to determine cash flow from the accounting statements of a typical company.

1. Cash flow is generated by the firm and paid to creditors and shareholders. It can be classified as:

   a. Cash flow from operations.

   b. Cash flow from changes in fixed assets.

   c. Cash flow from changes in working capital.

2. Calculations of cash flow are not difficult, but they require care and particular attention to detail in properly accounting for noncash expenses such as depreciation and deferred taxes. It is especially important that you do not confuse cash flow with changes in net working capital and net income.

CONCEPT QUESTIONS

1. **Liquidity** What does liquidity measure? Explain the trade-off a firm faces between high liquidity and low liquidity levels.

2. **Accounting and Cash Flows** Why is it that the revenue and cost figures shown on a standard income statement may not be representative of the actual cash inflows and outflows that occurred during the period?

3. **Accounting Statement of Cash Flows** Looking at the accounting statement of cash flows, what does the bottom-line number mean? How useful is this number for analyzing a company?

4. **Cash Flows** How do financial cash flows and the accounting statement of cash flows differ? Which is more useful when analyzing a company?

5. **Book Values versus Market Values** Under standard accounting rules, it is possible for a company's liabilities to exceed its assets. When this occurs, the owners' equity is negative. Can this happen with market values? Why or why not?

6. **Cash Flow from Assets** Suppose a company's cash flow from assets was negative for a particular period. Is this necessarily a good sign or a bad sign?

7. **Operating Cash Flow** Suppose a company's operating cash flow was negative for several years running. Is this necessarily a good sign or a bad sign?

8. **Net Working Capital and Capital Spending** Could a company's change in net working capital be negative in a given year? (*Hint:* Yes.) Explain how this might come about. What about net capital spending?

9. **Cash Flow to Stockholders and Creditors** Could a company's cash flow to stockholders be negative in a given year? (*Hint:* Yes.) Explain how this might come about. What about cash flow to creditors?

10. **Firm Values** In January 2018, GM announced that it was writing off $7 billion due to the loss in value of tax-deferred assets the company held. We would argue that GM's stockholders probably didn't suffer as a result of the reported loss. What do you think was the basis for our conclusion?

QUESTIONS AND PROBLEMS

1. **Building a Balance Sheet** Och, Inc., has current assets of $6,400, net fixed assets of $29,300, current liabilities of $5,100, and long-term debt of $11,800. What is the value of the shareholders' equity account for this firm? How much is net working capital?

2. **Building an Income Statement** Higgins, Inc., has sales of $517,400, costs of $296,300, depreciation expense of $42,300, interest expense of $20,400, and a tax rate of 21 percent. What is the net income for the firm? Suppose the company paid out $27,000 in cash dividends. What is the addition to retained earnings?

3. **Market Values and Book Values** Klingon Cruisers, Inc., purchased new cloaking machinery three years ago for $7.5 million. The machinery can be sold to the Romulans today for $5.6 million. Klingon's current balance sheet shows net fixed assets of $3.9 million, current liabilities of $1.125 million, and net working capital of $340,000. If all the current accounts were liquidated today, the company would receive $380,000 cash. What is the book value of Klingon's total assets today? What is the sum of the market value of NWC and market value of assets?

4. **Calculating Taxes** Timmy Tappan is single and had $189,000 in taxable income. Using the rates from Table 2.3 in the chapter, calculate his income taxes. What is the average tax rate? What is the marginal tax rate?

5. **Calculating OCF** Masters, Inc., has sales of $32,400, costs of $14,300, depreciation expense of $2,200, and interest expense of $1,160. If the tax rate is 23 percent, what is the operating cash flow, or OCF?

6. **Calculating Net Capital Spending** Bantam Egg's 2019 balance sheet showed net fixed assets of $3.82 million, and the 2020 balance sheet showed net fixed assets of $4.63 million. The company's 2020 income statement showed a depreciation expense of $405,000. What was the company's net capital spending for 2020?

7. **Building a Balance Sheet** The following table presents the long-term liabilities and stockholders' equity of Information Control Corp. one year ago:

Long-term debt	$29,600,000
Preferred stock	1,680,000
Common stock ($1 par value)	7,120,000
Capital surplus	32,800,000
Accumulated retained earnings	60,200,000

Basic
(Questions 1–10)

During the past year, the company issued 3.2 million shares of new stock at a total price of $20.8 million, and issued $7.6 million in new long-term debt. The company generated $12.24 million in net income and paid $2.48 million in dividends. Construct the current balance sheet reflecting the changes that occurred on the company's balance sheet during the year.

8. **Cash Flow to Creditors** The 2019 balance sheet of Dyrdek's Skate Shop, Inc., showed long-term debt of $2.16 million, and the 2020 balance sheet showed long-term debt of $2.28 million. The 2020 income statement showed an interest expense of $168,000. What was the firm's cash flow to creditors during 2020?

9. **Cash Flow to Stockholders** The 2019 balance sheet of Dyrdek's Skate Shop, Inc., showed $486,000 in the common stock account and $5.04 million in the additional paid-in surplus account. The 2020 balance sheet showed $536,000 and $5.56 million in the same two accounts, respectively. If the company paid out $245,000 in cash dividends during 2020, what was the cash flow to stockholders for the year?

10. **Calculating Total Cash Flows** Given the information for Dyrdek's Skate Shop, Inc., in the previous two problems, suppose you also know that the firm's net capital spending for 2020 was $575,000, and that the firm reduced its net working capital investment by $59,000. What was the firm's 2020 operating cash flow, or OCF?

Intermediate
(Questions 11–24)

11. **Cash Flows** Ritter Corporation's accountants prepared the following financial statements for year-end.

RITTER CORPORATION Income Statement 2020	
Revenue	$1,282
Expenses	945
Depreciation	92
EBT	$ 245
Tax	54
Net income	$ 191
Dividends	$ 58

RITTER CORPORATION Balance Sheets December 31		
	2019	2020
Assets		
Cash	$ 97	$ 112
Other current assets	304	318
Net fixed assets	828	988
Total assets	$1,229	$1,418
Liabilities and Equity		
Accounts payable	$ 354	$ 362
Long-term debt	0	48
Stockholders' equity	875	1,008
Total liabilities and equity	$1,229	$1,418

a. Explain the change in cash during the year 2020.

b. Determine the change in net working capital in 2020.

c. Determine the cash flow generated by the firm's assets during the year 2020.

12. **Cash Flow Identity**   Fizer, Inc., reported the following financial statements for the last two years. Construct the cash flow identity for the company. Explain what each number means.

FIZER, INC. 2020 Income Statement	
Sales	$632,790
Cost of goods sold	296,470
Selling & administrative	138,065
Depreciation	59,862
EBIT	$138,393
Interest	20,952
EBT	$117,441
Taxes	24,310
Net income	$ 93,131
Dividends	25,200
Addition to retained earnings	$ 67,931

FIZER, INC. Balance Sheet as of December 31, 2019			
Cash	$ 14,672	Accounts payable	$ 26,408
Accounts receivable	15,164	Long-term debt	148,700
Inventory	21,487	Owners' equity	249,975
Current assets	$ 51,323	Total liabilities and	
Net fixed assets	$373,760	owners' equity	$425,083
Total assets	$425,083		

FIZER, INC. Balance Sheet as of December 31, 2020			
Cash	$ 16,329	Accounts payable	$ 33,831
Accounts receivable	17,574	Long-term debt	$152,400
Inventory	25,753	Owners' equity	$321,906
Current assets	$ 59,656	Total liabilities and	
Net fixed assets	$448,481	owners' equity	$508,137
Total assets	$508,137		

13. **Cash Flow Identity**   The Stancil Corporation provided the following information:

Proceeds from long-term borrowing	$19,800
Proceeds from the sale of common stock	3,240
Purchases of fixed assets	23,100
Purchases of inventories	3,380
Payment of dividends	8,520
Payment of interest	2,460

What was the company's operating cash flow?

14. Building an Income Statement During the year, the Senbet Discount Tire Company had gross sales of $529,900. The company's cost of goods sold and selling expenses were $174,800 and $102,200, respectively. The company also had debt of $480,000, which carried an interest rate of 6 percent. Depreciation was $60,900. The tax rate was 24 percent.

     a. What was the company's net income?

     b. What was the company's operating cash flow?

15. Calculating Total Cash Flows Schwert Corp. shows the following information on its 2020 income statement: sales = $315,000; costs = $208,600; other expenses = $8,600; depreciation expense = $21,400; interest expense = $15,700; taxes = $12,747; dividends = $13,600. In addition, you're told that the firm issued $8,400 in new equity during 2020 and redeemed $11,900 in outstanding long-term debt.

     a. What was the 2020 operating cash flow?

     b. What was the 2020 cash flow to creditors?

     c. What was the 2020 cash flow to stockholders?

     d. If net fixed assets increased by $28,600 during the year, what was the addition to net working capital?

16. Using Income Statements Given the following information for O'Hara Marine Co., calculate the depreciation expense: sales = $69,480; costs = $34,320; addition to retained earnings = $9,420; dividends paid = $6,240; interest expense = $2,460; tax rate = 21 percent.

 17. Preparing a Balance Sheet Prepare a 2020 balance sheet for Jarrow Corp. based on the following information: cash = $117,600; patents and copyrights = $579,000; accounts payable = $300,300; accounts receivable = $165,900; tangible net fixed assets = $2,387,000; inventory = $269,500; notes payable = $118,000; accumulated retained earnings = $1,458,800; long-term debt = $1,389,500.

18. Residual Claims Prescott, Inc., is obligated to pay its creditors $13,500 very soon.

     a. What is the market value of the shareholders' equity if assets have a market value of $14,900?

     b. What if assets equal $10,700?

19. Net Income and OCF During 2020, Raines Umbrella Corp. had sales of $890,000. Cost of goods sold, administrative and selling expenses, and depreciation expenses were $604,000, $151,000, and $93,000, respectively. In addition, the company had an interest expense of $74,000 and a tax rate of 21 percent. (Assume that interest is fully deductible.)

     a. What was the company's net income for 2020?

     b. What was its operating cash flow?

     c. Explain your results in (a) and (b).

20. Accounting Values versus Cash Flows In the previous problem, suppose Raines Umbrella Corp. paid out $95,000 in cash dividends. Is this possible? If net capital spending and the change in net working capital were both zero, and if no new stock was issued during the year, what was the change in the firm's long-term debt account?

21. Calculating Cash Flows Stackhouse Industries had the following operating results for 2020: sales = $53,520; cost of goods sold = $36,800; depreciation expense = $5,560; interest expense = $1,260; dividends paid = $2,730. At the beginning of the year, net fixed assets were $33,020, current assets were $8,210, and current liabilities were $5,490. At the end of the year, net fixed assets were $42,730, current assets were $9,260, and current liabilities were $5,780. The tax rate was 25 percent.

     a. What was net income for 2020?

     b. What was the operating cash flow for 2020?

     c. What was the cash flow from assets for 2020? Is this possible? Explain.

d. If no new debt was issued during the year, what was the cash flow to creditors? What was the cash flow to stockholders? Explain and interpret the positive and negative signs of your answers in (a) through (d).

22. Calculating Cash Flows Consider the following abbreviated financial statements for Weston Enterprises:

WESTON ENTERPRISES 2019 and 2020 Partial Balance Sheets					
Assets			**Liabilities and Owners' Equity**		
	2019	2020		2019	2020
Current assets	$1,173	$1,260	Current liabilities	$ 523	$ 570
Net fixed assets	5,702	6,019	Long-term debt	3,168	3,399

WESTON ENTERPRISES 2020 Income Statement	
Sales	$17,259
Costs	5,113
Depreciation	1,472
Interest paid	618

a. What was owners' equity for 2019 and 2020?

b. What was the change in net working capital for 2020?

c. In 2020, the company purchased $3,050 in new fixed assets. How much in fixed assets did the company sell? What was the cash flow from assets for the year? The tax rate is 25 percent.

d. During 2020, the company raised $697 in new long-term debt. How much long-term debt must the company have paid off during the year? What was the cash flow to creditors?

Use the following information for Ingersoll, Inc., for Problems 23 and 24 (assume the tax rate is 25 percent):

	2019	2020
Sales	$ 48,892	$ 51,932
Depreciation	7,024	7,030
Cost of goods sold	20,628	23,277
Other expenses	3,986	3,331
Interest	2,518	3,770
Cash	25,636	26,227
Accounts receivable	33,940	38,237
Long-term debt	85,860	100,171
Net fixed assets	215,940	220,130
Accounts payable	32,819	30,767
Inventory	60,344	62,015
Dividends	5,900	8,600

23. Financial Statements Draw up an income statement and balance sheet for this company for 2019 and 2020.

24. Calculating Cash Flow For 2020, calculate the cash flow from assets, cash flow to creditors, and cash flow to stockholders.

25. Cash Flows You are researching Time Manufacturing and have found the following accounting statement of cash flows for the most recent year. You also know that the company paid $185 million in current taxes and had an interest expense of $96 million. Use the accounting statement of cash flows to construct the financial statement of cash flows.

Challenge
(Questions 25–26)

TIME MANUFACTURING	
Statement of Cash Flows	
(in $ millions)	
Operations	
Net income	$321
Depreciation	177
Deferred taxes	34
Changes in current assets and liabilities	
Accounts receivable	− 52
Inventories	41
Accounts payable	33
Accrued expenses	− 17
Other	4
Total cash flow from operations	$541
Investing activities	
Acquisition of fixed assets	−$332
Sale of fixed assets	42
Total cash flow from investing activities	−$290
Financing activities	
Retirement of long-term debt	−$195
Proceeds from long-term debt sales	105
Dividends	− 158
Repurchase of stock	− 26
Proceeds from new stock issue	50
Total cash flow from financing activities	−$224
Change in cash (on balance sheet)	$ 27

26. **Net Fixed Assets and Depreciation** On the balance sheet, the net fixed assets (NFA) account is equal to the gross fixed assets (FA) account, which records the acquisition cost of fixed assets, minus the accumulated depreciation (AD) account, which records the total depreciation taken by the firm against its fixed assets. Using the fact that NFA = FA − AD, show that the expression given in the chapter for net capital spending, $NFA_{end} - NFA_{beg} + D$ (where D is the depreciation expense during the year), is equivalent to $FA_{end} - FA_{beg}$.

WHAT'S ON THE WEB?

1. **Change in Net Working Capital** Find the most recent abbreviated balance sheets for General Dynamics at finance.yahoo.com. Enter the ticker symbol "GD" and follow the "Balance Sheet" link. Using the two most recent balance sheets, calculate the change in net working capital. What does this number mean?

2. **Book Values versus Market Values** The home page for The Coca-Cola Company can be found at www.coca-cola.com. Locate the most recent annual report, which contains a balance sheet for the company. What is the book value of equity for Coca-Cola? The market value of a company is the number of shares of stock outstanding times the price per share. This information can be found at finance.yahoo.com using the ticker symbol for Coca-Cola (KO). What is the market value of equity? Which number is more relevant for shareholders?

3. **Cash Flows to Stockholders and Creditors** Cooper Tire and Rubber Company provides financial information for investors on its website at www.coopertire.com. Follow the "Investors" link and find the most recent annual report. Using the consolidated statements of cash flows, calculate the cash flow to stockholders and the cash flow to creditors.

EXCEL MASTER IT! PROBLEM

Using Excel to find the marginal tax rate can be accomplished using the VLOOKUP function. However, calculating the total tax bill is a little more difficult. Below we have shown a copy of the IRS tax table for an individual for 2019 (the income thresholds are indexed to inflation and change through time):

ExcelMaster
coverage online
www.mhhe.com/RossCore6e

If Taxable Income Is Over:	But Not Over:	The Tax Is:
$ 0	$ 9,700	10% of the amount over $0
9,700	39,475	$970 plus 12% of the amount over $9,700
39,475	84,200	$4,543 plus 22% of the amount over $39,475
84,200	160,725	$14,382.50 plus 24% of the amount over $84,200
160,725	204,100	$32,748.50 plus 32% of the amount over $160,725
204,100	510,300	$46,628.50 plus 35% of the amount over $204,100
510,300		$153,789.50 plus 37% of the amount over $510,300

In reading this table, the marginal tax rate for taxable income less than $9,700 is 10 percent. If the taxable income is between $9,700 and $39,475, the tax bill is $970 plus the marginal taxes. The marginal taxes are calculated as the taxable income minus $9,700 times the marginal tax rate of 12 percent.

Below, we have the tax table for a married couple filing jointly:

If Taxable Income Is Greater Than Or Equal To:	But Less Than:	The Tax Rate Is:
$ 0	$ 19,400	10%
19,400	78,950	12
78,950	168,400	22
168,400	321,450	24
321,450	408,200	32
408,200	612,350	35
612,350		37

a. Create a tax table in Excel for a married couple similar to the individual tax table shown above. Your spreadsheet should then calculate the marginal tax rate, the average tax rate, and the tax bill for any level of taxable income input by a user.

b. For a taxable income of $355,000, what is the marginal tax rate?

c. For a taxable income of $355,000, what is the total tax bill?

d. For a taxable income of $355,000, what is the average tax rate?

CASH FLOWS AT EAST COAST YACHTS

Because of the dramatic growth at East Coast Yachts, Larissa decided that the company should be reorganized as a corporation (see our Chapter 1 Closing Case for more detail). Time has passed and, today, the company is publicly traded under the ticker symbol "ECY".

Dan Ervin was recently hired by East Coast Yachts to assist the company with its short-term financial planning and also to evaluate the company's financial performance. Dan graduated from college five years ago with a finance degree, and he has been employed in the treasury department of a Fortune 500 company since then.

The company's past growth has been somewhat hectic, in part due to poor planning. In anticipation of future growth, Larissa has asked Dan to analyze the company's cash flows. The company's financial statements are prepared by an outside auditor. Nearby you will find the most recent income statement and the balance sheets for the past two years.

EAST COAST YACHTS 2020 Income Statement	
Sales	$550,424,000
Cost of goods sold	397,185,000
Selling, general, and administrative	65,778,000
Depreciation	17,963,000
EBIT	$ 69,498,000
Interest expense	9,900,000
EBT	$ 59,598,000
Taxes (25%)	14,899,500
Net income	$ 44,698,500
Dividends	$ 19,374,500
Retained earnings	25,234,000

Larissa has also provided the following information. During the year, the company raised $36 million in new long-term debt and retired $20.3 million in long-term debt. The company also sold $21.8 million in new stock and repurchased $32.08 million. The company purchased $53.5 million in fixed assets and sold $5.046 million in fixed assets.

EAST COAST YACHTS Balance Sheet					
	2019	2020		2019	2020
Current assets			Current liabilities		
Cash and equivalents	$ 9,580,100	$10,107,000	Accounts payable	$38,133,900	$40,161,400
Accounts receivable	17,032,300	16,813,300	Accrued expenses	4,875,600	5,723,700
Inventories	15,382,000	18,135,700	Total current liabilities	$43,009,500	$45,885,100
Other	987,900	1,054,900			
Total current assets	$42,982,300	$46,110,900			

(Continued)

EAST COAST YACHTS Balance Sheet					
			Long-term debt	$136,674,000	$152,374,000
Fixed assets			Total long-term liabilities	$136,674,000	$152,374,000
Property, plant, and equipment	$364,255,000	$412,032,000			
Less accumulated depreciation	(84,489,000)	(102,452,000)			
Net property, plant, and equipment	$279,766,000	$309,580,000	Stockholders' equity		
Intangible assets and others	6,095,000	6,772,000	Preferred stock	$ 1,773,000	$ 1,773,000
Total fixed assets	$285,861,000	$316,352,000	Common stock	26,730,000	31,802,000
			Capital surplus	10,620,000	27,348,000
			Accumulated retained earnings	120,728,800	146,052,800
			Less treasury stock	(10,692,000)	(42,772,000)
			Total equity	$149,159,800	$164,203,800
Total assets	$328,843,300	$362,462,900	Total liabilities and shareholders' equity	$328,843,300	$362,462,900

Larissa has asked Dan to prepare the financial statement of cash flows and the accounting statement of cash flows. She has also asked you to answer the following questions:

1. How would you describe East Coast Yachts' cash flows?

2. Which cash flows statement more accurately describes the cash flows at the company?

3. In light of your previous answers, comment on Larissa's expansion plans.

3

Financial Statements Analysis and Financial Models

OPENING CASE

The price of a share of common stock in BJ's Wholesale Club closed at about $23 on January 2, 2019. At that price, BJ's had a price-earnings (PE) ratio of 20. That is, investors were willing to pay $20 for every dollar in income earned by BJ's. At the same time, investors were willing to pay $5, $11, and $164 for each dollar earned by Ford, Pfizer, and Cisco Systems, respectively. At the other extreme were Tesla and Qualcomm. Each had negative earnings for the previous year, yet Tesla was priced at about $310 per share and Qualcomm at about $57 per share. Because they had negative earnings, their PE ratios would have been negative, so they were not reported. At the time, the typical stock in the S&P 500 Index of large-company stocks was trading at a PE of about 19, or about 19 times earnings, as they say on Wall Street.

Price-earnings comparisons are examples of the use of financial ratios. As we will see in this chapter, there are a wide variety of financial ratios, all designed to summarize specific aspects of a firm's financial position. In addition to discussing how to analyze financial statements and compute financial ratios, we will have quite a bit to say about who uses this information and why.

Please visit us at corecorporatefinance.blogspot.com for the latest developments in the world of corporate finance.

3.1 FINANCIAL STATEMENTS ANALYSIS

ExcelMaster
coverage online
www.mhhe.com/RossCore6e

In Chapter 2, we discussed some of the essential concepts of financial statements and cash flows. This chapter continues where our earlier discussion left off. Our goal here is to expand your understanding of the uses (and abuses) of financial statement information.

A good working knowledge of financial statements is desirable because such statements, and numbers derived from those statements, are the primary means of communicating financial information both within the firm and outside the firm. In short, much of the language of business finance is rooted in the ideas we discuss in this chapter.

Clearly, one important goal of the accountant is to report financial information to the user in a form useful for decision making. Ironically, the information frequently does not come to the user in such a form. In other words, financial statements don't come with a user's guide. This chapter is a first step in filling this gap.

Standardizing Statements

One obvious thing we might want to do with a company's financial statements is to compare them to those of other, similar companies. We would immediately have a problem, however. It's almost impossible to directly compare the financial statements for two companies because of differences in size.

For example, Tesla and GM are obviously rivals in the auto market, but GM is larger, so it is difficult to compare them directly. For that matter, it's difficult even to compare financial statements from different points in time for the same company if the company's size has changed.

The size problem is compounded if we try to compare GM and, say, Toyota. If Toyota's financial statements are denominated in yen, then we have size *and* currency differences.

To start making comparisons, one obvious thing we might try to do is to somehow standardize the financial statements. One common and useful way of doing this is to work with percentages instead of total dollars. The resulting financial statements are called common-size statements. We consider these next.

Common-Size Balance Sheets

For easy reference, Prufrock Corporation's 2019 and 2020 balance sheets are provided in Table 3.1. Using these, we construct common-size balance sheets by expressing each item as a percentage of total assets. Prufrock's 2019 and 2020 common-size balance sheets are shown in Table 3.2.

Notice that some of the totals don't check exactly because of rounding. Also notice that the total change has to be zero because the beginning and ending numbers must add up to 100 percent.

In this form, financial statements are relatively easy to read and compare. For example, just looking at the two balance sheets for Prufrock, we see that current assets were 19.7 percent of total assets in 2020, up from 19.0 percent in 2019. Current liabilities declined from 16.1 percent to 15.1 percent of total liabilities and equity over that same time. Similarly, total equity rose from 68.2 percent of total liabilities and equity to 72.1 percent.

Overall, Prufrock's liquidity, as measured by current assets compared to current liabilities, increased over the year. Simultaneously, Prufrock's indebtedness diminished as a percentage of total assets. We might be tempted to conclude that the balance sheet has grown "stronger."

TABLE 3.1

PRUFROCK CORPORATION Balance Sheets as of December 31, 2019 and 2020 (in $ millions)		
Assets	**2019**	**2020**
Current assets		
Cash	$ 84	$ 98
Accounts receivable	165	188
Inventory	393	422
Total	$ 642	$ 708
Fixed assets		
Net plant and equipment	$2,731	$2,880
Total assets	$3,373	$3,588
Liabilities and Owners' Equity		
Current liabilities		
Accounts payable	$ 312	$ 344
Notes payable	231	196
Total	$ 543	$ 540
Long-term debt	$ 531	$ 460
Owners' equity		
Common stock and paid-in surplus	$ 500	$ 520
Retained earnings	1,799	2,068
Total	$2,299	$2,588
Total liabilities and owners' equity	$3,373	$3,588

TABLE 3.2

PRUFROCK CORPORATION Common-Size Balance Sheets December 31, 2019 and 2020			
Assets	2019	2020	Change
Current assets			
Cash	2.5%	2.7%	+ .2%
Accounts receivable	4.9	5.2	+ .3
Inventory	11.7	11.8	+ .1
Total	19.0	19.7	+ .7
Fixed assets			
Net plant and equipment	81.0	80.3	− .7
Total assets	100.0%	100.0%	.0%
Liabilities and Owners' Equity			
Current liabilities			
Accounts payable	9.2%	9.6%	+ .3%
Notes payable	6.8	5.5	−1.4
Total	16.1	15.1	−1.0
Long-term debt	15.7	12.8	−2.9
Owners' equity			
Common stock and paid-in surplus	14.8	14.5	− .3
Retained earnings	53.3	57.6	+4.3
Total	68.2	72.1	+4.0
Total liabilities and owners' equity	100.0%	100.0%	.0%

TABLE 3.3

Measures of Earnings

Investors and analysts look closely at the income statement for clues on how well a company has performed during a particular year. Here are some commonly used measures of earnings (numbers in millions).

Net Income The so-called bottom line, defined as total revenue minus total expenses. Net income for Prufrock in the latest period is $418 million. Net income reflects differences in a firm's capital structure and taxes as well as operating income. Interest expense and taxes are subtracted from operating income in computing net income. Shareholders look closely at net income because dividend payout and retained earnings are closely linked to net income.

EPS Net income divided by the number of shares outstanding. It expresses net income on a per-share basis. For Prufrock, the EPS = (Net income)/(Shares outstanding) = $418/33 = $12.67.

EBIT Earnings before interest expense and taxes. EBIT is usually called "income from operations" on the income statement and is income before unusual items, discontinued operations, or extraordinary items. To calculate EBIT, operating expenses are subtracted from total operations revenues. Analysts like EBIT because it abstracts from differences in earnings from a firm's capital structure (interest expense) and taxes. For Prufrock, EBIT is $691 million.

EBITDA Earnings before interest expense, taxes, depreciation, and amortization. EBITDA = EBIT + depreciation and amortization. Here amortization refers to a noncash expense similar to depreciation except it applies to an intangible asset (such as a patent), rather than a tangible asset (such as a machine). The word *amortization* here does not refer to the payment of debt. There is no amortization in Prufrock's income statement. For Prufrock, EBITDA = $691 + 276 = $967 million. Analysts like to use EBITDA because it adds back two noncash items (depreciation and amortization) to EBIT and thus is a better measure of before-tax operating cash flow.

Sometimes these measures of earnings are preceded by the letters LTM, meaning the last twelve months. For example, LTM EPS is the last 12 months of EPS and LTM EBITDA is the last 12 months of EBITDA. At other times, the letters TTM are used, meaning trailing 12 months. Needless to say, LTM is the same as TTM.

Common-Size Income Statements

Table 3.3 describes some commonly used measures of earnings. A useful way of standardizing the income statement shown in Table 3.4 is to express each item as a percentage of total sales, as illustrated for Prufrock in Table 3.5.

TABLE 3.4

PRUFROCK CORPORATION 2020 Income Statement (in $ millions)		
Sales		$2,311
Cost of goods sold		1,344
Depreciation		276
Earnings before interest and taxes		$ 691
Interest paid		141
Taxable income		$ 550
Taxes (24%)		132
Net income		$ 418
Dividends	$149	
Addition to retained earnings	269	

TABLE 3.5

PRUFROCK CORPORATION Common-Size Income Statement 2020		
Sales		100.0%
Cost of goods sold		58.2
Depreciation		11.9
Earnings before interest and taxes		29.9
Interest paid		6.1
Taxable income		23.8
Taxes (24%)		5.7
Net income		18.1%
Dividends	6.4%	
Addition to retained earnings	11.6	

This income statement tells us what happens to each dollar in sales. For Prufrock, interest expense eats up $.061 out of every sales dollar, and taxes take another $.057. When all is said and done, $.181 of each dollar flows through to the bottom line (net income), and that amount is split into $.116 retained in the business and $.064 paid out in dividends.

These percentages are useful in comparisons. For example, a relevant figure is the cost percentage. For Prufrock, $.582 of each $1.00 in sales goes to pay for goods sold. It would be interesting to compute the same percentage for Prufrock's main competitors to see how Prufrock stacks up in terms of cost control.

3.2 RATIO ANALYSIS

Another way of avoiding the problems involved in comparing companies of different sizes is to calculate and compare financial ratios. Such ratios are ways of comparing and investigating the relationships between different pieces of financial information. We cover some of the more common ratios next (there are many others we don't discuss here).

One problem with ratios is that different people and different sources frequently don't compute them in exactly the same way, and this leads to much confusion. The specific definitions we use here may or may not be the same as ones you have seen or will see elsewhere. If you are using ratios as tools for analysis, you should be careful to document how you calculate each one; and, if you are comparing your numbers to those of another source, be sure you know how their numbers are computed.

ExcelMaster
coverage online
www.mhhe.com/RossCore6e

We will defer much of our discussion of how ratios are used and some problems that come up with using them until later in the chapter. For now, for each ratio we discuss, several questions come to mind:

Go to www.reuters.com/finance and find the "Financials" link in a stock quote to examine comparative ratios for a huge number of companies.

1. How is it computed?
2. What is it intended to measure, and why might we be interested?
3. What is the unit of measurement?
4. What might a high or low value be telling us? How might such values be misleading?
5. How could this measure be improved?

Financial ratios are traditionally grouped into the following categories:

1. Short-term solvency, or liquidity, ratios.
2. Long-term solvency, or financial leverage, ratios.
3. Asset management, or turnover, ratios.
4. Profitability ratios.
5. Market value ratios.

We will consider each of these in turn. In calculating these numbers for Prufrock, we will use the ending balance sheet (2020) figures unless we explicitly say otherwise.

Short-Term Solvency or Liquidity Measures

As the name suggests, short-term solvency ratios as a group are intended to provide information about a firm's liquidity, and these ratios are sometimes called *liquidity measures.* The primary concern is the firm's ability to pay its bills over the short run without undue stress. Consequently, these ratios focus on current assets and current liabilities.

For obvious reasons, liquidity ratios are particularly interesting to short-term creditors. Because financial managers are constantly working with banks and other short-term lenders, an understanding of these ratios is essential.

One advantage of looking at current assets and liabilities is that their book values and market values are likely to be similar. Often (though not always), these assets and liabilities don't live long enough for the two to get seriously out of step. On the other hand, like any type of near-cash, current assets and liabilities can and do change fairly rapidly, so today's amounts may not be a reliable guide to the future.

CURRENT RATIO   One of the best-known and most widely used ratios is the *current ratio.* As you might guess, the current ratio is defined as:

$$\text{Current ratio} = \frac{\text{Current assets}}{\text{Current liabilities}} \tag{3.1}$$

For Prufrock, the 2020 current ratio is:

$$\text{Current ratio} = \frac{\$708}{\$540} = 1.31 \text{ times}$$

Because current assets and liabilities are, in principle, converted to cash over the following 12 months, the current ratio is a measure of short-term liquidity. The unit of measurement is either dollars or times. So, we could say Prufrock has $1.31 in current assets for every $1 in current liabilities, or we could say Prufrock has its current liabilities covered 1.31 times over.

To a creditor, particularly a short-term creditor such as a supplier, the higher the current ratio, the better. To the firm, a high current ratio indicates liquidity, but it also may indicate an inefficient use of cash and other short-term assets. Absent some extraordinary circumstances, we would expect to see a current ratio of at least 1; a current ratio of less than 1 would mean that net working capital (current assets less current liabilities) is negative. This would be unusual in a healthy firm, at least for most types of businesses.

The current ratio, like any ratio, is affected by various types of transactions. Suppose the firm borrows over the long term to raise money. The short-run effect would be an increase in cash from the issue proceeds and an increase in long-term debt. Current liabilities would not be affected, so the current ratio would rise.

EXAMPLE 3.1 — Current Events

Suppose a firm were to pay off some of its suppliers and short-term creditors. What would happen to the current ratio? Suppose a firm buys some inventory. What happens in this case? What happens if a firm sells some merchandise?

The first case is a trick question. What happens is that the current ratio moves away from 1. If it is greater than 1 (the usual case), it will get bigger, but if it is less than 1, it will get smaller. To see this, suppose the firm has $4 in current assets and $2 in current liabilities for a current ratio of 2. If we use $1 in cash to reduce current liabilities, the new current ratio is ($4 − 1)/($2 − 1) = 3. If we reverse the original situation to $2 in current assets and $4 in current liabilities, the change will cause the current ratio to fall to 1/3 from 1/2.

The second case is not quite as tricky. Nothing happens to the current ratio because cash goes down while inventory goes up—total current assets are unaffected.

In the third case, the current ratio would usually rise because inventory is normally shown at cost and the sale would normally be at something greater than cost (the difference is the markup). The increase in either cash or receivables is therefore greater than the decrease in inventory. This increases current assets, and the current ratio rises.

Finally, note that an apparently low current ratio may not be a bad sign for a company with a large reserve of untapped borrowing power.

QUICK (OR ACID-TEST) RATIO Inventory is often the least liquid current asset. It's also the one for which the book values are least reliable as measures of market value because the quality of the inventory isn't considered. Some of the inventory may later turn out to be damaged, obsolete, or lost.

More to the point, relatively large inventories are often a sign of short-term trouble. The firm may have overestimated sales and overbought or overproduced as a result. In this case, the firm may have a substantial portion of its liquidity tied up in slow-moving inventory.

To further evaluate liquidity, the *quick,* or *acid-test, ratio* is computed just like the current ratio, except inventory is omitted:

$$\text{Quick ratio} = \frac{\text{Current assets} - \text{Inventory}}{\text{Current liabilities}} \qquad (3.2)$$

Notice that using cash to buy inventory does not affect the current ratio, but it reduces the quick ratio. Again, the idea is that inventory is relatively illiquid compared to cash. For Prufrock, this ratio in 2020 was:

$$\text{Quick ratio} = \frac{\$708 - 422}{\$540} = .53 \text{ times}$$

The quick ratio here tells a somewhat different story than the current ratio because inventory accounts for more than half of Prufrock's current assets. To exaggerate the point, if this inventory consisted of, say, unsold nuclear power plants, then this would be a cause for concern.

To give an example of current versus quick ratios, based on recent financial statements, Walmart and Manpower Group, Inc., had current ratios of .85 and 1.39, respectively. However, Manpower carries no inventory to speak of, whereas Walmart's current assets are virtually all inventory. As a result, Walmart's quick ratio was only .22, and Manpower's was 1.39, the same as its current ratio.

CASH RATIO   A very short-term creditor might be interested in the *cash ratio:*

$$\text{Cash ratio} = \frac{\text{Cash}}{\text{Current liabilities}} \qquad (3.3)$$

You can verify that this works out to be .18 times for Prufrock.

Long-Term Solvency Measures

Long-term solvency ratios are intended to address the firm's long-run ability to meet its obligations or, more generally, its financial leverage. These ratios are sometimes called *financial leverage ratios* or just *leverage ratios.* We consider three commonly used measures and some variations.

TOTAL DEBT RATIO   The *total debt ratio* takes into account all debts of all maturities to all creditors. It can be defined in several ways, the easiest of which is:

$$\text{Total debt ratio} = \frac{\text{Total assets} - \text{Total equity}}{\text{Total assets}} \qquad (3.4)$$

$$= \frac{\$3,588 - 2,588}{\$3,588} = .28 \text{ times}$$

The online Women's Business Center has more information about financial statements, ratios, and small business topics at www.sba .gov/content/womens-business-resources.

In this case, an analyst might say that Prufrock uses 28 percent debt.[1] Whether this is high or low or whether it even makes any difference depends on whether capital structure matters, a subject we discuss in a later chapter.

Prufrock has $.28 in debt for every $1 in assets. Therefore, there is $.72 in equity (= $1 − .28) for every $.28 in debt. With this in mind, we can define two useful variations on the total debt ratio, the *debt-equity ratio* and the *equity multiplier:*

$$\text{Debt-equity ratio} = \text{Total debt}/\text{Total equity} \qquad (3.5)$$

$$= \$.28/\$.72 = .39 \text{ times}$$

$$\text{Equity multiplier} = \text{Total assets}/\text{Total equity} \qquad (3.6)$$

$$= \$1/\$.72 = 1.39 \text{ times}$$

The fact that the equity multiplier is 1 plus the debt-equity ratio is not a coincidence:

$$\text{Equity multiplier} = \text{Total assets}/\text{Total equity} = \$1/\$.72 = 1.39 \text{ times}$$

$$= (\text{Total equity} + \text{Total debt})/\text{Total equity}$$

$$= 1 + \text{Debt-equity ratio} = 1.39 \text{ times}$$

The thing to notice here is that given any one of these three ratios, you can immediately calculate the other two, so they all say exactly the same thing.

---

[1] Total equity here includes preferred stock, if there is any. An equivalent numerator in this ratio would be (Current liabilities + Long-term debt).

TIMES INTEREST EARNED Another common measure of long-term solvency is the *times interest earned* (TIE) *ratio.* Once again, there are several possible (and common) definitions, but we'll stick with the most traditional:

$$\text{Times interest earned ratio} = \frac{\text{EBIT}}{\text{Interest}} \tag{3.7}$$

$$= \frac{\$691}{\$141} = 4.90 \text{ times}$$

As the name suggests, this ratio measures how well a company has its interest obligations covered, and it is often called the *interest coverage ratio.* For Prufrock, the interest bill is covered 4.9 times over.

CASH COVERAGE A problem with the TIE ratio is that it is based on EBIT, which is not really a measure of cash available to pay interest. The reason is that depreciation and amortization, noncash expenses, have been deducted out. Because interest is most definitely a cash outflow (to creditors), one way to define the *cash coverage ratio* is:

$$\text{Cash coverage ratio} = \frac{\text{EBIT} + (\text{Depreciation and amortization})}{\text{Interest}} \tag{3.8}$$

$$= \frac{\$691 + 276}{\$141} = \frac{\$967}{\$141} = 6.86 \text{ times}$$

The numerator here, EBIT plus depreciation and amortization, is often abbreviated EBITDA (earnings before interest, taxes, depreciation, and amortization). It is a basic measure of the firm's ability to generate cash from operations, and it is frequently used as a measure of cash flow available to meet financial obligations.

More recently another long-term solvency measure is increasingly seen in financial statement analysis and in debt covenants. It uses EBITDA and interest-bearing debt. Specifically, for Prufrock:

$$\frac{\text{Interest-bearing debt}}{\text{EBITDA}} = \frac{\$196 \text{ million} + 460 \text{ million}}{\$967 \text{ million}} = .68 \text{ times}$$

Here we include notes payable (most likely notes payable is bank debt) and long-term debt in the numerator and EBITDA in the denominator. Values below 1 on this ratio are considered very strong and values above 5 are considered weak. However, a careful comparison with other comparable firms is necessary to properly interpret the ratio.

Asset Management or Turnover Measures

We next turn our attention to the efficiency with which Prufrock uses its assets. The measures in this section are sometimes called *asset management* or *utilization ratios.* The specific ratios we discuss can all be interpreted as measures of turnover. What they are intended to describe is how efficiently, or intensively, a firm uses its assets to generate sales. We first look at two important current assets: inventory and receivables.

INVENTORY TURNOVER AND DAYS' SALES IN INVENTORY During the year, Prufrock had a cost of goods sold of $1,344. Inventory at the end of the year was $422. With these numbers, *inventory turnover* can be calculated as:

$$\text{Inventory turnover} = \frac{\text{Cost of goods sold}}{\text{Inventory}} \tag{3.9}$$

$$= \frac{\$1,344}{\$422} = 3.18 \text{ times}$$

In a sense, we sold off, or turned over, the entire inventory 3.18 times during the year. As long as we are not running out of stock and thereby forgoing sales, the higher this ratio is, the more efficiently we are managing inventory.

If we know that we turned our inventory over 3.18 times during the year, we can immediately figure out how long it took us to turn it over on average. The result is the average *days' sales in inventory:*

$$\text{Days' sales in inventory} = \frac{365 \text{ days}}{\text{Inventory turnover}} \qquad (3.10)$$

$$= \frac{365}{3.18} = 114.61 \text{ days}$$

This tells us that, roughly speaking, inventory sits about 115 days, on average, before it is sold. Alternatively, assuming we used the most recent inventory and cost figures, it will take about 115 days to work off our current inventory.

For example, in late 2018, Mercedes-Benz USA had a 51-day supply of vehicles in inventory, less than the 60-day supply considered normal. This figure means that at the then-current rate of sales, it would have taken Mercedes-Benz 51 days to deplete the available supply, or, equivalently, that Mercedes-Benz had 51 days of sales in inventory. At the same time, Subaru had a 29-day inventory supply and Mitsubishi America's inventory level stood at 119 days. Of course, we could also examine these numbers on a per-model basis. For example, there was only a 56-day inventory for the Honda CR-V, while the Honda Accord had an inventory period of 113 days. Even worse, the Buick Cascada had an inventory level of 206 days.

RECEIVABLES TURNOVER AND DAYS' SALES IN RECEIVABLES   Our inventory measures give some indication of how fast we can sell products. We now look at how fast we collect on those sales. The *receivables turnover* is defined in the same way as inventory turnover:

$$\text{Receivables turnover} = \frac{\text{Sales}}{\text{Accounts receivable}} \qquad (3.11)$$

$$= \frac{\$2{,}311}{\$188} = 12.29 \text{ times}$$

Loosely speaking, we collected our outstanding credit accounts and lent the money again 12.29 times during the year.[2]

This ratio makes more sense if we convert it to days, so the *days' sales in receivables* is:

$$\text{Days' sales in receivables} = \frac{365 \text{ days}}{\text{Receivables turnover}} \qquad (3.12)$$

$$= \frac{365}{12.29} = 29.69 \text{ days}$$

Therefore, on average, we collect on our credit sales in about 30 days. For obvious reasons, this ratio is frequently called the *average collection period* (ACP). Also note that if we are using the most recent figures, we can say that we have 30 days' worth of sales currently uncollected.

---

[2] Here we have implicitly assumed that all sales are credit sales. If they were not, we would use total credit sales in these calculations, not total sales. Also, in making this calculation, we use the value of accounts receivable at the end of the accounting period. A common alternative is to use the average value of accounts receivable over the accounting period. The important point is to be consistent in your method of calculation over time and across firms.

Payables Turnover

Here is a variation on the receivables collection period. How long, on average, does it take for Prufrock Corporation to *pay* its bills? To answer, we need to calculate the accounts payable turnover rate using cost of goods sold. We will assume that Prufrock purchases everything on credit.

The cost of goods sold is $1,344, and accounts payable are $344. The turnover is therefore $1,344/$344 = 3.91 times. So, payables turned over about every 365/3.91 = 93.42 days. On average, then, Prufrock takes about 93 days to pay. As a potential creditor, we might take note of this fact.

TOTAL ASSET TURNOVER Moving away from specific accounts like inventory or receivables, we can consider an important "big picture" ratio, the *total asset turnover* ratio. As the name suggests, total asset turnover is:

$$\text{Total asset turnover} = \frac{\text{Sales}}{\text{Total assets}} \tag{3.13}$$

$$= \frac{\$2,311}{\$3,588} = .64 \text{ times}$$

In other words, for every dollar in assets, we generated $.64 in sales.

More Turnover

Suppose you find that a particular company generates $.40 in annual sales for every dollar in total assets. How often does this company turn over its total assets?

The total asset turnover here is .40 times per year. It takes 1/.40 = 2.5 years to turn assets over completely. The 2.5 number is frequently referred to as the firm's *capital intensity*.

Profitability Measures

The three types of measures we discuss in this section are probably the best-known and most widely used of all financial ratios. In one form or another, they are intended to measure how efficiently the firm uses its assets and how efficiently the firm manages its operations.

PROFIT MARGIN Companies pay a great deal of attention to their *profit margin*:

$$\text{Profit margin} = \frac{\text{Net income}}{\text{Sales}} \tag{3.14}$$

$$= \frac{\$418}{\$2,311} = .1809, \text{ or } 18.09\%$$

This tells us that Prufrock, in an accounting sense, generates a little more than 18 cents in net income for every dollar in sales.

EBITDA MARGIN   Another commonly used measure of profitability is the EBITDA margin. As mentioned, EBITDA is a measure of before-tax operating cash flow. It adds back non-cash expenses and does not include taxes or interest expense. As a consequence, EBITDA margin looks more directly at operating cash flows than does net income and does not include the effect of capital structure or taxes. For Prufrock, EBITDA margin is:

$$\frac{\text{EBITDA}}{\text{Sales}} = \frac{\$967 \text{ million}}{\$2,311 \text{ million}} = .4184, \text{ or } 41.84\%$$

All other things being equal, a relatively high margin is obviously desirable. This situation corresponds to low expense ratios relative to sales. However, we hasten to add that other things are often not equal.

For example, lowering our sales price will usually increase unit volume but will normally cause margins to shrink. Total profit (or, more importantly, operating cash flow) may go up or down, so the fact that margins are smaller isn't necessarily bad. After all, isn't it possible that, as the saying goes, "Our prices are so low that we lose money on everything we sell, but we make it up in volume"?[3]

Margins are very different for different industries. Grocery stores have a notoriously low profit margin, generally around 2 percent. In contrast, the profit margin for the pharmaceutical industry is about 18 percent. So, for example, it is not surprising that recent profit margins for Kroger and AbbVie were about 1.6 percent and 18.7 percent, respectively.

RETURN ON ASSETS   *Return on assets* (ROA) is a measure of profit per dollar of assets. It can be defined several ways,[4] but the most common is:

$$\text{Return on assets} = \frac{\text{Net income}}{\text{Total assets}} \tag{3.15}$$

$$= \frac{\$418}{\$3,588} = .1165, \text{ or } 11.65\%$$

RETURN ON EQUITY   *Return on equity* (ROE) is a measure of how the stockholders fared during the year. Because benefiting shareholders is our goal, ROE is, in an accounting sense, the true bottom-line measure of performance. ROE is usually measured as:

$$\text{Return on equity} = \frac{\text{Net income}}{\text{Total equity}} \tag{3.16}$$

$$= \frac{\$418}{\$2,588} = .1615, \text{ or } 16.15\%$$

Therefore, for every dollar in equity, Prufrock generated 16 cents in profit; but, again, this is correct only in accounting terms.

Because ROA and ROE are such commonly cited numbers, we stress that it is important to remember they are accounting rates of return. For this reason, these measures should properly be called *return on book assets* and *return on book equity.*

The fact that ROE exceeds ROA reflects Prufrock's use of financial leverage. We will examine the relationship between these two measures in the next section.

---

[3] No, it's not.

[4] For example, we might want a return on assets measure that is neutral with respect to capital structure (interest expense) and taxes. Such a measure for Prufrock would be:

$$\frac{\text{EBIT}}{\text{Total assets}} = \frac{\$691}{\$3,588} = .1926, \text{ or } 19.26\%$$

This measure has a very natural interpretation. If 19.26 percent exceeds Prufrock's borrowing rate, Prufrock will earn more money on its investments than it will pay out to its creditors. The surplus will be available to Prufrock's shareholders after adjusting for taxes.

Market Value Measures

Our final group of measures is based, in part, on information not necessarily contained in financial statements—the market price per share of the stock. Obviously, these measures can be calculated directly only for publicly traded companies.

We assume that Prufrock has 33 million shares outstanding and the stock sold for $88 per share at the end of the year. If we recall that Prufrock's net income was $418 million, then we can calculate that its earnings per share (EPS) was:

$$\text{EPS} = \frac{\text{Net income}}{\text{Shares outstanding}}$$
$$= \frac{\$418}{33} = \$12.67 \tag{3.17}$$

PRICE-EARNINGS RATIO The first of our market value measures, the *price-earnings* or *PE ratio* (or multiple), is defined as:

$$\text{PE ratio} = \frac{\text{Price per share}}{\text{Earnings per share}} \tag{3.18}$$
$$= \frac{\$88}{\$12.67} = 6.95 \text{ times}$$

In the vernacular, we would say that Prufrock shares sell for 6.95 times earnings, or we might say that Prufrock shares have, or "carry," a PE multiple of 6.95.

Because the PE ratio measures how much investors are willing to pay per dollar of current earnings, higher PEs are often taken to mean that the firm has significant prospects for future growth. Of course, if a firm had no or almost no earnings, its PE would probably be quite large; so, as always, care is needed in interpreting this ratio.

MARKET-TO-BOOK RATIO A second commonly quoted measure is the *market-to-book ratio*:

$$\text{Market-to-book ratio} = \frac{\text{Market value per share}}{\text{Book value per share}} \tag{3.19}$$
$$= \frac{\$88}{\$2,588/33} = \frac{\$88}{\$78.42} = 1.12 \text{ times}$$

Notice that book value per share is total equity (not just common stock) divided by the number of shares outstanding.

Book value per share is an accounting number that reflects historical costs. In a loose sense, the market-to-book ratio therefore compares the market value of the firm's investments to their cost. A value less than 1 could mean that the firm has not been successful overall in creating value for its stockholders.

MARKET CAPITALIZATION The market capitalization of a public firm is equal to the firm's stock market price per share multiplied by the number of shares outstanding. For Prufrock, this is:

$$\text{Price per share} \times \text{Shares outstanding} = \$88 \times 33 \text{ million} = \$2,904 \text{ million}$$

This is a useful number for potential buyers of Prufrock. A prospective buyer of all of the outstanding shares of Prufrock (in a merger or acquisition) would need to come up with at least $2,904 million plus a premium.

ENTERPRISE VALUE Enterprise value (EV) is a measure of firm value that is very closely related to market capitalization. Instead of focusing on only the market value of outstanding shares of stock, it measures the market value of outstanding shares of stock plus the market value of outstanding interest-bearing debt less cash on hand. We know the market capitalization of Prufrock, but we do not know the market value of its outstanding interest-bearing debt. In this situation, the common practice is to use the book value of outstanding interest-bearing debt less cash on hand as an approximation. For Prufrock, enterprise value is (in millions):

$$\text{EV} = \text{Market capitalization} + \text{Market value of interest-bearing debt} - \text{Cash} \qquad \textbf{(3.20)}$$
$$= \$2,904 + (\$196 + 460) - \$98 = \$3,462 \text{ million}$$

The purpose of the EV measure is to better estimate how much it would take to buy all of the outstanding stock of a firm and also to pay off the debt. The adjustment for cash is to recognize that if we were a buyer, the cash could be used immediately to buy back debt or pay a dividend.

ENTERPRISE VALUE MULTIPLES Financial analysts use valuation multiples based upon a firm's enterprise value when the goal is to estimate the value of the firm's total business rather than focusing on the value of its equity. To form an appropriate multiple, enterprise value is divided by EBITDA. For Prufrock, the enterprise value multiple is:

$$\text{EV multiple} = \frac{\text{EV}}{\text{EBITDA}} \qquad \textbf{(3.21)}$$
$$= \frac{\$3,462}{\$967} = 3.58 \text{ times}$$

The multiple is especially useful because it allows comparison of one firm with another when there are differences in capital structure (interest expense), taxes, or capital spending. The multiple is not directly affected by these differences.

Similar to PE ratios, we would expect a firm with high growth opportunities to have high EV multiples.

This completes our definition of some common ratios. We could tell you about more of them, but these are enough for now. We'll leave it here and go on to discuss some ways of using these ratios instead of how to calculate them. Table 3.6 summarizes some of the ratios we've discussed.

TABLE 3.6

Common Financial Ratios

I. Short-Term Solvency, or Liquidity, Ratios	III. Asset Utilization, or Turnover, Ratios
$\text{Current ratio} = \dfrac{\text{Current assets}}{\text{Current liabilities}}$	$\text{Inventory turnover} = \dfrac{\text{Cost of goods sold}}{\text{Inventory}}$
$\text{Quick ratio} = \dfrac{\text{Current assets} - \text{Inventory}}{\text{Current liabilities}}$	$\text{Days' sales in inventory} = \dfrac{365 \text{ days}}{\text{Inventory turnover}}$
$\text{Cash ratio} = \dfrac{\text{Cash}}{\text{Current liabilities}}$	$\text{Receivables turnover} = \dfrac{\text{Sales}}{\text{Accounts receivable}}$
II. Long-Term Solvency, or Financial Leverage, Ratios	$\text{Days' sales in receivables} = \dfrac{365 \text{ days}}{\text{Receivables turnover}}$
$\text{Total debt ratio} = \dfrac{\text{Total assets} - \text{Total equity}}{\text{Total assets}}$	$\text{Total asset turnover} = \dfrac{\text{Sales}}{\text{Total assets}}$
$\text{Debt-equity ratio} = \dfrac{\text{Total debt}}{\text{Total equity}}$	$\text{Capital intensity} = \dfrac{\text{Total assets}}{\text{Sales}}$
$\text{Equity multiplier} = \dfrac{\text{Total assets}}{\text{Total equity}}$	
$\text{Times interest earned ratio} = \dfrac{\text{EBIT}}{\text{Interest}}$	
$\text{Cash coverage ratio} = \dfrac{\text{EBITDA}}{\text{Interest}}$	*(Continued)*

IV. Profitability Ratios

$$\text{Profit margin} = \frac{\text{Net income}}{\text{Sales}}$$

$$\text{Return on assets (ROA)} = \frac{\text{Net income}}{\text{Total assets}}$$

$$\text{Return on equity (ROE)} = \frac{\text{Net income}}{\text{Total equity}}$$

$$\text{ROE} = \frac{\text{Net income}}{\text{Sales}} \times \frac{\text{Sales}}{\text{Assets}} \times \frac{\text{Assets}}{\text{Equity}}$$

V. Market Value Ratios

$$\text{Price-earnings ratio} = \frac{\text{Price per share}}{\text{Earnings per share}}$$

$$\text{Market-to-book ratio} = \frac{\text{Market value per share}}{\text{Book value per share}}$$

$$\text{EV multiple} = \frac{\text{Enterprise value}}{\text{EBITDA}}$$

EXAMPLE 3.4

Atlantic's and Pacific

Consider the following 2020 data for Atlantic's Companies and Pacific Depot (billions except for price and earnings per share):

	ATLANTIC'S COMPANIES, INC.	PACIFIC DEPOT, INC.
Sales	$48.3	$77.3
EBIT	$ 4.8	$ 7.3
Net income	$ 2.8	$ 4.4
Cash	$ .5	$ .5
Depreciation	$ 1.5	$ 1.9
Interest-bearing debt	$ 6.7	$13.4
Total assets	$30.9	$44.3
Price per share	$24	$27
Shares outstanding	1.5	1.7
Shareholder equity	$16.1	$17.7
Earnings per share	$ 1.87	$ 2.59

1. Determine the profit margin, ROE, market capitalization, enterprise value, PE multiple, and EV multiple for both Atlantic's and Pacific Depot.

	ATLANTIC'S COMPANIES, INC.	PACIFIC DEPOT, INC.
Equity multiplier	$30.9/$16.1 = 1.9	$44.3/$17.7 = 2.5
Asset turnover	$48.3/$30.9 = 1.6	$77.3/$44.3 = 1.7
Profit margin	$2.8/$48.3 = 5.8%	$4.4/$77.3 = 5.7%
ROE	$2.8/$16.1 = 17.4%	$4.4/$17.7 = 24.9%
Market capitalization	1.5 × $24 = $36 billion	1.7 × $27 = $45.9 billion
Enterprise value	(1.5 × $24) + 6.7 − .5 = $42.2 billion	(1.7 × $27) + 13.4 − .5 = $58.8 billion
PE multiple	$24/$1.87 = 12.8	27/$2.59 = 10.4
EBITDA	$4.8 + 1.5 = $6.3	$7.3 + 1.9 = $9.2
EV multiple	$42.2/$6.3 = 6.7	$58.8/$9.2 = 6.4

2. How would you describe these two companies from a financial point of view? These are similarly situated companies. In 2020, Pacific Depot had a higher ROE (partially because of using more debt and higher total asset turnover), but Atlantic's had slightly higher PE and EV multiples. Both companies' multiples were somewhat below the general market, raising questions about future growth prospects.

3.3 THE DUPONT IDENTITY

As we mentioned in discussing ROA and ROE, the difference between these two profitability measures reflects the use of debt financing or financial leverage. We illustrate the relationship between these measures in this section by investigating a famous way of decomposing ROE into its component parts.

A Closer Look at ROE

To begin, let's recall the definition of ROE:

$$\text{Return on equity} = \frac{\text{Net income}}{\text{Total equity}}$$

If we were so inclined, we could multiply this ratio by Assets/Assets without changing anything:

$$\text{Return on equity} = \frac{\text{Net income}}{\text{Total equity}} = \frac{\text{Net income}}{\text{Total equity}} \times \frac{\text{Assets}}{\text{Assets}}$$

$$= \frac{\text{Net income}}{\text{Assets}} \times \frac{\text{Assets}}{\text{Total equity}}$$

Notice that we have expressed the ROE as the product of two other ratios—ROA and the equity multiplier:

$$\text{ROE} = \text{ROA} \times \text{Equity multiplier} = \text{ROA} \times (1 + \text{Debt-equity ratio})$$

Looking back at Prufrock, for example, we see that the debt-equity ratio was .39 and ROA was 11.65 percent. Our work here implies that Prufrock's ROE, as we previously calculated, is:

$$\text{ROE} = .1165\% \times 1.39 = .1615, \text{ or } 16.15\%$$

The difference between ROE and ROA can be substantial, particularly for certain businesses. For example, based on recent financial statements, Bank of America had an ROA of only .82 percent, which is actually fairly typical for a bank. However, banks tend to borrow a lot of money, and, as a result, have relatively large equity multipliers. For Bank of America, ROE is about 6.71 percent, implying an equity multiplier of 8.18.

We can further decompose ROE by multiplying the top and bottom by total sales:

$$\text{ROE} = \frac{\text{Sales}}{\text{Sales}} \times \frac{\text{Net income}}{\text{Assets}} \times \frac{\text{Assets}}{\text{Total equity}}$$

If we rearrange things a bit, ROE is:

$$\text{ROE} = \underbrace{\frac{\text{Net income}}{\text{Sales}} \times \frac{\text{Sales}}{\text{Assets}}}_{\text{Return on assets}} \times \frac{\text{Assets}}{\text{Total equity}} \qquad (3.22)$$

$$= \text{Profit margin} \times \text{Total asset turnover} \times \text{Equity multiplier}$$

What we have now done is to partition ROA into its two component parts, profit margin and total asset turnover. The last expression of the preceding equation is called the DuPont identity after the DuPont Corporation, which popularized its use.

We can check this relationship for Prufrock by noting that the profit margin was 18.09 percent and the total asset turnover was .64. ROE should thus be:

ROE = Profit margin   × Total asset turnover × Equity multiplier
     = .1809   ×   .64   ×   1.39
     = .1615, or 16.15%

This 16.15 percent ROE is exactly what we had before.

The DuPont identity tells us that ROE is affected by three things:

1. Operating efficiency (as measured by profit margin).
2. Asset use efficiency (as measured by total asset turnover).
3. Financial leverage (as measured by the equity multiplier).

Weakness in either operating or asset use efficiency (or both) will show up in a diminished return on assets, which will translate into a lower ROE.

Considering the DuPont identity, it appears that the ROE could be leveraged up by increasing the amount of debt in the firm. However, notice that increasing debt also increases interest expense, which reduces profit margins, which acts to reduce ROE. So, ROE could go up or down, depending. More important, the use of debt financing has a number of other effects, and, as we discuss at some length in later chapters, the amount of leverage a firm uses is governed by its capital structure policy.

The decomposition of ROE we've discussed in this section is a convenient way of systematically approaching financial statement analysis. If ROE is unsatisfactory by some measure, then the DuPont identity tells you where to start looking for the reasons.

Amazon.com and Alibaba are among the most important internet marketplace companies in the world. They may be good examples of how DuPont analysis can be useful in helping to ask the right questions about a firm's financial performance. The DuPont breakdowns for Amazon.com and Alibaba are summarized in Table 3.7.

As you can see, in 2017, Amazon had an ROE of 15.0 percent, down from its ROE in 2015 of 16.7 percent. In contrast, also in 2017, Alibaba had an ROE of 15.7 percent, down from its ROE in 2015 of 16.7 percent. Given this information, it would appear that the two companies operate in a similar fashion, but as we see, that is not true.

TABLE 3.7

The DuPont Breakdown for Amazon.com and Alibaba

AMAZON.COM							
YEAR	ROE	=	PROFIT MARGIN	×	TOTAL ASSET TURNOVER	×	EQUITY MULTIPLIER
2017	15.0%	=	2.3%	×	1.355	×	4.74
2016	21.7%	=	3.1%	×	1.631	×	4.32
2015	16.7%	=	2.1%	×	1.653	×	4.84

ALIBABA							
YEAR	ROE	=	PROFIT MARGIN	×	TOTAL ASSET TURNOVER	×	EQUITY MULTIPLIER
2017	15.7%	=	27.6%	×	.312	×	1.82
2016	32.9%	=	70.7%	×	.278	×	1.68
2015	16.7%	=	31.8%	×	.298	×	1.76

Looking at the DuPont breakdown, Amazon's profit margin is in the 2 to 3 percent range, while Alibaba's profit has ranged from 27.6 percent to an astounding 70.7 percent. However, Amazon's ROE is similar to Alibaba's because Amazon has a higher asset utilization, as measured by total asset turnover, and higher leverage, as measured by the equity multiplier.

Problems with Financial Statement Analysis

We continue our chapter by discussing some additional problems that can arise in using financial statements. In one way or another, the basic problem with financial statement analysis is that there is no underlying theory to help us identify which quantities to look at and to guide us in establishing benchmarks.

As we discuss in other chapters, there are many cases in which financial theory and economic logic provide guidance in making judgments about value and risk. Little such help exists with financial statements. This is why we can't say which ratios matter the most and what a high or low value might be.

One particularly severe problem is that many firms are conglomerates, owning more or less unrelated lines of business. GE is a well-known example. The consolidated financial statements for such firms don't really fit any neat industry category. More generally, the kind of peer group analysis we have been describing is going to work best when the firms are strictly in the same line of business, the industry is competitive, and there is only one way of operating.

Another problem that is becoming increasingly common is that major competitors and natural peer group members in an industry may be scattered around the globe. The automobile industry is an obvious example. The problem here is that financial statements from outside the United States do not necessarily conform to GAAP. The existence of different standards and procedures makes it difficult to compare financial statements across national borders.

Even companies that are clearly in the same line of business may not be comparable. For example, electric utilities engaged primarily in power generation are all classified in the same group. This group is often thought to be relatively homogeneous. However, most utilities operate as regulated monopolies, so they don't compete much with each other, at least not historically. Many have stockholders, and many are organized as cooperatives with no stockholders. There are several different ways of generating power, ranging from hydroelectric to nuclear, so the operating activities of these utilities can differ quite a bit. Finally, profitability is strongly affected by the regulatory environment, so utilities in different locations can be similar but show different profits.

Several other general problems frequently crop up. First, different firms use different accounting procedures—for inventory, for example. This makes it difficult to compare statements. Second, different firms end their fiscal years at different times. For firms in seasonal businesses (such as a retailer with a large Christmas season), this can lead to difficulties in comparing balance sheets because of fluctuations in accounts during the year. Finally, for any particular firm, unusual or transient events, such as a one-time profit from an asset sale, may affect financial performance. Such events can give misleading signals as we compare firms. The nearby *Finance Matters* box discusses some issues along these lines.

WHAT'S IN A RATIO?

Abraham Briloff, a well-known financial commentator, famously remarked that "financial statements are like fine perfume: to be sniffed but not swallowed." As you have probably figured out by now, his point is that information gleaned from financial statements—and ratios and growth rates computed from that information—should be taken with a grain of salt.

For example, in early 2019, shares in cloud technology company GoDaddy had a PE ratio of about 88 times earnings. You would expect this stock to have a high growth rate, and indeed analysts thought so. The estimated earnings growth rate for GoDaddy for the next year was 42 percent. At the same time, Johnson & Johnson had a PE ratio of about 227, but analysts estimated an earnings growth rate of only 7 percent for the next year. Why is the PE so high? The answer is that Johnson & Johnson had low earnings the previous year. So, caution is warranted when looking at PE ratios.

Sears Holdings illustrates another issue. If you calculated its ROE in 2017, you would get about 10 percent, which is not too bad. What's strange is the company reported a loss of about $383 million during 2017! What's going on is that Sears had a book value of equity balance of *negative* $3.7 billion. In this situation, the more Sears loses, the higher the ROE becomes. Of course, Sears' market-to-book and PE ratios are also both negative. How do you interpret a negative PE? We're not really sure, either. Whenever a company has a negative book value of equity, it means that losses have been so large that book equity has been wiped out. In such cases, the ROE, PE ratio, and market-to-book ratio are often not reported because they are meaningless. Of course, for Sears, it was a really bad sign as the company declared bankruptcy in late 2018!

Even if a company's book equity is positive, you still have to be careful. For example, consider The Clorox Company, which had a market-to-book ratio of about 29 in late 2018. Because the market-to-book ratio measures the value created by the company for shareholders, this would seem to be a good sign. But a closer look shows that Clorox's book value of equity per share was negative $1.04 in 2012 and had risen to $5.67 in 2018. The low book value per share in 2012 had to do with accounting for stock repurchases made by the company, not gains or losses, but it nonetheless dramatically affected the market-to-book ratio.

Financial ratios are important tools used in evaluating companies of all types, but you cannot take a number as given. Instead, before doing any analysis, the first step is to ask whether the number actually makes sense.

3.4 FINANCIAL MODELS

Financial planning is another important use of financial statements. Most financial planning models output pro forma financial statements, where pro forma means "as a matter of form." In our case, this means that financial statements are the form we use to summarize the projected future financial status of a company.

ExcelMaster
coverage online

www.mhhe.com/RossCore6e

A Simple Financial Planning Model

We can begin our discussion of financial planning models with a relatively simple example. The Computerfield Corporation's financial statements from the most recent year are shown below.

Unless otherwise stated, the financial planners at Computerfield assume that all variables are tied directly to sales and current relationships are optimal. This means that all items will grow at exactly the same rate as sales. This is obviously oversimplified; we use this assumption only to make a point.

COMPUTERFIELD CORPORATION Financial Statements				
Income Statement		**Balance Sheet**		
Sales	$1,000	Assets	$500	Debt	$250
Costs	800			Equity	250
Net income	$ 200	Total	$500	Total	$500

Suppose sales increase by 20 percent, rising from $1,000 to $1,200. Planners would then also forecast a 20 percent increase in costs, from $800 to $800 × 1.2 = $960. The pro forma income statement would thus look like this:

Pro Forma Income Statement	
Sales	$1,200
Costs	960
Net income	$ 240

The assumption that all variables will grow by 20 percent lets us easily construct the pro forma balance sheet as well:

Pro Forma Balance Sheet			
Assets	$600 (+100)	Debt	$300 (+50)
		Equity	300 (+50)
Total	$600 (+100)	Total	$600 (+100)

PlanWare provides insight into cash flow forecasting at www.planware.org.

Notice we have increased every item by 20 percent. The numbers in parentheses are the dollar changes for the different items.

Now we have to reconcile these two pro forma statements. How, for example, can net income be equal to $240 and equity increase by only $50? The answer is that Computerfield must have paid out the difference of $240 − 50 = $190, possibly as a cash dividend. In this case dividends are the "plug" variable.

Suppose Computerfield does not pay out the $190. In this case, the addition to retained earnings is the full $240. Computerfield's equity will thus grow to $250 (the starting amount) plus $240 (net income), or $490, and debt must be retired to keep total assets equal to $600.

With $600 in total assets and $490 in equity, debt will have to be $600 − 490 = $110. Because we started with $250 in debt, Computerfield will have to retire $250 − 110 = $140 in debt. The resulting pro forma balance sheet would look like this:

Pro Forma Balance Sheet			
Assets	$600 (+100)	Debt	$110 (−140)
		Equity	490 (+240)
Total	$600 (+100)	Total	$600 (+100)

In this case, debt is the plug variable used to balance projected total assets and liabilities.

This example shows the interaction between sales growth and financial policy. As sales increase, so do total assets. This occurs because the firm must invest in net working capital and fixed assets to support higher sales levels. Because assets are growing, total liabilities and equity, the right side of the balance sheet, will grow as well.

The thing to notice from our simple example is that the way the liabilities and owners' equity change depends on the firm's financing policy and its dividend policy. The growth in assets requires that the firm decide on how to finance that growth. This is strictly a managerial decision. Note that in our example the firm needed no outside funds. This won't usually be the case, so we explore a more detailed situation in the next section.

The Percentage of Sales Approach

In the previous section, we described a simple planning model in which every item increased at the same rate as sales. This may be a reasonable assumption for some elements. For others, such as long-term borrowing, it probably is not: The amount of long-term borrowing is set by management, and it does not necessarily relate directly to the level of sales.

In this section, we describe an extended version of our simple model. The basic idea is to separate the income statement and balance sheet accounts into two groups, those that vary directly with sales and those that do not. Given a sales forecast, we will then be able to calculate how much financing the firm will need to support the predicted sales level.

The financial planning model we describe next is based on the percentage of sales approach. Our goal here is to develop a quick and practical way of generating pro forma statements. We defer discussion of some "bells and whistles" to a later section.

THE INCOME STATEMENT We start out with the most recent income statement for the Rosengarten Corporation, as shown in Table 3.8. Notice that we have still simplified things by including costs, depreciation, and interest in a single cost figure.

Rosengarten has projected a 25 percent increase in sales for the coming year, so we are anticipating sales of $1,000 \times 1.25 = $1,250. To generate a pro forma income statement, we assume that total costs will continue to run at $833/$1,000 = .833, or 83.3 percent of sales. With this assumption, Rosengarten's pro forma income statement is as shown in Table 3.9. The effect here of assuming that costs are a constant percentage of sales is to assume that the profit margin is constant. To check this, notice that the profit margin was $132/$1,000 = .132, or 13.2 percent. In our pro forma statement, the profit margin is $165/$1,250 = .132, or 13.2 percent; so it is unchanged.

Next, we need to project the dividend payment. This amount is up to Rosengarten's management. We will assume Rosengarten has a policy of paying out a constant fraction of net income in the form of a cash dividend. For the most recent year, the dividend payout ratio was:

$$\text{Dividend payout ratio} = \text{Cash dividends/Net income} \qquad (3.23)$$
$$= \$44/\$132 = .3333, \text{ or } 33.33\%$$

TABLE 3.8

ROSENGARTEN CORPORATION Income Statement		
Sales		$1,000
Costs (83.3% of sales)		833
Taxable income		$ 167
Taxes (21%)		35
Net income		$ 132
Dividends	$44	
Addition to retained earnings	88	

TABLE 3.9

ROSENGARTEN CORPORATION Pro Forma Income Statement	
Sales (projected)	$1,250
Costs (83.3% of sales)	1,041
Taxable income	$ 209
Taxes (21%)	44
Net income	$ 165

We can also calculate the ratio of the addition to retained earnings to net income:

Addition to retained earnings/Net income = $88/$132 = .6667, or 66.67%

This ratio is called the retention ratio or plowback ratio, and it is equal to 1 minus the dividend payout ratio because everything not paid out is retained. Assuming that the payout ratio is constant, the projected dividends and addition to retained earnings will be:

Projected dividends paid to shareholders = $165 × .3333 = $ 55
Projected addition to retained earnings = $165 × .6667 = ___110
$$\underline{\underline{\$165}}$$

THE BALANCE SHEET   To generate a pro forma balance sheet, we start with the most recent statement, as shown in Table 3.10.

On our balance sheet, we assume that some items vary directly with sales and others do not. For those items that vary with sales, we express each as a percentage of sales for the year just completed. When an item does not vary directly with sales, we write "n/a" for "not applicable."

For example, on the asset side, inventory is equal to 60 percent of sales (= $600/$1,000) for the year just ended. We assume this percentage applies to the coming year, so for each $1 increase in sales, inventory will rise by $.60. More generally, the ratio of total assets to sales for the year just ended is $3,000/$1,000 = 3, or 300 percent.

This ratio of total assets to sales is sometimes called the capital intensity ratio. It tells us the amount of assets needed to generate $1 in sales; the higher the ratio is, the more capital intensive is the firm. Notice also that this ratio is the reciprocal of the total asset turnover ratio we defined previously.

For Rosengarten, assuming that this ratio is constant, it takes $3 in total assets to generate $1 in sales (apparently Rosengarten is in a relatively capital-intensive business). Therefore, if sales are to increase by $100, Rosengarten will have to increase total assets by three times this amount, or $300.

On the liability side of the balance sheet, we show accounts payable varying with sales. The reason is that we expect to place more orders with our suppliers as sales volume increases, so payables will change "spontaneously" with sales. Notes payable, on the other

TABLE 3.10

ROSENGARTEN CORPORATION					
Balance Sheet					
Assets			**Liabilities and Owners' Equity**		
	$	**Percentage of Sales**		**$**	**Percentage of Sales**
Current assets			Current liabilities		
Cash	$ 160	16%	Accounts payable	$ 300	30%
Accounts receivable	440	44	Notes payable	100	n/a
Inventory	600	60	Total	$ 400	n/a
Total	$1,200	120	Long-term debt	$ 800	n/a
Fixed assets			Owners' equity		
Net plant and equipment	$1,800	180%	Common stock and paid-in surplus	$ 800	n/a
			Retained earnings	1,000	n/a
			Total	$1,800	n/a
Total assets	$3,000	300%	Total liabilities and owners' equity	$3,000	n/a

hand, represents short-term debt such as bank borrowing. This will not vary unless we take specific actions to change the amount, so we mark this item as "n/a."

Similarly, we use "n/a" for long-term debt because it won't automatically change with sales. The same is true for common stock and paid-in surplus. The last item on the right side, retained earnings, will vary with sales, but it won't be a simple percentage of sales. Instead, we will explicitly calculate the change in retained earnings based on our projected net income and dividends.

We can now construct a partial pro forma balance sheet for Rosengarten. We do this by using the percentages we have just calculated wherever possible to calculate the projected amounts. For example, net fixed assets are 180 percent of sales; so, with a new sales level of $1,250, the net fixed asset amount will be $1.80 \times \$1,250 = \$2,250$, representing an increase of $\$2,250 - 1,800 = \$450$ in plant and equipment. It is important to note that for items that don't vary directly with sales, we initially assume no change and write in the original amounts. The result is shown in Table 3.11. Notice that the change in retained earnings is equal to the $110 addition to retained earnings we calculated earlier.

Inspecting our pro forma balance sheet, we notice that assets are projected to increase by $750. However, without additional financing, liabilities and equity will increase by only $185, leaving a shortfall of $750 - 185 = \$565$. We label this amount *external financing needed* (EFN).

Rather than create pro forma statements, if we were so inclined, we could calculate EFN directly as follows:

$$EFN = \frac{\text{Assets}}{\text{Sales}} \times \Delta \text{Sales} - \frac{\text{Spontaneous liabilities}}{\text{Sales}} \times \Delta \text{Sales} - PM \qquad (3.24)$$
$$\times \text{Projected sales} \times (1 - d)$$

In this expression, "ΔSales" is the projected change in sales (in dollars). In our example projected sales for next year are $1,250, an increase of $250 over the previous year, so ΔSales = $250. By "Spontaneous liabilities," we mean liabilities that naturally move up and down with sales. For Rosengarten, the spontaneous liabilities are the $300 in accounts payable. Finally, *PM* and *d* are the profit margin and dividend payout ratios, which we previously calculated as

TABLE 3.11

ROSENGARTEN CORPORATION						
Partial Pro Forma Balance Sheet						
Assets			**Liabilities and Owners' Equity**			
	Projected	**Change from Previous Year**		**Projected**	**Change from Previous Year**	
Current assets			Current liabilities			
Cash	$ 200	$ 40	Accounts payable	$ 375	$ 75	
Accounts receivable	550	110	Notes payable	100	0	
Inventory	750	150	Total	$ 475	$ 75	
Total	$1,500	$300	Long-term debt	$ 800	$ 0	
Fixed assets			Owners' equity			
Net plant and equipment	$2,250	$450	Common stock and paid-in surplus	$ 800	$ 0	
			Retained earnings	1,110	110	
			Total	$1,910	$110	
Total assets	$3,750	$750	Total liabilities and owners' equity	$3,185	$185	
			External financing needed	$ 565	$565	

13.2 percent and 33 1/3 percent, respectively. Total assets and sales are $3,000 and $1,000, respectively, so we have:

$$EFN = \frac{\$3,000}{1,000} \times \$250 - \frac{\$300}{1,000} \times \$250 - .132 \times \$1,250 \times (1 - .3333) = \$565$$

In this calculation, notice that there are three parts. The first part is the projected increase in assets, which is calculated using the capital intensity ratio. The second is the spontaneous increase in liabilities. The third part is the product of profit margin and projected sales, which is projected net income, multiplied by the retention ratio. Thus, the third part is the projected addition to retained earnings.

A PARTICULAR SCENARIO   Our financial planning model now reminds us of one of those good news–bad news jokes. The good news is we're projecting a 25 percent increase in sales. The bad news is this isn't going to happen unless Rosengarten can somehow raise $565 in new financing.

This is a good example of how the planning process can point out problems and potential conflicts. If, for example, Rosengarten has a goal of not borrowing any additional funds and not selling any new equity, then a 25 percent increase in sales is probably not feasible.

If we take the need for $565 in new financing as given, we know that Rosengarten has three possible sources: short-term borrowing, long-term borrowing, and new equity. The choice of some combination among these three is up to management; we will illustrate only one of the many possibilities.

Suppose Rosengarten decides to borrow the needed funds. In this case, the firm might choose to borrow some over the short term and some over the long term. For example, current assets increased by $300 whereas current liabilities rose by only $75. Rosengarten could borrow $300 − 75 = $225 in short-term notes payable and leave total net working capital unchanged. With $565 needed, the remaining $565 − 225 = $340 would have to come from long-term debt. Table 3.12 shows the completed pro forma balance sheet for Rosengarten.

We have used a combination of short- and long-term debt as the plug here, but we emphasize that this is just one possible strategy; it is not necessarily the best one by any means. We could (and should) investigate many other scenarios. The various ratios we discussed earlier come in handy here. For example, with the scenario we have just examined, we would surely

TABLE 3.12

ROSENGARTEN CORPORATION Pro Forma Balance Sheet					
Assets			**Liabilities and Owners' Equity**		
	Projected	**Change from Previous Year**		**Projected**	**Change from Previous Year**
Current assets			Current liabilities		
Cash	$ 200	$ 40	Accounts payable	$ 375	$ 75
Accounts receivable	550	110	Notes payable	325	225
Inventory	750	150	Total	$ 700	$300
Total	$1,500	$300	Long-term debt	$1,140	$340
Fixed assets			Owners' equity		
Net plant and equipment	$2,250	$450	Common stock and paid-in surplus	$ 800	$ 0
			Retained earnings	1,110	110
			Total	$1,910	$110
Total assets	$3,750	$750	Total liabilities and owners' equity	$3,750	$750

want to examine the current ratio and the total debt ratio to see if we were comfortable with the new projected debt levels.

AN ALTERNATIVE SCENARIO The assumption that assets are a fixed percentage of sales is convenient, but it may not be suitable in many cases. In particular, note that we effectively assumed that Rosengarten was using its fixed assets at 100 percent of capacity because any increase in sales led to an increase in fixed assets. For most businesses, there would be some slack or excess capacity, and production could be increased by perhaps running an extra shift. According to the Federal Reserve, the overall capacity utilization for U.S. manufacturing companies in November 2018 was 78.5 percent, up from a recent low of 64.4 percent in June 2009.

If we assume that Rosengarten is operating at only 70 percent of capacity, then the need for external funds will be quite different. When we say "70 percent of capacity," we mean that the current sales level is 70 percent of the full-capacity sales level:

> **Current sales = $1,000 = .70 × Full-capacity sales**
> **Full-capacity sales = $1,000/.70 = $1,429**

This tells us that sales could increase by almost 43 percent—from $1,000 to $1,429—before any new fixed assets would be needed.

In our previous scenario, we assumed it would be necessary to add $450 in net fixed assets. In the current scenario, no spending on net fixed assets is needed because sales are projected to rise only to $1,250, which is substantially less than the $1,429 full-capacity level.

As a result, our original estimate of $565 in external funds needed is too high. We estimated that $450 in net new fixed assets would be needed. Instead, no spending on new net fixed assets is necessary. Thus, if we are currently operating at 70 percent capacity, we need only $565 − 450 = $115 in external funds. The excess capacity thus makes a considerable difference in our projections.

EXAMPLE 3.5

The Capital Intensity Ratio

Suppose Rosengarten is operating at 90 percent capacity. What would sales be at full capacity? What is the capital intensity ratio at full capacity? What is EFN in this case?

Full-capacity sales would be $1,000/.90 = $1,111. From Table 3.10, we know that fixed assets are $1,800. At full capacity, the ratio of fixed assets to sales is thus:

$$\frac{\text{Fixed assets}}{\text{Full-capacity sales}} = \frac{\$1,800}{\$1,111} = 1.62$$

So, Rosengarten needs $1.62 in fixed assets for every $1 in sales once it reaches full capacity. At the projected sales level of $1,250, then, it needs $1,250 × 1.62 = $2,025 in fixed assets. Compared to the $2,250 we originally projected, this is $225 less, so EFN is $565 − 225 = $340.

Current assets would still be $1,500, so total assets would be $1,500 + 2,025 = $3,525. The capital intensity ratio would thus be $3,525/$1,250 = 2.82, which is less than our original value of 3 because of the excess capacity.

3.5 EXTERNAL FINANCING AND GROWTH

Growth and the need for external financing are obviously related. All other things staying the same, the higher the rate of growth in sales or assets, the greater will be the need for external financing. In the previous section, we took a growth rate as given, and then we determined the amount of external financing needed to support that growth. In this section,

ExcelMaster
coverage online

www.mhhe.com/RossCore6e

we turn things around a bit. We will take the firm's financial policy as given and then examine the relationship between that financial policy and the firm's ability to finance new investments and thereby grow.

We emphasize that we are focusing on growth not because growth is an appropriate goal; instead, for our purposes, growth is a convenient means of examining the interactions between investment and financing decisions. In effect, we assume that the use of growth as a basis for planning is a reflection of the very high level of aggregation used in the planning process.

EFN and Growth

The first thing we need to do is establish the relationship between EFN and growth. To do this, we introduce the simplified income statement and balance sheet for the Hoffman Company in Table 3.13. Notice that we have simplified the balance sheet by combining short-term and long-term debt into a single total debt figure. Effectively, we are assuming that none of the current liabilities vary spontaneously with sales. This assumption isn't as restrictive as it sounds. If any current liabilities (such as accounts payable) vary with sales, we can assume that any such accounts have been netted out in current assets. Also, we continue to combine depreciation, interest, and costs on the income statement.

Suppose the Hoffman Company is forecasting next year's sales level at $600, a $100 increase. Notice that the percentage increase in sales is $100/$500 = 20 percent. Using the percentage of sales approach and the figures in Table 3.13, we can prepare a pro forma income statement and balance sheet as in Table 3.14. As Table 3.14 illustrates, at a 20 percent growth rate, Hoffman needs $100 in new assets. The projected addition to retained earnings is $52.8, so the external financing needed, EFN, is $100 − 52.8 = $47.2.

Notice that the debt-equity ratio for Hoffman was originally (from Table 3.13) equal to $250/$250 = 1.0. We will assume that the Hoffman Company does not wish to sell new equity. In this case, the $47.2 in EFN will have to be borrowed. What will the new debt-equity ratio be? From Table 3.14, we know that total owners' equity is projected at $302.8. The new total debt will be the original $250 plus $47.2 in new borrowing, or $297.2 total. The debt-equity ratio thus falls slightly from 1.0 to $297.2/$302.8 = .98.

TABLE 3.13

HOFFMAN COMPANY Income Statement and Balance Sheet				
INCOME STATEMENT				
Sales			$500	
Costs			412	
Taxable income			$ 88	
Taxes (25%)			22	
Net income			$ 66	
Dividends		$22		
Addition to retained earnings		44		

BALANCE SHEET					
Assets			**Liabilities and Owners' Equity**		
	$	**Percentage of Sales**		**$**	**Percentage of Sales**
Current assets	$200	40%	Total debt	$250	n/a
Net fixed assets	300	60	Owners' equity	250	n/a
Total assets	$500	100%	Total liabilities and owners' equity	$500	n/a

TABLE 3.14

HOFFMAN COMPANY		
Pro Forma Income Statement and Balance Sheet		
INCOME STATEMENT		
Sales (projected)		$600.0
Costs (82.4% of sales)		494.4
Taxable income		$105.6
Taxes (25%)		26.4
Net income		$ 79.2
Dividends	$26.4	
Addition to retained earnings	52.8	

BALANCE SHEET					
Assets			**Liabilities and Owners' Equity**		
	$	Percentage of Sales		$	Percentage of Sales
Current assets	$240.0	40%	Total debt	$250.0	n/a
Net fixed assets	360.0	60	Owners' equity	302.8	n/a
Total assets	$600.0	100%	Total liabilities and owners' equity	$552.8	n/a
			External financing needed	$ 47.2	n/a

Table 3.15 shows EFN for several different growth rates. The projected addition to retained earnings and the projected debt-equity ratio for each scenario are also given (you should probably calculate a few of these for practice). In determining the debt-equity ratios, we assumed that any needed funds were borrowed, and we also assumed any surplus funds were used to pay off debt. Thus, for the zero growth case the debt falls by $44, from $250 to $206. In Table 3.15, notice that the increase in assets required is equal to the original assets of $500 multiplied by the growth rate. Similarly, the addition to retained earnings is equal to the original $44 plus $44 times the growth rate.

Table 3.15 shows that for relatively low growth rates, Hoffman will run a surplus, and its debt-equity ratio will decline. Once the growth rate increases to about 10 percent, however, the surplus becomes a deficit. Furthermore, as the growth rate exceeds approximately 20 percent, the debt-equity ratio passes its original value of 1.0.

Figure 3.1 illustrates the connection between growth in sales and external financing needed in more detail by plotting asset needs and additions to retained earnings from Table 3.15 against the growth rates. As shown, the need for new assets grows at a much faster rate than the addition to retained earnings, so the internal financing provided by the addition to retained earnings rapidly disappears.

TABLE 3.15

Growth and Projected EFN for the Hoffman Company

Projected Sales Growth	Increase in Assets Required	Addition to Retained Earnings	External Financing Needed, EFN	Projected Debt-Equity Ratio
0%	$ 0	$44.0	−$44.0	.70
5	25	46.2	−21.2	.77
10	50	48.4	1.6	.84
15	75	50.6	24.4	.91
20	100	52.8	47.2	.98
25	125	55.0	70.0	1.05

FIGURE 3.1

Growth and Related
Financing Needed for the
Hoffman Company

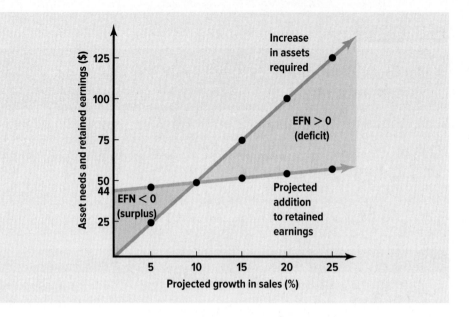

As this discussion shows, whether a firm runs a cash surplus or deficit depends on growth. Microsoft is a good example. Its revenue growth in the 1990s was amazing, averaging well over 30 percent per year for the decade. Growth slowed down noticeably over the 2000–2019 period, but, nonetheless, Microsoft's combination of growth and substantial profit margins led to enormous cash surpluses. In part because Microsoft paid relatively low dividends, the cash really piled up; in 2019, Microsoft's cash and short-term investment hoard exceeded $135 billion.

Financial Policy and Growth

Based on our preceding discussion, we see that there is a direct link between growth and external financing. In this section, we discuss two growth rates that are particularly useful in long-range planning.

THE INTERNAL GROWTH RATE   The first growth rate of interest is the maximum growth rate that can be achieved with no external financing of any kind. We will call this the internal growth rate because this is the rate the firm can maintain with internal financing only. In Figure 3.1, this internal growth rate is represented by the point where the two lines cross. At this point, the required increase in assets is exactly equal to the addition to retained earnings, and EFN is therefore zero. We have seen that this happens when the growth rate is slightly less than 10 percent. With a little algebra (see Problem 28 at the end of the chapter), we can define this growth rate more precisely as:

$$\text{Internal growth rate} = \frac{\text{ROA} \times b}{1 - \text{ROA} \times b} \tag{3.25}$$

where ROA is the return on assets we discussed earlier and b is the plowback, or retention, ratio, also defined earlier in this chapter.

For the Hoffman Company, net income was $66 and total assets were $500. ROA is thus $66/$500 = .132, or 13.2 percent. Of the $66 net income, $44 was retained, so the plowback ratio, b, is $44/$66 = .6667. With these numbers, we can calculate the internal growth rate as:

$$\begin{aligned}
\text{Internal growth rate} &= \frac{\text{ROA} \times b}{1 - \text{ROA} \times b} \\[6pt]
&= \frac{.132 \times .6667}{1 - .132 \times .6667} = .0965, \text{ or } 9.65\%
\end{aligned}$$

Thus, the Hoffman Company can expand at a maximum rate of 9.65 percent per year without external financing.

THE SUSTAINABLE GROWTH RATE   We have seen that if the Hoffman Company wishes to grow more rapidly than at a rate of 9.65 percent per year, external financing must be arranged. The second growth rate of interest is the maximum growth rate a firm can achieve with no external *equity* financing while it maintains a constant debt-equity ratio. This rate is commonly called the sustainable growth rate because it is the maximum rate of growth a firm can maintain without increasing its financial leverage.

There are various reasons why a firm might wish to avoid equity sales. For example, new equity sales can be expensive because of the substantial fees that may be involved. Alternatively, the current owners may not wish to bring in new owners or contribute additional equity. Why a firm might view a particular debt-equity ratio as optimal is discussed in later chapters; for now, we will take it as given.

Based on Table 3.15, the sustainable growth rate for Hoffman is approximately 20 percent because the debt-equity ratio is near 1.0 at that growth rate. The precise value can be calculated as follows (see Problem 28 at the end of the chapter):

$$\text{Sustainable growth rate} = \frac{\text{ROE} \times b}{1 - \text{ROE} \times b} \tag{3.26}$$

This is identical to the internal growth rate except that ROE, return on equity, is used instead of ROA.

For the Hoffman Company, net income was $66 and total equity was $250; ROE is thus $66/$250 = .264, or 26.4 percent. The plowback ratio, *b,* is still .6667, so we can calculate the sustainable growth rate as:

$$
\begin{aligned}
\text{Sustainable growth rate} &= \frac{\text{ROE} \times b}{1 - \text{ROE} \times b} \\
&= \frac{.264 \times .6667}{1 - .264 \times .6667} \\
&= .2136, \text{ or } 21.36\%
\end{aligned}
$$

Thus, the Hoffman Company can expand at a maximum rate of 21.36 percent per year without external equity financing.

EXAMPLE 3.6

Sustainable Growth

Suppose Hoffman grows at exactly the sustainable growth rate of 21.36 percent. What will the pro forma statements look like?

At a 21.36 percent growth rate, sales will rise from $500 to $606.8. The pro forma income statement will look like this:

HOFFMAN COMPANY Pro Forma Income Statement		
Sales (projected)		$606.8
Costs (82.4% of sales)		500.0
Taxable income		$106.8
Taxes (25%)		26.7
Net income		$ 80.1
Dividends	$26.7	
Addition to retained earnings	53.4	

(Continued)

We construct the balance sheet just as we did before. Notice, in this case, that owners' equity will rise from $250 to $303.4 because the addition to retained earnings is $53.4.

HOFFMAN COMPANY Pro Forma Balance Sheet					
Assets			**Liabilities and Owners' Equity**		
	$	**Percentage of Sales**		**$**	**Percentage of Sales**
Current assets	$242.7	40%	Total debt	$250.0	n/a
Net fixed assets	364.1	60	Owners' equity	303.4	n/a
Total assets	$606.8	100%	Total liabilities and owners' equity	$553.4	n/a
			External financing needed	$ 53.4	n/a

As illustrated, EFN is $53.4. If Hoffman borrows this amount, then total debt will rise to $303.4, and the debt-equity ratio will be exactly 1.0, which verifies our earlier calculation. At any other growth rate, something would have to change.

DETERMINANTS OF GROWTH   Earlier in this chapter, we saw that the return on equity, ROE, could be decomposed into its various components using the DuPont identity. Because ROE appears so prominently in the determination of the sustainable growth rate, it is obvious that the factors important in determining ROE are also important determinants of growth.

From our previous discussions, we know that ROE can be written as the product of three factors:

ROE = Profit margin × Total asset turnover × Equity multiplier

---

If we examine our expression for the sustainable growth rate, we see that anything that increases ROE will increase the sustainable growth rate by making the top larger and the bottom smaller. Increasing the plowback ratio will have the same effect.

Putting it all together, what we have is that a firm's ability to sustain growth depends explicitly on the following four factors:

1. *Profit margin:* An increase in profit margin will increase the firm's ability to generate funds internally and thereby increase its sustainable growth.
2. *Dividend policy:* A decrease in the percentage of net income paid out as dividends will increase the retention ratio. This increases internally generated equity and thus increases sustainable growth.
3. *Financial policy:* An increase in the debt-equity ratio increases the firm's financial leverage. Because this makes additional debt financing available, it increases the sustainable growth rate.
4. *Total asset turnover:* An increase in the firm's total asset turnover increases the sales generated for each dollar in assets. This decreases the firm's need for new assets as sales grow and thereby increases the sustainable growth rate. Notice that increasing total asset turnover is the same thing as decreasing capital intensity.

The sustainable growth rate is a very useful planning number. What it illustrates is the explicit relationship between the firm's four major areas of concern: its operating efficiency as measured by profit margin, its asset use efficiency as measured by total asset turnover, its dividend policy as measured by the retention ratio, and its financial policy as measured by the debt-equity ratio.

Profit Margins and Sustainable Growth

The Sandar Co. has a debt-equity ratio of .5, a profit margin of 3 percent, a dividend payout ratio of 40 percent, and a capital intensity ratio of 1. What is its sustainable growth rate? If Sandar desired a 10 percent sustainable growth rate and planned to achieve this goal by improving profit margins, what would you think?

ROE = .03 × 1 × 1.5 = .045, or 4.5%
Retention ratio = 1 − .40 = .60
Sustainable growth = .045(.60)/[1 − .045(.60)] = .0277, or 2.77%

For the company to achieve a 10 percent growth rate, the profit margin will have to rise. To see this, assume that sustainable growth is equal to 10 percent and then solve for profit margin, PM:

.10 = PM(1.5)(.6)/[1 − PM(1.5)(.6)]
PM = .1/.99 = .101, or 10.1%

For the plan to succeed, the necessary increase in profit margin is substantial, from below 3 percent to about 10 percent. This may not be feasible.

Given values for all four of these, there is only one growth rate that can be achieved. This is an important point, so it bears restating:

If a firm does not wish to sell new equity and its profit margin, dividend policy, financial policy, and total asset turnover (or capital intensity) are all fixed, then there is only one possible growth rate.

One of the primary benefits of financial planning is that it ensures internal consistency among the firm's various goals. The concept of the sustainable growth rate captures this element nicely. Also, we now see how a financial planning model can be used to test the feasibility of a planned growth rate. If sales are to grow at a rate higher than the sustainable growth rate, the firm must increase profit margins, increase total asset turnover, increase financial leverage, increase earnings retention, or sell new shares.

The two growth rates, internal and sustainable, are summarized in Table 3.16.

TABLE 3.16

Summary of Internal and Sustainable Growth Rates

I. Internal Growth Rate

$$\text{Internal growth rate} = \frac{\text{ROA} \times b}{1 - \text{ROA} \times b}$$

where

ROA = Return on assets = Net income/Total assets

b = Plowback (retention) ratio

b = Addition to retained earnings/Net income

The internal growth rate is the maximum growth rate that can be achieved with no external financing of any kind.

II. Sustainable Growth Rate

$$\text{Sustainable growth rate} = \frac{\text{ROE} \times b}{1 - \text{ROE} \times b}$$

where

ROE = Return on equity = Net income/Total equity

b = Plowback (retention) ratio

b = Addition to retained earnings/Net income

The sustainable growth rate is the maximum growth rate that can be achieved with no external equity financing while maintaining a constant debt-equity ratio.

A Note about Sustainable Growth Rate Calculations

Very commonly, the sustainable growth rate is calculated using just the numerator in our expression, ROE × b. This causes some confusion, which we can clear up here. The issue has to do with how ROE is computed. Recall that ROE is calculated as net income divided by total equity. If total equity is taken from an ending balance sheet (as we have done consistently, and is commonly done in practice), then our formula is the right one. However, if total equity is from the beginning of the period, then the simpler formula is the correct one.

In principle, you'll get exactly the same sustainable growth rate regardless of which way you calculate it (as long as you match up the ROE calculation with the right formula). In reality, you may see some differences because of accounting-related complications. By the way, if you use the average of beginning and ending equity (as some advocate), yet another formula is needed. All of our comments here apply to the internal growth rate as well.

3.6 SOME CAVEATS REGARDING FINANCIAL PLANNING MODELS

Financial planning models do not always ask the right questions. A primary reason is that they tend to rely on accounting relationships and not financial relationships. In particular, the three basic elements of firm value tend to get left out—namely, cash flow size, risk, and timing.

Because of this, financial planning models sometimes do not produce output that gives the user many meaningful clues about what strategies will lead to increases in value. Instead, they divert the user's attention to questions concerning the association of, say, the debt-equity ratio and firm growth.

The financial model we used for the Hoffman Company was simple—in fact, too simple. Our model, like many in use today, is really an accounting statement generator at heart. Such models are useful for pointing out inconsistencies and reminding us of financial needs, but they offer little guidance concerning what to do about these problems.

In closing our discussion, we should add that financial planning is an iterative process. Plans are created, examined, and modified over and over. The final plan will be a result negotiated between all the different parties to the process. In fact, long-term financial planning in most corporations relies on what might be called the Procrustes approach.[5] Upper-level management has a goal in mind, and it is up to the planning staff to rework and to ultimately deliver a feasible plan that meets that goal.

The final plan will therefore implicitly contain different goals in different areas and also satisfy many constraints. For this reason, such a plan need not be a dispassionate assessment of what we think the future will bring; it may instead be a means of reconciling the planned activities of different groups and a way of setting common goals for the future.

However it is done, the important thing to remember is that financial planning should not become a purely mechanical exercise. If it does, it will probably focus on the wrong things. Nevertheless, the alternative to planning is stumbling into the future. Perhaps the immortal Yogi Berra (the baseball catcher, not the cartoon character), said it best: "Ya gotta watch out if you don't know where you're goin'. You just might not get there."[6]

---

[5] In Greek mythology, Procrustes is a giant who seizes travelers and ties them to an iron bed. He stretches them or cuts off their legs as needed to make them fit the bed.

[6] We're not exactly sure what this means either, but we like the sound of it.

SUMMARY AND CONCLUSIONS

This chapter focuses on working with information contained in financial statements. Specifically, we studied standardized financial statements, ratio analysis, and long-term financial planning.

1. We explained that differences in firm size make it difficult to compare financial statements, and we discussed how to form common-size statements to make comparisons easier and more meaningful.

2. Evaluating ratios of accounting numbers is another way of comparing financial statement information. We defined a number of the most commonly used ratios, and we discussed the famous DuPont identity.

3. We showed how pro forma financial statements can be generated and used to plan for future financing needs.

After you have studied this chapter, we hope that you have some perspective on the uses and abuses of financial statement information. You should also find that your vocabulary of business and financial terms has grown substantially.

CONCEPT QUESTIONS

1. **Financial Ratio Analysis** A financial ratio by itself tells us little about a company because financial ratios vary a great deal across industries. There are two basic methods for analyzing financial ratios for a company: time trend analysis and peer group analysis. Why might each of these analysis methods be useful? What does each tell you about the company's financial health?

2. **Industry-Specific Ratios** So-called same-store sales are a very important measure for companies as diverse as McDonald's and Home Depot. As the name suggests, examining same-store sales means comparing revenues from the same stores or restaurants at two different points in time. Why might companies focus on same-store sales rather than total sales?

3. **Sales Forecast** Why do you think most long-term financial planning begins with sales forecasts? Put differently, why are future sales the key input?

4. **Sustainable Growth** In the chapter, we used Rosengarten Corporation to demonstrate how to calculate EFN. The ROE for Rosengarten is about 7.3 percent, and the plowback ratio is about 67 percent. If you calculate the sustainable growth rate for Rosengarten, you will find it is only 5.14 percent. In our calculation for EFN, we used a growth rate of 25 percent. Is this possible? (*Hint:* Yes. How?)

5. **EFN and Growth Rate** Broslofski Co. maintains a positive retention ratio and keeps its debt-equity ratio constant every year. When sales grow by 20 percent, the firm has a negative projected EFN. What does this tell you about the firm's sustainable growth rate? Do you know, with certainty, if the internal growth rate is greater than or less than 20 percent? Why? What happens to the projected EFN if the retention ratio is increased? What if the retention ratio is decreased? What if the retention ratio is zero?

6. **Common-Size Financials** One tool of financial analysis is common-size financial statements. Why do you think common-size income statements and balance sheets are used? Note that the accounting statement of cash flows is not converted into a common-size statement. Why do you think this is?

7. **Asset Utilization and EFN** One of the implicit assumptions we made in calculating the external funds needed was that the company was operating at full capacity. If the company is operating at less than full capacity, how will this affect the external funds needed?

Use the following information to answer the next five questions: A small business called The Grandmother Calendar Company began selling personalized photo calendar kits. The kits were a hit, and sales soon sharply exceeded forecasts. The rush of orders created a huge backlog, so the company leased more space and expanded capacity, but it still could not keep up with demand. Equipment failed from overuse and quality suffered. Working capital was drained to expand production, and, at the same time, payments from customers were often delayed until the product was shipped. Unable to deliver on orders, the company became so strapped for cash that employee paychecks began to bounce. Finally, out of cash, the company ceased operations entirely three years later.

8. **Product Sales** Do you think the company would have suffered the same fate if its product had been less popular? Why or why not?

9. **Cash Flow** The Grandmother Calendar Company clearly had a cash flow problem. In the context of the cash flow analysis we developed in Chapter 2, what was the impact of customers not paying until orders were shipped?

10. **Corporate Borrowing** If the firm was so successful at selling, why wouldn't a bank or some other lender step in and provide it with the cash it needed to continue?

11. **Cash Flow** Which is the biggest culprit here: too many orders, too little cash, or too little production capacity?

12. **Cash Flow** What are some of the actions that a small company like The Grandmother Calendar Company can take (besides expansion of capacity) if it finds itself in a situation in which growth in sales outstrips production?

13. **Comparing ROE and ROA** Both ROE and ROA measure profitability. Which one is more useful for comparing two companies? Why?

14. **Ratio Analysis** Consider the ratio EBITDA/Assets. What does this ratio tell us? Why might it be more useful than ROA in comparing two companies?

QUESTIONS AND PROBLEMS

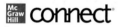

Basic
(Questions 1–10)

1. **DuPont Identity** If Hailey, Inc., has an equity multiplier of .85, total asset turnover of 2.10, and a profit margin of 5.97 percent, what is its ROE?

2. **Equity Multiplier and Return on Equity** Bello Company has a debt-equity ratio of .90. Return on assets is 7.7 percent, and total equity is $880,000. What is the equity multiplier? Return on equity? Net income?

3. **Using the DuPont Identity** Y3K, Inc., has sales of $5,930, total assets of $3,020, and a debt-equity ratio of .55. If its return on equity is 14 percent, what is its net income?

4. **EFN** The most recent financial statements for Locke, Inc., are shown here:

INCOME STATEMENT		BALANCE SHEET			
Sales	$45,000	Assets	$104,500	Debt	$ 28,200
Costs	36,100			Equity	76,300
Taxable income	$ 8,900	Total	$104,500	Total	$104,500
Taxes (24%)	2,136				
Net income	$ 6,764				

Assets and costs are proportional to sales; debt and equity are not. A dividend of $2,200 was paid, and the company wishes to maintain a constant payout ratio. Next year's sales are projected to be $53,100. What is the external financing needed?

5. Sales and Growth The most recent financial statements for Beckett Co. are shown here:

INCOME STATEMENT		BALANCE SHEET			
Sales	$74,300	Current assets	$ 20,000	Long term debt	$ 52,000
Costs	57,800	Fixed assets	146,000	Equity	114,000
Taxable income	$16,500	Total	$166,000	Total	$166,000
Taxes (21%)	3,465				
Net income	$13,035				

Assets and costs are proportional to sales. The company maintains a constant 30 percent dividend payout ratio and a constant debt-equity ratio. What is the maximum increase in sales that can be sustained assuming no new equity is issued?

6. Sustainable Growth If the SGS Corp. has an ROE of 13.8 percent and a payout ratio of 20 percent, what is its sustainable growth rate?

7. Sustainable Growth Assuming the following ratios are constant, what is the sustainable growth rate?

Total asset turnover	= 3.35
Profit margin	= 7.6%
Equity multiplier	= 1.25
Payout ratio	= 70%

8. Calculating EFN The most recent financial statements for Incredible Edibles, Inc., are shown here (assuming no income taxes):

INCOME STATEMENT		BALANCE SHEET			
Sales	$14,200	Assets	$29,100	Debt	$ 6,200
Costs	10,840			Equity	22,900
Net income	$ 3,360	Total	$29,100	Total	$29,100

Assets and costs are proportional to sales; debt and equity are not. No dividends are paid. Next year's sales are projected to be $16,472. What is the external financing needed?

9. External Funds Needed Cheryl Colby, CFO of Charming Florist Ltd., has created the firm's pro forma balance sheet for the next fiscal year. Sales are projected to grow by 15 percent to $179.4 million. Current assets, fixed assets, and short-term debt are 20 percent, 90 percent, and 15 percent of sales, respectively. The company pays out 40 percent of its net income in dividends. The company currently has $27.2 million of long-term debt, and $13 million in common stock par value. The profit margin is 10 percent.

  a. Construct the current balance sheet for the firm using the projected sales figure.

  b. Based on the sales growth forecast, how much does the company need in external funds for the upcoming fiscal year?

  c. Construct the firm's pro forma balance sheet for the next fiscal year and confirm the external funds needed that you calculated in part (b).

10. Sustainable Growth Rate The Cornelius Company has an ROE of 12.15 percent and a payout ratio of 30 percent.

  a. What is the company's sustainable growth rate?

  b. Can the company's actual growth rate be different from its sustainable growth rate? Why or why not?

  c. How can the company increase its sustainable growth rate?

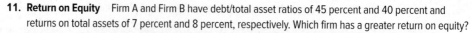

Intermediate
(Questions 11–23)

11. **Return on Equity**   Firm A and Firm B have debt/total asset ratios of 45 percent and 40 percent and returns on total assets of 7 percent and 8 percent, respectively. Which firm has a greater return on equity?

 12. **Ratios and Foreign Companies**   Prince Albert Canning PLC had a net loss of £21,435 on sales of £168,327. What was the company's profit margin? Does the fact that these figures are quoted in a foreign currency make any difference? Why? In dollars, sales were $214,496. What was the net loss in dollars?

13. **External Funds Needed**   The Optical Scam Company has forecast a sales growth rate of 18 percent for next year. The current financial statements are shown below. Current assets, fixed assets, and short-term debt are proportional to sales.

INCOME STATEMENT	
Sales	$34,700,000
Costs	27,100,000
Taxable income	$ 7,600,000
Taxes	1,748,000
Net income	$ 5,852,000
Dividends	$1,650,000
Addition to retained earnings	4,202,000

BALANCE SHEET			
Assets		**Liabilities and Equity**	
Current assets	$11,280,000	Short-term debt	$ 5,410,000
		Long-term debt	$ 8,080,000
Fixed assets	33,700,000		
		Common stock	$ 3,100,000
		Accumulated retained earnings	28,390,000
		Total equity	$31,490,000
Total assets	$44,980,000	Total liabilities and equity	$44,980,000

  a. Using the equation from the chapter, calculate the external funds needed for next year.

  b. Construct the firm's pro forma balance sheet for next year and confirm the external funds needed you calculated in part (a).

  c. Calculate the sustainable growth rate for the company.

  d. Can the company eliminate the need for external funds by changing its dividend policy? What other options are available to the company to meet its growth objectives?

14. **Days' Sales in Receivables**   A company has net income of $284,000, a profit margin of 8.1 percent, and an accounts receivable balance of $189,600. Assuming 80 percent of sales are on credit, what is the company's days' sales in receivables?

 15. **Ratios and Fixed Assets**   The Lawrence Company has a ratio of long-term debt to long-term debt plus equity of .45 and a current ratio of 1.35. Current liabilities are $1,380, sales are $10,530, profit margin is 7.5 percent, and ROE is 13.45 percent. What is the amount of the firm's net fixed assets?

16. **Calculating the Cash Coverage Ratio**   FVA Inc.'s net income for the most recent year was $32,145. The tax rate was 21 percent. The firm paid $8,640 in total interest expense and deducted $9,730 in depreciation expense. What was the cash coverage ratio for the year?

17. **Cost of Goods Sold**   Walker Corp. has current liabilities of $305,000, a quick ratio of .85, inventory turnover of 14.85, and a current ratio of 1.45. What is the cost of goods sold for the company?

18. Common-Size and Common-Base-Year Financial Statements In addition to common-size financial statements, common-base-year financial statements are often used. Common-base-year financial statements are constructed by dividing the current-year account value by the base-year account value. Thus, the result shows the growth rate in the account. Using the financial statements below, construct the common-size balance sheet and common-base-year balance sheet for the company. Use 2019 as the base year.

JARROW CORPORATION 2019 and 2020 Balance Sheets					
Assets			**Liabilities and Owners' Equity**		
	2019	**2020**		**2019**	**2020**
Current assets			Current liabilities		
Cash	$ 21,514	$ 25,878	Accounts receivable	$ 29,711	$ 37,027
Accounts receivable	34,278	36,993	Notes payable	37,514	45,397
Inventory	28,328	65,749	Total	$ 67,225	$ 82,424
Total	$ 84,120	$128,620	Long-term debt	$ 51,200	$ 80,500
			Owners' equity		
Fixed assets			Common stock and paid-in surplus	$ 63,000	$ 63,000
Net plant and equipment	$548,909	$563,412	Accumulated retained earnings	451,604	466,108
			Total	$514,604	$529,108
Total assets	$633,029	$692,032	Total liabilities and owners' equity	$633,029	$692,032

19. Full-Capacity Sales Allen Mfg., Inc., is currently operating at only 94 percent of fixed asset capacity. Current sales are $850,000. How fast can sales grow before any new fixed assets are needed?

20. Fixed Assets and Capacity Usage For the company in the previous problem, suppose fixed assets are currently $935,000 and sales are projected to grow to $925,000. How much in new fixed assets is required to support this growth in sales? Assume the company will operate at full capacity next year.

21. Calculating EFN The most recent financial statements for Retro Machine, Inc., follow. Sales for 2021 are projected to grow by 20 percent. Interest expense will remain constant; the tax rate and the dividend payout rate will also remain constant. Costs, other expenses, current assets, fixed assets, and accounts payable increase spontaneously with sales. If the firm is operating at full capacity and no new debt or equity is issued, what is the external financing needed to support the 20 percent growth rate in sales?

RETRO MACHINE INC. 2020 Income Statement	
Sales	$683,520
Costs	567,240
Other expenses	17,320
Earnings before interest and taxes	$ 98,960
Interest paid	15,780
Taxable income	$ 83,180
Taxes (21%)	17,468
Net income	$ 65,712
Dividends	$ 22,719
Addition to retained earnings	42,993

RETRO MACHINE, INC. Balance Sheet as of December 31, 2020			
Assets		**Liabilities and Owners' Equity**	
Current assets		Current liabilities	
Cash	$ 20,654	Accounts payable	$ 55,080
Accounts receivable	29,718	Notes payable	13,776
Inventory	70,966	Total	$ 68,856
Total	$121,338	Long-term debt	$127,000
Fixed assets		Owners' equity	
Net plant and equipment	$337,320	Common stock and paid-in surplus	$105,000
		Accumulated retained earnings	157,802
		Total	$262,802
Total assets	$458,658	Total liabilities and owners' equity	$458,658

22. **Capacity Usage and Growth**   In the previous problem, suppose the firm was operating at only 85 percent capacity in 2020. What is EFN now?

23. **Calculating EFN**   In Problem 21, suppose the firm wishes to keep its debt-equity ratio constant. What is EFN now?

Challenge
(Questions 24–30)

24. **EFN and Internal Growth**   Redo Problem 21 using sales growth rates of 15 and 25 percent in addition to 20 percent. Illustrate graphically the relationship between EFN and the growth rate, and use this graph to determine the relationship between them.

25. **EFN and Sustainable Growth**   Redo Problem 23 using sales growth rates of 30 and 35 percent in addition to 20 percent. Illustrate graphically the relationship between EFN and the growth rate, and use this graph to determine the relationship between them.

26. **Constraints on Growth**   Snell, Inc., wishes to maintain a growth rate of 10 percent per year and a debt-equity ratio of .35. The profit margin is 6.5 percent and the ratio of total assets to sales is constant at 2.1. Is this growth rate possible? To answer, determine what the dividend payout ratio must be. How do you interpret the result?

27. **EFN**   Define the following:

S = Previous year's sales

A = Total assets

E = Total equity

g = Projected growth in sales

PM = Profit margin

b = Retention (plowback) ratio

Assuming that all debt is constant, show that EFN can be written as:

$$EFN = -PM(S)b + [A - PM(S)b] \times g$$

Hint: Asset needs will equal $A \times g$. The addition to retained earnings will equal $PM(S)b \times (1 + g)$.

28. **Sustainable Growth Rate**   Based on the results in Problem 27, show that the internal and sustainable growth rates can be calculated as shown in equations 3.25 and 3.26. *Hint:* For the internal growth rate, set EFN equal to zero and solve for g.

29. **Sustainable Growth Rate**   In the chapter, we discussed one calculation of the sustainable growth rate as:

$$\text{Sustainable growth rate} = \frac{\text{ROE} \times b}{1 - \text{ROE} \times b}$$

In practice, probably the most commonly used calculation of the sustainable growth rate is ROE $\times$ b. This equation is identical to the two sustainable growth rate equations presented in the chapter if the ROE is calculated using the beginning of period equity. Derive this equation from the equation presented in the chapter.

30. **Sustainable Growth Rate**   Use the sustainable growth rate equations from the previous problem to answer the following questions. Grendl, Inc., had total assets of $410,000 and equity of $265,000 at the beginning of the year. At the end of the year, the company had total assets of $460,000. During the year, the company sold no new equity. Net income for the year was $75,000 and dividends were $32,000. What is the approximate sustainable growth rate for the company? What is the exact sustainable growth rate? What is the approximate sustainable growth rate if you calculate ROE based on the beginning of period equity? Is this number too high or too low? Why?

WHAT'S ON THE WEB?

1. **DuPont Identity**   You can find financial statements for The Walt Disney Company at Disney's home page, disney.com. For the three most recent years, calculate the DuPont identity for Disney. How has ROE changed over this period? How have changes in each component of the DuPont identity affected ROE over this period?

2. **Ratio Analysis**   You want to examine the financial ratios for Hilton Worldwide Holdings. Go to www.reuters.com and type in the ticker symbol for the company (HLT). Now find financial ratios for Hilton and the industry and sector averages for each ratio.

    a. What do TTM and MRQ mean?

    b. How do Hilton's recent profitability ratios compare to their values over the past five years? To the industry averages? To the sector averages? Which is the better comparison group for Hilton: the industry or sector averages? Why?

    c. In what areas does Hilton seem to outperform its competitors based on the financial ratios? Where does Hilton seem to lag behind its competitors?

3. **Applying Percentage of Sales**   Locate the most recent annual financial statements for DuPont at www.dupont.com under the "Investors" link. Locate the annual report. Using the growth in sales for the most recent year as the projected sales growth for next year, construct a pro forma income statement and balance sheet. Based on these projections, what are the external funds needed?

4. **Growth Rates**   You can find the home page for Caterpillar, Inc., at www.cat.com. Go to the web page and find the most recent annual report. Using the information from the financial statements, what is the sustainable growth rate?

RATIOS AND FINANCIAL PLANNING AT EAST COAST YACHTS

After Dan's analysis of East Coast Yachts's cash flow (at the end of our previous chapter), Larissa approached Dan about the company's performance and future growth plans. First, Larissa wants to find out how East Coast Yachts is performing relative to its peers. Additionally, she wants to find out the future financing necessary to fund the company's growth. In the past, East Coast Yachts experienced difficulty in financing its growth plan, in large part because of poor planning. In fact, the company had to turn down several large jobs because its facilities were unable to handle the additional demand. Larissa hoped that Dan would be able to estimate the amount of capital the company would have to raise next year so that East Coast Yachts would be better prepared to fund its expansion plans.

To get Dan started with his analyses, Larissa provided the following financial statements. Dan then gathered the industry ratios for the yacht manufacturing industry.

EAST COAST YACHTS 2020 Income Statement	
Sales	$550,424,000
Cost of goods sold	397,185,000
Selling, general, and administrative	65,778,000
Depreciation	17,963,000
EBIT	$ 69,498,000
Interest expense	9,900,000
EBT	$ 59,598,000
Taxes (25%)	14,899,500
Net income	$ 44,698,500
Dividends	$ 19,374,500
Retained earnings	25,324,000

EAST COAST YACHTS 2020 Balance Sheet				
Current assets			Current liabilities	
Cash and equivalents	$ 10,107,000		Accounts payable	$ 40,161,400
Accounts receivable	16,813,300		Accrued expenses	5,723,700
Inventory	18,135,700		Total current liabilities	$ 45,855,100
Other	1,054,900			
Total current assets	$ 46,110,900			
Fixed assets			Long-term debt	$152,374,000
Property, plant, and equipment	$412,032,000		Total long-term liabilities	$152,374,000
Less accumulated depreciation	(102,452,000)			
Net property, plant, and equipment	$309,580,000			
Intangible assets and others	6,772,000		Stockholders' equity	
Total fixed assets	$316,352,000		Preferred stock	$ 1,773,000
			Common stock	31,802,000
			Capital surplus	27,348,000

(Continued)

EAST COAST YACHTS		
2020 Balance Sheet		
	Accumulated retained earnings	146,052,800
	Less treasury stock	(42,772,000)
	Total equity	$164,203,800
Total assets $362,462,900	Total liabilities and shareholders' equity	$362,462,900

YACHT INDUSTRY RATIOS			
	Lower Quartile	**Median**	**Upper Quartile**
Current ratio	.86	1.51	1.97
Quick ratio	.43	.75	1.01
Total asset turnover	1.10	1.27	1.46
Inventory turnover	12.18	14.38	16.43
Receivables turnover	10.25	17.65	22.43
Debt ratio	.32	.56	.61
Debt-equity ratio	.83	1.13	1.44
Equity multiplier	1.83	2.13	2.44
Interest coverage	5.72	8.21	10.83
Profit margin	5.02%	7.48%	9.05%
Return on assets	7.05%	10.67%	14.16%
Return on equity	14.06%	19.32%	26.41%

1. East Coast Yachts uses a small percentage of preferred stock as a source of financing. In calculating the ratios for the company, should preferred stock be included as part of the company's total equity?

2. Calculate all of the ratios listed in the industry table for East Coast Yachts.

3. Compare the performance of East Coast Yachts to the industry as a whole. For each ratio, comment on why it might be viewed as positive or negative relative to the industry. Suppose you create an inventory ratio calculated as inventory divided by current liabilities. How would you interpret this ratio? How does East Coast Yachts compare to the industry average for this ratio?

4. Calculate the sustainable growth rate for East Coast Yachts. Calculate external funds needed (EFN) and prepare pro forma income statements and balance sheets assuming growth at precisely this rate. Recalculate the ratios in the previous question. What do you observe?

5. As a practical matter, East Coast Yachts is unlikely to be willing to raise external equity capital, in part because the shareholders don't want to dilute their existing ownership and control positions. However, East Coast Yachts is planning for a growth rate of 20 percent next year. What are your conclusions and recommendations about the feasibility of East Coast's expansion plans?

6. Most assets can be increased as a percentage of sales. For instance, cash can be increased by any amount. However, fixed assets often must be increased in specific amounts because it is impossible, as a practical matter, to buy part of a new plant or machine. In this case, a company has a "staircase" or "lumpy" fixed cost structure. Assume that East Coast Yachts is currently producing at 100 percent of capacity and sales are expected to grow at 20 percent. As a result, to expand production, the company must set up an entirely new line at a cost of $95,000,000. Prepare the pro forma income statement and balance sheet. What is the new EFN with these assumptions? What does this imply about capacity utilization for East Coast Yachts next year?

4 Discounted Cash Flow Valuation

The signing of big-name athletes is frequently accompanied by great fanfare, but the numbers are often misleading. For example, in late 2018, catcher Wilson Ramos reached a two-year deal with the New York Mets, signing a contract with a reported value of $19 million. Not bad, especially for someone who makes a living using the "tools of ignorance" (jock jargon for a catcher's equipment). Another example is the contract signed by Nathan Eovaldi of the Boston Red Sox, which had a stated value of $67.5 million.

It looks like Wilson and Nathan did pretty well, but the Washington Nationals spent a lot more as they signed pitcher Patrick Corbin to a contract that has a stated value of $140 million, but this amount was actually payable over several years. The contract called for $15 million for the first year, plus $125 million in future salary to be paid in the years 2020 through 2024. Nathan Eovaldi's payments were similarly spread over time, although his payments were only for four years. Because these contracts called for payments that are made at future dates, we must consider the time value of money, which means none of these players received the quoted amounts. How much did they really get? This chapter gives you the "tools of knowledge" to answer this question.

Please visit us at corecorporatefinance.blogspot.com for the latest developments in the world of corporate finance.

4.1 VALUATION: THE ONE-PERIOD CASE

Keith Vaughan is trying to sell a piece of raw land in Alaska. Yesterday, he was offered $10,000 for the property. He was about ready to accept the offer when another individual offered him $11,424. However, the second offer was to be paid a year from now. Keith has satisfied himself that both buyers are honest and financially solvent, so he has no fear that the offer he selects will fall through. These two offers are pictured as cash flows in Figure 4.1. Which offer should Mr. Vaughan choose?

Jim Ellis, Keith's financial adviser, points out that if Keith takes the first offer, he could invest the $10,000 in a bank at an insured rate of 12 percent.[1] At the end of one year, he would have:

$$\$10,000 + (.12 \times \$10,000) = \$10,000 \times 1.12 = \$11,200$$

Return of principal   Interest

Because this is less than the $11,424 Keith could receive from the second offer, Mr. Ellis recommends that he take the latter. This analysis uses the concept of **future value**, or **compound value**, which is the value of a sum after investing over one or more periods. The compound, or future value, of $10,000 at 12 percent is $11,200.

An alternative method employs the concept of **present value**. One can determine present value by asking the following question: How much money must Keith put in

---

[1] At this point, the savvy reader could ask where one could actually find guaranteed debt yielding 12 percent. One example is Puerto Rico's recent constitutionally guaranteed debt yielding a similar rate. However, in general, we concede that government guaranteed debt yielding double digits is very unusual and we should point out that Puerto Rico defaulted on its debt in July 2016.

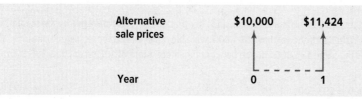

FIGURE 4.1

Cash Flow for Mr. Vaughan's Sale

the bank today at 12 percent so that he will have $11,424 next year? We can write this algebraically as:

PV × 1.12 = $11,424

We want to solve for present value (PV), the amount of money that yields $11,424 if invested at 12 percent today. Solving for PV, we have:

$$PV = \frac{\$11,424}{1.12} = \$10,200$$

The formula for PV can be written as:

Present Value of Investment $PV = \dfrac{C_1}{1+r}$, or   (4.1)

where C_1 is cash flow at Date 1 and r is the rate of return that Keith Vaughan requires on his land sale. It is sometimes referred to as the *discount rate.*

Present value analysis tells us that a payment of $11,424 to be received next year has a present value of $10,200 today. In other words, at a 12 percent interest rate, Mr. Vaughan is indifferent between $10,200 today or $11,424 next year. If you gave him $10,200 today, he could put it in the bank and receive $11,424 next year.

Because the second offer has a present value of $10,200, whereas the first offer is for only $10,000, present value analysis also indicates that Mr. Vaughan should take the second offer. In other words, both future value analysis and present value analysis lead to the same decision. As it turns out, present value analysis and future value analysis must always lead to the same decision.

As simple as this example is, it contains the basic principles that we will be working with over the next few chapters. We now use another example to develop the concept of net present value.

Present Value

Diane Badame, a financial analyst at Kaufman & Broad, a leading real estate firm, is thinking about recommending that Kaufman & Broad invest in a piece of land that costs $85,000. She is certain that next year the land will be worth $91,000, a sure $6,000 gain. Given that the guaranteed interest rate in the bank is 10 percent, should Kaufman & Broad undertake the investment in land? Ms. Badame's choice is described in Figure 4.2 with the cash flow time chart.

FIGURE 4.2   Cash Flows for Land Investment

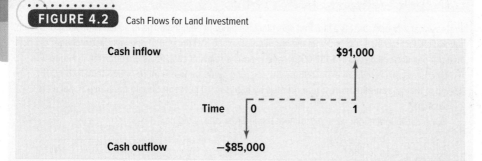

(Continued)

A moment's thought should be all it takes to convince her that this is not an attractive business deal. By investing $85,000 in the land, she will have $91,000 available next year. Suppose, instead, that Kaufman & Broad puts the same $85,000 into the bank. At the interest rate of 10 percent, this $85,000 would grow to:

$$(1 + .10) \times \$85,000 = \$93,500$$

next year.

It would be foolish to buy the land when investing the same $85,000 in the financial market would produce an extra $2,500 (that is, $93,500 from the bank minus $91,000 from the land investment).

This is a future value calculation.

Alternatively, she could calculate the present value of the sale price next year as:

$$\text{Present value} = \frac{\$91,000}{1.10} = \$82,727.27$$

Because the present value of next year's sales price is less than this year's purchase price of $85,000, present value analysis also indicates that she should not recommend purchasing the property.

Frequently, businesspeople want to determine the exact *cost* or *benefit* of a decision. The decision to buy this year and sell next year can be evaluated as:

Net Present Value of Investment:

$$-\$2,273 \quad = \quad \underset{\substack{\text{Cost of land} \\ \text{today}}}{-\$85,000} \quad + \quad \underset{\substack{\text{Present value of} \\ \text{next year's sales price}}}{\frac{\$91,000}{1.10}}$$

The formula for NPV can be written as:

$$\text{NPV} = -\text{Cost} + \text{PV} \tag{4.2}$$

Equation 4.2 says that the value of the investment is −$2,273, after stating all the benefits and all the costs as of Date 0. We say that −$2,273 is the **net present value (NPV)** of the investment. That is, NPV is the present value of future cash flows minus the present value of the cost of the investment. Because the net present value is negative, Diane Badame should not recommend purchasing the land.

Both the Vaughan and the Badame examples deal with perfect certainty. That is, Keith Vaughan knows with perfect certainty that he could sell his land for $11,424 next year. Similarly, Diane Badame knows with perfect certainty that Kaufman & Broad could receive $91,000 for selling its land. Unfortunately, businesspeople frequently do not know future cash flows with certainty. This uncertainty is treated in the next example.

EXAMPLE 4.2

Uncertainty and Valuation

Professional Artworks, Inc., is a firm that speculates in modern paintings. The manager is thinking of buying an original Picasso for $400,000 with the intention of selling it at the end of one year. The manager expects that the painting will be worth $480,000 in one year. The relevant cash flows are depicted in Figure 4.3.

Of course, this is only an expectation—the painting could be worth more or less than $480,000. Suppose the guaranteed interest rate granted by banks is 10 percent. Should the firm purchase the piece of art?

Our first thought might be to discount at the interest rate, yielding:

$$\frac{\$480,000}{1.10} = \$436,364$$

(*Continued*)

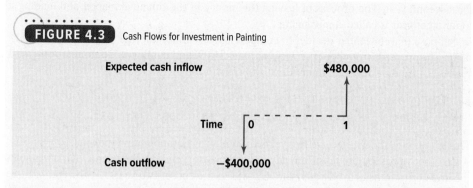

FIGURE 4.3 Cash Flows for Investment in Painting

Because $436,364 is greater than $400,000, it looks at first glance as if the painting should be purchased. However, 10 percent is the return we have assumed one can earn on a riskless investment. Because the painting is quite risky, a higher discount rate is called for. The manager chooses a rate of 25 percent to reflect this risk. In other words, he argues that a 25 percent expected return is fair compensation for an investment as risky as this painting.

The present value of the painting becomes:

$$\frac{\$480,000}{1.25} = \$384,000$$

Thus, the manager believes that the painting is currently overpriced at $400,000 and does not make the purchase.

The preceding analysis is typical of decision making in today's corporations, though real-world examples are, of course, much more complex. Unfortunately, any example with risk poses a problem not faced by a riskless example. In an example with riskless cash flows, the appropriate required return (i.e., discount rate) can be determined by checking the current returns on U.S. Treasury securities. Conceptually, the correct discount rate for a risky expected cash flow is the expected return available in the market on other investments of the same risks. This is the correct discount rate to apply because it represents the economic opportunity cost to investors. It is the expected return they will require before committing funding to an investment. However, the actual selection of the discount rate for a risky investment is quite a difficult task. We don't know at this point whether the discount rate on the painting should be 11 percent, 25 percent, 52 percent, or some other percentage.

Because the choice of a discount rate is so difficult, we merely wanted to broach the subject here. We must wait until the specific material on risk and return is covered in later chapters before a risk-adjusted analysis can be presented.

4.2 THE MULTIPERIOD CASE

The previous section presented the calculation of future value and present value for one period only. We will now perform the calculations for the multiperiod case.

ExcelMaster
coverage online
www.mhhe.com/RossCore6e

Future Value and Compounding

Suppose an individual were to make a loan of $1. At the end of the first year, the borrower would owe the lender the principal amount of $1 plus the interest on the loan at the interest rate of r. For the specific case where the interest rate is, say, 9 percent, the borrower owes the lender:

$1 × (1 + r) = $1 × 1.09 = $1.09

At the end of the year, though, the lender has two choices. She can either take the $1.09—or, more generally, $(1 + r)$—out of the financial market, or she can leave it in and lend it again for a second year. The process of leaving the money in the financial market and lending it for another year is called compounding.

Suppose that the lender decides to compound her loan for another year. She does this by taking the proceeds from her first one-year loan, $1.09, and lending this amount for the next year. At the end of next year, then, the borrower will owe her:

$$\$1 \times (1 + r) \times (1 + r) = \$1 \times (1 + r)^2 = 1 + 2r + r^2$$
$$\$1 \times (1.09) \times (1.09) = \$1 \times (1.09)^2 = \$1 + .18 + .0081 = \$1.1881$$

This is the total she will receive two years from now by compounding the loan.

In other words, by providing a ready opportunity for lending, the capital market enables the investor to transform $1 today into $1.1881 at the end of two years. At the end of three years, the total cash will be $1 \times 1.09^3 = \$1.2950$.

The most important point to notice is that the total amount that the lender receives is not just the $1 that she lent out plus two years' worth of interest on $1:

$$2 \times r = 2 \times \$.09 = \$.18$$

The lender also gets back an amount r^2, which is the interest in the second year on the interest that was earned in the first year. The term, $2 \times r$, represents simple interest over the two years, and the term, r^2, is referred to as the *interest on interest*. In our example, this latter amount is exactly:

$$r^2 = \$.09^2 = \$.0081$$

When cash is invested at compound interest, each interest payment is reinvested. With simple interest, the interest is not reinvested. Benjamin Franklin's statement, "Money makes money and the money that makes money makes more money," is a colorful way of explaining compound interest. The difference between compound interest and simple interest is illustrated in Figure 4.4. In this example, the difference does not amount to much because the loan is for $1. If the loan were for $1 million, the lender would receive $1,188,100 in two years' time. Of this amount, $8,100 is interest on interest. The lesson is that those small numbers beyond the decimal point can add up to big dollar amounts when the transactions are for big amounts. In addition, the longer-lasting the loan, the more important interest on interest becomes.

The general formula for an investment over many periods can be written as:

Future Value of an Investment FV $= C_0 \times (1 + r)^t$, or   (4.3)

FIGURE 4.4

Simple and Compound Interest

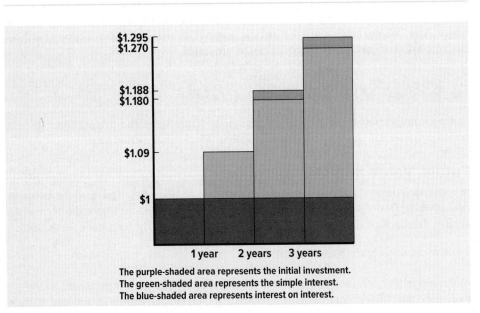

The purple-shaded area represents the initial investment.
The green-shaded area represents the simple interest.
The blue-shaded area represents interest on interest.

where C_0 is the cash to be invested at Date 0 (i.e., today), r is the interest rate per period, and t is the number of periods over which the cash is invested.

Interest on Interest

Suh-Pyng Ku has put $500 in a savings account at the First National Bank of Kent. The account earns 7 percent, compounded annually. How much will Ms. Ku have at the end of three years?

$$\$500 \times 1.07 \times 1.07 \times 1.07 = \$500 \times 1.07^3 = \$612.52$$

Figure 4.5 illustrates the growth of Ms. Ku's account.

FIGURE 4.5 Suh-Pyng Ku's Savings Account

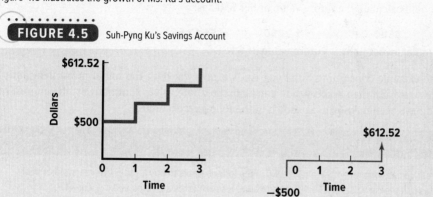

Compound Growth

Jay Ritter invested $1,000 in the stock of the SDH Company. The company pays a current dividend of $2, which is expected to grow by 20 percent per year for the next two years. What will the dividend of the SDH Company be after two years?

$$\$2 \times 1.20^2 = \$2.88$$

Figure 4.6 illustrates the increasing value of SDH's dividends.

FIGURE 4.6 The Growth of SDH Dividends

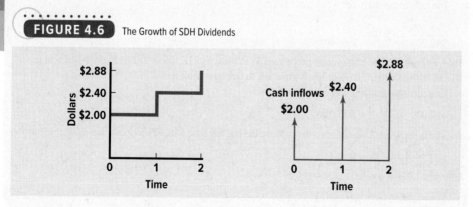

The two previous examples can be calculated in any one of four ways. The computations could be done by hand, by calculator, by spreadsheet, or with the help of a table. The appropriate table is Table A.3, which appears in the back of the text. This table presents the *future value of $1 at the end of* t *periods.* The table is used by locating the appropriate interest rate on the horizontal axis and the appropriate number of periods on the vertical axis.

For example, Suh-Pyng Ku would look at the following portion of Table A.3:

Period	Interest Rate		
	6%	7%	8%
1	1.0600	1.0700	1.0800
2	1.1236	1.1449	1.1664
3	1.1910	1.2250	1.2597
4	1.2625	1.3108	1.3605

She could calculate the future value of her $500 as:

$$\underset{\text{Initial investment}}{\$500} \quad \times \quad \underset{\text{Future value of \$1}}{1.2250} \quad = \$612.52$$

In the example concerning Suh-Pyng Ku, we gave you both the initial investment and the interest rate and then asked you to calculate the future value. Alternatively, the interest rate could have been unknown, as shown in the following example.

Finding the Rate

Gareth James, who recently won $10,000 in the lottery, wants to buy a car in five years. Gareth estimates that the car will cost $16,105 at that time. His cash flows are displayed in Figure 4.7.

FIGURE 4.7 Cash Flows for Purchase of Gareth James's Car

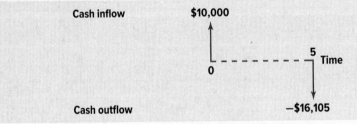

What interest rate must he earn to be able to afford the car?

The ratio of purchase price to initial cash is:

$$\frac{\$16,105}{\$10,000} = 1.6105$$

Thus, he must earn an interest rate that allows $1 to become $1.6105 in five years. Table A.3 tells us that an interest rate of 10 percent will allow him to purchase the car.

One can express the problem algebraically as:

$$\$10,000 \times (1 \times r)^5 = \$16,105$$

where r is the interest rate needed to purchase the car. Because $16,105/$10,000 = 1.6105, we have:

$$(1 + r)^5 = 1.6105$$

Either the table or a calculator solves for r.

The Power of Compounding: A Digression

Most people who have had any experience with compounding are impressed with its power over long periods of time. In fact, compound interest has been described as the "eighth wonder of the world" and "the most powerful force in the universe."[2] Take the stock market, for

[2] These quotes are often attributed to Albert Einstein (particularly the second one), but whether he really said either is unknown. The first quote is also often attributed to Baron Rothschild, John Maynard Keynes, Benjamin Franklin, and others.

example. Ibbotson and Sinquefield have calculated what the stock market returned, as a whole, from 1926 through 2018.[3] They find that one dollar placed in these stocks at the beginning of 1926 would have been worth $7,030.31 at the end of 2018. This is 9.99 percent compounded annually for 93 years, that is, $1.0999^{93} = $7,030.31$, ignoring a small rounding error.

The example illustrates the great difference between compound and simple interest. At 9.99 percent, simple interest on $1 is 9.99 cents a year (i.e., $.0999). Simple interest over 93 years is $9.29 (= 93 × $.0999). That is, an individual withdrawing .0999 cents every year would have withdrawn $9.29 (= 93 × $.0999) over 93 years. This is quite a bit below the $7,030.31 that was obtained by reinvestment of all principal and interest.

The results are more impressive over even longer periods of time. A person with no experience in compounding might think that the value of $1 at the end of 186 years would be twice the value of $1 at the end of 93 years, if the yearly rate of return stayed the same. Actually the value of $1 at the end of 186 years would be the *square* of the value of $1 at the end of 93 years. That is, if the annual rate of return remained the same, a $1 investment in common stocks should be worth $49,425,258.70 [$1 × (7,030.31 × 7,030.31)].

A few years ago, an archaeologist unearthed a relic stating that Julius Caesar lent the Roman equivalent of one penny to someone. Since there was no record of the penny ever being repaid, the archaeologist wondered what the interest and principal would be if a descendant of Caesar tried to collect from a descendant of the borrower in the 20th century. The archaeologist felt that a rate of 6 percent might be appropriate. To his surprise, the principal and interest due after more than 2,000 years was vastly greater than the entire wealth on earth.

The power of compounding can explain why the parents of well-to-do families frequently bequeath wealth to their grandchildren rather than to their children. That is, they skip a generation. The parents would rather make the grandchildren very rich than make the children moderately rich. We have found that in these families, the grandchildren have a more positive view of the power of compounding than do the children.

EXAMPLE 4.6

How Much for That Island?

Some people have said that it was the best real estate deal in history. Peter Minuit, director-general of New Netherlands, the Dutch West India Company's colony in North America, in 1626, allegedly bought Manhattan Island from native Americans for 60 guilders' worth of trinkets. This sounds cheap, but did the Dutch really get the better end of the deal? It is reported that 60 guilders was worth about $24 at the prevailing exchange rate. If the native Americans had sold the trinkets at a fair market value and invested the $24 at 5 percent (tax-free), it would now, about 393 years later, be worth about $5.1 billion. Today, Manhattan is undoubtedly worth more than $5.1 billion, and so, at a 5 percent rate of return, the native Americans got the worst of the deal. However, if invested at 10 percent, the amount of money they received would be worth about:

$$\$24(1 + r)^t = 24 \times 1.1^{393} = \$444.2 \text{ quadrillion}$$

This is a lot of money. In fact, $444.2 quadrillion is more than all the real estate in the world is worth today. Note that no one in the history of the world has ever been able to find an investment yielding 10 percent every year for 393 years.

Present Value and Discounting

We now know that an annual interest rate of 9 percent enables the investor to transform $1 today into $1.1881 two years from now. In addition, we would like to know:

How much would an investor need to lend today so that she could receive $1 two years from today?

---

[3] 2019 *SBBI Yearbook.*

FIGURE 4.8

Compounding and
Discounting

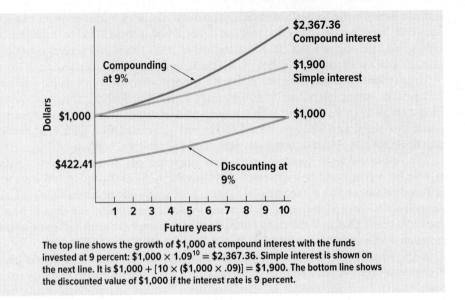

The top line shows the growth of $1,000 at compound interest with the funds invested at 9 percent: $1,000 \times 1.09^{10} = \$2,367.36$. Simple interest is shown on the next line. It is $1,000 + [10 \times (\$1,000 \times .09)] = \$1,900$. The bottom line shows the discounted value of $1,000 if the interest rate is 9 percent.

Algebraically, we can write this as:

$$PV \times 1.09^2 = \$1$$

In the preceding equation, PV stands for present value, the amount of money we must lend today in order to receive $1 in two years' time.

Solving for PV in this equation, we have:

$$PV = \frac{\$1}{1.1881} = \$.84$$

This process of calculating the present value of a future cash flow is called **discounting**. It is the opposite of compounding. The difference between compounding and discounting is illustrated in Figure 4.8.

To be certain that $.84 is in fact the present value of $1 to be received in two years, we must check whether or not, if we loaned out $.84 and rolled over the loan for two years, we would get exactly $1 back. If this were the case, the capital markets would be saying that $1 received in two years' time is equivalent to having $.84 today. Checking the exact numbers, we get:

$$\$.84168 \times 1.09 \times 1.09 = \$1$$

In other words, when we have capital markets with a sure interest rate of 9 percent, we are indifferent between receiving $.84 today or $1 in two years. We have no reason to treat these two choices differently from each other because if we had $.84 today and loaned it out for two years, it would return $1 to us at the end of that time. The value $(1/1.09^2)$ is called the **present value factor**. It is the factor used to calculate the present value of a future cash flow.

In the multiperiod case, the formula for PV can be written as:

Present Value of Investment:

$$PV = \frac{C_t}{(1 + r)^t} \tag{4.4}$$

where C_t is cash flow at Date t and r is the appropriate discount rate.

EXAMPLE 4.7

Multiperiod Discounting

Harry DeAngelo will receive $10,000 three years from now. Harry can earn 8 percent on his investments, so the appropriate discount rate is 8 percent. What is the present value of his future cash flow?

$$PV = \$10,000 \times \left(\frac{1}{1.08}\right)^3$$

$$= \$10,000 \times .7938$$

$$= \$7,938$$

Figure 4.9 illustrates the application of the present value factor to Harry's investment.

FIGURE 4.9 Discounting Harry DeAngelo's Opportunity

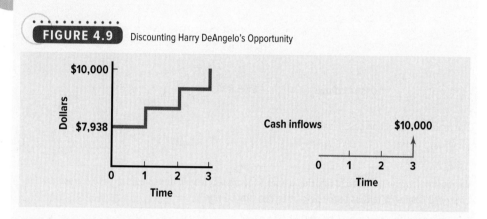

When his investments grow at an 8 percent rate of interest, Harry DeAngelo is equally inclined toward receiving $7,938 now and receiving $10,000 in three years' time. After all, he could convert the $7,938 he receives today into $10,000 in three years by lending it at an interest rate of 8 percent.

Harry DeAngelo could have reached his present value calculation in one of three ways. The computation could have been done by hand, by calculator, or with the help of Table A.1, which appears in the back of the text. This table presents *present value of $1 to be received after* t *periods.* The table is used by locating the appropriate interest rate on the horizontal and the appropriate number of periods on the vertical. For example, Harry DeAngelo would look at the following portion of Table A.1:

Period	Interest Rate		
	7%	8%	9%
1	.9346	.9259	.9174
2	.8734	.8573	.8417
3	.8163	.7938	.7722
4	.7629	.7350	.7084

The appropriate present value factor is .7938.

In the preceding example, we gave both the interest rate and the future cash flow. Alternatively, the interest rate could have been unknown.

EXAMPLE 4.8

Finding the Rate

A customer of the Beatty Corp. wants to buy a tugboat today. Rather than paying immediately, he will pay $150,000 in three years. It will cost the Beatty Corp. $115,830 to build the tugboat immediately. The relevant cash flows to Beatty Corp. are displayed in Figure 4.10. By charging what interest rate would the Beatty Corp. neither gain nor lose on the sale?

FIGURE 4.10 Cash Flows for Tugboat

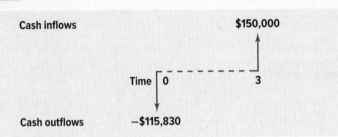

The ratio of construction cost to sale price is:

$$\frac{\$115,830}{\$150,000} = .7722$$

We must determine the interest rate that allows $1 to be received in three years to have a present value of $.7722. Table A.1 tells us that 9 percent is that interest rate.

Frequently, an investor or a business will receive more than one cash flow. The present value of the set of cash flows is the sum of the present values of the individual cash flows. This is illustrated in the following examples.

EXAMPLE 4.9

Cash Flow Valuation

Dennis Draper has won the Kentucky state lottery and will receive the following set of cash flows over the next two years:

Year	Cash Flow
1	$2,000
2	5,000

Mr. Draper can currently earn 6 percent in his money market account, so the appropriate discount rate is 6 percent. The present value of the cash flows is:

Year	Cash Flow × Present Value Factor = Present Value		
1	$2,000 \times \dfrac{1}{1.06}$	$= \$2,000 \times .9434$	$= \$1,887$
2	$\$5,000 \times \left(\dfrac{1}{1.06}\right)^{2}$	$= \$5,000 \times .8900$	$= 4,450$
		Total	$6,337$

In other words, Mr. Draper is equally inclined toward receiving $6,337 today and receiving $2,000 and $5,000 over the next two years, respectively.

NPV

Finance.com has an opportunity to invest in a new high-speed computer that costs $50,000. The computer will generate cash flows (from cost savings) of $25,000 one year from now, $20,000 two years from now, and $15,000 three years from now. The computer will be worthless after three years, and no additional cash flows will occur. Finance.com has determined that the appropriate discount rate is 7 percent for this investment. Should Finance.com make this investment in a new high-speed computer? What is the present value of the investment?

The cash flows and present value factors of the proposed computer are as follows:

	Cash Flows	Present Value Factor	
Year 0	−$50,000	1	$= 1$
1	25,000	$\dfrac{1}{1.07}$	$= .9346$
2	20,000	$\left(\dfrac{1}{1.07}\right)^2$	$= .8734$
3	15,000	$\left(\dfrac{1}{1.07}\right)^3$	$= .8163$

The present values of the cash flows are:

Cash flows × Present value factor = Present value

Year 0	−$50,000 × 1	=	−$50,000.00
1	$25,000 × .9346	=	23,364.49
2	$20,000 × .8734	=	17,468.77
3	$15,000 × .8163	=	12,244.47
		Total	$ 3,077.73

Finance.com should invest in a new high-speed computer because the present value of its future cash flows is greater than its cost. The NPV is $3,077.73.

The Algebraic Formula

To derive an algebraic formula for the net present value of a cash flow, recall that the PV of receiving a cash flow one year from now is:

$$PV = C_1/(1 + r)$$

and the PV of receiving a cash flow two years from now is:

$$PV = C_2/(1 + r)^2$$

We can write the NPV of a t-period project as:

$$NPV = -C_0 + \frac{C_1}{1 + r} + \frac{C_2}{(1 + r)^2} + \cdots + \frac{C_T}{(1 + r)^T} = -C_0 + \sum_{t=1}^{T} \frac{C_i}{(1 + r)^T} \qquad (4.5)$$

The initial flow, $-C_0$, is assumed to be negative because it represents an investment. The Σ is shorthand for the sum of the series.

We will close this section by answering the question we posed at the beginning of the chapter concerning baseball player Patrick Corbin's contract. The terms of the contract called for $15 million for the first year, $19 million in 2020, $24 million in 2021, $23 million in 2022, $24 million in 2023, and $35 million in 2024. If 12 percent is the appropriate interest rate, what kind of deal was Patrick pitched?

To answer, we can calculate the present value by discounting each year's salary back to the present as follows (notice we assume that all the payments are made at year-end and that 12 percent is the appropriate discount rate):

Year 1 (2019):	$\$15,000,000 \times 1/1.12^1 = \$13,392,857.14$
Year 2 (2020):	$\$19,000,000 \times 1/1.12^2 = \$15,146,683.67$
. . .	
Year 6 (2024):	$\$35,000,000 \times 1/1.12^6 = \$17,732,089.24$

If you fill in the missing rows and then add (do it for practice), you will see that Patrick's contract had a present value of about $91.59 million, or only about 65 percent of the stated $140 million value (but still pretty good).

As you have probably noticed, doing extensive present value calculations can get to be pretty tedious, so a nearby *Spreadsheet Techniques* box shows how we recommend doing them. As an application, we take a look at lottery payouts in a nearby *Finance Matters* box.

SPREADSHEET TECHNIQUES

How to Calculate Present Values with Multiple Future Cash Flows Using a Spreadsheet

We can set up a basic spreadsheet to calculate the present values of the individual cash flows as follows. Notice that we have calculated the present values one at a time and summed them.

	A	B	C	D	E
1					
2		Using a spreadsheet to value multiple future cash flows			
3					
4	What is the present value of $200 in one year, $400 the next year, $600 the next year, and				
5	$800 the last year if the discount rate is 12 percent?				
6					
7	Rate:	.12			
8					
9	Year	Cash flows	Present values	Formula used	
10	1	$200	$178.57	=PV($B$7,A10,0,−B10)	
11	2	$400	$318.88	=PV($B$7,A11,0,−B11)	
12	3	$600	$427.07	=PV($B$7,A12,0,−B12)	
13	4	$800	$508.41	=PV($B$7,A13,0,−B13)	
14					
15		Total PV:	**$1,432.93**	=SUM(C10:C13)	
16					
17	Notice the negative signs inserted in the PV formulas. These make the present values have				
18	positive signs. Also, the discount rate in cell B7 is entered as $B$7 (an "absolute" reference)				
19	because it is used over and over. We could have entered ".12" instead, but our approach is more				
20	flexible.				
21					
22					

If you or someone you know is a regular lottery player, you probably already understand that you are 1,300 times more likely to get struck by lightning than you are to win a big lottery jackpot. What are your odds of winning? Below you will find a table with your chances of winning the Mega Millions Lottery compared to other events.

Odds of winning a Mega Millions jackpot	1:302,575,350
Odds of being killed by lightning	1:218,106
Odds of being killed in an airplane	1:188,364
Odds of being killed by a dog attack	1:115,111
Odds of being killed by bees	1:46,452
Odds of being killed in a cataclysmic storm	1:31,394
Odds of being killed by electrocution	1:15,638
Odds of being killed by or in a car	1:103

Sweepstakes may have different odds than lotteries, but these odds may not be much better. At one time, the largest advertised potential grand prize ever was Pepsi's "Play for a Billion," which, you guessed it, had a $1 billion (*billion!*) prize. Not bad for a day's work, but you still had to read the fine print. It turns out that the winner would be paid $5 million per year for the next 20 years, $10 million per year for years 21 through 39, and a lump sum of $710 million in 40 years. From what you have learned, you know the value of the sweepstakes wasn't even close to $1 billion. In fact, at an interest rate of 10 percent, the present value is about $70.7 million.

Lottery jackpots are often paid out over 20 or more years, but the winner can usually choose to take a lump-sum cash payment instead. For example, in June 2018, a Hackensack, New Jersey, man won the $315 million Powerball lottery. He had the option of a single cash payment of $183 million or payments of $10.5 million over the next 30 years. In this case, he chose the cash option.

Some lotteries make your decision a little tougher. The Ontario Lottery will pay you either $2,000 a week for the rest of your life or $1.3 million now. (That's in Canadian dollars, or "loonies," by the way.) Of course, there is the chance you might die in the near future, so the lottery guarantees that your heirs will collect the $2,000 weekly payments until the 20th anniversary of the first payment, or until you would have turned 91, whichever comes first. This payout scheme complicates your decision quite a bit. If you live for only the 20-year minimum, the break-even interest rate between the two options is about 5.13 percent per year, compounded weekly. If you expect to live longer than the 20-year minimum, you might be better off accepting $2,000 per week for life. Of course, if you manage to invest the $1.3 million lump sum at a rate of return of about 8 percent per year (compounded weekly), you can have your cake and eat it too because the investment will return $2,000 at the end of each week forever! Taxes complicate the decision in this case because the lottery payments are all on an aftertax basis. Thus, the rates of return in this example would have to be aftertax as well.

4.3 COMPOUNDING PERIODS

So far we have assumed that compounding and discounting occur yearly. Sometimes compounding may occur more frequently than once a year. Imagine that a bank pays a 10 percent interest rate "compounded semiannually." This means that a $1,000 deposit in the bank would be worth $1,000 × 1.05 = $1,050 after six months, and $1,050 × 1.05 = $1,102.50 at the end of the year.

ExcelMaster
coverage online

www.mhhe.com/RossCore6e

The end-of-the-year wealth can be written as:

$$\$1{,}000\left(1+\frac{.10}{2}\right)^2 = \$1{,}000 \times 1.05^2 = \$1{,}102.50$$

Of course, a $1,000 deposit would be worth $1,100 (= $1,000 × 1.10) with yearly compounding. Note that the future value at the end of one year is greater with semiannual compounding than with yearly compounding. With yearly compounding, the original $1,000 remains the investment base for the full year. The original $1,000 is the investment base only for the first six months with semiannual compounding. The base over the second six months is $1,050. So, one gets *interest on interest* with semiannual compounding.

Because $1,000 × 1.1025 = $1,102.50, 10 percent compounded semiannually is the same as 10.25 percent compounded annually. In other words, a rational investor could not care less whether she is quoted a rate of 10 percent compounded semiannually or a rate of 10.25 percent compounded annually.

Quarterly compounding at 10 percent yields wealth at the end of one year of:

$$\$1{,}000\left(1+\frac{.10}{4}\right)^4 = \$1{,}103.81$$

More generally, compounding an investment m times a year provides end-of-year wealth of:

$$C_0\left(1+\frac{r}{m}\right)^m \tag{4.6}$$

where C_0 is the initial investment and r is the **annual percentage rate (APR)**. The APR is the annual interest rate without consideration of compounding. Banks and other financial institutions may use other names for the APR.[4]

---

[4] By law, lenders are required to report the APR on all loans. In this text, we compute the APR as the interest rate per period multiplied by the number of periods in a year. According to federal law, the APR is a measure of the cost of consumer credit expressed as a yearly rate and it includes interest and certain noninterest charges and fees. In practice, the APR can be much higher than the interest rate on the loan if the lender charges substantial fees that must be included in the federally mandated APR calculation.

EXAMPLE 4.12

Compounding Frequencies

If an annual percentage rate of 8 percent is compounded quarterly, what is the effective annual rate? Using Equation 4.7, we have:

$$\left(1 + \frac{r}{m}\right)^m - 1 = \left(1 + \frac{.08}{4}\right)^4 - 1 = .0824, \text{ or } 8.24\%$$

Referring back to our earlier example where $C_0 = \$1,000$ and $r = 10\%$, we can generate the following table:

C_0	Compounding Frequency (m)	C_1	Effective Annual Rate $= \left(1 + \frac{r}{m}\right)^m - 1$
$1,000	Yearly ($m = 1$)	$1,100.00	.10
1,000	Semiannually ($m = 2$)	1,102.50	.1025
1,000	Quarterly ($m = 4$)	1,103.81	.10381
1,000	Daily ($m = 365$)	1,105.16	.10516

Distinction between Annual Percentage Rate and Effective Annual Rate

The distinction between the annual percentage rate (APR) and the effective annual rate (EAR) is frequently quite troubling to students. One can reduce the confusion by noting that the APR becomes meaningful only if the compounding interval is given. For example, for an APR of 10 percent, the future value at the end of one year with semiannual compounding is $[1 + (.10/2)]^2 = 1.1025$. The future value with quarterly compounding is $[1 + (.10/4)]^4 = 1.1038$. If the APR is 10 percent but no compounding interval is given, one cannot calculate future value. In other words, one does not know whether to compound semiannually, quarterly, or over some other interval.

By contrast, the EAR is meaningful *without* a compounding interval. For example, an EAR of 10.25 percent means that a $1 investment will be worth $1.1025 in one year. One can think of this as an APR of 10 percent with semiannual compounding or an APR of 10.25 percent with annual compounding, or some other possibility.

There can be a big difference between an APR and an EAR when interest rates are high. For example, consider "payday loans." Payday loans are short-term loans made to consumers, often for less than two weeks. They are offered by companies such as Check Into Cash and Advance Financial. The loans work like this: You write a check today that is postdated. When the check date arrives, you go to the store and either pay the cash for the check or the company cashes the check. For example, in one particular state, Check Into Cash allows you to write a check for $117.64 dated 14 days in the future, for which they give you $100 today. So what are the APR and EAR of this arrangement? First, we need to find the interest rate, which we can find by the FV equation as follows:

$$FV = PV \times (1 + r)^1$$
$$\$117.64 = \$100 \times (1 + r)^1$$
$$1.1764 = (1 + r)$$
$$r = .1764, \text{ or } 17.64\%$$

That doesn't seem too bad until you remember this is the interest rate for *14 days*! The APR of the loan is:

$$\text{APR} = .1764 \times 365/14$$
$$\text{APR} = 4.5990, \text{ or } 459.90\%$$

And the EAR for this loan is:

$$\text{EAR} = (1 + \text{Quoted rate}/m)^m - 1$$
$$\text{EAR} = (1 + .1764)^{365/14} - 1$$
$$\text{EAR} = 68.0987, \text{ or } 6{,}809.87\%$$

Now that's an interest rate! To see what a difference a small variation in fees can make, Advance Financial will make you write a check for $110.72 for the same amount today. Check for yourself that the APR of this arrangement is 279.49 percent and the EAR is 1,322.45 percent. Still not a loan we would like to take out!

By law, lenders are required to report the APR on all loans. In this text, we compute the APR as the interest rate per period multiplied by the number of periods in a year. According to federal law, the APR is a measure of the cost of consumer credit expressed as a yearly rate, and it includes interest and certain noninterest charges and fees. In practice, the APR can be much higher than the interest rate on the loan if the lender charges substantial fees that must be included in the federally mandated APR calculation.

Compounding over Many Years

Equation 4.6 applies for an investment over one year. For an investment over one or more (t) years, the formula becomes:

Future Value with Compounding

$$FV = C_0 \left(1 + \frac{r}{m} \right)^{mt} \tag{4.8}$$

EXAMPLE 4.13

Multiyear Compounding

Harry DeAngelo is investing $5,000 at an annual percentage rate of 12 percent per year, compounded quarterly, for five years. What is his wealth at the end of five years?

Using Equation 4.8, his wealth is:

$$\$5{,}000 \times \left(1 + \frac{.12}{4} \right)^{4 \times 5} = \$5{,}000 \times 1.03^{20} = \$5{,}000 \times 1.8061 = \$9{,}030.56$$

Continuous Compounding

The previous discussion shows that one can compound much more frequently than once a year. One could compound semiannually, quarterly, monthly, daily, hourly, each minute, or even more often. The limiting case would be to compound every infinitesimal instant, which is commonly called continuous compounding. Surprisingly, banks and other financial institutions sometimes quote continuously compounded rates, which is why we study them.

Though the idea of compounding this rapidly may boggle the mind, a simple formula is involved. With continuous compounding, the value at the end of t years is expressed as:

$$C_0 \times e^{rt} \tag{4.9}$$

where C_0 is the initial investment, r is the annual percentage rate, and t is the number of years over which the investment runs. The number e is a constant and is approximately equal to 2.718. It is not an unknown like C_0, r, and t.

EXAMPLE 4.14

Continuous Compounding

Linda DeFond invested $1,000 at a continuously compounded rate of 10 percent for one year. What is the value of her wealth at the end of one year?

From Equation 4.9, we have:

$$\$1,000 \times e^{.10} = \$1,000 \times 1.1052 = \$1,105.20$$

This number can easily be read from our Table A.5. One merely sets r, the value on the horizontal dimension, to 10 percent and t, the value on the vertical dimension, to 1. For this problem, the relevant portion of the table is:

Period (t)	Continuously Compounded Rate (r)		
	9%	10%	11%
1	1.0942	1.1052	1.1163
2	1.1972	1.2214	1.2461
3	1.3100	1.3499	1.3910

Note that a continuously compounded rate of 10 percent is equivalent to an annually compounded rate of 10.52 percent. In other words, Linda DeFond would not care whether her bank quoted a continuously compounded rate of 10 percent or a 10.52 percent rate, compounded annually.

EXAMPLE 4.15

Continuous Compounding, Continued

Linda DeFond's brother, Mark, invested $1,000 at a continuously compounded rate of 10 percent for two years.

The appropriate equation here is:

$$\$1,000 \times e^{.10 \times 2} = \$1,000 \times e^{.20} = \$1,221.40$$

Using the portion of the table of continuously compounded rates reproduced above, we find the value to be 1.2214.

Figure 4.11 illustrates the relationship among annual, semiannual, and continuous compounding. Semiannual compounding gives rise to both a smoother curve and a higher ending value than does annual compounding. Continuous compounding has both the smoothest curve and the highest ending value of all.

EXAMPLE 4.16

Present Value with Continuous Compounding

The Michigan state lottery is going to pay you $1,000 at the end of four years. If the annual continuously compounded rate of interest is 8 percent, what is the present value of this payment?

$$\$1,000 \times \frac{1}{e^{.08 \times 4}} = \$1,000 \times \frac{1}{1.3771} = \$726.15$$

FIGURE 4.11

Annual, Semiannual, and Continuous Compounding

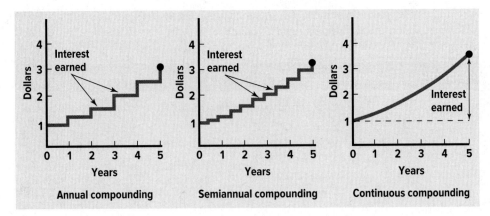

Annual compounding | Semiannual compounding | Continuous compounding

4.4 SIMPLIFICATIONS

The first part of this chapter has examined the concepts of future value and present value. Although these concepts allow one to answer a host of problems concerning the time value of money, the human effort involved can frequently be excessive. For example, consider a bank calculating the present value on a 20-year monthly mortgage. Because this mortgage has 240 (= 20 × 12) payments, a lot of time is needed to perform a conceptually simple task.

Because many basic finance problems are potentially so time-consuming, we seek simplifications in this section. We provide simplifying formulas for four classes of cash flow streams:

1. Perpetuity
2. Growing perpetuity
3. Annuity
4. Growing annuity

Perpetuity

A **perpetuity** is a constant stream of cash flows without end. If you are thinking that perpetuities have no relevance to reality, it will surprise you that there is a well-known case of an unending cash flow stream: the British bonds called *consols*. An investor purchasing a consol is entitled to receive yearly interest from the British government forever.

How can the price of a perpetuity be determined? Consider a perpetuity that makes a payment of C dollars each year and will do so forever. Applying the PV formula gives us:

$$PV = \frac{C}{1+r} + \frac{C}{(1+r)^2} + \frac{C}{(1+r)^3} + \cdots$$

where the dots at the end of the formula stand for the infinite string of terms that continues the formula. Series like the preceding one are called *geometric series*. It is well known that even though they have an infinite number of terms, the whole series has a finite sum because each term is only a fraction of the preceding term. Before turning to our calculus books, though, it is worth going back to our original principles to see if a bit of financial intuition can help us find the PV.

The present value of a perpetuity is the present value of all of its future payments. In other words, it is an amount of money that, if an investor had it today, would enable him to achieve the same pattern of expenditures that a perpetuity and its payments would. Suppose that an investor wanted to spend exactly C dollars each year. If he had a perpetuity, he could do this. How much money must he have today to spend the same amount? Clearly he would need exactly enough so that the interest on the money would be C dollars per year. If he had any more, he could spend more than C dollars each year. If he had any less, he would eventually run out of money spending C dollars per year.

The amount that will give the investor C dollars each year, and therefore the present value of a perpetuity, is:

$$PV = \frac{C}{r}$$ (4.10)

To confirm that this is the right answer, notice that if we lend the amount C/r, the interest it earns each year will be:

$$\text{Interest} = \frac{C}{r} \times r = C$$

which is exactly the perpetuity payment. To sum up, we have shown that for a perpetuity:

Formula for Present Value of a Perpetuity:

$$PV = \frac{C}{1+r} + \frac{C}{(1+r)^2} + \frac{C}{(1+r)^3} + \cdots$$

$$= \frac{C}{r}$$ (4.11)

It is comforting to know how easily we can use a bit of financial intuition to solve this mathematical problem.

EXAMPLE 4.17

Perpetuities

Consider a perpetuity paying $100 a year. If the relevant interest rate is 8 percent, what is the value of the perpetuity?

Using Equation 4.10, we have:

$$PV = \frac{\$100}{.08} = \$1,250$$

Now suppose that interest rates fall to 6 percent. Using Equation 4.10, the value of the perpetuity is:

$$PV = \frac{\$100}{.06} = \$1,666.67$$

Note that the value of the perpetuity rises with a drop in the interest rate. Conversely, the value of the perpetuity falls with a rise in the interest rate.

Growing Perpetuity

Imagine an apartment building where cash flows to the landlord after expenses will be $100,000 next year. These cash flows are expected to rise at 5 percent per year. Assuming that this rise will continue indefinitely, the cash flow stream is termed a **growing perpetuity**. The relevant interest rate is 11 percent. Therefore, the appropriate discount rate is 11 percent and the present value of the cash flows can be represented as:

$$PV = \frac{\$100,000}{1.11} + \frac{\$100,000(1.05)}{1.11^2} + \frac{\$100,000(1.05)^2}{1.11^3} + \cdots$$

$$+ \frac{\$100,000(1.05)^{T-1}}{1.11^T} + \cdots$$

Algebraically, we can write the formula as:

$$PV = \frac{C}{1+r} + \frac{C \times (1+g)}{(1+r)^2} + \frac{C \times (1+g)^2}{(1+r)^3} + \cdots + \frac{C \times (1+g)^{T-1}}{(1+r)^T} + \cdots$$

where C is the cash flow to be received one period from now; g is the rate of growth per period, expressed as a percentage; and r is the appropriate discount rate.

Fortunately, this formula reduces to the following simplification:

$$PV = \frac{C}{r - g} \tag{4.12}$$

From Equation 4.12, the present value of the cash flows from the apartment building is:

$$\frac{\$100,000}{.11 - .05} = \$1,666,667$$

There are three important points concerning the growing perpetuity formula:

1. *The Numerator.* The numerator in Equation 4.12 is the cash flow one period from now, not at Date 0. Consider the following example.

EXAMPLE 4.18

Paying Dividends

Rothstein Corporation is about to pay a dividend of $3.00 per share. Investors anticipate that the annual dividend will rise by 6 percent a year forever. The applicable discount rate is 11 percent. What is the price of the stock today?

The numerator in Equation 4.12 is the cash flow to be received next period. Because the growth rate is 6 percent, the dividend next year is $3.18 (= $3.00 × 1.06). The price of the stock today is:

$66.60	=	$3.00	+	$\dfrac{\$3.18}{.11 - .06}$
		Imminent dividend		Present value of all dividends beginning one year from now

The price of $66.60 includes both the dividend to be received immediately and the present value of all dividends beginning a year from now. Equation 4.12 only makes it possible to calculate the present value of all dividends beginning a year from now. Be sure you understand this example; test questions on this subject always seem to trip up a few of our students.

2. *The Discount Rate and the Growth Rate.* The discount rate r must be greater than the growth rate g for the growing perpetuity formula to work. Consider the case in which the growth rate approaches the discount rate in magnitude. Then the denominator in the growing perpetuity formula gets infinitesimally small and the present value grows infinitely large. The present value is in fact undefined when r is less than g.

3. *The Timing Assumption.* Cash generally flows into and out of real-world firms both randomly and nearly continuously. However, Equation 4.12 assumes that cash flows are received and disbursed at regular and discrete points in time. In the example of the apartment, we assumed that the net cash flows of $100,000 occurred only once a year. In reality, rent checks are commonly received every month. Payments for maintenance and other expenses may occur anytime within the year.

The growing perpetuity Equation 4.12 can be applied only by assuming a regular and discrete pattern of cash flow. Although this assumption is sensible because the formula saves so much time, the user should never forget that it is an assumption. This point will be mentioned again in the chapters ahead.

A few words should be said about terminology. Authors of financial textbooks generally use one of two conventions to refer to time. A minority of financial writers treat cash flows as being received on exact dates, for example, Date 0, Date 1, and so forth. Under this convention, Date 0 represents the present time. However, because a year is an interval, not a specific moment in time, the great majority of authors refer to cash flows that occur at the end of a year (or alternatively, the end of a *period*). Under this *end-of-the-year* convention, the end of Year 0 is the present, the end of Year 1 occurs one period from now, and so on. (The beginning of Year 0 has already passed and is not generally referred to.[5])

The interchangeability of the two conventions can be seen from the following chart:

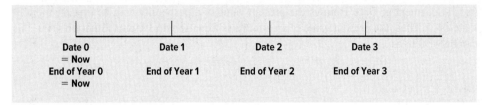

We strongly believe that the *dates convention* reduces ambiguity. However, we use both conventions because you are likely to see the *end-of-year convention* in later courses. In fact, both conventions may appear in the same example for the sake of practice.

Annuity

An **annuity** is a level stream of regular payments that lasts for a fixed number of periods. Not surprisingly, annuities are among the most common kinds of financial instruments. The pensions that people receive when they retire are often in the form of an annuity. Leases and mortgages are also often annuities.

To figure out the present value of an annuity we need to evaluate the following equation:

$$\frac{C}{1+r} + \frac{C}{(1+r)^2} + \frac{C}{(1+r)^3} + \cdots + \frac{C}{(1+r)^t}$$

The present value of only receiving the coupons for t periods must be less than the present value of a perpetuity, but how much less? To answer this we have to look at perpetuities a bit more closely.

Consider the following time chart:

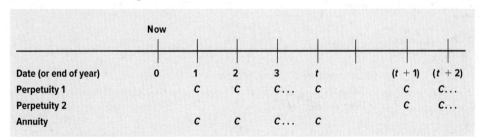

Perpetuity 1 is a perpetuity with its first payment at Date 1. The first payment of Perpetuity 2 occurs at Date $t + 1$.

The present value of having a cash flow of C at each of t dates is equal to the present value of Perpetuity 1 minus the present value of Perpetuity 2. The present value of Perpetuity 1 is given by:

$$PV = \frac{C}{r} \tag{4.13}$$

Perpetuity 2 is a perpetuity with its first payment at Date $t + 1$. From the perpetuity formula, this perpetuity will be worth C/r at Date t.[6] However, we do not want the value at Date t.

<hr>

[5] Sometimes financial writers merely speak of a cash flow in Year x. Although this terminology is ambiguous, such writers generally mean the *end of Year x.*

[6] Students frequently think that C/r is the present value at Date $t + 1$ because the perpetuity's first payment is at Date $t + 1$. However, the formula values the perpetuity as of one period prior to the first payment.

We want the value now; in other words, the present value at Date 0. We must discount C/r back by t periods. Therefore, the present value of Perpetuity 2 is:

$$PV = \frac{C}{r}\left[\frac{1}{(1+r)^t}\right] \qquad (4.14)$$

The present value of having cash flows for t years is the present value of a perpetuity with its first payment at Date 1 minus the present value of a perpetuity with its first payment at Date $t + 1$. Thus, the present value of an annuity is Equation 4.13 minus Equation 4.14. This can be written as:

$$\frac{C}{r} - \frac{C}{r}\left[\frac{1}{(1+r)^t}\right]$$

This simplifies to:

Formula for Present Value of Annuity:

$$PV = C\left[\frac{1}{r} - \frac{1}{r(1+r)^t}\right] \qquad (4.15)$$

This can also be written as:

$$PV = C\left[\frac{1 - \dfrac{1}{(1+r)^t}}{r}\right]$$

EXAMPLE 4.19

Lottery Valuation

Mark Young has just won the state lottery, paying $50,000 a year for 20 years. He is to receive his first payment a year from now. The state advertises this as the Million Dollar Lottery because $1,000,000 = $50,000 × 20. If the interest rate is 8 percent, what is the true value of the lottery?

Equation 4.15 yields:

$$\text{Present value of Million Dollar Lottery} = \$50,000 \times \left[\frac{1 - \dfrac{1}{(1.08)^{20}}}{.08}\right]$$

Periodic payment   Annuity factor
= $50,000   ×   9.8181
= $490,907.37

Rather than being overjoyed at winning, Mr. Young sues the state for misrepresentation and fraud. His legal brief states that he was promised $1 million but received only $490,907.37.

The term we use to compute the present value of the stream of level payments, C, for t years is called an **annuity factor**. The annuity factor in the current example is 9.8181. Because the annuity factor is used so often in PV calculations, we have included it in Table A.2 in the back of this book. The table gives the values of these factors for a range of interest rates, r, and maturity dates, t.

The annuity factor as expressed in the brackets of Equation 4.15 is a complex formula. For simplification, we may from time to time refer to the present value annuity factor as:

$$PVIFA_{r,t}$$

That is, the above expression stands for the present value of $1 a year for t years at an interest rate of r.

We can also provide a formula for the future value of an annuity:

Formula for Future Value of Annuity:

$$FV = C\left[\frac{(1+r)^t}{r} - \frac{1}{r}\right] = C\left[\frac{(1+r)^t - 1}{r}\right] \tag{4.16}$$

As with present value factors for annuities, we have compiled future value factors in Table A.4 in the back of this book. Of course, you can also use a spreadsheet, as we illustrate in the nearby *Spreadsheet Techniques* box.

Using a spreadsheet to find annuity present values goes like this:

	A	B	C	D	E	F	G
1							
2	Using a spreadsheet to find annuity present values						
3							
4	What is the present value of $500 per year for 3 years if the discount rate is 10 percent?						
5	We need to solve for the unknown present value, so we use the formula PV(rate, nper, pmt, fv).						
6							
7	Payment amount per period:	$500					
8	Number of payments:	3					
9	Discount rate:	.1					
10							
11	Annuity present value:	**$1,243.43**					
12							
13	The formula entered in cell B11 is =PV(B9,B8,-B7,0); notice that fv is zero and that						
14	pmt has a negative sign on it. Also notice that rate is entered as a decimal, not a percentage.						
15							
16							
17							

EXAMPLE 4.20

Retirement Investing

Suppose you put $3,000 per year into a Roth IRA. The account pays 6 percent per year. How much will you have when you retire in 30 years?

This question asks for the future value of an annuity of $3,000 per year for 30 years at 6 percent, which we can calculate as follows:

$$FV = C\left[\frac{(1+r)^t - 1}{r}\right] = \$3,000 \times \left[\frac{1.06^{30} - 1}{.06}\right]$$

$$= \$3,000 \times 79.0582$$

$$= \$237,174.56$$

So, you'll have close to a quarter million dollars in the account.

Our experience is that annuity formulas are not difficult, but tricky, for the beginning student. We present four tricks below.

TRICK 1: A DELAYED ANNUITY   One of the tricks in working with annuities or perpetuities is getting the timing exactly right. This is particularly true when an annuity or perpetuity begins at a date many periods in the future. We have found that even the brightest beginning student can make errors here. Consider the following example.

EXAMPLE 4.21

Delayed Annuities

Danielle Caravello will receive a four-year annuity of $500 per year, beginning at Date 6. If the interest rate is 10 percent, what is the present value of her annuity? This situation can be graphed as:

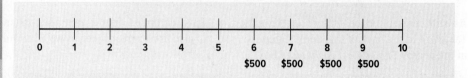

The analysis involves two steps:

1. Calculate the present value of the annuity using Equation 4.15. This is:

$$\$500 \times \left[\frac{1 - \dfrac{1}{1.10^4}}{.10}\right] = \$500 \times \text{PVIFA}_{10\%, 4}$$

$$= \$500 \times 3.1699$$

$$= \$1{,}584.93$$

Note that $1,584.93 represents the present value at Date 5.

Students frequently think that $1,584.93 is the present value at Date 6 because the annuity begins at Date 6. However, our formula values the annuity as of one period prior to the first payment. This can be seen in the most typical case where the first payment occurs at Date 1. The equation values the annuity as of Date 0 in that case.

2. Discount the present value of the annuity back to Date 0. That is:

$$\frac{\$1{,}584.93}{1.10^5} = \$984.12$$

Again, it is worthwhile mentioning that, because the annuity formula brings Danielle's annuity back to Date 5, the second calculation must discount over the remaining 5 periods. The two-step procedure is graphed in Figure 4.12.

FIGURE 4.12   Discounting Danielle Caravello's Annuity

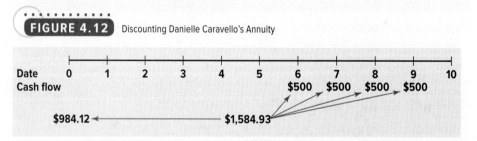

Step one: Discount the four payments back to Date 5 by using the annuity formula.
Step two: Discount the present value at Date 5 ($1,584.93) back to present value at Date 0.

TRICK 2: ANNUITY DUE   The annuity formula of Equation 4.15 assumes that the first annuity payment begins a full period from now. This type of annuity is sometimes called an *annuity in arrears* or an *ordinary annuity*. What happens if the annuity begins today, in other words, at Date 0?

EXAMPLE 4.22

Annuity Due

In a previous example, Mark Young received $50,000 a year for 20 years from the state lottery. In that example, he was to receive the first payment a year from the winning date. Let us now assume that the first payment occurs immediately. The total number of payments remains 20.

Under this new assumption, we have a 19-date annuity with the first payment occurring at Date 1 plus an extra payment at Date 0. The present value is:

$$\underset{\text{Payment at Date 0}}{\$50,000} + \underset{\text{19-year annuity}}{\$50,000 \times PVIFA_{8\%,19}}$$
$$= \$50,000 + (\$50,000 \times 9.6036)$$
$$= \$530,180$$

The present value in this example, $530,180, is greater than $490,907.37, the present value in the earlier lottery example. This is to be expected because the annuity of the current example begins earlier. An annuity with an immediate initial payment is called an *annuity in advance* or, more commonly, an *annuity due*. Always remember that Equation 4.15 and Table A.2 in this book refer to an *ordinary annuity*.

TRICK 3: THE INFREQUENT ANNUITY   The following example treats an annuity with payments occurring less frequently than once a year.

EXAMPLE 4.23

Infrequent Annuities

Ann Chen receives an annuity of $450, payable once every two years. The annuity stretches out over 20 years. The first payment occurs at Date 2, that is, two years from today. The annual interest rate is 6 percent.

The trick is to determine the interest rate over a two-year period. The interest rate over two years is:

$$(1.06 \times 1.06) - 1 = .1236, \text{ or } 12.36\%$$

That is, $100 invested over two years will yield $112.36.

What we want is the present value of a $450 annuity over 10 periods, with an interest rate of 12.36 percent per period. This is:

$$\$450 \times \left[\frac{1 - \frac{1}{(1 + .1236)^{10}}}{.1236} \right] = \$450 \times PVIFA_{12.36\%,10} = \$2,505.57$$

TRICK 4: EQUATING PRESENT VALUE OF TWO ANNUITIES   The following example equates the present value of inflows with the present value of outflows.

EXAMPLE 4.24

Working with Annuities

Harold and Helen Nash are saving for the college education of their newborn daughter, Susan. The Nashes estimate that college expenses will run $55,000 per year when their daughter reaches college in 18 years. The annual interest rate over the next few decades will be 14 percent. How much money must they deposit in the bank each year so that their daughter will be completely supported through four years of college?

To simplify the calculations, we assume that Susan is born today. Her parents will make the first of her four annual tuition payments on her 18th birthday. They will make equal bank deposits on each of her first 17 birthdays, but no deposit at Date 0. This is illustrated as:

(Continued)

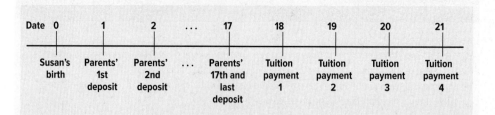

Date	0	1	2	...	17	18	19	20	21
	Susan's birth	Parents' 1st deposit	Parents' 2nd deposit	...	Parents' 17th and last deposit	Tuition payment 1	Tuition payment 2	Tuition payment 3	Tuition payment 4

Mr. and Ms. Nash will be making deposits to the bank over the next 17 years. They will be withdrawing $55,000 per year over the following four years. We can be sure they will be able to withdraw fully $55,000 per year if the present value of the deposits is equal to the present value of the four $55,000 withdrawals.

This calculation requires three steps. The first two determine the present value of the withdrawals. The final step determines yearly deposits that will have a present value equal to that of the withdrawals.

1. We calculate the present value of the four years at college using the annuity formula:

$$\$55,000 \times \left[\frac{1 - \frac{1}{(1.14)^4}}{.14}\right] = \$55,000 \times PVIFA_{14\%,4}$$

$$= \$55,000 \times 2.9137 = \$160,254.18$$

We assume that Susan enters college on her 18th birthday. Given our discussion in Trick 1, $160,254.18 represents the present value at Date 17.

2. We calculate the present value of the college education at Date 0 as:

$$\frac{\$160,254.18}{1.14^{17}} = \$17,275.35$$

3. Assuming that Helen and Harold Nash make deposits to the bank at the end of each of the 17 years, we calculate the annual deposit that will yield a present value of all deposits of $17,275.35. This is calculated as:

$$C \times PVIFA_{14\%,17} = \$17,275.35$$

Because $PVIFA_{14\%,17} = 6.3729$

$$C = \frac{\$17,275.35}{6.3729} = \$2,710.77$$

Thus, deposits of $2,710.77 made at the end of each of the first 17 years and invested at 14 percent will provide enough money to make tuition payments of $55,000 over the following four years. Alternatively, we could have set $160,254.18 as the future value of an annuity and solved for the payment that way. Do this yourself and see if you don't get the same annuity payment.

An alternative method would be to (1) calculate the present value of the tuition payments at Susan's 18th birthday and (2) calculate annual deposits such that the future value of the deposits at her 18th birthday equals the present value of the tuition payments at that date. Although this technique can also provide the right answer, we have found that it is more likely to lead to errors. Therefore, we only equate present values in our presentation.

Growing Annuity

Cash flows in business are very likely to grow over time, due either to real growth or to inflation. The growing perpetuity, which assumes an infinite number of cash flows, provides one formula to handle this growth. We now consider a *growing annuity*, which is a *finite* number of growing cash flows. Because perpetuities of any kind are rare, a formula for a growing annuity would be useful indeed. The formula is:

Formula for Present Value of Growing Annuity:

$$PV = C\left[\frac{1}{r-g} - \frac{1}{r-g} \times \left(\frac{1+g}{1+r}\right)^t\right] = C\left(\frac{1 - \left(\frac{1+g}{1+r}\right)^t}{r-g}\right) \tag{4.17}$$

where, as before, C is the payment to occur at the end of the first period; r is the interest rate; g is the rate of growth per period, expressed as a percentage; and t is the number of periods for the annuity.

EXAMPLE 4.25

Growing Annuities

Stuart Gabriel, a second-year MBA student, has just been offered a job at $80,000 a year. He anticipates his salary increasing by 9 percent a year until his retirement in 40 years. Given an interest rate of 20 percent, what is the present value of his lifetime salary?

We simplify by assuming he will be paid his $80,000 salary exactly one year from now, and that his salary will continue to be paid in annual installments. From Equation 4.17, the calculation is:

$$\begin{array}{l}\text{Present value}\\\text{of Stuart's}\\\text{lifetime salary}\end{array} = \$80,000 \times \left[\frac{1 - \left(\frac{1.09}{1.20}\right)^{40}}{.20 - .09}\right] = \$711,731$$

Though the growing annuity is quite useful, it is more tedious than the other simplifying formulas. Whereas most sophisticated calculators have special programs for perpetuity, growing perpetuity, and annuity, there is no special program for growing annuity. Because of this, you must calculate all the terms in Equation 4.17 directly.

EXAMPLE 4.26

More Growing Annuities

In a previous example, Harold and Helen Nash planned to make 17 identical payments in order to fund the college education of their daughter, Susan. Alternatively, imagine that they planned to increase their payments at 4 percent per year. What would their first payment be?

The first two steps of the previous Nash family example showed that the present value of the college costs was $17,275.35. These two steps would be the same here. However, the third step must be altered. Now we must ask, How much should their first payment be so that, if payments increase by 4 percent per year, the present value of all payments will be $17,275.35?

We set the growing annuity formula equal to $17,275.35 and solve for C.

$$C\left[\frac{1 - \left(\frac{1+g}{1+r}\right)^t}{r-g}\right] = C\left[\frac{1 - \left(\frac{1.04}{1.14}\right)^{17}}{.14 - .04}\right] = \$17,275.35$$

Here, $C = \$2,186.71$. Thus, the deposit on their daughter's first birthday is $2,186.71, the deposit on the second birthday is $2,274.17 (= 1.04 × $2,186.71), and so on.

4.5 LOAN TYPES AND LOAN AMORTIZATION

ExcelMaster
coverage online

www.mhhe.com/RossCore6e

Whenever a lender extends a loan, some provision will be made for repayment of the principal (the original loan amount). A loan might be repaid in equal installments, for example, or it might be repaid in a single lump sum. Because the way that the principal and interest are paid is up to the parties involved, there are actually an unlimited number of possibilities.

In this section, we describe a few forms of repayment that come up quite often, and more complicated forms can usually be built up from these. The three basic types of loans are pure discount loans, interest-only loans, and amortized loans. Working with these loans is a very straightforward application of the present value principles that we have already developed.

Pure Discount Loans

The *pure discount loan* is the simplest form of loan. With such a loan, the borrower receives money today and repays a single lump sum at some time in the future. A one-year, 10 percent pure discount loan, for example, would require the borrower to repay $1.10 in one year for every dollar borrowed today.

Because a pure discount loan is so simple, we already know how to value one. Suppose a borrower was able to repay $25,000 in five years. If we, acting as the lender, wanted a 12 percent interest rate on the loan, how much would we be willing to lend? Put another way, what value would we assign today to that $25,000 to be repaid in five years? Based on our previous work we know the answer is the present value of $25,000 at 12 percent for five years:

$$\text{Present value} = \$25,000/1.12^5$$
$$= \$25,000/1.7623$$
$$= \$14,186$$

Pure discount loans are common when the loan term is short, say a year or less. In recent years, they have become increasingly common for much longer periods.

EXAMPLE 4.27

Treasury Bills

When the U.S. government borrows money on a short-term basis (a year or less), it does so by selling what are called *Treasury bills,* or *T-bills* for short. A T-bill is a promise by the government to repay a fixed amount at some time in the future—for example, 3 months or 12 months.

Treasury bills are pure discount loans. If a T-bill promises to repay $10,000 in 12 months and the market interest rate is 7 percent, how much will the bill sell for in the market?

Because the going rate is 7 percent, the T-bill will sell for the present value of $10,000 to be repaid in one year at 7 percent:

Present value = $10,000/1.07 = $9,345.79

Interest-Only Loans

A second type of loan repayment plan calls for the borrower to pay interest each period and to repay the entire principal (the original loan amount) at some point in the future. Loans with such a repayment plan are called *interest-only loans.* Notice that if there is just one period, a pure discount loan and an interest-only loan are the same thing.

For example, with a three-year, 10 percent, interest-only loan of $1,000, the borrower would pay $1,000 × .10 = $100 in interest at the end of the first and second years. At the end of the third year, the borrower would return the $1,000 along with another $100 in interest for that year. Similarly, a 50-year interest-only loan would call for the borrower to pay interest every year for the next 50 years and then repay the principal. In the extreme, the borrower pays the interest every period forever and never repays any principal. As we discussed earlier in the chapter, the result is a perpetuity.

Most corporate bonds have the general form of an interest-only loan. Because we will be considering bonds in some detail in the next chapter, we will defer further discussion of them for now.

Amortized Loans

With a pure discount or interest-only loan, the principal is repaid all at once. An alternative is an *amortized loan,* with which the lender may require the borrower to repay parts of the loan amount over time. The process of providing for a loan to be paid off by making regular principal reductions is called *amortizing* the loan.

A simple way of amortizing a loan is to have the borrower pay the interest each period plus some fixed amount. This approach is common with medium-term business loans. For example, suppose a business takes out a $5,000, five-year loan at 9 percent. The loan agreement calls for the borrower to pay the interest on the loan balance each year and to reduce the loan balance each year by $1,000. Because the loan amount declines by $1,000 each year, it is fully paid in five years.

In the case we are considering, notice that the total payment will decline each year. The reason is that the loan balance goes down, resulting in a lower interest charge each year, whereas the $1,000 principal reduction is constant. For example, the interest in the first year will be $5,000 × .09 = $450. The total payment will be $1,000 + 450 = $1,450. In the second year, the loan balance is $4,000, so the interest is $4,000 × .09 = $360, and the total payment is $1,360. We can calculate the total payment in each of the remaining years by preparing a simple *amortization schedule* as follows:

Year	Beginning Balance	Total Payment	Interest Paid	Principal Paid	Ending Balance
1	$5,000	$1,450	$ 450	$1,000	$4,000
2	4,000	1,360	360	1,000	3,000
3	3,000	1,270	270	1,000	2,000
4	2,000	1,180	180	1,000	1,000
5	1,000	1,090	90	1,000	0
Totals		$6,350	$1,350	$5,000	

Notice that in each year, the interest paid is given by the beginning balance multiplied by the interest rate. Also notice that the beginning balance is given by the ending balance from the previous year.

Probably the most common way of amortizing a loan is to have the borrower make a single, fixed payment every period. Almost all consumer loans (such as car loans) and mortgages work this way. Suppose our five-year, 9 percent, $5,000 loan was amortized this way. How would the amortization schedule look?

We first need to determine the payment. From our discussion earlier in the chapter, we know that this loan's cash flows are in the form of an ordinary annuity. In this case, we can solve for the payment as follows:

$$\$5,000 = C \times \{[1 - (1/1.09^5)]/.09\}$$
$$= C \times [(1 - .6499)/.09]$$

This gives us:

$$C = \$5,000/3.8897$$
$$= \$1,285.46$$

The borrower will therefore make five equal payments of $1,285.46. Will this pay off the loan? We will check by filling in an amortization schedule.

In our previous example, we knew the principal reduction each year. We then calculated the interest owed to get the total payment. In this example, we know the total payment. We will thus calculate the interest and then subtract it from the total payment to calculate the principal portion in each payment.

In the first year, the interest is $450, as we calculated before. Because the total payment is $1,285.46, the principal paid in the first year must be:

$$\text{Principal paid} = \$1,285.46 - 450 = \$835.46$$

The ending loan balance is thus:

$$\text{Ending balance} = \$5,000 - 835.46 = \$4,164.54$$

The interest in the second year is $4,164.54 \times .09 = \$374.81$, and the loan balance declines by $1,285.46 - 374.81 = \$910.65$. We can summarize all of the relevant calculations in the following schedule:

Year	Beginning Balance	Total Payment	Interest Paid	Principal Paid	Ending Balance
1	$5,000.00	$1,285.46	$ 450.00	$ 835.46	$4,164.54
2	4,164.54	1,285.46	374.81	910.65	3,253.88
3	3,253.88	1,285.46	292.85	992.61	2,261.27
4	2,261.27	1,285.46	203.51	1,081.95	1,179.32
5	1,179.32	1,285.46	106.14	1,179.32	0.00
Totals		$6,427.31	$1,427.31	$5,000.00	

Because the loan balance declines to zero, the five equal payments do pay off the loan. Notice that the interest paid declines each period. This isn't surprising because the loan balance is going down. Given that the total payment is fixed, the principal paid must be rising each period. To see how to calculate this loan in Excel, see the upcoming *Spreadsheet Techniques* box.

Loan amortization is a common spreadsheet application. To illustrate, we will set up the problem that we examined earlier: a five-year, $5,000, 9 percent loan with constant payments. Our spreadsheet looks like this:

	A	B	C	D	E	F	G	H
1								
2				Using a spreadsheet to amortize a loan				
3								
4			Loan amount:	$5,000				
5			Interest rate:	.09				
6			Loan term:	5				
7			Loan payment:	**$1,285.46**				
8				Note: Payment is calculated using PMT(rate, nper, -pv, fv).				
9			*Amortization table:*					
10								
11		Year	Beginning	Total	Interest	Principal	Ending	
12			Balance	Payment	Paid	Paid	Balance	
13		1	$5,000.00	$1,285.46	$450.00	$835.46	$4,164.54	
14		2	4,164.54	1,285.46	374.81	910.65	3,253.88	
15		3	3,253.88	1,285.46	292.85	992.61	2,261.27	
16		4	2,261.27	1,285.46	203.51	1,081.95	1,179.32	
17		5	1,179.32	1,285.46	106.14	1,179.32	0.00	
18		Totals		6,427.31	1,427.31	5,000.00		
19								
20			*Formulas in the amortization table:*					
21								
22		Year	Beginning	Total	Interest	Principal	Ending	
23			Balance	Payment	Paid	Paid	Balance	
24		1	=+D4	=$D$7	=+$D$5*C13	=+D13-E13	=+C13-F13	
25		2	=+G13	=$D$7	=+$D$5*C14	=+D14-E14	=+C14-F14	
26		3	=+G14	=$D$7	=+$D$5*C15	=+D15-E15	=+C15-F15	
27		4	=+G15	=$D$7	=+$D$5*C16	=+D16-E16	=+C16-F16	
28		5	=+G16	=$D$7	=+$D$5*C17	=+D17-E17	=+C17-F17	
29								
30			Note: Totals in the amortization table are calculated using the SUM formula.					
31								

If you compare the two loan amortizations in this section, you will see that the total interest is greater for the equal total payment case: $1,427.31 versus $1,350. The reason for this is that the loan is repaid more slowly early on, so the interest is somewhat higher. This doesn't mean that one loan is better than the other; it means that one is effectively paid off faster than the other. For example, the principal reduction in the first year is $835.46 in the equal total payment case as compared to $1,000 in the first case.

EXAMPLE 4.28

Partial Amortization, or "Bite the Bullet"

A common arrangement in real estate lending might call for a 5-year loan with, say, a 15-year amortization. What this means is that the borrower makes a payment every month of a fixed amount based on a 15-year amortization. However, after 60 months, the borrower makes a single, much larger payment called a "balloon" or "bullet" to pay off the loan. Because the monthly payments don't fully pay off the loan, the loan is said to be partially amortized.

Suppose we have a $100,000 commercial mortgage with a 12 percent APR and a 20-year (240-month) amortization. Further suppose the mortgage has a five-year balloon. What will the monthly payment be? How big will the balloon payment be?

(Continued)

The monthly payment can be calculated based on an ordinary annuity with a present value of $100,000. There are 240 payments, and the interest rate is 1 percent per month. The payment is:

$$\$100,000 = C \times [(1 - 1/1.01^{240})/.01]$$
$$= C \times 90.8194$$
$$C = \$1,101.09$$

Now, there is an easy way and a hard way to determine the balloon payment. The hard way is to actually amortize the loan for 60 months to see what the balance is at that time. The easy way is to recognize that after 60 months, we have a 240 − 60 = 180-month loan. The payment is still $1,101.09 per month, and the interest rate is still 1 percent per month. The loan balance is thus the present value of the remaining payments:

$$\text{Loan balance} = \$1,101.09 \times [(1 - 1/1.01^{180})/.01]$$
$$= \$1,101.09 \times 83.3217$$
$$= \$91,744.33$$

The balloon payment is a substantial $91,744. Why is it so large? To get an idea, consider the first payment on the mortgage. The interest in the first month is $100,000 × .01 = $1,000. Your payment is $1,101.09, so the loan balance declines by only $101.09. Because the loan balance declines so slowly, the cumulative "pay down" over five years is not great.

We will close this section with an example that may be of particular relevance. Federal Stafford loans are an important source of financing for many college students, helping to cover the cost of tuition, books, new cars, condominiums, and many other things. Sometimes students do not seem to fully realize that Stafford loans have a serious drawback: They must be repaid in monthly installments, usually beginning six months after the student leaves school.

Some Stafford loans are subsidized, meaning that the interest does not begin to accrue until repayment begins (this is a good thing). If you are a dependent undergraduate student under this particular option, the total debt you can run up is, at most, $23,000. For loans between July 2018 and July 2019, the interest rate is 5.045 percent, or 5.045/12 = .4204 percent per month. Under the "standard repayment plan," the loans are amortized over 10 years (subject to a minimum payment of $50).

Suppose you max out borrowing under this program and also get stuck paying the maximum interest rate. Beginning six months after you graduate (or otherwise depart the ivory tower), what will your monthly payment be? How much will you owe after making payments for four years?

Given our earlier discussions, see if you don't agree that your monthly payment assuming a $23,000 total loan is $244.46 per month. Also, as explained in Example 4.28, after making payments for four years, you still owe the present value of the remaining payments. There are 120 payments in all. After you make 48 of them (the first four years), you have 72 to go. By now, it should be easy for you to verify that the present value of $244.46 per month for 72 months at .4204 percent per month is just over $15,000, so you still have a long way to go.

Of course, it is possible to rack up much larger debts. According to the Association of American Medical Colleges, students who borrowed to attend medical school and graduated in 2018 had an average student loan balance of $192,000. Ouch! How long will it take the average student to pay off her medical school loans?

Let's say she makes a monthly payment of $1,200, and the loan has an interest rate of 7 percent per year, or .5833 percent per month. See if you agree that it will take 466 months, or just about 39 years, to pay off the loan. Maybe MD really stands for "mucho debt!"

4.6 WHAT IS A FIRM WORTH?

Suppose you are in the business of trying to determine the value of small companies. (You are a business appraiser.) How can you determine what a firm is worth? One way to think about the question of how much a firm is worth is to calculate the present value of its future cash flows.

Let us consider the example of a firm that is expected to generate net cash flows (cash inflows minus cash outflows) of $5,000 in the first year and $2,000 for each of the next five years. The firm can be sold for $10,000 seven years from now. The owners of the firm would like to be able to make 10 percent on their investment in the firm.

The value of the firm is found by multiplying the net cash flows by the appropriate present value factor. The value of the firm is the sum of the present values of the individual net cash flows.

The present value of the net cash flows is given next.

End of Year	The Present Value of the Firm		
	Net Cash Flow of The Firm	Present Value Factor (10%)	Present Value of Net Cash Flows
1	$ 5,000	.90909	$ 4,545.45
2	2,000	.82645	1,652.89
3	2,000	.75131	1,502.63
4	2,000	.68301	1,366.03
5	2,000	.62092	1,241.84
6	2,000	.56447	1,128.95
7	10,000	.51316	5,131.58
		Present value of firm	$16,569.38

We can also use the simplifying formula for an annuity to give us:

$$\frac{\$5,000}{1.1} + \frac{\$2,000 \times \text{PVIFA}_{10\%,5}}{1.1} + \frac{\$10,000}{1.1^7} = \$16,569.38$$

Suppose you have the opportunity to acquire the firm for $12,000. Should you acquire the firm? The answer is yes because the NPV is positive.

$$\text{NPV} = \text{PV} - \text{Cost}$$
$$\$4,569.38 = \$16,569.38 - 12,000$$

The incremental value (NPV) of acquiring the firm is $4,569.38.

EXAMPLE 4.29

Firm Valuation

The Trojan Pizza Company is contemplating investing $1 million in four new outlets in Los Angeles. Andrew Lo, the firm's chief financial officer (CFO), has estimated that the investments will pay out cash flows of $200,000 per year for nine years and nothing thereafter. (The cash flows will occur at the end of each year, and there will be no cash flow after Year 9.) Mr. Lo has determined that the relevant discount rate for this investment is 15 percent. This is the rate of return that the firm can earn on comparable projects. Should the Trojan Pizza Company make the investments in the new outlets?

(Continued)

The decision can be evaluated as:

$$NPV = -\$1,000,000 + \frac{\$200,000}{1.15} + \frac{\$200,000}{1.15^2} + \cdots + \frac{\$200,000}{1.15^9}$$

$$= -\$1,000,000 + \$200,000 \times PVIFA_{15\%,9}$$

$$= -\$1,000,000 + \$954,316.78$$

$$= -\$45,683.22$$

The present value of the four new outlets is only $954,316.78. The outlets are worth less than they cost. The Trojan Pizza Company should not make the investment because the NPV is −$45,683.22. If the Trojan Pizza Company requires a 15 percent rate of return, the new outlets are not a good investment.

SUMMARY AND CONCLUSIONS

1. Two basic concepts, *future value* and *present value,* were introduced in the beginning of this chapter. With a 10 percent interest rate, an investor with $1 today can generate a future value of $1.10 in one year, $1.21 $(= \$1 \times 1.10^2)$ in two years, and so on. Conversely, present value analysis places a current value on a later cash flow. With the same 10 percent interest rate, a dollar to be received in one year has a present value of $.909 $(= \$1/1.10)$ in Year 0. A dollar to be received in two years has a present value of $.826 $(= \$1/1.10^2)$.

2. One commonly expresses the interest rate as, say, 12 percent per year. However, one can speak of the interest rate as 3 percent per quarter. Although the annual percentage rate remains 12 percent $(= 3 \text{ percent} \times 4)$, the effective annual interest rate is 12.55 percent $(= 1.03^4 - 1)$. In other words, the compounding process increases the future value of an investment. The limiting case is continuous compounding, where funds are assumed to be reinvested every infinitesimal instant.

3. A basic quantitative technique for financial decision making is net present value analysis. The net present value formula for an investment that generates cash flows (C_i) in future periods is:

$$NPV = -C_0 + \frac{C_1}{(1+r)} + \frac{C_2}{(1+r)^2} + \cdots + \frac{C_t}{(1+r)^t} = -C_0 + \sum_{i=1}^{t} \frac{C_i}{(1+r)^i}$$

The formula assumes that the cash flow at Date 0 is the initial investment (a cash outflow).

4. Frequently, the actual calculation of present value is long and tedious. The computation of the present value of a long-term mortgage with monthly payments is a good example of this. We presented four simplifying formulas:

$$\textbf{Perpetuity: } PV = \frac{C}{r}$$

$$\textbf{Growing perpetuity: } PV = \frac{C}{r-g}$$

$$\textbf{Annuity: } PV = C \left[\frac{1 - \dfrac{1}{(1+r)^t}}{r} \right]$$

$$\textbf{Growing annuity: } PV = C \left[\frac{1 - \left(\dfrac{1+g}{1+r}\right)^t}{r-g} \right]$$

5. We stressed a few practical considerations in the application of these formulas:

   a. The numerator in each of the formulas, C, is the cash flow to be received one period from now.

   b. Cash flows are generally irregular in practice. To avoid unwieldy problems, assumptions to create more regular cash flows are made both in this textbook and in the real world.

   c. A number of present value problems involve annuities (or perpetuities) beginning a few periods hence. Students should practice combining the annuity (or perpetuity) formula with the discounting formula to solve these problems.

   d. Annuities and perpetuities may have periods of every two or every n years, rather than once a year. The annuity and perpetuity formulas can easily handle such circumstances.

   e. One frequently encounters problems where the present value of one annuity must be equated with the present value of another annuity.

6. Many loans are annuities. The process of providing for a loan to be paid off gradually is called amortizing the loan, and we discussed how amortization schedules are prepared and interpreted.

CONCEPT QUESTIONS

1. **Compounding and Period**   As you increase the length of time involved, what happens to future values? What happens to present values?

2. **Interest Rates**   What happens to the future value of an annuity if you increase the rate r? What happens to the present value?

3. **Present Value**   Suppose two athletes sign 10-year contracts for $80 million. In one case, we're told that the $80 million will be paid in 10 equal installments. In the other case, we're told that the $80 million will be paid in 10 installments, but the installments will increase by 5 percent per year. Who got the better deal?

4. **APR and EAR**   Should lending laws be changed to require lenders to report EARs instead of APRs? Why or why not?

5. **Time Value**   On subsidized Stafford loans, a common source of financial aid for college students, interest does not begin to accrue until repayment begins. Who receives a bigger subsidy, a freshman or a senior? Explain.

Use the following information for Questions 6–10:

Toyota Motor Credit Corporation (TMCC), a subsidiary of Toyota Motor Corporation, offered some securities for sale to the public on March 28, 2008. Under the terms of the deal, TMCC promised to repay the owner of one of these securities $100,000 on March 28, 2038, but investors would receive nothing until then. Investors paid TMCC $24,099 for each of these securities, so they gave up $24,099 on March 28, 2008, for the promise of a $100,000 payment 30 years later.

6. **Time Value of Money**   Why would TMCC be willing to accept such a small amount today ($24,099) in exchange for a promise to repay about four times that amount ($100,000) in the future?

7. **Call Provisions**   TMCC has the right to buy back the securities on the anniversary date at a price established when the securities were issued (this feature is a term of this particular deal). What impact does this feature have on the desirability of this security as an investment?

8. **Time Value of Money**   Would you be willing to pay $24,099 today in exchange for $100,000 in 30 years? What would be the key considerations in answering yes or no? Would your answer depend on who is making the promise to repay?

9. **Investment Comparison**   Suppose that when TMCC offered the security for $24,099, the U.S. Treasury had offered an essentially identical security. Do you think it would have had a higher or lower price? Why?

10. **Length of Investment**   The TMCC security is bought and sold on the New York Stock Exchange. If you looked at the price today, do you think the price would exceed the $24,099 original price? Why? If you looked in the year 2025, do you think the price would be higher or lower than today's price? Why?

QUESTIONS AND PROBLEMS

Mc Graw Hill **connect**

1. **Simple Interest versus Compound Interest** First City Bank pays 7 percent simple interest on its savings account balances, whereas Second City Bank pays 7 percent interest compounded annually. If you made a $5,600 deposit in each bank, how much more money would you earn from your Second City Bank account at the end of 10 years?

Basic
(Questions 1–20)

2. **Calculating Future Values** Compute the future value of $4,375 compounded annually for:

   a. 10 years at 6 percent.

   b. 10 years at 8 percent.

   c. 20 years at 6 percent.

   d. Why is the interest earned in part (c) not twice the amount earned in part (a)?

3. **Calculating Present Values** For each of the following, compute the present value:

Present Value	Years	Interest Rate	Future Value
	9	7%	$ 10,971
	13	9	43,862
	16	14	754,500
	24	11	480,127

4. **Calculating Interest Rates** Solve for the unknown interest rate in each of the following:

Present Value	Years	Interest Rate	Future Value
$ 217	3		$ 284
432	10		1,250
41,000	16		173,864
54,382	19		425,600

5. **Calculating the Number of Periods** Solve for the unknown number of years in each of the following:

Present Value	Years	Interest Rate	Future Value
$ 625		7%	$ 1,284
810		10	4,341
18,400		8	234,162
21,500		13	215,000

6. **Calculating the Number of Periods** At 4.83 percent interest, how long does it take to double your money? To quadruple it?

7. **Calculating Present Values** Imprudential, Inc., has an unfunded pension liability of $450 million that must be paid in 20 years. To assess the value of the firm's stock, financial analysts want to discount this liability back to the present. If the relevant discount rate is 4.8 percent, what is the present value of this liability?

8. **Calculating Rates of Return** Although appealing to more refined tastes, art as a collectible has not always performed so profitably. In 2010, Deutscher-Menzies sold *Arkie Under the Shower*, a painting by renowned Australian painter Brett Whiteley, at auction for a price of $1,100,000. Unfortunately for the previous owner, he had purchased it three years earlier at a price of $1,680,000. What was his annual rate of return on this painting?

9. **Perpetuities**   An investor purchasing a British consol is entitled to receive annual payments from the British government forever. What is the price of a consol that pays $75 annually if the next payment occurs one year from today? The market interest rate is 3.1 percent.

 10. **Continuous Compounding**   Compute the future value of $2,430 continuously compounded for:

   a. Five years at an annual percentage rate of 14 percent.

   b. Three years at an annual percentage rate of 6 percent.

   c. Ten years at an annual percentage rate of 8 percent.

   d. Eight years at an annual percentage rate of 9 percent.

11. **Present Value and Multiple Cash Flows**   Machine Co. has identified an investment project with the following cash flows. If the discount rate is 5 percent, what is the present value of these cash flows? What is the present value at 13 percent? At 18 percent?

Year	Cash Flow
1	$ 655
2	945
3	1,960
4	2,380

12. **Present Value and Multiple Cash Flows**   Investment X offers to pay you $3,720 per year for nine years, whereas Investment Y offers to pay you $5,740 per year for five years. Which of these cash flow streams has the higher present value if the discount rate is 5 percent? If the discount rate is 21 percent?

13. **Calculating Annuity Present Value**   An investment offers $7,500 per year for 15 years, with the first payment occurring one year from now. If the required return is 6.8 percent, what is the value of the investment? What would the value be if the payments occurred for 40 years? For 75 years? Forever?

14. **Calculating Perpetuity Values**   The Perpetual Life Insurance Co. is trying to sell you an investment policy that will pay you and your heirs $15,000 per year forever. If the required return on this investment is 4.3 percent, how much will you pay for the policy? Suppose the company told you the policy costs $445,000. At what discount rate would this be a fair deal?

15. **Calculating EAR**   Find the EAR in each of the following cases:

APR	Number of Times Compounded	EAR
8.4%	Quarterly	
18.6	Monthly	
9.4	Daily	
7.8	Infinite	

16. **Calculating APR**   Find the APR in each of the following cases:

APR	Number of Times Compounded	EAR
	Semiannually	9.9%
	Monthly	11.4
	Weekly	15.5
	Infinite	16.3

17. **Calculating EAR**   First National Bank charges 14.8 percent compounded monthly on its business loans. First United Bank charges 15.1 percent compounded semiannually. As a potential borrower, which bank would you go to for a new loan?

18. Interest Rates Well-known financial writer Andrew Tobias argues that he can earn 177 percent per year buying wine by the case. Specifically, he assumes that he will consume one $10 bottle of fine Bordeaux per week for the next 12 weeks. He can either pay $10 per week or buy a case of 12 bottles today. If he buys the case, he receives a 10 percent discount, and, by doing so, earns the 177 percent. Assume he buys the wine and consumes the first bottle today. Do you agree with his analysis? Do you see a problem with his numbers?

19. Calculating Number of Periods One of your customers is delinquent on his accounts payable balance. You've mutually agreed to a repayment schedule of $350 per month. You will charge 1.3 percent per month interest on the overdue balance. If the current balance is $16,200, how long will it take for the account to be paid off?

20. Calculating EAR Friendly's Quick Loans, Inc., offers you "three for four or I knock on your door." This means you get $3 today and repay $4 when you get your paycheck in one week (or else). What's the effective annual return Friendly's earns on this lending business? If you were brave enough to ask, what APR would Friendly's say you were paying?

Intermediate
(Questions 21–52)

21. Future Value What is the future value in six years of $2,900 invested in an account with an annual percentage rate of 6.3 percent:

   a. Compounded annually?

   b. Compounded semiannually?

   c. Compounded monthly?

   d. Compounded continuously?

   e. Why does the future value increase as the compounding period shortens?

22. Simple Interest versus Compound Interest First Simple Bank pays 6.8 percent simple interest on its investment accounts. If First Complex Bank pays interest on its accounts compounded annually, what rate should the bank set if it wants to match First Simple Bank over an investment horizon of 10 years?

 23. Calculating Annuities You are planning to save for retirement over the next 30 years. To do this, you will invest $950 per month in a stock account and $375 per month in a bond account. The return of the stock account is expected to be an APR of 10.5 percent, and the bond account will earn an APR of 6.1 percent. When you retire, you will combine your money into an account with an APR of 6.9 percent. All interest rates are compounded monthly. How much can you withdraw each month from your account assuming a withdrawal period of 25 years?

24. Calculating Rates of Return Suppose an investment offers to triple your money in 12 months (don't believe it). What rate of return per quarter are you being offered?

25. Calculating Rates of Return You're trying to choose between two different investments, both of which have up-front costs of $45,000. Investment G returns $89,000 in five years. Investment H returns $210,000 in 11 years. Which of these investments has the higher return?

 26. Growing Perpetuities Mark Weinstein has been working on an advanced technology in laser eye surgery. His technology will be available in the near term. He anticipates his first annual cash flow from the technology to be $185,000, received three years from today. Subsequent annual cash flows will grow at 2.5 percent in perpetuity. What is the value today of the technology if the discount rate is 12 percent?

27. Perpetuities A prestigious investment bank designed a new security that pays a quarterly dividend of $1.45 in perpetuity. The first dividend occurs one quarter from today. What is the price of the security if the annual percentage rate is 4.9 percent, compounded quarterly?

28. Annuity Present Values What is the value today of an annuity of $7,200 per year, with the first cash flow received three years from today and the last one received 25 years from today? Use a discount rate of 7.4 percent.

29. Annuity Present Values What is the value today of a 15-year annuity that pays $950 a year? The annuity's first payment occurs six years from today. The annual interest rate is 9 percent for Years 1 through 5, and 12 percent thereafter.

30. Balloon Payments Mike Bayles has just arranged to purchase an $875,000 vacation home in the Bahamas with a 20 percent down payment. The mortgage has an APR of 5.8 percent, compounded monthly, and calls for equal monthly payments over the next 30 years. His first payment will be due one month from now. However, the mortgage has an eight-year balloon payment, meaning that the balance of the loan must be paid off at the end of Year 8. There were no other transaction costs or finance charges. How much will Mike's balloon payment be in eight years?

31. Calculating Interest Expense You receive a credit card application from Shady Banks Savings and Loan offering an introductory rate of 1.8 percent per year, compounded monthly for the first six months, increasing thereafter to 15 percent compounded monthly. Assuming you transfer the $9,000 balance from your existing credit card and make no subsequent payments, how much interest will you owe at the end of the first year?

32. Perpetuities King Pharmaceuticals is considering a drug project that costs $1.8 million today and is expected to generate end-of-year annual cash flows of $235,000 forever. At what discount rate would the company be indifferent between accepting or rejecting the project?

33. Growing Annuity Southern California Publishing Company is trying to decide whether or not to revise its popular textbook *Financial Psychoanalysis Made Simple*. It has estimated that the revision will cost $155,000. Cash flows from increased sales will be $43,000 the first year. These cash flows will increase by 5.5 percent per year. The book will go out of print five years from now. Assume that the initial cost is paid now and revenues are received at the end of each year. If the company requires a return of 11 percent for such an investment, should it undertake the revision?

 34. Growing Annuity Your job pays you only once a year, for all the work you did over the previous 12 months. Today, December 31, you just received your salary of $85,000 and you plan to spend all of it. However, you want to start saving for retirement beginning next year. You have decided that one year from today you will begin depositing 10 percent of your annual salary in an account that will earn 9.5 percent per year. Your salary will increase at 3.3 percent per year throughout your career. How much money will you have on the date of your retirement 35 years from today?

35. Present Value and Interest Rates What is the relationship between the value of an annuity and the level of interest rates? Suppose you just bought a 15-year annuity of $6,350 per year at the current interest rate of 10 percent per year. What happens to the value of your investment if interest rates suddenly drop to 5 percent? What if interest rates suddenly rise to 15 percent?

36. Calculating the Number of Payments You're prepared to make monthly payments of $245, beginning at the end of this month, into an account that pays an APR of 8.75 percent interest, compounded monthly. How many payments will you have made when your account balance reaches $25,000?

37. Calculating Annuity Present Values You want to borrow $135,000 from your local bank to buy a new sailboat. You can afford to make monthly payments of $2,650, but no more. Assuming monthly compounding, what is the highest APR you can afford on a 60-month loan?

38. Calculating Loan Payments You need a 30-year, fixed-rate mortgage to buy a new home for $245,000. Your mortgage bank will lend you the money at an APR of 5.1 percent. However, you can only afford monthly payments of $950, so you offer to pay off any remaining loan balance at the end of the loan in the form of a single balloon payment. How large will this balloon payment have to be for you to keep your monthly payments at $950?

 39. Present and Future Values The present value of the following cash flow stream is $5,800 when discounted at 7 percent annually. What is the value of the missing cash flow?

Year	Cash Flow
1	$1,300
2	?
3	1,900
4	2,450

40. Calculating Present Values You have just won the TVM Lottery. You will receive $1 million today plus another 10 annual payments that increase by $195,000 per year. Thus, in one year you receive $1.195 million. In two years, you get $1.39 million, and so on. If the appropriate discount rate is 7.3 percent, what is the value of your winnings today?

41. EAR versus APR You have just purchased a new warehouse. To finance the purchase, you've arranged for a 30-year mortgage loan for 80 percent of the $3.3 million purchase price. The monthly payment on this loan will be $16,250. What is the APR on this loan? The EAR?

42. Present Value and Break-Even Interest Consider a firm with a contract to sell an asset for $125,000 three years from now. The asset costs $87,000 to produce today. Given a relevant discount rate of 11 percent per year, will the firm make a profit on this asset? At what rate does the firm just break even?

43. Present Value and Multiple Cash Flows What is the value today of $4,100 per year, at a discount rate of 6.9 percent, if the first payment is received 7 years from now and the last payment is received 30 years from now?

44. Variable Interest Rates A 15-year annuity pays $1,750 per month, and payments are made at the end of each month. If the interest rate is 11.4 percent compounded monthly for the first seven years, and 8.6 percent compounded monthly thereafter, what is the value of the annuity today?

45. Comparing Cash Flow Streams You have your choice of two investment accounts. Investment A is a 15-year annuity that features end-of-month $1,050 payments and has an interest rate of 6.05 percent compounded monthly. Investment B is a continuously compounded lump-sum investment with an interest rate of 7 percent, also good for 15 years. How much money would you need to invest in B today for it to be worth as much as Investment A 15 years from now?

46. Calculating Present Value of a Perpetuity Given an interest rate of 7.6 percent per year, what is the value at $t = 7$ of a perpetual stream of $3,550 annual payments that begin at $t = 15$?

47. Calculating EAR A local finance company quotes an interest rate of 15.9 percent on one-year loans. So, if you borrow $27,000, the interest for the year will be $4,293. Because you must repay a total of $31,293 in one year, the finance company requires you to pay $31,293/12, or $2,607.75, per month over the next 12 months. Is the interest rate on the loan 15.9 percent? What rate would legally have to be quoted? What is the effective annual rate?

48. Calculating Present Values A five-year annuity of 10 $5,700 semiannual payments will begin 9 years from now, with the first payment coming 9.5 years from now. If the discount rate is 9 percent compounded monthly, what is the value of this annuity five years from now? What is the value three years from now? What is the current value of the annuity?

49. Calculating Annuities Due Suppose you are going to receive $16,000 per year for five years. The appropriate discount rate is 7.2 percent.
  a. What is the present value of the payments if they are in the form of an ordinary annuity? What is the present value if the payments are an annuity due?
  b. Suppose you plan to invest the payments for five years. What is the future value if the payments are an ordinary annuity? What if the payments are an annuity due?
  c. Which has the highest present value, the ordinary annuity or the annuity due? Which has the highest future value? Will this always be true?

50. Calculating Annuities Due You want to buy a new sports car from Muscle Motors for $76,000. The contract is in the form of a 60-month annuity due at an APR of 4.98 percent, compounded monthly. What will your monthly payment be?

51. Amortization with Equal Payments Prepare an amortization schedule for a three-year loan of $57,000. The interest rate is 9 percent per year, and the loan calls for equal annual payments. How much interest is paid in the third year? How much total interest is paid over the life of the loan?

52. Amortization with Equal Principal Payments Rework Problem 51 assuming that the loan agreement calls for a principal reduction of $19,000 every year instead of equal annual payments.

53. Calculating Annuities Due You want to lease a set of golf clubs from PGX Ltd. The lease contract is in the form of 24 equal monthly payments at an APR of 8.6 percent, compounded monthly. Because the clubs cost $4,600 retail, the company wants the present value of the lease payments to equal $4,600 and your first payment is due immediately. What will your monthly lease payments be?

Challenge
(Questions 53–80)

54. Annuities You are saving for the college education of your two children. They are 2 years apart in age; one will begin college 15 years from today and the other will begin 17 years from today. You estimate your children's college expenses to be $65,000 per year per child, payable at the beginning of each school year. The annual interest rate is 9.2 percent. How much money must you deposit in an account each year to fund your children's education? Your deposits begin 1 year from today. You will make your last deposit when your oldest child enters college. Assume your children will be on the four-year plan.

55. Growing Annuities Tom Adams has received a job offer from a large investment bank as a clerk to an associate banker. His base salary will be $75,000. He will receive his first annual salary payment one year from the day he begins to work. In addition, he will get an immediate $15,000 bonus for joining the company. His salary will grow at 3.2 percent each year. Each year he will receive a bonus equal to 10 percent of his salary. Mr. Adams is expected to work for 35 years. What is the present value of the offer if the discount rate is 9 percent?

56. Calculating Annuities You have recently won the super jackpot in the Set for Life Lottery. On reading the fine print, you discover that you have the following two options:

a. You will receive 31 annual payments of $400,000, with the first payment being delivered today. The income will be taxed at a rate of 36 percent. Taxes will be withheld when the checks are issued.

b. You will receive $1 million now and you will not have to pay taxes on this amount. In addition, beginning one year from today, you will receive $325,000 each year for 30 years. The cash flows from this annuity will be taxed at 36 percent.

Using a discount rate of 4.1 percent, which option should you select?

57. Calculating Growing Annuities You have 30 years left until retirement and want to retire with $2.5 million. Your salary is paid annually and you will receive $85,000 at the end of the current year. Your salary will increase at 3 percent per year, and you can earn a return of 9.7 percent on the money you invest. If you save a constant percentage of your salary, what percentage of your salary must you save each year?

58. Balloon Payments On September 1, 2017, Susan Chao bought a motorcycle for $43,000. She paid $2,000 down and financed the balance with a five-year loan at an APR of 5.8 percent compounded monthly. She started the monthly payments exactly one month after the purchase (i.e., October 1, 2017). Two years later, at the end of October 2019, Susan got a new job and decided to pay off the loan. If the bank charges her a 1 percent prepayment penalty based on the loan balance, how much must she pay the bank on November 1, 2019?

59. Calculating Annuity Values Bilbo Baggins wants to save money to meet three objectives. First, he would like to be able to retire 30 years from now with a retirement income of $24,000 per month for 20 years, with the first payment received 30 years and one month from now. Second, he would like to purchase a cabin in Rivendell in 10 years at an estimated cost of $375,000. Third, after he passes on at the end of the 20 years of withdrawals, he would like to leave an inheritance of $1 million to his nephew Frodo. He can afford to save $2,300 per month for the next 10 years. If he can earn an EAR of 11 percent before he retires and an EAR of 7 percent after he retires, how much will he have to save each month in Years 11 through 30?

60. **Calculating Annuity Values** After deciding to get a new car, you can either lease the car or purchase it with a three-year loan. The car you wish to buy costs $39,000. The dealer has a special leasing arrangement where you pay $3,000 today and $450 per month for the next three years. If you purchase the car, you will pay it off in monthly payments over the next three years at an APR of 4.1 percent, compounded monthly. You believe that you will be able to sell the car for $24,500 in three years. Should you buy or lease the car? What break-even resale price in three years would make you indifferent between buying and leasing?

61. **Calculating Annuity Values** An All-Pro defensive lineman is in contract negotiations. The team has offered the following salary structure:

Time	Salary
0	$10,000,000
1	7,400,000
2	7,400,000
3	7,700,000
4	8,500,000
5	10,400,000
6	11,900,000

All salaries are to be paid in a lump sum. The player has asked you as his agent to renegotiate the terms. He wants a signing bonus of $13 million payable today and a contract value increase of $3.5 million. He also wants an equal salary paid every three months, with the first paycheck three months from now. If the interest rate is an APR of 5 percent compounded daily, what is the amount of his quarterly check? Assume 365 days in a year.

62. **Discount Interest Loans** This question illustrates what is known as *discount interest.* Imagine you are discussing a loan with a somewhat unscrupulous lender. You want to borrow $20,000 for one year. The interest rate is 12.9 percent. You and the lender agree that the interest on the loan will be .129 × $20,000 = $2,580. So the lender deducts this interest amount from the loan up front and gives you $17,420. In this case, we say that the discount is $2,580. What's wrong here?

63. **Calculating Annuity Values** You are serving on a jury. A plaintiff is suing the city for injuries sustained after a freak street sweeper accident. In the trial, doctors testified that it will be five years before the plaintiff is able to return to work. The jury has already decided in favor of the plaintiff. You are the foreperson of the jury and propose that the jury give the plaintiff an award to cover the following: (1) The present value of two years' back pay. The plaintiff's annual salary for the last two years would have been $46,000 and $49,000, respectively. (2) The present value of five years' future salary. You assume the salary will be $53,000 per year. (3) $250,000 for pain and suffering. (4) $50,000 for court costs. Assume that the salary payments are equal amounts paid at the end of each month. If the interest rate you choose is an EAR of 9 percent, what is the size of the settlement? If you were the plaintiff, would you like to see a higher or lower interest rate?

64. **Calculating EAR with Points** You are looking at a one-year loan of $10,000. The interest rate is quoted as 13.4 percent plus two points. A *point* on a loan is 1 percent (one percentage point) of the loan amount. Quotes similar to this one are very common with home mortgages. The interest rate quotation in this example requires the borrower to pay two points to the lender up front and repay the loan later with 13.4 percent interest. What rate would you actually be paying here?

65. **Calculating EAR with Points** The interest rate on a one-year loan is quoted as 10.2 percent plus three points (see the previous problem). What is the EAR? Is your answer affected by the loan amount?

66. EAR versus APR There are two banks in the area that offer 30-year, $250,000 mortgages at 5.2 percent compounded monthly and charge a $3,100 loan application fee. However, the application fee charged by Insecurity Bank and Trust is refundable if the loan application is denied, whereas that charged by I. M. Greedy and Sons Mortgage Bank is not. The current disclosure law requires that any fees that will be refunded if the applicant is rejected be included in calculating the APR, but this is not required with nonrefundable fees (presumably because refundable fees are part of the loan rather than a fee). What are the EARs on these two loans? What are the APRs?

67. Calculating EAR with Add-On Interest This problem illustrates a deceptive way of quoting interest rates called *add-on interest*. Imagine that you see an advertisement for Crazy Judy's Stereo City that reads something like this: "$3,500 Instant Credit! 16.7% Simple Interest! Three Years to Pay! Low, Low Monthly Payments!" You're not exactly sure what all this means and somebody has spilled ink over the APR on the loan contract, so you ask the manager for clarification.

Judy explains that if you borrow $3,500 for three years at 16.7 percent interest, in three years you will owe:

$$\$3,500 \times 1.167^3 = \$3,500 \times 1.589324 = \$5,562.64$$

Now, Judy recognizes that coming up with $5,562.64 all at once might be a strain, so she lets you make "low, low monthly payments" of $5,562.64/36 = $154.52 per month, even though this is extra bookkeeping work for her.

Is the interest rate on this loan 16.7 percent? Why or why not? What is the APR on this loan? What is the EAR? Why do you think this is called add-on interest?

68. Growing Annuities You have successfully started and operated a company for the past 10 years. You have decided that it is time to sell your company and spend time on the beaches of Hawaii. A potential buyer is interested in your company, but he does not have the necessary capital to pay you a lump sum. Instead, he has offered $750,000 today and annuity payments for the balance. The first payment will be for $225,000 in three months. The payments will increase at 2.5 percent per quarter and a total of 25 quarterly payments will be made. If you require an EAR of 11 percent, how much are you being offered for your company?

69. Calculating the Number of Periods Your Christmas ski vacation was great, but it unfortunately ran a bit over budget. All is not lost because you just received an offer in the mail to transfer your $10,000 balance from your current credit card, which charges an annual rate of 18.2 percent, to a new credit card charging a rate of 7.9 percent. How much faster could you pay the loan off by making your planned monthly payments of $175 with the new card? What if there was a fee of 3 percent charged on any balances transferred?

70. Future Value and Multiple Cash Flows An insurance company is offering a new policy to its customers. Typically, the policy is bought by a parent or grandparent for a child at the child's birth. The details of the policy are as follows: The purchaser (say, the parent) makes the following six payments to the insurance company:

First birthday:	$700
Second birthday:	700
Third birthday:	800
Fourth birthday:	800
Fifth birthday:	900
Sixth birthday:	900

After the child's sixth birthday, no more payments are made. When the child reaches age 65, he or she receives $500,000. If the relevant interest rate is 10 percent for the first six years and 8 percent for all subsequent years, is the policy worth buying?

71. Annuity Present Values and Effective Rates You have just won the lottery. You will receive $5 million today, and then receive 40 payments of $1.95 million. These payments will start one year from now and will be paid every six months. A representative from Greenleaf Investments has offered to purchase all the payments from you for $39 million. If the appropriate interest rate is an APR of 8 percent compounded daily, should you take the offer? Assume there are 365 days per year.

72. **Calculating Interest Rates**   A financial planning service offers a college savings program. The plan calls for you to make six annual payments of $20,000 each, with the first payment occurring today, your child's 12th birthday. Beginning on your child's 18th birthday, the plan will provide $45,000 per year for four years. What return is this investment offering?

73. **Break-Even Investment Returns**   Your financial planner offers you two different investment plans. Plan X is a perpetuity with $15,000 annual payments. Plan Y is an annuity with 10 annual payments of $31,000. Both plans will make their first payment one year from today. At what discount rate would you be indifferent between these two plans?

74. **Perpetual Cash Flows**   What is the value of an investment that pays $45,000 every other year forever, if the first payment occurs one year from today and the discount rate is an APR of 11 percent compounded daily? What is the value today if the first payment occurs four years from today?

75. **Ordinary Annuities and Annuities Due**   As discussed in the text, an annuity due is identical to an ordinary annuity except that the periodic payments occur at the beginning of each period and not at the end of the period. Show that the relationship between the value of an ordinary annuity and the value of an otherwise equivalent annuity due is:

Annuity due value = Ordinary annuity value $\times (1 + r)$

Show this for both present and future values.

76. **Calculating Annuities**   You have just won the Life's Downhill After 30 lottery. The lottery payments will be made for the next 30 years. The payments are slightly unusual in that you will be paid $500,000 every 6 months starting 6 months from today, for a total of 60 payments. You will also receive $750,000 every 9 months starting 9 months from today, for a total of 40 payments. When the payments coincide, for example 18 months from today, you will receive both payments. If the interest rate is an APR of 8.1 percent compounded monthly, what is the present value of your winnings?

77. **Calculating EAR**   A check-cashing store is in the business of making personal loans to walk-up customers. The store makes only one-week loans at 4.9 percent interest per week.

   a.   What APR must the store report to its customers? What is the EAR that the customers are actually paying?

   b.   Now suppose the store makes one-week loans at 4.9 percent discount interest per week (see Question 62). What's the APR now? The EAR?

   c.   The check-cashing store also makes one-month add-on interest loans at 4.9 percent discount interest per week. Thus, if you borrow $100 for one month (four weeks), the interest will be ($100 $\times$ 1.049^4) − 100 = $21.09. Because this is discount interest, your net loan proceeds today will be $78.91. You must then repay the store $100 at the end of the month. To help you out, though, the store lets you pay off this $100 in installments of $25 per week. What is the APR of this loan? What is the EAR?

78. **Present Value of a Growing Perpetuity**   What is the equation for the present value of a growing perpetuity with a payment of C one period from today if the payments grow by C each period?

79. **Rule of 72**   A useful rule of thumb for the time it takes an investment to double with discrete compounding is the "Rule of 72." To use the Rule of 72, you divide 72 by the interest rate to determine the number of periods it takes for a value today to double. For example, if the interest rate is 6 percent, the Rule of 72 says it will take 72/6 = 12 years to double. This is approximately equal to the actual answer of 11.90 years. The Rule of 72 can also be applied to determine what interest rate is needed to double money in a specified period. This is a useful approximation for many interest rates and periods. At what rate is the Rule of 72 exact?

80. **Rule of 69.3**   A corollary to the Rule of 72 is the Rule of 69.3. The Rule of 69.3 is exactly correct except for rounding when interest rates are compounded continuously. Prove the Rule of 69.3 for continuously compounded interest.

WHAT'S ON THE WEB?

1. **Calculating Future Values**   Go to www.dinkytown.net and follow the "Investment Calculators" link. If you currently have $10,000 and invest this money at 9 percent, how much will you have in 30 years? Assume you will not make any additional contributions. How much will you have if you can earn 11 percent?

2. **Future Values and Taxes**   Taxes can greatly affect the future value of your investment. The website at www.fincalc.com has a financial calculator that adjusts your return for taxes. Suppose you have $50,000 to invest today. If you can earn a 12 percent return and make no additional deposits, how much will you have in 20 years? (Enter 0 percent as the tax rate.) Now, assume that your marginal tax rate is 27.5 percent. How much will you have at this tax rate?

EXCEL MASTER IT! PROBLEM

Excel is a great tool for solving problems, but with many time value of money problems, you may still need to draw a time line. For example, consider a classic retirement problem. A friend is celebrating her birthday and wants to start saving for her anticipated retirement. She has the following years to retirement and retirement spending goals:

ExcelMaster
coverage online

www.mhhe.com/RossCore6e

Years until retirement:	30
Amount to withdraw each year:	$90,000
Years to withdraw in retirement:	20
Interest rate:	8%

Because your friend is planning ahead, the first withdrawal will not take place until one year after she retires. She wants to make equal annual deposits into her account for her retirement fund.

a. If she starts making these deposits in one year and makes her last deposit on the day she retires, what amount must she deposit annually to be able to make the desired withdrawals at retirement?

b. Suppose your friend has just inherited a large sum of money. Rather than making equal annual payments, she has decided to make one lump-sum deposit today to cover her retirement needs. What amount does she have to deposit today?

c. Suppose your friend's employer will contribute to the account each year as part of the company's profit-sharing plan. In addition, your friend expects a distribution from a family trust several years from now. What amount must she deposit annually now to be able to make the desired withdrawals at retirement? The details are:

Employer's annual contribution:	$1,500
Years until trust fund distribution:	20
Amount of trust fund distribution:	$25,000

THE MBA DECISION

Ben Bates graduated from college six years ago with a finance undergraduate degree. Since graduation, he has been employed in the finance department at East Coast Yachts. Although he is satisfied with his current job, his goal is to become an investment banker. He feels that an MBA degree would allow him to achieve this goal. After examining schools, he has narrowed his choice to either Wilton University or Mount Perry College. Although internships are encouraged by both schools, to get class credit for the internship, no salary can be paid. Other than internships, neither school will allow its students to work while enrolled in its MBA program.

Ben's annual salary at East Coast Yachts is $57,000 per year, and his salary is expected to increase at 3 percent per year until retirement. He is currently 28 years old and expects to work for 40 more years. His current job includes a fully paid health insurance plan, and his current average tax rate is 26 percent. Ben has a savings account with enough money to cover the entire cost of his MBA program.

The Ritter College of Business at Wilton University is one of the top MBA programs in the country. The MBA degree requires two years of full-time enrollment at the university. The annual tuition is $63,000, payable at the beginning of each school year. Books and other supplies are estimated to cost $2,500 per year. Ben expects that after graduation from Wilton, he will receive a job offer for about $105,000 per year, with an $18,000 signing bonus. The salary at this job will increase at 4 percent per year. Because of the higher salary, his average income tax rate will increase to 31 percent.

The Bradley School of Business at Mount Perry College began its MBA program 16 years ago. The Bradley School is smaller and less well known than the Ritter College. Bradley offers an accelerated, one-year program, with a tuition cost of $75,000 to be paid upon matriculation. Books and other supplies for the program are expected to cost $3,500. Ben thinks that after graduation from Mount Perry, he will receive an offer of $88,000 per year, with a $15,000 signing bonus. The salary at this job will increase at 3.5 percent per year. His average income tax rate at this level of income will be 29 percent.

Both schools offer a health insurance plan that will cost $3,000 per year, payable at the beginning of the year. Ben also estimates that room and board expenses will cost $2,000 more per year at both schools than his current expenses, payable at the beginning of each year. The appropriate discount rate is 5.8 percent. Assume all salaries are paid at the end of each year.

1. How does Ben's age affect his decision to get an MBA?

2. What other, perhaps nonquantifiable factors, affect Ben's decision to get an MBA?

3. Assuming all salaries are paid at the end of each year, what is the best option for Ben—from a strictly financial standpoint?

4. In choosing between the two schools, Ben believes that the appropriate analysis is to calculate the future value of each option. How would you evaluate this statement?

5. What initial salary would Ben need to receive to make him indifferent between attending Wilton University and staying in his current position? Assume his tax rate after graduating from Wilton University will be 31 percent regardless of his income level.

6. Suppose that instead of being able to pay cash for his MBA, Ben must borrow the money. The current borrowing rate is 5.4 percent. How would this affect his decision to get an MBA?

Interest Rates and Bond Valuation

Generally, when you make an investment, you expect that you will get back more money in the future than you invested today. But in January 2019, that wasn't the case for many bond investors. The yields on 2-year and 5-year German government bonds were about negative .63 percent and negative .39 percent, respectively. The yields on 2-year and 5-year Japanese government bonds were slightly higher, at negative .15 percent and negative .16 percent, respectively. That month, over $11 trillion of government debt worldwide carried a negative yield. In fact, during 2016, the amount of debt worldwide with a negative yield reached a record $13.4 trillion! And negative yields were not restricted to government bonds, as at one point the yield on bonds issued by chocolate maker Nestlé and Deutsche Bank AG both traded with negative yields.

This chapter takes what we have learned about the time value of money and shows how it can be used to value one of the most common of all financial assets, a bond. It then discusses bond features, bond types, and the operation of the bond market. What we will see is that bond prices depend critically on interest rates, so we will go on to discuss some very fundamental issues regarding interest rates. Clearly, interest rates are important to everybody because they underlie what businesses of all types—small and large—must pay to borrow money.

Please visit us at corecorporatefinance.blogspot.com for the latest developments in the world of corporate finance.

Our goal in this chapter is to introduce you to bonds. We begin by showing how the techniques we developed in Chapter 4 can be applied to bond valuation. From there, we go on to discuss bond features and how bonds are bought and sold. One important thing we learn is that bond values depend, in large part, on interest rates. We therefore close out the chapter with an examination of interest rates and their behavior.

5.1 BONDS AND BOND VALUATION

When a corporation (or government) wishes to borrow money from the public on a long-term basis, it usually does so by issuing or selling debt securities that are generically called bonds. In this section, we describe the various features of corporate bonds and some of the terminology associated with bonds. We then discuss the cash flows associated with a bond and how bonds can be valued using our discounted cash flow procedure.

ExcelMaster
coverage online
www.mhhe.com/RossCore6e

Bond Features and Prices

A bond is normally an interest-only loan, meaning that the borrower will pay the interest every period, but none of the principal will be repaid until the end of the loan. For example, suppose the Beck Corporation wants to borrow $1,000 for 30 years. The interest rate on similar debt issued by similar corporations is 12 percent. Beck will thus pay $.12 \times \$1,000 = \$120$ in interest every year for 30 years. At the end of 30 years, Beck will repay the $1,000.

As this example suggests, a bond is a fairly simple financing arrangement. There is, however, a rich jargon associated with bonds, so we will use this example to define some of the more important terms.

In our example, the $120 regular interest payments that Beck promises to make are called the bond's *coupons*. Because the coupon is constant and paid every year, the type of bond we are describing is sometimes called a *level coupon bond*. The amount that will be repaid at the end of the loan is called the bond's *face value*, or *par value*. As in our example, this par value is usually $1,000 for corporate bonds, and a bond that sells for its par value is called a *par value bond*. Government bonds frequently have much larger face, or par, values. Finally, the annual coupon divided by the face value is called the *coupon rate* on the bond; in this case, because $120/$1,000 = .12, or 12 percent, the bond has a 12 percent coupon rate.

The number of years until the face value is paid is called the bond's time to *maturity*. A corporate bond will frequently have a maturity of 30 years when it is originally issued, but this varies. Once the bond has been issued, the number of years to maturity declines as time goes by.

Bond Values and Yields

As time passes, interest rates change in the marketplace. The cash flows from a bond, however, stay the same. As a result, the value of the bond will fluctuate. When interest rates rise, the present value of the bond's remaining cash flows declines and the bond is worth less. When interest rates fall, the bond is worth more.

To determine the value of a bond at a particular point in time, we need to know the number of periods remaining until maturity, the face value, the coupon, and the market interest rate for bonds with similar features. This interest rate required in the market on a bond is called the bond's *yield to maturity (YTM)*. This rate is sometimes called the bond's *yield* for short. Given all this information, we can calculate the present value of the cash flows as an estimate of the bond's current market value.

For example, suppose the Xanth (pronounced "zanth") Co. were to issue a bond with 10 years to maturity. The Xanth bond has an annual coupon of $80. (Most, but not all, straight coupon bonds in the United States pay interest semiannually. Practice differs around the world.) Similar bonds have a yield to maturity of 8 percent. Based on our preceding discussion, the Xanth bond will pay $80 per year for the next 10 years in coupon interest. In 10 years, Xanth will pay $1,000 to the owner of the bond. The cash flows from the bond are shown in Figure 5.1. What would this bond sell for?

As illustrated in Figure 5.1, the Xanth bond's cash flows have an annuity component (the coupons) and a lump sum (the face value paid at maturity). We thus estimate the market value of the bond by calculating the present value of these two components separately and adding the results together. First, at the going rate of 8 percent, the present value of the $1,000 paid in 10 years is:

$$\text{Present value} = \$1{,}000/1.08^{10} = \$1{,}000/2.1589 = \$463.19$$

FIGURE 5.1 Cash Flows for Xanth Co. Bond

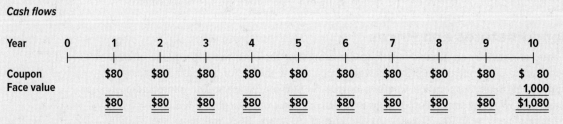

Cash flows

Year	0	1	2	3	4	5	6	7	8	9	10
Coupon		$80	$80	$80	$80	$80	$80	$80	$80	$80	$ 80
Face value											1,000
		$80	$80	$80	$80	$80	$80	$80	$80	$80	$1,080

As shown, the Xanth bond has an annual coupon of $80 and a face, or par, value of $1,000 paid at maturity in 10 years.

Second, the bond offers $80 per year for 10 years; the present value of this annuity stream is:

Annuity present value = $80 × (1 − 1/1.08^{10})/.08
= $80 × (1 − 1/2.1589)/.08
= $80 × 6.7101
= $536.81

We can now add the values for the two parts together to get the bond's value:

Total bond value = $463.19 + 536.81 = $1,000

This bond sells for exactly its face value. This is not a coincidence. The going interest rate in the market is 8 percent. Considered as an interest-only loan, what interest rate does this bond have? With an $80 coupon, this bond pays exactly 8 percent interest only when it sells for $1,000.

To illustrate what happens as interest rates change, suppose that a year has gone by. The Xanth bond now has 9 years to maturity. If the interest rate in the market has risen to 10 percent, what will the bond be worth? To find out, we repeat the present value calculations with 9 years instead of 10, and a 10 percent yield instead of an 8 percent yield. First, the present value of the $1,000 paid in 9 years at 10 percent is:

Present value = $1,000/1.10^9 = $1,000/2.3579 = $424.10

Second, the bond now offers $80 per year for nine years; the present value of this annuity stream at 10 percent is:

Annuity present value = $80 × (1 − 1/1.10^9)/.10
= $80 × (1 − 1/2.3579)/.10
= $80 × 5.7590
= $460.72

We can now add the values for the two parts together to get the bond's value:

Total bond value = $424.10 + 460.72 = $884.82

Therefore, the bond should sell for about $885. In the vernacular, we say that this bond, with its 8 percent coupon, is priced to yield 10 percent at $885.

The Xanth Co. bond now sells for less than its $1,000 face value. Why? The market interest rate is 10 percent. Considered as an interest-only loan of $1,000, this bond only pays 8 percent, its coupon rate. Because this bond pays less than the going rate, investors are willing to lend only something less than the $1,000 promised repayment. Because the bond sells for less than face value, it is said to be a *discount bond*.

A good bond site to visit is www.finra.org/investors/bonds, which has loads of useful information.

The only way to get the interest rate up to 10 percent is to lower the price to less than $1,000 so that the purchaser, in effect, has a built-in gain. For the Xanth bond, the price of $885 is $115 less than the face value, so an investor who purchased and kept the bond would get $80 per year and would have a $115 gain at maturity as well. This gain compensates the lender for the below-market coupon rate.

Another way to see why the bond is discounted by $115 is to note that the $80 coupon is $20 below the coupon on a newly issued par value bond, based on current market conditions. The bond would be worth $1,000 only if it had a coupon of $100 per year. In a sense, an investor who buys and keeps the bond gives up $20 per year for nine years. At 10 percent, this annuity stream is worth:

$$\text{Annuity present value} = \$20 \times (1 - 1/1.10^9)/.10$$
$$= \$20 \times 5.7590$$
$$= \$115.18$$

This is the amount of the discount.

Online bond calculators are available at personal.fidelity.com; interest rate information is available at money.cnn.com/data/bonds and www.bankrate.com.

What would the Xanth bond sell for if interest rates had dropped by 2 percent instead of rising by 2 percent? As you might guess, the bond would sell for more than $1,000. Such a bond is said to sell at a *premium* and is called a *premium bond*.

This case is the opposite of that of a discount bond. The Xanth bond now has a coupon rate of 8 percent when the market rate is only 6 percent. Investors are willing to pay a premium to get this extra coupon amount. In this case, the relevant discount rate is 6 percent, and there are nine years remaining. The present value of the $1,000 face amount is:

$$\text{Present value of face amount} = \$1,000/1.06^9 = \$1,000/1.6895 = \$591.90$$

The present value of the coupon stream is:

$$\text{Annuity present value} = \$80 \times (1 - 1/1.06^9)/.06$$
$$= \$80 \times (1 - 1/1.6895)/.06$$
$$= \$80 \times 6.8017$$
$$= \$544.14$$

We can now add the values for the two parts together to get the bond's value:

$$\text{Total bond value} = \$591.90 + 544.14 = \$1,136.03$$

Total bond value is therefore about $136 in excess of par value. Once again, we can verify this amount by noting that the coupon is now $20 too high, based on current market conditions. The present value of $20 per year for nine years at 6 percent is:

$$\text{Annuity present value} = \$20 \times (1 - 1/1.06^9)/.06$$
$$= \$20 \times 6.8017$$
$$= \$136.03$$

This is as we calculated.

Based on our examples, we can now write the general expression for the value of a bond. If a bond has (1) a face value of F paid at maturity, (2) a coupon of C paid per period, (3) t periods to maturity, and (4) a yield of r per period, its value is:

$$\text{Bond value} = C \times [1 - 1/(1 + r)^t]/r + F/(1 + r)^t \qquad [5.1]$$

Learn more about bonds at investorguide.com.

As we have illustrated in this section, bond prices and interest rates always move in opposite directions. When interest rates rise, a bond's value, like any other present value, will decline. Similarly, when interest rates fall, bond values rise. Even if we are considering a bond that is riskless in the sense that the borrower is certain to make all the payments, there is still risk in owning a bond. We discuss this next.

EXAMPLE 5.1

Semiannual Coupons

In practice, bonds issued in the United States usually make coupon payments twice a year. So, if an ordinary bond has a coupon rate of 14 percent, then the owner will get a total of $140 per year, but this $140 will come in two payments of $70 each. Suppose we are examining such a bond. The yield to maturity is quoted at 16 percent.

Bond yields are quoted like APRs; the quoted rate is equal to the actual rate per period multiplied by the number of periods. In this case, with a 16 percent quoted yield and semiannual payments, the true yield is 8 percent per six months. The bond matures in seven years. What is the bond's price? What is the effective annual yield on this bond?

Based on our discussion, we know the bond will sell at a discount because it has a coupon rate of 7 percent every six months when the market requires 8 percent every six months. So, if our answer exceeds $1,000, we know that we have made a mistake.

To get the exact price, we first calculate the present value of the bond's face value of $1,000 paid in seven years. This 7-year period has 14 periods of six months each. At 8 percent per period, the value is:

$$\text{Present value} = \$1,000/1.08^{14} = \$1,000/2.9372 = \$340.46$$

The coupons can be viewed as a 14-period annuity of $70 per period. At an 8 percent discount rate, the present value of such an annuity is:

$$\text{Annuity present value} = \$70 \times (1 - 1/1.08^{14})/.08$$
$$= \$70 \times 8.2442$$
$$= \$577.10$$

The total present value gives us what the bond should sell for:

$$\text{Total present value} = \$340.46 + 577.10 = \$917.56$$

To calculate the effective yield on this bond, note that 8 percent every six months is equivalent to:

$$\text{Effective annual rate} = 1.08^2 - 1 = .1664, \text{ or } 16.64\%$$

The effective yield, therefore, is 16.64 percent.

Interest Rate Risk

The risk that arises for bond owners from fluctuating interest rates is called *interest rate risk*. How much interest rate risk a bond has depends on how sensitive its price is to interest rate changes. This sensitivity directly depends on two things: the time to maturity and the coupon rate. As we will see momentarily, you should keep the following in mind when looking at a bond:

1. All other things being equal, the longer the time to maturity, the greater the interest rate risk.
2. All other things being equal, the lower the coupon rate, the greater the interest rate risk.

We illustrate the first of these two points in Figure 5.2. As shown, we compute and plot prices under different interest rate scenarios for 10 percent coupon bonds with maturities of 1 year and 30 years. We assume coupons are paid semiannually. Notice how the slope of the line connecting the prices is much steeper for the 30-year maturity than it is for the 1-year maturity. This steepness tells us that a relatively small change in interest rates will lead to a substantial change in the bond's value. In comparison, the 1-year bond's price is relatively insensitive to interest rate changes.

Intuitively, we can see that the reason that shorter-term bonds have less interest rate sensitivity is that a large portion of a bond's value comes from the $1,000 face amount. The present value of this amount isn't greatly affected by a small change in interest rates if

FIGURE 5.2

Interest Rate Risk and Time to Maturity

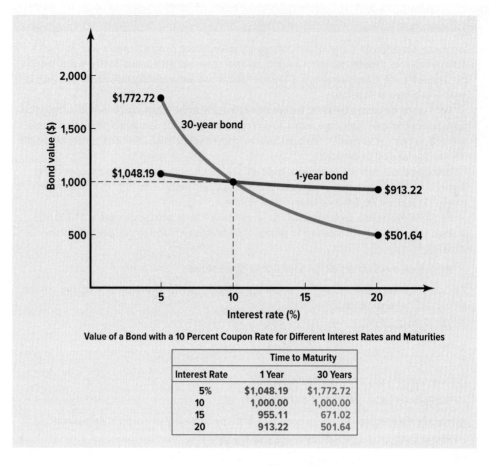

Value of a Bond with a 10 Percent Coupon Rate for Different Interest Rates and Maturities

	Time to Maturity	
Interest Rate	1 Year	30 Years
5%	$1,048.19	$1,772.72
10	1,000.00	1,000.00
15	955.11	671.02
20	913.22	501.64

the amount is to be received in one year. Even a small change in the interest rate, however, once it is compounded for 30 years, can have a significant effect on the present value. As a result, the present value of the face amount will be much more volatile with a longer-term bond.

The other thing to know about interest rate risk is that, like most things in finance and economics, it increases at a decreasing rate. In other words, if we compared a 10-year bond to a 1-year bond, we would see that the 10-year bond has much greater interest rate risk. However, if you were to compare a 20-year bond to a 30-year bond, you would find that while the 30-year bond has somewhat greater interest rate risk because it has a longer maturity, the difference in the risk would be fairly small.

The reason that bonds with lower coupons have greater interest rate risk is essentially the same. As we discussed earlier, the value of a bond depends on the present value of its coupons and the present value of the face amount. If two bonds with different coupon rates have the same maturity, then the value of the one with the lower coupon is proportionately more dependent on the face amount to be received at maturity. As a result, all other things equal, its value will fluctuate more as interest rates change. Put another way, the bond with the higher coupon has a larger cash flow early in its life, so its value is less sensitive to changes in the discount rate.

Bonds are rarely issued with maturities longer than 30 years. However, low interest rates have led to the issuance of bonds with much longer terms. In the 1990s, Walt Disney issued "Sleeping Beauty" bonds with a 100-year maturity. Similarly, BellSouth, Coca-Cola, and Dutch banking giant ABN AMRO all issued bonds with 100-year maturities. These companies evidently wanted to lock in the historical low interest rates for a *long* time. Before these issues, it appears the last time 100-year bonds were issued was in May 1954, by the Chicago and Eastern Railroad. And low interest rates in recent years have led to more 100-year bonds. Of course, there are even longer term bonds. In 2015, issuance of perpetual bonds hit a record. For example, French energy company Total issued $5.7 billion in perpetual bonds and Volkswagen issued $2.6 billion in perpetual debt.

We can illustrate the effect of interest rate risk using the 100-year BellSouth issue. The following table provides some basic information on this issue, along with its prices on December 31, 1995; July 31, 1996; and February 1, 2018.

Maturity	Coupon Rate	Price on 12/31/95	Price on 7/31/96	Percentage Change in Price 1995–96	Price on 2/1/18	Percentage Change in Price 1996–2018
2095	7.00%	$1,000.00	$800.00	−20.0%	$1,164.21	+45.5%

Several things emerge from this table. First, interest rates apparently rose between December 31, 1995, and July 31, 1996 (why?). After that, however, they fell (why?). The bond's price first lost 20 percent and then gained 45.5 percent. These swings illustrate that longer-term bonds have significant interest rate risk.

Finding the Yield to Maturity: More Trial and Error

Frequently, we will know a bond's price, coupon rate, and maturity date, but not its yield to maturity. For example, suppose we are interested in a six-year, 8 percent coupon bond with annual coupons. A broker quotes a price of $955.14. What is the yield on this bond?

We've seen that the price of a bond can be written as the sum of its annuity and lump-sum components. Knowing that there is an $80 coupon for six years and a $1,000 face value, we can say that the price is:

$$\$955.14 = \$80 \times [1 - 1/(1 + r)^6]/r + \$1,000/(1 + r)^6$$

where r is the unknown discount rate, or yield to maturity. We have one equation here and one unknown, but we cannot solve for r explicitly. The only way to find the answer is to use trial and error.

This problem is essentially identical to the one we examined in the last chapter when we tried to find the unknown interest rate on an annuity. However, finding the rate (or yield) on a bond is even more complicated because of the $1,000 face amount.

We can speed up the trial-and-error process by using what we know about bond prices and yields. In this case, the bond has an $80 coupon and is selling at a discount. We thus know that the yield is greater than 8 percent. If we compute the price at 10 percent:

$$\begin{aligned} \text{Bond value} &= \$80 \times (1 - 1/1.10^6)/.10 + \$1,000/1.10^6 \\ &= \$80 \times 4.3553 + \$1,000/1.7716 \\ &= \$912.89 \end{aligned}$$

At 10 percent, the value we calculate is lower than the actual price, so 10 percent is too high. The true yield must be somewhere between 8 and 10 percent. At this point, it's "plug and chug" to find the answer. You would probably want to try 9 percent next. If you did, you would see that this is in fact the bond's yield to maturity.

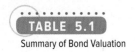

TABLE 5.1

Summary of Bond Valuation

I. Finding the Value of a Bond

Bond value = $C \times [1 - 1/(1 + r)^t]/r + F/(1 + r)^t$

where:

C = Coupon paid each period

r = Discount rate per period

t = Number of periods

F = Bond's face value

II. Finding the Yield on a Bond

Given a bond value, coupon, time to maturity, and face value, it is possible to find the implicit discount rate, or yield to maturity, by trial and error only. To do this, try different discount rates until the calculated bond value equals the given value (or let a spreadsheet or a financial calculator do it for you). Remember that increasing the rate decreases the bond value.

Current market rates are available at www. bankrate.com.

A bond's yield to maturity should not be confused with its current yield, which is a bond's annual coupon divided by its price. In the example we just worked, the bond's annual coupon was $80, and its price was $955.14. Given these numbers, we see that the current yield is $80/$955.14 = .0838, or 8.38 percent, which is less than the yield to maturity of 9 percent. The reason the current yield is too low is that it only considers the coupon portion of your return; it doesn't consider the built-in gain from the price discount. For a premium bond, the reverse is true, meaning that current yield would be higher because it ignores the built-in loss.

Our discussion of bond valuation is summarized in Table 5.1. A nearby *Spreadsheet Techniques* box shows how to find prices and yields the easy way.

EXAMPLE 5.2

Current Events

A bond has a quoted price of $1,080.42. It has a face value of $1,000, a semiannual coupon of $30, and a maturity of five years. What is its current yield? What is its yield to maturity? Which is bigger? Why?

Notice that this bond makes semiannual payments of $30, so the annual payment is $60. The current yield is thus $60/$1,080.42 = .0555, or 5.55 percent. To calculate the yield to maturity, refer back to Example 5.1. Now, in this case, the bond pays $30 every six months and it has 10 six-month periods until maturity. So, we need to find r as follows:

$$\$1,080.42 = \$30 \times [1 - 1/(1 + r)^{10}]/r + 1,000/(1 + r)^{10}$$

After some trial and error, we find that r is equal to 2.1 percent. But the tricky part is that this 2.1 percent is the yield *per six months*. We have to double it to get the yield to maturity, so the yield to maturity is 4.2 percent, which is less than the current yield. The reason is that the current yield ignores the built-in loss of the premium between now and maturity.

5.2 MORE ON BOND FEATURES

In this section, we continue our discussion of corporate debt by describing in some detail the basic terms and features that make up a typical long-term corporate bond. We discuss additional issues associated with long-term debt in subsequent sections.

Most spreadsheets have fairly elaborate routines available for calculating bond values and yields; many of these routines involve details that we have not discussed. However, setting up a simple spreadsheet to calculate prices or yields is straightforward, as our next two spreadsheets show:

	A	B	C	D	E	F	G	H
1								
2		**Using a spreadsheet to calculate bond values**						
3								
4	Suppose we have a bond with 22 years to maturity, a coupon rate of 8 percent, and a yield to							
5	maturity of 9 percent. If the bond makes semiannual payments, what is its price today?							
6								
7	Settlement date:	1/1/00						
8	Maturity date:	1/1/22						
9	Annual coupon rate:	.08						
10	Yield to maturity:	.09						
11	Face value (% of par):	100						
12	Coupons per year:	2						
13	Bond price (% of par):	**90.49**						
14								
15	The formula entered in cell B13 is =PRICE(B7,B8,B9,B10,B11,B12); notice that face value and bond							
16	price are given as a percentage of face value.							

	A	B	C	D	E	F	G	H
1								
2		**Using a spreadsheet to calculate bond yields**						
3								
4	Suppose we have a bond with 22 years to maturity, a coupon rate of 8 percent, and a price of							
5	$960.17. If the bond makes semiannual payments, what is its yield to maturity?							
6								
7	Settlement date:	1/1/00						
8	Maturity date:	1/1/22						
9	Annual coupon rate:	.08						
10	Bond price (% of par):	96.017						
11	Face value (% of par):	100						
12	Coupons per year:	2						
13	Yield to maturity:	**.084**						
14								
15	The formula entered in cell B13 is =YIELD(B7,B8,B9,B10,B11,B12); notice that face value and bond							
16	price are entered as a percentage of face value.							
17								

In our spreadsheets, notice that we had to enter two dates, a settlement date and a maturity date. The settlement date is the date you actually pay for the bond, and the maturity date is the day the bond actually matures. In most of our problems, we don't explicitly have these dates, so we have to make them up. For example, because our bond has 22 years to maturity, we picked 1/1/2000 (January 1, 2000) as the settlement date and 1/1/2022 (January 1, 2022) as the maturity date. Any two dates would do as long as they are exactly 22 years apart, but these are particularly easy to work with. Finally, notice that we had to enter the coupon rate and yield to maturity in annual terms and then explicitly provide the number of coupon payments per year.

Securities issued by corporations may be classified roughly as *equity securities* and *debt securities.* At the crudest level, a debt represents something that must be repaid; it is the result of borrowing money. When corporations borrow, they generally promise to make regularly scheduled interest payments and to repay the original amount borrowed (that is, the principal). The person or firm making the loan is called the *creditor,* or *lender.* The corporation borrowing the money is called the *debtor,* or *borrower.*

From a financial point of view, the main differences between debt and equity are the following:

1. Debt is not an ownership interest in the firm. Creditors generally do not have voting power.

2. The corporation's payment of interest on debt is considered a cost of doing business and is fully tax deductible. Dividends paid to stockholders are not tax deductible.

3. Unpaid debt is a liability of the firm. If it is not paid, the creditors can legally claim the assets of the firm. This action can result in liquidation or reorganization, two of the possible consequences of bankruptcy. Thus, one of the costs of issuing debt is the possibility of financial failure. This possibility does not arise when equity is issued.

Long-Term Debt: The Basics

Ultimately, all long-term debt securities are promises made by the issuing firm to pay principal when due and to make timely interest payments on the unpaid balance. Beyond this, there are a number of features that distinguish these securities from one another. We discuss some of these features next.

The maturity of a long-term debt instrument is the length of time the debt remains outstanding with some unpaid balance. Debt securities can be short term (with maturities of one year or less) or long term (with maturities of more than one year).[1] Short-term debt is sometimes referred to as *unfunded debt.*[2]

Debt securities are typically called *notes, debentures,* or *bonds.* Strictly speaking, a bond is a secured debt. However, in common usage, the word *bond* refers to all kinds of secured and unsecured debt. We will therefore continue to use the term generically to refer to long-term debt. Also, usually, the only difference between a note and a bond is the original maturity. Issues with an original maturity of 10 years or less are often called notes. Longer-term issues are called bonds.

The two major forms of long-term debt are public issue and privately placed. We concentrate on public-issue bonds. Most of what we say about them holds true for private-issue, long-term debt as well. The main difference between public-issue and privately placed debt is that the latter is directly placed with a lender and not offered to the public. Because this is a private transaction, the specific terms are up to the parties involved.

There are many other dimensions to long-term debt, including such things as security, call features, sinking funds, ratings, and protective covenants. The following table illustrates these features for a bond issued by CVS Health Corporation. If some of these terms are unfamiliar, have no fear. We will discuss them all presently.

---

[1] There is no universally agreed-upon distinction between short-term and long-term debt. In addition, people often refer to intermediate-term debt, which has a maturity of more than 1 year and less than 3 to 5, or even 10, years.

[2] The word *funding* is part of the jargon of finance. It generally refers to the long term. Thus, a firm planning to "fund" its debt requirements may be replacing short-term debt with long-term debt.

Features of a CVS Health Corporation Bond		
Term		**Explanation**
Amount of issue	$8 billion	The company issued $8 billion worth of bonds.
Date of issue	03/09/2018	The bonds were sold on 03/09/2018.
Maturity	03/25/2048	The bonds mature on 03/25/2048.
Face value	$2,000	The denomination of the bonds is $2,000.
Annual coupon	5.05%	Each bondholder will receive $101 per bond per year (5.05% of face value).
Offer price	99.430	The offer price will be 99.430% of the $2,000 face value, or $1,988.60, per bond.
Coupon payment dates	3/25, 9/25	Coupons of $101/2 = $50.50 will be paid on these dates.
Security	None	The bonds are not secured by specific assets.
Sinking fund	None	The bonds have no sinking fund.
Call provision	At any time	The bonds do not have a deferred call.
Call price	Treasury rate plus .30%	The bonds have a "make whole" call price.
Rating	S&P BBB, Moody's Baa2	The bonds have a medium-quality credit rating.

Many of these features will be detailed in the bond indenture, so we discuss this first.

The Indenture

The indenture is the written agreement between the corporation (the borrower) and its creditors. It is sometimes referred to as the *deed of trust*.[3] Usually, a trustee (a bank perhaps) is appointed by the corporation to represent the bondholders. The trust company must (1) make sure the terms of the indenture are obeyed, (2) manage the sinking fund (described in the following pages), and (3) represent the bondholders in default, that is, if the company defaults on its payments to them.

The bond indenture is a legal document. It can run several hundred pages and generally makes for very tedious reading. It is an important document, however, because it generally includes the following provisions:

1. The basic terms of the bonds.
2. The total amount of bonds issued.
3. A description of property used as security.
4. The repayment arrangements.
5. The call provisions.
6. Details of the protective covenants.

We discuss these features next.

TERMS OF A BOND   Corporate bonds usually have a par, or face, value (that is, a denomination) of $1,000, although par values of $2,000 like the CVS bond have become relatively common. Essentially, any par value is possible. For example, municipal bonds often have par values of $5,000 and Treasury bonds with par values of $10,000 or $100,000 are often sold. Par value is also called *principal value* and it is stated on the bond certificate. So, if a corporation wanted to borrow $1 million, 1,000 bonds with a par value of $1,000 would do the trick, as would 500 bonds with a $2,000 par value.

Corporate bonds are usually in registered form. For example, the indenture might read as follows:

> **Interest is payable semiannually on July 1 and January 1 of each year to the person in whose name the bond is registered at the close of business on June 15 or December 15, respectively.**

---

[3] The words *loan agreement* or *loan contract* are usually used for privately placed debt and term loans.

This means that the company has a registrar who will record the ownership of each bond and record any changes in ownership. The company will pay the interest and principal by check mailed directly to the address of the owner of record. A corporate bond may be registered and have attached "coupons." To obtain an interest payment, the owner must separate a coupon from the bond certificate and send it to the company registrar (the paying agent).

Alternatively, the bond could be in bearer form. This means that the certificate is the basic evidence of ownership, and the corporation will "pay the bearer." Ownership is not otherwise recorded, and, as with a registered bond with attached coupons, the holder of the bond certificate detaches the coupons and sends them to the company to receive payment.

There are two drawbacks to bearer bonds. First, they are difficult to recover if they are lost or stolen. Second, because the company does not know who owns its bonds, it cannot notify bondholders of important events. Bearer bonds were once the dominant type, but they are now much less common (in the United States) than registered bonds.

SECURITY   Debt securities are classified according to the collateral and mortgages used to protect the bondholder.

Collateral is a general term that frequently means securities (for example, bonds and stocks) that are pledged as security for payment of debt. For example, collateral trust bonds often involve a pledge of common stock held by the corporation. However, the term *collateral* is commonly used to refer to any asset pledged on a debt.

Mortgage securities are secured by a mortgage on the real property of the borrower. The property involved is usually real estate, for example, land or buildings. The legal document that describes the mortgage is called a *mortgage trust indenture* or *trust deed.*

Sometimes mortgages are on specific property, for example, a railroad car. More often, blanket mortgages are used. A blanket mortgage pledges all the real property owned by the company.[4]

Bonds frequently represent unsecured obligations of the company. A debenture is an unsecured bond, for which no specific pledge of property is made. The term note is generally used for such instruments if the maturity of the unsecured bond is less than 10 years when the bond is originally issued. Debenture holders have a claim only on property not otherwise pledged, in other words, the property that remains after mortgages and collateral trusts are taken into account.

The terminology that we use here and elsewhere in this chapter is standard in the United States. Outside the United States, these same terms can have different meanings. For example, bonds issued by the British government ("gilts") are called treasury "stock." Also, in the United Kingdom, a debenture is a *secured* obligation.

At the current time, public bonds issued in the United States by industrial and financial companies are typically debentures. However, most utility and railroad bonds are secured by a pledge of assets.

The Securities Industry and Financial Markets Association (SIFMA) site is www.sifma.org.

SENIORITY   In general terms, *seniority* indicates preference in position over other lenders, and debts are sometimes labeled as *senior* or *junior* to indicate seniority. Some debt is *subordinated,* as in, for example, a subordinated debenture.

In the event of default, holders of subordinated debt must give preference to other specified creditors. Usually, this means that the subordinated lenders will be paid off only after the specified creditors have been compensated. However, debt cannot be subordinated to equity.

REPAYMENT   Bonds can be repaid at maturity, at which time the bondholder will receive the stated, or face, value of the bond, or they may be repaid in part or in entirety before maturity. Early repayment in some form is more typical and is often handled through a sinking fund.

---

[4] Real property includes land and things "affixed thereto." It does not include cash or inventories.

A sinking fund is an account managed by the bond trustee for the purpose of repaying the bonds. The company makes annual payments to the trustee, who then uses the funds to retire a portion of the debt. The trustee does this by either buying up some of the bonds in the market or calling in a fraction of the outstanding bonds. This second option is discussed in the next section.

There are many different kinds of sinking fund arrangements, and the details would be spelled out in the indenture. For example:

1. Some sinking funds start about 10 years after the initial issuance.
2. Some sinking funds establish equal payments over the life of the bond.
3. Some high-quality bond issues establish payments to the sinking fund that are not sufficient to redeem the entire issue. As a consequence, there is the possibility of a large "balloon payment" at maturity.

THE CALL PROVISION   A call provision allows the company to repurchase, or "call," part or all of the bond issue at stated prices over a specific period. Corporate bonds are usually callable.

Generally, the call price is above the bond's stated value (that is, the par value). The difference between the call price and the stated value is the call premium. The amount of the call premium may become smaller over time. One arrangement is to initially set the call premium equal to the annual coupon payment and then make it decline to zero as the call date moves closer to the time of maturity.

Call provisions are often not operative during the first part of a bond's life. This makes the call provision less of a worry for bondholders in the bond's early years. For example, a company might be prohibited from calling its bonds for the first 10 years. This is a deferred call provision. During this period of prohibition, the bond is said to be call protected.

In recent years, a new type of call provision, a "make-whole" call, has become very widespread in the corporate bond market. With such a feature, bondholders receive approximately what the bonds are worth if they are called. Because bondholders don't suffer a loss in the event of a call, they are "made whole."

To determine the make-whole call price, we calculate the present value of the remaining interest and principal payments at a rate specified in the indenture. For example, looking at our CVS issue, we see that the discount rate is "Treasury rate plus .30%." What this means is that we determine the discount rate by first finding a U.S. Treasury issue with the same maturity. We calculate the yield to maturity on the Treasury issue and then add on an additional .30 percent to get the discount rate we use.

Notice that, with a make-whole call provision, the call price is higher when interest rates are lower and vice versa (why?). Also notice that, as is common with a make-whole call, the CVS issue does not have a deferred call feature. Why might investors not be too concerned about the absence of this feature?

PROTECTIVE COVENANTS   A protective covenant is that part of the indenture or loan agreement that limits certain actions a company might otherwise wish to take during the term of the loan. Protective covenants can be classified into two types: negative covenants and positive (or affirmative) covenants.

A *negative covenant* is a "thou shalt not" type of covenant. It limits or prohibits actions that the company might take. Here are some typical examples:

1. The firm must limit the amount of dividends it pays according to some formula.
2. The firm cannot pledge any assets to other lenders.
3. The firm cannot merge with another firm.
4. The firm cannot sell or lease any major assets without approval by the lender.
5. The firm cannot issue additional long-term debt.

Want detailed information
on the amount and terms
of the debt issued by a
particular firm? Check out
its latest financial statements by searching SEC
filings at www.sec.gov.

A *positive covenant* is a "thou shalt" type of covenant. It specifies an action that the company agrees to take or a condition the company must abide by. Here are some examples:

1. The company must maintain its working capital at or above some specified minimum level.
2. The company must periodically furnish audited financial statements to the lender.
3. The firm must maintain any collateral or security in good condition.

This is only a partial list of covenants; a particular indenture may feature many different ones.

5.3 BOND RATINGS

Firms frequently pay to have their debt rated. The two leading bond-rating firms are Moody's and Standard & Poor's (S&P). The debt ratings are an assessment of the creditworthiness of the corporate issuer. The definitions of creditworthiness used by Moody's and S&P are based on how likely the firm is to default and the protection creditors have in the event of a default.

Want to know what
criteria are commonly
used to rate corporate and
municipal bonds? Go to
www.standardandpoors
.com, www.moodys.com,
and www.fitchratings.com.

It is important to recognize that bond ratings are concerned only with the possibility of default. Earlier, we discussed interest rate risk, which we defined as the risk of a change in the value of a bond resulting from a change in interest rates. Bond ratings do not address this issue. As a result, the price of a highly rated bond can still be quite volatile.

Bond ratings are constructed from information supplied by the corporation and other sources. The rating classes and some information concerning them are shown in the following table.

	Investment-Quality Bond Ratings						Low-Quality, Speculative, and/or "Junk" Bond Ratings			
	High Grade		Medium Grade		Low Grade			Low Grade		
Standard & Poor's	AAA	AA	A	BBB	BB	B		CCC	CC	C	D
Moody's	AAA	AA	A	BAA	BA	B		CAA	CA	C	

Moody's	S&P	
Aaa	AAA	Debt rated Aaa and AAA has the highest rating. Capacity to pay interest and principal is extremely strong.
Aa	AA	Debt rated Aa and AA has a very strong capacity to pay interest and repay principal. Together with the highest rating, this group comprises the high-grade bond class.
A	A	Debt rated A has a strong capacity to pay interest and repay principal, although it is somewhat more susceptible to the adverse effects of changes in circumstances and economic conditions than debt in higher-rated categories.
Baa	BBB	Debt rated Baa and BBB is regarded as having an adequate capacity to pay interest and repay principal. Whereas it normally exhibits adequate protection parameters, adverse economic conditions or changing circumstances are more likely to lead to a weakened capacity to pay interest and repay principal for debt in this category than in higher-rated categories. These bonds are medium-grade obligations.
Ba; B Caa Ca C	BB; B CCC CC C	Debt rated in these categories is regarded, on balance, as predominantly speculative with respect to capacity to pay interest and repay principal in accordance with the terms of the obligation. BB and Ba indicate the lowest degree of speculation, and Ca, CC, and C the highest degree of speculation. Although such debt is likely to have some quality and protective characteristics, these are outweighed by large uncertainties or major risk exposures to adverse conditions. Issues rated C by Moody's are typically in default.
	D	Debt rated D is in default, and payment of interest and/or repayment of principal is in arrears.

Note: At times, both Moody's and S&P use adjustments (called notches) to these ratings. S&P uses plus and minus signs: A+ is the strongest A rating and A− the weakest. Moody's uses a 1, 2, or 3 designation, with 1 being the highest. Moody's has no D rating.

The highest rating a firm's debt can have is AAA or Aaa, and such debt is judged to be the best quality and to have the lowest degree of risk. For example, as of January 2019,

Microsoft and Johnson & Johnson were the only U.S.-based nonfinancial companies with a AAA credit rating. AA or Aa ratings indicate very good quality debt and are much more common.

A large part of corporate borrowing takes the form of low-grade, or "junk," bonds. If these low-grade corporate bonds are rated at all, they are rated below investment grade by the major rating agencies. Investment-grade bonds are bonds rated at least BBB by S&P or Baa by Moody's.

Rating agencies don't always agree. For example, some bonds are known as "crossover" or "5B" bonds. The reason is that they are rated triple-B (or Baa) by one rating agency and double-B (or Ba) by another, a "split rating." For example, in February 2016, India-based textile and chemical company Standard Industries sold an issue of 10-year notes rated BBB– by S&P and Ba2 by Moody's.

A bond's credit rating can change as the issuer's financial strength improves or deteriorates. For example, in January 2019, S&P cut the bond rating on PG&E from BBB– to B, lowering the company's bond rating from investment-grade to junk bond status. S&P cut PG&E's rating in large part due to potential liabilities from the November 2018 California wildfire. Bonds that drop into junk territory like this are called *fallen angels.*

Credit ratings are important because defaults really do occur, and when they do, investors can lose heavily. For example, in 2000, AmeriServe Food Distribution, Inc., which supplied restaurants such as Burger King with everything from burgers to giveaway toys, defaulted on $200 million in junk bonds. After the default, the bonds traded at just 18 cents on the dollar, leaving investors with a loss of more than $160 million.

Even worse in AmeriServe's case, the bonds had been issued only four months earlier, thereby making AmeriServe an NCAA champion. While that might be a good thing for a college basketball team such as the University of Kentucky Wildcats, in the bond market NCAA means "No Coupon At All," and it's not a good thing for investors.

Another good bond market site is money .cnn.com.

5.4 SOME DIFFERENT TYPES OF BONDS

Thus far, we have considered only "plain vanilla" corporate bonds. In this section, we briefly look at bonds issued by governments and also at bonds with unusual features.

Government Bonds

The biggest borrower in the world—by a wide margin—is everybody's favorite family member, Uncle Sam. In early 2019, the total debt of the U.S. government was about $22 *trillion,* or approximately $67,000 per citizen (and growing!). When the government wishes to borrow money for more than one year, it sells what are known as Treasury notes and bonds to the public (in fact, it does so every month). Currently, outstanding Treasury notes and bonds have original maturities ranging from 2 to 30 years.

Most U.S. Treasury issues are ordinary coupon bonds. There are two important things to keep in mind, however. First, U.S. Treasury issues, unlike essentially all other bonds, have no default risk because (we hope) the Treasury can always come up with the money to make the payments. Second, Treasury issues are exempt from state income taxes (though not federal income taxes). In other words, the coupons you receive on a Treasury note or bond are only taxed at the federal level.

State and local governments also borrow money by selling notes and bonds. Such issues are called *municipal* notes and bonds, or "munis." Unlike Treasury issues, munis have varying degrees of default risk, and, in fact, they are rated much like corporate issues. Also, they are almost always callable. The most intriguing thing about munis is that their coupons are exempt from federal income taxes (though not necessarily state income taxes), which makes them very attractive to high-income, high-tax-bracket investors.

If you're nervous about the level of debt piled up by the U.S. government, *don't* go to www.treasury. gov/resource-center or to www.usdebtclock.org! Learn all about government bonds at www. newyorkfed.org.

Because of the enormous tax break they receive, the yields on municipal bonds are much lower than the yields on taxable bonds. For example, in January 2019, long-term AAA-rated corporate bonds were yielding about 3.95 percent. At the same time, long-term AAA munis were yielding about 2.85 percent. Suppose an investor was in a 30 percent tax bracket. All else being the same, would this investor prefer a AAA corporate bond or a AAA municipal bond?

For information on municipal bonds, including prices, check out emma.msrb.org.

To answer, we need to compare the *aftertax* yields on the two bonds. Ignoring state and local taxes, the muni pays 2.85 percent on both a pretax and an aftertax basis. The corporate issue pays 3.95 percent before taxes, but it pays $.0395 \times (1 - .30) = .0277$, or 2.77 percent, once we account for the 30 percent tax bite. Given this, the muni bond has a slightly better yield.

EXAMPLE 5.3

Taxable versus Municipal Bonds

Suppose taxable bonds are currently yielding 8 percent, while at the same time, munis of comparable risk and maturity are yielding 6 percent. Which is more attractive to an investor in a 40 percent tax bracket? What is the break-even tax rate? How do you interpret this rate?

For an investor in a 40 percent tax bracket, a taxable bond yields $8\% \times (1 - .40) = 4.8$ percent after taxes, so the muni is much more attractive. The break-even tax rate is the tax rate at which an investor would be indifferent between a taxable and a nontaxable issue. If we let t^* stand for the break-even tax rate, then we can solve for it as follows:

$$.08 \times (1 - t^*) = .06$$
$$1 - t^* = .06/.08 = .75$$
$$t^* = .25$$

Thus, an investor in a 25 percent tax bracket would make 6 percent after taxes from either bond.

Zero Coupon Bonds

A bond that pays no coupons at all must be offered at a price that is much lower than its stated value. Such bonds are called zero coupon bonds, or just *zeroes*.[5]

Suppose the Eight-Inch Nails (EIN) Company issues a $1,000 face value, five-year zero coupon bond. The initial price is set at $508.35. Even though no interest payments are made on the bond, zero coupon bond calculations use semiannual periods to be consistent with coupon bond calculations. Using semiannual periods, it is straightforward to verify that, at this price, the bond yields 14 percent to maturity. The total interest paid over the life of the bond is $1,000 - 508.35 = $491.65.

For tax purposes, the issuer of a zero coupon bond deducts interest every year even though no interest is actually paid. Similarly, the owner must pay taxes on interest accrued every year, even though no interest is actually received.

The way in which the yearly interest on a zero coupon bond is calculated is governed by tax law. Before 1982, corporations could calculate the interest deduction on a straight-line basis. For EIN, the annual interest deduction would have been $491.65/5 = $98.33 per year.

Under current tax law, the implicit interest is determined by amortizing the loan. We do this by first calculating the bond's value at the beginning of each year. For example, after one year, the bond will have four years until maturity, so it will be worth $1,000/1.07^8 = $582.01; the value in two years will be $1,000/1.07^6 = $666.34; and so on. The implicit interest each year is the change in the bond's value for the year.

Notice that under the old rules, zero coupon bonds were more attractive for corporations because the deductions for interest expense were larger in the early years (compare the implicit interest expense with the straight-line expense).

---

[5] A bond issued with a very low coupon rate (as opposed to a zero coupon rate) is an original-issue-discount (OID) bond.

Under current tax law, EIN could deduct $73.66 (= $582.01 − 508.35) in interest paid the first year, and the owner of the bond would pay taxes on $73.66 of taxable income (even though no interest was actually received). This second tax feature makes taxable zero coupon bonds less attractive to individuals. However, they are still a very attractive investment for tax-exempt investors with long-term dollar-denominated liabilities, such as pension funds, because the future dollar value is known with relative certainty.

Some bonds are zero coupon bonds for only part of their lives. For example, at one time, General Motors had a debenture outstanding for which during the first 20 years of its life, no coupon payments would be made, but after 20 years, it would begin paying coupons at a rate of 7.75 percent per year, payable semiannually.

Floating-Rate Bonds

The conventional bonds we have talked about in this chapter have fixed-dollar obligations because the coupon rate is set as a fixed percentage of the par value. Similarly, the principal is set equal to the par value. Under these circumstances, the coupon payment and principal are completely fixed.

With *floating-rate bonds (floaters)*, the coupon payments are adjustable. The adjustments are tied to an interest rate index such as the Treasury bill interest rate or the 30-year Treasury bond rate.

The value of a floating-rate bond depends on exactly how the coupon payment adjustments are defined. In most cases, the coupon adjusts with a lag to some base rate. For example, suppose a coupon rate adjustment is made on June 1. The adjustment might be based on the simple average of Treasury bond yields during the previous three months. In addition, the majority of floaters have the following features:

1. The holder has the right to redeem his/her note at par on the coupon payment date after some specified amount of time. This is called a *put* provision, and it is discussed in the following section.

2. The coupon rate has a floor and a ceiling, meaning that the coupon is subject to a minimum and a maximum. In this case, the coupon rate is said to be "capped," and the upper and lower rates are sometimes called the *collar*.

A particularly interesting type of floating-rate bond is an *inflation-linked* bond. Such bonds have coupons that are adjusted according to the rate of inflation (the principal amount may be adjusted as well). The U.S. Treasury began issuing such bonds in January of 1997. The issues are sometimes called "TIPS," or Treasury Inflation-Protected Securities. Other countries, including Canada, Israel, and Britain, have issued similar securities.

Official information on U.S. inflation-indexed bonds is at www .treasurydirect.gov.

Other Types of Bonds

Many bonds have unusual or exotic features. For example, at one time, Berkshire Hathaway, the company run by the legendary Warren Buffett, issued bonds with a negative coupon. The buyers of these bonds also received the right to purchase shares of stock in Berkshire at a fixed price per share over the subsequent five years. Such a right, which is called a warrant, would be very valuable if the stock price climbed substantially (a later chapter discusses this subject in greater depth).

Bond features are really only limited by the imaginations of the parties involved. Unfortunately, there are far too many variations for us to cover in detail here. We therefore close out this section by mentioning only a few of the more common types. A nearby *Finance Matters* box has some additional discussion on more exotic bonds.

Income bonds are similar to conventional bonds, except that coupon payments are dependent on company income. Specifically, coupons are paid to bondholders only if the firm's income is sufficient. This would appear to be an attractive feature, but income bonds are not very common.

FINANCE MATTERS

BEAUTY IS IN THE EYE OF THE BONDHOLDER

Many bonds have unusual or exotic features. One of the most common types is an asset-backed, or securitized, bond. Mortgage-backed securities were big news in 2007. For several years, there had been rapid growth in so-called sub-prime mortgage loans, which are mortgages made to individuals with less than top-quality credit. However, a combination of cooling (and in some places dropping) housing prices and rising interest rates caused mortgage delinquencies and foreclosures to rise. This increase in problem mortgages caused a significant number of mortgage-backed securities to drop sharply in value and created huge losses for investors. Bondholders of a securitized bond receive interest and principal payments from a specific asset (or pool of assets) rather than a specific company. For example, at one point, rock legend David Bowie sold $55 million in bonds backed by future royalties from his albums and songs (that's some serious ch-ch-ch-change!). Owners of these "Bowie" bonds received the royalty payments, so if Bowie's record sales fell, there was a possibility the bonds could have defaulted. Other artists have sold bonds backed by future royalties, including James Brown, Iron Maiden, and the estate of the legendary Marvin Gaye.

Mortgage-backs are the best-known type of asset-backed security. With a mortgage-backed bond, a trustee purchases mortgages from banks and merges them into a pool. Bonds are then issued, and the bondholders receive payments derived from payments on the underlying mortgages. One unusual twist with mortgage bonds is that if interest rates decline, the bonds can actually decrease in value. This can occur because homeowners are likely to refinance at the lower rates, paying off their mortgages in the process. Securitized bonds are usually backed by assets with long-term payments, such as mortgages. However, there are bonds securitized by car loans and credit card payments, among other assets, and a growing market exists for bonds backed by automobile leases.

The reverse convertible is a relatively new type of structured note. This type generally offers a high coupon rate, but the redemption at maturity can be paid in cash at par value or paid in shares of stock. One recent General Motors (GM) reverse convertible had a coupon rate of 16 percent, which is a very high coupon rate in today's interest rate environment. However, at maturity, if GM's stock declined sufficiently, bondholders would receive a fixed number of GM shares that were worth less than par value. So, while the income portion of the bond return would be high, the potential loss in par value could easily erode the extra return.

CAT bonds are issued to cover insurance companies against natural catastrophes. The type of natural catastrophe is outlined in the bond's indenture. For example, about 30 percent of all CAT bonds protect against a North Atlantic hurricane. The way these issues are structured is that the borrowers can suspend payment temporarily (or even permanently) if they have significant hurricane-related losses. These CAT bonds may seem like pretty risky investments, and they can be, as losses have occurred. Perhaps the quickest loss was a CAT bond issued five weeks before the 2017 Mexican earthquake. The bond was a total loss.

Perhaps the most unusual bond (and certainly the most ghoulish) is the "death bond." Companies such as Stone Street Financial purchase life insurance policies from individuals who are expected to die within the next 10 years. They then sell bonds that are paid off from the life insurance proceeds received when the policyholders pass away. The return on the bonds to investors depends on how long the policyholders live. A major risk is that if medical treatment advances quickly, it will raise the life expectancy of the policyholders, thereby decreasing the return to the bondholder.

For a list of CAT bond defaults, go to http://www.artemis.bm/cat-bond-losses/.

A *convertible bond* can be swapped for a fixed number of shares of stock anytime before maturity at the holder's option. Convertibles are relatively common, but the number issued has been decreasing in recent years.

A *put bond* allows the *holder* to force the issuer to buy the bond back at a stated price. For example, International Paper Co. has bonds outstanding that allow the holder to force International Paper to buy the bonds back at 100 percent of the face value given that certain "risk" events happen. One such event is a change in credit rating from investment grade to lower than investment grade by Moody's or S&P. The put feature is therefore the reverse of the call provision.

Structured notes are bonds that are based on stocks, bonds, commodities, or currencies. One particular type of structured note has a return based on a stock market index. At expiration, if the stock index has declined, the bond returns the principal. However, if the stock index has increased, the bond will return a portion of the stock index return, say 80 percent. Another type of structured note will return twice the stock index return, but with the potential for loss of principal.

A given bond may have many unusual features. Two of the most recent exotic bonds are CoCo bonds, which have a coupon payment, and NoNo bonds, which are zero coupon bonds. CoCo and NoNo bonds are contingent convertible, putable, callable, subordinated bonds. The contingent convertible clause is similar to the normal conversion feature, except the contingent feature must be met. For example, a contingent feature may require that the company stock trade at 110 percent of the conversion price for 20 out of the most recent 30 days. Valuing a bond of this sort can be quite complex, and the yield to maturity calculation is often meaningless.

5.5 BOND MARKETS

Bonds are bought and sold in enormous quantities every day. You may be surprised to learn that the trading volume in bonds on a typical day is many, many times larger than the trading volume in stocks (by trading volume, we mean the amount of money that changes hands). Here is a finance trivia question: What is the largest securities market in the world? Most people would guess the New York Stock Exchange. In fact, the largest securities market in the world in terms of trading volume is the U.S. Treasury market, with an average daily volume over $500 billion.

ExcelMaster
coverage online
www.mhhe.com/RossCore6e

How Bonds Are Bought and Sold

Most trading in bonds takes place over the counter, or OTC. This means that there is no particular place where buying and selling occur. Instead, dealers around the country (and around the world) stand ready to buy and sell. The various dealers are connected electronically.

One reason the bond markets are so big is that the number of bond issues far exceeds the number of stock issues. There are two reasons for this. First, a corporation would typically have only one common stock issue outstanding (there are exceptions to this that we discuss in our next chapter). However, a single large corporation could easily have a dozen or more note and bond issues outstanding. Beyond this, federal, state, and local borrowing is enormous. For example, even a small city would usually have a wide variety of notes and bonds outstanding, representing money borrowed to pay for things like roads, sewers, and schools. When you think about how many small cities there are in the United States, you begin to get the picture!

Because the bond market is almost entirely OTC, it has historically had little or no *transparency*. A financial market is transparent if it is possible to easily observe its prices and trading volume. On the New York Stock Exchange, for example, it is possible to see the price and quantity for every single transaction. In contrast, in the bond market, it was often not possible to observe either. Transactions were privately negotiated between parties, and there was little or no centralized reporting of transactions.

Although the total volume of trading in bonds far exceeds that in stocks, only a very small fraction of the total bond issues that exist actually trade on a given day. This fact, combined with the historical lack of transparency in the bond market, meant that getting up-to-date prices on individual bonds was difficult or impossible, particularly for smaller corporate or municipal issues.

Bond Price Reporting

In 2002, transparency in the corporate bond market began to improve dramatically. Under new regulations, corporate bond dealers are now required to report trade information

To learn more about TRACE, visit www.finra.org.

through what is known as the Trade Report and Compliance Engine (TRACE). Now, essentially all publicly traded corporate bonds have trades reported by FINRA.

TRACE bond quotes are available at finra-markets.morningstar.com/MarketData/Default.jsp. We went to the site and entered "Deere" for the well-known manufacturer of green tractors. We found a total of eight bond issues outstanding. Below you can see the information we found for all of these bonds.

Issuer Name	Symbol	Callable	Sub-Product Type	Coupon	Maturity	Ratings Moody's®	Ratings S&P	Last Sale Price	Last Sale Yield
DEERE & CO	DE.GF		Corporate Bond	8.100	05/15/2030	A2	A	132.155	4.459
DEERE & CO	DE.GG		Corporate Bond	7.125	03/03/2031	A2	A	133.822	3.656
DEERE & CO	DE.LY		Corporate Bond	4.375	10/16/2019	A2	A	101.269	2.705
DEERE & CO	DE.LZ		Corporate Bond	5.375	10/16/2029	A2	A	114.052	3.778
DEERE & CO	DE3863463	Yes	Corporate Bond	2.600	06/08/2022	A2	A	98.328	3.119
DEERE & CO	DE3863464	Yes	Corporate Bond	3.900	06/09/2042	A2	A	98.076	4.027
DEERE & CO	DE.GB		Corporate Bond	8.500	01/09/2022	A2	A	115.746	2.984
DEERE & CO	DE.GC		Corporate Bond	6.550	10/01/2028	A2	A	122.309	3.789

If you go to the website and click on a particular bond, you will get a lot of information about the bond, including the credit rating, the call schedule, original issue information, and trade information. For example, when we checked, the first bond listed had not traded for two weeks.

As shown in Figure 5.3, the Financial Industry Regulatory Authority (FINRA) provides a daily snapshot of the data from TRACE by reporting the most active issues. The information reported is largely self-explanatory. Notice that the price of the first GE Capital bond listed decreased about .406 percent on this day. What do you think happened to the yield to maturity for this bond? Figure 5.3 focuses on the most active bonds with investment-grade ratings, but the most active high-yield and convertible bonds are also available on the website.

The Federal Reserve Bank of St. Louis maintains dozens of online files containing macroeconomic data as well as rates on U.S. Treasury issues. Go to fred.stlouisfed.org.

As we mentioned before, the U.S. Treasury market is the largest securities market in the world. As with bond markets in general, it is an OTC market, so there is limited transparency. However, unlike the situation with bond markets in general, trading in Treasury issues, particularly recently issued ones, is very heavy. Each day, representative prices for outstanding Treasury issues are reported.

FIGURE 5.3   Sample TRACE Bond Quotations

Most Active Investment Grade Bonds

Issuer Name	Symbol	Coupon	Maturity	Moody's®/S&P	High	Low	Last	Change	Yield%
GE CAP INTL FDG CO MEDIUM TERM NTS BOOK	GE4373444	2.342%	11/15/2020	Baa1/BBB+	97.46000	96.71200	96.83300	-0.406000	3.976232
COMCAST CORP NEW	CMCS4729173	4.700%	10/15/2048	A3/A-	98.00000	96.99300	97.19200	-0.477000	4.878992
PETROLEOS MEXICANOS	PEMX4606164	6.500%	03/13/2027	/	99.13500	95.78300	96.58700	-0.518000	7.045194
GE CAP INTL FDG CO MEDIUM TERM NTS BOOK	GE4373445	4.418%	11/15/2035	Baa1/BBB+	89.11900	86.09100	86.09100	-2.834139	5.705014
COMCAST CORP NEW	CMCS4729177	4.150%	10/15/2028	A3/A-	100.73100	98.93500	99.14800	-0.027000	4.255400
PETROLEOS MEXICANOS	PEMX4447364	6.750%	09/21/2047	Baa3/	87.97000	85.75000	86.00000	-0.200000	7.998419
GENERAL MTRS CO	GM4685729	5.000%	10/01/2028	Baa3/BBB	98.50000	94.82400	95.95600	1.382000	5.533966
COMCAST CORP NEW	CMCS4729172	4.600%	10/15/2038	A3/A-	98.62000	97.54600	97.93600	-0.189000	4.760990
COMCAST CORP NEW	CMCS4729176	3.950%	10/15/2025	A3/A-	101.79400	98.56200	99.89300	-0.101000	3.967165
GENERAL MTRS CO	GM4685730	5.950%	04/01/2049	Baa3/BBB	94.29400	92.89300	94.05200	2.306000	6.394972

Source: FINRA reported TRACE prices.

Treasury Bonds

FIGURE 5.4

Sample *Wall Street Journal* U.S. Treasury Bond Prices

Source: www.wsj.com, January 3, 2019.

Maturity	Coupon	Bid	Asked	Chg	Asked yield
3/31/2020	1.375	98.6563	98.6719	0.1328	2.472
5/15/2021	2.625	100.5625	100.5781	0.2578	2.371
2/29/2024	2.125	98.75	98.7656	0.5547	2.381
5/15/2025	2.125	98.1719	98.1875	0.6719	2.434
8/15/2026	6.75	129.6328	129.6484	0.8359	2.456
2/15/2027	2.25	98.1563	98.1719	0.7891	2.500
5/15/2028	2.875	102.6563	102.6719	0.8359	2.552
2/15/2029	5.25	123.6641	123.6797	1.0469	2.575
8/15/2029	6.125	132.7266	132.7891	1.1406	2.575
5/15/2030	6.25	135.7656	135.8281	1.1641	2.589
2/15/2031	5.375	128.6719	128.7344	1.1797	2.595
2/15/2036	4.5	125.4688	125.5313	1.5391	2.637
2/15/2037	4.75	129.7813	129.8438	1.6094	2.662
5/15/2037	5	133.6719	133.7344	1.6563	2.665
5/15/2038	4.5	126.875	126.9375	1.6328	2.704
2/15/2039	3.5	111.6172	111.6797	1.5078	2.741
8/15/2040	3.875	117.1563	117.2188	1.5938	2.807
11/15/2041	3.125	104.5547	104.6172	1.4609	2.849
5/15/2043	2.875	99.7969	99.8281	1.4922	2.885
5/15/2044	3.375	108.7969	108.8281	1.5625	2.882
11/15/2044	3	102.0625	102.0938	1.4766	2.884
2/15/2045	2.5	92.6953	92.7266	1.3984	2.899
5/15/2046	2.5	92.3594	92.3906	1.4141	2.905
8/15/2047	2.75	96.9844	97.0156	1.5313	2.904
11/15/2048	3.375	109.4766	109.5078	1.6563	2.897

Figure 5.4 shows a portion of the daily Treasury bond listings from the website wsj.com. Examine the entry that begins "5/15/2030." Reading from left to right, the "5/15/2030" tells us that the bond's maturity is May 15, 2030. The 6.25 is the bond's coupon rate.

The next two pieces of information are the **bid** and **asked prices**. In general, in any OTC or dealer market, the bid price represents what a dealer is willing to pay for a security, and the asked price (or "ask" price) is what a dealer is willing to take for it. The difference between the two prices is called the **bid-ask spread** (or "spread"), and it represents the dealer's profit.

Treasury prices are quoted as a percentage of face value. The bid price, or what a dealer is willing to pay, on the 5/15/2030 bond is 135.7656. With a $1,000 face value, this quote represents $1,357.656. The asked price, or the price at which the dealer is willing to sell the bond, is 135.8281, or $1,358.281.

The next number quoted is the change in the asked price from the previous day, measured as a percentage of face value, so this issue's asked price rose by 1.1641 percent, or $11.641, in value from the previous day. Finally, the last number reported is the yield to maturity, based on the asked price. Notice that this is a premium bond because it sells for more than its face value. Not surprisingly, its yield to maturity (2.589 percent) is less than its coupon rate (6.25 percent).

Current and historical Treasury yield information is available at www.publicdebt.treas.gov/.

The last bond listed, the 11/15/2048, is often called the "bellwether" bond. This bond's yield is the one that is usually reported in the evening news. So, for example, when you hear that long-term interest rates rose, what is really being said is that the yield on this bond went up (and its price went down).

If you examine the yields on the various issues in Figure 5.4, you will clearly see that they vary by maturity. Why this occurs and what it might mean are some of the things we discuss in our next section. Government (referred to as "sovereign") bond yields also vary by country of origin. Below we show the 10-year bond yields of several countries. The yields vary according to default risks and foreign exchange risks (to be discussed later in the text).

Selected International Government 10-Year Bond Yields	
	Yield (%)
Switzerland	−.28
Japan	−.01
Germany	.15
Canada	1.82
United States	2.55
Greece	4.37
India	7.43
Mexico	8.55
Brazil	9.15

Source: www.bloomberg.com, January 3, 2019.

EXAMPLE 5.4

Treasury Quotes

Locate the Treasury issue in Figure 5.4 that matures on May 15, 2021. What is its coupon rate? What is its bid price? What was the *previous day's* asked price?

The bond listed as 5/15/2021 is the one we seek. Its coupon rate is 2.625 percent of face value. The bid price is 100.5625, or 100.5625 percent of face value. The ask price is 100.5781, which is up by .2578 from the previous day. This means that the ask price on the previous day was equal to 100.5781 − .2578 = 100.3203.

A Note on Bond Price Quotes

If you buy a bond between coupon payment dates, the price you pay is usually more than the price you are quoted. The reason is that standard convention in the bond market is to quote prices net of "accrued interest," meaning that accrued interest is deducted to arrive at the quoted price. This quoted price is called the clean price. The price you actually pay, however, includes the accrued interest. This price is the dirty price, also known as the "full" or "invoice" price.

An example is the easiest way to understand these issues. Suppose you buy a bond with a 12 percent annual coupon, payable semiannually. You actually pay $1,080 for this bond, so $1,080 is the dirty, or invoice, price. Further, on the day you buy it, the next coupon is due in four months, so you are between coupon dates. Notice that the next coupon will be $60.

The accrued interest on a bond is calculated by taking the fraction of the coupon period that has passed, in this case two months out of six, and multiplying this fraction by the next coupon, $60. So, the accrued interest in this example is 2/6 × $60 = $20. The bond's quoted price (i.e., its clean price) would be $1,080 −20 = $1,060.[6]

5.6 INFLATION AND INTEREST RATES

So far, we haven't considered the role of inflation in our various discussions of interest rates, yields, and returns. Because this is an important consideration, we discuss the impact of inflation next.

Real versus Nominal Rates

In examining interest rates, or any other financial market rates such as discount rates, bond yields, rates of return, and required returns, it is often necessary to distinguish between real rates and nominal rates. Nominal rates are called *nominal* because they have not been adjusted for inflation. Real rates are rates that have been adjusted for inflation.

To see the effect of inflation, suppose prices are currently rising by 5 percent per year. In other words, the rate of inflation is 5 percent. An investment is available that will be worth $115.50 in one year. It costs $100 today. Notice that with a present value of $100 and a future value in one year of $115.50, this investment has a 15.5 percent rate of return. In calculating this 15.5 percent return, we did not consider the effect of inflation, however, so this is the nominal return.

What is the impact of inflation here? To answer, suppose pizzas cost $5 apiece at the beginning of the year. With $100, we can buy 20 pizzas. Because the inflation rate is 5 percent, pizzas will cost 5 percent more, or $5.25, at the end of the year. If we take the investment, how many pizzas can we buy at the end of the year? Measured in pizzas, what is the rate of return on this investment?

Our $115.50 from the investment will buy us $115.50/$5.25 = 22 pizzas. This is up from 20 pizzas, so our pizza rate of return is 10 percent. What this illustrates is that even though the nominal return on our investment is 15.5 percent, our buying power goes up by only 10 percent because of inflation. Put another way, we are really only 10 percent richer. In this case, we say that the real return is 10 percent.

Alternatively, we can say that with 5 percent inflation, each of the $115.50 nominal dollars we get is worth 5 percent less in real terms, so the real dollar value of our investment in a year is:

$$\$115.50/1.05 = \$110$$

What we have done is to *deflate* the $115.50 by 5 percent. Because we give up $100 in current buying power to get the equivalent of $110, our real return is again 10 percent. Because we have removed the effect of future inflation here, this $110 is said to be measured in current dollars.

The difference between nominal and real rates is important and bears repeating:

The nominal rate on an investment is the percentage change in the number of dollars you have.

The real rate on an investment is the percentage change in how much you can buy with your dollars, in other words, the percentage change in your buying power.

[6] The way accrued interest is calculated actually depends on the type of bond being quoted, for example, Treasury or corporate. The difference has to do with exactly how the fractional coupon period is calculated. In our example above, we implicitly treated the months as having exactly the same length (i.e., 30 days each, 360 days in a year), which is consistent with the way corporate bonds are quoted. In contrast, for Treasury bonds, actual day counts are used.

The Fisher Effect

Our discussion of real and nominal returns illustrates a relationship often called the Fisher effect (after the great economist Irving Fisher). Because investors are ultimately concerned with what they can buy with their money, they require compensation for inflation. Let R stand for the nominal rate and r stand for the real rate. The Fisher effect tells us that the relationship between nominal rates, real rates, and inflation can be written as:

$$1 + R = (1 + r) \times (1 + h) \tag{5.2}$$

where h is the inflation rate.

In the preceding example, the nominal rate was 15.50 percent and the inflation rate was 5 percent. What was the real rate? We can determine it by plugging in these numbers:

$$
\begin{aligned}
1 + .1550 &= (1 + r) \times (1 + .05) \\
1 + r &= 1.1550/1.05 = 1.10 \\
r &= .10, \text{ or } 10\%
\end{aligned}
$$

This real rate is the same as we had before. If we take another look at the Fisher effect, we can rearrange things a little as follows:

$$
\begin{aligned}
1 + R &= (1 + r) \times (1 + h) \\
R &= r + h + r \times h
\end{aligned}
\tag{5.3}
$$

What this tells us is that the nominal rate has three components. First, there is the real rate on the investment, r. Next, there is the compensation for the decrease in the value of the money originally invested because of inflation, h. The third component represents compensation for the fact that the dollars earned on the investment are also worth less because of the inflation.

This third component is usually small, so it is often dropped. The nominal rate is then approximately equal to the real rate plus the inflation rate:

$$R \approx r + h \tag{5.4}$$

Fisher's thinking is that investors are not foolish. They know that inflation reduces purchasing power, and, therefore, they will demand an increase in the nominal rate before lending money. Fisher's hypothesis, typically called the Fisher effect, can be stated as:

> A rise in the rate of inflation causes the nominal rate to rise just enough so that the real rate of interest is unaffected. In other words, the real rate is invariant to the rate of inflation.

EXAMPLE 5.5 The Fisher Effect

If investors require a 2 percent real rate of return, and the inflation rate is 8 percent, what must be the approximate nominal rate? The exact nominal rate?

First of all, the nominal rate is approximately equal to the sum of the real rate and the inflation rate: 2 percent + 8 percent = 10 percent. From the Fisher effect, we have:

$$
\begin{aligned}
1 + R &= (1 + r) \times (1 + h) \\
&= 1.02 \times 1.08 \\
&= 1.1016
\end{aligned}
$$

Therefore, the nominal rate will actually be closer to 10.16 percent. In this example, you can also see how negative nominal interests can come about, e.g., in the unusual situation when inflation rates are expected to be sufficiently negative.

It is important to note that financial rates, such as interest rates, discount rates, and rates of return, are almost always quoted in nominal terms. To remind you of this, we will henceforth use the symbol R instead of r in most of our discussions about such rates.

5.7 DETERMINANTS OF BOND YIELDS

We are now in a position to discuss the determinants of a bond's yield. As we will see, the yield on any particular bond is a reflection of a variety of factors, some common to all bonds and some specific to the issue under consideration.

ExcelMaster
coverage online
www.mhhe.com/RossCore6e

The Term Structure of Interest Rates

At any point in time, short-term and long-term interest rates will generally be different. Sometimes short-term rates are higher, sometimes lower. Figure 5.5 gives us a long-range perspective on this by showing about two centuries of short- and long-term U.S. Treasury interest rates. As shown, through time, the difference between short- and long-term rates has ranged from essentially zero to up to several percentage points, both positive and negative.

The relationship between short- and long-term interest rates is known as the **term structure of interest rates**. To be a little more precise, the term structure of interest rates tells us what *nominal* interest rates are on *default-free, pure discount* bonds of all maturities. These rates are, in essence, "pure" interest rates because they involve no risk of default and a single, lump-sum future payment. In other words, the term structure tells us the pure time value of money for different lengths of time.

When long-term rates are higher than short-term rates, we say that the term structure is upward sloping, and when short-term rates are higher, we say it is downward sloping. The term structure can also be "humped." When this occurs, it is usually because rates increase at first, but then begin to decline as we look at longer- and longer-term rates. The most

FIGURE 5.5 U.S. Interest Rates: 1800–2018

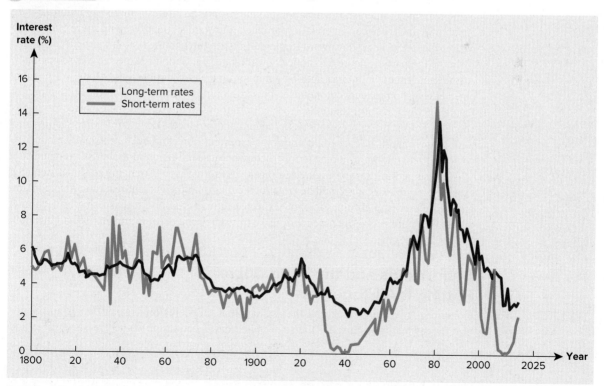

Source: Siegel, Jeremy J. *Stocks for the Long Run,* 4th ed. McGraw-Hill, 2008, updated by the authors.

common shape of the term structure, particularly in modern times, is upward sloping, but the degree of steepness has varied quite a bit.

What determines the shape of the term structure? There are three basic components. The first two are the ones we discussed in our previous section, the real rate of interest and the rate of inflation. The real rate of interest is the compensation investors demand for forgoing the use of their money. You can think of it as the pure time value of money after adjusting for the effects of inflation.

The real rate of interest is the basic component underlying every interest rate, regardless of the time to maturity. When the real rate is high, all interest rates will tend to be higher, and vice versa. Thus, the real rate doesn't really determine the shape of the term structure; instead, it mostly influences the overall level of interest rates.

In contrast, the prospect of future inflation very strongly influences the shape of the term structure. Investors thinking about loaning money for various lengths of time recognize that future inflation erodes the value of the dollars that will be returned. As a result, investors demand compensation for this loss in the form of higher nominal rates. This extra compensation is called the inflation premium.

If investors believe that the rate of inflation will be higher in the future, then long-term nominal interest rates will tend to be higher than short-term rates. Thus, an upward-sloping term structure may be a reflection of anticipated increases in inflation. Similarly, a downward-sloping term structure probably reflects the belief that inflation will be falling in the future.

The third, and last, component of the term structure has to do with interest rate risk. As we discussed earlier in the chapter, longer-term bonds have much greater risk of loss resulting from changes in interest rates than do shorter-term bonds. Investors recognize this risk, and they demand extra compensation in the form of higher rates for bearing it. This extra compensation is called the interest rate risk premium. The longer the term to maturity, the greater is the interest rate risk, so the interest rate risk premium increases with maturity. However, as we discussed earlier, interest rate risk increases at a decreasing rate, so the interest rate risk premium does as well.[7]

Putting the pieces together, we see that the term structure reflects the combined effect of the real rate of interest, the inflation premium, and the interest rate risk premium. Figure 5.6 shows how these can interact to produce an upward-sloping term structure (in the top part of Figure 5.6) or a downward-sloping term structure (in the bottom part).

In the top part of Figure 5.6, notice how the rate of inflation is expected to rise gradually. At the same time, the interest rate risk premium increases at a decreasing rate, so the combined effect is to produce a pronounced upward-sloping term structure. In the bottom part of Figure 5.6, the rate of inflation is expected to fall in the future, and the expected decline is enough to offset the interest rate risk premium and produce a downward-sloping term structure. Notice that if the rate of inflation was expected to decline by only a small amount, we could still get an upward-sloping term structure because of the interest rate risk premium.

We assumed in drawing Figure 5.6 that the real rate would remain the same. Actually, expected future real rates could be larger or smaller than the current real rate. Also, for simplicity, we used straight lines to show expected future inflation rates as rising or declining, but they do not necessarily have to look like this. They could, for example, rise and then fall, leading to a humped yield curve.

Bond Yields and the Yield Curve: Putting It All Together

Online yield curve information is available at www.bloomberg.com/markets.

Going back to Figure 5.4, recall that we saw that the yields on Treasury notes and bonds of different maturities are not the same. Each day, in addition to the Treasury prices and yields shown in Figure 5.4, the *Wall Street Journal* website provides a plot of Treasury yields

[7] In days of old, the interest rate risk premium was called a *liquidity premium*. Today, the term *liquidity premium* has an altogether different meaning, which we explore in our next section. Also, the interest rate risk premium is sometimes called a *maturity risk premium*. Our terminology is consistent with the modern view of the term structure.

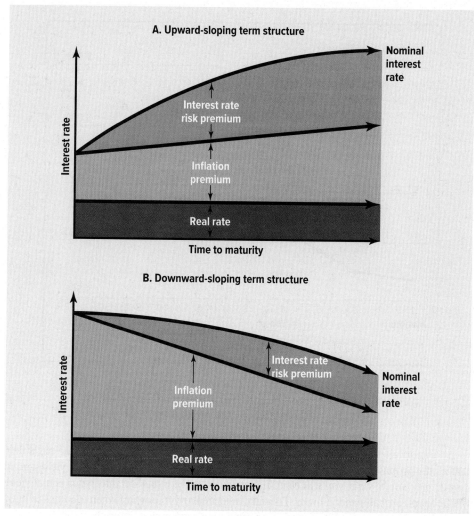

FIGURE 5.6

The Term Structure of
Interest Rates

A. Upward-sloping term structure

Nominal
interest
rate

Interest rate

Interest rate
risk premium

Inflation
premium

Real rate

Time to maturity

B. Downward-sloping term structure

Interest rate

Interest rate
risk premium

Nominal
interest
rate

Inflation
premium

Real rate

Time to maturity

relative to maturity. This plot is called the Treasury yield curve (or just the yield curve). Figure 5.7 shows the yield curve as of April 2019. Note, the yield curve available on the website will display both the current and previous year's yield curves.

As you probably now suspect, the shape of the yield curve is a reflection of the term structure of interest rates. In fact, the Treasury yield curve and the term structure of interest rates are almost the same thing. The only difference is that the term structure is based on pure discount bonds, whereas the yield curve is based on coupon bond yields. As a result, Treasury yields depend on the three components that underlie the term structure—the real rate, expected future inflation, and the interest rate risk premium.

Treasury notes and bonds have three important features that we need to remind you of: They are default-free, they are taxable, and they are highly liquid. This is not true of bonds in general, so we need to examine what additional factors come into play when we look at bonds issued by corporations or municipalities.

The first thing to consider is credit risk, that is, the possibility of default. Investors recognize that issuers other than the Treasury may or may not make all the promised payments on a bond, so they demand a higher yield as compensation for this risk. This extra compensation is called the default risk premium. Earlier in the chapter, we saw how bonds were rated based on their credit risk. What you will find if you start looking at bonds of different ratings is that lower-rated bonds have higher yields.

To see the current Treasury yield curve rates, check out the Data and Charts Center at www.treasury.gov.

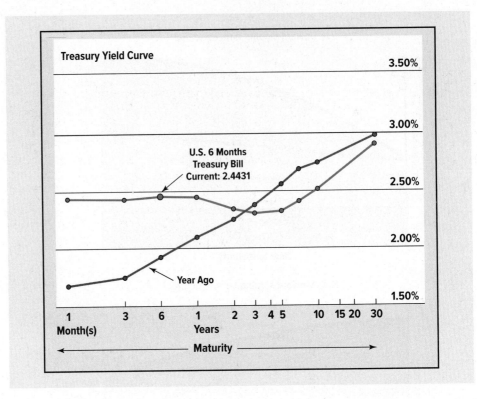

An important thing to recognize about a bond's yield is that it is calculated assuming that all the promised payments will be made. As a result, it is really a promised yield, and it may or may not be what you will earn. In particular, if the issuer defaults, your actual yield will be lower, probably much lower. This fact is particularly important when it comes to junk bonds. Thanks to a clever bit of marketing, such bonds are now commonly called high-yield bonds, which has a much nicer ring to it; but now you recognize that these are really high *promised* yield bonds.

Next, recall that we discussed earlier how municipal bonds are free from most taxes and, as a result, have much lower yields than taxable bonds. Investors demand the extra yield on a taxable bond as compensation for the unfavorable tax treatment. This extra compensation is the taxability premium.

Finally, bonds have varying degrees of liquidity. As we discussed earlier, there are an enormous number of bond issues, most of which do not trade on a regular basis. As a result, if you wanted to sell quickly, you would probably not get as good a price as you could otherwise. Investors prefer liquid assets to illiquid ones, so they demand a liquidity premium on top of all the other premiums we have discussed. As a result, all else being the same, less liquid bonds will have higher yields than more liquid bonds.

Conclusion

If we combine all of the things we have discussed regarding bond yields, we find that bond yields represent the combined effect of no fewer than six things. The first is the real rate of interest. On top of the real rate are five premiums representing compensation for (1) expected future inflation, (2) interest rate risk, (3) default risk, (4) taxability, and (5) lack of liquidity. As a result, determining the appropriate yield on a bond requires careful analysis of each of these effects.

SUMMARY AND CONCLUSIONS

This chapter has explored bonds, bond yields, and interest rates. We saw that:

1. Determining bond prices and yields is an application of basic discounted cash flow principles.

2. Bond values move in the direction opposite that of interest rates, leading to potential gains or losses for bond investors.

3. Bonds have a variety of features spelled out in a document called the indenture.

4. Bonds are rated based on their default risk. Some bonds, such as Treasury bonds, have no risk of default, whereas so-called junk bonds have substantial default risk.

5. A wide variety of bonds exist, many of which contain exotic or unusual features.

6. Almost all bond trading is OTC, with little or no market transparency in many cases. As a result, bond price and volume information can be difficult to find for some types of bonds.

7. Bond yields and interest rates reflect the effects of six different factors: the real interest rate and five premiums that investors demand as compensation for inflation, interest rate risk, default risk, taxability, and lack of liquidity.

CONCEPT QUESTIONS

1. **Treasury Bonds**   Is it true that a U.S. Treasury security is risk free?

2. **Interest Rate Risk**   Which has greater interest rate risk, a 30-year Treasury bond or a 30-year BB corporate bond?

3. **Treasury Pricing**   With regard to bid and ask prices on a Treasury bond, is it possible for the bid price to be higher? Why or why not?

4. **Yield to Maturity**   Treasury bid and ask quotes are sometimes given in terms of yields, so there would be a bid yield and an ask yield. Which do you think would be larger? Explain.

5. **Call Provisions**   A company is contemplating a long-term bond issue. It is debating whether or not to include a call provision. What are the benefits to the company from including a call provision? What are the costs? How do these answers change for a put provision?

6. **Coupon Rate**   How does a bond issuer decide on the appropriate coupon rate to set on its bonds? Explain the difference between the coupon rate and the required return on a bond.

7. **Real and Nominal Returns**   Are there any circumstances under which an investor might be more concerned about the nominal return on an investment than the real return?

8. **Bond Ratings**   Companies pay rating agencies such as Moody's and S&P to rate their bonds, and the costs can be substantial. However, companies are not required to have their bonds rated in the first place; doing so is strictly voluntary. Why do you think they do it?

9. **Bond Ratings**   Often, junk bonds are not rated. Why?

10. **Term Structure**   What is the difference between the term structure of interest rates and the yield curve?

11. **Crossover Bonds**   Looking back at the crossover bonds we discussed in the chapter, why do you think split ratings such as these occur?

12. **Municipal Bonds**   Why is it that municipal bonds are not taxed at the federal level but are taxable across state lines? Why is it that U.S. Treasury bonds are not taxable at the state level? (You may need to dust off the history books for this one.)

13. **Bond Market**   What are the implications for bond investors of the lack of transparency in the bond market?

14. **Treasury Market**   Take a look back at Figure 5.4. Notice the wide range of coupon rates. Why are they so different?

15. **Rating Agencies** A controversy erupted regarding bond-rating agencies when some agencies began to provide unsolicited bond ratings. Why do you think this is controversial?

16. **Bonds as Equity** The 100-year bonds we discussed in the chapter have something in common with junk bonds. Critics charge that, in both cases, the issuers are really selling equity in disguise. What are the issues here? Why would a company want to sell "equity in disguise"?

17. **Bond Prices versus Yields**

   a. What is the relationship between the price of a bond and its YTM?

   b. Explain why some bonds sell at a premium over par value while other bonds sell at a discount. What do you know about the relationship between the coupon rate and the YTM for premium bonds? What about for discount bonds? For bonds selling at par value?

   c. What is the relationship between the current yield and YTM for premium bonds? For discount bonds? For bonds selling at par value?

18. **Interest Rate Risk** All else being the same, which has more interest rate risk, a long-term bond or a short-term bond? What about a low coupon bond compared to a high coupon bond? What about a long-term, high coupon bond compared to a short-term, low coupon bond?

QUESTIONS AND PROBLEMS

Basic
(Questions 1–15)

1. **Valuing Bonds** What is the dollar price of a zero coupon bond with 21 years to maturity, semiannual compounding, and a par value of $1,000, if the YTM is:

   a. 4 percent

   b. 10 percent

   c. 14 percent

2. **Valuing Bonds** Microhard has issued a bond with the following characteristics:

   Par: $1,000

   Time to maturity: 18 years

   Coupon rate: 7 percent

   Semiannual payments

   Calculate the price of this bond if the YTM is:

   a. 7 percent

   b. 9 percent

   c. 5 percent

3. **Bond Yields** Qin Corp. issued 15-year bonds two years ago at a coupon rate of 5.1 percent. The bonds make semiannual payments. If these bonds currently sell for 96 percent of par value, what is the YTM?

4. **Coupon Rates** Lei Corporation has bonds on the market with 12.5 years to maturity, a YTM of 7.2 percent, a par value of $1,000, and a current price of $1,030. The bonds make semiannual payments. What must the coupon rate be on these bonds?

5. **Valuing Bonds** Even though most corporate bonds in the United States make coupon payments semiannually, bonds issued elsewhere often have annual coupon payments. Suppose a German company has a bond outstanding with a par value of €1,000, 16 years to maturity, and a coupon rate of 3.8 percent paid annually. If the yield to maturity is 3.1 percent, what is the current price of the bond?

6. **Bond Yields** A Japanese company has a bond outstanding that sells for 95.4 percent of its ¥100,000 par value. The bond has a coupon rate of 4.9 percent paid annually and matures in 18 years. What is the yield to maturity of this bond?

7. **Calculating Real Rates of Return**   If Treasury bills are currently paying 5.1 percent and the inflation rate is 2.9 percent, what is the approximate real rate of interest? The exact real rate?

8. **Inflation and Nominal Returns**   Suppose the real rate is 2.3 percent and the inflation rate is 3.5 percent. What rate would you expect to see on a Treasury bill?

9. **Nominal and Real Returns**   An investment offers a total return of 13.5 percent over the coming year. Powell Arms thinks the total real return on this investment will be only 8.6 percent. What does Powell believe the inflation rate will be over the next year?

10. **Nominal versus Real Returns**   Say you own an asset that had a total return last year of 10.9 percent. If the inflation rate last year was 3.8 percent, what was your real return?

11. **Zero Coupon Bonds**   You find a zero coupon bond with a par value of $10,000 and 13 years to maturity. If the yield to maturity on this bond is 4.9 percent, what is the dollar price of the bond? Assume semiannual compounding periods.

12. **Valuing Bonds**   Layton Corp. has a $2,000 par value bond outstanding with a coupon rate of 4.6 percent paid semiannually and 13 years to maturity. The yield to maturity of the bond is 3.8 percent. What is the dollar price of the bond?

13. **Valuing Bonds**   Union Local School District has bonds outstanding with a coupon rate of 3.9 percent paid semiannually and 16 years to maturity. The yield to maturity on these bonds is 4.2 percent and the bonds have a par value of $5,000. What is the price of the bonds?

14. **Using Treasury Quotes**   Locate the Treasury bond in Figure 5.4 that matures in May 2028. What is its coupon rate? What is its bid price? What was the previous day's asked price? Assume a par value of $1,000.

15. **Using Treasury Quotes**   Locate the Treasury bond in Figure 5.4 that matures in February 2039. Is this a premium or a discount bond? What is its current yield? What is its yield to maturity? What is the bid-ask spread in dollars? Assume a $1,000 par value.

16. **Bond Price Movements**   Miller Corporation has a premium bond making semiannual payments. The bond has a coupon rate of 7.4 percent, a YTM of 5.4 percent, and 13 years to maturity. The Modigliani Company has a discount bond making semiannual payments. This bond has a coupon rate of 5.4 percent, a YTM of 7.4 percent, and also 13 years to maturity. If interest rates remain unchanged, what do you expect the price of these bonds to be 1 year from now assuming both bonds have a par value of $1,000? In 3 years? In 8 years? In 12 years? In 13 years? What's going on here? Illustrate your answers by graphing bond prices versus time to maturity.

Intermediate
(Questions 16–25)

17. **Interest Rate Risk**   Laurel, Inc., and Hardy Corp. both have 7.3 percent coupon bonds outstanding, with semiannual interest payments, and both are currently priced at the par value of $1,000. The Laurel, Inc., bond has 4 years to maturity, whereas the Hardy Corp. bond has 23 years to maturity. If interest rates suddenly rise by 2 percent, what is the percentage change in the price of these bonds? If interest rates were to suddenly fall by 2 percent instead, what would the percentage change in the price of these bonds be then? Illustrate your answers by graphing bond prices versus YTM. What does this problem tell you about the interest rate risk of longer-term bonds?

18. **Interest Rate Risk**   The Faulk Corp. has a bond with a coupon rate of 6.4 percent outstanding. The Gonas Company has a bond with a coupon rate of 12.6 percent outstanding. Both bonds have 18 years to maturity, make semiannual payments, and have a YTM of 9.5 percent. If interest rates suddenly rise by 2 percent, what is the percentage change in the price of these bonds? What if interest rates suddenly fall by 2 percent instead? What does this problem tell you about the interest rate risk of lower coupon bonds?

19. **Bond Yields**   Stuart Software has 5.7 percent coupon bonds on the market with 11 years to maturity. The bonds make semiannual payments and currently sell for 93 percent of par. What is the current yield on the bonds? The YTM? The effective annual yield?

20. **Bond Yields**   Baxter Co. wants to issue new 20-year bonds for some much-needed expansion projects. The company currently has 5.6 percent coupon bonds on the market that sell for $1,094.30,

make semiannual payments, and mature in 20 years. What coupon rate should the company set on its new bonds if it wants them to sell at par? Both bonds have a par value of $1,000.

21. **Accrued Interest**   You purchase a bond with an invoice price of $945. The bond has a coupon rate of 5.6 percent, and there are two months to the next semiannual coupon date. What is the clean price of the bond?

22. **Accrued Interest**   You purchase a bond with a coupon rate of 7.1 percent and a clean price of $1,030. If the next semiannual coupon payment is due in four months, what is the invoice price?

23. **Finding the Bond Maturity**   Cavo Corp. has 6.3 percent coupon bonds making annual payments with a YTM of 7.14 percent. The current yield on these bonds is 6.95 percent. How many years do these bonds have left until they mature?

24. **Using Bond Quotes**   Suppose the following bond quote for IOU Corporation appears in the financial page of today's newspaper. Assume the bond has a face value of $1,000 and the current date is April 15, 2019. What is the yield to maturity of the bond? What is the current yield?

Company (Ticker)	Coupon	Maturity	Last Price	Last Yield	Est Vol (000s)
IOU (IOU)	5.400	Apr 15, 2038	96.425	??	1,827

25. **Finding the Maturity**   You've just found a 10 percent coupon bond on the market that sells for par value. What is the maturity on this bond?

Challenge
(Questions 26–34)

26. **Components of Bond Returns**   Bond P is a premium bond with a coupon of 7.8 percent. Bond D has a coupon rate of 4.2 percent and is currently selling at a discount. Both bonds make annual payments, have a YTM of 6 percent, and have eight years to maturity. What is the current yield for Bond P? For Bond D? If interest rates remain unchanged, what is the expected capital gains yield over the next year for Bond P? For Bond D? Explain your answers and the interrelationship among the various types of yields.

27. **Holding Period Yield**   You will earn the YTM on a bond if you hold the bond until maturity and if interest rates don't change. If you actually sell the bond before it matures, your realized return is known as the holding period yield (HPY).

    a. Suppose that today you buy a bond with an annual coupon rate of 5.4 percent for $945. The bond has 21 years to maturity. What rate of return do you expect to earn on your investment?

    b. Two years from now, the YTM on your bond has declined by 1 percent, and you decide to sell. What price will your bond sell for? What is the HPY on your investment? Compare this yield to the YTM when you first bought the bond. Why are they different?

28. **Valuing Bonds**   The Grimm Corporation has two different bonds currently outstanding. Bond M has a face value of $20,000 and matures in 20 years. The bond makes no payments for the first 6 years, then pays $800 every six months over the subsequent 8 years, and finally pays $1,000 every six months over the last 6 years. Bond N also has a face value of $20,000 and a maturity of 20 years; it makes no coupon payments over the life of the bond. If the required return on both these bonds is 5.3 percent compounded semiannually, what is the current price of Bond M? Of Bond N?

29. **Valuing the Call Feature**   At one point, some Treasury bonds were callable. Consider the prices on the following three Treasury issues as of February 24, 2019:

5.50	May 23	106.32150	106.37500	–.406	5.28
7.60	May 23	103.12000	103.50000	–.094	5.24
8.40	May 23	107.98750	108.21875	–.406	5.32

The bond in the middle is callable in February 2020. What is the implied value of the call feature? (*Hint:* Is there a way to combine the two noncallable issues to create an issue that has the same coupon as the callable bond?)

30. Treasury Bonds The following Treasury bond quote appeared in *The Wall Street Journal* on May 11, 2004:

| 9.125 | May 09 | 100.09375 | 100.125 | . . . | −2.15 |

Why would anyone buy this Treasury bond with a negative yield to maturity? How is this possible?

31. Real Cash Flows An engineer earned $26,300 per year when he began his career. Thirty years later, his annual salary was $105,350. The inflation index over this same period grew from 455.18 to 1,046.27. What was his real annual salary increase? What is his current salary in real terms?

32. Real Cash Flows When Marilyn Monroe died, ex-husband Joe DiMaggio vowed to place fresh flowers on her grave every Sunday as long as he lived. The week after she died in 1962, a bunch of fresh flowers that the former baseball player thought appropriate for the star cost about $5. Based on actuarial tables, "Joltin' Joe" could expect to live for 30 years after the actress died. Assume that the EAR is 5.9 percent. Also, assume that the price of the flowers will increase at 3.1 percent per year, when expressed as an EAR. Assuming that each year has exactly 52 weeks, what is the present value of this commitment? Joe began purchasing flowers the week after Marilyn died.

33. Real Cash Flows You are planning to save for retirement over the next 30 years. To save for retirement, you will invest $600 per month in a stock account in real dollars and $275 per month in a bond account in real dollars. The effective annual return of the stock account is expected to be 12 percent, and the bond account will have an annual return of 7 percent. When you retire, you will combine your money into an account with an effective annual return of 8 percent. The inflation rate over this period is expected to be 4 percent. How much can you withdraw each month from your account in real terms assuming a 25-year withdrawal period? What is the nominal dollar amount of your last withdrawal?

34. Real Cash Flows Paul Adams owns a health club in downtown Los Angeles. He charges his customers an annual fee of $900 and has an existing customer base of 575. Paul plans to raise the annual fee by 6 percent every year and expects the club membership to grow at a constant rate of 3 percent for the next five years. The overall expenses of running the health club are $95,000 a year and are expected to grow at the inflation rate of 2 percent annually. After five years, Paul plans to buy a luxury boat for $450,000, close the health club, and travel the world in his boat for the rest of his life. What is the annual amount that Paul can spend while on his world tour if he will have no money left in the bank when he dies? Assume Paul has a remaining life of 25 years and earns 9 percent on his savings.

WHAT'S ON THE WEB?

1. Bond Quotes You can find current bond prices at finra-markets.morningstar.com/MarketData/Default.jsp. You want to find the bond prices and yields for bonds issued by Clorox. You can enter the ticker symbol "CLX" to do a search. What is the shortest maturity bond issued by Clorox that is outstanding? What is the longest maturity bond? What is the credit rating for Clorox's bonds? Do all of the bonds have the same credit rating? Why do you think this is?

2. Yield Curves You can find information regarding the most current bond yields at money.cnn.com. Find the yield curve for U.S. Treasury bonds. What is the general shape of the yield curve? What does this imply about expected future inflation? Now graph the yield curve for AAA, AA, and A rated corporate bonds. Is the corporate yield curve the same shape as the Treasury yield curve? Why or why not?

3. Default Premiums The Federal Reserve Bank of St. Louis has files listing historical interest rates on its website www.stlouisfed.org. Find the link for "FRED" data. You will find listings for Moody's Seasoned Aaa Corporate Bond Yield and Moody's Seasoned Baa Corporate Bond Yield. A default premium can be calculated as the difference between the Aaa bond yield and the Baa bond yield. Calculate the default premium using these two bond indexes for the most recent 36 months. Is the default premium the same for every month? Why do you think this is?

EXCEL MASTER IT! PROBLEM

Companies often buy bonds to meet a future liability or cash outlay. Such an investment is called a *dedicated portfolio* because the proceeds of the portfolio are dedicated to the future liability. In such a case, the portfolio is subject to reinvestment risk. Reinvestment risk occurs because the company will be reinvesting the coupon payments it receives. If the YTM on similar bonds falls, these coupon payments will be reinvested at a lower interest rate, which will result in a portfolio value that is lower than desired at maturity. Of course, if interest rates increase, the portfolio value at maturity will be higher than needed.

Suppose Ice Cubes, Inc., has the following liability due in five years. The company is going to buy five-year bonds today to meet the future obligation. The liability and current YTM are below:

Amount of liability:	$100,000,000
Current YTM:	8%

a. At the current YTM, what is the face value of the bonds the company has to purchase today to meet its future obligation? Assume that the bonds in the relevant range will have the same coupon rate as the current YTM and these bonds make semiannual coupon payments.

b. Assume the interest rates remain constant for the next five years. Thus, when the company reinvests the coupon payments, it will reinvest at the current YTM. What is the value of the portfolio in five years?

c. Assume that immediately after the company purchases the bonds, interest rates either rise or fall by 1 percent. What is the value of the portfolio in five years under these circumstances?

One way to eliminate reinvestment risk is called *immunization*. Rather than buying bonds with the same maturity as the liability, the company instead buys bonds with the same duration as the liability. If you think about the dedicated portfolio, if the interest rate falls, the future value of the reinvested coupon payments decreases. However, as interest rates fall, the price of bonds increases. These effects offset each other in an immunized portfolio.

Another advantage of using duration to immunize a portfolio is that the duration of a portfolio is the weighted average of the duration of the assets in the portfolio. In other words, to find the duration of a portfolio, you take the weight of each asset multiplied by its duration and then sum the results.

d. What is the duration of the liability for Ice Cubes, Inc.?

e. Suppose the two bonds shown below are the only bonds available to immunize the liability. What face amount of each bond will the company need to purchase to immunize the portfolio?

	Bond A	Bond B
Settlement	1/1/2000	1/1/2000
Maturity	1/1/2003	1/1/2008
Coupon rate	7.00%	8.00%
YTM	7.50%	9.00%
Coupons per year	2	2

FINANCING EAST COAST YACHTS' EXPANSION PLANS WITH A BOND ISSUE

After Dan's EFN analysis for East Coast Yachts (see the Closing Case in Chapter 3), Larissa has decided to expand the company's operations. She has asked Dan to enlist an underwriter to help sell $45 million in new 30-year bonds to finance new construction. Dan has entered into discussions with Renata Harper, an underwriter from the firm of Crowe & Mallard, about which bond features East Coast Yachts should consider and also what coupon rate the issue will likely have. Although Dan is aware of bond features, he is uncertain as to the costs and benefits of some of them, so he isn't clear on how each feature would affect the coupon rate of the bond issue.

1. You are Renata's assistant, and she has asked you to prepare a memo to Dan describing the effect of each of the following bond features on the coupon rate of the bond. She would also like you to list any advantages or disadvantages of each feature.

   a. The security of the bond, that is, whether or not the bond has collateral.

   b. The seniority of the bond.

   c. The presence of a sinking fund.

   d. A call provision with specified call dates and call prices.

   e. A deferred call accompanying the above call provision.

   f. A make-whole call provision.

   g. Any positive covenants. Also, discuss several possible positive covenants East Coast Yachts might consider.

   h. Any negative covenants. Also, discuss several possible negative covenants East Coast Yachts might consider.

   i. A conversion feature (note that East Coast Yachts is not a publicly traded company).

   j. A floating rate coupon.

   Dan is also considering whether to issue coupon-bearing bonds or zero coupon bonds. The YTM on either bond issue will be 5.5 percent. The coupon bond would have a 5.5 percent coupon rate. The company's tax rate is 21 percent.

2. How many of the coupon bonds must East Coast Yachts issue to raise the $45 million? How many of the zeroes must it issue?

3. In 30 years, what will be the principal repayment due if East Coast Yachts issues the coupon bonds? What if it issues the zeroes?

4. What are the company's considerations in issuing a coupon bond compared to a zero coupon bond?

5. Suppose East Coast Yachts issues the coupon bonds with a make-whole call provision. The make-whole call rate is the Treasury rate plus .40 percent. If East Coast calls the bonds in seven years when the Treasury rate is 4.8 percent, what is the call price of the bond? What if it is 6.2 percent?

6. Are investors really made whole with a make-whole call provision?

7. After considering all the relevant factors, would you recommend a zero coupon issue or a regular coupon issue? Why? Would you recommend an ordinary call feature or a make-whole call feature? Why?

6

Stock Valuation

When the stock market closed on January 4, 2019, the common stock of oil company Marathon Petroleum was selling for $61.65 per share. On that same day, PriceSmart, the membership warehouse shopping company, closed at $60.58 per share, and business analytics company Omnicell closed at $60.50. Because the stock prices of these three companies were so similar, you might expect that they would be offering similar dividends to their stockholders, but you would be wrong. In fact, Marathon's annual dividend was $1.84 per share, PriceSmart's was $.70 per share, and Omnicell paid no dividends at all!

As we will see in this chapter, dividends currently being paid are one of the primary factors we look at when attempting to value common stocks. However, it is obvious from looking at Omnicell that current dividends are not the end of the story. This chapter explores dividends, stock values, and the connection between the two.

Please visit us at corecorporatefinance.blogspot.com for the latest developments in the world of corporate finance.

In our previous chapter, we introduced you to bonds and bond valuation. In this chapter, we turn to the other major source of financing for corporations, common and preferred stock. We first describe the cash flows associated with a share of stock and then go on to develop a very famous result, the dividend growth model. From there, we move on to examine various important features of common and preferred stock, focusing on shareholder rights. We close out the chapter with a discussion of how shares of stock are traded and how stock prices and other important information are reported in the financial press.

6.1 THE PRESENT VALUE OF COMMON STOCKS

Dividends versus Capital Gains

ExcelMaster
coverage online

www.mhhe.com/RossCore6e

Our goal in this section is to value common stocks. We learned in Chapter 5 that an asset's value is determined by the present value of its future cash flows. Investing in a stock can provide two kinds of cash flows. First, many stocks pay dividends on a regular basis. Second, the stockholder receives the sale price when she sells the stock. Thus, in order to value common stocks, we need to answer an interesting question: Is the value of a stock equal to:

1. The discounted present value of the sum of next period's dividend plus next period's stock price, or
2. The discounted present value of all future dividends?

This is the kind of question that students would love to see on a multiple-choice exam because both (1) and (2) are right.

To see that (1) and (2) are the same, let's start with an individual who will buy the stock and hold it for one year. In other words, she has a one-year *holding period.* In addition, she is willing to pay P_0 for the stock today. That is, she calculates:

$$P_0 = \frac{D_1}{1+R} + \frac{P_1}{1+R} \qquad [6.1]$$

D_1 is the dividend paid at year's end and P_1 is the price at year's end. P_0 is the present value of the common stock investment. The term in the denominator, R, is the appropriate discount rate for the stock.

That seems easy enough, but where does P_1 come from? P_1 is not pulled out of thin air. Rather, there must be a buyer at the end of Year 1 who is willing to purchase the stock for P_1. This buyer determines the price by:

$$P_1 = \frac{D_2}{1+R} + \frac{P_2}{1+R} \qquad [6.2]$$

Substituting the value of P_1 from Equation 6.2 into Equation 6.1 yields:

$$P_0 = \frac{1}{1+R}\left[D_1 + \left(\frac{D_2 + P_2}{1+R}\right)\right]$$

$$= \frac{D_1}{1+R} + \frac{D_2}{(1+R)^2} + \frac{P_2}{(1+R)^2} \qquad [6.3]$$

We can ask a similar question for Equation 6.3: Where does P_2 come from? An investor at the end of Year 2 is willing to pay P_2 because of the dividend and stock price at Year 3. This process can be repeated *ad nauseam.*[1] At the end, we are left with:

$$P_0 = \frac{D_1}{1+R} + \frac{D_2}{(1+R)^2} + \frac{D_3}{(1+R)^3} + \cdots = \sum_{t=1}^{\infty}\frac{D_t}{(1+R)^t} \qquad [6.4]$$

Thus the value of a firm's common stock to the investor is equal to the present value of all of the expected future dividends.

This is a very useful result. A common objection to applying present value analysis to stocks is that investors are too shortsighted to care about the long-run stream of dividends. These critics argue that an investor will generally not look past his or her time horizon. Thus, prices in a market dominated by short-term investors will reflect only near-term dividends. However, our discussion shows that a long-run dividend discount model holds even when investors have short-term time horizons. Although an investor may want to cash out early, she must find another investor who is willing to buy. The price this second investor pays is dependent on dividends after his date of purchase.

Valuation of Different Types of Stocks

The above discussion shows that the value of the firm is the present value of its future dividends. How do we apply this idea in practice? Equation 6.4 represents a very general model and is applicable regardless of whether the level of expected dividends is growing, fluctuating, or constant. The general model can be simplified if the firm's dividends are expected to follow some basic patterns: (1) zero growth, (2) constant growth, and (3) differential growth. These cases are illustrated in Figure 6.1.

---

[1] This procedure reminds us of the physicist lecturing on the origins of the universe. He was approached by an elderly gentleman in the audience who disagreed with the lecture. The attendee said that the universe rests on the back of a huge turtle. When the physicist asked what the turtle rested on, the gentleman said another turtle. Anticipating the physicist's objections, the attendee said, "Don't tire yourself out, young fellow. It's turtles all the way down."

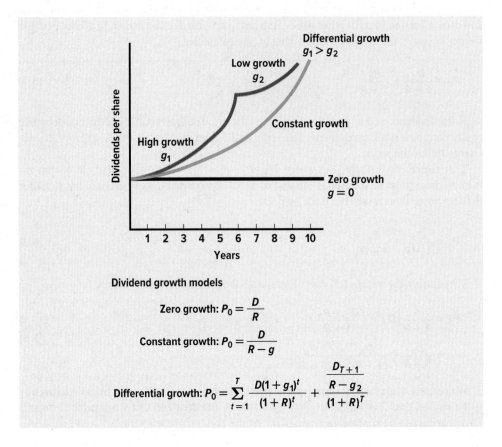

Dividend growth models

Zero growth: $P_0 = \dfrac{D}{R}$

Constant growth: $P_0 = \dfrac{D}{R-g}$

Differential growth: $P_0 = \displaystyle\sum_{t=1}^{T} \dfrac{D(1+g_1)^t}{(1+R)^t} + \dfrac{\dfrac{D_{T+1}}{R-g_2}}{(1+R)^T}$

CASE 1 (ZERO GROWTH)   The value of a stock with a constant dividend is given by:

$$P_0 = \dfrac{D_1}{1+R} + \dfrac{D_2}{(1+R)^2} + \cdots = \dfrac{D}{R}$$

Here it is assumed that $D_1 = D_2 = \cdots = D$. This is an application of the perpetuity formula from a previous chapter.

CASE 2 (CONSTANT GROWTH)   Dividends grow at rate g, as follows:

End of Year Dividend	1	2	3	4	...
	D_1	$D_1(1+g)$	$D_1(1+g)^2$	$D_1(1+g)^3$	

Note that D_1 is the dividend at the end of the first period.

Projected Dividends

EXAMPLE 6.1

Hampshire Products will pay a dividend of $4 per share a year from now. Financial analysts believe that dividends will rise at 6 percent per year for the foreseeable future. What is the dividend per share at the end of each of the first five years?

End of Year Dividend	1	2	3	4	5
	$4.00	$4 × 1.06 = $4.24	$4 × 1.06^2 = $4.4944	$4 × 1.06^3 = $4.7641	$4 × 1.06^4 = $5.0499

The value of a common stock with dividends growing at a constant rate is:

$$P_0 = \frac{D_1}{1+R} + \frac{D_1(1+g)}{(1+R)^2} + \frac{D_1(1+g)^2}{(1+R)^3} + \frac{D_1(1+g)^3}{(1+R)^4} + \cdots = \frac{D_1}{R-g}$$

where g is the growth rate. D_1 is the dividend on the stock at the end of the first period. This is the formula for the present value of a growing perpetuity, which we derived in a previous chapter.

EXAMPLE 6.2

Stock Valuation

Suppose an investor is considering the purchase of a share of the Utah Mining Company. The stock will pay a $3 dividend a year from today. This dividend is expected to grow at 10 percent per year ($g = 10\%$) for the foreseeable future. The investor thinks that the required return (R) on this stock is 15 percent, given her assessment of Utah Mining's risk. (We also refer to R as the discount rate of the stock.) What is the value of a share of Utah Mining Company's stock?

Using the constant growth formula of Case 2, we assess the value to be $60:

$$\$60 = \frac{\$3}{.15 - .10}$$

P_0 is quite dependent on the value of g. If g had been estimated to be 12.5 percent, the value of the share would have been:

$$\$120 = \frac{\$3}{.15 - .125}$$

The stock price doubles (from $60 to $120) when g only increases 25 percent (from 10 percent to 12.5 percent). Because of P_0's dependency on g, one must maintain a healthy sense of skepticism when using this constant growth of dividends model.

Furthermore, note that P_0 is equal to infinity when the growth rate, g, equals the discount rate, R. Because stock prices do not grow infinitely, an estimate of g greater than R implies an error in estimation. More will be said of this point later.

The assumption of steady dividend growth might strike you as peculiar. Why would the dividend grow at a constant rate? The reason is that, for many companies, steady growth in dividends is an explicit goal. For example, in 2018, Procter & Gamble, the Cincinnati-based maker of personal care and household products, increased its annual dividend by about 4 percent to $2.87 per share; this increase was notable because it was the 62nd in a row. The subject of dividend growth falls under the general heading of dividend policy, so we will defer further discussion of it to a later chapter.

CASE 3 (DIFFERENTIAL GROWTH)   In this case, an algebraic formula would be too unwieldy. Instead, we present examples.

EXAMPLE 6.3

Differential Growth

Consider the stock of Elixir Drug Company, which has a new back-rub ointment and is enjoying rapid growth. The dividend for a share of stock a year from today will be $1.15. During the next four years, the dividend will grow at 15 percent per year ($g_1 = 15\%$). After that, growth (g_2) will be equal to 10 percent per year. Can you calculate the present value of the stock if the required return (R) is 15 percent?

Figure 6.2 displays the growth in the dividends. We need to apply a two-step process to discount these dividends. We first calculate the present value of the dividends growing at 15 percent per year. That is, we first calculate the present value of the dividends at the end of each of the first five years. Second, we calculate the present value of the dividends beginning at the end of Year 6.

(Continued)

FIGURE 6.2 Growth in Dividends for Elixir Drug Company

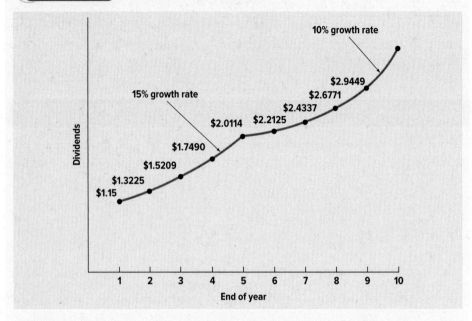

Calculate Present Value of First Five Dividends The present value of dividend payments in Years 1 through 5 is as follows:

Future Year	Growth Rate (g_1)	Expected Dividend	Present Value
1	.15	$1.1500	$1
2	.15	1.3225	1
3	.15	1.5209	1
4	.15	1.7490	1
5	.15	2.0114	1
Years 1–5	5		The present value of dividends = $5

The growing annuity formula of the previous chapter could normally be used in this step. However, note that dividends grow at 15 percent, which is also the discount rate. Because $g = R$, the growing annuity formula cannot be used in this example.

Calculate Present Value of Dividends Beginning at End of Year 6 This is the procedure for deferred perpetuities and deferred annuities that we mentioned in a previous chapter. The dividends beginning at the end of Year 6 are:

End of Year Dividend	6	7	8	9
	$D_5 \times (1 + g_2)$	$D_5 \times (1 + g_2)^2$	$D_5 \times (1 + g_2)^3$	$D_5 \times (1 + g_2)^4$
	2.0114×1.10	2.0114×1.10^2	2.0114×1.10^3	2.0114×1.10^4
	= $2.2125	= $2.4337	= $2.6771	= $2.9448

As stated in the previous chapter, the growing perpetuity formula calculates present value as of one year prior to the first payment. Because the payment begins at the end of Year 6, the present value formula calculates present value as of the end of Year 5.

The price at the end of Year 5 is given by:

$$P_5 = \frac{D_6}{R - g_2} = \frac{\$2.2125}{.15 - .10} = \$44.25$$

The present value of P_5 at the end of Year 0 is:

$$\frac{P_5}{(1+R)^5} = \frac{\$44.25}{1.15^5} = \$22$$

The present value of all dividends as of the end of Year 0 is $27 (= $22 + 5).

6.2 ESTIMATES OF PARAMETERS IN THE DIVIDEND DISCOUNT MODEL

The value of the firm is a function of its growth rate, g, and its discount rate, R. How does one estimate these variables?

Where Does g Come From?

The previous discussion on stocks assumed that dividends grow at the rate g. We now want to estimate this rate of growth. This section extends the discussion of growth contained in Chapter 3. Consider a business whose earnings next year are expected to be the same as earnings this year unless a net investment is made. This situation is likely to occur because net investment is equal to gross, or total, investment less depreciation. A net investment of zero occurs when total investment equals depreciation. If total investment is equal to depreciation, the firm's physical plant is maintained, consistent with no growth in earnings.

Net investment will be positive only if some earnings are not paid out as dividends, that is, only if some earnings are retained.[2] This leads to the following equation:

Earnings = Earnings + Retained × Return on	[6.5]
next this earnings retained	
year year this year earnings	
Increase in earnings	

The increase in earnings is a function of both the retained earnings and the return on the retained earnings.

We now divide both sides of Equation 6.5 by earnings this year, yielding:

$$\frac{\text{Earnings next year}}{\text{Earnings this year}} = \frac{\text{Earnings this year}}{\text{Earnings this year}} + \frac{\text{Retained earnings this year}}{\text{Earnings this year}}$$
$$\times \text{ Return on retained earnings} \qquad [6.6]$$

The left-hand side of Equation 6.6 is one plus the growth rate in earnings, which we write as $1 + g$. The ratio of retained earnings to earnings is called the retention ratio. Thus, we can write:

$1 + g = 1 +$ Retention ratio $\times$ Return on retained earnings   **[6.7]**

It is difficult for a financial analyst to determine the return to be expected on currently retained earnings because the details on forthcoming projects are not generally public information. However, it is frequently assumed that the projects selected in the current year have an anticipated return equal to returns from projects in other years. Here, we can estimate the anticipated return on current retained earnings by the historical return on equity, or ROE. After all, ROE is the return on the firm's entire equity, which is the return on the cumulation of all the firm's past projects.

---

[2] We ignore the possibility of the issuance of stocks or bonds in order to raise capital. These possibilities are considered in later chapters.

From Equation 6.7, we have a simple way to estimate growth:

Formula for Firm's Growth Rate:

g = Retention ratio $\times$ Return on retained earnings (ROE)   [6.8]

Previously g referred to growth in dividends. However, the growth in earnings is equal to the growth rate in dividends in this context because, as we will presently see, the ratio of dividends to earnings is held constant. In fact, as you have probably figured out, g is the sustainable growth rate we introduced in Chapter 3.

EXAMPLE 6.4

Earnings Growth

Pagemaster Enterprises just reported earnings of $2 million. It plans to retain 40 percent of its earnings. The historical return on equity (ROE) has been 16 percent, a figure that is expected to continue into the future. How much will earnings grow over the coming year?

We first perform the calculation without reference to Equation 6.8. Then we use Equation 6.8 as a check.

Calculation without Reference to Equation 6.8   The firm will retain $800,000 (= .40 × $2 million). Assuming that historical ROE is an appropriate estimate for future returns, the anticipated increase in earnings is:

$800,000 × .16 = $128,000

The percentage growth in earnings is:

$$\frac{\text{Change in earnings}}{\text{Total earnings}} = \frac{\$128{,}000}{\$2 \text{ million}} = .064$$

This implies that earnings in one year will be $2,128,000 (= $2,000,000 × 1.064).

Check Using Equation 6.8   We use g = Retention ratio × ROE. We have:

$g = .4 \times .16 = .064$, or 6.4%

Where Does *R* Come From?

Thus far, we have taken the required return, or discount rate R, as given. We will have quite a bit to say on this subject in later chapters. For now, we want to examine the implications of the dividend growth model for this required return. Earlier, we calculated P_0 as:

$P_0 = D_1/(R - g)$

Now let's assume we know P_0. If we rearrange this equation to solve for R, we get:

$R - g = D_1/P_0$

$R = D_1/P_0 + g$ [6.9]

This tells us that the total return, R, has two components. The first of these, D_1/P_0, is called the **expected dividend yield**. Because this is calculated as the expected cash dividend divided by the current price, it is conceptually similar to the current yield on a bond.

The second part of the total return is the growth rate, g. As we will verify shortly, the dividend growth rate is also the rate at which the stock price grows. Thus, this growth rate can be interpreted as the **capital gains yield**, that is, the rate at which the value of the invest-ment grows.

To illustrate the components of the required return, suppose we observe a stock selling for $20 per share. The next dividend will be $1 per share. You think that the dividend will grow by 10 percent per year more or less indefinitely. What return does this stock offer you if this is correct?

The dividend growth model calculates total return as:

$$R = \text{Dividend yield} + \text{Capital gains yield}$$
$$R = \quad D_1/P_0 \quad + \quad g$$

In this case, total return works out to be:

$$R = \$1/\$20 + .10$$
$$= .05 + .10$$
$$= .15, \text{ or } 15\%$$

This stock, therefore, has an expected return of 15 percent.

We can verify this answer by calculating the price in one year, P_1, using 15 percent as the required return. Based on the dividend growth model, this price is:

$$P_1 = D_1 \times (1 + g)/(R - g)$$
$$= \$1 \times 1.10/(.15 - .10)$$
$$= \$1.10/.05$$
$$= \$22$$

Notice that this $22 is $20 × 1.1, so the stock price has grown by 10 percent, as it should. If you pay $20 for the stock today, you will get a $1 dividend at the end of the year, and you will have a $22 − 20 = $2 gain. Your dividend yield is thus $1/$20 = .05, or 5 percent. Your capital gains yield is $2/$20 = .10, or 10 percent, so your total return would be 5 percent + 10 percent = 15 percent.

To get a feel for actual numbers in this context, consider that, according to the 2018 Value Line *Investment Survey,* Procter & Gamble's dividends were expected to grow by 5 percent over the next 5 or so years, compared to a historical growth rate of 5 percent over the preceding 5 years and 7.5 percent over the preceding 10 years. In 2018, the projected dividend for the coming year was given as $2.88. The stock price at that time was about $92 per share. What is the return investors require on P&G? Here, the dividend yield is 3.1 percent and the capital gains yield is 5 percent, giving a total required return of 8.1 percent on P&G stock.

Calculating the Required Return

Pagemaster Enterprises, the company examined in the previous example, has 1,000,000 shares of stock outstanding. The stock is selling at $10. What is the required return on the stock?

Because the retention ratio is 40 percent, the payout ratio is 60 percent (= 1 − Retention ratio). The payout ratio is the ratio of dividends/earnings. Because earnings a year from now will be $2,128,000 (= $2,000,000 × 1.064), dividends will be $1,276,800 (= .60 × $2,128,000). Dividends per share will be $1.28 (= $1,276,800/1,000,000). Given our previous result that $g = .064$, we calculate R from Equation 6.9 as follows:

$$\frac{\$1.28}{\$10.00} + .064 = .192, \text{ or } 19.2\%$$

A Healthy Sense of Skepticism

It is important to emphasize that our approach merely estimates g; our approach does not determine g precisely. We mentioned earlier that our estimate of g is based on a number of assumptions. For example, we assume that the return on reinvestment of future retained

FINANCE MATTERS

HOW FAST IS TOO FAST?

Growth rates are an important tool for evaluating a company and, as we have seen, an important part of valuing a company's stock. When you're thinking about (and calculating) growth rates, a little common sense goes a long way. For example, in 2018, retailing giant Walmart had about 785 million square feet of stores, distribution centers, and so forth in the United States. Suppose the company expected to increase its square footage by about 6 percent over the next year. This doesn't sound too outrageous, but can Walmart grow its square footage at 6 percent indefinitely?

Using the compound growth calculation we discussed in an earlier chapter, see if you agree that if Walmart grows at 6 percent per year over the next 202 years, the company will have more than 100 trillion square feet under roof, which is about the total land mass of the entire United States! In other words, if Walmart keeps growing at 6 percent, the entire country will eventually be one big Walmart. Scary.

Facebook is another example. The company had total revenues of about $1.97 billion in 2010 and $40.65 billion in 2017. This represents an annual rate of increase of 54 percent! How likely do you think it is that the company can continue this growth rate? If this growth continued, the company would have revenues of about $26.67 trillion in just 15 years, which exceeds the gross domestic product (GDP) of the United States. Obviously, Facebook's growth rate will slow substantially in the next several years.

What about growth in cash flow? As of the beginning of 2018, cash flow for internet travel booking website Priceline .com grew at an annual rate of about 37 percent for the previous 10 years. The company was expected to generate about $4.48 billion in cash flow for 2018. If Priceline.com's cash flow grew at the same rate for the next 19 years, the company would generate about $1.77 trillion per year, or slightly more than the $1.72 trillion of U.S. currency circulating in the world.

As these examples show, growth rates shouldn't just be extrapolated into the future. It is fairly easy for a small company to grow very fast. If a company has $100 in sales, it only has to increase sales by another $100 to have a 100 percent increase in sales. If the company's sales are $10 billion, it has to increase sales by another $10 billion to achieve the same 100 percent increase. So, long-term growth rate estimates must be chosen very carefully. As a rule of thumb, for really long-term growth rate estimates, you should probably assume that a company will not grow much faster than the economy as a whole, which is probably noticeably less than 5 percent (inflation adjusted).

earnings is equal to the firm's past ROE. We assume that the future retention ratio is equal to the past retention ratio. Our estimate for g will be off if these assumptions prove to be wrong.

Unfortunately, the determination of R is highly dependent on g. In the Pagemaster Enterprises example, if g is estimated to be 0, R equals 12.8 percent (= $1.28/$10). If g is estimated to be 12 percent, R equals 24.8 percent (= $1.28/$10 + .12). Thus, one should view estimates of R with a healthy sense of skepticism.

Because of the preceding, some financial economists generally argue that the estimation error for R for a single security is too large to be practical. Therefore, they suggest calculating the average R for an entire industry. This R would then be used to discount the dividends of a particular stock in the same industry.

One should be particularly skeptical of two polar cases when estimating R for individual securities. First, consider a firm currently paying no dividend. The stock price will be above zero because investors believe that the firm may initiate a dividend at some point or the firm may be acquired at some point. However, when a firm goes from no dividends to a positive number of dividends, the implied growth rate is infinite. Thus, Equation 6.9 must be used with extreme caution here, if at all—a point we emphasize later in this chapter.

Second, we mentioned earlier that the value of the firm is infinite when g is equal to R. Because prices for stocks do not grow infinitely, an analyst whose estimate of g for a particular firm is equal to or above R must have made a mistake. Most likely, the analyst's high estimate for g is correct for the next few years. However, firms cannot maintain an abnormally high growth rate forever. The analyst's error was to use a short-run estimate of g in a model requiring a perpetual growth rate. A nearby *Finance Matters* box discusses the consequences of long-term growth at unrealistic rates.

The No-Payout Firm

Students frequently ask the following question: If the dividend discount model is correct, why aren't no-payout stocks selling at zero? This is a good question and gets at the goals of the firm. A firm with many growth opportunities is faced with a dilemma. The firm can pay out cash now, or it can forgo cash payments now so that it can make investments that will generate even greater payouts in the future.[3] This is often a painful choice because a strategy of deferment may be optimal yet unpopular among certain stockholders.

Many firms choose to pay no cash to stockholders—and these firms sell at positive prices. For example, many internet firms, such as Alphabet, pay no cash to stockholders. Rational shareholders believe that either they will receive a payout at some point or they will receive something just as good. That is, the firm will be acquired in a merger, with the stockholders receiving either cash or shares of stock at that time.

Of course, the actual application of the dividend discount model is difficult for firms of this type. Clearly, the model for constant growth of payouts does not exactly apply. Though the differential growth model can work in theory, the difficulties of estimating the date of the first payout, the growth rate of payouts after that date, and the ultimate merger price make application of the model quite difficult in reality.

Empirical evidence suggests that firms with high growth rates are likely to have lower payouts, a result consistent with the above analysis. For example, consider Microsoft Corporation. The company started in 1975 and grew rapidly for many years. It paid its first dividend in 2003, though it was a billion-dollar company (in both sales and market value of stockholders' equity) prior to that date. Why did it wait so long to pay a dividend? It waited because it had so many positive growth opportunities, that is, new software products, to take advantage of.

6.3 COMPARABLES

So far in this chapter, we have valued stocks by discounting dividends (or total payouts). In addition to this approach, practitioners commonly value stocks by comparables. The comparables approach is similar to valuation in real estate. If your neighbor's home just sold for $200,000 and it has similar size and amenities to your home, your home is probably worth around $200,000 also. In the stock market, comparable firms are assumed to have similar *multiples.* To see how the comparables approach works, let's look at perhaps the most common multiple, the price-earnings (PE) multiple, or PE ratio.

Price-Earnings Ratio

Recall that a stock's price-earnings ratio is the ratio of the stock's price to its earnings per share. For example, if the stock of Sun Aerodynamic Systems (SAS) is selling at $27.00 per share and its earnings per share over the last year was $4.50, SAS's PE ratio would be 6 (= $27/$4.50).

It is generally assumed that similar firms have similar PE ratios. Imagine the average PE ratio across all publicly traded companies in the specialty retail industry is 12 and a particular company in the industry has earnings of $10 million. If this company is judged to be similar to the rest of the industry, one might estimate that company's value to be $120 million (= 12 × $10 million).

---

[3] A third alternative is to issue stock so that the firm has enough cash both to pay dividends and to invest. This possibility is explored in a later chapter.

Valuation via PE certainly looks easier than valuation via discounted cash flow (DCF) because the DCF approach calls for estimates of future cash flows. But is the PE approach better? That depends on the similarity across comparables.

On January 4, 2019, Alphabet's stock price was $1,071 and its EPS was $26.65, implying a PE ratio of about 40.2.[4] On the same day, Hewlett-Packard's PE was 11.2, Microsoft's was 41.9, and Apple's was 11.9. Why would stocks in the same industry trade at different PE ratios?

The dividend discount model (in Examples 6.1 and 6.2) implies that the PE ratio is related to growth opportunities.[5] As an example, consider two firms, each having just reported earnings per share of $1. However, one firm has many valuable growth opportunities, while the other firm has no growth opportunities at all. The firm with growth opportunities should sell at a higher price because an investor is buying both current income of $1 and growth opportunities. Suppose that the firm with growth opportunities sells for $16 and the other firm sells for $8. The $1 earnings per share number appears in the denominator of the PE ratio for both firms. Thus, the PE ratio is 16 for the firm with growth opportunities, but only 8 for the firm without the opportunities.

There are at least two additional factors explaining the PE ratio. The first is the discount rate, R. Because R appears in the denominator of the dividend discount model, the formula implies that the PE ratio is negatively related to the firm's discount rate. We have already suggested that the discount rate is positively related to the stock's risk or variability. Thus, the PE ratio is negatively related to the stock's risk. To see that this is a sensible result, consider two firms, A and B, behaving as cash cows. The stock market expects both firms to have annual earnings of $1 per share forever. However, the earnings of Firm A are known with certainty, while the earnings of Firm B are quite variable. A rational stockholder is likely to pay more for a share of Firm A because of the absence of risk. If a share of Firm A sells at a higher price and both firms have the same EPS, the PE ratio of Firm A must be higher.

The second additional factor concerns the firm's accounting method. As an example, consider two identical firms, C and D. Firm C uses LIFO and reports earnings of $2 per share.[6] Firm D uses the less conservative accounting assumptions of FIFO and reports earnings of $3 per share. The market knows that both firms are identical and prices both at $18 per share. The price-earnings ratio is 9 (= $18/$2) for Firm C and 6 (= $18/$3) for Firm D. Thus, the firm with the more conservative principles has the higher PE ratio.

In conclusion, we have argued that a stock's PE ratio is likely a function of three factors:

1. *Growth opportunities.* Companies with significant growth opportunities are likely to have high PE ratios.

2. *Risk.* Low-risk stocks are likely to have high PE ratios.

3. *Accounting practices.* Firms following conservative accounting practices will likely have high PE ratios.

---

[4] We just calculated PE as the ratio of current price to last year's EPS. Alternatively, PE can be computed as the ratio of current price to projected EPS over the next year.

[5] We can also use the constant growth version of the dividend discount model to solve for the price-earnings ratio. Recall that:

$$\text{Price per share} = \frac{D_1}{R-g}$$

If D_1 can be expressed as $\text{EPS}_1 \times (1-b)$, where EPS_1 is earnings per share in Time 1 and b is the plowback ratio (where $1-b$ is the dividend payout ratio), and $\text{EPS}_0(1+g) = \text{EPS}_1$, then:

$$\text{Price per share} = \frac{\text{EPS}_0(1+g)(1-b)}{R-g}$$

Dividing by EPS_0 yields:

$$\frac{\text{Price per share}}{\text{EPS}_0} = \frac{(1+g)(1-b)}{R-g}$$

[6] Recall from your accounting courses that in an inflationary environment, *FIFO* (*first-in, first-out*) accounting understates the true cost of inventory and hence inflates reported earnings. Inventory is valued according to more recent costs under *LIFO* (*last-in, first-out*), implying that reported earnings are lower here than they would be under FIFO. Thus, LIFO inventory accounting is a more *conservative* method than FIFO. Similar accounting leeway exists for construction costs (*completed contracts* versus *percentage-of-completion* methods) and depreciation (*accelerated depreciation* versus *straight-line depreciation*).

Which of these factors is most important in the real world? The consensus among finance professionals is that growth opportunities typically have the biggest impact on PE ratios. For example, high-tech companies generally have higher PE ratios than, say, utilities because utilities have fewer opportunities for growth, even though utilities typically have lower risk. And, within industries, differences in growth opportunities also generate the biggest differences in PE ratios. In our example at the beginning of this section, Alphabet's high PE is almost certainly due to its growth opportunities, not its low risk or its accounting conservatism. In fact, due to its relative youth, the risk of Alphabet is likely higher than the risk of many of its competitors. Hewlett-Packard's PE is lower than Alphabet's PE because Hewlett-Packard's growth opportunities are a small fraction of its existing business lines. However, Hewlett-Packard had a much higher PE decades ago, when it had huge growth opportunities but little in the way of existing business.

Thus, while multiples such as the PE ratio can be used to price stocks, care must be taken. Firms in the same industry are likely to have different multiples if they have different growth rates, risk levels, and accounting treatments. Average multiples should not be calculated across all firms in any industry. Rather, an average multiple should be calculated only across those firms in an industry with similar characteristics.

Enterprise Value Ratios

The PE ratio is an equity ratio. That is, the numerator is the price per share of stock and the denominator is the earnings per share of stock. In addition, practitioners often use ratios involving both equity and debt. Perhaps the most common is the enterprise value (EV) to EBITDA ratio. Enterprise value is equal to the market value of the firm's equity plus the market value of the firm's debt minus cash. Recall, EBITDA stands for earnings before interest, taxes, depreciation, and amortization.

For example, imagine that Illinois Food Products Co. (IFPC) has equity worth $800 million, debt worth $300 million, and cash of $100 million. The enterprise value here is $1 billion (= $800 + 300 − 100). Further imagine the firm has the following income statement:

ILLINOIS FOOD PRODUCTS CO. Income Statement ($ in millions)	
Revenue	$700
Cost of goods sold	500
Earnings before interest, taxes, depreciation, and amortization (EBITDA)	$200
Depreciation and amortization	100
Interest	24
Pretax income	76
Taxes (@ 21%)	16
Profit after taxes	$ 60

The EV to EBITDA ratio is 5 (= $1 billion/$200 million). Note that all the items in the income statement below EBITDA are ignored when calculating this ratio.

As with PE ratios, it is generally assumed that similar firms have similar EV/EBITDA ratios. For example, imagine that the average EV/EBITDA ratio in an industry is 6. If QRT Corporation, a firm in the industry with EBITDA of $50 million, is judged to be similar to the rest of the industry, its enterprise value might be estimated at $300 million (= 6 × $50). Now imagine that QRT has $75 million of debt and $25 million of cash. Given our estimate of QRT's enterprise value, QRT's stock would be worth $250 million (= $300 − 75 + 25).

A number of questions arise with value ratios:

1. Is there any advantage to the EV/EBITDA ratio over the PE ratio? Yes. Companies in the same industry may differ by leverage, i.e., the ratio of debt to equity. As you will learn in Chapter 14, leverage increases the risk of equity, impacting the discount rate, R. Thus, while firms in the same industry may be otherwise comparable, they are likely to have different PE ratios if they have different degrees of leverage. Because enterprise value includes debt and equity, the impact of leverage on the EV/EBITDA ratio is less.[7]

2. Why is EBITDA used in the denominator? The numerator and denominator of a ratio should be consistent. Because the numerator of the PE ratio is the price of a share of stock, it makes sense that the denominator is the earnings per share (EPS) of stock. That is, interest is specifically subtracted before EPS is calculated. By contrast, because EV involves the sum of debt and equity, it is sensible that the denominator is unaffected by interest payments. This is the case with EBITDA because, as its name implies, earnings are calculated before interest is taken out.

3. Why does the denominator ignore depreciation and amortization? Many practitioners argue that, because depreciation and amortization are not cash flows, earnings should be calculated before taking out depreciation and amortization. In other words, depreciation and amortization merely reflect the sunk cost of a previous purchase. However, this view is by no means universal. Others point out that depreciable assets will eventually be replaced in an ongoing business. Because depreciation charges reflect the cost of future replacement, it can be argued that these charges should be considered in a calculation of income.

4. What other denominators are used in value ratios? Among others, practitioners may use EBIT (earnings before interest and taxes), EBITA (earnings before interest, taxes, and amortization), and free cash flow.

5. Why is cash subtracted out? Many firms seem to hold amounts of cash well in excess of what is needed. For example, Microsoft held tens of billions of dollars in cash and short-term investments throughout the last decade, far more than many analysts believed was optimal. Because an enterprise value ratio should reflect the ability of productive assets to create earnings or cash flow, cash should be subtracted out when calculating the ratio. However, the viewpoint that all cash should be ignored can be criticized. Some cash holdings are necessary to run a business, and this amount of cash should be included in EV.

6.4 VALUING STOCKS USING FREE CASH FLOWS

So far in this chapter, we have discounted cash payouts to value a single share of stock and used the method of comparables. As an alternative, one can value stocks by discounting their cash flows using a "top down" approach.

As an example, consider Global Harmonic Control Systems (GHCS). Revenues, which are forecasted to be $500 million in one year, are expected to grow at 10 percent per year for the two years after that, 8 percent per year for the next two years, and 6 percent per year after that time. Expenses including depreciation are 60 percent of revenues. Net investment, including net working capital and capital spending less depreciation, is 10 percent of revenues. Because all costs are proportional to revenues, net cash flow (sometimes referred to as free cash flow) grows at the same rate as do revenues. GHCS is an all-equity firm with 12 million shares outstanding. A discount rate of 16 percent is appropriate for a firm of GHCS's risk.

[7] However, leverage does impact the ratio of EV to EBITDA to some extent. As we discuss in Chapter 14, leverage creates a tax shield, increasing EV. Because leverage should not impact EBITDA, the ratio should increase with leverage.

The relevant numbers for the first five years, rounded to two decimals, are:

	1	2	3	4	5
Revenues	$500.00	$550.00	$605.00	$653.40	$705.67
Expenses	300.00	330.00	363.00	392.04	423.40
Earnings before taxes	$200.00	$220.00	$242.00	$261.36	$282.27
Taxes (21%)	42.00	46.20	50.82	54.89	59.28
Earnings after taxes	$158.00	$173.80	$191.18	$206.47	$222.99
Net investment	50.00	55.00	60.50	65.34	70.57
Net cash flow	$108.00	$118.80	$130.68	$141.13	$152.43

Because net cash flow grows at 6 percent per year after Year 5, net cash flow in Year 6 is forecasted to be $161.57 (= $152.43 × 1.06). Using the growing perpetuity formula, we can calculate the present value as of Year 5 of all future cash flows to be $1,615.71 million [= $161.57/(.16 − .06)].

The present value as of today of that terminal value is:

$$\$1,615.71 \times \frac{1}{1.16^5} = \$769.26 \text{ million}$$

The present value of the net cash flows during the first five years is:

$$\frac{\$108}{1.16} + \frac{\$118.80}{1.16^2} + \frac{\$130.68}{1.16^3} + \frac{\$141.13}{1.16^4} + \frac{\$152.43}{1.16^5} = \$415.63 \text{ million}$$

Adding in the terminal value, today's value of the firm is $1,184.89 million (= $415.63 + 769.26). Given the number of shares outstanding, the price per share is $98.74 (= $1,184.89/12).

The above calculation assumes a growing perpetuity after Year 5. However, we pointed out in the previous section that stocks are often valued by multiples. An investor might estimate the terminal value of GHCS via a multiple, rather than the growing perpetuity formula. Suppose that the price-earnings ratio for comparable firms in GHCS's industry is 7.

Because earnings after tax in Year 5 are $222.99, using the PE multiple of 7, the value of the firm at Year 5 would be estimated as $1,560.95 million (= $222.99 × 7).

The firm's value today is:

$$\frac{\$108.00}{1.16} + \frac{\$118.80}{1.16^2} + \frac{\$130.68}{1.16^3} + \frac{\$141.13}{1.16^4} + \frac{\$152.43 + 1,560.95}{1.16^5} = \$1,158.82$$

With 12 million shares outstanding, the price per share of GHCS would be $96.57 (= $1,158.82/12).

Now we have two estimates of the value of a share of equity in GHCS. The different estimates reflect the different ways of calculating terminal value. Using the constant growth discounted cash flow method for terminal value, our estimate of the equity value per share of GHCS is $98.74; using the PE comparable method, our estimate is $96.57. There is no best method. If the comparable firms were all identical to GHCS, perhaps the PE method would be best. Unfortunately, firms are not identical. On the other hand, if we were very sure of the terminal date and the growth in subsequent cash flows, perhaps the constant growth method would be best. In practice, both methods are used.

Conceptually, the dividend discount model, the comparables method, and the free cash flow model are mutually consistent and can be used to determine the value of a share of stock.

In practice, the dividend discount model is especially useful for firms paying very steady dividends, and the comparables method is useful for firms with similar growth opportunities. The free cash flow model is helpful for non-dividend-paying firms with external financing needs.

6.5 SOME FEATURES OF COMMON AND PREFERRED STOCKS

In discussing common stock features, we focus on shareholder rights and dividend payments. For preferred stock, we explain what the "preferred" means, and we also debate whether preferred stock is really debt or equity.

Common Stock Features

The term common stock means different things to different people, but it is usually applied to stock that has no special preference either in receiving dividends or in bankruptcy.

SHAREHOLDER RIGHTS The conceptual structure of the corporation assumes that shareholders elect directors, who, in turn, hire management to carry out their directives. Shareholders, therefore, control the corporation through the right to elect the directors. Generally, only shareholders have this right.

Directors are elected each year at an annual meeting. Although there are exceptions (discussed next), the general idea is "one share, one vote" (not one shareholder, one vote). Corporate democracy is thus very different from our political democracy. With corporate democracy, the "golden rule" prevails absolutely.[8]

Directors are elected at an annual shareholders' meeting by a vote of the holders of a majority of shares who are present and entitled to vote. However, the exact mechanism for electing directors differs across companies. The most important difference is whether shares must be voted cumulatively or voted straight.

To illustrate the two different voting procedures, imagine that a corporation has two shareholders: Smith with 20 shares and Jones with 80 shares. Both want to be a director. Jones does not want Smith, however. We assume there are a total of four directors to be elected.

The effect of cumulative voting is to permit minority participation.[9] If cumulative voting is permitted, the total number of votes that each shareholder may cast is determined first. This is usually calculated as the number of shares (owned or controlled) multiplied by the number of directors to be elected.

With cumulative voting, the directors are elected all at once. In our example, this means that the top four vote recipients will be the new directors. A shareholder can distribute votes however he/she wishes.

Will Smith get a seat on the board? If we ignore the possibility of a five-way tie, then the answer is yes. Smith will cast $20 \times 4 = 80$ votes, and Jones will cast $80 \times 4 = 320$ votes. If Smith gives all his votes to himself, he is assured of a directorship. The reason is that Jones can't divide 320 votes among four candidates in such a way as to give all of them more than 80 votes, so Smith will finish fourth at worst.

In general, if there are N directors up for election, then $1/(N + 1)$ percent of the stock plus one share will guarantee you a seat. In our current example, this is $1/(4 + 1) = 20$ percent. So the more seats that are up for election at one time, the easier (and cheaper) it is to win one.

With straight voting, the directors are elected one at a time. Each time, Smith can cast 20 votes and Jones can cast 80. As a consequence, Jones will elect all of the candidates.

---

[8] The golden rule: Whosoever has the gold makes the rules.

[9] By minority participation, we mean participation by shareholders with relatively small amounts of stock.

Buying the Election

Stock in JRJ Corporation sells for $20 per share and features cumulative voting. There are 10,000 shares outstanding. If three directors are up for election, how much does it cost to ensure yourself a seat on the board?

The question here is how many shares of stock it will take to get a seat. The answer is 2,501, so the cost is 2,501 × $20 = $50,020. Why 2,501? Because there is no way the remaining 7,499 votes can be divided among three people to give all of them more than 2,501 votes. Suppose two people receive 2,502 votes and the first two seats. A third person can receive at most 10,000 − 2,502 − 2,502 − 2,501 = 2,495, so the third seat is yours.

The only way to guarantee a seat is to own 50 percent plus one share. This also guarantees that you will win every seat, so it's really all or nothing.

As we've illustrated, straight voting can "freeze out" minority shareholders; that is the reason many states have mandatory cumulative voting. In states where cumulative voting is mandatory, devices have been worked out to minimize its impact.

One such device is to stagger the voting for the board of directors. With staggered elections, only a fraction of the directorships are up for election at a particular time. Thus, if only two directors are up for election at any one time, it will take $1/(2 + 1) = .3333$, or 33.33 percent of the stock plus one share to guarantee a seat.

Overall, staggering has two basic effects:

1. Staggering makes it more difficult for a minority to elect a director when there is cumulative voting because there are fewer directors to be elected at one time.

2. Staggering makes takeover attempts less likely to be successful because it makes it more difficult to vote in a majority of new directors.

We should note that staggering may serve a beneficial purpose. It provides "institutional memory," that is, continuity on the board of directors. This may be important for corporations with significant long-range plans and projects.

PROXY VOTING   A *proxy* is the grant of authority by a shareholder to someone else to vote his/her shares. For convenience, much of the voting in large public corporations is actually done by proxy.

As we have seen, with straight voting, each share of stock has one vote. The owner of 10,000 shares has 10,000 votes. Large companies have hundreds of thousands or even millions of shareholders. Shareholders can come to the annual meeting and vote in person, or they can transfer their right to vote to another party.

Obviously, management always tries to get as many proxies as possible transferred to it. However, if shareholders are not satisfied with management, an "outside" group of shareholders can try to obtain votes via proxy. They can vote by proxy in an attempt to replace management by electing enough directors. The resulting battle is called a *proxy fight.*

CLASSES OF STOCK   Some firms have more than one class of common stock. Often, the classes are created with unequal voting rights. The Ford Motor Company, for example, has Class B common stock, which is not publicly traded (it is held by Ford family interests and trusts). This class has 40 percent of the voting power, even though it represents less than 10 percent of the total number of shares outstanding.

There are many other cases of corporations with different classes of stock. For example, Adolph Coors Class B shares, which were owned by the public, had no votes at all except in the case of a merger. (Adolph Coors later merged with Molson.) The CEO of cable TV giant Comcast, Brian Roberts, owned about .4 percent of the company's equity, but he had a third of all the votes, thanks to a special class of stock. Another good example is Alphabet, which became publicly owned in 2004. Alphabet initially had two classes of common stock, A and B (it has recently added a third class). The Class A shares are held by the public, and each share has one vote. The Class B shares are held by company insiders, and each Class B share has 10 votes. Then, in 2014, the company had a stock split of its Class B shares, creating Class C shares, which have no vote at all. As a result, Alphabet's founders and managers control the company.

Historically, the New York Stock Exchange did not allow companies to create classes of publicly traded common stock with unequal voting rights. Exceptions (e.g., Ford) appear to have been made. In addition, many non-NYSE companies have dual classes of common stock.

A primary reason for creating dual or multiple classes of stock has to do with control of the firm. If such stock exists, management of a firm can raise equity capital by issuing nonvoting or limited-voting stock while maintaining control.

The subject of unequal voting rights is controversial in the United States, and the idea of one share, one vote has a strong following and a long history. Interestingly, however, shares with unequal voting rights are quite common in the United Kingdom and elsewhere around the world.

OTHER RIGHTS   The value of a share of common stock in a corporation is directly related to the general rights of shareholders. In addition to the right to vote for directors, shareholders usually have the following rights:

1. The right to share proportionally in dividends paid.
2. The right to share proportionally in assets remaining after liabilities have been paid in a liquidation.
3. The right to vote on stockholder matters of great importance, such as a merger. Voting is usually done at the annual meeting or a special meeting.

In addition, stockholders sometimes have the right to share proportionally in any new stock sold. This is called the *preemptive right.*

Essentially, a preemptive right means that a company that wishes to sell stock must first offer it to the existing stockholders before offering it to the general public. The purpose is to give a stockholder the opportunity to protect his/her proportionate ownership in the corporation.

DIVIDENDS   A distinctive feature of corporations is that they have shares of stock on which they are authorized by law to pay dividends to their shareholders. Dividends paid to shareholders represent a return on the capital directly or indirectly contributed to the corporation by the shareholders. The payment of dividends is at the discretion of the board of directors.

Some important characteristics of dividends include the following:

1. Unless a dividend is declared by the board of directors of a corporation, it is not a liability of the corporation. A corporation cannot default on an undeclared dividend. As a consequence, corporations cannot become bankrupt because of nonpayment of dividends. The amount of the dividend and even whether it is paid are decisions based on the business judgment of the board of directors.
2. The payment of dividends by the corporation is not a business expense. Dividends are not deductible for corporate tax purposes. In short, dividends are paid out of the corporation's after-tax profits.
3. Dividends received by individual shareholders are taxable. In 2019, the tax rate on qualified dividends was 15 to 20 percent. However, corporations that own stock in other corporations are permitted to exclude 50 percent of the dividend amounts they receive and are taxed on only the remaining 50 percent (the 50 percent exclusion was reduced from 70 percent by the Tax Cuts and Jobs Act of 2017).[10]

---

[10] For the record, the 50 percent exclusion applies when the recipient owns less than 20 percent of the outstanding stock in a corporation. If a corporation owns more than 20 percent but less than 80 percent, the exclusion is 65 percent. If more than 80 percent is owned, the corporation can file a single "consolidated" return, and the exclusion is effectively 100 percent.

Preferred Stock Features

Preferred stock differs from common stock because it has preference over common stock in the payment of dividends and in the distribution of corporation assets in the event of liquidation. *Preference* means only that the holders of the preferred shares must receive a dividend (in the case of an ongoing firm) before holders of common shares are entitled to anything.

Preferred stock is a form of equity from a legal and tax standpoint. It is important to note, however, that holders of preferred stock sometimes have no voting privileges.

STATED VALUE   Preferred shares have a stated liquidating value, usually $100 per share. The cash dividend is described in terms of dollars per share. For example, a "$5 preferred" easily translates into a dividend yield of 5 percent of stated value.

CUMULATIVE AND NONCUMULATIVE DIVIDENDS   A preferred dividend is not like interest on a bond. The board of directors may decide not to pay the dividends on preferred shares, and their decision may have nothing to do with the current net income of the corporation.

Dividends payable on preferred stock are either *cumulative* or *noncumulative;* most are cumulative. If preferred dividends are cumulative and are not paid in a particular year, they will be carried forward as an *arrearage.* Usually, both the accumulated (past) preferred dividends and the current preferred dividends must be paid before the common shareholders can receive anything.

Unpaid preferred dividends are not debts of the firm. Directors elected by the common shareholders can defer preferred dividends indefinitely. However, in such cases, common shareholders must also forgo dividends. In addition, holders of preferred shares are sometimes granted voting and other rights if preferred dividends have not been paid for some time.

IS PREFERRED STOCK REALLY DEBT?   A good case can be made that preferred stock is really debt in disguise, a kind of equity bond. Preferred shareholders receive a stated dividend only, and if the corporation is liquidated, preferred shareholders get a stated value. Often, preferred stocks carry credit ratings much like those of bonds. Furthermore, preferred stock is sometimes convertible into common stock, and preferred stocks are often callable.

In addition, many issues of preferred stock have obligatory sinking funds. The existence of such a sinking fund effectively creates a final maturity because it means that the entire issue will ultimately be retired. For these reasons, preferred stock seems to be a lot like debt. However, for tax purposes, preferred dividends are treated like common stock dividends.

In the 1990s, firms began to sell securities that look a lot like preferred stock but are treated as debt for tax purposes. The new securities were given interesting acronyms like TOPrS (trust-originated preferred securities, or toppers), MIPS (monthly income preferred securities), and QUIPS (quarterly income preferred securities), among others. Because of various specific features, these instruments can be counted as debt for tax purposes, making the interest payments tax deductible. Payments made to investors in these instruments are treated as interest for personal income taxes for individuals. Until 2003, interest payments and dividends were taxed at the same marginal tax rate. When the tax rate on dividend payments was reduced, these instruments were not included, so individuals must still pay the higher income tax rate on dividend payments received from these instruments.

6.6 THE STOCK MARKETS

Stock markets consist of a primary market and a secondary market. In the primary, or new-issue market, shares of stock are first brought to the market and sold to investors. In the secondary market, existing shares are traded among investors.

ExcelMaster
coverage online

In the primary market, companies sell securities to raise money. We will discuss this process in detail in a later chapter. We therefore focus mainly on secondary market activity in this section. We conclude with a discussion of how stock prices are quoted in the financial press.

Dealers and Brokers

Because most securities transactions involve dealers and brokers, it is important to understand exactly what is meant by the terms *dealer* and *broker*. A **dealer** maintains an inventory and stands ready to buy and sell at any time. In contrast, a **broker** brings buyers and sellers together but does not maintain an inventory. Thus, when we speak of used car dealers and real estate brokers, we recognize that the used car dealer maintains an inventory, whereas the real estate broker does not.

In the securities markets, a dealer stands ready to buy securities from investors wishing to sell them and sell securities to investors wishing to buy them. Recall from our previous chapter that the price the dealer is willing to pay is called the *bid price*. The price at which the dealer will sell is called the *ask price* (sometimes called the *asked, offered,* or *offering price*). The difference between the bid and ask prices is called the *spread,* and it is the basic source of dealer profits.

Dealers exist in all areas of the economy, not just the stock markets. For example, your local college bookstore is probably both a primary and a secondary market textbook dealer. If you buy a new book, this is a primary market transaction. If you buy a used book, this is a secondary market transaction, and you pay the store's ask price. If you sell the book back, you receive the store's bid price, often half of the ask price. The bookstore's spread is the difference between the two prices.

How big is the bid-ask spread on your favorite stock? Check out the latest quotes at www.bloomberg.com.

In contrast, a securities broker arranges transactions between investors, matching investors wishing to buy securities with investors wishing to sell securities. The distinctive characteristic of security brokers is that they do not buy or sell securities for their own accounts. Facilitating trades by others is their business.

Organization of the NYSE

The New York Stock Exchange, or NYSE, has been popularly known as the Big Board. It has occupied its current location on Wall Street since the turn of the twentieth century. Measured in terms of dollar volume of activity and the total value of shares listed, it is the largest stock market in the world.

MEMBERS Historically, the NYSE had 1,366 exchange members. Prior to 2006, the exchange members were said to own "seats" on the exchange, and, collectively, the members of the exchange were also the owners. For this and other reasons, seats were valuable and were bought and sold fairly regularly. Seat prices reached a record $4 million in 2005.

In 2006, all of this changed when the NYSE became a publicly owned corporation. Naturally, its stock is listed on the NYSE. Now, instead of purchasing seats, exchange members must purchase trading licenses, the number of which is limited to 1,366. In 2019, a license would set you back a cool $50,000—per year. Having a license entitles you to buy and sell securities on the floor of the exchange. Different members play different roles in this regard.

On April 4, 2007, the NYSE grew even larger when it merged with Euronext to form NYSE Euronext. Euronext was a stock exchange in Amsterdam, with subsidiaries in Belgium, France, Portugal, and the United Kingdom. With the merger, NYSE Euronext became the world's first global exchange, with trading occurring 21 hours each business day. Further expansion occurred in 2008 when NYSE Euronext merged with the American Stock Exchange. Then, in November 2013, the acquisition of the NYSE by the Intercontinental Exchange (ICE) was completed. ICE, which was founded in May 2000, was originally a commodities exchange, but its rapid growth gave it the necessary $8.2 billion for the acquisition of the NYSE.

As we briefly describe how the NYSE operates, keep in mind that other markets owned by NYSE Euronext and ICE may function differently. What makes the NYSE somewhat unique is that it is a *hybrid market*. In a hybrid market, trading takes place both electronically and face-to-face.

With electronic trading, orders to buy and orders to sell are submitted to the exchange. Orders are compared by a computer and, whenever there is a match, the orders are executed with no human intervention. Most trades on the NYSE occur this way. For orders that are not handled electronically, the NYSE relies on its license holders. There are three different types of license holders: **designated market makers (DMMs)**, **floor brokers**, and **supplemental liquidity providers (SLPs)**.

DMMs, formerly known as "specialists," act as dealers in particular stocks. Typically, each stock on the NYSE is assigned to a single DMM. As a dealer, a DMM maintains a two-sided market, meaning that the DMM continually posts and updates bid and ask prices. By doing so, the DMM ensures that there is always a buyer or seller available, thereby promoting market liquidity.

Floor brokers execute trades for customers, trying to get the best price possible. Floor brokers are generally employees of large brokerage firms such as Merrill Lynch, the wealth management division of Bank of America. The interaction between floor brokers and DMMs is the key to nonelectronic trading on the NYSE. We discuss this interaction in detail in a moment.

SLPs are essentially investment firms that agree to be active participants in stocks assigned to them. Their job is to regularly make a one-sided market (i.e., offering to either buy or sell). They trade purely for their own accounts (using their own money), so they do not represent customers. They are given a small rebate on their buys and sells, which encourages them to be more aggressive. The NYSE's goal is to generate as much liquidity as possible, which makes it easier for ordinary investors to quickly buy and sell at prevailing prices. Unlike DMMs and floor brokers, SLPs do not operate on the floor of the stock exchange.

OPERATIONS   Now that we have a basic idea of how the NYSE is organized and who the major players are, we turn to the question of how trading actually takes place. Fundamentally, the business of the NYSE is to attract and process **order flow**. The term *order flow* means the flow of customer orders to buy and sell stocks. The customers of the NYSE are the millions of individual investors and tens of thousands of institutional investors who place their orders to buy and sell shares in NYSE-listed companies. The NYSE has been quite successful in attracting order flow. Currently, it is not unusual for well over a billion shares to change hands in a single day.

FLOOR ACTIVITY   It is quite likely that you have seen footage of the NYSE trading floor on television, or you may have visited the NYSE and viewed exchange floor activity from the visitors' gallery. Either way, you would have seen a big room, about the size of a basketball gym. This big room is called, technically, "the Big Room." There are a few other, smaller rooms that you normally don't see, one of which is called "the Garage" because that is what it was before it was taken over for trading.

On the floor of the exchange are a number of stations, each with a roughly figure-eight shape. Each of the stations is a **DMM's post**. These stations have multiple counters with numerous terminal screens above and on the sides. DMMs normally operate in front of their posts to monitor and manage trading in the stocks assigned to them. Clerical employees working for the DMMs operate behind the counter. Moving around the exchange floor are floor brokers, who receive customer orders, walk out to DMMs' posts where the orders can be executed, and return to confirm order executions and receive new customer orders.

To better understand activity on the NYSE trading floor, imagine yourself as a floor broker. Your phone clerk has just handed you an order to sell 20,000 shares of Walmart

Take a virtual field trip to the New York Stock Exchange at www.nyse.com.

for a customer of the brokerage company that employs you. The customer wants to sell the stock at the best possible price as soon as possible. You immediately walk (running violates exchange rules) to the DMM's post where Walmart stock is traded.

As you approach the DMM's post where Walmart is traded, you check the terminal screen for information on the current market price. The screen reveals that the last executed trade was at $60.25 and that the DMM is bidding $60 per share. You could immediately sell to the DMM at $60, but that would be too easy.

Instead, as the customer's representative, you are obligated to get the best possible price. It is your job to "work" the order, and your job depends on providing satisfactory order execution service. So, you look around for another broker who represents a customer who wants to buy Walmart stock. Luckily, you quickly find another broker at the DMM's post with an order to buy 20,000 shares. Noticing that the DMM is asking $60.10 per share, you both agree to execute your orders with each other at a price of $60.05. This price is exactly halfway between the DMM's bid and ask prices, and it saves each of your customers .05 × 20,000 = $1,000 as compared to dealing at the posted prices.

For a very actively traded stock, there may be many buyers and sellers around the DMM's post, and most of the trading will be done directly between brokers. This is called trading in the "crowd." In such cases, the DMM's responsibility is to maintain order and to make sure that all buyers and sellers receive a fair price. In other words, the DMM essentially functions as a referee.

More often, however, there will be no crowd at the DMM's post. Going back to our Walmart example, suppose you are unable to quickly find another broker with an order to buy 20,000 shares. Because you have an order to sell immediately, you may have no choice but to sell to the DMM at the bid price of $60. In this case, the need to execute an order quickly takes priority, and the DMM provides the liquidity necessary to allow immediate order execution.

NASDAQ Operations

In terms of total dollar volume of trading, the second largest stock market in the United States is NASDAQ (say "Naz-dak"). The somewhat odd name originally was an acronym for the National Association of Securities Dealers Automated Quotation system, but NASDAQ is now a name in its own right.

Introduced in 1971, the NASDAQ market is a computer network of securities dealers and others that disseminates timely security price quotes to computer screens worldwide. NASDAQ dealers act as market makers for securities listed on NASDAQ. As market makers, NASDAQ dealers post bid and ask prices at which they accept sell and buy orders, respectively. With each price quote, they also post the number of stock shares that they obligate themselves to trade at their quoted prices.

Like NYSE DMMs, NASDAQ market makers trade on an inventory basis, that is, using their inventory as a buffer to absorb buy and sell order imbalances. Unlike the NYSE DMM system, NASDAQ features multiple market makers for actively traded stocks. Thus, there are two key differences between the NYSE and NASDAQ:

1. NASDAQ is a computer network and has no physical location where trading takes place.
2. NASDAQ has a multiple market maker system rather than a DMM system.

Traditionally, a securities market largely characterized by dealers who buy and sell securities for their own inventories is called an over-the-counter (OTC) market. Consequently, NASDAQ is often referred to as an OTC market. However, in their efforts to promote a distinct image, NASDAQ officials prefer that the term OTC not be used when referring to the NASDAQ market. Nevertheless, old habits die hard, and many people still refer to NASDAQ as an OTC market.

FINANCE MATTERS

THE WILD, WILD WEST OF STOCK TRADING

Where do companies go when they can't (or don't want to) meet the listing requirements of the larger stock markets? Two options are the Over-the-Counter Bulletin Board (OTCBB) and OTC Markets, formerly Pink Sheets. These two electronic markets are part of the Wild, Wild West of stock trading. The somewhat odd names have simple explanations. The OTCBB began as an electronic bulletin board that was created to facilitate OTC trading in nonlisted stocks. The name "Pink Sheets" reflects the fact that, at one time, prices for such stocks were quoted on pink sheets of paper.

The well-known markets such as NASDAQ and the NYSE have relatively strict listing requirements. If a company fails to meet these requirements, it can be delisted. The OTCBB and the OTC Markets, on the other hand, have no listing requirements. The OTCBB does require that companies file financial statements with the SEC (or other relevant agency), but the OTC Markets does not.

Stocks traded on these markets often have very low prices and are frequently referred to as "penny stocks," "microcaps," or even "nanocaps." Relatively few brokers do any research on these companies, so information is often spread through word of mouth or the internet, not the most reliable of sources. In fact, for many stocks, these markets often look like big electronic rumor mills and gossip factories. To get a feel for what trading looks like, we captured a typical screen from the OTCBB website (finra-markets.morningstar.com/MarketData/EquityOptions/default.jsp):

OOTC Equity

Most Actives	% Gainers	% Losers	Exchange by	OOTC ▼		
Symbol			Last	Chg	Chg %	Vol (mil) ▼
LVGI	▲		0.0011	0.0006	120.0000	330.2571
WOGI	▼		0.0002	-0.0001	-33.3333	235.4207
PBYA	▲		0.0006	0.0003	98.3333	176.0571
NOUV	▲		0.0012	0.0001	9.0909	173.9192
HVCW	▼		0.0013	-0.0004	-24.1176	157.1892
QEDN	▲		0.0005	0.0001	25.0000	154.0043
USMJ	▼		0.0012	-0.0001	-7.6923	143.7611
PSRU	▲		0.0002	0.0000	0.0000	130.7167
MSPC	▲		0.0003	0.0000	0.0000	130.2494
WDBG	▼		0.0026	-0.0081	-75.7009	0.0000

OOTC Equity

Most Actives	% Gainers	% Losers	Exchange by	OOTC ▼		
Symbol			Last	Chg	Chg % ▼	Vol (mil)
CHHCF	▲		0.0500	0.0499	49900.0000	0.0122
COWI	▲		0.0001	0.0001	9900.0000	0.0100
DNAG	▲		0.0001	0.0001	9900.0000	0.1075
EURI	▲		0.0001	0.0001	9900.0000	0.0120
EVTI	▲		0.0001	0.0001	9900.0000	0.0050
MKRYF	▲		0.0001	0.0001	9900.0000	0.0060
PTTN	▲		0.0001	0.0001	9900.0000	0.5000
TXMC	▲		0.0001	0.0001	9900.0000	0.3000
AIXN	▲		1.0000	0.9890	8990.9091	0.0000
BAKPF	▲		0.0020	0.0019	1900.0000	0.0045

Source: FINRA

First, take a look at the returns. Limitless Venture Group (LGVI) had a return for the day of 120 percent! That's not something you see every day. Of course, the big return was generated with a whopping price increase of $.0006 per share. A stock listed on the OTCBB is often the most actively traded stock on any particular day. For example, by the end of this particular day, General Electric was the most active stock on the NYSE, trading about 154 million shares. On the OTCBB, Limitless Venture traded about 478 million shares by the end of the day. But, at an average price of, say, $.0008 per share, the total dollar volume in Limitless Venture was all of $382,000. In contrast, trades in General Electric amounted to about $1.3 billion.

The OTC Markets (www.otcmarkets.com) is operated by a privately owned company. To be listed on the OTC Markets, a company just has to find a market maker willing to trade in the company's stock. Companies list on the OTC Markets for various reasons. Small companies that do not wish to meet listing requirements are one type. Another is foreign companies that often list on the OTC Markets because they do not prepare their financial statements according to GAAP, a requirement for listing on U.S. stock exchanges. There are many companies that were formerly listed on bigger stock markets that were either delisted involuntarily or chose to "go dark" for various reasons, including, as we discussed in Chapter 1, the costs associated with Sarbox compliance.

All in all, the OTCBB and the OTC Markets can be pretty wild places to trade. Low stock prices allow for huge percentage returns on small stock price movements. Be advised, however, that attempts at manipulation and fraud are commonplace. Also, stocks on these markets are often thinly traded, meaning there is little volume. It is not unusual for a stock listed on either market to have no trades on a given day. Even two or three days in a row without a trade in a particular stock is not uncommon.

The NASDAQ is actually made up of three separate markets: the NASDAQ Global Select Market, the NASDAQ Global Market, and the NASDAQ Capital Market. As the market for NASDAQ's larger and more actively traded securities, the Global Select Market lists about 1,600 companies (as of 2018), including some of the best-known companies in the world, such as Microsoft and Intel. The NASDAQ Global Market companies are somewhat smaller in size, and NASDAQ lists about 860 of them. Finally, the smallest companies listed on NASDAQ are in the NASDAQ Capital Market; about 940 or so are currently listed. Of course, as Capital Market companies become more established, they may move up to the Global Market or Global Select Market.

NASDAQ (www.nasdaq.com) has a great website; check it out!

ECNS In a very important development in the late 1990s, the NASDAQ system was opened to so-called **electronic communications networks (ECNs)**. ECNs are basically websites that allow investors to trade directly with one another. Investor buy and sell orders placed on ECNs are transmitted to the NASDAQ and displayed along with market maker bid and ask prices. As a result, the ECNs open up the NASDAQ by essentially allowing individual investors, not just market makers, to enter orders. As a result, the ECNs act to increase liquidity and competition.

Of course, the NYSE and NASDAQ are not the only places stocks are traded. See our nearby *Finance Matters* box for a discussion of somewhat wilder markets.

Stock Market Reporting

In recent years, the reporting of stock prices and related information has increasingly moved from traditional print media, such as *The Wall Street Journal*, to various websites. Yahoo! Finance (finance.yahoo.com) is a good example. We went there and requested a stock quote on wholesale club Costco, which is listed on the NASDAQ. Here is a portion of what we found:

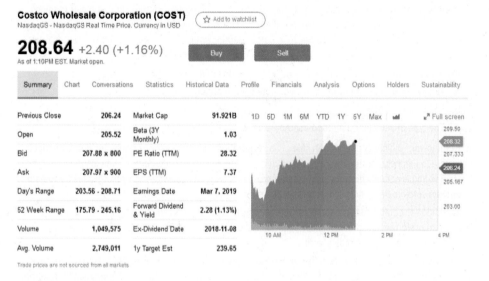

Source: finance.yahoo.com

Most of this information is self-explanatory. The most recent reported trade took place at 1:10 p.m. for $208.64. The reported change is from the previous day's closing price. The opening price is the first trade of the day. We see the bid and ask prices of $207.88 and $207.97, respectively, along with the market "depth," which is the number of shares sought at the bid price and offered at the ask price. The "1y Target Est" is the average estimated stock price one year ahead based on estimates from security analysts who follow the stock.

We are also shown the range of prices for this day, followed by the range over the previous 52 weeks. Volume is the number of shares traded today, followed by average daily volume over the last three months. Market cap is the number of shares outstanding (from the most recent quarterly financial statements) multiplied by the current price per share. P/E is the PE ratio we discussed earlier. The earnings per share (EPS) used in the calculation is "ttm," meaning "trailing twelve months." Finally, we have the dividend on the stock, which is actually the most recent quarterly dividend multiplied by 4, and the dividend yield. Notice that the yield is just the forward dividend divided by the stock price.

SUMMARY AND CONCLUSIONS

This chapter has covered the basics of stocks and stock valuations. The key points include:

1. A stock can be valued by discounting its dividends. We mention three types of situations:
   a. The case of zero growth of dividends.
   b. The case of constant growth of dividends.
   c. The case of differential growth.

2. An estimate of the growth rate of a stock is needed for the dividend discount model. A useful estimate of the growth rate is:

$$g = \text{Retention ratio} \times \text{Return on retained earnings (ROE)}$$

3. From accounting, we know that earnings are divided into two parts: dividends and retained earnings. Most firms continually retain earnings in order to create future dividends. One should not discount earnings to obtain price per share because part of earnings must be reinvested. Only dividends reach the stockholders, and only they should be discounted to obtain share price.

4. We suggest that a firm's price-earnings ratio is a function of three factors:
   a. The per-share amount of the firm's valuable growth opportunities.
   b. The risk of the stock.
   c. The type of accounting method used by the firm.

5. As the owner of shares of common stock in a corporation, you have various rights, including the right to vote to elect corporate directors. Voting in corporate elections can be either cumulative or straight. Most voting is actually done by proxy, and a proxy battle breaks out when competing sides try to gain enough votes to have their candidates for the board elected.

6. In addition to common stock, some corporations have issued preferred stock. The name stems from the fact that preferred stockholders must be paid first, before common stockholders can receive anything. Preferred stock has a fixed dividend.

7. The two biggest stock markets in the United States are the NYSE and the NASDAQ. We discussed the organization and operation of these two markets, and we saw how stock price information is reported.

CONCEPT QUESTIONS

1. **Stock Valuation**   Why does the value of a share of stock depend on dividends?
2. **Stock Valuation**   A substantial percentage of the companies listed on the NYSE and the NASDAQ don't pay dividends, but investors are nonetheless willing to buy shares in them. How is this possible given your answer to the previous question?
3. **Dividend Policy**   Referring to the previous questions, under what circumstances might a company choose not to pay dividends?
4. **Dividend Growth Model**   Under what two assumptions can we use the dividend growth model presented in the chapter to determine the value of a share of stock? Comment on the reasonableness of these assumptions.
5. **Common versus Preferred Stock**   Suppose a company has a preferred stock issue and a common stock issue. Both have just paid a $2 dividend. Which do you think will have a higher price, a share of the preferred or a share of the common?
6. **Dividend Growth Model**   Based on the dividend growth model, what are the two components of the total return on a share of stock? Which do you think is typically larger?
7. **Growth Rate**   In the context of the dividend growth model, is it true that the growth rate in dividends and the growth rate in the price of the stock are identical?
8. **Price-Earnings Ratio**   What are the three factors that determine a company's price-earnings ratio?
9. **Voting Rights**   When it comes to voting in elections, what are the differences between U.S. political democracy and U.S. corporate democracy?
10. **Corporate Ethics**   Is it unfair or unethical for corporations to create classes of stock with unequal voting rights?
11. **Voting Rights**   Some companies, such as Under Armour, have created classes of stock with no voting rights at all. Why would investors buy such stock?
12. **Stock Valuation**   Evaluate the following statement: Managers should not focus on the current stock value because doing so will lead to an overemphasis on short-term profits at the expense of long-term profits.

QUESTIONS AND PROBLEMS

Mc Graw Hill connect·

Basic
(Questions 1–13)

1. **Stock Values**   The Cricket Co. just paid a dividend of $3.14 per share on its stock. The dividends are expected to grow at a constant rate of 4 percent per year indefinitely. If investors require a return of 11 percent on the stock, what is the current price? What will the price be in 3 years? In 15 years?

2. **Stock Values**   The next dividend payment by Zone, Inc., will be $1.84 per share. The dividends are anticipated to maintain a growth rate of 4.4 percent forever. If the stock currently sells for $34 per share, what is the required return?

3. **Stock Values**   For the company in the previous problem, what is the dividend yield? What is the expected capital gains yield?

4. **Stock Values**   Romo Corporation will pay a dividend of $3.64 per share next year. The company pledges to increase its dividend by 4.3 percent per year indefinitely. If you require a return of 11 percent on your investment, how much will you pay for the company's stock today?

5. **Stock Valuation**   Douglas, Inc., is expected to maintain a constant 3.9 percent growth rate in its dividend indefinitely. If the company has a dividend yield of 5.6 percent, what is the required return on the company's stock?

6. **Stock Valuation**   Suppose you know that a company's stock currently sells for $76 per share and the required return on the stock is 10.8 percent. You also know that the total return on the stock is evenly divided between a capital gains yield and a dividend yield. If it's the company's policy to always maintain a constant growth rate in its dividends, what is the current dividend per share?

7. **Stock Valuation**   Griffith Corp. pays a constant $8.75 dividend on its stock. The company will maintain this dividend for the next eight years and will then cease paying dividends forever. If the required return on this stock is 10.9 percent, what is the current share price?

8. **Valuing Preferred Stock**   Ollie, Inc., has an issue of preferred stock outstanding that pays a dividend of $3.50 every year in perpetuity. If this issue currently sells for $96 per share, what is the required return?

9. **Growth Rate**   The newspaper reported last week that Jernigan Enterprises earned $31.5 million this year. The report also stated that the firm's return on equity is 13 percent. The firm retains 75 percent of its earnings. What is the firm's earnings growth rate? What will next year's earnings be?

10. **Stock Valuation and Required Return**   Red, Inc., Yellow Corp., and Blue Company each will pay a dividend of $3.08 next year. The growth rate in dividends for all three companies is 5 percent. The required return for each company's stock is 8 percent, 11 percent, and 14 percent, respectively. What is the stock price for each company? What do you conclude about the relationship between the required return and the stock price?

11. **Voting Rights**   After successfully completing your corporate finance class, you feel the next challenge ahead is to serve on the board of directors of Fitzpatrick Enterprises. Unfortunately, you will be the only person voting for you. If the company has 475,000 shares outstanding, and the stock currently sells for $46, how much will it cost you to buy a seat if the company uses straight voting?

12. **Voting Rights**   In the previous problem, assume that the company uses cumulative voting and there are four seats in the current election. How much will it cost you to buy a seat now?

13. **Stock Valuation and PE**   The Blooming Flower Co. has earnings of $4.21 per share. The benchmark PE for the company from a comparables analysis is 18. What stock price would you consider appropriate? What if the benchmark PE were 21?

Intermediate
(Questions 14–32)

14. **Stock Valuation**   BenchMark, Inc., just paid a dividend of $3.29 on its stock. The growth rate in dividends is expected to be a constant 4 percent per year indefinitely. Investors require a return of 15 percent on the stock for the first three years, a return of 13 percent for the next three years, and then a return of 10 percent thereafter. What is the current share price for the stock?

15. **Nonconstant Growth**   Metallica Bearings, Inc., is a young start-up company. No dividends will be paid on the stock over the next 9 years because the firm needs to plow back its earnings to fuel growth. The company will pay a dividend of $13 per share exactly 10 years from today and will increase the dividend by 5.5 percent per year thereafter. If the required return on this stock is 11 percent, what is the current share price?

16. **Nonconstant Dividends** Nelson, Inc., has an odd dividend policy. The company has just paid a dividend of $11 per share and has announced that it will increase the dividend by $3.50 per share for each of the next five years, and then never pay another dividend. If you require a return of 10 percent on the company's stock, how much will you pay for a share today?

 17. **Nonconstant Dividends** West Side Corporation is expected to pay the following dividends over the next four years: $15, $11, $9, and $2.65. Afterward, the company pledges to maintain a constant 5 percent growth rate in dividends forever. If the required return on the stock is 10 percent, what is the current share price?

18. **Differential Growth** Upton Co. is growing quickly. Dividends are expected to grow at 26 percent for the next three years, with the growth rate falling off to a constant 4.5 percent thereafter. If the required return is 10.4 percent and the company just paid a dividend of $2.45, what is the current share price?

19. **Differential Growth** Synovec Corp. is experiencing rapid growth. Dividends are expected to grow at 25 percent per year during the next three years, 17 percent over the following year, and then 4 percent per year indefinitely. The required return on this stock is 10 percent, and the stock currently sells for $71 per share. What is the projected dividend for the coming year?

20. **Negative Growth** Antiques R Us is a mature manufacturing firm. The company just paid a dividend of $14, but management expects to reduce the payout by 3 percent per year indefinitely. If you require a return of 9.6 percent on this stock, what will you pay for a share today?

21. **Finding the Dividend** Maddon Corporation stock currently sells for $57.13 per share. The market requires a return of 11 percent on the firm's stock. If the company maintains a constant 4 percent growth rate in dividends, what was the most recent dividend per share paid on the stock?

22. **Valuing Preferred Stock** Fifth National Bank just issued some new preferred stock. The issue will pay an annual dividend of $7 in perpetuity, beginning 10 years from now. If the market requires a return of 4.1 percent on this investment, how much does a share of preferred stock cost today?

23. **Using Stock Quotes** You have found the following stock quote for RJW Enterprises, Inc., in the financial pages of today's newspaper. What is the annual dividend? What was the closing price for this stock that appeared in yesterday's paper? If the company currently has 25 million shares of stock outstanding, what was net income for the most recent four quarters?

YTD %CHG	STOCK	SYM	YLD	PE	LAST	NET CHG
7.3	RJW Enterp.	RJW	2.4	22	43.23	.19

24. **Taxes and Stock Price** You own $100,000 worth of Smart Money stock. One year from now, you will receive a dividend of $3.15 per share. You will receive a dividend of $3.27 two years from now. You will sell the stock for $106 per share three years from now. Dividends are taxed at the rate of 20 percent. Assume there is no capital gains tax. The required aftertax rate of return is 9 percent. How many shares of stock do you own?

25. **Nonconstant Growth and Quarterly Dividends** Richard, Inc., will pay a quarterly dividend per share of $.61 at the end of each of the next 12 quarters. Thereafter, the dividend will grow at a quarterly rate of 1.1 percent forever. The appropriate rate of return on the stock is 11 percent, compounded quarterly. What is the current stock price?

26. **Finding the Dividend** Amos, Inc., is expected to pay equal dividends at the end of each of the next two years. Thereafter, the dividend will grow at a constant annual rate of 4 percent forever. The current stock price is $76. What is next year's dividend payment if the required rate of return is 9.8 percent?

 27. **Finding the Required Return** Juggernaut Satellite Corporation earned $36.3 million for the fiscal year ending yesterday. The firm also paid out 30 percent of its earnings as dividends yesterday. The firm will continue to pay out 30 percent of its earnings as annual, end-of-year dividends. The remaining 70 percent of earnings is retained by the company for use in projects. The company has 2.7 million shares of common stock outstanding. The current stock price is $116. The historical return on equity (ROE) of 12 percent is expected to continue in the future. What is the required rate of return on the stock?

28. **Dividend Growth** Four years ago, Bling Diamond, Inc., paid a dividend of $1.02 per share. The firm paid a dividend of $1.87 per share yesterday. Dividends will grow over the next five years at the same

rate they grew over the last four years. Thereafter, dividends will grow at 5 percent per year. What will the firm's cash dividend be in seven years?

29. **Price-Earnings Ratio** Consider Pacific Energy Company and U.S. Bluechips, Inc., both of which reported earnings of $1.4 million. Without new projects, both firms will continue to generate earnings of $1.4 million in perpetuity. Assume that all earnings are paid as dividends and that both firms require a return of 12 percent.

    a. What is the current PE for each company?

    b. Pacific Energy Company has a new project that will generate additional earnings of $330,000 each year in perpetuity. Calculate the new PE ratio of the company.

    c. U.S. Bluechips has a new project that will increase earnings by $660,000 each year in perpetuity. Calculate the new PE ratio of the company.

30. **Stock Valuation and PE** Sparrow Corp. currently has an EPS of $3.75, and the benchmark PE for the company is 18. Earnings are expected to grow at 6.5 percent per year.

    a. What is your estimate of the current stock price?

    b. What is the target stock price in one year?

    c. Assuming the company pays no dividends, what is the implied return on the company's stock over the next year? What does this tell you about the implicit stock return using PE valuation?

31. **Stock Valuation and EV** Bootstrap Corp. has yearly sales of $42.8 million and costs of $24.6 million. The company's balance sheet shows debt of $63 million and cash of $24 million. There are 960,000 shares outstanding, and the industry EV/EBITDA multiple is 7.5. What is the company's enterprise value? What is the stock price per share?

32. **Stock Valuation and Cash Flows** Anya Manufacturing has projected sales of $138 million next year. Costs are expected to be $77 million, and net investment is expected to be $11 million. Each of these values is expected to grow at 14 percent the following year, with the growth rate declining by 2 percent per year until the growth rate reaches 6 percent, where it is expected to remain indefinitely. There are 6.2 million shares of stock outstanding, and investors require a return of 12 percent on the company's stock. The corporate tax rate is 21 percent.

    a. What is your estimate of the current stock price?

    b. Suppose instead that you estimate the terminal value of the company using a PE multiple. The industry PE multiple is 12. What is your new estimate of the company's stock price?

33. **Capital Gains versus Income** Consider four different stocks, all of which have a required return of 16 percent and a most recent dividend of $4.15 per share. Stocks W, X, and Y are expected to maintain constant growth rates in dividends for the foreseeable future of 10 percent, 0 percent, and −5 percent per year, respectively. Stock Z is a growth stock that will increase its dividend by 30 percent for the next two years and then maintain a constant 8 percent growth rate thereafter. What is the dividend yield for each of these four stocks? What is the expected capital gains yield? Discuss the relationship among the various returns that you find for each of these stocks.

Challenge
(Questions 33–36)

34. **Stock Valuation** Most corporations pay quarterly dividends on their common stock rather than annual dividends. Barring any unusual circumstances during the year, the board raises, lowers, or maintains the current dividend once a year and then pays this dividend out in equal quarterly installments to its shareholders.

    a. Suppose a company currently pays an annual dividend of $3.24 on its common stock in a single annual installment, and management plans on raising this dividend by 4 percent per year indefinitely. If the required return on this stock is 11 percent, what is the current share price?

    b. Now suppose that the company in (a) actually pays its annual dividend in equal quarterly installments; thus, this company has just paid a dividend per share of $.81, as it has for the previous three quarters. What is your value for the current share price now? (*Hint:* Find the equivalent annual end-of-year dividend for each year.) Comment on whether you think this model of stock valuation is appropriate.

35. **Nonconstant Growth** Storico Co. just paid a dividend of $3.65 per share. The company will increase its dividend by 16 percent next year and will then reduce its dividend growth rate by 4 percentage

points per year until it reaches the industry average of 4 percent dividend growth, after which the company will keep a constant growth rate forever. If the required return on the company's stock is 10.5 percent, what will a share of stock sell for today?

36. **Nonconstant Growth**   This one's a little harder. Suppose the current share price for the firm in the previous problem is $81.15 and all the dividend information remains the same. What required return must investors be demanding on the company's stock? (*Hint:* Set up the valuation formula with all the relevant cash flows, and use trial and error to find the unknown rate of return.)

WHAT'S ON THE WEB?

1. **Dividend Discount Model**   According to the 2018 Value Line *Investment Survey,* the dividend growth rate for Johnson & Johnson (JNJ) is 8 percent. Find the current price quote and dividend information at finance.yahoo.com. If the growth rate given in the Value Line *Investment Survey* is correct, what is the required return for Johnson & Johnson? Does this number make sense to you?

EXCEL MASTER IT! PROBLEM

ExcelMaster
coverage online

www.mhhe.com/RossCore6e

In practice, the use of the dividend discount model is refined from the method we presented in the textbook. Many analysts will estimate the dividend for the next 5 years and then estimate a perpetual growth rate at some point in the future, typically 10 years. Rather than have the dividend growth fall dramatically from the fast growth period to the perpetual growth period, linear interpolation is applied. That is, the dividend growth is projected to fall by an equal amount each year. For example, if the high growth period is 15 percent for the next 5 years and the dividends are expected to fall to a 5 percent perpetual growth rate 5 years later, the dividend growth rate would decline by 2 percent each year.

The Value Line *Investment Survey* provides information for investors. Below, you will find information for Microsoft found in the 2018 edition of Value Line:

2019 dividend	$1.84
5-year dividend growth rate	12.5%

Although Value Line does not provide a perpetual growth rate or required return, we will assume they are:

Perpetual growth rate	4.5%
Required return	11.0%

a. Assume that the perpetual growth rate begins 11 years from now and use linear interpolation between the high growth rate and perpetual growth rate. Construct a table that shows the dividend growth rate and dividend each year. What is the stock price at Year 10? What is the stock price today?

b. How sensitive is the current stock price to changes in the perpetual growth rate? Graph the current stock price against the perpetual growth rate in 11 years to find out.

Instead of applying the constant dividend growth model to find the stock price in the future, analysts will often combine the dividend discount method with price ratio valuation, often with the PE ratio. Remember that the PE ratio is the price per share divided by the earnings per share. So, if we know what the PE ratio is, we can solve for the stock price. Suppose we also have the following information about Microsoft:

Payout ratio	30%
PE ratio at constant growth rate	17

c. Use the PE ratio to calculate the stock price when Microsoft reaches a perpetual growth rate in dividends. Now find the value of the stock today using the present value of the dividends during the nonconstant growth rate period and the price you calculated using the PE ratio.

d. How sensitive is the current stock price to changes in the PE ratio when the stock reaches the perpetual growth rate? Graph the current stock price against the PE ratio in 11 years to find out.

STOCK VALUATION AT RAGAN ENGINES

Larissa has been talking with the company's directors about the future of East Coast Yachts. To this point, the company has used outside suppliers for various key components of the company's yachts, including engines. Larissa has decided that East Coast Yachts should consider the purchase of an engine manufacturer to allow East Coast Yachts to better integrate its supply chain and get more control over engine features. After investigating several possible companies, Larissa feels that the purchase of Ragan Engines, Inc., is a possibility. She has asked Dan Ervin to analyze Ragan's value.

Ragan Engines, Inc., was founded nine years ago by a brother and sister—Carrington and Genevieve Ragan—and has remained a privately owned company. The company manufactures marine engines for a variety of applications. Ragan has experienced rapid growth because of a proprietary technology that increases the fuel efficiency of its engines with very little sacrifice in performance. The company is equally owned by Carrington and Genevieve. The original agreement between the siblings gave each 125,000 shares of stock.

Larissa has asked Dan to determine a value per share of Ragan stock. To accomplish this, Dan has gathered the following information about some of Ragan's competitors that are publicly traded:

	EPS	DPS	STOCK PRICE	ROE	R
Blue Ribband Motors Corp.	$1.24	$ .39	$20.10	11.00%	14.00%
Bon Voyage Marine, Inc.	1.55	.47	16.85	14.00	17.00
Nautilus Marine Engines	−.25	.67	31.60	N/A	13.00
Industry average	$ .85	$ .51	$22.85	12.50%	14.67%

Nautilus Marine Engines' negative earnings per share (EPS) was the result of an accounting write-off last year. Without the write-off, EPS for the company would have been $1.93. Last year, Ragan had an EPS of $3.65 and paid a dividend to Carrington and Genevieve of $195,000 each. The company also had a return on equity of 18 percent. Larissa tells Dan that a required return for Ragan of 13 percent is appropriate.

1. Assuming the company continues its current growth rate, what is the value per share of the company's stock?

2. Dan has examined the company's financial statements and those of its competitors. Although Ragan currently has a technological advantage, Dan's research indicates that Ragan's competitors are investigating other methods to improve efficiency. Given this, Dan believes that Ragan's technological advantage will last only for the next five years. After that period, the company's growth will likely slow to the industry average. Additionally, Dan believes that the required return the company uses is too high. He believes the industry average required return is more appropriate. Under Dan's assumptions, what is the estimated stock price?

3. What is the industry average price-earnings ratio? What is Ragan's price-earnings ratio? Comment on any differences and explain why they may exist.

4. Assume the company's growth rate slows to the industry average in five years. What future return on equity does this imply?

5. Carrington and Genevieve are not sure if they should sell the company. If they do not sell the company outright to East Coast Yachts, they would like to try and increase the value of the company's stock. In this case, they want to retain control of the company and do not want to sell stock to outside investors. They also feel that the company's debt is at a manageable level and do not want to borrow more money. What steps can they take to try and increase the price of the stock? Are there any conditions under which this strategy would not increase the stock price?

Net Present Value and Other Investment Rules

In March 2018, SoftBank, which is known for its large deals, signed a memorandum of understanding with Saudi Arabia to build a $200 billion solar power plant in that country. Of course, other companies announced new investments in 2018. Nauticol Energy announced plans to build a $2 billion methanol plant in Canada, and Formosa Chemical announced it would build a $9.4 billion chemical manufacturing plant in St. James Parish, Louisiana.

All three of these projects are examples of capital budgeting decisions. Decisions such as these, with price tags of up to $200 billion, are obviously major undertakings, and the risks and rewards must be carefully weighed. In this chapter, we discuss the basic tools used in making such decisions.

In Chapter 1, we saw that increasing the value of the stock in a company is the goal of financial management. Thus, what we need to know is how to tell whether a particular investment will achieve that or not. This chapter considers a variety of techniques that are used in practice for this purpose. More importantly, it shows how many of these techniques can be misleading, and it explains why the net present value approach is the right one.

Please visit us at corecorporatefinance.blogspot.com for the latest developments in the world of corporate finance.

7.1 WHY USE NET PRESENT VALUE?

ExcelMaster
coverage online

www.mhhe.com/RossCore6e

This chapter, as well as the next two, focuses on *capital budgeting,* the decision-making process for accepting or rejecting projects. This chapter develops the basic capital budgeting methods, leaving much of the practical application to Chapters 8 and 9. But we don't have to develop these methods from scratch. In Chapter 4, we pointed out that a dollar received in the future is worth less than a dollar received today. The reason, of course, is that today's dollar can be reinvested, yielding a greater amount in the future. And we showed in Chapter 4 that the exact worth of a dollar to be received in the future is its present value. Furthermore, Section 4.1 suggested calculating the net present value of any project. That is, the section suggested calculating the difference between the sum of the present values of the project's future cash flows and the initial cost of the project.

Find out more about capital budgeting for small businesses at www.missouribusiness.net.

The net present value (NPV) method is the first one to be considered in this chapter. We begin by reviewing the approach with a simple example. Next, we ask why the method leads to good decisions.

The basic investment rule can be generalized to:

Accept a project if the NPV is greater than zero.

Reject a project if the NPV is less than zero.

We refer to this as the NPV rule.

Now why does the NPV rule lead to good decisions? Consider the following two strategies available to the managers of Alpha Corporation:

1. Use $100 of corporate cash to invest in the project. The $107 will be paid as a dividend in one year.

2. Forgo the project and pay the $100 of corporate cash as a dividend today.

If Strategy 2 is employed, the stockholder might deposit the dividend in his bank for one year. With an interest rate of 6 percent, Strategy 2 would produce cash of $106 (= $100 × 1.06) at the end of the year. The stockholder would prefer Strategy 1 because Strategy 2 produces less than $107 at the end of the year.

Thus, our basic point is:

Accepting positive NPV projects benefits the stockholders.

EXAMPLE 7.1

Net Present Value

The Alpha Corporation is considering investing in a riskless project costing $100. The project receives $107 in one year and has no other cash flows. The discount rate is 6 percent.

The NPV of the project can be calculated as:

$$\$.94 = -\$100 + \frac{\$107}{1.06}$$

From Chapter 4, we know that the project should be accepted because its NPV is positive. Had the NPV of the project been negative, as would have been the case with an interest rate greater than 7 percent, the project should be rejected.

How do we interpret the exact NPV of $.94? This is the increase in the value of the firm from the project. For example, imagine that the firm today has productive assets worth $V and has $100 of cash. If the firm forgoes the project, the value of the firm today would be:

You can get a freeware NPV calculator at www.wheatworks.com.

$$\$V + \$100$$

If the firm accepts the project, the firm will receive $107 in one year but will have no cash today. Thus, the firm's value today would be:

$$\$V + \frac{\$107}{1.06}$$

The difference between the above equations is just $.94, the present value of Example 7.1. Thus:

The value of the firm rises by the NPV of the project.

Note that the value of the firm is the sum of the values of the different projects, divisions, or other entities within the firm. This property, called value additivity, is quite important. It implies that the contribution of any project to a firm's value is the NPV of the project. As we will see later, alternative methods discussed in this chapter do not generally have this nice property.

One detail remains. We assumed that the project was riskless, a rather implausible assumption. Future cash flows of real-world projects are invariably risky. In other words, cash flows can only be estimated, rather than known. Imagine that the managers of Alpha expect the cash flow of the project to be $107 next year. That is, the cash flow could be higher, say $117, or lower, say $97. With this slight change, the project is risky. Suppose the project is about as risky as the stock market as a whole, where the expected return this year is, say, 10 percent. Then 10 percent becomes the discount rate, implying that the NPV of the project would be:

$$-\$2.73 = -\$100 + \frac{\$107}{1.10}$$

Because the NPV is negative, the project should be rejected. This makes sense because a stockholder of Alpha receiving a $100 dividend today could invest it in the stock market, expecting a 10 percent return. Why accept a project with the same risk as the market but with an expected return of only 7 percent?

Conceptually, the discount rate on a risky project is the return that one can expect to earn on a financial asset of comparable risk. This discount rate is often referred to as an *opportunity cost* because corporate investment in the project takes away the stockholder's opportunity to invest the same cash in a financial asset. The calculation is by no means impossible. While we forgo the calculation in this chapter, we present it in Chapter 12.

Having shown that NPV is a sensible approach, how can we tell whether alternative methods are as good as NPV? The key to NPV is its three attributes:

1. *NPV Uses Cash Flows.* Cash flows from a project can be used for other corporate purposes (e.g., dividend payments, other capital budgeting projects, or payments of corporate interest). By contrast, earnings are an artificial construct. While earnings are useful to accountants, they should not be used in capital budgeting because they do not represent cash.

2. *NPV Uses All the Cash Flows of the Project.* Other approaches ignore cash flows beyond a particular date; beware of these approaches.

3. *NPV Discounts the Cash Flows Properly.* Other approaches may ignore the time value of money when handling cash flows. Beware of these approaches as well.

Calculating NPVs by hand can be tedious. A nearby *Spreadsheet Techniques* box shows how to do it the easy way and also illustrates an important caveat.

7.2 THE PAYBACK PERIOD METHOD

Defining the Rule

ExcelMaster
coverage online
www.mhhe.com/RossCore6e

One of the most popular alternatives to NPV is payback. Here is how payback works: Consider a project with an initial investment of −$50,000. Cash flows are $30,000, $20,000, and $10,000 in the first three years, respectively. These flows are illustrated in Figure 7.1. A useful way of writing investments like the preceding is with the notation:

(−$50,000, $30,000, $20,000, $10,000)

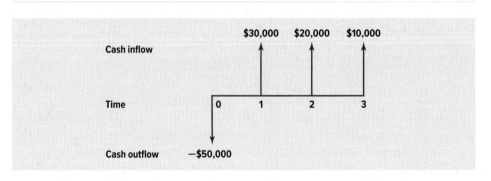

FIGURE 7.1

Cash Flows of an Investment Project

Spreadsheets are commonly used to calculate NPVs. Examining the use of spreadsheets in this context also allows us to issue an important warning. Consider the following:

	A	B	C	D	E	F	G	H
1								
2			Using a spreadsheet to calculate net present values					
3								
4	A project's cost is $10,000. The cash flows are $2,000 per year for the first two years,							
5	$4,000 per year for the next two, and $5,000 in the last year. The discount rate is							
6	10 percent; what's the NPV?							
7								
8		Year	Cash flow					
9		0	-$10,000		Discount rate =		10%	
10		1	2,000					
11		2	2,000		NPV =	$2,102.72	(wrong answer)	
12		3	4,000		NPV =	$2,312.99	(right answer)	
13		4	4,000					
14		5	5,000					
15								
16	The formula entered in cell F11 is =NPV(F9, C9:C14). However, this gives the wrong answer because the							
17	NPV function actually calculates present values, not *net* present values.							
18								
19	The formula entered in cell F12 is =NPV(F9, C10:C14) + C9. This gives the right answer because the							
20	NPV function is used to calculate the present value of the cash flows and then the initial cost is							
21	subtracted to calculate the answer. Notice that we added cell C9 because it is already negative.							

In our spreadsheet example, notice that we have provided two answers. The first answer is wrong even though we used the spreadsheet's NPV formula. What happened is that the "NPV" function in our spreadsheet is actually a PV function; unfortunately, one of the original spreadsheet programs many years ago got the definition wrong, and subsequent spreadsheets have copied it! Our second answer shows how to use the formula properly.

The example here illustrates the danger of blindly using calculators or computers without understanding what is going on; we shudder to think of how many capital budgeting decisions in the real world are based on incorrect use of this particular function.

The minus sign in front of the $50,000 reminds us that this is a cash outflow for the investor, and the commas between the different numbers indicate that they are received—or if they are cash outflows, that they are paid out—at different times. In this example, we are assuming that the cash flows occur one year apart, with the first one occurring the moment we decide to take on the investment.

The firm receives cash flows of $30,000 and $20,000 in the first two years, which add up to the $50,000 original investment. This means that the firm has recovered its investment within two years. In this case, two years is the *payback period* of the investment.

The payback period rule for making investment decisions is simple and potentially informative. The payback tells us when the cash outflow of an investment is "paid back" by cash inflows. If a particular cutoff date, say two years, is selected, all investment projects that have payback periods of two years or less are accepted and all of those that pay off in more than two years—if at all—are rejected.

Problems with the Payback Method

There are at least three problems with payback. To illustrate the first two problems, we consider the three projects in Table 7.1. All three projects have the same three-year payback period, so they should all be equally attractive—right?

Actually, they are not equally attractive, as can be seen by a comparison of different pairs of projects. To illustrate the payback period problems, consider Table 7.1. Suppose the expected return on comparable risky projects is 10 percent. Then we would use a discount rate of 10 percent for these projects. If so, the NPV would be $21.52, $26.26, and $53.58 for A, B,

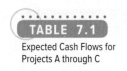
TABLE 7.1

Expected Cash Flows for
Projects A through C

Year	A	B	C
0	−$100	−$100	−$100
1	20	50	50
2	30	30	30
3	50	20	20
4	60	60	100
Payback period (years)	3	3	3

and C, respectively. When using the payback period, these projects are equal to one another, that is, they each have a payback period of three years. However, when considering all cash flows, B has a higher NPV than A because of the timing of cash flows within the payback period. And C has the highest NPV because of the $100 cash flow after the payback period.

PROBLEM 1: TIMING OF CASH FLOWS WITHIN THE PAYBACK PERIOD Let us compare Project A with Project B. In Years 1 through 3, the cash flows of Project A rise from $20 to $50, while the cash flows of Project B fall from $50 to $20. Because the large cash flow of $50 comes earlier with Project B, its net present value must be higher. Nevertheless, we saw above that the payback periods of the two projects are identical. Thus, a problem with the payback method is that it does not consider the timing of the cash flows within the payback period. This example shows that the payback method is inferior to NPV because, as we pointed out earlier, the NPV method discounts the cash flows properly.

PROBLEM 2: PAYMENTS AFTER THE PAYBACK PERIOD Now consider Projects B and C, which have identical cash flows within the payback period. However, Project C is clearly preferred because it has a cash flow of $100 in the fourth year. Thus, another problem with the payback method is that it ignores all cash flows occurring after the payback period. Because of the short-term orientation of the payback method, some valuable long-term projects are likely to be rejected. The NPV method does not have this flaw because, as we pointed out earlier, this method uses all the cash flows of the project.

PROBLEM 3: ARBITRARY STANDARD FOR PAYBACK PERIOD We do not need to refer to Table 7.1 when considering a third problem with the payback method. Capital markets help us estimate the discount rate used in the NPV method. The risk-free rate, perhaps proxied by the yield on a Treasury instrument, would be the appropriate rate for a riskless investment. Later chapters of this textbook show how to use returns in the capital markets in order to estimate the discount rate for a risky project. However, there is no comparable guide for choosing the payback cutoff date, so the choice is somewhat arbitrary.

Managerial Perspective

The payback method is often used by large, sophisticated companies when making relatively small decisions. The decision to build a small warehouse, for example, or to pay for a tune-up for a truck is the sort of decision that is often made by lower-level management. Typically, a manager might reason that a tune-up would cost, say, $200, and if it saved $120 each year in reduced fuel costs, it would pay for itself in less than two years. On such a basis the decision would be made.

Although the treasurer of the company might not have made the decision in the same way, the company endorses such decision making. Why would upper management condone or even encourage such retrograde activity in its employees? One answer would be that it is easy to make decisions using payback. Multiply the tune-up decision into 50 such decisions a month and the appeal of this simple method becomes clearer.

The payback method also has some desirable features for managerial control. As important as the investment decision itself is the company's ability to evaluate the manager's decision-making ability. Under the NPV method, a long time may pass before one can determine whether or not a decision was correct. With the payback method, we may know in a few years whether the manager's assessment of the cash flows was correct.

It has also been suggested that firms with good investment opportunities but no available cash may justifiably use payback. For example, the payback method could be used by small, privately held firms with good growth prospects but limited access to the capital markets. Quick cash recovery enhances the reinvestment possibilities for such firms.

Finally, practitioners often argue that standard academic criticisms of payback overstate any real-world problems with the method. For example, textbooks typically make fun of payback by positing a project with low cash inflows in the early years but a huge cash inflow right after the payback cutoff date. This project is likely to be rejected under the payback method, though its acceptance would, in truth, benefit the firm. Project C in our Table 7.1 is an example of such a project. Practitioners point out that the pattern of cash flows in these textbook examples is much too stylized to mirror the real world. In fact, a number of executives have told us that, for the overwhelming majority of real-world projects, both payback and NPV lead to the same decision. In addition, these executives indicate that, if an investment like Project C were encountered in the real world, decision makers would almost certainly make *ad hoc* adjustments to the payback rule so that the project would be accepted.

Notwithstanding all of the preceding rationale, it is not surprising to discover that as the decisions grow in importance, which is to say when firms look at bigger projects, NPV becomes the order of the day. When questions of controlling and evaluating the manager become less important than making the right investment decision, payback is used less frequently. For big-ticket decisions, such as whether or not to buy a machine, build a factory, or acquire a company, the payback method is seldom used.

Summary of Payback

The payback method differs from NPV and is therefore conceptually wrong. With its arbitrary cutoff date and its blindness to cash flows after that date, it can lead to some flagrantly foolish decisions if it is used too literally. Nevertheless, because of its simplicity, as well as its other advantages mentioned above, companies often use it as a screen for making the myriad minor investment decisions they continually face.

Although this means that you should be wary of trying to change approaches such as the payback method when you encounter them in companies, you should probably be careful not to accept the sloppy financial thinking they represent. After this course, you would do your company a disservice if you used payback instead of NPV when you had a choice.

7.3 THE DISCOUNTED PAYBACK PERIOD METHOD

ExcelMaster
coverage online
www.mhhe.com/RossCore6e

Aware of the pitfalls of payback, some decision makers use a variant called the discounted payback period method. Under this approach, we first discount the cash flows. Then we ask how long it takes for the discounted cash flows to equal the initial investment.

Suppose that the discount rate is 10 percent and the cash flows for a project are given by:

(−$100, $50, $50, $20)

This investment has a payback period of two years because the investment is paid back in that time.

To compute the project's discounted payback period, we first discount each of the cash flows at the 10 percent rate. These discounted cash flows are:

(−$100, $50/1.1, $50/1.1^2, $20/1.1^3) = (−$100, $45.45, $41.32, $15.03)

The discounted payback period of the original investment is the payback period for these discounted cash flows. The payback period for the discounted cash flows is slightly less than three years because the discounted cash flows over the three years are $101.80 (= \$45.45 + 41.32 + 15.03)$. As long as the cash flows are positive, the discounted payback period will never be smaller than the payback period because discounting reduces the value of the cash flows.

At first glance, discounted payback may seem like an attractive alternative, but on closer inspection we see that it has some of the same major flaws as payback. Like payback, discounted payback first requires us to make a somewhat magical choice of an arbitrary cutoff period, and then it ignores all of the cash flows after that date.

If we have already gone to the trouble of discounting the cash flows, any small appeal to simplicity or to managerial control that payback may have has been lost. We might as well add up all the discounted cash flows and use NPV to make the decision. Although discounted payback looks a bit like NPV, it is a poor compromise between the payback method and NPV.

7.4 THE AVERAGE ACCOUNTING RETURN METHOD

Defining the Rule

ExcelMaster coverage online

www.mhhe.com/RossCore6e

Another attractive, but fatally flawed, approach to capital budgeting is the **average accounting return**. The average accounting return is the average project earnings after taxes and depreciation, divided by the average book value of the investment during its life. In spite of its flaws, the average accounting return method is worth examining because it is sometimes used in the real world.

It is worth examining Table 7.2 carefully. In fact, the first step in any project assessment is a careful look at projected cash flows. First-year sales for the store are estimated to be $433,333. Before-tax cash flow will be $233,333. Sales are expected to rise and expenses are expected to fall in the second year, resulting in a before-tax cash flow of $300,000.

Competition from other stores and the loss in novelty will reduce before-tax cash flow to $166,667, $100,000, and $33,333, respectively, in the next three years.

To compute the average accounting return (AAR) on the project, we divide the average net income by the average amount invested. This can be done in three steps.

STEP 1: DETERMINING AVERAGE NET INCOME Net income in any year is net cash flow minus depreciation and taxes. Depreciation is not a cash outflow.[1] Rather, it is a charge reflecting the fact that the investment in the store becomes less valuable every year.

We assume the project has a useful life of five years, at which time it will be worthless. Because the initial investment is $500,000 and because it will be worthless in five years, we assume that it loses value at the rate of $100,000 each year. This steady loss in value of $100,000 is called straight-line depreciation. We subtract both depreciation and taxes from before-tax cash flow to derive net income, as shown in Table 7.2. Net income is $100,000 in the first year, $150,000 in Year 2, $50,000 in Year 3, $0 in Year 4, and −$50,000 in the last year. The average net income over the life of the project is therefore:

Average Net Income:

[$100,000 + 150,000 + 50,000 + 0 + (−50,000)]/5 = **$50,000**

STEP 2: DETERMINING AVERAGE INVESTMENT We stated earlier that, due to depreciation, the investment in the store becomes less valuable every year. Because depreciation is $100,000 per year, the value at the end of Year 0 is $500,000, the value at the end of Year 1 is $400,000, and so on. What is the average value of the investment over the life of the investment?

The mechanical calculation is:

Average Investment:

[$500,000 + 400,000 + 300,000 + 200,000 + 100,000 + 0)]/6 = **$250,000**

We divide by 6, and not 5, because $500,000 is what the investment is worth at the beginning of the five years and $0 is what it is worth at the beginning of the sixth year. In other words, there are six terms in the parentheses of the average investment equation.

STEP 3: DETERMINING AAR The average accounting return is:

$$\text{AAR} = \frac{\$50,000}{\$250,000} = .20, \text{ or } 20\%$$

If the firm had a targeted accounting rate of return greater than 20 percent, the project would be rejected, and if its targeted return were less than 20 percent, it would be accepted.

Analyzing the Average Accounting Return Method

By now you should be able to see what is wrong with the AAR method.

The most important flaw with AAR is that it does not work with the right raw materials. It uses the net income and book value of the investment, both of which come from the accounting books. Accounting numbers are somewhat arbitrary. For example, certain cash outflows, such as the cost of a building, are depreciated under current accounting rules. Other flows, such as maintenance, are expensed. In real-world situations, the decision to depreciate or expense an item involves judgment. Thus, the basic inputs of the AAR method, income and average investment, are affected by the accountant's judgment. Conversely, the NPV method uses cash flows. Accounting judgments do not affect cash flow.

Second, AAR takes no account of timing. In the previous example, the AAR would have been the same if the $100,000 net income in the first year had occurred in the last year. However, delaying an inflow for five years would have lowered the NPV of the investment. As mentioned earlier in this chapter, the NPV approach discounts properly.

---

[1] Depreciation will be treated in more detail in the next chapter.

Third, just as payback requires an arbitrary choice of the cutoff date, the AAR method offers no guidance on what the right targeted rate of return should be. In other words, the AAR is not a rate of return in any meaningful economic sense. Instead, it is the ratio of two accounting numbers, and it is not comparable to the returns offered, for example, in financial markets.[2]

Given these problems, is the AAR method employed in practice? Like the payback method, the AAR method (and variations of it) is frequently used as a "backup" to discounted cash flow methods. Perhaps this is so because it is easy to calculate and uses accounting numbers readily available from the firm's accounting system. In addition, both stockholders and the media pay a lot of attention to the overall profitability of a firm. Thus, some managers may feel pressured to select projects that are profitable in the near term, even if the projects come up short in terms of NPV. These managers may focus on the AAR of individual projects more than they should.

7.5 THE INTERNAL RATE OF RETURN

Now we come to the most important alternative to the NPV method, the internal rate of return, universally known as the IRR. The IRR is about as close as you can get to the NPV without actually being the NPV. The basic rationale behind the IRR method is that it provides a single number summarizing the merits of a project. That number does not depend on the various interest rates prevailing in the capital markets. That is why it is called the internal rate of return; the number is internal or intrinsic to the project and does not depend on anything except the cash flows of the project.

Consider the simple project (−$100, $110) in Figure 7.2. For a given rate, the net present value of this project can be described as:

$$NPV = -\$100 + \frac{\$110}{1 + R}$$

where R is the discount rate. What must the discount rate be to make the NPV of the project equal to zero?

We begin by using an arbitrary discount rate of 8 percent, which yields:

$$\$1.85 = -\$100 + \frac{\$110}{1.08}$$

Because the NPV in this equation is positive, we now try a higher discount rate, say, 12 percent. This yields:

$$-\$1.79 = -\$100 + \frac{\$110}{1.12}$$

Because the NPV in the equation above is negative, we lower the discount rate to, say, 10 percent. This yields:

$$0 = -\$100 + \frac{\$110}{1.10}$$

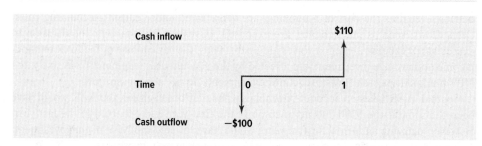

FIGURE 7.2

Cash Flows for a Simple Project

[2] The AAR is closely related to the return on assets, or ROA. In practice, the AAR is sometimes computed by first calculating the ROA for each year and then averaging the results. This produces a number that is similar, but not identical, to the one we computed.

Cash Flows for a More
Complex Project

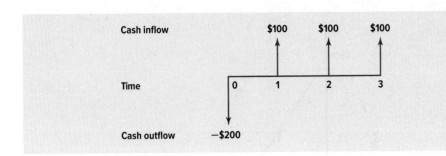

This trial-and-error procedure tells us that the NPV of the project is zero when R equals 10 percent.[3] Thus, we say that 10 percent is the project's **internal rate of return (IRR)**. In general, the IRR is the rate that causes the NPV of the project to be zero. The implication of this exercise is very simple. The firm should be equally willing to accept or reject the project if the discount rate is 10 percent. The firm should accept the project if the discount rate is below 10 percent. The firm should reject the project if the discount rate is above 10 percent.

The general IRR investment rule is clear:

Accept the project if IRR is greater than the discount rate. Reject the project if IRR is less than the discount rate.

We refer to this as the **basic IRR rule**. Now we can try the more complicated example (−$200, $100, $100, $100) in Figure 7.3.

As we did previously, let's use trial and error to calculate the internal rate of return. We try 20 percent and 30 percent, yielding:

Discount Rate	NPV
20%	$10.65
30	−18.39

After much more trial and error, we find that the NPV of the project is zero when the discount rate is 23.38 percent. Thus, the IRR is 23.38 percent. With a 20 percent discount rate, the NPV is positive and we would accept it. However, if the discount rate were 30 percent, we would reject it.

Algebraically, IRR is the unknown in the following equation:[4]

$$0 = -\$200 + \frac{\$100}{1 + IRR} + \frac{\$100}{(1 + IRR)^2} + \frac{\$100}{(1 + IRR)^3}$$

Figure 7.4 illustrates what the IRR of a project means. The figure plots the NPV as a function of the discount rate. The curve crosses the horizontal axis at the IRR of 23.38 percent because this is where the NPV equals zero.

It should also be clear that the NPV is positive for discount rates below the IRR and negative for discount rates above the IRR. This means that if we accept projects like this one when the discount rate is less than the IRR, we will be accepting positive NPV projects. Thus, the IRR rule coincides exactly with the NPV rule.

---

[3] Of course, we could have directly solved for R in this example after setting NPV equal to zero. However, with a long series of cash flows, one cannot generally directly solve for R. Instead, one is forced to use trial and error.

[4] One can derive the IRR directly for a problem with an initial outflow and up to two subsequent inflows. In the case of two subsequent inflows, for example, the quadratic formula is needed. In general, however, a calculator or spreadsheet is needed for an outflow and three or more subsequent inflows.

CHAPTER 7 Net Present Value and Other Investment Rules 203

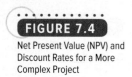
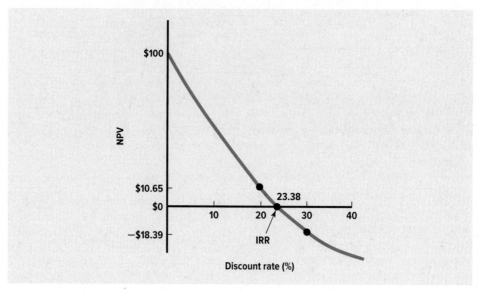

If this were all there were to it, the IRR rule would always coincide with the NPV rule. This would be a wonderful discovery because it would mean that just by computing the IRR for a project, we would be able to tell where it ranks among all of the projects we are considering. For example, if the IRR rule really works, a project with an IRR of 20 percent will always be better than one with an IRR of 15 percent.

But the world of finance is not so kind. Unfortunately, the IRR rule and the NPV rule are the same only for examples like the ones above. Several problems with the IRR approach occur in more complicated situations. In the real world, spreadsheets are used to avoid boring trial-and-error calculations. A nearby *Spreadsheet Techniques* box shows how.

SPREADSHEET TECHNIQUES **Calculating IRRs with a Spreadsheet**

Because IRRs are so tedious to calculate by hand, financial calculators and, especially, spreadsheets are generally used. The procedures used by various financial calculators are too different for us to illustrate here, so we will focus on using a spreadsheet. As the following example illustrates, using a spreadsheet is very easy.

	A	B	C	D	E	F	G	H
1								
2			Using a spreadsheet to calculate internal rates of return					
3								
4	Suppose we have a four-year project that costs $500. The cash flows over the four-year life will be							
5	$100, $200, $300, and $400. What is the IRR?							
6								
7		Year	Cash flow					
8		0	-$500					
9		1	100		IRR =	27.3%		
10		2	200					
11		3	300					
12		4	400					
13								
14								
15	The formula entered in cell F9 is =IRR(C8:C12). Notice that the Year 0 cash flow has a negative							
16	sign representing the initial cost of the project.							
17								

7.6 PROBLEMS WITH THE IRR APPROACH

Definition of Independent and Mutually Exclusive Projects

An independent project is one whose acceptance or rejection is independent of the acceptance or rejection of other projects. Imagine that McDonald's is considering putting a hamburger outlet on a remote island. Acceptance or rejection of this unit is likely to be unrelated to the acceptance or rejection of any other restaurant in its system. The remoteness of the outlet in question ensures that it will not pull sales away from other outlets.

Now consider the other extreme, mutually exclusive investments. What does it mean for two projects, A and B, to be mutually exclusive? You can accept A or you can accept B or you can reject both of them, but you cannot accept both of them. For example, A might be a decision to build an apartment complex on a corner lot that you own and B might be a decision to build a movie theater on the same lot.

We now present two general problems with the IRR approach that affect both independent and mutually exclusive projects. Then we deal with two problems affecting mutually exclusive projects only.

Two General Problems Affecting Both Independent and Mutually Exclusive Projects

We begin our discussion with Project A, which has the following cash flows:

(−$100, $130)

The IRR for Project A is 30 percent. Table 7.3 provides other relevant information on the project. The relationship between NPV and the discount rate is shown for this project in Figure 7.5. As you can see, the NPV declines as the discount rate rises.

PROBLEM 1: INVESTING OR FINANCING?   Now consider Project B, with cash flows of:

$100, −$130

These cash flows are exactly the reverse of the flows for Project A. In Project B, the firm receives funds first and then pays out funds later. While unusual, projects of this type do exist. Consider a corporation conducting a seminar where the participants pay in advance. Because large expenses are frequently incurred at the seminar date, cash inflows precede cash outflows.

TABLE 7.3   The Internal Rate of Return and Net Present Value

Dates:	Project A			Project B			Project C		
	0	1	2	0	1	2	0	1	2
Cash flows	−$100	$130		$100	−$130		−$100	$230	−$132
IRR		30%			30%		10%	and	20%
NPV@10%		$18.2			−$18.2			$0	
Accept if market rate		<30%			>30%		>10%	but	<20%
Financing or investing		Investing			Financing			Mixture	

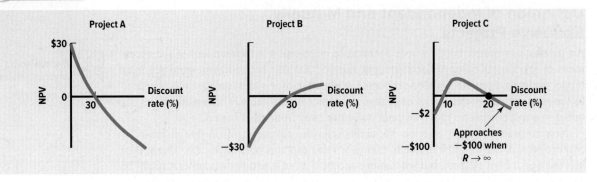

Consider our trial-and-error method to calculate IRR:

$$-\$4 = +\$100 - \frac{\$130}{1.25}$$

$$\$0 = +\$100 - \frac{\$130}{1.30}$$

$$\$3.70 = +\$100 - \frac{\$130}{1.35}$$

As with Project A, the internal rate of return is 30 percent. However, notice that the net present value is negative when the discount rate is below 30 percent. Conversely, the net present value is positive when the discount rate is above 30 percent. The decision rule is exactly the opposite of our previous result. For this type of a project, the rule is:

Accept the project when IRR is less than the discount rate. Reject the project when IRR is greater than the discount rate.

This unusual decision rule follows from the graph of Project B in Figure 7.5. The curve is upward sloping, implying that NPV is positively related to the discount rate.

The graph makes intuitive sense. Suppose that the firm wants to obtain $100 immediately. It can either (1) accept Project B or (2) borrow $100 from a bank. Thus, the project is actually a substitute for borrowing. In fact, because the IRR is 30 percent, taking on Project B is tantamount to borrowing at 30 percent. If the firm can borrow from a bank at, say, only 25 percent, it should reject the project. However, if a firm can only borrow from a bank at, say, 35 percent, it should accept the project. Thus, Project B will be accepted if and only if the discount rate is above the IRR.[5]

This should be contrasted with Project A. If the firm has $100 of cash to invest, it can either (1) accept Project A or (2) lend $100 to the bank. The project is actually a substitute for lending. In fact, because the IRR is 30 percent, taking on Project A is tantamount to lending at 30 percent. The firm should accept Project A if the lending rate is below 30 percent. Conversely, the firm should reject Project A if the lending rate is above 30 percent.

Because the firm initially pays out money with Project A but initially receives money with Project B, we refer to Project A as an *investing type project* and Project B as a

---

[5] This paragraph implicitly assumes that the cash flows of the project are risk-free. In this way, we can treat the borrowing rate as the discount rate for a firm needing $100. With risky cash flows, another discount rate would be chosen. However, the intuition behind the decision to accept when IRR is less than the discount rate would still apply.

financing type project. Investing type projects are the norm. Because the IRR rule is reversed for financing type projects, be careful when using it with this type of project.

PROBLEM 2: MULTIPLE RATES OF RETURN   Suppose the cash flows from a project are:

(−$100, $230, −$132)

Because this project has a negative cash flow, a positive cash flow, and another negative cash flow, we say that the project's cash flows exhibit two changes of signs, or "flip-flops." While this pattern of cash flows might look a bit strange at first, many projects require outflows of cash after receiving some inflows. An example would be a strip-mining project. The first stage in such a project is the initial investment in excavating the mine. Profits from operating the mine are received in the second stage. The third stage involves a further invest-ment to reclaim the land and satisfy the requirements of environmental protection legisla-tion. Cash flows are negative at this stage.

Projects financed by lease arrangements may produce a similar pattern of cash flows. Leases often provide substantial tax subsidies, generating cash inflows after an initial invest-ment. However, these subsidies decline over time, frequently leading to negative cash flows in later years. (The details of leasing will be discussed in a later chapter.)

It is easy to verify that this project has not one but two IRRs, 10 percent and 20 percent.[6] In a case like this, the IRR does not make any sense. What IRR are we to use, 10 percent or 20 percent? Because there is no good reason to use one over the other, IRR cannot be used here.

Why does this project have multiple rates of return? Project C generates multiple internal rates of return because both an inflow and an outflow occur after the initial investment. In general, these flip-flops or changes in signs produce multiple IRRs. In theory, a cash flow stream with K changes in signs can have up to K sensible internal rates of return (IRRs above −100 percent).[7] Therefore, because Project C has two changes in signs, it can have as many as two IRRs. As we pointed out, projects whose cash flows change signs repeatedly can occur in the real world.

NPV RULE   Of course, we should not be too worried about multiple rates of return. After all, we can always fall back on the NPV rule. Figure 7.5 plots the NPV of Project C (−$100, $230, −$132) as a function of the discount rate. As the figure shows, the NPV is zero at both 10 percent and 20 percent and negative outside the range. Thus, the NPV rule tells us to accept the project if the appropriate discount rate is between 10 percent and 20 percent. The project should be rejected if the discount rate lies outside of this range. Of course, if there is only one sign change in the project's cash flows, there can be at most one IRR.

---

[6] The calculations are:

$$-\$100 + \frac{\$230}{1.1} - \frac{\$132}{1.1^2}$$

$$0 = -\$100 + 209.09 - 109.09$$

and:

$$-\$100 + \frac{\$230}{1.2} - \frac{\$132}{1.2^2}$$

$$0 = -\$100 + 191.67 - 91.67$$

Thus, we have multiple rates of return.

[7] To be more precise, the number of possible IRRs comes from the great mathematician, philosopher, and financial analyst Descartes (of "I think; therefore, I am" fame). Descartes's Rule of Sign says that the maximum number of IRRs that are bigger than −100 percent is equal to the number of sign changes, or it differs from the number of sign changes by an even number. For example, if there are five sign changes, there are five IRRs, three IRRs, or one IRR. If there are two sign changes, there are either two IRRs or no IRRs.

GENERAL RULES   The following chart summarizes our rules:

Flows	Number of IRRs	IRR Criterion	NPV Criterion
First cash flow is negative and all remaining cash flows are positive.	1	Accept if IRR > R Reject if IRR < R	Accept if NPV > 0 Reject if NPV < 0
First cash flow is positive and all remaining cash flows are negative.	1	Accept if IRR < R Reject if IRR > R	Accept if NPV > 0 Reject if NPV < 0
Some cash flows after first cash flow are positive and some are negative.	May be more than 1	No valid IRR	Accept if NPV > 0 Reject if NPV < 0

Note that the NPV criterion is the same for each of the three cases. In other words, NPV analysis is always appropriate. Conversely, the IRR can be used only in certain cases. When it comes to NPV, the preacher's words, "You just can't lose with the stuff I use," clearly apply.

Problems Specific to Mutually Exclusive Projects

As mentioned earlier, two or more projects are mutually exclusive if the firm can, at most, accept only one of them. We now present two problems dealing with the application of the IRR approach to mutually exclusive projects. These two problems are quite similar, though logically distinct.

THE SCALE PROBLEM   A professor we know motivates class discussions on this topic with the statement: "Students, I am prepared to let one of you choose between two mutually exclusive 'business' propositions. Opportunity 1—You give me $1 now and I'll give you $1.50 back at the end of the class period. Opportunity 2—You give me $10 and I'll give you $11 back at the end of the class period. You can only choose one of the two opportunities. And you cannot choose either opportunity more than once. I'll pick the first volunteer."

Which would you choose? The correct answer is Opportunity 2.[8] To see this, look at the following chart:

	Cash Flow at Beginning of Class	Cash Flow at End of Class (90 Minutes Later)	NPV[9]	IRR
Opportunity 1	−$ 1	+$ 1.50	$ .50	50%
Opportunity 2	−10	+ 11.00	1.00	10

As we have stressed earlier in the text, one should choose the opportunity with the highest NPV. This is Opportunity 2 in the example. Or, as one of the professor's students explained it: "I'm bigger than the professor, so I know I'll get my money back. And I have $10 in my pocket right now so I can choose either opportunity. At the end of the class, I'll be able to buy a song on iTunes with Opportunity 2 and still have my original investment, safe and sound. The profit on Opportunity 1 buys only half a song."

This business proposition illustrates a defect with the internal rate of return criterion. The basic IRR rule indicates the selection of Opportunity 1 because the IRR is 50 percent. The IRR is only 10 percent for Opportunity 2.

Where does IRR go wrong? The problem with IRR is that it ignores issues of scale. While Opportunity 1 has a greater IRR, the investment is much smaller. In other words, the

---

[8] The professor uses real money here. Though many students have done poorly on the professor's exams over the years, no student ever chose Opportunity 1. The professor claims that his students are "money players."

[9] We assume a zero rate of interest because his class lasted only 90 minutes. It just seemed like a lot longer.

high percentage return on Opportunity 1 is more than offset by the ability to earn at least a decent return[10] on a much bigger investment under Opportunity 2.

Because IRR seems to be misguided here, can we adjust or correct it? We illustrate how in the next example.

NPV versus IRR

Stanley Jaffe and Sherry Lansing have just purchased the rights to *Corporate Finance: The Motion Picture*. They will produce this major motion picture on either a small budget or a big budget. The estimated cash flows are:

	Cash Flow at Date 0	Cash Flow at Date 1	NPV @25%	IRR
Small budget	−$10 million	$40 million	$22 million	300%
Large budget	−25 million	65 million	27 million	160

Because of high risk, a 25 percent discount rate is considered appropriate. Sherry wants to adopt the large budget because the NPV is higher. Stanley wants to adopt the small budget because the IRR is higher. Who is right?

For the reasons espoused in the classroom example above, NPV is correct. Hence, Sherry is right. However, Stanley is very stubborn where IRR is concerned. How can Sherry justify the large budget to Stanley using the IRR approach?

This is where *incremental IRR* comes in. Sherry calculates the incremental cash flows from choosing the large budget instead of the small budget as:

	Cash Flow at Date 0 (in $ millions)	Cash Flow at Date 1 (in $ millions)
Incremental cash flows from choosing large budget instead of small budget	−$25 − (−10) = −$15	$65 − 40 = $25

This chart shows that the incremental cash flows are −$15 million at Date 0 and $25 million at Date 1. Sherry calculates incremental IRR as:

Formula for Calculating the Incremental IRR:

$$0 = -\$15 \text{ million} + \frac{\$25 \text{ million}}{1 + IRR}$$

IRR equals 66.67 percent in this equation, implying that the incremental IRR is 66.67 percent. Incremental IRR is the IRR on the incremental investment from choosing the large project instead of the small project.

In addition, we can calculate the NPV of the incremental cash flows:

NPV of Incremental Cash Flows:

$$-\$15 \text{ million} + \frac{\$25 \text{ million}}{1.25} = \$5 \text{ million}$$

We know the small-budget picture would be acceptable as an independent project because its NPV is positive. We want to know whether it is beneficial to invest an additional $15 million in order to make the large-budget picture instead of the small-budget picture. In other words, is it beneficial to invest an additional $15 million in order to receive an

[10] A 10 percent return is more than decent over a 90-minute interval!

additional $25 million next year? First, the above calculations show the NPV on the incremental investment to be positive. Second, the incremental IRR of 66.67 percent is higher than the discount rate of 25 percent. For both reasons, the incremental investment can be justified. Hence, the large-budget movie should be made. The second reason is what Stanley needed to hear to be convinced.

In review, we can handle this example (or any mutually exclusive example) in one of three ways:

1. *Compare the NPVs of the Two Choices.* The NPV of the large-budget picture is greater than the NPV of the small-budget picture. That is, $27 million is greater than $22 million.

2. *Calculate the Incremental NPV from Making the Large-Budget Picture Instead of the Small-Budget Picture.* Because the incremental NPV equals $5 million, we choose the large-budget picture.

3. *Compare the Incremental IRR to the Discount Rate.* Because the incremental IRR is 66.67 percent and the discount rate is 25 percent, we take the large-budget picture.

All three approaches always give the same decision. However, we must not compare the IRRs of the two pictures. If we did, we would make the wrong choice. That is, we would accept the small-budget picture.

While students frequently think that problems of scale are relatively unimportant, the truth is just the opposite. A well-known chef on TV often says, "I don't know about your flour, but the flour I buy don't come seasoned." The same thing applies to capital budgeting. No real-world project comes in one clear-cut size. Many times, the firm has to determine the best size for the project. The movie budget of $25 million is not fixed in stone. Perhaps an extra $1 million to hire a bigger star or to film at a better location will increase the movie's gross. Similarly, an industrial firm must decide whether it wants a warehouse of, say, 500,000 square feet or 600,000 square feet. And, earlier in the chapter, we imagined McDonald's opening an outlet on a remote island. If it does this, it must decide how big the outlet should be. For almost any project, someone in the firm has to decide on its size, implying that problems of scale abound in the real world.

One final note here. Students often ask which project should be subtracted from the other in calculating incremental flows. Notice that we are subtracting the smaller project's cash flows from the bigger project's cash flows. This leaves an outflow at Date 0. We then use the basic IRR rule on the incremental flows.[11]

THE TIMING PROBLEM   Next we illustrate another, but quite similar, problem with the IRR approach when evaluating mutually exclusive projects.

EXAMPLE 7.4

Mutually Exclusive Investments

Suppose that the Kaufold Corporation has two alternative uses for a warehouse. It can store toxic waste containers (Investment A) or electronic equipment (Investment B). The cash flows are as follows:

	Cash Flow at Year				NPV			
Year:	0	1	2	3	@0%	@10%	@15%	IRR
Investment A	−$10,000	$10,000	$1,000	$ 1,000	$2,000	$669	$109	16.04%
Investment B	−10,000	1,000	1,000	12,000	4,000	751	−484	12.94

---

[11] Alternatively, we could have subtracted the larger project's cash flows from the smaller project's cash flows. This would have left an inflow at Date 0, making it necessary to use the IRR rule for financing situations. This would work, but we find it more confusing.

We find that the NPV of Investment B is higher with low discount rates, and the NPV of Investment A is higher with high discount rates. This is not surprising if you look closely at the cash flow patterns. The cash flows of A occur early, whereas the cash flows of B occur later. If we assume a high discount rate, we favor Investment A because we are implicitly assuming that the early cash flow (for example, $10,000 in Year 1) can be reinvested at that rate. Because most of Investment B's cash flows occur in Year 3, B's value is relatively high with low discount rates.

The patterns of cash flow for both projects appear in Figure 7.6. Project A has an NPV of $2,000 at a discount rate of zero. This is calculated by adding up the cash flows without discounting them. Project B has an NPV of $4,000 at the zero rate. However, the NPV of Project B declines more rapidly as the discount rate increases than does the NPV of Project A. As we mentioned above, this occurs because the cash flows of B occur later. Both projects have the same NPV at a discount rate of 10.55 percent. The IRR for a project is the rate at which the NPV equals zero. Because the NPV of B declines more rapidly, B actually has a lower IRR.

As with the movie example presented earlier, we can select the better project with one of three different methods:

1. *Compare the NPVs of the Two Projects.* Figure 7.6 aids our decision. If the discount rate is below 10.55 percent, one should choose Project B because B has a higher NPV. If the rate is above 10.55 percent, one should choose Project A because A has a higher NPV.

2. *Compare the Incremental IRR to the Discount Rate.* The above method employed NPV. Another way of determining that B is a better project is to subtract the cash flows of A from the cash flows of B and then to calculate the IRR. This is the incremental IRR approach we spoke of earlier.

   The incremental cash flows are:

| | | | | | | NPV of Incremental Cash Flows | | |
| | Year: | | | | | | | |
	0	1	2	3	Incremental IRR	@0%	@10%	@15%
B − A	0	−$9,000	0	$11,000	10.55%	$2,000	$83	−$593

This chart shows that the incremental IRR is 10.55 percent. In other words, the NPV on the incremental investment is zero when the discount rate is

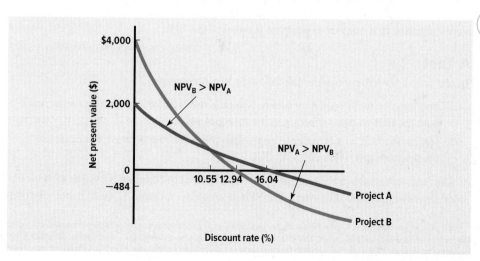

FIGURE 7.6

Net Present Value and the Internal Rate of Return for Mutually Exclusive Projects

10.55 percent. Thus, if the relevant discount rate is below 10.55 percent, Project B is preferred to Project A. If the relevant discount rate is above 10.55 percent, Project A is preferred to Project B.[12]

3. *Calculate the NPV on the Incremental Cash Flows.* Finally, one could calculate the NPV on the incremental cash flows. The chart that appears with the previous method displays these NPVs. We find that the incremental NPV is positive when the discount rate is either 0 percent or 10 percent. The incremental NPV is negative if the discount rate is 15 percent. If the NPV is positive on the incremental cash flows, one should choose B. If the NPV is negative, one should choose A.

In summary, the same decision is reached whether one (a) compares the NPVs of the two projects, (b) compares the incremental IRR to the relevant discount rate, or (c) examines the NPV of the incremental cash flows. However, as mentioned earlier, one should not compare the IRR of Project A with the IRR of Project B.

We suggested earlier that one should subtract the cash flows of the smaller project from the cash flows of the bigger project. What do we do here when the two projects have the same initial investment? Our suggestion in this case is to perform the subtraction so that the first nonzero cash flow is negative. In the Kaufold Corp. example, we achieved this by subtracting A from B. In this way, we can still use the basic IRR rule for evaluating cash flows.

The preceding examples illustrate problems with the IRR approach in evaluating mutually exclusive projects. Both the professor-student example and the motion picture example illustrate the problem that arises when mutually exclusive projects have different initial investments. The Kaufold Corp. example illustrates the problem that arises when mutually exclusive projects have different cash flow timing. When working with mutually exclusive projects, it is not necessary to determine whether it is the scale problem or the timing problem that exists. Very likely both occur in many real-world situations. Instead, the practitioner should use either an incremental IRR or an NPV approach.

Redeeming Qualities of IRR

IRR probably survives because it fills a need that NPV does not. People seem to want a rule that summarizes the information about a project in a single rate of return. This single rate provides people with a simple way of discussing projects. For example, one manager in a firm might say to another, "Remodeling the north wing has a 20 percent IRR."

To their credit, however, companies that employ the IRR approach seem to understand its deficiencies. For example, companies frequently restrict managerial projections of cash flows to be negative at the beginning and strictly positive later. In these cases, the IRR approach and the NPV approach are very often compatible. Perhaps, then, the ability of the IRR approach to capture a complex investment project in a single number and the ease of communicating that number explain the survival of the IRR.

A Test

To test your knowledge, consider the following two statements:

1. You must know the discount rate to compute the NPV of a project, but you compute the IRR without referring to the discount rate.
2. Hence, the IRR rule is easier to apply than the NPV rule because you don't use the discount rate when applying IRR.

The first statement is true. The discount rate is needed to compute NPV. The IRR is computed by solving for the rate where the NPV is zero. No mention is made of the discount

---

[12] In this example, we first showed that the NPVs of the two projects are equal when the discount rate is 10.55 percent. We next showed that the incremental IRR is also 10.55 percent. This is not a coincidence; this equality must always hold. The incremental IRR is the rate that causes the incremental cash flows to have zero NPV. The incremental cash flows have zero NPV when the two projects have the same NPV.

rate in the mere computation. However, the second statement is false. In order to apply IRR, you must compare the internal rate of return with the discount rate. Thus, the discount rate is needed for making a decision under either the NPV or IRR approach.

Modified IRR (MIRR)

To address some of the problems that can crop up with the standard IRR, it is often proposed that the modified IRR (MIRR) be used. As we will see, there are several different ways of calculating a modified IRR, or MIRR, but the idea is to modify the cash flows first and then calculate IRR using the modified cash flows.

To illustrate, let's examine a project with the following cash flows: (−$60, +$155, −$100). If you calculate the IRR for this project, you should get two IRRs, 25 percent and 33.33 percent. We next illustrate three different MIRRs, all of which have the property that only one answer will result, thereby eliminating the multiple IRR problem.

Method 1: The Discounting Approach   With the discounting approach, the idea is to discount all negative cash flows back to the present at the required return and add them to the initial cost. Then, calculate the IRR. Because only the first modified cash flow is negative, there will be only one IRR. The discount rate used might be the required return, or it might be some other externally supplied rate. We use the project's required return. If the required return on the project is 20 percent, then the modified cash flows look like this:

$$\text{Year 0: } -\$60 + \frac{-\$100}{1.20^2} = -\$129.44$$

Year 1: + $155
Year 2: $0

If you calculate the IRR of these modified cash flows, you should get 19.74 percent.

Method 2: The Reinvestment Approach   With the reinvestment approach, we compound all cash flows (positive and negative) except the first out to the end of the project's life and then calculate the IRR. In a sense, we are "reinvesting" the cash flows and not taking them out of the project until the very end. The rate we use could be the required return on the project, or it could be a separately specified "reinvestment rate." We use the project's required return. When we do, here are the modified cash flows:

Year 0: − $60
Year 1: $0
Year 2: − $100 + ($155 × 1.2) = $86

The MIRR on this set of cash flows is 19.72 percent, or a little lower than we found using the discounting approach.

Method 3: The Combination Approach   As the name suggests, the combination approach blends our first two methods. Negative cash flows are discounted back to the present, and positive cash flows are compounded to the end of the project. In practice, different discount or compounding rates might be used, but we again stick with the project's required return.

With the combination approach, the modified cash flows are as follows:

$$\text{Year 0: } -\$60 + \frac{-\$100}{1.20^2} = -\$129.44$$

Year 1: $0
Year 2: $155 × 1.2 = $186

See if you don't agree that the MIRR is 19.87, the highest of the three.

MIRR OR IRR: WHICH IS BETTER? MIRRs are controversial. At one extreme are those who claim that MIRRs are superior to IRRs, period. For example, by design, they clearly don't suffer from the multiple rate of return problem.

At the other end, detractors say that MIRR should stand for "meaningless internal rate of return." As our example makes clear, one problem with MIRRs is that there are different ways of calculating them and there is no clear reason to say one of our three methods is better than any other. The differences are small with our simple cash flows, but they could be much larger for a more complex project. Further, it's unclear how to interpret an MIRR. It may look like a rate of return, but it's a rate of return on a modified set of cash flows, not the project's actual cash flows.

We're not going to take sides. However, notice that calculating an MIRR requires discounting, compounding, or both, which leads to two obvious observations. First, if we have the relevant discount rate, why not calculate the NPV and be done with it? Second, because an MIRR depends on an externally supplied discount (or compounding) rate, the answer you get is not truly an "internal" rate of return, which, by definition, depends on only the project's cash flows.

We will take a stand on one issue that frequently comes up in this context. The value of a project does not depend on what the firm does with the cash flows generated by that project. A firm might use a project's cash flows to fund other projects, to pay dividends, or to buy an executive jet. It doesn't matter: How the cash flows are spent in the future does not affect their value today. As a result, there is generally no need to consider reinvestment of interim cash flows.

7.7 THE PROFITABILITY INDEX

ExcelMaster coverage online

www.mhhe.com/RossCore6e

Another method that is used to evaluate projects is called the profitability index. It is the ratio of the present value of the future expected cash flows after initial investment divided by the amount of the initial investment. The profitability index can be represented as:

$$\text{Profitability index (PI)} = \frac{\text{PV of cash flows subsequent to initial investment}}{\text{Initial investment}} \qquad [7.1]$$

EXAMPLE 7.5

Profitability Index

Hiram Finnegan, Inc. (HFI), applies a 12 percent discount rate to two investment opportunities:

Project	Cash Flows (in $ thousands)			PV @12% of Cash Flows Subsequent to Initial Investment (in $ thousands)	Profitability Index	NPV @12% (in $ thousands)
	C_0	C_1	C_2			
1	−$20	$70	$10	$70.5	3.52	$50.5
2	−10	15	40	45.3	4.53	35.3

Calculation of Profitability Index

The profitability index is calculated for Project 1 as follows. The present value of the cash flows after the initial investment is:

$$\$70.5 = \frac{\$70}{1.12} + \frac{\$10}{1.12^2}$$

The profitability index is obtained by dividing the result of the above equation by the initial investment of $20. This yields:

$$3.52 = \frac{\$70.5}{\$20}$$

APPLICATION OF THE PROFITABILITY INDEX   How do we use the profitability index? We consider three situations:

1. *Independent Projects.* Assume that HFI's two projects are independent. According to the NPV rule, both projects should be accepted because NPV is positive in each case. The profitability index (PI) is greater than 1 whenever the NPV is positive. Thus, the PI decision rule is:

   - Accept an independent project if PI > 1.
   - Reject if PI < 1.

2. *Mutually Exclusive Projects.* Let us now assume that HFI can accept only one of its two projects. NPV analysis says accept Project 1 because this project has the bigger NPV. Because Project 2 has the higher PI, the profitability index leads to the wrong selection.

   The problem with the profitability index for mutually exclusive projects is the same as the scale problem with the IRR that we mentioned earlier. Project 2 is smaller than Project 1. Because the PI is a ratio, this index misses the fact that Project 1 has a larger investment than Project 2 has. Thus, like IRR, PI ignores differences of scale for mutually exclusive projects.

   However, like IRR, the flaw with the PI approach can be corrected using incremental analysis. We write the incremental cash flows after subtracting Project 2 from Project 1 as follows:

Project	Cash Flows (in $ thousands)			PV @12% of Cash Flows Subsequent to Initial Investment (in $ thousands)	Profitability Index	NPV @12% (in $ thousands)
	C_0	C_1	C_2			
1 − 2	−$10	$55	−$30	$25.2	2.52	$15.2

Because the profitability index on the incremental cash flows is greater than 1.0, we should choose the bigger project, that is, Project 1. This is the same decision we get with the NPV approach.

3. *Capital Rationing.* The two cases above implicitly assumed that HFI could always attract enough capital to make any profitable investments. Now consider the case when the firm does not have enough capital to fund all positive NPV projects. This is the case of capital rationing.

   Imagine that the firm has a third project, as well as the first two. Project 3 has the following cash flows:

Project	Cash Flows (in $ thousands)			PV @12% of Cash Flows Subsequent to Initial Investment (in $ thousands)	Profitability Index	NPV @12% (in $ thousands)
	C_0	C_1	C_2			
3	−$10	−$5	$60	$43.4	4.34	$33.4

Further, imagine that (a) the projects of Hiram Finnegan, Inc., are independent, but (b) the firm has only $20 million to invest. Because Project 1 has an initial investment of $20 million, the firm cannot select both this project and another one. Conversely, because Projects 2 and 3 have initial investments of $10 million each, both these projects can be chosen. In other words, the cash constraint forces the firm to choose either Project 1 or Projects 2 and 3.

What should the firm do? Individually, Projects 2 and 3 have lower NPVs than Project 1 has. However, when the NPVs of Projects 2 and 3 are added together, the sum is higher than the NPV of Project 1. Thus, common sense dictates that Projects 2 and 3 should be accepted.

What does our conclusion have to say about the NPV rule or the PI rule? In the case of limited funds, we cannot rank projects according to their NPVs. Instead, we should rank them according to the ratio of present value to initial investment. This is the PI rule. Both Project 2 and Project 3 have higher PI ratios than does Project 1. Thus, they should be ranked ahead of Project 1 when capital is rationed.

The usefulness of the profitability index under capital rationing can be explained in military terms. The Pentagon speaks highly of a weapon with a lot of "bang for the buck." In capital budgeting, the profitability index measures the bang (the dollar return) for the buck invested. Hence, it is useful for capital rationing.

It should be noted that the profitability index does not work if funds are also limited beyond the initial time period. For example, if heavy cash outflows elsewhere in the firm were to occur at Year 1, Project 3, which also has a cash outflow at Year 1, might need to be rejected. In other words, the profitability index cannot handle capital rationing over multiple time periods.

In addition, what economists term *indivisibilities* may reduce the effectiveness of the PI rule. Imagine that HFI has $30 million available for capital investment, not just $20 million. The firm now has enough cash for Projects 1 and 2. Because the sum of the NPVs of these two projects is greater than the sum of the NPVs of Projects 2 and 3, the firm would be better served by accepting Projects 1 and 2. Because Projects 2 and 3 still have the highest profitability indexes, the PI rule now leads to the wrong decision. Why does the PI rule lead us astray here? The key is that Projects 1 and 2 use up all of the $30 million, while Projects 2 and 3 have a combined initial investment of only $20 million (= $10 + 10). If Projects 2 and 3 are accepted, the remaining $10 million must be left in the bank.

The above situation points out that care should be exercised when using the profitability index in the real world. Nevertheless, while not perfect, the profitability index goes a long way toward handling capital rationing.

7.8 THE PRACTICE OF CAPITAL BUDGETING

So far, this chapter has asked the question: Which capital budgeting methods should companies be using? An equally important question is: Which methods *are* companies using? Table 7.4 helps answer this question. As can be seen from the table, approximately three-quarters of U.S. and Canadian companies use the IRR and NPV methods. This is not surprising, given the theoretical advantages of these approaches. Over one-half of these companies use the payback method, a rather surprising result given the conceptual problems with this approach. And while discounted payback represents a theoretical improvement over regular payback, the usage here is far less. Perhaps companies are attracted to the user-friendly nature of payback. In addition, the flaws of this approach, as mentioned in the current chapter, may be relatively easy to correct. For example, while the payback method ignores all cash flows after the payback period, an alert manager can make ad hoc adjustments for a project with back-loaded cash flows.

Large firms often have huge capital budgets. For example, for 2019, Chevron announced that it expected to have about $20 billion in capital outlays during the year. This was the same as the amount spent in 2018 and up from the $18.8 billion in 2017. However, the 2019 capital outlay was still below the $22.4 billion spent in 2016. Other companies with large capital

	% Always or Almost Always
Internal rate of return (IRR)	75.6%
Net present value (NPV)	74.9
Payback method	56.7
Discounted payback	29.5
Accounting rate of return	20.3
Profitability index	11.9

Source: Graham, John R. and Campbell R. Harvey. "The Theory and Practice of Corporate Finance: Evidence from the Field." *Journal of Financial Economics* 60, no. 2–3 (May 2001): pp. 187–243. Adapted from Table 2. Based on a survey of 392 CFOs.

spending budgets were ConocoPhillips, which projected capital spending of about $6.1 billion for 2019, and Apple, which projected capital spending of about $14 billion in 2019.

Large-scale capital spending is often an industrywide occurrence. For example, in 2019, capital spending in the semiconductor industry was expected to be $107.1 billion. This sum represented a 15 percent increase compared to 2018. A large part of the industry spending was due to Samsung Electronics, which was expected to spend about $22.6 billion for the year.

According to information released by the Census Bureau in 2018, capital investment for the economy as a whole was $1.576 trillion in 2016, $1.642 trillion in 2015, and $1.507 trillion in 2014. The totals for the three years therefore exceeded $4.7 trillion!

Given the sums at stake, it is not too surprising that careful analysis of capital expenditures is something at which successful businesses seek to become adept.

One might expect the capital budgeting methods of large firms to be more sophisticated than the methods of small firms. After all, large firms have the financial resources to hire more sophisticated employees. Table 7.5 provides some support for this idea. Here, firms indicate frequency of use of the various capital budgeting methods on a scale of 0 (never) to 4 (always). Both the IRR and NPV methods are used more frequently, and payback less frequently, in large firms than in small firms. Conversely, large and small firms employ the last three approaches about equally.

The use of quantitative techniques in capital budgeting varies with the industry. As one would imagine, firms that are better able to estimate cash flows are more likely to use NPV. For example, estimation of cash flow in certain aspects of the oil business is quite feasible. Because of this, energy-related firms were among the first to use NPV analysis. Conversely, the cash flows in the motion-picture business are very hard to project. The grosses of the great hits like *Titanic, Harry Potter,* and *Star Wars* were far, far greater than anyone imagined. The big failures like *King Arthur: Legend of the Sword* and *Deepwater Horizon* were unexpected as well. Because of this, NPV analysis is frowned upon in the movie business.

How does Hollywood perform capital budgeting? The information that a studio uses to accept or reject a movie idea comes from the *pitch.* An independent movie producer

TABLE 7.5

Frequency of Use of Various
Capital Budgeting Methods

	Large Firms	Small Firms
Internal rate of return (IRR)	3.41	2.87
Net present value (NPV)	3.42	2.83
Payback method	2.25	2.72
Discounted payback	1.55	1.58
Accounting rate of return	1.25	1.41
Profitability index	.75	.88

Note: Firms indicate frequency of use on a scale from 0 (never) to 4 (always). Numbers in table are averages across respondents.
Source: Adapted from Table 2 from Graham, John R. and Campbell R. Harvey. "The Theory and Practice of Corporate Finance." *Journal of Financial Economics* 60, no. 2–3 (May 2001): pp. 187–243.

schedules an extremely brief meeting with a studio to pitch his or her idea for a movie. Consider the following four paragraphs of quotes concerning the pitch from the thoroughly delightful book *Reel Power.*[13]

"They [studio executives] don't want to know too much," says Ron Simpson. "They want to know concept. . . . They want to know what the three-liner is, because they want it to suggest the ad campaign. They want a title. . . . They don't want to hear any esoterica. And if the meeting lasts more than five minutes, they're probably not going to do the project."

"A guy comes in and says this is my idea: *'Jaws* on a spaceship,'" says writer Clay Frohman *(Under Fire).* "And they say, 'Brilliant, fantastic.' Becomes *Alien.* That is *Jaws* on a spaceship, ultimately. . . . And that's it. That's all they want to hear. Their attitude is 'Don't confuse us with the details of the story.'"

". . . Some high-concept stories are more appealing to the studios than others. The ideas liked best are sufficiently original that the audience will not feel it has already seen the movie, yet similar enough to past hits to reassure executives wary of anything too far-out. Thus, the frequently used shorthand: It's *Flashdance* in the country *(Footloose)* or *High Noon* in outer space *(Outland)*."

". . . One gambit not to use during a pitch," says executive Barbara Boyle, "is to talk about big box-office grosses your story is sure to make. Executives know as well as anyone that it's impossible to predict how much money a movie will make, and declarations to the contrary are considered pure malarkey."

[13] Excerpts from Mark Litwak, *Reel Power: The Struggle for Influence and Success in the New Hollywood* (New York: William Morrow and Company, Inc., 1986), pp. 73, 74, and 77.

SUMMARY AND CONCLUSIONS

1. In this chapter, we cover different investment decision rules. We evaluate the most popular alternatives to NPV: payback period, discounted payback period, accounting rate of return, internal rate of return, and profitability index. In doing so, we learn more about NPV.

2. While we find that the alternatives have some redeeming qualities, when all is said and done, they are not as good as the NPV rule.

3. Of the competitors to NPV, IRR must be ranked above both payback and accounting rate of return. In fact, IRR always reaches the same decision as NPV in the normal case where the initial outflows of an independent investment project are only followed by a series of inflows.

4. We classified the flaws of IRR into two types. First, we considered the general case applying to both independent and mutually exclusive projects. There appeared to be two problems here:

   a. Some projects have cash inflows followed by one or more outflows. The IRR rule is inverted here: One should accept when the IRR is below the discount rate.

   b. Some projects have a number of changes of sign in their cash flows. Here, there are likely to be multiple internal rates of return. The practitioner must use either NPV or modified internal rate of return in this case.

5. Next, we considered the specific problems with IRR for mutually exclusive projects. We showed that, due to differences either in size or in timing, the project with the highest IRR need not have the highest NPV. Hence, the IRR rule should not be applied. (Of course, NPV can still be applied.)

   However, we then calculated incremental cash flows. For ease of calculation, we suggested subtracting the cash flows of the smaller project from the cash flows of the larger project. In that way, the incremental initial cash flow is negative. One can always reach a correct decision by accepting the larger project if the incremental IRR is greater than the discount rate.

6. We describe capital rationing as the case where funds are limited to a fixed dollar amount. With capital rationing, the profitability index is a useful method of adjusting the NPV.

CONCEPT QUESTIONS

1. **Payback Period and Net Present Value**   If a project with conventional cash flows has a payback period less than the project's life, can you definitively state the algebraic sign of the NPV? Why or why not? If you know that the discounted payback period is less than the project's life, what can you say about the NPV? Explain.

2. **Net Present Value**   Suppose a project has conventional cash flows and a positive NPV. What do you know about its payback? Its discounted payback? Its profitability index? Its IRR? Explain.

3. **Comparing Investment Criteria**   Define each of the following investment rules and discuss any potential shortcomings of each. In your definition, state the criterion for accepting or rejecting independent projects under each rule.

   a. Payback period

   b. Average accounting return

   c. Internal rate of return

   d. Profitability index

   e. Net present value

4. **Payback and Internal Rate of Return**   A project has perpetual cash flows of C per period, a cost of I, and a required return of R. What is the relationship between the project's payback and its IRR? What implications does your answer have for long-lived projects with relatively constant cash flows?

5. **International Investment Projects**   In November 2018, Toyota and Mazda broke ground on a $1.6 billion plant to be operated jointly in Alabama. Toyota and Mazda apparently felt that they would be better able to compete and create value with U.S.-based facilities. Other companies such as Fujifilm and Swiss chemical company Lonza have reached similar conclusions and taken similar actions. What are some of the reasons that foreign manufacturers of products as diverse as automobiles, film, and chemicals might arrive at this same conclusion?

6. **Capital Budgeting Problems**   What are some of the difficulties that might come up in actual applications of the various criteria we discussed in this chapter? Which one would be the easiest to implement in actual applications? The most difficult?

7. **Capital Budgeting in Not-for-Profit Entities**   Are the capital budgeting criteria we discussed applicable to not-for-profit corporations? How should such entities make capital budgeting decisions? What about the U.S. government? Should it evaluate spending proposals using these techniques?

8. **Net Present Value**   The investment in Project A is $1 million, and the investment in Project B is $2 million. Both projects have a unique internal rate of return of 20 percent. Is the following statement true or false?

   For any discount rate from 0 percent to 20 percent, Project B has an NPV twice as great as that of Project A.

   Explain your answer.

9. **Net Present Value versus Profitability Index**   Consider the following two mutually exclusive projects available to Global Investments, Inc.

	C_0	C_1	C_2	Profitability Index	NPV
A	−$1,000	$1,000	$500	1.32	$322
B	−500	500	400	1.57	285

The appropriate discount rate for the projects is 10 percent. Global Investments chose to undertake Project A. At a luncheon for shareholders, the manager of a pension fund that owns a substantial amount of the firm's stock asks you why the firm chose Project A instead of Project B, when Project B has a higher profitability index.

How would you, the CFO, justify your firm's action? Are there any circumstances under which Global Investments should choose Project B?

10. **Internal Rate of Return**   Projects A and B have the following cash flows:

Year	Project A	Project B
0	−$1,000	−$2,000
1	C1A	C1B
2	C2A	C2B
3	C3A	C3B

a. If the cash flows from the projects are identical, which of the two projects would have a higher IRR? Why?

b. If C1B = 2C1A, C2B = 2C2A, and C3B = 2C3A, then is $IRR_A = IRR_B$?

11. **Net Present Value**   You are evaluating two projects, Project A and Project B. Project A has a short period of future cash flows, while Project B has relatively long future cash flows. Which project will be more sensitive to changes in the required return? Why?

12. **Modified Internal Rate of Return**   One of the less flattering interpretations of the acronym MIRR is "meaningless internal rate of return." Why do you think this term is applied to MIRR?

13. **Net Present Value**   One potential criticism of the net present value technique is that there is an implicit assumption that the intermediate cash flows of the project are reinvested at the required return. In other words, if you calculate the future value of the intermediate cash flows to the end of the project at the required return, sum the future values, and find the net present value of the two cash flows, you will get the same net present value as the original calculation. If the reinvestment rate used to calculate the future value is lower than the required return, the net present value will decrease. How would you evaluate this criticism?

14. **Internal Rate of Return**   One potential criticism of the internal rate of return technique is that there is an implicit assumption that the intermediate cash flows of the project are reinvested at the internal rate of return. In other words, if you calculate the future value of the intermediate cash flows to the end of the project at the required return, sum the future values, and calculate the internal rate of return of the two cash flows, you will get the same internal rate of return as the original calculation. If the reinvestment rate used to calculate the future value is different from the internal rate of return, the internal rate of return calculated for the two cash flows will be different. How would you evaluate this criticism?

QUESTIONS AND PROBLEMS

Mc Graw Hill **connect**

Basic

(Questions 1–10)

1. **Calculating Payback Period and NPV**   Greystone, Inc., has the following mutually exclusive projects.

Year	Project A	Project B
0	−$30,600	−$21,400
1	15,400	10,600
2	15,600	8,600
3	6,200	9,600

a. Suppose the company's payback period cutoff is two years. Which of these two projects should be chosen?

b. Suppose the company uses the NPV rule to rank these two projects. Which project should be chosen if the appropriate discount rate is 15 percent?

2. **Calculating Payback** An investment project provides cash inflows of $1,530 per year for eight years. What is the project payback period if the initial cost is $4,900? What if the initial cost is $7,900? What if it is $13,400?

3. **Calculating Discounted Payback** An investment project has annual cash inflows of $5,100, $5,700, $6,200, and $6,400, and a discount rate of 12 percent. What is the discounted payback period for these cash flows if the initial cost is $6,000? What if the initial cost is $9,500? What if it is $15,400?

4. **Calculating Discounted Payback** An investment project costs $15,500 and has annual cash flows of $4,400 for six years. What is the discounted payback period if the discount rate is 0 percent? What if the discount rate is 7 percent? If it is 21 percent?

5. **Average Accounting Return** Your firm is considering purchasing a machine with the following annual, end-of-year, book investment accounts.

	Year 0	Year 1	Year 2	Year 3	Year 4
Gross investment	$63,000	$63,000	$63,000	$63,000	$63,000
Less: Accumulated depreciation	0	15,750	31,500	47,250	63,000
Net investment	$63,000	$47,250	$31,500	$15,750	$ 0

The machine generates, on average, $6,100 per year in additional net income.

a. What is the average accounting return for this machine?

b. What three flaws are inherent in this decision rule?

6. **Average Accounting Return** The Mickelson Group has invested $34,000 in a high-tech project lasting three years. Depreciation is $9,600, $15,900, and $8,500 in Years 1, 2, and 3, respectively. The project generates earnings before tax of $3,560 each year. If the tax rate is 25 percent, what is the project's average accounting return (AAR)?

7. **Calculating IRR** Schaueffle Machines, Inc., has a project with the following cash flows.

Year	Cash Flows
0	−$20,300
1	9,600
2	13,700
3	5,800

The company evaluates all projects by applying the IRR rule. If the appropriate interest rate is 9 percent, should the company accept the project?

8. **Calculating IRR** Compute the internal rate of return for the cash flows of the following two projects.

	Cash Flows	
Year	Project A	Project B
0	−$8,100	−$5,400
1	2,900	2,200
2	4,600	2,700
3	3,100	2,300

9. **Calculating Profitability Index** Bill plans to open a self-serve grooming center in a storefront. The grooming equipment will cost $187,000. Bill expects aftertax cash inflows of $62,000 annually for seven years, after which he plans to scrap the equipment and retire to the beaches of Nevis. The first cash inflow occurs at the end of the first year. Assume the required return is 15 percent. What is the project's PI? Should it be accepted?

10. Calculating Profitability Index Suppose the following two independent investment opportunities are available to Woodland, Inc. The appropriate discount rate is 10 percent.

Year	Project Alpha	Project Beta
0	−$2,600	−$3,900
1	990	2,100
2	1,500	3,400
3	1,300	1,400

    a. Compute the profitability indexes for each of the two projects.

    b. Which project(s) should the company accept based on the profitability index rule?

Intermediate
(Questions 11–22)

11. Cash Flow Intuition A project has an initial cost of I, has a required return of R, and pays C annually for N years.

    a. Find C in terms of I and N such that the project has a payback period just equal to its life.

    b. Find C in terms of I, N, and R such that this is a profitable project according to the NPV decision rule.

    c. Find C in terms of I, N, and R such that the project has a benefit-cost ratio of 2.

12. Problems with IRR Suppose you are offered a project with the following payments.

Year	Cash Flows
0	$ 15,900
1	−5,900
2	−5,700
3	−4,900
4	−4,100

    a. What is the IRR of this offer?

    b. If the appropriate discount rate is 10 percent, should you accept this offer?

    c. If the appropriate discount rate is 20 percent, should you accept this offer?

    d. What is the NPV of the offer if the appropriate discount rate is 10 percent? 20 percent?

    e. Are the decisions under the NPV rule in part (d) consistent with those of the IRR rule?

 13. NPV versus IRR Consider the following cash flows on two mutually exclusive projects for the Bahamas Recreation Corporation. Both projects require an annual return of 15 percent.

Year	Deepwater Fishing	Submarine Ride
0	−$918,000	−$1,815,000
1	495,000	1,150,000
2	450,000	742,000
3	370,000	575,000

As a financial analyst for the company, you are asked the following questions.

    a. If your decision rule is to accept the project with the greater IRR, which project should you choose?

    b. Because you are fully aware of the IRR rule's scale problem, you calculate the incremental IRR for the cash flows. Based on your computation, which project should you choose?

    c. To be prudent, you compute the NPV for both projects. Which project should you choose? Is it consistent with the incremental IRR rule?

14. Problems with Profitability Index The Simpson Corporation is trying to choose between the following two mutually exclusive design projects:

Year	Cash Flow (I)	Cash Flow (II)
0	−$75,000	−$42,000
1	39,000	24,000
2	39,000	24,000
3	39,000	24,000

a. If the required return for both projects is 10 percent and the company applies the profitability index decision rule, which project should the firm accept?

b. If the company applies the NPV decision rule, which project should it choose?

c. Explain why your answers in (a) and (b) are different.

15. **Problems with IRR**   Bohrer Mining, Inc., is trying to evaluate a project with the following cash flows:

Year	Cash Flow
0	−$63,000,000
1	89,000,000
2	−11,000,000

a. If the project has a required return of 10 percent, should it accept this project? Why?

b. Compute the IRR for this project. How many IRRs are there? If you apply the IRR decision rule, should you accept the project or not? What's going on here?

 16. **Comparing Investment Criteria**   Mario Brothers, a game manufacturer, has a new idea for an adventure game. It can market the game either as a traditional board game or as a PC game, but not both. Consider the following cash flows of the two mutually exclusive projects. Assume the discount rate for both projects is 10 percent.

Year	Board Game	PC
0	−$380,000	−$625,000
1	292,000	396,000
2	165,000	319,000
3	107,000	204,000

a. Based on the payback period rule, which project should be chosen?

b. Based on the NPV, which project should be chosen?

c. Based on the IRR, which project should be chosen?

d. Based on the incremental IRR, which project should be chosen?

17. **Profitability Index versus NPV**   Broxton Group, a consumer electronics conglomerate, is reviewing its annual budget in wireless technology. It is considering investments in three different technologies to develop wireless communication devices. Consider the following cash flows of the three independent projects. Assume the discount rate is 10 percent. Further, the company has only $55 million to invest in new projects this year.

	Cash Flows (in $ millions)		
Year	L6	G5	WI-FI
0	−$20	−$35	−$55
1	15	23	23
2	13	29	42
3	9	21	39

a. Based on the profitability index decision rule, rank these investments.

b. Based on the NPV, rank these investments.

c. Based on your findings in (a) and (b), what would you recommend to the company's CEO, and why?

18. **Comparing Investment Criteria** Consider the following cash flows of two mutually exclusive projects for A-Z Motorcars. Assume the discount rate for both projects is 10 percent.

Year	AZM Mini-SUV	AZF Full-SUV
0	−$525,000	−$810,000
1	290,000	410,000
2	245,000	390,000
3	185,000	350,000

a. Based on the payback period, which project should be taken?

b. Based on the NPV, which project should be taken?

c. Based on the IRR, which project should be taken?

d. Based on the above analysis, is incremental IRR analysis necessary? If yes, please conduct the analysis.

19. **Comparing Investment Criteria** The treasurer of Tropical Fruits, Inc., has projected the cash flows of Projects A, B, and C as follows:

Year	Project A	Project B	Project C
0	−$300,000	−$525,000	−$300,000
1	203,000	360,000	210,000
2	203,000	360,000	185,000

Suppose the relevant discount rate is 12 percent per year.

a. Compute the profitability index for each of the three projects.

b. Compute the NPV for each of the three projects.

c. Suppose these three projects are independent. Which project(s) should the company accept based on the profitability index rule?

d. Suppose these three projects are mutually exclusive. Which project(s) should the company accept based on the profitability index rule?

e. Suppose the budget for these projects is $825,000. The projects are not divisible. Which project(s) should be accepted?

20. **Comparing Investment Criteria** Consider the following cash flows of two mutually exclusive projects for Spartan Rubber Company. Assume the discount rate for both projects is 10 percent.

Year	Dry Prepreg	Solvent Prepreg
0	−$2,160,000	−$1,100,000
1	828,000	678,000
2	546,000	492,000
3	1,680,000	408,000

a. Based on the payback period, which project should be taken?

b. Based on the NPV, which project should be taken?

c. Based on the IRR, which project should be taken?

d. Based on the above analysis, is incremental IRR analysis necessary? If yes, please conduct the analysis.

21. **Comparing Investment Criteria** Consider two mutually exclusive new product launch projects that Nagano Golf is considering. Assume the discount rate for both projects is 12 percent.

Project A: Nagano NP-30

Professional clubs that will take an initial investment of $1,320,000 at Time 0.

Introduction of new product at Year 6 will terminate further cash flows from this project.

Project B: Nagano NX-20

High-end amateur clubs that will take an initial investment of $910,000 at Time 0.

Introduction of new product at Year 6 will terminate further cash flows from this project.

Here are the cash flows:

Year	NP-30	NX-20
0	−$1,320,000	−$910,000
1	480,000	350,000
2	470,000	350,000
3	435,000	340,000
4	415,000	325,000
5	285,000	245,000

Please fill in the following table:

	NP-30	NX-20	Implications
NPV			
IRR			
Incremental IRR			
PI			

22. **Comparing Investment Criteria** Consider two mutually exclusive R&D projects that Savage Tech is considering. Assume the discount rate for both projects is 15 percent.

Project A: Server CPU .13 micron processing project

By shrinking the die size to .13 micron, the company will be able to offer server CPU chips with lower power consumption and heat generation, meaning faster CPUs.

Project B: New telecom chip project

Entry into this industry will require introduction of a new chip for cell phones. The know-how will require a larger amount of up-front capital, but success of the project will lead to large cash flows later on.

Year	A	B
0	−$1,030,000	−$1,725,000
1	495,000	518,000
2	495,000	565,000
3	390,000	578,000
4	295,000	783,000
5	203,000	762,000

Please fill in the following table:

	A	B	Implications
NPV			
IRR			
Incremental IRR			
PI			

Challenge
(Questions 23–30)

23. NPV and IRR   Anderson International Limited is evaluating a project in Erewhon. The project will create the following cash flows:

Year	Cash Flow
0	−$1,750,000
1	560,000
2	640,000
3	535,000
4	475,000

All cash flows will occur in Erewhon and are expressed in dollars. In an attempt to improve its economy, the Erewhonian government has declared that all cash flows created by a foreign company are "blocked" and must be reinvested with the government for one year. The reinvestment rate for these funds is 4 percent. If Anderson uses a required return of 11 percent on this project, what are the NPV and IRR of the project? Is the IRR you calculated the MIRR of the project? Why or why not?

24. Payback and NPV   An investment under consideration has a payback of six years and a cost of $745,000. If the required return is 12 percent, what is the worst-case NPV? The best-case NPV? Explain. Assume the cash flows are conventional.

25. Multiple IRRs   This problem is useful for testing the ability of financial calculators and computer software. Consider the following cash flows. How many different IRRs are there? (*Hint:* Search between 20 percent and 70 percent.) When should we take this project?

Year	Cash Flow
0	−$2,016
1	11,448
2	−24,280
3	22,800
4	−8,000

26. NPV Valuation   The Yurdone Corporation wants to set up a private cemetery business. According to the CFO, Barry M. Deep, business is "looking up." As a result, the cemetery project will provide a net cash inflow of $103,800 for the firm during the first year, and the cash flows are projected to grow at a rate of 3.5 percent per year forever. The project requires an initial investment of $1.55 million.

a. If the company requires a return of 10 percent on such undertakings, should the cemetery business be started?

b. The company is somewhat unsure about the assumption of a growth rate of 3.5 percent in its cash flows. At what constant growth rate would the company just break even if it still required a return of 10 percent on this investment?

27. Calculating IRR   The Utah Mining Corporation is set to open a gold mine near Provo, Utah. According to the treasurer, Monty Goldstein, "This is a golden opportunity." The mine will cost $3.5 million to open and will have an economic life of 11 years. It will generate a cash inflow of $605,000 at the end of the first year, and the cash inflows are projected to grow at 6 percent per year for the next 10 years. After 11 years, the mine will be abandoned. Abandonment costs will be $575,000 at the end of Year 11.

a. What is the IRR for the gold mine?

b. The company requires a return of 13 percent on such projects. Should the mine be opened?

28. Calculating IRR   Consider two projects, A and B. Project A's first cash flow is $7,000 and is received three years from today. Future cash flows for Project A grow by 3 percent in perpetuity. Project B's first cash flow is −$8,000, which occurs two years from today and will continue in perpetuity. Assume that the appropriate discount rate is 12 percent.

a. What is the present value of each project?

b. Suppose that the two projects are combined into one project, called C. What is the IRR of Project C?

c. What is the correct IRR rule for Project C?

29. Calculating Incremental Cash Flows   Darin Clay, the CFO of MakeMoney.com, has to decide between the following two projects:

Year	Project Million	Project Billion
0	$-\$1,500$	$-\$I_0$
1	$I_0 + 200$	$I_0 + 500$
2	1,200	1,500
3	1,500	2,000

The expected rate of return for either of the two projects is 12 percent. What is the range of initial investment (I_0) for which Project Billion is more financially attractive than Project Million?

30. Problems with IRR   Binomial Corp. has a project with the following cash flows:

Year	Cash Flow
0	$ 50,000
1	−61,000
2	41,000

What is the IRR of the project? What is happening here?

EXCEL MASTER IT! PROBLEM

As you have already seen, Excel does not have a function to calculate the payback period. We have shown three ways to calculate the payback period, but there are numerous other methods as well. Below, the cash flows for a project are shown. You need to calculate the payback period using two different methods.

ExcelMaster
coverage online

www.mhhe.com/RossCore6e

a. Calculate the payback period in a table. The first three columns of the table will be the year, the cash flow for that year, and the cumulative cash flow. The fourth column will show the whole year for the payback. In other words, if the payback period is three-plus years, this column will have a 3, otherwise it will be a 0. The next column will calculate the fractional part of the payback period, or else it will display 0. The last column will add the previous two columns and display the final payback period calculation. You should also have a cell that displays the final payback period by itself, and a cell that returns the correct accept or reject decision based on the payback criteria.

b. Write a nested IF statement that calculates the payback period using only the project cash flow column. The IF statement should return a value of "Never" if the project has no payback period. In contrast to the example we showed previously, the nested IF function should test for the payback period starting with shorter payback periods and working toward longer payback periods. Another cell should display the correct accept or reject decision based on the payback criteria.

t	Cash Flow
0	−$250,000
1	41,000
2	48,000
3	63,000
4	79,000
5	88,000
6	64,000
7	41,000
Required payback:	5

BULLOCK GOLD MINING

Seth Bullock, the owner of Bullock Gold Mining, is evaluating a new gold mine in South Dakota. Dan Dority, the company's geologist, has just finished his analysis of the mine site. He has estimated that the mine would be productive for eight years, after which the gold would be completely mined. Dan has taken an estimate of the gold deposits to Alma Garrett, the company's financial officer. Alma has been asked by Seth to perform an analysis of the new mine and present her recommendation on whether the company should open the new mine.

Alma has used the estimates provided by Dan to determine the revenues that could be expected from the mine. She has also projected the expense of opening the mine and the annual operating expenses. If the company opens the mine, it will cost $750 million today, and it will have a cash outflow of $105 million nine years from today in costs associated with closing the mine and reclaiming the area surrounding it. The expected cash flows each year from the mine are shown in the table that follows. Bullock has a 12 percent required return on all of its gold mines.

Year	Cash Flow
0	−$750,000,000
1	150,000,000
2	180,000,000
3	195,000,000
4	235,000,000
5	220,000,000
6	185,000,000
7	165,000,000
8	145,000,000
9	−105,000,000

1. Construct a spreadsheet to calculate the payback period, internal rate of return, modified internal rate of return, and net present value of the proposed mine.

2. Based on your analysis, should the company open the mine?

3. Bonus question: Most spreadsheets do not have a built-in formula to calculate the payback period. Write a VBA script that calculates the payback period for a project.

Making Capital Investment Decisions

Everyone knows that computer chips evolve quickly, getting smaller, faster, and cheaper. In fact, the famous Moore's Law (named after Intel cofounder Gordon Moore) predicts that the number of transistors placed on a chip will double every two years (and this prediction has held up very well since it was published in 1965). This growth often means that companies need to build new fabrication facilities. For example, in 2018, Samsung announced that it would start producing 7 nanometer (nm) chips at its $6 billion extreme ultraviolet lithography (EUV) line at the company's plant in Hwaseong. The 7 nm chips are faster and more energy efficient than previous chips. And although Moore's Law might be in jeopardy as the doubling has slowed down for many manufacturers, Samsung stated that it planned to build 4 nm chips beginning in 2020 and 3 nm chips in 2021.

This chapter follows up on our previous one by delving more deeply into capital budgeting and the evaluation of projects such as these chip manufacturing facilities. We identify the relevant cash flows of a project, including initial investment outlays, requirements for net working capital, and operating cash flows. Further, we look at the effects of depreciation and taxes. We also examine the impact of inflation and show how to consistently evaluate the NPV of a project.

Please visit us at corecorporatefinance.blogspot.com for the latest developments in the world of corporate finance.

8.1 INCREMENTAL CASH FLOWS

Cash Flows—Not Accounting Income

You may not have thought about it, but there is a big difference between corporate finance courses and financial accounting courses. Techniques in corporate finance generally use cash flows, whereas financial accounting generally stresses income or earnings numbers. Our text follows this tradition, as our net present value techniques discount cash flows, not earnings. When considering a single project, we discount the cash flows that the firm receives from the project. When valuing the firm as a whole, we discount the cash flows—not earnings—that an investor receives.

EXAMPLE 8.1

Relevant Cash Flows

The Weber-Decker Co. just paid $1 million in cash for a building as part of a new capital budgeting project. This entire $1 million is an immediate cash outflow. However, assuming straight-line depreciation over 20 years, only $50,000 (= $1 million/20) is considered an accounting expense in the current year. Current earnings are thereby reduced by only $50,000. The remaining $950,000 is expensed over the following 19 years. For capital budgeting purposes, the relevant cash outflow at Year 0 is the full $1 million, not the reduction in earnings of only $50,000.

Always discount cash flows, not earnings, when performing a capital budgeting or valuation calculation. Earnings do not represent real money. You can't spend out of earnings, you can't eat out of earnings, and you can't pay dividends out of earnings. You can only do these things out of cash flow.

In addition, it is not enough to use cash flows. In calculating the NPV of a project, only cash flows that are *incremental* to the project should be used. These cash flows are the changes in the firm's cash flows that occur as a direct consequence of accepting the project. That is, we are interested in the difference between the cash flows of the firm with the project and the cash flows of the firm without the project.

The use of incremental cash flows sounds easy enough, but pitfalls abound in the real world. We describe below how to avoid some of the pitfalls of determining incremental cash flows.

Sunk Costs

A sunk cost is a cost that has already occurred. Because sunk costs are in the past, they cannot be changed by the decision to accept or reject the project. Just as we "let bygones be bygones," we should ignore such costs. Sunk costs are not incremental cash outflows.

EXAMPLE 8.2

Sunk Costs

The General Milk Company is currently evaluating the NPV of establishing a line of chocolate milk. As part of the evaluation, the company had paid a consulting firm $100,000 to perform a test-marketing analysis. This expenditure was made last year. Is this cost relevant for the capital budgeting decision now confronting the management of General Milk Company?

The answer is no. The $100,000 is not recoverable, so the $100,000 expenditure is a sunk cost, or spilled milk. Of course, the decision to spend $100,000 for a marketing analysis was a capital budgeting decision itself and was perfectly relevant before it was sunk. Our point is that once the company incurred the expense, the cost became irrelevant for any future decision.

Opportunity Costs

Your firm may have an asset that it is considering selling, leasing, or employing elsewhere in the business. If the asset is used in a new project, potential revenues from alternative uses are lost. These lost revenues can meaningfully be viewed as costs. They are called opportunity costs because, by taking the project, the firm forgoes other opportunities for using the assets.

EXAMPLE 8.3

Opportunity Costs

Suppose the Weinstein Trading Company has an empty warehouse in Philadelphia that can be used to store a new line of electronic pinball machines. The company hopes to sell these machines to affluent Northeastern consumers. Should the warehouse be considered a cost in the decision to sell the machines?

The answer is yes. The company could sell the warehouse if it decides not to market the pinball machines. Thus, the sales price of the warehouse is an opportunity cost in the pinball machine decision.

Side Effects

Another difficulty in determining incremental cash flows comes from the side effects of the proposed project on other parts of the firm. A side effect is classified as either **erosion** or **synergy**. Erosion occurs when a new product reduces the sales and, hence, the cash flows, of existing products. Synergy occurs when a new product increases the cash flows of existing projects.

EXAMPLE 8.4

Erosion versus Synergy

Suppose the Innovative Motors Corporation (IMC) is determining the NPV of a new convertible sports car. Some of the customers who would purchase the car are owners of IMC's compact sedans. Are all sales and profits from the new convertible sports car incremental?

The answer is no because some of the cash flow represents transfers from other elements of IMC's product line. This is erosion, which must be included in the NPV calculation. Without taking erosion into account, IMC might erroneously calculate the NPV of the sports car to be, say, $100 million. If half the customers are transfers from the sedan and lost sedan sales have an NPV of −$150 million, the true NPV of the new convertible is −$50 million (= $100 million − 150 million).

IMC is also contemplating the formation of a racing team. The team is forecasted to lose money for the foreseeable future, with perhaps the best projection showing an NPV of −$35 million for the operation. However, IMC's managers are aware that the team will likely generate great publicity for all of IMC's products. A consultant estimates that the increase in cash flows elsewhere in the firm has a present value of $65 million. Assuming that the consultant's estimates of synergy are trustworthy, the net present value of the team is $30 million (= $65 million − 35 million). The managers should form the team.

Allocated Costs

Frequently a particular expenditure benefits a number of projects. Accountants allocate this cost across the different projects when determining income. However, for capital budgeting purposes, this **allocated cost** should be viewed as a cash outflow of a project only if it is an incremental cost of the project.

EXAMPLE 8.5

Allocated Cost

The Voetmann Consulting Corp. devotes one wing of its suite of offices to a library requiring a cash outflow of $100,000 a year in upkeep. A proposed capital budgeting project is expected to generate revenue equal to 5 percent of the overall firm's sales. An executive at the firm argues that $5,000 (= .05 × $100,000) should be viewed as the proposed project's share of the library's costs. Is this appropriate for capital budgeting?

The answer is no. One must ask the question: What is the difference between the cash flows of the entire firm with the project and the cash flows of the entire firm without the project? The firm will spend $100,000 on library upkeep whether or not the proposed project is accepted. Because acceptance of the proposed project does not affect this cash flow, the cash flow should be ignored when calculating the NPV of the project.

8.2 THE BALDWIN COMPANY: AN EXAMPLE

We next consider the example of a proposed investment in machinery and related items. Our example involves the Baldwin Company and colored bowling balls.

The Baldwin Company, originally established in 1965 to make footballs, is now a leading producer of tennis balls, baseballs, footballs, and golf balls. In 1973, the company introduced "High Flite," its first line of high-performance golf balls. The Baldwin management

ExcelMaster
coverage online

www.mhhe.com/RossCore6e

has sought opportunities in whatever businesses seem to have some potential for cash flow. In 2018, W. C. Meadows, vice president of the Baldwin Company, identified another segment of the sports ball market that looked promising and that he felt was not adequately served by larger manufacturers. That market was for brightly colored bowling balls, and he believed a large number of bowlers valued appearance and style above performance. He also believed that it would be difficult for competitors to take advantage of the opportunity because of both Baldwin's cost advantages and its highly developed marketing skills.

As a result, in early 2019, the Baldwin Company investigated the marketing potential of brightly colored bowling balls. Baldwin sent a questionnaire to consumers in three markets: Philadelphia, Los Angeles, and New Haven. The results of the three questionnaires were much better than expected and supported the conclusion that the brightly colored bowling balls could achieve a 10 to 15 percent share of the market. Of course, some people at Baldwin complained about the cost of the test marketing, which was $250,000. (As we shall see later, this is a sunk cost and should not be included in project evaluation.)

In any case, the Baldwin Company is now considering investing in a machine to produce bowling balls. The bowling balls would be manufactured in a building owned by the firm and located near Los Angeles. This building, which is vacant, and the land can be sold for $150,000 after taxes.

Working with his staff, Meadows is preparing an analysis of the proposed new product. He summarizes his assumptions as follows: The cost of the bowling ball machine is $100,000. The machine has an estimated market value at the end of five years of $30,000. Production by year during the five-year life of the machine is expected to be as follows: 5,000 units, 8,000 units, 12,000 units, 10,000 units, and 6,000 units. The price of bowling balls in the first year will be $20. The bowling ball market is highly competitive, so Meadows believes that the price of bowling balls will increase at only 2 percent per year, as compared to the anticipated general inflation rate of 5 percent. Conversely, the plastic used to produce bowling balls is rapidly becoming more expensive. Because of this, production cash outflows are expected to grow at 10 percent per year. First-year production costs will be $10 per unit. The corporate tax rate is 21 percent.

Net working capital is defined as the difference between current assets and current liabilities. Like any other manufacturing firm, Baldwin finds that it must maintain an investment in working capital. It will purchase raw materials before production and sale, giving rise to an investment in inventory. It will maintain cash as a buffer against unforeseen expenditures. And its credit sales will generate accounts receivable. Management determines that an immediate (Year 0) investment of $10,000 in the various items of working capital is required. The total net working capital for each subsequent year will be 10 percent of sales. Working capital is forecast to rise in the early years of the project but fall to $0 by the project's end. In other words, the investment in working capital is to be completely recovered by the end of the project's life.

Projections based on these assumptions and Meadows's analysis appear in Tables 8.1 through 8.4. In these tables all cash flows are assumed to occur at the end of the year. Because of the large amount of information in these tables, it is important to see how the tables are related. Table 8.1 shows the basic data for both investment and income. Supplementary schedules on operations and depreciation, as presented in Tables 8.2 and 8.3, help explain where the numbers in Table 8.1 come from. Our goal is to obtain projections of cash flow. The data in Table 8.1 are all that are needed to calculate the relevant cash flows, as shown in Table 8.4.

An Analysis of the Project

INVESTMENTS The investment outlays for the project are summarized in the top segment of Table 8.1. They consist of three parts:

1. *The Bowling Ball Machine.* The purchase requires an immediate (Year 0) cash outflow of $100,000. The firm realizes a cash inflow when the machine is sold in Year 5. These cash flows are shown in Line 1 of Table 8.1. As indicated in the footnote to the table, taxes are incurred when the asset is sold.

TABLE 8.1   The Worksheet for Cash Flows of the Baldwin Company (in $ thousands)

	Year 0	Year 1	Year 2	Year 3	Year 4	Year 5
Investments:						
(1) Bowling ball machine	−$100.00					$ 24.91*
(2) Accumulated depreciation		$ 20.00	$ 52.00	$ 71.20	$ 82.72	94.24
(3) Book value of machine (end of year)		80.00	48.00	28.80	17.28	5.76
(4) Opportunity cost (warehouse)	− 150.00					150.00
(5) Net working capital (end of year)	10.00	10.00	16.32	24.97	21.22	0
(6) Change in net working capital	− 10.00		− 6.32	− 8.65	3.75	21.22
(7) Total cash flow of investment [(1) + (4) + (6)]	− 260.00		− 6.32	− 8.65	3.75	196.13
Income:						
(8) Sales revenues		$100.00	$163.20	$249.70	$212.24	$129.89
(9) Operating costs		50.00	88.00	145.20	133.10	87.85
(10) Depreciation		20.00	32.00	19.20	11.52	$ 11.52
(11) Income before taxes [(8) − (9) − (10)]		$ 30.00	$ 43.20	$ 85.30	$ 67.62	$ 30.53
(12) Tax (21%)		6.30	9.07	17.91	14.20	6.41
(13) Net income		$ 23.70	$ 34.13	$ 67.38	$ 53.42	$ 24.12

*We assume that the ending market value of the capital investment at Year 5 is $30 (in thousands). The taxable amount is $24.24 (= $30 − 5.76). The aftertax salvage value is $30 − [.21 × ($30 − 5.76)] = $24.91.

2. *The Opportunity Cost of Not Selling the Warehouse.* If Baldwin accepts the bowling ball project, it will use a warehouse and land that could otherwise be sold. The estimated sales price of the warehouse and land is therefore included as an opportunity cost in Year 0, as presented in Line 4. Opportunity costs are treated as cash outflows for purposes of capital budgeting. However, note that if the project is accepted, management assumes that the warehouse will be sold for $150,000 (after taxes) in Year 5.

3. *The Investment in Working Capital.* Required working capital appears in Line 5. Working capital rises over the early years of the project as expansion occurs. However, all working capital is assumed to be recovered at the end, a common assumption in capital budgeting. In other words, all inventory is sold by the end, the cash balance maintained as a buffer is liquidated, and all accounts receivable are collected. Increases in working capital in the early years must be funded by cash generated elsewhere in the firm. Hence, these increases are viewed as cash outflows. To reiterate, it is the increase in working capital over a year that leads to a cash outflow in that year. Even if working capital is at a high level, there will be no cash outflow over a year if working capital stays constant over that year. Conversely, decreases in working capital in the later years are viewed as cash inflows. All of these cash flows are presented in Line 6. A more complete discussion of working capital is provided later in this section.

To recap, there are three investments in this example: the bowling ball machine (Line 1 in Table 8.1), the opportunity cost of the warehouse (Line 4), and the changes in working capital (Line 6). The total cash flow from the above three investments is shown in Line 7. The test-marketing cost of $250,000 is not included. The tests occurred in the past and should be viewed as a sunk cost.

INCOME AND TAXES   Next, the determination of income is presented in the bottom segment of Table 8.1. While we are ultimately interested in cash flow—not income—we need the income calculation in order to determine taxes. Lines 8 and 9 of Table 8.1 show sales

TABLE 8.2

Operating Revenues and
Costs of the Baldwin
Company

(1) Year	(2) Production	(3) Price	(4) Sales Revenues	(5) Cost per Unit	(6) Operating Costs
1	5,000	$20.00	$100,000	$10.00	$ 50,000
2	8,000	20.40	163,200	11.00	88,000
3	12,000	20.81	249,696	12.10	145,200
4	10,000	21.22	212,242	13.31	133,100
5	6,000	21.65	129,892	14.64	87,846

Prices rise at 2 percent per year.
Unit costs rise at 10 percent per year.

revenues and operating costs, respectively. The projections in these lines are based on the sales revenues and operating costs computed in Columns 4 and 6 of Table 8.2. The estimates of revenues and costs follow from assumptions made by the corporate planning staff at Baldwin. In other words, the estimates critically depend on the fact that product prices are projected to increase at 2 percent per year and costs per unit are projected to increase at 10 percent per year.

Depreciation of the $100,000 capital investment is shown in Line 10 of Table 8.1. Where do these numbers come from? Depreciation for tax purposes for U.S. companies is based on the Modified Accelerated Cost Recovery System (MACRS). Each asset is assigned a useful life under MACRS, with an accompanying depreciation schedule as shown in Table 8.3. The IRS ruled that Baldwin is to depreciate its capital investment over five years, so the second column of the table applies in this case. Because depreciation in the table is expressed as a percentage of the asset's cost, multiply the percentages in this column by $100,000 to arrive at depreciation in dollars.

Year	Recovery Period Class					
	3 Years	5 Years	7 Years	10 Years	15 Years	20 Years
1	.3333	.2000	.1429	.1000	.0500	.03750
2	.4445	.3200	.2449	.1800	.0950	.07219
3	.1481	.1920	.1749	.1440	.0855	.06677
4	.0741	.1152	.1249	.1152	.0770	.06177
5		.1152	.0893	.0922	.0693	.05713
6		.0576	.0892	.0737	.0623	.05285
7			.0893	.0655	.0590	.04888
8			.0446	.0655	.0590	.04522
9				.0656	.0591	.04462
10				.0655	.0590	.04461
11				.0328	.0591	.04462
12					.0590	.04461
13					.0591	.04462
14					.0590	.04461
15					.0591	.04462
16					.0295	.04461
17						.04462
18						.04461
19						.04462
20						.04461
21						.02231

Depreciation is expressed as a percent of the asset's cost. These schedules are based on the IRS Publication 946: *How to Depreciate Property*, and other details on depreciation are presented later in the chapter. Note that five-year depreciation actually carries over six years because the IRS assumes the purchase is made midyear.

Income before taxes is calculated in Line 11 of Table 8.1. Taxes are provided in Line 12 of this table, and net income is calculated in Line 13.

SALVAGE VALUE   In calculating depreciation under current tax law, the expected economic life and future value of an asset are not issues. As a result, the book value of an asset can differ substantially from its actual market value. For example, consider the bowling ball machine the Baldwin Company is considering for its new project. The book value after the first year is $100,000 less the first year's depreciation of $20,000, or $80,000. After six years, the book value of the machine is zero.

Suppose, at the end of the project, Baldwin sold the machine. At the end of the fifth year, the book value of the machine would be $5,760, but based on Baldwin's experience, it would probably be worth about $30,000. If the company actually sold it for this amount, then it would pay taxes at the ordinary income tax rate on the difference between the sale price of $30,000 and the book value of $5,760. With a 21 percent tax rate, the tax liability would be .21 × ($30,000 − 5,760) = $5,090. So, the aftertax salvage value of the equipment, a cash inflow to the company, would be $30,000 − 5,090 = $24,910. We would still use this same cash flow for this project even if Baldwin kept the machine to use in another project. In this case, the cash inflow in Year 5 for the machine would be an opportunity cost for this project, as well as for the other project.

Taxes must be paid in this case because the difference between the market value and the book value is "excess" depreciation, and it must be recaptured when the asset is sold. In this case, Baldwin would have overdepreciated the asset by $30,000 − 5,760 = $24,240. Because the depreciation was too high, the company paid too little in taxes.

Notice this is not a tax on a long-term capital gain. Further, what is and what is not a capital gain is ultimately up to taxing authorities, and the specific rules can be very complex. We will ignore capital gains taxes for the most part.

Finally, if the book value exceeds the market value, then the difference is treated as a loss for tax purposes. For example, if Baldwin sold the machine for $4,000, then the book value would exceed the market value by $1,760. In this case, a tax savings of .21 × $1,760 = $369.60 would occur.

CASH FLOW   Cash flow is finally determined in Table 8.4. We begin by reproducing Lines 8, 9, and 12 in Table 8.1 as Lines 1, 2, and 3 in Table 8.4. Operating cash flow, which is sales minus both operating costs and taxes, is provided in Line 4 of Table 8.4. Total investment cash flow, taken from Line 7 of Table 8.1, appears as Line 5 of Table 8.4. Cash flow from operations plus

. . . .

TABLE 8.4   Incremental Cash Flows for the Baldwin Company (in $ thousands)

	Year 0	Year 1	Year 2	Year 3	Year 4	Year 5
(1) Sales revenue [Line 8, Table 8.1]		$100.00	$163.20	$249.70	$212.24	$129.89
(2) Operating costs [Line 9, Table 8.1]		50.00	88.00	145.20	133.10	87.85
(3) Taxes [Line 12, Table 8.1]		6.30	9.07	17.91	14.20	6.41
(4) Operating cash flow [(1) − (2) − (3)]		$ 43.70	$ 66.13	$ 86.58	$ 64.94	$ 35.64
(5) Total cash flow of investment [Line 7, Table 8.1]	−$260.00		− 6.32	− 8.65	3.75	196.13
(6) Total cash flow of project [(4) + (5)]	−$260.00	$ 43.70	$ 59.81	$ 77.93	$ 68.69	$231.77
NPV @ 4% $155.81						
10 78.53						
15 28.97						
18.54 0						
20 −10.68						

total cash flow of the investment equals total cash flow of the project, which is displayed as Line 6 of Table 8.4. We should note that the cash flows we have calculated here are the cash flow from assets we calculated in Chapter 2.

NET PRESENT VALUE   The NPV of the Baldwin bowling ball project can be calculated from the cash flows in Line 6. This is often referred to as unlevered free cash flow. The word *unlevered* means that the cash flows are independent of any debt that may have been used to finance the project. The word *free* refers to the fact that these cash flows can be distributed to creditors and shareholders. As can be seen at the bottom of Table 8.4, the NPV is $78,533 if 10 percent is the appropriate discount rate and −$10,682 if 20 percent is the appropriate discount rate. If the discount rate is 18.54 percent, the project will have a zero NPV. In other words, the project's internal rate of return is 18.54 percent. If the discount rate of the Baldwin bowling ball project is above 18.54 percent, it should not be accepted because its NPV would be negative.

Which Set of Books?

It should be noted that the firm's management generally keeps two sets of books, one for the IRS (called the *tax books*) and another for its annual report (called the *stockholders' books*). The tax books follow the rules of the IRS. The stockholders' books follow the rules of the Financial Accounting Standards Board (FASB), the governing body in accounting. The two sets of rules differ widely in certain areas. For example, income on municipal bonds is ignored for tax purposes while being treated as income by the FASB. The differences almost always benefit the firm because the rules permit income on the stockholders' books to be higher than income on the tax books. That is, management can look profitable to the stockholders without needing to pay taxes on all of the reported profit. In fact, there are plenty of large companies that consistently report positive earnings to the stockholders while reporting losses to the IRS.

A Note on Net Working Capital

The investment in net working capital is an important part of any capital budgeting analysis. While we explicitly considered net working capital in Lines 5 and 6 of Table 8.1, students may be wondering where the numbers in these lines came from. Examples of investments in net working capital arise whenever (1) inventory is purchased, (2) cash is kept in the project as a buffer against unexpected expenditures, and (3) credit sales are made, generating accounts receivable rather than cash. This is reversed for credit purchases, which reduce net working capital and generate accounts payable. This investment in net working capital represents a cash outflow because cash generated elsewhere in the firm is tied up in the project.

To see how the investment in net working capital is built from its component parts, we focus on Year 1. We see in Table 8.1 that Baldwin's managers predict sales in Year 1 to be $100,000 and operating costs to be $50,000. If both the sales and costs were cash transactions, the firm would receive $50,000 (= $100,000 − 50,000). As stated earlier, this cash flow would occur at the end of Year 1.

Now let's give you more information. The managers:

1. Forecast that $9,000 of the sales will be on credit, implying that cash receipts at the end of Year 1 will be only $91,000 (= $100,000 − 9,000). The accounts receivable of $9,000 will be collected at the end of Year 2.
2. Believe that they can defer payment on $3,000 of the $50,000 of costs, implying that cash disbursements at the end of Year 1 will be only $47,000 (= $50,000 − 3,000). Baldwin will pay off the $3,000 of accounts payable at the end of Year 2.

3. Decide that inventory of $2,500 should be left on hand at the end of Year 1 to avoid stockouts (that is, running out of inventory).

4. Decide that cash of $1,500 should be earmarked for the project at the end of Year 1 to avoid running out of cash.

Thus, net working capital at the end of Year 1 is:

$$\underset{\substack{\text{Accounts} \\ \text{receivable}}}{\$9,000} \; - \; \underset{\substack{\text{Accounts} \\ \text{payable}}}{3,000} \; + \; \underset{\text{Inventory}}{2,500} \; + \; \underset{\text{Cash}}{1,500} \; = \; \underset{\substack{\text{Net working} \\ \text{capital}}}{\$10,000}$$

Because $10,000 of cash generated elsewhere in the firm must be used to offset this requirement for net working capital, Baldwin's managers correctly view the investment in net working capital as a cash outflow of the project. As the project grows over time, needs for net working capital increase. Changes in net working capital from year to year represent further cash flows, as indicated by the negative numbers for the first few years of Line 6 of Table 8.1. However, in the declining years of the project, net working capital is reduced—ultimately to zero. That is, accounts receivable are finally collected, the project's cash buffer is returned to the rest of the corporation, and all remaining inventory is sold off. This frees up cash in the later years, as indicated by positive numbers in Years 4 and 5 of Line 6.

Typically, corporate worksheets (such as Table 8.1) treat net working capital as a whole. The individual components of working capital (receivables, inventory, etc.) do not generally appear in the worksheets. However, you should remember that the working capital numbers in the worksheets are not pulled out of thin air. Rather, they result from a meticulous forecast of the components, as we illustrated for Year 1.

A Note on Depreciation

The Baldwin case made some assumptions about depreciation. Where did these assumptions come from? Depreciation rules are set forth in IRS Publication 946, entitled *How to Depreciate Property*. This publication sorts different property types into classes, thereby determining their depreciable lives for tax purposes. There are seven classes of depreciable property:

1. The three-year class includes certain specialized short-lived property. Tractor units and racehorses over two years old are among the very few items fitting into this class.

2. The five-year class includes (a) cars and trucks; (b) computers and peripheral equipment, as well as calculators, copiers, and typewriters; and (c) specific items used for research purposes.

3. The seven-year class includes office furniture, equipment, books, and single-purpose agricultural structures. It is also a catchall category because any asset not designated to be in another class is included here.

4. The 10-year class includes vessels, barges, tugs, and similar equipment related to water transportation.

5. The 15-year class encompasses a variety of specialized items. Included are equipment of telephone distribution plants and similar equipment used for voice and data communications, and sewage treatment plants.

6. The 20-year class includes farm buildings, sewer pipe, and other very long-lived equipment.

7. Real property that is depreciable is separated into two classes: residential and nonresidential. The cost of residential property is recovered over 27.5 years and nonresidential property over 39 years.

Items in the three-, five-, and seven-year classes are depreciated using the 200 percent declining-balance method, with a switch to straight-line depreciation at a point specified in the Tax Reform Act. Items in the 15- and 20-year classes are depreciated using the 150 percent declining-balance method, with a switch to straight-line depreciation at a specified point. All real estate is depreciated on a straight-line basis.

All calculations of depreciation include a half-year convention, which treats all property as if it were placed in service midyear. To be consistent, the IRS allows half a year of depreciation for the year in which property is disposed of or retired. The effect of this is to spread the deductions for property over one year more than the name of its class, for example, six tax years for five-year property.

For a number of years prior to 2018, various tax rules and regulations were enacted that allowed "bonus" depreciation. Based on the Protecting Americans from Tax Hikes (PATH) Act of 2015, the size of the bonus in 2017 was 50 percent. What this means is that a firm can take a depreciation deduction of 50 percent of the cost on an eligible asset in the first year and then depreciate the remaining 50 percent using the MACRS schedules as we have just described. Significantly, in late 2017, Congress passed the Tax Cuts and Jobs Act, which increased the bonus depreciation to 100 percent for 2018, lasting until the end of 2022. After that, it drops by 20 percent per year until it reaches zero after 2026. The implication is that most firms will not use the MACRS schedules until 2023 unless they wish to (taking the bonus depreciation is optional). Of course, future legislation may change things.

Interest Expense

It may have bothered you that interest expense was ignored in the Baldwin example. After all, many projects are at least partially financed with debt, particularly a bowling ball machine that is likely to increase the debt capacity of the firm. The reason is that adjustments for debt financing are generally reflected in the discount rate, not the cash flows. The treatment of debt in capital budgeting will be covered in Chapter 12. At this time, the full ramifications of debt financing are well beyond our current discussion.

8.3 INFLATION AND CAPITAL BUDGETING

**ExcelMaster
coverage online**

www.mhhe.com/RossCore6e

Inflation is an important fact of economic life, and it must be considered in capital budgeting. Capital budgeting requires data on cash flows as well as on interest rates. Like interest rates, cash flows can be expressed in either nominal or real terms. A **nominal cash flow** refers to the actual dollars to be received (or paid out). A **real cash flow** refers to the cash flow's purchasing power. Like most definitions, these definitions are best explained by examples.

EXAMPLE 8.6

Nominal versus Real Cash Flow

Burrows Publishing has just purchased the rights to the next book of famed romantic novelist Barbara Musk. Still unwritten, the book should be available to the public in four years. Currently, romantic novels sell for $10.00 in softcover. The publishers believe that inflation will be 6 percent per year over the next four years. Because romantic novels are so popular, the publishers anticipate that their prices will rise about 2 percent per year more than the inflation rate over the next four years. Burrows Publishing plans to sell the novel at a price of $13.60 (= $1.08^4 \times 10.00) four years from now, anticipating sales of 100,000 copies.

The expected cash flow in the fourth year of $1.36 million (= $13.60 \times 100,000$) is a nominal cash flow. That is, the firm expects to receive $1.36 million at that time. In other words, a nominal cash flow refers to the actual dollars to be received in the future.

The purchasing power of $1.36 million in four years is determined by deflating the $1.36 million at 6 percent for four years:

$$\$1.08 \text{ million} = \frac{\$1.36 \text{ million}}{1.06^4}$$

The figure $1.08 million is a real cash flow because it is expressed in terms of purchasing power.

EXAMPLE 8.7

Depreciation

EOBII Publishers, a competitor of Burrows, recently bought a printing press for $2,000,000 to be depreciated by the straight-line method over five years. This implies yearly depreciation of $400,000 (= $2,000,000/5). Is this $400,000 figure a real or a nominal quantity?

Depreciation is a nominal quantity because $400,000 is the actual tax deduction over each of the next four years. Depreciation becomes a real quantity if it is adjusted for purchasing power. Hence, $316,837 (= $400,000/1.06^4) is depreciation in the fourth year, expressed as a real quantity.

Discounting: Nominal or Real?

Our examples show that cash flows can be expressed in either nominal or real terms. Given these choices, how should one express discount rates and cash flows when performing capital budgeting?

Financial practitioners correctly stress the need to maintain consistency between cash flows and discount rates. That is:

> **Nominal cash flows must be discounted at the nominal rate.**
> **Real cash flows must be discounted at the real rate.**

As long as one is consistent, either approach is correct. In order to minimize computational error, it is generally advisable in practice to choose the approach that is easiest. This idea is illustrated in the following two examples.

EXAMPLE 8.8

Real and Nominal Discounting

Shields Electric forecasts the following nominal cash flows on a particular project:

Date	0	1	2
Cash Flow	−$1,000	$600	$650

The nominal discount rate is 14 percent, and the inflation rate is forecast to be 5 percent. What is the value of the project?

Using Nominal Quantities The NPV can be calculated as:

$$\$26.47 = -\$1,000 + \frac{\$600}{1.14} + \frac{\$650}{1.14^2}$$

The project should be accepted.

(Continued)

Using Real Quantities   The real cash flows are:

Date	0	1	2
Cash Flow	−$1,000	$571.43 $\left(=\dfrac{\$600}{1.05}\right)$	$589.57 $\left(=\dfrac{\$650}{1.05^2}\right)$

As we saw in an earlier chapter, from the Fisher equation, the real discount rate is 8.57143 percent (= 1.14/1.05 − 1).

The NPV can be calculated as:

$$\$26.47 = -\$1,000 + \frac{\$571.43}{1.0857143} + \frac{\$589.57}{1.0857143^2}$$

The NPV is the same whether cash flows are expressed in nominal or in real quantities. It must always be the case that the NPV is the same under the two different approaches.

Because both approaches always yield the same result, which one should be used? As mentioned above, use the approach that is simpler, since the simpler approach generally leads to fewer computational errors. Because the Shields Electric example begins with nominal cash flows, nominal quantities produce a simpler calculation here.

EXAMPLE 8.9

Real and Nominal NPV

Altshuler, Inc., generated the following forecast for a capital budgeting project:

	Year		
	0	1	2
Capital expenditure	$1,210		
Revenues (in real terms)		$1,900	$2,000
Cash expenses (in real terms)		950	1,000
Depreciation (straight line)		605	605

The president, David Altshuler, estimates inflation to be 10 percent per year over the next two years. In addition, he believes that the cash flows of the project should be discounted at the nominal rate of 15.5 percent. His firm's tax rate is 21 percent.

Mr. Altshuler forecasts all cash flows in nominal terms, leading to the following spreadsheet:

	Year		
	0	1	2
Capital expenditure	−$1,210		
Revenues		$2,090 (= $1,900 × 1.10)	$2,420 (= $2,000 × 1.10²)
Expenses		1,045 (= $950 × 1.10)	1,210 (= $1,000 × 1.10²)
Depreciation		605 (= $1,210/2)	605
Taxable income		$ 440	$ 605
Taxes (21%)		92	127
Net income		$ 348	$ 478
Depreciation		605	605
Cash flow		$ 953	$1,083

$$NPV = -\$1,210 + \frac{\$953}{1.155} + \frac{\$1,083}{1.155^2} = \$426.55$$

Mr. Altshuler's sidekick, Stuart Weiss, prefers working in real terms. He first calculates the real rate to be 5 percent (= 1.155/1.10 − 1). Next, he generates the following spreadsheet in real quantities:

	Year		
	0	1	2
Capital expenditure	−$1,210		
Revenues		$1,900	$2,000
Expenses		950	1,000
Depreciation		550 (= $605/1.1)	500 (= $605/1.1^2)
Taxable income		$ 400	$ 500
Taxes (21%)		84	105
Net income		$ 316	$ 395
Depreciation		550	500
Cash flow		$ 866	$ 895

$$NPV = -\$1,210 + \frac{\$866}{1.05} + \frac{\$895}{1.05^2} = \$426.55$$

In explaining his calculations to Mr. Altshuler, Mr. Weiss points out:

1. Because the capital expenditure occurs at Year 0 (today), its nominal value and its real value are equal.
2. Because yearly depreciation of $605 is a nominal value, one converts it to a real value by discounting at the inflation rate of 10 percent.

It is no coincidence that both Mr. Altshuler and Mr. Weiss arrive at the same NPV number. Both methods must always generate the same NPV.

8.4 ALTERNATIVE DEFINITIONS OF OPERATING CASH FLOW

The analysis we went through in the previous section is quite general and can be adapted to most capital investment problems. In the next section, we illustrate a particularly useful variation. Before we do so, we need to discuss the fact that there are different definitions of project operating cash flow that are commonly used, both in practice and in finance texts.

As we will see, the different approaches to operating cash flow that exist all measure the same thing. If they are used correctly, they all produce the same answer, and one is not necessarily any better or more useful than another. Unfortunately, the fact that alternative definitions are used does sometimes lead to confusion. For this reason, we examine several of these variations next to see how they are related.

In the discussion that follows, keep in mind that when we speak of cash flow, we literally mean dollars in less dollars out. This is all we are concerned with. Different definitions of operating cash flow amount to different ways of manipulating basic information about sales, costs, depreciation, and taxes to get at cash flow.

For a particular project and year under consideration, suppose we have the following estimates:

Sales	= **$1,500**
Costs	= **$700**
Depreciation	= **$600**

With these estimates, notice that EBIT is:

$$\begin{aligned} \text{EBIT} &= \text{Sales} - \text{Costs} - \text{Depreciation} \\ &= \$1{,}500 - 700 - 600 \\ &= \$200 \end{aligned}$$

Once again, we assume that no interest is paid, so the tax bill is:

$$\begin{aligned} \text{Taxes} &= \text{EBIT} \times T_C \\ &= \$200 \times .21 = \$42 \end{aligned}$$

where T_C, the corporate tax rate, is 21 percent.

When we put all of this together, we see that project operating cash flow, OCF, is:

$$\begin{aligned} \text{OCF} &= \text{EBIT} + \text{Depreciation} - \text{Taxes} \\ &= \$200 + 600 - 42 = \$758 \end{aligned}$$

It turns out there are some other ways to determine OCF that could be (and are) used. We consider these next.

The Bottom-Up Approach

Because we are ignoring any financing expenses, such as interest, in our calculations of project OCF, we can write project net income as:

$$\begin{aligned} \text{Project net income} &= \text{EBIT} - \text{Taxes} \\ &= \$200 - 42 \\ &= \$158 \end{aligned}$$

If we add the depreciation to both sides, we arrive at a slightly different and very common expression for OCF:

$$\begin{aligned} \text{OCF} &= \text{Net income} + \text{Depreciation} \\ &= \$158 + 600 \\ &= \$758 \end{aligned} \qquad [8.1]$$

This is the *bottom-up* approach. Here, we start with the accountant's bottom line (net income) and add back any noncash deductions such as depreciation. It is crucial to remember that this definition of operating cash flow as net income plus depreciation is correct only if there is no interest expense subtracted in the calculation of net income.

The Top-Down Approach

Perhaps the most obvious way to calculate OCF is:

$$\begin{aligned} \text{OCF} &= \text{Sales} - \text{Costs} - \text{Taxes} \\ &= \$1{,}500 - 700 - 42 = \$758 \end{aligned} \qquad [8.2]$$

This is the *top-down* approach, the second variation on the basic OCF definition. Here, we start at the top of the income statement with sales and work our way down to net cash flow by subtracting costs, taxes, and other expenses. Along the way, we leave out any strictly noncash items such as depreciation.

The Tax Shield Approach

The third variation on our basic definition of OCF is the *tax shield* approach. This approach will be very useful for some problems we consider in the next section. The tax shield definition of OCF is:

$$\text{OCF} = (\text{Sales} - \text{Costs}) \times (1 - T_C) + \text{Depreciation} \times T_C \qquad [8.3]$$

where T_C is again the corporate tax rate. Assuming that $T_C = 21$ percent, the OCF works out to be:

$$
\begin{aligned}
\text{OCF} &= (\$1{,}500 - 700) \times .79 + 600 \times .21 \\
&= \$632 + 126 \\
&= \$758
\end{aligned}
$$

This is as we had before.

This approach views OCF as having two components. The first part is what the project's cash flow would be if there were no depreciation expense. In this case, this would-have-been cash flow is $632.

The second part of OCF in this approach is the depreciation deduction multiplied by the tax rate. This is called the **depreciation tax shield**. We know that depreciation is a noncash expense. The only cash flow effect of deducting depreciation is to reduce our taxes, a benefit to us. At the current 21 percent corporate tax rate, every dollar in depreciation expense saves us 21 cents in taxes. So, in our example, the $600 depreciation deduction saves us $600 \times .21 = \$126$ in taxes.

Conclusion

Now that we've seen that all of these approaches are the same, you're probably wondering why everybody doesn't just agree on one of them. One reason is that different approaches are useful in different circumstances. The best one to use is whichever happens to be the most convenient for the problem at hand.

8.5 SOME SPECIAL CASES OF DISCOUNTED CASH FLOW ANALYSIS

ExcelMaster coverage online
www.mhhe.com/RossCore6e

To finish our chapter, we look at three common cases involving discounted cash flow analysis. The first case we consider comes up when a firm is involved in submitting competitive bids. The second case arises in choosing between equipment options with different economic lives. The third case is the decision to replace an old machine.

We could consider many other special cases, but these three are particularly important because problems similar to these are so common. Also, they illustrate some diverse applications of cash flow analysis and DCF valuation.

Setting the Bid Price

Early on, we used discounted cash flow analysis to evaluate a proposed new product. A somewhat different (and common) scenario arises when we must submit a competitive bid to win a job. Under such circumstances, the winner is whoever submits the lowest bid.

There is an old joke concerning this process: The low bidder is whoever makes the biggest mistake. This is called the winner's curse. In other words, if you win, there is a good chance you underbid. In this section, we look at how to go about setting the bid price to avoid the winner's curse. The procedure we describe is useful anytime we have to set a price on a product or service.

To illustrate how to go about setting a bid price, imagine we are in the business of buying stripped-down truck platforms and then modifying them to customer specifications for resale. A local distributor has requested bids for five specially modified trucks each year for the next four years, for a total of 20 trucks in all.

We need to decide what price per truck to bid. The goal of our analysis is to determine the lowest price we can profitably charge. This maximizes our chances of being awarded the contract while guarding against the winner's curse.

Suppose we can buy the truck platforms for $10,000 each. The facilities we need can be leased for $24,000 per year. The labor and material cost to do the modification works out to be about $4,000 per truck. Total cost per year will thus be $24,000 + 5 × ($10,000 + 4,000) = $94,000.

We will need to invest $60,000 in new equipment. This equipment will be depreciated straight-line to a zero salvage value over the four years. It will be worth about $5,000 at the end of that time. We will also need to invest $40,000 in raw materials inventory and other working capital items. The relevant tax rate is 21 percent. What price per truck should we bid if we require a 20 percent return on our investment?

We start by looking at the capital spending and net working capital investment. We have to spend $60,000 today for new equipment. The aftertax salvage value is $5,000(1 − .21) = $3,950. Furthermore, we have to invest $40,000 today in working capital. We will get this back in four years.

We can't determine the operating cash flow just yet because we don't know the sales price. Thus, if we draw a time line, here is what we have so far:

	Year				
	0	1	2	3	4
Operating cash flow		+OCF	+OCF	+OCF	+OCF
Change in NWC	−$ 40,000				$40,000
Capital spending	− 60,000				3,950
Total cash flow	−$100,000	+OCF	+OCF	+OCF	+OCF +$43,950

With this in mind, note that the key observation is the following: The lowest possible price we can profitably charge will result in a zero NPV at 20 percent. At that price, we earn exactly 20 percent on our investment.

Given this observation, we first need to determine what the operating cash flow must be for the NPV to equal zero. To do this, we calculate the present value of the $43,950 non-operating cash flow from the last year and subtract it from the $100,000 initial investment:

$$\$100,000 - 43,950/1.20^4 = \$100,000 - 21,195 = \$78,805$$

Once we have done this, our time line is as follows:

	Year				
	0	1	2	3	4
Total cash flow	−$78,805	+OCF	+OCF	+OCF	+OCF

As the time line suggests, the operating cash flow is now an unknown ordinary annuity amount. The four-year annuity factor for 20 percent is 2.58873, so we have:

$$\text{NPV} = 0 = -\$78,805 + \text{OCF} \times 2.58873$$

This implies that:

$$\text{OCF} = \$78,805/2.58873 = \$30,442$$

So, the operating cash flow needs to be $30,442 each year.

We're not quite finished. The final problem is to find out what sales price results in an operating cash flow of $30,442. The easiest way to do this is to recall that operating cash flow can be written as net income plus depreciation (the bottom-up definition). The depreciation here is $60,000/4 = $15,000. Given this, we can determine what net income must be:

$$\text{Operating cash flow} = \text{Net income} + \text{Depreciation}$$
$$\$30,442 = \text{Net income} + \$15,000$$
$$\text{Net income} = \$15,442$$

From here, we work our way backward up the income statement. If net income is $15,442, then our income statement is as follows:

Sales	?
Costs	$94,000
Depreciation	15,000
Taxes (21%)	?
Net income	$15,442

We can solve for sales by noting that:

$$\text{Net income} = (\text{Sales} - \text{Costs} - \text{Depreciation}) \times (1 - T_c)$$
$$\$15,442 = (\text{Sales} - \$94,000 - 15,000) \times (1 - .21)$$
$$\text{Sales} = \$15,442/.79 + 94,000 + 15,000$$
$$\text{Sales} = \$128,546$$

Sales per year must be $128,546. Because the contract calls for five trucks per year, the sales price has to be $128,546/5 = $25,709. It looks as though we need to bid about $25,700 per truck. At this price, were we to get the contract, our return would be about 20 percent.

Evaluating Equipment Options with Different Lives

Suppose a firm must choose between two machines of unequal lives. Both machines can do the same job, but they have different operating costs and will last for different time periods. An application of the NPV rule suggests taking the machine whose costs have the lower present value. This choice might be a mistake, however, because the lower-cost machine may need to be replaced before the other one.

Let's consider an example. The Downtown Athletic Club must choose between two mechanical tennis ball throwers. Machine A costs less than Machine B but will not last as long. The aftertax cash outflows from the two machines are:

Machine	Date				
	0	1	2	3	4
A	$500	$120	$ 120	$120	
B	600	100	100	100	$100

Machine A costs $500 and lasts three years. There will be aftertax maintenance expenses of $120 to be paid at the end of each of the three years. Machine B costs $600 and lasts four years. There will be aftertax maintenance expenses of $100 to be paid at the end of each of the four years. We place all costs in real terms, an assumption that greatly simplifies the analysis. Revenues per year are assumed to be the same, regardless of machine, so they are ignored in the analysis. Note that all numbers in the above chart are aftertax outflows.

To get a handle on the decision, let's take the present value of the costs of each of the two machines. Assuming a discount rate of 10 percent, we have:

$$\text{Machine A: } \$798.42 = \$500 + \frac{\$120}{1.1} + \frac{\$120}{1.1^2} + \frac{\$120}{1.1^3}$$

$$\text{Machine B: } \$916.99 = \$600 + \frac{\$100}{1.1} + \frac{\$100}{1.1^2} + \frac{\$100}{1.1^3} + \frac{\$100}{1.1^4}$$

Machine B has a higher present value of outflows. A naive approach would be to select Machine A because of its lower present value of costs. However, Machine B has a longer life, so perhaps its cost per year is actually lower.

How might one properly adjust for the difference in useful life when comparing the two machines? Perhaps the easiest approach involves calculating something called the *equivalent annual cost* of each machine. This approach puts costs on a per-year basis.

The above equation showed that payments of ($500, $120, $120, $120) are equivalent to a single payment of $798.42 at Date 0. We now wish to equate the single payment of $798.42 at Date 0 with a three-year annuity. Using techniques of previous chapters, we have:

$$\$798.42 = C \times \text{PVIFA}_{10\%,3}$$

Because $\text{PVIFA}_{10\%,3}$ equals 2.4869, C equals $321.06 (= $798.42/2.4869). Thus, a payment stream of ($500, $120, $120, $120) is equivalent to annuity payments of $321.06 made at the end of each year for three years. We refer to $321.06 as the equivalent annual cost of Machine A.

This idea is summarized in the chart below:

	Date			
	0	1	2	3
Cash outflows of Machine A	$500	$120	$120	$120
Equivalent annual cost of Machine A		321.06	321.06	321.06

The Downtown Athletic Club should be indifferent between cash outflows of ($500, $120, $120, $120) and cash outflows of ($0, $321.06, $321.06, $321.06). Alternatively, one can say that the purchase of the machine is financially equivalent to a rental agreement calling for annual lease payments of $321.06.

Now let's turn to Machine B. We calculate its equivalent annual cost from:

$$\$916.99 = C \times \text{PVIFA}_{10\%,4}$$

Because $\text{PVIFA}_{10\%,4}$ equals 3.1699, C equals $916.99/3.1699, or $289.28.

As we did above for Machine A, the following chart can be created for Machine B:

	Date				
	0	1	2	3	4
Cash outflows of Machine B	$600	$100	$100	$100	$100
Equivalent annual cost of Machine B		289.28	289.28	289.28	289.28

The decision is easy once the charts of the two machines are compared. Would you rather make annual lease payments of $321.06 or $289.28? Put this way, the problem becomes a no-brainer. Clearly, a rational person would rather pay the lower amount. Thus, Machine B is the preferred choice.

Two final remarks are in order. First, it is no accident that we specified the costs of the tennis ball machines in real terms. While Machine B would still have been the preferred machine had the costs been stated in nominal terms, the actual solution would have been much more difficult. As a general rule, always convert cash flows to real terms when working through problems of this type.

Second, the above analysis applies only if one anticipates that both machines can be replaced. The analysis would differ if no replacement were possible. Imagine that the only company that manufactured tennis ball throwers just went out of business and no new producers are expected to enter the field. In this case, Machine B would generate revenues in the fourth year whereas Machine A would not. Here, simple net present value analysis for mutually exclusive projects including both revenues and costs would be appropriate.

The General Decision to Replace

The previous analysis concerned the choice between Machine A and Machine B, both of which were new acquisitions. More typically, firms must decide when to replace an existing machine with a new one. This decision is actually quite straightforward. One should replace if the annual cost of the new machine is less than the annual cost of the old machine. As with much else in finance, an example clarifies this approach better than further explanation.

EXAMPLE 8.10

Replacement Decisions

Consider the situation of BIKE, which must decide whether to replace an existing machine. BIKE currently pays no taxes. The replacement machine costs $9,000 now and requires maintenance of $1,000 at the end of every year for eight years. At the end of eight years, the machine would be sold for $2,000.

The existing machine requires increasing amounts of maintenance each year, and its salvage value falls each year, as shown:

Year	Maintenance	Salvage
Present	$ 0	$4,000
1	1,000	2,500
2	2,000	1,500
3	3,000	1,000
4	4,000	0

This chart tells us that the existing machine can be sold for $4,000 now. If it is sold one year from now, the resale price will be $2,500, and $1,000 must be spent on maintenance during the year to keep it running. For ease of calculation, we assume that this maintenance fee is paid at the end of the year. The machine will last for four more years before it falls apart. In other words, salvage value will be zero at the end of Year 4. If BIKE faces an opportunity cost of capital of 15 percent, when should it replace the machine?

As we said above, our approach is to compare the annual cost of the replacement machine with the annual cost of the old machine. The annual cost of the replacement machine is its *equivalent annual cost* (EAC). Let's calculate that first.

(*Continued*)

Equivalent Annual Cost of New Machine   The present value of the cost of the replacement machine is as follows:

$$PV_{costs} = \$9,000 + \$1,000 \times PVIFA_{15\%,8} - \frac{\$2,000}{1.15^8}$$

$$= \$9,000 + \$1,000 \times 4.4873 - \$2,000/3.0590$$

$$= \$12,833.52$$

Notice that the $2,000 salvage value is an inflow. It is treated as a negative number in the above equation because it offsets the cost of the machine.

The EAC of a new machine equals:

$$PV/8\text{-year annuity factor at } 15\% = \frac{PV}{PVIFA_{15\%,8}} = \frac{\$12,833.52}{4.4873} = \$2,860$$

This calculation implies that buying a replacement machine is financially equivalent to renting this machine for $2,860 per year.

Cost of Old Machine   This calculation is a little trickier. If BIKE keeps the old machine for one year, the firm must pay maintenance costs of $1,000 a year from now. But this is not BIKE's only cost from keeping the machine for one year. BIKE will receive $2,500 at Year 1 if the old machine is kept for one year but would receive $4,000 today if the old machine were sold immediately. This reduction in sales proceeds is clearly a cost as well.

Thus, the PV of the costs of keeping the machine one more year before selling it equals:

$$\$4,000 + \frac{\$1,000}{1.15} - \frac{\$2,500}{1.15} = \$2,696$$

That is, if BIKE holds the old machine for one year, BIKE does not receive the $4,000 today. This $4,000 can be thought of as an opportunity cost. In addition, the firm must pay $1,000 a year from now. Finally, BIKE does receive $2,500 a year from now. This last item is treated as a negative number because it offsets the other two costs.

While we normally express cash flows in terms of present value, the analysis to come is made easier if we express the cash flow in terms of its future value one year from now. This future value is:

$$\$2,696 \times 1.15 = \$3,100$$

In other words, the cost of keeping the machine for one year is equivalent to paying $3,100 at the end of the year.[1]

Making the Comparison   Now let's review the cash flows. If we replace the machine immediately, we can view our annual expense as $2,860, beginning at the end of the year. This annual expense occurs forever if we replace the new machine every eight years. This cash flow stream can be written as:

	Year 1	Year 2	Year 3	Year 4	. . .
Expenses from replacing machine immediately	$2,860	$2,860	$2,860	$2,860	. . .

If we replace the old machine in one year, our expense from using the old machine for that final year can be viewed as $3,100, payable at the end of the year. After replacement, our annual expense is

---

[1] One caveat is in order. Perhaps the old machine's maintenance is high in the first year but drops after that. A decision to replace immediately might be premature in that case. Therefore, we need to check the cost of the old machine in future years.

The cost of keeping the existing machine a second year is:

$$PV \text{ of costs at Time 1} = \$2,500 + \frac{\$2,000}{1.15} - \frac{\$1,500}{1.15} = \$2,935$$

which has a future value of $3,375 (= $2,935 × 1.15).

The costs of keeping the existing machine for Years 3 and 4 are also greater than the EAC of buying a new machine. Thus, BIKE's decision to replace the old machine immediately is still valid.

$2,860, beginning at the end of two years. This annual expense occurs forever if we replace the new machine every eight years. This cash flow stream can be written as:

	Year 1	Year 2	Year 3	Year 4	...
Expenses from using old machine for one year and then replacing it	$3,100	$2,860	$2,860	$2,860	...

Put this way, the choice is a no-brainer. Anyone would rather pay $2,860 at the end of the year than $3,100 at the end of the year. Thus, BIKE should replace the old machine immediately in order to minimize the expense at Year 1.

Two final points should be made on the decision to replace. First, we have examined a situation where both the old machine and the replacement machine generate the same revenues. Because revenues are unaffected by the choice of machine, revenues do not enter into our analysis. This situation is common in business. For example, the decision to replace either the heating system or the air-conditioning system in one's home office will likely not affect firm revenues. However, sometimes revenues will be greater with a new machine. The above approach can easily be amended to handle differential revenues.

Second, we want to stress the importance of the above approach. Applications of the above approach are pervasive in business because every machine must be replaced at some point.

SUMMARY AND CONCLUSIONS

This chapter discusses a number of practical applications of capital budgeting.

1. Capital budgeting must be done on an incremental basis. This means that sunk costs must be ignored, while both opportunity costs and side effects must be considered.

2. In the Baldwin case, we computed NPV using the following two steps:
   a. Calculate the net cash flow from all sources for each period.
   b. Calculate the NPV using the cash flows calculated above.

3. Inflation must be handled consistently. One approach is to express both cash flows and the discount rate in nominal terms. The other approach is to express both cash flows and the discount rate in real terms. Conceptually, either approach yields the same NPV calculation. However, in practice, nominal values are mostly used.

4. There are different approaches to calculate operating cash flow that measure the same thing.

5. A firm should use the equivalent annual cost approach when choosing between two machines of unequal lives.

CONCEPT QUESTIONS

1. **Opportunity Cost**   In the context of capital budgeting, what is an opportunity cost?

2. **Incremental Cash Flows**   Which of the following should be treated as an incremental cash flow when computing the NPV of an investment?
   a. A reduction in the sales of a company's other products caused by the investment.
   b. An expenditure on plant and equipment that has not yet been made and will be made only if the project is accepted.
   c. Costs of research and development undertaken in connection with the product during the past three years.

d. Annual depreciation expense from the investment.

e. Dividend payments by the firm.

f. The resale value of plant and equipment at the end of the project's life.

g. Salary and medical costs for production personnel who will be employed only if the project is accepted.

3. **Incremental Cash Flows** Your company currently produces and sells steel shaft golf clubs. The board of directors wants you to consider the introduction of a new line of titanium bubble woods with graphite shafts. Which of the following costs are not relevant?

a. Land you already own that will be used for the project, but otherwise will be sold for $700,000, its market value.

b. A $300,000 drop in your sales of steel shaft clubs if the titanium woods with graphite shafts are introduced.

c. $200,000 spent on research and development last year on graphite shafts.

4. **Depreciation** Given the choice, would a firm prefer to use MACRS depreciation or straight-line depreciation? Why?

5. **Net Working Capital** In our capital budgeting examples, we assumed that a firm would recover all of the working capital it invested in a project. Is this a reasonable assumption? When might it not be valid?

6. **Stand-Alone Principle** Suppose a financial manager is quoted as saying, "Our firm uses the stand-alone principle. Because we treat projects like minifirms in our evaluation process, we include financing costs because they are relevant at the firm level." Critically evaluate this statement.

7. **Equivalent Annual Cost** When is EAC analysis appropriate for comparing two or more projects? Why is this method used? Are there any implicit assumptions required by this method that you find troubling? Explain.

8. **Cash Flow and Depreciation** "When evaluating projects, we're only concerned with the relevant incremental aftertax cash flows. Therefore, because depreciation is a noncash expense, we should ignore its effects when evaluating projects." Critically evaluate this statement.

9. **Capital Budgeting Considerations** A major college textbook publisher has an existing finance textbook. The publisher is debating whether or not to produce an "essentialized" version, meaning a shorter (and lower-priced) book. What are some of the considerations that should come into play?

To answer the next three questions, refer to the following example. In 2003, Porsche unveiled its new sports utility vehicle (SUV), the Cayenne. With a price tag of over $40,000, the original Cayenne went from 0 to 62 mph in 9.7 seconds. Porsche's decision to enter the SUV market was in response to the runaway success of other high-priced SUVs such as the Mercedes-Benz M-class. Vehicles in this class had generated years of very high profits. The Cayenne certainly spiced up the market, and Porsche subsequently introduced the Cayenne Turbo S, which goes from 0 to 62 mph in 3.7 seconds and has a top speed of 178 mph. The price tag for the Cayenne Turbo S in 2019? Over $125,000!

Some analysts questioned Porsche's entry into the luxury SUV market. The analysts were concerned not only that Porsche was a late entry into the market, but also that the introduction of the Cayenne would damage Porsche's reputation as a maker of high-performance automobiles.

10. **Erosion** In evaluating the Cayenne, would you consider the possible damage to Porsche's reputation as erosion?

11. **Capital Budgeting** Porsche was one of the last manufacturers to enter the sports utility vehicle market. Why would one company decide to proceed with a product when other companies, at least initially, decide not to enter the market?

12. **Capital Budgeting** In evaluating the Cayenne, what do you think Porsche needs to assume regarding the substantial profit margins that exist in this market? Is it likely that they will be maintained as the market becomes more competitive, or will Porsche be able to maintain the profit margin because of its image and the performance of the Cayenne?

QUESTIONS AND PROBLEMS

1. **Calculating Project NPV**   Avignon Restaurant is considering the purchase of a $37,000 soufflé maker. The soufflé maker has an economic life of six years and will be fully depreciated by the straight-line method. The machine will produce 2,300 soufflés per year, with each costing $2 to make and priced at $7. Assume that the discount rate is 14 percent and the tax rate is 21 percent. Should the company make the purchase?

Basic
(Questions 1–12)

2. **Calculating Project NPV**   The Fleming Company is considering a new investment. Financial projections for the investment are tabulated below. The corporate tax rate is 22 percent. Assume all sales revenue is received in cash, all operating costs and income taxes are paid in cash, and all cash flows occur at the end of the year. All net working capital is recovered at the end of the project.

	Year 0	Year 1	Year 2	Year 3	Year 4
Investment	$32,800	—	—	—	—
Sales revenue	—	$14,200	$15,900	$15,700	$12,900
Operating costs	—	2,100	2,100	2,100	2,100
Depreciation	—	8,200	8,200	8,200	8,200
Net working capital spending	450	175	250	275	?

a. Compute the incremental net income of the investment for each year.
b. Compute the incremental cash flows of the investment for each year.
c. Suppose the appropriate discount rate is 12 percent. What is the NPV of the project?

3. **Calculating Project NPV**   Down Under Boomerang, Inc., is considering a new three-year expansion project that requires an initial fixed asset investment of $3.75 million. The fixed asset will be depreciated straight-line to zero over its three-year tax life, after which time it will be worthless. The project is estimated to generate $3.07 million in annual sales, with costs of $1.51 million. The tax rate is 21 percent and the required return is 10 percent. What is the project's NPV?

4. **Calculating Project Cash Flow from Assets**   In the previous problem, suppose the project requires an initial investment in net working capital of $450,000 and the fixed asset will have a market value of $575,000 at the end of the project. What is the project's Year 0 net cash flow? Year 1? Year 2? Year 3? What is the new NPV?

5. **NPV and Modified ACRS**   In the previous problem, suppose the fixed asset actually falls into the three-year MACRS class. All the other facts are the same. What is the project's Year 1 net cash flow now? Year 2? Year 3? What is the new NPV?

6. **NPV and Bonus Depreciation**   In the previous problem, suppose the fixed asset actually qualifies for 100 percent bonus depreciation. All the other facts are the same. What is the project's Year 1 net cash flow now? Year 2? Year 3? What is the new NPV?

7. **Project Evaluation**   Your firm is contemplating the purchase of a new $655,000 computer-based order entry system. The system will be depreciated straight-line to zero over its five-year life. It will be worth $60,000 at the end of that time. You will save $215,000 before taxes per year in order processing costs, and you will be able to reduce working capital by $45,000 (this is a one-time reduction). If the tax rate is 22 percent, what is the IRR for this project?

8. **Project Evaluation**   Cori's Meats is looking at a new sausage system with an installed cost of $304,000. This cost will be depreciated straight-line to zero over the project's five-year life, at the end of which the sausage system can be scrapped for $30,000. The sausage system will save the firm $116,000 per year in pretax operating costs and the system requires an initial investment in net working capital of $15,000. If the tax rate is 23 percent and the discount rate is 10 percent, what is the NPV of this project?

9. **NPV and Bonus Depreciation** In the previous problem, suppose the fixed asset actually qualifies for 100 percent bonus depreciation. All the other facts are the same. What is the new NPV?

10. **Calculating Salvage Value** An asset used in a four-year project falls in the five-year MACRS class for tax purposes. The asset has an acquisition cost of $8.95 million and will be sold for $1.96 million at the end of the project. If the tax rate is 24 percent, what is the aftertax salvage value of the asset?

11. **Calculating NPV** Howell Petroleum is considering a new project that complements its existing business. The machine required for the project costs $3.57 million. The marketing department predicts that sales related to the project will be $1.95 million per year for the next four years, after which the market will cease to exist. The machine will be depreciated down to zero over its four-year economic life using the straight-line method. Cost of goods sold and operating expenses related to the project are predicted to be 30 percent of sales. The company also needs to add net working capital of $575,000 immediately. The additional net working capital will be recovered in full at the end of the project's life. The corporate tax rate is 21 percent. The required rate of return is 14 percent. Should the company proceed with the project?

12. **Calculating EAC** You are evaluating two different silicon wafer milling machines. The Techron I costs $490,000, has a three-year life, and has pretax operating costs of $90,000 per year. The Techron II costs $620,000, has a five-year life, and has pretax operating costs of $97,000 per year. For both milling machines, use straight-line depreciation to zero over the project's life and assume a salvage value of $76,000. If your tax rate is 21 percent and your discount rate is 14 percent, compute the EAC for both machines. Which do you prefer? Why?

Intermediate
(Questions 13–34)

13. **Cost-Cutting Proposals** Geller Machine Shop is considering a four-year project to improve its production efficiency. Buying a new machine press for $530,000 is estimated to result in $192,000 in annual pretax cost savings. The press falls in the MACRS five-year class, and it will have a salvage value at the end of the project of $45,000. The press also requires an initial investment in spare parts inventory of $15,000, along with an additional $4,000 in inventory for each succeeding year of the project. If the tax rate is 21 percent and the project's required return is 9 percent, should the company buy and install the machine press?

14. **NPV and Bonus Depreciation** In the previous problem, suppose the fixed asset actually qualifies for 100 percent bonus depreciation. All the other facts are the same. What is the new NPV?

15. **Comparing Mutually Exclusive Projects** Peyton Manufacturing is trying to decide between two different conveyor belt systems. System A costs $520,000, has a four-year life, and requires $145,000 in pretax annual operating costs. System B costs $695,000, has a six-year life, and requires $123,000 in pretax annual operating costs. Both systems are to be depreciated straight-line to zero over their lives and will have zero salvage value. Whichever system is chosen, it will not be replaced when it wears out. If the tax rate is 25 percent and the discount rate is 11 percent, which system should the firm choose?

16. **Comparing Mutually Exclusive Projects** Suppose in the previous problem that the company always needs a conveyor belt system; when one wears out, it must be replaced. Which system should the firm choose now?

17. **NPV and Bonus Depreciation** Eggz, Inc., is considering the purchase of new equipment that will allow the company to collect loose hen feathers for sale. The equipment will cost $425,000 and will be eligible for 100 percent bonus depreciation. The equipment can be sold for $45,000 at the end of the project in five years. Sales would be $275,000 per year, with annual fixed costs of $47,000 and variable costs equal to 35 percent of sales. The project would require an investment of $25,000 in NWC that would be returned at the end of the project. The tax rate is 22 percent and the required return is 9 percent. What is the project's NPV?

18. **Comparing Mutually Exclusive Projects** Vandalay Industries is considering the purchase of a new machine for the production of latex. Machine A costs $3.1 million and will last for six years. Variable costs are 35 percent of sales and fixed costs are $1.55 million per year. Machine B costs $4.9 million and will last for nine years. Variable costs for this machine are 30 percent and fixed costs are

$1.8 million per year. The sales for each machine will be $9.5 million per year. The required return is 10 percent and the tax rate is 21 percent. Both machines will be depreciated on a straight-line basis. If the company plans to replace the machine when it wears out on a perpetual basis, which machine should the company choose?

 19. **Capital Budgeting with Inflation**   Consider the following cash flows on two mutually exclusive projects:

Year	Project A	Project B
0	−$73,000	−$82,000
1	35,500	37,600
2	38,900	49,300
3	26,000	35,500

The cash flows of Project A are expressed in real terms while those of Project B are expressed in nominal terms. The appropriate nominal discount rate is 11 percent and the inflation rate is 4 percent. Which project should you choose?

20. **Inflation and Company Value**   Squirrel Spring Water, Inc., expects to sell 7.3 million bottles of drinking water each year in perpetuity. This year, each bottle will sell for $1.24 in real terms and will cost $.83 in real terms. Sales and costs occur at year-end. Revenues will rise at a real rate of 2 percent annually, while real costs will rise at a real rate of 1.5 percent annually. The real discount rate is 6 percent. The corporate tax rate is 21 percent. What is the company worth today?

 21. **Calculating Nominal Cash Flow**   Perkins, Inc., is considering an investment of $730,000 in an asset with an economic life of five years. The firm estimates that the nominal annual cash revenues and expenses at the end of the first year will be $285,000 and $86,000, respectively. Both revenues and expenses will grow thereafter at the annual inflation rate of 4 percent. The company will use the straight-line method to depreciate its asset to zero over five years. The salvage value of the asset is estimated to be $80,000 in nominal terms at that time. The one-time net working capital investment of $30,000 is required immediately and will be recovered at the end of the project. The tax rate is 22 percent. What is the project's total nominal cash flow from assets for each year?

22. **Cash Flow Valuation**   Sandbelt Industries runs a small manufacturing operation. For this fiscal year, it expects real net cash flows of $376,000. The company is an ongoing operation, but it expects competitive pressures to erode its real net cash flows at 2.6 percent per year in perpetuity. The appropriate real discount rate for the project is 2.9 percent. All net cash flows are received at year-end. What is the present value of the net cash flows from the company's operations?

23. **Equivalent Annual Cost**   SGS Golf Academy is evaluating different golf practice equipment. The "Dimple-Max" equipment costs $104,300, has a seven-year life, and costs $13,900 per year to operate. The relevant discount rate is 12 percent. Assume that the straight-line depreciation method is used and that the equipment is fully depreciated to zero. Furthermore, assume the equipment has a salvage value of $10,500 at the end of the project's life. The relevant tax rate is 23 percent. All cash flows occur at the end of the year. What is the EAC of this equipment?

24. **Equivalent Annual Cost**   Zoysia University must purchase mowers for its landscape department. The university can buy five EVF mowers that cost $6,800 each and have annual, year-end maintenance costs of $1,430 per mower. The EVF mowers will be replaced at the end of Year 4 and have no value at that time. Alternatively, Zoysia can buy six AEH mowers to accomplish the same work. The AEH mowers will be replaced after seven years. They cost $6,100 each and have annual, year-end maintenance costs of $1,570 per mower. Each AEH mower will have a resale value of $900 at the end of seven years. The university's opportunity cost of funds for this type of investment is 9 percent. Because the university is a nonprofit institution, it does not pay taxes. It is anticipated that whichever manufacturer is chosen now will be the supplier of future mowers. Would you recommend purchasing five EVF mowers or six AEH mowers?

25. **Calculating Project NPV** Hurzdan, Inc., is considering the purchase of a $755,000 computer with an economic life of five years. The computer will be fully depreciated over five years using the straight-line method. The market value of the computer will be $35,000 in five years. The computer will replace four office employees whose combined annual salaries are $185,000. The machine will also immediately lower the firm's required net working capital by $55,000. This amount of net working capital will need to be replaced once the machine is sold. The corporate tax rate is 21 percent. Is it worthwhile to buy the computer if the appropriate discount rate is 10 percent?

 26. **Calculating NPV and IRR for a Replacement** A firm is considering an investment in a new machine with a price of $9.26 million to replace its existing machine. The current machine has a book value of $2.48 million, and a market value of $4.16 million. The new machine is expected to have a four-year life, and the old machine has four years left in which it can be used. If the firm replaces the old machine with the new machine, it expects to save $2.1 million in operating costs each year over the next four years. Both machines will have no salvage value in four years. If the firm purchases the new machine, it will also need an investment of $165,000 in net working capital. The required return on the investment is 8 percent and the tax rate is 21 percent.

   a. What are the NPV and IRR of the decision to replace the old machine?

   b. Ignoring the time value of money, the new machine saves only $8.4 million over the next four years and has a cost of $9.26 million. How is it possible that the decision to replace the old machine has a positive NPV?

27. **Project Analysis and Inflation** Bing Enterprises, Inc., has been considering the purchase of a new manufacturing facility for $2.35 million. The facility is to be fully depreciated on a straight-line basis over seven years. It is expected to have no resale value after the seven years. Operating revenues from the facility are expected to be $1.025 million, in nominal terms, at the end of the first year. The revenues are expected to increase at the inflation rate of 5 percent. Production costs at the end of the first year will be $425,000, in nominal terms, and they are expected to increase at 4 percent per year. The real discount rate is 7 percent. The corporate tax rate is 23 percent. Should the company accept the project?

28. **Calculating Project NPV** With the growing popularity of casual surf print clothing, two recent MBA graduates decided to broaden this casual surf concept to encompass a "surf lifestyle for the home." With limited capital, they decided to focus on surf print table and floor lamps to accent people's homes. They projected unit sales of these lamps to be 10,200 in the first year, with growth of 7 percent each year for the next five years. Production of these lamps will require $65,000 in net working capital to start. The net working capital will be recovered at the end of the project. Total fixed costs are $285,000 per year, variable production costs are $18 per unit, and the units are priced at $67 each. The equipment needed to begin production will cost $545,000. The equipment will be depreciated using the straight-line method over a five-year life and is not expected to have a salvage value. The tax rate is 22 percent and the required rate of return is 15 percent. What is the NPV of this project?

29. **Calculating Project NPV** You have been hired as a consultant for Pristine Urban-Tech Zither, Inc. (PUTZ), manufacturers of fine zithers. The market for zithers is growing quickly. The company bought some land three years ago for $1.8 million in anticipation of using it as a toxic waste dump site but has recently hired another company to handle all toxic materials. Based on a recent appraisal, the company believes it could sell the land for $2.1 million on an aftertax basis. At the end of the project, the land could be sold for $2.35 million on an aftertax basis. The company also hired a marketing firm to analyze the zither market, at a cost of $275,000. An excerpt of the marketing report is as follows:

> The zither industry will have a rapid expansion in the next four years. With the brand name recognition that PUTZ brings to bear, we feel that the company will be able to sell 18,400, 26,100, 29,300, and 19,400 units each year for the next four years, respectively. Again, capitalizing on the name recognition of PUTZ, we feel that a premium price of $175 can be charged for each zither. Because zithers appear to be a fad, we feel at the end of the four-year period, sales should be discontinued.

PUTZ feels that fixed costs for the project will be $725,000 per year and variable costs are 15 percent of sales. The equipment necessary for production will cost $5.3 million and will be depreciated according to a three-year MACRS schedule. At the end of the project, the equipment can be scrapped for $500,000. Net working capital of $450,000 will be required immediately and will be recaptured at the end of the project. PUTZ has a tax rate of 21 percent and the required return on the project is 13 percent. What is the NPV of the project?

30. **NPV and Bonus Depreciation**   In the previous problem, suppose the fixed asset actually qualifies for 100 percent bonus depreciation. All the other facts are the same. What is the new NPV?

31. **Calculating Replacement NPV**   Pilot Plus Pens is deciding when to replace its old machine. The machine's current salvage value is $1.87 million. Its current book value is $1.14 million. If not sold, the old machine will require maintenance costs of $780,000 at the end of the year for the next five years. Depreciation on the old machine is $228,000 per year. At the end of five years, it will have a salvage value of $182,000 and a book value of $0. A replacement machine costs $4.37 million now and requires maintenance costs of $275,200 at the end of each year during its economic life of five years. At the end of the five years, the new machine will have a salvage value of $624,000. It will be fully depreciated by the straight-line method. Pilot will need to purchase this machine regardless of what choice it makes today. The corporate tax rate is 21 percent and the appropriate discount rate is 12 percent. The company is assumed to earn sufficient revenues to generate tax shields from depreciation. Should Pilot Plus Pens replace the old machine now or at the end of five years?

32. **Calculating EAC**   Gold Star Industries is contemplating a purchase of computers. The firm has narrowed its choices to the SAL 5000 and the HAL 1000. The company would need nine SALs, and each SAL costs $3,600 and requires $390 of maintenance each year. At the end of the computer's eight-year life, each one could be sold for $200. Alternatively, the company could buy seven HALs. Each HAL costs $4,300 and requires $355 of maintenance every year. Each HAL lasts for six years and has a resale value of $220 at the end of its economic life. The company will continue to purchase the model that it chooses today into perpetuity, and the tax rate is 23 percent. Assume that the maintenance costs occur at year-end. Depreciation is straight-line to zero. Which model should the company buy if the appropriate discount rate is 11 percent?

33. **EAC and Inflation**   Office Automation, Inc., must choose between two copiers, the XX40 or the RH45. The XX40 costs $2,400 and will last for three years. The copier will require a real aftertax cost of $160 per year after all relevant expenses. The RH45 costs $2,900 and will last five years. The real aftertax cost for the RH45 will be $255 per year. All cash flows occur at the end of the year. The inflation rate is expected to be 5 percent per year, and the nominal discount rate is 12 percent. Which copier should the company choose?

34. **Project Analysis and Inflation**   Merton Brothers, Inc., is considering investing in a machine to produce computer keyboards. The price of the machine will be $875,000 and its economic life is five years. The machine will be fully depreciated by the straight-line method. The machine will produce 17,000 keyboards each year. The price of each keyboard will be $91 in the first year and will increase by 5 percent per year. The production cost per keyboard will be $26 in the first year and will increase by 7 percent per year. The project will have an annual fixed cost of $785,000 and will require an immediate investment of $145,000 in net working capital. The corporate tax rate for the company is 21 percent. If the appropriate discount rate is 11 percent, what is the NPV of the investment?

35. **Project Evaluation**   Aria Acoustics, Inc. (AAI), projects unit sales for a new seven-octave voice emulation implant as follows:

Challenge
(Questions 35–45)

Year	Unit Sales
1	75,000
2	86,000
3	94,000
4	108,000
5	74,000

Production of the implants will require $1.4 million in net working capital to start and additional net working capital investments each year equal to 15 percent of the projected sales increase for the following year. Total fixed costs are $1.75 million per year, variable production costs are $135 per unit, and the units are priced at $315 each. The equipment needed to begin production has an installed cost of $28.4 million. Because the implants are intended for professional singers, this equipment is considered industrial machinery and thus qualifies as seven-year MACRS property. In five years, this equipment can be sold for about 20 percent of its acquisition cost. The tax rate is 21 percent and the required return on the project is 17 percent. Based on these project estimates, what is the NPV of the project? What is the IRR?

36. **Calculating Required Savings**   A proposed cost-saving device has an installed cost of $580,000. The device will be used in a five-year project but is classified as three-year MACRS property for tax purposes. The required initial net working capital investment is $40,000, the tax rate is 24 percent, and the project discount rate is 12 percent. The device has an estimated Year 5 salvage value of $45,000. What level of pretax cost savings do we require for this project to be profitable?

37. **Calculating a Bid Price**   Guthrie Enterprises needs someone to supply it with 165,000 cartons of machine screws per year to support its manufacturing needs over the next five years, and you've decided to bid on the contract. It will cost you $1.9 million to install the equipment necessary to start production; you'll depreciate this cost straight-line to zero over the project's life. You estimate that in five years, this equipment can be salvaged for $150,000. Your fixed production costs will be $315,000 per year, and your variable production costs should be $13.25 per carton. You also need an initial investment in net working capital of $175,000. If your tax rate is 21 percent and you require a return of 13 percent on your investment, what bid price should you submit?

38. **Financial Break-Even Analysis**   The technique for calculating a bid price can be extended to many other types of problems. Answer the following questions using the same technique as setting a bid price; that is, set the project NPV to zero and solve for the variable in question.

   a. In the previous problem, assume that the price per carton is $20 and find the project NPV. What does your answer tell you about your bid price? What do you know about the number of cartons you can sell and still break even? How about your level of costs?

   b. Solve the previous problem again with the price still at $20, but find the quantity of cartons per year that you can supply and still break even. (*Hint:* It's less than 165,000.)

   c. Repeat (b) with a price of $20 and a quantity of 165,000 cartons per year, and find the highest level of fixed costs you could afford and still break even. (*Hint:* It's more than $315,000.)

39. **Calculating a Bid Price**   Your company has been approached to bid on a contract to sell 20,000 voice recognition (VR) computer keyboards a year for four years. Due to technological improvements, beyond that time they will be outdated and no sales will be possible. The equipment necessary for the production will cost $5.4 million and will be depreciated on a straight-line basis to a zero salvage value. Production will require an investment in net working capital of $325,000, to be returned at the end of the project, and the equipment can be sold for $650,000 at the end of production. Fixed costs are $1.35 million per year, and variable costs are $135 per unit. In addition to the contract, you feel your company can sell 8,700, 10,400, 11,700, and 6,700 additional units to companies in other countries over the next four years, respectively, at a price of $275. This price is fixed. The tax rate is 23 percent, and the required return is 13 percent. Additionally, the president of the company will only undertake the project if it has an NPV of $500,000. What bid price should you set for the contract?

40. **Replacement Decisions**   Suppose we are thinking about replacing an old computer with a new one. The old one cost us $344,000; the new one will cost $371,000. The new machine will be depreciated straight-line to zero over its five-year life. It will probably be worth about $36,000 after five years.

   The old computer is being depreciated at a rate of $32,000 per year. It will be completely written off in three years. If we don't replace it now, we will have to replace it in two years. We can sell it now for $132,000; in two years, it will probably be worth $20,000. The new machine will save us $55,000 per year in operating costs. The tax rate is 21 percent and the discount rate is 11 percent.

a. Suppose we recognize that if we don't replace the computer now, we will be replacing it in two years. Should we replace it now or should we wait? (*Hint:* What we effectively have here is a decision either to "invest" in the old computer—by not selling it—or to invest in the new one. Notice that the two investments have unequal lives.)

b. Suppose we only consider whether or not we should replace the old computer now without worrying about what's going to happen in two years. What are the relevant cash flows? Should we replace it or not? (*Hint:* Consider the net change in the firm's aftertax cash flows if we do the replacement.)

41. Project Analysis Benson Enterprises is evaluating alternative uses for a three-story manufacturing and warehousing building that it has purchased for $2.8 million. The company can continue to rent the building to the present occupants for $85,000 per year. The present occupants have indicated an interest in staying in the building for at least another 15 years. Alternatively, the company could modify the existing structure and use it for its own manufacturing and warehousing needs. Benson's production engineer feels the building could be adapted to handle one of two new product lines. The cost and revenue data for the two product alternatives are as follows:

	Product A	Product B
Initial cash outlay for building modifications	$148,000	$170,000
Initial cash outlay for equipment	305,000	365,000
Annual pretax cash revenues (generated for 15 years)	395,000	484,000
Annual pretax expenditures (generated for 15 years)	235,000	295,000

The building will be used for only 15 years for either Product A or Product B. After 15 years, the building will be too small for efficient production of either product line. At that time, Benson plans to rent the building to firms similar to the current occupants. To rent the building again, Benson will need to restore the building to its present layout. The estimated cash cost of restoring the building if Product A has been undertaken is $85,000. If Product B has been manufactured, the cash cost will be $100,000. These cash costs can be deducted for tax purposes in the year the expenditures occur.

Benson will depreciate the original building shell over a 39-year life to zero, regardless of which alternative it chooses. The building modifications and equipment purchases for either product are estimated to have a 15-year life. They will be depreciated by the straight-line method. The firm's tax rate is 21 percent, and its required rate of return on such investments is 12 percent.

Assume all cash flows occur at the end of the year. The initial outlays for modifications and equipment will occur today and the restoration outlays will occur at the end of Year 15. Which use of the building would you recommend to management?

42. Project Analysis and Inflation The Biological Insect Control Corporation (BICC) has hired you as a consultant to evaluate the NPV of its proposed toad ranch. BICC plans to breed toads and sell them as ecologically desirable insect control mechanisms. They anticipate that the business will continue into perpetuity. Following the negligible start-up costs, BICC expects the following nominal cash flows at the end of the year:

Revenues	$315,000
Labor costs	236,000
Other costs	71,000

The company will lease machinery for $95,000 per year. The lease payments start at the end of Year 1 and are expressed in nominal terms. Revenues will increase by 2 percent per year in real terms. Labor costs will increase by 1 percent per year in real terms. Other costs will decrease by 1 percent per year in real terms. The rate of inflation is expected to be 4 percent per year. The required rate of return is 7 percent in real terms. The company has a tax rate of 22 percent. All cash flows occur at year-end. What is the NPV of the proposed toad ranch today?

43. **Project Analysis and Inflation**   Sony International has an investment opportunity to produce a new stereo HDTV. The required investment on January 1 of this year is $95 million. The firm will depreciate the investment to zero using the straight-line method over four years. The investment has no resale value after completion of the project. The tax rate is 21 percent. The price of the product will be $515 per unit, in real terms, and will not change over the life of the project. Labor costs for Year 1 will be $20.43 per hour in real terms, and will increase at 2 percent per year in real terms. Energy costs for Year 1 will be $6.25 per physical unit, in real terms, and will increase at 3 percent per year in real terms. The inflation rate is 4 percent per year. Revenues are received and costs are paid at year-end. Refer to the table below for the production schedule.

	Year 1	Year 2	Year 3	Year 4
Physical production, in units	160,000	185,000	245,000	140,000
Labor input, in hours	2,150,000	2,470,000	2,950,000	1,950,000
Energy input, in physical units	180,000	215,000	280,000	167,500

The real discount rate for the project is 8 percent. Calculate the NPV of this project.

44. **Project Analysis and Inflation**   After extensive medical and marketing research, Pill, Inc., believes it can penetrate the pain reliever market. It is considering two alternative products. The first is to produce a medication for headache pain. The second is a pill for headache and arthritis pain. Both products would be introduced at a price of $7.85 per package in real terms. The headache-only medication is projected to sell 3.8 million packages a year, while the headache and arthritis remedy would sell 4.5 million packages a year. Cash costs of production in the first year are expected to be $3.40 per package in real terms for the headache-only brand. Production costs are expected to be $3.95 in real terms for the headache and arthritis pill. All prices and costs are expected to rise at the general inflation rate of 4 percent.

   Either product requires further investment. The headache-only pill could be produced using equipment costing $30 million. That equipment would last three years and have no resale value. The machinery required to produce the broader remedy would cost $34 million and last three years. The firm expects that equipment to have a $1 million resale value (in real terms) at the end of Year 3.

   The company uses straight-line depreciation. The firm faces a corporate tax rate of 21 percent and believes that the appropriate real discount rate is 6 percent. Which pain reliever should the firm produce?

45. **Calculating Project NPV**   J. Smythe, Inc., manufactures fine furniture. The company is deciding whether to introduce a new mahogany dining room table set. The set will sell for $6,500, including a set of eight chairs. The company feels that sales will be 2,150, 2,230, 2,560, 2,180, and 1,740 sets per year for the next five years, respectively. Variable costs will amount to 35 percent of sales and fixed costs are $4.5 million per year. The new dining room table sets will require inventory amounting to 10 percent of sales, produced and stockpiled in the year prior to sales. It is believed that the addition of the new table set will cause a loss of sales of 250 dining room table sets per year of the oak tables the company produces. These table sets sell for $4,900 and have variable costs of 40 percent of sales. The inventory for the oak table is also 10 percent. The company believes that sales of the oak table will be discontinued after three years. J. Smythe currently has excess production capacity. If the company buys the necessary equipment today, it will cost $12.9 million. However, the excess production capacity means the company can produce the new table without buying the new equipment. The company controller has said that the current excess capacity will end in two years with current production. This means that if the company uses the current excess capacity for the new table, it will be forced to spend the $12.9 million in two years to accommodate the increased sales of its current products. In five years, the new equipment will have a market value of $1.75 million if purchased today, and $7.5 million if purchased in two years. The equipment is depreciated on a seven-year MACRS schedule. The company has a tax rate of 24 percent, and the required return for the project is 14 percent.

   a. Should the company undertake the new project?

   b. Can you perform an IRR analysis on this project? How many IRRs would you expect to find?

   c. How would you interpret the profitability index?

EXCEL MASTER IT! PROBLEM

After extensive research and development, Goodweek Tires, Inc., has recently developed a new tire, the SuperTread, and must decide whether to make the investment necessary to produce and market it. The tire would be ideal for drivers doing a large amount of wet weather and off-road driving in addition to normal freeway usage. The research and development costs so far have totaled about $10 million. The SuperTread would be put on the market beginning this year, and Goodweek expects it to stay on the market for a total of four years. Test marketing costing $5 million has shown that there is a significant market for a SuperTread-type tire.

ExcelMaster
coverage online

www.mhhe.com/RossCore6e

As a financial analyst at Goodweek Tires, you have been asked by your CFO, Adam Smith, to evaluate the SuperTread project and provide a recommendation on whether to go ahead with the investment. Except for the initial investment that will occur immediately, assume all cash flows will occur at year-end.

Goodweek must initially invest $120 million in production equipment to make the SuperTread. This equipment can be sold for $51 million at the end of four years. Goodweek intends to sell the SuperTread to two distinct markets:

1. The Original Equipment Manufacturer (OEM) Market. The OEM market consists primarily of the large automobile companies (e.g., General Motors) that buy tires for new cars. In the OEM market, the SuperTread is expected to sell for $36 per tire. The variable cost to produce each tire is $18.

2. The Replacement Market. The replacement market consists of all tires purchased after the automobile has left the factory. This market allows for higher margins, and Goodweek expects to sell the SuperTread for $59 per tire there. Variable costs are the same as in the OEM market.

Goodweek Tires intends to raise prices at 1 percent above the inflation rate; variable costs will also increase 1 percent above the inflation rate. In addition, the SuperTread project will incur $25 million in marketing and general administration costs the first year. This cost is expected to increase at the inflation rate in subsequent years.

Goodweek's corporate tax rate is 21 percent. Annual inflation is expected to remain constant at 3.25 percent. The company uses a 15.9 percent discount rate to evaluate new product decisions.

Automotive industry analysts expect automobile manufacturers to produce 2 million new cars this year and project that production will grow at 2.5 percent per year thereafter. Each new car needs four tires (the spare tires are undersized and are in a different category). Goodweek Tires expects the SuperTread to capture 11 percent of the OEM market. Industry analysts estimate that the replacement tire market size will be 16 million tires this year and that it will grow at 2 percent annually. Goodweek expects the SuperTread to capture an 8 percent market share. The appropriate depreciation schedule for the equipment is the seven-year MACRS schedule. The immediate initial working capital requirement is $11 million. Thereafter, the net working capital requirements will be 15 percent of sales.

    a. What is the profitability index of the project?

    b. What is the IRR of the project?

    c. What is the NPV of the project?

    d. At what OEM price would Goodweek Tires be indifferent to accepting the project? Assume the replacement market price is constant.

    e. At what level of variable costs per unit would Goodweek Tires be indifferent to accepting the project?

EXPANSION AT EAST COAST YACHTS

Because East Coast Yachts is producing at full capacity, Larissa has decided to have Dan examine the feasibility of a new manufacturing plant. This expansion would represent a major capital outlay for the company. A preliminary analysis of the project has been conducted at a cost of $1.2 million. This analysis determined that the new plant will require an immediate outlay of $55 million and an additional outlay of $30 million in one year. The company has received a special tax dispensation that will allow the building and equipment to be depreciated on a 20-year MACRS schedule.

Because of the time necessary to build the new plant, no sales will be possible for the next year. Two years from now, the company will have partial-year sales of $18 million. Sales in the following four years will be $27 million, $35 million, $39 million, and $43 million. Because the new plant will be more efficient than East Coast Yachts's current manufacturing facilities, variable costs are expected to be 60 percent of sales, and fixed costs will be $3.5 million per year. The new plant will also require net working capital amounting to 8 percent of sales for the next year.

Dan realizes that sales from the new plant will continue into the indefinite future. Because of this, he believes the cash flows after Year 5 will continue to grow at 3 percent indefinitely. The company's tax rate is 21 percent and the required return is 11 percent.

Larissa would like Dan to analyze the financial viability of the new plant and calculate the profitability index, NPV, and IRR. Also, Larissa has instructed Dan to disregard the value of the land that the new plant will require. East Coast Yachts already owns it, and, as a practical matter, it will go unused indefinitely. She has asked Dan to discuss this issue in his report.

BETHESDA MINING COMPANY

Bethesda Mining is a midsized coal mining company with 20 mines located in Ohio, Pennsylvania, West Virginia, and Kentucky. The company operates deep mines as well as strip mines. Most of the coal mined is sold under contract, with excess production sold on the spot market.

The coal mining industry, especially high-sulfur coal operations such as Bethesda, has been hard-hit by environmental regulations. Recently, however, a combination of increased demand for coal and new pollution reduction technologies has led to an improved market demand for high-sulfur coal. Bethesda has just been approached by Mid-Ohio Electric Company with a request to supply coal for its electric generators for the next four years. Bethesda Mining does not have enough excess capacity at its existing mines to guarantee the contract. The company is considering opening a strip mine in Ohio on 5,000 acres of land purchased 10 years ago for $5.4 million. Based on a recent appraisal, the company feels it could receive $7.3 million on an aftertax basis if it sold the land today.

Strip mining is a process where the layers of topsoil above a coal vein are removed and the exposed coal is removed. Some time ago, the company would remove the coal and leave the land in an unusable condition. Changes in mining regulations now force a company to reclaim the land; that is, when the mining is completed, the land must be restored to near its original condition. The land can then be used for other purposes. As they are currently operating at full capacity, Bethesda will need to purchase additional equipment, which will cost $43 million. The equipment will be depreciated on a seven-year MACRS schedule. The contract only runs for four years. At that time, the coal from the site will be entirely mined. The company feels that the equipment can be sold for 60 percent of its initial purchase price. However, Bethesda plans to open another strip mine at that time and will use the equipment at the new mine.

The contract calls for the delivery of 500,000 tons of coal per year at a price of $57 per ton. Bethesda Mining feels that coal production will be 750,000 tons, 810,000 tons, 830,000 tons, and 720,000 tons, respectively, over the next four years. The excess production will be sold in the spot market at an average of $45 per ton. Variable costs amount to $16 per ton and fixed costs are $3.7 million per year. The mine will require a net working capital investment of 5 percent of sales. The NWC will be built up in the year prior to the sales.

Bethesda will be responsible for reclaiming the land at termination of the mining. This will occur in Year 5. The company uses an outside company for reclamation of all the company's strip mines. It is estimated the cost of reclamation will be $3.9 million. After the land is reclaimed, the company plans to donate the land to the state for use as a public park and recreation area as a condition to receive the necessary mining permits. This will occur in Year 5 and result in a charitable expense deduction of $7.3 million. Bethesda faces a 21 percent tax rate and has a 12 percent required return on new strip mine projects. Assume a loss in any year will result in a tax credit.

You have been approached by the president of the company with a request to analyze the project. Calculate the payback period, profitability index, net present value, and internal rate of return for the new strip mine. Should Bethesda Mining take the contract and open the mine?

Risk Analysis, Real Options, and Capital Budgeting

Even having a major star is no guarantee of success for a movie release. In 2018, the film *Gotti*, which starred John Travolta, slept with the fishes as it debuted with a 0.0 rating on Rotten Tomatoes. The critics all said, "fuhgeddaboudit!" Fortunately for the production company, Oasis Films, the film didn't lose a lot of money (it only cost $10 million to make). Not all films are as lucky. Take *Monster Trucks,* the children's film about the monsters that live in trucks. According to critics, just watching the movie amounted to a crushing experience. One called it a "clueless family caper." Another was even more harsh, saying, "*Monster Trucks* is a wreck, fueled by the crazy belief that noise and repetition can disguise the lack of credible writing, directing, acting, and FX."

Looking at the numbers, Paramount Pictures spent close to $125 million making the movie, plus millions more for marketing and distribution. Paramount was so negative about movie ticket sales that it wrote off $115 million before the movie was released! And the movie subsequently crashed, pulling in only $64.5 million worldwide. Of course, there are movies that do quite well. Also in 2018, the superhero hit *Black Panther* raked in about $1.4 billion worldwide at a production cost of about $200 million.

Obviously, Paramount Pictures didn't *plan* to lose $60 or so million on *Monster Trucks,* but it happened. As the money poured into *Monster Trucks* shows, projects don't always go as companies think they will. This chapter explores how this can happen, and what companies can do to analyze and possibly avoid these situations.

Please visit us at corecorporatefinance.blogspot.com for the latest developments in the world of corporate finance.

9.1 DECISION TREES

ExcelMaster
coverage online

www.mhhe.com/RossCore6e

There is usually a sequence of decisions in NPV project analysis. This section introduces the device of **decision trees** for identifying these sequential decisions.

Imagine you are the treasurer of the Solar Electronics Corporation (SEC), and the engineering group has recently developed the technology for solar-powered jet engines. The jet engine is to be used with 150-passenger commercial airplanes. The marketing staff has proposed that SEC develop some prototypes and conduct test marketing of the engine. A corporate planning group, including representatives from production, marketing, and engineering, estimates that this preliminary phase will take a year and will cost $100 million. Furthermore, the group believes there is a 75 percent chance that the marketing tests will prove successful.

If the initial marketing tests are successful, SEC can go ahead with full-scale production. This investment phase will cost $1,500 million. Production and sales will occur over the next five years. The preliminary cash flow projection appears in Table 9.1. Should SEC go ahead with investment and production on the jet engine, the NPV (in millions) at a discount rate of 15 percent is:

$$\text{NPV} = -\$1,500 + \$900 \times \text{PVIFA}_{15\%,5}$$
$$= \$1,518$$

Investment	Year 1	Years 2–6
Revenues		$6,000
Variable costs		3,000
Fixed costs		1,940
Depreciation		300
Pretax profit		$ 760
Tax (21%)		160
Net income		$ 600
Cash flow		$ 900
Initial investment cost	−$1,500	

TABLE 9.1

Cash Flow Forecasts for Solar Electronics Corporation's Jet Engine Base Case (in $ millions)*

* Assumptions: (1) Investment is depreciated in Years 2 through 6 using the straight-line method; (2) the company receives no tax benefits on initial development costs.

Note that the NPV is calculated as of Year 1, the date at which the investment of $1,500 million is made. Later, we bring this number back to Year 0.

If the initial marketing tests are unsuccessful, SEC's $1,500 million investment has an NPV of −$3,611 million. This figure is also calculated as of Year 1. (To save space, we will not provide the raw numbers leading to this calculation.)

Figure 9.1 displays the problem concerning the jet engine as a decision tree. If SEC decides to conduct test marketing, there is a 75 percent probability that the test marketing will be successful. If the tests are successful, the firm faces a second decision: whether to invest $1,500 million in a project that yields a $1,518 million NPV or to stop. If the tests are unsuccessful, the firm faces a different decision: whether to invest $1,500 million in a project that yields a −$3,611 million NPV or to stop.

FIGURE 9.1

Decision Tree (in $ millions) for SEC

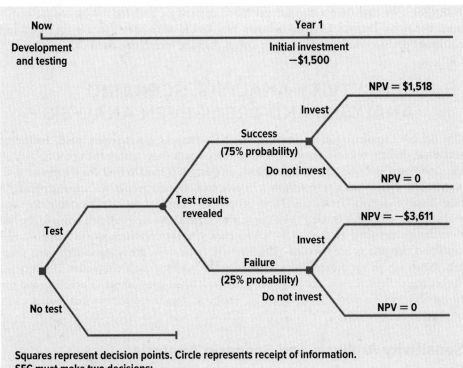

Squares represent decision points. Circle represents receipt of information.
SEC must make two decisions:
1. Whether to develop and test engine.
2. Whether to invest for full-scale production.

To review, SEC has the following two decisions to make:

1. Whether to develop and test the solar-powered jet engine.
2. Whether to invest for full-scale production following the results of the test.

One makes decisions in reverse order with decision trees. Thus we analyze the second-stage investment of $1,500 million first. If the tests are successful, should SEC make the second-stage investment? The answer is obviously yes because $1,518 million is greater than zero. If the tests are unsuccessful, should the second-stage investment be made? Just as obviously, the answer is no because −$3,611 million is below zero.

Now we move back to the first stage, where the decision boils down to the question: Should SEC invest $100 million now to obtain a 75 percent chance of $1,518 million one year later? The expected payoff evaluated at Year 1 (in millions) is:

$$
\begin{array}{c}
\begin{array}{c}\text{Expected}\\\text{payoff}\end{array} = \left(\begin{array}{ccc}\text{Probability}&&\text{Payoff}\\\text{of}&\times&\text{if}\\\text{success}&&\text{successful}\end{array}\right) + \left(\begin{array}{ccc}\text{Probability}&&\text{Payoff}\\\text{of}&\times&\text{if}\\\text{failure}&&\text{failure}\end{array}\right)\\[6pt]
= \quad (.75 \quad \times \quad \$1{,}518) \quad + \quad (.25 \quad \times \quad \$0)\\[4pt]
= \quad \$1{,}139
\end{array}
$$

The NPV of testing computed at Year 0 (in millions) is:

$$
\begin{array}{l}
\text{NPV} = -\$100 + \dfrac{\$1{,}139}{1.15}\\[8pt]
\quad\quad = \$890
\end{array}
$$

Because the NPV is a positive number, the firm should test the market for solar-powered jet engines.

WARNING   We have used a discount rate of 15 percent for both the testing and the investment decisions. Perhaps a higher discount rate should have been used for the initial test marketing decision, which is likely to be riskier than the investment decision.

9.2 SENSITIVITY ANALYSIS, SCENARIO ANALYSIS, AND BREAK-EVEN ANALYSIS

ExcelMaster
coverage online
www.mhhe.com/RossCore6e

One point we emphasize in this book is that NPV analysis is a superior capital budgeting technique. In fact, because the NPV approach uses cash flows rather than profits, uses all the cash flows, and discounts the cash flows properly, it is hard to find any theoretical fault with it. However, in our conversations with practical businesspeople, we hear the phrase "a false sense of security" frequently. These people point out that the documentation for capital budgeting proposals is often quite impressive. Cash flows are projected down to the last thousand dollars (or even the last dollar) for each year (or even each month). Opportunity costs and side effects are handled quite properly. Sunk costs are ignored—also quite properly. When a high net present value appears at the bottom, one's temptation is to say yes immediately. Nevertheless, the projected cash flow often goes unmet in practice, and the firm ends up with a money loser. A nearby *Finance Matters* box discusses some recent cases of plans gone awry.

Sensitivity Analysis and Scenario Analysis

How can the firm get the net present value technique to live up to its potential? One approach is **sensitivity analysis** (a.k.a. *what-if analysis* and *bop analysis*[1]), which examines

[1] Bop stands for best, optimistic, pessimistic.

WHEN THINGS GO WRONG . . .

If you think about it, the decision by a company to acquire another company is a capital budgeting decision. One important difference, however, is that an acquisition may be more expensive than a typical project and possibly much more expensive. Of course, as with any other project, acquisitions can fail. When they do, the losses can be huge.

In April 2016, AbbVie purchased Stemcentrx for $5.8 billion in cash and stock. The main product Stemcentrx had at the time was a lung cancer therapy called Rova-T. The new therapy showed great promise, as indicated by the price paid for Stemcentrx. Unfortunately, within two years, the drug failed its late-stage trial. As a result, in January 2019, AbbVie was forced to write off $4 billion related to the acquisition of Stemcentrx.

In another example, Verizon felt that it should compete with content providers Facebook, Google, and Amazon. As a result, Verizon purchased AOL in 2015 for $4.4 billion and Yahoo! for $4.5 billion in 2017. These two companies were combined into Verizon's Oath division. Unfortunately, things didn't go as planned. The revenues and earnings from Oath never reached Verizon's goals. As a result, in December 2018, Verizon wrote off $4.6 billion relating to Oath. In fact, as we will describe, problems with AOL began much earlier.

One of the largest acquisitions in U.S. history was America Online's (AOL's) purchase of Time Warner in 2001. AOL purchased Time Warner under the assumption that AOL was part of the "new economy" and primed for fast growth. Time Warner was the "old" communications company, owning cable stations and a music label, among other things.

But things didn't work as planned. Infighting among employees from the two companies hurt production and morale. In 2002, accounting irregularities were uncovered at AOL, and, as a result of the acquisition costs, the company was saddled with massive debt. To make matters worse, AOL began to lose customers and money. Although AOL was the acquirer, and once dominant partner, things got so bad at AOL that the company changed its name back to Time Warner. To cap things off, in 2002, Time Warner wrote off a stunning $54 billion in assets associated with the acquisition, which was, at the time, the largest such write-off in history.

how sensitive a particular NPV calculation is to changes in underlying assumptions. We illustrate the technique with Solar Electronics's solar-powered jet engine from the previous section. As pointed out earlier, the cash flow forecasts for this project appear in Table 9.1. We begin by considering the assumptions underlying the revenues, costs, and aftertax cash flows shown in the table.

REVENUES Sales projections for the proposed jet engine have been estimated by the marketing department as:

$$\frac{\text{Number of jet}}{\text{engines sold}} = \text{Market share} \times \frac{\text{Size of jet}}{\text{engine market}}$$

$$3,000 = .30 \times 10,000$$

$$\text{Sales revenues} = \frac{\text{Number of jet}}{\text{engines sold}} \times \frac{\text{Price per}}{\text{engine}}$$

$$\$6,000 \text{ million} = 3,000 \times \$2 \text{ million}$$

Thus, it turns out that the revenue estimates depend on three assumptions:

1. Market share.
2. Size of jet engine market.
3. Price per engine.

COSTS Financial analysts frequently divide costs into two types: variable costs and fixed costs. Variable costs change as the output changes, and they are zero when production is zero. Costs of direct labor and raw materials are usually variable. It is common to assume that a variable cost is constant per unit of output, implying that total variable costs are proportional to the level of production. For example, if direct labor is variable and one unit of final output requires $10 of direct labor, then 100 units of final output should require $1,000 of direct labor.

Fixed costs are not dependent on the amount of goods or services produced during the period. Fixed costs are usually measured as costs per unit of time, such as rent per month or salaries per year. Naturally, fixed costs are not fixed forever. They are only fixed over a predetermined time period.

The engineering department has estimated variable costs to be $1 million per engine. Fixed costs are $1,940 million per year. The cost breakdowns are:

Variable cost	=	Variable cost per unit	×	Number of jet engines sold
$3,000 million	=	$1 million	×	3,000
Total cost before taxes =		Variable cost	+	Fixed cost
$4,940 million		= $3,000 million	+	1,940 million

The above estimates for market size, market share, price, variable cost, and fixed cost, as well as the estimate of initial investment, are presented in the middle column of Table 9.2. These figures represent the firm's expectations or best estimates of the different parameters. For purposes of comparison, the firm's analysts prepared both optimistic and pessimistic forecasts for the different variables. These are also provided in the table.

Standard sensitivity analysis calls for an NPV calculation for all three possibilities of a single variable, along with the expected forecast for all other variables. This procedure is illustrated in Table 9.3. Consider the NPV calculation of $9,463 million provided in the

TABLE 9.2

Different Estimates for Solar Electronics's Solar Jet Engine

Variable	Pessimistic	Expected or Best	Optimistic
Market size (per year)	5,000	10,000	20,000
Market share	20%	30%	50%
Price	$1.9 million	$2 million	$2.2 million
Variable cost (per engine)	$1.2 million	$1 million	$.8 million
Fixed cost (per year)	$2,000 million	$1,940 million	$1,740 million
Investment	$1,900 million	$1,500 million	$1,000 million

TABLE 9.3

NPV Calculations as of Year 1 (in $ millions) for the Solar Jet Engine Using Sensitivity Analysis

	Pessimistic	Expected or Best	Optimistic
Market size	−$2,454*	$1,518	$9,463
Market share	−1,130*	1,518	6,815
Price	724	1,518	3,107
Variable cost	−71*	1,518	3,107
Fixed cost	1,359	1,518	2,048
Investment	1,175	1,518	1,948

Under sensitivity analysis, one input is varied while all other inputs are assumed to meet expectations. For example, an NPV of −$2,454 occurs when the pessimistic forecast of 5,000 is used for market size. However, the expected forecasts from Table 9.2 are used for all other variables when −$2,454 is generated.

* We assume that the other divisions of the firm are profitable, implying that a loss on this project can offset income elsewhere in the firm, thereby reducing the overall taxes of the firm.

upper right-hand corner of this table. This occurs when the optimistic forecast of 20,000 units per year is used for market size. However, the expected forecasts from Table 9.2 are employed for all other variables when the $9,463 million figure is generated. Note that the same number of $1,518 million appears in each row of the middle column of Table 9.3. This occurs because the expected forecast is used for the variable that was singled out, as well as for all other variables.

Table 9.3 can be used for a number of purposes. First, taken as a whole, the table can indicate whether NPV analysis should be trusted. In other words, it reduces the false sense of security we spoke of earlier. Suppose that NPV is positive when the expected forecast for each variable is used. However, further suppose that every number in the pessimistic column is highly negative and every number in the optimistic column is highly positive. Even a single error in this forecast greatly alters the estimate, making one leery of the net present value approach. A conservative manager might well scrap the entire NPV analysis in this situation. Fortunately, this does not seem to be the case in Table 9.3 because all but three of the numbers are positive. Managers viewing the table will likely consider NPV analysis to be useful for the solar-powered jet engine.

Second, sensitivity analysis shows where more information is needed. For example, an error in the estimate of investment appears to be relatively unimportant because, even under the pessimistic scenario, the NPV of $1,175 million is still highly positive. By contrast, the pessimistic forecast for market share leads to a negative NPV of –$1,130 million, and a pessimistic forecast for market size leads to a substantially negative NPV of –$2,454 million. Because the effect of incorrect estimates on revenues is so much greater than the effect of incorrect estimates on costs, more information on the factors determining revenues might be needed.

Because of these advantages, sensitivity analysis is widely used in practice. Graham and Harvey[2] report that slightly over 50 percent of the 392 firms in their sample subject their capital budgeting calculations to sensitivity analysis. This number is particularly large when one considers that only about 75 percent of the firms in their sample use NPV analysis.

Unfortunately, sensitivity analysis also suffers from some drawbacks. For example, sensitivity analysis may unwittingly increase the false sense of security among managers. Suppose all pessimistic forecasts yield positive NPVs. A manager might feel that there is no way the project can lose money. Of course, the forecasters may have an optimistic view of a pessimistic forecast. To combat this, some companies do not treat optimistic and pessimistic forecasts subjectively. Rather, their pessimistic forecasts are always, say, 20 percent less than expected. Unfortunately, the cure in this case may be worse than the disease because a deviation of a fixed percentage ignores the fact that some variables are easier to forecast than others.

In addition, sensitivity analysis treats each variable in isolation when, in reality, the different variables are likely to be related. If ineffective management allows costs to get out of control, it is likely that variable costs, fixed costs, and investment will all rise above expectations at the same time. If the market is not receptive to a solar plane, both market share and price should decline together.

Managers frequently perform scenario analysis, a variant of sensitivity analysis, to minimize this problem. This approach examines a number of different likely scenarios, where each scenario involves a confluence of factors. As a simple example, consider the effect of a few airline crashes. These crashes are likely to reduce flying in total, thereby limiting the demand for any new engines. Furthermore, even if the crashes did not involve solar-powered aircraft, the public could become more averse to any innovative and controversial technologies. Hence, SEC's market share might fall as well. Perhaps the cash flow calculations would

[2] See Figure 2 of John Graham and Campbell Harvey, "The Theory and Practice of Corporate Finance: Evidence from the Field," *Journal of Financial Economics* 60, no. 2–3 (2001), pp. 187–243.

TABLE 9.4

Cash Flow Forecast
(in millions) under the
Scenario of a Plane Crash*

	Year 1	Years 2–6
Revenues		$2,800
Variable costs		1,400
Fixed costs		1,940
Depreciation		300
Pretax profit		−$ 840
Tax (21%)†		− 176
Net profit		−$ 664
Cash flow		−$ 364
Initial investment cost	−$1,500	

* Assumptions are:

| Market size | 7,000 (70 percent of expectation) |
| Market share | 20% (2/3 of expectation) |

Forecasts for all other variables are the expected forecasts as given in Table 9.2.
† Tax loss offsets income elsewhere in firm.

look like those in Table 9.4 under the scenario of a plane crash. Given the calculations in the table, the NPV (in millions) would be:

$$-\$2{,}719 = -\$1{,}500 - \$364 \times PVIFA_{15\%,5}$$

A series of scenarios like this might illuminate issues concerning the project better than the standard application of sensitivity analysis would.

Break-Even Analysis

Our discussion of sensitivity analysis and scenario analysis suggests that there are many ways to examine variability in forecasts. We now present another approach, break-even analysis. As its name implies, this approach determines the sales needed to break even. The approach is a useful complement to sensitivity analysis because it also sheds light on the severity of incorrect forecasts. We calculate the break-even point in terms of both accounting profit and net present value.

ACCOUNTING PROFIT   Net profit under four different sales forecasts is:

Unit Sales	Net Profit (in $ millions)
0	−$1,770
1,000	− 980
3,000	600
10,000	6,130

A more complete presentation of costs and revenues appears in Table 9.5.

We plot the revenues, costs, and profits under the different assumptions about sales in Figure 9.2. The revenue and cost curves cross at 2,240 jet engines. This is the break-even point, that is, the point where the project generates no profits or losses. As long as sales are above 2,240 jet engines, the project will make a profit.

TABLE 9.5 Revenues and Costs of Project under Different Sales Assumptions (in $ millions, except unit sales)

| Year 1 | | | | | | Year 2–6 | | | | |
Initial Invest-ment	Annual Unit Sales	Revenues	Variable Costs	Fixed Costs	Depreciation	Taxes* (21%)	Net Income	Operating Cash Flows	NPV (Evaluated Year 1)
$1,500	0	$ 0	$ 0	$1,940	$300	− $470	−$1,770	−$1,470	−$ 6,426
1,500	1,000	2,000	1,000	1,940	300	− 260	− 980	− 680	− 3,778
1,500	3,000	6,000	3,000	1,940	300	160	600	900	1,518
1,500	10,000	20,000	10,000	1,940	300	1,630	6,130	6,430	$20,056

*Loss is incurred in the first two rows. For tax purposes, this loss offsets income elsewhere in the firm.

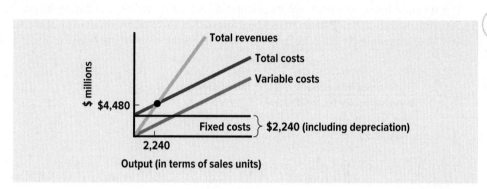

FIGURE 9.2

Break-Even Point Using Accounting Numbers

This break-even point can be calculated very easily. Because the sales price is $2 million per engine and the variable cost is $1 million per engine,[3] the difference per engine is:

(Sales price − Variable cost) = $2 million − 1 million

= $1 million

This aftertax difference is called the contribution margin because each additional engine contributes this amount to pretax profit.

Fixed costs are $1,940 million and depreciation is $300 million, implying that the pretax sum of these costs is:

Fixed costs + Depreciation = $1,940 million + 300 million = $2,240 million

That is, the firm incurs costs of $2,240 million, regardless of the number of sales. Because each engine contributes $1 million, sales must reach the following level to offset the above costs:

Accounting Profit Break-Even Point:

$$\frac{\text{(Fixed costs + Depreciation)}}{\text{(Sales price − Variable costs)}} = \frac{\$2,240 \text{ million}}{\$1 \text{ million}} = 2,240$$

Thus, 2,240 engines must be sold in order to not lose money on an accounting basis.

[3] Though the previous section considered both optimistic and pessimistic forecasts for sales price and variable cost, break-even analysis uses just the expected, or best, estimates of these variables.

FINANCIAL BREAK-EVEN As we have stated many times in the text, we are more interested in present value than we are in net profits. Therefore, we must calculate the present value of the cash flows. Given a discount rate of 15 percent, we have:

Unit Sales	NPV (in $ millions)
0	−$6,426
1,000	− 3,778
3,000	1,518
10,000	20,056

These NPV calculations are reproduced from the last column of Table 9.5. We can see that the NPV is negative if SEC produces 1,000 jet engines and positive if it produces 3,000 jet engines. Obviously, the zero NPV point occurs between 1,000 and 3,000 jet engines.

The financial break-even point can be calculated very easily. The firm originally invested $1,500 million. This initial investment can be expressed as a five-year equivalent annual cost (EAC), determined by dividing the initial investment by the appropriate five-year annuity factor:

$$\text{EAC} = \frac{\text{Initial investment}}{\text{5-year annuity factor at 15\%}} = \frac{\text{Initial investment}}{\text{PVIFA}_{15\%,5}}$$

$$= \frac{\$1,500 \text{ million}}{3.3522} = \$447.5 \text{ million}$$

Note that the EAC of $447.5 million is greater than the yearly depreciation of $300 million. This must occur since the calculation of EAC implicitly assumes that the $1,500 million investment could have been invested at 15 percent.

Aftertax costs, regardless of output, can be viewed as:

$$\underset{\text{million}}{\$1,917.1} = \text{EAC} + \underset{\text{costs}}{\text{Fixed}} \times (1 - T_c) - \text{Depreciation} \times T_c$$

$$= \underset{\text{million}}{\$447.5} + \underset{\text{million}}{\$1,940} \times .79 - \underset{\text{million}}{\$300} \times .21$$

That is, in addition to the initial investment's equivalent annual cost of $447.5 million, the firm pays fixed costs each year and receives a depreciation tax shield each year. The depreciation tax shield is written as a negative number because it offsets the costs in the equation. Because each engine contributes $.79 million to aftertax profit, it will take the following sales to offset the above costs:

Financial Break-Even Point:

$$\frac{\text{EAC} + \text{Fixed costs} \times (1 - T_c) - \text{Depreciation} \times T_c}{(\text{Sales price} - \text{Variable costs}) \times (1 - T_c)} = \frac{\$1,917.1 \text{ million}}{\$.79 \text{ million}} = 2,426.68$$

About 2,427 engines must be sold to reach the financial break-even point.

Why is the accounting break-even point different from the financial break-even point? When we use accounting profit as the basis for the break-even calculation, we subtract depreciation. Depreciation for the solar jet engine project is $300 million. If 2,240 solar jet engines are sold, SEC will generate sufficient revenues to cover the $300 million depreciation expense plus other costs. Unfortunately, at this level of sales, SEC will not cover the economic opportunity costs of the $1,500 million laid out for the investment. If we take into account that the $1,500 million could have been invested at 15 percent, the true annual cost of the investment is $447.5 million and not $300 million. Depreciation understates the true costs of recovering the initial investment. Thus, companies that break even on an accounting basis are really losing money. They are losing the opportunity cost of the initial investment.

9.3 MONTE CARLO SIMULATION

ExcelMaster
coverage online
www.mhhe.com/RossCore6e

Both sensitivity analysis and scenario analysis attempt to answer the question, "What if?" However, while both analyses are frequently used in the real world, each has its own limitations. Sensitivity analysis allows only one variable to change at a time. By contrast, many variables are likely to move at the same time in the real world. Scenario analysis follows specific scenarios, such as changes in inflation, government regulation, or the number of competitors. While this methodology is often quite helpful, it cannot cover all sources of variability. In fact, projects are likely to exhibit a lot of variability under just one economic scenario.

Monte Carlo simulation is a further attempt to model real-world uncertainty. This approach takes its name from the famous European casino because it analyzes projects the way one might analyze gambling strategies. Imagine a serious blackjack player who wonders if he should take a third card whenever his first two cards total 16. Most likely, a formal mathematical model would be too complex to be practical here. However, he could play thousands of hands in a casino, sometimes drawing a third card when his first two cards add to 16 and sometimes not drawing that third card. He could compare his winnings (or losings) under the two strategies in order to determine which was better. Of course, because he would probably lose a lot of money performing this test in a real casino, simulating the results from the two strategies on a computer might be cheaper. Monte Carlo simulation of capital budgeting projects is in this spirit.

Imagine that Backyard Barbeques, Inc. (BBI), a manufacturer of both charcoal and gas grills, has the blueprint for a new grill that cooks with compressed hydrogen. The CFO, Edward H. Comiskey, being dissatisfied with simpler capital budgeting techniques, wants a Monte Carlo simulation for this new grill. A consultant specializing in the Monte Carlo approach, Les Mauney, takes him through the five basic steps of the method.

For a demonstration of a spreadsheet application of Monte Carlo analysis, go to www.crystalball.com.

Step 1: Specify the Basic Model

Les Mauney breaks up cash flow into three components: annual revenue, annual costs, and initial investment. The revenue in any year is viewed as:

$$
\begin{array}{c}
\text{Number of grills sold} \\
\text{by entire industry}
\end{array}
\times
\begin{array}{c}
\text{Market share of BBI's} \\
\text{hydrogen grill (in percent)}
\end{array}
\times
\begin{array}{c}
\text{Price per} \\
\text{hydrogen grill}
\end{array}
$$

The cost in any year is viewed as:

$$
\text{Fixed manufacturing costs} + \text{Variable manufacturing costs} \\
+ \text{Marketing costs} + \text{Selling costs}
$$

Initial investment is viewed as:

$$
\text{Cost of patent} + \text{Test-marketing costs} + \text{Cost of production facility}
$$

Step 2: Specify a Distribution for Each Variable in the Model

Here comes the hard part. Let's start with revenue, which has three components in the equation above. The consultant first models overall market size, that is, the number of grills sold by the entire industry. The trade publication *Outdoor Food (OF)* reported that 10 million grills of all types were sold in the continental United States last year and it forecasts sales of 10.5 million next year. Mr. Mauney, using *OF*'s forecast and his own intuition, creates the following distribution for next year's sales of grills by the entire industry:

Probability		20%	60%	20%
Next Year's Industrywide Unit Sales		10 million	10.5 million	11 million

The tight distribution here reflects the slow but steady historical growth in the grill market.

Les Mauney realizes that estimating the market share of BBI's hydrogen grill is more difficult. Nevertheless, after a great deal of analysis, he determines the distribution of next year's market share to be:

Probability	10%	20%	30%	25%	10%	5%
Market Share of BBI's Hydrogen Grill Next Year	1%	2%	3%	4%	5%	8%

While the consultant assumed a symmetrical distribution for industrywide unit sales, he believes a skewed distribution makes more sense for the project's market share. In his mind, there is always the small possibility that sales of the hydrogen grill will really take off.

The above forecasts assume that unit sales for the overall industry are unrelated to the project's market share. In other words, the two variables are independent of each other. Mr. Mauney reasons that, while an economic boom might increase industrywide grill sales and a recession might decrease them, the project's market share is unlikely to be related to economic conditions.

Now Mr. Mauney must determine the distribution of price per grill. Mr. Comiskey, the CFO, informs him that the price will be in the area of $200 per grill, given what other competitors are charging. However, the consultant believes that the price per hydrogen grill will almost certainly depend on the size of the overall market for grills. As in any business, you can usually charge more if demand is high.

After rejecting a number of complex models for price, Mr. Mauney settles on the following specification:

$$\text{Next year's price per hydrogen grill} = \$190 + \$1 \times \text{Industrywide unit sales (in millions)} +/-\$3$$

The grill price in the above equation is dependent on the unit sales of the industry. In addition, random variation is modeled via the term "+/– $3," where a drawing of +$3 and a drawing of –$3 each occurs 50 percent of the time. For example, if industrywide unit sales are 11 million, the price per grill would be either:

$$\$190 + 11 + 3 = \$204 \quad (50\% \text{ probability})$$
$$\$190 + 11 - 3 = \$198 \quad (50\% \text{ probability})$$

The consultant now has distributions for each of the three components of next year's revenue. However, he needs distributions for future years as well. Using forecasts from *Outdoor Food* and other publications, Mr. Mauney forecasts the distribution of growth rates for the entire industry over the second year to be:

Probability	20%	60%	20%
Growth Rate of Industrywide Unit Sales in Second Year	1%	3%	5%

Given both the distribution of next year's industrywide unit sales and the distribution of growth rates for this variable over the second year, we can generate the distribution of industrywide unit sales for the second year. A similar extension should give Mr. Mauney a distribution for later years as well, though we won't go into the details here. And, just as the consultant extended the first component of revenue (industrywide unit sales) to later years, he would want to do the same thing for market share and unit price.

The above discussion shows how the three components of revenue can be modeled. Step 2 would be complete once the components of cost and of investment are modeled in a similar way. Special attention must be paid to the interactions between variables here because ineffective management will likely allow the different cost components to rise together. However, because you are probably getting the idea now, we will skip the rest of this step.

Step 3: The Computer Draws One Outcome

As we said above, next year's revenue in our model is the product of three components. Imagine that the computer randomly picks industrywide unit sales of 10 million, a market share for BBI's hydrogen grill of 2 percent, and a +$3 random price variation. Given these drawings, next year's price per hydrogen grill will be:

$$\$190 + 10 + 3 = \$203$$

and next year's revenue for BBI's hydrogen grill will be:

$$10 \text{ million} \times .02 \times \$203 = \$40.6 \text{ million}$$

Of course, we are not done with the entire outcome yet. We would have to perform drawings for revenue in each future year. In addition, we would perform drawings for costs in each future year. Finally, a drawing for initial investment would have to be made as well. In this way, a single outcome would generate a cash flow from the project in each future year.

How likely is it that the specific outcome above would be drawn? We can answer this because we know the probability of each component. Because industry sales of 10 million units have a 20 percent probability, a market share of 2 percent also has a 20 percent probability, and a random price variation of +$3 has a 50 percent probability, the probability of these three drawings together in the same outcome is:

$$.02 = .20 \times .20 \times .50$$

Of course, the probability would get even smaller once drawings for future revenues, future costs, and the initial investment are included in the outcome.

This step generates the cash flow for each year from a single outcome. What we are ultimately interested in is the distribution of cash flow each year across many outcomes. We ask the computer to randomly draw over and over again to give us this distribution, which is what is done in the next step.

Step 4: Repeat the Procedure

While the above three steps generate one outcome, the essence of Monte Carlo simulation is repeated outcomes. Depending on the situation, the computer may be called on to generate thousands or even millions of outcomes. The result of all these drawings is a distribution of cash flow for each future year. This distribution is the basic output of Monte Carlo simulation.

Consider Figure 9.3. Here, repeated drawings have produced the simulated distribution of the third year's cash flow. There would be, of course, a distribution like the one in this figure for each future year. This leaves us with one more step.

Step 5: Calculate NPV

Given the distribution of cash flow for the third year in Figure 9.3, one can determine the expected cash flow for this year. In a similar manner, one can also determine the expected cash flow for each future year and can then calculate the net present value of the project by discounting these expected cash flows at an appropriate rate.

Monte Carlo simulation is often viewed as a step beyond either sensitivity analysis or scenario analysis. Interactions between the variables are explicitly specified in Monte Carlo; so, at least in theory, this methodology provides a more complete analysis. And, as a by-product, having to build a precise model deepens the forecaster's understanding of the project.

FIGURE 9.3

Simulated Distribution of
the Third Year's Cash Flow
for BBI's New Hydrogen Grill

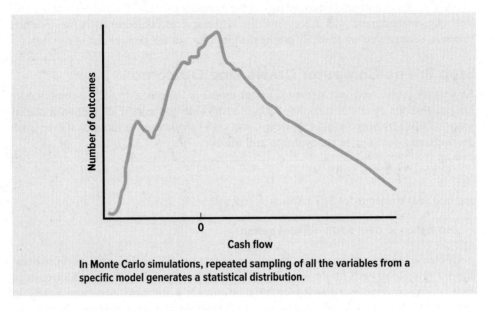

In Monte Carlo simulations, repeated sampling of all the variables from a specific model generates a statistical distribution.

Because Monte Carlo simulations have been around since at least the 1940s, you might think that most firms would be performing them by now. Surprisingly, this does not seem to be the case. In our experience, executives are frequently skeptical of all the complexity. It is difficult to model either the distributions of each variable or the interactions between variables. In addition, the computer output is often devoid of economic intuition. Thus, while Monte Carlo simulations are used in certain real-world situations, the approach is not likely to be "the wave of the future." In fact, Graham and Harvey[4] report that only about 15 percent of the firms in their sample use capital budgeting simulations.

9.4 REAL OPTIONS

In Chapter 7, we stressed the superiority of net present value (NPV) analysis over other approaches when valuing capital budgeting projects. However, both scholars and practitioners have pointed out problems with NPV. The basic idea here is that NPV analysis, as well as all the other approaches in Chapter 7, ignores the adjustments that a firm can make after a project is accepted. These adjustments are called **real options**. In this respect, NPV underestimates the true value of a project. NPV's conservatism here is best explained through a series of examples.

The Option to Expand

Conrad Willig, an entrepreneur, recently learned of a chemical treatment that causes water to freeze at 100 degrees Fahrenheit rather than 32 degrees. Of all the many practical applications for this treatment, Mr. Willig liked the idea of hotels made of ice more than anything else. Conrad estimated the annual cash flows from a single ice hotel to be $2 million, based on an initial investment of $12 million. He felt that 20 percent was an appropriate discount rate, given the risk of this new venture. Assuming that the cash flows were perpetual, Mr. Willig determined the NPV of the project to be:

$$-\$12,000,000 + \$2,000,000/.20 = -\$2 \text{ million}$$

Most entrepreneurs would have rejected this venture, given its negative NPV. But Conrad was not your typical entrepreneur. He reasoned that NPV analysis missed a hidden

---

[4] See Figure 2 of Graham and Harvey, "The Theory and Practice of Corporate Finance."

FIGURE 9.4

Decision Tree for Ice Hotel

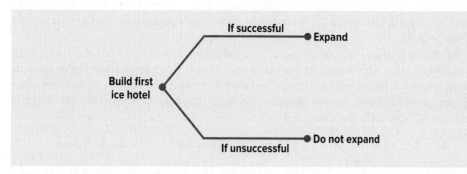

source of value. While he was pretty sure that the initial investment would cost $12 million, there was some uncertainty concerning annual cash flows. His cash flow estimate of $2 million per year actually reflected his belief that there was a 50 percent probability that annual cash flows would be $3 million and a 50 percent probability that annual cash flows would be $1 million.

The NPV calculations for the two forecasts are:

> **Optimistic forecast: − $12 million + $3 million/.20 = $3 million**
> **Pessimistic forecast: − $12 million + $1 million/.20 = − $7 million**

On the surface, this new calculation doesn't seem to help Mr. Willig very much because an average of the two forecasts yields an NPV for the project of:

> **.50 × $3 million + .50 × (−$7 million) = − $2 million**

which is the value he calculated in the first place.

However, if the optimistic forecast turns out to be correct, Mr. Willig would want to expand. If he believes that there are, say, 10 locations in the country that can support an ice hotel, the true NPV of the venture would be:

> **.50 × 10 × $3 million + .50 × (−$7 million) = $11.5 million**

The idea here, which is represented in Figure 9.4, is both basic and universal. The entrepreneur has the option to expand if the pilot location is successful. For example, think of all the people that start restaurants, most of them ultimately failing. These individuals are not necessarily overly optimistic. They may realize the likelihood of failure but go ahead anyway because of the small chance of starting the next McDonald's or Burger King.

The Option to Abandon

Managers also have the option to abandon existing projects. While abandonment may seem cowardly, it can often save companies a great deal of money. Because of this, the option to abandon increases the value of any potential project.

The above example of ice hotels, which illustrated the option to expand, can also illustrate the option to abandon. To see this, imagine that Mr. Willig now believes that there is a 50 percent probability that annual cash flows will be $6 million and a 50 percent probability that annual cash flows will be −$2 million. The NPV calculations under the two forecasts become:

> **Optimistic forecast: − $12 million + $6 million/.2 = $18 million**
> **Pessimistic forecast: − $12 million − $2 million/.2 = − $22 million**

yielding an NPV for the project of:

> **.50 × $18 million + .50 × (− $22 million) = − $2 million**

Furthermore, now imagine that Mr. Willig wants to own, at most, one ice hotel, implying that there is no option to expand. Because the NPV here is negative, it looks as if he will not build the hotel.

But things change when we consider the abandonment option. As of Date 1, the entrepreneur will know which forecast has come true. If cash flows equal those under the optimistic forecast, Conrad will keep the project alive. If, however, cash flows equal those under the pessimistic forecast, he will abandon the hotel. Knowing these possibilities ahead of time, the NPV of the project becomes:

$$.50 \times \$18 \text{ million} + .50 \times (-\$12 \text{ million} - \$2 \text{ million}/1.20) = \$2.17 \text{ million}$$

Because Conrad abandons after experiencing the cash flow of −$2 million at Date 1, he does not have to endure this outflow in any of the later years. Because the NPV is now positive, Conrad will accept the project.

The example here is clearly a stylized one. While many years may pass before a project is abandoned in the real world, our ice hotel was abandoned after one year. And, while salvage values generally accompany abandonment, we assumed no salvage value for the ice hotel. Nevertheless, abandonment options are pervasive in the real world.

For example, consider the moviemaking industry, which we discussed to open the chapter. As shown in Figure 9.5, movies begin with either the purchase or development of a script. A completed script might cost a movie studio a few million dollars and potentially lead to actual production. However, the great majority of scripts (perhaps well in excess of 80 percent) are abandoned. Why would studios abandon scripts that they had commissioned in the first place? While the studios know ahead of time that only a few scripts will be promising, they don't know which ones. Thus, they cast a wide net, commissioning many scripts to get a few good ones. And the studios must be ruthless with the bad scripts because the expenditure on a script pales in comparison to the huge losses from producing a bad movie.

The few lucky scripts will then move into production, where costs might be budgeted in the tens of millions of dollars, if not much more. At this stage, the dreaded phrase is that on-location production gets "bogged down," creating cost overruns. But the studios are equally ruthless here. Should these overruns become excessive, production is likely to be abandoned in midstream. Interestingly, abandonment almost always occurs due to high costs, not due to the fear that the movie won't be able to find an audience. Little information on that score will be obtained until the movie is actually released.

FIGURE 9.5

The Abandonment Option in the Movie Industry

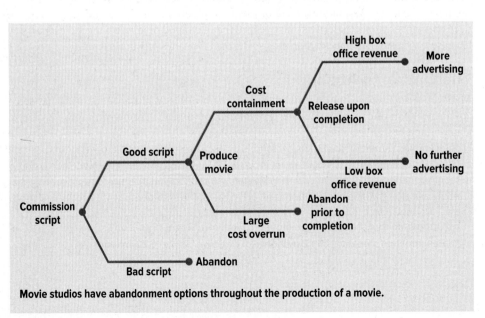

Movie studios have abandonment options throughout the production of a movie.

Release of the movie is accompanied by significant advertising expenditures, perhaps in the range of $10 to $20 million. Box office success in the first few weeks is likely to lead to further advertising expenditures. Again, the studio has the option, but not the obligation, to increase advertising here.

Moviemaking is one of the riskiest businesses around, with studios receiving hundreds of millions of dollars in a matter of weeks from a blockbuster while receiving practically nothing during this period from a flop. The above abandonment options control costs that might otherwise bankrupt the industry.

To illustrate some of these ideas, consider the case of Euro Disney. The deal to open Euro Disney occurred in 1987, and the park opened its doors outside of Paris in 1992. Disney's management thought Europeans would go goofy over the new park, but trouble soon began. The number of visitors never met expectations, in part because the company priced tickets too high. Disney also decided not to serve alcohol in a country that was accustomed to wine with meals. French labor inspectors fought Disney's strict dress codes, and so on.

After several years of operations, the park began serving wine in its restaurants, lowered ticket prices, and made other adjustments. In other words, management exercised its option to reformulate the product. The park began to make a small profit. Then the company exercised the option to expand by adding a "second gate," which was another theme park next to Euro Disney named Walt Disney Studios. The second gate was intended to encourage visitors to extend their stays. But the new park flopped. The reasons ranged from high ticket prices to attractions geared toward Hollywood rather than European filmmaking, labor strikes in Paris, and a summer heat wave.

By the summer of 2003, Euro Disney was close to bankruptcy again. Executives discussed a range of options. These options ranged from letting the company go broke (the option to abandon) to pulling the Disney name from the park. In 2005, the company finally agreed to a restructuring with the help of the French government.

The whole idea of managerial options was summed up aptly by Jay Rasulo, the overseer of Disney's theme parks, when he said, "One thing we know for sure is that you never get it 100 percent right the first time. We open every one of our parks with the notion that we're going to add content." In 2017, the resort posted revenues of $6.5 billion and a net income of $1.8 billion. And then, in 2018, Walt Disney announced plans to invest €2 billion in the renamed Disneyland Paris.

A recent example of the option to abandon occurred in 2018 when Intel announced that it would shut down the New Devices Group, which had only been in existence for five years. The division was in charge of developing wearables, including a pair of lightweight smart glasses. Intel had sunk hundreds of millions of dollars into the division, including the 2014 purchase of Basis for $100 million and the 2015 purchase of Recon for $150 million. Intel apparently learned that breaking into the wearables market was more difficult than it first believed.

Timing Options

One often finds urban land that has been vacant for many years. Yet this land is bought and sold from time to time. Why would anyone pay a positive price for land that has no source of revenue? Certainly one could not arrive at this positive value through NPV analysis. However, the paradox can easily be explained in terms of real options.

Suppose that the land's highest and best use is as an office building. Total construction costs for the building are estimated to be $1 million. Currently, net rents (after all costs) are estimated to be $90,000 per year in perpetuity and the discount rate is 10 percent. The NPV of this proposed building would be:

$$-\$1 \text{ million} + \$90,000/.10 = -\$100,000$$

FIGURE 9.6

Decision Tree for Vacant
Land

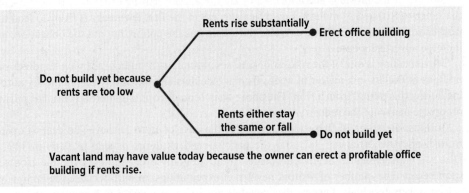

Vacant land may have value today because the owner can erect a profitable office building if rents rise.

Because this NPV is negative, one would not currently want to build. In addition, it appears as if the land is worthless. However, suppose that the federal government is planning various urban revitalization programs for the city. Office rents will likely increase if the programs succeed. In this case, the property's owner might want to erect the office building after all. Conversely, office rents will remain the same, or even fall, if the programs fail. The owner will not build in this case.

We say that the property owner has a *timing option*. While he does not currently want to build, he will want to build in the future should rents in the area rise substantially. This timing option explains why vacant land often has value. While there are costs, such as taxes, from holding raw land, the value of an office building after a substantial rise in rents may more than offset these holding costs. Of course, the exact value of the vacant land depends on both the probability of success in the revitalization program and the extent of the rent increase. Figure 9.6 illustrates this timing option.

Mining operations almost always provide timing options as well. Suppose you own a copper mine where the cost of mining each ton of copper exceeds the sales revenue. It's a no-brainer to say that you would not want to mine the copper currently. And because there are costs of ownership such as property taxes, insurance, and security, you might actually want to pay someone to take the mine off your hands. However, we would caution you not to do so hastily. Copper prices in the future might very well increase enough so that production is profitable. Given that possibility, you could likely find someone to pay a positive price for the property today.

SUMMARY AND CONCLUSIONS

This chapter discusses a number of practical applications of capital budgeting.

1. Though NPV is the best capital budgeting approach conceptually, it has been criticized in practice for providing managers with a false sense of security. Sensitivity analysis shows NPV under varying assumptions, giving managers a better feel for the project's risks. Unfortunately, sensitivity analysis modifies only one variable at a time, while many variables are likely to vary together in the real world. Scenario analysis examines a project's performance under different scenarios (e.g., war breaking out or oil prices skyrocketing). Finally, managers want to know how bad forecasts must be before a project loses money. Break-even analysis calculates the sales figure at which the project breaks even. Though break-even analysis is frequently performed on an accounting profit basis, we suggest that a net present value basis is more appropriate.

2. Monte Carlo simulation begins with a model of the firm's cash flows, based on both the interactions between different variables and the movement of each individual variable over time. Random sampling generates a distribution of these cash flows for each period, leading to a net present value calculation.

3. We analyze the hidden options in capital budgeting, such as the option to expand, the option to abandon, and timing options.

CONCEPT QUESTIONS

1. **Forecasting Risk**   What is forecasting risk? In general, would the degree of forecasting risk be greater for a new product or a cost-cutting proposal? Why?

2. **Sensitivity Analysis and Scenario Analysis**   What is the essential difference between sensitivity analysis and scenario analysis?

3. **Marginal Cash Flows**   A co-worker claims that looking at all this marginal this and incremental that is just a bunch of nonsense, and states: "Listen, if our average revenue doesn't exceed our average cost, then we will have a negative cash flow, and we will go broke!" How do you respond?

4. **Break-Even Point**   As a shareholder of a firm that is contemplating a new project, would you be more concerned with the accounting break-even point, the cash break-even point (i.e., the point at which operating cash flow is zero), or the financial break-even point? Why?

5. **Break-Even Point**   Assume a firm is considering a new project that requires an initial investment and has equal sales and costs over its life. Will the project reach the accounting, cash, or financial break-even point first? Which will it reach next? Last? Will this ordering always apply?

6. **Real Options**   Why does traditional NPV analysis tend to underestimate the true value of a capital budgeting project?

7. **Real Options**   The Mango Republic has just liberalized its markets and is now permitting foreign investors. Tesla Manufacturing has analyzed starting a project in the country and has determined that the project has a negative NPV. Why might the company go ahead with the project? What type of option is most likely to add value to this project?

8. **Sensitivity Analysis and Break-Even**   How does sensitivity analysis interact with break-even analysis?

9. **Option to Wait**   An option can often have more than one source of value. Consider a logging company. The company can log the timber today or wait another year (or more) to log the timber. What advantages would waiting one year potentially have?

10. **Project Analysis**   You are discussing a project analysis with a co-worker. The project involves real options, such as expanding the project if successful, or abandoning the project if it fails. Your co-worker makes the following statement: "This analysis is ridiculous. We looked at expanding or abandoning the project in two years, but there are many other options we should consider. For example, we could expand in one year, and expand further in two years. Or we could expand in one year, and abandon the project in two years. There are too many options for us to examine. Because of this, anything this analysis would give us is worthless." How would you evaluate this statement? Considering that with any capital budgeting project there are an infinite number of real options, when do you stop the option analysis on an individual project?

QUESTIONS AND PROBLEMS

1. **Sensitivity Analysis and Break-Even Point**   We are evaluating a project that costs $772,000, has an eight-year life, and has no salvage value. Assume that depreciation is straight-line to zero over the life of the project. Sales are projected at 96,000 units per year. Price per unit is $39, variable cost per unit is $21, and fixed costs are $1.35 million per year. The tax rate is 21 percent, and we require a return of 15 percent on this project.

   a. Calculate the accounting break-even point.
   b. Calculate the base-case cash flow and NPV. What is the sensitivity of NPV to changes in the sales figure? Explain what your answer tells you about a 500-unit decrease in projected sales.
   c. What is the sensitivity of OCF to changes in the variable cost figure? Explain what your answer tells you about a $1 decrease in estimated variable costs.

2. **Scenario Analysis**   In the previous problem, suppose the projections given for price, quantity, variable costs, and fixed costs are all accurate to within ±10 percent. Calculate the best-case and worst-case NPV figures.

Mc Graw Hill connect

Basic
(Questions 1–10)

3. **Calculating Break-Even**   In each of the following cases, find the unknown variable. Ignore taxes.

Accounting Break-Even	Unit Price	Unit Variable Cost	Fixed Costs	Depreciation
96,200	$37	$23	$740,000	?
12,318	?	49	855,000	$725,000
7,583	127	?	245,000	143,000

4. **Financial Break-Even**   Jed's Cars, Inc., just purchased a $538,000 machine to produce toy cars. The machine will be fully depreciated by the straight-line method over its five-year economic life. Each toy sells for $34. The variable cost per toy is $9, and the firm incurs fixed costs of $365,000 each year. The corporate tax rate for the company is 22 percent. The appropriate discount rate is 10 percent. What is the financial break-even point for the project?

5. **Option to Wait**   Your company is deciding whether to invest in a new machine. The new machine will increase cash flow by $495,000 per year. You believe the technology used in the machine has a 10-year life; in other words, no matter when you purchase the machine, it will be obsolete 10 years from today. The machine is currently priced at $2.7 million. The cost of the machine will decline by $205,000 per year until it reaches $1.47 million, where it will remain. If your required return is 12 percent, should you purchase the machine? If so, when should you purchase it?

6. **Decision Trees**   Ang Electronics, Inc., has developed a new HD DVD. If the HD DVD is successful, the present value of the payoff (at the time the product is brought to market) is $24 million. If the HD DVD fails, the present value of the payoff is $6.5 million. If the product goes directly to market, there is a 55 percent chance of success. Alternatively, the company can delay the launch by one year and spend $1.8 million to test-market the HD DVD. Test-marketing would allow the firm to improve the product and increase the probability of success to 75 percent. The appropriate discount rate is 11 percent. Should the firm conduct test-marketing?

7. **Decision Trees**   The manager for a growing firm is considering the launch of a new product. If the product goes directly to market, there is a 40 percent chance of success. For $60,000, the manager can conduct a focus group that will increase the product's chance of success to 60 percent. Alternatively, the manager has the option to pay a consulting firm $355,000 to research the market and refine the product. The consulting firm successfully launches new products 85 percent of the time. If the firm successfully launches the product, the payoff will be $1.23 million. If the product is a failure, the NPV is $0. Which action will result in the highest expected payoff to the firm?

8. **Decision Trees**   B&B has a new baby powder ready to market. If the firm goes directly to the market with the product, there is only a 60 percent chance of success. However, the firm can conduct customer segment research, which will take a year and cost $650,000. By going through research, the company will be able to better target potential customers and will increase the probability of success to 75 percent. If successful, the baby powder will bring a present value profit (at time of initial selling) of $29 million. If unsuccessful, the present value profit is only $5.7 million. Should the firm conduct customer segment research or go directly to market? The appropriate discount rate is 12 percent.

9. **Financial Break-Even Analysis**   You are considering investing in a company that cultivates abalone for sale to local restaurants. Use the following information:

Sales price per abalone	= $52.25
Variable costs per abalone	= $14.60
Fixed costs per year	= $580,000
Depreciation per year	= $65,000
Tax rate	= 21%

The discount rate for the company is 13 percent, the initial investment in equipment is $455,000, and the project's economic life is seven years. Assume the equipment is depreciated on a straight-line basis over the project's life.

    a. What is the accounting break-even level for the project?

    b. What is the financial break-even level for the project?

10. Financial Break-Even   Chartreuse Co. has purchased a brand new machine to produce its High Flight line of shoes. The machine has an economic life of six years. The depreciation schedule for the machine is straight-line with no salvage value. The machine costs $735,000. The sales price per pair of shoes is $94, while the variable cost is $26. Fixed costs of $475,000 per year are attributed to the machine. The corporate tax rate is 23 percent and the appropriate discount rate is 12 percent. What is the financial break-even point?

11. Break-Even Intuition   Consider a project with a required return of *R* percent that costs $1 and will last for *N* years. The project uses straight-line depreciation to zero over the *N*-year life; there are neither salvage value nor net working capital requirements.

Intermediate
(Questions 11–25)

    a. At the accounting break-even level of output, what is the IRR of this project? The payback period? The NPV?

    b. At the cash break-even level of output, what is the IRR of this project? The payback period? The NPV?

    c. At the financial break-even level of output, what is the IRR of this project? The payback period? The NPV?

12. Sensitivity Analysis   Consider a four-year project with the following information: initial fixed asset investment = $385,000; straight-line depreciation to zero over the four-year life; zero salvage value; price = $26; variable costs = $17; fixed costs = $395,000; quantity sold = 73,000 units; tax rate = 22 percent. How sensitive is OCF to changes in quantity sold?

13. Project Analysis   You are considering a new product launch. The project will cost $830,000, have a four-year life, and have no salvage value; depreciation is straight-line to zero. Sales are projected at 250 units per year; price per unit will be $18,300, variable cost per unit will be $13,200, and fixed costs will be $595,000 per year. The required return on the project is 15 percent, and the relevant tax rate is 21 percent.

    a. Based on your experience, you think the unit sales, variable cost, and fixed cost projections given here are probably accurate to within ±10 percent. What are the upper and lower bounds for these projections? What is the base-case NPV? What are the best-case and worst-case scenarios?

    b. Evaluate the sensitivity of your base-case NPV to changes in fixed costs.

    c. What is the accounting break-even level of output for this project?

14. Project Analysis   McGilla Golf has decided to sell a new line of golf clubs. The clubs will sell for $850 per set and have a variable cost of $445 per set. The company has spent $150,000 for a marketing study that determined the company will sell 45,000 sets per year for seven years. The marketing study also determined that the company will lose sales of 12,000 sets of its high-priced clubs. The high-priced clubs sell at $1,300 and have variable costs of $720. The company will also increase sales of its cheap clubs by 10,000 sets. The cheap clubs sell for $415 and have variable costs of $185 per set. The fixed costs each year will be $6.2 million. The company has also spent $1 million on research and development for the new clubs. The plant and equipment required will cost $14.5 million and will be depreciated on a straight-line basis. The new clubs will also require an increase in net working capital of $2.1 million that will be returned at the end of the project. The tax rate is 21 percent, and the cost of capital is 14 percent. Calculate the payback period, the NPV, and the IRR.

15. Scenario Analysis   In the previous problem, you feel that the units sold, variable costs, and fixed costs are accurate to within only ±10 percent. What are the best-case and worst-case NPVs? (*Hint:* The price and variable costs for the two existing sets of clubs are known with certainty; only the sales gained or lost are uncertain.)

16. Sensitivity Analysis   McGilla Golf (see Problem 14) would like to know the sensitivity of NPV to changes in the price of the new clubs and the quantity of new clubs sold. What is the sensitivity of the NPV to each of these variables?

17. Abandonment Value   We are examining a new project. We expect to sell 14,000 units per year at $64 net cash flow apiece for the next 10 years. In other words, the annual operating cash flow is projected to be $64 × 14,000 = $896,000. The relevant discount rate is 11 percent, and the initial investment required is $3.95 million.

    a. What is the base-case NPV?

    b. After the first year, the project can be dismantled and sold for $1.75 million. If expected sales are revised based on the first year's performance, when would it make sense to abandon the investment? In other words, at what level of expected sales would it make sense to abandon the project?

    c. Explain how the $1.75 million abandonment value can be viewed as the opportunity cost of keeping the project in one year.

18. Abandonment   In the previous problem, suppose you think it is likely that expected sales will be revised upward to 19,000 units if the first year is a success and revised downward to 3,700 units if the first year is not a success.

    a. If success and failure are equally likely, what is the NPV of the project? Consider the possibility of abandonment in answering.

    b. What is the value of the option to abandon?

19. Abandonment and Expansion   In the previous problem, suppose the scale of the project can be doubled in one year in the sense that twice as many units can be produced and sold. Naturally, expansion would only be desirable if the project were a success. This implies that if the project is a success, projected sales after expansion will be 28,000. Again assuming that success and failure are equally likely, what is the NPV of the project? Note that abandonment is still an option if the project is a failure. What is the value of the option to expand?

20. Break-Even Analysis   Your buddy comes to you with a surefire way to make some quick money and help pay off your student loans. His idea is to sell T-shirts with the words "I get" on them. "You get it?" He says, "You see all those bumper stickers and T-shirts that say, 'got milk' or 'got surf.' So this says, 'I get.' It's funny! All we have to do is buy a used silk screen press for $10,500 and we are in business!" Assume there are no fixed costs, and you depreciate the $10,500 in the first period. Taxes are 21 percent.

    a. What is the accounting break-even point if each shirt costs $3.85 to make and you can sell them for $14 apiece?

    b. Now assume one year has passed and you have sold 5,000 shirts! You find out that the Dairy Farmers of America have copyrighted the "got milk" slogan and are requiring you to pay $25,000 to continue operations. You expect this craze will last for another three years and that your discount rate is 12 percent. What is the financial break-even point for your enterprise now?

21. Decision Trees   Young screenwriter Carl Draper has just finished his first script. It has action, drama, and humor, and he thinks it will be a blockbuster. He takes the script to every motion picture studio in town and tries to sell it, but to no avail. Finally, ACME studios offers to buy the script, for either (a) $50,000 or (b) 1 percent of the movie's profits. There are two decisions the studio will have to make. First is to decide if the script is good or bad, and second if the movie is good or bad. There is a 90 percent chance that the script is bad. If it is bad, the studio does nothing more and throws the script out. If the script is good, the studio will shoot the movie. After the movie is shot, the studio will review it, and there is a 70 percent chance that the movie is bad. If the movie is bad, the movie will not be promoted and will not turn a profit. If the movie is good, the studio will promote heavily and the average profit for this type of movie is $120 million. Carl rejects the $50,000 and says he wants the 1 percent of profits. Was this a good decision by Carl?

22. Accounting Break-Even   Samuelson, Inc., has just purchased a $726,000 machine to produce calculators. The machine will be fully depreciated by the straight-line method over its economic life of five years and will produce 45,000 calculators each year. The variable production cost per calculator is $12.70, and total fixed costs are $875,000 per year. The corporate tax rate for the company is 21 percent. For the firm to break even in terms of accounting profit, how much should the firm charge per calculator?

23. Abandonment Decisions   Tag Products, Inc., is considering a new product launch. The firm expects to have an annual operating cash flow of $6.8 million for the next 10 years. The required return for this project is 14 percent. The initial investment is $27.5 million. Assume that the project has no salvage value at the end of its economic life.

a. What is the NPV of the new product?

b. After the first year, the project can be dismantled and sold for $17 million. If the estimates of remaining cash flows are revised based on the first year's experience, at what level of expected cash flows does it make sense to abandon the project?

24. **Expansion Decisions**   Applied Nanotech is thinking about introducing a new surface cleaning machine. The marketing department has come up with the estimate that the company can sell 10 units per year at $153,000 net cash flow per unit for the next five years. The engineering department has come up with the estimate that developing the machine will take a $5.9 million initial investment. The finance department has estimated that a discount rate of 13 percent should be used.

a. What is the base-case NPV?

b. If unsuccessful, after the first year the project can be dismantled and will have an aftertax salvage value of $3.1 million. Also, after the first year, expected cash flows will be revised up to 20 units per year or to 0 units, with equal probability. What is the revised NPV?

25. **Scenario Analysis**   You are the financial analyst for a tennis racket manufacturer. The company is considering using a graphite-like material in its tennis rackets. The company has estimated the information in the table below about the market for a racket with the new material. The company expects to sell the racket for five years. The equipment required for the project has no salvage value and will be depreciated on a straight-line basis. The required return for projects of this type is 13 percent, and the company has a 23 percent tax rate. Should you recommend the project?

	Pessimistic	Expected	Optimistic
Market size	81,000	97,000	112,000
Market share	14%	17%	19%
Selling price	110	$ 116	$ 119
Variable costs per year	$ 38	$ 36	$ 34
Fixed costs per year	$ 615,000	$ 575,000	$ 550,000
Initial investment	$1,550,000	$1,450,000	$1,350,000

26. **Scenario Analysis**   Consider a project to supply Detroit with 35,000 tons of machine screws annually for automobile production. You will need an initial $6.5 million investment in threading equipment to get the project started; the project will last for five years. The accounting department estimates that annual fixed costs will be $850,000 and that variable costs should be $124 per ton; accounting will depreciate the initial fixed asset investment straight-line to zero over the five-year project life. It also estimates a salvage value of $400,000 after dismantling costs. The marketing department estimates that the automakers will let the contract at a selling price of $219 per ton. The engineering department estimates you will need an initial net working capital investment of $550,000. You require a return of 13 percent and face a marginal tax rate of 24 percent on this project.

Challenge
(Questions 26–30)

a. What is the estimated OCF for this project? The NPV? Should you pursue this project?

b. Suppose you believe that the accounting department's initial cost and salvage value projections are accurate only to within ±15 percent; the marketing department's price estimate is accurate only to within ±10 percent; and the engineering department's net working capital estimate is accurate only to within ±5 percent. What is your worst-case scenario for this project? Your best-case scenario? Do you still want to pursue the project?

27. **Sensitivity Analysis**   In Problem 26, suppose you're confident about your own projections, but you're a little unsure about Detroit's actual machine screw requirement. What is the sensitivity of the project OCF to changes in the quantity supplied? What about the sensitivity of NPV to changes in quantity supplied? Given the sensitivity number you calculated, is there some minimum level of output below which you wouldn't want to operate? Why?

28. **Abandonment Decisions**   Consider the following project for Hand Clapper, Inc. The company is considering a four-year project to manufacture clap-command garage door openers. This project requires an initial investment of $12.7 million that will be depreciated straight-line to zero over the project's life.

An initial investment in net working capital of $2.028 million is required to support spare parts inventory; this cost is fully recoverable whenever the project ends. The company believes it can generate $10.99 million in pretax revenues with $4.524 million in total pretax operating costs. The tax rate is 21 percent and the discount rate is 16 percent. The market value of the equipment over the life of the project is as follows:

Year	Market Value (in $ millions)
1	$8.80
2	7.96
3	5.30
4	0.00

a. Assuming the company operates this project for four years, what is the NPV?

b. Now compute the project NPVs assuming the project is abandoned after only one year, after two years, and after three years. What economic life for this project maximizes its value to the firm? What does this problem tell you about not considering abandonment possibilities when evaluating projects?

29. **Abandonment Decisions**   First Person Games, Inc., has hired you to perform a feasibility study of a new video game that requires an initial investment of $3.7 million. The company expects a total annual operating cash flow of $600,000 for the next 10 years. The relevant discount rate is 11 percent. Cash flows occur at year-end.

a. What is the NPV of the new video game?

b. After one year, the estimate of remaining annual cash flows will either be revised upward to $940,000 or revised downward to $340,000. Each revision has an equal probability of occurring. At that time, the video game project can be sold for $2.46 million after taxes. What is the revised NPV given that the firm can abandon the project after one year?

30. **Financial Break-Even**   The Cornchopper Company is considering the purchase of a new harvester. The company has hired you to determine the break-even purchase price in terms of present value of the harvester. This break-even purchase price is the price at which the project's NPV is zero. Base your analysis on the following facts:

- The new harvester is not expected to affect revenues, but pretax operating expenses will be reduced by $9,000 per year for 10 years.
- The old harvester is now 5 years old, with 10 years of its scheduled life remaining. It was originally purchased for $67,000 and has been depreciated by the straight-line method.
- The old harvester can be sold for $21,000 today.
- The new harvester will be depreciated by the straight-line method over its 10-year life.
- The corporate tax rate is 21 percent.
- The firm's required rate of return is 13 percent.
- The initial investment, the proceeds from selling the old harvester, and any resulting tax effects occur immediately.
- All other cash flows occur at year-end.
- The market value of each harvester at the end of its economic life is zero.

EXCEL MASTER IT! PROBLEM

ExcelMaster
coverage online

www.mhhe.com/RossCore6e

Dahlia Simmons, CFO of Ulrich Enterprises, is analyzing a new project to sell solar-powered batteries for cell phones. Dahlia has estimated the following probability distributions for the variables in the project:

Probability	10%	30%	40%	20%		
Industry Demand	80 million	95 million	108 million	124 million		
Probability	5%	20%	20%	25%	20%	10%
Ulrich Market Share	1%	2%	3%	4%	10%	6%

Probability	20%	70%	10%	
Initial Cost	$60 million	$65 million	$72 million	

Probability	20%	65%	15%	
Variable Cost per Unit	$24	$26	$29	

Probability	15%	25%	40%	20%
Industry Demand	$20 million	$24 million	$27 million	$31 million

The unit price depends on the industry demand because a greater demand will result in a higher price. Dahlia determines that the price per unit will be given by the equation:

Price = Industry demand/2,000,000 +/− $2

The random "+/−$2" term represents an increase or decrease in price according to the following distribution:

Probability	45%	55%
Price Randomness	−$2	$2

The length of the project, tax rate, and required return are:

Project length (years):	6
Tax rate:	21%
Required return:	14%

a. Create a Monte Carlo simulation for the project with at least 500 runs. Calculate the IRR for each run. Note that the IRR function in Excel will return an error if the IRR of the project is too low. For example, if both the initial cash flow and the operating cash flows are negative, the IRR is less than −100 percent. This is not a problem when you are calculating the IRR one time because you can see the IRR is too low, but when you are running 500 or more iterations, it can create a problem when you try to summarize the results. Because of this issue, you should create an IF statement that tests whether the operating cash flow divided by the absolute value of the initial investment is less than .10. If this is the case, the cell will return an IRR of −99.99 percent; if this is not the case, the cell will calculate the IRR.

b. Create a graph of the distribution of the IRRs from the Monte Carlo simulation for different ranges of IRR.

c. Create a graph for the cumulative probability function for the IRR distribution.

CLOSING CASE

BUNYAN LUMBER, LLC

Bunyan Lumber, LLC, harvests timber and delivers logs to timber mills for sale. The company was founded 70 years ago by Pete Bunyan. The current CEO is Paula Bunyan, the granddaughter of the founder. The company is currently evaluating a 6,500-acre forest it owns in Oregon. Paula has asked Hunter Holland, the company's finance officer, to evaluate the project. Paula's concern is when the company should harvest the timber.

Lumber is sold by the company for its "pond value." Pond value is the amount a mill will pay for a log delivered to the mill location. The price paid for logs delivered to a mill is quoted in dollars per thousands of board feet (MBF), and the price depends on the grade of the logs. The forest Bunyan Lumber is evaluating was planted by the company 20 years ago and is made up entirely of Douglas fir trees. The table below shows the current price per MBF for the three grades of timber the company feels will come from the stand:

Timber Grade	Price per MBF
1P	$735
2P	710
3P	697

Hunter believes that the pond value of lumber will increase at the inflation rate. The company is planning to thin the forest today, and it expects to realize a positive cash flow of $3,500 per acre from thinning. The thinning is done to increase the growth rate of the remaining trees, and it is always done 20 years following a planting.

The major decision the company faces is when to log the forest. When the company logs the forest, it will immediately replant saplings, which will allow for a future harvest. The longer the forest is allowed to grow, the larger the harvest becomes per acre. Additionally, an older forest has a higher grade of timber. Hunter has compiled the following table with the expected harvest per acre in thousands of board feet, along with the breakdown of the timber grade.

Years from Today to Begin Harvest	Harvest (MBF) per Acre	Timber Grade		
		1P	2P	3P
20	15.7	20%	41%	39%
25	23.4	23	45	32
30	27.8	27	47	26
35	29.6	29	49	22

The company expects to lose 5 percent of the timber it cuts due to defects and breakage.

The forest will be clear-cut when the company harvests the timber. This method of harvesting allows for faster growth of replanted trees. All of the harvesting, processing, replanting, and transportation are to be handled by subcontractors hired by Bunyan Lumber. The cost of the logging is expected to be $160 per MBF. A road system has to be constructed and is expected to cost $65 per MBF, on average. Sales preparation and administrative costs, excluding office overhead costs, are expected to be $22 per MBF.

As soon as the harvesting is complete, the company will reforest the land. Reforesting costs include the following:

	Per Acre Cost
Excavator piling	$170
Broadcast burning	295
Site preparation	155
Planting costs	305

All costs are expected to increase at the inflation rate.

Assume all cash flows occur at the year of harvest. For example, if the company begins harvesting the timber 20 years from today, the cash flow from the harvest will be received 20 years from today. When the company logs the land, it will immediately replant the land with new saplings. The harvest period chosen will be repeated for the foreseeable future. The company's nominal required return is 10 percent, and the inflation rate is expected to be 3.7 percent per year. Bunyan Lumber has a 21 percent tax rate.

Clear-cutting is a controversial method of forest management. To obtain the necessary permits, Bunyan Lumber has agreed to contribute to a conservation fund every time it harvests the lumber. If the company harvested the forest today, the required contribution would be $5 million. The company has agreed that the required contribution will grow by 3.2 percent per year. When should the company harvest the forest?

Risk and Return: Lessons from Market History

10

OPENING CASE

With the S&P 500 Index down about 6.2 percent, and the NASDAQ Composite Index down about 3.9 percent in 2018, overall stock market performance was pretty poor. However, investors in cloud communications company Twilio had to be happy about the 278 percent gain that stock delivered, and investors in identity solutions company Okta weren't hiding the company's 149 percent gain. Of course, not all stocks increased in value during the year. Stock in beauty and makeup supplier Coty fell about 67 percent during the year, and stock in General Electric dropped about 57 percent.

These examples show that there were tremendous potential profits to be made during 2018, but there was also the risk of losing money, and lots of it. So what should you, as a stock market investor, expect when you invest your own money? In this chapter, we study nine decades of market history to find out.

Please visit us at corecorporatefinance.blogspot.com for the latest developments in the world of corporate finance.

10.1 RETURNS

Dollar Returns

Suppose the Video Concept Company has several thousand shares of stock outstanding and you are a shareholder. You purchased shares of stock in the company at the beginning of the year; it is now year-end and you want to figure out how well you have done on your investment. The return you get on an investment in stocks, like that in bonds or any other investment, comes in two forms.

First, over the year most companies pay dividends to shareholders. As the owner of stock in the Video Concept Company, you are a part owner of the company. If the company is profitable, it may distribute some of its profits to the shareholders. Therefore, as the owner of shares of stock, you will receive some cash, called a *dividend,* during the year. This cash is the *income component* of your return. In addition to the dividend, the other part of your return is the *capital gain*—or, if it is negative, the *capital loss* (negative capital gain)—on the investment.

Suppose we are considering the cash flows of the investment in Figure 10.1 and you purchased 100 shares of stock at the beginning of the year at a price of $37 per share. Your total investment, then, would be:

$$C_0 = \$37 \times 100 = \$3,700$$

ExcelMaster coverage online
www.mhhe.com/RossCore6e

How did the market do today? Find out at finance.yahoo.com.

FIGURE 10.1

Dollar Returns

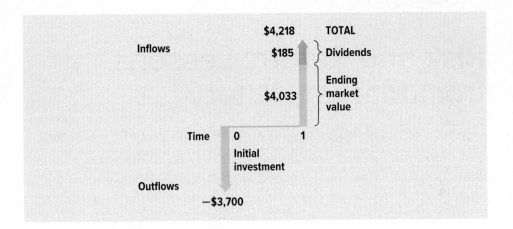

Over the year, the stock paid a dividend of $1.85 per share. During the year, then, you would have received income of:

Dividends = $1.85 × 100 = $185

Lastly, at the end of the year the market price of the stock is $40.33 per share. Because the stock increased in price, you have a capital gain of:

Gain = ($40.33 − 37) × 100 = $333

The capital gain, like the dividend, is part of the return that shareholders require to maintain their investment in the Video Concept Company. Of course, if the price of Video Concept stock had dropped in value to, say, $34.78, you would have recorded a capital loss of:

Loss = ($34.78 − 37) × 100 = − $222

The *total dollar return* on your investment is the sum of the dividend income and the capital gain or loss on the investment:

Total dollar return = Dividend income + Capital gain (or loss)   [10.1]

(From now on we will refer to *capital losses* as *negative capital gains* and not distinguish them.) In our first example, the total dollar return is given by:

Total dollar return = $185 + 333 = $518

Notice that if you sold the stock at the end of the year, your total amount of cash would be the initial investment plus the total dollar return. In the preceding example, you would have:

Total cash if stock is sold = Initial investment + Total dollar return
= $3,700 + 518
= $4,218

As a check, notice that this is the same as the proceeds from the sale of stock plus the dividends:

Proceeds from stock sale + Dividends
= $40.33 × 100 + $185
= $4,033 + 185
= $4,218

Suppose, however, that you hold your Video Concept stock and don't sell it at year-end. Should you still consider the capital gain as part of your return? Does this violate our previous present value rule that only cash matters?

The answer to the first question is a strong yes, and the answer to the second question is an equally strong no. The capital gain is every bit as much a part of your return as is the dividend, and you should certainly count it as part of your total return. That you have decided to hold on to the stock and not sell or realize the gain or the loss in no way changes the fact that, if you want to, you could get the cash value of the stock. After all, you could always sell the stock at year-end and immediately buy it back. The total amount of cash you would have at year-end would be the $518 gain plus your initial investment of $3,700. You would not lose this return when you bought back 100 shares of stock. In fact, you would be in exactly the same position as if you had not sold the stock (assuming, of course, that there are no tax consequences and no brokerage commissions from selling the stock).

Percentage Returns

It is more convenient to summarize the information about returns in percentage terms than in dollars because the percentages apply to any amount invested. The question we want to answer is: How much return do we get for each dollar invested? To find this out, let t stand for the year, let P_t be the price of the stock at the beginning of the year, and let D_{t+1} be the dividend paid on the stock during the year. Consider the cash flows in Figure 10.2.

In our example, the price at the beginning of the year was $37 per share and the dividend paid during the year on each share was $1.85. Hence the percentage income return, sometimes called the *dividend yield,* is:

Go to www.finviz.com/ map.ashx for a chart that shows today's returns by market sector.

$$\text{Dividend yield} = D_{t+1}/P_t \qquad [10.2]$$
$$= \$1.85/\$37$$
$$= .05, \text{ or } 5\%$$

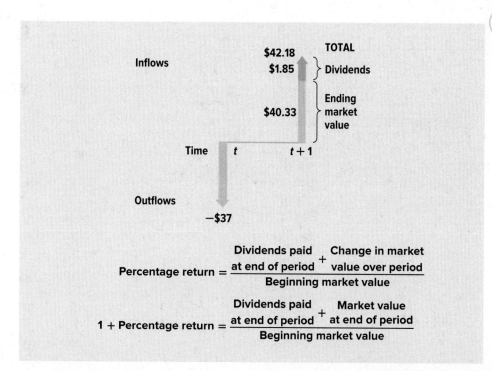

$$\text{Percentage return} = \frac{\text{Dividends paid at end of period} + \text{Change in market value over period}}{\text{Beginning market value}}$$

$$1 + \text{Percentage return} = \frac{\text{Dividends paid at end of period} + \text{Market value at end of period}}{\text{Beginning market value}}$$

FIGURE 10.2

Percentage Returns

The **capital gain** (or loss) is the change in the price of the stock divided by the initial price. Letting P_{t+1} be the price of the stock at year-end, the capital gain can be computed:

$$\text{Capital gain} = (P_{t-1} - P_t)/P_t \qquad [10.3]$$
$$= (\$40.33 - 37)/\$37$$
$$= \$3.33/\$37$$
$$= .09, \text{ or } 9\%$$

Combining these two results, we find that the *total return* on the investment in Video Concept stock over the year, which we will label R_{t+1}, was:

$$R_{t+1} = \frac{D_{t+1}}{P_t} + \frac{(P_{t+1} - P_t)}{P_t} \qquad [10.4]$$
$$= 5\% + 9\%$$
$$= 14\%$$

From now on we will refer to returns in percentage terms.

To give a more concrete example, stock in pharmaceutical company Eli Lilly began 2018 at $84.46 per share. The company paid dividends of $2.25 during 2018, and the stock price at year-end was $115.72. What was the return for the year? For practice, see if you agree that the answer is 39.68 percent. Of course, negative returns occur as well. For example, in 2018, investment management company Invesco's stock price at the beginning of the year was $36.54 per share, and dividends of $1.61 were paid. The stock ended the year at $16.74 per share. Verify that the loss was 49.78 percent for the year.

EXAMPLE 10.1 Calculating Returns

Suppose a stock begins the year with a price of $25 per share and ends with a price of $35 per share. During the year it paid a $2 dividend per share. What are its dividend yield, capital gain, and total return for the year? The cash flows in Figure 10.3 are:

$$R_1 = \frac{D_1}{P_0} + \frac{P_1 - P_0}{P_0}$$
$$= \frac{\$2}{\$25} + \frac{\$35 - 25}{\$25} = \frac{\$12}{\$25}$$
$$= .08 + .40 = .48, \text{ or } 48\%$$

FIGURE 10.3 An Investment Example

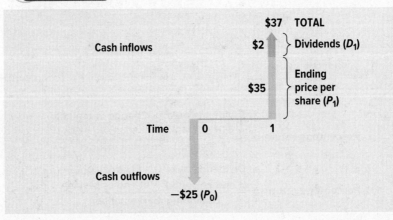

$37   TOTAL

Cash inflows $2   } Dividends ($D_1$)

                      $35 } Ending price per share (P_1)

Time   0   1

Cash outflows

−$25 ($P_0$)

Thus, the stock's dividend yield, capital gain yield, and total return are 8 percent, 40 percent, and 48 percent, respectively.

Suppose you had $5,000 invested. The total dollar return you would have received on an investment in the stock is $5,000 × .48 = $2,400. If you know the total dollar return on the stock, you do not need to know how many shares you would have had to purchase to figure out how much money you would have made on the $5,000 investment. You just use the total dollar return.

10.2 HOLDING PERIOD RETURNS

A famous set of studies dealing with rates of return on common stocks, bonds, and Treasury bills was conducted by Roger Ibbotson and Rex Sinquefield.[1] They present year-by-year historical rates of return for the following five important types of financial instruments in the United States:

ExcelMaster
coverage online
www.mhhe.com/RossCore6e

For more on market history, visit www.global-financialdata.com.

1. *Large-Company Common Stocks.* The common stock portfolio is based on the Standard & Poor's (S&P) composite index. At present, the S&P composite includes 500 of the largest (in terms of market value) stocks in the United States.

2. *Small-Company Common Stocks.* This is a portfolio corresponding to the bottom fifth of stocks traded on the New York Stock Exchange, in which stocks are ranked by market value (i.e., the price of the stock multiplied by the number of shares outstanding).

3. *Long-Term Corporate Bonds.* This is a portfolio of high-quality corporate bonds with a 20-year maturity.

4. *Long-Term U.S. Government Bonds.* This is based on U.S. government bonds with a maturity of 20 years.

5. *U.S. Treasury Bills.* This is based on Treasury bills with a one-month maturity.

None of the returns are adjusted for taxes or transactions costs. In addition to the year-by-year returns on financial instruments, the year-to-year change in the consumer price index is computed. This is a basic measure of inflation. Year-by-year real returns can be calculated by subtracting annual inflation.

Before looking closely at the different portfolio returns, we graphically present the returns and risks available from U.S. capital markets in the 93-year period from 1926 to 2018. Figure 10.4 shows the growth of $1 invested at the beginning of 1926. Notice that the vertical axis is logarithmic, so that equal distances measure the same percentage change. The figure shows that if $1 were invested in large-company common stocks and all dividends were reinvested, the dollar would have grown to $7,030.31 by the end of 2018. The biggest growth was in the small stock portfolio. If $1 were invested in small stocks in 1926, the investment would have grown to $32,645.08. However, when you look carefully at Figure 10.4, you can see great variability in the returns on small stocks, especially in the earlier part of the period. A dollar in long-term government bonds was very stable as compared with a dollar in common stocks. Figures 10.5 to 10.8 plot each year-to-year percentage return as a vertical bar drawn from the horizontal axis for large-company common stocks, small-company stocks, long-term government bonds and Treasury bills, and inflation, respectively.

[1] The first article was Roger Ibbotson and Rex Sinquefield, "Stocks, Bonds, Bills, and Inflation: Year-by-Year Historical Returns (1926–1974)," *Journal of Business* 49, no. 1 (1976), pp. 11–47.

FIGURE 10.4   Wealth Indexes of Investments in the U.S. Capital Markets (Year-End 1925 = $1.00)

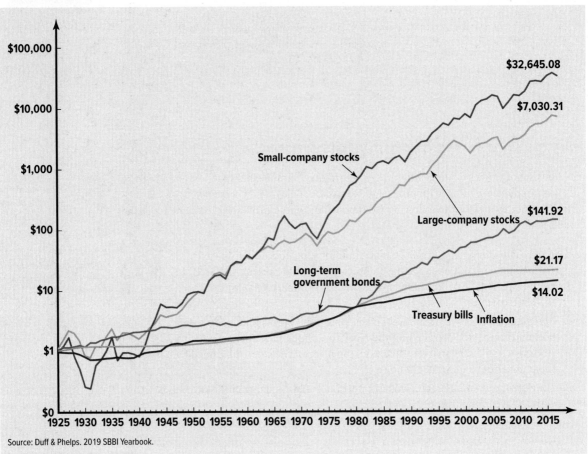

Source: Duff & Phelps. 2019 SBBI Yearbook.

FIGURE 10.5   Year-by-Year Total Returns on Large-Company Common Stocks

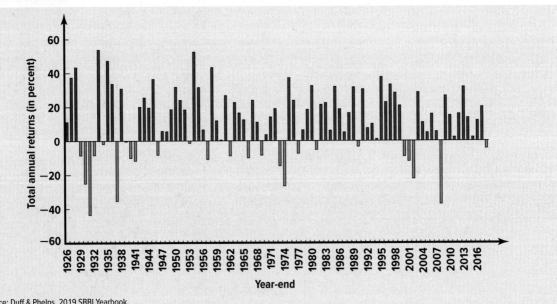

Source: Duff & Phelps. 2019 SBBI Yearbook.

FIGURE 10.6 Year-by-Year Total Returns on Small-Company Stocks

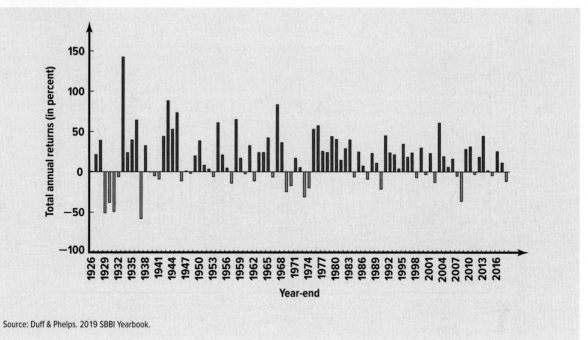

Source: Duff & Phelps. 2019 SBBI Yearbook.

Figure 10.4 gives the growth of a dollar investment in the stock market from 1926 through 2018. In other words, it shows what the worth of the investment would have been if the dollar had been left in the stock market and if each year the dividends from the previous year had been reinvested in more stock. If R_t is the return in Year t (expressed in decimals), the value you would have at the end of Year T is the product of 1 plus the return in each of the years:

$$(1 + R_1) \times (1 + R_2) \times \cdots \times (1 + R_t) \times \cdots \times (1 + R_T)$$

For example, if the returns were 11 percent, −5 percent, and 9 percent in a three-year period, an investment of $1 at the beginning of the period would be worth:

$$\$1 \times (1 + R_1) \times (1 + R_2) \times (1 + R_3) = (1 + .11) \times (1 - .05) \times (1 + .09)$$
$$= 1.11 \times .95 \times 1.09$$
$$= \$1.15$$

Go to bigcharts.
marketwatch.com to see
both intraday and long-
term charts.

at the end of the three years. Notice that .15, or 15 percent, is the total return and that it includes the return from reinvesting the first-year dividends in the stock market for two more years and reinvesting the second-year dividends for the final year. The 15 percent is called a three-year **holding period return**. Table 10.1 gives the annual returns each year for selected investments from 1926 to 2018. From this table, you can determine holding period returns for any combination of years.

FIGURE 10.7 Year-by-Year Total Returns on Bonds and Bills

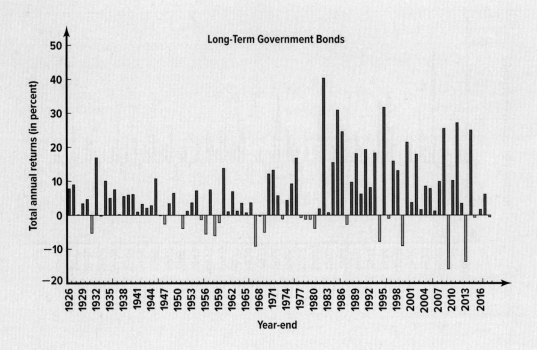

Source: Duff & Phelps. 2019 SBBI Yearbook.

FIGURE 10.8 Year-by-Year Inflation

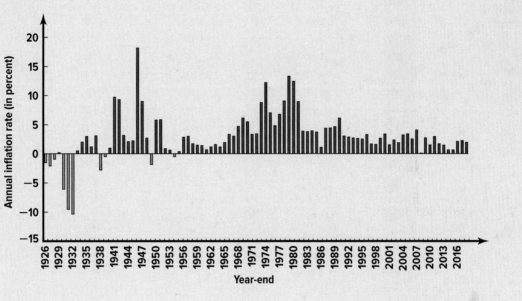

Source: Duff & Phelps. 2019 SBBI Yearbook.

TABLE 10.1

Year-by-Year Total Returns, 1926–2018

Source: Duff & Phelps. 2019 SBBI Yearbook.

Year	Large-Company Stocks	Long-Term Government Bonds	U.S. Treasury Bills	Consumer Price Index
1926	11.62%	7.77%	3.27%	−1.49%
1927	37.49	8.93	3.12	−2.08
1928	43.61	.10	3.56	−.97
1929	−8.42	3.42	4.75	.20
1930	−24.90	4.66	2.41	−6.03
1931	−43.34	−5.31	1.07	−9.52
1932	−8.19	16.84	.96	−10.30
1933	53.99	−.07	.30	.51
1934	−1.44	10.03	.16	2.03
1935	47.67	4.98	.17	2.99
1936	33.92	7.52	.18	1.21
1937	−35.03	.23	.31	3.10
1938	31.12	5.53	−.02	−2.78
1939	−.41	5.94	.02	−.48
1940	−9.78	6.09	.00	.96
1941	−11.59	.93	.06	9.72
1942	20.34	3.22	.27	9.29
1943	25.90	2.08	.35	3.16
1944	19.75	2.81	.33	2.11
1945	36.44	10.73	.33	2.25
1946	−8.07	−.10	.35	18.16

(Continued)

TABLE 10.1

Year-by-Year Total Returns, 1926–2018

(Continued)

Year	Large-Company Stocks	Long-Term Government Bonds	U.S. Treasury Bills	Consumer Price Index
1947	5.71	−2.62	.50	9.01
1948	5.50	3.40	.81	2.71
1949	18.79	6.45	1.10	−1.80
1950	31.71	.06	1.20	5.79
1951	24.02	−3.93	1.49	5.87
1952	18.37	1.16	1.66	.88
1953	−.99	3.64	1.82	.62
1954	52.62	7.19	.86	−.50
1955	31.56	−1.29	1.57	.37
1956	6.56	−5.59	2.46	2.86
1957	−10.78	7.46	3.14	3.02
1958	43.36	−6.09	1.54	1.76
1959	11.96	−2.26	2.95	1.50
1960	.47	13.78	2.66	1.48
1961	26.89	.97	2.13	.67
1962	−8.73	6.89	2.73	1.22
1963	22.80	1.21	3.12	1.65
1964	16.48	3.51	3.54	1.19
1965	12.45	.71	3.93	1.92
1966	−10.06	3.65	4.76	3.35
1967	23.98	−9.18	4.21	3.04
1968	11.06	−.26	5.21	4.72
1969	−8.50	−5.07	6.58	6.11
1970	3.86	12.11	6.52	5.49
1971	14.30	13.23	4.39	3.36
1972	18.99	5.69	3.84	3.41
1973	−14.69	−1.11	6.93	8.80
1974	−26.47	4.35	8.00	12.20
1975	37.23	9.20	5.80	7.01
1976	23.93	16.75	5.08	4.81
1977	−7.16	−.69	5.12	6.77
1978	6.57	−.1.18	7.18	9.03
1979	18.61	−1.23	10.38	13.31
1980	32.50	−3.95	11.24	12.40
1981	−4.92	1.86	14.71	8.94
1982	21.55	40.36	10.54	3.87
1983	22.56	.65	8.80	3.80
1984	6.27	15.48	9.85	3.95
1985	31.73	30.97	7.72	3.77
1986	18.67	24.53	6.16	1.13
1987	5.25	−2.71	5.47	4.41
1988	16.61	9.67	6.35	4.42
1989	31.69	18.11	8.37	4.65
1990	−3.10	6.18	7.81	6.11
1991	30.47	19.30	5.60	3.06

(Continued)

Year	Large-Company Stocks	Long-Term Government Bonds	U.S. Treasury Bills	Consumer Price Index
1992	7.62	8.05	3.51	2.90
1993	10.08	18.24	2.90	2.75
1994	1.32	−7.77	3.90	2.67
1995	37.58	31.67	5.60	2.54
1996	22.96	−.93	5.21	3.32
1997	33.36	15.85	5.26	1.70
1998	28.58	13.06	4.86	1.61
1999	21.04	−8.96	4.68	2.68
2000	−9.10	21.48	5.89	3.39
2001	−11.89	3.70	3.83	1.55
2002	−22.10	17.84	1.65	2.38
2003	28.68	1.45	1.02	1.88
2004	10.88	8.51	1.20	3.26
2005	4.91	7.81	2.98	3.42
2006	15.79	1.19	4.80	2.54
2007	5.49	9.88	4.66	4.08
2008	−37.00	25.87	1.60	.09
2009	26.46	−14.90	.10	2.72
2010	15.06	10.14	.12	1.50
2011	2.11	27.10	.04	2.96
2012	16.00	3.43	.06	1.74
2013	32.39	−12.78	.02	1.51
2014	13.69	24.71	.02	.76
2015	1.38	−.65	.02	.73
2016	11.96	1.75	.20	2.07
2017	21.83	6.24	.80	2.11
2018	−4.38	−.57	1.81	1.91

TABLE 10.1

Year-by-Year Total Returns, 1926–2018

(*Concluded*)

10.3 RETURN STATISTICS

The history of capital market returns is too complicated to be handled in its undigested form. To use the history, we must first find some manageable ways of describing it, dramatically condensing the detailed data into a few simple statements.

This is where two important numbers summarizing the history come in. The first and most natural number is some single measure that best describes the past annual returns on the stock market. In other words, what is our best estimate of the return that an investor could have realized in a particular year over the 1926 to 2018 period? This is the *average return*.

Figure 10.9 plots the histogram of the yearly stock market returns. This plot is the frequency distribution of the numbers. The height of the graph gives the number of sample observations in the range on the horizontal axis.

Given a frequency distribution like that in Figure 10.9, we can calculate the average, or mean, of the distribution. To compute the average of the distribution, we add up all of the values and divide by the total (T) number (93 in our case because we have 93 years of data). The bar over the R is used to represent the mean, and the formula is the ordinary formula for the average:

$$\text{Mean} = \overline{R} = \frac{(R_1 + \cdots + R_T)}{T} \tag{10.5}$$

ExcelMaster
coverage online

www.mhhe.com/RossCore6e

••••••••••
FIGURE 10.9   Histogram of Returns on Common Stocks, 1926–2018

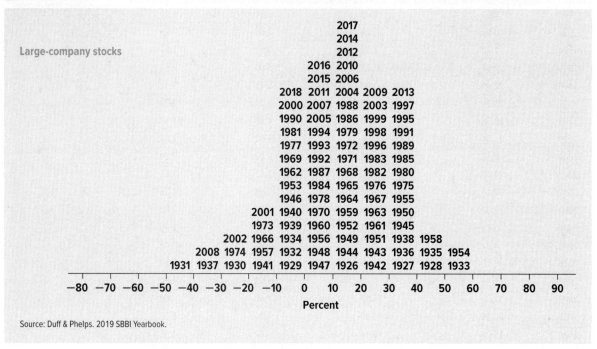

Source: Duff & Phelps. 2019 SBBI Yearbook.

The mean return of the portfolio of large-company stocks from 1926 to 2018 is 11.9 percent.

EXAMPLE 10.2

Calculating Average Returns

Suppose the returns on common stock over a four-year period are .1370, .3580, .4514, and −.0888, respectively. The average, or mean, return over these four years is:

$$\overline{R} = \frac{.1370 + .3580 + .4514 - .0888}{4} = .2144, \text{ or } 21.44\%$$

10.4 AVERAGE STOCK RETURNS AND RISK-FREE RETURNS

Now that we have computed the average return on the stock market, it seems sensible to compare it with the returns on other securities. The most obvious comparison is with the low-variability returns in the government bond market. These are free of most of the volatility we see in the stock market.

The government borrows money by issuing bonds, which the investing public holds. As we discussed in an earlier chapter, these bonds come in many forms, and the ones we will look at here are called *Treasury bills,* or *T-bills.* Once a week the government sells some bills at an auction. A typical bill is a pure discount bond that will mature in a year or less.

TABLE 10.2 Total Annual Returns, 1926–2018

Series	Average Return	Standard Deviation	Distribution
Small-company stocks	16.2%	31.6%	
Large-company stocks	11.9	19.8	
Long-term corporate bonds	6.3	8.4	
Long-term government bonds	5.9	9.8	
Intermediate-term government bonds	5.2	5.6	
U.S. Treasury bills	3.4	3.1	
Inflation	3.0	4.0	

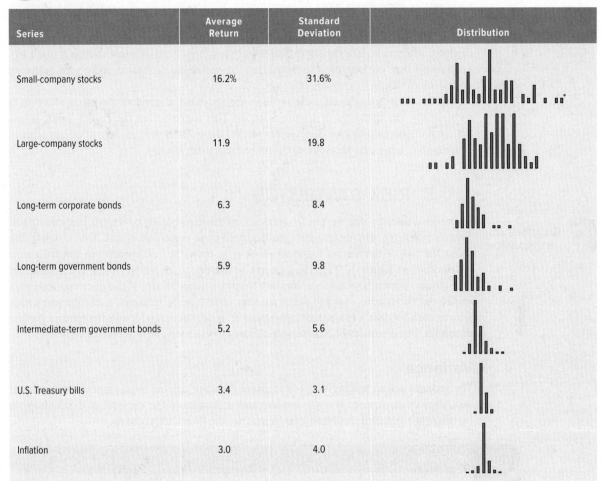

* The 1933 small-company stock total return was 142.9 percent.

Source: Duff & Phelps. 2019 SBBI Yearbook.

Because the government can raise taxes to pay for the debt it incurs—a trick that many of us would like to be able to perform—this debt is virtually free of the risk of default. Thus, we will call this the *risk-free return* over a short time (one year or less).

An interesting comparison, then, is between the virtually risk-free return on T-bills and the very risky return on the portfolios of common stocks. This difference between risky returns and risk-free returns is often called the *excess return on the risky asset.* It is called *excess* because it is the additional return resulting from the riskiness of common stocks and is interpreted as an equity **risk premium**.

Table 10.2 shows the average stock return, bond return, T-bill return, and inflation rate for the period from 1926 through 2018. From this we can derive excess returns. The average excess return from the portfolio of large-company common stocks for the entire period was 8.5 percent (= 11.9 percent − 3.4 percent).

One of the most significant observations of stock market data is this long-run excess of the stock return over the risk-free return. An investor for this period was rewarded for investing in the stock market with an extra or excess return over what would have been achieved by investing in T-bills.

Why was there such a reward? Does it mean that it never pays to invest in T-bills and that someone who invested in them instead of in a portfolio of common stocks needs a course in finance? A complete answer to these questions lies at the heart of modern finance, and Chapter 11 is devoted entirely to this. However, part of the answer can be found in the variability of the various types of investments. We see in Table 10.1 many years when an investment in T-bills achieved higher returns than an investment in large-company common stocks. Also, we note that the returns from an investment in common stocks are frequently negative, whereas an investment in T-bills only produces a small negative return one time. So, we now turn our attention to measuring the variability of returns and an introductory discussion of risk.

We first look more closely at Table 10.2. We see that the standard deviation of T-bills is substantially less than that of common stocks. This suggests that the risk of T-bills is less than that of common stocks. Because the answer depends on the riskiness of investments in common stock, we next turn our attention to measuring this risk.

10.5 RISK STATISTICS

ExcelMaster
coverage online
www.mhhe.com/RossCore6e

The second number that we use to characterize the distribution of returns is a measure of the risk in returns. There is no universally agreed-upon definition of risk. One way to think about the risk of returns on common stock is in terms of how spread out the frequency distributions in Figure 10.9 are. The spread, or dispersion, of a distribution is a measure of how much a particular return can deviate from the mean return. If the distribution is very spread out, the returns that will occur are very uncertain. By contrast, a distribution whose returns are all within a few percentage points of each other is tight, and the returns are less uncertain. The measures of risk we will discuss are variance and standard deviation.

Variance

For an easy-to-read review of basic stats, check out www.robert-niles.com/stats.

The **variance** and its square root, the **standard deviation**, are the most common measures of variability or dispersion. We will use Var and σ^2 to denote the variance and SD and σ to represent the standard deviation. σ is, of course, the Greek letter sigma.

EXAMPLE 10.3   **Volatility**

Suppose the returns on common stocks over a four-year period are (in decimals) .1370, .3580, .4514, and −.0888, respectively. The variance of this sample is computed as:

$$\text{Var} = \frac{1}{T-1}[(R_1 - \bar{R})^2 + \cdots + (R_T - \bar{R})^2] \qquad [10.6]$$

$$.0582 = \frac{1}{3}[(.1370 - .2144)^2 + (.3580 - .2144)^2$$

$$+ (.4514 - .2144)^2 + (-.0888 - .2144)^2]$$

$$\text{SD} = \sqrt{.0582} = .2413, \text{ or } 24.13\%$$

This formula tells us just what to do: Take the T individual returns ($R_1, R_2, \ldots$) and subtract the average return $\bar{R}$, square the result, and add them up. Finally, this total must be divided by the number of returns less one ($T - 1$). The standard deviation is always just the square root of the variance.

Using the stock returns for the 93-year period from 1926 through 2018 in the above formula, the resulting standard deviation of large-company stock returns is 19.8 percent. The standard deviation is the standard statistical measure of the spread of a sample, and it will be the measure we use most of the time. Its interpretation is facilitated by a discussion of the normal distribution.

Standard deviations are widely reported for mutual funds. For example, the Fidelity Magellan Fund is one of the largest mutual funds in the United States. How volatile is it? To find out, we went to www.morningstar.com, entered the ticker symbol FMAGX, and hit the "Ratings & Risk" link. Here is what we found:

MPT Statistics FMAGX

| 3-Year | 5-Year | 10-Year | 15-Year |

3-Year Trailing	Index	R-Squared	Beta	Alpha	Treynor Ratio	Currency
vs. Best-Fit Index						
FMAGX	Morningstar US Large Cap TR USD	95.68	1.11	-1.82	—	USD
vs. Standard Index						
FMAGX	S&P 500 TR USD	95.10	1.09	-1.23	12.72	USD
Category: LG	S&P 500 TR USD	83.99	1.05	0.78	14.79	USD

02/28/2019

Volatility Measures FMAGX

| 3-Year | 5-Year | 10-Year | 15-Year |

3-Year Trailing	Standard Deviation	Return	Sharpe Ratio	Sortino Ratio	Bear Market Percentile Rank
FMAGX	12.57	15.14	1.09	1.62	—
S&P 500 TR USD	11.21	15.28	1.22	1.88	—
Category: LG	13.06	16.81	1.17	1.90	—

Source: www.morningstar.com, March 24, 2019.

Over the last three years, the standard deviation of the return on the Fidelity Magellan Fund was 12.57 percent. When you consider the average stock has a standard deviation of about 50 percent, this seems like a low number, but the Magellan Fund is a relatively well-diversified portfolio, so this is an illustration of the power of diversification, a subject we will discuss in detail later. The mean is the average return, so, over the last three years, investors in the Magellan Fund gained a 15.14 percent return per year. Also under the Volatility Measures section, you will see the Sharpe ratio. The Sharpe ratio is calculated as the risk premium of the asset divided by the standard deviation. As such, it is a measure of return to the level of risk taken (as measured by standard deviation). This ratio is 1.09 for the period covered. The "beta" for the Fidelity Magellan Fund is 1.11. We will have more to say about this number—lots more—in the next chapter.

Normal Distribution and Its Implications for Standard Deviation

A large enough sample drawn from a normal distribution looks like the bell-shaped curve drawn in Figure 10.10. As you can see, this distribution is *symmetric* about its mean, not *skewed,* and has a much cleaner shape than the actual distributions of yearly returns drawn in Figure 10.9. Of course, if we had been able to observe stock market returns for 1,000 years, we might have filled in a lot of the jumps and jerks in Figure 10.9 and had a smoother curve.

FIGURE 10.10

The Normal Distribution

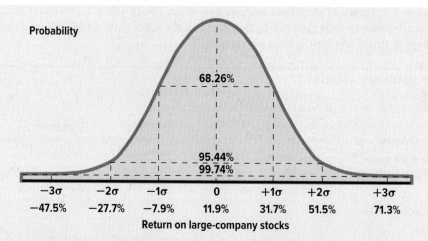

In the case of a normal distribution, there is a **68.26** percent probability that a return will be within one standard deviation of the mean. In this example, there is a **68.26** percent probability that a yearly return will be between **−7.9** percent and **31.7** percent.

There is a **95.44** percent probability that a return will be within two standard deviations of the mean. In this example, there is a **95.44** percent probability that a yearly return will be between **−27.7** percent and **51.5** percent.

Finally, there is a **99.74** percent probability that a return will be within three standard deviations of the mean. In this example, there is a **99.74** percent probability that a yearly return will be between **−47.5** percent and **71.3** percent.

In classical statistics, the normal distribution plays a central role, and the standard deviation is the usual way to represent the spread of a normal distribution. For the normal distribution, the probability of having a return that is above or below the mean by a certain amount depends only on the standard deviation. For example, the probability of having a return that is within one standard deviation of the mean of the distribution is approximately .68, or 2/3, and the probability of having a return that is within two standard deviations of the mean is approximately .95.

The 19.8 percent standard deviation we found for the portfolio of large-company stock returns from 1926 through 2018 can now be interpreted in the following way: If stock returns are roughly normally distributed, the probability that a yearly return will fall within 19.8 percent of the mean of 11.9 percent will be approximately 2/3. That is, about 2/3 of the yearly returns will be between −7.9 percent and 31.7 percent. (Note that −7.9% = 11.9% − 19.8% and 31.7% = 11.9% + 19.8%.) The probability that the return in any year will fall within two standard deviations is about .95. That is, about 95 percent of yearly returns will be between −27.7 percent and 51.5 percent.

10.6 THE U.S. EQUITY RISK PREMIUM: HISTORICAL AND INTERNATIONAL PERSPECTIVES

So far in this chapter we have studied the United States in the period from 1926 to 2018. As we have discussed, the historical U.S. stock market risk premium has been substantial. Of course, anytime we use the past to predict the future, there is a danger that the past period isn't representative of what the future will hold. Perhaps U.S. investors got lucky over this period and earned particularly large returns. Data from earlier years for the United States is available, though it is not of the same quality. With that caveat in mind, researchers have tracked returns

TABLE 10.3

World Stock Market
Capitalization, select
markets, 2017

Source: data.worldbank.org/
indicator/CM.MKT.LCAP.CD,
March 24, 2019.

Country	$ in trillions	Percent
United States	$32.1	40.5%
China	8.7	11.0
Euro area	7.9	10.0
Japan	6.2	7.9
Hong Kong	4.4	5.5
Canada	2.4	3.0
India	2.3	2.9
World	$72.2	80.8%

TABLE 10.4

Annualized Equity Risk
Premiums and Sharpe
Ratios for 17 Countries,
1900–2010

*Germany omits 1922–1923.
Source: Dimson, Elroy, Paul
Marsh, and Michael Staunton.
"The Worldwide Equity
Premium: A Smaller Puzzle." In
Handbook of the Equity Risk
Premium, edited by Rajnish
Mehra. Amsterdam: Elsevier,
2007. As updated by the
authors.

Country	Historical Equity Risk Premiums (%) (1)	Standard Deviation (%) (2)	The Sharpe Ratio (1)/(2)
Denmark	4.6%	20.5%	.22
Switzerland	5.1	18.9	.27
Ireland	5.3	21.5	.25
Spain	5.4	21.9	.25
Belgium	5.5	24.7	.22
Canada	5.6	17.2	.33
Norway	5.9	26.5	.22
United Kingdom	6.0	19.9	.30
Netherlands	6.5	22.8	.29
Sweden	6.6	22.1	.30
United States	7.2	19.8	.36
South Africa	8.3	22.1	.37
Australia	8.3	17.6	.47
France	8.7	24.5	.36
Japan	9.0	27.7	.32
Germany*	9.8	31.8	.31
Italy	9.8	32.0	.31

back to 1802, and the U.S. equity risk premium in the pre-1926 era was smaller. Using the U.S. return data from 1802, the historical equity risk premium was 5.2 percent.[2]

Also, we have not looked at other major countries. Actually, more than half of the value of tradeable stock is not in the United States. From Table 10.3, we can see that while the total world stock market capitalization was $72.2 trillion in 2017, about 41 percent was in the United States. Thanks to Dimson, Marsh, and Staunton, data from earlier periods and other countries are now available to help us take a closer look at equity risk premiums. Table 10.4 and Figure 10.11 show the historical stock market risk premiums for 17 countries around the world in the period from

[2] Jeremy J. Siegel has estimated the U.S. equity risk premium with data from 1802. As can be seen in the following table, from 1802 to 2008, the historical equity risk premium was 5.2 percent.

	Average Returns 1802–2008 (%)
Common stock	9.5
Treasury bills	4.3
Equity risk premium	5.2

Source: Adopted and updated from Jeremy Siegel, Stocks for the Long Run, 4th ed. (New York: McGraw-Hill, 2008).

FIGURE 10.11 Stock Market Risk Premiums for 17 Countries: 1900–2010

Source: Dimson, Elroy, Paul Marsh, and Michael Staunton. "The Worldwide Equity Premium: A Smaller Puzzle." In *Handbook of the Equity Risk Premium*, edited by Rajnish Mehra. Amsterdam: Elsevier, 2007. As updated by the authors.

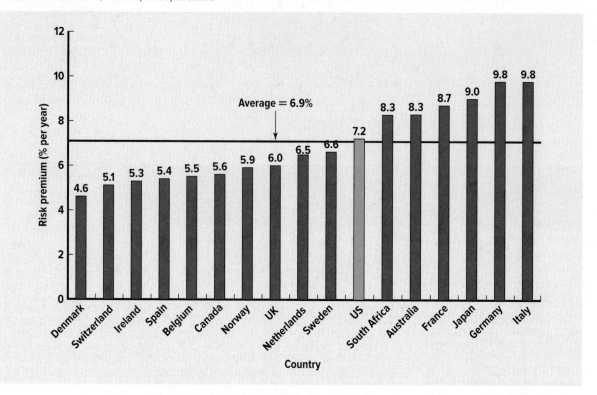

1900 to 2010. Looking at the numbers, the U.S. historical equity risk premium is the seventh highest at 7.2 percent (which differs from our earlier estimate because of the different time periods examined). The overall world average risk premium is 6.9 percent. It seems clear that U.S. investors did well, but not exceptionally so relative to many other countries. The top-performing countries according to the Sharpe ratio were the United States, Australia, France, and South Africa, while the worst performers were Belgium, Norway, and Denmark. Germany, Japan, and Italy might make an interesting case study because they have the highest stock returns over this period (despite World Wars I and II), but also the highest risk.

So what is a good estimate of the U.S. equity risk premium going forward? Unfortunately, nobody can know for sure what investors expect in the future. If history is a guide, the expected U.S. equity risk premium could be 7.2 percent based upon estimates from 1900 to 2010. We should also be mindful that the average world equity risk premium was 6.9 percent over this same period. On the other hand, the more recent periods (1926–2018) suggest higher estimates of the U.S. equity risk premium, and earlier periods going back to 1802 suggest lower estimates.

The standard error (SE) helps with the issue of how much confidence we can have in our historical average of 7.2 percent. The SE is the standard deviation of the historical risk premium and is given the following formula:

$$\text{SE} = \text{SD}(\bar{R}) = \frac{\text{SD}(R)}{\sqrt{\text{The number of observations}}} \qquad [10.7]$$

If we assume that the distribution of returns is normal and that each year's return is independent of all the others, we know there is a 95.4 percent probability that the true mean return is within two standard errors of the historical average.

More specifically, the 95.4 percent confidence interval for the true equity risk premium is the historical average return ± (2 × standard error). From 1900 to 2010, the historical equity risk premium of U.S. stocks was 7.2 percent and the standard deviation was 19.8 percent. Therefore, 95.4 percent of the time the true equity risk premium should be within 3.4 and 11 percent:

$$7.2 \pm 2 \left(\frac{19.8}{\sqrt{110}} \right) = 7.2 \pm 2 \left(\frac{19.8}{10.5} \right) = 7.2 \pm 3.8$$

In other words, we can be 95.4 percent confident that our estimate of the U.S. equity risk premium from historical data is in the range from 3.4 percent to 11 percent.

Taking a slightly different approach, Ivo Welch asked the opinions of 226 financial economists regarding the future U.S. equity risk premium, and the median response was 7 percent.[3]

We are comfortable with an estimate based on the historical U.S. equity risk premium of about 7 percent, but estimates of the future U.S. equity risk premium that are somewhat higher or lower could be reasonable if we have good reason to believe the past is not representative of the future.[4] The bottom line is that any estimate of the future equity risk premium will involve assumptions about the future risk environment as well as the amount of risk aversion of future investors.

10.7 2008: A YEAR OF FINANCIAL CRISIS

The year 2008 entered the record books as one of the worst years for stock market investors in U.S. history. How bad was it? The widely followed S&P 500 Index, which tracks the total market value of 500 of the largest U.S. corporations, decreased 37 percent for the year. Of the 500 stocks in the index, 485 were down for the year.

Over the period 1926–2008, only the year 1931 had a lower return than 2008 (−44 percent versus −37 percent). Making matters worse, the downdraft continued with a further decline of 25.1 percent through March 9, 2009. In all, from November 2007 (when the decline began) through March 9, 2009, the S&P 500 lost 56.8 percent of its value. Fortunately for investors, things turned around dramatically for the rest of the year. From March 9, 2009, to December 31, 2009, the market gained about 65 percent!

Figure 10.12 shows the month-by-month performance of the S&P 500 during 2008. As indicated, returns were negative in 8 of the 12 months. Most of the decline occurred in the fall, with investors losing almost 17 percent in October alone. Small stocks fared no better. They also fell 37 percent for the year (with a 21 percent drop in October), their worst performance since losing 58 percent in 1937.

As Figure 10.12 suggests, stock prices were highly volatile at the end of the year—more than has been generally true historically. Oddly, the S&P had 126 up days and 126 down days (remember the markets are closed weekends and holidays). Of course, the down days were much worse on average.

The drop in stock prices was a global phenomenon, and many of the world's major markets declined by much more than the S&P. China, India, and Russia, for example, all experienced declines of more than 50 percent. Tiny Iceland saw share prices drop by more than 90 percent for the year. Trading on the Icelandic exchange was temporarily suspended on October 9. In what has to be a modern record for a single day, stocks fell by 76 percent when trading resumed on October 14.

---

[3] For example, see Ivo Welch, "Views of Financial Economists on the Equity Risk Premium and Other Issues," *Journal of Business* 73, no. 4 (2000), pp. 501–537.

[4] In Elroy Dimson, Paul Marsh, and Mike Staunton, "The Worldwide Equity Premium: A Smaller Puzzle," from *Handbook of the Equity Risk Premium*, ed. R. Mehra (Amsterdam: Elsevier, 2007), the authors argue that a good estimate of the world equity risk premium going forward should be about 5 percent, largely because of nonrecurring factors that positively affected worldwide historical returns. However, it could be argued that the global financial crisis of 2008–2009 was a negative shock to the stock market that has increased the equity risk premium from its historical levels.

FIGURE 10.12

S&P 500 Monthly Returns, 2008

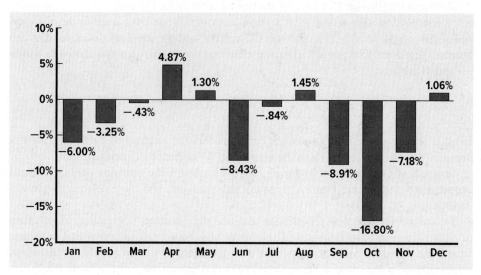

Did any types of securities perform well in 2008? The answer is yes because, as stock values declined, bond values increased, particularly U.S. Treasury bonds. In fact, long-term Treasury bonds gained 20 percent, while shorter-term Treasury bonds were up 13 percent. Higher-quality long-term corporate bonds did less well but still managed to achieve a positive return of about 9 percent. These returns were especially impressive considering that the rate of inflation, as measured by the CPI, was very close to zero.

Of course, stock prices can be volatile in both directions. From March 2009 through February 2011, a period of about 700 days, the S&P 500 doubled in value. This climb was the fastest doubling since 1936, when the S&P did it in just 500 days.

What lessons should investors take away from this recent bit of capital market history? First, and most obviously, stocks have significant risk! But there is a second, equally important lesson. Depending on the mix, a diversified portfolio of stocks and bonds probably would have suffered in 2008, but the losses would have been much smaller than those experienced by an all-stock portfolio. Finally, because of increased volatility and heightened risk aversion, many have argued that the equity risk premium going forward is probably (at least temporarily) somewhat higher than has been true historically.

10.8 MORE ON AVERAGE RETURNS

Thus far in this chapter, we have looked closely at simple average returns. But there is another way of computing an average return. The fact that average returns are calculated two different ways leads to some confusion, so our goal in this section is to explain the two approaches and also the circumstances under which each is appropriate.

Arithmetic versus Geometric Averages

Let's start with a simple example. Suppose you buy a particular stock for $100. Unfortunately, the first year you own it, it falls to $50. The second year you own it, it rises back to $100, leaving you where you started (no dividends were paid).

What was your average return on this investment? Common sense seems to say that your average return must be exactly zero since you started with $100 and ended with $100. But if we calculate the returns year by year, we see that you lost 50 percent the first year (you lost half of your money). The second year, you made 100 percent (you doubled your money). Your average return over the two years was thus (−50 percent + 100 percent)/2 = 25 percent!

So which is correct, 0 percent or 25 percent? The answer is that both are correct; they just answer different questions. The 0 percent is called the geometric average return.

The 25 percent is called the *arithmetic average return*. The geometric average return answers the question, *"What was your average compound return per year over a particular period?"* The arithmetic average return answers the question, *"What was your return in an average year over a particular period?"*

Notice that, in previous sections, the average returns we calculated were all arithmetic averages, so we already know how to calculate them. What we need to do now is (1) learn how to calculate geometric averages and (2) learn the circumstances under which one average is more meaningful than the other.

Calculating Geometric Average Returns

First, to illustrate how we calculate a geometric average return, suppose a particular investment had annual returns of 10 percent, 12 percent, 3 percent, and −9 percent over the last four years. The geometric average return over this four-year period is calculated as $(1.10 \times 1.12 \times 1.03 \times .91)^{1/4} - 1 = .0366$, or 3.66 percent. In contrast, the average arithmetic return we have been calculating is $(.10 + .12 + .03 - .09)/4 = .04$, or 4.0 percent.

In general, if we have T years of returns, the geometric average return over these T years is calculated using this formula:

$$\text{Geometric average return} = \left[(1 + R_1) \times (1 + R_2) \times \cdots \times (1 + R_T)\right]^{1/T} - 1 \qquad [10.8]$$

This formula tells us that four steps are required:

1. Take each of the T annual returns $R_1, R_2, \ldots, R_T$ and add 1 to each (after converting them to decimals!).
2. Multiply all the numbers from Step 1 together.
3. Take the result from Step 2 and raise it to the power of $1/T$.
4. Finally, subtract 1 from the result of Step 3. The result is the geometric average return.

EXAMPLE 10.4

Calculating the Geometric Average Return

Calculate the geometric average return for S&P 500 large-cap stocks for a five-year period using the numbers given here.

First, convert percentages to decimal returns, add 1, and then calculate their product:

S&P 500 Returns	Product
.1375	1.1375
.3570	×1.3570
.4508	×1.4508
−.0880	× .9120
−.2513	× .7487
	1.5291

Notice that the number 1.5291 is what our investment is worth after five years if we started with a $1 investment. The geometric average return is then calculated as:

Geometric average return = $1.5291^{1/5} - 1 = .0887$, or 8.87%

The geometric average return is about 8.87 percent in this example. Here is a tip: If you are using a financial calculator, you can put $1 in as the present value, $1.5291 as the future value, and 5 as the number of periods. Then, solve for the unknown rate. You should get the same answer we did.

TABLE 10.5

Geometric versus
Arithmetic Average Returns:
1926–2018

Source: Duff & Phelps. 2019
SBBI Yearbook.

Series	Geometric Average	Arithmetic Average	Standard Deviation
Small-company stocks	11.8%	16.2%	31.6%
Large-company stocks	10.0	11.9	19.8
Long-term corporate bonds	5.9	6.3	8.4
Long-term government bonds	5.5	5.9	9.8
Intermediate-term government bonds	5.1	5.2	5.6
U.S. Treasury bills	3.3	3.4	3.1
Inflation	2.9	3.0	4.0

One thing you may have noticed in our examples thus far is that the geometric average returns seem to be smaller. It turns out that this will always be true (as long as the returns are not all identical, in which case the two "averages" would be the same). To illustrate, Table 10.5 shows the arithmetic averages and standard deviations from Table 10.2, along with the geometric average returns.

As shown in Table 10.5, the geometric averages are all smaller, but the magnitude of the difference varies quite a bit. The reason is that the difference is greater for more volatile investments. In fact, there is a useful approximation. The geometric average return is approximately equal to the arithmetic average return minus half the variance. For example, looking at the large-company stocks, the arithmetic average is 11.9 percent and the standard deviation is .198, implying that the variance is .0392. The approximate geometric average is thus $11.9 - \frac{1}{2}(3.92) = 9.94$ percent, which is quite close to the actual value.

EXAMPLE 10.5

More Geometric Averages

Take a look back at Figure 10.4. There, we showed the value of a $1 investment after 93 years. Use the value for the small-company stock investment to check the geometric average in Table 10.5.

In Figure 10.4, the small-company investment grew to $32,645.08 over 93 years. The geometric average return is thus:

Geometric average return $= 32,645.08^{1/93} - 1 = .118$, or 11.8%

This 11.8% is the value shown in Table 10.5. For practice, check some of the other numbers in Table 10.5 the same way.

Arithmetic Average Return or Geometric Average Return?

When we look at historical returns, the difference between the geometric and arithmetic average returns isn't too hard to understand. To put it slightly differently, the geometric average tells you what you actually earned per year on average, compounded annually. This fact makes the geometric average return a very useful measure of past performance. The arithmetic average tells you what you earned in a typical year. This fact makes the arithmetic average return a very useful measure of expected future yearly returns. You should use whichever one answers the question you want answered.

A somewhat trickier question concerns forecasting the long-run future, and there's a lot of confusion about this point among analysts and financial planners. The problem is this:

If we have *estimates* of both the arithmetic and geometric average yearly returns, then the arithmetic average is probably too high for longer periods and the geometric average is probably too low.[5]

---

[5] This result is due to Marshall Blume, "Unbiased Estimates of Long-Run Expected Rates of Return," *Journal of the American Statistical Association* 69, no. 347 (1974), pp. 634–38. He shows that a good estimate of long-run returns is a weighted average of the arithmetic yearly average and the geometric yearly average. Another way of thinking about estimating an investment's return over a particular future horizon is to recall from your statistics class that the arithmetic average is a "sample" mean. As such, it provides an unbiased estimate of the underlying true mean. To use the arithmetic average to estimate the future returns, we must make sure the historical returns are measured using the same interval as the future forecasting period. For example, we could use yearly (annual) returns to estimate next year's return. The arithmetic average would be a good basis for forecasting the next two-year returns if two-year holding period returns were used. We also must be confident that the past distribution of returns is the same as that of the future.

SUMMARY AND CONCLUSIONS

1. This chapter presents returns for a number of different asset classes. The general conclusion is that stocks have outperformed bonds over most of the 20th century, though stocks have also exhibited more risk.

2. The statistical measures in this chapter are necessary building blocks for the material of the next three chapters. In particular, standard deviation and variance measure the variability of the return on an individual security and on portfolios of securities. In the next chapter, we will argue that standard deviation and variance are appropriate measures of the risk of an individual security if an investor's portfolio is composed of that security only.

3. Both arithmetic and geometric averages are commonly reported. The chapter explains how both are calculated and interpreted.

CONCEPT QUESTIONS

1. **Investment Selection** Given that Twilio was up by 278 percent for 2018, why didn't all investors hold Twilio?

2. **Investment Selection** Given that Coty was down by 67 percent for 2018, why did some investors hold the stock? Why didn't they sell out before the price declined so sharply?

3. **Risk and Return** We have seen that over long periods of time stock investments have tended to substantially outperform bond investments. However, it is not at all uncommon to observe investors with long horizons holding their investments entirely in bonds. Are such investors irrational?

4. **Stocks versus Gambling** Critically evaluate the following statement: Playing the stock market is like gambling. Such speculative investing has no social value, other than the pleasure people get from this form of gambling.

5. **Effects of Inflation** Look at Table 10.1 and Figure 10.7 in the text. When were T-bill rates at their highest over the period from 1926 through 2018? Why do you think they were so high during this period? What relationship underlies your answer?

6. **Risk Premiums** Is it possible for the risk premium to be negative before an investment is undertaken? Can the risk premium be negative after the fact? Explain.

7. **Returns** Two years ago, General Materials's and Standard Fixtures's stock prices were the same. During the first year, General Materials's stock price increased by 10 percent while Standard Fixtures's stock price decreased by 10 percent. During the second year, General Materials's stock price decreased by 10 percent and Standard Fixtures's stock price increased by 10 percent. Do these two stocks have the same price today? Explain.

8. **Returns**   Two years ago, the Lake Minerals and Small Town Furniture stock prices were the same. The average annual return for both stocks over the past two years was 10 percent. Lake Minerals's stock price increased 10 percent each year. Small Town Furniture's stock price increased 25 percent in the first year and lost 5 percent last year. Do these two stocks have the same price today?

9. **Arithmetic versus Geometric Returns**   What is the difference between arithmetic and geometric returns? Suppose you have invested in a stock for the last 10 years. Which number is more important to you, the arithmetic or geometric return?

10. **Historical Returns**   The historical asset class returns presented in the chapter are not adjusted for inflation. What would happen to the estimated risk premium if we did account for inflation? The returns are also not adjusted for taxes. What would happen to the returns if we accounted for taxes? What would happen to the volatility?

QUESTIONS AND PROBLEMS

Basic
(Questions 1–18)

1. **Calculating Returns**   Suppose a stock had an initial price of $76 per share, paid a dividend of $1.31 per share during the year, and had an ending share price of $87. Compute the total percentage return.

2. **Calculating Yields**   In Problem 1, what was the dividend yield? The capital gains yield?

3. **Calculating Returns**   Rework Problems 1 and 2 assuming the ending share price is $64.

4. **Calculating Returns**   Suppose you bought a bond with a coupon rate of 5.2 percent one year ago for $1,015. The bond sells for $1,032 today. The bond pays annual coupons.

   a. Assuming a $1,000 face value, what was your total dollar return on this investment over the past year?

   b. What was your total nominal rate of return on this investment over the past year?

   c. If the inflation rate last year was 3.2 percent, what was your total real rate of return on this investment?

5. **Nominal versus Real Returns**   What was the arithmetic average annual return on large-company stocks from 1926 through 2018:

   a. In nominal terms?

   b. In real terms?

6. **Bond Returns**   What is the historical real return on long-term government bonds? On long-term corporate bonds?

 7. **Calculating Returns and Variability**   Using the following returns, calculate the average returns, the variances, and the standard deviations for X and Y.

	Returns	
Year	X	Y
1	19%	38%
2	13	16
3	8	19
4	−9	−27
5	17	18

8. **Risk Premiums**   Refer to Table 10.1 in the text and look at the period from 1973 through 1978.

   a. Calculate the arithmetic average returns for large-company stocks and T-bills over this time period.

   b. Calculate the standard deviation of the returns for large-company stocks and T-bills over this time period.

   c. Calculate the observed risk premium in each year for the large-company stocks versus the T-bills. What was the arithmetic average risk premium over this period? What was the standard deviation of the risk premium over this period?

9. **Calculating Returns and Variability**   You've observed the following returns on Bennington Corporation's stock over the past five years: 21 percent, −11 percent, 8 percent, 17 percent, and 13 percent.

   a. What was the arithmetic average return on the company's stock over this five-year period?

   b. What was the variance of the company's stock returns over this period? The standard deviation?

10. **Calculating Real Returns and Risk Premiums**   In Problem 9, suppose the average inflation rate over this period was 2.6 percent and the average T-bill rate over the period was 3.25 percent.

    a. What was the average real return on the company's stock?

    b. What was the average nominal risk premium on the company's stock?

11. **Calculating Real Rates**   Given the information in Problem 10, what was the average real risk-free rate over this time period? What was the average real risk premium?

12. **Holding Period Return**   A stock has had returns of −13.18 percent, 17.63 percent, 24.87 percent, 8.32 percent, and 13.41 percent over the past five years, respectively. What was the holding period return for the stock?

13. **Calculating Returns**   You purchased a zero coupon bond one year ago for $425.32. The market interest rate is now 4.3 percent. If the bond had 20 years to maturity when you originally purchased it, what was your total return for the past year? Assume a par value of $1,000 and semiannual compounding.

14. **Calculating Returns**   You bought a share of 2.8 percent preferred stock for $94.16 last year. The market price for your stock is now $96.20. The par value is $100. What is your total return for last year?

15. **Calculating Returns**   You bought a stock three months ago for $61.18 per share. The stock paid no dividends. The current share price is $64.32. What is the APR of your investment? The EAR?

16. **Calculating Real Returns**   Refer to Table 10.1. What was the average real return for Treasury bills from 1926 through 1932?

 17. **Return Distributions**   Refer back to Table 10.2. What range of returns would you expect to see 68 percent of the time for long-term corporate bonds? What about 95 percent of the time?

18. **Return Distributions**   Refer back to Table 10.2. What range of returns would you expect to see 68 percent of the time for large-company stocks? What about 95 percent of the time?

19. **Calculating Returns and Variability**   You find a certain stock that had returns of 13 percent, 9 percent, −7 percent, and 11 percent for four of the last five years. If the average return of the stock over this period was 10.35 percent, what was the stock's return for the missing year? What is the standard deviation of the stock's returns?

Intermediate
(Questions 19–24)

 20. **Arithmetic and Geometric Returns**   A stock has had returns of −24 percent, 32 percent, 17 percent, −6 percent, 29 percent, and 13 percent over the last six years. What are the arithmetic and geometric average returns for the stock?

21. **Arithmetic and Geometric Returns** A stock has had the following year-end prices and dividends:

Year	Price	Dividend
0	$64.27	—
1	68.95	$.95
2	76.38	1.15
3	71.27	1.40
4	85.16	1.65
5	95.87	1.85

What are the arithmetic and geometric average returns for the stock?

22. **Calculating Returns** Refer to Table 10.1 in the text and look at the period from 1973 through 1980.

 a. Calculate the average return for Treasury bills and the average annual inflation rate (consumer price index) for this period.

 b. Calculate the standard deviation of Treasury bill returns and inflation over this time period.

 c. Calculate the real return for each year. What is the average real return for Treasury bills?

 d. Many people consider Treasury bills to be risk-free. What do these calculations tell you about the potential risks of Treasury bills?

23. **Calculating Investment Returns** You bought one of Elkins Manufacturing Co.'s 5.4 percent coupon bonds one year ago for $1,030. These bonds make annual payments, mature eight years from now, and have a par value of $1,000. Suppose you decide to sell your bonds today, when the required return on the bonds is 5.1 percent. If the inflation rate was 2.9 percent over the past year, what would be your total real return on the investment?

24. **Using Return Distributions** Suppose the returns on long-term government bonds are normally distributed. Based on the historical record, what is the approximate probability that your return on these bonds will be less than −3.9 percent in a given year? What range of returns would you expect to see 95 percent of the time? What range would you expect to see 99 percent of the time?

Challenge
(Questions 25–28)

25. **Using Return Distributions** Assuming that the returns from holding small-company stocks are normally distributed, what is the approximate probability that your money will double in value in a single year? Triple in value?

26. **Distributions** In the previous problem, what is the probability that the return is less than −100 percent? (Think.) What are the implications for the distribution of returns?

27. **Using Probability Distributions** Suppose the returns on large-company stocks are normally distributed. Based on the historical record, use the NORMDIST function in Excel® to determine the probability that in any given year you will lose money by investing in common stock.

28. **Using Probability Distributions** Suppose the returns on long-term corporate bonds and T-bills are normally distributed. Based on the historical record, use the NORMDIST function in Excel® to answer the following questions:

 a. What is the probability that in any given year, the return on long-term corporate bonds will be greater than 10 percent? Less than 0 percent?

 b. What is the probability that in any given year, the return on T-bills will be greater than 10 percent? Less than 0 percent?

 c. In 1979, the return on long-term corporate bonds was −4.18 percent. How likely is it that such a low return will recur at some point in the future? T-bills had a return of 10.38 percent in this same year. How likely is it that such a high return on T-bills will recur at some point in the future?

WHAT'S ON THE WEB?

1. **Market Risk Premium**   You want to find the current market risk premium. Go to money.cnn.com and find current interest rates. What is the shortest maturity interest rate shown? What is the interest rate for this maturity? Using the large-company stock return in Table 10.5, what is the current market risk premium? What assumption are you making when calculating the risk premium?

2. **Historical Interest Rates**   Go to the Federal Reserve Bank of St. Louis website at www.stlouisfed.org and search for "Treasury." You will find a list of links for different historical interest rates. Follow the "10-Year Treasury Constant Maturity Rate" link and you will find the monthly 10-year Treasury note interest rates. Calculate the average annual 10-year Treasury interest rate for 2018 and 2019. How does the 10-year Treasury interest rate compare to the numbers found in Table 10.2. Do you expect this relationship to always hold? Why or why not?

EXCEL MASTER IT! PROBLEM

As we have seen, over the 1926–2018 period, small-company stocks had the highest return and the highest risk, while U.S. Treasury bills had the lowest return and the lowest risk. While we certainly hope you have a 93-year holding period, it is likely your investment horizon will be somewhat shorter. One way risk and return are examined over shorter investment periods is by using rolling returns and standard deviations. Suppose you have a series of annual returns and you want to calculate a three-year rolling average return. You would calculate the first rolling average at Year 3 using the returns for the first three years. The next rolling average would be calculated using the returns from Years 2, 3, and 4, and so on.

ExcelMaster
coverage online

www.mhhe.com/RossCore6e

a. Using the annual returns for large-company stocks and Treasury bills, calculate both the 5- and 10-year rolling average returns and standard deviations.

b. Over how many 5-year periods did Treasury bills outperform large-company stocks? Over how many 10-year periods?

c. Over how many 5-year periods did Treasury bills have a larger standard deviation than large-company stocks? Over how many 10-year periods?

d. Graph the rolling 5-year and 10-year average returns for large-company stocks and Treasury bills.

e. What conclusions do you draw from the above results?

CLOSING CASE

A JOB AT EAST COAST YACHTS, PART 1

You recently graduated from college, and your job search led you to East Coast Yachts. Because you felt the company's business was seaworthy, you accepted a job offer. The first day on the job, while you are finishing your employment paperwork, Dan Ervin, who works in finance, stops by to inform you about the company's 401(k) plan.

A 401(k) plan is a retirement plan offered by many companies. Such plans are tax-deferred savings vehicles, meaning that any deposits you make into the plan are deducted from your current pretax income, so no current taxes are paid on the money. For example, assume your salary will be $50,000 per year. If you contribute $3,000 to the 401(k) plan, you will only pay taxes on $47,000 in income. There are also no taxes paid on any capital gains or income while you are invested in the plan, but you do pay taxes when you withdraw money at retirement. As is fairly common, the company also has a 5 percent match. This means that the company will match your contribution up to 5 percent of your salary, but you must contribute to get the match.

The 401(k) plan has several options for investments, most of which are mutual funds. A mutual fund is a portfolio of assets. When you purchase shares in a mutual fund, you are actually purchasing partial owner-ship of the fund's assets. The return of the fund is the weighted average of the return of the assets owned by the fund, minus any expenses. The largest expense is typically the management fee, paid to the fund manager. The management fee is compensation for the manager, who makes all of the investment decisions for the fund.

East Coast Yachts uses Bledsoe Financial Services as its 401(k) plan administrator. The investment options offered for employees are discussed below.

Company Stock   One option in the 401(k) plan is stock in East Coast Yachts. The company is currently privately held. However, when you interviewed with the owner, Larissa Warren, she informed you the company stock was expected to go public in the next three to four years. Until then, a company stock price is set each year by the board of directors.

Bledsoe S&P 500 Index Fund   This mutual fund tracks the S&P 500. Stocks in the fund are weighted exactly the same as the S&P 500. This means the fund return is approximately the return on the S&P 500, minus expenses. Because an index fund purchases assets based on the composition of the index it is follow-ing, the fund manager is not required to research stocks and make investment decisions. The result is that the fund expenses are usually low. The Bledsoe S&P 500 Index Fund charges expenses of .15 percent of assets per year.

Bledsoe Small-Cap Fund   This fund primarily invests in small-capitalization stocks. As such, the returns of the fund are more volatile. The fund can also invest 10 percent of its assets in companies based outside the United States. This fund charges 1.70 percent in expenses.

Bledsoe Large-Company Stock Fund   This fund invests primarily in large-capitalization stocks of compa-nies based in the United States. The fund is managed by Evan Bledsoe and has outperformed the market in six of the last eight years. The fund charges 1.50 percent in expenses.

Bledsoe Bond Fund   This fund invests in long-term corporate bonds issued by U.S.-domiciled compa-nies. The fund is restricted to investments in bonds with an investment-grade credit rating. This fund charges 1.40 percent in expenses.

Bledsoe Money Market Fund   This fund invests in short-term, high-credit-quality debt instruments, which include Treasury bills. As such, the return on the money market fund is only slightly higher than the return on Treasury bills. Because of the credit quality and short-term nature of the investments, there is only a very slight risk of a negative return. The fund charges .60 percent in expenses.

1. What advantages do the mutual funds offer compared to the company stock?

2. Assume that you invest 5 percent of your salary and receive the full 5 percent match from East Coast Yachts. What EAR do you earn from the match? What conclusions do you draw about matching plans?

3. Assume you decide you should invest at least part of your money in large-capitalization stocks of companies based in the United States. What are the advantages and disadvantages of choosing the Bledsoe Large-Company Stock Fund compared to the Bledsoe S&P 500 Index Fund?

4. The returns on the Bledsoe Small-Cap Fund are the most volatile of all the mutual funds offered in the 401(k) plan. Why would you ever want to invest in this fund? When you examine the expenses of the mutual funds, you will notice that this fund also has the highest expenses. Does this affect your decision to invest in this fund?

5. A measure of risk-adjusted performance that is often used is the Sharpe ratio. The Sharpe ratio is calculated as the risk premium of an asset divided by its standard deviation. The standard deviation and return of the funds over the past 10 years are listed below. Calculate the Sharpe ratio for each of these

funds. Assume that the expected return and standard deviation of the company stock will be 15 percent and 65 percent, respectively. Calculate the Sharpe ratio for the company stock. How appropriate is the Sharpe ratio for these assets? When would you use the Sharpe ratio? Assume the risk-free rate was 2.76 percent.

	10-Year Annual Return	Standard Deviation
Bledsoe S&P 500 Index Fund	11.85%	23.85%
Bledsoe Small-Cap Fund	15.32	29.62
Bledsoe Large-Company Stock Fund	10.73	26.73
Bledsoe Bond Fund	8.04	10.34

6. What portfolio allocation would you choose? Why? Explain your thinking carefully.

Return and Risk: The Capital Asset Pricing Model (CAPM)

OPENING CASE

In early 2019, PG&E, Netflix, and Amazon.com all made major announcements. Following such events, stock prices tend to change, and it was no different in these cases.

PG&E, the California utility company, announced it was filing for bankruptcy. The company's stock jumped about 16 percent on the day. For Netflix, the company announced 8.8 million new subscribers, resulting in a record number of subscriptions. This meant the company's streaming services were used in about 10 percent of U.S. households. Its stock dropped almost 4 percent on the news. Amazon.com announced that its earnings per share for the fourth quarter of 2018 were $6.04, compared to the estimate of $5.68, but the company's stock fell more than 5 percent.

PG&E's announcement seems like bad news, but its stock rose. The news from Netflix and Amazon.com seems good, but their stock prices fell. So when is good news really good news? The answer is fundamental to understanding risk and return, and—the good news is—this chapter explores it in some detail.

Please visit us at corecorporatefinance.blogspot.com for the latest developments in the world of corporate finance.

11.1 INDIVIDUAL SECURITIES

In the first part of Chapter 11, we will examine the characteristics of individual securities. In particular, we will discuss:

1. *Expected Return.* This is the return that an individual expects a stock to earn over the next period. Of course, because this is only an expectation, the actual return may be either higher or lower. An individual's expectation may be the average return per period a security has earned in the past. Alternatively, it may be based on a detailed analysis of a firm's prospects, on some computer-based model, or on special (or inside) information.

2. *Variance and Standard Deviation.* There are many ways to assess the volatility of a security's return. One of the most common is variance, which is a measure of the squared deviations of a security's return from its expected return. Standard deviation is the square root of the variance.

3. *Covariance and Correlation.* Returns on individual securities are related to one another. Covariance is a statistic that measures the interrelationship between two securities. Alternatively, this relationship can be restated in terms of the correlation between the two securities. Covariance and correlation are building blocks to an understanding of the beta coefficient.

11.2 EXPECTED RETURN, VARIANCE, AND COVARIANCE

Expected Return and Variance

Suppose financial analysts believe that there are four unequally likely states of the economy next year: depression, recession, normal, and boom times. The returns on the Supertech Company, R_{Super}, are expected to follow the economy closely, while the returns on the Slowpoke Company, R_{Slow}, are not. The return predictions are as follows:

State of Economy	Probability of State of Economy	Supertech Returns R_{Super}	Slowpoke Returns R_{Slow}
Depression	.10	−30%	0%
Recession	.20	−10	5
Normal	.50	20	20
Boom	.20	50	−5

Variance can be calculated in four steps.[1] An additional step is needed to calculate standard deviation. The calculations are presented in Table 11.1. The steps are:

1. Calculate the expected returns, $E(R_{Super})$ and $E(R_{Slow})$, by multiplying each possible return by the probability that it occurs, and then add them up:

Supertech
$E(R_{Super}) = .10(−.30) + .20(−.10) + .50(.20) + .20(.50) = .15$, or 15%

Slowpoke
$E(R_{Slow}) = .10(.00) + .20(.05) + .50(.20) + .20(−.05) = .10$, or 10%

---

2. As shown in the fourth column of Table 11.1, we next calculate the deviation of each possible return from the expected returns for the two companies.

3. Next, take the deviations from the fourth column and square them, as we have done in the fifth column.

4. Finally, multiply each squared deviation by its associated probability and add the products up. As shown in Table 11.1, we get a variance of .0585 for Supertech and .0110 for Slowpoke.

5. As always, to get the standard deviations, we just take the square roots of the variances:

Supertech
$SD(R_{Super}) = \sigma_{Super} = \sqrt{.0585} = .242$, or 24.2%

Slowpoke
$SD(R_{Slow}) = \sigma_{Slow} = \sqrt{.0110} = .105$, or 10.5%

---

[1] Notice we have a different variance calculation in this chapter. In Chapter 10, we were estimating the population variance from a sample of historical returns. In this chapter, we are calculating the population variance from a known distribution.

TABLE 11.1 Calculating Variance and Standard Deviation

(1) State of Economy	(2) Probability of State of Economy	(3) Rate of Return	(4) Deviation from Expected Return	(5) Squared Value of Deviation	(6) Product (2) × (5)
Supertech (Expected Return = .15)					
		R_{Super}	$R_{Super} - E(R_{Super})$	$[R_{Super} - E(R_{Super})]^2$	
Depression	.10	−.30	−.45	.2025	.02025
Recession	.20	−.10	−.25	.0625	.01250
Normal	.50	.20	.05	.0025	.00125
Boom	.20	.50	.35	.1225	.02450
				$Var(R_{Super}) = \sigma^2_{Super} =$	.05850
Slowpoke (Expected Return = .10)					
		R_{Slow}	$R_{Slow} - E(R_{Slow})$	$[R_{Slow} - E(R_{Slow})]^2$	
Depression	.10	.00	−.10	.0100	.00100
Recession	.20	.05	−.05	.0025	.00050
Normal	.50	.20	.10	.0100	.00500
Boom	.20	−.05	−.15	.0225	.00450
				$Var(R_{Slow}) = \sigma^2_{Slow} =$	.01100

Covariance and Correlation

Variance and standard deviation measure the variability of individual stocks. We now wish to measure the relationship between the return on one stock and the return on another. Enter covariance and correlation.

Covariance and correlation measure how two random variables are related. We explain these terms by extending our Supertech and Slowpoke example presented earlier.

EXAMPLE 11.1

Calculating Covariance and Correlation

We have already calculated the expected returns and standard deviations for both Supertech and Slowpoke. In addition, we calculated the deviation of each possible return from the expected return for each firm. Using these data, covariance can be calculated in two steps. An extra step is needed to calculate correlation.

1. For each state of the economy, multiply Supertech's deviation from its expected return and Slowpoke's deviation from its expected return together. For example, Supertech's rate of return in a depression is −.30, which is −.45 (= −.30 − .15) from its expected return. Slowpoke's rate of return in a depression is .00, which is −.10 (= .00 − .10) from its expected return. Multiplying the two deviations together yields .0450 [= (−.45) × (−.10)]. The actual calculations are given in the last column of Table 11.2. This procedure can be written algebraically as:

$$[R_{Super} - E(R_{Super})] \times [R_{Slow} - E(R_{Slow})] \tag{11.1}$$

where R_{Super} and R_{Slow} are the returns on Supertech and Slowpoke. $E(R_{Super})$ and $E(R_{Slow})$ are the expected returns on the two securities.

TABLE 11.2 Calculating Covariance and Correlation

(1) State of Economy	(2) Probability of State of Economy	(3) Deviations from Expected Returns Supertech	(4) Slowpoke	(5) Product of Deviation	(6) Product (2) × (5)
Depression	.10	−.45	−.10	.0450	.0045
Recession	.20	−.25	−.05	.0125	.0025
Normal	.50	.05	.10	.0050	.0025
Boom	.20	.35	−.15	−.0525	−.0105
				$\mathrm{Cov}(R_{Super}, R_{Slow}) = \sigma_{A,B} =$	−.0010

2. Once we have the products of the deviations, we multiply each one by its associated probability and sum to get the covariance.

Note that we represent the covariance between Supertech and Slowpoke as either $\mathrm{Cov}(R_{Super}, R_{Slow})$ or $\sigma_{Super,Slow}$. Equation 11.1 illustrates the intuition of covariance. Suppose Supertech's return is generally above its average when Slowpoke's return is above its average, and Supertech's return is generally below its average when Slowpoke's return is below its average. This is indicative of a positive relationship between the two returns. Note that the term in Equation 11.1 will be positive in any state where both returns are above their averages. In addition, Equation 11.1 will still be positive in any state where both terms are below their averages. Thus, a positive relationship between the two returns will give rise to a positive value for covariance.

Conversely, suppose Supertech's return is generally above its average when Slowpoke's return is below its average, and Supertech's return is generally below its average when Slowpoke's return is above its average. This is indicative of a negative relationship between the two returns. Note that the term in Equation 11.1 will be negative in any state where one return is above its average and the other return is below its average. Thus, a negative relationship between the two returns will give rise to a negative value for covariance.

Finally, suppose there is no relation between the two returns. In this case, knowing whether the return on Supertech is above or below its expected return tells us nothing about the return on Slowpoke. In the covariance formula, there will be no tendency for the deviations to be positive or negative together. On average, they will tend to offset each other and cancel out, making the covariance zero.

Of course, even if the two returns are unrelated to each other, the covariance formula will not equal zero exactly in any actual history. This is due to sampling error; randomness alone will make the calculation positive or negative. But for a historical sample that covers a sufficient period of time, if the two returns are not related to each other, we should expect the covariance to be about zero.

Our covariance calculation seems to capture what we are looking for. If the two returns are positively related to each other, they will have a positive covariance, and if they are negatively related to each other, the covariance will be negative. Last, and very important, if they are unrelated, the covariance should be zero.

The covariance we calculated is −.001. A negative number like this implies that the return on one stock is likely to be above its average when the return on the other stock is below its average, and vice versa. However, the size of the number is difficult to interpret. Like the variance figure, the covariance is in squared deviation units. Until we can put it in perspective, we don't know what to make of it.

We solve the problem by computing the correlation.

3. To calculate the correlation, divide the covariance by the product of the standard deviations of the two securities. For our example, we have:

$$\rho_{Super,Slow} = \mathrm{Corr}(R_{Super}, R_{Slow}) = \frac{\mathrm{Cov}(R_{Super}, R_{Slow})}{\sigma_{Super} \times \sigma_{Slow}} = \frac{-.001}{.242 \times .105} = -.039 \qquad [11.2]$$

(Continued)

where σ_{Super} and σ_{Slow} are the standard deviations of Supertech and Slowpoke, respectively. Note that we represent the correlation between Supertech and Slowpoke either as $Corr(R_{Super}, R_{Slow})$ or $\rho_{Super,Slow}$. Note also that the ordering of the two variables is unimportant. That is, the correlation of Supertech with Slowpoke is equal to the correlation of Slowpoke with Supertech. More generally, $Corr(R_A, R_B) = Corr(R_B, R_A)$ or $\rho_{A,B} = \rho_{B,A}$. The same is true for covariance.

Because the standard deviation is always positive, the sign of the correlation between two variables must be the same as that of the covariance between the two variables. If the correlation is positive, we say that the variables are positively correlated; if it is negative, we say that they are negatively correlated; and if it is zero, we say that they are uncorrelated. Furthermore, it can be proved that the correlation is always between $+1$ and -1. This is due to the standardizing procedure of dividing by the product of the two standard deviations.

We can compare the correlation between different pairs of securities. For example, it turns out that the correlation between General Motors and Ford is much higher than the correlation between General Motors and IBM. Hence, we can state that the first pair of securities is more interrelated than the second pair.

Figure 11.1 shows the three benchmark cases for two assets, A and B. The figure shows two assets with return correlations of $+1$, -1, and 0. This implies perfect positive correlation, perfect negative correlation, and no correlation, respectively. The graphs in the figure plot the separate returns on the two securities through time.

FIGURE 11.1 Examples of Different Correlation Coefficients—Graphs Plotting the Separate Returns on the Two Securities through Time

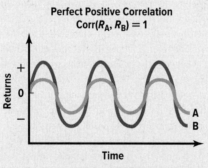

Perfect Positive Correlation
$Corr(R_A, R_B) = 1$

Both the return on Security A and the return on Security B are higher than average at the same time. Both the return on Security A and the return on Security B are lower than average at the same time.

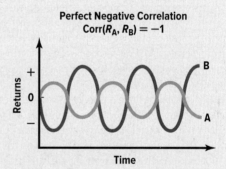

Perfect Negative Correlation
$Corr(R_A, R_B) = -1$

Security A has a higher-than-average return when Security B has a lower-than-average return, and vice versa.

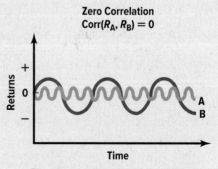

Zero Correlation
$Corr(R_A, R_B) = 0$

The return on Security A is completely unrelated to the return on Security B.

11.3 THE RETURN AND RISK FOR PORTFOLIOS

Suppose that an investor has estimates of the expected returns and standard deviations on individual securities and the correlations between securities. How then does the investor choose the best combination, or *portfolio*, of securities to hold? Obviously, the investor would like a portfolio with a high expected return and a low standard deviation of return. It is therefore worthwhile to consider:

1. The relationship between the expected return on individual securities and the expected return on a portfolio made up of these securities.
2. The relationship between the standard deviations of individual securities, the correlations between these securities, and the standard deviation of a portfolio made up of these securities.

In order to analyze the above two relationships, we will continue with our example of Supertech and Slowpoke.

ExcelMaster
coverage online
www.mhhe.com/RossCore6e

The Expected Return on a Portfolio

The formula for the expected return on a portfolio is very simple:

> The expected return on a portfolio is a weighted average of the expected returns on the individual securities.

RELEVANT DATA FROM EXAMPLE OF SUPERTECH AND SLOWPOKE

Item	Symbol	Value
Expected return on Supertech	$E(R_{Super})$	.15, or 15%
Expected return on Slowpoke	$E(R_{Slow})$	.10, or 10%
Variance of Supertech	σ^2_{Super}	.0585
Variance of Slowpoke	σ^2_{Slow}	.0110
Standard deviation of Supertech	σ_{Super}	.242, or 24.2%
Standard deviation of Slowpoke	σ_{Slow}	.105, or 10.5%
Covariance between Supertech and Slowpoke	$\sigma_{Super, Slow}$	−.001
Correlation between Supertech and Slowpoke	$\rho_{Super, Slow}$	−.039

EXAMPLE 11.2

Portfolio Expected Returns

Consider Supertech and Slowpoke. From the preceding box, we find that the expected returns on these two securities are 15 percent and 10 percent, respectively.

The expected return on a portfolio of these two securities alone can be written as:

Expected return on portfolio $= X_{Super} (.15) + X_{Slow} (.10) = R_P$

where X_{Super} is the percentage of the portfolio in Supertech and X_{Slow} is the percentage of the portfolio in Slowpoke. If the investor with $100 invests $60 in Supertech and $40 in Slowpoke, the expected return on the portfolio can be written as:

Expected return on portfolio $= .6 \times .15 + .4 \times .10 = .13$, or 13%

Algebraically, we can write:

Expected return on portfolio $= X_A E(R_A) + X_B E(R_B) = E(R_P)$ [11.3]

where X_A and X_B are the proportions of the total portfolio, or portfolio weights, in Assets A and B, respectively. Because our investor can only invest in two securities, $X_A + X_B$ must equal 1, or 100 percent. $E(R_A)$ and $E(R_B)$ are the expected returns on the two securities.

Now consider two stocks, each with an expected return of 10 percent. The expected return on a portfolio composed of these two stocks must be 10 percent, regardless of the proportions of the two stocks held. This result may seem obvious at this point, but it will become important later. The result implies that you do not reduce or dissipate your expected return by investing in a number of securities. Rather, the expected return on your portfolio is a weighted average of the expected returns on the individual assets in the portfolio.

Variance and Standard Deviation of a Portfolio

THE VARIANCE The formula for the variance of a portfolio composed of two securities, A and B, is:

The Variance of the Portfolio:

$$\text{Var (portfolio)} = X_A^2\sigma_A^2 + 2X_AX_B\sigma_{A,B} + X_B^2\sigma_B^2 \qquad [11.4]$$

Note that there are three terms on the right-hand side of the equation (in addition to X_A and X_B, the investment proportions). The first term involves the variance of A (σ_A^2), the second term involves the covariance between the two securities ($\sigma_{A,B}$), and the third term involves the variance of B (σ_B^2). As stated earlier in this chapter, $\sigma_{A,B} = \sigma_{B,A}$. That is, the ordering of the variables is not relevant when expressing the covariance between two securities.

The formula indicates an important point. The variance of a portfolio depends on both the variances of the individual securities and the covariance between the two securities. The variance of a security measures the variability of an individual security's return. Covariance measures the relationship between the two securities. For given variances of the individual securities, a positive relationship or covariance between the two securities increases the variance of the entire portfolio. A negative relationship or covariance between the two securities decreases the variance of the entire portfolio. This important result seems to square with common sense. If one of your securities tends to go up when the other goes down, or vice versa, your two securities are offsetting each other. You are achieving what we call a *hedge* in finance, and the risk of your entire portfolio will be lower. However, if both your securities rise and fall together, you are not hedging at all. Hence, the risk of your entire portfolio will be higher.

The variance formula for our two securities, Supertech and Slowpoke, is:

$$\text{Var (portfolio)} = X_{\text{Super}}^2\sigma_{\text{Super}}^2 + 2X_{\text{Super}}X_{\text{Slow}}\sigma_{\text{Super,Slow}} + X_{\text{Slow}}^2\sigma_{\text{Slow}}^2$$

Given our earlier assumption that an individual with $100 invests $60 in Supertech and $40 in Slowpoke, $X_{\text{Super}} = .6$ and $X_{\text{Slow}} = .4$. Using this assumption and the relevant data from the previous box, the variance of the portfolio is:

$$.0223 = .36 \times .0585 + 2 \times [.6 \times .4 \times (-.001)] + .16 \times .0110$$

STANDARD DEVIATION OF A PORTFOLIO We can now determine the standard deviation of the portfolio's return. This is:

$$\sigma_P = \text{SD (portfolio)} = \sqrt{\text{Var (portfolio)}} \qquad [11.5]$$
$$= \sqrt{.0223} = .1495, \text{ or } 14.95\%$$

The interpretation of the standard deviation of the portfolio is the same as the interpretation of the standard deviation of an individual security. The expected return on our portfolio is 13 percent. A return of -1.95 percent ($= 13\% - 14.95\%$) is one standard deviation below the mean, and a return of 27.95 percent ($= 13\% + 14.95\%$) is one standard deviation above the mean. If the return on the portfolio is normally distributed, a return between -1.95 percent and $+27.95$ percent occurs about 68 percent of the time.[2]

---

[2] There are only four possible returns for Supertech and Slowpoke, so neither security possesses a normal distribution. Thus, probabilities would be somewhat different in our example.

THE DIVERSIFICATION EFFECT   It is instructive to compare the standard deviation of the portfolio with the standard deviation of the individual securities. The weighted average of the standard deviations of the individual securities is:

$$\text{Weighted average of standard deviations} = X_{Super}\sigma_{Super} + X_{Slow}\sigma_{Slow} \qquad [11.6]$$
$$.187 = .6 \times .242 + .4 \times .105$$

One of the most important results in this chapter concerns the difference between Equations 11.5 and 11.6. In our example, the standard deviation of the portfolio is less than a weighted average of the standard deviations of the individual securities.

We pointed out earlier that the expected return on the portfolio is a weighted average of the expected returns on the individual securities. Thus, we get a different type of result for the standard deviation of a portfolio than we do for the expected return on a portfolio.

It is generally argued that our result for the standard deviation of a portfolio is due to diversification. For example, Supertech and Slowpoke are slightly negatively correlated ($\rho = -.039$). Supertech's return is likely to be a little below average if Slowpoke's return is above average. Similarly, Supertech's return is likely to be a little above average if Slowpoke's return is below average. Thus, the standard deviation of a portfolio composed of the two securities is less than a weighted average of the standard deviations of the two securities.

The above example has negative correlation. Clearly, there will be less benefit from diversification if the two securities exhibit positive correlation. How high must the positive correlation be before all diversification benefits vanish?

To answer this question, let us rewrite Equation 11.4 in terms of correlation rather than covariance. First, note that the covariance can be rewritten as:

$$\sigma_{Super,\ Slow} = \rho_{Super,\ Slow}\sigma_{Super}\sigma_{Slow} \qquad [11.7]$$

The formula states that the covariance between any two securities is the correlation between the two securities multiplied by the standard deviations of each. In other words, covariance incorporates both (1) the correlation between the two assets and (2) the variability of each of the two securities as measured by standard deviation.

From our calculations earlier in this chapter, we know that the correlation between the two securities is $-.039$. Thus, the variance of our portfolio can be expressed as:

Variance of the portfolio's return:
$$= X_{Super}^2\ \sigma_{Super}^2 + 2X_{Super}X_{Slow}\rho_{Super,\ Slow}\sigma_{Super}\sigma_{Slow} + X_{Slow}^2\sigma_{Slow}^2 \qquad [11.8]$$
$$.0223 = .36 \times .0585 + 2 \times .6 \times .4 \times (-.039) \times .242 \times .105$$
$$+ .16 \times .0110$$

The middle term on the right-hand side is now written in terms of correlation, ρ, not covariance.

Suppose $\rho_{Super,\ Slow} = 1$, the highest possible value for correlation. Assume all the other parameters in the example are the same. The variance of the portfolio is:

Variance of the $= .035 = .36 \times .0585 + 2 \times .6 \times .4 \times 1 \times .242 \times .105$
portfolio's return $+ .16 \times .0110$

The standard deviation is:

$$\text{Standard deviation of portfolio's return} = \sqrt{.035} = .187, \text{ or } 18.7\%$$

Note that this calculation of the standard deviation and Equation 11.6 are equal. That is, the standard deviation of a portfolio's return is equal to the weighted average of the standard deviations of the individual returns when $\rho = 1$. Inspection of Equation 11.8 indicates

Asset	Standard Deviation
S&P 500 Index	13.33%
Johnson & Johnson	14.64
Pfizer	17.31
Microsoft	21.95
Boeing	25.41
General Electric	28.81
Amazon.com	29.57
American Express	36.21
Ford	50.40
Advanced Micro Devices	61.36

that the variance and, hence, the standard deviation of the portfolio must fall as the correlation drops below 1. This leads to the following result:

> As long as ρ < 1, the standard deviation of a portfolio of two securities is less than the weighted average of the standard deviations of the individual securities.

In other words, the diversification effect applies as long as there is less than perfect correlation (as long as ρ < 1). Thus, our Supertech-Slowpoke example is a case of overkill. We illustrated diversification by an example with negative correlation. We could have illustrated diversification by an example with positive correlation—as long as it was not perfect positive correlation.

AN EXTENSION TO MANY ASSETS   The preceding insight can be extended to the case of many assets. That is, as long as correlations between pairs of securities are less than 1, the standard deviation of a portfolio of many assets is less than the weighted average of the standard deviations of the individual securities.

Now consider Table 11.3, which shows the standard deviation (based on annual returns) of the Standard & Poor's 500 Index and the standard deviations of some of the individual securities listed in the index over a recent 10-year period. Note that all of the individual securities in the table have higher standard deviations than that of the index. In general, the standard deviations of most of the individual securities in an index will be above the standard deviation of the index itself, although a few of the securities could have lower standard deviations than that of the index.

11.4 THE EFFICIENT SET

The Two-Asset Case

Our results on expected returns and standard deviations are graphed in Figure 11.2. In the figure, there is a dot labeled Slowpoke and a dot labeled Supertech. Each dot represents both the expected return and the standard deviation for an individual security. As can be seen, Supertech has both a higher expected return and a higher standard deviation.

The box or "□" in the graph represents a portfolio with 60 percent invested in Supertech and 40 percent invested in Slowpoke. You will recall that we have previously calculated both the expected return and the standard deviation for this portfolio.

The choice of 60 percent in Supertech and 40 percent in Slowpoke is just one of an infinite number of portfolios that can be created. The set of portfolios is sketched by the curved line in Figure 11.3.

Consider Portfolio 1. This is a portfolio composed of 90 percent Slowpoke and 10 percent Supertech. Because it is weighted so heavily toward Slowpoke, it appears close

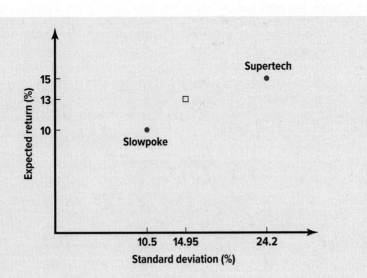

FIGURE 11.2

Expected Returns and
Standard Deviations for
Supertech, Slowpoke, and
a Portfolio Composed of
60 Percent in Supertech and
40 Percent in Slowpoke

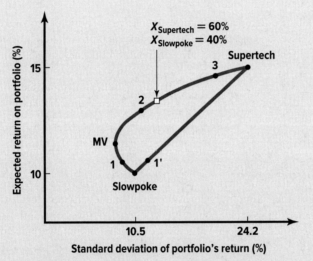

FIGURE 11.3

Set of Portfolios Composed
of Holdings in Supertech
and Slowpoke (correlation
between the two securities
is −.039)

Portfolio 1 is composed of 90 percent Slowpoke and 10 percent Supertech ($\rho = -.039$).

Portfolio 2 is composed of 50 percent Slowpoke and 50 percent Supertech ($\rho = -.039$).

Portfolio 3 is composed of 10 percent Slowpoke and 90 percent Supertech ($\rho = -.039$).

Portfolio 1′ is composed of 90 percent Slowpoke and 10 percent Supertech ($\rho = 1$).

Point MV denotes the minimum variance portfolio. This is the portfolio with the lowest possible variance. By definition, the same portfolio must also have the lowest possible standard deviation.

to the Slowpoke point on the graph. Portfolio 2 is higher on the curve because it is composed of 50 percent Slowpoke and 50 percent Supertech. Portfolio 3 is close to the Supertech point on the graph because it is composed of 90 percent Supertech and 10 percent Slowpoke.

There are a few important points concerning this graph:

1. We argued that the diversification effect occurs whenever the correlation between the two securities is below 1. The correlation between Supertech and Slowpoke is −.039. The diversification effect can be illustrated by comparison with the straight line between the Supertech point and the Slowpoke point.

The straight line represents points that would have been generated had the correlation coefficient between the two securities been 1. The diversification effect is illustrated in the figure because the curved line is always to the left of the straight line. Consider Point 1′. This represents a portfolio composed of 90 percent Slowpoke and 10 percent Supertech if the correlation between the two is exactly 1. We argue that there is no diversification effect if $\rho = 1$. However, the diversification effect applies to the curved line because Point 1 has the same expected return as Point 1′ but has a lower standard deviation. (Points 2′ and 3′ are omitted to reduce the clutter of Figure 11.3.)

Though the straight line and the curved line are both represented in Figure 11.3, they do not simultaneously exist in the same world. Either $\rho = -.039$ and the curve exists or $\rho = 1$ and the straight line exists. In other words, though an investor can choose between different points on the curve if $\rho = -.039$, she cannot choose between points on the curve and points on the straight line.

2. Point MV represents the minimum variance portfolio. This is the portfolio with the lowest possible variance. By definition, this portfolio must also have the lowest possible standard deviation. (The term *minimum variance portfolio* is standard in the literature, and we will use that term. Perhaps minimum standard deviation would actually be better because standard deviation, not variance, is measured on the horizontal axis of Figure 11.3.)

To find the mean variance optimal portfolio for any two stocks, go to www. wolframalpha.com and enter the ticker symbols.

3. An individual contemplating an investment in a portfolio of Slowpoke and Supertech faces an **opportunity set** or **feasible set** represented by the curved line in Figure 11.3. That is, he can achieve any point on the curve by selecting the appropriate mix between the two securities. He cannot achieve any point above the curve because he cannot increase the return on the individual securities, decrease the standard deviations of the securities, or decrease the correlation between the two securities. Neither can he achieve points below the curve because he cannot lower the returns on the individual securities, increase the standard deviations of the securities, or increase the correlation. (Of course, he would not want to achieve points below the curve, even if he were able to do so.)

Were he relatively tolerant of risk, he might choose Portfolio 3. In fact, he could even choose the end point by investing all his money in Supertech. An investor with less tolerance for risk might choose Portfolio 2. An investor wanting as little risk as possible would choose MV, the portfolio with minimum variance or minimum standard deviation.

4. Note that the curve is backward bending between the Slowpoke point and MV. This indicates that, for a portion of the feasible set, standard deviation actually decreases as one increases expected return. Students frequently ask, "How can an increase in the proportion of the risky security, Supertech, lead to a reduction in the risk of the portfolio?"

This surprising finding is due to the diversification effect. The returns on the two securities are negatively correlated with each other. One security tends to go up when the other goes down and vice versa. Thus, an addition of a small amount of Supertech acts as a hedge to a portfolio composed only of Slowpoke. The risk of the portfolio is reduced, implying backward bending. Actually, backward bending always occurs if $\rho \leq 0$. It may or may not occur when $\rho > 0$. Of course, the curve bends backward only for a portion of its length. As one continues to increase the percentage of Supertech in the portfolio, the high standard deviation of this security eventually causes the standard deviation of the entire portfolio to rise.

5. No investor would want to hold a portfolio with an expected return below that of the minimum variance portfolio. For example, no investor would choose Portfolio 1. This portfolio has less expected return but more standard deviation than the minimum variance portfolio. We say that portfolios such as Portfolio 1

FIGURE 11.4

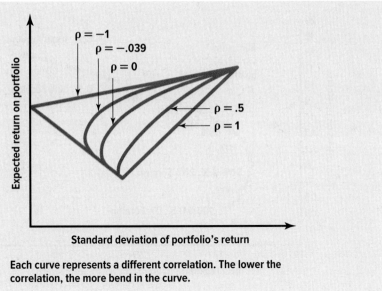

Each curve represents a different correlation. The lower the
correlation, the more bend in the curve.

are *dominated* by the minimum variance portfolio. Though the entire curve from Slowpoke to Supertech is called the *feasible set,* investors only consider the curve from MV to Supertech. Hence, the curve from MV to Supertech is called the efficient set or the efficient frontier.

You can find out more
about the efficient fron-
tier on the web at www
.efficientfrontier.com.

Figure 11.3 represents the opportunity set where $\rho = -.039$. It is worthwhile to examine Figure 11.4, which shows different curves for different correlations. As can be seen, the lower the correlation, the more bend there is in the curve. This indicates that the diversification effect rises as ρ declines. The greatest bend occurs in the limiting case where $\rho = -1$. This is perfect negative correlation. While this extreme case where $\rho = -1$ seems to fascinate students, it has little practical importance. Most pairs of securities exhibit positive correlation. Strong negative correlations, let alone perfect negative correlations, are uncommon occurrences for ordinary securities such as stocks and bonds.

Note that there is only one correlation between a pair of securities. We stated earlier that the correlation between Slowpoke and Supertech is $-.039$. Thus, the curve in Figure 11.3 representing this correlation is the correct one, and the other curves in Figure 11.4 should be viewed as merely hypothetical.

The graphs we examined are not mere intellectual curiosities. Rather, efficient sets can easily be calculated in the real world. As mentioned earlier, data on returns, standard deviations, and correlations are generally taken from past observations, though subjective notions can be used to determine the values of these parameters as well. Once the parameters have been determined, any one of a whole host of software packages can be purchased to generate an efficient set. However, the choice of the preferred portfolio within the efficient set is up to you. As with other important decisions like what job to choose, what house or car to buy, and how much time to allocate to this course, there is no computer program to choose the preferred portfolio.

An efficient set can be generated where the two individual assets are portfolios themselves. For example, the two assets in Figure 11.5 are a diversified portfolio of American stocks and a diversified portfolio of foreign stocks. Expected returns, standard deviations, and the correlation coefficient were calculated over the recent past. No subjectivity entered the analysis. The U.S. stock portfolio with a standard deviation of about .17 is less risky than the foreign stock portfolio, which has a standard deviation of about .22. However,

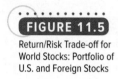

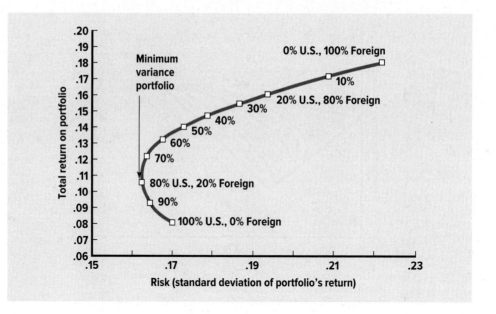

combining a small percentage of the foreign stock portfolio with the U.S. portfolio actually reduces risk, as can be seen by the backward-bending nature of the curve. In other words, the diversification benefits from combining two different portfolios more than offset the introduction of a riskier set of stocks into one's holdings. The minimum variance portfolio occurs with about 80 percent of one's funds in U.S. stocks and about 20 percent in foreign stocks. Addition of foreign securities beyond this point increases the risk of one's entire portfolio.

The backward-bending curve in Figure 11.5 is important information that has not bypassed American money managers. In recent years, pension fund and mutual fund managers in the United States have sought out investment opportunities overseas. Another point worth pondering concerns the potential pitfalls of using only past data to estimate future returns. The stock markets of many foreign countries have had phenomenal growth in the past 40 years. Thus, a graph like Figure 11.5 makes a large investment in these foreign markets seem attractive. However, because abnormally high returns cannot be sustained forever, some subjectivity must be used when forecasting future expected returns.

The Efficient Set for Many Securities

The previous discussion concerned two securities. We found that a simple curve shows all the possible portfolios. Because investors generally hold more than two securities, we should look at the same graph when more than two securities are held. The shaded area in Figure 11.6 represents the opportunity set or feasible set when many securities are considered. The shaded area represents all the possible combinations of expected return and standard deviation for a portfolio. For example, in a universe of 100 securities, Point 1 might represent a portfolio of, say, 40 securities. Point 2 might represent a portfolio of 80 securities. Point 3 might represent a different set of 80 securities, or the same 80 securities held in different proportions, or something else. Obviously, the combinations are virtually endless. However, note that all possible combinations fit into a confined region. No security or combination of securities can fall outside of the shaded region. That is, no one can choose a portfolio with an expected return above that given by the shaded region. Furthermore, no one can choose a portfolio with a standard deviation below that given in the shaded area. Perhaps more surprisingly, no one can choose an expected return below that given in the curve.

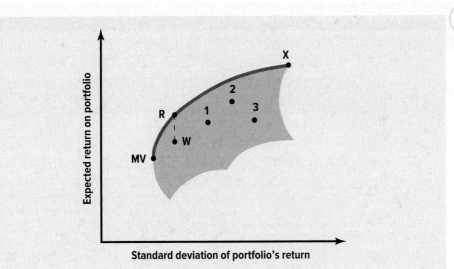

In other words, the capital markets actually prevent a self-destructive person from taking on a guaranteed loss.[3]

So far, Figure 11.6 is different from the earlier graphs. When only two securities are involved, all the combinations lie on a single curve. Conversely, with many securities the combinations cover an entire area. However, notice that an individual will want to be somewhere on the upper edge between MV and X. The upper edge, which we indicate in Figure 11.6 by a thick curve, is called the *efficient set.* Any point below the efficient set would receive less expected return and the same standard deviation as a point on the efficient set. For example, consider R on the efficient set and W directly below it. If W contains the risk you desire, you should choose R instead in order to receive a higher expected return.

In the final analysis, Figure 11.6 is quite similar to Figure 11.3. The efficient set in Figure 11.3 runs from MV to Supertech. It contains various combinations of the securities Supertech and Slowpoke. The efficient set in Figure 11.6 runs from MV to X. It contains various combinations of many securities. The fact that a whole shaded area appears in Figure 11.6 but not in Figure 11.3 is not an important difference; no investor would choose any point below the efficient set in Figure 11.6 anyway.

We mentioned before that an efficient set for two securities can be traced out easily in the real world. The task becomes more difficult when additional securities are included because the number of calculations quickly becomes huge. As a result, hand calculations are impractical for more than a few securities. A number of software packages allow the calculation of an efficient set for portfolios of moderate size. By all accounts, these packages sell quite briskly, so our discussion above would appear to be important in practice.

11.5 RISKLESS BORROWING AND LENDING

Figure 11.6 assumes that all the securities on the efficient set are risky. Alternatively, an investor could combine a risky investment with an investment in a riskless or risk-free security, such as an investment in U.S. Treasury bills. This is illustrated in the following example:

---

[3] Of course, someone dead set on parting with his money can do so. For example, he can trade frequently without purpose, so that commissions more than offset the positive expected returns on the portfolio.

EXAMPLE 11.3

Riskless Lending and Portfolio Risk

Ms. Bagwell is considering investing in the common stock of Merville Enterprises. In addition, Ms. Bagwell will either borrow or lend at the risk-free rate. The relevant parameters are:

	Common Stock of Merville	Risk-Free Asset
Expected return	14%	10%
Standard deviation	.20	0

Suppose Ms. Bagwell chooses to invest a total of $1,000, $350 of which is to be invested in Merville Enterprises and $650 placed in the risk-free asset. The expected return on her total investment is a weighted average of the two returns:

Expected return on portfolio composed of one riskless and one risky asset $= .35 \times .14 + .65 \times .10 = .114$, or 11.4%

Because the expected return on the portfolio is a weighted average of the expected return on the risky asset (Merville Enterprises) and the risk-free return, the calculation is analogous to the way we treated two risky assets. In other words, Equation 11.3 applies here.

Using Equation 11.4, the formula for the variance of the portfolio can be written as:

$$X^2_{Merville}\sigma^2_{Merville} + 2X_{Merville}X_{Risk\text{-}free}\sigma_{Merville, Risk\text{-}free} + X^2_{Risk\text{-}free}\sigma^2_{Risk\text{-}free}$$

However, by definition, the risk-free asset has no variability. Thus, both $\sigma_{Merville, Risk\text{-}free}$ and $\sigma^2_{Risk\text{-}free}$ are equal to zero, reducing the above expression to:

Variance of portfolio composed of one riskless and one risky asset $= X^2_{Merville}\,\sigma^2_{Merville}$ [11.9]

$$= .35^2 \times .20^2$$
$$= .0049$$

The standard deviation of the portfolio is:

Standard deviation of portfolio composed of one riskless and one risky asset $= X_{Merville}\,\sigma_{Merville}$ [11.10]

$$= \sqrt{.0049}$$
$$= .07$$

The relationship between risk and expected return for one risky and one riskless asset can be seen in Figure 11.7. Ms. Bagwell's split of 35-65 percent between the two assets is represented on a straight line between the risk-free rate and a pure investment in Merville Enterprises. Note that, unlike the case of two risky assets, the opportunity set is straight, not curved.

Suppose that, alternatively, Ms. Bagwell borrows $200 at the risk-free rate. Combining this with her original sum of $1,000, she invests a total of $1,200 in Merville. Her expected return would be:

Expected return on portfolio formed by borrowing to invest in risky asset $= 1.20 \times .14 + (-.2 \times .10) = .148$, or 14.8%

Here, she invests 120 percent of her original investment of $1,000 by borrowing 20 percent of her original investment. Note that the return of 14.8 percent is greater than the 14 percent expected return on Merville Enterprises. This occurs because she is borrowing at 10 percent to invest in a security with an expected return greater than 10 percent.

The standard deviation is:

Standard deviation of portfolio formed by borrowing to invest in risky asset $= 1.20 \times .2 = .24$, or 24%

FIGURE 11.7 Relationship between Expected Return and Risk for a Portfolio of One Risky Asset and One Riskless Asset

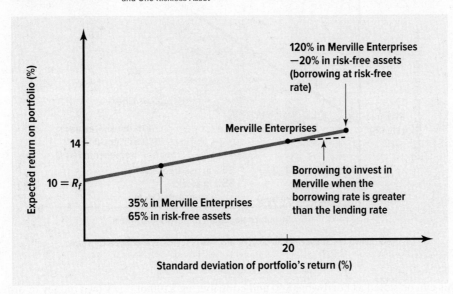

The standard deviation of 24 percent is greater than 20 percent, the standard deviation of the Merville investment, because borrowing increases the variability of the investment. This investment also appears in Figure 11.7.

So far, we have assumed that Ms. Bagwell is able to borrow at the same rate at which she can lend.[4] Now let us consider the case where the borrowing rate is above the lending rate. The dotted line in Figure 11.7 illustrates the opportunity set for borrowing opportunities in this case. The dotted line is below the solid line because a higher borrowing rate lowers the expected return on the investment.

The Optimal Portfolio

The previous section concerned a portfolio formed between one riskless asset and one risky asset. In reality, an investor is likely to combine an investment in the riskless asset with a *portfolio* of risky assets. This is illustrated in Figure 11.8.

Consider Point Q, representing a portfolio of securities. Point Q is in the interior of the feasible set of risky securities. Let us assume the point represents a portfolio of 30 percent AT&T, 45 percent General Electric (GE), and 25 percent IBM stock. Individuals combining investments in Q with investments in the riskless asset would achieve points along the straight line from R_f to Q. We refer to this as Line I. For example, Point 1 on the line represents a portfolio of 70 percent in the riskless asset and 30 percent in stocks represented by Q. An investor with $100 who chooses Point 1 as his portfolio would put $70 in the riskless asset and $30 in Q. This can be restated as $70 in the riskless asset, $9 (= .3 × $30) in AT&T, $13.50 (= .45 × $30) in GE, and $7.50 (= .25 × $30) in IBM. Point 2 also represents a portfolio of the risk-free asset and Q, with more (65 percent) being invested in Q.

Point 3 is obtained by borrowing to invest in Q. For example, an investor with $100 of his own would borrow $40 from the bank or broker in order to invest $140 in Q.

---

[4] Surprisingly, this appears to be a decent approximation because a large number of investors are able to borrow from a brokerage firm (called *going on margin*) when purchasing stocks. The borrowing rate here is very near the riskless rate of interest, particularly for large investors.

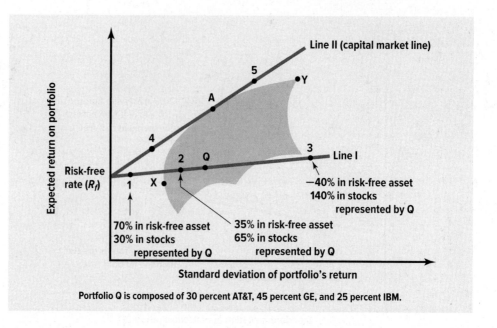

FIGURE 11.8

Relationship between Expected Return and Standard Deviation for an Investment in a Combination of Risky Securities and the Riskless Asset

Portfolio Q is composed of 30 percent AT&T, 45 percent GE, and 25 percent IBM.

This can be stated as borrowing $40 and contributing $100 of one's own money in order to invest $42 (= .3 × $140) in AT&T, $63 (= .45 × $140) in GE, and $35 (= .25 × $140) in IBM.

The above investments can be summarized as:

	Point Q	Point 1 (Lending $70)	Point 3 (Borrowing $40)
AT&T	$ 30	$ 9.00	$ 42
GE	45	13.50	63
IBM	25	7.50	35
Risk-free	0	70.00	− 40
Total investment	$100	$100.00	$100

Though any investor can obtain any point on Line I, no point on the line is optimal. To see this, consider Line II, a line running from R_f through A. Point A represents a portfolio of risky securities. Line II represents portfolios formed by combinations of the risk-free asset and the securities in A. Points between R_f and A are portfolios in which some money is invested in the riskless asset and the rest is placed in A. Points past A are achieved by borrowing at the riskless rate to buy more of A than one could with one's original funds alone.

As drawn, Line II is tangent to the efficient set of risky securities. Whatever point an individual can obtain on Line I, he can obtain a point with the same standard deviation and a higher expected return on Line II. In fact, because Line II is tangent to the efficient set of risky assets, it provides the investor with the best possible opportunities. In other words, Line II can be viewed as the efficient set of all assets, both risky and riskless. An investor with a fair degree of risk aversion might choose a point between R_f and A, perhaps Point 4. An individual with less risk aversion might choose a point closer to A or even beyond A. For example, Point 5 corresponds to an individual borrowing money to increase his investment in A.

The graph illustrates an important point. With riskless borrowing and lending, the portfolio of risky assets held by any investor would always be Point A. Regardless of the investor's tolerance for risk, he would never choose any other point on the efficient set of risky assets (represented by Curve XAY) nor any point in the interior of the feasible region. Rather, he would combine the securities of A with the riskless assets if he had high aversion to risk. He would borrow the riskless asset to invest more funds in A if he had low aversion to risk.

This result establishes what financial economists call the separation principle. That is, the investor's investment decision consists of two separate steps:

1. After estimating (*a*) the expected returns and variances of individual securities and (*b*) the covariances between pairs of securities, the investor calculates the efficient set of risky assets, represented by Curve XAY in Figure 11.8. He then determines Point A, the tangency between the risk-free rate and the efficient set of risky assets (Curve XAY). Point A represents the portfolio of risky assets that the investor will hold. This point is determined solely from his estimates of returns, variances, and covariances. No personal characteristics, such as degree of risk aversion, are needed in this step.

2. The investor must now determine how he will combine Point A, his portfolio of risky assets, with the riskless asset. He might invest some of his funds in the riskless asset and some in Portfolio A. He would end up at a point on the line between R_f and A in this case. Alternatively, he might borrow at the risk-free rate and contribute some of his own funds as well, investing the sum in Portfolio A. In this case, he would end up at a point on Line II beyond A. His position in the riskless asset, that is, his choice of where on the line he wants to be, is determined by his internal characteristics, such as his ability to tolerate risk.

11.6 ANNOUNCEMENTS, SURPRISES, AND EXPECTED RETURNS

Now that we know how to construct portfolios and evaluate their returns, we begin to describe more carefully the risks and returns associated with individual securities. Thus far, we have measured volatility by looking at the difference between the actual return on an asset or portfolio, *R,* and the expected return, E(*R*). We now look at why those deviations exist.

Expected and Unexpected Returns

To begin, for concreteness, we consider the return on the stock of a company called Flyers. What will determine this stock's return in, say, the coming year?

The return on any stock traded in a financial market is composed of two parts. First, the normal, or expected, return from the stock is the part of the return that shareholders in the market predict or expect. This return depends on the information shareholders have that bears on the stock, and it is based on the market's understanding today of the important factors that will influence the stock in the coming year.

The second part of the return on the stock is the uncertain, or risky, part. This is the portion that comes from unexpected information revealed within the year. A list of all possible sources of such information would be endless, but here are a few examples:

News about Flyers's research.

Government figures released on gross domestic product (GDP).

The results from the latest arms control talks.

The news that Flyers's sales figures are higher than expected.

A sudden, unexpected drop in interest rates.

Based on this discussion, one way to express the return on Flyers's stock in the coming year would be:

| Total return = Expected return + Unexpected return | [11.11] |
| $R = E(R) + U$ | |

where R stands for the actual total return in the year, $E(R)$ stands for the expected part of the return, and U stands for the unexpected part of the return. What this says is that the actual return, R, differs from the expected return, $E(R)$, because of surprises that occur during the year. In any given year, the unexpected return will be positive or negative, but, through time, the average value of U will be zero. This means that, on average, the actual return equals the expected return.

Announcements and News

We need to be careful when we talk about the effect of news items on the return. For example, suppose Flyers's business is such that the company prospers when GDP grows at a relatively high rate and suffers when GDP is relatively stagnant. In this case, in deciding what return to expect this year from owning stock in Flyers, shareholders either implicitly or explicitly must think about what GDP is likely to be for the year.

When the government actually announces GDP figures for the year, what will happen to the value of Flyers's stock? Obviously, the answer depends on what figure is released. More to the point, however, the impact depends on how much of that figure is new information.

At the beginning of the year, market participants will have some idea or forecast of what the yearly GDP will be. To the extent that shareholders have predicted GDP, that prediction will already be factored into the expected part of the return on the stock, $E(R)$. On the other hand, if the announced GDP is a surprise, then the effect will be part of U, the unanticipated portion of the return. As an example, suppose shareholders in the market had forecast that the GDP increase this year would be .5 percent. If the actual announcement this year is exactly .5 percent, the same as the forecast, then the shareholders don't really learn anything, and the announcement isn't news. There will be no impact on the stock price as a result. This is like receiving confirmation of something that you suspected all along; it doesn't reveal anything new.

A common way of saying that an announcement isn't news is to say that the market has already "discounted" the announcement. The use of the word *discount* here is different from the use of the term in computing present values, but the spirit is the same. When we discount a dollar in the future, we say it is worth less to us because of the time value of money. When we discount an announcement or a news item, we say that it has less of an impact on the market because the market already knew much of it.

Going back to Flyers, suppose the government announces that the actual GDP increase during the year has been 1.5 percent. Now shareholders have learned something, namely, that the increase is one percentage point higher than they had forecast. This difference between the actual result and the forecast, one percentage point in this example, is sometimes called the *innovation* or the *surprise*.

This distinction explains why what seems to be good news can actually be bad news (and vice versa). For example, to open the chapter we compared PG&E, Netflix, and Amazon.com. For PG&E, the company was being blamed for starting a California wildfire, and it faced a potential liability of $30 billion. The bankruptcy allowed time for the company to deal with claims filed by consumers. Additionally, bankruptcy could force California to pass legislation to allow the company to pass the costs of claims on to customers and permit the company to rework existing renewable energy contracts, which were some of the most expensive in the country. For Netflix, although the company had a record number of new subscribers, revenue came in at $4.19 billion, slightly less than the estimate of $4.21 billion. The company had also announced a price hike one week earlier, which is generally an indication of strong growth, so investors may have been expecting better results. In Amazon.com's case, the company also beat revenue, another positive sign. However, the growth rate in earnings was lower than in previous years. The company also announced that capital spending for 2019 would increase. Investors may have felt that these new investments would be in lower return ventures.

To summarize, an announcement can be broken into two parts, the anticipated, or expected, part and the surprise, or innovation:

$$\text{Announcement} = \text{Expected part} + \text{Surprise} \qquad [11.12]$$

The expected part of any announcement is the part of the information that the market uses to form the expectation, $E(R)$, of the return on the stock. The surprise is the news that influences the unanticipated return on the stock, U. Henceforth, when we speak of news, we will mean the surprise part of an announcement and not the portion that the market has expected and therefore already discounted.

11.7 RISK: SYSTEMATIC AND UNSYSTEMATIC

The unanticipated part of the return, that portion resulting from surprises, is the true risk of any investment. After all, if we always receive exactly what we expect, then the investment is perfectly predictable and, by definition, risk-free. In other words, the risk of owning an asset comes from surprises—unanticipated events.

There are important differences, though, among various sources of risk. Look back at our previous list of news stories. Some of these stories are directed specifically at Flyers, and some are more general. Which of the news items are of specific importance to Flyers?

Announcements about interest rates or GDP are clearly important for nearly all companies, whereas the news about Flyers's research or sales is of specific interest to Flyers. We will distinguish between these two types of events because, as we shall see, they have very different implications.

Systematic and Unsystematic Risk

The first type of surprise, the one that affects a large number of assets, we will label systematic risk. A systematic risk is one that influences a large number of assets, each to a greater or lesser extent. Because systematic risks have marketwide effects, they are sometimes called *market risks* (or correlated risks).

The second type of surprise we will call unsystematic risk. An unsystematic risk is one that affects a single asset or a small group of assets. Because these risks are unique to individual companies or assets, they are sometimes called *unique* or *asset-specific risks* (or uncorrelated risks). We will use these terms interchangeably.

As we have seen, uncertainties about general economic conditions, such as GDP, interest rates, or inflation, are examples of systematic risks. These conditions affect nearly all companies to some degree. An unanticipated increase, or surprise, in inflation, for example, affects wages and the costs of the supplies that companies buy; it affects the value of the assets that companies own; and it affects the prices at which companies sell their products. Forces such as these, to which all companies are susceptible, are the essence of systematic risk.

In contrast, the announcement of an oil strike by a company will primarily affect that company and, perhaps, a few others (such as primary competitors and suppliers). It is unlikely to have much of an effect on the world oil market, however, or on the affairs of companies not in the oil business, so this is an unsystematic event.

Systematic and Unsystematic Components of Return

The distinction between a systematic risk and an unsystematic risk is never really as exact as we make it out to be. Even the most narrow and peculiar bit of news about a company ripples through the economy. This is true because every enterprise, no matter how tiny, is a part of the economy. It's like the tale of a kingdom that was lost because one horse lost a shoe. This is mostly hairsplitting, however. Some risks are clearly much more general than others. We'll see some evidence on this point in just a moment.

The distinction between the types of risk allows us to break down the surprise portion, U, of the return on the Flyers stock into two parts. Earlier, we had the actual return broken down into its expected and surprise components:

$$R = E(R) + U$$

We now recognize that the total surprise component for Flyers, U, has a systematic and an unsystematic component, so:

$$R = E(R) + \text{Systematic portion} + \text{Unsystematic portion} \qquad [11.13]$$

To see why the distinction between systematic and unsystematic risks is important, we need to return to the subject of portfolio risk.

11.8 DIVERSIFICATION AND PORTFOLIO RISK

For more on risk and diversification, visit www.investopedia.com/university.

We've seen earlier that portfolio risks can, in principle, be quite different from the risks of the assets that make up the portfolio. We now look more closely at the riskiness of an individual asset versus the risk of a portfolio of many different assets. We will once again examine some market history to get an idea of what happens with actual investments in U.S. capital markets.

The Effect of Diversification: Another Lesson from Market History

In our previous chapter, we saw that the standard deviation of the annual return on a portfolio of 500 large common stocks has historically been about 20 percent per year. Does this mean that the standard deviation of the annual return on a typical stock in that group of 500 is about 20 percent? As you might suspect by now, the answer is no. This is an extremely important observation.

To allow examination of the relationship between portfolio size and portfolio risk, Table 11.4 illustrates typical average annual standard deviations for equally weighted portfolios that contain different numbers of randomly selected NYSE securities.

In Column 2 of Table 11.4, we see that the standard deviation for a "portfolio" of one security is about 49 percent. What this means is that if you randomly selected a single NYSE stock and put all your money into it, your standard deviation of return would typically be a substantial 49 percent per year. If you were to randomly select two stocks and invest half your money in each, your standard deviation would be about 37 percent, on average, and so on.

The important thing to notice in Table 11.4 is that the standard deviation declines as the number of securities is increased. By the time we have 100 randomly chosen stocks, the portfolio's standard deviation has declined by about 60 percent, from 49 percent to about 20 percent. With 500 securities, the standard deviation is 19.27 percent, similar to the 19.8 percent we saw in our previous chapter for the large common stock portfolio. The small difference exists because the portfolio securities and time periods examined are not identical.

The Principle of Diversification

Figure 11.9 illustrates the point we've been discussing. What we have plotted is the standard deviation of return versus the number of stocks in the portfolio. Notice in Figure 11.9 that the benefit in terms of risk reduction from adding securities drops off as we add more and more.

(1)	(2)	(3)
Number of Stocks in Portfolio	**Average Standard Deviation of Annual Portfolio Returns**	**Ratio of Portfolio Standard Deviation to Standard Deviation of a Single Stock**
1	49.24%	1.00
2	37.36	.76
4	29.69	.60
6	26.64	.54
8	24.98	.51
10	23.93	.49
20	21.68	.44
30	20.87	.42
40	20.46	.42
50	20.20	.41
100	19.69	.40
200	19.42	.39
300	19.34	.39
400	19.29	.39
500	19.27	.39
1,000	19.21	.39

TABLE 11.4

Standard Deviations of Annual Portfolio Returns

Sources: Statman, Meir. "How Many Stocks Make a Diversified Portfolio?" *Journal of Financial and Quantitative Analysis* 22, no. 3 (1987): pp. 353–63. Derived from Elton, Edwin J., and Martin J. Gruber. "Risk Reduction and Portfolio Size: An Analytic Solution," *Journal of Business* 50, no. 4 (1977): pp. 415–37.

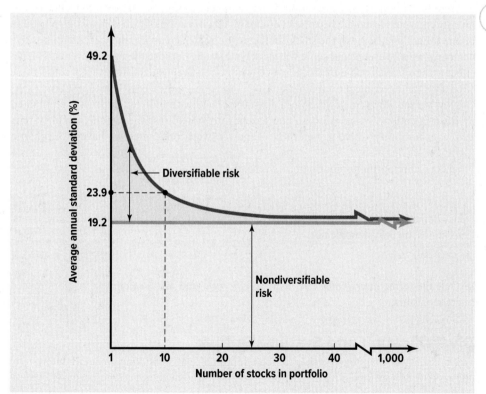

FIGURE 11.9

Portfolio Diversification

By the time we have 10 securities, most of the effect is already realized, and by the time we get to 30 or so, there is very little remaining benefit.

Figure 11.9 illustrates two key points. First, some of the riskiness associated with individual assets can be eliminated by forming portfolios. The process of spreading an investment across assets (and thereby forming a portfolio) is called *diversification.* The principle of diversification tells us that spreading an investment across many assets will eliminate some of the risk. The purple shaded area in Figure 11.9, labeled "Diversifiable risk," is the part that can be eliminated by diversification.

The second point is equally important. There is a minimum level of risk that cannot be eliminated by diversifying. This minimum level is labeled "Nondiversifiable risk" in Figure 11.9. Taken together, these two points are another important lesson from capital market history: Diversification reduces risk, but only up to a point. Put another way, some risk is diversifiable and some is not.

To give a recent example of the impact of diversification, the Dow Jones Industrial Average (DJIA), which is a widely followed stock market index of 30 large, well-known U.S. stocks, was down about 3.5 percent in 2018. As we saw in our previous chapter, this loss represents a poor year for a portfolio of large-cap stocks. The biggest individual winners for the year were Merck (up 40 percent) and Pfizer (up 25 percent). Of course, not all 30 stocks were up: The losers included Goldman Sachs (down 34 percent) and DowDuPont (down 23 percent). Again, the lesson is clear: Diversification reduces exposure to extreme outcomes, both good and bad.

Diversification and Unsystematic Risk

From our discussion of portfolio risk, we know that some of the risk associated with individual assets can be diversified away and some cannot. We are left with an obvious question: Why is this so? It turns out that the answer hinges on the distinction we made earlier between systematic and unsystematic risk.

Here is the important observation: If we only held a single stock, then the value of our investment would fluctuate because of company-specific events. If we hold a large portfolio, on the other hand, some of the stocks in the portfolio will go up in value because of positive company-specific events and some will go down in value because of negative events. The net effect on the overall value of the portfolio will be relatively small, however, because these effects will tend to cancel each other out.

Now we see why some of the variability associated with individual assets is eliminated by diversification. When we combine assets into portfolios, the unique, or unsystematic, events—both positive and negative—tend to "wash out" once we have more than a few assets.

This is an important point that bears repeating:

> Unsystematic risk is essentially eliminated by diversification, so a portfolio with many assets has almost no unsystematic risk.

In fact, the terms *diversifiable risk, asset-specific risk,* and *unsystematic risk* are often used interchangeably.

Diversification and Systematic Risk

We've seen that unsystematic risk can be eliminated by diversifying. What about systematic risk? Can it also be eliminated by diversification? The answer is no because, by definition, a systematic risk affects almost all assets to some degree. As a result, no matter how many assets we put into a portfolio, the systematic risk doesn't go away. Thus, for obvious reasons, the terms *systematic risk, market risk,* and *nondiversifiable risk* are used interchangeably.

Because we have introduced so many different terms, it is useful to summarize our discussion before moving on. What we have seen is that the total risk of an investment, as measured by the standard deviation of its returns, can be written as:

$$\text{Total risk} = \text{Systematic risk} + \text{Unsystematic risk} \qquad [11.14]$$

For a well-diversified portfolio, the unsystematic risk is negligible. For such a portfolio, essentially all of the risk is systematic.

11.9 MARKET EQUILIBRIUM

Definition of the Market Equilibrium Portfolio

Financial economists often imagine a world where all investors possess the same estimates on expected returns, variances, and covariances. Though this can never be literally true, it can be thought of as a useful simplifying assumption in a world where investors have access to similar sources of information. This assumption is called homogeneous expectations.[5]

ExcelMaster
coverage online
www.mhhe.com/RossCore6e

If all investors had homogeneous expectations, Figure 11.8 would be the same for all individuals. That is, all investors would sketch out the same efficient set of risky assets because they would be working with the same inputs. This efficient set of risky assets is represented by the Curve XAY. Because the same risk-free rate would apply to everyone, all investors would view Point A as the portfolio of risky assets to be held.

This Point A takes on great importance because all investors would purchase the risky securities that it represents. Those investors with a high degree of risk aversion might combine A with an investment in the riskless asset, achieving Point 4, for example. Others with low aversion to risk might borrow to achieve, say, Point 5. Because this is a very important conclusion, we restate it:

In a world with homogeneous expectations, all investors would hold the portfolio of risky assets represented by Point A.

If all investors choose the same portfolio of risky assets, it is possible to determine what that portfolio is. Common sense tells us that it is a market value–weighted portfolio of all existing securities. It is the market portfolio. In terms of our discussion of diversification, the market portfolio is perfectly diversified by having eliminated all unsystematic risk.

In practice, financial economists use a broad-based index such as the Standard & Poor's (S&P) 500 as a proxy for the market portfolio. Of course, all investors do not hold the same portfolio. However, we know that a large number of investors hold diversified portfolios, particularly when mutual funds or pension funds are included. A broad-based index is a good proxy for the highly diversified portfolios of many investors.

Definition of Risk When Investors Hold the Market Portfolio

The previous section states that many investors hold diversified portfolios similar to broad-based indexes. This result allows us to be more precise about the risk of a security in the context of a diversified portfolio.

Researchers have shown that the best measure of the risk of a security in a large portfolio is the *beta* of the security. We illustrate beta by an example.

[5] The assumption of homogeneous expectations states that all investors have the same beliefs concerning returns, variances, and covariances. It does not say that all investors have the same aversion to risk.

EXAMPLE 11.4

Beta

Consider the following possible returns both on the stock of Jelco, Inc., and on the market:

State	Type of Economy	Return on Market	Return on Jelco, Inc.
I	Bull	15%	25%
II	Bull	15	15
III	Bear	−5	−5
IV	Bear	−5	−15

Though the return on the market has only two possible outcomes (15% and −5%), the return on Jelco has four possible outcomes. It is helpful to consider the expected return on a security for a given return on the market. Assuming each state is equally likely, we have:

Type of Economy	Return on Market	Expected Return on Jelco, Inc.
Bull	15%	20% = 25% × .50 + 15% × .50
Bear	−5	−10% = −5% × .50 + (−15%) × .50

Jelco, Inc., responds to market movements because its expected return is greater in bullish states than in bearish states. We now calculate exactly how responsive the security is to market movements. The market's return in a bullish economy is 20 percent [= 15% − (−5%)] greater than the market's return in a bearish economy. However, the expected return on Jelco in a bullish economy is 30 percent [= 20% − (−10%)] greater than its expected return in a bearish state. Thus, Jelco, Inc., has a responsiveness coefficient of 1.5 (= 30%/20%).

This relationship appears in Figure 11.10. The returns for both Jelco and the market in each state are plotted as four points. In addition, we plot the expected return on the security for each of the two

FIGURE 11.10 Performance of Jelco, Inc., and the Market Portfolio

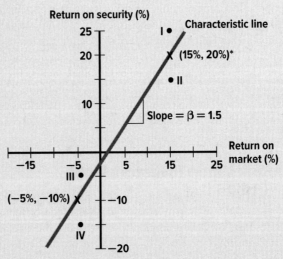

The two points marked X represent the expected return on Jelco for each possible outcome of the market portfolio. The expected return on Jelco is positively related to the return on the market. Because the slope is 1.5, we say that Jelco's beta is 1.5. Beta measures the responsiveness of the security's return to movements in the market.

*(15%, 20%) refers to the point where the return on the market is 15 percent and the return on the security is 20 percent.

Stock	Beta
Dominion Energy	.22
Johnson & Johnson	.62
Kellogg Company	.64
General Motors	.99
Apple	1.11
Cisco Systems	1.12
Fastenal	1.29
Amazon.com	1.83

TABLE 11.5

Estimates of Beta for Selected Individual Stocks

The beta is defined as $Cov(R_j, R_M)/Var(R_M)$, where $Cov(R_j, R_M)$ is the covariance of the return on an individual stock, R_j, and the return on the market, R_M. $Var(R_M)$ is the variance of the return on the market, R_M.

Source: finance.yahoo.com. 2019.

possible returns on the market. These two points, each of which we designate by an X, are joined by a line called the characteristic line of the security. The slope of the line is 1.5, the number calculated in the previous paragraph. This responsiveness coefficient of 1.5 is the beta of Jelco.

The interpretation of beta from Figure 11.10 is intuitive. The graph tells us that the returns of Jelco are magnified 1.5 times over those of the market. When the market does well, Jelco's stock is expected to do even better. When the market does poorly, Jelco's stock is expected to do even worse. Now imagine an individual with a portfolio near that of the market who is considering the addition of Jelco to his portfolio. Because of Jelco's *magnification factor* of 1.5, he will view this stock as contributing much to the risk of the portfolio. (We will show shortly that the beta of the average security in the market is 1.) Jelco contributes more to the risk of a large, diversified portfolio than does an average security because Jelco is more responsive to movements in the market.

Further insight can be gleaned by examining securities with negative betas. One should view these securities as either hedges or insurance policies. The security is expected to do well when the market does poorly and vice versa. Because of this, adding a negative beta security to a large, diversified portfolio actually reduces the risk of the portfolio.[6]

Table 11.5 presents empirical estimates of betas for individual securities. As can be seen, some securities are more responsive to the market than others. For example, Cisco has a beta of 1.12. This means that, for every 1 percent movement in the market, Cisco is expected to move 1.12 percent in the same direction. Conversely, Kellogg has a beta of only .64. This means that, for every 1 percent movement in the market, Kellogg is expected to move .64 percent in the same direction.

We can summarize our discussion of beta by saying:

Beta measures the responsiveness of a security to movements in the market portfolio.

You can find beta estimates at many sites on the web. One of the best is finance.yahoo.com. We went there and entered the ticker symbol FNMA for Fannie Mae and followed the "Statistics" link. Here is part of what we found:

Betas are easy to find on the internet. Try finance. yahoo.com and money .cnn.com.

Stock Price History

Beta (3Y Monthly)	1.71
52-Week Change [3]	16.82%

[6] Unfortunately, empirical evidence shows that virtually no stocks have negative betas.

Management Effectiveness

Return on Assets (ttm)	0.18%
Return on Equity (ttm)	116.65%

Balance Sheet

Total Cash (mrq)	94.91B
Total Cash Per Share (mrq)	16.54
Total Debt (mrq)	3.37T
Total Debt/Equity (mrq)	48,382.02
Current Ratio (mrq)	86.49
Book Value Per Share (mrq)	-23.17

The reported beta for Fannie Mae Corporation is 1.71, which means Fannie Mae has about 1.71 times the systematic risk of the average stock. Fannie Mae has a return on equity of about 117 percent, which is outstanding. However, digging into the numbers, Fannie Mae has a negative book value of equity stemming from an accumulation of losses. The company lost money over the previous year, which resulted in a positive ROE. In fact, the more money Fannie Mae loses, the higher its ROE! In all, Fannie Mae seems to be a good candidate for a high beta. For more about "real-world" betas, see the nearby *Finance Matters* box.

The Formula for Beta

Our discussion so far has stressed the intuition behind beta. The actual definition of beta is:

$$\beta_i = \frac{Cov(R_i, R_M)}{\sigma^2(R_M)} \qquad [11.15]$$

For more on beta, visit
money.msn.com.

where $Cov(R_i, R_M)$ is the covariance between the return on Asset i and the return on the market portfolio and $\sigma^2(R_M)$ is the variance of the market. This formula reinforces the notion that the risk of an individual security does not depend on its own variance (or standard deviation), only on its covariance with the market.

One useful property is that the average beta across all securities, when weighted by the proportion of each security's market value to that of the market portfolio, is 1. That is:

$$\sum_{i=1}^{N} X_i \beta_i = 1 \qquad [11.16]$$

where X_i is the proportion of Security i's market value to that of the entire market and N is the number of securities in the market.

Equation 11.16 is intuitive, once you think about it. If you weight all securities by their market values, the resulting portfolio is the market. By definition, the beta of the market portfolio is 1. That is, for every 1 percent movement in the market, the market must move 1 percent—by definition.

A Test

We have put these questions on past corporate finance examinations:

1. What sort of investor rationally views the variance (or standard deviation) of an individual security's return as the security's proper measure of risk?

2. What sort of investor rationally views the beta of a security as the security's proper measure of risk?

BETA, BETA, WHO'S GOT THE BETA?

Based on what we've studied so far, you can see that beta is a pretty important topic. You might wonder then, are all published betas created equal? Read on for a partial answer to this question.

We did some checking on betas and found some interesting results. The Value Line *Investment Survey* is one of the best-known sources for information on publicly traded companies. However, with the explosion of online investing, there has been a corresponding increase in the amount of investment information available online. We decided to compare the betas presented by Value Line to those reported by Yahoo! Finance (finance.yahoo.com), Google (finance.google.com), and CNN Money (money.cnn.com). What we found leads to an important note of caution.

Consider Microsoft, with its beta reported on the internet as 1.28, which is larger than Value Line's beta of 1.00. Microsoft wasn't the only stock that showed a divergence in betas from different sources. In fact, for most of the technology companies we looked at, Value Line reported betas that were significantly lower than their online cousins. For example, the online beta for Cisco Systems was 1.22, but Value Line reported 1.05. The online beta for eBay was 1.49 versus a Value Line beta of 1.00. Value Line's betas are not always lower. For example, the online beta for Adobe (maker of the ubiquitous Acrobat software) was .80, compared to Value Line's 1.10.

We also found some unusual, and even hard-to-believe, estimates for beta. Caesars Entertainment had a very low online beta of .01, while Value Line reported Caesars's beta as 1.60. The online estimate for Southern Company was .03, compared to Value Line's .54. Perhaps the most outrageous reported betas were the online betas for SPO Global and Sunnylife Global, with betas of 155.23 and −263.53 (notice the negative sign!), respectively. Value Line did not report a beta for these companies. How do you suppose we should interpret a beta of −263.53?

There are a few lessons to be learned from all of this. First, not all betas are created equal. Some are computed using weekly returns and some using daily returns. Some are computed using 60 months of stock returns; some consider more or fewer returns. Some betas are computed by comparing the stock to the S&P 500 Index, while others use alternative indexes. Finally, some reporting firms (including Value Line) make adjustments to raw betas to reflect information other than just the fluctuation in stock prices.

The second lesson is perhaps more subtle and comes from the betas of SPO Global and Sunnylife Global. We are interested in knowing what the beta of the stock will be in the future, but betas have to be estimated using historical data. Anytime we use the past to predict the future, there is the danger of a poor estimate. In our case, it is very unlikely that SPO Global has a beta anything like 155.23 or that Sunnylife Global has a beta of −263.53. Instead, the estimates are almost certainly poor ones. The moral of the story is that, as with any financial tool, beta is not a black box that should be taken without question.

A good answer might be something like the following:

A rational, risk-averse investor views the variance (or standard deviation) of her portfolio's return as the proper measure of the risk of her portfolio. If for some reason or another the investor can hold only one security, the variance of that security's return becomes the variance of the portfolio's return. Hence, the variance of the security's return is the security's proper measure of risk.

If an individual holds a diversified portfolio, she still views the variance (or standard deviation) of her portfolio's return as the proper measure of the risk of her portfolio. However, she is no longer interested in the variance of each individual security's return. Rather, she is interested in the contribution of an individual security to the variance of the portfolio.

Under the assumption of homogeneous expectations, all individuals hold the market portfolio. Thus, we measure risk as the contribution of an individual security to the variance of the market portfolio. This contribution, when standardized properly, is the beta of the security. While very few investors hold the market portfolio exactly, many hold reasonably diversified portfolios. These portfolios are close enough to the market portfolio so that the beta of a security is likely to be a reasonable measure of its risk.

11.10 RELATIONSHIP BETWEEN RISK AND EXPECTED RETURN (CAPM)

It is commonplace to argue that the expected return on an asset should be positively related to its risk. That is, individuals will hold a risky asset only if its expected return compensates for its risk. In this section, we estimate expected returns on individual securities.

Expected Return on Individual Security

What is the expected return on an individual security? We start with the intuition that the expected return on an individual security can be represented as $E(R_i) = R_f +$ Risk premium. In words, the expected return on any individual security (or portfolio) is the sum of the risk-free rate plus some compensation for systematic risk. We have argued that the beta of a security is the appropriate measure of risk in a large, diversified portfolio. Because most investors are diversified, the expected return on a security should be positively related to its beta. This is illustrated in Figure 11.11.

Actually, financial economists can be more precise about the relationship between expected return and beta. They posit that, under plausible conditions, the relationship between expected return and beta can be represented by the following equation:

For more on CAPM and the equity risk premium, visit www.investopedia.com/terms/c/capm.asp.

Capital Asset Pricing Model:

$$E(R) = R_f + \beta \times [E(R_M) - R_f] \qquad [11.17]$$

| Expected return on a security | = | Risk-free rate | + | Beta of the security | × | Difference between expected return on market and risk-free rate, or the market risk premium |

This formula, which is called the **capital asset pricing model** (or CAPM for short), implies that the expected return on a security is linearly related to its beta. Because the average return on the market has been higher than the average risk-free rate over long periods of

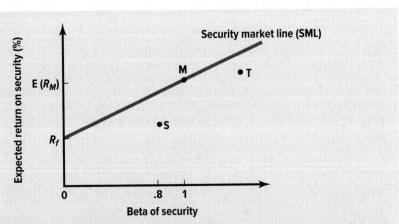

FIGURE 11.11

Relationship between Expected Return on an Individual Security and Beta of the Security

The security market line (SML) is the graphical depiction of the capital asset pricing model (CAPM). The expected return on a stock with a beta of 0 is equal to the risk-free rate. The expected return on a stock with a beta of 1 is equal to the expected return on the market.

time, the market risk premium $E(R_M) - R_f$ is presumably positive. Thus, the formula implies that the expected return on a security is positively related to its beta. The formula can be illustrated by assuming a few special cases:

- *Assume that* $\beta = 0$. Here $E(R) = R_f$, that is, the expected return on the security is equal to the risk-free rate. Because a security with zero beta has no relevant risk, its expected return should equal the risk-free rate.

- *Assume that* $\beta = 1$. Equation 11.17 reduces to $E(R) = E(R_M)$. That is, the expected return on the security is equal to the expected return on the market. This makes sense because the beta of the market portfolio is also 1.

Equation 11.17 can be represented graphically by the upward-sloping line in Figure 11.11. Note that the line begins at R_f and rises to $E(R_M)$ when beta is 1. This line is frequently called the **security market line (SML)**.

As with any line, the SML has both a slope and an intercept. R_f, the risk-free rate, is the intercept. Because the beta of a security is the horizontal axis, $E(R_M) - R_f$ is the slope. The line will be upward sloping as long as the expected return on the market is greater than the risk-free rate. Because the market portfolio is a risky asset, theory suggests that its expected return is above the risk-free rate. As mentioned, the empirical evidence of the previous chapter showed that the average return per year on the market portfolio (e.g., U.S. large-company stocks) from 1900–2010 was 7.2 percent above the risk-free rate.

EXAMPLE 11.5

CAPM

The stock of Aardvark Enterprises has a beta of 1.5, and that of Zebra Enterprises has a beta of .7. The risk-free rate is assumed to be 3 percent, and the difference between the expected return on the market and the risk-free rate is assumed to be 8 percent. The expected returns on the two securities are:

Expected Return for Aardvark
$15.0\% = 3\% + 1.5 \times 8\%$

Expected Return for Zebra
$8.6\% = 3\% + .7 \times 8\%$

Three additional points concerning the CAPM should be mentioned:

1. *Linearity.* The intuition behind an upwardly sloping curve is clear. Because beta is the appropriate measure of risk, high-beta securities should have an expected return above that of low-beta securities. However, both Figure 11.11 and Equation 11.17 show something more than an upwardly sloping curve; the relationship between expected return and beta corresponds to a straight line.

   It is easy to show that the line of Figure 11.11 is straight. To see this, consider Security S with, say, a beta of .8. This security is represented by a point below the security market line in the figure. Any investor could duplicate the beta of Security S by buying a portfolio with 20 percent in the risk-free asset and 80 percent in a security with a beta of 1. However, the homemade portfolio would itself lie on the SML. In other words, the portfolio dominates Security S because the portfolio has a higher expected return and the same beta.

Now consider Security T with, say, a beta greater than 1. This security is also below the SML in Figure 11.11. Any investor could duplicate the beta of Security T by borrowing to invest in a security with a beta of 1. This portfolio must also lie on the SML, thereby dominating Security T.

Because no one would hold either S or T, their stock prices would drop. This price adjustment would raise the expected returns on the two securities. The price adjustment would continue until the two securities lay on the security market line. The preceding example considered two overpriced stocks and a straight SML. Securities lying above the SML are *underpriced.* Their prices must rise until their expected returns lie on the line. If the SML is itself curved, many stocks would be mispriced. In equilibrium, all securities would be held only when prices changed so that the SML became straight. In other words, linearity would be achieved.

2. *Portfolios as Well as Securities.* Our discussion of the CAPM considered individual securities. Does the relationship in Figure 11.11 and Equation 11.17 hold for portfolios as well?

Yes. To see this, consider a portfolio formed by investing equally in our two securities, Aardvark and Zebra. The expected return on the portfolio is:

Expected Return on Portfolio:
$$11.8\% = .5 \times 15.0\% + .5 \times 8.6\%$$

The beta of the portfolio is a weighted average of the betas of the two securities. Thus, we have:

Beta of Portfolio:
$$1.1 = .5 \times 1.5 + .5 \times .7$$

Under the CAPM, the expected return on the portfolio is:

$$11.8\% = 3\% + 1.1 \times 8\%$$

Because the expected return in Equation 11.17 is the same as the expected return in the above equation, the example shows that the CAPM holds for portfolios as well as for individual securities.

3. *A Potential Confusion.* Students often confuse the SML in Figure 11.11 with Line II in Figure 11.8. Actually, the lines are quite different. Line II traces the efficient set of portfolios formed from both risky assets and the riskless asset. Each point on the line represents an entire portfolio. Point A is a portfolio composed entirely of risky assets. Every other point on the line represents a portfolio of the securities in A combined with the riskless asset. The axes on Figure 11.8 are the expected return on a portfolio and the standard deviation of a portfolio. Individual securities do not lie along Line II.

The SML in Figure 11.11 relates expected return to beta. Figure 11.11 differs from Figure 11.8 in at least two ways. First, beta appears in the horizontal axis of Figure 11.11, but standard deviation appears in the horizontal axis of Figure 11.8. Second, the SML in Figure 11.11 holds both for all individual securities and for all possible portfolios, whereas Line II in Figure 11.8 holds only for efficient portfolios.

We stated earlier that, under homogeneous expectations, Point A in Figure 11.8 becomes the market portfolio. In this situation, Line II is referred to as the **capital market line (CML).**

SUMMARY AND CONCLUSIONS

This chapter sets forth the fundamentals of modern portfolio theory. Our basic points are these:

1. This chapter shows us how to calculate the expected return and variance for individual securities, and the covariance and correlation for pairs of securities. Given these statistics, the expected return and variance for a portfolio of two securities, A and B, can be written as:

$$\text{Expected return on portfolio} = X_A E(R_A) + X_B E(R_B)$$
$$\text{Variance of portfolio return} = X_A^2 \sigma_A^2 + 2X_A X_B \sigma_{A,B} + X_B^2 \sigma_B^2$$

2. In our notation, X stands for the portfolio weight of a security in the portfolio. By varying X, one can trace out the efficient set of portfolios. We graphed the efficient set for the two-asset case as a curve, pointing out that the degree of curvature or bend in the graph reflects the diversification effect: the lower the correlation between the two securities, the greater the bend. The same general shape of the efficient set holds in a world of many assets.

3. A diversified portfolio can eliminate only some, not all, of the risk associated with individual securities. The reason is that part of the risk with an individual asset is unsystematic, meaning essentially unique to that asset. In a well-diversified portfolio, these unsystematic risks tend to cancel out. Systematic, or market, risks are not diversifiable.

4. The efficient set of risky assets can be combined with riskless borrowing and lending. In this case, a rational investor will always choose to hold the portfolio of risky securities represented by Point A in Figure 11.8. Then he can either borrow or lend at the riskless rate to achieve any desired point on Line II in the figure.

5. The contribution of a security to the risk of a large, well-diversified portfolio is proportional to the covariance of the security's return with the market's return. This contribution, when standardized, is called the beta. The beta of a security can also be interpreted as the responsiveness of a security's return to that of the market.

6. The CAPM states that:

$$E(R) = R_f + \beta \left[E(R_M) - R_f \right]$$

In other words, the expected return on a security is positively (and linearly) related to the security's beta.

CONCEPT QUESTIONS

1. **Diversifiable and Nondiversifiable Risks** In broad terms, why is some risk diversifiable? Why are some risks nondiversifiable? Does it follow that an investor can control the level of unsystematic risk in a portfolio, but not the level of systematic risk?

2. **Information and Market Returns** Suppose the government announces that, based on a just-completed survey, the growth rate in the economy is likely to be 2 percent in the coming year, as compared to 5 percent for the year just completed. Will security prices increase, decrease, or stay the same following this announcement? Does it make any difference whether or not the 2 percent figure was anticipated by the market? Explain.

3. **Systematic versus Unsystematic Risk** Classify the following events as mostly systematic or mostly unsystematic. Is the distinction clear in every case?
   a. Short-term interest rates increase unexpectedly.
   b. The interest rate a company pays on its short-term debt borrowing is increased by its bank.
   c. Oil prices unexpectedly decline.
   d. An oil tanker ruptures, creating a large oil spill.
   e. A manufacturer loses a multimillion-dollar product liability suit.
   f. A Supreme Court decision substantially broadens producer liability for injuries suffered by product users.

4. **Systematic versus Unsystematic Risk** Indicate whether the following events might cause stocks in general to change price, and whether they might cause Big Widget Corp.'s stock to change price.

   a. The government announces that inflation unexpectedly jumped by 2 percent last month.
   b. Big Widget's quarterly earnings report, just issued, generally fell in line with analysts' expectations.
   c. The government reports that economic growth last year was at 3 percent, which generally agreed with most economists' forecasts.
   d. The directors of Big Widget die in a plane crash.
   e. Congress approves changes to the tax code that will increase the top marginal corporate tax rate. The legislation had been debated for the previous six months.

5. **Expected Portfolio Returns** If a portfolio has a positive investment in every asset, can the expected return on the portfolio be greater than that on every asset in the portfolio? Can it be less than that on every asset in the portfolio? If you answer yes to one or both of these questions, give an example to support your answer.

6. **Diversification** True or false: The variances of the individual assets in the portfolio are the most important characteristic in determining the expected return of a well-diversified portfolio. Explain.

7. **Portfolio Risk** If a portfolio has a positive investment in every asset, can the standard deviation on the portfolio be less than that on every asset in the portfolio? What about the portfolio beta?

8. **Beta and CAPM** Is it possible that a risky asset could have a beta of zero? Explain. Based on the CAPM, what is the expected return on such an asset? Is it possible that a risky asset could have a negative beta? What does the CAPM predict about the expected return on such an asset? Can you give an explanation for your answer?

9. **Corporate Downsizing** In recent years, it has been common for companies to experience significant stock price changes in reaction to announcements of massive layoffs. Critics charge that such events encourage companies to fire longtime employees and that Wall Street is cheering them on. Do you agree or disagree?

10. **Earnings and Stock Returns** As indicated by a number of examples in this chapter, earnings announcements by companies are closely followed by, and frequently result in, share price revisions. Two issues should come to mind. First, earnings announcements concern past periods. If the market values stocks based on expectations of the future, why are numbers summarizing past performance relevant? Second, these announcements concern accounting earnings. Going back to Chapter 2, such earnings may have little to do with cash flow, so, again, why are they relevant?

11. **Covariance** Briefly explain why the covariance of a security with the rest of a well-diversified portfolio is a more appropriate measure of the risk of the security than the security's variance.

12. **Beta** Consider the following quotation from a leading investment manager: "The shares of Mid-South Electric have traded close to $12 for most of the past three years. Because Mid-South's stock has demonstrated very little price movement, the stock has a low beta. Tech Flyer, on the other hand, has traded as high as $150 and as low as its current $75. Because Tech Flyer's stock has demonstrated a large amount of price movement, the stock has a very high beta." Do you agree with this analysis? Explain.

13. **Risk** A broker has advised you not to invest in oil industry stocks because they have high standard deviations. Is the broker's advice sound for a risk-averse investor like yourself? Why or why not?

14. **Security Selection** Is the following statement true or false? A risky security cannot have an expected return that is less than the risk-free rate because no risk-averse investor would be willing to hold this asset in equilibrium. Explain.

QUESTIONS AND PROBLEMS

Basic
(Questions 1–19)

1. **Determining Portfolio Weights**   What are the portfolio weights for a portfolio that has 165 shares of Stock A that sell for $41 per share and 280 shares of Stock B that sell for $29 per share?

2. **Portfolio Expected Return**   You own a portfolio that has $4,260 invested in Stock A and $6,490 invested in Stock B. If the expected returns on these stocks are 8.4 percent and 12.3 percent, respectively, what is the expected return on the portfolio?

3. **Portfolio Expected Return**   You own a portfolio that is 45 percent invested in Stock X, 35 percent invested in Stock Y, and 20 percent invested in Stock Z. The expected returns on these three stocks are 9.2 percent, 11.8 percent, and 14.3 percent, respectively. What is the expected return on the portfolio?

4. **Portfolio Expected Return**   You have $10,000 to invest in a stock portfolio. Your choices are Stock X with an expected return of 11.9 percent and Stock Y with an expected return of 9.7 percent. If your goal is to create a portfolio with an expected return of 10.3 percent, how much money will you invest in Stock X? In Stock Y?

5. **Calculating Expected Return**   Based on the following information, calculate the expected return.

State of Economy	Probability of State of Economy	Rate of Return If State Occurs
Recession	.35	−.14
Normal	.50	.16
Boom	.15	.43

6. **Calculating Returns and Standard Deviations**   Based on the following information, calculate the expected return and standard deviation for the two stocks.

State of Economy	Probability of State of Economy	Rate of Return If State Occurs	
		Stock A	Stock B
Recession	.10	.01	−.19
Normal	.60	.09	.11
Boom	.30	.13	.37

7. **Calculating Returns and Standard Deviations**   Based on the following information, calculate the expected return and standard deviation of the following stock.

State of Economy	Probability of State of Economy	Rate of Return If State Occurs
Depression	.10	−.243
Recession	.20	−.116
Normal	.45	.138
Boom	.25	.328

8. **Calculating Expected Returns**   A portfolio is invested 20 percent in Stock G, 65 percent in Stock J, and 15 percent in Stock K. The expected returns on these stocks are 8.6 percent, 10.8 percent, and 13.4 percent, respectively. What is the portfolio's expected return? How do you interpret your answer?

9. **Returns and Standard Deviations**   Consider the following information:

State of Economy	Probability of State of Economy	Rate of Return If State Occurs		
		Stock A	Stock B	Stock C
Boom	.15	.24	.43	.36
Good	.45	.11	.19	.15
Poor	.35	.03	−.16	−.04
Bust	.05	−.09	−.29	−.08

a. Your portfolio is invested 35 percent each in A and C, and 30 percent in B. What is the expected return of the portfolio?

b. What is the variance of this portfolio? The standard deviation?

10. **Calculating Portfolio Betas** You own a stock portfolio invested 15 percent in Stock Q, 20 percent in Stock R, 30 percent in Stock S, and 35 percent in Stock T. The betas for these four stocks are .83, 1.24, 1.13, and 1.41, respectively. What is the portfolio beta?

11. **Calculating Portfolio Betas** You own a portfolio equally invested in a risk-free asset and two stocks. If one of the stocks has a beta of 1.27 and the total portfolio is equally as risky as the market, what must the beta be for the other stock in your portfolio?

12. **Using CAPM** A stock has a beta of 1.08, the expected return on the market is 10.9 percent, and the risk-free rate is 2.7 percent. What must the expected return on this stock be?

13. **Using CAPM** A stock has an expected return of 10.9 percent, the risk-free rate is 3.1 percent, and the market risk premium is 6.9 percent. What must the beta of this stock be?

14. **Using CAPM** A stock has an expected return of 9.7 percent, its beta is .89, and the risk-free rate is 2.9 percent. What must the expected return on the market be?

15. **Using CAPM** A stock has an expected return of 11.5 percent, its beta is 1.09, and the expected return on the market is 10.8 percent. What must the risk-free rate be?

16. **Portfolio Returns** Using information from the previous chapter on capital market history, determine the return on a portfolio that is equally invested in large-company stocks and long-term government bonds. What is the return on a portfolio that is equally invested in small-company stocks and Treasury bills?

 17. **Using the SML** Asset W has an expected return of 10.8 percent and a beta of 1.15. If the risk-free rate is 2.7 percent, complete the following table for portfolios of Asset W and a risk-free asset. Illustrate the relationship between portfolio expected return and portfolio beta by plotting the expected returns against the betas. What is the slope of the line that results?

Percentage of Portfolio in Asset W	Portfolio Expected Return	Portfolio Beta
0%		
25		
50		
75		
100		
125		
150		

 18. **Reward-to-Risk Ratios** Stock Y has a beta of 1.15 and an expected return of 12.6 percent. Stock Z has a beta of .83 and an expected return of 9.5 percent. If the risk-free rate is 4.3 percent and the market risk premium is 6.7 percent, are these stocks correctly priced?

19. **Reward-to-Risk Ratios** In the previous problem, what would the risk-free rate have to be for the two stocks to be correctly priced?

Intermediate
(Questions 20–32)

20. **Using CAPM** A stock has a beta of 1.13 and an expected return of 11.8 percent. A risk-free asset currently earns 2.6 percent.

a. What is the expected return on a portfolio that is equally invested in the two assets?

b. If a portfolio of the two assets has a beta of .5, what are the portfolio weights?

c. If a portfolio of the two assets has an expected return of 10 percent, what is its beta?

d. If a portfolio of the two assets has a beta of 2.26, what are the portfolio weights? How do you interpret the weights for the two assets in this case? Explain.

21. **CAPM** Using the CAPM, show that the ratio of the risk premiums on two assets is equal to the ratio of their betas.

22. **Portfolio Returns and Deviations** Consider the following information on three stocks:

State of Economy	Probability of State of Economy	Rate of Return If State Occurs		
		Stock A	Stock B	Stock C
Boom	.30	.26	.33	.50
Normal	.55	.14	.15	.02
Bust	.15	−.03	−.18	−.45

a. If your portfolio is invested 25 percent each in A and B and 50 percent in C, what is the portfolio expected return? The variance? The standard deviation?
b. If the expected T-bill rate is 4.10 percent, what is the expected risk premium on the portfolio?
c. If the expected inflation rate is 3.50 percent, what are the approximate and exact expected real returns on the portfolio? What are the approximate and exact expected real risk premiums on the portfolio?

23. **Analyzing a Portfolio** You want to create a portfolio equally as risky as the market, and you have $1 million to invest. Given this information, fill in the rest of the following table:

Asset	Investment	Beta
Stock A	$265,000	.87
Stock B	$390,000	1.18
Stock C		1.30
Risk-free asset		

24. **Analyzing a Portfolio** You have $100,000 to invest in a portfolio containing Stock X and Stock Y. Your goal is to create a portfolio that has an expected return of 12.1 percent. If Stock X has an expected return of 11.3 percent and a beta of 1.15, and Stock Y has an expected return of 9.1 percent and a beta of .85, how much money will you invest in Stock Y? How do you interpret your answer? What is the beta of your portfolio?

25. **Covariance and Correlation** Based on the following information, calculate the expected return and standard deviation of each of the following stocks. Assume each state of the economy is equally likely to happen. What are the covariance and correlation between the returns of the two stocks?

State of Economy	Return on Stock A	Return on Stock B
Bear	−.068	−.087
Normal	.104	−.019
Bull	.241	.432

26. **Covariance and Correlation** Based on the following information, calculate the expected return and standard deviation for each of the following stocks. What are the covariance and correlation between the returns of the two stocks?

State of Economy	Probability of State of Economy	Return on Stock J	Return on Stock K
Bear	.15	−.140	.023
Normal	.60	.103	.097
Bull	.25	.328	.032

27. **Portfolio Standard Deviation**   Security F has an expected return of 11 percent and a standard deviation of 47 percent per year. Security G has an expected return of 14 percent and a standard deviation of 63 percent per year.

   a. What is the expected return on a portfolio composed of 65 percent of Security F and 35 percent of Security G?

   b. If the correlation between the returns of Security F and Security G is .15, what is the standard deviation of the portfolio described in part (a)?

28. **Portfolio Standard Deviation**   Suppose the expected returns and standard deviations of Stocks A and B are $E(R_A) = .10$, $E(R_B) = .13$, $\sigma_A = .41$, and $\sigma_B = .59$, respectively.

   a. Calculate the expected return and standard deviation of a portfolio that is composed of 40 percent A and 60 percent B when the correlation between the returns on A and B is .5.

   b. Calculate the standard deviation of a portfolio that is composed of 40 percent A and 60 percent B when the correlation coefficient between the returns on A and B is $-.5$.

   c. How does the correlation between the returns on A and B affect the standard deviation of the portfolio?

29. **Correlation and Beta**   You have been provided the following data on the securities of three firms, the market portfolio, and the risk-free asset:

Security	Expected Return	Standard Deviation	Correlation*	Beta
Firm A	.11	.36	(i)	.97
Firm B	.14	(ii)	.38	1.24
Firm C	.13	.42	.41	(iii)
The market portfolio	.12	.19	(iv)	(v)
The risk-free asset	.03	(vi)	(vii)	(viii)

*With the market portfolio.

   a. Fill in the missing values in the table.

   b. Is the stock of Firm A correctly priced according to the capital asset pricing model (CAPM)? What about the stock of Firm B? Firm C? If these securities are not correctly priced, what is your investment recommendation for someone with a well-diversified portfolio?

30. **CML**   The market portfolio has an expected return of 10.7 percent and a standard deviation of 19 percent. The risk-free rate is 3.2 percent.

   a. What is the expected return on a well-diversified portfolio with a standard deviation of 24 percent?

   b. What is the standard deviation of a well-diversified portfolio with an expected return of 15 percent?

31. **Beta and CAPM**   A portfolio that combines the risk-free asset and the market portfolio has an expected return of 6 percent and a standard deviation of 11 percent. The risk-free rate is 2.9 percent, and the expected return on the market portfolio is 12 percent. Assume the capital asset pricing model holds. What expected rate of return would a security earn if it had a .55 correlation with the market portfolio and a standard deviation of 50 percent?

32. **Beta and CAPM**   Suppose the risk-free rate is 2.1 percent and the market portfolio has an expected return of 11.1 percent. The market portfolio has a variance of .0387. Portfolio Z has a correlation coefficient with the market of .29 and a variance of .3287. According to the capital asset pricing model, what is the expected return on Portfolio Z?

Challenge
(Questions 33–38)

33. **Systematic versus Unsystematic Risk**   Consider the following information on Stocks I and II:

State of Economy	Probability of State of Economy	Rate of Return If State Occurs	
		Stock I	Stock II
Recession	.20	.07	−.27
Normal	.50	.18	.12
Irrational exuberance	.30	.09	.31

The market risk premium is 7.5 percent, and the risk-free rate is 3 percent. Which stock has the most systematic risk? Which one has the most unsystematic risk? Which stock is "riskier"? Explain.

34. SML Suppose you observe the following situation:

Security	Beta	Expected Return
Pete Corp.	1.13	.1165
Repete Co.	.92	.0988

Assume these securities are correctly priced. Based on the CAPM, what is the expected return on the market? What is the risk-free rate?

35. Covariance and Portfolio Standard Deviation There are three securities in the market. The following chart shows their possible payoffs.

State	Probability of Outcome	Return on Security 1	Return on Security 2	Return on Security 3
1	.15	.20	.20	.05
2	.35	.15	.10	.10
3	.35	.10	.15	.15
4	.15	.05	.05	.20

a. What are the expected return and standard deviation of each security?
b. What are the covariances and correlations between the pairs of securities?
c. What are the expected return and standard deviation of a portfolio with half of its funds invested in Security 1 and half in Security 2?
d. What are the expected return and standard deviation of a portfolio with half of its funds invested in Security 1 and half in Security 3?
e. What are the expected return and standard deviation of a portfolio with half of its funds invested in Security 2 and half in Security 3?
f. What do your answers in parts (a), (c), (d), and (e) imply about diversification?

36. SML Suppose you observe the following situation:

State of Economy	Probability of State	Return If State Occurs	
		Stock A	Stock B
Bust	.20	−.09	−.11
Normal	.60	.11	.12
Boom	.20	.39	.27

a. Calculate the expected return on each stock.
b. Assuming the capital asset pricing model holds and Stock A's beta is greater than Stock B's beta by .34, what is the expected market risk premium?

37. Standard Deviation and Beta There are two stocks in the market: Stock A and Stock B. The price of Stock A today is $67. The price of Stock A next year will be $40 if the economy is in a recession, $76 if the economy is normal, and $89 if the economy is expanding. The probabilities of recession, normal times, and expansion are .10, .65, and .25, respectively. Stock A pays no dividends and has a correlation of .73 with the market portfolio. Stock B has a standard deviation of 63 percent, a correlation with the market portfolio of .35, and a correlation with Stock A of .50. The market portfolio has a standard deviation of 20 percent. The risk-free rate is 4 percent and the market risk premium is 7.5 percent. Assume the CAPM holds.

a. If you are a typical, risk-averse investor with a well-diversified portfolio, which stock would you prefer? Why?

b. What are the expected return and standard deviation of a portfolio consisting of 70 percent of Stock A and 30 percent of Stock B?

c. What is the beta of the portfolio in part (b)?

38. **Minimum Variance Portfolio**   Assume Stocks A and B have the following characteristics:

Stock	Expected Return (%)	Standard Deviation (%)
A	13	34
B	11	58

The covariance between the returns on the two stocks is .01.

a. Suppose an investor holds a portfolio consisting of only Stock A and Stock B. Find the portfolio weights, X_A and X_B, such that the variance of his portfolio is minimized. (*Hint:* Remember that the sum of the two weights must equal 1.)

b. What is the expected return on the minimum variance portfolio?

c. If the covariance between the returns on the two stocks is $-.15$, what are the minimum variance weights?

d. What are the variance and standard deviation of the portfolio in part (c)?

WHAT'S ON THE WEB?

1. **Expected Return**   You want to find the expected return for Honeywell using the CAPM. First you need the market risk premium. Go to money.cnn.com and find the current interest rate for three-month Treasury bills. Use the historic market risk premium from Chapter 10 as the market risk premium. Next, go to finance.yahoo.com, enter the ticker symbol HON for Honeywell, and find the beta for Honeywell. What is the expected return for Honeywell using the CAPM? What assumptions have you made to arrive at this number?

2. **Portfolio Beta**   You have decided to invest in an equally weighted portfolio consisting of American Express, Procter & Gamble, Home Depot, and DowDuPont and need to find the beta of your portfolio. Go to finance.yahoo.com and find the beta for each of the companies. What is the beta for your portfolio?

3. **Beta**   Which companies currently have the highest and lowest betas? Go to finance.yahoo.com and find the "Screeners" link. Enter 0 as the maximum beta and search. How many stocks currently have a beta less than or equal to 0? What is the lowest beta? Go back to the stock screener and enter 3 as the minimum. How many stocks have a beta above 3? What stock has the highest beta?

4. **Security Market Line**   Go to finance.yahoo.com and enter the ticker symbol IP for International Paper. Follow the "Statistics" link to get the beta for the company. Next, find the estimated (or "target") price in 12 months according to market analysts. Using the current share price and the mean target price, compute the expected return for this stock. Don't forget to include the expected dividend payments over the next year. Now go to money.cnn.com and find the current interest rate for three-month Treasury bills. Using this information, calculate the expected return on the market using the reward-to-risk ratio. Does this number make sense? Why or why not?

EXCEL MASTER IT! PROBLEM

ExcelMaster
coverage online

www.mhhe.com/RossCore6e

The CAPM is one of the most thoroughly researched models in financial economics. When beta is estimated in practice, a variation of CAPM called the *market model* is often used. To derive the market model, we start with the CAPM:

$$E(R_i) = R_f \times \beta \, [E(R_M) - R_f]$$

Because CAPM is an equation, we can subtract the risk-free rate from both sides, which gives us:

$$E(R_i) - R_f = \beta \, [E(R_M) - R_f]$$

This equation is deterministic; that is, it is exact. In a regression, we realize that there is some indeterminate error. We need to formally recognize this in the equation by adding epsilon, which represents this error:

$$E(R_i) - R_f = \beta \, [E(R_M) - R_f] + \varepsilon$$

Finally, think of the above equation in a regression. Because there is no intercept in the equation, the intercept is zero. However, when we estimate the regression equation, we can add an intercept term, which we will call alpha:

$$E(R_i) - R_f = \alpha_i + \beta \, [E(R_M) - R_f] + \varepsilon$$

This equation is often called the market model, though it is not the only equation with that name, which is a source of confusion. The intercept term is known as Jensen's alpha, and it represents the excess return. If CAPM holds exactly, this intercept should be zero. If you think of alpha in terms of the SML, if the alpha is positive, the stock plots above the SML; if the alpha is negative, the stock plots below the SML.

a. You want to estimate the market model for an individual stock and a mutual fund. First, go to finance.yahoo.com and download the adjusted prices for the last 61 months for an individual stock, a mutual fund, and the S&P 500. Next, go to the Federal Reserve Bank of St. Louis website at www.stlouisfed.org. You should find the FRED® database there. Look for the 1-Month Treasury Constant Maturity Rate and download the data. This series will be the proxy for the risk-free rate. When using this rate, you should be aware that this interest rate is the annualized interest rate. Because we are using monthly stock returns, you will need to adjust the 1-month T-bill rate. For the stock and mutual fund you select, estimate the beta and alpha using the market model. When you estimate the regression model, find the box that says "Residuals" and check this box when you do each regression. Because you are saving the residuals, you may want to save the regression output in a new worksheet.

1. Are the alpha and beta for each regression statistically different from zero?
2. How do you interpret the alpha and beta for the stock and the mutual fund?
3. Which of the two regression estimates has the highest R-squared? Is this what you would have expected? Why?

b. In part (a), you asked Excel to return the residuals of the regression, which is the epsilon in the regression equation. If you remember back to basic statistics, the residuals are the distance from each observation to the regression line. In this context, the residuals are the part of the monthly return that is not explained by the market model estimate. The residuals can be used to calculate the appraisal ratio, which is the alpha divided by the standard deviation of the residuals.

1. What do you think the appraisal ratio is intended to measure?
2. Calculate the appraisal ratios for the stock and the mutual fund. Which has a better appraisal ratio?
3. Often, the appraisal ratio is used to evaluate the performance of mutual fund managers. Why do you think the appraisal ratio is used more often for mutual funds, which are portfolios, than for individual stocks?

A JOB AT EAST COAST YACHTS, PART 2

You are discussing your 401(k) with Dan Ervin when he mentions that Sarah Brown, a representative from Bledsoe Financial Services, is visiting East Coast Yachts today. You decide that you should meet with Sarah, so Dan sets up an appointment for you later in the day.

When you sit down with Sarah, she discusses the various investment options available in the company's 401(k) account. You mention to Sarah that you researched East Coast Yachts before you accepted your new job. You are confident in management's ability to lead the company. Analysis of the company has led to your belief that the company is growing and will achieve a greater market share in the future. You also feel you should support your employer. Given these considerations, along with the fact that you are a conservative investor, you are leaning toward investing 100 percent of your 401(k) account in East Coast Yachts.

Assume the risk-free rate is the historical average risk-free rate (in Chapter 10). The correlation between the bond fund and the large-cap stock fund is .16. (*Note:* The spreadsheet graphing and "Solver" functions may assist you in answering the following questions.)

1. Considering the effects of diversification, how should Sarah respond to the suggestion that you invest 100 percent of your 401(k) account in East Coast Yachts stock?

2. After hearing Sarah's response to investing your 401(k) account entirely in East Coast Yachts stock, she has convinced you that this may not be the best alternative. Because you are a conservative investor, you tell Sarah that a 100 percent investment in the bond fund may be the best alternative. Is it?

3. Using the returns for the Bledsoe Large-Cap Stock Fund and the Bledsoe Bond Fund, graph the opportunity set of feasible portfolios.

4. After examining the opportunity set, you notice that you can invest in a portfolio consisting of the bond fund and the large-cap stock fund that will have exactly the same standard deviation as the bond fund. This portfolio will also have a greater expected return. What are the portfolio weights and expected return of this portfolio?

5. Examining the opportunity set, notice there is a portfolio that has the lowest standard deviation. This is the minimum variance portfolio. What are the portfolio weights, expected return, and standard deviation of this portfolio? Why is the minimum variance portfolio important?

6. A measure of risk-adjusted performance that is often used is the Sharpe ratio. The Sharpe ratio is calculated as the risk premium of an asset divided by its standard deviation. The portfolio with the highest possible Sharpe ratio on the opportunity set is called the Sharpe optimal portfolio. What are the portfolio weights, expected return, and standard deviation of the Sharpe optimal portfolio? How does the Sharpe ratio of this portfolio compare to the Sharpe ratio of the bond fund and the large-cap stock fund? Do you see a connection between the Sharpe optimal portfolio and the CAPM? What is the connection?

Risk, Cost of Capital, and Valuation

OPENING CASE

With over 115,000 employees on five continents, Germany-based BASF is a major international company. It operates in a variety of industries, including agriculture, oil and gas, chemicals, and plastics. In an attempt to increase value, BASF launched Vision 2020, a comprehensive plan that included all functions within the company and challenged and encouraged all employees to act in an entrepreneurial manner. The major financial component of the strategy was that the company expected to earn its weighted average cost of capital, or WACC, plus a premium. So, what exactly is the WACC?

The WACC is the minimum return a company needs to earn to satisfy all of its investors, including stockholders, bondholders, and preferred stockholders. In 2018, for example, BASF pegged its cost of capital at 10 percent, the same rate it used in 2016 and 2017. This target was down from the WACC of 11 percent used from 2012 to 2015. In this chapter, we learn how to compute a firm's cost of capital and find out what it means to the firm and its investors. We will also learn when to use the firm's cost of capital and, perhaps more important, when not to use it.

Please visit us at corecorporatefinance.blogspot.com for the latest developments in the world of corporate finance.

The goal of this chapter is to determine the rate at which cash flows of risky projects are to be discounted. Projects are financed with equity, debt, and other sources, and we must estimate the cost of each of these sources in order to determine the appropriate discount rate. We begin with the cost of equity capital. Because the analysis here builds on beta and the capital asset pricing model, we discuss beta in depth, including its calculation, its intuition, and its determinants. We next discuss the cost of debt and the cost of preferred stock. These costs serve as building blocks for the weighted average cost of capital (WACC), which is used to discount cash flows. We calculate the WACC for a real-world company, Eastman Chemical Co. Finally, we introduce flotation costs.

12.1 THE COST OF EQUITY

Whenever a firm has extra cash, it can take one of two actions. It can pay out the cash directly to its investors. Alternatively, the firm can invest the extra cash in a project, paying out the future cash flows of the project. Which action would the investors prefer? If an investor can reinvest the cash in a financial asset (a stock or bond) with the same risk as that of the project, investors would desire the alternative with the highest expected return. In other words, the project should be undertaken only if its expected return is greater than that of a financial asset of comparable risk. This idea is illustrated in Figure 12.1. Our discussion implies a very simple capital budgeting rule:

> **The discount rate of a project should be the expected return on a financial asset of comparable risk.**

FIGURE 12.1

Choices of a Firm with Extra Cash

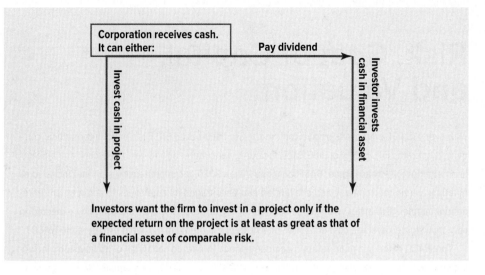

Investors want the firm to invest in a project only if the expected return on the project is at least as great as that of a financial asset of comparable risk.

There are various synonyms for the discount rate. For example, the discount rate is often called the *required return* on the project. This is an appropriate name because the project should be accepted only if the project generates a return above what is required. Alternatively, the discount rate of the project is said to be its *cost of capital.* This name is also appropriate because the project must earn enough to pay its suppliers of capital. Our book will use these three terms—the discount rate, the required return, and the cost of capital—synonymously.

Now imagine that all projects of the firm have the same risk. In that case, one could say that the discount rate is equal to the cost of capital for the firm as a whole. And, if the firm is all equity, the discount rate is also equal to the firm's cost of equity capital.

12.2 ESTIMATING THE COST OF EQUITY WITH THE CAPM

It's one thing to define the cost of equity, as we have done above. It's quite another to estimate it. The problem is that stockholders do not tell the firm what their required returns are. So, what do we do? Luckily, the capital asset pricing model (CAPM) can be used to estimate the required return.

Under the CAPM, the expected return on the stock can be written as:

$$R_S = R_f + \beta \times (R_M - R_f) \tag{12.1}$$

where R_f is the risk-free rate and $R_M - R_f$ is the difference between the expected return on the market portfolio and the riskless rate. Recall that this difference is often called the expected excess market return or market risk premium. Note we have dropped the bar denoting expectations from our expression to simplify the notation, but remember that we are always thinking about expected returns with the CAPM.

The expected return on the stock in Equation 12.1 is based on the stock's risk, as measured by beta. Alternatively, we could say that this expected return is the required return on the stock, based on the stock's risk. Similarly, this expected return can be viewed as the firm's cost of equity.

While academics have long argued for the use of the CAPM in valuation, how prevalent is this approach in practice? One study[1] finds that almost three-fourths of U.S. companies use the CAPM in valuation, indicating that industry has largely adopted the approach of this, and many other, textbooks.

We now have the tools to estimate a firm's cost of equity. To do this, we need to know three things:

1. The risk-free rate, R_f.
2. The market risk premium, $R_M - R_f$.
3. The stock beta, β.

EXAMPLE 12.1

Cost of Equity

Suppose the stock of the Quatram Company, a publisher of college textbooks, has a beta (β) of 1.3. The firm is 100 percent equity financed; that is, it has no debt. Quatram is considering a number of capital budgeting projects that will double its size. Because these new projects are similar to the firm's existing ones, the average beta on the new projects is assumed to be equal to Quatram's existing beta. The risk-free rate is 5 percent. What is the appropriate discount rate for these new projects, assuming a market risk premium of 8.4 percent?

We estimate the cost of equity, R_S, for Quatram as:

$$R_S = .05 + .084 \times 1.3$$
$$= .1592, \text{ or } 15.92\%$$

Two key assumptions were made in this example: (1) The beta risk of the new projects is the same as the risk of the firm and (2) the firm is all equity financed. Given these assumptions, it follows that the cash flows of the new projects should be discounted at the 15.92 percent rate.

EXAMPLE 12.2

Project Evaluation and Beta

Alpha Air Freight is an all-equity firm with a beta of 1.21. The market risk premium is 9.5 percent and the risk-free rate is 5 percent. We can determine the expected return on the common stock of Alpha Air Freight from Equation 12.1. We find that the expected return is:

$$.05 + 1.21 \times .095 = .16495, \text{ or } 16.495\%$$

Because this is the return that shareholders can expect in the financial markets on a stock with a β of 1.21, it is the return they expect on Alpha Air Freight's stock.

Suppose Alpha is evaluating the following independent projects:

Project	Project's Beta (β)	Project's Expected Cash Flows Next Year	Project's Internal Rate of Return	Project's NPV When Cash Flows Are Discounted at 16.495%	Accept or Reject
A	1.21	$140	40%	$20.2	Accept
B	1.21	120	20	3.0	Accept
C	1.21	110	10	−5.6	Reject

(Continued)

---

[1] John R. Graham and Campbell R. Harvey, "The Theory and Practice of Corporate Finance: Evidence from the Field," *Journal of Financial Economics* 60, no. 2–3 (2001), pp. 187–246. Graham and Harvey report in their Table 3 that 73.49 percent of the companies in their sample use the CAPM for capital budgeting.

Each project initially costs $100. All projects are assumed to have the same risk as the firm as a whole. Because the cost of equity is 16.495 percent, projects in an all-equity firm are discounted at this rate. Projects A and B have positive NPVs, and C has a negative NPV. Thus, only A and B will be accepted. This result is illustrated in Figure 12.2.

FIGURE 12.2 Using the Security Market Line to Estimate the Risk-Adjusted Discount Rate for Risky Projects

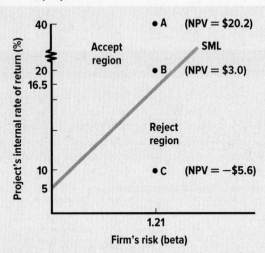

The diagonal line represents the relationship between the cost of equity and the firm's beta. An all-equity firm should accept a project whose internal rate of return is greater than the cost of equity, and should reject a project whose internal rate of return is less than the cost of equity.

In the previous two examples, the values for the risk-free rate, the market risk premium, and the firm's beta were assumed. How would we go about estimating these parameters in practice? We will investigate each of these parameters in turn.

The Risk-Free Rate

While no bond is completely free of the risk of default, Treasury bills and bonds in the United States are about as close to this ideal as possible. No U.S. Treasury instrument has ever defaulted.

However, as we learned from Chapter 5, there is a whole term structure of interest rates, where the yield on any U.S. Treasury instrument is a function of that instrument's maturity. Which maturity should have its yield serve as the risk-free rate? Unfortunately there is no airtight answer to this question. The CAPM is a period-by-period model, so a good case can be made that a short-term rate should be chosen, such as the one-year U.S. Treasury bill rate. For simplicity, we will usually adopt this convention.[2] In practice, firms frequently use a U.S. Treasury rate that matches the maturity of a particular project or investment. When appropriate we will use this approach—particularly for very long-lived investments.

[2] The problem is that projects typically have long lives, so, using the short-term rate approach, the average one-year rate anticipated over the life of the project, rather than today's one-year rate, is potentially more accurate.

How can we estimate this expected one-year rate? We can use the current one-year Treasury bill rate and assume it will be the same over the life of the project. This is our convention. On the other hand, the anticipated average one-year rate can be estimated from the term structure. Table 10.2 shows that, over the period from 1926 to 2018, the average return on 20-year bonds was 5.9%, and the average return on one-year Treasury bills was 3.4%. Thus, the term premium, as it is called, was 5.9% − 3.4% = 2.5%. This positive term premium is not surprising because we know that the term structure of interest rates typically slopes upward. As of one recent date, the yield on a 20-year Treasury bond was about 2.5%. This yield should reflect both the average one-year interest rate over the next 20 years and the term premium. Thus, one can argue that the average one-year interest rate expected over the next 20 years is 2.5% − 2.5% = 0.0%. Alternatively, the CAPM suggests we should use a Treasury security whose maturity matches the investment horizon of investors. Unfortunately, no one agrees on what horizon that is.

Market Risk Premium

METHOD 1: USING HISTORICAL DATA   Much of Chapter 10 was devoted to the calculation of historical rates of return and the market risk premium. The chapter settled on an estimate of 7 percent for the premium, though this number should not be interpreted as definitive. Next we need a risk-free rate. The current one-year Treasury bill is about 2.4 percent.

As a quick example, consider an all-equity company with a beta of 1.5. Given our parameters, its cost of capital would be:

$$.024 + 1.5 \times .07 = .1290, \text{ or } 12.90\%$$

METHOD 2: USING THE DIVIDEND DISCOUNT MODEL (DDM)   Earlier in this chapter, we referenced a study indicating that most corporations use the CAPM for capital budgeting. Does the CAPM imply that risk premiums must be calculated from past returns, as we did above? The answer is no. There is another method, based on the dividend discount model of an earlier chapter, for estimating the risk premium.

In Chapter 6, we pointed out that the price of a share of stock is equal to the present value of all of its future dividends. Furthermore, we noted in that chapter that, if the firm's dividends are expected to grow at a constant rate, g, the price of a share of stock today, P_0, can be written as:

$$P_0 = \frac{D_1}{R - g}$$

where D_1 is the dividend per share to be received next year, R is the discount rate, and g is the constant annual rate of growth in dividends. This equation can be rearranged, yielding:

$$R = \frac{D_1}{P_0} + g$$

In words, the annual return on a stock is the sum of the dividend yield ($= D_1/P_0$) over the next year plus the annual growth rate in dividends.

Just as this formula can be used to estimate the total return on a stock, it can be used to estimate the total return on the market as a whole. The first term on the right-hand side is easy to estimate because a number of print and web services calculate the dividend yield for the market. For example, as this is written, the average dividend yield across all stocks in the Standard & Poor's (S&P) 500 Index was about 2.1 percent. We will use this number in our forecasts.

Next, we need an estimate of the per-share growth rate in dividends across all companies in the market. Security analysts, who are typically employees of investment banking houses, money management firms, and independent research organizations, study individual securities, industries, and the overall stock market. As part of their work, they forecast dividends and earnings, as well as make stock recommendations. For example, suppose the numbers in the Value Line (VL) *Investment Survey* imply a five-year growth rate in dividends for VL's Industrial Composite Index of about 6 percent per year. With a dividend yield of 2.1 percent, the expected return on the market becomes 2.1% + 6% = 8.1%. Given our one-year yield on Treasury bills of 2.4 percent, the market risk premium would be 8.1% −2.4% = 5.7%, a number somewhat below the 7 percent provided by Method 1.

For our firm with a beta of 1.5, the cost of capital becomes:

$$.024 + 1.5 \times .057 = .1095, \text{ or } 10.95\%$$

Of course, Value Line is just one source for forecasts. More likely, a firm would either rely on a consensus of many forecasts or use its own subjective growth estimate.

Academics have, nevertheless, long preferred the historical market risk premium for its objectivity. Because historical returns have been precisely measured, there is little room for subjective judgment. By contrast, estimation of future dividend growth in the DDM is more subjective. However, the subjective nature of the DDM approach is not meant as a criticism. Proponents of using the DDM point out that returns in the long run can only come from the current dividend yield and future dividend growth. Anyone who thinks that long-run stock returns will exceed the sum of these two components is fooling himself.[3] The expression, "You can't squeeze blood out of a turnip," applies here.

12.3 ESTIMATION OF BETA

In the previous section, we assumed that the beta of the company was known. Of course, beta must be estimated in the real world. We pointed out earlier that the beta of a security is the standardized covariance of a security's return with the return on the market portfolio. As we have seen, the formula for Security i is:

$$\text{Beta of Security } i = \frac{\text{Cov}(R_i, R_M)}{\text{Var}(R_M)} = \frac{\sigma_{i,M}}{\sigma_M^2} \qquad [12.2]$$

In words, the beta is the covariance of a security with the market, divided by the variance of the market. Because we calculated both covariance and variance in earlier chapters, calculating beta involves no new material.

Measuring Company Betas

The basic method of measuring company betas is to estimate:

$$\frac{\text{Cov}(R_i, R_M)}{\text{Var}(R_M)}$$

using $t = 1, 2, \ldots, T$ observations.

Problems

1. Betas may vary over time.
2. The sample size may be inadequate.
3. Betas are influenced by changing financial leverage and business risk.

Solutions

1. Problems 1 and 2 can be moderated by more sophisticated statistical techniques.
2. Problem 3 can be lessened by adjusting for changes in business and financial risk.
3. Look at average beta estimates of several comparable firms in the industry.

Real-World Betas

It is instructive to see how betas are determined for real-world companies. Figure 12.3 plots monthly returns for four large firms against monthly returns on the Standard & Poor's (S&P) 500 Index. Using a standard regression technique, we fit a straight line through the data points. The result is called the "characteristic" line for the security. The slope of the characteristic line is beta. Though we have not shown it in the figure, we can also determine the intercept (commonly called alpha) of the characteristic line by regression.

We use five years of monthly data for each plot. Although this choice is arbitrary, it is in line with calculations performed in the real world. Practitioners know that the accuracy of the beta coefficient is suspect when too few observations are used. Conversely, because firms may change their industry over time, observations from the distant past are out of date.

---

[3] For example, see Jay Ritter, "The Biggest Mistakes We Teach," *Journal of Financial Research* 25, no. 2 (June 2002), pp. 159–68; Eugene Fama and Kenneth French, "The Equity Premium," *Journal of Finance* 57, no. 2 (2002), pp. 637–59; and Ravi Jagannathan, Ellen R. McGrattan, and Anna Scherbina, "The Declining U.S. Equity Premium," *Federal Reserve Bank of Minneapolis Quarterly Review* 24, no. 4 (2000), pp. 3–19.

FIGURE 12.3 Plots of Five Years of Monthly Returns (2014–2018) on Four Individual Securities against Five Years of Monthly Returns on the Standard & Poor's (S&P) 500 Index

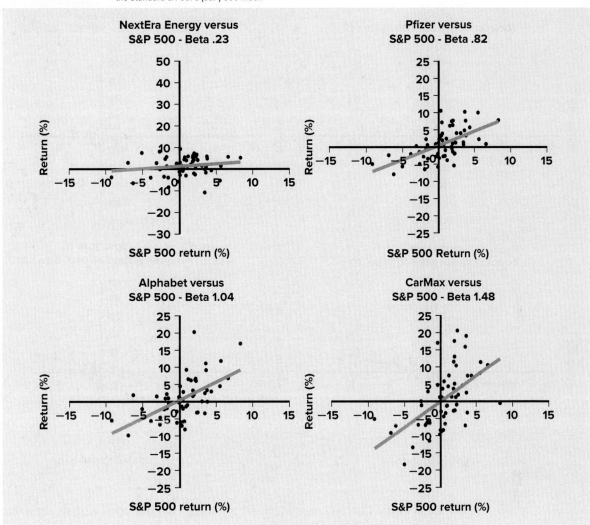

We stated in a previous chapter that the average beta across all stocks in an index is 1. Of course, this need not be true for a subset of the index. For example, of the four securities in Figure 12.3, two have betas above 1 and two have betas below 1. Because beta is a measure of the risk of a single security for someone holding a large, diversified portfolio, our results indicate that NextEra Energy has relatively low risk and CarMax has relatively high risk.

Stability of Beta

We have stated that the beta of a firm is likely to change if the firm changes its industry. It is also interesting to ask the reverse question: Does the beta of a firm stay the same if its industry stays the same?

Take the case of Microsoft, which has remained in the same industry for many decades. Figure 12.4 plots the returns on Microsoft and the returns on the S&P 500 for four successive five-year periods. As can be seen from the figure, Microsoft's beta varies from period to period. However, this movement in beta is probably nothing more than random variation.[4] Thus, for practical purposes, Microsoft's beta has been very stable over the two decades

[4] More precisely, we can say that the beta coefficients over the four periods are not statistically different from each other.

FIGURE 12.4 Plots of Monthly Returns on Microsoft against Returns on the Standard & Poor's 500 Index for Four Consecutive Five-Year Periods

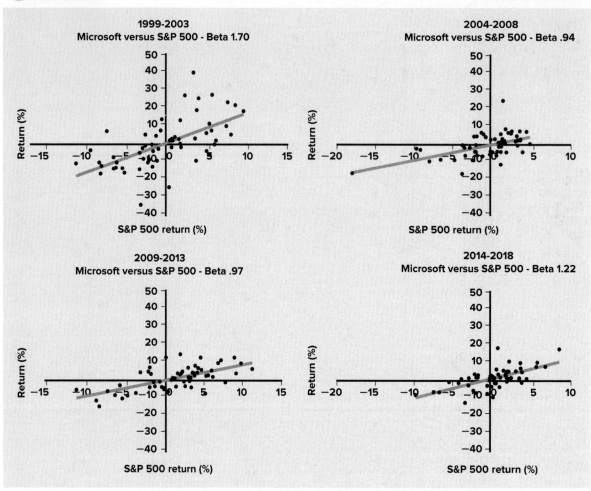

covered in Figure 12.4. Although Microsoft is just one company, most analysts argue that betas are generally stable for firms remaining in the same industry.

However, this is not to say that, as long as a firm stays in the same industry, its beta will never change. Changes in product lines, changes in technology, or changes in the market may affect a firm's beta. Furthermore, as we will show in a later section, an increase in the leverage of a firm (i.e., the amount of debt in its capital structure) will increase the firm's beta.

Using an Industry Beta

Our approach to estimating the beta of a company from its own past data may seem like common sense. However, it is frequently argued that a firm's beta can be better estimated by involving the whole industry. Consider Table 12.1, which shows the betas of some prominent firms in the software industry. The average beta across all of the firms in the table is 1.04. Imagine a financial executive at Fiserv trying to estimate the firm's beta. Because beta estimation is subject to large, random variation in this volatile industry, the executive may be uncomfortable with the estimate of .76. However, the error in beta estimation on a single stock is much higher than the error for a portfolio of securities. Thus, the executive of Fiserv may prefer the average industry beta of 1.04 as the estimate of its own firm's beta.[5]

---

[5] Actually, one should adjust for leverage before averaging betas, though not much is gained unless leverage ratios differ significantly. Adjustment for leverage will be discussed in later chapters.

TABLE 12.1

Betas for Firms in the
Computer Software Industry

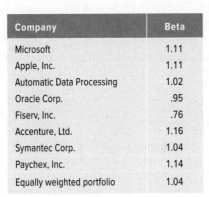

Company	Beta
Microsoft	1.11
Apple, Inc.	1.11
Automatic Data Processing	1.02
Oracle Corp.	.95
Fiserv, Inc.	.76
Accenture, Ltd.	1.16
Symantec Corp.	1.04
Paychex, Inc.	1.14
Equally weighted portfolio	1.04

Assuming a risk-free rate of 2.40 percent and a risk premium of 7 percent, Fiserv might estimate its cost of equity as:

$$.024 + .76 \times .07 = .0772, \text{ or } 7.72\%$$

However, if Fiserv believed the industry beta contained less estimation error, it could estimate its cost of equity as:

$$.024 + 1.04 \times .07 = .0965, \text{ or } 9.65\%$$

The difference is about 2 percent, which could make a significant difference in accepting or rejecting a project. If the difference were small, it would likely not affect the decision.

While there is no formula for selecting the right beta, there is a very simple guideline. If you believe that the operations of a firm are similar to the operations of the rest of the industry, you should use the industry beta to reduce estimation error.[6] However, if an executive believes that the operations of the firm are fundamentally different from those in the rest of the industry, the firm's beta should be used.

When we discussed financial statement analysis in Chapter 3, we noted that a problem frequently comes up in practice—namely, what is the industry? For example, Value Line's *Investment Survey* categorizes Accenture, Ltd., as a computer software company, whereas online financial providers such as www.reuters.com/finance categorize the same company in the business services industry, so more than a little care must be taken in using the industry approach.

12.4 DETERMINANTS OF BETA

The regression analysis approach in Section 12.3 doesn't tell us where beta comes from. Of course, the beta of a stock does not come out of thin air. Rather, it is determined by the characteristics of the firm. We consider three factors: the cyclical nature of revenues, operating leverage, and financial leverage.

Cyclicality of Revenues

The revenues of some firms are quite cyclical. That is, these firms do well in the expansion phase of the business cycle and do poorly in the contraction phase. Empirical evidence suggests high-tech firms, retailers, and automotive firms fluctuate with the business cycle. Firms in industries such as utilities, railroads, food, and airlines are less dependent on the cycle. Because beta measures the responsiveness of a stock's return to the market's return, it is not surprising that highly cyclical stocks have high betas.

[6] As we will see later, an adjustment must be made when the debt level in the industry is different from that of the firm. However, we ignore this adjustment here because firms in the software industry generally have little debt.

It is worthwhile to point out that cyclicality is not the same as variability. For example, a moviemaking firm has highly variable revenues because hits and flops are not easily predicted. However, because the revenues of a studio are more dependent on the quality of its releases than the phase of the business cycle, motion picture companies are not particularly cyclical. In other words, stocks with high standard deviations need not have high betas, a point we have stressed before.

Operating Leverage

We distinguished fixed costs from variable costs in Chapter 9. At that time, we mentioned that fixed costs do not change as quantity changes. Conversely, variable costs increase as the quantity of output rises. Firms often face a trade-off between fixed and variable costs. For example, a firm can build its own factory, incurring a high level of fixed costs in the process. Alternatively, the firm can outsource production to a supplier, typically generating lower fixed costs but higher variable costs. Fixed costs tend to magnify the impact of sales cyclicality. Fixed costs must be paid, even at a low level of sales, leaving the firm with the possibility of large losses. And with fixed costs replacing variable costs, any additional sales generate low marginal costs, leaving the firm with a substantial increase in profit.

Firms with high fixed costs and low variable costs are generally said to have high operating leverage. Conversely, firms with low fixed and high variable costs have low operating leverage. Operating leverage magnifies the effect of the cyclicality of a firm's revenues on beta. That is, a firm with a given sales cyclicality will increase its beta if fixed costs replace variable costs in its production process.

Financial Leverage and Beta

As suggested by their names, operating leverage and financial leverage are analogous concepts. Operating leverage refers to the firm's fixed costs of production. Financial leverage is the extent to which a firm relies on debt, and a levered firm is a firm with some debt in its capital structure. Because a levered firm must make interest payments regardless of the firm's sales, financial leverage refers to the firm's fixed costs of finance.

Just as an increase in operating leverage increases beta, an increase in financial leverage (i.e., an increase in debt) increases beta. To see this point, consider a firm with some debt and some equity in its capital structure. Further, imagine an individual who owns all the firm's debt and all its equity. In other words, this individual owns the entire firm. What is the beta of her portfolio of the firm's debt and equity?

As with any portfolio, the beta of this portfolio is a weighted average of the betas of the individual items in the portfolio. Let B stand for the market value of the firm's debt and S stand for the market value of the firm's equity. We have:

$$\beta_{Portfolio} = \beta_{Asset} = \frac{S}{B + S} \times \beta_{Equity} + \frac{B}{B + S} \times \beta_{Debt} \qquad [12.3]$$

where β_{Equity} is the beta of the stock of the levered firm. Notice that the beta of debt, β_{Debt}, is multiplied by $B/(B + S)$, the percentage of debt in the capital structure. Similarly, the beta of equity is multiplied by the percentage of equity in the capital structure. Because the portfolio contains both the debt of the firm and the equity of the firm, the beta of the portfolio can be thought of as the beta of the common stock had the firm been all equity. In practice, this beta is called the asset beta because its value is dependent only on the assets of the firm.

The beta of debt is very low in practice. If we make the common assumption that the beta of debt is zero, we have:

$$\beta_{Asset} = \frac{S}{B + S} \times \beta_{Equity} \qquad [12.4]$$

Because $S/(B + S)$ must be below 1 for a levered firm, it follows that $\beta_{Asset} < \beta_{Equity}$. Rearranging this equation, we have:

$$\beta_{Equity} = \beta_{Asset}\left(1 + \frac{B}{S}\right)$$

The equity beta will always be greater than the asset beta with financial leverage (assuming the asset beta is positive).[7] In other words, the equity beta of a levered firm will always be greater than the equity beta of an otherwise identical all-equity firm.

Which beta does regression analysis estimate, the asset beta or the equity beta? Regression, as performed in Section 12.3 and also in the real world, provides us with an equity beta because the technique uses stock returns as inputs. We must transform this equity beta using Equation 12.4 to arrive at the asset beta. (Of course, the two betas are the same for an all-equity firm.)

EXAMPLE 12.3

Asset versus Equity Betas

Consider a tree-growing company, Rapid Cedars, Inc., which is currently all equity and has a beta of .8. The firm has decided to move to a capital structure of one part debt to two parts equity. Because the firm is staying in the same industry, its asset beta should remain at .8. However, assuming a zero beta for its debt, its equity beta would become:

$$\beta_{Equity} = \beta_{Asset}\left(1 + \frac{B}{S}\right)$$

$$1.2 = .8\left(1 + \frac{1}{2}\right)$$

If the firm had one part debt to one part equity in its capital structure, its equity beta would be:

$$1.6 = .8\,(1 + 1)$$

However, as long as it stayed in the same industry, its asset beta would remain at .8. The effect of leverage, then, is to increase the equity beta.

12.5 DIVIDEND DISCOUNT MODEL

In Section 12.2, we showed how the CAPM could be used to determine a firm's cost of equity. Among other inputs, we needed an estimate of the market risk premium. One approach used the dividend discount model (DDM) to forecast the expected return on the market as a whole, leading to an estimate of this risk premium. We now use the DDM to estimate the expected return on an individual stock directly.

Our discussion in Section 12.2 on the DDM led to the following formula:

$$R = \frac{D_1}{P_0} + g$$

where P is the price per share of a stock, D_1 is the dividend per share to be received next year, R is the discount rate, and g is the constant annual growth rate in dividends per share. The equation tells us that the discount rate on a stock is equal to the sum of the stock's

---

[7] It can be shown that the relationship between a firm's asset beta and its equity beta with corporate taxes is:

$$\beta_{Equity} = \beta_{Asset}\left[1 + (1 - T_C)\frac{B}{S}\right]$$

In this expression, T_C is the corporate tax rate. Tax effects are considered in more detail in a later chapter.

dividend yield $(= D_1/P_0)$ and its growth rate of dividends. Thus, in order to apply the DDM to a particular stock, we must estimate both the dividend yield and the growth rate.

The dividend yield is relatively easy to forecast. Security analysts routinely provide forecasts of next year's dividend for many stocks. Alternatively, we can set next year's dividend as the product of last year's dividend and $1 + g$, using approaches to estimate g that we describe below. The price per share of any publicly traded stock can generally be determined from either financial newspapers or the web.

The growth rate of dividends can be estimated in one of three ways. First, we can calculate the firm's historical growth rate in dividends from past data. For some firms, this historical growth rate may be a serviceable, though clearly imperfect, estimate of the future growth rate. Second, in Chapter 6, we argued that the growth rate in dividends can be expressed as:

---

g = Retention ratio × ROE

---

where the retention ratio is the ratio of retained earnings to earnings and ROE stands for return on equity. Return on equity is the ratio of earnings to the last period's accounting book value of the firm's equity. All the variables needed to estimate both the retention ratio and ROE can be found on a firm's income statement and balance sheet. Third, security analysts commonly provide forecasts of future growth. However, analysts' estimates are generally for five-year growth rates in earnings, while the DDM requires long-term growth rates in dividends.

As an example of the third approach, the consensus five-year forecast for annual earnings growth, as recently reported on finance.yahoo.com, was 9.84 percent for Eastman Chemical Co. The company's dividend yield was 3.18 percent, implying an expected rate of return, and therefore a cost of equity, of $3.18\% + 9.84\% = 13.02\%$ for Eastman. We should note that a perpetual growth rate of 9.84 percent is almost certainly too high.

The above discussion shows how one can use the DDM to estimate a firm's cost of equity. How accurate is this approach compared to the CAPM? We examine this question in the section below.

Comparison of DDM and CAPM

Both the dividend discount model and the capital asset pricing model are internally consistent models. Nevertheless, academics have generally favored the CAPM over the DDM. In addition, one study[8] reported that slightly fewer than three-fourths of companies use the CAPM to estimate the cost of equity, while slightly fewer than one-sixth of companies use the dividend discount model to do so. Why has the pendulum swung over to the CAPM? The CAPM has two primary advantages: It explicitly adjusts for risk and it is applicable to firms that pay no dividends or whose dividend growth is difficult to estimate. The primary advantage of the DDM is its simplicity. Unfortunately, the DDM is only useful for firms that pay steady dividends.

While no one, to our knowledge, has done a systematic comparison of the two approaches, the DDM appears to contain more measurement error than does the CAPM. The problem is that one is estimating the growth rate of an individual company in the DDM, and each of our suggested approaches to estimate g is fraught with potential measurement error for single firms.[9]

---

[8] John R. Graham and Campbell R. Harvey, "The Theory and Practice of Corporate Finance: Evidence from the Field," *Journal of Financial Economics* 60, no. 2-3 (2001), pp. 187–243.

[9] Of course, there is more to the story because we have to estimate three parameters for the CAPM (risk-free rate, market risk premium, and beta), each one of which contains error. Beta estimation is generally considered the problem here because we need a beta for each company. However, as mentioned earlier in the chapter, analysts frequently calculate average betas across the different companies in an industry in order to reduce measurement error. The presumption is that the betas of different firms in an industry are similar. By contrast, we should not calculate average values of g across the different firms in an industry. Even though these firms are in the same industry, their growth rates can differ widely.

12.6 COST OF CAPITAL FOR DIVISIONS AND PROJECTS

Previous sections of this chapter all assumed that the risk of a potential project is equal to the risk of the existing firm. How should we estimate the discount rate for a project whose risk differs from that of the firm? The answer is that each project should be discounted at a rate commensurate with its own risk. For example, let's assume that we use the CAPM to determine the discount rate.[10] If a project's beta differs from that of the firm, the project's cash flows should be discounted at a rate commensurate with the project's own beta. This is an important point because firms frequently speak of a *corporate discount rate.* (As mentioned earlier, *required return* and *cost of capital* are frequently used synonymously.) Unless all projects in the corporation are of the same risk, choosing the same discount rate for all projects is incorrect.

The above paragraph considered the discount rates of individual projects. The same message would apply for whole divisions. If a corporation has a number of divisions, each in a different industry, it would be a mistake to assign the same discount rate to each division.

Project Risk

D. D. Ronnelley Co., a publishing firm, is considering a project in computer software. Noting that computer software companies have high betas, the publishing firm views the software venture as more risky than the rest of its business. It should discount the project at a rate commensurate with the risk of software companies. For example, it might use the average beta of a portfolio of publicly traded software firms. Instead, if all projects in D. D. Ronnelley Co. were discounted at the same rate, a bias would result. The firm would accept too many high-risk projects (software ventures) and reject too many low-risk projects (books and magazines). This point is illustrated in Figure 12.5.

FIGURE 12.5 Relationship between the Firm's Cost of Capital and the Security Market Line (SML)

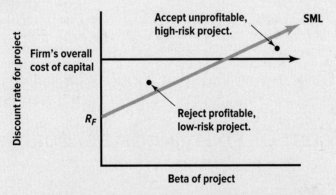

A single cost of capital for all projects in a firm, as indicated by the horizontal line in the figure, may lead to incorrect capital budgeting decisions. Projects with high risk, such as the software venture for D. D. Ronnelley Co., should be discounted at a high rate. By using the firm's cost of capital, the firm is likely to accept too many high-risk projects.

Projects with low risk should be discounted at a low rate. By using the firm's cost of capital, the firm is likely to reject too many low-risk projects.

---

[10] For simplicity, we consider only the CAPM in this section. However, a similar approach would apply if the cost of capital were determined from the DDM.

The D. D. Ronnelley (DDR) example points out that we should discount a project at a rate commensurate with the risk of the project's cash flows. However, practitioners should be concerned with three issues here. First, they must choose the appropriate industry. While this may seem to be an easy task, the problem is that companies often have more than one line of business. Suppose that DDR was considering a project in the movie industry, not in computer software. Their first thought might be to look at the betas of the largest and most important companies in the film industry. The six biggest studios are Warner Brothers, Columbia, Universal, Paramount, 21st Century Fox, and Disney. However, the first two studios are owned by AT&T and Sony, respectively. These parent corporations are diversified, with movies making up only a small portion of total revenues. Comcast, Viacom, and 21st Century Fox, the respective owners of the next three studios, are also heavily involved in news, sports, cable television, and network ownership. And while the parent of the sixth studio has the same Walt Disney name, it too is quite diversified, with holdings in television, radio, theme parks, and cruise ships. With all this diversification, it would likely be quite difficult to determine the beta of a pure moviemaking company from the betas of the six parents. Analysts often talk about identifying *pure plays,* or other companies that specialize only in projects similar to the project your firm is considering. Pure plays are easier to find in some situations than in others.

Second, even if all companies in a particular industry are pure plays, the beta of a new project may be greater than the beta of existing firms because a new project is likely to be particularly responsive to economy-wide movements. For example, a start-up computer venture may fail in a recession while IBM, Microsoft, or Oracle will still be around. Conversely, in an expansion, the venture may grow faster than the older computer firms.

Fortunately, a slight adjustment is all that is needed here. The new venture should be assigned a somewhat higher beta than that of the industry to reflect added risk. The adjustment is necessarily ad hoc, so no formula can be given. Our experience indicates that this approach is in widespread practice today.

Third, a problem arises for the rare project constituting its own industry. For example, consider the firms providing consumer shopping by television. Today, we can obtain a reasonable estimate for the beta of this industry because a few of the firms have publicly traded stock. However, when the ventures began in the 1980s, any beta estimate was suspect. At that time, no one knew whether shopping by TV belonged in the television industry, in the retail industry, or in an entirely new industry.

What beta should be used when the project constitutes its own industry? Earlier in this chapter we mentioned three determinants of beta: Cyclicality of revenues, operating leverage, and financial leverage. Comparing the values of these three determinants for the project in question to the values for other firms should provide at least a general feel for the project's beta.

12.7 COST OF FIXED INCOME SECURITIES

In this section, we examine the cost of both debt and preferred stock. We consider the cost of debt first.

Cost of Debt

The cost of equity is often difficult to estimate. The task generally involves a fair amount of data gathering, and the end result is often measured with error. Fortunately, the cost of debt is much easier to determine; it is the cost of borrowing. The firm can generally obtain this information either by checking the yield on publicly traded bonds or by talking to commercial and investment bankers.

Two years ago, the Ritter Manufacturing Corp. (RMC) issued $100 million of debt with a 7 percent coupon. While the bonds were initially issued at par, rising interest rates over the last two years have caused them to sell at a discount. The yield on the bonds is currently 8 percent. In order to finance expansion, RMC is considering another large issue of bonds. What is the cost of the new debt?

The cost of the new debt should be around 8 percent. If the old bonds are selling at 8 percent, the new debt will not sell at a lower yield. The 7 percent is merely a historical number, often called the *embedded cost* of the debt, with no relevance today.

Alternatively, perhaps a firm is issuing debt for the first time. Here, the firm's investment banker can generally indicate to the firm's managers what the yield on the prospective bonds will be. That yield can be used as an estimate of the cost of debt.[11] Or perhaps the company will take out a loan with a commercial bank. Again, the borrowing rate on the prospective loan is the cost of debt.

There is only one complication that needs to be discussed. We have ignored taxes so far, obviously an assumption at odds with reality. Under U.S. tax law, interest payments are tax deductible. Consider the following example where two firms, Unlevered Corp. and Levered Corp., differ only in debt. Unlevered Corp. has no debt and Levered Corp. has $100 of debt with an interest rate of 10 percent.

Unlevered Corp.		Levered Corp.	
Revenue	$180.0	Revenue	$180
Expenses	70.0	Expenses	70
Pretax earnings	$110.0	Earnings before interest and taxes	$110
Taxes (21% rate)	23.1	Interest (10% on $100 borrowed)	10
Aftertax earnings	$ 86.9	Pretax earnings	$100
		Taxes (21% rate)	21
		Aftertax earnings	$ 79

While the Levered Corp. must pay $10 of interest per year, its aftertax earnings are only $7.9 (= $86.9 − 79) less than those of the Unlevered Corp. Why? Because the interest payments are tax deductible. That is, while Levered Corp.'s pretax earnings are $10 (= $110 − 100) less than those of Unlevered Corp., Levered Corp. pays $2.1 (= $23.1 − 21) less in taxes than does Unlevered Corp.

The $7.9 reduction of aftertax earnings is 7.9 percent of the $100 that Levered Corp. borrowed. Thus, the aftertax cost of debt is 7.9 percent. In general, the aftertax cost of debt can be written as:

$$\text{Aftertax cost of debt} = (1 - T_C) \times \text{Borrowing rate}$$
$$.079, \text{ or } 7.9\% = (1 - .21) \times .10$$

Why have we tax-adjusted the cost of debt but not the cost of equity? Because, while firms can deduct their interest payments before paying taxes, dividends are not tax deductible.

Cost of Preferred Stock

The name *preferred stock* is an unfortunate one because preferred stock is probably more similar to bonds than to common stock. Preferred stock pays a constant dividend in perpetuity. Interest payments on bonds are quite similar to dividends on preferred stock, though almost all bonds have a finite maturity. By contrast, dividends on common stock are not constant over time.

---

[11] A caveat is in order here. The current market yield will be higher than the return bondholders can expect to receive because of the possibility of default. For investment grade bonds, the probability of default is negligible. However, for noninvestment grade bonds, the adjustments for the probability of default could be important.

Suppose a share of the preferred stock of Polytech, Inc., is selling at $17.16 and pays a dividend of $1.50 per year. Because preferred stocks are perpetuities, they should be priced using the perpetuity formula, $PV = C/R_P$, where PV is the present value, or price; C is the cash to be received each year; and R_P is the yield, or rate of return. Rearranging, we have:

$$R_P = C/PV$$

For this preferred issue, the rate of return is .087, or 8.7% (= $1.50/$17.16). The cost of preferred stock is this rate of return.

Why don't we tax-adjust the cost of preferred stock the way we did the cost of debt? We don't tax-adjust here because dividend payments on preferred stock are not tax deductible.

12.8 THE WEIGHTED AVERAGE COST OF CAPITAL

Sections 12.1 and 12.2 showed how to estimate the discount rate when a project is all equity financed. In this section, we discuss an adjustment when the project is financed with both debt and equity.

Suppose a firm uses both debt and equity to finance its investments. If the firm pays R_B for its debt financing and R_S for its equity, what is the overall, or average, cost of its capital? The cost of equity is R_S, as discussed in earlier sections. The cost of debt is the firm's borrowing rate, R_B, which we can often observe by looking at the yield to maturity on the firm's debt. If a firm uses both debt and equity, the cost of capital is a weighted average of each. This works out to be:

$$\frac{S}{S+B} \times R_S + \frac{B}{S+B} \times R_B$$

The weights in the formula are, respectively, the proportion of total value represented by equity:

$$\frac{S}{S+B}$$

and the proportion of total value represented by debt:

$$\frac{B}{S+B}$$

This is only natural. If the firm had issued no debt and was therefore an all-equity firm, its average cost of capital would equal its cost of equity, R_S. At the other extreme, if the firm had issued so much debt that its equity was valueless, it would be an all-debt firm, and its average cost of capital would be its cost of debt, R_B.

Interest is tax deductible at the corporate level, as stated in the previous section. The aftertax cost of debt is:

$$\text{Cost of debt (after corporate tax)} = R_B \times (1 - T_C)$$

where T_C is the corporation's tax rate.

Assembling these results, we get the average cost of capital (after tax) for the firm.[12]

$$\text{Average cost of capital} = \frac{S}{S+B} \times R_s + \frac{B}{S+B} \times R_B \times (1 - T_C) \qquad [12.5]$$

Because the average cost of capital weighs the cost of equity and the cost of debt, it is usually referred to as the weighted average cost of capital, or WACC, and from now on we will use this term.

EXAMPLE 12.5

WACC

Consider a firm whose debt has a market value of $40 million and whose stock has a market value of $60 million (3 million outstanding shares of stock, each selling for $20 per share). The firm pays a 5 percent rate of interest on its new debt and has a beta of 1.41. The corporate tax rate is 21 percent. Assume that the security market line (SML) holds, the risk premium on the market is 9.5 percent, and the current Treasury bill rate is 1 percent. What is this firm's WACC?

To compute the WACC using Equation 12.5, we must know (1) the aftertax cost of debt, $R_B \times (1 - T_C)$; (2) the cost of equity, R_S; and (3) the proportions of debt and equity used by the firm. These three values are determined next:

1. The pretax cost of debt is 5 percent, implying an aftertax cost of 3.95 percent $[= 5\% \times (1 - .21)]$.
2. We calculate the cost of equity capital by using the SML:

$$\begin{aligned}R_S &= R_f + \beta \times [R_M - R_f] \\ &= .01 + 1.41 \times .095 \\ &= .1440, \text{ or } 14.40\%\end{aligned}$$

3. We compute the proportions of debt and equity from the market values of debt and equity. Because the market value of the firm is $100 million (= $40 million + 60 million), the proportions of debt and equity are 40 and 60 percent, respectively.

The cost of equity, R_S, is 14.40 percent, and the aftertax cost of debt, $R_B \times (1 - T_C)$, is 3.95 percent. B is $40 million and S is $60 million. Therefore:

$$\begin{aligned}\text{WACC} &= \frac{S}{B+S} \times R_S + \frac{B}{B+S} \times R_B \times (1 - T_C) \\ &= \left(\frac{60}{100} \times .1440\%\right) + \left(\frac{40}{100} \times .0395\%\right) = .1022, \text{ or } 10.22\%\end{aligned}$$

The above calculations are presented in table form below:

(1) Financing Components	(2) Market Values	(3) Weight	(4) Cost of Capital (After Corporate Tax)	(5) Weighted Cost of Capital
Debt	$ 40,000,000	.40	$.05 \times (1 - .21) = .0395$, or 3.95%	1.58%
Equity	60,000,000	.60	$.01 + 1.41 \times .095 = .1440$, or 14.40%	8.64
	$100,000,000	1.00		10.22%

---

[12] For simplicity, Equation 12.5 ignores preferred stock financing. With the addition of preferred stock, the formula becomes:

$$\begin{aligned}\text{Average cost of captial} &= \frac{S}{S+B+P} \times R_S + \frac{B}{S+B+P} + R_S \times (1 - T_C) \\ &\quad + \frac{P}{S+B+P} \times R_p\end{aligned}$$

where R_P is the cost of preferred stock.

The weights used in the previous example are market value weights. Market value weights are more appropriate than book value weights because the market values of the securities are closer to the actual dollars that would be received from their sale. In fact, it is better to think in terms of target market weights. These are the market weights expected to prevail over the life of the firm or project.

12.9 VALUATION WITH THE WACC

Now we are in a position to use the weighted average cost of capital, WACC, to value both projects and entire firms. Our interpretation of WACC is that it is the overall expected return the firm must earn on its existing assets to maintain its value. The WACC reflects the risk and the capital structure of the firm's existing assets. As a result, the WACC is an appropriate discount rate for the firm or for a project that is a replica of the firm.

Project Evaluation and the WACC

When valuing a project, we start by determining the correct discount rate and use discounted cash flow to determine NPV.

Suppose a firm has both a current and a target debt-equity ratio of .6, a cost of debt of 5.15 percent, and a cost of equity of 10 percent. The corporate tax rate is 21 percent. What is the firm's weighted average cost of capital?

Our first step calls for transforming the debt-equity (B/S) ratio to a debt-value ratio. A B/S ratio of .6 implies 6 parts debt for 10 parts equity. Because value is equal to the sum of the debt plus the equity, the debt-value ratio is $6/(6 + 10) = .375$. Similarly, the equity-value ratio is $10/(6 + 10) = .625$. The WACC will then be:

$$\text{WACC} = \frac{S}{S + B} \times R_S + \frac{B}{S + B} \times R_B \times (1 - T_C)$$

$$= .625 \times .10 + .375 \times .0515 \times .79 = .0778, \text{ or } 7.78\%$$

Suppose the firm is considering taking on a warehouse renovation costing $60 million that is expected to yield cost savings of $12 million a year for six years. Using the NPV equation and discounting the six years of expected cash flows from the renovation at the WACC, We have:

$$\text{NPV} = -\$60 + \frac{\$12}{(1 + \text{WACC})} + \cdots + \frac{\$12}{(1 + \text{WACC})^6}$$

$$= -\$60 + \$12 \times \frac{\left[1 - \left(\frac{1}{1.0778}\right)^6\right]}{.0778}$$

$$= -\$60 + \$12 \times 4.6545$$

$$= -\$4.15$$

Should the firm take on the warehouse renovation? The project has a negative NPV using the firm's WACC. This means that the financial markets offer superior investments in the same risk class, namely, the firm's risk class. The answer is clear: The firm should reject the project.

Of course, we are assuming that the project is in the same risk class as the firm.

Firm Valuation with the WACC

When valuing a complete business enterprise, our approach is the same as the one used for individual capital projects like the warehouse renovation, except that we use a horizon, and this complicates the calculations. Specifically, we use the firm's weighted average cost of capital as our discount rate, and we set up the usual discounted cash flow model by forecasting the firm's entire net cash flow (sometimes called distributable cash flow, free cash flow, or total cash flow of the firm) up to a horizon along with a terminal value of the firm:

$$PV_0 = \frac{CF_1}{1 + WACC} + \frac{CF_2}{(1 + WACC)^2} + \frac{CF_3}{(1 + WACC)^3} + \cdots + \frac{CF_T + TV_T}{(1 + WACC)^T}$$

Consistent with the differential growth version of the dividend discount model, the terminal value (TV)[13] is estimated by assuming a constant perpetual growth rate for cash flows beyond the horizon, T, so that:

$$TV_T = \frac{CF_{T+1}}{WACC - g_{CF}} = \frac{CF_T(1 + g_{CF})}{WACC - g_{CF}}$$

where CF is the net cash flows and is equal to earnings before interest and taxes (EBIT), minus taxes, minus capital spending, minus increases in net working capital plus depreciation;[14] g_{CF} is the growth rate of cash flow beyond T; and WACC is the weighted average cost of capital.

Consider the Good Food Corporation, a public company headquartered in Barstow, California, that is currently a leading global food service retailer. It operates about 10,000 restaurants in 100 countries. Good Food serves a value-based menu focused on hamburgers and french fries. The company has $4 billion in market-valued debt and $2 billion in market-valued common stock. Its tax rate is 20 percent. Good Food has estimated its cost of debt as 5 percent and its cost of equity as 10 percent. Its weighted average cost of capital is equal to:

Financial Component	Market Values	Weights	Cost of Capital	Weighted Average
Debt	$4 billion	.6667	5%(1 − .2) = 4%	.6667 × 4%
Equity	2 billion	.3333	10%	.3333 × 10%
	$6 billion			6% = the weighted average cost of capital

Good Food is seeking to grow by acquisition, and the investment bankers of Good Food have identified a potential acquisition candidate, Happy Meals, Inc. Happy Meals is currently a private firm with no publicly tradable common stock but it has the same product mix as Good Food and is a direct competitor to Good Food in many markets. It operates about 4,000 restaurants, mostly in North America and Europe. Happy Meals has $1,318.8 million of debt outstanding with its market value the same as the book value.[15] It has 12.5 million shares outstanding. Because Happy Meals is a private firm, we have no stock market price to rely on for our valuation. Happy Meals expects its EBIT to grow 10 percent a year for the next five years. Increases in net working capital and capital spending are both expected to be 24 percent of EBIT. Depreciation will be 8 percent of EBIT. The perpetual growth rate in cash flow after five years is estimated to be 2 percent.

[13] The terminal date is often referred to as the horizon. In general, we choose a horizon whenever we can assume cash flow grows at a constant rate perpetually thereafter. By using the word *terminal*, we do not rule out the firm continuing to exist. Instead, we are attempting to simplify the cash flow estimation process.

[14] This definition of cash flow is the same one we used to determine the NPV of capital investments in Chapter 8.

[15] Sometimes analysts refer to a firm's net debt, which is the market value of debt minus excess cash. Neither Good Food nor Happy Meals has excess cash.

If Good Food acquires Happy Meals, Good Food analysts estimate the net cash flows from Happy Meals (in $ millions) would be (rounding to one decimal):

Year	1	2	3	4	5
Earnings before interest and taxes (EBIT)	$150	$165	$181.5	$199.7	$219.6
− Taxes (20%)	30	33	36.3	39.9	43.9
= Earnings after taxes	$120	$132	$145.2	$159.7	$175.7
+ Depreciation	12	13.2	14.5	16	17.6
− Capital spending	36	39.6	43.6	47.9	52.7
− Increases in net working capital	36	39.6	43.6	47.9	52.7
= Net cash flows (CF)	$ 60	$ 66.0	$ 72.6	$ 79.9	$ 87.8

We start our calculations by computing a terminal value of Happy Meals as:

$$TV_5 = \frac{\$87.8 \times 1.02}{.06 - .02} = \$2,240.1$$

Next, we compute the present value of Happy Meals to be:

$$PV_0 = \frac{\$60}{1.06} + \frac{\$66}{1.06^2} + \frac{\$72.6}{1.06^3} + \frac{\$79.9}{1.06^4} + \frac{\$87.8}{1.06^5} + \frac{\$2,240.1}{1.06^5} = \$1,979.1$$

The present value of net cash flows in Years 1 to 5 is $305.2, and the value today of the terminal value is:

$$\$2,240.1 \times \left(\frac{1}{1.06}\right)^5 = \$1,673.9$$

so the total value of the company is $305.2 + 1,673.9 = $1,979.1.

To find the value of equity, we subtract the value of debt, which gives us $1,979.1 − 1,318.8 = $660.3. To find the equity value per share, we divide the value of equity by the number of shares outstanding: $660.3/12.5 = $52.83. Good Food will find Happy Meals an attractive acquisition candidate for payments of less than $52.83 per share (the lower the better).

In doing our valuation of Happy Meals, Inc., it is important to remember that we have assumed that Happy Meals is a pure play for Good Food. Our weighted average cost of capital method only works if Happy Meals has the same business risks as Good Food and the debt-equity ratio will remain the same.

The above calculations assume a growing perpetuity after Year 5 (i.e., the horizon). However, we pointed out in Chapter 3 and Chapter 7 that firms as a whole are often valued by multiples. The most common multiple for overall firm valuation is the enterprise value to EBITDA multiple (i.e., EV/EBITDA). For example, the analysts at Good Food might estimate the terminal value of Happy Meals via an EV/EBITDA multiple, rather than a growing perpetuity. To see how this might work, suppose the EV/EBITDA multiple for comparable firms in the food service industry is 10. The EBITDA for Happy Meals in Year 5 will be equal to EBIT + depreciation, or $237.2 (= $219.6 + 17.6). Using the EV/EBITDA multiple of 10, the value of Happy Meals in Year 5 can be estimated as $2,371.8. The present value of Happy Meals using the EV/EBITDA multiple for terminal value would be:

$$PV_0 = \frac{\$60}{1.06} + \frac{\$66}{1.06^2} + \frac{\$72.6}{1.06^3} + \frac{\$79.9}{1.06^4} + \frac{\$87.8}{1.06^5} + \frac{\$2,371.8}{1.06^5} = \$2,077.6$$

The value of the equity of Happy Meals can be estimated as:

PV (of entire firm) less debt = $2,077.6 − 1,318.8 = $758.8

With 12.5 million shares outstanding, the value of a share of equity would be:

$758.8/12.5 = $60.70

Now we have two estimates of the value of a share of equity in Happy Meals. The different estimates reflect the different ways of calculating terminal value. Using the constant growth discounted cash flow method for terminal value, our estimate of the equity value per share of Happy Meals is $52.83, and using the EV/EBITDA comparable firm method, our estimate is $60.70. As mentioned in Chapter 7, there is no perfect method. If the comparable firms were all identical to Happy Meals, perhaps the EV/EBITDA method would be best. Unfortunately firms are not identical. On the other hand, if we were very sure of the terminal date and the growth in subsequent cash flows, perhaps the constant growth method would be best. Both methods are used in practice.

12.10 ESTIMATING EASTMAN CHEMICAL'S COST OF CAPITAL

In our previous sections, we calculated the cost of capital in examples. A nearby *Finance Matters* box shows the cost of capital for petroleum companies. We will now calculate the cost of capital for Eastman Chemical Co., a leading international chemical company and maker of plastics for soft drink containers and other uses. Eastman Chemical was created in 1994 when its former parent company, Eastman Kodak, split off the division as a separate company.

ExcelMaster
coverage online
www.mhhe.com/RossCore6e

Eastman's Cost of Equity

Our first stop for Eastman is finance.yahoo.com (ticker symbol: "EMN"). As of January 2019, some of the relevant data are in the next two tables.

Eastman Chemical Company (EMN)
NYSE - NYSE Delayed Price. Currency in USD

80.86 +2.80 (+3.59%)
At close: January 25 4:02PM EST

Summary   Chart   Conversations   Statistics

Stock Price History

Beta (3Y Monthly)	0.98
52-Week Change [3]	-22.89%
S&P500 52-Week Change [3]	-7.40%
52 Week High [3]	112.45
52 Week Low [3]	67.40
50-Day Moving Average [3]	74.14
200-Day Moving Average [3]	87.50

FINANCE MATTERS

THE COST OF CAPITAL, TEXAS STYLE

We have seen how the WACC is used in the corporate world. It is also used by state governments to value property for tax purposes. Property valuation can be tricky. The value of a home depends on what it could be sold for, which is not too hard to estimate, but how do you value an oil or gas field? For the Texas Comptroller of Public Accounts, the answer is to estimate the present value of the future cash flows of the property. As you know by now, the cost of capital depends on the use of funds, not the source of funds. So, Texas calculates the WACC for companies in the oil industry and adjusts the industry average WACC for company-specific factors. The table below shows the state's calculations for integrated oil companies.

Company Name	Total Capital	Total Equity	Total Convertible Preferred Stock	Total Long-Term Debt	Equity % of Capital	Convertible Preferred Stock % of Capital	Long-Term Debt % of Capital	Beta Factor	After Income Tax Cost of Equity, %	Before Income Tax Cost of Equity, %	Cost Of Convertible Preferred Stock %	Cost of Debt %	Before Income Tax WACC %
Anadarko	$44,019,112,000	$28,472,112,000	$0	$15,547,000,000	64.68	0.000	35.32	1.65	12.88	16.31	0.00	4.53	12.15
Apache	$24,017,914,358	$16,083,914,358	$0	$7,934,000,000	66.97	0.000	33.03	1.55	12.27	15.53	0.00	4.22	11.80
Cabot	$14,391,379,700	$13,173,488,700	$0	$1,217,891,000	91.54	0.000	8.46	1.05	9.22	11.67	0.00	5.57	11.16
Chevron	$272,020,628,983	$238,449,628,983	$0	$33,571,000,000	87.66	0.000	12.34	1.20	10.14	12.83	0.00	2.91	11.61
Cimarex	$13,131,241,322	$11,644,321,322	$0	$1,486,920,000	88.68	0.000	11.32	1.40	11.36	14.38	0.00	3.27	13.12
Conoco Phillips	$81,739,410,969	$64,611,410,969	$0	$17,128,000,000	79.05	0.000	20.95	1.40	11.36	14.38	0.00	3.78	12.16
Devon	$32,026,000,000	$21,735,000,000	$0	$10,291,000,000	67.87	0.000	32.13	1.80	13.80	17.46	0.00	3.98	13.13
Encana	$17,168,423,000	$12,971,423,000	$0	$4,197,000,000	75.55	0.000	24.45	1.70	13.19	16.69	0.00	4.59	13.73
Energen	$6,374,933,370	$5,592,072,370	$0	$782,861,000	87.72	0.000	12.28	1.70	13.19	16.69	0.00	4.88	15.24
EOG	$68,454,268,243	$62,423,432,243	$0	$6,030,836,000	91.19	0.000	8.81	1.45	11.66	14.76	0.00	3.26	13.75
Exxon Mobil	$378,955,960,000	$354,549,960,000	$0	$24,406,000,000	93.56	0.000	6.44	0.95	8.61	10.90	0.00	3.15	10.40
Hess	$21,398,595,104	$14,955,595,104	$46,000,000	$6,397,000,000	69.89	0.002	29.89	1.65	12.88	16.31	8.00	5.17	12.96
Marathon	$19,884,500,000	$14,390,500,000	$0	$5,494,000,000	72.37	0.000	27.63	1.90	14.41	18.24	0.00	4.20	14.36
Murphy	$8,264,907,707	$5,358,387,707	$0	$2,906,520,000	64.83	0.000	35.17	1.65	12.88	16.31	0.00	4.50	12.15
Noble	$21,023,329,846	$14,277,329,846	$0	$6,746,000,000	67.91	0.000	32.09	1.50	11.97	15.15	0.00	4.42	11.70
Occidental	$65,685,598,354	$56,357,598,354	$0	$9,328,000,000	85.80	0.000	14.20	1.15	9.83	12.45	0.00	3.07	11.11
Pioneer	$31,700,101,411	$29,417,101,411	$0	$2,283,000,000	92.80	0.000	7.20	1.45	11.66	14.76	0.00	3.59	13.96
TOTAL	$1,120,256,304,368	$964,463,276,368	$46,000,000	$155,747,028,000	1348.06	0.002	351.73	25.15	201.30	254.81	8.00	69.09	214.48
ENTRIES					17	1	17	17	17	17	1	17	17
AVERAGE					79.30	0.002	20.69	1.48	11.84	14.99	8.00	4.06	12.62
STANDARD DEVIATION					10.99	0.001	10.98	0.27	1.62	2.06	1.94	0.78	1.31

As you can see, the WACC numbers for the companies are similar. ExxonMobil has the lowest WACC at 10.40 percent and Energen has the highest at 15.24 percent, but most other companies are in the 11 to 13 percent range. The average WACC for a company in this industry is 12.62 percent, with a standard deviation of 1.31 percent. When Texas uses this calculation, a 2 percent adjustment factor is added, plus any property-specific risk adjustment. The range used by the state for 2018 was 14.62 percent to 20.81 percent, before any property-specific factors.

Notice that the Texas Comptroller of Public Accounts calculated these numbers on a pretax, rather than aftertax, basis. In other words, the state did not account for the tax deductibility of interest payments in this calculation. The reason is that the state adjusts the cost of capital for taxes on a company-by-company basis.

The market capitalization of EMN's equity, which is share price times the number of shares outstanding, is $11.324 billion.

To estimate Eastman's cost of equity, we will assume a market risk premium of 7 percent and a risk-free rate of 2.40 percent. Eastman's beta on finance.yahoo.com is .98.

Using Eastman's beta in the CAPM to estimate the cost of equity,[16] we find:

$$R_S = .024 + .98 \times .07 = .0926, \text{ or } 9.26\%$$

Eastman's Cost of Debt   Eastman has 12 long-term bond issues that account for essentially all of its long-term debt. To calculate the cost of debt, we will have to combine these 12 issues and compute a weighted average. We went to finra-markets.morningstar.com/BondCenter/Default.jsp to find quotes on the bonds. We should note here that finding the yield to maturity for all of a company's outstanding bond issues on a single day is unusual. In our previous discussion on bonds, we found that the bond market is not as liquid as the stock market; on many days, individual bond issues may not trade. To find the book value of the bonds, we go to www.sec.gov and find the most recent 10-Q (or 10-K) report. The basic information is as follows:

Coupon Rate	Maturity	Book Value (Face Value, in $ millions)	Price (% of Par)	Yield to Maturity
5.50%	2019	$250	102.252%	3.25%
2.70	2020	798	99.908	2.80
4.50	2021	185	102.269	3.13
3.60	2022	739	100.550	3.42
1.50	2023	865	90.737	3.79
7.25	2024	198	113.898	4.15
7.625	2024	43	116.540	4.45
3.80	2025	688	97.750	4.22
1.875	2026	572	83.479	4.52
7.60	2027	195	118.411	4.81
4.80	2042	493	94.790	5.19
4.65	2044	872	92.964	5.15

To calculate the weighted average cost of debt, we take the percentage of the total debt represented by each issue and multiply by the yield on the issue. We then add to get the overall weighted average debt cost. We use both book values and market values here for comparison. The results of the calculations are as follows:

Coupon Rate	Book Value (Face Value, in $ millions)	Percentage of Total	Market Value (in $ millions)	Percentage of Total	Yield to Maturity	Book Values	Market Values
5.50%	$ 250	.04	$ 255.63	.04	3.25%	.14%	.15%
2.70	798	.14	797.27	.14	2.80	.38	.39
4.50	185	.03	189.20	.03	3.13	.10	.10
3.60	739	.13	743.06	.13	3.42	.43	.45
1.50	865	.15	784.88	.14	3.79	.56	.52
7.25	198	.03	225.52	.04	4.15	.14	.16
7.625	43	.01	50.11	.01	4.45	.03	.04
3.80	688	.12	672.52	.12	4.22	.49	.50
1.875	572	.10	477.50	.08	4.52	.44	.38
7.60	195	.03	230.90	.04	4.81	.16	.19
4.80	493	.08	467.31	.08	5.19	.43	.42
4.65	872	.15	810.65	.14	5.15	.76	.73
Total	$5,898	1.00	$5,704.55	1.00		4.05%	4.04%

[16] Alternatively, one might use an average beta across all companies in the chemical industry, after properly adjusting for leverage. Some argue this averaging approach provides more accuracy because errors in beta estimation for a single firm are reduced.

As these calculations show, Eastman's cost of debt is 4.05 percent on a book value basis and 4.04 percent on a market value basis. Thus, for Eastman, whether market values or book values are used makes little difference. The reason is that the market values and book values are similar. This will often be the case and explains why companies frequently use book values for debt in WACC calculations. We will, however, use market values in our calculations because the market reflects current values.

Eastman's WACC   We now have the various pieces necessary to calculate Eastman's WACC. First, we need to calculate the capital structure weights. The market values of Eastman's debt and equity are $5.705 billion and $11.324 billion, respectively. The total value of the firm is $17.028 billion, implying that the debt and equity weights are $5.705/$17.028 = .335 and $11.324/$17.028 = .665, respectively. Assuming a tax rate of 21 percent, Eastman's WACC is:

$$\text{WACC} = .335 \times .0404 \times (1 - .21) + .665 \times .0926 = .0723, \text{ or } 7.23\%$$

12.11 FLOTATION COSTS AND THE WEIGHTED AVERAGE COST OF CAPITAL

So far, we have not included issue costs in our discussion of the weighted average cost of capital. When projects are funded by stocks and bonds, the firm will incur these costs, which are commonly called *flotation costs.*

Sometimes it is suggested that the firm's WACC should be adjusted upward to reflect flotation costs. This is really not the best approach because the required return on an investment depends on the risk of the investment, not the source of the funds. This is not to say that flotation costs should be ignored. Because these costs arise as a consequence of the decision to undertake a project, they are relevant cash flows. We therefore briefly discuss how to include them in project analysis.

The Basic Approach

We start with a simple case. The Spatt Company, an all-equity firm, has a cost of equity of 20 percent. Because this firm is 100 percent equity, its WACC and its cost of equity are the same. Spatt is contemplating a large-scale $100 million expansion of its existing operations. The expansion would be funded by selling new stock.

Based on conversations with its investment banker, Spatt believes its flotation costs will run 10 percent of the amount issued. This means that Spatt's proceeds from the equity sale will be only 90 percent of the amount sold. When flotation costs are considered, what is the cost of the expansion?

Spatt needs to sell enough equity to raise $100 million after covering the flotation costs. In other words:

$$\$100 \text{ million} = (1 - .10) \times \text{Amount raised}$$
$$\text{Amount raised} = \$100 \text{ million}/.90 = \$111.11 \text{ million}$$

Spatt's flotation costs are thus $11.11 million and the true cost of the expansion is $111.11 million including flotation costs.

Things are only slightly more complicated if the firm uses both debt and equity. Suppose Spatt's target capital structure is 60 percent equity, 40 percent debt. The flotation costs associated with equity are still 10 percent, but the flotation costs for debt are less—say 5 percent.

Earlier, when we had different capital costs for debt and equity, we calculated a weighted average cost of capital using the target capital structure weights. Here, we will do much the same thing. We can calculate an overall, or weighted average, flotation cost, f_A, by multiplying the flotation cost for stock, f_S, by the percentage of stock (S/V), and the flotation cost for bonds, f_B, by the percentage of bonds (B/V), and then adding the two together:

$$f_A = S/V \times f_S + B/V \times f_B \qquad \text{[12.6]}$$
$$= .60 \times .10 + .40 \times .05$$
$$= .08, \text{ or } 8\%$$

The weighted average flotation cost is thus 8 percent. What this tells us is that for every dollar in outside financing needed for new projects, the firm must actually raise $\$1/(1 - .08) =$ $\$1.087$. In our example, the project cost is $\$100$ million when we ignore flotation costs. If we include them, then the true cost is $\$100$ million/$(1 - f_A) = \$100$ million/.92 = $\$108.7$ million.

In taking issue costs into account, the firm must be careful not to use the wrong weights. The firm should use the target weights, even if it can finance the entire cost of the project with either debt or equity. The fact that a firm can finance a specific project with debt or equity is not directly relevant. If a firm has a target debt-equity ratio of 1, for example, but chooses to finance a particular project with all debt, it will have to raise additional equity later on to maintain its target debt-equity ratio. To take this into account, the firm should always use the target weights in calculating the flotation cost.

EXAMPLE 12.6

Calculating the Weighted Average Flotation Cost

The Weinstein Corporation has a target capital structure of 80 percent equity and 20 percent debt. The flotation costs for equity issues are 20 percent of the amount raised; the flotation costs for debt issues are 6 percent. If Weinstein needs $\$65$ million for a new manufacturing facility, what is the true cost including flotation costs?

We first calculate the weighted average flotation cost, f_A:

$$f_A = S/V \times f_S + B/V \times f_B$$
$$= .80 \times .20 + .20 \times .06$$
$$= .172, \text{ or } 17.2\%$$

The weighted average flotation cost is 17.2 percent. The project cost is $\$65$ million without flotation costs. If we include them, then the true cost is $\$65$ million/$(1 - f_A) = \$65$ million/.828 = $\$78.5$ million, again illustrating that flotation costs can be a considerable expense.

Flotation Costs and NPV

To illustrate how flotation costs can be included in an NPV analysis, suppose the Tripleday Printing Company is currently at its target debt-equity ratio of 100 percent. It is considering building a new $\$500,000$ printing plant in Kansas. This new plant is expected to generate aftertax cash flows of $\$73,150$ per year forever. The tax rate is 21 percent. There are two financing options:

1. A $\$500,000$ new issue of common stock: The issuance costs of the new common stock would be about 10 percent of the amount raised. The required return on the company's new equity is 20 percent.

2. A $\$500,000$ issue of 30-year bonds: The issuance costs of the new debt would be 2 percent of the proceeds. The company can raise new debt at 10 percent.

What is the NPV of the new printing plant?

To begin, because printing is the company's main line of business, we will use the company's weighted average cost of capital, WACC, to value the new printing plant:

$$\text{WACC} = S/V \times R_S + B/V \times R_B \times (1 - T_C)$$
$$= .50 \times .20 + .50 \times .10 \times (1 - .21)$$
$$= .1395, \text{ or } 13.95\%$$

Because the cash flows are $73,150 per year forever, the PV of the cash flows at 13.95 percent per year is:

$$PV = \frac{\$73,150}{.1395} = \$524.373$$

If we ignore flotation costs, the NPV is:

$$NPV = \$524.373 - 500,000 = \$24.373$$

With no flotation costs, the project generates an NPV that is greater than zero, so it should be accepted.

What about financing arrangements and issue costs? Because new financing must be raised, the flotation costs are relevant. From the information given, we know that the flotation costs are 2 percent for debt and 10 percent for equity. Because Tripleday uses equal amounts of debt and equity, the weighted average flotation cost, f_A, is:

$$f_A = S/V \times f_S + B/V \times f_B$$
$$= .50 \times .10 + .50 \times .02$$
$$= .06, \text{ or } 6\%$$

Remember, the fact that Tripleday can finance the project with all debt or all equity is irrelevant. Because Tripleday needs $500,000 to fund the new plant, the true cost, once we include flotation costs, is $500,000/(1 - f_A) = \$500,000/.94 = \$531,915$. Because the PV of the cash flows is $524,373, the plant has an NPV of $524,373 - 531,915 = -\$7,542$, so the company should reject the project under these conditions.

Internal Equity and Flotation Costs

Our discussion of flotation costs to this point implicitly assumed that firms always have to raise the capital needed for new investments. In reality, most firms rarely sell equity at all. Instead, their internally generated cash flow is sufficient to cover the equity portion of their capital spending. Only the debt portion must be raised externally.

The use of internal equity doesn't change our approach. However, we now assign a value of zero to the flotation cost of equity because there is no such cost. In our Tripleday example, the weighted average flotation cost would therefore be:

$$f_A = S/V \times f_S + B/V \times f_B$$
$$= .50 \times 0 + .50 \times .02$$
$$= .01, \text{ or } 1\%$$

Notice that whether equity is generated internally or externally makes a big difference because external equity has a relatively high flotation cost.

SUMMARY AND CONCLUSIONS

Earlier chapters on capital budgeting assumed that projects generate riskless cash flows. The appropriate discount rate in that case is the riskless interest rate. Of course, most cash flows from real-world capital budgeting projects are risky. This chapter discussed the discount rate when cash flows are risky.

1. A firm with excess cash can either pay a dividend or make a capital expenditure. Because stockholders can reinvest the dividend in risky financial assets, the expected return on a capital budgeting project should be at least as great as the expected return on a financial asset of comparable risk.

2. The expected return on any asset is dependent on its beta. Thus, we showed how to estimate the beta of a stock. The appropriate procedure employs regression analysis on historical returns.

3. Both beta and covariance measure the responsiveness of a security to movements in the market. Correlation and beta measure different concepts. Beta is the slope of the regression line and correlation is the tightness of fit around the regression line.

4. We considered the case of a project with beta risk equal to that of the firm. If the firm is unlevered, the discount rate on the project is equal to:

$$R_f + \beta \times (R_M - R_f)$$

where R_M is the expected return on the market portfolio and R_f is the risk-free rate. In words, the discount rate on the project is equal to the CAPM's estimate of the expected return on the security.

5. The beta of a company is a function of a number of factors. Perhaps the three most important are:
   - Cyclicality of revenues.
   - Operating leverage.
   - Financial leverage.

6. If the project's beta differs from that of the firm, the discount rate should be based on the project's beta. We can generally estimate the project's beta by determining the average beta of the project's industry.

7. Sometimes we cannot use the average beta of the project's industry as an estimate of the beta of the project. For example, a new project may not fall neatly into any existing industry. In this case, we can estimate the project's beta by considering the project's cyclicality of revenues and its operating leverage. This approach is qualitative.

8. If a firm uses debt, the discount rate to use is the WACC. To calculate WACC, we must estimate the cost of equity and the cost of debt applicable to a project. If the project is similar to the firm, the cost of equity can be estimated using the SML for the firm's equity. Conceptually, a dividend growth model could be used as well, though it is likely to be far less accurate in practice.

9. New projects are often funded by bonds and stock. The costs of issuance, generally called flotation costs, should be included in any NPV analysis.

CONCEPT QUESTIONS

1. **Project Risk**   If you can borrow all the money you need for a project at 6 percent, doesn't it follow that 6 percent is your cost of capital for the project?

2. **WACC and Taxes**   Why do we use an aftertax figure for cost of debt but not for cost of equity?

3. **SML Cost of Equity Estimation**   If you use the stock beta and the security market line to compute the discount rate for a project, what assumptions are you implicitly making?

4. **SML Cost of Equity Estimation**   What are the advantages of using the SML approach to finding the cost of equity? What are the disadvantages? What are the specific pieces of information needed to use this method? Are all of these variables observable, or do they need to be estimated? What are some of the ways in which you could get these estimates?

5. **Cost of Debt Estimation**   How do you determine the appropriate cost of debt for a company? Does it make a difference if the company's debt is privately placed as opposed to being publicly traded? How would you estimate the cost of debt for a firm whose only debt issues are privately held by institutional investors?

6. **Cost of Capital**   Suppose Tom O'Bedlam, president of Bedlam Products, Inc., has hired you to determine the firm's cost of debt and cost of equity.
   a. The stock currently sells for $50 per share, and the dividend per share will probably be about $5. Tom argues, "It will cost us $5 per share to use the stockholders' money this year, so the cost of equity is equal to 10 percent (= $5/$50)." What's wrong with this conclusion?
   b. Based on the most recent financial statements, Bedlam Products' total liabilities are $8 million. Total interest expense for the coming year will be about $1 million. Tom therefore reasons, "We owe $8 million, and we will pay $1 million interest. Therefore, our cost of debt is obviously $1 million/$8 million = .125, or 12.5 percent." What's wrong with this conclusion?

c. Based on his own analysis, Tom is recommending that the company increase its use of equity financing because "debt costs 12.5 percent, but equity only costs 10 percent; thus equity is cheaper." Ignoring all the other issues, what do you think about the conclusion that the cost of equity is less than the cost of debt?

7. **Company Risk versus Project Risk**   Both Dow Chemical Company, a large natural gas user, and Superior Oil, a major natural gas producer, are thinking of investing in natural gas wells near Houston. Both are all equity financed companies. Dow and Superior are looking at identical projects. They've analyzed their respective investments, which would involve a negative cash flow now and positive expected cash flows in the future. These cash flows would be the same for both firms. No debt would be used to finance the projects. Both companies estimate that their projects would have a net present value of $1 million at an 18 percent discount rate and a −$1.1 million NPV at a 22 percent discount rate. Dow has a beta of 1.25, whereas Superior has a beta of .75. The expected risk premium on the market is 8 percent, and risk-free bonds are yielding 12 percent. Should either company proceed? Should both? Explain.

8. **Divisional Cost of Capital**   Under what circumstances would it be appropriate for a firm to use different costs of capital for its different operating divisions? If the overall firm WACC was used as the hurdle rate for all divisions, would the riskier divisions or the more conservative divisions tend to get most of the investment projects? Why? If you were to try to estimate the appropriate cost of capital for different divisions, what problems might you encounter? What are two techniques you could use to develop a rough estimate for each division's cost of capital?

9. **Leverage**   Consider a levered firm's projects that have similar risks to the firm as a whole. Is the discount rate for the projects higher or lower than the rate computed using the security market line? Why?

10. **Beta**   What factors determine the beta of a stock? Define and describe each.

QUESTIONS AND PROBLEMS

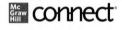

Basic
(Questions 1–15)

1. **Calculating Cost of Equity**   The Angelina Corporation's common stock has a beta of 1.08. If the risk-free rate is 3.7 percent and the expected return on the market is 10 percent, what is the company's cost of equity?

2. **Calculating Cost of Debt**   J&R Renovation, Inc., is trying to determine its cost of debt. The firm has a debt issue outstanding with 14 years to maturity that is quoted at 95 percent of face value. The issue makes semiannual payments and has a coupon rate of 5.9 percent annually. What is the company's pretax cost of debt? If the tax rate is 21 percent, what is the aftertax cost of debt?

3. **Calculating Cost of Debt**   Marysa Corp. issued a 30-year, 5.8 percent semiannual bond seven years ago. The bond currently sells for 97 percent of its face value. The company's tax rate is 21 percent.

a. What is the pretax cost of debt?

b. What is the aftertax cost of debt?

c. Which is more relevant, the pretax or the aftertax cost of debt? Why?

4. **Calculating Cost of Debt**   For the firm in the previous problem, suppose the book value of the debt issue is $65 million. In addition, the company has a second debt issue on the market, a zero coupon bond with 12 years left to maturity; the book value of this issue is $50 million and the bonds sell for 67 percent of par. What is the company's total book value of debt? The total market value? What is your best estimate of the aftertax cost of debt now?

5. **Calculating WACC**   Croft Corporation has a target capital structure of 75 percent common stock and 25 percent debt. Its cost of equity is 11.2 percent, and the cost of debt is 5.8 percent. The tax rate is 21 percent. What is the company's WACC?

6. **Taxes and WACC**   Bento, Inc., has a target debt-equity ratio of .80. Its cost of equity is 12 percent, and its cost of debt is 7 percent. If the tax rate is 21 percent, what is the company's WACC?

7. **Finding the Capital Structure**   Fama's Llamas has a weighted average cost of capital of 8.6 percent. The company's cost of equity is 11.2 percent and its pretax cost of debt is 6.4 percent. The tax rate is 21 percent. What is the company's debt-equity ratio?

8. **Book Value versus Market Value**   Pandora Manufacturing has 5.8 million shares of common stock outstanding. The current share price is $52, and the book value per share is $4. The company also has two bond issues outstanding. The first bond issue has a face value of $50 million, a coupon rate of 6.1 percent, and sells for 108.3 percent of par. The second issue has a face value of $40 million, has a coupon rate of 6.3 percent, and sells for 108.9 percent of par. The first issue matures in 8 years, the second in 27 years.

    a. What are the company's capital structure weights on a book value basis?
    b. What are the company's capital structure weights on a market value basis?
    c. Which are more relevant, the book or market value weights? Why?

9. **Calculating the WACC**   In the previous problem, suppose the company's stock has a beta of 1.20. The risk-free rate is 3.1 percent, and the market risk premium is 6.5 percent. Assume that the overall cost of debt is the weighted average implied by the two outstanding debt issues. Both bonds make semiannual payments. The tax rate is 21 percent. What is the company's WACC?

10. **WACC**   Butler, Inc., has a target debt-equity ratio of .45. Its WACC is 9.6 percent and the tax rate is 21 percent.

    a. If the company's cost of equity is 12.4 percent, what is its pretax cost of debt?
    b. If instead you know that the aftertax cost of debt is 5.7 percent, what is the cost of equity?

11. **Finding the WACC**   Given the following information for Tara Ita Power Co., find the WACC. Assume the company's tax rate is 21 percent.

Debt:	7,000 5 percent coupon bonds outstanding, $1,000 par value, 20 years to maturity, selling for 105 percent of par; the bonds make semiannual payments.
Common stock:	180,000 shares outstanding, selling for $58 per share; the beta is .85.
Market:	6.5 percent market risk premium and 4.3 percent risk-free rate.

12. **Finding the WACC**   Brodsky Metals Corporation has 8.1 million shares of common stock outstanding and 150,000 5.8 percent semiannual bonds outstanding, par value $1,000 each. The common stock currently sells for $41 per share and has a beta of 1.08. The bonds have 20 years to maturity and sell for 104 percent of par. The market risk premium is 7 percent, T-bills are yielding 3.1 percent, and the tax rate is 23 percent.

    a. What is the firm's market value capital structure?
    b. If the company is evaluating a new investment project that has the same risk as the firm's typical project, what rate should the firm use to discount the project's cash flows?

13. **SML and WACC**   An all-equity firm is considering the following projects:

Project	Beta	IRR
W	.85	10.4%
X	.95	10.6
Y	1.20	11.9
Z	1.35	14.1

The T-bill rate is 3.5 percent, and the expected return on the market is 11 percent.

    a. Which projects have a higher expected return than the firm's 11 percent cost of capital?
    b. Which projects should be accepted?
    c. Which projects would be incorrectly accepted or rejected if the firm's overall cost of capital was used as a hurdle rate?

14. Calculating Flotation Costs Suppose your company needs $45 million to build a new assembly line. Your target debt-equity ratio is .45. The flotation cost for new equity is 7 percent, but the flotation cost for debt is only 3 percent. Your boss has decided to fund the project by borrowing money because the flotation costs are lower and the needed funds are relatively small.

   a. What do you think about the rationale behind borrowing the entire amount?

   b. What is your company's weighted average flotation cost, assuming all equity is raised externally?

   c. What is the true cost of building the new assembly line after taking flotation costs into account? Does it matter in this case that the entire amount is being raised from debt?

 15. Calculating Flotation Costs Southern Star Company needs to raise $75 million to start a new project and will raise the money by selling new bonds. The company will generate no internal equity for the foreseeable future. The company has a target capital structure of 65 percent common stock, 5 percent preferred stock, and 30 percent debt. Flotation costs for issuing new common stock are 7 percent; for new preferred stock, 4 percent; and for new debt, 3 percent. What is the initial cost figure the company should use when evaluating its project?

Intermediate
(Questions 16–21)

16. WACC and NPV Pink, Inc., is considering a project that will result in initial aftertax cash savings of $4.1 million at the end of the first year, and these savings will grow at a rate of 3 percent per year indefinitely. The firm has a target debt-equity ratio of .55, a cost of equity of 11.7 percent, and an aftertax cost of debt of 4.9 percent. The cost-saving proposal is somewhat riskier than the usual projects the firm undertakes; management uses the subjective approach and applies an adjustment factor of +2 percent to the cost of capital for such risky projects. Under what circumstances should the company take on the project?

17. Preferred Stock and WACC The IPO Investment Bank has the following financing outstanding. What is the WACC for the company?

Debt:	80,000 bonds with a coupon rate of 5.8 percent and a current price quote of 106.4; the bonds have 20 years to maturity. 230,000 zero coupon bonds with a price quote of 14.3 and 30 years until maturity. Both bonds have a par value of $1,000 and semiannual coupons.
Preferred stock:	150,000 shares of 3.8 percent preferred stock with a current price of $81 and a par value of $100.
Common stock:	2,300,000 shares of common stock; the current price is $68, and the beta of the stock is 1.09.
Market:	The corporate tax rate is 23 percent, the market risk premium is 7 percent, and the risk-free rate is 3.2 percent.

18. Flotation Costs Tube, Inc., recently issued new securities to finance a new TV show. The project cost $29 million, and the company paid $1.57 million in flotation costs. In addition, the equity issued had a flotation cost of 7 percent of the amount raised, whereas the debt issued had a flotation cost of 3 percent of the amount raised. If the company issued new securities in the same proportion as its target capital structure, what is the company's target debt-equity ratio?

19. Calculating the Cost of Equity Benton Industries stock has a beta of 1.15. The company just paid a dividend of $.95, and the dividends are expected to grow at 3.9 percent per year. The expected return on the market is 11 percent, and Treasury bills are yielding 4.3 percent. The current price of the company's stock is $71.

   a. Calculate the cost of equity using the DDM.

   b. Calculate the cost of equity using the SML method.

   c. Why do you think your estimates in (a) and (b) are so different?

20. Firm Valuation Schultz Industries is considering the purchase of Arras Manufacturing. Arras is currently a supplier for Schultz, and the acquisition would allow Schultz to better control its material supply. The current cash flow from assets for Arras is $7.3 million. The cash flows are expected to grow at 9 percent for the next five years before leveling off to 4 percent for the indefinite future. The cost of capital for Schultz and Arras is 12 percent and 10 percent, respectively. Arras currently has 1.9 million shares of stock outstanding and $30 million in debt outstanding. What is the maximum price per share Schultz should pay for Arras?

21. Firm Valuation Happy Times, Inc., wants to expand its party stores into the Southeast. In order to establish an immediate presence in the area, the company is considering the purchase of the privately held Joe's Party Supply. Happy Times currently has debt outstanding with a market value of $95 million and a YTM of 6 percent. The company's market capitalization is $340 million and the required return on equity is 11 percent. Joe's currently has debt outstanding with a market value of $26.5 million. The EBIT for Joe's next year is projected to be $10.3 million. EBIT is expected to grow at 10 percent per year for the next five years before slowing to 3 percent in perpetuity. Net working capital, capital spending, and depreciation as a percentage of EBIT are expected to be 9 percent, 15 percent, and 8 percent, respectively. Joe's has 1.85 million shares outstanding and the tax rate for both companies is 21 percent.

    a. Based on these estimates, what is the maximum share price that Happy Times should be willing to pay for Joe's?

    b. After examining your analysis, the CFO of Happy Times is uncomfortable using the perpetual growth rate in cash flows. Instead, she feels that the terminal value should be estimated using the EV/EBITDA multiple. If the appropriate EV/EBITDA multiple is 8, what is your new estimate of the maximum share price for the purchase?

22. Flotation Costs and NPV Photochronograph Corporation (PC) manufactures time series photographic equipment. It is currently at its target debt-equity ratio of .45 and is considering building a new $40 million manufacturing facility. This new plant is expected to generate aftertax cash flows of $5.4 million a year in perpetuity. The company raises all equity from outside financing. There are three financing options:

Challenge
(Questions 22–24)

    1. *A new issue of common stock:* The flotation costs of the new common stock would be 8 percent of the amount raised. The required return on the company's new equity is 13 percent.

    2. *A new issue of 20-year bonds:* The flotation costs of the new bonds would be 4 percent of the proceeds. If the company issues these new bonds at an annual coupon rate of 7 percent, they will sell at par.

    3. *Increased use of accounts payable financing:* Because this financing is part of the company's ongoing daily business, it has no flotation costs, and the company assigns it a cost that is the same as the overall firm WACC. Management has a target ratio of accounts payable to long-term debt of .20. (Assume there is no difference between the pretax and aftertax accounts payable cost.)

What is the NPV of the new plant? Assume that the company has a 21 percent tax rate.

23. Flotation Costs Trower Corp. has a debt-equity ratio of .65. The company is considering a new plant that will cost $145 million to build. When the company issues new equity, it incurs a flotation cost of 7 percent. The flotation cost on new debt is 2.5 percent. What is the initial cost of the plant if the company raises all equity externally? What if it typically uses 60 percent retained earnings? What if all equity investments are financed through retained earnings?

24. Project Evaluation This is a comprehensive project evaluation problem bringing together much of what you have learned in this and previous chapters. Suppose you have been hired as a financial consultant to Defense Electronics, Inc. (DEI), a large, publicly traded firm that is the market share leader in radar detection systems (RDSs). The company is looking at setting up a manufacturing plant overseas to produce a new line of RDSs. This will be a five-year project. The company bought some land three years ago for $7.5 million in anticipation of using it as a toxic dump site for waste chemicals, but it built a piping system to safely discard the chemicals instead. The land was appraised last week for $7.1 million. In five years, the aftertax value of the land will be $7.4 million, but the company expects to keep the land for a future project. The company wants to build its new manufacturing plant on this land; the plant and equipment will cost $45 million to build. The following market data on DEI's securities is current:

Debt:	280,000 6.4 percent coupon bonds outstanding, 25 years to maturity, selling for 103 percent of par; the bonds have a $1,000 par value each and make semiannual payments.
Common stock:	9,800,000 shares outstanding, selling for $73 per share; the beta is 1.20.
Preferred stock:	450,000 shares of 5.10 percent preferred stock outstanding, selling for $87 per share and having a par value of $100.
Market:	7.5 percent expected market risk premium; 3.2 percent risk-free rate.

DEI uses G.M. Wharton as its lead underwriter. Wharton charges DEI spreads of 6.5 percent on new common stock issues, 4.5 percent on new preferred stock issues, and 3 percent on new debt issues. Wharton has included all direct and indirect issuance costs (along with its profit) in setting these spreads. Wharton has recommended to DEI that it raise the funds needed to build the plant by issuing new shares of common stock. DEI's tax rate is 24 percent. The project requires $1.4 million in initial net working capital investment to get operational. Assume Wharton raises all equity for new projects externally.

a. Calculate the project's initial Time 0 cash flow, taking into account all side effects.

b. The new RDS project is somewhat riskier than a typical project for DEI, primarily because the plant is being located overseas. Management has told you to use an adjustment factor of +2 percent to account for this increased riskiness. Calculate the appropriate discount rate to use when evaluating DEI's project.

c. The manufacturing plant has an eight-year tax life, and DEI uses straight-line depreciation. At the end of the project (that is, the end of Year 5), the plant and equipment can be scrapped for $8.5 million. What is the aftertax salvage value of this plant and equipment?

d. The company will incur $8.1 million in annual fixed costs. The plan is to manufacture 18,000 RDSs per year and sell them at $12,900 per machine; the variable production costs are $11,250 per RDS. What is the annual operating cash flow (OCF) from this project?

e. DEI's comptroller is primarily interested in the impact of DEI's investments on the bottom line of reported accounting statements. What will you tell her is the accounting break-even quantity of RDSs sold for this project?

f. Finally, DEI's president wants you to throw all your calculations, assumptions, and everything else into the report for the chief financial officer; all he wants to know is what the RDS project's internal rate of return (IRR) and net present value (NPV) are. What will you report?

EXCEL MASTER IT! PROBLEM

www.mhhe.com/RossCore6e

You want to calculate the WACC for auto parts retailer AutoZone (AZO). Complete the following steps to construct a spreadsheet that can be updated.

a. Using an input for the ticker symbol, create hyperlinks to the web pages that you will need to find all of the information necessary to calculate the cost of equity. Use a market risk premium of 7 percent when using CAPM.

b. Create hyperlinks to go to the FINRA bond quote website and the SEC EDGAR database and find the information for the company's bonds. Create a table that calculates the cost of debt for the company. Assume the tax rate is 21 percent.

c. Finally, calculate the market value weights for debt and equity. What is the WACC for AutoZone?

THE COST OF CAPITAL FOR SWAN MOTORS

You have recently been hired by Swan Motors, Inc. (SMI), in its relatively new treasury management department. SMI was founded eight years ago by Joe Swan. Joe found a method to manufacture a cheaper battery with much greater energy density than was previously possible, giving a car powered by the battery a range of 700 miles before requiring a charge. The cars manufactured by SMI are midsized and carry a price that allows the company to compete with other mainstream auto manufacturers. The company is privately owned by Joe and his family, and it had sales of $97 million last year.

SMI primarily sells to customers who buy the cars online, although it does have a limited number of company-owned dealerships. The customer selects any customization and makes a deposit of 20 percent of the purchase price. After the order is taken, the car is made to order, typically within 45 days. SMI's growth to date has come from its profits. When the company had sufficient capital, it would expand production. Relatively little formal analysis has been used in its capital budgeting process. Joe has just read about capital budgeting techniques and has come to you for help. For starters, the company has never attempted to determine its cost of capital, and Joe would like you to perform the analysis. Because the company is privately owned, it is difficult to determine the cost of equity for the company. Joe wants you to use the pure play approach to estimate the cost of capital for SMI, and he has chosen Tesla Motors as a representative company. The following questions will lead you through the steps to calculate this estimate.

1. Most publicly traded corporations are required to submit 10-Q (quarterly) and 10-K (annual) reports to the SEC detailing their financial operations over the previous quarter or year, respectively. These corporate filings are available on the SEC website at www.sec.gov. Go to the SEC website and enter "TSLA" for Tesla in the "Search for Company Filings" link. Find the most recent 10-Q or 10-K and download the form. Look on the balance sheet to find the book value of debt and the book value of equity. If you look further down the report, you should find a section titled either "Long-Term Debt" or "Long-Term Debt and Interest Rate Risk Management" that will list a breakdown of Tesla's long-term debt.

2. To estimate the cost of equity for Tesla, go to finance.yahoo.com and enter the ticker symbol "TSLA." Follow the various links to find answers to the following questions: What is the most recent stock price listed for Tesla? What is the market value of equity, or market capitalization? How many shares of stock does Tesla have outstanding? What is the beta for Tesla? Now go back to finance.yahoo.com and follow the "Bonds" link. What is the yield on three-month Treasury bills? Using a 7 percent market risk premium, what is the cost of equity for Tesla using the CAPM?

3. Go to www.reuters.com and find the list of competitors in the industry. Find the beta for each of these competitors, and then calculate the industry average beta. Using the industry average beta, what is the cost of equity? Does it matter if you use the beta for Tesla or the beta for the industry in this case?

4. You now need to calculate the cost of debt for Tesla. Go to http://finra-markets.morningstar.com/BondCenter/Default.jsp, enter Tesla as the company, and find the yield to maturity for each of Tesla's bonds. What is the weighted average cost of debt for Tesla using the book value weights and the market value weights? Does it make a difference in this case if you use book value weights or market value weights?

5. You now have all the necessary information to calculate the weighted average cost of capital for Tesla. Calculate the weighted average cost of capital for Tesla using book value weights and market value weights, assuming Tesla has a 21 percent tax rate. Which cost of capital number is more relevant?

6. You used Tesla as a representative company to estimate the cost of capital for SMI. What are some of the potential problems with this approach in this situation? What improvements might you suggest?

13

Efficient Capital Markets and Behavioral Challenges

The decade of the 2000s proved to be one of the more interesting in stock market history. Following a spectacular rise in the late 1990s, the NASDAQ lost about 40 percent of its value in 2000, followed by another 30 percent in 2001. The ISDEX, an index of internet-related stocks, rose from 100 in January 1996 to 1,100 in February 2000, a gain of about 1,000 percent! It then fell like a rock to 600 by May 2000. The end of the decade saw almost exactly the reverse. From January 2008 through March 9, 2009, the S&P 500 lost about 57 percent of its value. Of course, from that point through February 2011, a period of about 700 days, the S&P 500 doubled in value. This climb was the fastest doubling of the S&P since 1936, when it doubled in just 500 days.

The performance of the NASDAQ in the late 1990s, and particularly the rise and fall of internet stocks, has been described by many as one of the greatest market "bubbles" in history. The argument is that prices were inflated to economically ridiculous levels before investors came to their senses, which then caused the bubble to pop and prices to plunge. Debate over whether the stock market of the late 1990s really was a bubble has generated much controversy. Similarly, the reasons behind the market's collapse in 2008 and its subsequent rebound in 2009 and early 2010 are being hotly debated. In this chapter, we will discuss the competing ideas, present some evidence on both sides, and then examine the implications for financial managers.

Please visit us at corecorporatefinance.blogspot.com for the latest developments in the world of corporate finance.

13.1 A DESCRIPTION OF EFFICIENT CAPITAL MARKETS

If capital markets are efficient, corporate managers cannot create value by fooling investors, and market values reflect underlying intrinsic values. The key to understanding the concept of the efficient market is the relationship between market values and information.

An efficient capital market is one in which stock prices fully reflect available information. To illustrate how an efficient market works, suppose the F-stop Camera Corporation (FCC) is attempting to develop a camera that will double the speed of the auto-focusing system now available. FCC believes this research has a positive NPV.

Now consider a share of stock in FCC. What determines the willingness of investors to hold shares of FCC at a particular price? One important factor is the probability that FCC will be the first company to develop the new auto-focusing system. In an efficient market, we would expect the price of the shares of FCC to increase if this probability increases.

Suppose FCC hires a well-known scientist to develop the new auto-focusing system. In an efficient market, what will happen to FCC's share price when this is announced? If the well-known scientist is paid a salary that fully reflects his or her contribution to the firm, the price of the stock will not necessarily change. Suppose, instead, that hiring the scientist is a positive NPV transaction. In this case, the price of shares in FCC will increase because the firm can pay the scientist a salary below his or her true value to the company.

When will the increase in the price of FCC's shares take place? Assume that the hiring announcement is made in a press release on Wednesday morning. In an efficient market, the price of shares in FCC will immediately adjust to this new information. Investors should not be able to buy the stock on Wednesday afternoon and make a profit on Thursday. This would imply that it took the stock market a day to realize the implication of the FCC press release. The efficient market hypothesis predicts that the price of shares of FCC stock on Wednesday afternoon will already reflect the information contained in the Wednesday morning press release.

The **efficient market hypothesis (EMH)** has implications for investors and for firms:

- Because information is reflected in prices immediately, investors should only expect to obtain a normal rate of return. Awareness of information when it is released does an investor no good. The price adjusts before the investor has time to trade on it.

- Firms should expect to receive fair value for securities that they sell. *Fair* means that the price they receive for the securities they issue is the present value. Thus, valuable financing opportunities that arise from fooling investors are unavailable in efficient capital markets.

Figure 13.1 presents several possible adjustments in stock prices. The solid line represents the path taken by the stock in an efficient market. In this case, the price adjusts immediately to the new information with no further price changes. The dotted line depicts a delayed reaction. Here it takes the market 30 days to fully absorb the information. Finally, the broken line illustrates an overreaction and subsequent correction back

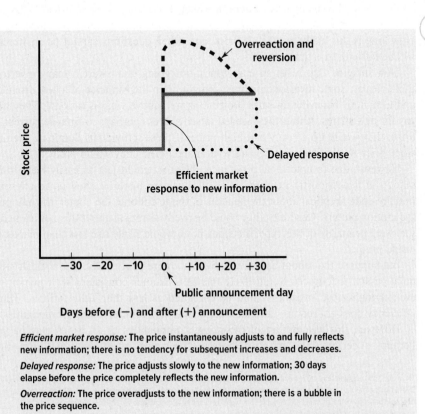

FIGURE 13.1

Reaction of Stock Price to New Information in Efficient and Inefficient Markets

Overreaction and reversion

Delayed response

Efficient market response to new information

Stock price

−30 −20 −10 0 +10 +20 +30

Public announcement day

Days before (−) and after (+) announcement

Efficient market response: The price instantaneously adjusts to and fully reflects new information; there is no tendency for subsequent increases and decreases.

Delayed response: The price adjusts slowly to the new information; 30 days elapse before the price completely reflects the new information.

Overreaction: The price overadjusts to the new information; there is a bubble in the price sequence.

to the true price. The broken line and the dotted line show the paths that the stock price might take in an inefficient market. If the price of the stock were to take several days to adjust, trading profits would be available to investors who suitably timed their purchases and sales.[1]

Foundations of Market Efficiency

Figure 13.1 shows the consequences of market efficiency. But what are the conditions that *cause* market efficiency? Andrei Shleifer argues that there are three conditions, any one of which will lead to efficiency: (1) rationality, (2) independent deviations from rationality, and (3) arbitrage.[2] A discussion of these conditions follows.

RATIONALITY Imagine that all investors are rational. When new information is released in the marketplace, all investors will adjust their estimates of stock prices in a rational way. In our example, investors will use the information in FCC's press release, in conjunction with existing information on the firm, to determine the NPV of FCC's new venture. If the information in the press release implies that the NPV of the venture is $10 million and there are 2 million shares, investors will calculate that the NPV is $5 per share. While FCC's old price might be, say, $40, no one would now transact at that price. Anyone interested in selling would only sell at a price of at least $45 (= $40 + 5). And anyone interested in buying would now be willing to pay up to $45. In other words, the price would rise by $5. And the price would rise immediately because rational investors would see no reason to wait before trading at the new price.

Of course, we all know times when family members, friends, and, yes, even we seem to behave less than perfectly rational. Thus, perhaps it is too much to ask that all investors behave rationally. But the market will still be efficient if the following scenario holds.

INDEPENDENT DEVIATIONS FROM RATIONALITY Suppose that FCC's press release is not all that clear. How many new cameras are likely to be sold? At what price? What is the likely cost per camera? Will other camera companies be able to develop competing products? How long is this likely to take? If these, and other, questions cannot be answered easily, it will be difficult to estimate NPV.

Now imagine that, with so many questions going unanswered, many investors do not think clearly. Some investors might get caught up in the romance of a new product, hoping, and ultimately believing, in sales projections well above what is rational. They would overpay for new shares. And if they needed to sell shares (perhaps to finance current consumption), they would do so only at a high price. If these individuals dominate the market, the stock price would likely rise beyond what market efficiency would predict.

However, due to emotional resistance, investors could just as easily react to new information in a pessimistic manner. After all, business historians tell us that investors were initially quite skeptical about the benefits of the telephone, the copier, the automobile, and the motion picture. Certainly, they could be overly skeptical about this new camera. If investors were primarily of this type, the stock price would likely rise less than market efficiency would predict.

But suppose that about as many individuals were irrationally optimistic as were irrationally pessimistic. Prices would likely rise in a manner consistent with market efficiency, even though most investors would be classified as less than fully rational. Thus, market efficiency does not require rational individuals, only countervailing irrationalities.

However, this assumption of offsetting irrationalities at all times may be unrealistic. Perhaps, at certain times, most investors are swept away by excessive optimism and, at other

---

[1] Now you should understand the following short story. A student was walking down the hall with his finance professor when they both saw a $20 bill on the ground. As the student bent down to pick it up, the professor shook his head slowly and, with a look of disappointment on his face, said patiently to the student, "Don't bother. If it were really there, someone else would have already picked it up."

[2] Andrei Shleifer, *Inefficient Markets: An Introduction to Behavioral Finance* (Oxford: Oxford University Press, 2000).

times, are caught in the throes of extreme pessimism. But even here, there is an assumption that will produce efficiency.

ARBITRAGE   Imagine a world with two types of individuals: the irrational amateurs and the rational professionals. The amateurs get caught up in their emotions, at times believing irrationally that a stock is undervalued and at other times believing the opposite. If the passions of the different amateurs do not cancel each other out, these amateurs, by themselves, would tend to carry stocks either above or below their efficient prices.

Now let's bring in the professionals. Suppose professionals go about their business methodically and rationally. They study companies thoroughly, they evaluate the evidence objectively, they estimate stock prices coldly and clearly, and they act accordingly. If a stock is underpriced, they would buy it. If overpriced, they would sell it. And their confidence would likely be greater than that of the amateurs. While an amateur might risk only a small sum, these professionals might risk large ones, knowing as they do that the stock is mispriced. Furthermore, they would be willing to rearrange their entire portfolio in search of a profit. If they find that General Motors is underpriced, they might sell the Ford stock they own in order to buy GM. *Arbitrage* is the word that comes to mind here because arbitrage generates profit from the simultaneous purchase and sale of different, but substitute, securities. If the arbitrage of professionals dominates the speculation of amateurs, markets will still be efficient.

13.2 THE DIFFERENT TYPES OF EFFICIENCY

In our previous discussion, we assumed that the market responds immediately to all available information. In actuality, certain information may affect stock prices more quickly than other information. To handle differential response rates, researchers separate information into different types. The most common classification system identifies three types: information on past prices, publicly available information, and all information. The effect of these three information sets on prices is examined next.

The Weak Form

Imagine a trading strategy that recommends buying a stock after it has gone up three days in a row and recommends selling a stock after it has gone down three days in a row. This strategy uses information based only on past prices. It does not use any other information, such as earnings, forecasts, merger announcements, or money supply figures. A capital market is said to be *weakly efficient,* or to satisfy weak form efficiency, if it fully incorporates the information in past stock prices. Thus, the above strategy would not be able to generate profits if weak form efficiency holds.

Weak form efficiency is about the weakest type of efficiency that we would expect a financial market to display because historical price information is the easiest kind of information about a stock to acquire. If it were possible to make extraordinary profits by finding patterns in stock price movements, everyone would do it, and any profits would disappear in the scramble.

This effect of competition can be seen in Figure 13.2. Suppose the price of a stock displays a cyclical pattern, as indicated by the wavy curve. Shrewd investors would buy at the low points, forcing those prices up. Conversely, they would sell at the high points, forcing prices down. Via competition, cyclical regularities would be eliminated, leaving only random fluctuations.

The Semistrong and Strong Forms

If weak form efficiency is controversial, even more contentious are the two stronger types of efficiency, semistrong form efficiency and strong form efficiency. A market is semistrong form

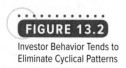

FIGURE 13.2

Investor Behavior Tends to
Eliminate Cyclical Patterns

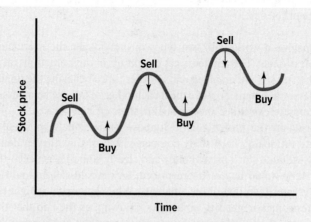

If a stock's price follows a cyclical pattern, the pattern will be quickly
eliminated in an efficient market. A random pattern will emerge as
investors buy at the trough and sell at the peak of a cycle.

efficient if prices reflect (incorporate) all publicly available information, including information such as published accounting statements for the firm as well as historical price information. A market is strong form efficient if prices reflect all information, public or private.

The information set of past prices is a subset of the information set of publicly available
information, which in turn is a subset of all information. This is shown in Figure 13.3. Thus,
strong form efficiency implies semistrong form efficiency, and semistrong form efficiency
implies weak form efficiency. The distinction between semistrong form efficiency and weak
form efficiency is that semistrong form efficiency requires not only that the market be efficient with respect to historical price information, but that all of the information available to
the public be reflected in prices.

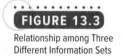

FIGURE 13.3

Relationship among Three
Different Information Sets

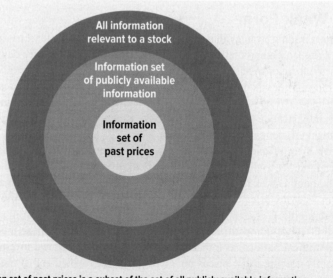

The information set of past prices is a subset of the set of all publicly available information,
which in turn is a subset of all information. If today's price reflects only information on past
prices, the market is weak form efficient. If today's price reflects all publicly available information, the market is semistrong form efficient. If today's price reflects all information, both
public and private, the market is strong form efficient.

Semistrong form efficiency implies weak form efficiency, and strong form efficiency implies
semistrong form efficiency.

To illustrate the different forms of efficiency, imagine an investor who always sold a particular stock after its price had risen. A market that was only weak form efficient and not semistrong form efficient would still prevent such a strategy from generating positive profits. According to weak form efficiency, a recent price rise does not imply that the stock is overvalued.

Now consider a firm reporting increased earnings. An individual might consider investing in the stock after hearing of the news release giving this information. However, if the market is semistrong form efficient, the price should rise immediately upon the news release. Thus, the investor would end up paying the higher price, eliminating all chance for profit.

At the furthest end of the spectrum is strong form efficiency. This form says that anything that is pertinent to the value of the stock and that is known to at least one investor is, in fact, fully incorporated into the stock price. A strict believer in strong form efficiency would deny that an insider who knew whether a company mining operation had struck gold could profit from that information. Such a devotee of the strong form efficient market hypothesis might argue that as soon as the insider tried to trade on his or her information, the market would recognize what was happening, and the price would shoot up before he or she could buy any of the stock. Believers in strong form efficiency argue that there are no secrets, and as soon as the gold is discovered, the secret gets out.

One reason to expect that markets are weak form efficient is that it is so cheap and easy to find patterns in stock prices. Anyone who can program a computer and knows a little bit of statistics can search for such patterns. It stands to reason that if there were such patterns, people would find and exploit them, in the process causing them to disappear.

Semistrong form efficiency, though, implies more sophisticated investors than does weak form efficiency. An investor must be skilled at economics and statistics, and steeped in the idiosyncrasies of individual industries and companies. Furthermore, to acquire and use such skills requires talent, ability, and time. In the jargon of the economist, such an effort is costly and the ability to be successful at it is probably in scarce supply.

As for strong form efficiency, this is farther down the road than semistrong form efficiency. It is difficult to believe that the market is so efficient that someone with valuable inside information cannot prosper from it. And empirical evidence tends to be unfavorable to this form of market efficiency.

Some Common Misconceptions about the Efficient Market Hypothesis

No idea in finance has attracted as much attention as that of efficient markets, and not all of the attention has been flattering. To a certain extent, this is because much of the criticism has been based on a misunderstanding of what the hypothesis does and does not say. We illustrate three misconceptions below.

THE EFFICACY OF DART THROWING   When the notion of market efficiency was first publicized and debated in the popular financial press, it was often characterized by the following quote: ". . . throwing darts at the financial page will produce a portfolio that can be expected to do as well as any managed by professional security analysts."[3,4] This is almost, but not quite, true.

All the efficient market hypothesis really says is that, on average, the manager will not be able to achieve an abnormal or excess return. The excess return is defined with respect

---

[3] Malkiel, Burton G. *A Random Walk Down Wall Street,* 12th ed. (New York: W.W. Norton & Company, 2019).

[4] Older articles often referred to the benchmark of "dart-throwing monkeys." As government involvement in the securities industry grew, the benchmark was often restated as "dart-throwing congressmen."

to some benchmark expected return, such as that from the security market line (SML) of Chapter 11. The investor must still decide how risky a portfolio he or she wants. In addition, a random dart thrower might wind up with all of the darts sticking into one or two high-risk stocks that deal in genetic engineering. Would you really want all of your stock investments in two such stocks?

The failure to understand this has often led to confusion about market efficiency. Sometimes it is wrongly argued that market efficiency means that it does not matter what you do because the efficiency of the market will protect the unwary. However, someone once remarked, "The efficient market protects the sheep from the wolves, but nothing can protect the sheep from themselves."

What efficiency does say is that the price that a firm obtains when it sells a share of its stock is a fair price in the sense that it reflects the value of that stock given the information that is available about it. Shareholders need not worry that they are paying too much for a stock with a low dividend or some other characteristic because the market has already incorporated it into the price. However, investors still have to worry about such things as their level of risk exposure and their degree of diversification.

PRICE FLUCTUATIONS   Much of the public is skeptical of efficiency because stock prices fluctuate from day to day. However, daily price movement is in no way inconsistent with efficiency; a stock in an efficient market adjusts to new information by changing price. A great deal of new information comes into the stock market each day. In fact, the absence of daily price movements in a changing world might suggest an inefficiency.

STOCKHOLDER DISINTEREST   Many laypersons are skeptical that the market price can be efficient if only a fraction of the outstanding shares changes hands on any given day. However, the number of traders in a stock on a given day is generally far less than the number of people following the stock. This is true because an individual will trade only when his appraisal of the value of the stock differs enough from the market price to justify incurring brokerage commissions and other transaction costs. Furthermore, even if the number of traders following a stock is small relative to the number of outstanding shareholders, the stock can be expected to be efficiently priced as long as a number of interested traders use the publicly available information. That is, the stock price can reflect the available information even if many stockholders never follow the stock and are not considering trading in the near future.

13.3 THE EVIDENCE

The evidence on the efficient market hypothesis is extensive, with studies covering the broad categories of weak form, semistrong form, and strong form efficiency. In the first category, we investigate whether stock price changes are random. We review both *event studies* and studies of the performance of mutual funds in the second category. In the third category, we look at the performance of corporate insiders.

The Weak Form

Weak form efficiency implies that a stock's price movement in the past is unrelated to its price movement in the future. The work of Chapter 11 allows us to test this implication. In that chapter, we discussed the concept of correlation between the returns on two different stocks. For example, the correlation between the return on General Motors and the return on Ford is likely to be relatively high because both stocks are in the same industry. Conversely, the correlation between the return on General Motors and the return on the stock of, say, a European fast-food chain is likely to be low.

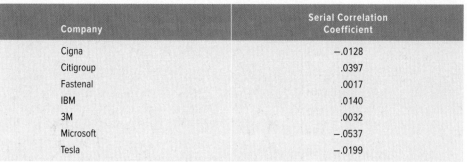

Company	Serial Correlation Coefficient
Cigna	−.0128
Citigroup	.0397
Fastenal	.0017
IBM	.0140
3M	.0032
Microsoft	−.0537
Tesla	−.0199

Fastenal's coefficient of .0017 is slightly positive, implying that a positive return today makes a positive return tomorrow slightly more likely. Cigna's coefficient is negative, implying that a negative return today makes a positive return tomorrow slightly more likely. However, the coefficients are so small relative to estimation error and transaction costs that the results are generally considered to be consistent with efficient capital markets.

Financial economists frequently speak of serial correlation, which involves only one security. This is the correlation between the current return on a security and the return on the same security over a later period. A positive coefficient of serial correlation for a particular stock indicates a tendency toward *continuation*. That is, a higher-than-average return today is likely to be followed by higher-than-average returns in the future. Similarly, a lower-than-average return today is likely to be followed by lower-than-average returns in the future.

A negative coefficient of serial correlation for a particular stock indicates a tendency toward *reversal*. A higher-than-average return today is likely to be followed by lower-than-average returns in the future. Similarly, a lower-than-average return today is likely to be followed by higher-than-average returns in the future. Both significantly positive and significantly negative serial correlation coefficients are indications of market inefficiencies; in either case, returns today can be used to predict future returns.

Serial correlation coefficients for stock returns near zero would be consistent with weak form efficiency. Thus, a current stock return that is higher than average is as likely to be followed by lower-than-average returns as by higher-than-average returns. Similarly, a current stock return that is lower than average is as likely to be followed by higher-than-average returns as by lower-than-average returns.

Table 13.1 shows the serial correlation for daily stock price changes for seven large U.S. companies. These coefficients indicate whether or not there are relationships between yesterday's return and today's return. As can be seen, the correlation coefficients for three of the companies are negative, implying that a higher-than-average return today makes a lower-than-average return tomorrow slightly more likely. Conversely, the correlation coefficients for the other four companies are slightly positive, implying that a higher-than-average return today makes a higher-than-average return tomorrow slightly more likely.

However, because correlation coefficients can, in principle, vary between −1 and 1, the reported coefficients are quite small. In fact, the coefficients are so small relative to both estimation errors and transaction costs that the results are generally considered to be consistent with weak form efficiency.

The weak form of the efficient market hypothesis has been tested in many other ways as well. Our view of the literature is that the evidence, taken as a whole, is consistent with weak form efficiency.

This finding raises an interesting thought: If price changes are truly random, why do so many believe that prices follow patterns? The work of both psychologists and statisticians suggests that most people do not know what randomness looks like. For example, consider Figure 13.4. The top graph was generated by a computer using random numbers. Yet, we have found that people examining the chart generally see patterns. Different people see

FIGURE 13.4

Simulated and Actual Stock
Price Movements

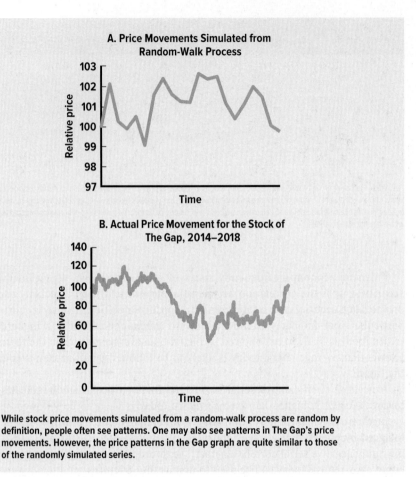

While stock price movements simulated from a random-walk process are random by definition, people often see patterns. One may also see patterns in The Gap's price movements. However, the price patterns in the Gap graph are quite similar to those of the randomly simulated series.

different patterns and forecast different future price movements. However, in our experience, viewers are all quite confident of the patterns they see.

Next, consider the bottom graph, which tracks actual movements in The Gap's stock price. This graph may look quite nonrandom to some, suggesting weak form inefficiency. However, statistical tests indicate that it indeed behaves like a purely random series. Thus, in our opinion, people claiming to see patterns in stock price data are probably seeing optical illusions.

The Semistrong Form

The semistrong form of the efficient market hypothesis implies that prices should reflect all publicly available information. We present two types of tests of this form.

EVENT STUDIES   The *abnormal return* (AR) on a given stock for a particular day can be calculated by subtracting the market's return on the same day (R_M)—as measured by a broad-based index such as the S&P composite index—from the actual return (R) on the stock for that day. We write this algebraically as:

$$AR = R - R_M$$

The following system will help us understand tests of the semistrong form:

Information released at Time $t - 1 \rightarrow AR_{t-1}$
Information released at Time $t \rightarrow AR_t$
Information released at Time $t + 1 \rightarrow AR_{t+1}$

FIGURE 13.5 Cumulative Abnormal Returns for Companies Announcing Dividend Omissions

Source: Szewczyk, Samuel H., George P. Tsetsekos, and Zaher Z. Zantout. "Do Dividend Omissions Signal Future Earnings or Past Earnings?" *Journal of Investing* 40, no. 1 (1997): pp. 40–53.

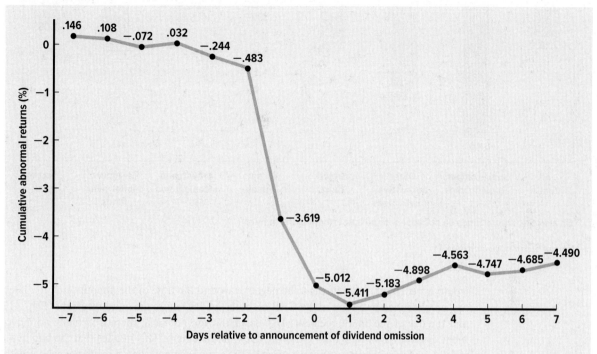

Cumulative abnormal returns (CARs) fall on both the day before the announcement and the day of the announcement of dividend omissions. CARs have very little movement after the announcement date. This pattern is consistent with market efficiency.

The arrows indicate that the abnormal return in any time period is related only to the information released during that period.

According to the efficient market hypothesis, a stock's abnormal return at Time t, AR_t, should reflect the release of information at the same time, t. Any information released before then should have no effect on abnormal returns in this period because all of its influence should have been felt before. In other words, an efficient market would already have incorporated previous information into prices. Because a stock's return today cannot depend on what the market does not yet know, information that will be known only in the future cannot influence the stock's return either. Hence, the arrows point in the direction that is shown, with information in any one time period affecting only that period's abnormal return. *Event studies* are statistical studies that examine whether the arrows are as shown or whether the release of information influences returns on other days.

These studies also speak of *cumulative abnormal returns* (CARs), as well as abnormal returns (ARs). As an example, consider a firm with ARs of 1 percent, −3 percent, and 6 percent for Dates −1, 0, and 1 relative to a corporate announcement. The CARs for Dates −1, 0, and 1 would be 1 percent, −2 percent [= 1 percent + (−3 percent)], and 4 percent [= 1 percent + (−3 percent) + 6 percent], respectively.

As an example, consider the study by Szewczyk, Tsetsekos, and Zantout[5] on dividend omissions. Figure 13.5 shows the plot of CARs for a sample of companies announcing dividend omissions. Because dividend omissions are generally considered to be bad events, we

[5] Samuel H. Szewczyk, George P. Tsetsekos, and Zaher Z. Zantout, "Do Dividend Omissions Signal Future Earnings or Past Earnings?," *Journal of Investing* 40, no. 1 (1997), pp. 40–53.

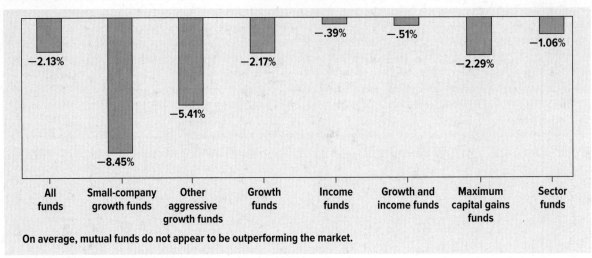

FIGURE 13.6 Annual Return Performance* of Different Types of U.S. Mutual Funds Relative to a Broad-Based Market Index (1963–1998)

Source: Table 2 of Pastor, Lubos, and Robert F. Stambaugh. "Mutual Fund Performance and Seemingly Unrelated Assets." *Journal of Financial Economics* 63, no. 3 (2003): pp. 315–49.

				–.39%	–.51%		–1.06%
–2.13%			–2.17%			–2.29%	
		–5.41%					
	–8.45%						
All funds	Small-company growth funds	Other aggressive growth funds	Growth funds	Income funds	Growth and income funds	Maximum capital gains funds	Sector funds

On average, mutual funds do not appear to be outperforming the market.

* Performance is relative to the market model.

would expect abnormal returns to be negative around the time of the announcements. They are, as evidenced by a drop in the CAR on both the day before the announcement (Day −1) and the day of the announcement (Day 0).[6] However, note that there is virtually no movement in the CARs in the days following the announcement. This implies that the bad news is fully incorporated into the stock price by the announcement day, a result consistent with market efficiency.

Over the years, this type of methodology has been applied to a large number of events. Announcements of dividends, earnings, mergers, capital expenditures, and new issues of stock are a few examples of the vast literature in the area. The early event study tests generally supported the view that the market is semistrong form (and therefore also weak form) efficient. However, a number of more recent studies present evidence that the market does not impound all relevant information immediately. Some conclude from this that the market is not efficient. Others argue that this conclusion is unwarranted, given statistical and methodological problems in the studies. This issue will be addressed in more detail later in the chapter.

THE RECORD OF MUTUAL FUNDS If the market is efficient in the semistrong form, then no matter what publicly available information mutual fund managers rely on to pick stocks, their average returns should be the same as those of the average investor in the market as a whole. We can test efficiency, then, by comparing the performance of these professionals with that of a market index.

Consider Figure 13.6, which presents the performance of various types of mutual funds relative to the stock market as a whole. The far left of the figure shows that the universe of

[6] An astute reader may wonder why the abnormal return is negative on Day −1, as well as on Day 0. To see why, first note that the announcement date is generally taken in academic studies to be the publication date of the story in *The Wall Street Journal (WSJ)*. Then consider a company announcing a dividend omission via a press release at noon on Tuesday. The stock should fall on Tuesday. The announcement will be reported in the *WSJ* on Wednesday because the Tuesday edition of the *WSJ* has already been printed. For this firm, the stock price falls on the day before the announcement in the *WSJ*.

Alternatively, imagine another firm announcing a dividend omission via a press release on Tuesday at 8 p.m. Since the stock market is closed at that late hour, the stock price will fall on Wednesday. Because the *WSJ* will report the announcement on Wednesday, the stock price falls on the day of the announcement in the *WSJ*.

Since firms may either make announcements during trading hours or after trading hours, stocks should fall on both Day −1 and Day 0 relative to publication in the *WSJ*.

all funds covered in the study underperforms the market by 2.13 percent per year, after an appropriate adjustment for risk. Thus, rather than outperforming the market, the evidence shows underperformance. This underperformance holds for a number of types of funds as well. Returns in this study are net of fees, expenses, and commissions, so fund returns would be higher if these costs were added back. However, the study shows no evidence that funds, as a whole, are beating the market.

Perhaps nothing rankles successful stock market investors more than to have some professor tell them that they are not necessarily smart, just lucky. However, while Figure 13.6 represents only one study, there have been many papers on mutual funds. The overwhelming evidence here is that mutual funds, on average, do not beat broad-based indexes.

By and large, mutual fund managers rely on publicly available information. Thus, the finding that they do not outperform market indexes is consistent with semistrong form and weak form efficiency.

However, this evidence does not imply that mutual funds are bad investments for individuals. Though these funds fail to achieve better returns than some indexes of the market, they do permit the investor to buy a portfolio that has a large number of stocks in it (the phrase *a well-diversified portfolio* is often used). They might also be very good at providing a variety of services such as keeping custody and records of all the stocks.

The Strong Form

Even the strongest adherents to the efficient market hypothesis would not be surprised to find that markets are inefficient in the strong form. After all, if an individual has information that no one else has, it is likely that she can profit from it.

One group of studies of strong form efficiency investigates insider trading. Insiders in firms have access to information that is not generally available. But if the strong form of the efficient market hypothesis holds, they should not be able to profit by trading on their information. A government agency, the Securities and Exchange Commission, requires insiders in companies to reveal any trading they might do in their own company's stock. By examining the record of such trades, we can see whether they made abnormal returns. A number of studies support the view that these trades were abnormally profitable. Thus, strong form efficiency does not seem to be substantiated by the evidence.

13.4 THE BEHAVIORAL CHALLENGE TO MARKET EFFICIENCY

In Section 13.1, we presented Prof. Shleifer's three conditions, any one of which will lead to market efficiency. In that section, we made a case that at least one of the conditions is likely to hold in the real world. However, there is definitely disagreement here. Many members of the academic community (including Prof. Shleifer) argue that none of the three conditions are likely to hold in reality. This point of view is based on what is called *behavioral finance.* Let us examine the behavioral view on each of these three conditions.

Rationality

Are people really rational? Not always. Just travel to Atlantic City or Las Vegas to see people gambling, sometimes with large sums of money. The casino's take implies a negative expected return for the gambler. Because gambling is risky and has a negative expected return, it can never be on the efficient frontier discussed in Chapter 11. In addition, gamblers will often bet on black at a roulette table after black has occurred a number of consecutive times, thinking that the run will continue. This strategy is faulty because roulette tables have no memory.

But, of course, gambling is only a sideshow as far as finance is concerned. Do we see irrationality in financial markets as well? The answer may very well be yes. Many investors do not achieve the degree of diversification that they should. Others trade frequently, generating both commissions and taxes. In fact, taxes can be handled optimally by selling losers and holding on to winners. While some individuals invest with tax minimization in mind, plenty of them do the opposite. Many are more likely to sell their winners than their losers, a strategy leading to high tax payments. The behavioral view is not that all investors are irrational. Rather, it is that some, perhaps many, investors are.

Independent Deviations from Rationality

Are deviations from rationality generally random, thereby likely to cancel out in a whole population of investors? To the contrary, psychologists have long argued that people deviate from rationality in accordance with a number of basic principles. While not all of these principles have an application to finance and market efficiency, at least two seem to do so.

The first principle, called *representativeness,* can be explained with the gambling example used above. The gambler who believes a run of black will continue is in error because, in reality, the probability of a black spin is still only about 50 percent. Gamblers behaving in this way exhibit the psychological trait of representativeness. That is, they draw conclusions from insufficient data. In other words, the gambler believes the small sample he observed is more representative of the population than it really is.

How is this related to finance? Perhaps a market dominated by representativeness leads to bubbles. People see a sector of the market, for example, internet stocks, having a short history of high revenue growth and extrapolate that it will continue forever. When the growth inevitably stalls, prices have nowhere to go but down.

The second principle is *conservatism,* which means that people are too slow in adjusting their beliefs to new information. Suppose that your goal since childhood was to become a dentist. Perhaps you came from a family of dentists, perhaps you liked the security and relatively high income that comes with that profession, or perhaps teeth always fascinated you. As things stand now, you could probably look forward to a long and productive career in that occupation. However, suppose that a new drug was developed that would prevent tooth decay. That drug would clearly reduce, or even eliminate, the demand for dentists. How quickly would you realize the implications as stated here? If you were emotionally attached to dentistry, you might adjust your beliefs very slowly. Family and friends could tell you to switch out of predental courses in college, but you might not be psychologically ready to do that. Instead, you might cling to your rosy view of dentistry's future.

Perhaps there is a relationship to finance here. For example, many studies report that prices seem to adjust slowly to the information contained in earnings announcements. Could it be that, because of conservatism, investors are slow in adjusting their beliefs to new information? More will be said on this in the next section.

Arbitrage

In Section 13.1, we suggested that professional investors, knowing that securities are mispriced, could buy the underpriced ones while selling correctly priced (or even overpriced) substitutes. This might well undo any mispricing caused by emotional amateurs.

However, trading of this sort is likely to be more risky than it appears at first glance. Suppose professionals generally believed that McDonald's stock was underpriced. They would buy it, while selling their holdings in, say, Burger King and Wendy's. However, if amateurs were taking opposite positions, prices would adjust to correct levels only if the positions of amateurs were small relative to those of the professionals. In a world of many amateurs, a few professionals would have to take big positions to bring prices into line, perhaps even engaging heavily in short selling. Buying large amounts of one stock and short selling large amounts of another stock is quite risky, even if the two stocks are in the same industry. Here, unanticipated bad news about McDonald's and unanticipated good news about the other two stocks would cause the professionals to register large losses.

In addition, if amateurs mispriced McDonald's today, what is to prevent McDonald's from being even more mispriced tomorrow? This risk of further mispricing, even in the presence of no new information, may also cause professionals to cut back their arbitrage positions. As an example, imagine a shrewd professional who believed internet stocks were overpriced in 1998. Had he bet on a decline at that time, he would have lost in the near term because prices rose through March of 2000. Yet, he would have eventually made money because prices later fell. However, near-term risk may reduce the size of arbitrage strategies.

In conclusion, the arguments presented here suggest that the theoretical underpinnings of the efficient capital markets hypothesis, presented in Section 13.1, might not hold in reality. That is, investors may be irrational, irrationality may be related across investors rather than canceling out across investors, and arbitrage strategies may involve too much risk to eliminate market efficiencies.

13.5 EMPIRICAL CHALLENGES TO MARKET EFFICIENCY

Section 13.3 presented empirical evidence supportive of market efficiency. We now present evidence challenging this hypothesis. (Adherents of market efficiency generally refer to results of this type as *anomalies*.)

1. *Limits to Arbitrage.* Royal Dutch Petroleum and Shell Transport merged their interests in 1907, with all subsequent cash flows being split on a 60 percent–40 percent basis between the two companies. However, both companies continued to be publicly traded. One might imagine that the market value of Royal Dutch would always be 1.5 (= 60/40) times that of Shell. That is, if Royal Dutch ever became overpriced, rational investors would buy Shell instead of Royal Dutch. If Royal Dutch were underpriced, investors would buy Royal Dutch. In addition, arbitrageurs would go further by buying the underpriced security and selling the overpriced security short.

   However, Figure 13.7 shows that Royal Dutch and Shell rarely traded at parity over the 1962 to 2005 period (the companies discontinued separate

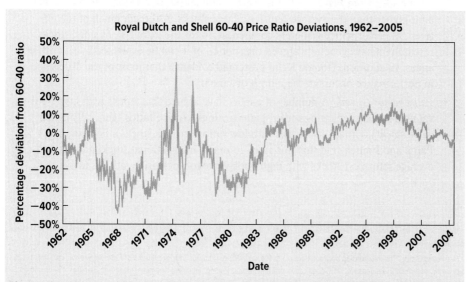

FIGURE 13.7

Deviations of the Ratio of the Market Value of Royal Dutch to the Market Value of Shell, from Parity

Source: Author calculations.

Royal Dutch and Shell 60-40 Price Ratio Deviations, 1962–2005

Apparently, arbitrage is unable to keep the ratio of the market value of Royal Dutch to the market value of Shell at parity.

trading in 2005). Why would these deviations occur? As stated in the previous section, behavioral finance suggests that there are limits to arbitrage. That is, an investor buying the overpriced asset and selling the underpriced asset does not have a sure thing. Deviations from parity could actually *increase* in the short run, implying losses for the arbitrageur. The well-known statement, "Markets can stay irrational longer than you can stay solvent," attributed to John Maynard Keynes, applies here. Thus, risk considerations may force arbitrageurs to take positions that are too small to move prices back to parity. A nearby *Finance Matters* box discusses another recent example of relative mispricing between two stocks.

2. *Earnings Surprises.* Common sense suggests that prices should rise when earnings are reported to be higher than expected and prices should fall when the reverse occurs. However, market efficiency implies that prices will adjust immediately to the announcement, while behavioral finance would predict another pattern. Chan, Jegadeesh, and Lakonishok rank companies by the extent of their *earnings surprise,* that is, the difference between current quarterly earnings and quarterly earnings four quarters ago, divided by the standard deviation of quarterly earnings.[7] They form a portfolio of companies with the most extreme positive surprises and another portfolio of companies with the most extreme negative surprises. Figure 13.8 shows returns from buying the two portfolios. As can be seen, prices adjust slowly to the earnings announcements, with the portfolio with the positive surprises outperforming the portfolio with the negative surprises over both the next six months and the next year. Many other researchers obtain similar results.

   Why do prices adjust slowly? Behavioral finance suggests that investors exhibit conservatism here, as they are slow to adjust to the information contained in the announcements.

3. *Size.* In 1981, two important papers presented evidence that, in the United States, the returns on stocks with small market capitalizations were greater than the returns on stocks with large market capitalizations over most of the 20th century.[8] The studies have since been replicated over different time periods and in different countries. For example, Figure 13.9 shows average annual returns over the period from 1963 to 1995 for five portfolios of U.S. stocks ranked on size. As can be seen from Figure 13.9, the average annual return on small stocks is quite a bit higher than the average return on large stocks. Although much of the differential performance is merely compensation for the extra risk of small stocks, researchers have generally argued that not all of it can be explained by risk differences. In addition, Donald Keim presented evidence that most of the difference in performance occurs in the month of January.[9]

4. *Value versus Growth.* A number of papers have argued that stocks with high book-value-to-stock-price ratios and/or high earnings-to-price ratios (generally called *value stocks*) outperform stocks with low ratios (growth stocks). For example, Fama and French find that, for 12 of 13 major international stock markets, the average return on stocks with high book-value-to-stock-price ratios is above the

---

[7] Louis K.C. Chan, Narasimhan Jegadeesh, and Josef Lakonishok, "Momentum Strategies," *Journal of Finance* 51, no. 5 (1996), pp. 1681–713.

[8] See Rolf W. Banz, "The Relationship between Return and Market Value of Common Stocks," *Journal of Financial Economics* 9, no. 1 (1981), pp. 3–18; and Marc R. Reinganum, "Misspecification of Capital Asset Pricing: Empirical Anomalies Based on Earnings' Yields and Market Values," *Journal of Financial Economics* 9, no. 1 (1981), pp. 19–46.

[9] Donald B. Keim, "Size-Related Anomalies and Stock Return Seasonality: Further Empirical Evidence," *Journal of Financial Economics* 12, no. 1 (1983), pp. 13–32.

FINANCE MATTERS

CAN STOCK MARKET INVESTORS ADD AND SUBTRACT?

On March 2, 2000, 3Com, a profitable provider of computer networking products and services, sold 5 percent of one of its subsidiaries to the public via an initial public offering (IPO). At the time, the subsidiary was known as Palm (it has since been acquired by Hewlett-Packard).

3Com planned to distribute the remaining Palm shares to 3Com shareholders at a later date. Under the plan, if you owned one share of 3Com, you would receive 1.5 shares of Palm. So, after 3Com sold part of Palm via the IPO, investors could buy Palm shares directly or indirectly by purchasing shares of 3Com and waiting.

What makes this case interesting is what happened in the days that followed the Palm IPO. If you owned one 3Com share, you would be entitled, eventually, to 1.5 shares of Palm. Therefore, each 3Com share should be worth *at least* 1.5 times the value of each Palm share. We say at least because the other parts of 3Com were profitable. As a result, each 3Com share should have been worth much more than 1.5 times the value of one Palm share. But, as you might guess, things did not work out this way.

The day before the Palm IPO, shares in 3Com sold for $104.13. After the first day of trading, Palm closed at $95.06 per share. Multiplying $95.06 by 1.5 results in $142.59, which is the minimum value one would expect to pay for 3Com. But the day Palm closed at $95.06, 3Com shares closed at $81.81, more than $60 lower than the price implied by Palm. It gets stranger.

A 3Com price of $81.81 when Palm was selling for $95.06 implies that the market valued the rest of 3Com's businesses (per share) at $81.81 − 142.59 = −$60.78. Given the number of 3Com shares outstanding at the time, this means the market placed a negative value of about $22 billion for the rest of 3Com's businesses. Of course, a stock price cannot be negative. This means, then, that the price of Palm relative to 3Com was much too high.

To profit from this mispricing, investors would purchase shares of 3Com and sell shares of Palm. This trade is a no-brainer. In a well-functioning market, arbitrage traders would force the prices into alignment quite quickly. What happened?

As you can see in the accompanying figure, the market valued 3Com and Palm shares in such a way that the non-Palm part of 3Com had a negative value for about two months, from March 2, 2000, until May 8, 2000. Thus, the pricing error was corrected by market forces, but not instantly, which is consistent with the existence of limits to arbitrage.

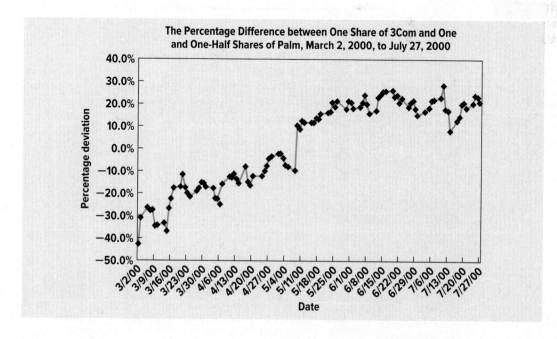

The Percentage Difference between One Share of 3Com and One and One-Half Shares of Palm, March 2, 2000, to July 27, 2000

FIGURE 13.8

Returns to Two Investment
Strategies Based on
Earnings Surprise

Source: Adapted from
Table 3 of Chan, Louis K.C.,
Narasimhan Jegadeesh, and
Josef Lakonishok. "Momentum
Strategies." *Journal of
Finance* 51, no. 5 (1996),
pp. 1681–1713.

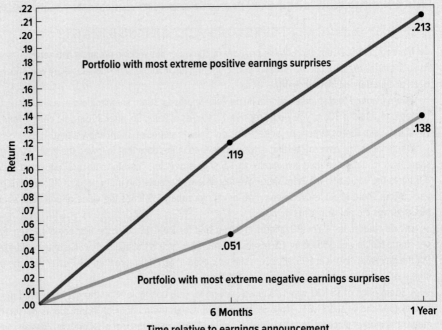

This figure compares returns to a strategy of buying stocks with extremely high positive earnings
surprises (the difference between current quarterly earnings and quarterly earnings four quarters ago,
divided by the standard deviation of quarterly earnings) to returns to a strategy of buying stocks with
extremely high negative earnings surprises. The graph shows a slow adjustment to the information in the
earnings announcement.

FIGURE 13.9

Annual Stock Returns on
Portfolios Sorted by Size
(Market Capitalization)

Source: Loughran, Tim. "Book-to-
Market Across Firm Size, Exchange
and Seasonality: Is There an
Effect?" *Journal of Financial and
Quantitative Analysis* 32, no. 3
(1997): pp. 249–68.

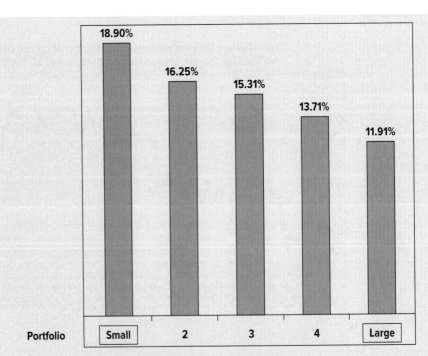

Historically, the average return on small stocks has been above the average return on large stocks.

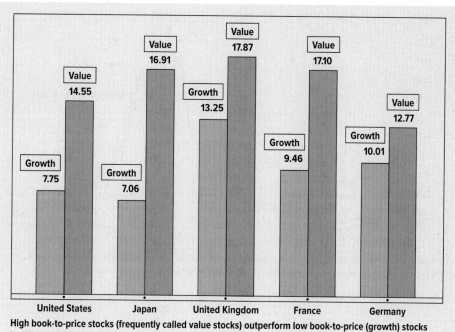

FIGURE 13.10

Annual U.S. Dollar Returns* (in percent) on Low Book-to-Price Firms and High Book-to-Price Firms in Selected Countries

Source: Fama, Eugene F., and Kenneth R. French. "Value Versus Growth: The International Evidence." *Journal of Finance* 53, no. 6 (1998): pp. 1975–99.

High book-to-price stocks (frequently called value stocks) outperform low book-to-price (growth) stocks in different countries.

* Returns are expressed as the excess over the return on U.S. Treasury bills.

average return on stocks with low book-value-to-stock-price ratios.[10] Figure 13.10 shows these returns for five large stock markets. Value stocks have outperformed growth stocks in each of these five markets.

Because the return difference is so large and because the above ratios can be obtained so easily for individual stocks, the results may constitute strong evidence against market efficiency. However, a number of papers suggest that the unusual returns are due to biases in the commercial databases or to differences in risk, not to a true inefficiency.[11] Because the debate revolves around arcane statistical issues, we will not pursue the issue further. However, it is safe to say that no conclusion is warranted at this time. As with so many other topics in finance and economics, further research is needed.

5. *Crashes and Bubbles.* The stock market crash of October 19, 1987, is extremely puzzling. The market dropped between 20 percent and 25 percent on a Monday following a weekend during which little surprising news was released. A drop of this magnitude for no apparent reason is not consistent with market efficiency. Because the crash of 1929 is still an enigma, it is doubtful that the more recent 1987 debacle will be explained anytime soon. The recent comments of an eminent historian are apt here: When asked what, in his opinion, the effect of the French Revolution of 1789 was, he replied that it was too early to tell.

Perhaps the two stock market crashes are evidence consistent with the bubble theory of speculative markets. That is, security prices sometimes move wildly above their true values. Eventually, prices fall back to their original levels, causing great losses for investors. Consider, for example, the behavior of internet

[10] Taken from Table III of Eugene F. Fama and Kenneth R. French, "Value versus Growth: The International Evidence," *Journal of Finance* 53, no. 6 (1998), pp. 1975–99.

[11] For example, see S. P. Kothari, Jay Shanken, and Richard G. Sloan, "Another Look at the Cross-Section of Expected Stock Returns," *Journal of Finance* 50, no. 1 (1995), pp. 185–224; and Eugene F. Fama and Kenneth R. French, "Multifactor Explanations of Asset Pricing Anomalies," *Journal of Finance* 51, no. 1 (1996), pp. 55–84.

FIGURE 13.11

Value of Index of Internet Stocks

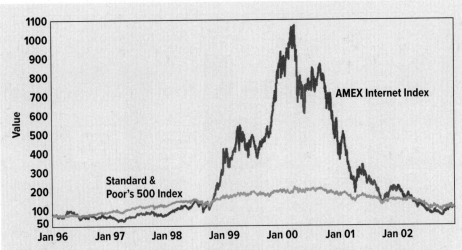

The index of internet stocks rose over 10-fold from the beginning of 1996 to its high in March 2000 before falling to approximately its original level in 2002.

stocks in the late 1990s. Figure 13.11 shows values of an index of internet stocks from 1996 through 2002. The index rose over 10-fold from January 1996 to its high in March 2000, before retreating to approximately its original level in 2002. For comparison, the figure also shows price movement for the Standard & Poor's 500 Index. While this index rose and fell over the same period, the price movement was quite muted, relative to that of internet stocks.[12]

Many commentators describe the rise and fall of internet stocks as a *bubble*. Is it correct to do so? Unfortunately, there is no precise definition of the term. Some academics argue that the price movement in the figure is consistent with rationality. Prices rose initially, they say, because it appeared that the internet would soon capture a large chunk of international commerce. Prices fell when later evidence suggested this would not occur quite so quickly. However, others argue that the initial rosy scenario was never supported by the facts. Rather, prices rose due to nothing more than "irrational exuberance."

13.6 REVIEWING THE DIFFERENCES

It is fair to say that the controversy over efficient capital markets has yet to be resolved. Rather, academic financial economists have sorted themselves into three camps, with some adhering to market efficiency, some believing in behavioral finance, and others (perhaps the majority) not yet convinced that either side has won the argument. This state of affairs is certainly different from, say, 30 years ago, when market efficiency went unchallenged. In addition, the controversy here is perhaps the most contentious of any area of financial economics.

Because of the controversy, it does not appear that our textbook, or any textbook, can easily resolve the differing points of view. However, we can illustrate the differences between the two camps by relating the two psychological principles mentioned earlier, representativeness and conservatism, to stock returns.

[12] More recently, many have suggested that the Standard & Poor's 500 Index experienced a bubble. It more than doubled in value from October 2002 to October 2007. But from November 2007 to March 2009, the Index lost more than 50 percent of its value. Of course, then it doubled again in value from March 2009 through February 2011, a period of 700 days.

Representativeness

This principle implies overweighting the results of small samples, as with the gambler who thinks a few consecutive spins of black on the roulette wheel make black a more likely outcome than red on the next spin. Financial economists have argued that representativeness leads to overreaction in stock returns. We mentioned earlier that financial bubbles are likely overreactions to news. Internet companies showed great revenue growth for a short time in the late 1990s, causing many to believe that this growth would continue indefinitely. Stock prices rose (too much) at this point. When, at last, investors realized that this growth could not be sustained, prices plummeted.

Conservatism

This principle states that individuals adjust their beliefs too slowly to new information. A market composed of this type of investor would likely lead to stock prices that underreact in the presence of new information. The example concerning earnings surprises may well illustrate this underreaction. Prices rose slowly following announcements of positive earnings surprises. Announcements of negative surprises had a similar, but opposite, reaction.

The two academic camps have different views of these results. The efficient market believers stress that representativeness and conservatism have opposite implications for stock prices. Which principle, they ask, should dominate in any particular situation? In other words, why should investors overreact to news about internet stocks but underreact to earnings news? Fama reviews the academic studies on anomalies, finding that about half of them show overreaction and about half show underreaction.[13] He concludes that this evidence is consistent with the market efficiency hypothesis that anomalies are chance events. In addition, he argues that behavioral finance must do better at specifying which types of information should lead to overreaction and which to underreaction before one rejects market efficiency in favor of behavioral finance.

Adherents of behavioral finance see things a little differently. First, they point out that, as discussed in Section 13.4, the three theoretical foundations of market efficiency appear to be violated in the real world. Second, there are too many anomalies, with a number of them being replicated in out-of-sample tests. This argues against anomalies being mere chance events. Finally, though the field has not yet determined why either overreaction or underreaction should dominate in a particular situation, much progress has already been made in a short period of time.

What is the bottom line? It is important to reiterate that the efficient market hypothesis doesn't say that market prices are correct with perfect foresight or hindsight. Clearly, most stocks were overvalued in 2008 given the events that unfolded (i.e., the financial crisis). This situation is not necessarily inconsistent with efficient markets. In extremely volatile markets, market prices can be very "wrong" with hindsight. We will conclude by suggesting that markets are very efficient much of the time but not all of the time; bubbles may appear with hindsight. The question is, are these bubbles evidence that market prices are not good estimates of intrinsic value?

13.7 IMPLICATIONS FOR CORPORATE FINANCE

So far, the chapter has examined both theoretical arguments and empirical evidence concerning efficient markets. We now ask the question: Does market efficiency have any relevance for corporate financial managers? The answer is that it does. Below we consider four implications of efficiency for managers.

---

[13] Eugene F. Fama, "Market Efficiency, Long-Term Returns, and Behavioral Finance," *Journal of Financial Economics* 49, no. 3 (1998), pp. 283–306.

1. Accounting Choices, Financial Choices, and Market Efficiency

The accounting profession provides firms with a significant amount of leeway in their reporting practices. For example, companies may choose between the last-in, first-out (LIFO) or the first-in, first-out (FIFO) method in valuing inventories. They may choose either the percentage-of-completion or the completed-contract method for construction projects. They may depreciate physical assets by either accelerated or straight-line depreciation.

Managers clearly prefer high stock prices to low stock prices. Should managers use the leeway in accounting choices to report the highest possible income? Not necessarily, if markets are efficient. That is, accounting choice should not affect stock price if two conditions hold. First, enough information must be provided in the annual report so that financial analysts can construct earnings under the alternative accounting methods. This appears to be the case for many, though not necessarily all, accounting choices. Second, the market must be efficient in the semistrong form. In other words, the market must appropriately use all of this accounting information in determining the market price.

Of course, the issue of whether accounting choice affects stock price is ultimately an empirical matter. A number of academic papers have addressed this issue, and the evidence does not suggest that managers can boost stock price through accounting practices. In other words, the market appears efficient enough to see through different accounting choices.

One caveat is called for here. Our discussion specifically assumed that financial analysts can construct earnings under the alternative accounting methods. However, companies like Enron, WorldCom, Global Crossing, and Xerox reported fraudulent numbers in recent years. There was no way for financial analysts to construct alternative earnings numbers because these analysts were unaware how the reported numbers were determined. So it was not surprising that the prices of these stocks initially rose well above fair value. Yes, managers can boost prices in this way—as long as they are willing to serve time once they are caught!

Is there anything else that investors can be expected to see through in an efficient market? Consider stock splits and stock dividends. Today Amarillo Corporation has 1 million shares outstanding and reports $10 million of earnings. In the hopes of boosting its stock price, the firm's chief financial officer (CFO), Ms. Green, recommends to the board of directors that Amarillo have a 2-for-1 stock split. That is, a shareholder with 100 shares prior to the split would have 200 shares after the split. The CFO contends that each investor would feel richer after the split because he would own more shares.

However, this thinking runs counter to market efficiency. A rational investor knows that he would own the same proportion of the firm after the split as before the split. For example, our investor with 100 shares owns 1/10,000 (= 100/1 million) of Amarillo's shares prior to the split. His share of the earnings would be $1,000 (= $10 million/10,000). While he would own 200 shares after the split, there would now be 2 million shares outstanding. Thus, he still would own 1/10,000 of the firm. His share of the earnings would still be $1,000 because the stock split would not affect the earnings of the entire firm.

2. The Timing Decision

Imagine a firm whose managers are contemplating the date to issue equity. This decision is frequently called the *timing* decision. If managers believe that their stock is overpriced, they are likely to issue equity immediately. Here, they are creating value for their current stockholders because they are selling stock for more than it is worth. Conversely, if the managers believe that their stock is underpriced, they are more likely to wait, hoping that the stock price will eventually rise to its true (i.e., intrinsic) value.

However, if markets are efficient, securities are neither overpriced nor underpriced. Because efficiency implies that stock is sold for its true worth, the timing decision becomes unimportant. Figure 13.12 shows three possible stock price adjustments to the issuance of new stock.

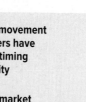

FIGURE 13.12

Three Stock Price
Adjustments after Issuing
Equity

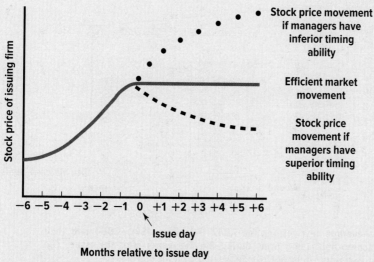

Stock price movement
if managers have
inferior timing
ability

Efficient market
movement

Stock price
movement if
managers have
superior timing
ability

Stock price of issuing firm

−6 −5 −4 −3 −2 −1 0 +1 +2 +3 +4 +5 +6

Issue day

Months relative to issue day

Studies show that stock is more likely to be issued after stock prices have increased. No inferences on market efficiency can be drawn from this result. Rather, market efficiency implies that the stock price of the issuing firm, on average, neither rises nor falls (relative to stock market indexes) after issuance of stock.

Of course, market efficiency is ultimately an empirical issue. Surprisingly, recent research has called market efficiency into question. Ritter presents evidence that the annual returns over the five years following an initial public offering (IPO) are about 2 percent less for the issuing company than the returns on a nonissuing company of similar book-to-market ratio.[14] Annual returns over this period following a seasoned equity offering (SEO) are between 3 percent and 4 percent less for the issuing company than for a comparable non-issuing company. A company's first public offering is called an IPO, and all subsequent offerings are termed SEOs. The upper half of Figure 13.13 shows average annual returns of both IPOs and their control group, and the lower half of the figure shows average annual returns of both SEOs and their control group.

The evidence in Ritter's paper suggests that corporate managers issue SEOs when the company's stock is overpriced. In other words, managers appear to time the market success-fully. The evidence that managers time their IPOs is less compelling because returns following IPOs are closer to those of their control group.

Does the ability of a corporate official to issue an SEO when the security is overpriced indicate that the market is inefficient in the semistrong form or the strong form? The answer is actually somewhat more complex than it may first appear. On one hand, officials are likely to have special information that the rest of us do not have, suggesting that the market need only be inefficient in the strong form. On the other hand, if the market were truly semistrong efficient, the price would drop immediately and completely upon the announce-ment of an upcoming SEO. That is, rational investors would realize that stock is being issued because corporate officials have special information that the stock is overpriced. Indeed, many empirical studies report a price drop on the announcement date. However, Figure 13.13 indicates that there is a further price drop in the subsequent years, suggesting that the market is inefficient in the semistrong form.

If firms can time the issuance of common stock, perhaps they can also time the repurchase of stock. Here, a firm would like to repurchase when its stock is undervalued. Ikenberry,

---

[14] Jay Ritter, "Investment Banking and Securities Issuance," chap. 5 in *Handbook of the Economics of Finance,* ed. George Constantinides, Milton Harris, and René Stulz (Amsterdam: North Holland, 2003).

FIGURE 13.13

Returns on Initial Public Offerings (IPOs) and Seasoned Equity Offerings (SEOs) in Years Following Issue

Source: Ritter, Jay. "Investment Banking and Securities Issuance." Chap. 5 in Handbook of the Economics of Finance, edited by George Constantinides, Milton Harris, and Rene Stulz. Amsterdam: North Holland, 2003.

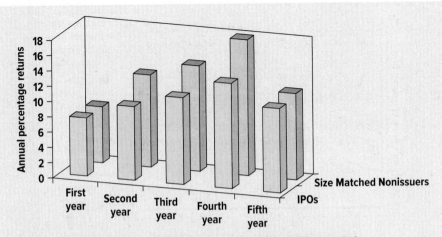

The average raw returns for 7,042 IPOs from 1970–2000 and their matching nonissuing firms during the five years after the issue. The first-year return does not include the return on the day of issue.

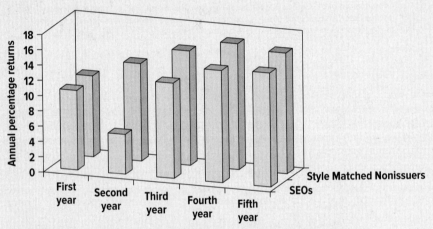

The average raw returns for 7,502 SEOs from 1970–2000 and their matching nonissuing firms during the five years after the issue. The first-year return does not include the return on the day of issue. On average, IPOs underperform their control groups by about 2% per year in the five years following issuance. SEOs underperform by about 3%–4% per year.

Lakonishok, and Vermaelen find that stock returns of repurchasing firms are abnormally high in the two years following repurchase, suggesting that timing is effective here.[15]

As is always the case, empirical research is never ultimately settled. However, in our opinion, the evidence strongly suggests that managers successfully engage in timing. If this conclusion stands the test of time, it would constitute evidence against market efficiency.

3. Speculation and Efficient Markets

We normally think of individuals and financial institutions as the primary speculators in financial markets. However, industrial corporations speculate as well. For example, many companies make interest rate bets. If the managers of a firm believe that interest rates are

[15] David Ikenberry, Josef Lakonishok, and Theo Vermaelen, "Market Underreaction to Open Market Share Repurchases," *Journal of Financial Economics* 39, nos. 2–3 (1995), pp. 181–208.

likely to rise, they have an incentive to borrow because the present value of the liability will fall with the rate increase. In addition, these managers will have an incentive to borrow long term rather than short term in order to lock in the low rates for a longer period of time. The thinking can get more sophisticated. Suppose that the long-term rate is already higher than the short-term rate. The manager might argue that this differential reflects the market's view that rates will rise. However, perhaps he anticipates a rate increase even greater than what the market anticipates, as implied by the upward-sloping term structure. Again, the manager will want to borrow long term rather than short term.

Firms also speculate in foreign currencies. Suppose that the CFO of a multinational corporation based in the United States believes that the euro will decline relative to the dollar. He would probably issue euro-denominated debt rather than dollar-denominated debt because he expects the value of the foreign liability to fall. Conversely, he would issue debt domestically if he believes foreign currencies will appreciate relative to the dollar.

We are perhaps getting a little ahead of our story because the subtleties of the term structure and exchange rates are treated in other chapters, not this one. However, the big-picture question is this: What does market efficiency have to say about the above activity? The answer is quite clear. If financial markets are efficient, managers should not waste their time trying to forecast the movements of interest rates and foreign currencies. Their forecasts will likely be no better than chance. And they will be using up valuable executive time. This is not to say, however, that firms should flippantly pick the maturity or the denomination of their debt in a random fashion. A firm must choose these parameters carefully. However, the choice should be based on other rationales, not on an attempt to beat the market. For example, a firm with a project lasting five years might decide to issue five-year debt. A firm might issue yen-denominated debt because it anticipates expanding into Japan in a big way.

The same thinking applies to acquisitions. Many corporations buy up other firms because they think these targets are underpriced. Unfortunately, the empirical evidence suggests that the market is too efficient for this type of speculation to be profitable. And the acquirer never pays just the current market price. The bidding firm must pay a premium above market to induce a majority of shareholders of the target firm to sell their shares. However, this is not to say that firms should never be acquired. Rather, one should consider an acquisition if there are benefits, that is, synergies, from the union. Improved marketing, economies in production, replacement of bad management, and even tax reduction are typical synergies. These synergies are distinct from the perception that the acquired firm is underpriced.

One caveat should be mentioned. We talked earlier about empirical evidence suggesting that SEOs are timed to take advantage of overpriced stock. This makes sense because managers are likely to know more about their own firm than the market does. However, while managers may very well have special information about their own firm, it is unlikely that they have special information about interest rates, foreign currencies, and other firms. There are too many participants in these markets, many of whom are devoting all of their time to forecasting. Managers typically spend most of their time running their own firms, with only a small amount devoted to studying financial markets.

4. Information in Market Prices

The previous section argued that it is quite difficult to forecast future market prices. However, the current and past prices of any asset are known—and of great use. Consider, for example, Becher's study of bank mergers.[16] The author finds that stock prices of acquired banks rise about 23 percent, on average, upon the first announcement of a merger. This is not surprising because companies are generally bought out at a premium above current stock price. However, the same study shows that prices of acquiring banks fall almost 5 percent, on average, upon the same announcement. This is pretty strong evidence that bank mergers do

---

[16] David A. Becher, "The Valuation Effects of Bank Mergers," *Journal of Corporate Finance* 6, no. 2 (2000), pp. 189–214.

FIGURE 13.14

Stock Performance Prior to Forced Departures of Management

Source: Warner, Jerold B., Ross L. Watts, and Karen H. Wruck. "Stock Prices and Top Management Changes." *Journal of Financial Economics* 20 (January–March 1988): pp. 461–92.

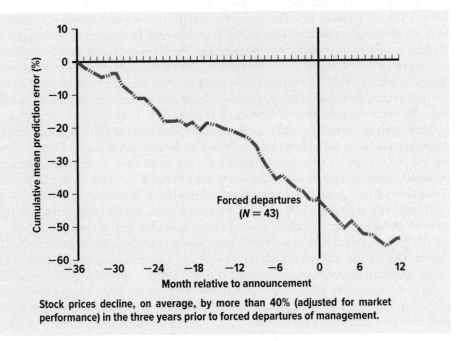

Stock prices decline, on average, by more than 40% (adjusted for market performance) in the three years prior to forced departures of management.

not benefit, and may even hurt, acquiring companies. The reason for this result is unclear, though perhaps acquirers overpay for acquisitions. Regardless of the reason, the implication is clear. A bank should think deeply before making an acquisition of another bank.

Furthermore, suppose you are the CFO of a company whose stock price drops much more than 5 percent upon announcement of an acquisition. The market is telling you that the merger is quite bad for your firm. Serious consideration should be given to canceling the merger, even if, prior to the announcement, you thought the merger was a good idea.

Of course, mergers are only one type of corporate event. Managers should pay attention to the stock price reaction to any of their announcements, whether it concerns a new venture, a divestiture, a restructuring, or something else.

This is not the only way in which corporations can use the information in market prices. Suppose you are on the board of directors of a company whose stock price has declined precipitously since the current chief executive officer (CEO) was hired. In addition, the prices of competitors have risen over the same time. Though there may be extenuating circumstances, this can be viewed as evidence that the CEO is doing a poor job. Perhaps he should be fired. If this seems harsh, consider that Warner, Watts, and Wruck find a strong negative correlation between managerial turnover and prior stock performance.[17] Figure 13.14 shows that stocks fall, on average, about 40 percent in price (relative to market movements) in the three years prior to the forced departure of a top manager.

If managers are fired for bad stock price performance, perhaps they are rewarded for stock price appreciation. Hall and Liebman state:

> Our main empirical finding is that CEO wealth often changes by millions of dollars for typical changes in firm value. For example, the median total compensation for CEOs is about $1 million if their firm's stock has a 30th percentile annual return (−7.0 percent) and is $5 million if the firm's stock has a 70th percentile annual return (20.5 percent). Thus, there is a difference of about $4 million in compensation for achieving a moderately above average performance relative to a moderately below average performance.[18]

[17] Jerold B. Warner, Ross L. Watts, and Karen H. Wruck, "Stock Prices and Top Management Changes," *Journal of Financial Economics* 20 (January–March 1988), pp. 461–92.

[18] Hall, Brian J., and Jeffrey B. Liebman. "Are CEOs Really Paid Like Bureaucrats?" *Quarterly Journal of Economics* (August 1998), p. 654.

Market efficiency implies that stock prices reflect all available information. We recommend using this information as much as possible in corporate decisions. And, at least with respect to executive firings and executive compensation, it looks as if real-world corporations do pay attention to market prices. The following box summarizes some key issues in the efficient market debate:

EFFICIENT MARKET HYPOTHESIS: A SUMMARY

Does Not Say

- Prices are uncaused.
- Investors are foolish and too stupid to be in the market.
- All shares of stock have the same expected returns.
- Investors should throw darts to select stocks.
- There is no upward trend in stock prices.

Does Say

- Prices reflect underlying value.
- Financial managers cannot time stock and bond sales.
- Managers cannot profitably speculate in foreign currencies.
- Managers cannot boost stock prices through creative accounting.

Why Doesn't Everybody Believe It?

- There are optical illusions, mirages, and apparent patterns in charts of stock market returns.
- The truth is less interesting.
- There is evidence against efficiency:
  - Two different, but financially identical, classes of stock of the same firm selling at different prices.
  - Earnings surprises.
  - Small versus large stocks.
  - Value versus growth stocks.
  - Crashes and bubbles.

Three Forms

Weak form: Current prices reflect past prices; chartism (technical analysis) is useless.

Semistrong form: Prices reflect all public information; most financial analysis is useless.

Strong form: Prices reflect all that is knowable; nobody consistently makes superior profits.

SUMMARY AND CONCLUSIONS

1. An efficient financial market processes the information available to investors and incorporates it into the prices of securities. Market efficiency has two general implications. First, in any given time period, a stock's abnormal return depends on information or news received by the market in that period. Second, an investor who uses the same information as the market cannot expect to earn abnormal returns. In other words, systems for playing the market are doomed to fail.

2. What information does the market use to determine prices? The weak form of the efficient market hypothesis says that the market uses the past history of prices and is therefore efficient with respect to these past prices. This implies that stock selection based on patterns of past stock price movements is no better than random stock selection.

3. The semistrong form states that the market uses all publicly available information in setting prices.

4. Strong form efficiency states that the market uses all of the information that anybody knows about stocks, even inside information.

5. Much evidence from different financial markets supports weak form and semistrong form efficiency but not strong form efficiency.

6. Behavioral finance states that the market is not efficient. Adherents argue that:

   a. Investors are not rational.

   b. Deviations from rationality are similar across investors.

   c. Arbitrage, being costly, will not eliminate inefficiencies.

7. Behaviorists point to many studies, including those showing that small stocks outperform large stocks, value stocks outperform growth stocks, and stock prices adjust slowly to earnings surprises, as empirical confirmation of their beliefs.

8. Four implications of market efficiency for corporate finance are:

   a. Managers cannot fool the market through creative accounting.

   b. Firms cannot successfully time issues of debt and equity.

   c. Managers cannot profitably speculate in foreign currencies and other instruments.

   d. Managers can reap many benefits by paying attention to market prices.

CONCEPT QUESTIONS

1. **Firm Value**   What rule should a firm follow when making financing decisions? How can firms create valuable financing opportunities?

2. **Efficient Market Hypothesis**   Define the three forms of market efficiency.

3. **Efficient Market Hypothesis**   Which of the following statements are true about the efficient market hypothesis?

   a. It implies perfect forecasting ability.

   b. It implies that prices reflect all available information.

   c. It implies an irrational market.

   d. It implies that prices do not fluctuate.

   e. It results from keen competition among investors.

4. **Market Efficiency Implications**   Explain why a characteristic of an efficient market is that investments in that market have zero NPVs.

5. **Efficient Market Hypothesis**   A stock market analyst is able to identify mispriced stocks by comparing the average price for the last 10 days to the average price for the last 60 days. If this is true, what do you know about the market?

6. **Semistrong Efficiency**   If a market is semistrong form efficient, is it also weak form efficient? Explain.

7. **Efficient Market Hypothesis**   What are the implications of the efficient market hypothesis for investors who buy and sell stocks in an attempt to "beat the market"?

8. **Stocks versus Gambling**   Critically evaluate the following statement: Playing the stock market is like gambling. Such speculative investing has no social value, other than the pleasure people get from this form of gambling.

9. Efficient Market Hypothesis There are several celebrated investors and stock pickers frequently mentioned in the financial press who have recorded huge returns on their investments over the past two decades. Is the success of these particular investors an invalidation of the EMH? Explain.

10. Efficient Market Hypothesis For each of the following scenarios, discuss whether profit opportunities exist from trading in the stock of the firm under the conditions that (1) the market is not weak form efficient, (2) the market is weak form but not semistrong form efficient, (3) the market is semistrong form but not strong form efficient, and (4) the market is strong form efficient.

a. The stock price has risen steadily each day for the past 30 days.

b. The financial statements for a company were released three days ago, and you believe you've uncovered some anomalies in the company's inventory and cost control reporting techniques that are causing the firm's true liquidity strength to be understated.

c. You observe that the senior management of a company has been buying a lot of the company's stock on the open market over the past week.

Use the following information for the next two questions:

Technical analysis is a controversial investment practice. Technical analysis covers a wide array of techniques, which are all used in an attempt to predict the direction of a particular stock or the market. Technical analysts look at two major types of information: historical stock prices and investor sentiment. A technical analyst would argue these two information sets provide information on the future direction of a particular stock or the market as a whole.

11. Technical Analysis What would a technical analyst say about market efficiency?

12. Investor Sentiment A technical analysis tool that is sometimes used to predict market movements is an investor sentiment index. AAII, the American Association of Individual Investors, publishes an investor sentiment index based on a survey of its members. In the table below you will find the percentage of investors who were bullish, bearish, or neutral during a four-week period.

Week	Bullish	Bearish	Neutral
1	37%	25%	38%
2	52	14	34
3	29	35	36
4	43	26	31

What is the investor sentiment index intended to capture? How might it be useful in technical analysis?

13. Performance of the Pros In the mid- to late-1990s, the performance of the pros was unusually poor—on the order of 90 percent of all equity mutual funds underperformed a passively managed index fund. How does this bear on the issue of market efficiency?

14. Efficient Markets A hundred years ago or so, companies did not compile annual reports. Even if you owned stock in a particular company, you were unlikely to be allowed to see the balance sheet and income statement for the company. Assuming the market is semistrong form efficient, what does this say about market efficiency then compared to now?

15. Efficient Market Hypothesis Aerotech, an aerospace technology research firm, announced this morning that it has hired the world's most knowledgeable and prolific space researchers. Before today, Aerotech's stock had been selling for $100. Assume that no other information is received over the next week and the stock market as a whole does not move.

   a. What do you expect will happen to Aerotech's stock?

   b. Consider the following scenarios:

     i. The stock price jumps to $118 on the day of the announcement. In subsequent days it floats up to $123, then falls back to $116.

     ii. The stock price jumps to $116 and remains at that level.

     iii. The stock price gradually climbs to $116 over the next week.

   Which scenario(s) indicates market efficiency? Which do not? Why?

16. **Efficient Market Hypothesis**   When the 56-year-old founder of Gulf & Western, Inc., died of a heart attack, the stock price immediately jumped from $18.00 a share to $20.25, a 12.5 percent increase. This is evidence of market inefficiency because an efficient stock market would have anticipated his death and adjusted the price beforehand. Assume that no other information is received and the stock market as a whole does not move. Is this statement about market efficiency true or false? Explain.

17. **Efficient Market Hypothesis**   Today, the following announcement was made: "Early today the Justice Department reached a decision in the Universal Product Care (UPC) case. UPC has been found guilty of discriminatory practices in hiring. For the next five years, UPC must pay $2 million each year to a fund representing victims of UPC's policies." Assuming the market is efficient, should investors not buy UPC stock after the announcement because the litigation will cause an abnormally low rate of return? Explain.

18. **Efficient Market Hypothesis**   Newtech Corp. is going to adopt a new chip-testing device that can greatly improve its production efficiency. Do you think the lead engineer can profit from purchasing the firm's stock before the news release on the device? After reading the announcement in *The Wall Street Journal,* should you be able to earn an abnormal return from purchasing the stock if the market is efficient?

19. **Efficient Market Hypothesis**   TransTrust Corp. has changed how it accounts for inventory. Taxes are unaffected, although the resulting earnings report released this quarter is 20 percent higher than what it would have been under the old accounting system. There is no other surprise in the earnings report, and the change in the accounting treatment was publicly announced. If the market is efficient, will the stock price be higher when the market learns that the reported earnings are higher?

20. **Efficient Market Hypothesis**   The Durkin Investing Agency has been the best stock picker in the country for the past two years. Before this rise to fame, the Durkin newsletter had 200 subscribers. Those subscribers beat the market consistently, earning substantially higher returns after adjustment for risk and transaction costs. Subscriptions have skyrocketed to 10,000. Now, when the Durkin Investing Agency recommends a stock, the price instantly rises several points. The subscribers currently earn only a normal return when they buy recommended stock because the price rises before anybody can act on the information. Briefly explain this phenomenon. Is Durkin's ability to pick stocks consistent with market efficiency?

21. **Efficient Market Hypothesis**   Your broker commented that well-managed firms are better investments than poorly managed firms. As evidence, your broker cited a recent study examining 100 small manufacturing firms that eight years earlier had been listed in an industry magazine as the best-managed small manufacturers in the country. In the ensuing eight years, the 100 firms listed have not earned more than the normal market return. Your broker continued to say that if the firms were well managed, they should have produced better-than-average returns. If the market is efficient, do you agree with your broker?

22. **Efficient Market Hypothesis**   A famous economist just announced in *The Wall Street Journal* his findings that the recession is over and the economy is again entering an expansion. Assume market efficiency. Can you profit from investing in the stock market after you read this announcement?

23. **Efficient Market Hypothesis**   Suppose the market is semistrong form efficient. Can you expect to earn excess returns if you make trades based on:

   a.   Your broker's information about record earnings for a stock?

   b.   Rumors about a merger of a firm?

   c.   Yesterday's announcement of a successful new product test?

24. **Efficient Market Hypothesis**   Imagine that a particular macroeconomic variable that influences your firm's net earnings is positively serially correlated. Assume market efficiency. Would you expect price changes in your stock to be serially correlated? Why or why not?

25. **Efficient Market Hypothesis**   The efficient market hypothesis implies that all mutual funds should obtain the same expected risk-adjusted returns. Therefore, we can pick mutual funds at random. Is this statement true or false? Explain.

26. **Efficient Market Hypothesis**   Assume that markets are efficient. During a trading day, American Golf, Inc., announces that it has lost a contract for a large golfing project that, prior to the news, it was widely believed to have secured. If the market is efficient, how should the stock price react to this information if no additional information is released?

27. **Efficient Market Hypothesis**   Prospectors, Inc., is a publicly traded gold prospecting company in Alaska. Although the firm's searches for gold usually fail, the prospectors occasionally find a rich vein of ore. What pattern would you expect to observe for Prospectors's cumulative abnormal returns if the market is efficient?

28. **Evidence on Market Efficiency**   Some people argue that the efficient market hypothesis cannot explain the 1987 market crash or the high price-to-earnings ratio of internet stocks during the late 1990s. What alternative hypothesis is currently used for these two phenomena?

QUESTIONS AND PROBLEMS

1. **Cumulative Abnormal Returns**   Delta, United, and American Airlines announced purchases of planes on July 18 (7/18), February 12 (2/12), and October 7 (10/7), respectively. Given the information below, calculate the cumulative abnormal return (CAR) for these stocks as a group. Graph the result and provide an explanation. All of the stocks have a beta of 1.0, and no other announcements are made.

Basic
(Questions 1–4)

| | Delta | | | United | | | American | |
Date	Market Return	Company Return	Date	Market Return	Company Return	Date	Market Return	Company Return
7/12	−.3	−.5	2/8	−.9	−1.1	10/1	.5	.3
7/13	.0	.2	2/9	−1.0	−1.1	10/2	.4	.6
7/16	.5	.7	2/10	.4	.2	10/3	1.1	1.1
7/17	−.5	−.3	2/11	.6	.8	10/6	.1	−.3
7/18	−2.2	1.1	2/12	−.3	−.1	10/7	−2.2	−.3
7/19	−.9	−.7	2/15	1.1	1.2	10/8	.5	.5
7/20	−1.0	−1.1	2/16	.5	.5	10/9	−.3	−.2
7/23	.7	.5	2/17	−.3	−.2	10/10	.3	.1
7/24	.2	.1	2/18	.3	.2	10/13	.0	−.1

2. **Cumulative Abnormal Returns**   The following diagram shows the cumulative abnormal returns (CARs) for 386 oil exploration companies announcing oil discoveries over the period from 1950 to 1980. Month 0 in the diagram is the announcement month. Assume that no other information is received and the stock market as a whole does not move. Is the diagram consistent with market efficiency? Why or why not?

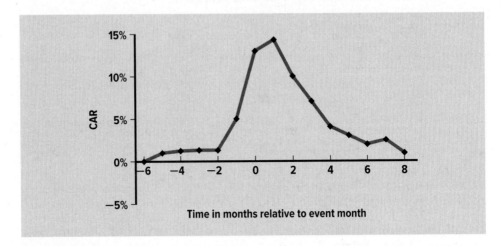

3. **Cumulative Abnormal Returns**   The following figures present the results of four cumulative abnormal return (CAR) studies. Indicate whether the results of each study support, reject, or are inconclusive about the semistrong form of the efficient market hypothesis. In each figure, Time 0 is the date of an event.

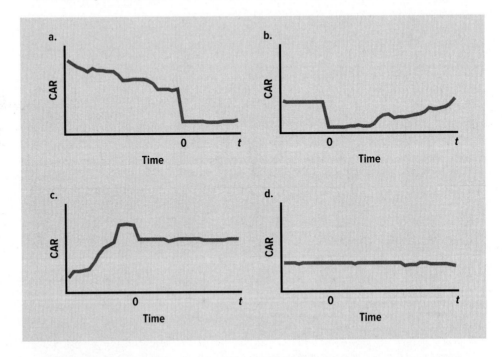

4. **Cumulative Abnormal Returns**   A study analyzed the behavior of the stock prices of firms that had lost antitrust cases. Included in the diagram are all firms that lost the initial court decision, even if the decision was later overturned on appeal. The event at Time 0 is the initial, pre-appeal court decision. Assume no other information was released, aside from that disclosed in the initial trial. The stock prices all have a beta of 1. Is the diagram consistent with market efficiency? Why or why not?

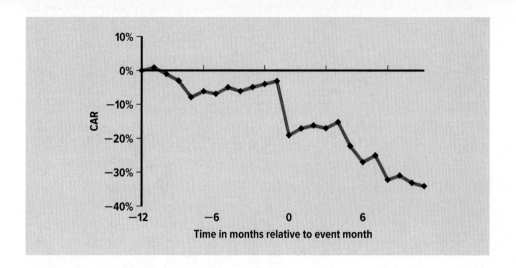

WHAT'S ON THE WEB?

1. **Cumulative Abnormal Returns** On March 22, 2015, Lumber Liquidators (LL) announced that it agreed to pay $2.5 million to California to settle charges related to the use of formaldehyde in the company's laminate flooring sourced in China. In addition to the settlement, the company agreed to ensure that its products complied with the California Air Resources Board formaldehyde level. Investors cheered the news and the stock rose about 16 percent on the day. Go to finance.yahoo.com and find the historical stock prices for the company 15 days before and 15 days after March 22, 2015. Construct the cumulative abnormal return compared to the S&P 500 Index. What does the trading volume look like over this same period?

CLOSING CASE

YOUR 401(k) ACCOUNT AT EAST COAST YACHTS

You have been at your job with East Coast Yachts for a week now and have decided you need to sign up for the company's 401(k) plan. Even after your discussion with Sarah Brown, the Bledsoe Financial Services representative, you are still unsure as to which investment option you should choose. Recall that the options available to you are stock in East Coast Yachts, the Bledsoe S&P 500 Index Fund, the Bledsoe Small-Cap Fund, the Bledsoe Large-Company Stock Fund, the Bledsoe Bond Fund, and the Bledsoe Money Market Fund. You have decided that you should invest in a diversified portfolio, with 70 percent of your investment in equity, 25 percent in bonds, and 5 percent in the money market fund. You have also decided to focus your equity investment on large-cap stocks, but you are debating whether to select the S&P 500 Index Fund or the Large-Company Stock Fund.

In thinking it over, you understand the basic difference in the two funds. One is a purely passive fund that replicates a widely followed large-cap index, the S&P 500, and has low fees. The other is actively managed with the intention that the skill of the portfolio manager will result in improved performance relative to an index. Fees are higher in the latter fund. You're not certain of which way to go, so you ask Dan Ervin, who works in the company's finance area, for advice.

After discussing your concerns, Dan gives you some information comparing the performance of equity mutual funds and the Vanguard 500 Index Fund. The Vanguard 500 is one of the world's largest equity index mutual funds. It replicates the S&P 500, and its return is only negligibly different from the S&P 500. Fees are very low. As a result, the Vanguard 500 is essentially identical to the Bledsoe S&P 500 Index Fund offered in the 401(k) plan, but it has been in existence for much longer, so you can study its track record for over two decades. The graph below summarizes Dan's comments by showing the percentage of equity mutual funds that outperformed the Vanguard 500 Fund over the previous 10 years.[19] So, for example, from January 1989 to December 1998, only about 16 percent of equity mutual funds outperformed the Vanguard 500. Dan suggests that you study the graph and answer the following questions:

1. What implications do you draw from the graph for mutual fund investors?
2. Is the graph consistent or inconsistent with market efficiency? Explain carefully.
3. What investment decision would you make for the equity portion of your 401(k) account? Why?

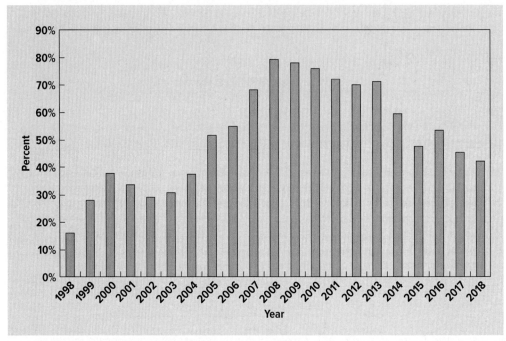

Source: Author calculations using data from the Center for Research in Security Prices (CRSP) Survivor Bias-Free U.S. Mutual Fund Database.

[19] Note that this graph is not hypothetical; it reflects the actual performance of the Vanguard 500 Index Fund relative to a very large population of diversified equity mutual funds. Specialty funds, such as international funds, are excluded. All returns are net of management fees but do not include sales charges (which are known as "loads"), if any. As a result, the performance of actively managed funds is overstated.

Capital Structure: Basic Concepts

OPENING CASE

In addition to lowering the corporate tax rate from 35 percent to 21 percent, the Tax Cuts and Jobs Act of 2017, which was passed that December, limited the tax deductibility of interest expense. The deduction of interest expense is now capped at 30 percent of "adjustable tax income," roughly equivalent to earnings before interest and taxes. Earlier in 2017, with the new law being discussed, corporations responded. For example, BHP announced plans to repurchase $2.5 billion of its bonds, Walmart repurchased $8.5 billion of its debt, and Sprint repurchased $1 billion of its debt. In fact, through the middle of October 2017, U.S. corporations announced plans to repurchase $178.5 billion in debt, more than double the $80 billion of repurchases for the same period in 2016, and way more than the $18 billion in 2014.

So why did these companies decide to repurchase debt? A firm's choice of debt or equity is known as a capital structure decision, and the deductibility of interest expense is an important part of this decision. In this chapter, we discuss the basic ideas underlying capital structures and how firms choose them.

Please visit us at corecorporatefinance.blogspot.com for the latest developments in the world of corporate finance.

14.1 THE CAPITAL STRUCTURE QUESTION AND THE PIE THEORY

How should a firm choose its debt-equity ratio? We call our approach to the capital structure question the **pie model**. If you are wondering why we chose this name, take a look at Figure 14.1. The pie in question is the sum of the financial claims of the firm, which are debt and equity in this case. We define the value of the firm to be this sum. Hence, the value of the firm, V, is:

$$V = B + S \qquad [14.1]$$

where B is the market value of the debt and S is the market value of the equity. Figure 14.1 presents two possible ways of slicing this pie between stock and debt: 40 percent–60 percent and 60 percent–40 percent. If the goal of the management of the firm is to make the firm as valuable as possible, then the firm should pick the debt-equity ratio that makes the pie—the total value—as big as possible.

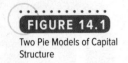

FIGURE 14.1

Two Pie Models of Capital Structure

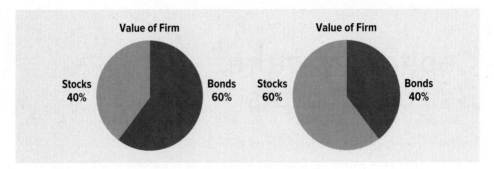

This discussion begs two important questions:

1. Why should the stockholders in the firm care about maximizing the value of the entire firm? After all, the value of the firm is, by definition, the sum of both the debt and the equity. Instead, why should the stockholders not prefer the strategy that maximizes their interests only?

2. What is the ratio of debt to equity that maximizes the shareholders' interests?

Let us examine each of the two questions in turn.

14.2 MAXIMIZING FIRM VALUE VERSUS MAXIMIZING STOCKHOLDER INTERESTS

The following example illustrates that the capital structure that maximizes the value of the firm is the one that financial managers should choose for the shareholders.

EXAMPLE 14.1

Debt and Firm Value

Suppose the market value of the J. J. Sprint Company is $1,000. The company currently has no debt, and each of J. J. Sprint's 100 shares of stock sells for $10. A company such as J. J. Sprint with no debt is called an *unlevered* company. The company plans to borrow $500 and pay the $500 proceeds to shareholders as an extra cash dividend of $5 per share. After the issuance of debt, the firm becomes *levered*. The investments of the firm will not change as a result of this transaction. What will the value of the firm be after the proposed restructuring?

Management recognizes that, by definition, only one of three outcomes can occur from restructuring. Firm value after restructuring can be either (1) greater than the original firm value of $1,000, (2) equal to $1,000, or (3) less than $1,000. After consulting with investment bankers, management believes that restructuring will not change firm value more than $250 in either direction. Thus, it views firm values of $1,250, $1,000, and $750 as the relevant range. The original capital structure and these three possibilities under the new capital structure are presented next.

	No Debt (Original Capital Structure)	Value of Debt plus Equity after Payment of Dividend (Three Possibilities)		
		1	2	3
Debt	$ 0	$ 500	$ 500	$500
Equity	1,000	750	500	250
Firm value	$1,000	$1,250	$1,000	$750

Note that the value of equity is below $1,000 under any of the three possibilities. This can be explained in one of two ways. First, the table shows the value of the equity after the extra cash dividend is paid. Because cash is paid out, a dividend represents a partial liquidation of the firm. Consequently, there is less value in the firm for the equityholders after the dividend payment. Second, in the event of a future liquidation, stockholders will be paid only after bondholders have been paid in full. Thus, the debt is an encumbrance of the firm, reducing the value of the equity.

Of course, management recognizes that there are infinite possible outcomes. The above three are to be viewed as representative outcomes only. We can now determine the payoff to stockholders under the three possibilities.

	Payoff to Shareholders after Restructuring		
	1	2	3
Capital gains	−$250	−$500	−$750
Dividends	500	500	500
Net gain or loss to stockholders	$250	$ 0	−$250

No one can be sure ahead of time which of the three outcomes will occur. However, imagine that managers believe that Outcome 1 is most likely. They should definitely restructure the firm because the stockholders would gain $250. That is, although the price of the stock declines by $250 to $750, they receive $500 in dividends. Their net gain is $250 (= −$250 + 500). Also, notice that the value of the firm would rise by $250 (= $1,250 − 1,000).

Alternatively, imagine that managers believe that Outcome 3 is most likely. In this case, they should not restructure the firm because the stockholders would expect a $250 loss. That is, the stock falls by $750 to $250 and they receive $500 in dividends. Their net loss is −$250 (= −$750 + 500). Also, notice that the value of the firm would change by −$250 (= $750 − 1,000).

Finally, imagine that the managers believe that Outcome 2 is most likely. Restructuring would not affect the stockholders' interest because the net gain to stockholders in this case is zero. Also, notice that the value of the firm is unchanged if Outcome 2 occurs.

This example explains why managers should attempt to maximize the value of the firm. In other words, it answers Question 1 in Section 14.1. We find in this example that:

Managers should choose the capital structure that they believe will have the highest firm value because this capital structure will be most beneficial to the firm's stockholders.[1]

Clearly J. J. Sprint should borrow $500 if it expects Outcome 1. Note, however, that this example does not tell us which of the three outcomes is most likely to occur. Thus, it does not tell us whether debt should be added to J. J. Sprint's capital structure. In other words, it does not answer Question 2 in Section 14.1. This second question is treated in the next section.

---

[1] This result may not hold exactly in a more complex case where debt has a significant possibility of default. Issues of default are treated in the next chapter.

14.3 FINANCIAL LEVERAGE AND FIRM VALUE: AN EXAMPLE

Leverage and Returns to Shareholders

ExcelMaster
coverage online
www.mhhe.com/RossCore6e

The previous section shows that the capital structure producing the highest firm value is the one that maximizes shareholder wealth. In this section, we wish to determine that optimal capital structure. We begin by illustrating the effect of capital structure on returns to stockholders. We will use a detailed example that we encourage students to study carefully. Once we have this example under our belts, we will be ready to determine the optimal capital structure.

Trans Am Corporation currently has no debt in its capital structure. The firm is considering issuing debt to buy back some of its equity. Both its current and proposed capital structures are presented in Table 14.1. The firm's assets are $8,000. There are 400 shares of the all-equity firm, implying a market value per share of $20. The proposed debt issue is for $4,000, leaving $4,000 in equity. The interest rate is 10 percent.

The effect of economic conditions on earnings per share is shown in Table 14.2 for the current capital structure (all-equity). Consider first the middle column, where earnings are expected to be $1,200. Because assets are $8,000, the return on assets (ROA) is 15 percent (= $1,200/$8,000). Because assets equal equity for this all-equity firm, return on equity (ROE) is also 15 percent. Earnings per share (EPS) are $3.00 (= $1,200/400). Similar calculations yield EPS of $1.00 and $5.00 in the cases of recession and expansion, respectively.

The case of leverage is presented in Table 14.3. ROA in the three economic states is identical in Tables 14.2 and 14.3 because this ratio is calculated before interest is considered. Because debt is $4,000 here, interest is $400 (= .10 × $4,000). Thus, earnings after interest are $800 (= $1,200 − 400) in the expected case. Because equity is $4,000, ROE is 20 percent (= $800/$4,000). Earnings per share are $4.00 (= $800/200). Similar calculations yield earnings of $0 and $8.00 for recession and expansion, respectively.

Tables 14.2 and 14.3 show that the effect of financial leverage depends on the company's earnings before interest. If earnings before interest are equal to $1,200, the return on equity (ROE) is higher under the proposed structure. If earnings before interest are equal to $400, the ROE is higher under the current structure.

TABLE 14.1

Financial Structure of Trans Am Corporation

	Current	Proposed
Assets	$8,000	$8,000
Debt	$ 0	$4,000
Equity (market and book)	$8,000	$4,000
Interest rate	10%	10%
Market value/share	$ 20	$ 20
Shares outstanding	400	200

TABLE 14.2

Trans Am's Current Capital Structure: No Debt

	Recession	Expected	Expansion
Return on assets (ROA)	5%	15%	25%
Earnings	$400	$1,200	$2,000
Return on equity (ROE) = Earnings/Equity	5%	15%	25%
Earnings per share (EPS)	$1.00	$3.00	$5.00

	Recession	Expected	Expansion
Return on assets (ROA)	5%	15%	25%
Earnings before interest (EBI)	$400	$1,200	$2,000
Interest	400	400	400
Earnings after interest	$ 0	$ 800	$1,600
Return on equity (ROE) = Earnings after interest/Equity	0%	20%	40%
Earnings per share (EPS)	$0	$4.00	$8.00

TABLE 14.3

Trans Am's Proposed Capital Structure: Debt = $4,000

This idea is represented in Figure 14.2. The solid line represents the case of no leverage. The line begins at the origin, indicating that earnings per share (EPS) would be zero if earnings before interest (EBI) were zero. The EPS rises in tandem with a rise in EBI.

The dotted line represents the case of $4,000 of debt. Here, EPS is negative if EBI is zero. This follows because $400 of interest must be paid regardless of the firm's profits.

Now consider the slopes of the two lines. The slope of the dotted line (the line with debt) is higher than the slope of the solid line. This occurs because the levered firm has fewer shares of stock outstanding than the unlevered firm. Therefore, any increase in EBI leads to a greater rise in EPS for the levered firm because the earnings increase is distributed over fewer shares of stock.

Because the dotted line has a lower intercept but a higher slope, the two lines must intersect. The break-even point occurs at $800 of EBI. Were earnings before interest to be $800, both firms would produce $2 of EPS. Because $800 is the break-even point, earnings above $800 lead to greater EPS for the levered firm. Earnings below $800 lead to greater EPS for the unlevered firm.

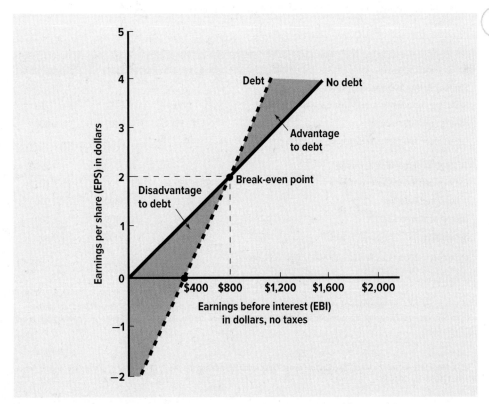

FIGURE 14.2

Financial Leverage: EPS and EBI for the Trans Am Corporation

The Choice between Debt and Equity

Tables 14.2 and 14.3 and Figure 14.2 are important because they show the effect of leverage on earnings per share. Students should study the tables and figure until they feel comfortable with the calculation of each number in them. However, we have not yet presented the punch line. That is, we have not yet stated which capital structure is better for Trans Am.

At this point, many students believe that leverage is beneficial because EPS is expected to be $4.00 with leverage and only $3.00 without leverage. However, leverage also creates risk. Note that in a recession, EPS is higher ($1.00 versus $0) for the unlevered firm. Thus, a risk-averse investor might prefer the all-equity firm, while a less risk-averse investor might prefer leverage. Given this ambiguity, which capital structure is better?

Modigliani and Miller (MM or M&M) have a convincing argument that a firm cannot change the total value of its outstanding securities by changing the proportions of its capital structure. In other words, the value of the firm is always the same under different capital structures. In still other words, no capital structure is any better or worse than any other capital structure for the firm's stockholders. This rather pessimistic result is the famous MM Proposition I.[2]

Their argument compares a simple strategy, which we call Strategy A, with a two-part strategy, which we call Strategy B. Both of these strategies for shareholders of Trans Am are illuminated in Table 14.4. Let us now examine the first strategy.

STRATEGY A—BUY 100 SHARES OF THE LEVERED EQUITY

The first line in the top panel of Table 14.4 shows EPS for the proposed levered equity in the three economic states. The second line shows the earnings in the three states for an individual buying 100 shares. The next line shows that the cost of these 100 shares is $2,000.

Let us now consider the second strategy, which has two parts to it:

<table>
<tr><td></td><td>Recession</td><td>Expected</td><td>Expansion</td></tr>
<tr><td colspan="4">Strategy A: Buy 100 Shares of Levered Equity</td></tr>
<tr><td>EPS of levered equity (taken from last line of Table 14.3)</td><td>$0</td><td>$4</td><td>$8</td></tr>
<tr><td>Earnings per 100 shares</td><td>$0</td><td>$400</td><td>$800</td></tr>
<tr><td>Initial cost = 100 shares @ $20/share = $2,000</td><td></td><td></td><td></td></tr>
<tr><td colspan="4">Strategy B: Homemade Leverage</td></tr>
<tr><td>Earnings per 200 shares in current</td><td>$1 × 200 =</td><td>$3 × 200 =</td><td>$5 × 200 =</td></tr>
<tr><td>   unlevered Trans Am</td><td>$200</td><td>$600</td><td>$1,000</td></tr>
<tr><td>Interest at 10% on $2,000</td><td>200</td><td>200</td><td>200</td></tr>
<tr><td>Net earnings</td><td>$0</td><td>$400</td><td>$800</td></tr>
<tr><td colspan="4">Initial cost = 200 shares @ $20 share − $2,000 = $2,000
      Cost of stock   Amount
                             borrowed</td></tr>
</table>

TABLE 14.4

Payoff and Cost to Shareholders of Trans Am Corporation under the Proposed Structure and under the Current Structure with Homemade Leverage

Investor receives the same payoff whether she (1) buys shares in a levered corporation or (2) buys shares in an unlevered firm and borrows on personal account. Her initial investment is the same in either case. Thus, the firm neither helps nor hurts her by adding debt to the capital structure.

[2] Franco Modigliani and Merton Miller, "The Cost of Capital, Corporation Finance and the Theory of Investment," *American Economic Review* 47, no. 3 (1958), pp. 261–97.

STRATEGY B—HOMEMADE LEVERAGE

1. Borrow $2,000 from either a bank or, more likely, a brokerage house. (If the brokerage house is the lender, we say that this activity is *going on margin*.)
2. Use the borrowed proceeds plus your own investment of $2,000 (a total of $4,000) to buy 200 shares of the current unlevered equity at $20 per share.

The bottom panel of Table 14.4 shows payoffs under Strategy B, which we call the *homemade leverage* strategy. First, observe the middle column, which indicates that 200 shares of the unlevered equity are expected to generate $600 of earnings. Assuming that the $2,000 is borrowed at a 10 percent interest rate, the interest expense is $200 (= .10 × $2,000). Thus, the net earnings are expected to be $400. A similar calculation generates net earnings of either $0 or $800 in recession or expansion, respectively.

Now, let us compare these two strategies, both in terms of net earnings and in terms of initial cost. The top panel of the table shows that Strategy A generates earnings of $0, $400, and $800 in the three states. The bottom panel of the table shows that Strategy B generates the same net earnings in the three states.

The top panel of the table shows that Strategy A involves an initial cost of $2,000. Similarly, the bottom panel shows an identical net cost of $2,000 for Strategy B.

This shows a very important result. Both the cost and the payoff from the two strategies are the same. Thus, one must conclude that Trans Am is neither helping nor hurting its stockholders by restructuring. In other words, an investor is not receiving anything from corporate leverage that she could not receive on her own.

Note that, as shown in Table 14.1, the equity of the unlevered firm is valued at $8,000. Because the equity of the levered firm is $4,000 and its debt is $4,000, the value of the levered firm is also $8,000. Now suppose that, for whatever reason, the value of the levered firm were actually greater than the value of the unlevered firm. Here, Strategy A would cost more than Strategy B. In this case, an investor would prefer to borrow on his own account and invest in the stock of the unlevered firm. He would get the same net earnings each year as if he had invested in the stock of the levered firm. However, his cost would be less. The strategy would not be unique to our investor. Given the higher value of the levered firm, no rational investor would invest in the stock of the levered firm. Anyone desiring shares in the levered firm would get the same dollar return more cheaply by borrowing to finance a purchase of the unlevered firm's shares. The equilibrium result would be, of course, that the value of the levered firm would fall and the value of the unlevered firm would rise until they became equal. At this point, individuals would be indifferent between Strategy A and Strategy B.

This example illustrates the basic result of MM and is, as we have noted, commonly called their Proposition I. We restate this proposition as:

> **MM Proposition I (no taxes): The value of the levered firm is the same as the value of the unlevered firm.**

This is generally considered the beginning point of modern managerial finance. Before MM, the effect of leverage on the value of the firm was considered complex and convoluted. Modigliani and Miller showed a blindingly simple result: If levered firms are priced too high, rational investors will borrow on their personal accounts to buy shares in unlevered firms. This substitution is often called homemade leverage. As long as individuals borrow (and lend) on the same terms as the firms, they can duplicate the effects of corporate leverage on their own.

The example of Trans Am Corporation shows that leverage does not affect the value of the firm. Because we showed earlier that stockholders' welfare is directly related to the firm's value, changes in capital structure cannot affect the stockholders' welfare.

A Key Assumption

The MM result hinges on the assumption that individuals can borrow as cheaply as corporations. If, alternatively, individuals can only borrow at a higher rate, one can easily show that corporations can increase firm value by borrowing.

Is this assumption of equal borrowing costs a good one? Individuals who want to buy stock and borrow can do so by establishing a margin account with a brokerage firm. Under this arrangement, the brokerage firm loans the individual a portion of the purchase price. For example, the individual might buy $10,000 of stock by investing $6,000 of her own funds and borrowing $4,000 from the brokerage firm. Should the stock be worth $9,000 on the next day, the individual's net worth or equity in the account would be $5,000 (= $9,000 − 4,000).[3]

The brokerage firm fears that a sudden price drop will cause the equity in the individual's account to be negative, implying that the brokerage firm may not get her loan repaid in full. To guard against this possibility, stock exchange rules require that the individual make additional cash contributions (replenish her margin account) as the stock price falls. Because (1) the procedures for replenishing the account have developed over many years and (2) the brokerage firm holds the stock as collateral, there is little default risk to the brokerage firm.[4] In particular, if margin contributions are not made on time, the brokerage firm can sell the stock in order to satisfy her loan. Therefore, brokerage firms generally charge low interest, with many rates being only slightly above the risk-free rate.

By contrast, corporations frequently borrow using illiquid assets (e.g., plant and equipment) as collateral. The costs to the lender of initial negotiation and ongoing supervision, as well as of working out arrangements in the event of financial distress, can be quite substantial. Thus, it is difficult to argue that individuals must borrow at higher rates than corporations.

14.4 MODIGLIANI AND MILLER: PROPOSITION II (NO TAXES)

Risk to Equityholders Rises with Leverage

At a Trans Am corporate meeting, a corporate officer said, "Well, maybe it does not matter whether the corporation or the individual levers—as long as some leverage takes place. Leverage benefits investors. After all, an investor's expected return rises with the amount of the leverage present." He then pointed out that, as shown in Tables 14.2 and 14.3, the expected return on unlevered equity is 15 percent while the expected return on levered equity is 20 percent.

However, another officer replied, "Not necessarily. Though the expected return rises with leverage, the risk rises as well." This point can be seen from an examination of Tables 14.2 and 14.3. With earnings before interest (EBI) varying between $400 and $2,000, EPS for the stockholders of the unlevered firm varies between $1.00 and $5.00. EPS for the stockholders of the levered firm varies between $0 and $8.00. This greater range for the EPS of the levered firm implies greater risk for the levered firm's stockholders. In other words, levered stockholders have better returns in good times than do unlevered stockholders, but they have worse returns in bad times. The two tables also show greater range for the ROE of the levered firm's stockholders. The above interpretation concerning risk applies here as well.

---

[3] We are ignoring the one-day interest charge on the loan.

[4] Had this text been published before October 19, 1987, when stock prices declined by more than 20 percent in a single day, we might have used the phrase "virtually no" risk instead of "little" risk.

The same insight can be taken from Figure 14.2. The slope of the line for the levered firm is greater than the slope of the line for the unlevered firm. This means that the levered stockholders have better returns in good times than do unlevered stockholders but worse returns in bad times, implying greater risk with leverage. In other words, the slope of the line measures the risk to stockholders because the slope indicates the responsiveness of EPS to changes in firm performance (earnings before interest).

Proposition II: Required Return to Equityholders Rises with Leverage

Because levered equity has greater risk, it should have a greater expected return as compensation. In our example, the market requires only a 15 percent expected return for the unlevered equity, but it requires a 20 percent expected return for the levered equity.

This type of reasoning allows us to develop MM Proposition II. Here, MM argue that the expected return on equity is positively related to leverage because the risk to equityholders increases with leverage.

To develop this position, recall that the firm's weighted average cost of capital, WACC, can be written as:[5]

$$\text{WACC} = \frac{S}{B+S} \times R_S + \frac{B}{B+S} \times R_B \qquad [14.2]$$

where:

R_B = The cost of debt
R_S = The expected return on equity or stock, also called the cost of equity or the required return on equity
WACC = The firm's weighted average cost of capital
B = The value of the firm's debt or bonds
S = The value of the firm's stock or equity

Equation 14.2 is quite intuitive. It says that a firm's weighted average cost of capital is a weighted average of its cost of debt and its cost of equity. The weight applied to debt is the proportion of debt in the capital structure, and the weight applied to equity is the proportion of equity in the capital structure. Calculations of the WACC from Equation 14.2 for both the unlevered and the levered firm are presented in Table 14.5.

TABLE 14.5

Cost of Capital Calculations for Trans Am

$$\text{WACC} = \frac{S}{B+S} \times R_S + \frac{B}{B+S} \times R_B$$

Unlevered firm: $15\% = \dfrac{\$8,000}{\$8,000} \times 15\%^* + \dfrac{0}{\$8,000} \times 10\%^\dagger$

Levered firm: $15\% = \dfrac{\$4,000}{\$8,000} \times 20\%^{**} + \dfrac{\$4,000}{\$8,000} \times 10\%^\dagger$

*From the "Expected" column in Table 14.2, we learn that expected earnings for the unlevered firm are $1,200. From Table 14.1, we learn that equity for the unlevered firm is $8,000. Thus, R_S for the unlevered firm is:

$$\frac{\text{Expected earnings}}{\text{Equity}} = \frac{\$1,200}{\$8,000} = .15, \text{ or } 15\%$$

**From the "Expected" column in Table 14.3, we learn that expected earnings after interest for the levered firm are $800. From Table 14.1, we learn that equity for the levered firm is $4,000. Thus, R_S for the levered firm is:

$$\frac{\text{Expected earnings after interest}}{\text{Equity}} = \frac{\$800}{\$4,000} = .20, \text{ or } 20\%$$

† 10% is the cost of debt.

[5] Because we do not have taxes here, the cost of debt is R_B, not $R_B(1 - T_C)$ as it was in Chapter 12.

An implication of MM Proposition I is that the WACC is a constant for a given firm, regardless of the capital structure.[6] For example, Table 14.5 shows that the WACC for Trans Am is 15 percent, with or without leverage.

Let us now define R_0 to be the *cost of capital for an all-equity firm*. For the Trans Am Corp., R_0 is calculated as:

$$R_0 = \frac{\text{Expected earnings of unlevered firm}}{\text{Unlevered equity}} = \frac{\$1,200}{\$8,000} = .15, \text{ or } 15\%$$

As can be seen from Table 14.5, WACC is equal to R_0 for Trans Am. In fact, WACC must always equal R_0 in a world without corporate taxes.

Proposition II states the expected return of equity, R_S, in terms of leverage. The exact relationship, derived by setting WACC $= R_0$ and then rearranging Equation 14.2, is:

MM Proposition II (no taxes):

$$R_S = R_0 + (R_0 - R_B)\frac{B}{S} \qquad [14.3]$$

Equation 14.3 implies that the required return on equity is a linear function of the firm's debt-equity ratio. Examining Equation 14.3, we see that if R_0 exceeds the debt rate, R_B, then the cost of equity rises with increases in the debt-equity ratio, B/S. Normally, R_0 should exceed R_B. That is, because even unlevered equity is risky, it should have an expected return greater than that of riskless debt. Note that Equation 14.3 holds for Trans Am in its levered state:

$$.20, \text{ or } 20\% = .15 + \frac{\$4,000}{\$4,000}(.15 - .10)$$

Figure 14.3 graphs Equation 14.3. As you can see, we have plotted the relation between the cost of equity, R_S, and the debt-equity ratio, B/S, as a straight line. What we witness in Equation 14.3 and illustrate in Figure 14.3 is the effect of leverage on the cost of equity.

FIGURE 14.3

The Cost of Equity, the Cost of Debt, and the Weighted Average Cost of Capital: MM Proposition II with No Corporate Taxes

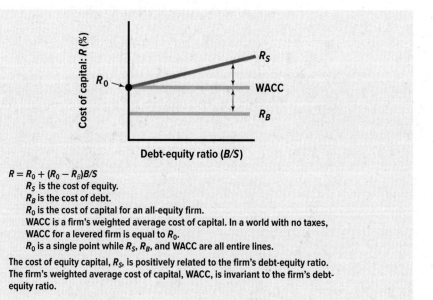

$R = R_0 + (R_0 - R_B)B/S$
R_S is the cost of equity.
R_B is the cost of debt.
R_0 is the cost of capital for an all-equity firm.
WACC is a firm's weighted average cost of capital. In a world with no taxes, WACC for a levered firm is equal to R_0.
R_0 is a single point while R_S, R_B, and WACC are all entire lines.

The cost of equity capital, R_S, is positively related to the firm's debt-equity ratio. The firm's weighted average cost of capital, WACC, is invariant to the firm's debt-equity ratio.

---

[6] This statement holds in a world of no taxes. It does not hold in a world with taxes, a point to be brought out later in this chapter (see Figure 14.6).

As the firm raises the debt-equity ratio, each dollar of equity is levered with additional debt. This raises the risk of equity and therefore the required return, R_S, on the equity.

Figure 14.3 also shows that the WACC is unaffected by leverage, a point we made above. It is important for students to realize that R_0, the cost of capital for an all-equity firm, is represented by a single dot on the graph. By contrast, WACC is an entire line.

MM Propositions I and II

Luteran Motors, an all-equity firm, has expected earnings of $10 million per year in perpetuity. The firm pays all of its earnings out as dividends, so that the $10 million may also be viewed as the stockholders' expected cash flow. There are 10 million shares outstanding, implying expected annual cash flow of $1 per share. The cost of capital for this unlevered firm is 10 percent. In addition, the firm will soon build a new plant for $4 million. The plant is expected to generate additional cash flow of $1 million per year. These figures can be described as:

Current Company	New Plant
Cash flow: $10 million	Initial outlay: $4 million
Number of outstanding shares: 10 million	Additional annual cash flow: $1 million

The project's net present value is:

$$-\$4 \text{ million} + \frac{\$1 \text{ million}}{.1} = \$6 \text{ million}$$

assuming that the project is discounted at the same rate as the firm as a whole. Before the market knows of the project, the market value balance sheet of the firm is:

LUTERAN MOTORS	
Balance Sheet (all Equity)	
Old assets: $\frac{\$10 \text{ million}}{.1} = \$100$ million	Equity $100 million
	(10 million shares of stock)

The value of the firm is $100 million because the cash flow of $10 million per year is capitalized (discounted) at 10 percent. A share of stock sells for $10 (= $100 million/10 million) because there are 10 million shares outstanding.

The market value balance sheet is a useful tool of financial analysis. Because students are often thrown off guard by it initially, we recommend extra study here. The key is that the market value balance sheet has the same form as the balance sheet that accountants use. That is, assets are placed on the left-hand side, whereas liabilities and owners' equity are placed on the right-hand side. In addition, the left-hand side and the right-hand side must be equal. The difference between a market value balance sheet and the accountant's balance sheet is in the numbers. Accountants value items in terms of historical cost (original purchase price less depreciation), whereas financial analysts value items in terms of market value.

The firm will issue $4 million of either equity or debt. Let us consider the effect of equity and debt financing in turn.

Stock Financing   Imagine that the firm announces that in the near future, it will raise $4 million in equity in order to build a new plant. The stock price, and therefore the value of the firm, will rise to reflect the positive net present value of the plant. According to efficient markets, the increase occurs immediately. That is, the rise occurs on the day of the announcement, not on the date of

(Continued)

either the onset of construction of the plant or the forthcoming stock offering. The market value balance sheet becomes:

LUTERAN MOTORS Balance Sheet (upon announcement of equity issue to construct plant)			
Old assets	$100 million	Equity	$106 million
			(10 million shares of stock)
NPV of plant:			
$-\$4 \text{ million} + \dfrac{\$1 \text{ million}}{.1} =$	6 million		
Total assets	$106 million		

Note that the NPV of the plant is included in the market value balance sheet. Because the new shares have not yet been issued, the number of outstanding shares remains 10 million. The price per share has now risen to $10.60 (= $106 million/10 million) to reflect news concerning the plant.

Shortly thereafter, $4 million of stock is issued or floated. Because the stock is selling at $10.60 per share, 377,358 (= $4 million/$10.60) shares of stock are issued. Imagine that funds are put in the bank temporarily before being used to build the plant. The market value balance sheet becomes:

LUTERAN MOTORS Balance Sheet (upon issuance of stock but before construction begins on plant)			
Old assets	$100 million	Equity	$110 million
			(10,377,358 shares of stock)
NPV of plant:	6 million		
Proceeds from new issue of stock (currently placed in bank)	4 million		
Total assets	$110 million		

The number of shares outstanding is now 10,377,358 because 377,358 new shares were issued. The price per share is $10.60 (= $110,000,000/10,377,358). Note that the price has not changed. This is consistent with efficient capital markets because the stock price should only move due to new information.

Of course, the funds are placed in the bank only temporarily. Shortly after the new issue, the $4 million is given to a contractor who builds the plant. To avoid problems in discounting, we assume that the plant is built immediately. The balance sheet then becomes:

LUTERAN MOTORS Balance Sheet (upon completion of the plant)			
Old assets	$100 million	Equity	$110 million
			(10,377,358 shares of stock)
PV of plant: $\dfrac{\$1 \text{ million}}{.1} =$	10 million		
Total assets	$110 million		

Though total assets do not change, the composition of the assets does change. The bank account has been emptied to pay the contractor. The present value of cash flows of $1 million a year from the plant is reflected as an asset worth $10 million. Because the building expenditures of $4 million have already been paid, they no longer represent a future cost. Hence, they no longer reduce the value of the plant. According to efficient capital markets, the price per share of stock remains $10.60.

Expected yearly cash flow from the firm is $11 million, $10 million of which comes from the old assets and $1 million from the new. The expected return to equityholders is:

$$R_S = \frac{\$11 \text{ million}}{\$110 \text{ million}} = .10, \text{ or } 10\%$$

Because the firm is all equity, $R_S = R_0 = .10$.

Debt Financing   Alternatively, imagine the firm announces that, in the near future, it will borrow $4 million at 6 percent to build a new plant. This implies yearly interest payments of $240,000 (= $4,000,000 × .06). Again, the stock price rises immediately to reflect the positive net present value of the plant. Thus, we have:

LUTERAN MOTORS Balance Sheet (upon announcement of debt issue to construct plant)			
Old assets	$100 million	Equity	$106 million
			(10 million shares of stock)
NPV of plant:			
$-\$4 \text{ million} + \dfrac{\$1 \text{ million}}{.1} =$	6 million		
Total assets	$106 million		

The value of the firm is the same as in the equity financing case because (1) the same plant is to be built and (2) MM proved that debt financing is neither better nor worse than equity financing.

At some point, $4 million of debt is issued. As before, the funds are placed in the bank temporarily. The market value balance sheet becomes:

LUTERAN MOTORS Balance Sheet (upon issuance but before construction begins on plant)			
Old assets	$100 million	Debt	$ 4 million
NPV of plant:	6 million	Equity	$106 million
			(10 million shares of stock)
Proceeds from debt issue (currently invested in bank)	4 million		
Total assets	$110 million	Debt plus equity	$110 million

Note that debt appears on the right-hand side of the balance sheet. The stock price is still $10.60, in accordance with our discussion of efficient capital markets.

Finally, the contractor receives $4 million and builds the plant. The market value balance sheet becomes:

LUTERAN MOTORS Balance Sheet (upon completion of the plant)			
Old assets	$100 million	Debt	$4 million
PV of plant	10 million	Equity	$106 million
			(10 million shares of stock)
Total assets	$110 million	Debt plus equity	$110 million

(*Continued*)

The only change here is that the bank account has been depleted to pay the contractor. The equityholders expect yearly cash flow after interest of:

$$
\begin{array}{ccccccc}
\$10{,}000{,}000 & + & 1{,}000{,}000 & - & 240{,}000 & = & \$10{,}760{,}000 \\
\text{Cash flow on} & & \text{Cash flow on} & & \text{Interest} & & \\
\text{old assets} & & \text{new assets} & & (\$4\text{ million} \times .06) & &
\end{array}
$$

The equityholders expect to earn a return of:

$$
\frac{\$10{,}760{,}000}{\$106{,}000{,}000} = .1015, \text{ or } 10.15\%
$$

This return of 10.15 percent for levered equityholders is higher than the 10 percent return for the unlevered equityholders. This result is sensible because, as we argued earlier, levered equity is riskier. In fact, the return of 10.15 percent should be exactly what MM Proposition II predicts. This prediction can be verified by plugging values into Equation 14.3:

$$
R_S = R_0 + \frac{B}{S} \times (R_0 - R_B)
$$

Doing so, we obtain:

$$
.1015, \text{ or } 10.15\% = .10 + \frac{\$4{,}000{,}000}{\$106{,}000{,}000} \times (.10 - .06)
$$

This example was useful for two reasons. First, we wanted to introduce the concept of market value balance sheets, a tool that will prove useful elsewhere in the text. Among other things, this technique allows one to calculate the price per share of a new issue of stock. Second, the example illustrates three aspects of Modigliani and Miller:

1. The example is consistent with MM Proposition I because the value of the firm is $110 million after either equity or debt financing.
2. Students are often more interested in stock price than in firm value. We show that the stock price is always $10.60, regardless of whether debt or equity financing is used.
3. The example is consistent with MM Proposition II. The expected return to equityholders rises from 10 to 10.15 percent, just as Equation 14.3 states. This rise occurs because the equityholders of a levered firm face more risk than do the equityholders of an unlevered firm.

MM: An Interpretation

The Modigliani-Miller results indicate that managers cannot change the value of a firm by repackaging the firm's securities. Though this idea was considered revolutionary when it was originally proposed in the late 1950s, the MM approach and proof have since met with wide acclaim.[7]

MM argue that the firm's overall cost of capital cannot be reduced as debt is substituted for equity, even though debt appears to be cheaper than equity. The reason for this is that as the firm adds debt, the remaining equity becomes more risky. As this risk rises, the cost of equity capital rises as a result. The increase in the cost of the remaining equity capital offsets the higher proportion of the firm financed by low-cost debt. In fact, MM prove that the two effects exactly offset each other, so that both the value of the firm and the firm's overall cost of capital are invariant to leverage.

MM use an interesting analogy to food. They consider a dairy farmer with two choices. On the one hand, he can sell whole milk. On the other hand, by skimming, he can sell a combination of cream and low-fat milk. Though the farmer can get a high price for the cream, he gets a low price for the low-fat milk, implying no net gain. In fact, imagine that the proceeds from the whole-milk strategy were less than those from the cream/low-fat milk strategy. Arbitrageurs would buy the whole milk, perform the skimming operation themselves, and

---

[7] Both Merton Miller and Franco Modigliani were awarded separate Nobel Prizes, in part for their work on capital structure.

resell the cream and low-fat milk separately. Competition between arbitrageurs would tend to boost the price of whole milk until proceeds from the two strategies became equal. Thus, the value of the farmer's milk is invariant to the way in which the milk is packaged.

Food found its way into this chapter earlier, when we viewed the firm as a pie. MM argue that the size of the pie does not change, no matter how stockholders and bondholders divide it. MM say that a firm's capital structure is irrelevant; it is what it is by some historical accident. The theory implies that firms' debt-equity ratios could be anything. They are what they are because of whimsical and random managerial decisions about how much to borrow and how much stock to issue.

Although scholars are always fascinated with far-reaching theories, students are perhaps more concerned with real-world applications. Do real-world managers follow MM by treating capital structure decisions with indifference? Unfortunately for the theory, virtually all companies in certain industries, such as banking, choose high debt-equity ratios. Conversely, companies in other industries, such as pharmaceuticals, choose low debt-equity ratios. In fact, almost any industry has a debt-equity ratio to which companies in that industry tend to adhere. Thus, companies do not appear to be selecting their degree of leverage in a frivolous or random manner. Because of this, financial economists (including MM themselves) have argued that real-world factors may have been left out of the theory.

Though many of our students have argued that individuals can only borrow at rates above the corporate borrowing rate, we disagreed with this argument earlier in the chapter. But when we look elsewhere for unrealistic assumptions in the theory, we find two:[8]

1. Taxes were ignored.
2. Bankruptcy costs and other agency costs were not considered.

We turn to taxes in the next section. Bankruptcy costs and other agency costs will be treated in the next chapter. A summary of the main Modigliani-Miller results without taxes is presented in the nearby boxed section.

14.5 TAXES

The Basic Insight

The previous part of this chapter showed that firm value is unrelated to debt in a world without taxes. We now show that, in the presence of corporate taxes, the firm's value is positively related to its debt. The basic intuition can be seen from a pie chart, such as the

---

[8] MM were aware of both of these issues, as can be seen in their original paper.

FIGURE 14.4

Two Pie Models of Capital
Structure under Corporate
Taxes

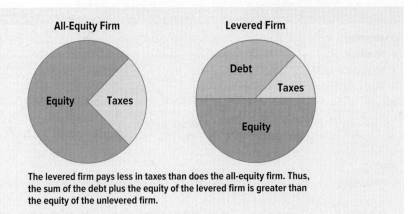

All-Equity Firm   **Levered Firm**

The levered firm pays less in taxes than does the all-equity firm. Thus,
the sum of the debt plus the equity of the levered firm is greater than
the equity of the unlevered firm.

one in Figure 14.4. Consider the all-equity firm on the left. Here, both equityholders and the IRS have claims on the firm. The value of the all-equity firm is, of course, that part of the pie owned by the equityholders. The proportion going to taxes is a cost.

The pie on the right for the levered firm shows three claims: equityholders, debtholders, and taxes. The value of the levered firm is the sum of the value of the debt and the value of the equity. In selecting between the two capital structures in the picture, a financial manager should select the one with the higher value. Assuming that the total area is the same for both pies,[9] value is maximized for the capital structure paying the least in taxes. In other words, the manager should choose the capital structure that the IRS hates the most.

We will show that due to a quirk in U.S. tax law, the proportion of the pie allocated to taxes is less for the levered firm than it is for the unlevered firm. Thus, managers should select high leverage.

EXAMPLE 14.3

Taxes and Cash Flow

The Water Products Company has a corporate tax rate, T_C, of 21 percent and expected earnings before interest and taxes (EBIT) of $1 million each year. Its entire earnings after taxes are paid out as dividends.

The firm is considering two alternative capital structures. Under Plan I, Water Products would have no debt in its capital structure. Under Plan II, the company would have $4,000,000 of debt, B. The cost of debt, R_B, is 10 percent.

The chief financial officer for Water Products makes the following calculations:

	Plan I	Plan II
Earnings before interest and corporate taxes (EBIT)	$1,000,000	$1,000,000
Interest $(R_B B)$	0	400,000
Earnings before taxes (EBT $= \text{EBIT} - R_B B$)	$1,000,000	$ 600,000
Taxes $(T_C = 21\%)$	210,000	126,000
Earnings after corporate taxes EAT $= (\text{EBIT} - R_B B) \times (1 - T_C)$	$ 790,000	$ 474,000
Total cash flow to both stockholders and bondholders $[\text{EBIT} \times (1 - T_C) + T_C R_B B]$	$ 790,000	$ 874,000

The most relevant numbers for our purposes are the two on the bottom line. Dividends, which are equal to earnings after taxes in this example, are the cash flow to stockholders, and interest is the cash flow to bondholders. Here, we see that more cash flow reaches the owners of the firm

[9] Under the MM propositions developed earlier, the two pies should be of the same size.

(both stockholders and bondholders) under Plan II. The difference is $84,000 (= $874,000 − 790,000). It does not take one long to realize the source of this difference. The IRS receives less taxes under Plan II ($126,000) than it does under Plan I ($210,000). The difference here is $84,000 (= $210,000 − 126,000).

This difference occurs because the way the IRS treats interest is different from the way it treats earnings going to stockholders.[10] Interest totally escapes corporate taxation, whereas earnings after interest but before corporate taxes (EBT) are taxed at the 21 percent rate.

Present Value of the Tax Shield

The discussion above shows a tax advantage to debt or, equivalently, a tax disadvantage to equity. We now want to value this advantage. The dollar interest is:

$$\text{Interest} = \underset{\text{Interest rate}}{R_B} \times \underset{\text{Amount borrowed}}{B}$$

This interest is $400,000 (= 10 percent × $4,000,000) for Water Products. All this interest is tax deductible. That is, whatever the taxable income of Water Products would have been without the debt, the taxable income is now $400,000 less with the debt.

Because the corporate tax rate is 21 percent in our example, the reduction in corporate taxes is $84,000 (= .21 × $400,000). This number is identical to the reduction in corporate taxes calculated previously.

Algebraically, the reduction in corporate taxes is:

$$\underset{\text{Corporate tax rate}}{T_C} \times \underset{\text{Dollar amount of interest}}{R_B B} \qquad \qquad \text{[14.4]}$$

That is, whatever taxes a firm would pay each year without debt, the firm will pay $T_C R_B B$ less with debt of B. Equation 14.4 is often called the *tax shield from debt*. Note that it is an annual amount.

As long as the firm expects to be in a positive tax bracket, we can assume that the cash flow in Equation 14.4 has the same risk as the interest on the debt. Thus, its value can be determined by discounting at the cost of debt, R_B. Assuming that the cash flows are perpetual, the present value of the tax shield is:

$$\frac{T_C R_B B}{R_B} = T_C B$$

Value of the Levered Firm

We have just calculated the present value of the tax shield from debt. Our next step is to calculate the value of the levered firm. The annual aftertax cash flow of an unlevered firm is:

$$\text{EBIT} \times (1 - T_C)$$

where EBIT is earnings before interest and taxes. The value of an unlevered firm (that is, a firm with no debt) is the present value of EBIT × (1 − T_C):

$$V_U = \frac{\text{EBIT} \times (1 - T_C)}{R_0}$$

---

[10] Note that stockholders actually receive more under Plan I ($790,000) than under Plan II ($474,000). Students are often bothered by this because it seems to imply that stockholders are better off without leverage. However, remember that there are more shares outstanding in Plan I than in Plan II. A full-blown model would show that earnings per share are higher with leverage.

where:

$$V_U = \text{Present value of an unlevered firm}$$
$$\text{EBIT} \times (1 - T_C) = \text{Firm cash flows after corporate taxes}$$
$$T_C = \text{Corporate tax rate}$$
$$R_0 = \text{The cost of capital to an all-equity firm. As can be seen}$$
$$\text{from the formula, } R_0 \text{ now discounts aftertax cash flows.}$$

As shown previously, leverage increases the value of the firm by the tax shield, which is $T_C B$ for perpetual debt. Thus, we merely add this tax shield to the value of the unlevered firm to get the value of the levered firm.

We can write this algebraically as:

MM Proposition I with corporate taxes:

$$V_L = \frac{\text{EBIT} \times (1 - T_C)}{R_0} + \frac{T_C R_B B}{R_B} = V_U + T_C B \qquad [14.5]$$

Equation 14.5 is MM Proposition I under corporate taxes. The first term in Equation 14.5 is the value of the cash flows of the firm with no debt tax shield. In other words, this term is equal to V_U, the value of the all-equity firm. The value of the levered firm is the value of an all-equity firm plus $T_C B$, the tax rate times the value of the debt. $T_C B$ is the present value of the tax shield in the case of perpetual cash flows. Because the tax shield increases with the amount of debt, the firm can raise its total cash flow and its value by substituting debt for equity.

EXAMPLE 14.4

MM with Corporate Taxes

Divided Airlines is currently an unlevered firm. The company expects to generate $126.58 in earnings before interest and taxes (EBIT) in perpetuity. The corporate tax rate is 21 percent, implying after tax earnings of $100. All earnings after tax are paid out as dividends.

The firm is considering a capital restructuring to allow $200 of debt. Its cost of debt capital is 10 percent. Unlevered firms in the same industry have a cost of equity capital of 20 percent. What will the new value of Divided Airlines be?

FIGURE 14.5 The Effect of Financial Leverage on Firm Value: MM with Corporate Taxes in the Case of Divided Airlines

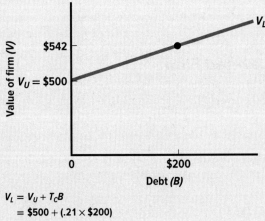

$$V_L = V_U + T_C B$$
$$= \$500 + (.21 \times \$200)$$
$$= \$542$$

Debt reduces Divided's tax burden. As a result, the value of the firm is positively related to debt.

The value of Divided Airlines will be equal to:

$$V_L = \frac{EBIT \times (1 - T_C)}{R_0} + T_C B$$

$$= \frac{\$100}{.20} + (.21 \times \$200)$$

$$= \$500 + 42$$

$$= \$542$$

The value of the levered firm is $542, which is greater than the unlevered value of $500. Because $V_L = B + S$, the value of levered equity, S, is equal to $542 - 200 = \$342$. The value of Divided Airlines as a function of leverage is illustrated in Figure 14.5.

Expected Return and Leverage under Corporate Taxes

MM Proposition II under no taxes posits a positive relationship between the expected return on equity and leverage. This result occurs because the risk of equity increases with leverage. The same intuition also holds in a world of corporate taxes. The exact formula in a world of corporate taxes is:

MM Proposition II with corporate taxes:

$$R_S = R_0 + \frac{B}{S} \times (1 - T_C) \times (R_0 - R_B) \qquad [14.6]$$

Applying the formula to Divided Airlines, we get:

$$R_S = .20 + \frac{\$200}{\$342} \times (1 - .21) \times (.20 - .10) = .2462, \text{ or } 24.62\%$$

This calculation is illustrated in Figure 14.6.

Whenever $R_0 > R_B$, R_S increases with leverage, a result that we also found in the no-tax case. As stated earlier in this chapter, R_0 should exceed R_B. That is, because equity (even unlevered equity) is risky, it should have an expected return greater than that on the less-risky debt.

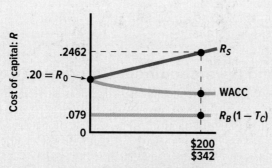

$$R_S = R_0 + (1 - T_C)(R_0 - R_B)B/S = .20 + \left(.79 \times .10 \times \frac{\$200}{\$342}\right) = .2462, \text{ or } 24.62\%$$

Financial leverage adds risk to the firm's equity. As compensation, the cost of equity rises with the firm's risk. Note that R_0 is a single point, while R_S, $R_B(1 - T_C)$, and WACC are all entire lines.

Let's check our calculations by determining the value of the levered equity in another way. The algebraic formula for the value of levered equity is:

$$S = \frac{(EBIT - R_B B) \times (1 - T_C)}{R_S}$$

The numerator is the expected cash flow to levered equity after interest and taxes. The denominator is the rate at which the cash flow to equity is discounted.

For Divided Airlines we get:

$$\frac{(\$126.58 - .10 \times \$200)(1 - .21)}{.2462} = \$342$$

This is the same result we obtained earlier.

The Weighted Average Cost of Capital (WACC) and Corporate Taxes

In Chapter 12, we defined the weighted average cost of capital (with corporate taxes) as follows (note that $V_L = S + B$):

$$WACC = \frac{S}{V_L} R_S + \frac{B}{V_L} R_B (1 - T_C)$$

Note that the cost of debt capital, R_B, is multiplied by $(1 - T_C)$ because interest is tax deductible at the corporate level. However, the cost of equity, R_S, is not multiplied by this factor because dividends are not deductible. In the no-tax case, WACC is not affected by leverage. This result is reflected in Figure 14.3, which we discussed earlier. However, because debt is tax advantaged relative to equity, it can be shown that WACC declines with leverage in a world with corporate taxes. This result can be seen in Figure 14.6.

For Divided Airlines, WACC is equal to:

$$WACC = \left(\frac{\$342}{\$542} \times .2462\right) + \left(\frac{\$200}{\$542} \times .10 \times .79\right) = .1845, \text{ or } 18.45\%$$

Divided Airlines has reduced its WACC from 20 percent with no debt to 18.45 percent with debt. This result is intuitively pleasing because it suggests that when a firm lowers its WACC, the firm's value will increase. Using the WACC approach, we can confirm that the value of Divided Airlines is $542:

$$V_L = \frac{EBIT \times (1 - T_C)}{WACC} = \frac{\$100}{.1845} = \$542$$

Stock Price and Leverage under Corporate Taxes

At this point, students often believe the numbers—or at least are too intimidated to dispute them. However, they sometimes think we have asked the wrong question. "Why are we choosing to maximize the value of the firm?" they will say. "If managers are looking out for the stockholders' interests, why aren't they trying to maximize stock price?" If this question occurred to you, you have come to the right section.

Our response is twofold: First, we showed in the first section of this chapter that the capital structure that maximizes firm value is also the one that most benefits the interests of the stockholders.

However, that general explanation is not always convincing to students. As a second procedure, we calculate the stock price of Divided Airlines both before and after the exchange of debt for stock. We do this by presenting a set of market value balance sheets. The market value balance sheet for the company in its all-equity form can be represented as:

DIVIDED AIRLINES Balance Sheet (all-equity firm)			
Physical assets:		Equity	$500
$\frac{\$126.58}{.20} \times (1 - .21) = \$500$			(100 shares)

Assuming that there are 100 shares outstanding, each share is worth $5 = $500/100.

Next, imagine the company announces that, in the near future, it will issue $200 of debt to buy back $200 of stock. We know from our previous discussion that the value of the firm will rise to reflect the tax shield of debt. If we assume that capital markets efficiently price securities, the increase occurs immediately. That is, the rise occurs on the day of the announcement, not on the date of the debt-for-equity exchange. The market value balance sheet now becomes:

DIVIDED AIRLINES Balance Sheet (upon announcement of debt issue)			
Physical assets:	$500	Equity	$542
			(100 shares)
Present value of tax shield:			
$T_C B = .21 \times \$200 =$	42		
Total assets	$542		

Note that the debt has not yet been issued. Therefore, only equity appears on the right-hand side of the balance sheet. Each share is now worth $542/100 = $5.42, implying that the stockholders have benefited by $42. The equityholders gain because they are the owners of a firm that has improved its financial policy.

The introduction of the tax shield to the balance sheet is perplexing to many students. Although physical assets are tangible, the ethereal nature of the tax shield bothers these students. However, remember that an asset is any item with value. The tax shield has value because it reduces the stream of future taxes. The fact that one cannot touch the shield in the way that one can touch a physical asset is a philosophical, not financial, consideration.

At some point, the exchange of debt for equity occurs. Debt of $200 is issued, and the proceeds are used to buy back shares. How many shares of stock are repurchased? Because shares are now selling at $5.42 each, the number of shares that the firm acquires is $200/$5.42 = 36.90. This leaves 63.10 (= 100 − 36.90) shares of stock outstanding. The market value balance sheet is now:

DIVIDED AIRLINES Balance Sheet (after exchange has taken place)			
Physical assets:	$500	Equity	$342
			(100 − 36.90 = 63.10 shares)
Present value of tax shield	42	Debt	200
Total assets	$542	Debt plus equity	$542

Each share of stock is worth $342/63.10 = $5.42 after the exchange. Notice that the stock price does not change on the exchange date. As we mentioned above, the stock price moves on the date of the announcement only. Because the shareholders participating in the exchange receive a price equal to the market price per share after the exchange, they do not care whether they exchange their stock or not.

This example was provided for two reasons. First, it shows that an increase in the value of the firm from debt financing leads to an increase in the price of the stock. In fact, the stockholders capture the entire $42 tax shield. Second, we wanted to provide more work with market value balance sheets.

A summary of the main results of Modigliani-Miller with corporate taxes is presented in the following boxed section:

Summary of Modigliani-Miller Propositions with Corporate Taxes

Assumptions

- Corporations are taxed at the rate T_C on earnings after interest.
- No transaction costs.
- Individuals and corporations borrow at same rate.

Results

Proposition I: $V_L = V_U + T_C B$ (for a firm with perpetual debt)

Proposition II: $R_S = R_0 + \dfrac{B}{S}(1 - T_C)(R_0 - R_B)$

Intuition

Proposition I: Because corporations can deduct interest payments but not dividend payments, corporate leverage lowers tax payments.

Proposition II: The cost of equity rises with leverage because the risk to equity rises with leverage.

SUMMARY AND CONCLUSIONS

1. We began our discussion of the capital structure decision by arguing that the particular capital structure that maximizes the value of the firm is also the one that provides the most benefit to the stockholders.

2. In a world of no taxes, the famous Proposition I of Modigliani and Miller proves that the value of the firm is unaffected by the debt-equity ratio. In other words, a firm's capital structure is a matter of indifference in that world. The authors obtain their results by showing that either a high or a low corporate ratio of debt to equity can be offset by homemade leverage. The result hinges on the assumption that individuals can borrow at the same rate as corporations, an assumption we believe to be quite plausible.

3. MM's Proposition II in a world without taxes states that:

$$R_S = R_0 + \frac{B}{S}(R_0 - R_B)$$

This implies that the expected rate of return on equity (also called the cost of equity or the required return on equity) is positively related to the firm's leverage. This makes intuitive sense because the risk of equity rises with leverage, a point illustrated by Figure 14.2.

4. While the above work of MM is quite elegant, it does not explain the empirical findings on capital structure very well. MM imply that the capital structure decision is a matter of indifference, while the decision appears to be a weighty one in the real world. To achieve real-world applicability, we next considered corporate taxes.

5. In a world with corporate taxes but no bankruptcy costs, firm value is an increasing function of leverage. The formula for the value of the firm is:

$$V_L = V_U + T_C B$$

Expected return on levered equity can be expressed as:

$$R_S = R_0 + (1 - T_C) \times (R_0 - R_B) \times \frac{B}{S}$$

Here, value is positively related to leverage. This result implies that firms should have a capital structure almost entirely composed of debt. Because real-world firms select more moderate levels of debt, the next chapter considers modifications to the results of this chapter.

CONCEPT QUESTIONS

1. **MM Assumptions**   List the three assumptions that lie behind the Modigliani-Miller theory in a world without taxes. Are these assumptions reasonable in the real world? Explain.

2. **MM Propositions**   In a world with no taxes, no transaction costs, and no costs of financial distress, is the following statement true, false, or uncertain? If a firm issues equity to repurchase some of its debt, the price per share of the firm's stock will rise because the shares are less risky. Explain.

3. **MM Propositions**   In a world with no taxes, no transaction costs, and no costs of financial distress, is the following statement true, false, or uncertain? Moderate borrowing will not increase the required return on a firm's equity. Explain.

4. **MM Propositions**   What is the quirk in the tax code that makes a levered firm more valuable than an otherwise identical unlevered firm?

5. **Business Risk versus Financial Risk**   Explain what is meant by business and financial risk. Suppose Firm A has greater business risk than Firm B. Is it true that Firm A also has a higher cost of equity capital? Explain.

6. **MM Propositions**   How would you answer in the following debate?

   Q: Isn't it true that the riskiness of a firm's equity will rise if the firm increases its use of debt financing?

   A: Yes, that's the essence of MM Proposition II.

   Q: And isn't it true that, as a firm increases its use of borrowing, the likelihood of default increases, thereby increasing the risk of the firm's debt?

   A: Yes.

   Q: In other words, increased borrowing increases the risk of the equity and the debt?

   A: That's right.

   Q: Well, given that the firm uses only debt and equity financing, and given that the risks of both are increased by increased borrowing, does it not follow that increasing debt increases the overall risk of the firm and therefore decreases the value of the firm?

   A: ??

7. **Optimal Capital Structure**   Is there an easily identifiable debt-equity ratio that will maximize the value of a firm? Why or why not?

8. **Financial Leverage**   Why is the use of debt financing referred to as financial leverage?

9. **Homemade Leverage**   What is homemade leverage?

10. **Capital Structure Goal**   What is the basic goal of financial management with regard to capital structure?

QUESTIONS AND PROBLEMS

1. **EBIT and Leverage**   Fowler, Inc., has no debt outstanding and a total market value of $325,000. Earnings before interest and taxes, EBIT, are projected to be $31,000 if economic conditions are normal. If there is strong expansion in the economy, then EBIT will be 25 percent higher. If there is a recession, then EBIT will be 30 percent lower. The firm is considering a debt issue of $105,000 with an interest rate of 6 percent. The proceeds will be used to repurchase shares of stock. There are currently 5,000 shares outstanding. Ignore taxes for this problem. Assume the stock price is constant under all scenarios.

   a. Calculate earnings per share, EPS, under each of the three economic scenarios before any debt is issued. Also, calculate the percentage changes in EPS when the economy expands or enters a recession.

   b. Repeat part (a) assuming that the firm goes through with recapitalization. What do you observe?

2. **EBIT, Taxes, and Leverage**   Repeat parts (a) and (b) in Problem 1 assuming the firm has a tax rate of 21 percent.

Basic
(Questions 1–16)

3. **ROE and Leverage** Suppose the firm in Problem 1 has a market-to-book ratio of 1.0.

   a. Calculate return on equity, ROE, under each of the three economic scenarios before any debt is issued. Also, calculate the percentage changes in ROE for economic expansion and recession, assuming no taxes.

   b. Repeat part (a) assuming the firm goes through with the proposed recapitalization.

   c. Repeat parts (a) and (b) of this problem assuming the firm has a tax rate of 21 percent.

4. **Break-Even EBIT** Kuchar Corporation is comparing two different capital structures, an all-equity plan, Plan I, and a levered plan, Plan II. Under Plan I, the company would have 125,000 shares of stock outstanding. Under Plan II, there would be 90,000 shares of stock outstanding and $1,197,000 in debt outstanding. The interest rate on the debt is 7 percent and there are no taxes.

   a. If EBIT is $250,000, which plan will result in the higher EPS?

   b. If EBIT is $350,000, which plan will result in the higher EPS?

   c. What is the break-even EBIT?

5. **MM and Stock Value** In Problem 4, use MM Proposition I to find the price per share of equity under each of the two proposed plans. What is the value of the firm?

6. **Break-Even EBIT and Leverage** Coldstream Corp. is comparing two different capital structures. Plan I would result in 4,950 shares of stock and $10,255 in debt. Plan II would result in 4,500 shares of stock and $23,440 in debt. The interest rate on the debt is 7 percent.

   a. Ignoring taxes, compare both of these plans to an all-equity plan assuming that EBIT will be $8,400. The all-equity plan would result in 5,300 shares of stock outstanding. Which of the three plans has the highest EPS? The lowest?

   b. In part (a), what are the break-even levels of EBIT for each plan as compared to that for an all-equity plan? Is one higher than the other? Why?

   c. Ignoring taxes, when will EPS be identical for Plans I and II?

   d. Repeat parts (a), (b), and (c) assuming that the corporate tax rate is 21 percent. Are the break-even levels of EBIT different from before? Why or why not?

7. **Leverage and Stock Value** Ignoring taxes in Problem 6, what is the price per share of equity under Plan I? Plan II? What principle is illustrated by your answers?

8. **Homemade Leverage** FCOJ, Inc., a prominent consumer products firm, is debating whether or not to convert its all-equity capital structure to one that is 35 percent debt. Currently, there are 7,100 shares outstanding and the price per share is $55. EBIT is expected to remain at $36,000 per year forever. The interest rate on new debt is 8 percent, and there are no taxes.

   a. Ms. Brown, a shareholder of the firm, owns 100 shares of stock. What is her cash flow under the current capital structure, assuming the firm has a dividend payout rate of 100 percent?

   b. What will Ms. Brown's cash flow be under the proposed capital structure of the firm? Assume that she keeps all 100 of her shares.

   c. Suppose the company does convert, but Ms. Brown prefers the current all-equity capital structure. Show how she could unlever her shares of stock to re-create the original capital structure.

   d. Using your answer to part (c), explain why the company's choice of capital structure is irrelevant.

9. **Homemade Leverage and WACC** ABC Co. and XYZ Co. are identical firms in all respects except for their capital structures. ABC is all-equity financed with $550,000 in stock. XYZ uses both stock and perpetual debt; its stock is worth $275,000 and the interest rate on its debt is 8 percent. Both firms expect EBIT to be $60,000. Ignore taxes.

   a. Richard owns $20,000 worth of XYZ's stock. What rate of return is he expecting?

   b. Show how Richard could generate exactly the same cash flows and rate of return by investing in ABC and using homemade leverage.

   c. What is the cost of equity for ABC? What is it for XYZ?

   d. What is the WACC for ABC? For XYZ? What principle have you illustrated?

10. **MM**   Nolan Corp. uses no debt. The weighted average cost of capital is 8.9 percent. If the current market value of the equity is $47.8 million and there are no taxes, what is EBIT?

11. **MM and Taxes**   In the previous question, suppose the corporate tax rate is 23 percent. What is EBIT in this case? What is the WACC? Explain.

12. **Calculating WACC**   Weston Industries has a debt-equity ratio of 1.4. Its WACC is 8.3 percent, and its cost of debt is 5.4 percent. The corporate tax rate is 24 percent.

   a. What is the company's cost of equity capital?

   b. What is the company's unlevered cost of equity capital?

   c. What would the cost of equity be if the debt-equity ratio were 2? What if it were 1? What if it were zero?

13. **Calculating WACC**   Shadow Corp. has no debt but can borrow at 5.75 percent. The firm's WACC is currently 8.9 percent, and the tax rate is 22 percent.

   a. What is the firm's cost of equity?

   b. If the firm converts to 25 percent debt, what will its cost of equity be?

   c. If the firm converts to 50 percent debt, what will its cost of equity be?

   d. What is the firm's WACC in part (b)? In part (c)?

14. **MM and Taxes**   Cede & Co. expects its EBIT to be $92,600 every year forever. The firm can borrow at 7 percent. The firm currently has no debt, and its cost of equity is 14 percent. If the tax rate is 22 percent, what is the value of the firm? What will the value be if the firm borrows $165,000 and uses the proceeds to repurchase shares?

15. **MM and Taxes**   In Problem 14, what is the cost of equity after recapitalization? What is the WACC? What are the implications for the firm's capital structure decision?

16. **MM Proposition I**   Levered, Inc., and Unlevered, Inc., are identical in every way except their capital structures. Each company expects to earn $235,000 before interest per year in perpetuity, with each company distributing all its earnings as dividends. Levered's perpetual debt has a market value of $290,000 and costs 8 percent per year. Levered has 18,000 shares outstanding, currently worth $64 per share. Unlevered has no debt and 23,000 shares outstanding, currently worth $66 per share. Neither firm pays taxes. Is Levered's stock a better buy than Unlevered's stock?

17. **MM**   Tool Manufacturing has an expected EBIT of $51,600 in perpetuity and a tax rate of 24 percent. The firm has $90,000 in outstanding debt at an interest rate of 6.5 percent, and its unlevered cost of capital is 11 percent. What is the value of the firm according to MM Proposition I with taxes? Should the firm change its debt-equity ratio if the goal is to maximize the value of the firm? Explain.

Intermediate
(Questions 17–26)

18. **Firm Value**   Full Moon Corporation expects an EBIT of $28,650 every year forever. The company currently has no debt, and its cost of equity is 12.8 percent. The corporate tax rate is 23 percent.

   a. What is the current value of the company?

   b. Suppose the company can borrow at 7.1 percent. What will the value of the firm be if the company takes on debt equal to 50 percent of its unlevered value? What if it takes on debt equal to 100 percent of its unlevered value?

   c. What will the value of the firm be if the company takes on debt equal to 50 percent of its levered value? What if the company takes on debt equal to 100 percent of its levered value?

19. **MM Proposition I with Taxes**   The Maxwell Company is financed entirely with equity. The company is considering a loan of $525,000. The loan will be repaid in equal principal installments over the next two years, and it has an interest rate of 7 percent. The company's tax rate is 23 percent. According to MM Proposition I with taxes, what would be the increase in the value of the company after the loan?

20. **MM Proposition I without Taxes** Alpha Corporation and Beta Corporation are identical in every way except their capital structures. Alpha Corporation, an all-equity firm, has 21,000 shares of stock outstanding, currently worth $23 per share. Beta Corporation uses leverage in its capital structure. The market value of Beta's debt is $90,000, and its cost of debt is 7 percent. Each firm is expected to have earnings before interest of $76,000 in perpetuity. Neither firm pays taxes. Assume that every investor can borrow at 7 percent per year.

    a. What is the value of Alpha Corporation?

    b. What is the value of Beta Corporation?

    c. What is the market value of Beta Corporation's equity?

    d. How much will it cost to purchase 20 percent of each firm's equity?

    e. Assuming each firm meets its earnings estimates, what will be the dollar return to each purchase in part (d) over the next year?

    f. Construct an investment strategy in which an investor purchases 20 percent of Alpha's equity and replicates both the cost and dollar return of purchasing 20 percent of Beta's equity.

    g. Is Alpha's equity more or less risky than Beta's equity? Explain.

21. **Cost of Capital** Jenkins, Inc., has equity with a market value of $6.4 million and debt with a market value of $2.6 million. The cost of the debt is 7.5 percent per year. Treasury bills that mature in one year yield 4 percent per year, and the expected return on the market portfolio over the next year is 11 percent. The beta of the company's equity is 1.10. The firm pays no taxes.

    a. What is the company's debt-equity ratio?

    b. What is the company's weighted average cost of capital?

    c. What is the cost of capital for an otherwise identical all-equity firm?

22. **Homemade Leverage** The Veblen Company and the Knight Company are identical in every respect except that Veblen is not levered. The Knight Company's 6 percent bonds sell at par value. Financial information for the two firms appears below. All earnings streams are perpetuities. Neither firm pays taxes. Both firms distribute all earnings available to common stockholders immediately.

	Veblen	Knight
Projected operating income	$ 425,000	$ 425,000
Year-end interest on debt	0	99,000
Market value of stock	2,850,000	1,650,000
Market value of debt	0	1,650,000

    a. An investor who is able to borrow at 6 percent per year wishes to purchase 5 percent of Knight's equity. Can he increase his dollar return by purchasing 5 percent of Veblen's equity if he borrows so that the initial net costs of the two strategies are the same?

    b. Given the two investment strategies in (a), which will investors choose? When will this process cease?

23. **MM Propositions** Arya Corporation is planning to repurchase part of its common stock by issuing corporate debt. As a result, the firm's debt-equity ratio is expected to rise from 20 percent to 35 percent. The firm currently has $4.15 million worth of debt outstanding. The cost of this debt is 7 percent per year. The firm expects to have EBIT of $2.73 million per year in perpetuity and pays no taxes.

    a. What is the market value of the firm before and after the repurchase announcement?

    b. What is the expected return on the firm's equity before the announcement of the stock repurchase plan?

    c. What is the expected return on the equity of an otherwise identical all-equity firm?

    d. What is the expected return on the firm's equity after the announcement of the stock repurchase plan?

24. **Stock Value and Leverage** Green Manufacturing, Inc., plans to announce that it will issue $1.9 million of perpetual debt and use the proceeds to repurchase common stock. The bonds will sell at par with an annual coupon rate of 6 percent. The company is currently an all-equity firm worth $8.1 million with 250,000 shares

of common stock outstanding. After the sale of the bonds, the company will maintain the new capital structure indefinitely. The company currently generates annual pretax earnings of $1.86 million. This level of earnings is expected to remain constant in perpetuity. The corporate tax rate is 24 percent.

a. What is the expected return on equity before the announcement of the debt issue?

b. Construct the market value balance sheet before the announcement of the debt issue. What is the price per share of the firm's equity?

c. Construct the market value balance sheet immediately after the announcement of the debt issue.

d. What is the stock price per share immediately after the repurchase announcement?

e. How many shares will the company repurchase as a result of the debt issue? How many shares of common stock will remain after the repurchase?

f. Construct the market value balance sheet after the restructuring.

g. What is the required return on the company's equity after the restructuring?

25. **MM with Taxes** Williamson, Inc., has a debt-equity ratio of 1.8. The company's weighted average cost of capital is 9.1 percent and its pretax cost of debt is 5.6 percent. The corporate tax rate is 21 percent.

a. What is the company's cost of equity capital?

b. What is the company's unlevered cost of equity capital?

c. What would the company's weighted average cost of capital be if the debt-equity ratio were .60? What if it were 1.25?

26. **EBIT, Taxes, and Leverage** Repeat parts (a) and (b) in Problem 2 assuming the firm has a tax rate of 21 percent. Assume that the stock price will increase upon the announcement of the debt offering.

27. **Weighted Average Cost of Capital** In a world of corporate taxes only, show that the WACC can be written as WACC $= R_0 \times [1 - T_C(B/V)]$.

Challenge
(Questions 27–31)

28. **Cost of Equity and Leverage** Assuming a world of corporate taxes only, show that the cost of equity, R_S, is as given in the chapter by MM Proposition II with corporate taxes.

29. **Business and Financial Risk** Assume a firm's debt is risk-free, so that the cost of debt equals the risk-free rate, R_F. Define β_A as the firm's *asset* beta, that is, the systematic risk of the firm's assets. Define β_S to be the beta of the firm's equity. Use the capital asset pricing model, CAPM, along with MM Proposition II to show that $\beta_S = \beta_A \times (1 + B/S)$, where B/S is the debt-equity ratio. Assume the tax rate is zero.

30. **Stockholder Risk** Suppose a firm's business operations are such that they mirror movements in the economy as a whole very closely, that is, the firm's asset beta is 1.0. Use the result of the previous problem to find the equity beta for this firm for debt-equity ratios of 0, 1, 5, and 20. What does this tell you about the relationship between capital structure and shareholder risk? How is the shareholders' required return on equity affected? Explain.

31. **Unlevered Cost of Equity** Beginning with the cost of capital equation, that is:

$$\text{WACC} = \frac{S}{B+S}R_S + \frac{B}{B+S}R_B$$

show that the cost of equity capital for a levered firm can be written as:

$$R_S = R_0 + \frac{B}{S}(R_0 - R_B)$$

WHAT'S ON THE WEB?

1. **Capital Structure** Go to www.reuters.com and enter the ticker symbol "AMGN" for Amgen, a biotechnology company. Find the long-term debt-equity and total debt-equity ratios. How does Amgen compare to the industry and sector in these areas? Now answer the same question for Edison International (EIX), the parent company of Southern California Edison, a utility company. How do the capital structures of Amgen and Edison International compare? Can you think of possible explanations for the difference between these two companies?

2. **Capital Structure**   Go to finance.yahoo.com and find the "Equity Screener" link. How many companies have debt-equity ratios greater than 2? Greater than 5? Greater than 10? What company has the highest debt-equity ratio? What is the ratio? Now find how many companies have a negative debt-equity ratio. What is the lowest debt-equity ratio? What does it mean if a company has a negative debt-equity ratio?

CLOSING CASE

STEPHENSON REAL ESTATE RECAPITALIZATION

Stephenson Real Estate Company was founded 25 years ago by the current CEO, Robert Stephenson. The company purchases real estate, including land and buildings, and rents the property to tenants. The company has shown a profit every year for the past 18 years, and the shareholders are satisfied with the company's management. Prior to founding Stephenson Real Estate, Robert was the founder and CEO of a failed alpaca farming operation. The resulting bankruptcy made him extremely averse to debt financing. As a result, the company is entirely equity financed, with 16 million shares of common stock outstanding. The stock currently trades at $46.75 per share.

Stephenson is evaluating a plan to purchase a huge tract of land in the southeastern United States for $95 million. The land will subsequently be leased to tenant farmers. This purchase is expected to increase Stephenson's annual pretax earnings by $20.2 million in perpetuity. Kim Weyand, the company's new CFO, has been put in charge of the project. Kim has determined that the company's current cost of capital is 10.5 percent. She feels that the company would be more valuable if it included debt in its capital structure, so she is evaluating whether the company should issue debt to entirely finance the project. Based on some conversations with investment banks, she thinks that the company can issue bonds at par value with a 7 percent coupon rate. Based on her analysis, she also believes that a capital structure in the range of 70 percent equity/30 percent debt would be optimal. If the company goes beyond 30 percent debt, its bonds would carry a lower rating and a much higher coupon because the possibility of financial distress and the associated costs would rise sharply. Stephenson has a 21 percent corporate tax rate (state and federal).

1. If Stephenson wishes to maximize its total market value, would you recommend that it issue debt or equity to finance the land purchase? Explain.
2. Construct Stephenson's market value balance sheet before it announces the purchase.
3. Suppose Stephenson decides to issue equity to finance the purchase.
   a. What is the net present value of the project?
   b. Construct Stephenson's market value balance sheet after it announces that the firm will finance the purchase using equity. What would be the new price per share of the firm's stock? How many shares will Stephenson need to issue in order to finance the purchase?
   c. Construct Stephenson's market value balance sheet after the equity issue but before the purchase has been made. How many shares of common stock does Stephenson have outstanding? What is the price per share of the firm's stock?
   d. Construct Stephenson's market value balance sheet after the purchase has been made.
4. Suppose Stephenson decides to issue debt in order to finance the purchase.
   a. What will the market value of the Stephenson company be if the purchase is financed with debt?
   b. Construct Stephenson's market value balance sheet after both the debt issue and the land purchase. What is the price per share of the firm's stock?
5. Which method of financing maximizes the per-share stock price of Stephenson's equity?

Capital Structure: Limits to the Use of Debt

No matter how you look at it, 2018 was a tough year for brick-and-mortar retailers. Although it was widely expected, in October 2018, 125-year-old retailer Sears was forced to file for bankruptcy. The company was struggling due to declining sales and a large debt load. Of course, Sears was not alone: Since 2015, about 57 large retailers have filed for bankruptcy, including Mattress Firm, Nine West, and Radio Shack. Retailers were not alone in filing for bankruptcy in 2018 as Southeastern Grocers, owner of Winn-Dixie and Bi-Lo, was also forced to file. The company was able to reduce its debt by $600 million in bankruptcy. The company also closed about 100 stores. Management believed these changes would allow the company to operate profitably going forward.

As these situations point out, there is a limit to the financial leverage a company can use, and a risk of too much leverage is bankruptcy. In this chapter, we discuss the costs associated with bankruptcies and how companies attempt to avoid this process.

Please visit us at corecorporatefinance.blogspot.com for the latest developments in the world of corporate finance.

15.1 COSTS OF FINANCIAL DISTRESS

One limiting factor affecting the amount of debt a firm might use comes in the form of *bankruptcy costs*. As the debt-equity ratio rises, so too does the probability that the firm will be unable to pay its bondholders what was promised to them. When this happens, ownership of the firm's assets is ultimately transferred from the stockholders to the bondholders.

In principle, a firm becomes bankrupt when the value of its assets equals the value of its debt. When this occurs, the value of equity is zero, and the stockholders turn over control of the firm to the bondholders. When this takes place, the bondholders hold assets whose value is exactly equal to what is owed on the debt. In a perfect world, there are no costs associated with this transfer of ownership, and the bondholders don't lose anything.

This idealized view of bankruptcy is not, of course, what happens in the real world. Ironically, it is expensive to go bankrupt. As we discuss, the costs associated with bankruptcy may eventually offset the tax-related gains from leverage.

Direct Bankruptcy Costs

When the value of a firm's assets equals the value of its debt, then the firm is economically bankrupt in the sense that the equity has no value. However, the formal turning over of the assets to the bondholders is a legal process, not an economic one. There are legal and administrative costs to bankruptcy, and it has been remarked that bankruptcies are to lawyers what blood is to sharks.

To give you some idea of the costs associated with a bankruptcy, consider the case of financial giant Lehman Brothers, which filed for bankruptcy in September 2008. Three-and-a-half years later, Lehman emerged from bankruptcy as a liquidating company whose main business was paying back its creditors and investors. In 2019, the Federal Reserve Bank of New York released the final cost of Lehman's bankruptcy. Compensation and benefits were $1.97 billion, professional and consulting fees were $2.56 billion, and other operating expenses were $1.37 billion, for total bankruptcy costs of $5.9 billion. In general, bankruptcy costs range between 1.4 percent and 3.4 percent of pre-bankruptcy value. Lehman's pre-bankruptcy value was about $300 billion, so its costs were about 2 percent of value. The next largest bankruptcy-related fees appear to have been paid to those involved in the Enron bankruptcy, where fees reached a mere $1 billion. In comparison, the WorldCom and General Motors bankruptcies appear to have only cost about $600 million.

Because of the expenses associated with bankruptcy, bondholders won't get all that they are owed. Some fraction of the firm's assets will "disappear" in the legal process of going bankrupt. These are the legal and administrative expenses associated with the bankruptcy proceeding. We call these costs direct bankruptcy costs.

These direct bankruptcy costs are a disincentive to debt financing. If a firm goes bankrupt, then, suddenly, a piece of the firm disappears. This amounts to a bankruptcy "tax." So, a firm faces a trade-off: Borrowing saves a firm money on its corporate taxes, but the more a firm borrows, the more likely it is that the firm will become bankrupt and have to pay the bankruptcy tax.

Indirect Bankruptcy Costs

Because it is expensive to go bankrupt, a firm will spend resources to avoid doing so. When a firm is having significant problems in meeting its debt obligations, we say that it is experiencing financial distress. Some financially distressed firms ultimately file for bankruptcy, but most do not because they are able to recover or otherwise survive.

The costs of avoiding a bankruptcy filing incurred by a financially distressed firm are called indirect bankruptcy costs. We use the term financial distress costs to refer generically to the direct and indirect costs associated with going bankrupt and/or avoiding a bankruptcy filing.

Cutler and Summers examine the costs of the well-publicized Texaco bankruptcy.[1] In January 1984, Pennzoil reached what it believed to be a binding agreement to acquire three-sevenths of Getty Oil. However, less than a week later, Texaco acquired all of Getty at a higher per-share price. Pennzoil then sued Getty for breach of contract. Because Texaco had previously indemnified Getty against litigation, Texaco became liable for damages.

In November 1985, the Texas State Court awarded damages of $12 billion to Pennzoil, although this amount was later reduced. As a result, Texaco filed for bankruptcy. Cutler and Summers identify nine important events over the course of the litigation. They find that Texaco's market value (stock price times number of shares outstanding) fell a cumulative $4.1 billion over these events, whereas Pennzoil's value rose only $682 million. Thus, Pennzoil gained about one-sixth of what Texaco lost, resulting in a net loss to the two firms of almost $3.5 billion.

What could explain this net loss? Cutler and Summers suggest that it is likely due to costs that Texaco and Pennzoil incurred from the litigation and subsequent bankruptcy. The authors argue that direct bankruptcy fees represent only a small part of these costs, estimating Texaco's aftertax legal expenses to be about $165 million. Legal costs to Pennzoil were more difficult to assess because Pennzoil's lead lawyer, Joe Jamail, stated publicly that he had no set fee. However, using a clever statistical analysis, the authors estimate his fee to be about $200 million. Thus, one must search elsewhere for the bulk of the costs.

---

[1] David M. Cutler and Lawrence H. Summers, "The Costs of Conflict Resolution and Financial Distress: Evidence from the Texaco-Pennzoil Litigation," *RAND Journal of Economics* 19, no. 2 (1988), pp. 157–72.

Indirect costs of financial distress may be the culprit here. An affidavit by Texaco stated that, following the lawsuit, some of its suppliers were demanding cash payments. Other suppliers halted or canceled shipments of crude oil. Certain banks restricted Texaco's use of futures contracts on foreign exchange. The affidavit stressed that these constraints were reducing Texaco's ability to run its business, leading to deterioration of its financial condition. Could these sorts of indirect costs explain the $3.5 billion disparity between Texaco's drop and Pennzoil's rise in market value? Unfortunately, although it is quite likely that indirect costs play a role here, there is no way to obtain a decent, quantitative estimate for them.

Agency Costs

When a firm has debt, conflicts of interest arise between stockholders and bondholders. Because of this, stockholders are tempted to pursue selfish strategies. These conflicts of interest, which are magnified when financial distress is incurred, impose agency costs on the firm. We describe three kinds of selfish strategies that stockholders use to hurt the bondholders and help themselves. These strategies are costly because they will lower the market value of the whole firm.

Selfish Investment Strategy 1: Incentive to Take Large Risks   Firms near bankruptcy often take great chances because they believe that they are playing with someone else's money. To see this, imagine a levered firm considering two mutually exclusive projects, a low-risk one and a high-risk one. There are two equally likely outcomes, recession and boom. The firm is in such dire straits that should a recession hit, it will come near to bankruptcy with one project and actually fall into bankruptcy with the other. The cash flows for the entire firm if the low-risk project is taken can be described as:

		Value of Entire Firm If Low-Risk Project Is Chosen				
	Probability	Value of Firm	=	Stock	+	Bonds
Recession	.5	$100	=	$ 0	+	$100
Boom	.5	200	=	100	+	100

If a recession occurs, the value of the firm will be $100, and if a boom happens, the value of the firm will be $200. The expected value of the firm is $150 (= .5 × $100 + .5 × $200).

The firm has promised to pay bondholders $100. Shareholders will obtain the difference between the total payoff and the amount paid to the bondholders. In other words, the bondholders have the prior claim on the payoffs, and the shareholders have the residual claim.

Now suppose that another, riskier project can be substituted for the low-risk project. The payoffs and probabilities are as follows:

		Value of Entire Firm If High-Risk Project Is Chosen				
	Probability	Value of Firm	=	Stock	+	Bonds
Recession	.5	$ 50	=	$ 0	+	$ 50
Boom	.5	240	=	140	+	100

The expected value of the firm is $145 (= .5 × $50 + .5 × $240), which is lower than the expected value of the firm with the low-risk project. Thus, the low-risk project would be accepted if the firm were all equity. However, note that the expected value of the stock is $70 (= .5 × 0 + .5 × $140) with the high-risk project, but only $50 (= .5 × 0 + .5 × $100) with the low-risk project. Given the firm's present levered state, stockholders will select the high-risk project, even though the high-risk project has a lower NPV.

The key is that, relative to the low-risk project, the high-risk project increases firm value in a boom and decreases firm value in a recession. The increase in value in a boom is captured by the stockholders because the bondholders are paid in full (they receive $100) regardless of which project is accepted. Conversely, the drop in value in a recession is lost by the bondholders because they are paid in full with the low-risk project but receive only $50 with the high-risk one. The stockholders will receive nothing in a recession anyway, whether the high-risk or low-risk project is selected. Thus, financial economists argue that stockholders expropriate value from the bondholders by selecting high-risk projects.

A story, perhaps apocryphal, illustrates this idea. It seems that Federal Express was near financial collapse within a few years of its inception. The founder, Frederick Smith, took $20,000 of corporate funds to Las Vegas in despair. He won at the gaming tables, providing enough capital to allow the firm to survive. Had he lost, the banks would have received $20,000 less when the firm reached bankruptcy.

Selfish Investment Strategy 2: Incentive Toward Underinvestment   Stockholders of a firm with a significant probability of bankruptcy often find that new investment helps the bondholders at the stockholders' expense. The simplest case might be a real estate owner facing imminent bankruptcy. If he took $100,000 out of his own pocket to refurbish the building, he could increase the building's value by, say, $150,000. Though this investment has a positive net present value, he will turn it down if the increase in value cannot prevent bankruptcy. "Why," he asks, "should I use my own funds to improve the value of a building that the bank will soon repossess?"

This idea is formalized by the following simple example. Consider a firm with $4,000 of principal and interest payments due at the end of the year. It will be pulled into bankruptcy by a recession because its cash flows will be only $2,400 in that state. The firm's cash flows are presented in the left-hand side of Table 15.1. The firm could avoid bankruptcy in a recession by raising new equity to invest in a new project. The project costs $1,000 and brings in $1,700 in either state, implying a positive net present value. Clearly it would be accepted in an all-equity firm.

However, the project hurts the stockholders of the levered firm. To see this, imagine the old stockholders contribute the $1,000 themselves.[2] The expected value of the stockholders' interest without the project is $500 (= .5 × $1,000 + .5 × 0). The expected value with the project is $1,400 (= .5 × $2,700 + .5 × $100). The stockholders' interest rises by only $900 (= $1,400 − 500) while costing $1,000.

TABLE 15.1

Example Illustrating Incentive to Underinvest

	Firm without Project		Firm with Project	
	Boom	Recession	Boom	Recession
Firm cash flows	$5,000	$2,400	$6,700	$4,100
Bondholders' claim	4,000	2,400	4,000	4,000
Stockholders' claim	$1,000	$ 0	$2,700	$ 100

The project has positive NPV. However, much of its value is captured by bondholders. Rational managers, acting in the stockholders' interest, will reject the project.

[2] The same qualitative results will be obtained if the $1,000 is raised from new stockholders. However, the arithmetic becomes much more difficult because we must determine how many new shares are issued.

The key is that the stockholders contribute the full $1,000 investment, but the stockholders and bondholders share the benefits. The stockholders take the entire gain if boom times occur. Conversely, the bondholders reap most of the cash flow from the project in a recession.

The discussion of selfish Strategy 1 is quite similar to the discussion of selfish Strategy 2. In both cases, an investment strategy for the levered firm is different from the one for the unlevered firm. Thus, leverage results in distorted investment policy. Whereas the unlevered corporation always chooses projects with positive net present values, the levered firm may deviate from this policy.

Selfish Investment Strategy 3: Milking the Property   Another strategy is to pay out extra dividends or other distributions in times of financial distress, leaving less in the firm for the bondholders. This is known as *milking the property,* a phrase taken from real estate. Strategies 2 and 3 are very similar. In Strategy 2, the firm chooses not to raise new equity. Strategy 3 goes one step further because equity is actually withdrawn through the dividend.

SUMMARY OF SELFISH STRATEGIES   The above distortions occur only when there is a probability of bankruptcy or financial distress. Thus, these distortions should not affect, say, IBM because bankruptcy is not a realistic possibility for a diversified blue-chip firm such as this. In other words, IBM's debt will be virtually risk-free, regardless of the projects it accepts. The same argument could be made for regulated companies that are protected by state utility commissions. However, smaller firms in risky industries, such as solar energy, might be very much affected by these distortions. Firms in the solar energy industry generally have significant potential future investment opportunities as compared to assets in place and face intense competition and uncertain future revenues. Because the distortions are related to financial distress, we have included them in our discussion of the indirect costs of financial distress. For firms that face these distortions, debt will be difficult and costly to obtain. These firms will have low leverage ratios.

Who pays for the cost of selfish investment strategies? We argue that it is ultimately the stockholders. Rational bondholders know that, when financial distress is imminent, they cannot expect help from stockholders. Rather, stockholders are likely to choose investment strategies that reduce the value of the bonds. Bondholders protect themselves accordingly by raising the interest rate that they require on bonds. Because the stockholders must pay these high rates, they ultimately bear the costs of selfish strategies. The relationship between stockholders and bondholders is very similar to the relationship between Errol Flynn and David Niven, good friends and movie stars in the 1930s. Niven reportedly said that the good thing about Flynn was that you knew exactly where you stood with him. When you needed his help, you could always count on him to let you down.

15.2 CAN COSTS OF DEBT BE REDUCED?

As U.S. senators are prone to say, "A billion here, a billion there. Pretty soon it all adds up."[3] Each of the costs of financial distress we mentioned previously is substantial in its own right. The sum of them may affect debt financing severely. Thus, managers have an incentive to reduce these costs. We now turn to some of their methods. However, it should be mentioned at the outset that the methods below can, at most, reduce the costs of debt. They cannot eliminate them entirely.

---

[3] The original quote is generally attributed to Senator Everett Dirksen, though whether he actually said it is unknown.

Protective Covenants

As we discussed in a previous chapter, loan agreements and bond indentures frequently include protective covenants. These covenants should reduce the costs of bankruptcy, ultimately increasing the value of the firm. Thus, stockholders are likely to favor all reasonable covenants. To see this, consider three choices by stockholders to reduce bankruptcy costs:

1. *Issue No Debt.* Because of the tax advantages to debt, this is a very costly way of avoiding conflicts.
2. *Issue Debt with No Restrictive and Protective Covenants.* In this case, bondholders will demand high interest rates to compensate for the unprotected status of their debt.
3. *Write Protective and Restrictive Covenants into the Loan Contracts.* If the covenants are clearly written, the creditors may receive protection without large costs being imposed on the shareholders. The creditors will gladly accept a lower interest rate.

Thus, bond covenants, even if they reduce flexibility, can increase the value of the firm. They can be the lowest-cost solution to the stockholder-bondholder conflict. A list of typical bond covenants and their uses appears in Table 15.2.

Consolidation of Debt

One reason bankruptcy costs are so high is that different creditors (and their lawyers) contend with each other. This problem can be alleviated by proper arrangement of bondholders and stockholders. For example, perhaps one, or at most a few, lenders can shoulder the entire debt. Should financial distress occur, negotiating costs are minimized under this arrangement. In addition, bondholders can purchase stock. In this way, stockholders and debtholders are not pitted against each other because they are not separate entities. This appears to be the approach in Japan, where large banks generally take significant stock positions in the firms to which they lend money. Debt-equity ratios in Japan are far higher than those in the United States.

TABLE 15.2

Bond Covenants

Covenant Type	Shareholder Action or Firm Circumstances	Reason for Covenant
Financial statement signals: 1. Working capital requirement 2. Interest coverage 3. Minimum net worth	As the firm approaches financial distress, shareholders may want firm to make high-risk investments.	Shareholders lose value before bankruptcy; bondholders are hurt much more in bankruptcy than shareholders (limited liability); bondholders are hurt by distortion of investment that leads to increases in risk.
Restrictions on asset disposition: 1. Limit dividends 2. Limit sale of assets 3. Collateral and mortgages	Shareholders attempt to transfer corporate assets to themselves.	This limits the ability of shareholders to transfer assets to themselves and to underinvest.
Restrictions on switching assets	Shareholders attempt to increase risk of firm.	Increased firm risk helps shareholders; bondholders are hurt by distortion of investment that leads to increases in risk.
Dilution: 1. Limit on leasing 2. Limit on further borrowing	Shareholders may attempt to issue new debt of equal or greater priority.	This restricts dilution of the claim of existing bondholders.

15.3 INTEGRATION OF TAX EFFECTS AND FINANCIAL DISTRESS COSTS

Modigliani and Miller argue that the firm's value rises with leverage in the presence of corporate taxes. Because this implies that all firms should choose maximum debt, the theory does not predict the behavior of firms in the real world. Other authors have suggested that bankruptcy and related costs reduce the value of the levered firm.

The integration of tax effects and distress costs appears in Figure 15.1. At the top of the figure, the diagonal straight line represents the value of the firm in a world without bankruptcy costs. The ∩-shaped curve represents the value of the firm with these costs. This curve rises as the firm moves from all equity to a small amount of debt. Here, the present value of the distress costs is minimal because the probability of distress is so small. However, as more and more debt is added, the present value of these costs rises at an increasing rate. At some point, the increase in the present value of these costs from an additional dollar of debt equals the increase in the present value of the tax shield. This is the debt level maximizing the value of the firm and is represented by B^* in Figure 15.1. In other words, B^* is the optimal amount of debt. Bankruptcy costs increase faster than the tax shield beyond this point, implying a reduction in firm value from further leverage. At the

FIGURE 15.1

The Optimal Amount of Debt and the Value of the Firm

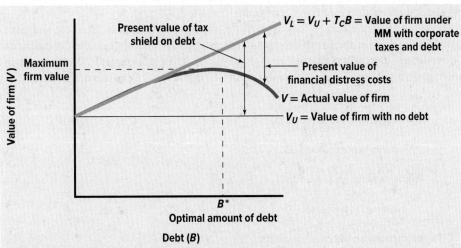

The tax shield increases the value of the levered firm. Financial distress costs lower the value of the levered firm. The two offsetting factors produce an optimal amount of debt at B^*.

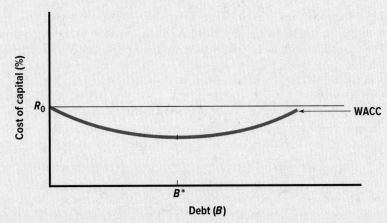

According to the static theory, the WACC falls initially because of the tax advantage of debt. Beyond point B^*, it begins to rise because of financial distress costs.

bottom of Figure 15.1, the weighted average cost of capital (WACC) goes down as debt is added to the capital structure. After reaching B^*, the weighted average cost of capital goes up. The optimal amount of debt also produces the lowest weighted average cost of capital.

Our discussion implies that a firm's capital structure decisions involve a trade-off between the tax benefits of debt and the costs of financial distress. In fact, this approach is frequently called the *trade-off* or the *static trade-off* theory of capital structure. The implication is that there is an optimum amount of debt for any individual firm. This amount of debt becomes the firm's target debt level. This optimum is frequently referred to as the firm's *debt capacity*. Because financial distress costs cannot be expressed in a precise way, no formula has yet been developed to determine a firm's optimal debt level exactly. However, the last section of this chapter offers some rules of thumb for selecting a debt-equity ratio in the real world. Our situation reminds us of a quote attributed to John Maynard Keynes. He reputedly said that, although most historians would agree that Queen Elizabeth I was both a better monarch and an unhappier woman than Queen Victoria, no one has yet been able to express the statement in a precise and rigorous formula.

Pie Again

Critics of the Modigliani-Miller (MM) theory often say that MM fails when we add such real-world issues as taxes and bankruptcy costs. Taking that view, however, blinds critics to the real value of the MM theory. The pie approach offers a more constructive way of thinking about these matters and the role of capital structure.

Taxes are another claim on the cash flows of the firm. Let G (for government and taxes) stand for the value of the firm's taxes. Bankruptcy costs are also another claim on the cash flows. Let us label their value with an L (for lawyers). The pie theory says that these claims are paid from only one source, the cash flows (CF) of the firm. Algebraically, we must have:

CF = Payments to stockholders (*S*)

\+

Payments to bondholders (*B*)

\+

Payments to the government (*G*)

\+

Payments to lawyers (*L*)

\+

Payments to any and all other claimants

to the cash flows of the firm

Figure 15.2 shows the new pie. No matter how many slices we take and no matter who gets them, they must still add up to the total cash flow. The total value of the firm, V_T, is unaltered by the capital structure. Now, however, we must be broader in our definition of the firm's value:

$$V_T = S + B + G + L$$

We previously wrote the firm's value as:

$$S + B$$

when we ignored taxes and bankruptcy costs.

We have not even begun to exhaust the list of financial claims to the firm's cash flows. To give an unusual example, everyone reading this book has an economic claim to the cash flows of General Motors. After all, if you are injured in an accident, you might sue GM.

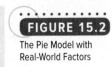

FIGURE 15.2

The Pie Model with
Real-World Factors

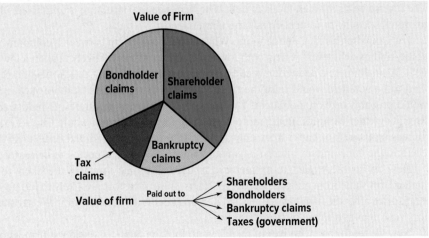

Win or lose, GM will expend resources dealing with the matter. If you think this is far-fetched and unimportant, ask yourself what GM might be willing to pay every man, woman, and child in the country to have them promise that they would never sue GM, no matter what happened. The law does not permit such payments, but that does not mean that a value to all of those potential claims does not exist. We guess that it would run into the billions of dollars, and, for GM or any other company, there should be a slice of the pie labeled *LS* for "potential lawsuits."

This is the essence of the MM intuition and theory: V is $V(CF)$ and depends on the total cash flow of the firm. The capital structure cuts it into slices.

There is, however, an important difference between claims such as those of stockholders and bondholders on the one hand and those of government and potential litigants in lawsuits on the other. The first set of claims are marketed claims, and the second set are nonmarketed claims. One difference is that the marketed claims can be bought and sold in financial markets, and the nonmarketed claims cannot.

When we speak of the value of the firm, we are referring to the value of the marketed claims, V_M, and not the value of nonmarketed claims, V_N. What we have shown is that the total value:

$$V_T = S + B + G + L$$
$$= V_M + V_N$$

is unaltered. But, as we saw, the value of the marketed claims, V_M, can change with changes in the capital structure.

By the pie theory, any increase in V_M must imply an identical decrease in V_N. Rational financial managers will choose a capital structure to maximize the value of the marketed claims, V_M. Equivalently, rational managers will work to minimize the value of the nonmarketed claims, V_N. These are taxes and bankruptcy costs in the previous example, but they also include all the other nonmarketed claims such as the *LS* claim.

15.4 SIGNALING

The previous section pointed out that the corporate leverage decision involves a trade-off between a tax subsidy and financial distress costs. This idea was graphed in Figure 15.1, where the marginal tax subsidy of debt exceeds the distress costs of debt for low levels of debt.

The reverse holds for high levels of debt. The firm's capital structure is optimized where the marginal tax subsidy to debt equals the marginal cost.

Let's explore this idea a little more. What is the relationship between a company's profitability and its debt level? A firm with low anticipated profits will likely take on a low level of debt. A small interest deduction is all that is needed to offset all of this firm's pretax profits. And too much debt would raise the firm's expected distress costs. A more successful firm would probably take on more debt. This firm could use the extra interest to reduce the taxes from its greater earnings. Being more financially secure, this firm would find its extra debt increasing the risk of bankruptcy only slightly. In other words, rational firms raise debt levels (and the concomitant interest payments) when profits are expected to increase.

How do investors react to an increase in debt? Rational investors are likely to infer a higher firm value from a higher debt level. Thus, these investors are likely to bid up a firm's stock price after the firm has, say, issued debt in order to buy back equity. We say that investors view debt as a *signal* of firm value.

Now we get to the incentives of managers to fool the public. Consider a firm whose level of debt is optimal. That is, the marginal tax benefit of debt exactly equals the marginal distress costs of debt. However, imagine that the firm's manager desires to increase the firm's current stock price, perhaps because he knows that many of his stockholders want to sell their stock soon. This manager might want to increase the level of debt to make investors think that the firm is more valuable than it really is. If the strategy works, investors will push up the price of the stock.

The above implies that firms can fool investors by taking on some additional leverage. Now let's ask the big question. Are there benefits to extra debt but no costs, implying that all firms will take on as much debt as possible? The answer, fortunately, is that there are costs as well. Imagine that a firm has issued extra debt to fool the public. At some point, the market will learn that the company is not that valuable after all. At this time, the stock price should actually fall below what it would have been had the debt never been increased. Why? Because the firm's debt level is now above the optimal level. That is, the marginal tax benefit of debt is below the marginal cost of debt. Thus, if the current stockholders plan to sell, say, half of their shares now and retain the other half, an increase in debt will help them on immediate sales but likely hurt them on later ones.

Now here is the important point: We said earlier that, in a world where managers do not attempt to fool investors, valuable firms issue more debt than less valuable ones. It turns out that, even when managers attempt to fool investors, the more valuable firms will still want to issue more debt than the less valuable firms. That is, while all firms will increase debt levels somewhat to fool investors, the cost of extra debt prevents the less valuable firms from issuing more debt than the more valuable firms issue. Thus, investors can still treat debt level as a signal of firm value. In other words, investors can still view an announcement of debt as a positive sign for the firm.

The above is a simplified example of debt signaling, and one can argue that it is too simplified. For example, perhaps the stockholders of some firms want to sell most of their stock immediately while the stockholders of other firms want to sell only a little of theirs now. It is impossible to tell here whether the firms with the most debt are the most valuable or merely the ones with the most impatient stockholders. Because other objections can be brought up as well, signaling theory is best validated by empirical evidence. And, fortunately, the empirical evidence tends to support the theory.

For example, consider the evidence concerning exchange offers. Firms often change their debt levels through exchange offers, of which there are two types. The first type of offer allows stockholders to exchange some of their stock for debt, thereby increasing leverage. The second type allows bondholders to exchange some of their debt for stock, decreasing leverage. Figure 15.3 shows the stock price behavior of firms that change their proportions of debt and equity via exchange offers. The purple line in the figure indicates that stock prices rise substantially on the date when an exchange offering increasing leverage is announced.

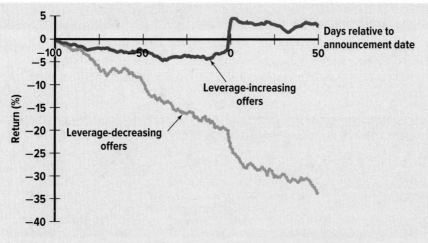

FIGURE 15.3

Stock Returns at the Time of Announcements of Exchange Offers

Source: Shah, Kshitij. "The Nature of Information Conveyed by Pure Capital Structure Changes." *Journal of Financial Economics* 36, no. 1 (1994), pp. 89–126.

Exchange offers change the debt-equity ratios of firms. The graph shows that stock prices increase for firms whose exchange offers increase leverage. Conversely, stock prices decrease for firms whose offers decrease leverage.

(This date is referred to as Date 0 in the figure.) Conversely, the blue line in the figure indicates that stock prices fall substantially when an offer decreasing leverage is announced.

The market infers from an increase in debt that the firm is better off, leading to a stock price rise. Conversely, the market infers the reverse from a decrease in debt, leading to a stock price fall. Thus, we say that managers signal information when they change leverage.

15.5 SHIRKING, PERQUISITES, AND BAD INVESTMENTS: A NOTE ON AGENCY COST OF EQUITY

The previous section introduced the static trade-off model, where a rise in debt increases both the tax shield and the costs of distress. We now extend the trade-off model by considering an important agency cost of equity. A discussion of this cost of equity is contained in a well-known quote from Adam Smith.[4]

> The directors of such [joint-stock] companies, however, being the managers rather of other people's money than of their own, it cannot well be expected, that they should watch over it with the same anxious vigilance with which the partners in a private copartnery frequently watch over their own. Like the stewards of a rich man, they are apt to consider attention to small matters as not for their master's honor, and very easily give themselves a dispensation from having it. Negligence and profusion, therefore, must always prevail, more or less, in the management of the affairs of such a company.

This elegant prose can be restated in modern-day vocabulary. An individual will work harder for a firm if she is one of its owners rather than just an employee. In addition, the individual will work harder if she owns a large percentage of the company rather than a small percentage. This idea has an important implication for capital structure, which we illustrate with the following example.

---

[4] Adam Smith. *The Wealth of Nations* [1776]. Ed. Edwin Cannan. New York: Modern Library, 1937, p. 700. As quoted in Michael C. Jensen and William H. Meckling, "Theory of the Firm: Managerial Behavior, Agency Costs and Ownership Structure," *Journal of Financial Economics* 3, no. 4 (1976), pp. 305–60.

EXAMPLE 15.1

Shirking and Perks

Ms. Pagell is an owner-entrepreneur running a computer services firm worth $1 million. She currently owns 100 percent of the firm. Because of the need to expand, she must raise another $2 million. She can either issue $2 million of debt at 12 percent interest or issue $2 million in stock. The cash flows under the two alternatives are presented below:

	Debt Issue				Stock Issue			
	Cash Flow	Interest	Cash Flow to Equity	Cash Flow to Ms. Pagell (100% of Equity)	Cash Flow	Interest	Cash Flow to Equity	Cash Flow to Ms. Pagell (33$\frac{1}{3}$% of Equity)
6-hour days	$300,000	$240,000	$ 60,000	$ 60,000	$300,000	0	$300,000	$100,000
10-hour days	400,000	240,000	160,000	160,000	400,000	0	400,000	133,333

Like any entrepreneur, Ms. Pagell can choose the degree of intensity with which she works. In our example, she can work either a 6- or a 10-hour day. With the debt issue, the extra work brings her $100,000 (= $160,000 − 60,000) more income. However, let's assume that with a stock issue she retains only a one-third interest in the equity. Here, the extra work brings her merely $33,333 (= $133,333 − 100,000). Being only human, she is likely to work harder if she issues debt. In other words, she has more incentive to *shirk* if she issues equity.

In addition, she is likely to obtain more *perquisites* (a big office, a company car, more expense account meals) if she issues stock. If she is a one-third stockholder, two-thirds of these costs are paid for by the other stockholders. If she is the sole owner, any additional perquisites reduce her equity stake alone.

Finally, she is more likely to take on capital budgeting projects with negative net present values. It might seem surprising that a manager with any equity interest at all would take on negative NPV projects because the stock price would clearly fall here. However, managerial salaries generally rise with firm size, indicating that managers have an incentive to accept some unprofitable projects after all the profitable ones have been taken on. That is, when an unprofitable project is accepted, the loss in stock value to a manager with only a small equity interest may be less than the increase in salary. In fact, it is our opinion that losses from accepting bad projects are far greater than losses from either shirking or excessive perquisites. Hugely unprofitable projects have bankrupted whole firms, something that even the largest of expense accounts is unlikely to do.

Thus, as the firm issues more equity, our entrepreneur will likely increase leisure time, work-related perquisites, and unprofitable investments. These three items are called agency costs because managers of the firm are agents of the stockholders.[5]

This example is quite applicable to a small company considering a large stock offering. Because a manager-owner will greatly dilute his or her share of the total equity in this case, a significant drop in work intensity or a significant increase in fringe benefits is possible. However, the example may be less applicable for a large corporation with many stockholders. For example, consider a large company such as General Electric issuing stock for the umpteenth time. The typical manager there already has such a small percentage stake in the firm that any temptation for negligence has probably been experienced before. An additional offering cannot be expected to increase this temptation.

---

[5] As previously discussed (see Chapter 1), agency costs are generally defined as the costs from conflicts of interest among stockholders, bondholders, and managers.

Who bears the burden of these agency costs? If the new stockholders invest with their eyes open, they do not. Knowing that Ms. Pagell may work shorter hours, they will pay only a low price for the stock. Thus, it is the owner who is hurt by agency costs. However, Ms. Pagell can protect herself to some extent. Just as stockholders reduce bankruptcy costs through protective covenants, an owner may allow monitoring by new stockholders. However, though proper reporting and surveillance may reduce the agency costs of equity, these techniques are unlikely to eliminate them.

It is commonly suggested that leveraged buyouts (LBOs) significantly reduce the cost of equity. In an LBO, a purchaser (usually a team of existing management) buys out the stockholders at a price above the current market. In other words, the company goes private because the stock is placed in the hands of only a few people. Because the managers now own a substantial chunk of the business, they are likely to work harder than when they were hired hands.[6]

Effect of Agency Costs of Equity on Debt-Equity Financing

The preceding discussion on the agency costs of equity should be viewed as an extension of the static trade-off model. That is, we stated in Section 15.3 that the change in the value of the firm when debt is substituted for equity is the difference between (1) the tax shield on debt and (2) the increase in the costs of financial distress (including the agency costs of debt). Now the change in the value of the firm is (1) the tax shield on debt plus (2) the reduction in the agency costs of equity minus (3) the increase in the costs of financial distress (including the agency costs of debt). The optimal debt-equity ratio would be higher in a world with agency costs of equity than in a world without these costs. However, because costs of financial distress are so significant, the costs of equity do not imply 100 percent debt financing.

Free Cash Flow

Any reader of murder mysteries knows that a criminal must have both motive and opportunity. The above discussion was about motive. Managers with only a small ownership interest have an incentive for wasteful behavior. For example, they bear only a small portion of the costs of, say, excessive expense accounts, and reap all of the benefits.

Now let's talk about opportunity. A manager can only pad his expense account if the firm has the cash flow to cover it. Thus, we might expect to see more wasteful activity in a firm with a capacity to generate large cash flows than in one with a capacity to generate only small flows. This very simple idea is formally called the *free cash flow hypothesis*.

A fair amount of academic work supports the hypothesis. For example, a frequently cited paper found that firms with high free cash flow are more likely to make bad acquisitions than firms with low free cash flow.[7]

The hypothesis has important implications for capital structure. Because dividends leave the firm, they reduce free cash flow. Thus, according to the free cash flow hypothesis, an increase in dividends should benefit the stockholders by reducing the ability of managers to pursue wasteful activities. Furthermore, because interest and principal also leave the firm,

---

[6] One professor we know introduces his classes to LBOs by asking the students three questions:

    1. How many of you have ever owned your own car?

    2. How many of you have ever rented a car?

    3. How many of you took better care of the car you owned than the car you rented?

Just as it is human nature to take better care of your own car, it is human nature to work harder when you own more of the company.

[7] Larry H.P. Lang, Reneé M. Stulz, and Ralph A. Walkling, "Managerial Performance, Tobin's Q, and the Gains from Successful Tender Offers," *Journal of Financial Economics* 24, no. 1 (1989), pp. 137–54.

debt reduces free cash flow as well. In fact, interest and principal should have a greater effect than dividends on the free-spending ways of managers because bankruptcy will occur if the firm is unable to make future debt payments. By contrast, a future dividend reduction will cause fewer problems for managers because the firm has no legal obligation to pay dividends. Because of this, the free cash flow hypothesis argues that a shift from equity to debt will boost firm value.

In summary, the free cash flow hypothesis provides still another reason for firms to issue debt. We previously discussed the cost of equity; new equity dilutes the holdings of managers with equity interests, increasing their motive to waste corporate resources. We now state that debt reduces free cash flow because the firm must make interest and principal payments. The free cash flow hypothesis implies that debt reduces the opportunity for managers to waste resources.

15.6 THE PECKING-ORDER THEORY

Although the trade-off theory has dominated corporate finance circles for a long time, attention is also being paid to the *pecking-order theory*. To understand this view of the world, let's put ourselves in the position of a corporate financial manager whose firm needs new capital. The manager faces a choice between issuing debt and issuing equity. Previously, we evaluated the choice in terms of tax benefits, distress costs, and agency costs. However, there is one consideration that we have so far neglected: timing.

Imagine the manager saying:

> I want to issue stock in one situation only—when it is overvalued. If the stock of my firm is selling at $50 per share, but I think that it is actually worth $60, I will not issue stock. I would actually be giving new stockholders a gift because they would receive stock worth $60, but would only have to pay $50 for it. More importantly, my current stockholders would be upset because the firm would be receiving $50 in cash but giving away something worth $60. So if I believe that my stock is undervalued, I would issue bonds. Bonds, particularly those with little or no risk of default, are likely to be priced correctly. Their value is primarily determined by the marketwide interest rate, a variable that is publicly known.
>
> But suppose that our stock is selling at $70. Now I'd like to issue stock. If I can get some fool to buy our stock for $70 while the stock is really only worth $60, I will be making $10 for our current shareholders.

Although this may strike you as a cynical view, it seems to square well with reality. Before the United States adopted insider trading and disclosure laws, many managers were alleged to have unfairly trumpeted their firm's prospects prior to equity issuance. And, even today, managers seem more willing to issue equity after the price of their stock has risen than after their stock has fallen in price. Thus, timing might be an important motive in equity issuance, perhaps even more important than those motives in the trade-off theory. After all, the firm in the preceding example immediately makes $10 by properly timing the issuance of equity. Ten dollars' worth of agency and bankruptcy cost reduction might take many years to realize.

The key that makes the example work is asymmetric information; the manager must know more about his firm's prospects than does the typical investor. If the manager's estimate of the true worth of the company is no better than the estimate of a typical investor, any attempts by the manager to time the issuance of equity will fail. This assumption of asymmetry is quite plausible. Managers should know more about their company than do outsiders because managers work at the company every day. One caveat is that some managers are perpetually optimistic about their firm, blurring good judgment.

But we are not done with this example yet; we must consider the investor. Imagine an investor saying:

> I make investments carefully because it involves my hard-earned money. However, even with all the time I put into studying stocks, I can't possibly know what the managers themselves know.

After all, I've got a day job to be concerned with. So, I watch what the managers do. If a firm issues stock, the firm was likely overvalued beforehand. If a firm issues debt, it was likely undervalued.

When we look at both issuers and investors, we see a kind of poker game, with each side trying to outwit the other. There are two prescriptions to the issuer in this poker game. The first one, which is fairly straightforward, is to issue debt instead of equity when the stock is undervalued. The second, which is more subtle, is to issue debt also when the firm is overvalued. After all, if a firm issues equity, investors will infer that the stock is overvalued. They will not buy it until the stock has fallen enough to eliminate any advantage from equity issuance. In fact, only the most overvalued firms have any incentive to issue equity. Should even a moderately overpriced firm issue equity, investors will infer that this firm is among the most overpriced, causing the stock to fall more than is deserved. Thus, the end result is that virtually no one will issue equity.

This result that essentially all firms should issue debt is clearly an extreme one. It is as extreme as (1) the Modigliani-Miller (MM) result that, in a world without taxes, firms are indifferent to capital structure and (2) the MM result that, in a world of corporate taxes but no financial distress costs, all firms should be 100 percent debt financed. Perhaps we in finance have a penchant for extreme models!

But just as one can temper MM's conclusions by combining financial distress costs with corporate taxes, we can temper those of the pure pecking-order theory. This pure version assumes that timing is the financial manager's only consideration. In reality, a manager must consider taxes, financial distress costs, and agency costs as well. Thus, a firm may issue debt only up to a point. If financial distress becomes a real possibility beyond that point, the firm may issue equity instead.

Rules of the Pecking Order

The above discussion presented the basic ideas behind the pecking-order theory. What are the practical implications of the theory for financial managers? The theory provides the following two rules for the real world.

RULE #1: USE INTERNAL FINANCING For expository purposes, we have oversimplified by comparing equity to risk-free debt. Managers cannot use special knowledge of their firm to determine if this type of debt is mispriced because the price of risk-free debt is determined solely by the marketwide interest rate. However, in reality, corporate debt has the possibility of default. Thus, just as managers have a tendency to issue equity when they think it is overvalued, managers also have a tendency to issue debt when they think it is overvalued.

When would managers view their debt as overvalued? Probably in the same situations when they think their equity is overvalued. For example, if the public thinks that the firm's prospects are rosy but the managers see trouble ahead, these managers would view their debt—as well as their equity—as being overvalued. That is, the public might see the debt as nearly risk-free, whereas the managers see a strong possibility of default.

Thus, investors are likely to price a debt issue with the same skepticism that they have when pricing an equity issue. The way managers get out of this box is to finance projects out of retained earnings. You don't have to worry about investor skepticism if you can avoid going to investors in the first place. Thus, the first rule of the pecking order is:

Use internal financing.

RULE #2: ISSUE SAFE SECURITIES FIRST Although investors fear mispricing of both debt and equity, the fear is much greater for equity. Corporate debt still has relatively little risk compared to equity because, if financial distress is avoided, investors receive a fixed return. Thus, the pecking-order theory implies that, if outside financing is required, debt should be issued before equity. Only when the firm's debt capacity is reached should the firm consider equity.

Of course, there are many types of debt. For example, because convertible debt is more risky than straight debt, the pecking-order theory implies that one should issue straight debt before issuing convertibles. Thus, the second rule of the pecking-order theory is:

Issue the safest securities first.

Implications

There are a number of implications associated with the pecking-order theory that are at odds with the trade-off theory:

1. *There Is No Target Amount of Leverage.* According to the trade-off theory, each firm balances the benefits of debt, such as the tax shield, with the costs of debt, such as distress costs. The optimal amount of leverage occurs where the marginal benefit of debt equals the marginal cost of debt.

   By contrast, the pecking-order theory does not imply a target amount of leverage. Rather, each firm chooses its leverage ratio based on financing needs. Firms first fund projects out of retained earnings. This should lower the percentage of debt in the capital structure because profitable, internally funded projects raise both the book value and the market value of equity. Additional cash needs are met with debt, clearly raising the debt level. However, at some point the debt capacity of the firm may be exhausted, giving way to equity issuance. Thus, the amount of leverage is determined by the happenstance of available projects. Firms do not pursue a target ratio of debt to equity.

2. *Profitable Firms Use Less Debt.* Profitable firms generate cash internally, implying less need for outside financing. Because firms desiring outside capital turn to debt first, profitable firms end up relying on less debt. The trade-off theory does not have this implication. The greater cash flow of more profitable firms creates greater debt capacity. These firms will use that debt capacity to capture the tax shield and the other benefits of leverage.

3. *Companies Like Financial Slack.* The pecking-order theory is based on the difficulties of obtaining financing at a reasonable cost. A skeptical investing public thinks a stock is overvalued if the managers try to issue more of it, thereby leading to a stock-price decline. Because this happens with bonds only to a lesser extent, managers rely first on bond financing. However, firms can only issue so much debt before encountering the potential costs of financial distress.

   Wouldn't it be easier to have the cash ahead of time? This is the idea behind *financial slack.* Because firms know that they will have to fund profitable projects at various times in the future, they accumulate cash today. They are then not forced to go to the capital markets when a project comes up. However, there is a limit to the amount of cash a firm will want to accumulate. As mentioned earlier in this chapter, too much free cash may tempt managers to pursue wasteful activities.

15.7 HOW FIRMS ESTABLISH CAPITAL STRUCTURE

The theories of capital structure are among the most elegant and sophisticated in the field of finance. Financial economists should (and do!) pat themselves on the back for contributions in this area. However, the practical applications of the theories are less than fully satisfying. Consider that our work on net present value produced an exact formula for evaluating projects. Prescriptions for capital structure under either the trade-off model or the pecking-order theory are vague by comparison. No exact formula is available for evaluating the optimal debt-equity ratio. Because of this, we turn to evidence from the real world.

The following empirical regularities are worth considering when formulating capital structure policy:

1. *Most Nonfinancial Corporations Have Relatively Low Debt-Asset Value Ratios.* How much debt is used in the real world? Figure 15.4 shows the median debt-to-value ratio, defined as book value of debt to market value of the firm, in each of 39 different countries. This ratio ranges from slightly over 50 percent for Korea to slightly under 10 percent for Australia. The ratio for U.S. companies is the fourth lowest.

    Should we view these ratios as being high or low? Because academics generally see corporate tax reduction as a chief motivation for debt, we might wonder if real-world companies issue enough debt to greatly reduce, if not downright eliminate, corporate taxes. The empirical evidence suggests that this is not the case. For example, corporate income taxes in the United States for 2017 were about $297 billion. Most large U.S. public companies pay some income taxes, but a few do not.[8] Thus, it is clear that corporations do not issue debt up to the point

FIGURE 15.4 Median Leverage Ratio of Sample Firms in 39 Different Countries (1991–2006)

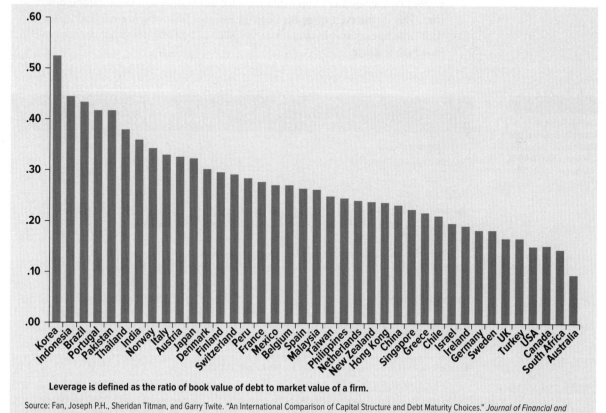

Leverage is defined as the ratio of book value of debt to market value of a firm.

Source: Fan, Joseph P.H., Sheridan Titman, and Garry Twite. "An International Comparison of Capital Structure and Debt Maturity Choices." *Journal of Financial and Quantitative Analysis* 47, no. 1 (2012), pp. 23–56.

[8] For example, in 2014, there were 15 Fortune 500 companies (the largest U.S. public firms by sales) that paid no income taxes. *The Fiscal Times,* April 9, 2015.

where tax shelters are completely used up.[9] There are clearly limits to the amount of debt corporations can issue, perhaps because of the financial distress costs discussed earlier in this chapter.

2. *A Number of Firms Use No Debt.* Strebulaev and Yang examined the capital structures of large U.S. public firms from 1962 to 2009 and found 10.2 percent, on average, had zero debt and about 22 percent had less than 5 percent debt.[10] Bessler, Drobetz, Haller and Meier looked at zero-debt firms in the G7 countries (U.S., U.K., Canada, France, Germany, Italy, and Japan). Their overall findings were similar to the U.S. findings: namely about 10 percent of G7 firms over an 11-year period used no debt. Both studies found zero-debt behavior to be significant and showed no tendency to decrease over time.[11]

Zero-debt behavior is evident even when firms have cash balances, pay high taxes, and pay high dividends. Typically the top management in these firms has high equity ownership. Furthermore, there is significantly greater family involvement. Clearly, management and governance characteristics are related to the zero-debt behavior, but financial distress appears not to be a major factor.

Thus, a possible story emerges. Control is important to the top managers of all equity firms but they are less diversified than managers of similar, but levered, firms. Because of this, leverage represents an added but unwanted risk.

3. *There Are Differences in the Capital Structures of Different Industries.* There are significant interindustry differences in debt ratios that persist over time. As can be seen in Table 15.3, debt ratios tend to be quite low in high-growth industries with ample future investment opportunities, such as the drug and electronics industries. This is true even when the need for external financing is great. Industries with large investments in tangible assets, such as building construction, tend to have high leverage.

TABLE 15.3

Capital Structure Ratios for Selected U.S. Nonfinancial Industries (medians), Five-Year Average

	Debt* as a Percentage of the Market Value of Equity and Debt (Industry Medians)
High Leverage	
Radio and television broadcasting stations	59.60
Air transport	45.89
Hotels and motels	45.55
Building construction	42.31
Natural gas distribution	33.11
Low Leverage	
Electronic equipment	10.58
Computers	9.53
Educational services	8.93
Drugs	8.79
Biological products	8.05

*Debt is defined as the total of short-term debt and long-term debt.
Source: Ibbotson 2011 Cost of Capital Yearbook (Chicago: Morningstar, 2011).

[9] For further insight, see John Graham, "How Big Are the Tax Benefits of Debt?," *Journal of Finance* 55, no. 5 (2000), pp. 1901–41.
[10] Ilya Strebulaev and Baozhong Yang, "The Mystery of Zero Leverage Firms,"*The Journal of Financial Economics* 109, vol. 1 (2013), pp. 1–23. See also Anup Agrawal and Nandu Nagarajan, "Corporate Capital Structure, Agency Costs, and Ownership Control: The Case of All Equity Firms,"*Journal of Finance* 45, no. 4 (1990), pp. 1325–31.
[11] Wolfgang Bessler, Wolfgang Drobetz, Rebekka Haller, and Iwan Meier, "The International Zero Leverage Phenomenon," *Journal of Corporate Finance* 23 (2015), pp. 196–221. In addition, they find more zero-debt behavior in countries with capital-market-oriented financial systems, common law regimes, and high creditor protection (e.g., the U.K.) and less zero-debt behavior in countries with a bank-oriented financial system, civil law regime, and low creditor protection.

To give a more specific example of industry effects, we looked up some capital structure information on Johnson & Johnson (JNJ) and Consolidated Edison (ED) using the "Financials" area of www.reuters.com. Johnson & Johnson's capital structure looks like this (note that leverage ratios are expressed as percentages on this site):

	Company	industry	sector
Quick Ratio (MRQ)	1.40	2.65	2.63
Current Ratio (MRQ)	1.72	3.71	3.68
LT Debt to Equity (MRQ)	45.62	7.50	9.53
Total Debt to Equity (MRQ)	48.36	10.94	13.39
Interest Coverage (TTM)	42.55	40.82	33.85

For every dollar of equity, Johnson & Johnson has long-term debt of $.4562 and total debt of $.4836. Compare this result to Consolidated Edison:

	Company	industry	sector
Quick Ratio (MRQ)	0.56	1.33	2.31
Current Ratio (MRQ)	0.62	1.40	2.44
LT Debt to Equity (MRQ)	97.44	145.23	108.51
Total Debt to Equity (MRQ)	113.05	177.60	126.57
Interest Coverage (TTM)	4.48	5.74	13.34

For every dollar of equity, Consolidated Edison has $.9744 of long-term debt and total debt of $1.1305. When we examine the industry and sector averages, the differences are again apparent. The pharmaceutical industry, on average, has only $.0750 of long-term debt and $.1094 of total debt for every dollar of equity. By comparison, the electric utility industry on average has $1.4523 of long-term debt and $1.7760 of total debt for every dollar of equity. Thus, we see that choice of capital structure is a management decision, but it is clearly also influenced by industry characteristics.

4. *Most Corporations Employ Target Debt-Equity Ratios.* Graham and Harvey asked 392 chief financial officers (CFOs) whether their firms use target debt-equity ratios, with the results being presented in Figure 15.5.[12] As can be seen, the great majority of the firms use targets, though the strictness of the targets varies across

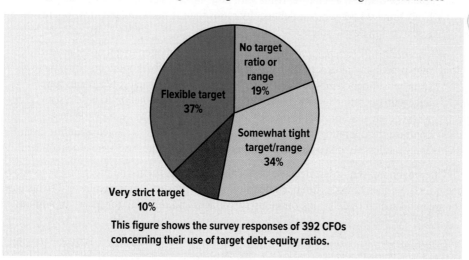

This figure shows the survey responses of 392 CFOs concerning their use of target debt-equity ratios.

FIGURE 15.5

Survey Results on the Use of Target Debt-Equity Ratios

Source: Graham, John R., and Campbell R. Harvey. "The Theory and Practice of Corporate Finance." *Journal of Financial Economics* 60, no. 2–3 (2001): pp. 187–243.

---

[12] John R. Graham and Campbell R. Harvey, "The Theory and Practice of Corporate Finance," *Journal of Financial Economics* 60, no. 2–3 (2001), pp. 187–243.

companies. Only 19 percent of the firms avoid target ratios. Results elsewhere in the paper indicate that large firms are more likely than small firms to employ these targets. The CFOs did not specify what they meant by either *flexible* or *strict* targets. However, elsewhere in the study the respondents indicated that, by and large, they did not rebalance in response to changes in their firm's stock price, suggesting flexibility in target ratios.

5. *Capital Structures of Individual Firms Can Vary Significantly over Time.* While Graham and Harvey report that most firms use target leverage ratios, a recent paper nevertheless concludes that capital structures of individual firms often vary widely over time.[13] Consider Figure 15.6, which presents leverage ratios for General Motors, IBM, and Eastman Kodak from 1926 to 2008. Both book leverage (total book value of debt divided by total assets) and market leverage (total book value of debt divided by total book debt plus market value of common stock) are shown. Regardless of the measure, all three companies display significant variations in leverage. Large variations in individual firm leverage over time is evidence that variations in individual firm investment opportunities and the need for financing are important determinants of capital structure and of the importance of financial slack (i.e., firms borrow money when they have projects worth spending it on).[14]

How should companies establish target debt-equity ratios? While there is no mathematical formula for establishing a target ratio, we present four important factors affecting the ratio:

- *Flexibility.* Establishing a firm's capital structure will probably include some kind of a debt-equity target. However, the targeting should allow for a wide range of variation and adjustments over time.

- *Taxes.* As we pointed out earlier, firms can deduct interest for tax purposes only to the extent of their profits before interest. Thus, highly profitable firms are more likely to have larger target ratios than less profitable firms.[15]

- *Types of Assets.* Financial distress is costly with or without formal bankruptcy proceedings. The costs of financial distress depend on the types of assets that the firm has. For example, if a firm has a large investment in land, buildings, and other tangible assets, it will have smaller costs of financial distress than a firm with a large investment in research and development. Research and development typically has less resale value than land; thus, most of its value disappears in financial distress. Therefore, firms with large investments in tangible assets are likely to have higher target debt-equity ratios than firms with large investments in research and development.

- *Uncertainty of Operating Income.* Firms with uncertain operating income have a high probability of experiencing financial distress, even without debt. Thus, these firms must finance mostly with equity. For example, pharmaceutical firms have uncertain operating income because no one can predict whether today's research will generate new, profitable drugs. Consequently, these firms issue little debt. By contrast, the operating income of firms in regulated industries, such as utilities, generally has low volatility. Relative to other industries, utilities use a great deal of debt.

One final note is in order. Because no formula supports them, the preceding points may seem too nebulous to assist financial decision making. Instead, many real-world firms base their capital structure decisions on industry averages and the need for a certain amount of

---

[13] Harry DeAngelo and Richard Roll, "How Stable Are Corporate Capital Structures?," *Journal of Finance* 70, no. 1 (2015), pp. 373–418.

[14] See also Harry DeAngelo, Linda DeAngelo, and Toni M. Whited, "Capital Structure Dynamics and Transitory Debt," *Journal of Financial Economics* 99, no. 2 (2011), pp. 235–61.

[15] By contrast, the pecking-order theory argues that profitable firms will employ less debt because they can invest out of retained earnings. However, the pecking-order theory argues against the use of target ratios in the first place.

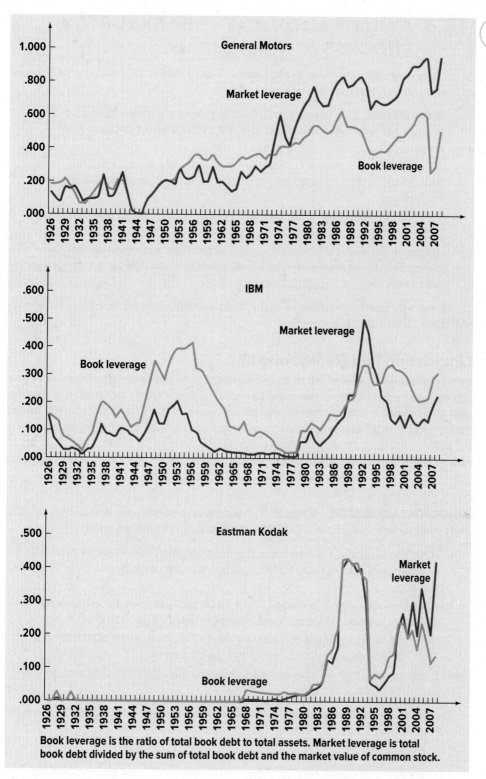

FIGURE 15.6

Leverage Ratios of General Motors, IBM, and Eastman Kodak over Time

Source: DeAngelo, Harry, and Richard Roll. "How Stable Are Corporate Capital Structures?" *Journal of Finance* 70, no. 1 (2015), pp. 373–418. Figure 1.

Book leverage is the ratio of total book debt to total assets. Market leverage is total book debt divided by the sum of total book debt and the market value of common stock.

financial slack. This may strike some as a cowardly approach, but it at least keeps firms from deviating far from accepted practice. After all, the existing firms in any industry are the survivors. Therefore we should pay at least some attention to their decisions. However, firms sometimes deviate substantially from their target capital structure, especially when there is a need to issue transitory debt because of positive NPV investment opportunities.

15.8 A QUICK LOOK AT THE BANKRUPTCY PROCESS

As we have discussed, one of the consequences of using debt is the possibility of financial distress, which can be defined in several ways:

The SEC provides a good overview of the bankruptcy process: www.sec.gov.

1. *Business Failure.* This term is usually used to refer to a situation in which a business has terminated with a loss to creditors, but even an all-equity firm can fail.

2. *Legal Bankruptcy.* Firms or creditors bring petitions to a federal court for bankruptcy. Bankruptcy is a legal proceeding for liquidating or reorganizing a business.

3. *Technical Insolvency.* Technical insolvency occurs when a firm is unable to meet its financial obligations.

4. *Accounting Insolvency.* Firms with negative net worth are insolvent on the books. This happens when the total book liabilities exceed the book value of the total assets.

We now very briefly discuss some of the terms and more relevant issues associated with bankruptcy and financial distress.

Liquidation and Reorganization

Firms that cannot or choose not to make contractually required payments to creditors have two basic options: liquidation or reorganization. Liquidation means termination of the firm as a going concern and involves selling off the assets of the firm. The proceeds, net of selling costs, are distributed to creditors in order of established priority. Reorganization is the option of keeping the firm a going concern; it often involves issuing new securities to replace old securities. Both liquidation and reorganization are the result of a bankruptcy proceeding. Which occurs depends on whether the firm is worth more "dead or alive."

BANKRUPTCY LIQUIDATION Chapter 7 of the Federal Bankruptcy Reform Act of 1978 deals with "straight" liquidation. The following sequence of events is typical:

1. A petition is filed in a federal court. Corporations may file a voluntary petition, or involuntary petitions may be filed against the corporation by several of its creditors.

2. A trustee-in-bankruptcy is elected by the creditors to take over the assets of the debtor corporation. The trustee will attempt to liquidate the assets.

3. When the assets are liquidated, after payment of the bankruptcy administration costs, the proceeds are distributed among the creditors.

4. If any proceeds remain, after expenses and payments to creditors, they are distributed to the shareholders.

The distribution of the proceeds of the liquidation occurs according to the following priority list:

1. Administrative expenses associated with the bankruptcy.
2. Other expenses arising after the filing of an involuntary bankruptcy petition but before the appointment of a trustee.
3. Wages, salaries, and commissions.
4. Contributions to employee benefit plans.
5. Consumer claims.
6. Government tax claims.

7. Payment to unsecured creditors.

8. Payment to preferred stockholders.

9. Payment to common stockholders.

This priority list for liquidation is a reflection of the absolute priority rule (APR). The higher a claim is on this list, the more likely it is to be paid. In many of these categories, there are various limitations and qualifications that we omit for the sake of brevity.

Two qualifications to this list are in order. The first concerns secured creditors. Such creditors are entitled to the proceeds from the sale of the security and are outside this ordering. However, if the secured property is liquidated and provides insufficient cash to cover the amount owed, the secured creditors join with unsecured creditors in dividing the remaining liquidated value. In contrast, if the secured property is liquidated for proceeds greater than the secured claim, the net proceeds are used to pay unsecured creditors and others. The second qualification to the APR is that, in reality, what happens and who gets what in the event of bankruptcy are subject to much negotiation, and, as a result, the APR is frequently not followed.

BANKRUPTCY REORGANIZATION   Corporate reorganization takes place under Chapter 11 of the Federal Bankruptcy Reform Act of 1978. The general objective of a proceeding under Chapter 11 is to plan to restructure the corporation with some provision for repayment of creditors. The typical sequence of events is as follows:

> Get the latest on bankruptcy at www .bankruptcydata.com.

1. A voluntary petition can be filed by the corporation, or an involuntary petition can be filed by creditors.

2. A federal judge either approves or denies the petition. If the petition is approved, a time for filing proofs of claims is set.

3. In most cases, the corporation (the "debtor in possession") continues to run the business.

4. The corporation (and, in certain cases, the creditors) submits a reorganization plan.

5. Creditors and shareholders are divided into classes. A class of creditors accepts the plan if a majority of the class agrees to the plan.

6. After its acceptance by creditors, the plan is confirmed by the court.

7. Payments in cash, property, and securities are made to creditors and shareholders. The plan may provide for the issuance of new securities.

8. For some fixed length of time, the firm operates according to the provisions of the reorganization plan.

The corporation may wish to allow the old stockholders to retain some participation in the firm. Needless to say, this may involve some protest by the holders of unsecured debt. In some cases, the bankruptcy procedure is needed to invoke the "cram-down" power of the bankruptcy court. Under certain circumstances, a class of creditors can be forced to accept a bankruptcy plan even if they vote not to approve it, hence the remarkably apt description "cram-down."

So-called prepackaged bankruptcies are a relatively common phenomenon. What happens is that the corporation secures the necessary approval of a bankruptcy plan from a majority of its creditors first, and then it files for bankruptcy. As a result, the company enters bankruptcy and reemerges almost immediately.

For example, on March 21, 2018, Southeastern Grocers, owner of Winn-Dixie and Bi-Lo grocery stores, filed a prepack bankruptcy. Under the terms of the deal, the company's debt was reduced by $600 million, and creditors were given an equity stake in the company when it emerged from bankruptcy. The entire bankruptcy process took about two months.

In 2005, Congress passed the most significant overhaul of U.S. bankruptcy laws in the last 25 years, the Bankruptcy Abuse Prevention and Consumer Protection Act of 2005

(BAPCPA). Most of the changes were aimed at individual debtors, but corporations were also affected. Before BAPCPA, a bankrupt company had the exclusive right to submit reorganization plans to the bankruptcy court. It has been argued that this exclusivity is one reason some companies have remained in bankruptcy for so long. Under the new law, after 18 months, creditors can submit their own plan for the court's consideration.

One controversial change made by BAPCPA has to do with so-called key employee retention plans, or KERPs. Strange as it may sound, bankrupt companies routinely give bonus payments to executives, even though the executives may be the same ones who led the company into bankruptcy in the first place. Such bonuses are intended to keep valuable employees from moving to more successful firms, but critics have argued they are often abused. The new law permits KERPs only if the employee in question actually has a job offer from another company.

Recently, Section 363 of the bankruptcy code has been in the news. In a traditional Chapter 11 filing, the bankruptcy plan is described to creditors and shareholders in a prospectuslike disclosure. The plan must then be approved by a vote involving the interested parties. A Section 363 bankruptcy is more like an auction. An initial bidder, known as a *stalking horse*, bids on all or part of the bankrupt company's assets. Other bidders are then invited into the process to determine the highest bid for the company's assets. The main advantage of a Section 363 bankruptcy is speed. Because a traditional bankruptcy requires the approval of interested parties, it is not uncommon for the process to take several years, whereas a Section 363 bankruptcy is generally much quicker. For example, in the middle of 2009, both General Motors and Chrysler sped through the bankruptcy process in less than 45 days with the help of Section 363 sales.

Financial Management and the Bankruptcy Process

It may seem a little odd, but the right to go bankrupt is very valuable. There are several reasons why this is true. First of all, from an operational standpoint, when a firm files for bankruptcy, there is an immediate "stay" on creditors, usually meaning that payments to creditors will cease and creditors will have to await the outcome of the bankruptcy process to find out if and how much they will be paid. This stay gives the firm time to evaluate its options, and it prevents what is usually termed a "race to the courthouse steps" by creditors and others.

Beyond this, some bankruptcy filings are actually strategic actions intended to improve a firm's competitive position, and firms have filed for bankruptcy even though they were not insolvent at the time. Probably the most famous example is Continental Airlines. In 1983, following deregulation of the airline industry, Continental found itself competing with newly established airlines that had much lower labor costs. Continental filed for reorganization under Chapter 11 even though it was not insolvent.

Continental argued that, based on pro forma data, it would become insolvent in the future, and a reorganization was therefore necessary. By filing for bankruptcy, Continental was able to terminate its existing labor agreements, lay off large numbers of workers, and slash wages for the remaining employees. In other words, at least in the eyes of critics, Continental essentially used the bankruptcy process as a vehicle for reducing labor costs. Congress subsequently modified bankruptcy laws to make it more difficult, though not impossible, for companies to abrogate a labor contract through the bankruptcy process. Continental merged with United Airlines in 2010.

Other famous examples of strategic bankruptcies exist. For example, Manville (then known as Johns-Manville) and Dow Corning filed for bankruptcy because of expected future losses resulting from litigation associated with asbestos and silicone breast implants, respectively. In fact, by 2019, over 100 companies had filed for Chapter 11 bankruptcy because of asbestos litigation. In 2001, for example, W.R. Grace, a well-known chemical and plastics company, threw in the towel and filed for bankruptcy. Six years later, in November

2007, the company filed a reorganization plan with the bankruptcy court. At that time, the company reported that it had incurred $21.3 million in bankruptcy-related expenses in the third quarter of 2007 alone, up from $12 million in the third quarter of 2006. Estimates of the total costs related to asbestos bankruptcy litigation for all firms involved put the bill at over $200 billion. Other notable companies that have filed for bankruptcy due to the asbestos nightmare include Congoleum, Federal-Mogul, and two subsidiaries of Halliburton.

Agreements to Avoid Bankruptcy

When a firm defaults on an obligation, it can avoid a bankruptcy filing. Because the legal process of bankruptcy can be lengthy and expensive, it is often in everyone's best interest to devise a "workout" that avoids a bankruptcy filing. Much of the time, creditors can work with the management of a company that has defaulted on a loan contract. Voluntary arrangements to restructure or "reschedule" the company's debt can be and often are made. This may involve extension, which postpones the date of payment, or composition, which involves a reduced payment.

SUMMARY AND CONCLUSIONS

1. We mentioned in the last chapter that according to theory, firms should create all-debt capital structures under corporate taxation. Because firms generally assume moderate amounts of debt in the real world, the theory must have been missing something at that point. We state in this chapter that costs of financial distress cause firms to restrain their issuance of debt. These costs are of two types: direct and indirect. Lawyers' and accountants' fees during the bankruptcy process are examples of direct costs. We mention four examples of indirect costs:

   - Impaired ability to conduct business.
   - Incentive to take on risky projects.
   - Incentive toward underinvestment.
   - Distribution of funds to stockholders prior to bankruptcy.

2. Because the above costs are substantial and the stockholders ultimately bear them, firms have an incentive for cost reduction. We suggest two cost reduction techniques:

   - Protective covenants.
   - Consolidation of debt.

3. Because costs of financial distress can be reduced but not eliminated, firms will not finance entirely with debt. Figure 15.1 illustrates the relationship between firm value and debt. In the figure, firms select the debt-equity ratio at which firm value is maximized.

4. Signaling theory argues that profitable firms are likely to increase their leverage because the extra interest payments will offset some of the pretax profits. Rational stockholders will infer higher firm value from a higher debt level. Thus, investors view debt as a signal of firm value.

5. Managers who own a small proportion of a firm's equity can be expected to work less, maintain more lavish expense accounts, and accept more pet projects with negative NPVs than managers who own a large proportion of equity. Because new issues of equity dilute a manager's percentage interest in the firm, the above agency costs are likely to increase when a firm's growth is financed through new equity rather than through new debt.

6. The pecking-order theory implies that managers prefer internal to external financing. If external financing is required, managers tend to choose the safest securities, such as debt. Firms may accumulate slack to avoid external financing.

7. Debt-equity ratios vary across industries. We present three factors determining the target debt-equity ratio:

   a. *Taxes.* Firms with high taxable income should rely more on debt than firms with low taxable income.

   b. *Types of Assets.* Firms with a high percentage of intangible assets such as research and development should have low debt. Firms with primarily tangible assets should have higher debt.

   c. *Uncertainty of Operating Income.* Firms with high uncertainty of operating income should rely mostly on equity.

8. We closed the chapter with a brief look at the bankruptcy process and some financial aspects of bankruptcy.

CONCEPT QUESTIONS

1. **Bankruptcy Costs**   What are the direct and indirect costs of bankruptcy? Briefly explain each.

2. **Stockholder Incentives**   Do you agree or disagree with the following statement: A firm's stockholders will never want the firm to invest in projects with negative net present values. Why?

3. **Capital Structure Decisions**   Due to large losses incurred in the past several years, a firm has $2 billion in tax loss carryforwards. This means that the next $2 billion of the firm's income will be free from corporate income taxes. Security analysts estimate that it will take many years for the firm to generate $2 billion in earnings. The firm has a moderate amount of debt in its capital structure. The firm's CEO is deciding whether to issue debt or equity in order to raise the funds needed to finance an upcoming project. Which method of financing would you recommend? Why?

4. **Cost of Debt**   What steps can stockholders take to reduce the costs of debt?

5. **MM and Bankruptcy Costs**   How do the existence of financial distress costs and agency costs affect Modigliani and Miller's theory in a world where corporations pay taxes?

6. **Agency Costs of Equity**   What are the sources of the agency costs of equity?

7. **Observed Capital Structures**   Refer to the observed capital structures given in Table 15.3 of the text. What do you notice about the types of industries with respect to their average debt-equity ratios? Are certain types of industries more likely to be highly leveraged than others? What are some possible reasons for this observed segmentation? Do the operating results and tax history of the firms play a role? How about their future earnings prospects? Explain.

8. **Bankruptcy and Corporate Ethics**   As mentioned in the text, some firms have filed for bankruptcy because of actual or likely litigation-related losses. Is this a proper use of the bankruptcy process?

9. **Bankruptcy and Corporate Ethics**   Firms sometimes use the threat of a bankruptcy filing to force creditors to renegotiate terms. Critics argue that in such cases, the firm is using bankruptcy laws "as a sword rather than a shield." Is this an ethical tactic?

10. **Bankruptcy and Corporate Ethics**   As mentioned in the text, Continental Airlines filed for bankruptcy, at least in part, as a means of reducing labor costs. Whether this move was ethical or proper was hotly debated. Give both sides of the argument.

QUESTIONS AND PROBLEMS

Basic
(Questions 1–5)

1. **Firm Value**   Connor Corp. has an EBIT of $535,000 per year that is expected to continue in perpetuity. The unlevered cost of equity for the company is 13.2 percent, and the corporate tax rate is 21 percent. The company also has a perpetual bond issue outstanding with a market value of $950,000.

   a. What is the value of the company?

   b. The CFO of the company informs the company president that the value of the company is $3.3 million. Is the CFO correct?

2. **Agency Costs**   Tom Scott is the owner, president, and primary salesperson for Scott Manufacturing. Because of this, the company's profits are driven by the amount of work Tom does. If he works 40 hours each week, the company's EBIT will be $415,000 per year, and if he works a 50-hour week, the company's EBIT will be $560,000 per year. The company is currently worth $2.9 million. The company needs a cash infusion of $1.6 million, and it can issue equity or issue debt with an interest rate of 8 percent. Assume there are no corporate taxes.

   a. What are the cash flows to Tom under each scenario?

   b. Under which form of financing is Tom likely to work harder?

   c. What specific new costs will occur with each form of financing?

3. **Capital Structure and Growth**   Edwards Construction currently has debt outstanding with a market value of $340,000 and a cost of 6 percent. The company has an EBIT of $20,400 that is expected to continue in perpetuity. Assume there are no taxes.

   a. What is the value of the company's equity? What is the debt-to-value ratio?

   b. What are the equity value and debt-to-value ratio if the company's growth rate is 2 percent?

   c. What are the equity value and debt-to-value ratio if the company's growth rate is 4 percent?

4. **Nonmarketed Claims**   Hominy, Inc., has debt outstanding with a face value of $2.15 million. The value of the firm if it were entirely financed by equity would be $11.4 million. The company also has 195,000 shares of stock outstanding that sell at a price of $47 per share. The corporate tax rate is 21 percent. What is the decrease in the value of the company due to expected bankruptcy costs?

5. **Capital Structure and Nonmarketed Claims**   Suppose the president of the company in the previous problem stated that the company should increase the amount of debt in its capital structure because of the tax-advantaged status of its interest payments. His argument is that this action would increase the value of the company. How would you respond?

6. **Costs of Financial Distress**   Steinberg Corporation and Dietrich Corporation are identical firms except that Dietrich is more levered. Both companies will remain in business for one more year. The companies' economists agree that the probability of the continuation of the current expansion is 80 percent for the next year, and the probability of a recession is 20 percent. If the expansion continues, each firm will generate earnings before interest and taxes (EBIT) of $2.6 million. If a recession occurs, each firm will generate earnings before interest and taxes (EBIT) of $725,000. Steinberg's debt obligation requires the firm to pay $640,000 at the end of the year. Dietrich's debt obligation requires the firm to pay $1.1 million at the end of the year. Neither firm pays taxes. Assume a discount rate of 12 percent.

Intermediate
(Questions 6–8)

   a. What are the current market values of Steinberg's equity and debt? What about those for Dietrich?

   b. Steinberg's CEO recently stated that Steinberg's value should be higher than Dietrich's because the firm has less debt, and, therefore, less bankruptcy risk. Do you agree or disagree with this statement?

7. **Agency Costs**   Sheaves Corporation economists estimate that a good business environment and a bad business environment are equally likely for the coming year. Management must choose between two mutually exclusive projects. Assume that the project chosen will be the firm's only activity and that the firm will close one year from today. The firm is obligated to make a $12,000 payment to bondholders at the end of the year. The projects have the same systematic risk but different volatilities. Consider the following information pertaining to the two projects:

Economy	Probability	Low-Volatility Project Payoff	High-Volatility Project Payoff
Bad	.50	$12,000	$11,400
Good	.50	12,800	13,300

   a. What is the expected value of the firm if the low-volatility project is undertaken? What if the high-volatility project is undertaken? Which of the two strategies maximizes the expected value of the firm?

b. What is the expected value of the firm's equity if the low-volatility project is undertaken? What is it if the high-volatility project is undertaken?

c. Which project would the firm's stockholders prefer? Explain.

d. Suppose bondholders are fully aware that stockholders might choose to maximize equity value rather than total firm value and opt for the high-volatility project. To minimize this agency cost, the firm's bondholders decide to use a bond covenant to stipulate that the bondholders can demand a higher payment if the firm chooses to take on the high-volatility project. What payment to bondholders would make stockholders indifferent between the two projects?

8. **Financial Distress** Mid States Company is a regional chain department store. It will remain in business for one more year. The probability of a boom year is 60 percent and the probability of a recession is 40 percent. It is projected that the company will generate a total cash flow of $53 million in a boom year and $31 million in a recession. The company's required debt payment at the end of the year is $39 million. The market value of the company's outstanding debt is $34 million. The company pays no taxes.

a. What payoff do bondholders expect to receive in the event of a recession?

b. What is the promised return on the company's debt?

c. What is the expected return on the company's debt?

Challenge
(Questions 9–10)

9. **Personal Taxes, Bankruptcy Costs, and Firm Value** When personal taxes on interest income and bankruptcy costs are considered, the general expression for the value of a levered firm in a world in which the tax rate on equity distributions equals zero is:

$$V_L = V_U + \left[1 - \left(\frac{1 - T_C}{1 - T_B} \right) \right] \times B - C(B)$$

where:

V_L = the value of a levered firm
V_U = the value of an unlevered firm
B = the value of the firm's debt
T_C = the tax rate on corporate income
T_B = the personal tax rate on interest income
$C(B)$ = the present value of the costs of financial distress

a. In their no-tax model, what do Modigliani and Miller assume about T_C, T_B, and $C(B)$? What do these assumptions imply about a firm's optimal debt-equity ratio?

b. In their model with corporate taxes, what do Modigliani and Miller assume about T_C, T_B, and $C(B)$? What do these assumptions imply about a firm's optimal debt-equity ratio?

c. Consider an all-equity firm that is certain to be able to use interest deductions to reduce its corporate tax bill. If the corporate tax rate is 25 percent, the personal tax rate on interest income is 20 percent, and there are no costs of financial distress, by how much will the value of the firm change if it issues $1.2 million in debt and uses the proceeds to repurchase equity?

d. Consider another all-equity firm that does not pay taxes due to large tax loss carry forwards from previous years. The personal tax rate on interest income is 20 percent, and there are no costs of financial distress. What would be the change in the value of this firm from adding $1 of perpetual debt rather than $1 of equity?

10. **Personal Taxes, Bankruptcy Costs, and Firm Value** Overnight Publishing Company (OPC) has $1.7 million in excess cash. The firm plans to use this cash either to retire all of its outstanding debt or to repurchase equity. The firm's debt is held by one institution that is willing to sell it back to OPC for $1.7 million. The institution will not charge OPC any transaction costs. Once OPC becomes an all-equity firm, it will remain unlevered forever. If OPC does not retire the debt, the company will use the $1.7 million in cash to buy back some of its stock on the open market. Repurchasing stock also has no transaction costs. The company will generate $795,000 of annual earnings before interest and taxes in perpetuity

regardless of its capital structure. The firm immediately pays out all earnings as dividends at the end of each year. OPC is subject to a corporate tax rate of 24 percent, and the required rate of return on the firm's unlevered equity is 14 percent. The personal tax rate on interest income is 25 percent, and there are no taxes on equity distributions. Assume there are no bankruptcy costs.

a. What is the value of the company if it chooses to retire all of its debt and become an unlevered firm?

b. What is the value of the company if it decides to repurchase stock instead of retiring its debt? (*Hint:* Use the equation for the value of a levered firm with personal tax on interest income from the previous problem.)

c. Assume that expected bankruptcy costs have a present value of $425,000. How does this influence the company's decision?

CLOSING CASE

DUGAN CORPORATION'S CAPITAL BUDGETING

Sam Dugan is the founder and CEO of Dugan Restaurants, Inc., a regional company. Sam is considering opening several new restaurants. Sally Thornton, the company's CFO, has been put in charge of the capital budgeting analysis. She has examined the potential for the company's expansion and determined that the success of the new restaurants will depend critically on the state of the economy next year and over the next few years.

Dugan currently has a bond issue outstanding with a face value of $9.3 million that is due in one year. Covenants associated with this bond issue prohibit the issuance of any additional debt. This restriction means that the expansion will be entirely financed with equity at a cost of $3.7 million. Sally has summarized her analysis in the following table, which shows the value of the company in each state of the economy next year, both with and without expansion.

Economic Growth	Probability	Without Expansion	With Expansion
Low	.30	$ 6,900,000	$ 8,400,000
Normal	.50	12,000,000	17,200,000
High	.20	16,000,000	20,700,000

1. What is the expected value of the company in one year, with and without expansion? Would the company's stockholders be better off with or without expansion? Why?

2. What is the expected value of the company's debt in one year, with and without the expansion?

3. One year from now, how much value creation is expected from the expansion? How much value is expected for stockholders? Bondholders?

4. If the company announces that it is not expanding, what do you think will happen to the price of its bonds? What will happen to the price of the bonds if the company does expand?

5. If the company opts not to expand, what are the implications for the company's future borrowing needs? What are the implications if the company does expand?

6. Because of the bond covenant, the expansion would have to be financed with equity. How would it affect your answer if the expansion were financed with cash on hand instead of new equity?

16 Dividends and Other Payouts

Any way you look at it, 2018 was a great year for dividend payments. During the year, 415 companies in the S&P 500 paid out about $456.3 billion in dividends, a record aggregate dividend payment. This payout was an increase from the previous records of $419.8 billion in 2017 and $397.2 billion in 2016. Companies with large dividends paid during the year included Apple, with total dividends paid of $13.7 billion, and AT&T and Microsoft, which both paid about $13.9 billion.

Please visit us at corecorporatefinance.blogspot.com for the latest developments in the world of corporate finance.

16.1 DIFFERENT TYPES OF DIVIDENDS

The term *dividend* usually refers to a cash distribution of earnings. If a distribution is made from sources other than current or accumulated retained earnings, the term *distribution* rather than dividend is used. However, it is acceptable to refer to a distribution from earnings as a *dividend* and a distribution from capital as a *liquidating dividend*. More generally, any direct payment by the corporation to the shareholders may be considered part of dividend policy.

The most common type of dividend is in the form of cash. Public companies usually pay regular cash dividends four times a year. Sometimes firms will pay a regular cash dividend and an *extra cash dividend*. Paying a cash dividend reduces the corporate cash and retained earnings shown in the balance sheet—except in the case of a liquidating dividend (where paid-in capital may be reduced).

Another type of dividend is paid out in shares of stock. This dividend is referred to as a stock dividend. It is not a true dividend because no cash leaves the firm. Rather, a stock dividend increases the number of shares outstanding, thereby reducing the value of each share. A stock dividend is commonly expressed as a ratio. With a 2 percent stock dividend, a shareholder receives one new share for every 50 currently owned.

When a firm declares a stock split, it increases the number of shares outstanding. Because each share is now entitled to a smaller percentage of the firm's cash flow, the stock price should fall. If the managers of a firm whose stock is selling at $90 declare a 3:1 stock split, the price of a share of stock should fall to about $30. A stock split strongly resembles a stock dividend except that it is usually much larger.

16.2 STANDARD METHOD OF CASH DIVIDEND PAYMENT

The decision to pay a dividend rests in the hands of the board of directors of the corporation. A dividend is distributable to shareholders of record on a specific date. When a dividend has been declared, it becomes a liability of the firm and cannot be easily rescinded by the corporation. The amount of the dividend is expressed as dollars per share (*dividend per share*), as a percentage of the market price (*dividend yield*), or as a percentage of earnings per share (*dividend payout*).

The mechanics of a dividend payment can be illustrated by the example in Figure 16.1 and the following chronology:

1. *Declaration Date.* On January 15 (the declaration date), the board of directors passes a resolution to pay a dividend of $1 per share on February 16 to all holders of record on January 30.

2. *Date of Record.* The corporation prepares a list on January 30 of all individuals believed to be stockholders as of this date. The word *believed* is important here because the dividend will not be paid to those individuals whose notification of purchase is received by the company after January 30.

3. *Ex-Dividend Date.* The SEC mandates a $t + 2$ settlement procedure for stocks. What this means is that if an investor purchases a stock on Wednesday, he or she will pay for it on Friday. For dividend payments, all brokerage firms entitle stockholders to receive the dividend if they purchased the stock one business day before the date of record. The day before the date of record, which is January 29 in our example, is called the *ex-dividend date.* Before this date, the stock is said to trade *cum dividend.*

4. *Date of Payment.* The dividend checks are mailed to the stockholders on February 16.

Obviously, the ex-dividend date is important because an individual purchasing the security before the ex-dividend date will receive the current dividend, whereas another individual purchasing the security on or after this date will not receive the dividend. The stock price will therefore fall on the ex-dividend date (assuming no other events occur). It is worthwhile to note that this drop is an indication of efficiency, not inefficiency, because the market rationally attaches value to a cash dividend. In a world with neither taxes nor transaction costs, the stock price would be expected to fall by the amount of the dividend:

Before ex-dividend date	Price = $(P + 1)$
On or after ex-dividend date	Price = P

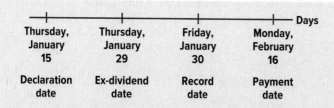

1. *Declaration date*: The board of directors declares a payment of dividends.
2. *Ex-dividend date*: A share of stock becomes ex dividend on the date the seller is entitled to keep the dividend; under SEC rules, shares are traded ex dividend on and after the first business day before the record date.
3. *Record date*: The declared dividends are distributable to shareholders of record on a specific date.
4. *Payment date*: The dividend checks are mailed to shareholders of record.

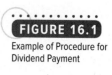

Example of Procedure for Dividend Payment

FIGURE 16.2

Price Behavior around the
Ex-Dividend Date for a $1
Cash Dividend

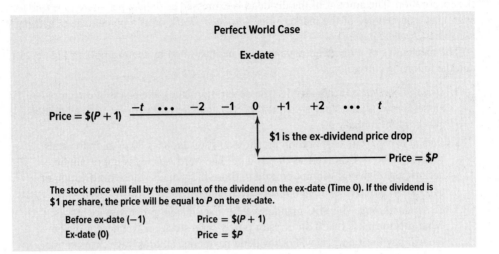

Perfect World Case

Ex-date

The stock price will fall by the amount of the dividend on the ex-date (Time 0). If the dividend is
$1 per share, the price will be equal to P on the ex-date.

Before ex-date (-1)   Price = $\$(P + 1)$
Ex-date (0)   Price = $\$P$

This is illustrated in Figure 16.2.

The amount of the price drop may depend on tax rates. For example, consider the case with no capital gains taxes. On the day before a stock goes ex dividend, shareholders must decide to either (1) buy the stock immediately and pay tax on the forthcoming dividend or (2) buy the stock tomorrow, thereby missing the dividend. If all investors are in the 15 percent tax bracket and the quarterly dividend is $1, the stock price should fall by $.85 on the ex-dividend date. That is, if the stock price falls by this amount on the ex-dividend date, purchasers will receive the same return from either strategy.

As an example of the price drop on the ex-dividend date, we examine the large dividend paid by Warrior Met Coal, operator of coal mines in Alabama, in November 2017. The dividend was $11.21 per share at a time when the stock price was around $30, so the dividend was about 40 percent of the total stock price, a truly special dividend.

The stock went ex dividend on November 24, 2017. The stock price chart below shows the change in Warrior stock four days prior to the ex-dividend date and on the ex-dividend date.

The stock closed at $29.90 on November 22 (November 23 was a holiday) and opened at $18.65 on November 24—a drop of $11.25. With a 20 percent tax rate on dividends, we would have expected a drop of about $9, so the actual price dropped more than we would have expected. We discuss dividends and taxes in more detail in a subsequent section.

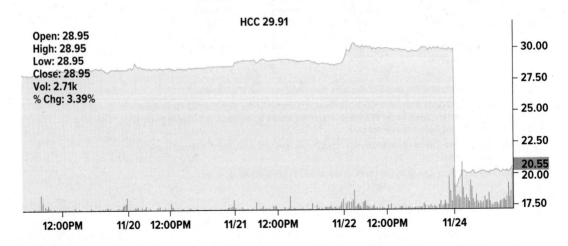

16.3 THE BENCHMARK CASE: AN ILLUSTRATION OF THE IRRELEVANCE OF DIVIDEND POLICY

A powerful argument can be made that dividend policy does not matter. This will be illustrated with the Bristol Corporation. Bristol is an all-equity firm started 10 years ago. The current financial managers know at the present time (Date 0) that the firm will dissolve in one year (Date 1). At Date 0 the managers are able to forecast cash flows with perfect certainty. The managers know that the firm will receive a cash flow of $10,000 immediately and another $10,000 next year. Bristol has no additional positive NPV projects.

Current Policy: Dividends Set Equal to Cash Flow

At the present time, dividends (D) at each date are set equal to the cash flow of $10,000. The value of the firm can be calculated by discounting these dividends. This value is expressed as:

$$V_0 = D_0 + \frac{D_1}{1 + R_S} \qquad\qquad [16.1]$$

where D_0 and D_1 are the cash flows paid out in dividends and R_S is the discount rate. The first dividend is not discounted because it will be paid immediately.

Assuming $R_S = 10$ percent, the value of the firm is:

$$\$19{,}090.91 = \$10{,}000 + \frac{\$10{,}000}{1.1}$$

If 1,000 shares are outstanding, the value of each share is:

$$\$19.09 = \$10 + \frac{\$10}{1.1}$$

To simplify the example, we assume that the ex-dividend date is the same as the date of payment. After the imminent dividend is paid, the stock price will immediately fall to $9.09 (= $19.09 − 10). Several members of the board of Bristol have expressed dissatisfaction with the current dividend policy and have asked you to analyze an alternative policy.

Alternative Policy: Initial Dividend Is Greater Than Cash Flow

Another policy is for the firm to pay a dividend of $11 per share immediately, which is, of course, a total dividend payout of $11,000. Because the cash flow is only $10,000, the extra $1,000 must be raised in one of a few ways. Perhaps the simplest would be to issue $1,000 of bonds or stock now (at Date 0). Assume that stock is issued and the new stockholders will desire enough cash flow at Date 1 to let them earn the required 10 percent return on their Date 0 investment. The new stockholders will demand $1,100 of the Date 1 cash flow, leaving only $8,900 to the old stockholders. The dividends to the old stockholders will be:

	Date 0	Date 1
Aggregate dividends to old stockholders	$11,000	$8,900
Dividends per share	11.00	8.90

The present value of the dividends per share is therefore:

$$\$19.09 = \$11 + \frac{\$8.90}{1.1}$$

Students often find it instructive to determine the price at which the new stock is issued. Because the new stockholders are not entitled to the immediate dividend, they would pay $8.09 (= $8.90/1.1) per share. Thus, 123.60 (= $1,000/$8.09) new shares are issued.

The Indifference Proposition

Note that the values given in the previous example by the current policy and the alternative policy are equal. This leads to the initially surprising conclusion that the change in dividend policy did not affect the value of a share of stock. However, upon reflection, the result seems quite sensible. The new stockholders are parting with their money at Date 0 and receiving it back with the appropriate return at Date 1. In other words, they are taking on a zero NPV investment. As illustrated in Figure 16.3, old stockholders are receiving additional funds at Date 0 but must pay the new stockholders their money with the appropriate return at Date 1. Because the old stockholders must pay back principal plus the appropriate return, the act of issuing new stock at Date 0 will not increase or decrease the value of the old stockholders' holdings. That is, they are giving up a zero NPV investment to the new stockholders. An increase in dividends at Date 0 leads to the necessary reduction of dividends at Date 1, so the value of the old stockholders' holdings remains unchanged.

This illustration is based on the pioneering work of Miller and Modigliani (MM). Although our presentation is in the form of a numerical example, the MM paper[1] proves that investors are indifferent to dividend policy in a more general setting.

FIGURE 16.3

Current and Alternative Dividend Policies

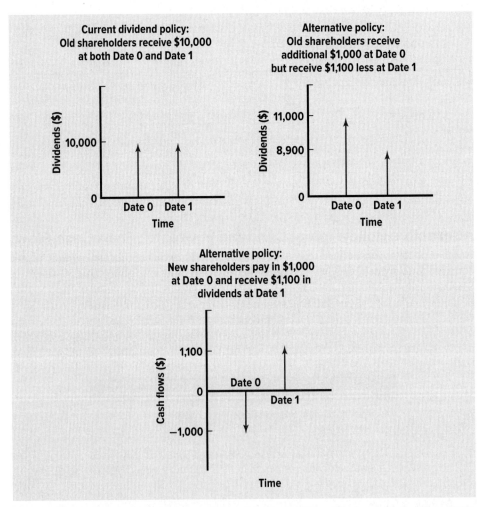

[1] Merton H. Miller and Franco Modigliani, "Dividend Policy, Growth, and the Valuation of Shares," *The Journal of Business* 34, no. 4 (1961), pp. 411–33.

Homemade Dividends

To illustrate the indifference investors have toward dividend policy in our example, we used present value equations. An alternative and perhaps more intuitively appealing explanation avoids the mathematics of discounted cash flows.

Suppose Investor X prefers dividends per share of $10 at both Dates 0 and 1. Would she be disappointed when informed that the firm's management is adopting the alternative dividend policy (dividends of $11 and $8.90 on the two dates, respectively)? Not necessarily, because she could easily reinvest the $1 of unneeded funds received on Date 0, yielding an incremental return of $1.10 at Date 1. Thus, she would receive her desired net cash flow of $11 − 1 = $10 at Date 0 and $8.90 + 1.10 = $10 at Date 1.

Conversely, imagine Investor Z, preferring $11 of cash flow at Date 0 and $8.90 of cash flow at Date 1, who finds that management will pay dividends of $10 at both Dates 0 and 1. Here he can sell off shares of stock at Date 0 to receive the desired amount of cash flow. That is, if he sells off shares (or fractions of shares) at Date 0 totaling $1, his cash flow at Date 0 becomes $10 + 1 = $11. Because a $1 sale of stock at Date 0 will reduce his dividends by $1.10 at Date 1, his net cash flow at Date 1 would be $10 − 1.10 = $8.90.

The example illustrates how investors can make homemade dividends. In this instance, corporate dividend policy is being undone by a potentially dissatisfied stockholder. This homemade dividend is illustrated by Figure 16.4. Here, the firm's cash flows of $10 per share at both Dates 0 and 1 are represented by Point A. This point also represents the initial dividend payout. However, as we just saw, the firm could alternatively pay out $11 per share at Date 0 and $8.90 per share at Date 1, a strategy represented by Point B. Similarly, by either issuing new stock or buying back old stock, the firm could achieve a dividend payout represented by any point on the diagonal line.

The previous paragraph describes the choices available to the managers of the firm. The same diagonal line also represents the choices available to the shareholder. For example, if the shareholder receives a per-share dividend distribution of ($11, $8.90), he or she can either reinvest some of the dividends to move down and to the right on the graph or sell off shares of stock and move up and to the left.

FIGURE 16.4

Homemade Dividends: A Trade-off between Dividends per Share at Date 0 and Dividends per Share at Date 1

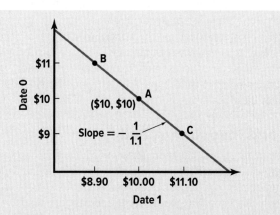

The graph illustrates both (1) how managers can vary dividend policy and (2) how individuals can undo the firm's dividend policy.

Managers varying dividend policy. A firm paying out all cash flows immediately is at Point A on the graph. The firm could achieve Point B by issuing stock to pay extra dividends or achieve Point C by buying back old stock with some of its cash.

Individuals undoing the firm's dividend policy. Suppose the firm adopts the dividend policy represented by Point B: dividends per share of $11 at Date 0 and $8.90 at Date 1. An investor can reinvest $1 of the dividends at 10 percent, which will place her at Point A. Suppose, alternatively, the firm adopts the dividend policy represented by Point A. An individual can sell off $1 of stock at Date 0, placing him at Point B. No matter what dividend policy the firm establishes, a shareholder can undo it.

The implications of the graph can be summarized in two sentences:

1. By varying dividend policy, the managers can achieve any payout along the diagonal line in Figure 16.4.
2. Either by reinvesting excess dividends at Date 0 or by selling off shares of stock at this date, any individual investor can achieve any net cash payout along the diagonal line.

Thus, because both the corporation and the individual investor can move only along the diagonal line, dividend policy in this model is irrelevant. The changes the managers make in dividend policy can be undone by an individual who, by either reinvesting dividends or selling off stock, can move to a desired point on the diagonal line.

A Test

You can test your knowledge of this material by examining these true statements:

1. Dividends are relevant.
2. Dividend policy is irrelevant.

The first statement follows from common sense. Clearly, investors prefer higher dividends to lower dividends at any single date if the dividend level is held constant at every other date. In other words, if the dividend per share at a given date is raised while the dividend per share for each other date is held constant, the stock price will rise. This act can be accomplished by management decisions that improve productivity, increase tax savings, or strengthen product marketing. In fact, you may recall in Chapter 6 we argued that the value of a firm's equity is equal to the discounted present value of all its future dividends.

The second statement is understandable once we realize that dividend policy cannot raise the dividend per share at one date while holding the dividend level per share constant at all other dates. Rather, dividend policy merely establishes the trade-off between dividends at one date and dividends at another date. As we saw in Figure 16.4, an increase in Date 0 dividends can be accomplished only by a decrease in Date 1 dividends. The extent of the decrease is such that the present value of all dividends is not affected.

Thus, in this simple world, dividend policy does not matter. That is, managers choosing either to raise or to lower the current dividend do not affect the current value of their firm. The above theory is a powerful one, and the work of MM is generally considered a classic in modern finance. With relatively few assumptions, a rather surprising result is shown to be perfectly true. Because we want to examine many real-world factors ignored by MM, their work is only a starting point in this chapter's discussion of dividends. The next part of the chapter investigates these real-world considerations.

Dividends and Investment Policy

The preceding argument shows that an increase in dividends through issuance of new shares neither helps nor hurts the stockholders. Similarly, a reduction in dividends through a share repurchase neither helps nor hurts stockholders.

What about reducing capital expenditures to increase dividends? Earlier chapters show that a firm should accept all positive net present value projects. To do otherwise reduces the value of the firm. Thus, we have an important point:

> Firms should never give up a positive NPV project to increase a dividend (or to pay a dividend for the first time).

This idea was implicitly considered by Miller and Modigliani. One of the assumptions underlying their dividend irrelevance proposition was, "The investment policy of the firm is set ahead of time and is not altered by changes in dividend policy."

16.4 REPURCHASE OF STOCK

Instead of paying dividends, a firm may use cash to repurchase shares of its own stock. Share repurchases have taken on increased importance in recent years. Consider Figure 16.5, which shows the aggregate dollar amounts of dividends, repurchases, and earnings for large U.S. firms in the years from 2004 to 2017. As can be seen, the amount of repurchases was more than the amount of dividends up to 2008. However, the amount of dividends exceeded the amount of repurchases in late 2008 and 2009. This trend reversed after 2009. Notice also from Figure 16.5 that there is "stickiness" to repurchases and dividend payouts. In late 2008 when aggregate corporate earnings turned negative, the level of dividends and share repurchases did not change much. More generally, the volatility of aggregate earnings has been greater than that of dividends and share repurchases.

Share repurchases are typically accomplished in one of three ways. First, companies may purchase their own stock, just as anyone would buy shares of a particular stock. In these *open market purchases,* the firm does not reveal itself as the buyer. Thus, the seller does not know whether the shares were sold back to the firm or to another investor.

Second, the firm could institute a *tender offer.* Here, the firm announces to all of its stockholders that it is willing to buy a fixed number of shares at a specific price. For example, suppose Arts and Crafts (A&C), Inc., has 1 million shares of stock outstanding, with a stock price of $50 per share. The firm makes a tender offer to buy back 300,000 shares at $60 per share. A&C chooses a price above $50 to induce shareholders to sell—that is, tender—their shares. In fact, if the tender price is set high enough, shareholders may want to sell more than the 300,000 shares. In the extreme case where all outstanding shares are tendered, A&C will buy back 3 out of every 10 shares that a shareholder has. On the other hand, if shareholders do not tender enough shares, the offer can be canceled. A method

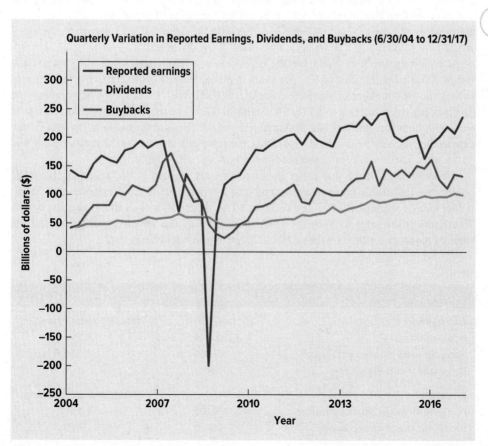

FIGURE 16.5

Earnings, Dividends, and Net Repurchases for U.S. Industrial Firms

Source: Standard & Poor's, S&P Dow Jones Indices.

related to a tender offer is the *Dutch auction*. Here, the firm does not set a fixed price for the shares to be sold. Instead, the firm conducts an auction in which it bids for shares. The firm announces the number of shares it is willing to buy back at various prices, and shareholders indicate how many shares they are willing to sell at the various prices. The firm will then pay the lowest price that will achieve its goal.

Finally, firms may repurchase shares from specific individual stockholders, a procedure called a *targeted repurchase*. Suppose the International Biotechnology Corporation purchased approximately 10 percent of the outstanding stock of the Prime Robotics Company (P-R Co.) in April at around $38 per share. At that time, International Biotechnology announced to the Securities and Exchange Commission that it might eventually try to take control of P-R Co. In May, P-R Co. repurchased the International Biotechnology holdings at $48 per share, well above the market price at that time. This offer was not extended to other shareholders.

Companies engage in targeted repurchases for a variety of reasons. In some rare cases, a single large stockholder can be bought out at a price lower than that in a tender offer. The legal fees in a targeted repurchase may also be lower than those in a more typical buyback. In addition, the shares of large stockholders are often repurchased to avoid a takeover unfavorable to management.

We now consider an example of a repurchase presented in the theoretical world of a perfect capital market. We next discuss real-world factors involved in the repurchase decision.

Dividend versus Repurchase: Conceptual Example

Imagine that Telephonic Industries has excess cash of $300,000 (or $3 per share) and is considering an immediate payment of this amount as an extra dividend. The firm forecasts that, after the dividend, earnings will be $450,000 per year, or $4.50 for each of the 100,000 shares outstanding. Because the price-earnings ratio is 6 for comparable companies, the shares of the firm should sell for $27 (= $4.50 × 6) after the dividend is paid. These figures are presented in the top half of Table 16.1. Because the dividend is $3 per share, the stock would have sold for $30 a share before payment of the dividend.

Alternatively, the firm could use the excess cash to repurchase some of its own stock. Imagine that a tender offer of $30 per share is made. Here, 10,000 shares are repurchased so that the total number of shares remaining is 90,000. With fewer shares outstanding, the earnings per share will rise to $5 (= $450,000/90,000). The price-earnings ratio remains at 6 because both the business and financial risks of the firm are the same in the repurchase case as they were in the dividend case. Thus, the price of a share after the repurchase is $30 (= $5 × 6). These results are presented in the bottom half of Table 16.1.

If commissions, taxes, and other imperfections are ignored in our example, the stockholders are indifferent between a dividend and a repurchase. With dividends, each stockholder owns a share worth $27 and receives $3 in dividends, so that the total value is $30. This figure is the same as both the amount received by the selling stockholders and the value of the stock for the remaining stockholders in the repurchase case.

TABLE 16.1

Dividend versus Repurchase Example for Telephonic Industries

	For Entire Firm	Per Share
Extra Dividend		**(100,000 shares outstanding)**
Proposed dividend	$ 300,000	$ 3.00
Forecasted annual earnings after dividend	450,000	4.50
Market value of stock after dividend	2,700,000	27.00
Repurchase		**(90,000 shares outstanding)**
Forecasted annual earnings after repurchase	$ 450,000	$ 5.00
Market value of stock after repurchase	2,700,000	30.00

This example illustrates the important point that, in a perfect market, the firm is indifferent between a dividend payment and a share repurchase. This result is quite similar to the indifference propositions established by MM for debt versus equity financing and for dividends versus capital gains.

You may often read in the popular financial press that a repurchase agreement is beneficial because earnings per share increase. Earnings per share do rise for Telephonic Industries if a repurchase is substituted for a cash dividend: The EPS is $4.50 after a dividend and $5 after the repurchase. This result holds because the drop in shares after a repurchase implies a reduction in the denominator of the EPS ratio.

However, the financial press frequently places undue emphasis on EPS figures in a repurchase agreement. Given the irrelevance propositions we have discussed, the increase in EPS here is not beneficial. Table 16.1 shows that, in a perfect capital market, the total value to the stockholder is the same under the dividend payment strategy as under the repurchase strategy.

Dividends versus Repurchases: Real-World Considerations

We previously referred to Figure 16.5, which showed growth in share repurchases relative to dividends. In fact, most firms that pay dividends also repurchase shares of stock. This suggests that repurchasing shares of stock is not always a substitute for paying dividends but rather a complement to it. For example, recently the number of U.S. industrial firms that pay dividends only or repurchase only is about the same as the number of firms paying both dividends and repurchasing shares. Why do some firms choose repurchases over dividends? Here are perhaps five of the most common reasons.

1. FLEXIBILITY   Firms often view dividends as a commitment to their stockholders and are quite hesitant to reduce an existing dividend. Repurchases do not represent a similar commitment. Thus, a firm with a permanent increase in cash flow is likely to increase its dividend. Conversely, a firm whose cash flow increase is only temporary is likely to repurchase shares of stock.

2. EXECUTIVE COMPENSATION   Executives are frequently given stock options as part of their overall compensation. Let's revisit the Telephonic Industries example of Table 16.1, where the firm's stock was selling at $30 when the firm was considering either a dividend or a repurchase. Further imagine that Telephonic had granted 1,000 stock options to its CEO, Ralph Taylor, two years earlier. At that time, the stock price was, say, only $20. This means that Mr. Taylor can buy 1,000 shares for $20 a share at any time between the grant of the options and their expiration, a procedure called *exercising* the options. His gain from exercising is directly proportional to the rise in the stock price above $20. As we saw in the example, the price of the stock would fall to $27 following a dividend but would remain at $30 following a repurchase. The CEO would clearly prefer a repurchase to a dividend because the difference between the stock price and the exercise price of $20 would be $10 (= $30 − 20) following the repurchase but only $7 (= $27 − 20) following the dividend. Existing stock options will always have greater value when the firm repurchases shares instead of paying a dividend because the stock price will be greater after a repurchase than after a dividend.

3. OFFSET TO DILUTION   In addition, the exercise of stock options increases the number of shares outstanding. In other words, exercise causes dilution of the stock. Firms frequently buy back shares of stock to offset this dilution. However, it is hard to argue that this is a valid reason for repurchase. As we showed in Table 16.1, repurchase is neither better nor worse for the stockholders than a dividend. Our argument holds whether or not stock options have been exercised previously.

4. UNDERVALUATION   Many companies buy back stock because they believe that a repurchase is their best investment. This occurs more frequently when managers believe that the stock price is temporarily depressed.

The fact that some companies repurchase their stock when they believe it is undervalued does not imply that the management of the company must be correct; only empirical studies can make this determination. The immediate stock market reaction to the announcement of a stock repurchase is usually quite favorable. In addition, some empirical work has shown that the long-term stock price performance of securities after a buyback is better than the stock price performance of comparable companies that do not repurchase.

5. TAXES Because taxes for both dividends and share repurchases are treated in depth in the next section, suffice it to say at this point that repurchases provide a tax advantage over dividends.

16.5 PERSONAL TAXES, ISSUANCE COSTS, AND DIVIDENDS

The model we used in Section 16.3 to determine the level of dividends assumed that there were no taxes, no transaction costs, and no uncertainty. It concluded that dividend policy is irrelevant. Although this model helps us to grasp some fundamentals of dividend policy, it ignores many real-world factors. It is now time to investigate these practical considerations. We first examine the effect of taxes on the level of a firm's dividends.

In the United States, historically, dividends have been taxed as ordinary income (at ordinary income tax rates). In 2003, under President George W. Bush, this changed dramatically. Tax rates on dividends and capital gains were lowered from a maximum in the 35–39 percent range to 15 percent, giving corporations a much larger tax incentive to pay dividends. In 2019, the tax rate on dividends was 0 percent, 15 percent, or 20 percent, depending on the individual's marginal tax rate.

Firms without Sufficient Cash to Pay a Dividend

It is simplest to begin with a firm without cash and owned by a single entrepreneur. If this firm should decide to pay a dividend of $100, it must raise capital. The firm might choose among a number of different stock and bond issues in order to pay the dividend. For simplicity, we assume that the entrepreneur contributes cash to the firm by issuing stock to himself. This transaction, diagrammed in the left-hand side of Figure 16.6, would clearly be a wash in a world of no taxes: $100 cash goes into the firm when stock is issued and is

FIGURE 16.6

Firm Issues Stock in Order to Pay a Dividend

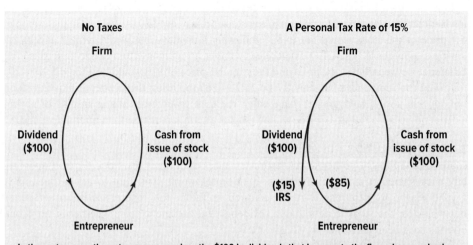

In the no-tax case, the entrepreneur receives the $100 in dividends that he gave to the firm when purchasing stock. The entire operation is called a *wash;* in other words, it has no economic effect. With taxes, the entrepreneur still receives $100 in dividends. However, he must pay $15 in taxes to the IRS. The entrepreneur loses and the IRS wins when a firm issues stock to pay a dividend.

immediately paid out as a dividend. Thus, the entrepreneur neither benefits nor loses when the dividend is paid, a result consistent with Miller-Modigliani.

Now assume that dividends are taxed at the owner's personal tax rate of 15 percent. The firm still receives $100 upon issuance of stock. However, the entrepreneur does not get to keep the full $100 dividend. Instead, the dividend payment is taxed, implying that the owner receives only $85 net after tax. Thus, the entrepreneur loses $15.

Though the example is clearly contrived and unrealistic, similar results can be reached for more plausible situations. Thus, financial economists generally agree that, in a world of personal taxes, one should not issue stock to pay a dividend.

The direct costs of issuance will add to this effect. Investment bankers must be paid when new capital is raised. Thus, the net receipts due to the firm from a new issue are less than 100 percent of total capital raised. Because the size of new issues can be lowered by a reduction in dividends, we have another argument in favor of a low-dividend policy.

Of course, our advice not to finance dividends through new stock issues might need to be modified somewhat in the real world. A company with a large and steady cash flow for many years in the past might be paying a regular dividend. If the cash flow unexpectedly dried up for a single year, should new stock be issued so that dividends could be continued? While our above discussion would imply that new stock should not be issued, many managers might issue the stock anyway for practical reasons. In particular, stockholders appear to prefer dividend stability. Thus, managers might be forced to issue stock to achieve this stability, knowing full well the adverse tax consequences.

Firms with Sufficient Cash to Pay a Dividend

The previous discussion argues that, in a world with personal taxes, one should not issue stock to pay a dividend. Does the tax disadvantage of dividends imply the stronger policy, "Never pay dividends in a world with personal taxes"?

We argue below that this prescription does not necessarily apply to firms with excess cash. To see this, imagine a firm with $1 million in extra cash after selecting all positive NPV projects and determining the level of prudent cash balances. The firm might consider the following alternatives to a dividend:

1. *Select Additional Capital Budgeting Projects.* Because the firm has taken all the available positive NPV projects already, it must invest its excess cash in negative NPV projects. This is clearly a policy at variance with the principles of corporate finance.

    In spite of our distaste for this policy, researchers have suggested that many managers purposely take on negative NPV projects in lieu of paying dividends. The idea here is that managers would rather keep the funds in the firm because their prestige, pay, and perquisites are often tied to the firm's size. While managers may help themselves here, they are hurting stockholders. We broached this subject in a previous chapter, and we will have more to say about it later in this chapter.

2. *Acquire Other Companies.* To avoid the payment of dividends, a firm might use excess cash to acquire another company. This strategy has the advantage of acquiring profitable assets. However, a firm often incurs heavy costs when it embarks on an acquisition program. In addition, acquisitions are invariably made above the market price. Premiums of 20 to 80 percent are not uncommon. Because of this, a number of researchers have argued that mergers are not generally profitable to the acquiring company, even when firms are merged for a valid business purpose. Therefore, a company making an acquisition merely to avoid a dividend is unlikely to succeed.

3. *Purchase Financial Assets.* Deciding whether to invest in financial assets or to pay a dividend is a complex question, depending on the tax rate of the firm, the marginal tax rates of its investors, and the application of the dividend exclusion. While there are likely many real-world situations where the numbers favor investment in financial assets, few companies actually seem to hoard cash in this

FINANCE MATTERS

STOCK BUYBACKS: NO END IN SIGHT

The year 2018 was a great year for stock repurchases. For the 12 months ending in September 2018, repurchases by S&P 500 companies totaled a record $750.4 billion, up an astounding 44.9 percent from the $517.7 billion for the same period in 2017. Total announced buybacks for 2018, that is, buybacks companies announced would take place in the future, were about $1.1 trillion. For the past several years, share repurchases have been so large that U.S. corporations bought back more shares than they sold. In other words, aggregate net equity raised by U.S. corporations was negative.

Some companies appear to have become serial repurchasers. For example, ExxonMobil suspended its repurchase program in late 2017. However, from 2008 to 2017, ExxonMobil repurchased about $180 billion of its stock. In 2018, ExxonMobil stated that, in the near term, it would only use buybacks to offset dilution related to employee stock option and purchase programs. Microsoft is another serial repurchaser. During its 2018 fiscal year, the company repurchased about $4.5 billion of its stock. It had repurchased about $122 billion over the 2008–2018 period. One of the more interesting serial repurchasers is AutoZone. The company had about 125 million shares outstanding in 2002, but thanks to buybacks, the number of shares outstanding has been reduced to about 25 million in early 2019.

Stock buybacks have evolved to the point where they are used for other purposes. For example, in January 2005, consumer products giant Procter & Gamble (P&G) announced that it was purchasing razor manufacturer Gillette for $54 billion. The purchase was paid for entirely by stock in P&G. This is important because if a company acquires another company for cash, the shareholders of the acquired company are forced to pay taxes. If shareholders receive stock, no taxes are due. What made the deal unique was that P&G announced at the same time that it would repurchase from $18 to $22 billion in stock. Thus, P&G essentially paid about 60 percent in stock and 40 percent in cash, but the way the deal was structured made it look like a 100 percent stock acquisition to Gillette's stockholders.

Stock buybacks can represent a large percentage of a company's equity. For example, in 2018, the Clorox Company announced plans to repurchase $2 billion worth of its shares. Although the amount of the buyback may not be as large as some, it represented about 10 percent of the company's outstanding shares. Later that year, oil and gas company Hess Corporation announced a $1 billion stock buyback, which represented about 7 percent of its shares.

In early 2019, politicians on the left and the right got in the news by attacking stock buybacks. For example, Bernie Sanders and Chuck Schumer proposed that a company should only be allowed to buy back its own stock if certain conditions were met, such as an employee wage of $15 per hour. And Marco Rubio announced he would propose a tax on buybacks that would be similar to the tax on dividends for investors. Of course, as these suggestions have come from politicians, they may reflect a poor understanding of stock buybacks (they should probably read this chapter before passing any legislation).

We haven't discussed what happens to the stock when a company does a buyback. There are actually several things the company can do. Many companies keep the stock and use the shares for employee stock option plans. When employee stock options are exercised by the employee, new shares are created, which increases the number of shares of stock outstanding. By using the repurchased shares, the company does not need to issue any new shares. A company can also keep the repurchased stock for itself as Treasury stock. Finally, the company can cancel the stock completely. In essence, it destroys the repurchased shares, which reduces the number of shares outstanding.

manner without limit. The reason is that Section 532 of the Internal Revenue Code penalizes firms exhibiting "improper accumulation of surplus." Thus, in the final analysis, the purchase of financial assets, like selecting negative NPV projects and acquiring other companies, does not obviate the need for companies with excess cash to pay dividends.

4. *Repurchase Shares.* The example we described in the previous section showed that investors are indifferent between share repurchases and dividends in a world without taxes and transaction costs. However, under current tax law, stockholders generally prefer a repurchase to a dividend.

As an example, consider an individual receiving a dividend of $1 on each of 100 shares of a stock. With a 15 percent tax rate, that individual would pay taxes of $15 on the dividend. Selling shareholders would pay lower taxes if the firm repurchased $100 of existing shares. This occurs because taxes are paid only on the profit from a sale. The individual's gain on a sale would be only $40 if the shares sold for $100 were originally purchased for, say, $60. The capital gains tax would be $6 (= .15 × $40), a number below the tax on dividends of $15. Note that the tax from a repurchase is less than the tax on a dividend even though the same 15 percent tax rate applies to both the repurchase and the dividend.

In fact, of all the alternatives to dividends mentioned in this section, the strongest case can be made for repurchases. A nearby *Finance Matters* box contains more on recent repurchase activity.

Summary on Personal Taxes

This section suggests that, because of personal taxes, firms have an incentive to reduce dividends. For example, they might increase capital expenditures, acquire other companies, or purchase financial assets. However, due to financial considerations and legal constraints, rational firms with large cash flows will likely exhaust these activities with plenty of cash left over for dividends.

It is harder to explain why firms pay dividends instead of repurchasing shares. The tax savings from buybacks are significant, and fear of either the SEC or the IRS seems overblown. Academics are of two minds here. Some argue that corporations were slow to grasp the benefits from repurchases. However, because the idea has firmly caught on, the trend toward replacement of dividends with buybacks will continue. One might even conjecture that dividends will be as unimportant in the future as repurchases were in the past. Conversely, others argue that companies have paid dividends all along for good reason. Perhaps the legal hassles, particularly from the IRS, are significant after all. Or there may be other, more subtle benefits from dividends. We consider potential benefits of dividends in the next section.

16.6 REAL-WORLD FACTORS FAVORING A HIGH-DIVIDEND POLICY

In the previous section, we pointed out that taxes must be paid by the recipient of a dividend. Because the tax rate on dividends is above the effective tax rate on capital gains, financial managers will seek out ways to reduce dividends. While we discussed the problems with taking on more capital budgeting projects, acquiring other firms, and hoarding cash, we stated that a share repurchase has many of the benefits of a dividend with less of a tax disadvantage. In this section, we consider reasons why a firm might pay its shareholders high dividends, even in the presence of personal taxes on these dividends.

Desire for Current Income

It has been argued that many individuals desire current income. The classic example is the group of retired people and others living on fixed incomes, proverbially known as "widows and orphans." The argument further states that these individuals would bid up the stock price should dividends rise and bid down the stock price should dividends fall.

Miller and Modigliani point out that this argument does not hold in their theoretical model. An individual preferring high current cash flow but holding low-dividend securities could easily sell off shares to provide the necessary funds. Thus, in a world of no transaction costs, a high current dividend policy would be of no value to the stockholder.

However, the current income argument does have relevance in the real world. The sale of stock involves brokerage fees and other transaction costs—direct cash expenses that could be avoided by an investment in high-dividend securities. In addition, the expenditure of one's time when selling securities might further lead many investors to buy high-dividend securities.

However, to put this argument in perspective, it should be remembered that financial intermediaries such as mutual funds can perform repackaging transactions at low cost. Such intermediaries could buy low-dividend stocks and, by a controlled policy of realizing gains, pay their investors at a higher rate.

Behavioral Finance

Suppose it turned out that the transaction costs in selling no-dividend securities could not account for the preference of investors for dividends. Would there still be a reason for high dividends? We introduced the topic of behavioral finance in an earlier chapter, pointing out that the ideas of behaviorists represent a strong challenge to the theory of efficient capital markets. It turns out that behavioral finance also has an argument for high dividends.

The basic idea here concerns self-control, a concept that, though quite important in psychology, has received virtually no emphasis in finance. While we cannot review all that psychology has to say about self-control, let's focus on one example—losing weight. Suppose Alfred Martin, a college student, just got back from the Christmas break more than a few pounds heavier than he would like. Everyone would probably agree that diet and exercise are the two ways to lose weight. But how should Alfred put this approach into practice? We'll focus on exercise, though the same principle would apply to diet as well. One way, let's call it the economists' way, would involve trying to make rational decisions. Each day, Al would balance the costs and the benefits of exercising. Perhaps he would choose to exercise on most days because losing the weight is important to him. However, when he is too busy with exams, he might rationally choose not to exercise because he cannot afford the time. And he wants to be socially active as well, so he may rationally choose to avoid exercise on days when parties and other social commitments become too time-consuming.

This seems sensible—at first glance. The problem is that he must make a choice every day and there may be too many days when his lack of self-control gets the better of him. He may tell himself that he doesn't have the time to exercise on a particular day because he is starting to find exercise boring, not because he really doesn't have the time. Before long, he is avoiding exercise on most days—and overeating in reaction to the guilt from not exercising!

What does this have to do with dividends? Investors must also deal with self-control. Suppose a retiree wants to consume $20,000 a year from savings. On one hand, she could buy stocks with a dividend yield high enough to generate $20,000 in dividends. On the other hand, she could place her savings in no-dividend stocks, selling off $20,000 each year for consumption. Though these two approaches seem equivalent financially, the second one may allow for too much leeway. If lack of self-control gets the better of her, she might sell off too much, leaving little for her later years. Better, perhaps, to short-circuit this possibility by investing in dividend-paying stocks, with a strict personal rule of never "dipping into principal." While behaviorists do not claim that this approach is for everyone, they argue that enough people think this way to explain why firms pay dividends, even though, as we said earlier, dividends are tax disadvantaged.

Does behavioral finance argue for increased stock repurchases as well as increased dividends? The answer is no because investors will sell the stock that firms repurchase. As we said above, selling stock involves too much leeway. Investors might sell too many shares of stock, leaving little for the later years. Thus, the behaviorist argument may explain why companies pay dividends in a world with personal taxes.

Agency Costs

Although stockholders, bondholders, and management form firms for mutually beneficial reasons, one party may later gain at another's expense. For example, take the potential conflict between bondholders and stockholders. Bondholders would like stockholders to leave as much cash as possible in the firm so that this cash would be available to pay the bondholders during times of financial distress. Conversely, stockholders would like to keep this extra cash for themselves. That's where dividends come in. Managers, acting on behalf of the stockholders, may pay dividends to keep the cash away from the bondholders. In other words, a dividend can be viewed as a wealth transfer from bondholders to stockholders. Of course, bondholders know of the propensity of stockholders to transfer money out of the firm. To protect themselves, bondholders frequently create loan agreements stating that dividends can be paid only if the firm has earnings, cash flow, and working capital above prespecified levels.

Although the managers may be looking out for the stockholders in any conflict with bondholders, the managers may pursue selfish goals at the expense of stockholders in other situations. As discussed in an earlier chapter, managers might pad expense accounts, take on pet projects with negative NPVs, or not work very hard. Managers find it easier to pursue these selfish goals when the firm has plenty of free cash flow. After all, one cannot squander funds if the funds are not available in the first place. And that is where dividends come in. It has been suggested that dividends can serve as a way for the board of directors to reduce agency costs. By paying dividends equal to the amount of "surplus" cash flow, a firm can reduce management's ability to squander the firm's resources.

While the above discussion suggests a reason for increased dividends, the same argument applies to share repurchases as well. Managers, acting on behalf of stockholders, can just as easily keep cash from bondholders through repurchases as through dividends. And the board of directors, also acting on behalf of stockholders, can reduce the cash available to spendthrift managers just as easily through repurchases as through dividends. Thus, the presence of agency costs is not an argument for dividends over repurchases. Rather, agency costs imply firms may well increase either dividends or share repurchases rather than hoard large amounts of cash.

Information Content of Dividends and Dividend Signaling

While there are many things researchers do not know about dividends, there is one thing that we know for sure: The stock price of a firm will generally rise when the firm announces an increase in the dividend and will generally fall when a dividend reduction is announced. The question is: How should one interpret this fact? Consider the following three positions on dividends:

1. From the homemade dividend argument of MM, dividend policy is irrelevant, given that future earnings (and cash flows) are held constant.
2. Because of tax effects, a firm's stock price is negatively related to the current dividend when future earnings (or cash flows) are held constant.
3. Because of stockholders' desire for current income, a firm's stock price is positively related to its current dividend, even when future earnings (or cash flows) are held constant.

At first glance, the empirical evidence that stock prices rise when dividend increases are announced may seem consistent with Position 3 and inconsistent with Positions 1 and 2. In fact, many writers have argued this. However, other authors have countered that the observation itself is consistent with all three positions. They point out that companies do not like to cut a dividend. Thus, firms will raise the dividend only when future earnings, cash flow, and so on are expected to rise enough so that the dividend is not likely to be reduced later to its original level. A dividend increase is management's *signal* to the market that the firm is expected to do well.

It is the expectation of good times, and not only the stockholders' affinity for current income, that raises the stock price. The rise in the stock price following the dividend signal is called the information content effect of the dividend. To recapitulate, imagine that the stock price is unaffected or even negatively affected by the level of dividends, given that future earnings (or cash flows) are held constant. Nevertheless, the information content effect implies that the stock price may rise when dividends are raised—if dividends simultaneously cause stockholders to increase their expectations of future earnings and cash flows.

16.7 THE CLIENTELE EFFECT: A RESOLUTION OF REAL-WORLD FACTORS?

In the previous two sections, we pointed out that the existence of personal taxes favors a low-dividend policy, whereas other factors favor high dividends. The financial profession had hoped that it would be easy to determine which of these sets of factors dominates. Unfortunately, after years of research, no one has been able to conclude which of the two is more important. This is surprising: We might be skeptical that the two sets of factors would cancel each other out so perfectly.

However, one particular idea, known as the *clientele effect,* implies that the two sets of factors are likely to cancel each other out after all. To understand this idea, let's separate investors in high tax brackets from those in low tax brackets. Individuals in high tax brackets likely prefer either no, or low, dividends. Low tax bracket investors generally fall into three categories. First, there are individual investors in low brackets. They are likely to prefer some dividends if they desire current income. Second, pension funds pay no taxes on either dividends or capital gains. Because they face no tax consequences, pension funds will also prefer dividends if they have a preference for current income. Finally, corporations can exclude at least 50 percent of their dividend income but cannot exclude any of their capital gains. Thus, corporations are likely to prefer high-dividend stocks, even without a preference for current income.

Suppose that 40 percent of all investors prefer high dividends and 60 percent prefer low dividends, yet only 20 percent of firms pay high dividends while 80 percent pay low dividends. Here, the high-dividend firms will be in short supply, implying that their stock should be bid up while the stock of low-dividend firms should be bid down.

However, the dividend policies of all firms need not be fixed in the long run. In this example, we would expect enough low-dividend firms to increase their payout so that 40 percent of the firms pay high dividends and 60 percent of the firms pay low dividends. After this adjustment, no firm will gain from changing its dividend policy. Once payouts of corporations conform to the desires of stockholders, no single firm can affect its market value by switching from one dividend strategy to another.

Clienteles are likely to form in the following way:

Group	Stocks
Individuals in high tax brackets	Zero- to low-payout stocks
Individuals in low tax brackets	Low- to medium-payout stocks
Tax-free institutions	Medium-payout stocks
Corporations	High-payout stocks

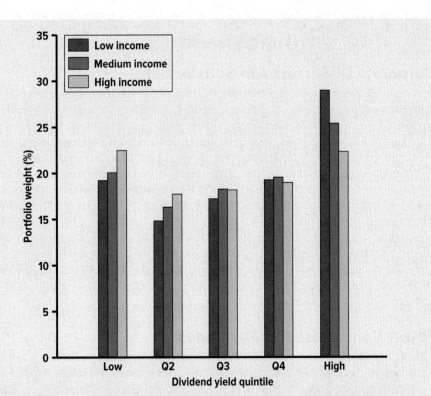

FIGURE 16.7

Preferences of Investors for Dividend Yield

Source: Graham, John R., and Alok Kumar. "Do Dividend Clienteles Exist? Evidence on Dividend Preferences of Retail Investors." *Journal of Finance* 60, no. 3 (2006): pp. 1305–36.

All stocks are ranked on their dividend yields and placed into five quintile portfolios. The figure shows the weight of each quintile in the portfolios of low-, medium-, and high-income investors. Relative to those with lower income, high-income investors place a greater percentage of their assets in low-dividend stocks and a smaller percentage in high-dividend stocks.

To see if you understand the clientele effect, consider the following statement: "In a world where many investors like high dividends, a firm can boost its share price by increasing its dividend payout ratio." True or false?

The statement is likely to be false. As long as there are already enough high-dividend firms to satisfy dividend-loving investors, a firm will not be able to boost its share price by paying high dividends. A firm can boost its stock price only if an *unsatisfied* clientele exists.

Our discussion of clienteles followed from the fact that tax brackets vary across investors. If shareholders care about taxes, stocks should attract clienteles based on dividend yield. Is there any evidence that this is the case?

Consider Figure 16.7. Here, John Graham and Alok Kumar[2] rank common stocks by their dividend yields (the ratio of dividend to stock price) and place them into five portfolios, called quintiles. The bottom quintile contains the 20 percent of stocks with the lowest dividend yields; the next quintile contains the 20 percent of stocks with the next lowest dividend yields; and so on. The figure shows the weight of each quintile in the portfolios of low-, medium-, and high-income investors. As can be seen, relative to low-income investors, high-income investors put a greater percentage of their assets into low-dividend securities. Conversely, again relative to low-income investors, high-income investors put a smaller percentage of their assets into high-dividend securities.

[2] John R. Graham and Alok Kumar, "Do Dividend Clienteles Exist? Evidence on Dividend Preferences of Retail Investors," *Journal of Finance* 60, no. 3 (2006), pp. 1305–36.

16.8 WHAT WE KNOW AND DO NOT KNOW ABOUT DIVIDEND POLICY

Corporate Dividends Are Substantial

We pointed out earlier in the chapter that dividends are tax disadvantaged relative to capital gains because dividends are taxed upon payment whereas taxes on capital gains are deferred until sale. Nevertheless, dividends in the U.S. economy are substantial. For example, consider Figure 16.8, which shows the ratio of aggregate dividends to aggregate earnings for all U.S. firms from 1980 to 2016. The ratio has generally been above 50 percent.

We might argue that the taxation on dividends is actually minimal, perhaps because dividends are paid primarily to individuals in low tax brackets (currently the tax rate on cash dividends is 15 percent for all but the highest earners; the top rate is 20 percent for the highest earners) or because institutions such as pension funds, which pay no taxes, are the primary recipients. However, Peterson, Peterson, and Ang conducted an in-depth study of dividends for one representative year, 1979.[3] They found that about two-thirds of dividends went to individuals and that the average marginal tax bracket for these individuals was about 40 percent. Thus, we must conclude that large amounts of dividends are paid, even in the presence of substantial taxation.

Fewer Companies Pay Dividends

Although dividends are substantial, Fama and French (FF) point out that the percentage of companies paying dividends has fallen over the last few decades.[4] FF argue that the decline was caused primarily by an explosion of small, currently unprofitable companies that have recently listed on various stock exchanges. For the most part, firms of this type do not pay dividends. Figure 16.9 shows that the proportion of dividend payers among U.S. industrial firms dropped substantially from 1980 to about 2002.

This figure, presented in a paper by DeAngelo, DeAngelo, and Skinner,[5] also shows an increase in the proportion of dividend payers after 2002. One obvious explanation is the cut in the maximum tax rate on dividends to 15 percent, signed into law in May 2003. However,

FIGURE 16.8

Ratio of Aggregate Dividends to Aggregate Earnings for All U.S. Firms: 1980 to 2016

Source: The Bureau of Economic Analysis, November 2017.

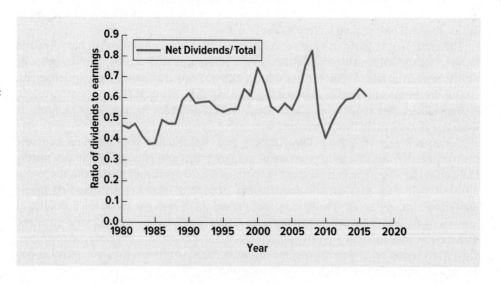

[3] Pamela P. Peterson, David R. Peterson, and James S. Ang, "Direct Evidence on the Marginal Rate of Taxation on Dividend Income," *Journal of Financial Economics* 14, no. 2 (1985), pp. 267–82.

[4] Eugene F. Fama and Kenneth R. French, "Disappearing Dividends: Changing Firm Characteristics or Lower Propensity to Pay?," *Journal of Financial Economics* 60, no. 1 (2001), pp. 3–43.

[5] Harry DeAngelo, Linda DeAngelo, and Douglas J. Skinner, "Corporate Payout Policy," *Foundations and Trends in Finance* 3, no. 2–3 (2008), pp. 95–287.

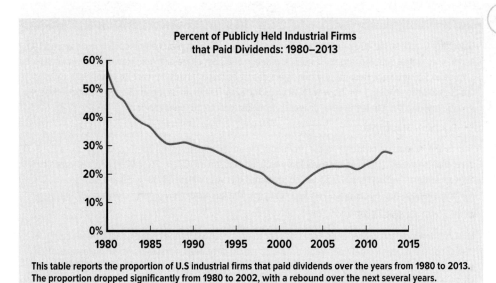

FIGURE 16.9

Proportion of Dividend Payers among All Publicly Held U.S. Industrial Firms

Source: DeAngelo, Harry, Linda DeAngelo, and Douglas J. Skinner. "Corporate Payout Policy." *Foundations and Trends in Finance* 3, no. 2–3 (2008): pp. 95–287. Data updated by DeAngelo, DeAngelo, and Skinner.

Percent of Publicly Held Industrial Firms that Paid Dividends: 1980–2013

This table reports the proportion of U.S industrial firms that paid dividends over the years from 1980 to 2013. The proportion dropped significantly from 1980 to 2002, with a rebound over the next several years.

DeAngelo, DeAngelo, and Skinner downplay the effect of the tax cut, suggesting a number of other reasons.

Figure 16.9 does not imply that dividends across all firms declined from 1980 to 2002. DeAngelo, DeAngelo, and Skinner[6] point out that while small firms have shied away from dividends, the largest firms have substantially increased their dividends over recent decades. This increase has created such concentration in dividends that the 25 top dividend-paying firms accounted for more than 50 percent of aggregate dividends in the United States in 2013. DeAngelo and colleagues suggest, "Industrial firms exhibit a two-tier structure in which a small number of firms with very high earnings generates the majority of earnings and dominates the dividend supply, while the majority of firms has, at best, a modest impact on aggregate earnings and dividends."

Corporations Smooth Dividends

In 1956, John Lintner made two important observations concerning dividend policy that still ring true.[7] First, real-world companies typically set long-term target ratios of dividends to earnings. A firm is likely to set a low target ratio if it has many positive NPV projects relative to available cash flow and a high ratio if it has few positive NPV projects. Second, managers know that only part of any change in earnings is likely to be permanent. Because managers need time to assess the permanence of any earnings increase, dividend changes appear to lag earnings changes by a number of periods.

Taken together, Lintner's observations suggest that two parameters describe dividend policy: the target payout ratio (t) and the speed of adjustment of current dividends to the target (s). Dividend changes will tend to conform to the following model:

$$\text{Dividend change} \equiv D_1 - D_0 = s \times (tEPS_1 - D_0) \tag{16.2}$$

where D_1 and D_0 are dividends in the next year and dividends in the current year, respectively. EPS_1 is earnings per share in the next year.

---

[6] Harry DeAngelo, Linda DeAngelo, and Douglas J. Skinner, "Are Dividends Disappearing? Dividend Concentration and the Consolidation of Earnings," *Journal of Financial Economics* 72, no. 3 (2004), pp. 425–56.

[7] John Lintner, "Distribution of Incomes of Corporations among Dividends, Retained Earnings, and Taxes," *American Economic Review* 46, no. 2 (1956), pp. 97–113.

EXAMPLE 16.1

Dividend Smoothing

Calculator Graphics, Inc. (CGI), has a target payout ratio of .30. Last year's earnings per share were $10, and in accordance with the target, CGI paid dividends of $3 per share last year. However, earnings have jumped to $20 this year. Because the managers do not believe that this increase is permanent, they do not plan to raise dividends all the way to $6 (= .30 × $20). Rather, their speed of adjustment coefficient, s, is .5, implying that the increase in dividends from last year to this year will be:

$$.5 \times (\$6 - 3) = \$1.50$$

That is, the increase in dividends is the product of the speed of adjustment coefficient, .50, times the difference between what dividends would be with full adjustment [$6 (= .30 × $20)] and last year's dividends. Dividends will increase by $1.50, so dividends this year will be $4.50 (= $3 + 1.50).

Now suppose that earnings stay at $20 next year. The increase in dividends next year will be:

$$.5 \times (\$6 - 4.50) = \$.75$$

In words, the increase in dividends from this year to next year will be the speed of adjustment coefficient (.50) times the difference between what dividends would have been next year with full adjustment ($6) and this year's dividends ($4.50). Because dividends will increase by $.75, dividends next year will be $5.25 (= $4.50 + .75). In this way, dividends will slowly rise every year if earnings in all future years remain at $20. However, dividends will reach $6 only at infinity.

The limiting cases in Equation 16.2 occur when $s = 1$ and $s = 0$. If $s = 1$, the actual change in dividends will be equal to the target change in dividends. Here, full adjustment occurs immediately. If $s = 0$, $D_1 = D_0$. In other words, there is no change in dividends at all. Real-world companies can be expected to set s between 0 and 1.

An implication of Lintner's model is that the dividends-to-earnings ratio rises when a company begins a period of bad times and the ratio falls when a company starts a period of good times. Thus, dividends display less variability than do earnings. In other words, firms smooth dividends.

THE PROS AND CONS OF PAYING DIVIDENDS	
Pros	**Cons**
1. Dividends may appeal to investors who desire stable cash flow but do not want to incur the transaction costs from periodically selling shares of stock.	1. Dividends traditionally have been taxed as ordinary income.
2. Behavioral finance argues that investors with limited self-control can meet current consumption needs with high-dividend stocks while adhering to the policy of never dipping into principal.	2. Dividends can reduce internal sources of financing. Dividends may force the firm to forgo positive NPV projects or to rely on costly external equity financing.
3. Managers, acting on behalf of stockholders, can pay dividends in order to keep cash from bondholders.	3. Once established, dividend cuts are hard to make without adversely affecting a firm's stock price.
4. The board of directors, acting on behalf of stockholders, can use dividends to reduce the cash available to spendthrift managers.	
5. Managers may increase dividends to signal their optimism concerning future cash flow.	

Some Survey Evidence about Dividends

A recent study surveyed a large number of financial executives regarding dividend policy. One of the questions asked was this: "Do these statements describe factors that affect your company's dividend decisions?" Table 16.2 shows some of the results.

Policy Statements	Percentage Who Agree or Strongly Agree
1. We try to avoid reducing dividends per share.	93.8%
2. We try to maintain a smooth dividend from year to year.	89.6
3. We consider the level of dividends per share that we have paid in recent quarters.	88.2
4. We are reluctant to make dividend changes that might have to be reversed in the future.	77.9
5. We consider the change or growth in dividends per share.	66.7
6. We consider the cost of raising external capital to be smaller than the cost of cutting dividends.	42.8
7. We pay dividends to attract investors subject to "prudent man" investment restrictions.	41.7

* Survey respondents were asked the question, "Do these statements describe factors that affect your company's dividend decisions?"

TABLE 16.2

Survey Responses on Dividend Decisions*

Source: Brav, Alon, John R. Graham, Campbell R. Harvey, and Roni Michaely. "Payout Policy in the 21st Century." *Journal of Financial Economics* 77, no. 3 (2005): pp. 483–527.

Policy Statements	Percentage Who Think This Is Important or Very Important
1. Maintaining consistency with our historic dividend policy.	84.1%
2. Stability of future earnings.	71.9
3. A sustainable change in earnings.	67.1
4. Attracting institutional investors to purchase our stock.	52.5
5. The availability of good investment opportunities for our firm to pursue.	47.6
6. Attracting retail investors to purchase our stock.	44.5
7. Personal taxes our stockholders pay when receiving dividends.	21.1
8. Flotation costs to issuing new equity.	9.3

* Survey respondents were asked the question, "How important are the following factors to your company's dividend decisions?"

TABLE 16.3

Survey Responses on Dividend Decisions*

Source: Alon Brav, John R. Graham, Campbell R. Harvey, and Roni Michaely. "Payout Policy in the 21st Century," *Journal of Financial Economics* 77, no. 3 (2005), pp. 483–527.

As shown in Table 16.2, financial managers are very disinclined to cut dividends. Moreover, they are very conscious of their previous dividends and desire to maintain a relatively steady dividend. In contrast, the cost of external capital and the desire to attract "prudent man" investors (those with fiduciary duties) are less important.

Table 16.3 is drawn from the same survey, but here the responses are to the question, "How important are the following factors to your company's dividend decisions?" Not surprisingly given the responses in Table 16.2 and our earlier discussion, the highest priority is maintaining a consistent dividend policy. The next several items are also consistent with our previous analysis. Financial managers are very concerned about earnings stability and future earnings levels in making dividend decisions, and they consider the availability of good investment opportunities. Survey respondents also believed that attracting both institutional and individual (retail) investors was relatively important.

In contrast to our discussion in the earlier part of this chapter of taxes and flotation costs, the financial managers in this survey did not think that personal taxes paid on dividends by shareholders are very important. And even fewer think that equity flotation costs are relevant.

16.9 PUTTING IT ALL TOGETHER

Much of what we have discussed in this chapter (and much of what we know about dividends from decades of research) can be pulled together and summarized in the following six points:[8]

---

[8] This list is distilled in part from a longer list in Harry DeAngelo and Linda DeAngelo, "Payout Policy Pedagogy: What Matters and Why," *European Financial Management* 13, no. 1 (2007), pp. 11–27.

1. Aggregate dividend and stock repurchases are massive, and they have increased steadily in nominal and real terms over the years.
2. Cash dividends and repurchases are heavily concentrated among a relatively small number of large, mature firms.
3. Managers are very reluctant to cut dividends, normally doing so only due to firm-specific problems.
4. Managers smooth dividends, raising them slowly and incrementally as earnings grow.
5. Stock prices react to unanticipated changes in dividends.
6. The magnitude of stock repurchases tends to vary with transitory earnings.

The challenge now is to fit these six pieces into a reasonably coherent picture. With regard to payouts in general, meaning the combination of stock repurchases and cash dividends, a simple life cycle theory fits Points 1 and 2. The key ideas are straightforward. First, relatively young firms with less available cash generally should not make cash distributions. They need the cash to fund positive NPV projects (and flotation costs discourage the raising of outside cash).

However, as a firm survives and matures, it begins to generate free cash flow (which, you will recall, is internally generated cash flow beyond that needed to fund profitable investment activities). Significant free cash flow can lead to agency problems if it is not distributed. Managers may become tempted to pursue empire building or otherwise spend the excess cash in ways not in the shareholders' best interests. Thus, firms come under shareholder pressure to make distributions rather than hoard cash. And, consistent with what we observe, we expect large firms with a history of profitability to make large distributions.

Thus, the life cycle theory says that firms trade off the agency costs of excess cash retention against the potential future costs of external equity financing. A firm should begin making distributions when it generates sufficient internal cash flow to fund its investment needs now and into the foreseeable future.

The more complex issue concerns the type of distribution—cash dividends or repurchase. The tax argument in favor of repurchases is a clear and strong one. Repurchases are a much more flexible option (and managers greatly value financial flexibility), so the question is: Why would firms ever choose a cash dividend?

If we are to answer this question, we have to ask a different question. What can a cash dividend accomplish that a share repurchase cannot? One answer is that when a firm makes a commitment to pay a cash dividend now and into the future, it sends a two-part signal to the markets. As we have already discussed, one signal is that the firm anticipates being profitable, with the ability to make the payments on an ongoing basis. Note that a firm cannot benefit by trying to fool the market in this regard because the firm would ultimately be punished when it couldn't make the dividend payment (or couldn't make it without relying on external financing). Thus, a cash dividend may let a firm distinguish itself from less profitable rivals.

A second, and more subtle, signal takes us back to the agency problem of free cash flow. By committing to pay cash dividends now and in the future, the firm signals that it won't be hoarding cash (or at least not as much cash), thereby reducing agency costs and enhancing shareholder wealth.

This two-part signaling story is consistent with Points 3 to 5, but an obvious objection remains. Why don't firms commit to a policy of setting aside whatever money would be used to pay dividends and use it instead to buy back shares? After all, either way, a firm is committing to pay out cash to shareholders.

A fixed repurchase strategy suffers from two drawbacks. The first is verifiability. A firm could announce an open market repurchase and then not do it. By suitably fudging its books, it would be some time before the deception was discovered. Thus, it would be necessary for shareholders to develop a monitoring mechanism, meaning some sort of way for stockholders to know for sure that the repurchase was in fact done. Such a mechanism wouldn't be difficult to build (it could be a simple trustee relationship such as we observe in the bond markets), but it currently does not exist. Of course, a tender offer repurchase needs little or no verification, but such offers have expenses associated with them. The beauty of a cash dividend is that it needs no monitoring. A firm is forced to cut and mail checks four times a year, year in and year out.

CHARACTERISTICS OF A SENSIBLE PAYOUT POLICY

- Over time, pay out all free cash flows.
- Avoid cutting positive NPV projects to pay dividends or buy back shares.
- Do not initiate dividends until the firm is generating substantial free cash flow.
- Set the current regular dividend consistent with a long-run target payout ratio.
- Set the level of dividends low enough to avoid expensive future external financing.
- Use repurchases to distribute transitory cash flow increases.

A second objection to a fixed repurchase strategy is more controversial. Suppose managers, as insiders, are better able than stockholders to judge whether their stock price is too high or too low. (Note that this idea does not conflict with semistrong market efficiency if inside information is the reason.) In this case, a fixed repurchase commitment forces management to buy back stock even in circumstances when the stock is overvalued. In other words, it forces management into making negative NPV investments.

More research on the cash dividend versus share repurchase question is needed, but the historical trend seems to be favoring continued growth in repurchases relative to dividends. Total corporate payouts seem to be relatively stable over time, but repurchases are becoming a larger portion of that total. The split reached about 50-50 in the latter part of the 1990s, but it looks like aggregate repurchases have recently passed aggregate dividends.

One aspect of aggregate cash dividends that has not received much attention is that there may be a strong legacy effect. Before 1982, the regulatory status of stock repurchases was somewhat murky, creating a significant disincentive. In 1982, the SEC, after years of debate, created a clear set of guidelines for firms to follow, thereby making repurchases much more attractive.

The legacy effect arises because many of the giant firms that pay such a large portion of aggregate dividends were paying dividends before (and perhaps long before) 1982. To the extent that these firms are unwilling to cut their dividends, aggregate cash dividends will be large, but only because of a "lock-in" effect for older firms. If locked-in, legacy payers account for much of the aggregate dividend, what we should observe is (1) a sharply reduced tendency for maturing firms to initiate dividends and (2) a growth in repurchases relative to cash dividends over time. We actually do see evidence of both of these trends.

16.10 STOCK DIVIDENDS AND STOCK SPLITS

Stock splits and stock dividends have essentially the same impact on the corporation and the shareholder: They increase the number of shares outstanding and reduce the value per share. The accounting treatment is not the same, however, and it depends on two things: (1) whether the distribution is a stock split or a stock dividend and (2) the size of the stock dividend if it is called a dividend.

By convention, stock dividends of less than 20 to 25 percent are called *small stock dividends*. The accounting procedure for such a dividend is discussed next. A stock dividend greater than this value of 20 to 25 percent is called a *large stock dividend*. Large stock dividends are not uncommon. For example, in March 2018, insurance company Aflac completed a 100 percent stock split, and in February 2018, wine and spirits company Brown-Forman completed a 400 percent stock dividend.

EXAMPLE OF A STOCK DIVIDEND   The Peterson Co., a consulting firm specializing in difficult accounting problems, has 10,000 shares of stock outstanding, each selling at $66. The total market value of the equity is $66 × 10,000 = $660,000. With a 10 percent stock dividend, each stockholder receives one additional share for each 10 owned, and the total number of shares outstanding after the dividend is 11,000.

Before the stock dividend, the equity portion of Peterson's balance sheet might look like this:

Common stock ($1 par, 10,000 shares outstanding)	$ 10,000
Capital in excess of par value	200,000
Retained earnings	290,000
Total owners' equity	$500,000

A seemingly arbitrary accounting procedure is used to adjust the balance sheet after a small stock dividend. Because 1,000 new shares are issued, the common stock account is increased by $1,000 (1,000 shares at $1 par value each), for a total of $11,000. The market price of $66 is $65 greater than the par value, so the "excess" of $65 × 1,000 shares = $65,000 is added to the capital surplus account (capital in excess of par value), producing a total of $265,000.

Total owners' equity is unaffected by the stock dividend because no cash has come in or out, so retained earnings are reduced by the entire $66,000, leaving $224,000. The net effect of these machinations is that Peterson's equity accounts now look like this:

Common stock ($1 par, 11,000 shares outstanding)	$ 11,000
Capital in excess of par value	265,000
Retained earnings	224,000
Total owners' equity	$500,000

EXAMPLE OF A STOCK SPLIT   A stock split is conceptually similar to a stock dividend, but it is commonly expressed as a ratio. For example, in a three-for-two split, each shareholder receives one additional share of stock for each two held originally, so a three-for-two split amounts to a 50 percent stock dividend. Again, no cash is paid out, and the percentage of the entire firm that each shareholder owns is unaffected.

The accounting treatment of a stock split is a little different from (and simpler than) that of a stock dividend. Suppose Peterson decides to declare a two-for-one stock split. The number of shares outstanding will double to 20,000, and the par value will be halved to $.50 per share. The owners' equity after the split is represented as:

Common stock ($.50 par, 20,000 shares outstanding)	$ 10,000
Capital in excess of par value	200,000
Retained earnings	290,000
Total owners' equity	$500,000

Note that, for all three of the categories, the figures on the right are completely unaffected by the split. The only changes are in the par value per share and the number of shares outstanding. Because the number of shares has doubled, the par value of each is cut in half.

For a list of recent stock splits, try www.stocksplits.net.

EXAMPLE OF A LARGE STOCK DIVIDEND   In our example, if a 100 percent stock dividend were declared, 10,000 new shares would be distributed, so 20,000 shares would be outstanding. At a $1 par value per share, the common stock account would rise by $10,000, for a total of $20,000. The retained earnings account would be reduced by $10,000, leaving $280,000. The result would be the following:

Common stock ($1 par, 20,000 shares outstanding)	$ 20,000
Capital in excess of par value	200,000
Retained earnings	280,000
Total owners' equity	$500,000

Value of Stock Splits and Stock Dividends

The laws of logic tell us that stock splits and stock dividends can (1) leave the value of the firm unaffected, (2) increase its value, or (3) decrease its value. Unfortunately, the issues are complex enough that one cannot easily determine which of the three relationships holds.

THE BENCHMARK CASE   A strong case can be made that stock dividends and splits do not change either the wealth of any shareholder or the wealth of the firm as a whole. In our preceding example, the equity had a total market value of $660,000. With the small stock dividend, the number of shares increased to 11,000, so it seems that each would be worth $660,000/11,000 = $60.

A shareholder who had 100 shares worth $66 each before the dividend would have 110 shares worth $60 each afterwards. The total value of the stock is $6,600 either way, so the stock dividend doesn't really have any economic effect.

After the stock split, there are 20,000 shares outstanding, so each should be worth $660,000/20,000 = $33. In other words, the number of shares doubles and the price halves. From these calculations, it appears that stock dividends and splits are just paper transactions.

Although these results are relatively obvious, there are reasons that are often given to suggest that there may be some benefits to these actions. The typical financial manager is aware of many real-world complexities, and for that reason, the stock split or stock dividend decision is not treated lightly in practice.

POPULAR TRADING RANGE   Proponents of stock dividends and stock splits frequently argue that a security has a proper trading range and that firms should use stock dividends and splits to keep the price in that range. For example, in early 2003, Microsoft announced a 2-for-1 stock split. This was the ninth split for Microsoft since the company went public in 1986. The stock had split 3-for-2 on two occasions and 2-for-1 a total of seven times. So, for every share of Microsoft you owned in 1986 when the company first went public, you would own 288 shares as of the most recent stock split in 2003. Similarly, since Walmart went public in 1970, it has split its stock 2-for-1 11 times, and Apple has split 7-for-1 once and 2-for-1 three times since going public in 1987. For a really long history of splits, consider Procter & Gamble, which has split 5-for-1 twice, 1.5-for-1 once, and 2-for-1 eight times since 1920. Each share of P&G purchased prior to the company's first split would have become 9,600 shares along the way.

Although this argument of a trading range is a popular one, its validity is questionable for a number of reasons. Mutual funds, pension funds, and other institutions have steadily increased their trading activity since World War II and now handle a sizable percentage of total trading volume (on the order of 80 percent of NYSE trading volume, for example). Because these institutions buy and sell in huge amounts, the individual share price is of little concern.

Furthermore, we sometimes observe share prices that are quite large that do not appear to cause problems. To take an extreme case, consider the Swiss chocolatier Lindt. In February 2019, Lindt shares were selling for around 72,000 Swiss francs each, or about $71,600. A round lot would have cost a cool $7.16 million. This is fairly expensive, but also consider Berkshire Hathaway, the company run by legendary investor Warren Buffett. In February 2019, the company's stock price was about $308,000, down from its all-time high of $335,900.

There is some evidence that stock splits may actually decrease the liquidity of the company's shares. Following a two-for-one split, the number of shares traded should more than double if liquidity is increased by the split. This doesn't appear to happen, and the reverse is sometimes observed.

Reverse Splits

A less frequently encountered financial maneuver is the reverse split. For example, in December 2018, Spirit Realty Company underwent a 1-for-5 reverse stock split, and about the same time, oil and gas exploration company Sylios Corporation announced a truly large 1-for-4,000 reverse stock split. In a 1-for-5 reverse stock split, each investor exchanges 5 old shares for 1 new one. The par value is increased fivefold in the process.

Given real-world imperfections, three related reasons are cited for reverse splits. First, transaction costs to shareholders may be less after the reverse split. Second, the liquidity and marketability of a company's stock might be improved when its price is raised to the popular trading range. Third, stocks selling at prices below a certain level are not considered respectable, meaning that investors underestimate these firms' earnings, cash flow, growth, and stability. Some financial analysts argue that a reverse split can achieve instant respectability. As was the case with stock splits, none of these reasons are particularly compelling, especially not the third one.

There are two other reasons for reverse splits. First, stock exchanges have minimum price per share requirements. A reverse split may bring the stock price up to such a minimum. For example, NASDAQ delists companies whose stock price drops below $1 per share for 30 days. Following the collapse of the internet boom in 2001–2002, a large number of internet-related companies found themselves in danger of being delisted and used reverse splits to boost their stock prices. Second, companies sometimes perform reverse splits and, at the same time, buy out any stockholders who end up with less than a certain number of shares.

For example, in July 2018, shareholders of performance fluid company GlyEco approved a reverse/forward split. In this case, the company would complete a 1-for-500 reverse stock split. The company would repurchase all shares held by stockholders with less than one share of stock, thereby eliminating small shareholders (and reducing the total number of shareholders). The purpose of the reverse split was to reduce the number of shares outstanding from 166.6 million shares to 1.33 million shares. What made the proposal especially imaginative was that immediately after the reverse split, the company would complete a 4-for-1 ordinary split to bring the stock price back down!

SUMMARY AND CONCLUSIONS

1. The dividend policy of the firm is irrelevant in a perfect capital market because the shareholder can effectively undo the firm's dividend strategy. If a shareholder receives a greater dividend than desired, he or she can reinvest the excess. Conversely, if the shareholder receives a smaller dividend than desired, he or she can sell off extra shares of stock. This argument is due to MM and is similar to their homemade leverage concept, discussed in a previous chapter.

2. Stockholders will be indifferent between dividends and share repurchases in a perfect capital market.

3. Because dividends are taxed, firms have an incentive to use share repurchases instead of paying cash dividends, and the evidence suggests they are increasingly choosing to do so.

4. The life cycle theory of cash distributions says that firms trade off the agency costs of excess cash holdings against the potential future costs of external equity financing. A firm should begin making distributions when it generates sufficient internal cash flow to fund its equity investment needs now and into the foreseeable future (and not before).

5. Consistent with the life cycle theory, aggregate distributions in the U.S. are huge and growing, but they are heavily concentrated in a relatively small number of large, mature firms.

6. Managers smooth dividends, raising them slowly and incrementally. They are very reluctant to cut dividends, normally doing so only in response to firm-specific problems.

7. Stock prices react to unanticipated changes in dividends.

8. Why a firm would pay a cash dividend at all (instead of doing a repurchase) is a challenging question. One reason is that doing so signals a commitment to making payments in the future (and having the funds to do so). Such signaling may let a firm distinguish itself from its less profitable rivals and also reassure market participants about the firm's reported earnings.

CONCEPT QUESTIONS

1. **Dividend Policy Irrelevance**   How is it possible that dividends are so important, but at the same time, dividend policy is irrelevant?

2. **Stock Repurchases**   What is the impact of a stock repurchase on a company's debt ratio? Does this suggest another use for excess cash?

3. **Dividend Policy**   It is sometimes suggested that firms should follow a "residual" dividend policy. With such a policy, the main idea is that a firm should focus on meeting its investment needs and maintaining its desired debt-equity ratio. Having done so, any leftover, or residual, income is paid out as dividends. What do you think would be the chief drawback to a residual dividend policy?

4. **Dividend Chronology**   On Tuesday, December 12, Hometown Power Co.'s board of directors declares a dividend of 75 cents per share payable on Wednesday, January 17, to shareholders of record as of Wednesday, January 3. When is the ex-dividend date? If a shareholder buys stock before that date, who gets the dividends on those shares, the buyer or the seller?

5. **Alternative Dividends**   Some corporations, like one British company that offers its large shareholders free crematorium use, pay dividends in kind (that is, offer their services to shareholders at below-market cost). Should mutual funds invest in stocks that pay these dividends in kind? (The fundholders do not receive these services.)

6. **Dividends and Stock Price**   If increases in dividends tend to be followed by (immediate) increases in share prices, how can it be said that dividend policy is irrelevant?

7. **Dividends and Stock Price**   Last month, Central Virginia Power Company, which had been having trouble with cost overruns on a nuclear power plant that it had been building, announced that it

was "temporarily suspending payments due to the cash flow crunch associated with its investment program." The company's stock price dropped from $28.50 to $25 when this announcement was made. How would you interpret this change in the stock price (that is, what would you say caused it)?

8. **Dividend Reinvestment Plans**   The DRK Corporation has recently developed a dividend reinvestment plan, or DRIP. The plan allows investors to reinvest cash dividends automatically in DRK in exchange for new shares of stock. Over time, investors in DRK will be able to build their holdings by reinvesting dividends to purchase additional shares of the company.

Over 1,000 companies offer dividend reinvestment plans. Most companies with DRIPs charge no brokerage or service fees. In fact, the shares of DRK will be purchased at a 10 percent discount from the market price.

A consultant for DRK estimates that about 75 percent of DRK's shareholders will take part in this plan. This is somewhat higher than the average.

Evaluate DRK's dividend reinvestment plan. Will it increase shareholder wealth? Discuss the advantages and disadvantages involved here.

9. **Dividend Policy**   For initial public offerings of common stock, 2018 was a fairly ordinary year, with about $33.5 billion raised by the process. Relatively few of the 134 firms involved paid cash dividends. Why do you think that most chose not to pay cash dividends?

10. **Investment and Dividends**   The Phew Charitable Trust pays no taxes on its capital gains or on its dividend income or interest income. Would it be irrational for it to have low-dividend, high-growth stocks in its portfolio? Would it be irrational for it to have municipal bonds in its portfolio? Explain.

Use the following information to answer the next two questions:

Historically, the U.S. tax code treated dividend payments made to shareholders as ordinary income. Thus, dividends were taxed at the investor's marginal tax rate, which was as high as 38.6 percent in 2002. Capital gains were taxed at a capital gains tax rate, which was the same for most investors and fluctuated through the years. In 2002, the capital gains tax rate stood at 20 percent. In an effort to stimulate the economy, President George W. Bush presided over a tax plan overhaul that included changes in dividend and capital gains tax rates. The new tax plan, which was implemented in 2003, called for a 15 percent tax rate on both dividends and capital gains for investors in higher tax brackets. In 2013, the tax rate became 20 percent for the very highest earners. For very low tax bracket investors, the tax rate on dividends and capital gains was set at 5 percent through 2007, dropping to zero in 2008.

11. **Ex-Dividend Stock Prices**   How do you think this tax law change affects ex-dividend stock prices?

12. **Stock Repurchases**   How do you think this tax law change affects the relative attractiveness of stock repurchases compared to dividend payments?

13. **Dividends and Stock Value**   The growing perpetuity model expresses the value of a share of stock as the present value of the expected dividends from that stock. How can you conclude that dividend policy is irrelevant when this model is valid?

14. **Bird-in-the-Hand Argument**   The bird-in-the-hand argument, which states that a dividend today is safer than the uncertain prospect of a capital gain tomorrow, is often used to justify high dividend payout ratios. Explain the fallacy behind this argument.

15. **Dividends and Income Preference**   The desire for current income is not a valid explanation for preference for high current dividend policy, as investors can always create homemade dividends by selling a portion of their stocks. Is this statement true or false? Why?

16. **Dividends and Clientele**   Cap Henderson owns Neotech stock because its price has been steadily rising over the past few years, and he expects this performance to continue. Cap is trying to convince Widow Jones to purchase some Neotech stock, but she is reluctant because Neotech has never paid a dividend. She depends on steady dividends to provide her with income.

a. What preferences are these two investors demonstrating?

b. What argument should Cap use to convince Widow Jones that Neotech stock is the stock for her?

c. Why might Cap's argument not convince Widow Jones?

17. **Dividends and Taxes** Your aunt is in a high tax bracket and would like to minimize the tax burden of her investment portfolio. She is willing to buy and sell in order to maximize her aftertax returns, and she has asked for your advice. What would you suggest she do?

18. **Dividends versus Capital Gains** If the market places the same value on $1 of dividends as on $1 of capital gains, then firms with different payout ratios will appeal to different clienteles of investors. One clientele is as good as another; therefore, a firm cannot increase its value by changing its dividend policy. Yet empirical investigations reveal a strong correlation between dividend payout ratios and other firm characteristics. For example, small, rapidly growing firms that have recently gone public almost always have payout ratios that are zero; all earnings are reinvested in the business. Explain this phenomenon if dividend policy is irrelevant.

19. **Dividends and Company Life Cycle** How does the life cycle of a company help explain dividend payments? What evidence is there to suggest that the company's life cycle, at least in part, explains dividend payments?

20. **Dividends versus Share Repurchases** Because it can be shown that share repurchases have exactly the same wealth effect for shareholders in the absence of taxes and are more beneficial when we account for taxes, why don't all companies repurchase shares instead of paying dividends?

QUESTIONS AND PROBLEMS

1. **Dividends and Taxes** Schultz, Inc., has declared a dividend of $5.60 per share. Suppose capital gains are not taxed, but dividends are taxed at 25 percent. New IRS regulations require that taxes be withheld at the time the dividend is paid. The company's stock sells for $81 per share and is about to go ex dividend. What do you think the ex-dividend price will be?

Basic
(Questions 1–10)

 2. **Stock Dividends** The owners' equity accounts for Southern Lights International are shown here:

Common stock ($1 par value)	$ 22,000
Capital surplus	95,000
Retained earnings	632,800
Total owners' equity	$749,800

   a. If the company's stock currently sells for $33 per share and a 10 percent stock dividend is declared, how many new shares will be distributed? Show how the equity accounts would change.

   b. If the company declared a 25 percent stock dividend, how would the accounts change?

3. **Stock Splits** For the company in Problem 2, show how the equity accounts will change if:

   a. The company declares a 4-for-1 stock split. How many shares are outstanding now? What is the new par value per share?

   b. The company declares a 1-for-5 reverse stock split. How many shares are outstanding now? What is the new par value per share?

 4. **Stock Splits and Stock Dividends** Roll Corporation (RC) currently has 365,000 shares of stock outstanding that sell for $87 per share. Assuming no market imperfections or tax effects exist, what will the share price be after:

   a. RC has a 5-for-3 stock split?

   b. RC has a 15 percent stock dividend?

   c. RC has a 42.5 percent stock dividend?

   d. RC has a 4-for-7 reverse stock split?

   Determine the new number of shares outstanding in parts (a) through (d).

5. **Regular Dividends** The balance sheet for Kare Corp. is shown here in market value terms. There are 6,400 shares of stock outstanding.

Market Value Balance Sheet			
Cash	$ 46,000	Equity	$251,000
Fixed assets	205,000		
Total	$251,000	Total	$251,000

The company has declared a dividend of $1.90 per share. The stock goes ex dividend tomorrow. Ignoring any tax effects, what is the stock selling for today? What will it sell for tomorrow? What will the balance sheet look like after the dividends are paid?

6. **Share Repurchase** In the previous problem, suppose the company has announced it is going to repurchase $12,160 worth of stock. What effect will this transaction have on the equity of the firm? How many shares will be outstanding? What will the price per share be after the repurchase? Ignoring tax effects, show how the share repurchase is effectively the same as a cash dividend.

7. **Stock Dividends** The market value balance sheet for Desktop Manufacturing is shown here. The company has declared a 25 percent stock dividend. The stock goes ex dividend tomorrow (the chronology for a stock dividend is similar to that for a cash dividend). There are 19,000 shares of stock outstanding. What will the ex-dividend price be?

Market Value Balance Sheet			
Cash	$153,000	Debt	$127,000
Fixed assets	603,000	Equity	629,000
Total	$756,000	Total	$756,000

8. **Stock Dividends** The company with the common equity accounts shown here has declared a stock dividend of 12 percent at a time when the market value of its stock is $73 per share. What effects on the equity accounts will the distribution of the stock dividend have?

Common stock ($1 par value)	$ 120,000
Capital surplus	912,300
Retained earnings	2,347,200
Total owners' equity	$3,379,500

9. **Stock Splits** In the previous problem, suppose the company instead decides on a 5-for-1 stock split. The firm's 74 cent per share cash dividend on the new (post-split) shares represents an increase of 10 percent over last year's dividend on the pre-split stock. What effect does this have on the equity accounts? What was last year's dividend per share?

10. **Dividends and Stock Price** The Spector Company currently has 65,000 outstanding shares selling at $87 each. The firm is contemplating the declaration of a dividend of $9 at the end of the fiscal year that just began. Assume there are no taxes on dividends. Answer the following questions based on the Miller and Modigliani model.

a. What will be the price of the stock on the ex-dividend date if the dividend is declared?

b. What will be the price of the stock at the end of the year if the dividend is not declared?

c. If the company makes $1.8 million of new investments at the beginning of the period, earns net income of $1.05 million, and pays the dividend at the end of the year, how many shares of new stock must the firm issue to meet its funding needs?

d. Is it realistic to use the MM model in the real world to value stock? Why or why not?

11. **Homemade Dividends**   You own 1,000 shares of stock in Avondale Corporation. You will receive a $2.34 per share dividend in one year. In two years, the company will pay a liquidating dividend of $74 per share. The required return on the stock is 14 percent. What is the current share price of your stock (ignoring taxes)? If you would rather have equal dividends in each of the next two years, show how you can accomplish this by creating homemade dividends. (*Hint:* Dividends will be in the form of an annuity.)

Intermediate
(Questions 11–16)

12. **Homemade Dividends**   In the previous problem, suppose you want only $200 total in dividends the first year. What will your homemade dividend be in two years?

13. **Stock Repurchase**   Iron Corporation is evaluating an extra dividend versus a share repurchase. In either case, $11,008 would be spent. Current earnings are $4.50 per share, and the stock currently sells for $89 per share. There are 4,300 shares outstanding. Ignore taxes and other imperfections in answering the first two questions.

a. Evaluate the two alternatives in terms of the effect on the price per share of the stock and shareholder wealth.

b. What will be the effect on the company's EPS and PE ratio under the two different scenarios?

c. In the real world, which of these actions would you recommend? Why?

14. **Dividends and Firm Value**   The net income of Steel City Corporation is $130,000. The company has 30,000 outstanding shares, and a 100 percent payout policy. The expected value of the firm one year from now is $2.43 million. The appropriate discount rate is 11 percent, and there are no taxes.

a. What is the current value of the company assuming the current dividend has not yet been paid?

b. What is the ex-dividend price of the company's stock if the board follows its current policy?

c. At the dividend declaration meeting, several board members claimed that the dividend is too meager and is probably depressing the company's stock price. They proposed that the company sell enough new shares to finance a dividend of $5.40.

i. Comment on the claim that the low dividend is depressing the stock price. Support your argument with calculations.

ii. If the proposal is adopted, at what price will the new shares sell and how many shares will be sold?

15. **Dividend Policy**   White Chocolate Co. has a current period cash flow of $1.35 million and pays no dividends. The present value of the company's future cash flows is $17.8 million. The company is entirely financed with equity and has 315,000 shares outstanding. Ignore taxes.

a. What is the share price of the company's stock?

b. Suppose the board of directors of the company announces its plan to pay out 50 percent of its current cash flow as cash dividends to its shareholders. How can a shareholder who owns 1,000 shares of the stock achieve a zero payout policy on his own?

16. **Dividend Smoothing**   The Sharpe Co. just paid a dividend of $2.34 per share of stock. Its target payout ratio is 50 percent. The company expects to have earnings per share of $6.10 one year from now.

a. If the adjustment rate is .3 as defined in the Lintner model, what is the dividend one year from now?

b. If the adjustment rate is .6 instead, what is the dividend one year from now?

c. Which adjustment rate is more conservative? Why?

17. **Expected Return, Dividends, and Taxes**   The Gecko Company and the Gordon Company are two firms whose business risk is the same but have different dividend policies. Gecko pays no dividend, whereas Gordon has an expected dividend yield of 2.5 percent. Suppose the capital gains tax rate is zero,

Challenge
(Questions 17–20)

whereas the dividend tax rate is 25 percent. Gecko has an expected earnings growth rate of 14 percent annually, and its stock price is expected to grow at this same rate. If the aftertax expected returns on the two stocks are equal because they are in the same risk class, what is the pretax required return on Gordon's stock?

18. **Dividends and Taxes**   As discussed in the text, in the absence of market imperfections and tax effects, we would expect the share price to decline by the amount of the dividend payment when the stock goes ex dividend. Once we consider the role of taxes, however, this is not necessarily true. One model has been proposed that incorporates tax effects into determining the ex-dividend price:[9]

$$(P_0 - P_X)/D = (1 - T_P)/(1 - T_G)$$

where P_0 is the price just before the stock goes ex, P_X is the ex-dividend share price, D is the amount of the dividend per share, T_P is the relevant marginal personal tax rate on dividends, and T_G is the effective marginal tax rate on capital gains.

a. If $T_P = T_G = 0$, how much will the share price fall when the stock goes ex?

b. If $T_P = 15$ percent and $T_G = 0$, how much will the share price fall?

c. If $T_P = 15$ percent and $T_G = 20$ percent, how much will the share price fall?

d. Suppose the only owners of stock are corporations. Recall that corporations get at least a 50 percent exemption from taxation on the dividend income they receive, but they do not get such an exemption on capital gains. If the corporation's income and capital gains tax rates are both 21 percent, how much will the share price fall?

e. What does this problem tell you about real-world tax considerations and the dividend policy of the firm?

19. **Dividends versus Reinvestment**   National Business Machine Co. (NBM) has $2.6 million of extra cash after taxes have been paid. NBM has two choices to make use of this cash. One alternative is to invest the cash in financial assets. The resulting investment income will be paid out as a special dividend at the end of three years. In this case, the firm can invest in Treasury bills yielding 1.6 percent or in 4.3 percent preferred stock. IRS regulations allow the company to exclude from taxable income 50 percent of the dividends received from investing in another company's stock. Another alternative is to pay out the cash now as dividends. This would allow the shareholders to invest on their own in Treasury bills with the same yield or in preferred stock. The corporate tax rate is 21 percent. Assume the investor has a 35 percent personal income tax rate, which is applied to interest income and preferred stock dividends. The personal dividend tax rate is 15 percent on common stock dividends. Should the cash be paid today or in three years? Which of the two options generates the higher aftertax income for the shareholders?

20. **Dividends versus Reinvestment**   After completing its capital spending for the year, Carlson Manufacturing has $1,000 extra cash. The company's managers must choose between investing the cash in Treasury bonds that yield 3.5 percent or paying out the cash to investors who would invest in the bonds themselves.

a. If the corporate tax rate is 21 percent, what personal tax rate would make the investors equally willing to receive the dividend or to let the company invest the money?

b. Is the answer to (a) reasonable? Why or why not?

c. Suppose the only investment choice is a preferred stock that yields 6.2 percent. The corporate dividend exclusion of 50 percent applies. What personal tax rate will make the stockholders indifferent to the outcome of the company's dividend decision?

d. Is this a compelling argument for a low dividend payout ratio? Why or why not?

[9] Edwin J. Elton and Martin J. Gruber, "Marginal Stockholder Tax Rates and the Clientele Effect," *Review of Economics and Statistics* 52, no. 1 (1970), pp. 68–74.

WHAT'S ON THE WEB?

1. **Dividend Reinvestment Plans** Dividend reinvestment plans (DRIPs) permit shareholders to automatically reinvest cash dividends in the company. To find out more about DRIPs, go to www.fool.com and answer the following questions. What are the advantages Motley Fool lists for DRIPs? What are the different types of DRIPs? What is a direct purchase plan? How does a direct purchase plan differ from a DRIP?

2. **Dividends** Go to www.dividend.com and find how many companies went "ex" on this day. What is the largest declared dividend? For the stocks going "ex" today, what is the longest time until the payable date?

3. **Stock Splits** Go to www.stocksplits.net and find the stock splits today. How many stock splits are listed? How many are reverse splits? What are the largest split and the largest reverse split in terms of shares? Pick a company and follow the link. What type of information do you find?

4. **Dividend Yields** Which stock has the highest dividend yield? To answer this (and more), go to finance.yahoo.com and find the stock screener. Find out how many stocks have a dividend yield above 3 percent and how many have a dividend yield above 5 percent. Now find out how many stocks have an annual dividend above $2 and how many have an annual dividend above $4.

5. **Stock Splits** How many times has IBM's stock split? Go to the Investor Relations section at www.ibm.com to find out. When did IBM's stock first split? What was the split? When was the most recent stock split?

CLOSING CASE

ELECTRONIC TIMING, INC.

Electronic Timing, Inc. (ETI), is a small company founded 15 years ago by electronics engineers Tom Miller and Jessica Kerr. ETI manufactures integrated circuits to capitalize on the complex mixed-signal design technology and has recently entered the market for frequency timing generators, or silicon timing devices, which provide the timing signals or "clocks" necessary to synchronize electronic systems. Its clock products originally were used in PC video graphics applications, but the market subsequently expanded to include motherboards, PC peripheral devices, and other digital consumer electronics, such as digital television boxes and game consoles. ETI also designs and markets custom application-specific integrated circuits (ASICs) for industrial customers. The ASIC's design combines analog and digital, or mixed-signal, technology. In addition to Tom and Jessica, Nolan Pittman, who provided capital for the company, is the third primary owner. Each owns 25 percent of the one million shares outstanding. The company has several other individuals, including current employees, who own the remaining shares.

Recently, the company designed a new computer motherboard. The company's design is both more efficient and less expensive to manufacture, and the ETI design is expected to become standard in many personal computers. After investigating the possibility of manufacturing the new motherboard, ETI determined that the costs involved in building a new plant would be prohibitive. The owners also decided that they were unwilling to bring in another large outside owner. Instead, ETI sold the design to an outside firm. The sale of the motherboard design was completed for an aftertax payment of $30 million.

1. Tom believes the company should use the extra cash to pay a special one-time dividend. How will this proposal affect the stock price? How will it affect the value of the company?

2. Jessica believes that the company should use the extra cash to pay off debt and upgrade and expand its existing manufacturing capability. How would Jessica's proposals affect the company?

3. Nolan is in favor of a share repurchase. He argues that a repurchase will increase the company's PE ratio, return on assets, and return on equity. Are his arguments correct? How will a share repurchase affect the value of the company?

4. Another option discussed by Tom, Jessica, and Nolan would be to begin a regular dividend payment to shareholders. How would you evaluate this proposal?

5. One way to value a share of stock is the dividend growth, or growing perpetuity, model. Consider the following: The dividend payout ratio is one minus b, where b is the retention or plowback ratio. So, the dividend next year will be the earnings next year, E_1, times one minus the retention ratio. The most commonly used equation to calculate the sustainable growth rate is the return on equity times the retention ratio. Substituting these relationships into the dividend growth model, we get the following equation to calculate the price of a share of stock today:

$$P_0 = \frac{E_1(1 - b)}{R_S - \text{ROE} \times b}$$

What are the implications of this result in terms of whether the company should pay a dividend or upgrade and expand its manufacturing capability? Explain.

6. Does the question of whether the company should pay a dividend depend on whether the company is organized as a corporation or an LLC?

Options and Corporate Finance

17

On February 6, 2019, the closing stock prices for ConocoPhillips, Starbucks, and Dunkin' Donuts were $69.11, $68.85, and $68.84, respectively. Each company had a call option trading on the Chicago Board Options Exchange with a $65 strike price and an expiration date of March 22—44 days away. Given how close the stock prices are, you might expect that the prices on these call options would be similar, but they were not. The ConocoPhillips options sold for $5.65, Starbucks options traded at $4.40, and Dunkin' Donuts options traded at $3.40. Why would options on these three similarly priced stocks be priced so differently when the strike prices and the time to expiration were exactly the same? A big reason is that the volatility of the underlying stock is an important determinant of an option's underlying value, and in fact, these three stocks had very different volatilities. In this chapter, we will explore this issue—and many others—in much greater depth using the Nobel Prize-winning Black-Scholes option pricing model.

Please visit us at corecorporatefinance.blogspot.com for the latest developments in the world of corporate finance.

OPENING CASE

17.1 OPTIONS

An **option** is a contract giving its owner the right to buy or sell an asset at a fixed price on or before a given date. For example, an option on a building might give the buyer the right to buy the building for $1 million on or anytime before the Saturday prior to the third Wednesday in January 2022. Options are a unique type of financial contract because they give the buyer the right, but not the *obligation,* to do something. The buyer uses the option only if it is advantageous to do so; otherwise the option can be thrown away.

There is a special vocabulary associated with options. Here are some important definitions:

1. **Exercising the option** The act of buying or selling the underlying asset via the option contract is referred to as *exercising the option.*
2. **Strike or exercise price** The fixed price in the option contract at which the holder can buy or sell the underlying asset is called the *strike price* or *exercise price.*
3. **Expiration date** The maturity date of the option is referred to as the *expiration date.* After this date, the option is dead.
4. **American and European options** An American option may be exercised anytime up to the expiration date. A European option differs from an American option in that it can be exercised only on the expiration date.

The Options Industry Council has lots of educational material at www.optionseducation.org.

17.2 CALL OPTIONS

The most common type of option is a **call option**. A call option gives the owner the right to buy an asset at a fixed price during a particular time period. There is no restriction on the kind of asset, but the most common ones traded on exchanges are options on stocks and bonds.

For example, call options on IBM stock can be purchased on the Chicago Board Options Exchange. IBM does not issue (that is, sell) call options on its common stock. Instead, individual investors are the original buyers and sellers of call options on IBM common stock. A representative call option on IBM stock enables an investor to buy 100 shares of IBM on or before July 15, at an exercise price of $100. This is a valuable option if there is some probability that the price of IBM common stock will exceed $100 on or before July 15.

The Value of a Call Option at Expiration

What is the value of a call option contract on common stock at expiration? The answer depends on the value of the underlying stock at expiration.

Let's continue with the IBM example. Suppose the stock price is $130 at expiration. The buyer[1] of the call option has the right to buy the underlying stock at the exercise price of $100. In other words, he has the right to exercise the call. Having the right to buy something for $100 when it is worth $130 is obviously a good thing. The value of this right is $30 (= $130 − 100) on the expiration day.[2]

The call would be worth even more if the stock price were higher on the expiration day. For example, if IBM were selling for $150 on the date of expiration, the call would be worth $50 (= $150 − 100) at that time. In fact, the call's value increases $1 for every $1 rise in the stock price.

If the stock price is greater than the exercise price, we say that the call is *in the money.* Of course, it is also possible that the value of the common stock will turn out to be less than the exercise price. In this case, we say that the call is *out of the money.* The holder will not exercise in this case. For example, if the stock price at the expiration date is $90, no rational investor would exercise. Why pay $100 for stock worth only $90? Because the option holder has no obligation to exercise the call, she can walk away from the option. As a consequence, if IBM's stock price is less than $100 on the expiration date, the value of the call option will be $0. In this case, the value of the call option is not the difference between IBM's stock price and $100, as it would be if the holder of the call option had the obligation to exercise the call.

The payoff of a call option at expiration is:

	Payoff on the Expiration Date	
	If Stock Price Is Less than $100	If Stock Price Is Greater than $100
Call option value	$0	Stock price − $100

Figure 17.1 plots the value of the call at expiration against the value of IBM's stock. It is referred to as the *hockey stick diagram* of call option values. If the stock price is less than $100, the call is out of the money and worthless. If the stock price is greater than $100, the

---

[1] We use *buyer, owner,* and *holder* interchangeably.

[2] This example assumes that the call lets the holder purchase one share of stock at $100. In reality, one call option contract would let the holder purchase 100 shares. The profit would then equal $3,000 = [($130 − 100) × 100].

FIGURE 17.1

The Value of a Call Option
on the Expiration Date

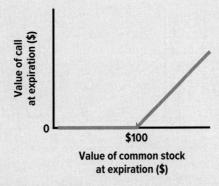

A call option gives the owner the right to buy an asset at a fixed
price during a particular time period. If IBM's stock price is greater
than $100 at the expiration date, the call's value is:

Stock price − $100

If IBM's stock price is less than $100 at this time, the value of the
call is $0.

call is in the money and its value rises one-for-one with increases in the stock price. Notice
that the call can never have a negative value. It is a *limited liability instrument,* which means
that all the holder can lose is the initial amount she paid for it.

EXAMPLE 17.1

Call Option Payoffs

Suppose Mr. Optimist holds a one-year call option on TIX common stock. It is a European call option
and can be exercised at $150. Assume that the expiration date has arrived. What is the value of the
TIX call option on the expiration date? If TIX is selling for $200 per share, Mr. Optimist can exercise the
option—purchase TIX at $150—and then immediately sell the share at $200. Mr. Optimist will have made
$50 (= $200 − 150).

Instead, assume that TIX is selling for $100 per share on the expiration date. If Mr. Optimist still
holds the call option, he will throw it out. The value of the TIX call on the expiration date will be $0 in
this case.

17.3 PUT OPTIONS

A **put option** can be viewed as the opposite of a call option. Just as a call gives the holder the
right to buy the stock at a fixed price, a put gives the holder the right to sell the stock for a
fixed exercise price.

The Value of a Put Option at Expiration

The circumstances that determine the value of the put are the opposite of those for a call
option because a put option gives the holder the right to sell shares. Let us assume that the
exercise price of the put is $50 and the stock price at expiration is $40. The owner of this
put option has the right to sell the stock for more than it is worth, something that is clearly
profitable. That is, he can buy the stock at the market price of $40 and immediately sell it
at the exercise price of $50, generating a profit of $10 (= $50 − 40). Thus, the value of the
option at expiration must be $10.

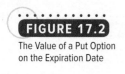
FIGURE 17.2

The Value of a Put Option
on the Expiration Date

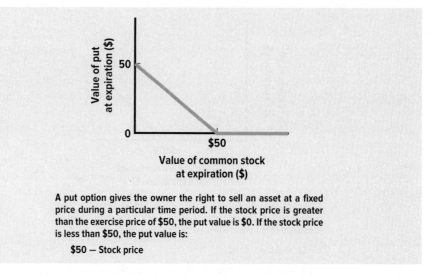

A put option gives the owner the right to sell an asset at a fixed
price during a particular time period. If the stock price is greater
than the exercise price of $50, the put value is $0. If the stock price
is less than $50, the put value is:

$50 − Stock price

The profit would be greater still if the stock price were lower. If the stock price were only $30, the value of the option would be $20 (= $50 − 30). In fact, for every $1 that the stock price declines at expiration, the value of the put rises by $1.

However, suppose that the stock at expiration is trading at $60—or any price above the exercise price of $50. The owner of the put would not want to exercise here. It is a losing proposition to sell stock for $50 when it trades in the open market at $60. Instead, the owner of the put will walk away from the option. That is, he will let the put option expire.

The payoff of this put option is:

	Payoff on the Expiration Date	
	If Stock Price Is Less than $50	If Stock Price Is Greater than $50
Put option value	$50 − Stock price	$0

Figure 17.2 plots the values of a put option for all possible values of the underlying stock. It is instructive to compare Figure 17.2 with Figure 17.1 for the call option. The call option is valuable whenever the stock is above the exercise price, and the put is valuable when the stock price is below the exercise price.

EXAMPLE 17.2

Put Option Payoffs

Ms. Pessimist feels quite certain that BMI will fall from its current $160 per-share price. She buys a put. Her put option contract gives her the right to sell a share of BMI stock at $150 one year from now. If the price of BMI is $200 on the expiration date, she will tear up the put option contract because it is worthless. That is, she will not want to sell stock worth $200 for the exercise price of $150.

On the other hand, if BMI is selling for $100 on the expiration date, she will exercise the option. In this case, she can buy a share of BMI in the market for $100 per share and turn around and sell the share at the exercise price of $150. Her profit will be $50 (= $150 − 100). The value of the put option on the expiration date therefore will be $50.

17.4 SELLING OPTIONS

An investor who sells (or *writes*) a call on common stock promises to deliver shares of the common stock if required to do so by the call option holder. Notice that the seller is obligated to do so.

If, at the expiration date, the price of the common stock is greater than the exercise price, the holder will exercise the call and the seller must give the holder shares of stock in exchange for the exercise price. The seller loses the difference between the stock price and the exercise price. Assume that the stock price is $60 and the exercise price is $50. Knowing that exercise is imminent, the option seller buys stock in the open market at $60. Because she is obligated to sell at $50, she loses $10 (= $50 − 60). Conversely, if at the expiration date the price of the common stock is below the exercise price, the call option will not be exercised and the seller's liability is zero.

Why would the seller of a call place himself in such a precarious position? After all, the seller loses money if the stock price ends up above the exercise price and he merely avoids losing money if the stock price ends up below the exercise price. The answer is that the seller is paid to take this risk. On the day that the option transaction takes place, the seller receives the price that the buyer pays.

Now, let's look at the seller of puts. An investor who sells a put on common stock agrees to purchase shares of common stock if the put holder should so request. The seller loses on this deal if the stock price falls below the exercise price and the holder puts the stock to the seller. Assume that the stock price is $40 and the exercise price is $50. The holder of the put will exercise in this case. In other words, he will sell the underlying stock at the exercise price of $50. This means that the seller of the put must buy the underlying stock at the exercise price of $50. Because the stock is only worth $40, the loss here is $10 (= $40 − 50).

The values of the "sell-a-call" and "sell-a-put" positions are depicted in Figure 17.3. The graph on the left-hand side of the figure shows that the seller of a call loses nothing when the stock price at expiration is below $50. However, the seller loses a dollar for every dollar that the stock rises above $50. The graph in the center of the figure shows that the seller of a put loses nothing when the stock price at the expiration date is above $50. However, the seller loses a dollar for every dollar that the stock falls below $50.

It is worthwhile to spend a few minutes comparing the graphs in Figure 17.3 to those in Figures 17.1 and 17.2. The graph of selling a call (the graph in the left-hand side of Figure 17.3) is the mirror image of the graph of buying a call (Figure 17.1).[3] This

Check out this option exchange: www.cmegroup.com.

FIGURE 17.3 The Payoffs to Sellers of Calls and Puts and Buyers of Common Stock

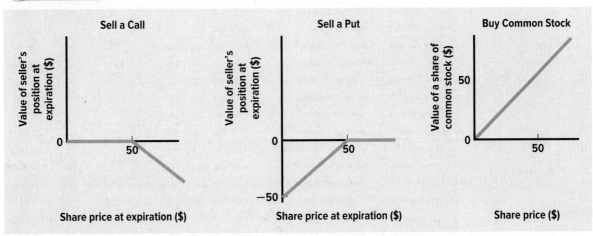

[3] Actually, because of differing exercise prices, the two graphs are not quite mirror images of each other. The exercise price in Figure 17.1 is $100 and the exercise price in Figure 17.3 is $50.

occurs because options are a zero-sum game. The seller of a call loses what the buyer makes. Similarly, the graph of selling a put (the middle graph in Figure 17.3) is the mirror image of the graph of buying a put (Figure 17.2). Again, the seller of a put loses what the buyer makes.

Figure 17.3 also shows the value at expiration of buying common stock. Notice that buying the stock is the same as buying a call option on the stock with an exercise price of $0. This is not surprising. If the exercise price is $0, the call holder can buy the stock for nothing, which is really the same as owning it.

17.5 OPTION QUOTES

Now that we understand the definitions for calls and puts, let's see how these options are quoted. Table 17.1 presents information on Goldman Sachs options expiring in March 2019, obtained from finance.yahoo.com. At the time of these quotes, Goldman Sachs was selling for $196.62.

The top half of the table presents call option quotes; put option quotes are featured in the section below. The first column of the table contains ticker symbols, which uniquely indicate the underlying stock, the type of option, the expiration date, and the strike price. The second column shows the date and time of the last trade, followed by the strike price. Next, we have the most recent prices on the options (Last Price), the bid and ask prices, and the change from the previous day (Change). Note that option prices are quoted on a per-option

For more on option ticker symbols, go to the "Symbol Directory" link under "Trading Resources" at www.cboe.com.

TABLE 17.1

Information on the Options of Goldman Sachs

Source: Yahoo! Finance.

Contract Name	Last Trade Date	Strike ∧	Last Price	Bid	Ask	Change	% Change	Volume	Open Interest	Implied Volatility
GS190322C00187500	2019-02-01 3:18PM EST	187.50	12.90	12.75	13.00	0.00	-	1	1	28.52%
GS190322C00192500	2019-02-01 1:04PM EST	192.50	10.45	9.15	9.35	0.00	-	5	5	26.36%
GS190322C00197500	2019-02-05 10:08AM EST	197.50	6.20	6.05	6.45	+0.13	+2.14%	1	35	25.21%
GS190322C00205000	2019-02-05 1:37PM EST	205.00	2.93	2.92	3.15	-0.15	-4.87%	21	27	23.37%
GS190322C00207500	2019-02-04 3:59PM EST	207.50	2.36	2.17	2.44	0.00	-	4	18	23.16%
GS190322C00210000	2019-02-05 11:08AM EST	210.00	1.89	1.64	1.84	-0.47	-19.92%	3	2	22.86%
GS190322C00212500	2019-02-05 1:18PM EST	212.50	1.20	1.21	1.38	-0.09	-6.98%	15	6	22.71%
GS190322C00215000	2019-02-04 3:23PM EST	215.00	0.93	0.87	1.00	0.00	-	-	12	22.44%
GS190322C00222500	2019-02-01 3:03PM EST	222.50	0.48	0.33	0.41	0.00	-	1	1	22.68%

Puts for March 22, 2019

Contract Name	Last Trade Date	Strike ∧	Last Price	Bid	Ask	Change	% Change	Volume	Open Interest	Implied Volatility
GS190322P00165000	2019-02-05 10:06AM EST	165.00	0.40	0.36	0.42	-0.14	-25.93%	100	100	31.01%
GS190322P00167500	2019-02-05 10:16AM EST	167.50	0.51	0.46	0.53	-0.02	-3.77%	100	101	30.30%
GS190322P00170000	2019-02-01 3:03PM EST	170.00	0.91	0.57	0.65	0.00	-	1	1	29.44%
GS190322P00172500	2019-02-04 11:37AM EST	172.50	0.95	0.68	0.78	0.00	-	10	110	28.41%
GS190322P00177500	2019-02-04 11:34AM EST	177.50	1.47	1.05	1.21	0.00	-	1	2	26.92%
GS190322P00180000	2019-02-05 12:50PM EST	180.00	1.39	1.32	1.52	-0.30	-17.75%	2	11	26.29%
GS190322P00185000	2019-02-04 12:08PM EST	185.00	2.56	2.06	2.29	0.00	-	-	11	24.68%
GS190322P00187500	2019-01-31 1:31PM EST	187.50	3.68	2.57	2.86	0.00	-	-	1	24.13%
GS190322P00190000	2019-01-31 1:09PM EST	190.00	4.45	3.30	3.40	0.00	-	-	16	22.99%
GS190322P00192500	2019-01-31 11:56AM EST	192.50	4.71	4.05	4.15	0.00	-	-	2	22.22%
GS190322P00195000	2019-02-05 10:06AM EST	195.00	4.88	4.95	5.15	-0.37	-7.05%	1	210	21.85%
GS190322P00197500	2019-02-05 10:06AM EST	197.50	5.95	6.00	6.25	-0.55	-8.46%	1	33	21.25%
GS190322P00200000	2019-02-04 11:01AM EST	200.00	8.85	7.20	7.50	0.00	-	1	12	20.58%
GS190322P00202500	2019-02-01 11:01AM EST	202.50	9.00	8.75	9.10	0.00	-	1	1	20.57%
GS190322P00205000	2019-02-01 9:51AM EST	205.00	10.90	10.15	10.65	0.00	-	1	1	19.68%
GS190322P00217500	2019-02-01 2:17PM EST	217.50	21.30	20.50	21.25	0.00	-	10	10	18.99%

basis, but trading actually occurs in standardized contracts, where each contract calls for the purchase (for calls) or sale (for puts) of 100 shares. Thus, the call option with a strike price of $192.50 last traded at $10.45 per option, or $1,045 per contract. Volume shows the number of contracts traded this day, and Open Interest is the number of contracts currently outstanding. We'll have more to say about the implied volatility later.

17.6 COMBINATIONS OF OPTIONS

ExcelMaster
coverage online

www.mhhe.com/RossCore6e

Puts and calls can serve as building blocks for more complex option contracts. For example, Figure 17.4 illustrates the payoff from buying a put option on a stock and simultaneously buying the stock.

If the share price is greater than the exercise price, the put option is worthless, and the value of the combined position is equal to the value of the common stock. If instead the exercise price is greater than the share price, the decline in the value of the shares will be exactly offset by the rise in value of the put.

The strategy of buying a put and buying the underlying stock is called a *protective put.* It is as if one is buying insurance for the stock. The stock can always be sold at the exercise price, regardless of how far the market price of the stock falls.

Note that the combination of buying a put and buying the underlying stock has the same shape in Figure 17.4 as the call purchase in Figure 17.1. To pursue this point, let's consider the graph for buying a call, which is shown at the far left of Figure 17.5. This

FIGURE 17.4 Payoff to the Combination of Buying a Put and Buying the Underlying Stock

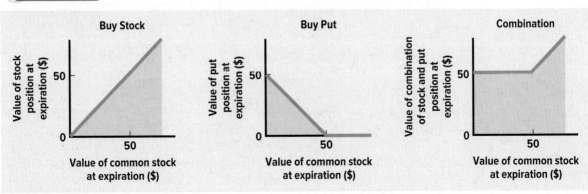

FIGURE 17.5 Payoff to the Combination of Buying a Call and Buying a Zero Coupon Bond

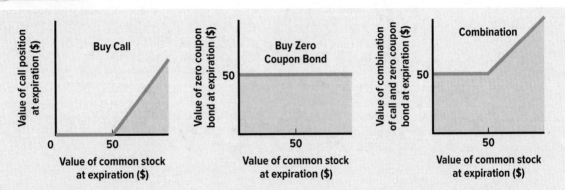

The graph of buying a call and buying a zero coupon bond is the same as the graph of buying a put and buying the stock in Figure 17.4.

graph is the same as Figure 17.1, except that the exercise price is $50 here. Now let's try the strategy of:

(Leg A) Buying a call.

(Leg B) Buying a risk-free, zero coupon bond (i.e., a T-bill), with a face value of $50 that matures on the same day that the option expires.

We have drawn the graph of Leg A of this strategy at the far left of Figure 17.5, but what does the graph of Leg B look like? It looks like the middle graph of the figure. That is, anyone buying this zero coupon bond will be guaranteed to get $50, regardless of the price of the stock at expiration.

What does the graph of simultaneously buying both Leg A and Leg B of this strategy look like? It looks like the far-right graph of Figure 17.5. That is, the investor receives a guaranteed $50 from the bond, regardless of what happens to the stock. In addition, the investor receives a payoff from the call of $1 for every $1 that the price of the stock rises above the exercise price of $50.

The far-right graph of Figure 17.5 looks exactly like the far-right graph of Figure 17.4. Thus, an investor gets the same payoff from the strategy of Figure 17.4 and the strategy of Figure 17.5, regardless of what happens to the price of the underlying stock. In other words, the investor gets the same payoff from:

1. Buying a put and buying the underlying stock.
2. Buying a call and buying a risk-free, zero coupon bond.

If investors have the same payoffs from the two strategies, the two strategies must have the same cost. Otherwise, all investors will choose the strategy with the lower cost and avoid the strategy with the higher cost. This leads to the interesting result that:

$$\underbrace{\text{Price of underlying stock} + \text{Price of put}}_{\text{Cost of first strategy}} = \underbrace{\text{Price of call} + \text{Present value of exercise price}}_{\text{Cost of second strategy}} \qquad [17.1]$$

This relationship is known as **put-call parity** and is one of the most fundamental relationships concerning options. It says that there are two ways of buying a protective put. You can buy a put and buy the underlying stock simultaneously. Here, your total cost is the price of the underlying stock plus the price of the put. Or you can buy a call and buy a zero coupon bond. Here, your total cost is the price of the call plus the price of the zero coupon bond. The price of the zero coupon bond is equal to the present value of the exercise price, that is, the present value of $50 in our example.

Equation 17.1 is a very precise relationship. It holds only if the put and the call have both the same exercise price and the same expiration date. In addition, the maturity date of the zero coupon bond must be the same as the expiration date of the options.

To see how fundamental put-call parity is, let's rearrange the formula, yielding:

$$\text{Price of underlying stock} = \text{Price of call} - \text{Price of put} + \text{Present value of exercise price}$$

This relationship now states that you can replicate the purchase of a share of stock by buying a call, selling a put, and buying a zero coupon bond. (Note that, because a minus sign comes before "Price of put," the put is sold, not bought.) Investors in this three-legged strategy are said to have purchased a *synthetic stock*.

Let's do one more transformation:

$$\text{Price of underlying stock} - \text{Price of call} = -\text{Price of put} + \text{Present value of exercise price}$$

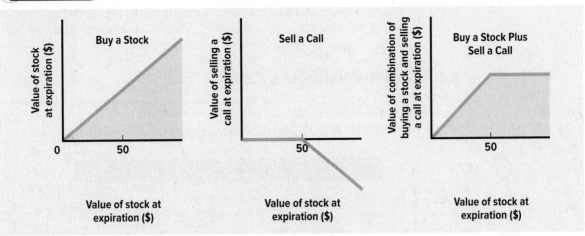

Many investors like to buy a stock and write a call on the stock simultaneously. This is a conservative strategy known as a *covered call.* The preceding put-call parity relationship tells us that this strategy is equivalent to selling a put and buying a zero coupon bond. Figure 17.6 develops the graph for the covered call. You can verify that the covered call can be replicated by selling a put and simultaneously buying a zero coupon bond.

Of course, there are other ways of rearranging the basic put-call relationship. For each rearrangement, the strategy on the left-hand side is equivalent to the strategy on the right-hand side. The beauty of put-call parity is that it shows how any strategy in options can be achieved in two different ways.

To test your understanding of put-call parity, suppose shares of stock in Joseph-Belmont, Inc., are selling for $80. A three-month call option with an $85 strike price goes for $6. The risk-free rate is .5 percent per month. What's the value of a three-month put option with an $85 strike price?

We can rearrange the put-call parity relationship to solve for the price of the put as follows:

$$\text{Price of put} = -\text{Price of underlying stock} + \text{Price of call} + \text{Present value of strike price}$$
$$= -\$80 + \$6 + \$85/1.005^3$$
$$= \$9.74$$

As illustrated, the value of the put is $9.74.

EXAMPLE 17.3

A Synthetic T-bill

Suppose that shares of stock in Smolira Corp. are selling for $110. A call option on Smolira with one year to maturity and a $110 strike price sells for $15. A put with the same terms sells for $5. What's the risk-free rate?

To answer, we need to use put-call parity to determine the price of a risk-free, zero coupon bond:

$$\text{Price of underlying stock} + \text{Price of put} - \text{Price of call} = \text{Present value of exercise price}$$

Plugging in the numbers, we get:

$$\$110 + 5 - 15 = \$100$$

Because the present value of the $110 strike price is $100, the implied risk-free rate is obviously 10 percent.

17.7 VALUING OPTIONS

In the last section, we determined what options are worth on the expiration date. Now, we wish to determine the value of options when you buy them well before expiration.[4] We begin by considering the lower and upper bounds on the value of a call.

Bounding the Value of a Call

LOWER BOUND   Consider an American call that is in the money prior to expiration. Assume that the stock price is $60 and the exercise price is $50. In this case, the option cannot sell below $10. To see this, note the simple strategy if the option sells at, say, $9.

Date		Transaction	
Today	(1)	Buy call.	−$ 9
Today	(2)	Exercise call—that is, buy underlying stock at exercise price.	−$50
Today	(3)	Sell stock at current market price.	+$60
Arbitrage profit			+$ 1

The type of profit that is described in this transaction is an *arbitrage* profit. Arbitrage profits come from transactions that have no risk or cost and cannot occur regularly in normal, well-functioning financial markets. The excess demand for these options would quickly force the option price up to at least $10 (= $60 − 50).

Of course, the price of the option is likely to be above $10. Investors will rationally pay more than $10 because of the possibility that the stock will rise above $60 before expiration. Suppose the call actually sells for $12. In this case, we say that the *intrinsic value* of the option is $10, meaning it must always be worth at least this much. The remaining $12 − 10 = $2 is called the *time premium,* and it represents the extra that investors are willing to pay because of the possibility that the stock price will rise before the option expires.

UPPER BOUND   Is there an upper boundary for the option price as well? It turns out that the upper boundary is the price of the underlying stock. That is, an option to buy common stock cannot have a greater value than the common stock itself. A call option can be used to buy common stock with a payment of an exercise price. It would be foolish to buy stock this way if the stock could be purchased directly at a lower price.

The upper and lower bounds are represented in Figure 17.7. In addition, these bounds are summarized in the bottom half of Table 17.2.

The Factors Determining Call Option Values

The previous discussion indicated that the price of a call option must fall somewhere in the shaded region of Figure 17.7. We now will determine more precisely where in the shaded region it should be. The factors that determine a call's value can be broken into two sets. The first set contains the features of the option contract. The two basic contractual features are the expiration date and the exercise price. The second set of factors affecting the call price concerns characteristics of the stock and the market.

EXERCISE PRICE   An increase in the exercise price reduces the value of the call. Imagine that there are two calls on a stock selling at $60. The first call has an exercise price of $50 and

---

[4] Our discussion in this section is of American options because they are more commonly traded in the real world. As necessary, we will indicate differences for European options.

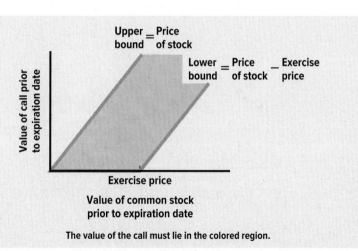

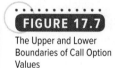
FIGURE 17.7
The Upper and Lower
Boundaries of Call Option
Values

The value of the call must lie in the colored region.

Increase in	Call Option*	Put Option*
Value of underlying asset (stock price)	+	−
Exercise price	−	+
Stock volatility	+	+
Interest rate	+	−
Time to expiration date	+	+

TABLE 17.2
Factors Affecting American
Option Values

In addition to the preceding, we have presented the following four relationships for American calls:

1. The call price can never be greater than the stock price (*upper bound*).
2. The call price can never be less than either zero or the difference between the stock price and the exercise price (*lower bound*).
3. The call is worth zero if the stock is worth zero.
4. When the stock price is much greater than the exercise price, the call price tends toward the difference between the stock price and the present value of the exercise price.

* The signs (+, −) indicate the effect of the variables on the value of the option. For example, the two +s for stock volatility indicate that an increase in volatility will increase both the value of a call and the value of a put.

the second one has an exercise price of $40. Which call would you rather have? Clearly, you would rather have the call with an exercise price of $40 because that one is $20 (= $60 − 40) in the money. In other words, the call with an exercise price of $40 should sell for more than an otherwise identical call with an exercise price of $50.

EXPIRATION DATE   The value of an American call option must be at least as great as the value of an otherwise identical option with a shorter term to expiration. Consider two American calls: One has a maturity of nine months and the other expires in six months. Obviously, the nine-month call has the same rights as the six-month call, and it also has an additional three months within which these rights can be exercised. It cannot be worth less and will generally be more valuable.[5]

STOCK PRICE   Other things being equal, the higher the stock price, the more valuable the call option will be. For example, if a stock is worth $80, a call with an exercise price of $100 isn't worth very much. If the stock soars to $120, the call becomes much more valuable.

---

[5] This relationship need not hold for a European call option. Consider a firm with two otherwise identical European call options, one expiring at the end of May and the other expiring a few months later. Further assume that a huge dividend is paid in early June. If the first call is exercised at the end of May, its holder will receive the underlying stock. If he does not sell the stock, he will receive the large dividend shortly thereafter. However, the holder of the second call will receive the stock through exercise after the dividend is paid. Because the market knows that the holder of this option will miss the dividend, the value of the second call option could be less than the value of the first.

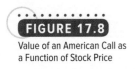

FIGURE 17.8

Value of an American Call as
a Function of Stock Price

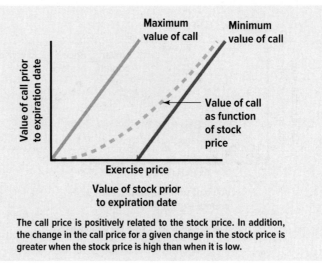

Maximum
value of call

Minimum
value of call

Value of call
as function
of stock
price

Value of call prior
to expiration date

Exercise price

Value of stock prior
to expiration date

The call price is positively related to the stock price. In addition,
the change in the call price for a given change in the stock price is
greater when the stock price is high than when it is low.

Now consider Figure 17.8, which shows the relationship between the call price and the
stock price prior to expiration. The curve indicates that the call price increases as the stock
price increases. Furthermore, it can be shown that the relationship is represented not by a
straight line, but by a convex curve. That is, the increase in the call price for a given change
in the stock price is greater when the stock price is high than when the stock price is low.

There are two special items of note regarding the curve in Figure 17.8:

1. *The Stock Is Worthless.* The call must be worthless if the underlying stock is worthless. That is, if the stock has no chance of attaining any value, it is not worthwhile
   to pay the exercise price in order to obtain the stock.

2. *The Stock Price Is Very High Relative to the Exercise Price.* In this situation, the owner of
   the call knows that he will end up exercising the call. He can view himself as the owner
   of the stock now, with one difference. He must pay the exercise price at expiration.

Thus, the value of his position, that is, the value of the call, is:

Stock price − Present value of exercise price

These two points are summarized in the bottom half of Table 17.2.

THE KEY FACTOR: THE VARIABILITY OF THE UNDERLYING ASSET The greater the variability
of the underlying asset, the more valuable the call option will be. Consider the following
example. Suppose that just before the call expires, the stock price will be either $100 with
probability .5 or $80 with probability .5. What will be the value of a call with an exercise price
of $110? Clearly, it will be worthless because no matter what happens to the stock, its price
will always be below the exercise price.

Now let us see what happens if the stock is more variable. Suppose that we add $20 to
the best case and take $20 away from the worst case. Now the stock has a one-half chance
of being worth $60 and a one-half chance of being worth $120. We have spread the stock
returns, but, of course, the expected value of the stock has stayed the same:

$$(1/2 \times \$80) + (1/2 \times \$100) = \$90 = (1/2 \times \$60) + (1/2 \times \$120)$$

Notice that the call option has value now because there is a one-half chance that the
stock price will be $120, or $10 above the exercise price of $110. This illustrates a very
important point. There is a fundamental distinction between holding an option on an underlying asset and holding the underlying asset. If investors in the marketplace are risk-averse,

For an option-oriented
site focusing on
volatilities, visit
www.ivolatility.com.

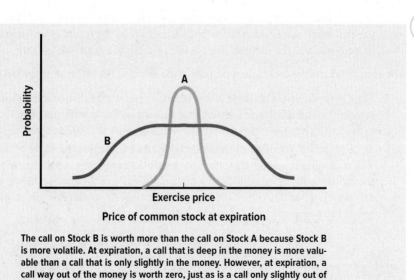

Distribution of Common Stock Price at Expiration for Both Stock A and Stock B. Options on the Two Stocks Have the Same Exercise Price.

The call on Stock B is worth more than the call on Stock A because Stock B is more volatile. At expiration, a call that is deep in the money is more valuable than a call that is only slightly in the money. However, at expiration, a call way out of the money is worth zero, just as is a call only slightly out of the money.

a rise in the variability of the stock will decrease its market value. However, the holder of a call receives payoffs from the positive tail of the probability distribution. As a consequence, a rise in the variability in the underlying stock increases the market value of the call.

This result can also be seen in Figure 17.9. Consider two stocks, A and B, each of which is normally distributed. For each security, the figure illustrates the probability of different stock prices on the expiration date.[6] As can be seen from the figure, Stock B has more volatility than does Stock A. This means that Stock B has a higher probability of both abnormally high returns and abnormally low returns. Let us assume that options on each of the two securities have the same exercise price. To option holders, a return much below average on Stock B is no worse than a return only moderately below average on Stock A. In either situation, the option expires out of the money. However, to option holders, a return much above average on Stock B is better than a return only moderately above average on Stock A. Because a call's price at the expiration date is the difference between the stock price and the exercise price, the value of the call on Stock B at expiration will be higher in this case.

THE INTEREST RATE   Call prices are also a function of the level of interest rates. Buyers of calls do not pay the exercise price until they exercise the option, if they do so at all. The ability to delay payment is more valuable when interest rates are high and less valuable when interest rates are low. Thus, the value of a call is positively related to interest rates.

A Quick Discussion of Factors Determining Put Option Values

Given our extended discussion of the factors influencing a call's value, we can examine the effect of these factors on puts very easily. Table 17.2 summarizes the five factors influencing the prices of both American calls and American puts. The effect of three factors on puts is the opposite of the effect of these three factors on calls:

1. *Value of Underlying Asset.* The put's market value decreases as the stock price increases because puts are in the money when the stock sells below the exercise price.

2. *Exercise Price.* The value of a put with a high exercise price is greater than the value of an otherwise identical put with a low exercise price for the reason given in (1).

[6] This graph assumes that, for each security, the exercise price is equal to the expected stock price. This assumption is employed merely to facilitate the discussion. It is not needed to show the relationship between a call's value and the volatility of the underlying stock.

CHAPTER 17 Options and Corporate Finance   527

3. *Interest Rate.* A high interest rate adversely affects the value of a put. The ability to sell a stock at a fixed exercise price sometime in the future is worth less if the present value of the exercise price is diminished by a high interest rate.

The effect of the other two factors on puts is the same as the effect of these factors on calls:

4. *Time to Expiration.* The value of an American put with a distant expiration date is greater than an otherwise identical put with an earlier expiration.[7] The longer time to maturity gives the put holder more flexibility, just as it did in the case of a call.

5. *Stock Volatility.* Volatility of the underlying stock increases the value of the put. The reasoning is analogous to that for a call. At expiration, a put that is way in the money is more valuable than a put only slightly in the money. However, at expiration, a put way out of the money is worth zero, just as is a put only slightly out of the money.

17.8 AN OPTION PRICING FORMULA

ExcelMaster coverage online
www.mhhe.com/RossCore6e

We have explained qualitatively that the value of a call option is a function of five variables:

1. The current price of the underlying asset, which for stock options is the price of a share of common stock.
2. The exercise price.
3. The time to expiration date.
4. The variance of the underlying asset's rate of return.
5. The risk-free interest rate.

It is time to replace the qualitative model with a precise option valuation model. The model we choose is the famous Black-Scholes option pricing model. You can put numbers into the Black-Scholes model and get option values back.

The Black-Scholes model is represented by a rather imposing formula.[8] A derivation of the formula is not practical in this textbook, as many students will be happy to learn. However, some appreciation for the achievement as well as some intuitive understanding is in order.

In the early chapters of this book, we showed how to discount capital budgeting projects using the net present value formula. We also used this approach to value stocks and bonds. Why, students sometimes ask, can't the same NPV formula be used to value puts and calls? It is a good question because the earliest attempts at valuing options used NPV. Unfortunately, the attempts were not successful because no one could determine the appropriate discount rate. An option is generally riskier than the underlying stock, but no one knew exactly how much riskier.

Fischer Black and Myron Scholes attacked the problem by pointing out that a strategy of borrowing to finance a stock purchase duplicates the risk of a call. Then, knowing the price of a stock already, one can determine the price of a call such that its return is identical to that of the stock-with-borrowing alternative.

We illustrate the intuition behind the Black-Scholes approach by considering a simple example where a combination of a call and a stock eliminates all risk. This example works because we let the future stock price be one of only two values. Hence, the example is called a *two-state option model.* By eliminating the possibility that the stock price can take on other values, we are able to duplicate the call exactly.

---

[7] Though this result must hold in the case of an American put, it need not hold for a European put.

[8] Fischer Black and Myron Scholes, "The Pricing of Options and Corporate Liabilities," *Journal of Political Economy* 81, no. 3 (1973), pp. 637–54.

A Two-State Option Model

Consider the following example. Suppose the current market price of a stock is $50 and the stock will sell for either $60 or $40 at the end of the year. Further, imagine a call option on this stock with a one-year expiration date and a $50 exercise price. Investors can borrow at 10 percent. Our goal is to determine the value of the call.

In order to value the call correctly, we need to examine two strategies. The first is to buy the call. The second is to:

a. Buy one-half a share of stock.

b. Borrow $18.18, implying a payment of principal and interest at the end of the year of $20 (= $18.18 × 1.10).

As you will see shortly, the cash flows from the second strategy exactly match the cash flows from buying a call. (A little later, we will show how we came up with the exact fraction of a share of stock to buy and the exact borrowing amount.) Because the cash flows match, we say that we are duplicating the call with the second strategy.

At the end of the year, the future payoffs are set out as follows:

	Future Payoffs	
Initial Transactions	If Stock Price Is $60	If Stock Price Is $40
1. Buy a call	$60 − 50 = $10	$ 0
2. Buy $\frac{1}{2}$ share of stock	$\frac{1}{2} \times \$60 =$ $30	$\frac{1}{2} \times \$40 =$ $20
Borrow $18.18 at 10%	−($18.18 × 1.10) = −$20	−$20
Total from stock and borrowing strategy	$10	$ 0

Note that the future payoff structure of the "buy-a-call" strategy is duplicated by the strategy of "buy stock" and "borrow." That is, under either strategy, an investor would end up with $10 if the stock price rose and $0 if the stock price fell. Thus, these two strategies are equivalent as far as traders are concerned.

If two strategies always have the same cash flows at the end of the year, how must their initial costs be related? The two strategies must have the same initial cost. Otherwise, there will be an arbitrage possibility. We can calculate this cost for our strategy of buying stock and borrowing. This cost is:

Buy $\frac{1}{2}$ share of stock	$\frac{1}{2} \times \$50 =$	$25.00
Borrow $18.18		−18.18
		$ 6.82

Because the call option provides the same payoffs at expiration as does the strategy of buying stock and borrowing, the call must be priced at $6.82. This is the value of the call option in a market without arbitrage profits.

We left two issues unexplained in the preceding example.

DETERMINING THE DELTA How did we know to buy one-half a share of stock in the duplicating strategy? Actually, the answer is easier than it might at first appear. The call price at the end of the year will be either $10 or $0, whereas the stock price will be either $60 or $40. Thus, the call price has a potential swing of $10 (= $10 − 0) next period, whereas the stock price has a potential swing of $20 (= $60 − 40). We can write this in terms of the following ratio:

$$\text{Delta} = \frac{\text{Swing of call}}{\text{Swing of stock}} = \frac{\$10 - 0}{\$60 - 40} = \frac{1}{2}$$

As indicated, this ratio is called the *delta* of the call. In words, a $1 swing in the price of the stock gives rise to a $.50 swing in the price of the call. Because we are trying to duplicate the call with the stock, it seems sensible to buy one-half a share of stock instead of buying one call. In other words, the risk of buying one-half a share of stock should be the same as the risk of buying one call.

DETERMINING THE AMOUNT OF BORROWING   How did we know how much to borrow? Buying one-half a share of stock brings us either $30 or $20 at expiration, which is exactly $20 more than the payoffs of $10 and $0, respectively, from the call. To duplicate the call through a purchase of stock, we should also borrow enough money so that we have to pay back exactly $20 of interest and principal. This amount of borrowing is the present value of $20, which is $18.18 (= $20/1.10).

Now that we know how to determine both the delta and the amount of borrowing, we can write the value of the call as:

$$\text{Value of call} = \text{Stock price} \times \text{Delta} - \text{Amount borrowed} \qquad [17.2]$$

$$\$6.82 \quad = \quad \$50 \quad \times \quad \frac{1}{2} \quad - \quad \$18.18$$

We will find this intuition very useful in explaining the Black-Scholes model.

RISK-NEUTRAL VALUATION   Before leaving this example, we should comment on a remarkable feature. We found the exact value of the option without even knowing the probability that the stock would go up or down! If an optimist thought the probability of an up move was very high and a pessimist thought it was very low, they would still agree on the option value. How could that be? The answer is that the current $50 stock price already balances the views of the optimist and the pessimist. The option reflects that balance because its value depends on the stock price.

This insight provides us with another approach to valuing the call. If we don't need the probabilities of the two states to value the call, perhaps we can select any probabilities we want and still come up with the right answer. Suppose we selected probabilities such that the return on the stock is equal to the risk-free rate of 10 percent. We know that the stock return given a rise is 20 percent (= $60/$50 − 1) and the stock return given a fall is −20 percent (= $40/$50 − 1). Thus, we can solve for the probability of a rise necessary to achieve an expected return of 10 percent as:

$$10\% = \text{Probability of a rise} \times 20\% + (1 - \text{Probability of a rise}) \times - 20\%$$

Solving this formula, we find that the probability of a rise is 3/4 and the probability of a fall is 1/4. If we apply these probabilities to the call, we can value it as:

$$\text{Value of call} = \frac{\frac{3}{4} \times \$10 + \frac{1}{4} \times \$0}{1.10} = \$6.82$$

the same value that we got from the duplicating approach.

Why did we select probabilities such that the expected return on the stock is 10 percent? We wanted to work with the special case where investors are *risk-neutral*. This case occurs when the expected return on any asset (including both the stock and the call) is equal to the risk-free rate. In other words, this case occurs when investors demand no additional compensation beyond the risk-free rate, regardless of the risk of the asset in question.

What would have happened if we had assumed that the expected return on the stock was greater than the risk-free rate? The value of the call would still be $6.82. However, the calculations would be more difficult. For example, if we assumed that the expected return on the stock was, say, 11 percent, we would have had to derive the expected return on the call. Although the expected return on the call would be higher than 11 percent, it would take a lot of work to determine it precisely. Why do any more work than you have to? Because we can't think of any good reason, we (and most other financial economists) choose to assume risk-neutrality.

Thus, the preceding material allows us to value a call in the following two ways:

1. Determine the cost of a strategy to duplicate the call. This strategy involves an investment in a fractional share of stock financed by partial borrowing.

2. Calculate the probabilities of a rise and a fall under the assumption of risk-neutrality. Use those probabilities, in conjunction with the risk-free rate, to discount the payoffs of the call at expiration.

The Black-Scholes Model

The preceding example illustrates the duplicating strategy. Unfortunately, a strategy such as this will not work in the real world over, say, a one-year time frame because there are many more than two possibilities for next year's stock price. However, the number of possibilities is reduced as the time period is shortened. In fact, the assumption that there are only two possibilities for the stock price over the next infinitesimal instant is quite plausible.[9]

In our opinion, the fundamental insight of Black and Scholes is to shorten the time period. They show that a specific combination of stock and borrowing can indeed duplicate a call over an infinitesimal time horizon. Because the price of the stock will change over the first instant, another combination of stock and borrowing is needed to duplicate the call over the second instant and so on. By adjusting the combination from moment to moment, one can continually duplicate the call. It may boggle the mind that a formula can (1) determine the duplicating combination at any moment and (2) value the option based on this duplicating strategy. Suffice it to say that their dynamic strategy allows one to value a call in the real world, just as we showed how to value a call in the two-state model.

This is the basic intuition behind the Black-Scholes model. Because the actual derivation of their formula is, alas, far beyond the scope of this text, we present the formula itself. The equation is:

$$C = SN(d_1) - Ee^{-Rt}N(d_2) \hspace{4cm} [17.3]$$

where:

$$d_1 = [\ln(S/E) + (R + \sigma^2/2)t]/\sqrt{\sigma^2 t}$$
$$d_2 = d_1 - \sqrt{\sigma^2 t}$$

This equation for the value of a call, C, is one of the most complex in finance. However, it involves only five parameters:

1. S = Current stock price.
2. E = Exercise price of call.
3. R = Annual risk-free rate of return, continuously compounded.
4. σ^2 = Variance (per year) of the continuous return on the stock.
5. t = Time (in years) to expiration date.

There's a Black-Scholes calculator (and a lot more) at www.option-price.com.

[9] A full treatment of this assumption can be found in John C. Hull, *Options, Futures and Other Derivatives,* 10th ed. (Upper Saddle River, NJ: Pearson, 2017).

The small e in the formula is the mathematical constant 2.71828. . . . In addition, there is the statistical concept:

> $N(d)$ = Probability that a standardized, normally distributed, random
> variable will be less than or equal to d

Rather than discuss the formula in its algebraic state, we illustrate the formula with an example:

EXAMPLE 17.4

Black-Scholes

Consider Private Equipment Company (PEC). On October 4, the PEC April 49 call option has a closing value of $4. The stock itself is selling at $50. The option has 199 days to expiration (maturity date = April 21 next year). The annual risk-free interest rate, continuously compounded, is 7 percent.

This information determines three variables directly:

1. The stock price, S, is $50.
2. The exercise price, E, is $49.
3. The risk-free rate, R, is .07.

In addition, the time to maturity, t, can be calculated quickly: The formula calls for t to be expressed in years.

4. We express the 199-day interval in years as $t = 199/365$.

In the real world, an option trader would know S and E exactly. Traders generally view U.S. Treasury bills with the same maturity as the options as risk-free, so a current quote from *The Wall Street Journal* or a similar source would be obtained for the interest rate. The trader would also know (or could count) the number of days to expiration exactly. Thus, the fraction of a year to expiration, t, could be calculated quickly.

The problem comes in determining the variance of the stock's return. The formula calls for the variance between the purchase date of October 4 and the expiration date. Unfortunately, this represents the future, so the correct value for variance is not available. Instead, traders frequently estimate variance from past data, just as we calculated variance in an earlier chapter. In addition, some traders may use intuition to adjust their estimate. For example, if anticipation of an upcoming event is currently increasing the volatility of the stock, the trader might adjust her estimate of variance upward to reflect this. (This problem was severe right after the October 19, 1987, crash and the market crash in 2008. The stock market was quite risky in the aftermath, so estimates using precrash data were too low.)

The above discussion was intended merely to mention the difficulties in variance estimation, not to present a solution. For our purposes, we assume that a trader has come up with an estimate of variance.

5. The variance of PEC has been estimated to be .09 per year.

Using the above five parameters, we calculate the Black-Scholes value of the PEC option in three steps:

Step 1: *Calculate d_1 and d_2.* These values can be determined by a straightforward, albeit tedious, insertion of our parameters into the basic formula. We get:

$$d_1 = \left[\ln\left(\frac{S}{E}\right) + (R + \sigma^2/2)t\right]/\sqrt{\sigma^2 t}$$

$$= \left[\ln\left(\frac{50}{49}\right) + (.07 + .09/2) \times \frac{199}{365}\right]/\sqrt{.09 \times \frac{199}{365}}$$

$$= [.0202 + .0627]/.2215$$

$$= .3742$$

$$d_2 = d_1 - \sqrt{\sigma^2 t}$$

$$= .1527$$

FIGURE 17.10 Graph of Cumulative Probability

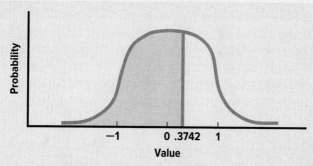

The shaded area represents cumulative probability. Because the probability is .6459 that a drawing from the standard normal distribution will be below .3742, we say that N(.3742) = .6459. That is, the cumulative probability of .3742 is .6459.

Step 2: *Calculate N(d_1) and N(d_2).* The values N(d_1) and N(d_2) can best be understood by examining Figure 17.10. The figure shows the normal distribution with an expected value of 0 and a standard deviation of 1. This is frequently called the **standardized normal distribution**. We mentioned in an earlier chapter that the probability that a drawing from this distribution will be between −1 and +1 (within one standard deviation of its mean, in other words) is 68.26 percent.

Now let us ask a different question. What is the probability that a drawing from the standardized normal distribution will be below a particular value? For example, the probability that a drawing will be below 0 is clearly 50 percent because the normal distribution is symmetric. Using statistical terminology, we say that the **cumulative probability** of 0 is 50 percent. Statisticians also say that N(0) = 50%. It turns out that:

$$N(d_1) = N(.3742) = .6459$$
$$N(d_2) = N(.1527) = .5607$$

The first value means that there is a 64.59 percent probability that a drawing from the standardized normal distribution will be below .3742. The second value means that there is a 56.07 percent probability that a drawing from the standardized normal distribution will be below .1527. More generally, N(d) is the notation that a drawing from the standardized normal distribution will be below d. In other words, N(d) is the cumulative probability of d. Note that d_1 and d_2 in our example are slightly above zero, so N(d_1) and N(d_2) are slightly greater than .50.

Perhaps the easiest way to determine N(d_1) and N(d_2) is from the Excel function NORMSDIST. In our example, NORMSDIST(.3742) and NORMSDIST(.1527) are .6459 and .5607, respectively.

We can also determine the cumulative probability from Table 17.3. For example, consider $d = .37$. This can be found in the table as .3 on the vertical and .07 on the horizontal. The value in the table for $d = .37$ is .1443. This value is not the cumulative probability of .37. One must first make an adjustment to determine cumulative probability. That is:

$$N(.37) = .50 + .1443 = .6443$$
$$N(-.37) = .50 - .1443 = .3557$$

Unfortunately, our table handles only two significant digits, whereas our value of .3742 has four significant digits. Hence, we must interpolate to find N(.3742). Because N(.37) = .6443 and N(.38) = .6480, the difference between the two values is .0037 (= .6480 − .6443). Because .3742 is 42 percent of the way between .37 and .38, we interpolate as:[10]

$$N(.3742) = .6443 + .42 \times .0037 = .6459$$

(Continued)

---

[10] This method is called *linear interpolation*. It is only one of a number of possible methods of interpolation.

TABLE 17.3 Cumulative Probabilities of the Standard Normal Distribution Function

d	.00	.01	.02	.03	.04	.05	.06	.07	.08	.09
.0	.0000	.0040	.0080	.0120	.0160	.0199	.0239	.0279	.0319	.0359
.1	.0398	.0438	.0478	.0517	.0557	.0596	.0636	.0675	.0714	.0753
.2	.0793	.0832	.0871	.0910	.0948	.0987	.1026	.1064	.1103	.1141
.3	.1179	.1217	.1255	.1293	.1331	.1368	.1406	.1443	.1480	.1517
.4	.1554	.1591	.1628	.1664	.1700	.1736	.1772	.1808	.1844	.1879
.5	.1915	.1950	.1985	.2019	.2054	.2088	.2123	.2157	.2190	.2224
.6	.2257	.2291	.2324	.2357	.2389	.2422	.2454	.2486	.2517	.2549
.7	.2580	.2611	.2642	.2673	.2704	.2734	.2764	.2794	.2823	.2852
.8	.2881	.2910	.2939	.2967	.2995	.3023	.3051	.3078	.3106	.3133
.9	.3159	.3186	.3212	.3238	.3264	.3289	.3315	.3340	.3365	.3389
1.0	.3413	.3438	.3461	.3485	.3508	.3531	.3554	.3577	.3599	.3621
1.1	.3643	.3665	.3686	.3708	.3729	.3749	.3770	.3790	.3810	.3830
1.2	.3849	.3869	.3888	.3907	.3925	.3944	.3962	.3980	.3997	.4015
1.3	.4032	.4049	.4066	.4082	.4099	.4115	.4131	.4147	.4162	.4177
1.4	.4192	.4207	.4222	.4236	.4251	.4265	.4279	.4292	.4306	.4319
1.5	.4332	.4345	.4357	.4370	.4382	.4394	.4406	.4418	.4429	.4441
1.6	.4452	.4463	.4474	.4484	.4495	.4505	.4515	.4525	.4535	.4545
1.7	.4554	.4564	.4573	.4582	.4591	.4599	.4608	.4616	.4625	.4633
1.8	.4641	.4649	.4656	.4664	.4671	.4678	.4686	.4693	.4699	.4706
1.9	.4713	.4719	.4726	.4732	.4738	.4744	.4750	.4756	.4761	.4767
2.0	.4773	.4778	.4783	.4788	.4793	.4798	.4803	.4808	.4812	.4817
2.1	.4821	.4826	.4830	.4834	.4838	.4842	.4846	.4850	.4854	.4857
2.2	.4861	.4866	.4830	.4871	.4875	.4878	.4881	.4884	.4887	.4890
2.3	.4893	.4896	.4898	.4901	.4904	.4906	.4909	.4911	.4913	.4916
2.4	.4918	.4920	.4922	.4925	.4927	.4929	.4931	.4932	.4934	.4936
2.5	.4938	.4940	.4941	.4943	.4945	.4946	.4948	.4949	.4951	.4952
2.6	.4953	.4955	.4956	.4957	.4959	.4960	.4961	.4962	.4963	.4964
2.7	.4965	.4966	.4967	.4968	.4969	.4970	.4971	.4972	.4973	.4974
2.8	.4974	.4975	.4976	.4977	.4977	.4978	.4979	.4979	.4980	.4981
2.9	.4981	.4982	.4982	.4982	.4984	.4984	.4985	.4985	.4986	.4986
3.0	.4987	.4987	.4987	.4988	.4988	.4989	.4989	.4989	.4990	.4990

$N(d)$ represents areas under the standard normal distribution function. Suppose that $d_1 = .24$. This table implies a cumulative probability of $.5000 + .0948 = .5948$. If d_1 is equal to .2452, we must estimate the probability by interpolating between $N(.25)$ and $N(.24)$.

Step 3: *Calculate C.* We have:

$$C = S \times [N(d_1)] - Ee^{-Rt} \times [N(d_2)]$$
$$= \$50 \times [N(d_1)] - \$49 \times \left[e^{-.07\times(199/365)}\right] \times N(d_2)$$
$$= (\$50 \times .6459) - (\$49 \times .9626 \times .5607)$$
$$= \$32.295 - 26.445$$
$$= \$5.85$$

The estimated price of $5.85 is greater than the $4 actual price, implying that the call option is under-priced. A trader believing in the Black-Scholes model would buy a call. Of course, the Black-Scholes model is fallible. Perhaps the disparity between the model's estimate and the market price reflects error in the trader's estimate of variance.

The previous example stressed the calculations involved in using the Black-Scholes formula. Is there any intuition behind the formula? Yes, and that intuition follows from the stock purchase and borrowing strategy in our binomial example. The Black-Scholes equation is:

$$C = S \times N(d_1) - Ee^{-Rt} N(d_2)$$

which is exactly analogous to Equation 17.2:

Value of call = Stock price × Delta − Amount borrowed

that we presented in the binomial example. It turns out that $N(d_1)$ is the delta in the Black-Scholes formula. $N(d_1)$ is .6459 in the previous example. In addition, $Ee^{-Rt}N(d_2)$ is the amount that an investor must borrow to duplicate a call. In the previous example, this value is $26.45 (= $49 × .9626 × .5607). Thus, the model tells us that we can duplicate the call of the preceding example by both:

Another good options calculator can be found at http://quantcalc.net/ Margrabe.html.

1. Buying .6459 share of stock.
2. Borrowing $26.45.

It is no exaggeration to say that the Black-Scholes formula is among the most important contributions in finance. It allows anyone to calculate the value of an option given a few parameters. The attraction of the formula is that four of the parameters are observable: the current price of stock, S; the exercise price, E; the interest rate, R; and the time to expiration date, t. Only one of the parameters must be estimated: the variance of return, σ^2.

To see how truly attractive this formula is, note what parameters are not needed. First, the investor's risk aversion does not affect the option value. The formula can be used by anyone, regardless of willingness to bear risk. Second, it does not depend on the expected return on the stock! Investors with different assessments of the stock's expected return will nevertheless agree on the call price. As in the two-state example, this is because the call depends on the stock price, and that price already balances investors' divergent views.

Implied Standard Deviations

Thus far, we have focused on using Black-Scholes to calculate option values, but there is another important use. Of the five factors that determine an option's value, four can be directly observed: the stock price, the strike price, the risk-free rate, and the life of the option. Only the standard deviation must be estimated.

The standard deviation we use in Black-Scholes is a prediction of what the standard deviation of the underlying asset's return is going to be over the life of the option. Often, we already know the value of an option because we observe its price in the financial markets. In such cases, we can use the value of the option, along with the four observable inputs, to back out a value for the standard deviation. When we solve for the standard deviation this way, the result is called the implied standard deviation or ISD (which some people pronounce as "iz-dee"), also known as the implied volatility. We should note that you cannot solve directly for the ISD, so we have to use trial and error.

If you want to find the ISD for the overall stock market, you can do so easily. The volatility index, or VIX, is the implied volatility on S&P 500 options for the next 30 days. It is often viewed as a "fear gauge" because a higher VIX implies that the market expects a higher volatility in the next 30 days. Historically, the VIX has been 15 to 20, although it climbed into the 80s during the market turmoil of 2008. To allow investors to trade on volatility, exchange-traded futures and options are available on the VIX index. Here is a question for you: Suppose you were to calculate the ISD of a VIX option. What would this number mean?

17.9 VALUATION OF EQUITY AND DEBT IN A LEVERAGED FIRM

In our earlier chapter about options, we pointed out that the equity in a leveraged corporation (a corporation that has borrowed money) can be viewed as a call option on the assets of the business. The reason is that when a debt comes due, the stockholders have the option to pay off the debt, and thereby acquire the assets free and clear, or else default. The act of paying off the debt amounts to exercising an in-the-money call option to acquire the assets. Defaulting amounts to letting an out-of-the-money call option expire. In this section, we expand on the idea of equity as a call option in several ways.

Valuing the Equity in a Leveraged Firm

Consider a firm that has a single zero coupon bond issue outstanding with a face value of $10 million. It matures in six years. The firm's assets have a current *market* value of $12 million. The volatility (standard deviation) of the return on the firm's assets is 40 percent per year. The continuously compounded risk-free rate is 6 percent. What is the current market value of the firm's equity? Its debt? What is its continuously compounded cost of debt?

What this case amounts to is that the stockholders have the right, but not the obligation, to pay $10 million in six years. If they do, they get the assets of the firm. If they don't, they default and get nothing. So, the equity in the firm is a call option with a strike price of $10 million.

Using the Black-Scholes formula in this case can be a little confusing because now we are solving for the stock price. The symbol C is the value of the stock, and the symbol S is the value of the firm's assets. With this in mind, we can value the equity of the firm by plugging the numbers into the Black-Scholes OPM with $S = \$12$ million and $E = \$10$ million. When we do so, we get $6.554 million as the value of the equity, with a delta of .852.

Now that we know the value of the equity, we can calculate the value of the debt using the standard balance sheet identity. The firm's assets are worth $12 million and the equity is worth $6.554 million, so the debt is worth $12 - 6.554 = \$5.446$ million.

To calculate the firm's continuously compounded cost of debt, we observe that the present value is $5.446 million and the future value in six years is the $10 million face value. We need to solve for a continuously compounded rate, R_D, as follows:

$$\$5.446 = \$10 \times e^{-R_D(6)}$$
$$.5446 = e^{-R_D(6)}$$
$$R_D = -1/6 \times \ln(.5446)$$
$$= .10$$

So, the firm's cost of debt is 10 percent, compared to a risk-free rate of 6 percent. The extra 4 percent is the default risk premium—that is, the extra compensation the bondholders demand because of the risk that the firm will default and bondholders will receive assets worth less than $10 million.

We also know that the delta of the option here is .852. How do we interpret this? In the context of valuing equity as a call option, the delta tells us what happens to the value of the equity when the value of the firm's assets changes. This is an important consideration. Suppose the firm undertakes a project with an NPV of $100,000, meaning that the value of the firm's assets will rise by $100,000. We now see that the value of the stock will rise (approximately) by only $.852 \times \$100,000 = \$85,162.$[11] Why?

The reason is that the firm has made its assets more valuable, which means default is less likely to occur in the future. As a result, the bonds gain value, too. How much do they gain? The answer is $100,000 - 85,162 = \$14,838$—in other words, whatever value the stockholders don't get.

---

[11] Delta is used to evaluate the effect of a small change in the underlying asset's value, so it might look like we shouldn't use it to evaluate a shift of $100,000. "Small" is relative, however, and $100,000 is small relative to the $12 million total asset value.

Equity as a Call Option

Consider a firm that has a single zero coupon bond issue outstanding with a face value of $40 million. It matures in five years. The risk-free rate is 4 percent. The firm's assets have a current market value of $35 million, and the firm's equity is worth $15 million. If the firm takes a project with a $200,000 NPV, approximately how much will the stockholders gain?

To answer this question, we need to know the delta, so we need to calculate $N(d_1)$. To do this, we need to know the relevant standard deviation, which we don't have. We do have the value of the option ($15 million), though, so we can calculate the ISD. If we use $C = \$15$ million, $S = \$35$ million, and $E = \$40$ million along with the risk-free rate of 4 percent and time to expiration of five years, we find that the ISD is 48.1 percent. With this value, the delta is .725; so, if $200,000 in value is created, the stockholders will get 72.5 percent of it, or about $145,000.

Options and the Valuation of Risky Bonds

Let's continue with the case we just examined of a firm with $12 million in assets and a six-year, zero coupon bond with a face value of $10 million. Given the other numbers, we showed that the bonds were worth $5.446 million. Suppose that the holders of these bonds wish to eliminate the risk of default. In other words, the holders want to turn their risky bonds into risk-free bonds. How can they do this?

The answer is that the bondholders can do a protective put along the lines we described earlier in the chapter. In this case, the bondholders want to make sure their bonds will never be worth less than the face value of $10 million, so the bondholders need to purchase a put option with a six-year life and a $10 million face value. The put option is an option to sell the assets of the firm for $10 million.

Remember that if the assets of the firm are worth more than $10 million in six years, the shareholders will pay the $10 million. If the assets are worth less than $10 million, the stockholders will default, and the bondholders will receive the assets of the firm. At that point, however, the bondholders will exercise their put and sell the assets for $10 million. Either way, the bondholders get $10 million.

What we have discovered is that a risk-free bond is the same thing as a combination of a risky bond and a put option on the assets of the firm, with a matching maturity and a strike price equal to the face value of the bond:

Value of risky bond + Put option = Value of risk-free bond [17.4]

In our example, the face value of the debt is $10 million, and the risk-free rate is 6 percent, so the value of the bonds if they were risk-free would be:

Value of risk-free bonds = $10 million $\times e^{-.06(6)}$
= $6.977 million

If we compare this to the value of the risky bonds, $5.446 million, we see that the put option is worth $6.977 - 5.446 = \$1.531$ million. Notice that the value of the risk-free bonds is also the present value of the strike price at the risk-free rate.

We can check that this put value is correct. We know the value of the underlying assets is $12 million, the value of the call option (the stock) is $6.554 million, and the present value of the strike price is $6.977 million. Using the PCP condition:

$P = \$6.977 + 6.554 - 12$
$= \$1.531$ million

which is exactly what we calculated.

We can restate our result here as follows:

$$\text{Value of risky bond} = \text{Value of risk-free bond} - \text{Put option} \qquad [17.5]$$
$$= E \times e^{-Rt} - P$$

This shows us that anything that increases the value of the put option *decreases* the value of the firm's bonds. With this in mind, we can use the PCP condition to bring together a lot of our discussion in this chapter (and this book!).

Using the PCP condition, we can write:

$$S = C + E \times e^{-Rt} - P$$

Remember that, in this case, the stock is the underlying asset. Now, if we are thinking of the stock in a firm as being a call option on the assets of the firm, here is how we would interpret this:

$$\text{Value of assets (S)} = \text{Value of stock (C)} + (E \times e^{-Rt} - P) \qquad [17.6]$$

where E, the strike price, is the face value of the firm's debt. Notice that, as we have just seen, the term in parentheses is the value of the firm's risky bonds, so this expression is really the balance sheet identity:

$$\text{Value of assets (S)} = \text{Value of stock (C)} + \text{Value of bonds } (E \times e^{-Rt} - P) \qquad [17.7]$$

The PCP condition and the balance sheet identity say the same thing, but recognizing the nature of the option-like features of the equity and debt in a leveraged firm leads to a far richer understanding of corporate finance. We illustrate some important examples in the next section.

17.10 OPTIONS AND CORPORATE DECISIONS: SOME APPLICATIONS

In this section, we explore the implications of options analysis in two key areas: capital budgeting and mergers. We start with mergers and show a very surprising result. We then go on to show that the net present value rule has some important wrinkles in a leveraged firm.

Mergers and Diversification

Elsewhere in our book, we discuss mergers and acquisitions. There we mention that diversification is frequently cited as a reason for two firms to merge. Is diversification a good reason to merge? It might seem so. After all, in an earlier chapter, we spent a lot of time explaining why diversification is very valuable for investors in their own portfolios because of the elimination of unsystematic risk.

To investigate this issue, let's consider two companies, Sunshine Swimwear (SS) and Polar Winterwear (PW). For obvious reasons, both companies have seasonal cash flows; in their respective off-seasons, both companies worry about cash flow. If the two companies were to merge, the combined company would have a much more stable cash flow. In other words, a merger would diversify away some of the seasonal variation and, in fact, would make bankruptcy much less likely.

Notice that the operations of the two firms are very different, so the proposed merger is a purely "financial" merger. This means there are no "synergies" or other value-creating possibilities except possible gains from risk reduction. Here is some premerger information:

	Sunshine Swimwear	Polar Winterwear
Market value of assets	$30 million	$10 million
Face value of pure discount debt	$12 million	$ 4 million
Debt maturity	3 years	3 years
Asset return standard deviation	50 percent	60 percent

The risk-free rate, continuously compounded, is 5 percent. Given this, we can calculate the following (check these for practice):

	Sunshine Swimwear	Polar Winterwear
Market value of equity	$20.424 million	$7.001 million
Market value of debt	$ 9.576 million	$2.999 million

If you check these, you may get slightly different answers if you use Table 17.3 (we used an options calculator).

After the merger, the combined firm's assets will be the sum of the premerger values, $30 + 10 = $40, because no value was created or destroyed. Similarly, the total face value of the debt is now $16 million. However, we will assume that the combined firm's asset return standard deviation is 40 percent. This is lower than for either of the two individual firms because of the diversification effect.

So, what is the impact of this merger? To find out, we compute the postmerger value of the equity. Based on our discussion, here is the relevant information:

	Combined Firm
Market value of assets	$40 million
Face value of pure discount debt	$16 million
Debt maturity	3 years
Asset return standard deviation	40 percent

Once again, we can calculate equity and debt values:

	Combined Firm
Market value of equity	$26.646 million
Market value of debt	$13.354 million

What we notice is that this merger is a terrible idea, at least for the stockholders! Before the merger, the stock in the two separate firms was worth a total of $20.424 + 7.001 = $27.425 million, compared to only $26.646 million postmerger, so the merger vaporized $27.425 − 26.646 = $.779 million, or almost $800,000, in equity.

Where did nearly $800,000 in equity go? It went to the bondholders. Their bonds were worth $9.576 + 2.999 = $12.575 million before the merger and $13.354 million after, a gain of exactly $.779 million. This merger neither created nor destroyed value, but it shifted it from the stockholders to the bondholders.

Our example shows that pure financial mergers are a bad idea, and it also shows why. The diversification works in the sense that it reduces the volatility of the firm's return on assets. This risk reduction benefits the bondholders by making default less likely. This is sometimes called the *coinsurance effect*. Essentially, by merging, the firms insure each other's bonds. The bonds are less risky, and they rise in value. If the bonds increase in value, and there is no net increase in asset values, then the equity must decrease in value. So, pure financial mergers are good for creditors, but not stockholders.

Another way to see this is that because the equity is a call option, a reduction in return variance on the underlying asset has to reduce its value. The reduction in value in the case of a purely financial merger has an interesting interpretation. The merger makes default (and bankruptcy) less likely to happen. That is obviously a good thing from a bondholder's perspective, but why is it a bad thing from a stockholder's perspective? The answer is simple: The right to go bankrupt is a valuable stockholder option. A purely financial merger reduces the value of that option.

Options and Capital Budgeting

In our earlier chapter about options, we discussed the many options embedded in capital budgeting decisions, including the option to wait, the option to abandon, and others. To add to these option-related issues, we now consider two additional issues. What we show is that, for a leveraged firm, the shareholders might prefer a lower NPV project to a higher one. We then show that they might even prefer a negative NPV project to a positive NPV project.

As usual, we will illustrate these points first with an example. Here is the basic background information for the firm:

Market value of assets	$20 million
Face value of pure discount debt	$40 million
Debt maturity	5 years
Asset return standard deviation	50 percent

The risk-free rate is 4 percent. As we have now done many times, we can calculate equity and debt values:

Market value of equity	$ 5.744
Market value of debt	$14.256

This firm has a fairly high degree of leverage; the debt-equity ratio based on market values is $14.256/$5.744 = 2.48$, or 248 percent. This is high, but not unheard of. Notice also that the option here is out of the money; as a result, the delta is .547.

The firm has two mutually exclusive investments under consideration. They both must be taken now or never, so there is no timing issue. The projects affect both the market value of the firm's assets and the firm's asset return standard deviation as follows:

	Project A	Project B
NPV (millions)	$ 4	$ 2
Market value of firm's assets ($20 + NPV)	$24	$22
Firm's asset return standard deviation	40 percent	60 percent

Which project is better? It is obvious that Project A has the higher NPV, but by now you are wary of the change in the firm's asset return standard deviation. One project reduces it; the other increases it. To see which project the stockholders like better, we have to go through our (by now) very familiar calculations:

	Project A	Project B
Market value of equity	$ 5.965	$ 8.751
Market value of debt	$18.035	$13.249

There is a dramatic difference between the two projects. Project A benefits both the stockholders and the bondholders, but most of the gain goes to the bondholders. Project B has a huge impact on the value of the equity, plus it reduces the value of the debt. Clearly, the stockholders prefer B.

What are the implications of our analysis? We have discovered two things. First, when the equity has a delta significantly smaller than 1.0, any value created will go partially to bondholders. Second, stockholders have a strong incentive to increase the variance of the return on the firm's assets. More specifically, stockholders will have a strong preference for variance-increasing projects as opposed to variance-decreasing ones, even if that means a lower NPV.

Let's do one final example. Here is a different set of numbers:

Market value of assets	$ 20 million
Face value of pure discount debt	$100 million
Debt maturity	5 years
Asset return standard deviation	50 percent

The risk-free rate is 4 percent, so the equity and debt values are:

Market value of equity	$ 2.012 million
Market value of debt	$17.988 million

Notice that the change from our previous example is that the face value of the debt is now $100 million, so the option is far out of the money. The delta is only .241, so most of any value created will go to the bondholders.

The firm has an investment under consideration that must be taken now or never. The project affects both the market value of the firm's assets and the firm's asset return standard deviation as follows:

Project NPV	−$ 1 million
Market value of firm's assets ($20 million + NPV)	$19 million
Firm's asset return standard deviation	70 percent

The project has a negative NPV, but it increases the standard deviation of the firm's return on assets. If the firm takes the project, here is the result:

Market value of equity	$ 4.834 million
Market value of debt	$14.166 million

This project more than doubles the value of the equity! Once again, what we are seeing is that stockholders have a strong incentive to increase volatility, particularly when the option is far out of the money. What is happening is that the shareholders have relatively little to lose because bankruptcy is the likely outcome. As a result, there is a strong incentive to go for a long shot, even if that long shot has a negative NPV. It's a bit like using your very last dollar on a lottery ticket. It's a bad investment, but there aren't a lot of other options!

SUMMARY AND CONCLUSIONS

This chapter serves as an introduction to options.

1. The most familiar options are puts and calls. These options give the holder the right to sell or buy shares of common stock at a given exercise price. American options can be exercised any time up to and including the expiration date. European options can be exercised only on the expiration date.

2. We showed that a strategy of buying a stock and buying a put is equivalent to a strategy of buying a call and buying a zero coupon bond. From this, the put-call parity relationship was established:

$$\underset{\text{stock}}{\text{Value of}} + \underset{\text{put}}{\text{Value of}} - \underset{\text{call}}{\text{Value of}} = \underset{\text{exercise price}}{\text{Present value of}}$$

3. The value of an option depends on five factors:

   a. The price of the underlying asset.

   b. The exercise price.

   c. The expiration date.

   d. The variability of the underlying asset's return.

   e. The interest rate on risk-free bonds.

   The Black-Scholes model can determine the intrinsic price of an option from these five factors.

4. The positions of stockholders and bondholders can be described in terms of calls and puts.

CONCEPT QUESTIONS

1. **Options** What is a call option? A put option? Under what circumstances might you want to buy each? Which one has greater potential profit? Why?

2. **Options** Complete the following sentence for each of these investors:

   a. A buyer of call options

   b. A buyer of put options

   c. A seller (writer) of call options

   d. A seller (writer) of put options

   "The (buyer/seller) of a (put/call) option (pays/receives) money for the (right/obligation) to (buy/sell) a specified asset at a fixed price for a fixed length of time."

3. **American and European Options** What is the difference between an American option and a European option?

4. **Intrinsic Value** What is the intrinsic value of a call option? Of a put option? How do we interpret this value?

5. **Option Pricing** You notice that shares of stock in the Patel Corporation are going for $50 per share. Call options with an exercise price of $35 per share are selling for $10. What's wrong here? Describe how you can take advantage of this mispricing if the option expires today.

6. **Options and Stock Risk** If the risk of a stock increases, what is likely to happen to the price of call options on the stock? To the price of put options? Why?

7. **Option Rise** True or false: The unsystematic risk of a share of stock is irrelevant in valuing the stock because it can be diversified away; therefore, it is also irrelevant for valuing a call option on the stock. Explain.

8. **Option Pricing** Suppose a certain stock currently sells for $30 per share. If a put option and a call option are available with $30 exercise prices, which do you think will sell for more, the put or the call? Explain.

9. **Option Price and Interest Rates** Suppose the interest rate on T-bills suddenly and unexpectedly rises. All other things being the same, what is the impact on call option values? On put option values?

10. **Contingent Liabilities** When you take out an ordinary student loan, it is often the case that whoever holds that loan is given a guarantee by the U.S. government, meaning that the government will make up any payments you skip. This is just one example of the many loan guarantees made by the U.S. government. Such guarantees don't show up in calculations of government spending or in official deficit figures. Why not? Should they show up?

11. **Options and Expiration Dates** What is the impact of lengthening the time to expiration on an option's value? Explain.

12. **Options and Stock Price Volatility** What is the impact of an increase in the volatility of the underlying stock's return on an option's value? Explain.

13. **Insurance as an Option** An insurance policy is considered analogous to an option. From the policyholder's point of view, what type of option is an insurance policy? Why?

14. **Equity as a Call Option** It is said that the equityholders of a levered firm can be thought of as holding a call option on the firm's assets. Explain what is meant by this statement.

15. **Option Valuation and NPV** You are CEO of Titan Industries and have just been awarded a large number of employee stock options. The company has two mutually exclusive projects available. The first project has a large NPV and will reduce the total risk of the company. The second project has a small NPV and will increase the total risk of the company. You have decided to accept the first project when you remember your employee stock options. How might this affect your decision?

16. **Put-Call Parity** You find a put and a call with the same exercise price and maturity. What do you know about the relative prices of the put and call? Prove your answer and provide an intuitive explanation.

17. **Put-Call Parity** A put and a call have the same maturity and strike price. If they have the same price, which one is in the money? Prove your answer and provide an intuitive explanation.

18. **Put-Call Parity** One thing put-call parity tells us is that given any three of a stock, a call, a put, and a T-bill, the fourth can be synthesized, or replicated, using the other three. For example, how can we replicate a share of stock using a call, a put, and a T-bill?

QUESTIONS AND PROBLEMS

1. **Understanding Option Quotes** Use the option quote information shown here to answer the questions that follow. The stock is currently selling for $77.

Basic
(Questions 1–14)

Option and NY Close	Expiration	Strike Price	Calls		Puts	
			Vol.	Last	Vol.	Last
RWJ						
	Mar	75	230	1.90	160	.80
	Apr	75	170	6.00	127	1.40
	Jul	75	139	8.05	43	3.90
	Oct	75	60	10.20	11	3.65

a. Are the call options in the money? What is the intrinsic value of an RWJ Corp. call option?

b. Are the put options in the money? What is the intrinsic value of an RWJ Corp. put option?

c. Two of the options are clearly mispriced. Which ones? At a minimum, what should the mispriced options sell for? Explain how you could profit from the mispricing in each case.

2. **Calculating Payoffs** Use the option quote information shown below to answer the questions that follow. The stock is currently selling for $93.

Option and NY Close	Expiration	Strike Price	Calls		Puts	
			Vol.	Last	Vol.	Last
Macrosoft						
	Feb	90	85	2.85	40	1.13
	Mar	90	61	5.25	22	4.05
	May	90	22	7.78	11	5.94
	Aug	90	3	10.20	3	9.12

a. Suppose you buy 10 contracts of the February 90 call option. How much will you pay, ignoring commissions?

b. In part (a), suppose that Macrosoft stock is selling for $96 per share on the expiration date. How much is your options' investment worth? What if the terminal stock price is $107? Explain.

c. Suppose you buy 10 contracts of the August 90 put option. What is your maximum gain? On the expiration date, Macrosoft is selling for $83 per share. How much is your options' investment worth? What is your net gain?

d. In part (c), suppose you sell 10 of the August 90 put contracts. What is your net gain or loss if Macrosoft is selling for $88 at expiration? For $98? What is the break-even price, that is, the terminal stock price that results in a zero profit?

3. **Put-Call Parity**   A stock is currently selling for $51 per share. A call option with an exercise price of $55 sells for $2.79 and expires in three months. If the risk-free rate of interest is 3.9 percent per year, compounded continuously, what is the price of a put option with the same exercise price?

4. **Put-Call Parity**   A put option that expires in five months with an exercise price of $60 sells for $3.19. The stock is currently priced at $57, and the risk-free rate is 4.1 percent per year, compounded continuously. What is the price of a call option with the same exercise price?

5. **Put-Call Parity**   A put option and a call option with an exercise price of $50 and three months to expiration sell for $3.87 and $4.89, respectively. If the risk-free rate is 2.7 percent per year, compounded continuously, what is the current stock price?

6. **Put-Call Parity**   A put option and a call option with an exercise price of $80 expire in four months and sell for $7.05 and $11.74, respectively. If the stock is currently priced at $84.17, what is the annual continuously compounded rate of interest?

7. **Black-Scholes**   What are the prices of a call option and a put option with the following characteristics?

$$
\begin{aligned}
\text{Stock price} &= \$79 \\
\text{Exercise price} &= \$75 \\
\text{Risk-free rate} &= 4\% \text{ per year, compounded continuously} \\
\text{Maturity} &= 3 \text{ months} \\
\text{Standard deviation} &= 47\% \text{ per year}
\end{aligned}
$$

8. **Black-Scholes**   What are the prices of a call option and a put option with the following characteristics?

$$
\begin{aligned}
\text{Stock price} &= \$87 \\
\text{Exercise price} &= \$90 \\
\text{Risk-free rate} &= 3\% \text{ per year, compounded continuously} \\
\text{Maturity} &= 2 \text{ months} \\
\text{Standard deviation} &= 49\% \text{ per year}
\end{aligned}
$$

9. **Delta**   What are the deltas of a call option and a put option with the following characteristics? What does the delta of the option tell you?

$$
\begin{aligned}
\text{Stock price} &= \$68 \\
\text{Exercise price} &= \$60 \\
\text{Risk-free rate} &= 5\% \text{ per year, compounded continuously} \\
\text{Maturity} &= 9 \text{ months} \\
\text{Standard deviation} &= 43\% \text{ per year}
\end{aligned}
$$

10. **Black-Scholes and Asset Value**   You own a lot in Key West, Florida, that is currently unused. Similar lots have recently sold for $1.1 million. Over the past five years, the price of land in the area has increased 7 percent per year, with an annual standard deviation of 25 percent. A buyer has recently approached you and wants an option to buy the land in the next 12 months for $1.3 million. The risk-free rate of interest is 5 percent per year, compounded continuously. How much should you charge for the option?

11. **Black-Scholes and Asset Value**   In the previous problem, suppose you wanted the option to sell the land to the buyer in one year. Assuming all the facts are the same, describe the transaction that would occur today. What is the price of the transaction today?

12. **Time Value of Options** You are given the following information concerning options on a particular stock:

$$
\begin{aligned}
\text{Stock price} &= \$68 \\
\text{Exercise price} &= \$70 \\
\text{Risk-free rate} &= 4\% \text{ per year, compounded continuously} \\
\text{Maturity} &= 6 \text{ months} \\
\text{Standard deviation} &= 54\% \text{ per year}
\end{aligned}
$$

a. What is the intrinsic value of the call option? Of the put option?

b. What is the time value of the call option? Of the put option?

c. Does the call or the put have the larger time value component? Would you expect this to be true in general?

13. **Risk-Neutral Valuation** A stock is currently priced at $66. The stock will either increase or decrease by 13 percent over the next year. There is a call option on the stock with a strike price of $60 and one year until expiration. If the risk-free rate is 6 percent, what is the risk-neutral value of the call option?

14. **Risk-Neutral Valuation** In the previous problem, assume the risk-free rate is only 4 percent. What is the risk-neutral value of the option now? What happens to the risk-neutral probabilities of a stock price increase and a stock price decrease?

15. **Black-Scholes** A call option matures in six months. The underlying stock price is $75, and the stock's return has a standard deviation of 20 percent per year. The risk-free rate is 4 percent per year, compounded continuously. If the exercise price is $0, what is the price of the call option?

Intermediate
(Questions 15–25)

16. **Black-Scholes** A call option has an exercise price of $70 and matures in six months. The current stock price is $74, and the risk-free rate is 4 percent per year, compounded continuously. What is the price of the call if the standard deviation of the stock is 0 percent per year?

17. **Black-Scholes** A stock is currently priced at $35. A call option with an expiration of one year has an exercise price of $40. The risk-free rate is 3 percent per year, compounded continuously, and the standard deviation of the stock's return is infinitely large. What is the price of the call option?

18. **Equity as an Option** Sunburn Sunscreen has a zero coupon bond issue outstanding with a face value of $12,000 that matures in one year. The current market value of the firm's assets is $13,800. The standard deviation of the return on the firm's assets is 32 percent per year, and the annual risk-free rate is 6 percent per year, compounded continuously. Based on the Black-Scholes model, what is the market value of the firm's equity and debt?

19. **Equity as an Option and NPV** Suppose the firm in the previous problem is considering two mutually exclusive investments. Project A has an NPV of $800, and Project B has an NPV of $1,300. As a result of taking Project A, the standard deviation of the return on the firm's assets will increase to 50 percent per year. If Project B is taken, the standard deviation will fall to 23 percent per year.

a. What is the value of the firm's equity and debt if Project A is undertaken? If Project B is undertaken?

b. Which project would the stockholders prefer? Can you reconcile your answer with the NPV rule?

c. Suppose the stockholders and bondholders are in fact the same group of investors. Would this affect your answer to (b)?

d. What does this problem suggest to you about stockholder incentives?

20. **Equity as an Option** Frostbite Thermalwear has a zero coupon bond issue outstanding with a face value of $20,000 that matures in one year. The current market value of the firm's assets is $21,900. The standard deviation of the return on the firm's assets is 34 percent per year, and the annual risk-free rate is 6 percent per year, compounded continuously. Based on the Black-Scholes model, what is the market value of the firm's equity and debt? What is the firm's continuously compounded cost of debt?

21. **Equity as an Option and NPV** A company has a single zero coupon bond outstanding that matures in 10 years and has a face value of $10 million. The current value of the company's assets is $8.8 million, and the standard deviation of the return on the firm's assets is 47 percent per year. The risk-free rate is 6 percent per year, compounded continuously.

    a. What is the current market value of the company's equity?

    b. What is the current market value of the company's debt?

    c. What is the company's continuously compounded cost of debt?

    d. The company has a new project available. The project has an NPV of $1.1 million. If the company undertakes the project, what will be the new market value of equity? Assume volatility is unchanged.

    e. Assuming the company undertakes the new project and does not borrow any additional funds, what is the new continuously compounded cost of debt? What is happening here?

22. **Two-State Option Pricing Model** Ken is interested in buying a European call option written on Southeastern Airlines, Inc., a non-dividend-paying common stock, with a strike price of $70 and one year until expiration. Currently, the company's stock sells for $74 per share. In one year, the stock will be trading at either $85 per share or $59 per share. Ken is able to borrow and lend at the risk-free EAR of 5.5 percent.

    a. What should the call option sell for today?

    b. If no options currently trade on the stock, is there a way to create a synthetic call option with identical payoffs to the call option described above? If there is, how would you do it?

    c. How much does the synthetic call option cost? Is this greater than, less than, or equal to what the actual call option costs? Does this make sense?

23. **Two-State Option Pricing Model** Rob wishes to buy a European put option on BioLabs, Inc., a non-dividend-paying common stock, with a strike price of $70 and six months until expiration. The company's common stock is currently selling for $66 per share, and will either rise to $79 or fall to $58 in six months. Rob can borrow and lend at the risk-free EAR of 4.3 percent.

    a. What should the put option sell for today?

    b. If no options currently trade on the stock, is there a way to create a synthetic put option with identical payoffs to the put option described above? If there is, how would you do it?

    c. How much does the synthetic put option cost? Is this greater than, less than, or equal to what the actual put option costs? Does this make sense?

24. **Two-State Option Pricing Model** Maverick Manufacturing, Inc., must purchase gold in three months for use in its operations. Maverick's management has estimated that if the price of gold were to rise above $1,390 per ounce, the firm would go bankrupt. The current price of gold is $1,330 per ounce. The firm's chief financial officer believes that the price of gold will either rise to $1,490 per ounce or fall to $1,140 per ounce over the next three months. Management wishes to eliminate any risk of the firm going bankrupt. The company can borrow and lend at the risk-free EAR of 4 percent.

    a. Should the company buy a call option or a put option on gold? In order to avoid bankruptcy, what strike price and time to expiration would the company like this option to have?

    b. How much should such an option sell for in the open market?

    c. If no options currently trade on gold, is there a way for the company to create a synthetic option with identical payoffs to the option described above? If there is, how would the firm do it?

    d. How much does the synthetic option cost? Is this greater than, less than, or equal to what the actual option costs? Does this make sense?

25. **Black-Scholes and Collar Cost** An investor is said to take a position in a "collar" if she buys the asset, buys an out-of-the-money put option on the asset, and sells an out-of-the-money call option on the asset. The two options should have the same time to expiration. Suppose Marie wishes to purchase a collar on Hollywood, Inc., a non-dividend-paying common stock, with six months until expiration. She would like the put to have a strike price of $55 and the call to have a strike price of $65. The current price of the stock is $59 per share. Marie can borrow and lend at the continuously compounded risk-free rate of 4.7 percent per year, and the annual standard deviation of the stock's return is 45 percent.

Use the Black-Scholes model to calculate the total cost of the collar that Marie is interested in buying. What is the effect of the collar?

26. **Mergers and Equity as an Option**   Suppose Sunburn Sunscreen (Problem 18) and Frostbite Thermalwear (Problem 20) have decided to merge. Because the two companies have seasonal sales, the combined firm's return on assets will have a standard deviation of 16 percent per year.

Challenge
(Questions 26–35)

   a.   What is the combined value of equity in the two existing companies? Value of debt?

   b.   What is the value of the new firm's equity? Value of debt?

   c.   What was the gain or loss for shareholders? For bondholders?

   d.   What happened to shareholder value here?

27. **Debt Valuation and Time to Maturity**   Eagle Industries has a zero coupon bond issue that matures in two years with a face value of $100,000. The current value of the company's assets is $81,000, and the standard deviation of the return on assets is 60 percent per year.

   a.   Assume the risk-free rate is 5 percent per year, compounded continuously. What is the value of a risk-free bond with the same face value and maturity as the company's bond?

   b.   What price would the bondholders have to pay for a put option on the firm's assets with a strike price equal to the face value of the debt?

   c.   Using the answers from (a) and (b), what is the value of the firm's debt? What is the continuously compounded yield on the company's debt?

   d.   From an examination of the value of the assets of the company, and the fact that the debt must be repaid in two years, it seems likely that the company will default on its debt. Management has approached bondholders and proposed a plan whereby the company would repay the same face value of debt, but the repayment would not occur for five years. What is the value of the debt under the proposed plan? What is the new continuously compounded yield on the debt? Explain why this occurs.

28. **Debt Valuation and Asset Variance**   Watson Corp. has a zero coupon bond that matures in five years with a face value of $85,000. The current value of the company's assets is $69,000, and the standard deviation of its return on assets is 50 percent per year. The risk-free rate is 6 percent per year, compounded continuously.

   a.   What is the value of a risk-free bond with the same face value and maturity as the current bond?

   b.   What is the value of a put option on the firm's assets with a strike price equal to the face value of the debt?

   c.   Using the answers from (a) and (b), what is the value of the firm's debt? What is the continuously compounded yield on the company's debt?

   d.   Assume the company can restructure its assets so that the standard deviation of its return on assets increases to 60 percent per year. What happens to the value of the debt? What is the new continuously compounded yield on the debt? Reconcile your answers in (c) and (d).

   e.   What happens to bondholders if the company restructures its assets? What happens to shareholders? How does this create an agency problem?

29. **Two-State Option Pricing and Corporate Valuation**   Masters Real Estate, Inc., a construction firm financed by both debt and equity, is undertaking a new project. If the project is successful, the value of the firm in one year will be $110 million, but if the project is a failure, the firm will only be worth $70 million. The company's current value is $96 million, a figure that includes the prospects for the new project. The company has outstanding zero coupon bonds due in one year with a face value of $89 million. Treasury bills that mature in one year yield an EAR of 7 percent. The company pays no dividends.

   a.   Use the two-state option pricing model to calculate the current value of the company's debt and equity.

   b.   Suppose the company has 300,000 shares of common stock outstanding. What is the price per share of the firm's equity?

c. Compare the market value of the company's debt to the present value of an equal amount of debt that is riskless with one year until maturity. Is the firm's debt worth more than, less than, or the same as the riskless debt? Does this make sense? What factors might cause these two values to be different?

d. Suppose that in place of the project described above, the company's management decides to undertake a project that is even more risky. The value of the firm will either increase to $125 million or decrease to $60 million by the end of the year. Surprisingly, management concludes that the value of the company today will remain at exactly $96 million if this risky project is substituted for the less risky one. Use the two-state option pricing model to determine the value of the firm's debt and equity if the firm plans on undertaking this new project. What is the stock price if the firm undertakes this project? Which project do bondholders prefer?

30. Black-Scholes and Dividends   In addition to the five factors discussed in the chapter, dividends also affect the price of an option. The Black-Scholes option pricing model with dividends is:

$$C = S \times e^{-dt} \times N(d_1) - E \times e^{-Rt} \times N(d_2)$$
$$d_1 = [\ln(S/E) + (R - d + \sigma^2/2) \times t]/(\sigma \times \sqrt{t})$$
$$d_2 = d_1 - \sigma \times \sqrt{t}$$

All of the variables are the same as the Black-Scholes model without dividends except for the variable d, which is the continuously compounded dividend yield on the stock.

a. What effect do you think the dividend yield will have on the price of a call option? Explain.

b. A stock is currently priced at $96 per share, the standard deviation of its return is 50 percent per year, and the risk-free rate is 5 percent per year, compounded continuously. What is the price of a call option with a strike price of $95 and a maturity of 4 months if the stock has a dividend yield of 2 percent per year?

31. Put-Call Parity and Dividends   The put-call parity condition is altered when dividends are paid. The dividend-adjusted put-call parity formula is:

$$S \times e^{-dt} + P = E \times e^{-Rt} + C$$

where d is again the continuously compounded dividend yield.

a. What effect do you think the dividend yield will have on the price of a put option? Explain.

b. From the previous question, what is the price of a put option with the same strike price and time to expiration as the call option?

32. Put Delta   The delta for a put option is $N(d_1) - 1$. Is this the same thing as $-N(-d_1)$? (*Hint:* Yes, but why?)

33. Black-Scholes Put Pricing Model   Use the Black-Scholes model for pricing a call, put-call parity, and the previous question to show that the Black-Scholes model for directly pricing a put can be written as:

$$P = E \times e^{-Rt} \times N(-d_2) - S \times N(-d_1)$$

34. Black-Scholes   A stock is currently priced at $50. The stock will never pay a dividend. The risk-free rate is 12 percent per year, compounded continuously, and the standard deviation of the stock's return is 60 percent. A European call option on the stock has a strike price of $100 and no expiration date, meaning that it has an infinite life. Based on Black-Scholes, what is the value of the call option? Do you see a paradox here? Do you see a way out of the paradox?

35. Delta   You purchase one call and sell one put with the same strike price and expiration date. What is the delta of your portfolio? Why?

WHAT'S ON THE WEB?

1. **Black-Scholes**   Go to www.option-price.com. Find the stock option calculator. The call option and put option on a stock expire in 30 days. The strike price is $50 and the current stock price is $51.20. The standard deviation of the stock is 60 percent per year, and the risk-free rate is 4.8 percent per year, compounded continuously. What are the prices of the call and the put? What are the deltas?

2. **Black-Scholes**   Go to www.cboe.com, and find the options calculator. A stock is currently priced at $93 per share, and its return has a standard deviation of 48 percent per year. Options are available with an exercise price of $90, and the risk-free rate is 5.2 percent per year, compounded continuously. What are the prices of the call and the put that expire next month? What are the deltas? How do your answers change for an exercise price of $95?

3. **Black-Scholes with Dividends**   Recalculate the first two problems assuming a dividend yield of 2 percent per year. How does this change your answers? Can you explain why dividends have the effect they do?

EXCEL MASTER IT! PROBLEM

In addition to spinners and scroll bars, there are numerous other controls in Excel. For this assignment, you need to build a Black-Scholes option pricing model spreadsheet using several of these controls.

ExcelMaster
coverage online

www.mhhe.com/RossCore6e

a. Buttons are always used in sets. Using buttons permits you to check an option, and the spreadsheet will use that input. In this case, you need to create two buttons, one for a call option and one for a put option. When using the spreadsheet, if you click the call option, the spreadsheet will calculate a call price, and if you click the put option, it will calculate the price of a put. Notice on the next spreadsheet that cell B20 is empty. This cell should change names. The names should be "Call option price" and "Put option price." In the price cell, only the price for the call option or put option is displayed depending on which button is selected. For the button, use the button under Form Controls.

b. A combo box uses a drop-down menu with values entered by the spreadsheet developer. One advantage of a combo box is that the user can either choose values from the drop-down menu or enter another value. In this case, you want to create one combo box for the stock price and a separate combo box for the strike price. On the right-hand side of the spreadsheet, we have values for the drop-down menu. These values should be created in an array before the combo box is inserted. To create an ActiveX combo box, go to Developer, Insert, and select Combo Box from the ActiveX Controls menu. After you draw the combo box, right-click on the box, select Properties, and enter the LinkedCell, which is the cell where you want the output displayed, and the ListFillRange, which is the range that contains the list of values you want displayed in the drop-down menu.

c. In contrast to a combo box, a list box permits the user to scroll through a list of possible values that are predetermined by the spreadsheet developer. No other values can be entered. You need to create a list box for the interest rate using the interest rate array on the right-hand side of the spreadsheet. To insert a list box, go to Developer, Insert, and choose the List Box from the ActiveX Controls. To enter the linked cell and array of values, right-click on List Box and select Properties from the menu. We should note here that to edit both the combo box and list box you will need to make sure that Design Mode is checked on the Developer tab.

EXOTIC CUISINES EMPLOYEE STOCK OPTIONS

As a newly minted MBA, you've taken a management position with Exotic Cuisines, Inc., a restaurant chain that just went public last year. The company's restaurants specialize in exotic main dishes, using ingredients such as alligator, buffalo, and ostrich. A concern you had going in was that the restaurant business is very risky. However, after some due diligence, you discovered a common misperception about the restaurant industry. It is widely thought that 90 percent of new restaurants close within three years; however, recent evidence suggests the failure rate is closer to 60 percent over three years. So, it is a risky business, although not as risky as you originally thought.

During your interview process, one of the benefits mentioned was employee stock options. Upon signing your employment contract, you received options with a strike price of $50 for 10,000 shares of company stock. As is fairly common, your stock options have a three-year vesting period and a 10-year expiration, meaning that you cannot exercise the options for a period of three years, and you lose them if you leave before they vest. After the three-year vesting period, you can exercise the options at any time. Thus, the employee stock options are European (and subject to forfeit) for the first three years and American afterward. Of course, you cannot sell the options, nor can you enter into any sort of hedging agreement. If you leave the company after the options vest, you must exercise within 90 days or forfeit.

Exotic Cuisines stock is currently trading at $21.32 per share, a slight increase from the initial offering price last year. There are no market-traded options on the company's stock. Because the company has only been traded for about a year, you are reluctant to use the historical returns to estimate the standard deviation of the stock's return. However, you have estimated that the average annual standard deviation for restaurant company stocks is about 55 percent. Because Exotic Cuisines is a newer restaurant chain, you decide to use a 65 percent standard deviation in your calculations. The company is relatively young, and you expect that all earnings will be reinvested back into the company for the near future. Therefore, you expect no dividends will be paid for at least the next 10 years. A three-year Treasury note currently has a yield of 1.5 percent, and a 10-year Treasury note has a yield of 2.6 percent.

1. You're trying to value your options. What minimum value would you assign? What is the maximum value you would assign?

2. Suppose that, in three years, the company's stock is trading at $60. At that time, should you keep the options or exercise them immediately? What are some of the important determinants in making such a decision?

3. Your options, like most employee stock options, are not transferable or tradeable. Does this have a significant effect on the value of the options? Why?

4. Why do you suppose employee stock options usually have a vesting provision? Why must they be exercised shortly after you depart the company even after they vest?

5. A controversial practice with employee stock options is repricing. What happens is that a company experiences a stock price decrease, which leaves employee stock options far out of the money or "underwater." In such cases, many companies have "repriced" or "restruck" the options, meaning that the company leaves the original terms of the option intact but lowers the strike price. Proponents of repricing argue that because the option is very unlikely to end in the money due to the stock price decline, the motivational force is lost. Opponents argue that repricing is in essence a reward for failure. How do you evaluate this argument? How does the possibility of repricing affect the value of an employee stock option at the time it is granted?

6. As we have seen, much of the volatility in a company's stock price is due to systematic or marketwide risks. Such risks are beyond the control of a company and its employees. What are the implications for employee stock options? In light of your answer, can you recommend an improvement over traditional employee stock options?

Short-Term Finance and Planning

Most often, when news breaks about a firm's cash position, it's because the company is running low on cash. However, that wasn't the case for many companies in early 2019. Automobile company Ford, for example, had a cash balance of $23 billion, or about $6 per share. What's so striking about that amount is the stock was trading for only about $8.50 per share, so Ford's cash per share was only a little less than its stock price, normally not a good sign. Other companies also had large amounts of cash. For example, Microsoft had a cash balance of about $133.7 billion. But no company came close to investment bank Goldman Sachs, with a cash hoard of $469 billion. In examining these numbers, it is clear that these companies certainly had ample cash reserves; in fact, the word *enormous* might be more appropriate. Why would these firms hold such large quantities of cash? To find out, this chapter explores short-term finance and examines optimal investments in current assets such as cash.

Please visit us at corecorporatefinance.blogspot.com for the latest developments in the world of corporate finance.

To this point, we have described many of the decisions of long-term finance, such as those of capital budgeting, dividend policy, and financial structure. In this chapter, we begin to discuss short-term finance. Short-term finance is primarily concerned with the analysis of decisions that affect current assets and current liabilities.

Frequently, the term *net working capital* is associated with short-term financial decision making. As we have described in previous chapters, net working capital is the difference between current assets and current liabilities. Often, short-term financial management is called *working capital management.* These terms mean the same thing.

There is no universally accepted definition of short-term finance. The most important difference between short-term and long-term finance is in the timing of cash flows. Short-term financial decisions typically involve cash inflows and outflows that occur within a year or less. For example, short-term financial decisions are involved when a firm orders raw materials, pays in cash, and anticipates selling finished goods in one year for cash. In contrast, long-term financial decisions are involved when a firm purchases a special machine that will reduce operating costs over, say, the next five years.

> Interested in a career in short-term finance? Visit the Association for Financial Professionals (AFP) website at www.afponline.org.

What types of questions fall under the general heading of short-term finance? To name just a very few:

1. What is a reasonable level of cash to keep on hand (in a bank) to pay bills?
2. How much should the firm borrow in the short term?
3. How much credit should be extended to customers?

This chapter introduces the basic elements of short-term financial decisions. First, we discuss the short-term operating activities of the firm. We then identify some alternative short-term financial policies. Finally, we outline the basic elements in a short-term financial plan and describe short-term financing instruments.

18.1 TRACING CASH AND NET WORKING CAPITAL

In this section, we examine the components of cash and net working capital as they change from one year to the next. We have already discussed various aspects of this subject in Chapters 2 and 3. We briefly review some of that discussion as it relates to short-term financing decisions. Our goal is to describe the short-term operating activities of the firm and their impact on cash and working capital.

To begin, recall that current assets are cash and other assets that are expected to convert to cash within the year. Current assets are presented on the balance sheet in order of their accounting liquidity—the ease with which they can be converted to cash and the time it takes to convert them. Four of the most important items found in the current asset section of a balance sheet are cash and cash equivalents, marketable securities, accounts receivable, and inventories.

Analogous to their investment in current assets, firms use several kinds of short-term debt, called current liabilities. Current liabilities are obligations that are expected to require cash payment within one year (or within the operating period if it is longer than one year). Three major items found as current liabilities are accounts payable, expenses payable (including accrued wages and taxes), and notes payable.

Because we want to focus on changes in cash, we start off by defining cash in terms of the other elements of the balance sheet. This lets us isolate the cash account and explore the impact on cash from the firm's operating and financing decisions. The basic balance sheet identity can be written as:

$$\text{Net working capital} + \text{Fixed assets} = \text{Long-term debt} + \text{Equity} \qquad \text{[18.1]}$$

Net working capital is cash plus other current assets, less current liabilities, that is:

$$\text{Net working capital} = \text{Cash} + \text{Other current assets} - \text{Current liabilities} \qquad \text{[18.2]}$$

If we substitute this for net working capital in the basic balance sheet identity and rearrange things a bit, we see that cash is:

$$\text{Cash} = \text{Long-term debt} + \text{Equity} + \text{Current liabilities}$$
$$- \text{Current assets other than cash} - \text{Fixed assets} \qquad \text{[18.3]}$$

This tells us in general terms that some activities naturally increase cash and some activities decrease it. We can list these various activities, along with an example of each, as follows:

ACTIVITIES THAT INCREASE CASH

Increasing long-term debt (borrowing over the long term)

Increasing equity (selling some stock)

Increasing current liabilities (getting a 90-day loan)

Decreasing current assets other than cash (selling some inventory for cash)

Decreasing fixed assets (selling some property)

ACTIVITIES THAT DECREASE CASH

Decreasing long-term debt (paying off a long-term debt)

Decreasing equity (repurchasing some stock)

Decreasing current liabilities (paying off a 90-day loan)

Increasing current assets other than cash (buying some inventory for cash)

Increasing fixed assets (buying some property)

Notice that our two lists are exact opposites. For example, floating a long-term bond issue increases cash (at least until the money is spent). Paying off a long-term bond issue decreases cash.

Activities that increase cash are called *sources of cash*. Those activities that decrease cash are called *uses of cash*. Looking back at our list, we see that sources of cash always involve increasing a liability (or equity) account or decreasing an asset account. This makes sense because increasing a liability means that we have raised money by borrowing it or by selling an ownership interest in the firm. A decrease in an asset means that we have sold or otherwise liquidated an asset. In either case, there is a cash inflow.

Uses of cash are just the reverse. A use of cash involves decreasing a liability by paying it off, perhaps, or increasing assets by purchasing something. Both of these activities require that the firm spend some cash.

Sources and Uses

Here is a quick check of your understanding of sources and uses of cash. If accounts payable go up by $100, does this indicate a source or a use? What if accounts receivable go up by $100?

Accounts payable are what we owe our suppliers. This is a short-term debt. If it rises by $100, we have effectively borrowed the money, which is a source of cash. Receivables are what our customers owe to us, so an increase of $100 in accounts receivable means that we have loaned the money; this is a use of cash.

18.2 THE OPERATING CYCLE AND THE CASH CYCLE

The primary concern in short-term finance is the firm's short-run operating and financing activities. For a typical manufacturing firm, these short-run activities might consist of the following sequence of events and decisions:

Event	Decision
1. Buying raw materials	1. How much inventory to order
2. Paying cash	2. Whether to borrow or draw down cash balances
3. Manufacturing the product	3. What choice of production technology to use
4. Selling the product	4. Whether credit should be extended to a particular customer
5. Collecting cash	5. How to collect

These activities create patterns of cash inflows and cash outflows. These cash flows are both unsynchronized and uncertain. They are unsynchronized because, for example, the payment of cash for raw materials does not happen at the same time as the receipt of cash from selling the product. They are uncertain because future sales and costs cannot be precisely predicted.

Defining the Operating and Cash Cycles

We can start with a simple case. One day, call it Day 0, we purchase $1,000 worth of inventory on credit. We pay the bill 30 days later, and after 30 more days, someone buys the

$1,000 in inventory for $1,400. Our buyer does not actually pay for another 45 days. We can summarize these events chronologically as follows:

Day	Activity	Cash Effect
0	Acquire inventory	None
30	Pay for inventory	−$1,000
60	Sell inventory on credit	None
105	Collect on sale	+$1,400

THE OPERATING CYCLE   There are several things to notice in our example. First, the entire cycle, from the time we acquire some inventory to the time we collect the cash, takes 105 days. This is called the operating cycle.

As we illustrate, the operating cycle is the length of time it takes to acquire inventory, sell it, and collect for it. This cycle has two distinct components. The first part is the time it takes to acquire and sell the inventory. This period, a 60-day span in our example, is called the inventory period. The second part is the time it takes to collect on the sale, 45 days in our example. This is called the accounts receivable period.

Based on our definitions, the operating cycle is the sum of the inventory and accounts receivable periods:

$$\text{Operating cycle} = \text{Inventory period} + \text{Accounts receivable period} \qquad [18.4]$$
$$105 \text{ days} = 60 \text{ days} + 45 \text{ days}$$

What the operating cycle describes is how a product moves through the current asset accounts. The product begins life as inventory, it is converted to a receivable when it is sold, and it is finally converted to cash when we collect from the sale. Notice that, at each step, the asset is moving closer to cash.

THE CASH CYCLE   The second thing to notice is that the cash flows and other events that occur are not synchronized. For example, we don't actually pay for the inventory until 30 days after we acquire it. The intervening 30-day period is called the accounts payable period. Next, we spend cash on Day 30, but we don't collect until Day 105. Somehow, we have to arrange to finance the $1,000 for $105 - 30 = 75$ days. This period is called the cash cycle.

The cash cycle, therefore, is the number of days that pass before we collect the cash from a sale, measured from when we actually pay for the inventory. Notice that, based on our definitions, the cash cycle is the difference between the operating cycle and the accounts payable period:

$$\text{Cash cycle} = \text{Operating cycle} - \text{Accounts payable period} \qquad [18.5]$$
$$75 \text{ days} = 105 \text{ days} - 30 \text{ days}$$

Figure 18.1 depicts the short-term operating activities and cash flows for a typical manufacturing firm by way of a cash flow time line, which presents the operating cycle and the cash cycle in graphical form. In Figure 18.1, the need for short-term financial management is suggested by the gap between the cash inflows and the cash outflows. This is related to the lengths of the operating cycle and the accounts payable period.

The gap between short-term inflows and outflows can be filled either by borrowing or by holding a liquidity reserve in the form of cash or marketable securities. Alternatively, the gap can be shortened by changing the inventory, receivable, and payable periods. These are all managerial options that we discuss in the following sections.

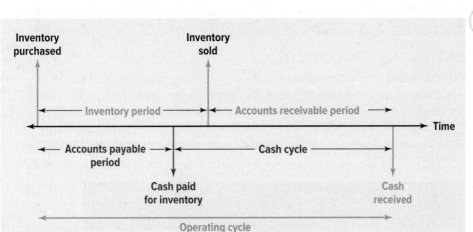

The operating cycle is the time period from inventory purchase until the receipt of cash. (The operating cycle may not include the time from placement of the order until arrival of the stock.) The cash cycle is the time period from when cash is paid out to when cash is received.

Internet-based bookseller and retailer Amazon.com provides an interesting example of the importance of managing the cash cycle. In early 2019, the market value of Amazon was higher than (in fact more than 1,700 times as much as) that of Barnes & Noble, king of the brick-and-mortar bookstores.

How could Amazon be worth so much more? There are multiple reasons, but short-term management is one factor. During 2018, Amazon turned over its inventory about 8 times per year, 3 times faster than Barnes & Noble, so its inventory period is dramatically shorter. Even more striking, Amazon charges a customer's credit card when it ships a product, and it usually gets paid by the credit card firm within a day. This means Amazon has a *negative* cash cycle! In fact, during 2018, Amazon's cash cycle was negative 29 days. Every sale therefore generates a cash inflow that can be put to work immediately. Our nearby *Finance Matters* box discusses the cash cycle and operating cycle for several industries, as well as for some specific companies.

The Operating Cycle and the Firm's Organization Chart

Before we examine the operating and cash cycles in greater detail, it is useful for us to take a look at the people involved in managing a firm's current assets and liabilities. As Table 18.1 illustrates, short-term financial management in a large corporation involves a number of different financial and nonfinancial managers. Examining Table 18.1, we see that selling on credit involves at least three different entities: the credit manager, the marketing manager, and the controller. Of these three, only two are responsible to the vice president of finance (the marketing function is usually associated with the vice president of marketing). Thus, there is the potential for conflict, particularly if different managers concentrate on only part of the picture. For example, if marketing is trying to land a new account, it may seek more liberal credit terms as an inducement. However, this may increase the firm's investment in receivables or its exposure to bad-debt risk, and conflict can result.

Calculating the Operating and Cash Cycles

In our example, the lengths of time that made up the different periods were obvious. If all we have is financial statement information, we will have to do a little more work. We illustrate these calculations next.

FINANCE MATTERS

A LOOK AT OPERATING AND CASH CYCLES

In 2018, *CFO* magazine and The Hackett Group published their annual survey of working capital for various industries. The results of this survey highlight the marked differences in cash and operating cycles across industries. The table below shows four different industries and the median operating and cash cycles for each. Of these, the airline industry has the lowest operating and cash cycles. Looking at the components, it is surprising that the receivables period is as long as 14 days for the airline industry (most customers prepay for flights). For example, the receivables period for Delta is one of the longest in the industry at 21 days.

	Receivables Period (Days)	Inventory Period (Days)	Operating Cycle (Days)	Payables Period (Days)	Cash Cycle (Days)
Aerospace & defense	67	83	150	38	112
Homebuilding	2	365	367	21	346
Airlines	14	10	24	24	0
Internet software	60	0	60	48	12

Compared to the airline industry, the homebuilding industry has a much longer operating cycle. Its long inventory period is the major cause. However, this does not necessarily mean the homebuilding industry is less efficient. It takes a while to build a home, sell it, and then collect. In addition, companies often purchase land in tracts, so the land may be carried in inventory until a house can be built and sold.

We've seen that operating and cash cycles can vary quite a bit across industries, but these cycles also can be different for companies within the same industry. Below you will find the operating and cash cycles for selected companies within the beverage industry. As you can see, there are major differences. Molson Brewing and Pepsico have the best operating and cash cycles in the industry, while Coca-Cola and Monster have the worst operating and cash cycles.

	Receivables Period (Days)	Inventory Period (Days)	Operating Cycle (Days)	Payables Period (Days)	Cash Cycle (Days)
Molson Brewing	24	38	62	99	−37
Pepsico	34	41	75	93	−18
Coca-Cola	38	80	118	69	49
Monster Beverage	49	79	128	74	54

By examining all parts of the cash cycle, you can see where a company is performing well or poorly, as the case may be. As we have noted, Molson and Pepsico have shorter operating cycles. When we dig deeper, the reason becomes apparent: Although both companies have a shorter receivables period, the inventory period is one-half as long as that for Coca-Cola and Monster Beverage. Molson and Pepsico also have a payables period of about three months, which results in a negative cash conversion cycle for each.

While Pepsico and Coca-Cola are direct competitors, Molson may not be in the same industry, so whether Molson is comparable to Pepsico and Coca-Cola is not quite as clear. The lesson here is that when you look at the operating and cash cycles, consider that each is really a financial ratio. As with any financial ratio, firm and industry characteristics will have an effect, so take care in the interpretation and also take care to choose genuine peer firms for any comparative analyses.

TABLE 18.1

Managers Who Deal with
Short-Term Financial
Problems

Title of Manager	Duties Related to Short-Term Financial Management	Assets/Liabilities Influenced
Cash manager	Collection, concentration, disbursement; short-term investments; short-term borrowing; banking relations	Cash, marketable securities, short-term loans
Credit manager	Monitoring and control of accounts receivable; credit policy decisions	Accounts receivable
Marketing manager	Credit policy decisions	Accounts receivable
Purchasing manager	Decisions on purchases, suppliers; may negotiate payment terms	Inventory, accounts payable
Production manager	Setting of production schedules and materials requirements	Inventory, accounts payable
Payables manager	Decisions on payment policies and on whether to take discounts	Accounts payable
Controller	Accounting information on cash flows; reconciliation of accounts payable; application of payments to accounts receivable	Accounts receivable, accounts payable

To begin, we need to determine various things such as how long it takes, on average, to sell inventory and how long it takes, on average, to collect. We start by gathering some balance sheet information such as the following (in thousands):

Item	Beginning	Ending	Average
Inventory	$2,000	$3,000	$2,500
Accounts receivable	1,600	2,000	1,800
Accounts payable	750	1,000	875

Also, from the most recent income statement, we might have the following figures (in thousands):

Net sales	$11,500
Cost of goods sold	8,200

We now need to calculate some financial ratios. We discussed these in some detail in Chapter 3; here, we just define and use them as needed.

THE OPERATING CYCLE   First of all, we need the inventory period. We spent $8.2 million on inventory (our cost of goods sold). Our average inventory was $2.5 million. We thus turned our inventory over $8.2/$2.5 = 3.28 times during the year:[1]

$$\text{Inventory turnover} = \frac{\text{Cost of goods sold}}{\text{Average inventory}}$$

$$= \frac{\$8.2 \text{ million}}{\$2.5 \text{ million}} = 3.28 \text{ times}$$

Loosely speaking, this tells us that we bought and sold off our inventory 3.28 times during the year. This means that, on average, we held our inventory for:

$$\text{Inventory period} = \frac{365 \text{ days}}{\text{Inventory turnover}}$$

$$= \frac{365}{3.28} = 111.3 \text{ days}$$

---

[1] Notice that in calculating inventory turnover here, we use the average inventory instead of using the ending inventory as we did in Chapter 3. Both approaches are used in the real world. To gain some practice using average figures, we will stick with this approach in calculating various ratios throughout this chapter.

So, the inventory period is about 111 days. On average, in other words, inventory sat for about 111 days before it was sold.[2]

Similarly, receivables averaged $1.8 million, and sales were $11.5 million. Assuming that all sales were credit sales, the receivables turnover is:[3]

$$\text{Receivables turnover} = \frac{\text{Credit sales}}{\text{Average accounts receivable}}$$

$$= \frac{\$11.5 \text{ million}}{\$1.8 \text{ million}} = 6.39 \text{ times}$$

If we turn over our receivables 6.39 times, then the receivables period is:

$$\text{Receivables period} = \frac{365 \text{ days}}{\text{Receivables turnover}}$$

$$= \frac{365}{6.39} = 57.1 \text{ days}$$

The receivables period is also called the *days' sales in receivables* or the *average collection period*. Whatever it is called, it tells us that our customers took an average of 57 days to pay.

The operating cycle is the sum of the inventory and receivables periods:

$$\text{Operating cycle} = \text{Inventory period} + \text{Accounts receivable period}$$

$$= 111 \text{ days} + 57 \text{ days} = 168 \text{ days}$$

This tells us that, on average, 168 days elapse between the time we acquire inventory and, having sold it, collect for the sale.

THE CASH CYCLE   We now need the payables period. From the information given earlier, we know that average payables were $875,000 and cost of goods sold was $8.2 million. Our payables turnover is:

$$\text{Payables turnover} = \frac{\text{Cost of goods sold}}{\text{Average payables}}$$

$$= \frac{\$8.2 \text{ million}}{\$.875 \text{ million}} = 9.37 \text{ times}$$

The payables period is:

$$\text{Payables period} = \frac{365 \text{ days}}{\text{Payables turnover}}$$

$$= \frac{365}{9.37} = 38.9 \text{ days}$$

Thus, we took an average of 39 days to pay our bills.

Finally, the cash cycle is the difference between the operating cycle and the payables period:

$$\text{Cash cycle} = \text{Operating cycle} - \text{Accounts payables period}$$

$$= 168 \text{ days} - 39 \text{ days} = 129 \text{ days}$$

So, on average, there is a 129-day delay between the time we pay for merchandise and the time we collect on the sale.

---

[2] This measure is conceptually identical to the days' sales in inventory figure we discussed in Chapter 3.

[3] If less than 100 percent of our sales were credit sales, then we would need a little more information, namely, credit sales for the year. See Chapter 3 for more discussion of this measure.

EXAMPLE 18.2

The Operating and Cash Cycles

You have collected the following information for the Slowpay Company.

Item	Beginning	Ending
Inventory	$5,000	$7,000
Accounts receivable	1,600	2,400
Accounts payable	2,700	4,800

Credit sales for the year just ended were $50,000, and cost of goods sold was $30,000. How long does it take Slowpay to collect on its receivables? How long does merchandise stay around before it is sold? How long does Slowpay take to pay its bills?

We can first calculate the three turnover ratios:

Inventory turnover = $30,000/$6,000 = 5 times
Receivables turnover = $50,000/$2,000 = 25 times
Payables turnover = $30,000/$3,750 = 8 times

We use these to get the various periods:

Inventory period = 365/5 = 73 days
Receivables period = 365/25 = 14.6 days
Payables period = 365/8 = 45.6 days

All told, Slowpay collects on a sale in 14.6 days, inventory sits around for 73 days, and bills get paid after about 46 days. The operating cycle here is the sum of the inventory and receivables periods: 73 + 14.6 = 87.6 days. The cash cycle is the difference between the operating cycle and the payables period: 87.6 − 45.6 = 42 days.

Interpreting the Cash Cycle

Our examples show that the cash cycle depends on the inventory, receivables, and payables periods. The cash cycle increases as the inventory and receivables periods get longer. It decreases if the company is able to defer payment of payables and thereby lengthen the payables period.

Unlike Amazon, most firms have a positive cash cycle, and they thus require financing for inventories and receivables. The longer the cash cycle, the more financing is required. Also, changes in the firm's cash cycle are often monitored as an early-warning measure. A lengthening cycle can indicate that the firm is having trouble moving inventory or collecting on its receivables. Such problems can be masked, at least partially, by an increased payables cycle, so both cycles should be monitored.

The link between the firm's cash cycle and its profitability can be easily seen by recalling that one of the basic determinants of profitability and growth for a firm is its total asset turnover, which is defined as Sales/Total assets. In Chapter 3, we saw that the higher this ratio is, the greater is the firm's accounting return on assets, ROA, and return on equity, ROE. Thus, all other things being the same, the shorter the cash cycle is, the lower is the firm's investment in inventories and receivables. As a result, the firm's total assets are lower, and total turnover is higher.

18.3 SOME ASPECTS OF SHORT-TERM FINANCIAL POLICY

The short-term financial policy that a firm adopts will be reflected in at least two ways:

1. *The Size of the Firm's Investment in Current Assets.* This is usually measured relative to the firm's level of total operating revenues. A *flexible,* or accommodative,

short-term financial policy would maintain a relatively high ratio of current assets to sales. A *restrictive* short-term financial policy would entail a low ratio of current assets to sales.[4]

2. *The Financing of Current Assets.* This is measured as the proportion of short-term debt (that is, current liabilities) and long-term debt used to finance current assets. A restrictive short-term financial policy means a high proportion of short-term debt relative to long-term financing, and a flexible policy means less short-term debt and more long-term debt.

If we take these two areas together, we see that a firm with a flexible policy would have a relatively large investment in current assets, and it would finance this investment with relatively less in short-term debt. The net effect of a flexible policy is thus a relatively high level of net working capital. Put another way, with a flexible policy, the firm maintains a higher overall level of liquidity.

The Size of the Firm's Investment in Current Assets

Short-term financial policies that are flexible with regard to current assets include such actions as:

1. Keeping large balances of cash and marketable securities.
2. Making large investments in inventory.
3. Granting liberal credit terms, which results in a high level of accounts receivable.

Restrictive short-term financial policies would be just the opposite:

1. Keeping low cash balances and making little investment in marketable securities.
2. Making small investments in inventory.
3. Allowing few or no credit sales, thereby minimizing accounts receivable.

Determining the optimal level of investment in short-term assets requires an identification of the different costs of alternative short-term financing policies. The objective is to trade off the cost of a restrictive policy against the cost of a flexible one to arrive at the best compromise.

Current asset holdings are highest with a flexible short-term financial policy and lowest with a restrictive policy. So, flexible short-term financial policies are costly in that they require a greater investment in cash and marketable securities, inventory, and accounts receivable. However, we expect that future cash inflows will be higher with a flexible policy. For example, sales are stimulated by the use of a credit policy that provides liberal financing to customers. A large amount of finished inventory on hand ("on the shelf") enables quick delivery service to customers and may increase sales. Similarly, a large inventory of raw materials may result in fewer production stoppages because of inventory shortages.

A more restrictive short-term financial policy probably reduces future sales to levels below those that would be achieved under flexible policies. It is also possible that higher prices can be charged to customers under flexible working capital policies. Customers may be willing to pay higher prices for the quick delivery service and more liberal credit terms implicit in flexible policies.

Managing current assets can be thought of as involving a trade-off between costs that rise and costs that fall with the level of investment. Costs that rise with increases in the level of investment in current assets are called **carrying costs**. The larger the investment a firm makes in its current assets, the higher its carrying costs will be. Costs that fall with increases in the level of investment in current assets are called **shortage costs**.

---

[4] Some people use the term *conservative* in place of *flexible* and the term *aggressive* in place of *restrictive*.

In a general sense, carrying costs are the opportunity costs associated with current assets. The rate of return on current assets is very low when compared to that on other assets. For example, the rate of return on U.S. Treasury bills is usually a good deal less than 5 percent. This is very low compared to the rate of return firms would like to achieve overall. (U.S. Treasury bills are an important component of cash and marketable securities.)

Shortage costs are incurred when the investment in current assets is low. If a firm runs out of cash, it will be forced to sell marketable securities. Of course, if a firm runs out of cash and cannot readily sell marketable securities, it may have to borrow or default on an obligation. This situation is called a *cash-out*. A firm may lose customers if it runs out of inventory (a *stockout*) or if it cannot extend credit to customers.

More generally, there are two kinds of shortage costs:

1. *Trading, or Order, Costs.* Order costs are the costs of placing an order for more cash (brokerage costs, for example) or more inventory (production setup costs, for example).
2. *Costs Related to Lack of Safety Reserves.* These are costs of lost sales, lost customer goodwill, and disruption of production schedules.

The top part of Figure 18.2 illustrates the basic trade-off between carrying costs and shortage costs. On the vertical axis, we have costs measured in dollars, and on the horizontal axis, we have the amount of current assets. Carrying costs start out at zero when current assets are zero and then climb steadily as current assets grow. Shortage costs start out very high and then decline as we add current assets. The total cost of holding current assets is the sum of the two. Notice how the combined costs reach a minimum at CA*. This is the optimal level of current assets.

Optimal current asset holdings are highest under a flexible policy. This policy is one in which the carrying costs are perceived to be low relative to shortage costs. This is Case A in Figure 18.2. In comparison, under restrictive current asset policies, carrying costs are perceived to be high relative to shortage costs, resulting in lower current asset holdings. This is Case B in Figure 18.2.

Alternative Financing Policies for Current Assets

In previous sections, we looked at the basic determinants of the level of investment in current assets, and we thus focused on the asset side of the balance sheet. Now we turn to the financing side of the question. Here we are concerned with the relative amounts of short-term and long-term debt, assuming that the investment in current assets is constant.

AN IDEAL CASE We start off with the simplest possible case: an "ideal" economy. In such an economy, short-term assets can always be financed with short-term debt, and long-term assets can be financed with long-term debt and equity. In this economy, net working capital is always zero.

Consider a simplified case for a grain elevator operator. Grain elevator operators buy crops after harvest, store them, and sell them during the year. They have high inventories of grain after the harvest and end up with low inventories just before the next harvest.

Bank loans with maturities of less than one year are used to finance the purchase of grain and the storage costs. These loans are paid off from the proceeds of the sale of grain.

The situation is shown in Figure 18.3. Long-term assets are assumed to grow over time, whereas current assets increase at the end of the harvest and then decline during the year. Short-term assets end up at zero just before the next harvest. Current (short-term) assets are financed by short-term debt, and long-term assets are financed with long-term debt

FIGURE 18.2

Carrying Costs and
Shortage Costs

Short-Term Financial Policy: The Optimal Investment in Current Assets

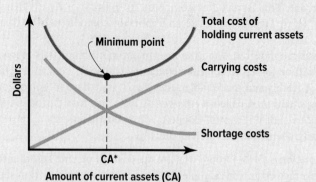

CA* represents the optimal amount of current assets.
Holding this amount minimizes total costs.

Carrying costs increase with the level of investment in current assets. They include the costs of maintaining economic value and opportunity costs. Shortage costs decrease with increases in the level of investment in current assets. They include trading costs and the costs related to being short of the current asset (for example, being short of cash). The firm's policy can be characterized as flexible or restrictive.

A. Flexible Policy

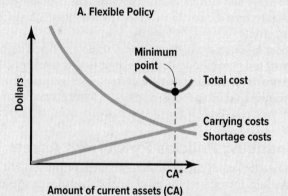

A flexible policy is most appropriate when carrying costs are low relative to shortage costs.

B. Restrictive Policy

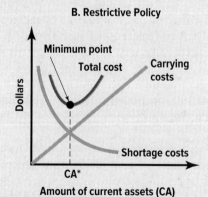

A restrictive policy is most appropriate when carrying costs are high relative to shortage costs.

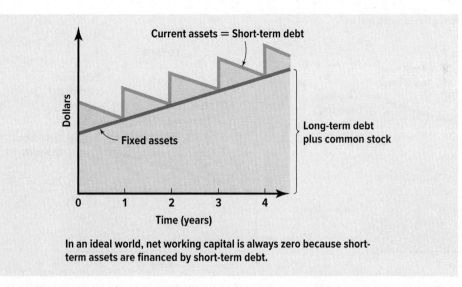

FIGURE 18.3

Financing Policy for an Ideal
Economy

In an ideal world, net working capital is always zero because short-term assets are financed by short-term debt.

and equity. Net working capital—current assets minus current liabilities—is always zero. Figure 18.3 displays a "sawtooth" pattern that we will see again when we get to our discussion on cash management in the next chapter. For now, we need to discuss some alternative policies for financing current assets under less idealized conditions.

DIFFERENT POLICIES FOR FINANCING CURRENT ASSETS In the real world, it is not likely that current assets will ever drop to zero. For example, a long-term rising level of sales will result in some permanent investment in current assets. Moreover, the firm's investments in long-term assets may show a great deal of variation.

A growing firm can be thought of as having a total asset requirement consisting of the current assets and long-term assets needed to run the business efficiently. The total asset requirement may exhibit change over time for many reasons, including (1) a general growth trend, (2) seasonal variation around the trend, and (3) unpredictable day-to-day and month-to-month fluctuations. This fluctuation is depicted in Figure 18.4. (We have not tried to show the unpredictable day-to-day and month-to-month variations in the total asset requirement.)

The peaks and valleys in Figure 18.4 represent the firm's total asset needs through time. For example, for a lawn and garden supply firm, the peaks might represent inventory buildups prior to the spring selling season. The valleys would come about because of lower off-season inventories. There are two strategies such a firm might consider to meet its

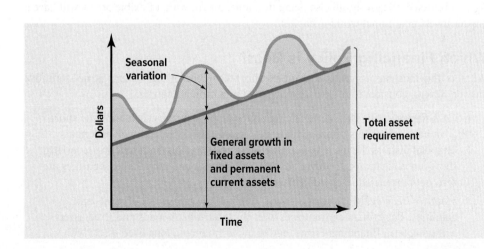

FIGURE 18.4

The Total Asset Requirement
over Time

FIGURE 18.5   Alternative Asset Financing Policies

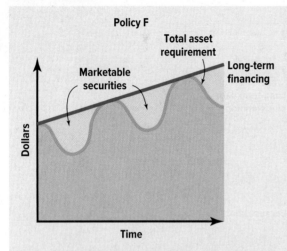

Policy F always implies a short-term cash surplus and a large investment in cash and marketable securities.

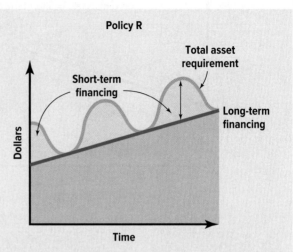

Policy R uses long-term financing for permanent asset requirements only and short-term borrowing for seasonal variations.

cyclical needs. First, the firm could keep a relatively large pool of marketable securities. As the need for inventory and other current assets began to rise, the firm would sell off marketable securities and use the cash to purchase whatever was needed. Once the inventory was sold and inventory holdings began to decline, the firm would reinvest in marketable securities. This approach is the flexible policy illustrated in Figure 18.5 as Policy F. Notice that the firm essentially uses a pool of marketable securities as a buffer against changing current asset needs.

At the other extreme, the firm could keep relatively little in marketable securities. As the need for inventory and other assets began to rise, the firm would borrow the needed cash on a short-term basis. The firm would repay the loans as the need for assets cycled back down. This approach is the restrictive policy illustrated in Figure 18.5 as Policy R.

In comparing the two strategies illustrated in Figure 18.5, notice that the chief difference is the way in which the seasonal variation in asset needs is financed. In the flexible case, the firm finances internally, using its own cash and marketable securities. In the restrictive case, the firm finances the variation externally, borrowing the needed funds on a short-term basis. As we discussed previously, all else being the same, a firm with a flexible policy will have a greater investment in net working capital.

Which Financing Policy Is Best?

What is the most appropriate amount of short-term borrowing? There is no definitive answer. Several considerations must be included in a proper analysis:

1. *Cash Reserves.* The flexible financing policy implies surplus cash and little short-term borrowing. This policy reduces the probability that a firm will experience financial distress. Firms may not have to worry as much about meeting recurring, short-run obligations. However, investments in cash and marketable securities are zero net present value investments at best.

2. *Maturity Hedging.* Most firms attempt to match the maturities of assets and liabilities. They finance inventories with short-term bank loans and fixed assets with long-term financing. Firms tend to avoid financing long-lived assets with

FIGURE 18.6

A Compromise Financing
Policy

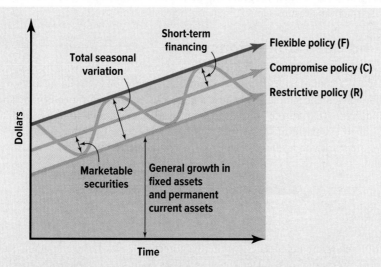

With a compromise policy, the firm keeps a reserve of liquidity that it uses
to initially finance seasonal variations in current asset needs. Short-term
borrowing is used when the reserve is exhausted.

short-term borrowing. This type of maturity mismatching would necessitate
frequent refinancing and is inherently risky because short-term interest rates are
more volatile than longer-term rates.

3. *Relative Interest Rates.* Short-term interest rates are usually lower than long-term
rates. This implies that it is, on average, more costly to rely on long-term borrowing than short-term borrowing.

The two policies we depict in Figure 18.5 are, of course, extreme cases. With F, the firm
never does any short-term borrowing, and with R, the firm never has a cash reserve (an
investment in marketable securities). Figure 18.6 illustrates these two policies along with a
compromise, Policy C.

With this compromise approach, the firm borrows in the short term to cover peak
financing needs, but it maintains a cash reserve in the form of marketable securities during
slow periods. As current assets build up, the firm draws down this reserve before doing any
short-term borrowing. This allows for some run-up in current assets before the firm has to
resort to short-term borrowing.

Current Assets and Liabilities in Practice

Short-term assets represent a significant portion of a typical firm's overall assets. For U.S.
manufacturing, mining, and trade corporations, current assets were about 50 percent of
total assets in the 1960s. Today, this figure is closer to 40 percent. Most of the decline is due
to more efficient cash and inventory management. Over this same period, current liabilities
rose from about 20 percent of total liabilities and equity to almost 30 percent. The result is
that liquidity (as measured by the ratio of net working capital to total assets) has declined,
signaling a move to more restrictive short-term policies.

18.4 THE CASH BUDGET

The **cash budget** is a primary tool in short-run financial planning. It allows the financial
manager to identify short-term financial needs and opportunities. An important function of
the cash budget is to help the manager explore the need for short-term borrowing. The idea

ExcelMaster
coverage online

www.mhhe.com/RossCore6e

of the cash budget is simple: It records estimates of cash receipts (cash in) and disbursements (cash out). The result is an estimate of the cash surplus or deficit.

Sales and Cash Collections

We start with an example involving the Fun Toys Corporation. We will prepare a quarterly cash budget. We could just as well use a monthly, weekly, or even daily basis. We choose quarters for convenience and also because a quarter is a common short-term business planning period. (Note that, throughout this example, all figures are in millions of dollars.)

All of Fun Toys's cash inflows come from the sale of toys. Cash budgeting for Fun Toys must therefore start with a sales forecast for the coming year, by quarter:

	Q1	Q2	Q3	Q4
Sales (in $millions)	$200	$300	$250	$400

Note that these are predicted sales, so there is forecasting risk here, and actual sales could be higher or lower. Fun Toys started the year with accounts receivable equal to $120.

Fun Toys has a 45-day receivables, or average, collection period. This means that half of the sales in a given quarter will be collected the following quarter. This happens because sales made during the first 45 days of a quarter will be collected in that quarter, whereas sales made in the second 45 days will be collected in the next quarter. Note that we are assuming that each quarter has 90 days, so the 45-day collection period is the same as a half-quarter collection period.

Based on the sales forecasts, we now need to estimate Fun Toys's projected cash collections. First, any receivables that we have at the beginning of a quarter will be collected within 45 days, so all of them will be collected sometime during the quarter. Second, as we discussed, any sales made in the first half of the quarter will be collected, so total cash collections are:

$$\text{Cash collection} = \text{Beginning accounts receivable} + 1/2 \times \text{Sales} \qquad [18.6]$$

For example, in the first quarter, cash collections would be the beginning receivables of $120 plus half of sales, $1/2 \times \$200 = \$100$, for a total of $220.

Because beginning receivables are all collected along with half of sales, ending receivables for a particular quarter will be the other half of sales. First-quarter sales are projected at $200, so ending receivables will be $100. This will be the beginning receivables in the second quarter. Cash collections in the second quarter will thus be $100 plus half of the projected $300 in sales, or $250 total.

Continuing this process, we can summarize Fun Toys's projected cash collections as shown in Table 18.2. In this table, collections are shown as the only source of cash. Of course, this need not be the case. Other sources of cash could include asset sales, investment income, and receipts from planned long-term financing.

TABLE 18.2

Cash Collection for Fun Toys (in $ millions)

	Q1	Q2	Q3	Q4
Beginning receivables	$120	$100	$150	$125
Sales	200	300	250	400
Cash collections	−220	−250	−275	−325
Ending receivables	$100	$150	$125	$200

Collections = Beginning receivables + 1/2 × Sales
Ending receivables = Beginning receivables + Sales − Collections
= 1/2 × Sales

Cash Outflows

Next, we consider cash disbursements, or payments. These come in four basic categories:

1. *Payments of Accounts Payable.* These are payments for goods or services rendered by suppliers, such as raw materials. Generally, these payments will be made sometime after purchases.

2. *Wages, Taxes, and Other Expenses.* This category includes all other regular costs of doing business that require actual expenditures. Depreciation, for example, is often thought of as a regular cost of business, but it requires no cash outflow and is not included.

3. *Capital Expenditures.* These are payments of cash for long-lived assets.

4. *Long-Term Financing Expenses.* This category includes, for example, interest payments on long-term debt outstanding and dividend payments to shareholders.

Fun Toys's purchases from suppliers (in dollars) in a quarter are equal to 60 percent of the next quarter's predicted sales. Fun Toys's payments to suppliers are equal to the previous quarter's purchases, so the accounts payable period is 90 days. In the quarter just ended, Fun Toys ordered .60 × $200 = $120 in supplies. This will actually be paid in the first quarter (Q1) of the coming year.

Wages, taxes, and other expenses are routinely 20 percent of sales; interest and dividends are currently $20 per quarter. In addition, Fun Toys plans a major plant expansion (a capital expenditure) costing $100 in the second quarter. If we put all this information together, the cash outflows are as shown in Table 18.3.

The Cash Balance

The predicted *net cash inflow* is the difference between cash collections and cash disbursements. The net cash inflow for Fun Toys is shown in Table 18.4. What we see immediately is that there is a cash surplus in the first and third quarters and a cash deficit in the second and fourth.

We will assume that Fun Toys starts the year with a $20 cash balance. Furthermore, Fun Toys maintains a $10 minimum cash balance to guard against unforeseen contingencies and forecasting errors. So, the company starts the first quarter with $20 in cash. This amount rises by $40 during the quarter, and the ending balance is $60. Of this, $10 is reserved as a minimum, so we subtract it out and find that the first quarter surplus is $60 − 10 = $50.

Fun Toys starts the second quarter with $60 in cash (the ending balance from the previous quarter). There is a net cash inflow of −$110, so the ending balance is $60 − 110 = −$50. We need another $10 as a buffer, so the total deficit is −$60. These calculations and those for the last two quarters are summarized in Table 18.5.

	Q1	Q2	Q3	Q4
Payment of accounts (60% of sales)	$120	$180	$150	$240
Wages, taxes, other expenses	40	60	50	80
Capital expenditures	0	100	0	0
Long-term financing expenses (interest and dividends)	20	20	20	20
Total cash disbursements	$180	$360	$220	$340

TABLE 18.3
Cash Disbursements for Fun Toys (in $ millions)

	Q1	Q2	Q3	Q4
Total cash collections	$220	$250	$275	$325
Total cash disbursements	180	360	220	340
Net cash inflow	$ 40	−$110	$ 55	−$ 15

TABLE 18.4
Net Cash Inflow for Fun Toys (in $ millions)

TABLE 18.5

Cash Balance for Fun Toys (in $ millions)

	Q1	Q2	Q3	Q4
Beginning cash balance	$20	$ 60	−$50	$ 5
Net cash inflow	40	− 110	55	− 15
Ending cash balance	$60	−$ 50	$ 5	−$10
Minimum cash balance	− 10	− 10	− 10	− 10
Cumulative surplus (deficit)	$50	−$ 60	−$ 5	−$20

At the end of the second quarter, Fun Toys has a cash shortfall of $60. This occurs because of the seasonal pattern of sales (higher toward the end of the second quarter), the delay in collections, and the planned capital expenditure.

The cash situation at Fun Toys is projected to improve to a $5 deficit in the third quarter, but by year's end, Fun Toys still has a $20 deficit. Without some sort of financing, this deficit will carry over into the next year. We explore this subject in the next section.

For now, we can make the following general comments on Fun Toys's cash needs:

1. Fun Toys's large outflow in the second quarter is not necessarily a sign of trouble. It results from delayed collections on sales and a planned capital expenditure (presumably a worthwhile one).

2. The figures in our example are based on a forecast. Sales could be much worse (or better) than the forecasted figures.

18.5 SHORT-TERM BORROWING

Fun Toys has a short-term financing problem. It cannot meet the forecasted cash outflows in the second quarter using internal sources. How it will finance that shortfall depends on its financial policy. With a very flexible policy, Fun Toys might seek up to $60 million in long-term debt financing.

In addition, note that much of the cash deficit comes from the large capital expenditure. Arguably, this is a candidate for long-term financing. Nonetheless, because we have discussed long-term financing elsewhere, we will concentrate here on four short-term borrowing options: (1) unsecured borrowing, (2) secured borrowing, (3) commercial paper, and (4) trade credit.

Unsecured Loans

The most common way to finance a temporary cash deficit is to arrange a short-term unsecured bank loan. Firms that use short-term bank loans often arrange for a line of credit. A line of credit is an agreement under which a firm is authorized to borrow up to a specified amount. To ensure that the line is used for short-term purposes, the lender will sometimes require the borrower to pay the line down to zero and keep it there for some period during the year, typically 60 days (called a *cleanup period*).

Short-term lines of credit are classified as either *committed* or *noncommitted*. The latter type is an informal arrangement that allows firms to borrow up to a previously specified limit without going through the normal paperwork (much as they would with a credit card). A *revolving credit arrangement* (or just *revolver*) is similar to a line of credit, but it is usually open for two or more years, whereas a line of credit would usually be evaluated on an annual basis.

Committed lines of credit are more formal legal arrangements and usually involve a commitment fee paid by the firm to the bank (usually the fee is on the order of .25 percent of the total committed funds per year). The interest rate on the line of credit is usually set equal to the bank's prime lending rate plus an additional percentage, and the rate will usually float. A firm that pays a commitment fee for a committed line of credit is essentially buying insurance to guarantee that the bank can't back out of the agreement (absent some material change in the borrower's status).

COMPENSATING BALANCES   As a part of a credit line or other lending arrangement, banks will sometimes require that the firm keep some amount of money on deposit. This is called a compensating balance. A compensating balance is some of the firm's money kept by the bank in low-interest or non-interest-bearing accounts. By leaving these funds with the bank and receiving little or no interest, the firm further increases the effective interest rate earned by the bank on the line of credit, thereby "compensating" the bank. A compensating balance might be on the order of 2 to 5 percent of the amount borrowed.

Firms also use compensating balances to pay for noncredit bank services such as cash management services. A traditionally contentious issue is whether the firm should pay for bank credit and noncredit services with fees or with compensating balances. Most major firms have now negotiated for banks to use the corporation's collected funds for compensation and use fees to cover any shortfall. Arrangements such as this one and some similar approaches discussed in the next chapter make the subject of minimum balances less of an issue than it once was.

COST OF A COMPENSATING BALANCE   A compensating balance requirement has an obvious opportunity cost because the money often must be deposited in an account with a zero or low interest rate. Suppose that we have a $100,000 line of credit with a 10 percent compensating balance requirement. This means that 10 percent of the amount actually used must be left on deposit in a non-interest-bearing account.

The quoted interest rate on the credit line is 16 percent. Suppose we need $54,000 to purchase some inventory. How much do we have to borrow? What interest rate are we effectively paying?

If we need $54,000, we have to borrow enough so that $54,000 is left over after we take out the 10 percent compensating balance:

$54,000 = (1 − .10) × Amount borrowed
$60,000 = $54,000/.90 = Amount borrowed

The interest on the $60,000 for one year at 16 percent is $60,000 × .16 = $9,600. We're actually only getting $54,000 to use, so the effective interest rate is:

Effective interest rate = Interest paid/Amount available
= $9,600/$54,000
= .1778, or 17.78%

Notice that what effectively happens here is that we pay 16 cents in interest on every 90 cents we borrow because we don't get to use the 10 cents tied up in the compensating balance. The interest rate is thus .16/.90 = 17.78 percent, as we calculated.

Several points bear mentioning. First, compensating balances are usually computed as a monthly average of the daily balances. This means that the effective interest rate may be lower than our example illustrates. Second, it has become common for compensating balances to be based on the *unused* amount of the credit line. The requirement of such a balance amounts to an implicit commitment fee. Third, and most important, the details of short-term business lending arrangements are highly negotiable. Banks will generally work with firms to design a package of fees and interest.

LETTERS OF CREDIT   A *letter of credit* is a common arrangement in international finance. With a letter of credit, the bank issuing the letter promises to make a loan if certain conditions are met. Typically, the letter guarantees payment on a shipment of goods provided that the goods arrive as promised. A letter of credit can be revocable (subject to cancellation) or irrevocable (not subject to cancellation if the specified conditions are met).

Secured Loans

Banks and other finance companies often require security for a short-term loan just as they do for a long-term loan. Security for short-term loans usually consists of accounts receivable, inventories, or both.

ACCOUNTS RECEIVABLE FINANCING   Accounts receivable financing involves either *assigning* receivables or *factoring* receivables. Under assignment, the lender has the receivables as security, but the borrower is still responsible if a receivable can't be collected. With *conventional factoring*, the receivable is discounted and sold to the lender (the factor). Once it is sold, collection is the factor's problem, and the factor assumes the full risk of default on bad accounts. With *maturity factoring*, the factor forwards the money on an agreed-upon future date.

Factors play a particularly important role in the retail industry. Retailers in the clothing business, for example, must buy large amounts of new clothes at the beginning of the season. Because this is typically a long time before they have sold anything, they wait to pay their suppliers, sometimes 30 to 60 days. If an apparel maker can't wait that long, it turns to factors, who buy the receivables and take over collection. In fact, the garment industry accounts for about 80 percent of all factoring in the United States.

One of the newest types of factoring is called *credit card receivable funding* or *business cash advances.* The way business cash advances work is that a company goes to a factor and receives cash up front. From that point on, a portion of each credit card sale (perhaps 6 to 8 percent) is routed directly to the factor by the credit card processor until the loan is paid off. This arrangement may be attractive to small businesses in particular, but it can be expensive. The typical premium on the advance is about 35 percent—meaning that with a $100,000 loan, $135,000 must be repaid within a relatively short period.

Purchase order financing (or just PO financing) is a popular form of factoring used by small and midsize companies. In a typical scenario, a small business receives a firm order from a customer, but it doesn't have sufficient funds to pay the supplier that manufactures the product. With PO financing, the factor pays the supplier. When the sale is completed and the seller is paid, the factor is repaid. A typical interest rate on purchase order factoring is 3.5 percent for the first 30 days, then 1.25 percent every 10 days thereafter, an annual interest rate of more than 50 percent.

EXAMPLE 18.3

Cost of Factoring

For the year just ended, LuLu's Pies had an average of $50,000 in accounts receivable. Credit sales were $500,000. LuLu's factors its receivables by discounting them 3 percent, in other words, by selling them for 97 cents on the dollar. What is the effective interest rate on this source of short-term financing?

To determine the interest rate, we first have to know the accounts receivable, or average collection, period. During the year, LuLu's turned over its receivables $500,000/$50,000 = 10 times. The average collection period is therefore 365/10 = 36.5 days.

The interest paid here is a form of discount interest (discussed in Chapter 4). In this case, LuLu's is paying 3 cents in interest on every 97 cents of financing. The interest rate per 36.5 days is thus .03/.97 = 3.09 percent. The APR is 10 × 3.09 percent = 30.9 percent, but the effective annual rate is:

$$\text{EAR} = 1.0309^{10} - 1 = .356, \text{ or } 35.6\%$$

Factoring is a relatively expensive source of money in this case.

We should note that, if the factor takes on the risk of default by a buyer, then the factor is providing insurance as well as immediate cash. More generally, the factor essentially takes over the firm's credit operations. This can result in a significant savings. The interest rate we calculated is therefore overstated, particularly if default is a significant possibility.

INVENTORY LOANS   Inventory loans, short-term loans to purchase inventory, come in three basic forms: blanket inventory liens, trust receipts, and field warehouse financing:

1. *Blanket Inventory Lien.* A blanket lien gives the lender a lien against all the borrower's inventories (the blanket "covers" everything).

2. *Trust Receipt.* A trust receipt is a device by which the borrower holds specific inventory in "trust" for the lender. Automobile dealer financing, for example, is done by use of trust receipts. This type of secured financing is also called *floor planning,* in reference to inventory on the showroom floor. However, it is somewhat cumbersome to use trust receipts for, say, wheat grain.

3. *Field Warehouse Financing.* In field warehouse financing, a public warehouse company (an independent company that specializes in inventory management) acts as a control agent to supervise the inventory for the lender.

Commercial Paper

There are a variety of other sources of short-term funds employed by corporations. One of the most important, especially for certain very large corporations, is *commercial paper.*

Commercial paper consists of short-term notes issued by large and highly rated firms. Typically, these notes are of short maturity, ranging up to 270 days (beyond that limit, the firm must file a registration statement with the SEC). Because the firm issues these directly and because it usually backs the issue with a special bank line of credit, the interest rate the firm obtains is often significantly below the rate a bank would charge for a direct loan.

Trade Credit

Another very important source of short-term financing for firms of all sizes is *trade credit,* meaning accounts payable. Such payables amount to money borrowed from suppliers, and small firms in particular rely heavily on suppliers for short-term credit. Trade credit is important for large firms as well; retailing giant Walmart uses more trade credit than it does money borrowed from banks.

UNDERSTANDING TRADE CREDIT TERMS   The easiest way to understand trade credit terms is to consider an example. For bulk candy, terms of 2/10, net 60, might be quoted.[5] This means that customers have 60 days from the invoice date (discussed next) to pay the full amount. However, if payment is made within 10 days, a 2 percent cash discount can be taken.

Consider a buyer who places an order for $1,000, and assume that the terms of the sale are 2/10, net 60. The buyer has the option of paying $1,000 × (1 − .02) = $980 in 10 days, or paying the full $1,000 in 60 days. If the terms were stated as just net 30, then the customer would have 30 days from the invoice date to pay the entire $1,000, and no discount would be offered for early payment.

In general, credit terms are interpreted in the following way:

(Take this discount off the invoice price)/(if you pay in this many days),

(or else pay the full invoice amount in this many days)

Thus, 5/10, net 45, means take a 5 percent discount from the full price if you pay within 10 days, or else pay the full amount in 45 days.

CASH DISCOUNTS   As we have seen, cash discounts are often part of the terms of sale. The practice of granting discounts for cash purchases in the United States dates to the Civil War and is widespread today. One reason discounts are offered is to speed up

---

[5] The terms of sale cited from specific industries in this section and elsewhere are drawn from Theodore N. Beckman, *Credits and Collections: Management and Theory* (New York: McGraw-Hill, 1962).

the collection of receivables and reduce the amount of credit being offered (and the potential losses from defaults).

Notice that when a cash discount is offered, the credit is essentially free during the discount period. The buyer pays for the credit only after the discount expires. With 2/10, net 30, a rational buyer either pays in 10 days to make the greatest possible use of the free credit or pays in 30 days to get the longest possible use of the money in exchange for giving up the discount. So, by giving up the discount, the buyer effectively gets $30 - 10 = 20$ days' credit.

Another reason for cash discounts is that they provide a way of charging higher prices to customers who have had credit extended to them. In this sense, cash discounts are a convenient way of charging for the credit granted to customers.

In our examples, it might seem that the discounts are rather small. With 2/10, net 30, for example, early payment only gets the buyer a 2 percent discount. Does this provide a significant incentive for early payment? The answer is yes because the implicit interest rate is extremely high.

To see why the discount is important, we will calculate the cost to the buyer of *not* paying early. To do this, we will find the interest rate that the buyer is effectively paying for the trade credit. Suppose the order is for $1,000. The buyer can pay $980 in 10 days or wait another 20 days and pay $1,000. It's obvious that the buyer is effectively borrowing $980 for 20 days and paying $20 in interest on the "loan." What's the interest rate?

With $20 in interest on $980 borrowed, the rate is $20/$980 = .020408, or 2.0408 percent. This is relatively low, but remember that this is the rate per 20-day period. There are $365/20 = 18.25$ such periods in a year, so, by not taking the discount, the buyer is paying an effective annual rate of:

$$EAR = 1.020408^{18.25} - 1 = .446, \text{ or } 44.6\%$$

From the buyer's point of view, this is an expensive source of financing!

Given that the interest rate is so high here, it is unlikely that the seller benefits from early payment. Ignoring the possibility of default by the buyer, the decision by a customer to forgo the discount almost surely works to the seller's advantage.

What's the Rate?

Ordinary tiles are often sold with terms of 3/30, net 60. What effective annual rate does a buyer pay by not taking the discount? What would the APR be if one were quoted?

Here we have 3 percent discount interest on $60 - 30 = 30$ days' credit. The rate per 30 days is $.03/.97 = .03093$, or 3.093 percent. There are $365/30 = 12.17$ such periods in a year, so the effective annual rate is:

$$EAR = 1.03093^{12.17} - 1 = .449, \text{ or } 44.9\%$$

The APR, as always, would be calculated by multiplying the rate per period by the number of periods:

$$APR = .03093 \times 12.17 = .376, \text{ or } 37.6\%$$

An interest rate calculated like this APR is often quoted as the cost of the trade credit and, as this example illustrates, can seriously understate the true cost.

18.6 A SHORT-TERM FINANCIAL PLAN

To illustrate a completed short-term financial plan, we will assume that Fun Toys arranges to borrow any needed funds on a short-term basis. The interest rate is a 20 percent APR, and it is calculated on a quarterly basis. From Chapter 4, we know that the rate is 20 percent/4 = 5 percent per quarter. We will assume that Fun Toys starts the year with no short-term debt.

TABLE 18.6

Short-Term Financial Plan
for Fun Toys (in $ millions)

	Q1	Q2	Q3	Q4
Beginning cash balance	$20	$ 60	$10	$10.0
Net cash inflow	40	−110	55	−15.0
New short-term borrowing	—	60	—	15.4
Interest on short-term borrowing	—	—	− 3	− .4
Short-term borrowing repaid	—	—	−52	—
Ending cash balance	$60	$ 10	$10	$10.0
Minimum cash balance	− 10	− 10	−10	−10.0
Cumulative surplus (deficit)	$50	$ 0	$ 0	$ 0.0
Beginning short-term borrowing	0	0	60	8.0
Change in short-term debt	0	60	−52	15.4
Ending short-term debt	$ 0	$ 60	$ 8	$23.4

From Table 18.5, we know that Fun Toys has a second-quarter deficit of $60 million. The firm will have to borrow this amount. Net cash inflow in the following quarter is $55 million. The firm will now have to pay $60 million × .05 = $3 million in interest out of that, leaving $52 million to reduce the borrowing.

Fun Toys still owes $60 million − 52 million = $8 million at the end of the third quarter. Interest in the last quarter will thus be $8 million × .05 = $.4 million. In addition, net inflows in the last quarter are −$15 million, so the company will have to borrow a total of $15.4 million, bringing total borrowing up to $15.4 million + 8 million = $23.4 million. Table 18.6 extends Table 18.5 to include these calculations.

Notice that the ending short-term debt is just equal to the cumulative deficit for the entire year, $20 million, plus the interest paid during the year, $3 million + .4 million = $3.4 million, for a total of $23.4 million.

Our plan is very simple. For example, we ignored the fact that the interest paid on the short-term debt is tax deductible. We also ignored the fact that the cash surplus in the first quarter would earn some interest (which would be taxable). We could add on a number of refinements. Even so, our plan highlights the fact that in about 90 days, Fun Toys will need to borrow $60 million or so on a short-term basis. It's time to start lining up the source of the funds.

Our plan also illustrates that financing the firm's short-term needs will cost about $3.4 million in interest (before taxes) for the year. This is a starting point for Fun Toys to begin evaluating alternatives to reduce this expense. For example, can the $100 million planned expenditure be postponed or spread out? At 5 percent per quarter, short-term credit is expensive.

Also, if Fun Toys's sales are expected to keep growing, then the deficit of $20 million-plus will probably also keep growing, and the need for additional financing will be permanent. Fun Toys may wish to think about raising money on a long-term basis to cover this need.

SUMMARY AND CONCLUSIONS

1. This chapter has introduced the management of short-term finance. Short-term finance involves short-lived assets and liabilities. We trace and examine the short-term sources and uses of cash as they appear on the firm's financial statements. We see how current assets and current liabilities arise in the short-term operating activities and the cash cycle of the firm.

2. Managing short-term cash flows involves the minimizing of costs. The two major costs are carrying costs, the return forgone by keeping too much invested in short-term assets such as cash, and shortage costs,

the costs of running out of short-term assets. The objective of managing short-term finance and doing short-term financial planning is to find the optimal trade-off between these two costs.

3. In an ideal economy, the firm could perfectly predict its short-term uses and sources of cash, and net working capital could be kept at zero. In the real world, cash and net working capital provide a buffer that lets the firm meet its ongoing obligations. The financial manager seeks the optimal level of each of the current assets.

4. The financial manager can use the cash budget to identify short-term financial needs. The cash budget tells the manager what borrowing is required or what lending will be possible in the short run. The firm has available to it a number of possible ways of acquiring funds to meet short-term shortfalls, including unsecured and secured loans, commercial paper, and trade credit.

CONCEPT QUESTIONS

1. **Operating Cycle**   What are some of the characteristics of a firm with a long operating cycle?

2. **Cash Cycle**   What are some of the characteristics of a firm with a long cash cycle?

3. **Sources and Uses**   For the year just ended, you have gathered the following information on the Holly Corporation:

   a. A $200 dividend was paid.

   b. Accounts payable increased by $500.

   c. Fixed asset purchases were $900.

   d. Inventories increased by $625.

   e. Long-term debt decreased by $1,200.

   Label each as a source or use of cash and describe its effect on the firm's cash balance.

4. **Cost of Current Assets**   Loft Manufacturing, Inc., has recently installed a just-in-time (JIT) inventory system. Describe the effect this is likely to have on the company's carrying costs, shortage costs, and operating cycle.

5. **Operating and Cash Cycles**   Is it possible for a firm's cash cycle to be longer than its operating cycle? Explain why or why not.

6. **Shortage Costs**   What are the costs of shortages? Describe them.

7. **Reasons for Net Working Capital**   In an ideal economy, net working capital is always zero. Why might net working capital be positive in a real economy?

   Use the following information to answer Questions 8–12:

   Last month, BlueSky Airline announced that it would stretch out its bill payments to 45 days from 30 days. The reason given was that the company wanted to "control costs and optimize cash flow." The increased payables period will be in effect for all of the company's 4,000 suppliers.

8. **Operating and Cash Cycles**   What impact did this change in payables policy have on BlueSky's operating cycle? Its cash cycle?

9. **Operating and Cash Cycles**   What impact did the announcement have on BlueSky's suppliers?

10. **Corporate Ethics**   Is it ethical for large firms to unilaterally lengthen their payables periods, particularly when dealing with smaller suppliers?

11. **Payables Period**   Why don't all firms increase their payables periods to shorten their cash cycles?

12. **Payables Period**   BlueSky lengthened its payables period to "control costs and optimize cash flow." Exactly what is the cash benefit to BlueSky from this change?

QUESTIONS AND PROBLEMS

Basic
(Questions 1–16)

1. **Changes in the Cash Account** Indicate the impact of the following corporate actions on cash, using the letter *I* for an increase, the letter *D* for a decrease, or the letter *N* when no change occurs.

   a. A dividend is paid with funds received from a sale of debt.

   b. Real estate is purchased and paid for with short-term debt.

   c. Inventory is bought on credit.

   d. A short-term bank loan is repaid.

   e. Next year's taxes are prepaid.

   f. Preferred stock is redeemed.

   g. Sales are made on credit.

   h. Interest on long-term debt is paid.

   i. Payments for previous sales are collected.

   j. The accounts payable balance is reduced.

   k. A dividend is paid.

   l. Production supplies are purchased and paid for with a short-term note.

   m. Utility bills are paid.

   n. Cash is paid for raw materials purchased for inventory.

   o. Marketable securities are sold.

2. **Cash Equation** Geller Corp. has a book value of equity of $12,490. Long-term debt is $7,230. Net working capital, other than cash, is $3,155. Fixed assets are $15,120. How much cash does the company have? If current liabilities are $2,160, what are current assets?

3. **Changes in the Operating Cycle** Indicate the effect that the following will have on the operating cycle. Use the letter *I* to indicate an increase, the letter *D* for a decrease, and the letter *N* for no change.

   a. Receivables average goes up.

   b. Credit repayment times for customers are increased.

   c. Inventory turnover goes from 3 times to 6 times.

   d. Payables turnover goes from 6 times to 11 times.

   e. Receivables turnover goes from 7 times to 9 times.

   f. Payments to suppliers are accelerated.

4. **Changes in Cycles** Indicate the impact of the following on the cash and operating cycles, respectively. Use the letter *I* to indicate an increase, the letter *D* for a decrease, and the letter *N* for no change.

   a. The terms of cash discounts offered to customers are made less favorable.

   b. The cash discounts offered by suppliers are increased; thus, payments are made earlier.

   c. An increased number of customers begin to pay in cash instead of with credit.

   d. Fewer raw materials than usual are purchased.

   e. A greater percentage of raw material purchases are paid for with credit.

   f. More finished goods are produced for inventory instead of for order.

5. **Calculating Cash Collections** The Litzenberger Company has projected the following quarterly sales amounts for the coming year:

	Q1	Q2	Q3	Q4
Sales	$740	$830	$880	$960

a. Accounts receivable at the beginning of the year are $325. The company has a 45-day collection period. Calculate cash collections in each of the four quarters by completing the following:

	Q1	Q2	Q3	Q4
Beginning receivables				
Sales				
Cash collections				
Ending receivables				

b. Rework (a) assuming a collection period of 60 days.

c. Rework (a) assuming a collection period of 30 days.

6. **Calculating Cycles** Consider the following financial statement information for the Emma Corporation:

Item	Beginning		Ending
Inventory	$17,453		$19,281
Accounts receivable	14,087		15,314
Accounts payable	15,387		16,822
Net sales		$418,276	
Cost of goods sold		234,912	

All sales are on credit. Calculate the operating and cash cycles. How do you interpret your answer?

7. **Factoring Receivables** Your firm has an average collection period of 34 days. Current practice is to factor all receivables immediately at a discount of 1.2 percent. What is the effective cost of borrowing in this case? Assume that default is extremely unlikely.

 8. **Calculating Payments** Lewellen Products has projected the following sales for the coming year:

	Q1	Q2	Q3	Q4
Sales	$1,260	$1,370	$1,240	$1,510

Sales in the year following this one are projected to be 15 percent greater in each quarter.

a. Calculate payments to suppliers assuming that the company places orders during each quarter equal to 30 percent of projected sales for the next quarter. Assume that the company pays immediately. What is the payables period in this case?

	Q1	Q2	Q3	Q4
Payment of accounts	$	$	$	$

b. Rework (a) assuming a 90-day payables period.

	Q1	Q2	Q3	Q4
Payment of accounts	$	$	$	$

c. Rework (a) assuming a 60-day payables period.

	Q1	Q2	Q3	Q4
Payment of accounts	$	$	$	$

9. **Calculating Payments** The Thakor Corporation's purchases from suppliers in a quarter are equal to 75 percent of the next quarter's forecasted sales. The payables period is 60 days. Wages, taxes, and other expenses are 20 percent of sales, and interest and dividends are $170 per quarter. No capital expenditures are planned.

   Projected quarterly sales are:

	Q1	Q2	Q3	Q4
Sales	$1,840	$1,970	$2,090	$2,360

Sales for the first quarter of the following year are projected at $2,010. Calculate the company's cash outlays by completing the following:

	Q1	Q2	Q3	Q4
Payment of accounts				
Wages, taxes, other expenses				
Long-term financing expenses (interest and dividends)				
Total				

10. **Calculating Cash Collections** The following is the sales budget for Shleifer, Inc., for the first quarter of 2020:

	January	February	March
Sales budget	$337,000	$398,000	$431,000

Credit sales are collected as follows:

   65 percent in the month of the sale
   20 percent in the month after the sale
   15 percent in the second month after the sale

The accounts receivable balance at the end of the previous quarter was $208,000 ($143,000 of which was uncollected December sales).

   a. Compute the sales for November.

   b. Compute the sales for December.

   c. Compute the cash collections from sales for each month from January through March.

11. **Calculating the Cash Budget** Here are some important figures from the budget of Cornell, Inc., for the second quarter of 2020:

	April	May	June
Credit sales	$467,000	$545,000	$582,500
Credit purchases	230,600	315,200	320,400
Cash disbursements			
Wages, taxes, and expenses	68,300	84,600	101,200
Interest	18,900	18,900	18,900
Equipment purchases	131,400	173,600	–

The company predicts that 5 percent of its credit sales will never be collected, 35 percent of its sales will be collected in the month of the sale, and the remaining 60 percent will be collected in the following month. Credit purchases will be paid in the month following the purchase.

In March 2020, credit sales were $435,000 and credit purchases were $234,200. Using this information, complete the following cash budget:

	April	May	June
Beginning cash balance	$265,000		
Cash receipts			
Cash collections from credit sales			
Total cash available			
Cash disbursements			
Purchases			
Wages, taxes, and expenses			
Interest			
Equipment purchases			
Total cash disbursements			
Ending cash balance			

12. **Sources and Uses** Following are the most recent balance sheets for Country Kettles, Inc. Excluding accumulated depreciation, determine whether each item is a source or a use of cash, and the amount.

Country Kettles, Inc. Balance Sheet (in $ thousands)		
	2019	2020
Assets		
Cash	$ 65,373	$ 74,187
Accounts receivable	163,031	161,368
Inventories	139,024	156,216
Property, plant, and equipment	413,424	478,814
Less: Accumulated depreciation	109,570	140,105
Total assets	$671,282	$730,480
Liabilities and Equity		
Accounts payable	$106,810	$109,664
Accrued expenses	20,614	22,552
Long-term debt	78,474	75,038
Common stock	66,935	74,405
Accumulated retained earnings	398,449	448,821
Total liabilities and equity	$671,282	$730,480

13. **Cash Discounts** You place an order for 425 units of inventory at a unit price of $108. The supplier offers terms of 1/10, net 30.

   a. How long do you have to pay before the account is overdue? If you take the full period, how much should you remit?

   b. What is the discount being offered? How quickly must you pay to get the discount? If you do take the discount, how much should you remit?

   c. If you don't take the discount, how much interest are you paying implicitly? How many days' credit are you receiving?

14. **Terms of Sale**   A firm offers terms of 1/10, net 30. What effective annual interest rate does the firm earn when a customer does not take the discount? Without doing any calculations, explain what will happen to this effective rate if:

   a. The discount is changed to 3 percent.

   b. The credit period is increased to 45 days.

   c. The discount period is increased to 15 days.

15. **Size of Accounts Receivable**   Essence of Skunk Fragrances, Ltd., sells 4,100 units of its perfume collection each year at a price per unit of $435. All sales are on credit with terms of 1/10, net 40. The discount is taken by 65 percent of the customers. What is the amount of the company's accounts receivable? In reaction to sales by its main competitor, Sewage Spray, Essence of Skunk is considering a change in its credit policy to terms of 2/10, net 30, to preserve its market share. How will this change in policy affect accounts receivable?

16. **ACP and Receivables Turnover**   Lupo, Inc., has an average collection period of 34 days. Its average daily investment in receivables is $109,000. What are annual credit sales? What is the receivables turnover?

17. **Costs of Borrowing**   You've worked out a line of credit arrangement that allows you to borrow up to $65 million at any time. The interest rate is .53 percent per month. In addition, 4 percent of the amount that you borrow must be deposited in a non-interest-bearing account. Assume that your bank uses compound interest on its line of credit loans.

Intermediate
(Questions 17–20)

   a. What is the effective annual interest rate on this lending arrangement?

   b. Suppose you need $30 million today and you repay it in six months. How much interest will you pay?

18. **Costs of Borrowing**   A bank offers your firm a revolving credit arrangement for up to $50 million at an interest rate of 1.71 percent per quarter. The bank also requires you to maintain a compensating balance of 5 percent against the unused portion of the credit line, to be deposited in a non-interest-bearing account. Assume you have a short-term investment account at the bank that pays .81 percent per quarter, and assume that the bank uses compound interest on its revolving credit loans.

   a. What is your effective annual interest rate (an opportunity cost) on the revolving credit arrangement if your firm does not use it during the year?

   b. What is your effective annual interest rate on the lending arrangement if you borrow $35 million immediately and repay it in one year?

   c. What is your effective annual interest rate if you borrow $50 million immediately and repay it in one year?

19. **Calculating the Cash Budget**   Wildcat, Inc., has estimated sales (in millions) for the next four quarters as:

	Q1	Q2	Q3	Q4
Sales	$176	$159	$209	$242

   Sales for the first quarter of the year after this one are projected at $193 million. Accounts receivable at the beginning of the year were $69 million. Wildcat has a 45-day collection period.

   Wildcat's purchases from suppliers in a quarter are equal to 45 percent of the next quarter's forecasted sales, and suppliers are normally paid in 36 days. Wages, taxes, and other expenses run about 30 percent of sales. Interest and dividends are $16 million per quarter.

   Wildcat plans a major capital outlay in the second quarter of $55 million. Finally, the company started the year with a cash balance of $40 million and wishes to maintain a minimum balance of $20 million.

a. Complete a cash budget for Wildcat by filling in the following:

Wildcat, Inc. Cash Budget (in $ millions)	Q1	Q2	Q3	Q4
Beginning cash balance	$40			
Net cash inflow				
Ending cash balance				
Minimum cash balance	20			
Cumulative surplus (deficit)				

b. Assume that Wildcat can borrow any needed funds on a short-term basis at a rate of 3 percent per quarter and can invest any excess funds in short-term marketable securities at a rate of 2 percent per quarter. Prepare a short-term financial plan by filling in the following schedule. What is the net cash cost (total interest paid minus total investment income earned) for the year?

Wildcat, Inc. Short-Term Financial Plan (in $ millions)	Q1	Q2	Q3	Q4
Minimum cash balance	$20			
Net cash inflow				
New short-term investments				
Income from short-term investments				
Short-term investments sold				
New short-term borrowing				
Interest on short-term borrowing				
Short-term borrowing repaid				
Ending cash balance				
Minimum cash balance	20			
Cumulative surplus (deficit)				
Beginning short-term investments				
Ending short-term investments				
Beginning short-term debt				
Ending short-term debt				

20. Cash Management Policy Rework Problem 19 assuming:

a. Wildcat maintains a minimum cash balance of $30 million.

b. Wildcat maintains a minimum cash balance of $10 million.

Based on your answers in (a) and (b), do you think the firm can boost its profit by changing its cash management policy? Are there other factors that must be considered as well? Explain.

Challenge
(Questions 21–22)

21. Costs of Borrowing In exchange for a $300 million fixed commitment line of credit, your firm has agreed to do the following:

1. Pay 1.95 percent per quarter on any funds actually borrowed.

2. Maintain a compensating balance of 5 percent on any funds actually borrowed.

3. Pay an up-front commitment fee of .195 percent of the amount of the line.

Based on this information, answer the following:

a. Ignoring the commitment fee, what is the effective annual interest rate on this line of credit?

b. Suppose your firm immediately uses $125 million of the line and pays it off in one year. What is the effective annual interest rate on this loan?

22. Costs of Borrowing   DeAngelo Bank offers your firm a discount interest loan with an interest rate of 9.1 percent for up to $20 million, and in addition requires you to maintain a compensating balance of 4.5 percent against the amount borrowed. What is the effective annual interest rate on this lending arrangement?

WHAT'S ON THE WEB?

1. Cash Cycle   Go to www.reuters.com. You will need to find the most recent annual income statement and two most recent balance sheets for Stryker (SYK) and Estée Lauder (EL). Both companies are in the S&P 500 Index. SYK is a medical technology company, while ELP is a manufacturer and marketer of beauty and related products. Calculate the cash cycle for each company and comment on any similarities or differences.

2. Operating Cycle   Using the information you gathered in the previous problem, calculate the operating cycle for each company. What are the similarities or differences? Is this what you would expect from companies in each of these industries?

EXCEL MASTER IT! PROBLEM

Heidi Pedersen, treasurer for Wood Products, Inc., has just been asked by Justin Wood, the company's president, to prepare a memo detailing the company's ending cash balance for the next three months. Below, you will see the relevant estimates for this period.

ExcelMaster
coverage online

www.mhhe.com/RossCore6e

	July	August	September
Credit sales	$1,275,800	$1,483,500	$1,096,300
Credit purchases	765,480	890,160	657,780
Cash disbursements			
Wages, taxes, and expenses	348,600	395,620	337,150
Interest	29,900	29,900	29,900
Equipment	0	158,900	96,300
Credit sales collections:			
Collected in month of sale:	35%		
Collected month after sale:	60%		
Never collected:	5%		
June credit sales:	$1,135,020		
June credit purchases:	$ 681,012		
Beginning cash balance:	$ 425,000		

All credit purchases are paid in the month after the purchase.

a. Complete the cash budget for Wood Products for the next three months.

b. Heidi knows that the cash budget will become a standard report completed before each quarter. To help reduce the time to prepare the report each quarter, she would like a memo with the appropriate information in Excel linked to the memo. Prepare a memo to Justin that will automatically update when the values are changed in Excel.

KEAFER MANUFACTURING WORKING CAPITAL MANAGEMENT

You have recently been hired by Keafer Manufacturing to work in its newly established treasury department. Keafer Manufacturing is a small company that produces highly customized cardboard boxes in a variety of sizes for different purchasers. Adam Keafer, the owner of the company, works primarily in the sales and production areas of the company. Currently, the company basically puts all receivables in one pile and all payables in another, and a part-time bookkeeper periodically comes in and attacks the piles. Because of this disorganized system, the finance area needs work, and that's what you've been brought in to do.

The company currently has a cash balance of $170,000, and it plans to purchase new machinery in the third quarter at a cost of $325,000. The purchase of the machinery will be made with cash because of the discount offered for a cash purchase. Adam wants to maintain a minimum cash balance of $130,000 to guard against unforeseen contingencies. All of Keafer's sales to customers and purchases from suppliers are made with credit, and no discounts are offered or taken.

The company had the following sales each quarter of the year just ended:

	Q1	Q2	Q3	Q4
Gross sales	$893,000	$924,000	$996,000	$858,000

After some research and discussions with customers, you're projecting that sales will be 8 percent higher in each quarter next year. Sales for the first quarter of the following year are also expected to grow at 8 percent. You calculate that Keafer currently has an accounts receivable period of 57 days and an accounts receivable balance of $683,000. However, 10 percent of the accounts receivable balance is from a company that has just entered bankruptcy, and it is likely that this portion will never be collected.

You've also calculated that Keafer typically orders supplies each quarter in the amount of 50 percent of the next quarter's projected gross sales, and suppliers are paid in 53 days, on average. Wages, taxes, and other costs run about 25 percent of gross sales. The company has a quarterly interest payment of $190,000 on its long-term debt. Finally, the company uses a local bank for its short-term financial needs. It currently pays 1.2 percent per quarter on all short-term borrowing and maintains a money market account that pays .5 percent per quarter on all short-term deposits.

Adam has asked you to prepare a cash budget and short-term financial plan for the company under the current policies. He has also asked you to prepare additional plans based on changes in several inputs.

1. Use the numbers given to complete the cash budget and short-term financial plan.
2. Rework the cash budget and short-term financial plan assuming Keafer changes to a minimum cash balance of $100,000.
3. Rework the sales budget assuming an 11 percent growth rate in sales and a 5 percent growth rate in sales. Assume a $100,000 target cash balance.
4. Assuming the company's sales grow at 8 percent, what target cash balance would result in a zero need for short-term financing? To answer this question, you may need to set up a spreadsheet and use the "Solver" function.
5. You have looked at competitors' credit policies and have determined that the industry standard credit policy is 1/10, net 45. The interpretation of these credit terms is that a purchaser will receive a 1 percent discount on sales if it pays within 10 days. If the purchaser does not pay within 10 days, the full sales price is due in 45 days. You want to examine how a switch to this credit policy would affect your cash budget and short-term financial plan. If this credit policy is implemented, you estimate that 25 percent of all customers will take advantage of it, and the accounts receivable period will decline to 38 days. Rework the cash budget and short-term financial plan under the new credit policy and a minimum cash balance of $100,000. What interest rate is implied by the credit terms?
6. You have talked to the company's main supplier about the credit terms Keafer receives. The supplier has stated that it would be willing to offer new credit terms of 2/15, net 40. The interpretation of these credit terms is that Keafer will receive a 2 percent discount on sales if it pays within 15 days. If it does not pay within 15 days, the full sales price will be due in 40 days. What interest rate are the suppliers offering the company? Rework the cash budget and short-term financial plan assuming you take the credit terms on all orders and the minimum cash balance is $100,000.

Raising Capital

On April 3, 2018, digital music company Spotify went public in an unusual manner. Typically, when a company goes public, it hires investment banks, or underwriters, to help sell the company's stock. In the initial public offering (IPO), the underwriter sells the shares to the public, and the proceeds of the sale go to the company, minus any underwriter commission. But in Spotify's case, the company elected to do a "direct listing." It received no funds from selling stock to the public; instead, shares held by company insiders and investors became directly tradeable on the NYSE. What was even more unique about this IPO is that about seven months later, Spotify announced a $1 billion stock buyback.

Generally, companies undertake an IPO to raise funds from new investors. The current U.S. record holder is credit card giant Visa, which raised $17.9 billion in its 2008 IPO. In this chapter, we will examine the process by which companies sell stock to the public, the costs of doing so, and the role of investment banks in the process.

Businesses large and small have one thing in common: They need long-term capital. This chapter describes how they get it. We pay particular attention to what is probably the most important stage in a company's financial life cycle, the initial public offering. Such offerings are the process by which companies convert from being privately owned to being publicly owned. For many, starting a company, growing it, and taking it public is the ultimate entrepreneurial dream.

Please visit us at corecorporatefinance.blogspot.com for the latest developments in the world of corporate finance.

This chapter examines how firms raise capital. The financing method is generally tied to the firm's life cycle. Start-up firms are often financed via venture capital. As firms grow, they may want to "go public." A firm's first public offering is called an IPO, which stands for initial public offering. Later offerings are called SEOs, for seasoned equity offerings. This chapter follows the life cycle of the firm, covering venture capital, IPOs, and SEOs. Debt financing is discussed toward the end of the chapter.[1]

19.1 EARLY-STAGE FINANCING AND VENTURE CAPITAL

One day, you and a friend have a great idea for a new computer software product that will help users communicate using the next-generation meganet. Filled with entrepreneurial zeal, you christen the product Megacomm and set about bringing it to market.

Working nights and weekends, you are able to create a prototype of your product. It doesn't actually work, but at least you can show it around to illustrate your idea. To actually develop the product, you need to hire programmers, buy computers, rent office space,

---

[1] We are indebted to Jay R. Ritter of the University of Florida and M. Shane Hadden of *The Currency Report* (www.globalcurrencyreport.com) for helpful comments and suggestions on this chapter.

and so on. Unfortunately, because you are both MBA students, your combined assets are not sufficient to fund a pizza party, much less a start-up company. You need what is often referred to as OPM—other people's money.

Your first thought might be to approach a bank for a loan. You would probably discover, however, that banks are generally not interested in making loans to start-up companies with no assets (other than an idea) run by fledgling entrepreneurs with no track record. Instead you search for other sources of capital.

One group of potential investors goes by the name of angel investors, or just angels. They may be friends and family, with little knowledge of your product's industry and little experience backing start-up companies. However, some angels are more knowledgeable individuals, or groups of individuals, who have invested in a number of previous ventures.

Venture Capital

Alternatively, you might seek funds in the venture capital (VC) market. While venture capital does not have a precise definition, venture capitalists share some common characteristics. Three characteristics are particularly important:[2]

1. *VCs Are Financial Intermediaries That Raise Funds from Outside Investors.* VC firms are typically organized as limited partnerships. As with any limited partnership, limited partners invest with the general partner, who makes the investment decisions. The limited partners are frequently institutional investors, such as pension plans, endowments, and corporations. Wealthy individuals and families are often limited partners as well. This characteristic separates VCs from angels because angels typically invest just their own money. In addition, corporations sometimes set up internal venture capital divisions to fund fledgling firms. However, Metrick and Yasuda point out that because these divisions invest the funds of their corporate parent, rather than the funds of others, they are not—in spite of their name—venture capitalists.

2. *VCs Play an Active Role in Overseeing, Advising, and Monitoring the Companies in Which They Invest.* For example, members of venture capital firms frequently join the board of directors. The principals in VC firms are generally quite experienced in business. By contrast, while entrepreneurs at the helm of start-up companies may be bright, creative, and knowledgeable about their products, they often lack much business experience.

3. *VCs Generally Do Not Want to Own the Investment Forever.* Rather, VCs look for an exit strategy, such as taking the investment public (a topic we discuss in the next section) or selling it to another company. Corporate venture capital does not share this characteristic because corporations are frequently content to have the investment stay on the books of the internal VC division indefinitely.

This last characteristic is quite important in determining the nature of typical VC investments. A firm must be a certain size to either go public or be easily sold. Because the investment is generally small initially, it must possess great growth potential; many businesses do not. For example, imagine an individual who wants to open a gourmet restaurant. If the owner is a true "foodie" with no desire to expand beyond one location, it is unlikely the restaurant will ever become large enough to go public. By contrast, firms in high-tech fields often have significant growth potential, and many VC firms specialize in this area.

Figure 19.1 shows VC investments by industry. As can be seen, a large percentage of these investments are in high-tech fields.

How often do VC investments have successful exits? While data on exits are difficult to come by, Figure 19.2 shows outcomes for over 11,000 companies funded in the 1990s.

---

[2] These characteristics are discussed in depth in Andrew Metrick and Ayako Yasuda, *Venture Capital and the Finance of Innovation*, 2nd ed. (Hoboken, NJ: John Wiley and Sons, 2011).

FIGURE 19.1

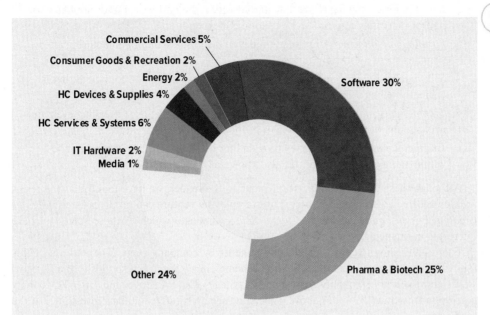

FIGURE 19.1

Venture Capital Investments in 2017 by Industry Sector

Source: National Venture Capital Association Yearbook 2018.

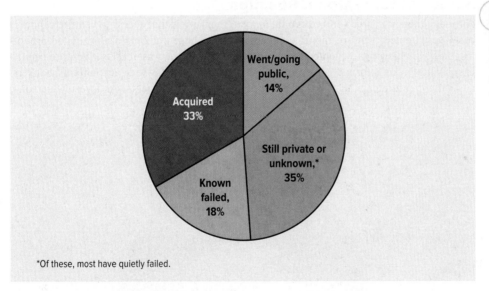

FIGURE 19.2

Exit Funnel Outcomes of the 11,686 Companies First Funded from 1991 to 2000

Source: National Venture Capital Association.

As can be seen, nearly 50 percent (= 14% + 33%) went public or were acquired. However, the internet bubble reached its peak in early 2000, so the period covered in the figure may have been an unusual one.

Stages of Financing

Both practitioners and scholars frequently speak of stages in venture capital financing. Well-known classifications for these stages are as follows:[3]

1. *Seed Money Stage.* A small amount of financing needed to prove a concept or develop a product. Marketing is not included in this stage.

---

[3] Albert V. Bruno and Tyzoon T. Tyebjee, "The Entrepreneur's Search for Capital," *Journal of Business Venturing* 1, no. 1 (1985), pp. 61–74; see also Paul Gompers and Josh Lerner, *The Venture Capital Cycle,* 2nd ed. (Cambridge, MA: MIT Press, 2006).

2. *Start-Up.* Financing for firms that started within the past year. Funds are likely to pay for marketing and product development expenditures.

3. *First-Round Financing.* Additional money to begin sales and manufacturing after a firm has spent its start-up funds.

4. *Second-Round Financing.* Funds earmarked for working capital for a firm that is currently selling its product but still losing money.

5. *Third-Round Financing.* Financing for a company that is at least breaking even and is contemplating an expansion. This round is also known as *mezzanine financing*.

6. *Fourth-Round Financing.* Money provided for firms that are likely to go public within half a year. This round is also known as *bridge financing*.

Although these categories may seem vague to the reader, we have found that the terms are well accepted within the industry. For example, the venture capital firms listed in *Pratt's Guide to Private Equity & Venture Capital Sources* indicate which of these stages they are interested in financing.[4]

Figure 19.3 shows venture capital investments by company stage. The authors of this figure use a slightly different classification scheme. *Angel/Seed* corresponds to the first two stages above. *Early VC* roughly corresponds to Stages 3 and 4 above, and *Later VC* roughly corresponds to Stages 5 and 6 above. As can be seen, venture capitalists invest little at the seed stage.

Some Venture Capital Realities

Although there is a large venture capital market, the truth is that access to venture capital is really very limited. Venture capital companies receive huge numbers of unsolicited proposals, the vast majority of which end up in the circular file (the wastebasket). Venture capitalists rely heavily on informal networks of engineers, scientists, lawyers, accountants, bankers, and other venture capitalists to help identify potential investments. As a result, personal

FIGURE 19.3

2017 Venture Capital Investment by Company Stage

Source: National Venture Capital Association Yearbook 2018.

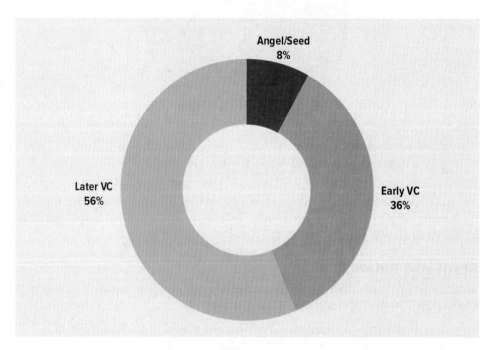

Angel/Seed
8%

Later VC
56%

Early VC
36%

[4] *Pratt's Guide to Private Equity and Venture Capital Sources* (2019), available at PE Hub Network, https://www.pehub.com/pratts/.

contacts are important in gaining access to the venture capital market; it is very much an "introduction" market.

Another fact about venture capital is that it is incredibly expensive. In a typical deal, the venture capitalist will demand (and get) 40 percent or more of the equity in the company. The venture capitalist will frequently hold voting convertible preferred stock, which gives various priorities in the event that the company is sold or liquidated. The venture capitalist will typically demand (and get) several seats on the company's board of directors and may even appoint one or more members of senior management.

Crowdfunding

On April 5, 2012, the JOBS Act was signed into law. A provision of this act allowed companies to raise money through crowdfunding, the effort of individuals to raise money in small amounts. Crowdfunding was first used to underwrite the U.S. tour of British rock band Marillion, but the JOBS Act allows companies to sell equity by crowdfunding. Originally, the JOBS Act allowed a company to issue up to $1 million in securities in a 12-month period, although this limit was raised to $5 million in 2015.

We should make an important distinction about two types of crowdfunding—*project crowdfunding* and *equity crowdfunding.* As an example of project crowdfunding, consider the card game Exploding Kittens, which exploded on the crowdfunding website Kickstarter and raised $8.8 million from about 220,000 backers. During the crowdfunding campaign, the company presold card decks. Every backer was shipped a deck of cards for the game, beginning about six months after the campaign ended. In this case, the backers were purchasers, not investors. This type of crowdfunding also has become a popular way to raise money for charitable causes. In contrast, with equity crowdfunding, the backers receive equity in the company. In May 2016, Regulation CF (also known as Title III of the JOBS Act) kicked in, which allows small investors access to new crowdfunding "portals." Previously, investors in crowdfunding had to be "accredited." For an individual, this requirement translates to more than $1 million in net worth or more than $200,000 in income for two of the past three years. Regulation CF allows investors with less than $100,000 in income or assets to invest at least $2,000 per year, up to a maximum of $5,000.

To sell securities through Regulation CF, a company must file a form with the SEC. This filing makes the company eligible to list its securities on a crowdfunding portal that is approved by FINRA (the Financial Industry Regulatory Authority), the same agency we mentioned earlier in the textbook for bond price reporting. Crowdfunding portals are already specializing. For example, there are portals that specialize in only accredited investors, all investors, or real estate, to name just a few.

> Check out two of the more well-known project and charitable crowdfunding websites at www.kickstarter.com and www.gofundme.com.

Initial Coin Offerings

In addition to sales of traditional debt and equity, a company can raise funds by selling tokens. These tokens often grant the holder the right to use the company's service in the future. For example, a company building a railroad may issue a token that can be used as a train ticket after the railroad is built.

Token sales occur on digital currency platforms and can be easily transferred on the platform or converted to U.S. dollars on specialized token exchanges. This liquidity has made tokens a popular means of funding since their introduction in 2015. Tokens are now purchased by both customers and investors, who may never use the token for the service being offered.

> See upcoming ICOs at tokenmarket.net/ico-calendar.

The initial sale of a token on a digital currency platform is often called an *initial coin offering,* or ICO (to sound like IPO). Many start-up companies are now choosing to raise funding through an ICO rather than the traditional venture capital channels. The most common platform for issuing new tokens is Ethereum, but there are many competitors. In 2018, there were 1,251 ICOs with a total value of about $7.7 billion.

> The SEC has some warnings on ICOs at www.sec.gov/news/public-statement/statement-clayton-2017-12-11.

Token sales are most popular among companies that are building services based on blockchain technology. This technology is at the heart of bitcoin and other cryptocurrencies. A blockchain is a timestamped ledger of transactions that is kept among a network of users without centralized control. It is similar to a traditional database, except that cryptography is used to make it infeasible to change the data once they are added to the chain. Many industries, including finance, are now updating their recordkeeping infrastructures with blockchain technology.

See the market value of tokens at coinmarketcap .com.

Token sales also can serve as an effective marketing tool. This is especially true if the business benefits from network effects as the potential for price appreciation in the tokens attracts new customers. The increase in customers increases the value of the service, which in turn increases the value of the tokens. For example, Civic is building a blockchain-based identity platform, and its currency is used to purchase identity verification services from trusted parties. The company raised $33 million in June 2017 through an ICO of the CVC token. The total value of the tokens at the end of 2017 was $224 million. In an indication of the volatility of tokens, the value dropped to less than $17 million by early 2019.

19.2 SELLING SECURITIES TO THE PUBLIC: THE BASIC PROCEDURE

We discuss the process of selling (issuing) securities to the public in the next several sections, paying particular attention to the process of going public.

Find out what firms are going public this week at marketwatch.com.

There are many rules and regulations surrounding the process of selling securities. The Securities Act of 1933 is the origin of federal regulations for all new interstate securities issues. The Securities Exchange Act of 1934 is the basis for regulating securities already outstanding. The Securities and Exchange Commission, or SEC, administers both acts.

There is a series of steps involved in issuing securities to the public. In general terms, the basic procedure is as follows:

1. Management's first step in issuing any securities to the public is to obtain approval from the board of directors. In some cases, the number of authorized shares of common stock must be increased. This requires a vote of the shareholders.

2. The firm must prepare a registration statement and file it with the SEC. With just a few exceptions, the registration statement is required for all public, interstate issues of securities.

Normally, a registration statement contains many pages of financial information, including a financial history, details of the existing business, proposed financing, and plans for the future.

3. The SEC examines the registration statement during a waiting period. During this time, the firm may distribute copies of a preliminary prospectus. The prospectus contains much of the information put into the registration statement, and it is given to potential investors by the firm. The preliminary prospectus is sometimes called a red herring, in part because bold red letters are printed on the cover.

A registration statement becomes effective on the 20th day after its filing unless the SEC sends a *letter of comment* suggesting changes. In that case, after the changes are made, the 20-day waiting period starts again. It is important to note that the SEC does not consider the economic merits of the proposed sale; it merely makes sure that various rules and regulations are followed. Also, the SEC generally does not check the accuracy or truthfulness of information in the prospectus.

The registration statement does not initially contain the price of the new issue. Usually, a price amendment is filed at or near the end of the waiting period, and the registration becomes effective.

4. The company cannot sell the securities during the waiting period. However, oral offers can be made.

5. On the effective date of the registration statement, a price is determined and a full-fledged selling effort gets under way. A final prospectus must accompany the delivery of securities or confirmation of sale, whichever comes first.

Tombstone advertisements (or *tombstones*) are used by underwriters after the waiting period. An example is reproduced in Figure 19.4. The tombstone contains the name of the issuer (the World Wrestling Federation, or WWF, in this case). It provides some information about the issue, and it lists the investment banks (the underwriters) that are involved with selling the issue. The role of the investment banks in selling securities is discussed more fully in the following pages.

The investment banks are divided into groups called *brackets* on the tombstone, based on their participation in the issue, and the names of the banks are listed alphabetically within each bracket. The brackets are often viewed as a kind of pecking order. In general, the higher the bracket, the greater is the underwriter's prestige.

19.3 ALTERNATIVE ISSUE METHODS

When a company decides to issue a new security, it can sell it as a public issue or a private issue. In the case of a public issue, the firm is required to register the issue with the SEC. Not all offerings of securities must be registered with the SEC. The most common exemptions from the registration requirements for stock offerings include:[5]

1. Private offerings to a limited number of persons or institutions.

2. Offerings of limited size.

3. Intrastate offerings.

Learn more about exempt offerings at www.sec .gov/smallbusiness/ exemptofferings.

For equity sales, there are two kinds of public issues: a general cash offer and a rights offer (or *rights offering*). With a cash offer, securities are offered to the general public on a "first-come, first-served" basis. With a rights offer, securities are initially offered only to existing owners. Rights offers are fairly common in other countries, but they are relatively rare in the United States, particularly in recent years. We therefore focus on cash offers in this chapter.

The first public equity issue that is made by a company is referred to as an initial public offering, an IPO, or an *unseasoned new issue*. This issue occurs when a company decides to go public. Obviously, all initial public offerings are cash offers. If the firm's existing shareholders wanted to buy the shares, the firm wouldn't have to sell them publicly in the first place.

A seasoned equity offering (SEO) is a new issue for a company with securities that have been previously issued. The terms *secondary* and *follow-on offering* are also commonly used. A seasoned equity offering of common stock can be made by using a cash offer or a rights offer.

---

[5] A variety of different arrangements can be made for private equity issues. Selling unregistered securities avoids the costs of complying with the Securities Exchange Act of 1934. Regulation significantly restricts the resale of unregistered equity securities. For example, the purchaser may be required to hold the securities for at least two years. Many of the restrictions were significantly eased in 1990 for very large institutional investors, however. The private placement of bonds is discussed in a later section.

FIGURE 19.4

An Example of a Tombstone Advertisement

This announcement is neither an offer to sell nor a solicitation of an offer to buy any of these securities. The offering is made only by the Prospectus.

New Issue

11,500,000 Shares

World Wrestling Federation Entertainment, Inc.

Class A Common Stock

Price $17.00 Per Share

Copies of the Prospectus may be obtained in any State in which this announcement is circulated from only such of the Underwriters, including the undersigned, as may lawfully offer these securities in such State.

U.S. Offering

9,200,000 Shares

This portion of the underwriting is being offered in the United States and Canada.

Bear, Stearns & Co. Inc.

Credit Suisse First Boston

Merrill Lynch & Co.

Wit Capital Corporation

Allen & Company Incorporated	Banc of America Securities LLC	Deutsche Banc Alex. Brown
Donaldson, Lufkin & Jenrette	A.G. Edwards & Sons, Inc.	Hambrecht & Quist ING Barings
Prudential Securities	SG Cowen Wassertein Perella Securities, Inc.	Advest, Inc.
Axiom Capital Management, Inc.	Blackford Securities Corp.	J.C. Bradford & Co.
Joseph Charles & Assoc., Inc.	Chatsworth Securities LLC	Gabelli & Company, Inc.
Gaines, Berland Inc. Jefferies & Company, Inc.	Josephthal & Co. Inc.	Neuberger Berman, LLC
Raymond James & Associates, Inc.		Sanders Morris Mundy
Tucker Anthony Cleary Gull		Wachovia Securities, Inc.

International Offering

2,300,000 Shares

This portion of the underwriting is being offered outside of the United States and Canada.

Bear, Stearns International Limited

Credit Suisse First Boston

Merrill Lynch International

TABLE 19.1

The Methods of
Issuing New Securities

Method	Type	Definition
Public		
Traditional negotiated cash offer	Firm commitment cash offer	Company negotiates an agreement with an investment banker to underwrite and distribute the new shares. A specified number of shares are bought by underwriters and sold at a higher price.
	Best efforts cash offer	Company has investment bankers sell as many of the new shares as possible at the agreed-upon price. There is no guarantee concerning how much cash will be raised. Some best efforts offerings do not use an underwriter.
	Dutch auction cash offer	Company has investment bankers auction shares to determine the highest offer price obtainable for a given number of shares to be sold.
Privileged subscription	Direct rights offer	Company offers the new stock directly to its existing shareholders.
	Standby rights offer	Like the direct rights offer, this contains a privileged subscription arrangement with existing shareholders. The net proceeds are guaranteed by the underwriters.
Nontraditional cash offer	Shelf cash offer	Qualifying companies can authorize all the shares they expect to sell over a two-year period and sell them when needed.
	Competitive firm cash offer	Company can elect to award the underwriting contract through a public auction instead of negotiation.
Private	Direct placement	Securities are sold directly to the purchaser, who, at least until recently, generally could not resell the securities for at least two years.

These methods of issuing new securities are shown in Table 19.1. Notice, we didn't include the direct listing method, which Spotify used to list its stock, because the company doesn't issue new shares in a direct listing.

19.4 UNDERWRITERS

If the public issue of securities is a cash offer, underwriters are usually involved. Underwriting is an important line of business for large investment firms such as Goldman Sachs. Underwriters perform services such as the following for corporate issuers:

1. Formulating the method used to issue the securities.
2. Pricing the new securities.
3. Selling the new securities.

Typically, the underwriter buys the securities for less than the offering price and accepts the risk of not being able to sell them. The difference between the underwriter's buying price and the offering price is called the spread, or *discount*. It is the basic compensation received by the underwriter. Sometimes the underwriter will get noncash compensation in the form of warrants and stock in addition to the spread.[6]

Underwriters combine to form an underwriting group called a syndicate to share the risk and to help sell the issue. In a syndicate, one or more managers arrange the offering. This manager is designated as the lead manager, or principal manager. The lead manager typically has the responsibility of pricing the securities. The other underwriters in the syndicate serve primarily to distribute the issue.

---

[6] Warrants are essentially options to buy stock at a fixed price for some fixed period of time.

Choosing an Underwriter

A firm can offer its securities to the highest bidding underwriter on a *competitive offer* basis, or it can negotiate directly with an underwriter. In most cases, companies usually do new issues of debt and equity on a *negotiated offer* basis.

There is evidence that competitive underwriting is cheaper to use than negotiated underwriting, and the underlying reasons for the dominance of negotiated underwriting in the United States are the subject of ongoing debate.

Types of Underwriting

Three basic types of underwriting are involved in a cash offer: firm commitment, best efforts, and Dutch auction.

FIRM COMMITMENT UNDERWRITING   In firm commitment underwriting, the issuer sells the entire issue to the underwriters, who then attempt to resell it. This is the most prevalent type of underwriting in the United States. This is really a purchase-resale arrangement, and the underwriters' fee is the spread. For a new issue of seasoned equity, the underwriters can look at the market price to determine what the issue should sell for, and most such new issues are firm commitments.

If the underwriter cannot sell all of the issue at the agreed-upon offering price, it may have to lower the price on the unsold shares. Nonetheless, with firm commitment underwriting, the issuer receives the agreed-upon amount, and all the risk associated with selling the issue is transferred to the underwriter.

Because the offering price usually isn't set until the underwriters have investigated how receptive the market is to the issue, this risk is usually minimal. Also, because the offering price usually is not set until just before selling commences, the issuer doesn't know precisely what its net proceeds will be until that time.

To determine the offering price, the underwriter will meet with potential buyers, typically large institutional buyers such as mutual funds. Often, the underwriter and company management will do presentations in multiple cities, pitching the stock in what is known as a *road show.* Potential buyers provide information on the price they would be willing to pay and the number of shares they would purchase at a particular price. This process of soliciting information about buyers and the prices and quantities they would demand is known as *bookbuilding.* As we will see, despite the bookbuilding process, underwriters frequently get the price wrong, or so it seems.

Of course, there are risks to the underwriters in a firm commitment offering. In November 2018, Credit Suisse underwrote a 10-million-share secondary offering for Canada Goose, known for its expensive coats and parkas. When the offering was made, in an unrelated incident, Huawei Technologies' finance chief was arrested in Vancouver, sparking a diplomatic dispute between Canada and China. The arrest led to a Chinese boycott of Canadian brands, sending Canada Goose shares down by 20 percent. Credit Suisse was forced to sell the shares at a loss to the offering price, or risk a further decline in the stock price. Reportedly, Credit Suisse lost $60 million on the transaction.

BEST EFFORTS UNDERWRITING   In best efforts underwriting, the underwriter is legally bound to use "best efforts" to sell the securities at the agreed-upon offering price. Beyond this, the underwriter does not guarantee any particular amount of money to the issuer. This form of underwriting has become uncommon in recent years; firm commitments are now the dominant form.

DUTCH AUCTION UNDERWRITING   With Dutch auction underwriting, the underwriter does not set a fixed price for the shares to be sold. Instead, the underwriter conducts an auction in which investors bid for shares. The offer price is determined based on the submitted bids.

A Dutch auction is also known by the more descriptive name *uniform price auction.* This approach to selling securities to the public is relatively new in the IPO market and has not been widely used there, but it is very common in the bond markets. For example, it is the sole procedure used by the U.S. Treasury to sell enormous quantities of notes, bonds, and bills to the public.

The best way to understand a Dutch or uniform price auction is to consider a simple example. Suppose the Rial Company wants to sell 400 shares to the public. The company receives five bids as follows:

Bidder	Quantity	Price
A	100 shares	$16
B	100 shares	14
C	200 shares	12
D	100 shares	12
E	200 shares	10

Thus, Bidder A is willing to buy 100 shares at $16 each, Bidder B is willing to buy 100 shares at $14, and so on. The Rial Company examines the bids to determine the highest price that will result in all 400 shares being sold. So, for example, at $14, A and B would buy only 200 shares, so that price is too high. Working our way down, all 400 shares won't be sold until we hit a price of $12, so $12 will be the offer price in the IPO. Bidders A through D will receive shares; Bidder E will not.

There are two additional important points to observe in our example: First, all the winning bidders will pay $12, even Bidders A and B, who actually bid a higher price. The fact that all successful bidders pay the same price is the reason for the name "uniform price auction." The idea in such an auction is to encourage bidders to bid aggressively by providing some protection against bidding a price that is too high.

Second, notice that at the $12 offer price, there are actually bids for 500 shares, which exceeds the 400 shares Rial wants to sell. Thus, there has to be some sort of allocation. How this is done varies a bit, but in the IPO market, the approach has been to compute the ratio of shares offered to shares bid at the offer price or better, which, in our example, is $400/500 = .8$, and allocate bidders that percentage of their bids. In other words, Bidders A through D would each receive 80 percent of the shares they bid at a price of $12 per share.

Learn all about Dutch auction IPOs at www.wrhambrecht.com.

The Green Shoe Provision

Many underwriting contracts contain a Green Shoe provision (sometimes called the *over-allotment option*), which gives the members of the underwriting group the option to purchase additional shares from the issuer at the offering price.[7] Essentially all IPOs and SEOs include this provision, but ordinary debt offerings generally do not. The stated reason for the Green Shoe option is to cover excess demand and oversubscriptions. Green Shoe options usually last for about 30 days and involve no more than 15 percent of the newly issued shares.

The Aftermarket

The period after a new issue is initially sold to the public is referred to as the *aftermarket.* The lead underwriter frequently will "stabilize," or support, the market price for a relatively short time following the offering. This is done by actually selling 115 percent of the issue. If the price rises in the aftermarket, the underwriter will exercise the Green Shoe option to

---

[7] The term *Green Shoe provision* sounds quite exotic, but the origin is relatively mundane. The term comes from the name of the Green Shoe Manufacturing Company, which, in 1963, was the first issuer to grant such an option.

purchase the extra 15 percent needed. If the price declines, however, the underwriter will step in and buy the stock in the open market, thereby supporting the price. In this second case, the underwriter allows the Green Shoe option to expire.[8] For example, when Facebook went public in May 2012, lead underwriter Morgan Stanley was forced to step in and stabilize the stock price. Even though the stock opened at $42.05, it quickly fell to $38 less than an hour after trading on the stock began. At that point, Morgan Stanley stepped in and began buying shares of the stock to create a floor of $38 per share.

Lockup Agreements

Although they are not required by law, almost all underwriting contracts contain so-called lockup agreements. Such agreements specify how long insiders must wait after an IPO before they can sell some or all of their stock. Lockup periods have become fairly standardized in recent years at 180 days. Thus, following an IPO, insiders can't cash out until six months have gone by, which ensures that they maintain a significant economic interest in the company going public.

Lockup periods are also important because it is not unusual for the number of locked-up shares to exceed the number of shares held by the public, sometimes by a substantial multiple. On the day the lockup period expires, there is the possibility that a large number of shares will hit the market on the same day and thereby depress values. The evidence suggests that, on average, venture capital-backed companies are particularly likely to experience a loss in value on the lockup expiration day.

Learn more about investment banks at Morgan Stanley's website: www.morganstanley.com/what-we-do/investment-banking.

The Quiet Period

From the time a company begins to seriously consider an IPO until 40 calendar days following an IPO, the SEC requires that a firm and its managing underwriters observe a "quiet period." This means that all communications with the public must be limited to ordinary announcements and other purely factual matters. The SEC's logic is that all relevant information should be contained in the prospectus. An important result of this requirement is that the underwriters' analysts are prohibited from making recommendations to investors. As soon as the quiet period ends, however, the managing underwriters typically publish research reports, usually accompanied by a favorable "buy" recommendation.

Firms that don't stay quiet can have their IPOs delayed. For example, just before Google's IPO, an interview with cofounders Sergey Brin and Larry Page appeared in *Playboy*. The interview almost caused a postponement of the IPO, but Google was able to amend its prospectus in time (by including the article!). However, in May 2004, Salesforce.com's IPO was delayed because an interview with CEO Marc Benioff appeared in *The New York Times*. Salesforce.com finally went public two months later.

19.5 IPOs AND UNDERPRICING

Determining the correct offering price is the most difficult thing an underwriter must do for an initial public offering. The issuing firm faces a potential cost if the offering price is set too high or too low. If the issue is priced too high, it may be unsuccessful and have to be withdrawn. If the issue is priced below the true market value, the issuer's existing shareholders will experience an opportunity loss when they sell their shares for less than they are worth.

Underpricing is fairly common. It obviously helps new shareholders earn a higher return on the shares they buy. However, the existing shareholders of the issuing firm are not helped by underpricing. For example, consider the Anaplan IPO on October 12, 2018. Anaplan, a cloud software company, sold 15.5 million shares at a price of $17. The stock really moved,

---

[8] Occasionally, the price of a security falls dramatically when the underwriter ceases to stabilize the price. In such cases, Wall Street humorists (the ones who didn't buy any of the stock) have referred to the period following the aftermarket as the aftermath.

jumping to $24.30 by the end of the day, an increase of about 43 percent. On the basis of these numbers, Anaplan's stock was underpriced by about $7.30 per share, which means the company missed out on an additional $113.2 million, a large sum considering the company raised only $263.5 million.

Dutch auctions are supposed to eliminate this kind of "pop" in first-day prices. Google sold 19.6 million shares at a price of $85 in a Dutch auction IPO. However, the stock closed at $100.34 on the first day, an increase of 18 percent, so Google missed out on an additional $300 million.

One of the biggest dollar amounts "left on the table" occurred in 1999 when eToys went public, offering 8.2 million shares. The stock jumped $57 above the offer price on the first day, which meant eToys left about half a billion dollars on the table! eToys could have used the money; it filed for bankruptcy less than two years later. In May 2002, the company sued its lead underwriter, claiming the offer price was deliberately set too low.

Of course, not all IPOs increase in price on the first day. For example, security company ADT went public on January 19, 2018, at a price of $14. The company's stock opened at $12.65 and dropped to $12.00 before closing at $12.39 by the end of the day, a drop of about 12 percent from the IPO price.

IPO information is ubiquitous on the World Wide Web. Two sites of interest are IPO Home at www.renaissancecapital .com and at www .ipocentral.com.

Evidence on Underpricing

Figure 19.5 provides a more general illustration of the underpricing phenomenon. What is shown is the month-by-month history of underpricing for SEC-registered IPOs.[9] The period covered is 1960 through 2018. Figure 19.6 presents the number of offerings in each month for the same period.

FIGURE 19.5 Average Initial Returns by Month for SEC-Registered Initial Public Offerings: 1960–2018

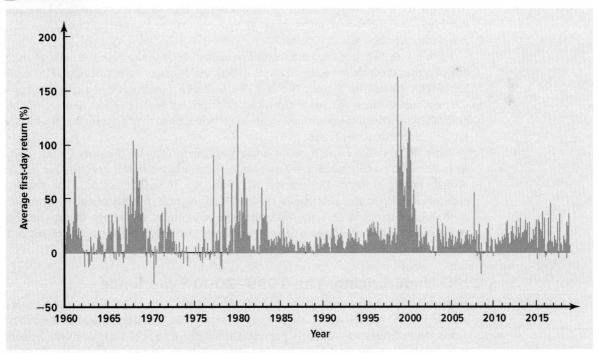

Source: Ibbotson, Roger G., Jody L. Sindelar, and Jay R. Ritter. "The Market's Problems with the Pricing of Initial Public Offerings." *Journal of Applied Corporate Finance* 7, no. 1 (1994): pp. 66–74, as updated by the authors.

[9] The discussion in this section draws on Jay R. Ritter, "Initial Public Offerings," *Contemporary Finance Digest* 2, no. 1 (1998), pp. 5–30.

FIGURE 19.6 Number of Offerings by Month for SEC-Registered Initial Public Offerings: 1960–2018

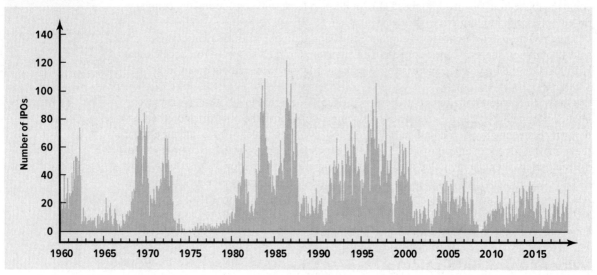

Source: Ibbotson, Roger G., Jody L. Sindelar, and Jay R. Ritter. "The Market's Problems with the Pricing of Initial Public Offerings." *Journal of Applied Corporate Finance* 7, no. 1 (1994): pp. 66–74, as updated by the authors.

Figure 19.5 shows that underpricing can be quite dramatic, exceeding 100 percent in some months. In such months, the average IPO more than doubled in value, sometimes in a matter of hours. Also, the degree of underpricing varies through time, and periods of severe underpricing ("hot issue" markets) are followed by periods of little underpricing ("cold issue" markets). For example, in the 1980s, the average IPO was underpriced by 7.3 percent. For 1999–2000, IPOs were underpriced by 64.5 percent, on average, and for 2001–2018, average underpricing was 21.3 percent.

From Figure 19.6, it is apparent that the number of IPOs is also highly variable through time. Further, there are pronounced cycles in both the degree of underpricing and the number of IPOs. Comparing Figures 19.5 and 19.6, we see that increases in the number of new offerings tend to follow periods of significant underpricing by roughly 6 to 12 months. This probably occurs because companies decide to go public when they perceive that the market is highly receptive to new issues.

Table 19.2 contains a year-by-year summary of underpricing for the years 1980 to 2018. As indicated, a grand total of 8,497 companies were included in this analysis. The degree of underpricing averaged 17.9 percent overall for the 39 years examined. The smallest underpricing during this period was 1984, with an increase in value of only 3.7 percent. At the other extreme, in 1999, the 476 issues were underpriced, on average, by a remarkable 71.2 percent. The nearby *Finance Matters* box shows that IPO underpricing is not just confined to the United States; instead, it seems to be a global phenomenon.

IPO Underpricing: The 1999–2000 Experience

Table 19.2, along with Figures 19.5 and 19.6, shows that 1999 and 2000 were extraordinary years in the IPO market. About 850 companies went public, and the average first-day return across the two years was about 65 percent. During this time, 194 IPOs doubled, or more than doubled, in value on the first day. In contrast, only 39 did so in the preceding 24 years combined. One company, VA Linux, shot up 698 percent!

The dollar amount raised in 2000, $64.80 billion, was a record, which topped the $64.67 billion in 1999. The underpricing was so severe in 1999 that companies left $37 billion "on the table," which was substantially more than in 1990 through 1998 combined, and in 2000,

Year	Number of Offerings*	Average First-Day Returns (%)†	Gross Proceeds ($ billions)‡
1980	71	14.3	.91
1981	193	5.9	2.31
1982	77	11.0	1.00
1983	451	9.9	8.89
1984	171	3.7	2.02
1985	186	6.4	4.09
1986	393	6.1	13.40
1987	285	5.6	11.68
1988	105	5.5	3.88
1989	116	8.0	5.81
1990	110	10.8	4.27
1991	286	11.9	15.39
1992	412	10.3	22.69
1993	510	12.7	31.44
1994	402	9.6	17.17
1995	461	21.2	27.95
1996	677	17.2	42.05
1997	474	14.0	31.76
1998	281	21.9	33.65
1999	476	71.2	64.67
2000	380	56.4	64.80
2001	79	14.2	34.24
2002	66	9.1	22.03
2003	63	11.7	9.54
2004	173	12.3	31.19
2005	159	10.3	28.23
2006	157	12.1	30.48
2007	1,159	14.0	35.66
2008	21	5.7	22.76
2009	41	9.8	13.17
2010	91	9.4	29.82
2011	81	13.9	26.97
2012	93	17.8	31.11
2013	157	21.1	38.75
2014	206	15.5	42.20
2015	118	19.2	22.00
2016	75	14.6	12.52
2017	107	13.0	22.99
2018	134	18.6	33.45
1980–1989	2,048	7.2	53.99
1990–1998	3,613	14.8	226.38
1999–2000	856	64.6	129.47
2001–2018	1,980	14.3	487.10
1980–2018	**8,497**	**17.9**	**896.95**

TABLE 19.2

Number of Offerings, Average First-Day Returns, and Gross Proceeds of Initial Public Offerings: 1980–2018

Source: Professor Jay R. Ritter, University of Florida.

* The number of offerings excludes IPOs with an offer price of less than $5.00, ADRs, best efforts, units, Regulation A offers (small issues, raising less than $1.5 million during the 1980s), real estate investment trusts (REITs), partnerships, and closed-end funds. Banks and S&Ls and non-CRSP-listed IPOs are included.

† First-day returns are computed as the percentage return from the offering price to the first closing market price.

‡ Gross proceeds data are from Securities Data Co., and they exclude overallotment options but include the international tranche, if any. No adjustments for inflation have been made.

FINANCE MATTERS

IPO UNDERPRICING AROUND THE WORLD

The United States is not the only country in which initial public offerings (IPOs) of common stock are underpriced. The phenomenon exists in every country with a stock market, although the extent of underpricing varies from country to country.

In general, countries with developed capital markets have more moderate underpricing than in emerging markets. During the internet bubble of 1999–2000, however, underpricing in the developed capital markets increased dramatically. In the United States, for example, the average first-day return during 1999–2000 was 65 percent. At the same time underpricing in the developed capital markets increased, the underpricing of IPOs sold to residents of China moderated. The Chinese average has come down to a mere 158 percent, which is lower than it had been in the early and mid-1990s. After the bursting of the internet bubble in mid-2000, the level of underpricing in the United States, Germany, and other developed capital markets has returned to more traditional levels.

The table below gives a summary of the average first-day returns on IPOs in a number of countries around the world, with the figures collected from a number of studies by various authors.

Country	Sample Size	Time Period	Avg. Initial Return	Country	Sample Size	Time Period	Avg. Initial Return
Argentina	26	1991–2013	4.2%	Korea	1,758	1980–2014	58.8
Australia	1,562	1976–2011	21.8	Malaysia	562	1980–2018	51.0
Austria	103	1971–2013	6.4	Mauritius	40	1989–2005	15.2
Belgium	154	1984–2017	11.0	Mexico	149	1987–2017	9.9
Brazil	303	1979–2018	30.3	Netherlands	212	1982–2017	13.3
Bulgaria	9	2004–2007	36.5	New Zealand	242	1979–2013	18.6
Canada	758	1971–2017	6.4	Nigeria	125	1989–2017	12.8
Chile	86	1982–2018	6.9	Norway	266	1984–2018	6.7
China	3,554	1990–2017	157.7	Philippines	173	1987–2018	17.3
Cyprus	73	1997–2012	20.3	Poland	309	1991–2014	12.7
Denmark	173	1984–2017	7.4	Portugal	33	1992–2017	11.5
Egypt	74	1990–2017	9.4	Russia	64	1999–2013	3.3
Finland	168	1971–2013	16.9	Saudi Arabia	80	2003–2011	239.8
France	834	1983–2017	9.7	Singapore	687	1973–2017	25.8
Germany	779	1978–2014	23.0	South Africa	316	1980–2013	17.4
Greece	373	1976–2013	50.8	Spain	143	1986–2013	10.3
Hong Kong	2,042	1980–2017	44.5	Sri Lanka	105	1987–2008	33.5
India	3,145	1990–2014	85.2	Sweden	405	1980–2015	25.9
Indonesia	531	1990–2017	26.4	Switzerland	164	1983–2013	27.3
Iran	279	1991–2004	22.4	Taiwan	1,620	1980–2013	38.1
Ireland	38	1991–2013	21.6	Thailand	697	1987–2018	40.0
Israel	348	1990–2006	13.8	Turkey	404	1990–2014	9.6
Italy	312	1985–2013	15.2	United Kingdom	4,932	1959–2012	16.0
Japan	3,488	1970–2016	44.7	United States	13,314	1960–2018	16.8
Jordan	53	1999–2008	149.0				

Source: Professor Jay R. Ritter, University of Florida.

the amount was about $30 billion. In other words, over the two-year period, companies missed out on $67 billion because of underpricing.

October 19, 1999, was one of the more memorable days during this time. The World Wrestling Federation (WWF) (now known as World Wrestling Entertainment, or WWE) and Martha Stewart Omnimedia both went public, so it was Martha Stewart versus "Stone Cold" Steve Austin. When the closing bell rang, it was a clear smackdown as Martha Stewart gained 98 percent on the first day, compared to 48 percent for the WWF.

The IPO market cooled off considerably in 2001. Many observers now refer to the 1999–2000 period as the internet "bubble" period. The word *bubble* in this context refers to a situation in which prices are bid up to irrational, and unsustainable, levels. During 1999, for example, 323 of the companies that went public were considered internet IPOs, meaning companies that did most (or all) of their business on the internet, or companies whose products were used for computers or networks. By April 2001, of the 1999 internet IPOs, only 12, or 4 percent, were trading above their offer price, and only four, or 1 percent, were trading above their first-day close. Was it really a bubble? Let us say that, at a minimum, there were instances of valuations that are very hard to reconcile with economic reality.

Why Does Underpricing Exist?

Based on the evidence we've examined, an obvious question is why does underpricing continue to exist? As we discuss, there are various explanations, but, to date, there is a lack of complete agreement among researchers as to which is correct.

We present some pieces of the underpricing puzzle by stressing two important caveats to our preceding discussion. First, the average figures we have examined tend to obscure the fact that much of the apparent underpricing is attributable to the smaller, more highly speculative issues. This point is illustrated in Table 19.3, which shows the extent of underpricing for about 8,500 firms during the period from 1980 through 2018. Here, the firms are grouped based on their total sales in the 12 months prior to the IPO.

As illustrated in Table 19.3, there is a tendency for underpricing to be more pronounced for firms with relatively small pre-IPO sales. These firms tend to be young firms, and such young firms can be very risky investments. Arguably, they must be significantly underpriced, on average, just to attract investors, and this is one explanation for the underpricing phenomenon.

The second caveat is that relatively few IPO buyers will actually get the initial high average returns observed in IPOs, and many will actually lose money. Although it is true that, on

TABLE 19.3 Average First-Day Returns, Categorized by Sales, for IPOs: 1980–2018*

Annual Sales of Issuing Firms	1980–1989		1990–1998		1999–2000		2001–2018	
	Number of Firms	First-Day Average Return	Number of Firms	First-Day Average Return	Number of Firms	First-Day Average Return	Number of Firms	First-Day Average Return
$0 ≤ sales < $10m	425	10.3%	741	17.2%	331	68.9%	429	10.0%
$10m ≤ sales < $20m	242	8.6	393	18.5	138	81.4	85	13.5
$20m ≤ sales < $50m	501	7.8	789	18.8	154	75.5	228	15.7
$50m ≤ sales < $100m	356	6.3	590	12.8	86	62.2	293	20.8
$100m ≤ sales < $200m	234	5.1	454	11.8	56	35.8	259	19.5
$200m ≤ sales	290	3.4	646	8.7	91	25.0	686	11.9
All	2,048	7.2%	3,613	14.8%	856	64.6%	1,980	14.3%

* Sales, measured in millions, are for the last 12 months prior to going public. All sales have been converted into dollars of 2003 purchasing power using the Consumer Price Index. There are 8,178 IPOs, after excluding IPOs with an offer price of less than $5.00 per share, units, REITs, SPACs, ADRs, closed-end funds, banks and S&Ls, firms not listed on CRSP within six months of the offer date, and natural resources partnerships. The average first-day return is 18.0 percent.

Source: Professor Jay R. Ritter, University of Florida.

average, IPOs have positive initial returns, a significant fraction of them have price drops. Furthermore, when the price is too low, the issue is often "oversubscribed." This means investors will not be able to buy all of the shares they want, and the underwriters will allocate the shares among investors.

The average investor will find it difficult to get shares in a "successful" offering (one in which the price increases) because there will not be enough shares to go around. On the other hand, an investor blindly submitting orders for IPOs tends to get more shares in issues that go down in price.

To illustrate, consider this tale of two investors. Smith knows very accurately what the Bonanza Corporation is worth when its shares are offered. She is confident that the shares are underpriced. Jones knows only that IPOs are usually underpriced. Armed with this information, Jones decides to buy 1,000 shares of every IPO. Does he actually earn an abnormally high return on the initial offering?

The answer is no, and at least one reason is Smith. Knowing about the Bonanza Corporation, Smith invests all her money in its IPO. When the issue is oversubscribed, the underwriters have to somehow allocate the shares between Smith and Jones. The net result is that when an issue is underpriced, Jones doesn't get to buy as much of it as he wanted.

Smith also knows that the Blue Sky Corporation IPO is overpriced. In this case, she avoids its IPO altogether, and Jones ends up with a full 1,000 shares. To summarize this tale, Jones gets fewer shares when more knowledgeable investors swarm to buy an underpriced issue and gets all he wants when the smart money avoids the issue.

This is an example of a "winner's curse," and it is thought to be another reason why IPOs have such a large average return. When the average investor "wins" and gets the entire allocation, it may be because those who knew better avoided the issue. The only way underwriters can counteract the winner's curse and attract the average investor is to underprice new issues (on average) so that the average investor still makes a profit.

A final reason for underpricing is that the underpricing is a kind of insurance for the investment banks. Conceivably, an investment bank could be sued successfully by angry customers if it consistently overpriced securities. Underpricing guarantees that, at least on average, customers will come out ahead.[10]

The Partial Adjustment Phenomenon

When a company files its registration statement with the SEC, it will at some point in the process indicate a range of stock prices between which it expects to offer shares. This range is called the "file price range," or words to that effect. A file price range of $10 to $12 is common, but many others exist. For example, the Anaplan IPO filings, which we mentioned earlier, indicated a maximum anticipated price of $15.

Just before a company's shares are sold to investors, the final IPO offer price is determined. As shown in Section A of Table 19.4, that price can be above, within, or below the price range originally indicated by the company. Over the period 1980–2018, 46 percent of IPOs were within the file range, with 28 percent below and 26 percent above.

Section B of Table 19.4 illustrates an interesting and very clear pattern. IPO underpricing is much more severe when an offer is priced above the file range. Again over the 1980–2018 period, IPOs that priced above the file range were underpriced by 50 percent, on average, compared to only 3 percent for firms priced below it. The 1999–2000 period again stands out. Issues that "went off" above the file range were underpriced by an average of 122 percent!

---

[10] Some researchers have hypothesized that overenthusiasm and optimism among individual investors can explain high first-day returns. For example, see Jay Ritter and Ivo Welch, "A Review of IPO Activity, Pricing and Allocations," *Journal of Finance* 45, no. 4 (2002), pp. 1795–828. See also Francesca Cornelli, David Goldreich, and Alexander Ljungqvist, "Investor Sentiment and Pre-IPO Markets," *Journal of Finance* 61, no. 3 (2006), pp. 1187–216. In addition, Gerard Hoberg, "The Underwriter Persistence Phenomenon," *Journal of Finance* 62, no. 3 (2007), pp. 1169–206, concludes that high-underpricing underwriters are not "lowballing" issuers but instead have access to superior information and use this advantage.

A: Percentage of IPOs Relative to File Price Range			
	Below	**Within**	**Above**
1980–1989	30%	57%	13%
1990–1998	27	49	24
1999–2000	18	38	44
2001–2018	34	45	21
1980–2018	28	46	26

B: Average First-Day Returns Relative to File Price Range			
	Below	**Within**	**Above**
1980–1989	0%	6%	20%
1990–1998	4	11	31
1999–2000	8	26	122
2001–2018	4	11	37
1980–2018	3	11	50

TABLE 19.4

IPO Underpricing and File Price Range

This pattern is known as the "partial adjustment" phenomenon. The name refers to the fact that when firms raise their IPO offer prices, they only do so partially, meaning that they don't move the price high enough. In Anaplan's case, the final offer price was $17, at the top of the $15 to $17 price range. This price range was a revision of the originally announced $13 to $15 price range: The stock jumped 43 percent on the first day of trading.

Why does the partial adjustment phenomenon exist? The answer is unknown. The question is related to the broader question of why IPO underpricing exists, which we consider next.

19.6 WHAT CFOS SAY ABOUT THE IPO PROCESS

In an IPO, a firm accomplishes two important things: raising capital and becoming a public company. The two major benefits to a firm going public are the better ability to raise capital and better ability of shareholders to diversify. However, there are substantial costs to being a public company in the United States. We have described the statutory disclosure requirements monitored by the Securities and Exchange Commission. More recently, there are the requirements of the Sarbanes-Oxley Act for more accountability in corporate governance.

In 2000–2002, a large number of CFOs whose firms had recently gone public were asked about their firms' motives. Figure 19.7 describes their responses. The motives that were cited the most for going public were the creation of public shares for use in future acquisitions and establishing a market value for the firm. Diversification was also seen as a benefit.

The CFOs were also asked to describe their perceptions of IPO underpricing. Figure 19.8 shows the results of the survey. The most cited reason for IPO underpricing was to compensate investors for taking the risk of the IPO, followed by the increase of the post-issue trading volume for the stock. The reasons are consistent with our story of Ms. Smith and Mr. Jones and underwriting risk, but they also show that the quality and liquidity of the aftermarket are important.

FIGURE 19.7 Survey Evidence on the Motivations for Going Public

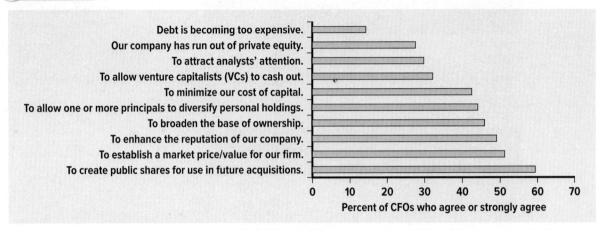

Source: Brau, James C., and Stanley E. Fawcett. "Evidence on What CFOs Think About the IPO Process: Practice, Theory and Managerial Implications." *Journal of Applied Corporate Finance* 18, no. 3 (2006): pp. 107–17.

FIGURE 19.8 CFO Perceptions of IPO Underpricing

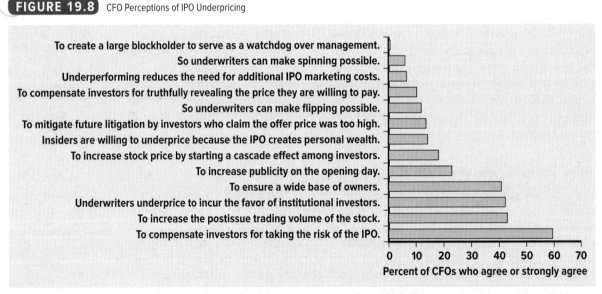

Source: Brau, James C., and Stanley E. Fawcett. "Evidence on What CFOs Think About the IPO Process: Practice, Theory and Managerial Implications." *Journal of Applied Corporate Finance* 18, no. 3 (2006): pp. 107–17.

19.7 SEOs AND THE VALUE OF THE FIRM

We now turn to a consideration of seasoned equity offerings (SEOs), which, as we discussed earlier, are offerings by firms that already have outstanding securities. It seems reasonable to believe that new long-term financing is arranged by firms after positive net present value projects are put together. As a consequence, when the announcement of external financing is made, the firm's market value should go up. Interestingly, this is not what happens. Stock prices tend to decline following the announcement of a new equity issue, although they tend not to change much following a debt announcement. A number of researchers have studied this issue. Plausible reasons for this strange result include the following:

1. *Managerial Information.* If management has superior information about the market value of the firm, it may know when the firm is overvalued. If it does, it will attempt to issue new shares of stock when the market value exceeds the correct value. This will benefit existing shareholders. However, the potential new shareholders are not stupid, and they will anticipate this superior information and discount it in lower market prices at the new issue date.

2. *Debt Usage.* A company's issuing new equity may reveal that the company has too much debt or too little liquidity. One version of this argument says that the equity issue is a bad signal to the market. After all, if the new projects are favorable ones, why should the firm let new shareholders in on them? It could just issue debt and let the existing shareholders have all the gain.

3. *Issue Costs.* As we discuss next, there are substantial costs associated with selling securities.

The drop in value of the existing stock following the announcement of a new issue is an example of an indirect cost of selling securities. This drop might typically be on the order of 3 percent for an industrial corporation (and somewhat smaller for a public utility), so, for a large company, it can represent a substantial amount of money. We label this drop the *abnormal return* in our discussion of the costs of new issues that follows.

19.8 THE COST OF ISSUING SECURITIES

Issuing securities to the public isn't free, and the costs of different methods are important determinants of which is used. These costs associated with *floating* a new issue are generically called *flotation costs*. In this section, we take a closer look at the flotation costs associated with equity sales to the public.

The costs of selling stock are classified in the following table and fall into six categories: (1) the spread, (2) other direct expenses, (3) indirect expenses, (4) abnormal returns (discussed previously), (5) underpricing, and (6) the Green Shoe option.

	The Costs of Issuing Securities
1. Spread	The spread consists of direct fees paid by the issuer to the underwriting syndicate—the difference between the price the issuer receives and the offer price.
2. Other direct expenses	These are direct costs incurred by the issuer that are not part of the compensation to underwriters. These costs include filing fees, legal fees, and taxes—all reported on the prospectus.
3. Indirect expenses	These costs are not reported on the prospectus and include the cost of management time spent working on the new issue.
4. Abnormal returns	In a seasoned issue of stock, the price of the existing stock drops on average by 3 percent upon the announcement of the issue. This drop is called the abnormal return.
5. Underpricing	For initial public offerings, losses arise from selling the stock below the true value.
6. Green Shoe option	The Green Shoe option gives the underwriters the right to buy additional shares at the offer price to cover overallotments.

Table 19.5 reports direct costs as a percentage of the gross amount raised for IPOs, SEOs, straight (ordinary) bonds, and convertible bonds sold by U.S. companies over the 19-year period from 1990 through 2008. These are direct costs only. Not included are indirect expenses, the cost of the Green Shoe provision, underpricing (for IPOs), and abnormal returns (for SEOs).

As Table 19.5 shows, the direct costs alone can be very large, particularly for smaller issues (less than $10 million). On a smaller IPO, for example, the total direct costs amount to 25.22 percent of the amount raised. This means that if a company sells $10 million in stock,

• • • • • • •
TABLE 19.5

Direct Costs as a Percentage of Gross Proceeds for Equity (IPOs and SEOs) and Straight and Convertible Bonds Offered by Domestic Operating Companies: 1990–2008

Proceeds (in $ millions)	IPOs				SEOs			
	Number of Issues	Gross Spread	Other Direct Expense	Total Direct Cost	Number of Issues	Gross Spread	Other Direct Expense	Total Direct Cost
2.00–9.99	1,007	9.40%	15.82%	25.22%	515	8.11%	26.99%	35.11%
10.00–19.99	810	7.39	7.30	14.69	726	6.11	7.76	13.86
20.00–39.99	1,422	6.96	7.06	14.03	1,393	5.44	4.10	9.54
40.00–59.99	880	6.89	2.87	9.77	1,129	5.03	8.93	13.96
60.00–79.99	522	6.79	2.16	8.94	841	4.88	1.98	6.85
80.00–99.99	327	6.71	1.84	8.55	536	4.67	2.05	6.72
100.00–199.99	702	6.39	1.57	7.96	1,372	4.34	.89	5.23
200.00–499.99	440	5.81	1.03	6.84	811	3.72	1.22	4.94
500.00 and up	155	5.01	.49	5.50	264	3.10	.27	3.37
Total/Average	**6,265**	**7.19%**	**3.18%**	**10.37%**	**7,587**	**5.02%**	**2.68%**	**7.69%**
	Straight Bonds				Convertible Bonds			
2.00–9.99	3,962	1.64	2.40	4.03	14	6.39	3.43	9.82
10.00–19.99	3,400	1.50	1.71	3.20	23	5.52	3.09	8.61
20.00–39.99	2,690	1.25	.92	2.17	30	4.63	1.67	6.30
40.00–59.99	3,345	.81	.79	1.59	35	3.49	1.04	4.54
60.00–79.99	891	1.65	.80	2.44	60	2.79	.62	3.41
80.00–99.99	465	1.41	.57	1.98	16	2.30	.62	2.92
100.00–199.99	4,949	1.61	.52	2.14	82	2.66	.42	3.08
200.00–499.99	3,305	1.38	.33	1.71	46	2.65	.33	2.99
500.00 and up	1,261	.61	.15	.76	7	2.16	.13	2.29
Total/Average	**24,268**	**1.38%**	**.61%**	**2.00%**	**313**	**3.07%**	**.85%**	**3.92%**

Source: Inmoo, Lee, Scott Lochhead, Jay Ritter, and Quanshui Zhao. "The Costs of Raising Capital." *Journal of Financial Research* 19, no. 1 (1996): pp. 59–74. Calculations and updates by the authors.

FINANCE MATTERS

ANATOMY OF AN IPO

On July 21, 2018, i3 Verticals, the Nashville-based payment and software solutions company, went public via an IPO. i3 Verticals issued 6.65 million shares of stock at a price of $13 each. The lead underwriters on the IPO were Cowen, Raymond James, and KeyBanc Capital Markets.

Even though the IPO raised a gross sum of $86,450,000, i3 Verticals got to keep only $80,398,500 after expenses. The biggest expense was the 7 percent underwriter spread, which is ordinary for an offering of this size. i3 Verticals sold each of the 6.65 million shares to the underwriters for $12.09, and the underwriters in turn sold the shares to the public for $13 each.

But wait—there's more. i3 Verticals spent $12,378 in SEC registration fees, $17,750 in FINRA filing fees, and $125,000 to be listed on the NASDAQ. The company also spent $1,827,366 in legal fees, $989,578 on accounting to obtain the necessary audits, $4,500 for a transfer agent to physically transfer the shares and maintain a list of shareholders, $190,230 for printing and engraving expenses, and, finally, $169,924 in miscellaneous expenses.

As i3 Verticals' outlays show, an IPO can be a costly undertaking! In the end, i3 Verticals' expenses totaled $9.4 million, of which $6.07 million went to the underwriters and $3.3 million went to other parties. All told, the total cost to i3 Verticals was about 12 percent of the issue proceeds.

it will only net about $7.5 million; the other $2.5 million goes to cover the underwriter spread and other direct expenses. Typical underwriter spreads on an IPO range from about 5 percent for large offerings to 10 percent for small offerings, but for about half of the IPOs in Table 19.5, the spread is exactly 7 percent, so this is, by far, the most common spread. A nearby *Finance Matters* box provides a detailed example for a particular company.

Overall, four clear patterns emerge from Table 19.5. First of all, with the possible exception of straight debt offerings (about which we will have more to say later), there are substantial economies of scale. The underwriter spreads are smaller on larger issues, and the other direct costs fall sharply as a percentage of the amount raised, a reflection of the mostly fixed nature of such costs. Second, the costs associated with selling debt are substantially less than the costs of selling equity. Third, IPOs have higher expenses than SEOs, but the difference is not as great as might originally be guessed. Finally, straight bonds are cheaper to float than convertible bonds.

As we have discussed, the underpricing of IPOs is an additional cost to the issuer. To give a better idea of the total cost of going public, Table 19.6 combines the information in

Proceeds (in $ millions)	Number of Issues	Gross Spread	Other Direct Expense	Total Direct Cost	Underpricing
2.00–9.99	1,007	9.40%	15.82%	25.22%	20.42%
10.00–19.99	810	7.39	7.30	14.69	10.33
20.00–39.99	1,422	6.96	7.06	14.03	17.03
40.00–59.99	880	6.89	2.87	9.77	28.26
60.00–79.99	522	6.79	2.16	8.94	28.36
80.00–99.99	327	6.71	1.84	8.55	32.92
100.00–199.99	702	6.39	1.57	7.96	21.55
200.00–499.99	440	5.81	1.03	6.84	6.19
500.00 and up	155	5.01	.49	5.50	6.64
Total/Average	**6,265**	**7.19%**	**3.18%**	**10.37%**	**19.34%**

TABLE 19.6

Direct and Indirect Costs, in Percentages, of Equity IPOs: 1990–2008

Source: Inmoo, Lee, Scott Lochhead, Jay Ritter, and Quanshui Zhao. "The Costs of Raising Capital." *Journal of Financial Research* 19, no. 1 (1996): pp. 59–74. Calculations and updates by the authors.

Table 19.5 for IPOs with data on the underpricing experienced by these firms. Comparing the total direct costs (in the fifth column) to the underpricing (in the sixth column), we see that they tend to be similar in size, so the direct costs are only about half of the total for small issues. Overall, across all size groups, the total direct costs amount to 10 percent of the amount raised and the underpricing amounts to 19 percent.

Finally, with regard to debt offerings, there is a general pattern in issue costs that is somewhat obscured in Table 19.5. Recall from Chapter 5 that bonds carry different credit ratings. Higher-rated bonds are said to be investment grade, whereas lower-rated bonds are noninvestment grade. Table 19.7 contains a breakdown of direct costs for bond issues after the investment and noninvestment grades have been separated.

Table 19.7 clarifies three things regarding debt issues. First, there are substantial economies of scale here. Second, investment-grade issues have much lower direct costs, particularly for straight bonds. Finally, there are relatively few noninvestment-grade issues in the smaller size categories, reflecting the fact that such issues are more commonly handled as private placements.

19.9 RIGHTS

When new shares of common stock are offered to the general public in a seasoned new equity issue, the proportionate ownership of existing shareholders is likely to be reduced. However, if a preemptive right is contained in the firm's articles of incorporation, the firm must first offer any new issue of common stock to existing shareholders. This assures each owner of his or her proportionate share.

An issue of common stock to existing stockholders is called a *rights offering*. Here each shareholder is issued an option to buy a specified number of new shares from the firm at a specified price within a specified time, after which the rights expire. For example, a firm whose stock is selling at $30 may let current stockholders buy a fixed number of shares at $10 per share within two months. The terms of the option are evidenced by certificates known as *share warrants* or *rights*. Such rights are often traded on securities exchanges or over the counter.

The Mechanics of a Rights Offering

We illustrate the mechanics of a rights offering by considering National Power Company. National Power has 1 million shares outstanding and the stock is selling at $20 per share, implying a market capitalization of $20 million. The company plans to raise $5 million of new equity funds by a rights offering.

The process of issuing rights differs from the process of issuing shares of stock for cash. Existing stockholders are notified that they have been given one right for each share of stock they own. Exercise occurs when a shareholder sends payment to the firm's subscription agent (usually a bank) and turns in the required number of rights. Shareholders of National Power will have several choices: (1) subscribe for the full number of entitled shares, (2) order all the rights sold, or (3) do nothing and let the rights expire.

The management of National Power must answer the following questions:

1. What price should the existing shareholders be allowed to pay for a share of new stock?
2. How many rights will be required to purchase one share of stock?
3. What effect will the rights offering have on the existing price of the stock?

Subscription Price

In a rights offering, the subscription price is the price that existing shareholders are allowed to pay for a share of stock. A rational shareholder will subscribe to the rights offering only if the subscription price is below the market price of the stock on the offer's expiration date.

TABLE 19.7

Average Gross Spreads and Total Direct Costs for Domestic Debt Issues: 1990–2008

Convertible Bonds

Proceeds (in $ millions)	Investment Grade				Junk or Not Rated			
	Number of Issues	Gross Spread	Other Direct Expense	Total Direct Cost	Number of Issues	Gross Spread	Other Direct Expense	Total Direct Cost
2.00–9.99	—	—	—	—	14	6.39%	3.43%	9.82%
10.00–19.99	1	14.12%	1.87%	15.98%	23	5.52	3.09	8.61
20.00–39.99	—	—	—	—	30	4.63	1.67	6.30
40.00–59.99	3	1.92	.51	2.43	35	3.49	1.04	4.54
60.00–79.99	6	1.65	.44	2.09	60	2.79	.62	3.41
80.00–99.99	4	.89	.27	1.16	16	2.30	.62	2.92
100.00–199.99	27	2.22	.33	2.55	82	2.66	.42	3.08
200.00–499.99	27	2.03	.19	2.22	46	2.65	.33	2.99
500.00 and up	11	1.94	.13	2.06	7	2.16	.13	2.29
Total/Average	**79**	**2.15%**	**.29%**	**2.44%**	**313**	**3.31%**	**.98%**	**4.29%**

Straight Bonds

Proceeds (in $ millions)	Investment Grade				Junk or Not Rated			
	Number of Issues	Gross Spread	Other Direct Expense	Total Direct Cost	Number of Issues	Gross Spread	Other Direct Expense	Total Direct Cost
2.00–9.99	2,709	.62%	1.28%	1.90%	1,253	2.77%	2.50%	5.27%
10.00–19.99	2,564	.59	1.17	1.76	836	3.15	1.97	5.12
20.00–39.99	2,400	.63	.74	1.37	290	3.07	1.13	4.20
40.00–59.99	3,146	.40	.52	.92	199	2.93	1.20	4.14
60.00–79.99	792	.58	.38	.96	99	3.12	1.16	4.28
80.00–99.99	385	.66	.29	.96	80	2.73	.93	3.66
100.00–199.99	4,427	.54	.25	.79	522	2.73	.68	3.41
200.00–499.99	3,031	.52	.25	.76	274	2.59	.39	2.98
500.00 and up	1,207	.31	.08	.39	54	2.38	.25	2.63
Total/Average	**20,661**	**.52%**	**.35%**	**.87%**	**3,607**	**2.76%**	**.81%**	**3.57%**

Source: Inmoo, Lee, Scott Lochhead, Jay Ritter, and Quanshui Zhao. "The Costs of Raising Capital." *Journal of Financial Research* 19, no. 1 (1996): pp. 59–74. Calculations and updates by the authors.

For example, if the stock price at expiration is $13 and the subscription price is $15, no rational shareholder will subscribe. Why pay $15 for something worth $13? National Power chooses a price of $10, which is well below the current market price of $20. As long as the market price does not fall by half before expiration, the rights offering will succeed.

Number of Rights Needed to Purchase a Share

National Power wants to raise $5 million in new equity. With a subscription price of $10, it must issue 500,000 new shares. This can be determined by dividing the total amount to be raised by the subscription price:

$$\text{Number of new shares} = \frac{\text{Funds to be raised}}{\text{Subscription price}} = \frac{\$5,000,000}{\$10} = 500,000 \text{ shares}$$

Because stockholders typically get one right for each share of stock they own, 1 million rights will be issued by National Power. To determine how many rights must be exercised to get one share of stock, we can divide the number of existing (or old) outstanding shares of stock by the number of new shares:

$$\frac{\text{Number of rights needed}}{\text{to buy a share of stock}} = \frac{\text{"Old" shares}}{\text{"New" shares}} = \frac{1,000,000}{500,000} = 2 \text{ rights}$$

A shareholder must give up two rights plus $10 to receive a share of new stock. If all the stockholders do this, National Power will raise the required $5 million.

Given that National Power wants to raise $5 million, the number of new shares and the number of rights needed to buy one new share follow from the subscription price, as indicated below.

Subscription Price	Number of New Shares	Number of Rights Needed to Buy a Share of Stock
$20	250,000 (= $5,000,000/$20)	4 (= 1,000,000/250,000)
10	500,000 (= $5,000,000/$10)	2 (= 1,000,000/500,000)
5	1,000,000 (= $5,000,000/$5)	1 (= 1,000,000/1,000,000)

As can be seen, a lower subscription price leads the firm both to issue more shares and to reduce the number of rights needed to buy one share.

Effect of Rights Offering on Price of Stock

Rights clearly have value. In the case of National Power, the right to be able to buy a share of stock worth $20 for $10 is valuable.

Suppose a shareholder of National Power owns two shares of stock just before the rights offering. This situation is depicted in Table 19.8. Initially, the price of National Power is $20 per share, so the shareholder's total holding is worth $2 \times \$20 = \$40$. The stockholder who has two shares will receive two rights. The National Power rights offer gives shareholders with two rights the opportunity to purchase one additional share for $10. The holding of the shareholder who exercises these rights and buys the new share would increase to three shares. The value of the new holding would be $40 + 10 = $50 (the $40 initial value plus the $10 paid to the company). Because the stockholder now holds three shares, the price per share would drop to $50/3 = $16.67.

The difference between the old share price of $20 and the new share price of $16.67 reflects the fact that the old shares carried rights to subscribe to the new issue. The difference must be equal to the value of one right—that is, $20 − 16.67 = $3.33.

We also can calculate the value of a right in another way. The rights offer lets an individual pay $10 for a share worth $16.67, generating a gain of $6.67. Because the individual

	The Shareholder
Initial position	
Number of shares	2
Share price	$20
Value of holding	$40
Terms of offer	
Subscription price	$10
Number of rights issued	2
Number of rights for a share	2
After offer	
Number of shares	3
Value of holding	$50
Share price	$16.67
Value of a right	
Old price − New price	$20 − 16.67 = $3.33
$\dfrac{\text{New price} - \text{Subscription price}}{\text{Number of rights for a share}}$	($16.67 − 10)/2 = $3.33

needs two rights for this transaction, a rational individual would be willing to pay as much as $3.33 (= $6.67/2) for a single right.

As we learned of an ex-dividend date in the previous chapter, there is an **ex-rights date** here. An individual buying the stock prior to the ex-rights date will receive the rights when they are distributed. An individual buying the stock on or after the ex-rights date will not receive the rights. In our example, the price of the stock prior to the ex-rights date is $20. An individual buying on or after the ex-rights date is not entitled to the rights. The price on or after the ex-rights date is $16.67.

Table 19.9 shows what happens to National Power. If all shareholders exercise their rights, the number of shares will increase to 1.5 million and the value of the firm will increase to $25 million. After the rights offering, the value of each share will drop to $16.67 (= $25 million/1.5 million).

•••••••••
TABLE 19.9

National Power Company
Rights Offering

	The Company
Initial position	
Number of shares	1 million
Share price	$20
Value of firm	$20 million
Terms of offer	
Subscription price	$10
Number of rights issued	1 million
Number of rights for a share	2
After offer	
Number of shares	1.5 million
Share price	$16.67
Value of firm	$25 million
Value of one right	$20 − 16.67 = $3.33
	or ($16.67 − 10)/2 = $3.33

An investor holding no shares of National Power stock who wants to subscribe to the new issue can do so by buying rights. An outside investor buying two rights will pay $3.33 × 2 = $6.67. If the investor exercises the rights at a subscription cost of $10, the total cost would be $10 + 6.67 = $16.67. In return for this expenditure, the investor will receive a share of the new stock, which is worth $16.67.

Of course, outside investors can also buy National Power stock directly at $16.67 per share. In an efficient stock market, it will make no difference whether new stock is obtained via rights or via direct purchase.

Effects on Shareholders

Shareholders can exercise their rights or sell them. In either case, the stockholder will neither win nor lose by the rights offering. The hypothetical holder of two shares of National Power has a portfolio worth $40. On the one hand, if the shareholder exercises the rights, she ends up with three shares worth a total of $50. In other words, by spending $10, the investor increases the value of the holding by $10, which means that she is neither better nor worse off.

On the other hand, a shareholder who sells the two rights for $3.33 each obtains $3.33 × 2 = $6.67 in cash. Because the two shares are each worth $16.67, the holdings are valued at:

Shares = 2 × $16.67 =	$33.33
Sold rights = 2 × $ 3.33 =	$ 6.67
Total	= $40.00

The new $33.33 market value plus $6.67 in cash is exactly the same as the original holding of $40. Thus, stockholders can neither lose nor gain from exercising or selling rights.

It is obvious that the new market price of the firm's stock will be lower after the rights offering than it was before the rights offering. The lower the subscription price, the greater the price decline of a rights offering. However, our analysis shows that the stockholders have suffered no loss because of the rights offering.

There is one last issue. How do we set the subscription price in a rights offering? If you think about it, you will see that the subscription price really should not matter. It has to be below the market price of the stock for the rights to have value, but beyond that, the price is arbitrary. In principle, it could be as low as we cared to make it as long as it is not zero.

The Underwriting Arrangements

Undersubscription can occur if investors throw away rights or if bad news causes the market price of the stock to fall below the subscription price. To ensure against these possibilities, rights offerings are typically arranged by standby underwriting. Here the underwriter makes a firm commitment to purchase the unsubscribed portion of the issue at the subscription price less a take-up fee. The underwriter usually receives a standby fee as compensation for this risk-bearing function.

In practice, the subscription price is usually set well below the current market price, making the probability of a rights failure quite small. Though a small percentage (less than 10 percent) of shareholders fail to exercise valuable rights, shareholders are usually allowed to purchase unsubscribed shares at the subscription price. This oversubscription privilege makes it unlikely that the corporate issuer would need to turn to its underwriter for help.

The Rights Puzzle

If corporate executives are rational, they will raise equity in the cheapest manner. However, the evidence on issuance costs suggests that issues of pure rights should dominate. Surprisingly, almost all new equity issues in the United States are sold without rights. On the other hand, rights offerings are very significant around the world. This is generally viewed as an anomaly in the finance profession, though a few explanations have been advanced.

The arguments include these: (a) The proceeds of underwritten issues are available sooner than are the proceeds from a rights offer; (b) underwriters provide a wider distribution of ownership than would be possible with a rights offering; (c) consulting advice from investment bankers may be beneficial; (d) stockholders find exercising rights a nuisance; (e) the risk that the market price might fall below the subscription price is significant; and (f) in direct underwriting, the underwriter "certifies" that the offering price is consistent with the true value of the issue.

19.10 DILUTION

A subject that comes up quite a bit in discussions involving the selling of securities is dilution. Dilution refers to a loss in existing shareholders' value. There are several kinds:

1. Dilution of percentage ownership.
2. Dilution of market value.
3. Dilution of book value and earnings per share.

The differences between these three types can be a little confusing, and there are some common misconceptions about dilution, so we discuss it in this section.

Dilution of Proportionate Ownership

The first type of dilution can arise whenever a firm sells shares to the general public. For example, Joe Smith owns 5,000 shares of Merit Shoe Company. Merit Shoe currently has 50,000 shares of stock outstanding; each share gets one vote. Joe thus controls 10 percent (= 5,000/50,000) of the votes and gets 10 percent of the dividends.

If Merit Shoe issues 50,000 new shares of common stock to the public via a general cash offer, Joe's ownership in Merit Shoe may be diluted. If Joe does not participate in the new issue, his ownership will drop to 5 percent (= 5,000/100,000). Notice that the value of Joe's shares is unaffected; he just owns a smaller percentage of the firm.

Because a rights offering would ensure Joe Smith an opportunity to maintain his proportionate 10 percent share, dilution of the ownership of existing shareholders can be avoided by using a rights offering.

Dilution of Value: Book versus Market Values

We now examine dilution of value by looking at some accounting numbers. We do this to illustrate a fallacy concerning dilution; we do not mean to suggest that accounting value dilution is more important than market value dilution. As we illustrate, quite the reverse is true.

Suppose Upper States Manufacturing (USM) wants to build a new electricity-generating plant to meet future anticipated demands. As shown in Table 19.10, USM currently has 1 million shares outstanding and no debt. Each share is selling for $5, and the company has a $5 million market value. USM's book value is $10 million total, or $10 per share.

USM has experienced a variety of difficulties in the past, including cost overruns, regulatory delays in building a nuclear-powered electricity-generating plant, and below-normal profits. These difficulties are reflected in the fact that USM's market-to-book ratio is $5/$10 = .50 (successful firms rarely have market prices below book values).

Net income for USM is currently $1 million. With 1 million shares, earnings per share are $1, and the return on equity is 10 percent (= $1/$10). USM thus sells for five times earnings (the price-earnings ratio is 5). USM has 200 shareholders, each of whom holds 5,000 shares. The new plant will cost $2 million, so USM will have to issue 400,000 new shares ($5 × 400,000 = $2 million). There will thus be 1.4 million shares outstanding after the issue.

| | Initial | After Taking on New Project | |
		With Dilution	With No Dilution
Number of shares	1,000,000	1,400,000	1,400,000
Book value	$10,000,000	$12,000,000	$12,000,000
Book value per share (B)	$10	$8.57	$8.57
Market value	$5,000,000	$6,000,000	$8,000,000
Market price (P)	$5	$4.29	$5.71
Net income	$1,000,000	$1,200,000	$1,600,000
Return on equity (ROE)	.10	.10	.1333
Earnings per share (EPS)	$1	$.857	$1.14
EPS/P	.20	.20	.20
P/EPS	5	5	5
P/B	.5	.5	.67
Project cost $2,000,000		NPV = −$1,000,000	NPV = $1,000,000

The ROE on the new plant is expected to be the same as for the company as a whole. In other words, net income is expected to go up by .10 × $2 million = $200,000. Total net income will thus be $1.2 million. The following will result if the plant is built:

1. With 1.4 million shares outstanding, EPS will be $1.2/1.4 = $.857, down from $1.

2. The proportionate ownership of each old shareholder will drop to .36 percent (= 5,000/1.4 million) from .50 percent.

3. If the stock continues to sell for five times earnings, then the value will drop to 5 × $.857 = $4.29, representing a loss of $.71 per share.

4. The total book value will be the old $10 million plus the new $2 million, for a total of $12 million. Book value per share will fall to $12 million/1.4 million = $8.57.

If we take this example at face value, then dilution of proportionate ownership, accounting dilution, and market value dilution all occur. USM's stockholders appear to suffer significant losses.

A MISCONCEPTION   Our example appears to show that selling stock when the market-to-book ratio is less than 1 is detrimental to stockholders. Some managers claim that the resulting dilution occurs because EPS will go down whenever shares are issued when the market value is less than the book value.

When the market-to-book ratio is less than 1, increasing the number of shares does cause EPS to go down. Such a decline in EPS is accounting dilution, and accounting dilution will always occur under these circumstances.

Is it also true that market value dilution will necessarily occur? The answer is no. There is nothing incorrect about our example, but why the market price decreased is not obvious. We discuss this next.

THE CORRECT ARGUMENTS   In this example, the market price falls from $5 per share to $4.29. This is true dilution, but why does it occur? The answer has to do with the new project. USM is going to spend $2 million on the new plant. However, as shown in Table 19.10, the total market value of the company is going to rise from $5 million to $6 million, an increase of only $1 million. This means that the NPV of the new project is −$1 million. With 1.4 million shares, the loss per share is $1/1.4 = $.71, as we calculated before.

So, true dilution takes place for the shareholders of USM because the NPV of the project is negative, not because the market-to-book ratio is less than 1. This negative NPV causes the market price to drop, and the accounting dilution has nothing to do with it.

Suppose the new project has a positive NPV of $1 million. The total market value rises by $2 million + 1 million = $3 million. As shown in Table 19.10 (third column), the price per share rises to $5.71. Notice that accounting dilution still takes place because the book value per share still falls, but there is no economic consequence of that fact. The market value of the stock rises.

The $.71 increase in share value comes about because of the $1 million NPV, which amounts to an increase in value of about $.71 per share. Also, as shown, if the ratio of price to EPS remains at 5, then EPS must rise to $1.14 (= $5.71/5). Total earnings (net income) rise to $1.6 million ($1.14 per share × 1.4 million shares). Finally, ROE will rise to 13.33% (= $1.6 million/$12 million).

19.11 ISSUING LONG-TERM DEBT

The general procedures followed in a public issue of bonds are the same as those for stocks. The issue must be registered with the SEC, there must be a prospectus, and so on. The registration statement for a public issue of bonds, however, is different from the one for common stock. For bonds, the registration statement must indicate an indenture.

Another important difference is that more than 50 percent of all debt is issued privately. There are two basic forms of direct private long-term financing: term loans and private placement.

Term loans are direct business loans. These loans have maturities of between one year and five years. Most term loans are repayable during the life of the loan. The lenders include commercial banks, insurance companies, and other lenders that specialize in corporate finance. Private placements are very similar to term loans except that the maturities are longer.

The important differences between direct private long-term financing and public issues of debt are:

1. A direct long-term loan avoids the cost of Securities and Exchange Commission registration.
2. Direct placement is likely to have more restrictive covenants.
3. It is easier to renegotiate a term loan or a private placement in the event of a default. It is harder to renegotiate a public issue because hundreds of holders are usually involved.
4. Life insurance companies and pension funds dominate the private-placement segment of the bond market. Commercial banks are significant participants in the term-loan market.
5. The costs of distributing bonds are lower in the private market.

The interest rates on term loans and private placements are often higher than those on an equivalent public issue. This difference may reflect the trade-off between a higher interest rate and more flexible arrangements in the event of financial distress, as well as the lower costs associated with private placements.

An additional, and very important, consideration is that the flotation costs associated with selling debt are much less than the comparable costs associated with selling equity.

19.12 SHELF REGISTRATION

To simplify the procedures for issuing securities, in March 1982, the SEC adopted Rule 415 on a temporary basis, and it was made permanent in November 1983. Rule 415 allows shelf registration. Both debt and equity securities can be shelf registered.

Shelf registration permits a corporation to register an offering that it reasonably expects to sell within the next two years and then sell the issue whenever it wants during that two-year period. In July 2018, data analytics company Helios and Matheson announced a shelf registration to sell up to $1.2 billion of debt, preferred stock, common stock, subscription rights, units, and warrants. According to the registration documents filed by the company, the use of the proceeds would be announced if the shelf registration was offered.

Not all companies can use Rule 415. The primary qualifications are:

1. The company must be rated investment grade.
2. The firm cannot have defaulted on its debt in the past three years.
3. The aggregate market value of the firm's outstanding stock must be more than $150 million.
4. The firm must not have had a violation of the Securities Act of 1934 in the past three years.

The rule has been controversial. Arguments have been constructed against shelf registration:

1. The costs of new issues might go up because underwriters might not be able to provide as much current information to potential investors as they would otherwise, so investors would pay less. The expense of selling the issue piece by piece might therefore be higher than that of selling it all at once.
2. Some investment bankers have argued that shelf registration will cause a "market overhang" that will depress market prices. In other words, the possibility that the company could increase the supply of stock at any time will have a negative impact on the current stock price. There is little evidence to support this position, however.

In addition to shelf registrations, companies also sell stock through continuous equity offerings, also known as *dribble programs,* or *at-the-market* offerings. In a dribble program, the company registers the stock with the SEC through a variety of different methods and sells the shares in dribbles as it sees fit. In other words, the company sells the stock on the secondary market like any other investor would.

SUMMARY AND CONCLUSIONS

This chapter has looked at how corporate securities are issued. The following are the main points:

1. The venture capital market is a primary source of financing for new high-risk companies.
2. The costs of issuing securities can be quite large. They are much lower (as a percentage) for larger issues.
3. Firm commitment underwriting is far more prevalent for large issues than best efforts underwriting. This is probably connected to the uncertainty of smaller issues. For a given size offering, the direct expenses of best efforts underwriting and firm commitment underwriting are of the same magnitude.
4. The direct and indirect costs of going public can be substantial. However, once a firm is public, it can raise additional capital with much greater ease.

CONCEPT QUESTIONS

1. **Debt versus Equity Offering Size**   In the aggregate, debt offerings are much more common than equity offerings and typically much larger as well. Why?
2. **Debt versus Equity Flotation Costs**   Why are the costs of selling equity so much larger than the costs of selling debt?

3. **Bond Ratings and Flotation Costs**   Why do noninvestment-grade bonds have much higher direct costs than investment-grade issues?

4. **Underpricing in Debt Offerings**   Why is underpricing not a great concern with bond offerings?

Use the following information to answer the next three questions.

In September 2018, ticketing and events company Eventbrite went public. Assisted by investment banks Goldman Sachs, JP Morgan, and others, Eventbrite sold 10 million shares at $23 each, thereby raising a total of $230 million. By the end of the first day of trading, the stock jumped to $36.50 per share, down from a high of $39.30. Based on the end-of-day numbers, Eventbrite shares were apparently underpriced by about $13.50 each, meaning that the company missed out on an additional $135 million.

5. **IPO Pricing**   The Eventbrite IPO was underpriced by about 59 percent. Should Eventbrite be upset at Goldman Sachs and JP Morgan over the underpricing?

6. **IPO Pricing**   In the previous question, how would it affect your thinking to know that the company was incorporated in 2016, had only $202 million in revenues in 2017, and had a net loss of $39 million?

7. **IPO Pricing**   In the previous two questions, how would it affect your thinking to know that insiders owned 10 percent of the company's Class A stock and all of the company's Class B stock, controlling 98.5 percent of the voting rights?

8. **Cash Offer versus Rights Offer**   McCanless International is planning to raise fresh equity capital by selling a large new issue of common stock. McCanless is currently a publicly traded corporation, and it is trying to choose between an underwritten cash offer and a rights offering (not underwritten) to current shareholders. McCanless's management is interested in minimizing the selling costs and has asked you for advice on the choice of issue methods. What is your recommendation and why?

9. **IPO Underpricing**   In 1980, a certain assistant professor of finance bought 12 initial public offerings of common stock. He held each of these for approximately one month and then sold. The investment rule he followed was to submit a purchase order for every firm commitment initial public offering of oil and gas exploration companies. There were 22 of these offerings, and he submitted a purchase order for approximately $1,000 in stock for each of the companies. With 10 of these, no shares were allocated to this assistant professor. With 5 of the 12 offerings that were purchased, fewer than the requested number of shares were allocated.

The year 1980 was very good for oil and gas exploration company owners: On average, for the 22 companies that went public, the stocks were selling for 80 percent above the offering price a month after the initial offering date. The assistant professor looked at his performance record and found that the $8,400 invested in the 12 companies had grown to $10,000, representing a return of only about 20 percent (commissions were negligible). Did he have bad luck, or should he have expected to do worse than the average initial public offering investor? Explain.

10. **IPO Pricing**   The following material represents the cover page and summary of the prospectus for the initial public offering of the Pest Investigation Control Corporation (PICC), which is going public tomorrow with a firm commitment initial public offering managed by the investment banking firm of Erlanger and Ritter. Answer the following questions:

   a. Assume that you know nothing about PICC other than the information contained in the prospectus. Based on your knowledge of finance, what is your prediction for the price of PICC tomorrow? Provide a short explanation of why you think this will occur.

   b. Assume that you have several thousand dollars to invest. When you get home from class tonight, you find that your stockbroker, whom you have not talked to for weeks, has called. She has left a message that PICC is going public tomorrow and that she can get you several hundred shares at the offering price if you call her back first thing in the morning. Discuss the merits of this opportunity.

PROSPECTUS   PICC

200,000 shares

PEST INVESTIGATION CONTROL CORPORATION

Of the shares being offered hereby, all 200,000 are being sold by the Pest Investigation Control Corporation, Inc. ("the Company"). Before the offering, there has been no public market for the shares of PICC, and no guarantee can be given that any such market will develop.

These securities have not been approved or disapproved by the SEC nor has the commission passed upon the accuracy or adequacy of this prospectus. Any representation to the contrary is a criminal offense.

	Price to Public	Underwriting Discount	Proceeds to Company*
Per share	$11.00	$1.10	$9.90
Total	$2,200,000	$220,000	$1,980,000

*Before deducting expenses estimated at $27,000 and payable by the Company.

This is an initial public offering. The common shares are being offered, subject to prior sale, when, as, and if delivered to and accepted by the Underwriters and subject to approval of certain legal matters by their Counsel and by Counsel for the Company The Underwriters reserve the right to withdraw, cancel, or modify such offer and to reject offers in whole or in part.

Erlanger and Ritter, Investment Bankers
July 12, 2020
Prospectus Summary

The Company	The Pest Investigation Control Corporation (PICC) breeds and markets toads and tree frogs as ecologically safe insect-control mechanisms.
The Offering	200,000 shares of common stock, no par value.
Listing	The Company will seek listing on NASDAQ and will trade over the counter.
Shares Outstanding	As of June 30, 2020, 400,000 shares of common stock were outstanding. After the offering, 600,000 shares of common stock will be outstanding.
Use of Proceeds	To finance expansion of inventory and receivables and general working capital, and to pay for country club memberships for certain finance professors.

Selected Financial Information
(amounts in $ thousands except per-share data)

	Fiscal Year Ended June 30				As of June 30, 2020	
	2018	2019	2020		Actual	As Adjusted for This Offering
Revenues	$60.00	$120.00	$240.00	Working capital	$ 8	$1,961
Net earnings	3.80	15.90	36.10	Total assets	511	2,464
Earnings per share	.01	.04	.09	Stockholders' equity	423	2,376

QUESTIONS AND PROBLEMS

Basic
(Questions 1–8)

1. **Rights Offerings**   Simpkins, Inc., is proposing a rights offering. Presently, there are 425,000 shares outstanding at $65 each. There will be 90,000 new shares offered at $57 each.

   a. What is the new market value of the company?

   b. How many rights are associated with one of the new shares?

   c. What is the ex-rights price?

   d. What is the value of a right?

   e. Why might a company have a rights offering rather than a general cash offer?

2. **Rights Offering** The Clifford Corporation has announced a rights offer to raise $50 million for a new journal, the *Journal of Financial Excess*. This journal will review potential articles after the author pays a nonrefundable reviewing fee of $5,000 per page. The stock currently sells for $37 per share, and there are 2.7 million shares outstanding.

   a. What is the maximum possible subscription price? What is the minimum?

   b. If the subscription price is set at $32 per share, how many shares must be sold? How many rights will it take to buy one share?

   c. What is the ex-rights price? What is the value of a right?

   d. Show how a shareholder with 1,000 shares before the offering and no desire (or money) to buy additional shares is not harmed by the rights offer.

3. **Rights** Blue Shoe Co. has concluded that additional equity financing will be needed to expand operations and that the needed funds will be best obtained through a rights offering. It has correctly determined that as a result of the rights offering, the share price will fall from $67 to $64.60 ($67 is the "rights-on" price; $64.60 is the ex-rights price, also known as the *when-issued* price). The company is seeking $12 million in additional funds with a per-share subscription price equal to $40. How many shares are there currently, before the offering? (Assume that the increment to the market value of the equity equals the gross proceeds from the offering.)

4. **IPO Underpricing** The Koepka Co. and the Woods Co. have both announced IPOs at $30 per share. One of these is undervalued by $7, and the other is overvalued by $4, but you have no way of knowing which is which. You plan on buying 1,000 shares of each issue. If an issue is underpriced, it will be rationed, and only half your order will be filled. If you could get 1,000 shares in Koepka and 1,000 shares in Woods, what would your profit be? What profit do you actually expect? What principle have you illustrated?

5. **Calculating Flotation Costs** The Trafford Corporation needs to raise $60 million to finance its expansion into new markets. The company will sell new shares of equity via a general cash offering to raise the needed funds. If the offer price is $29 per share and the company's underwriters charge a spread of 7 percent, how many shares need to be sold?

6. **Calculating Flotation Costs** In the previous problem, if the SEC filing fee and associated administrative expenses of the offering are $1.3 million, how many shares need to be sold?

7. **Calculating Flotation Costs** The Cypress Co. has just gone public. Under a firm commitment agreement, the company received $20.46 for each of the 12 million shares sold. The initial offering price was $22 per share, and the stock rose to $27.85 per share in the first few minutes of trading. The company paid $1.65 million in direct legal and other costs and $375,000 in indirect costs. What was the flotation cost as a percentage of funds raised?

8. **Price Dilution** Choi, Inc., has 125,000 shares of stock outstanding. Each share is worth $58, so the company's market value of equity is $7.25 million. Suppose the firm issues 33,750 new shares at the following prices: $58, $55, and $51. What will the effect be of each of these alternative offering prices on the existing price per share?

9. **Dilution** Stencil, Inc., wishes to expand its facilities. The company currently has 6.8 million shares outstanding and no debt. The stock sells for $65 per share, but the book value per share is $20. Net income for the company is currently $11.5 million. The new facility will cost $30 million, and it will increase net income by $675,000.

   Intermediate
   (Questions 9–16)

   a. Assuming a constant price-earnings ratio, what will the effect be of issuing new equity to finance the investment? To answer, calculate the new book value per share, the new total earnings, the new EPS, the new stock price, and the new market-to-book ratio. What is going on here?

   b. What would the new net income for the company have to be for the stock price to remain unchanged?

10. Dilution The Metallica Heavy Metal Mining (MHMM) Corporation wants to diversify its operations. Some recent financial information for the company is shown here:

Stock price	$75
Number of shares	65,000
Total assets	$9,400,000
Total liabilities	$4,100,000
Net income	$980,000

The company is considering an investment that has the same PE ratio as the firm. The cost of the investment is $1.5 million, and it will be financed with a new equity issue. The return on the investment will equal the company's current ROE. What will happen to the book value per share, the market value per share, and the EPS? What is the NPV of this investment? Does dilution take place?

11. Dilution In the previous problem, what would the ROE on the investment have to be if we wanted the price after the offering to be $75 per share? Assume the PE ratio remains constant. What is the NPV of this investment? Does any dilution take place?

12. Rights A company's stock currently sells for $68 per share. Last week the firm issued rights to raise new equity. To purchase a new share, a stockholder must remit $6 and three rights.

   a. What is the ex-rights stock price?

   b. What is the price of one right?

   c. When will the price drop occur? Why will it occur then?

13. Rights Naccarato Corp.'s stock is currently selling at $31 per share. There are 1.45 million shares outstanding. The firm is planning to raise $2.8 million to finance a new project. What are the ex-rights stock price, the value of a right, and the appropriate subscription prices under the following scenarios?

   a. Two shares of outstanding stock are entitled to purchase one additional share of the new issue.

   b. Four shares of outstanding stock are entitled to purchase one additional share of the new issue.

   c. How does the stockholders' wealth change from part (a) to part (b)?

14. Rights Kiser Mfg. is considering a rights offer. The company has determined that the ex-rights price will be $53. The current price is $58 per share, and there are 9.2 million shares outstanding. The rights offer would raise a total of $45 million. What is the subscription price?

15. Value of a Right Show that the value of a right can be written as

$$\text{Value of a right} = P_{RO} - P_X = (P_{RO} - P_S)/(N + 1)$$

where P_{RO}, P_S, and P_X stand for the "rights-on" price, the subscription price, and the ex-rights price, respectively, and N is the number of rights needed to buy one new share at the subscription price.

16. Valuing a Right Cimaroli Inventory Systems, Inc., has announced a rights offer. The company has announced that it will take four rights to buy a new share in the offering at a subscription price of $40. At the close of business the day before the ex-rights day, the company's stock sells for $75 per share. The next morning, you notice that the stock sells for $68 per share and the rights sell for $6 each. Are the stock and/or the rights correctly priced on the ex-rights day? Describe a transaction in which you could use these prices to create an immediate profit.

EAST COAST YACHTS GOES PUBLIC

Larissa Warren and Dan Ervin have been discussing the future of East Coast Yachts. The company has been experiencing fast growth, and the future looks like clear sailing. However, the fast growth means that the company's growth can no longer be funded by internal sources, so Larissa and Dan have decided the time is right to take the company public. To this end, they have entered into discussions with the investment bank of Crowe & Mallard. The company has a working relationship with Renata Harper, the underwriter who assisted with the company's previous bond offering. Crowe & Mallard have helped numerous small companies in the IPO process, so Larissa and Dan feel confident with this choice.

Renata begins by telling Larissa and Dan about the process. Although Crowe & Mallard charged an underwriter fee of 4 percent on the bond offering, the underwriter fee is 7 percent on all initial stock offerings of the size of East Coast Yachts's initial offering. Renata tells Larissa and Dan that the company can expect to pay about $1,600,000 in legal fees and expenses, $15,000 in SEC registration fees, and $20,000 in other filing fees. Additionally, to be listed on the NASDAQ, the company must pay $100,000. There are also transfer agent fees of $9,500 and engraving expenses of $540,000. The company should also expect to pay $125,000 for other expenses associated with the IPO.

Finally, Renata tells Larissa and Dan that to file with the SEC, the company must provide three years' worth of audited financial statements. She is unsure of the costs of the audit. Dan tells Renata that the company provides audited financial statements as part of its bond indenture, and the company pays $300,000 per year for the outside auditor.

1. At the end of the discussion, Dan asks Renata about the Dutch auction IPO process. What are the differences in the expenses to East Coast Yachts if it uses a Dutch auction IPO versus a traditional IPO? Should the company go public with a Dutch auction or use a traditional underwritten offering?

2. During the discussion of the potential IPO and East Coast Yachts's future, Dan states that he feels the company should raise $60 million. However, Larissa points out that if the company needs more cash soon, a secondary offering close to the IPO would be potentially problematic. Instead, she suggests that the company should raise $90 million in the IPO. How can we calculate the optimal size of the IPO? What are the advantages and disadvantages of increasing the size of the IPO to $90 million?

3. After deliberation, Larissa and Dan have decided that the company should use a firm commitment offering with Crowe & Mallard as the lead underwriter. The IPO will be for $70 million. Ignoring underpricing, how much will the IPO cost the company as a percentage of the funds received?

4. Many of the employees of East Coast Yachts have shares of stock in the company because of an existing employee stock purchase plan. To sell the stock, the employees can tender their shares to be sold in the IPO at the offering price, or the employees can retain their stock and sell it in the secondary market after East Coast Yachts goes public (once the 180-day lockup period expires). Larissa asks you to advise the employees about which option is better. What would you suggest to the employees?

20 International Corporate Finance

In Chapter 18, we mentioned the cash balances held by several large companies, but we didn't mention that much of that cash was held overseas. For example, Apple led the way with over $250 billion in overseas cash, followed by Microsoft ($130 billion) and Alphabet ($94 billion). Before 2018, companies like Apple had a strong tax incentive to keep huge cash hoards outside the United States. All of that changed with the signing of the Tax Cuts and Jobs Act of 2017, which ushered in big changes in the way U.S. corporations are taxed on their overseas operations. In this chapter, we discuss this topic, along with the important roles played by currencies, exchange rates, and other features of the international finance landscape.

Please visit us at corecorporatefinance.blogspot.com for the latest developments in the world of corporate finance.

Corporations with significant foreign operations are often called *international corporations* or *multinationals*. Such corporations must consider many financial factors that do not directly affect purely domestic firms. These include foreign exchange rates, differing interest rates from country to country, complex accounting methods for foreign operations, foreign tax rates, and foreign government intervention.

The basic principles of corporate finance still apply to international corporations; like domestic companies, these firms seek to invest in projects that create more value for the shareholders than they cost and to arrange financing that raises cash at the lowest possible cost. In other words, the net present value principle holds for both foreign and domestic operations, although it is usually more complicated to apply the NPV rule to foreign investments.

One of the most significant complications of international finance is foreign exchange. The foreign exchange markets provide important information and opportunities for an international corporation when it undertakes capital budgeting and financing decisions. As we will discuss, international exchange rates, interest rates, and inflation rates are closely related. We will spend much of this chapter exploring the connection between these financial variables.

We won't have much to say here about the role of cultural and social differences in international business. Neither will we be discussing the implications of differing political and economic systems. These factors are of great importance to international businesses, but it would take another book to do them justice. Consequently, we will focus only on some purely financial considerations in international finance and some key aspects of foreign exchange markets.

20.1 TERMINOLOGY

A common buzzword for the student of business finance is *globalization*. The first step in learning about the globalization of financial markets is to conquer the new vocabulary. As with any specialty, international finance is rich in jargon. Accordingly, we get started on the subject with a highly eclectic vocabulary exercise.

The terms that follow are presented alphabetically, and they are not all of equal importance. We choose these particular ones because they appear frequently in the financial press or because they illustrate the colorful nature of the language of international finance.

1. An **American Depositary Receipt (ADR)** is a security issued in the United States that represents shares of a foreign stock, allowing that stock to be traded in the United States. Foreign companies use ADRs, which are issued in U.S. dollars, to expand the pool of potential U.S. investors. ADRs are available in two forms for a large and growing number of foreign companies: company sponsored, which are listed on an exchange, and unsponsored, which usually are held by the investment bank that makes a market in the ADR. Both forms are available to individual investors, but only company-sponsored issues are quoted daily in newspapers.

   See www.adr.com for more on ADRs.

2. The **cross-rate** is the implicit exchange rate between two currencies (usually non-U.S.) when both are quoted in some third currency, usually the U.S. dollar.

3. A **Eurobond** is a bond issued in multiple countries but denominated in a single currency, usually the issuer's home currency. Such bonds have become an important way to raise capital for many international companies and governments. Eurobonds are issued outside the restrictions that apply to domestic offerings and are syndicated and traded mostly from London. However, trading can and does take place anywhere there is a buyer and a seller.

4. **Eurocurrency** is money deposited in a financial center outside of the country whose currency is involved. For instance, Eurodollars—the most widely used Eurocurrency—are U.S. dollars deposited in banks outside the U.S. banking system.

5. **Foreign bonds**, unlike Eurobonds, are issued in a single country and are usually denominated in that country's currency. Often, the country in which these bonds are issued will draw distinctions between them and bonds issued by domestic issuers, including different tax laws, restrictions on the amount issued, and tougher disclosure rules.

   Foreign bonds often are nicknamed for the country where they are issued: Yankee bonds (United States), samurai bonds (Japan), Rembrandt bonds (the Netherlands), bulldog bonds (Britain), and dim sum bonds (yuan-denominated bonds issued in Hong Kong). Partly because of tougher regulations and disclosure requirements, the foreign bond market hasn't grown in past years with the vigor of the Eurobond market.

6. **Gilts**, technically, are British and Irish government securities, although the term also includes issues of local British authorities and some overseas public sector offerings.

7. The **London Interbank Offered Rate (LIBOR)** is the rate that most international banks charge one another for loans of Eurodollars overnight in the London market. LIBOR is a cornerstone in the pricing of money market issues and other short-term debt issues by both government and corporate borrowers. Interest rates are frequently quoted as some spread over LIBOR, and they then float with the LIBOR rate. Although LIBOR has long been a widely used interest rate, because of various scandals, financial regulators have undertaken the search for a replacement. A leading candidate is known as the Secured Overnight Financing Rate (SOFR).

   For current LIBOR rates, see www.bloomberg.com.

8. There are two basic kinds of **swaps**: interest rate and currency. An interest rate swap occurs when two parties exchange a floating-rate payment for a fixed-rate payment or vice versa. Currency swaps are agreements to deliver one currency in exchange for another. Often, both types of swaps are used in the same transaction when debt denominated in different currencies is swapped.

20.2 FOREIGN EXCHANGE MARKETS AND EXCHANGE RATES

ExcelMaster
coverage online
www.mhhe.com/RossCore6e

The foreign exchange market is undoubtedly the world's largest financial market. It is the market where one country's currency is traded for another's. Most of the trading takes place in a few currencies: the U.S. dollar ($), the British pound sterling (£), the Japanese yen (¥), and the euro (€). Table 20.1 lists some of the more common currencies and their symbols.

The foreign exchange market is an over-the-counter market, so there is no single location where traders get together. Instead, market participants are located in the major commercial and investment banks around the world. They communicate using computer terminals, telephones, and other telecommunications devices. For example, one communications network for foreign transactions is maintained by the Society for Worldwide Interbank Financial Telecommunication (SWIFT), a Belgian not-for-profit cooperative. Using data transmission lines, a bank in New York can send messages to a bank in London via SWIFT regional processing centers.

The many different types of participants in the foreign exchange market include the following:

Visit SWIFT at www.swift
.com.

1. Importers who pay for goods using foreign currencies.
2. Exporters who receive foreign currency and may want to convert to the domestic currency.
3. Portfolio managers who buy or sell foreign stocks and bonds.
4. Foreign exchange brokers who match buy and sell orders.
5. Traders who "make a market" in foreign currencies.
6. Speculators who try to profit from changes in exchange rates.

TABLE 20.1

International Currency Symbols

Country	Currency	Symbol
Australia	Dollar	A$
Canada	Dollar	Can$
Denmark	Krone	DKr
EMU*	Euro	€
India	Rupee	RS
Iran	Rial	RI
Japan	Yen	¥
Kuwait	Dinar	KD
Mexico	Peso	Ps
Norway	Krone	NKr
Saudi Arabia	Riyal	SR
Singapore	Dollar	S$
South Africa	Rand	R
Sweden	Krona	SKr
Switzerland	Franc	Fr
United Kingdom	Pound	£
United States	Dollar	$

* European Economic and Monetary Union.

Exchange Rates

An **exchange rate** is the price of one country's currency expressed in terms of another country's currency. In practice, almost all trading of currencies takes place in terms of the U.S. dollar. For example, both the Swiss franc and the Japanese yen are traded with their prices quoted in U.S. dollars. Exchange rates are constantly changing.

EXCHANGE RATE QUOTATIONS   Figure 20.1 reproduces exchange rate quotations as they appeared on www.wsj.com and www.barchart.com in 2019. The first column (labeled "in USD equiv") gives the number of dollars it takes to buy one unit of foreign currency. Because this is the price in dollars of a foreign currency, it is called a *direct* or *American quote* (remember that "Americans are direct"). For example, the Australian dollar is quoted at .7093, which means that you can buy one Australian dollar with U.S. $.7093.

The second column shows the *indirect, or European, exchange rate* (even though the currency may not be European). This is the amount of foreign currency per U.S. dollar. The Australian dollar is quoted here at 1.4098, so you can get 1.4098 Australian dollars for one U.S. dollar. Naturally, this second exchange rate is the reciprocal of the first one (possibly with a small rounding error), 1/.7093 = 1.4098.

Get up-to-the minute exchange rates at www.xe.com and www.exchangerate.com.

You can also find exchange rates on a number of websites. Suppose you have just returned from your dream vacation to Jamaica and feel rich because you have 10,000 Jamaican dollars left over. You now need to convert these to U.S. dollars. How much will you have? We went to www.xe.com and used the currency converter on the site to find out. This is what we found:

Source: XE.com Inc.

Looks like you left Jamaica just before you ran out of money.

EXAMPLE 20.1

A Yen for Euros

Suppose you have $1,000. Based on the rates in Figure 20.1, how many Japanese yen can you get? Alternatively, if a Porsche costs €100,000 (recall that € is the symbol for the euro), how many dollars will you need to buy it?

The exchange rate in terms of yen per dollar (second column) is 111.74. Your $1,000 will thus get you:

$1,000 × 111.74 yen per $1 = 111,740 yen

Because the exchange rate in terms of dollars per euro (first column) is 1.1340, you will need:

€100,000 × $1.1340 per € = $113,400

CROSS-RATES AND TRIANGLE ARBITRAGE   Using the U.S. dollar as the common denominator in quoting exchange rates greatly reduces the number of possible cross-currency quotes. With five major currencies, there would potentially be 10 exchange rates instead of four.[1] Also, the fact that the dollar is used throughout cuts down on inconsistencies in the exchange rate quotations.

---

[1] There are four exchange rates instead of five because one exchange rate would involve the exchange of a currency for itself. More generally, it might seem that there should be 25 exchange rates with five currencies. There are 25 different combinations, but of these, 5 involve the exchange of a currency for itself. Of the remaining 20, half are redundant because they are just the reciprocals of another exchange rate. Of the remaining 10, 6 can be eliminated by using a common denominator.

FIGURE 20.1 Exchange Rate Quotations

Americas	USD equiv	Currency per US dollar
Argentina peso	0.0251	39.823
Brazil real	0.2649	3.7756
Canada dollar	0.7517	1.3303
Chile peso	0.001515	660.2
Ecuador US dollar	1	1
Mexico peso	0.0518	19.2971
Uruguay peso	0.03059	32.69
Asia-Pacific		
Australian dollar	0.7093	1.4098
1-mos forward	0.7058	1.4168
3-mos forward	0.6996	1.4294
6-mos forward	0.7073	1.4138
China yuan	0.1491	6.7071
Hong Kong dollar	0.1274	7.8492
India rupee	0.0141	70.9
Indonesia rupiah	0.0000708	14130
Japan yen	0.008949	111.74
1-mos forward	0.009229	111.77
3-mos forward	0.009749	111.82
6-mos forward	0.009109	111.90
Kazakhstan tenge	0.00266	376.22
Macau pataca	0.1238099	8.077
Malaysia ringgit	0.2452	4.079
New Zealand dollar	0.6824	1.4654
Pakistan rupee	0.00716	139.76
Philippines peso	0.0193	51.811
Singapore dollar	0.7383	1.3545
South Korea won	0.0008877	1126.46
Sri Lanka rupee	0.0055624	179.78
Taiwan dollar	0.03243	30.84
Thailand baht	0.03139	31.86
Vietnam dong	0.0000431	23200

Americas	USD equiv	Currency per US dollar
Europe		
Bulgaria lev	0.57958	1.725
Croatia kuna	0.1526	6.554
Czech Rep. koruna	0.04423	22.607
Denmark krone	0.1520	6.5799
Euro area euro	1.1340	0.8819
Hungary forint	0.0035917	278.42
Iceland krona	0.008307	120.38
Norway krone	0.1157	8.6448
Poland zloty	0.2638	3.7915
Romania leu	0.2393	4.178
Russia ruble	0.01521	65.741
Sweden krona	0.1071	9.3371
Switzerland franc	1.0011	0.9989
1-mos forward	1.0042	0.9958
3-mos forward	1.0097	0.9904
6-mos forward	1.0185	0.9818
Turkey lira	0.186	5.3776
Ukraine hryvnia	0.0373	26.83
U.K. pound	1.3178	0.7588
1-mos forward	1.3157	0.7601
3-mos forward	1.3118	0.7623
6-mos forward	1.3058	0.7658
Middle East/Africa		
Bahrain dinar	2.6523	0.377
Egypt pound	0.0571	17.522
Israel shekel	0.2758	3.6252
Kuwait dinar	3.2945	0.3035
Oman sul rial	2.59737	0.39
Qatar rial	0.2748	3.6387
Saudia Arabia riyal	0.2666	3.7505
South Africa rand	0.0703	14.2209

Earlier, we defined the cross-rate as the exchange rate for a non-U.S. currency expressed in terms of another non-U.S. currency. Suppose we observe the following for the euro (€) and the Swiss franc (Fr):

€ per $1 = 1.00
Fr per $1 = 2.00

Suppose the cross-rate is quoted as:

€ per Fr = .40

What do you think?

The cross-rate here is inconsistent with the exchange rates. To see this, suppose you have $100. If you convert this to Swiss francs, you will receive:

$100 × Fr 2 per $1 = Fr 200

If you convert this to euros at the cross-rate, you will have:

Fr 200 × €.4 per Fr 1 = €80

However, if you convert your dollars to euros without going through Swiss francs, you will have:

$100 × €1 per $1 = €100

What we see is that the euro has two prices, €1 per $1 and €.80 per $1, with the price we pay depending on how we get the euros.

To make money, we want to buy low and sell high. The important thing to note is that euros are cheaper if you buy them with dollars because you get 1 euro instead of .8. You should proceed as follows:

1. Buy 100 euros for $100.
2. Use the 100 euros to buy Swiss francs at the cross-rate. Because it takes .4 euro to buy a Swiss franc, you will receive €100/.4 = Fr 250.
3. Use the Fr 250 to buy dollars. Because the exchange rate is Fr 2 per dollar, you receive Fr 250/2 = $125, for a round-trip profit of $25.
4. Repeat Steps 1 through 3.

This particular activity is called *triangle arbitrage* because the arbitrage involves moving through three different exchange rates:

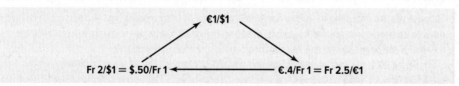

To prevent such opportunities, it is not difficult to see that because a dollar will buy you either 1 euro or 2 Swiss francs, the cross-rate must be:

(€1/$1)/(Fr 2/$1) = €1/Fr 2

That is, the cross-rate must be 1 euro per 2 Swiss francs. If it were anything else, there would be a triangle arbitrage opportunity.

EXAMPLE 20.2

Shedding Some Pounds

Suppose the exchange rates for the British pound and Swiss franc are:

>   Pounds per $1 = .60
>   Fr per $1 = 2.00

The cross-rate is three francs per pound. Is this consistent? Explain how to go about making some money.

The cross-rate should be Fr 2.00/£.60 = Fr 3.33 per pound. You can buy a pound for Fr 3 in one market, and you can sell a pound for Fr 3.33 in another. So we want to first get some francs, then use the francs to buy some pounds, and then sell the pounds. Assuming you have $100, you could:

1. Exchange dollars for francs: $100 × 2 = Fr 200.
2. Exchange francs for pounds: Fr 200/3 = £66.67.
3. Exchange pounds for dollars: £66.67/.60 = $111.11.

This would result in an $11.11 round-trip profit per $100 used.

For international news and events, visit www .ft.com.

TYPES OF TRANSACTIONS   There are two basic types of trades in the foreign exchange market: spot trades and forward trades. A spot trade is an agreement to exchange currency "on the spot," which actually means that the transaction will be completed or settled within two business days. The exchange rate on a spot trade is called the spot exchange rate. Implicitly, all of the exchange rates and transactions we have discussed so far have referred to the spot market.

A forward trade is an agreement to exchange currency at some time in the future. The exchange rate that will be used is agreed upon today and is called the forward exchange rate. A forward trade will normally be settled sometime in the next 12 months.

If you look back at Figure 20.1, you will see forward exchange rates quoted for some of the major currencies. For example, the spot exchange rate for the Swiss franc is Fr 1 = $1.0011. The 180-day (6-month) forward exchange rate is Fr 1 = $1.0185. This means that you can buy a Swiss franc today for $1.0011 or you can agree to take delivery of a Swiss franc in 180 days and pay $1.0185 at that time.

Notice that the Swiss franc is more expensive in the forward market ($1.0185 versus $1.0011). Because the Swiss franc is more expensive in the future than it is today, it is said to be selling at a *premium* relative to the dollar. For the same reason, the dollar is said to be selling at a *discount* relative to the Swiss franc.

Why does the forward market exist? One answer is that it allows businesses and individuals to lock in a future exchange rate today, thereby eliminating any risk from unfavorable shifts in the exchange rate.

EXAMPLE 20.3

Looking Forward

Suppose you are expecting to receive a million British pounds in six months, and you agree to a forward trade to exchange your pounds for dollars. Based on Figure 20.1, how many dollars will you get in six months? Is the pound selling at a discount or a premium relative to the dollar?

In Figure 20.1, the spot exchange rate and the 180-day forward rate in terms of dollars per pound are $1.3178 = £1 and $1.3058 = £1, respectively. If you expect £1 million in 180 days, then you will get £1 million × $1.3058 per pound = $1.3058 million. Because it is less expensive to buy a pound in the forward market than in the spot market ($1.3178 versus $1.3058), the pound is said to be selling at a discount relative to the dollar.

As we mentioned earlier, it is standard practice around the world (with a few exceptions) to quote exchange rates in terms of the U.S. dollar. This means that rates are quoted as the amount of currency per U.S. dollar. For the remainder of this chapter, we will stick with this form. Things can get extremely confusing if you forget this. Thus, when we say things like "the exchange rate is expected to rise," it is important to remember that we are talking about the exchange rate quoted as units of foreign currency per dollar.

20.3 PURCHASING POWER PARITY

Now that we have discussed what exchange rate quotations mean, we can address an obvious question: What determines the level of the spot exchange rate? In addition, because we know that exchange rates change through time, we can ask the related question: What determines the rate of change in exchange rates? At least part of the answer in both cases goes by the name of purchasing power parity (PPP), the idea that the exchange rate adjusts to keep purchasing power constant among currencies. As we discuss next, there are two forms of PPP, *absolute* and *relative*.

Absolute Purchasing Power Parity

The basic idea behind *absolute purchasing power parity* is that a commodity costs the same regardless of what currency is used to purchase it or where it is selling. This is a very straightforward concept. If a beer costs £2 in London, and the exchange rate is £.60 per dollar, then a beer costs £2/.60 = $3.33 in New York. In other words, absolute PPP says that $1 will buy you the same number of, say, cheeseburgers anywhere in the world.

More formally, let S_0 be the spot exchange rate between the British pound and the U.S. dollar today (Time 0), and remember that we are quoting exchange rates as the amount of foreign currency per dollar. Let P_{US} and P_{UK} be the current U.S. and British prices, respectively, on a particular commodity, say, apples. Absolute PPP says that:

$$P_{UK} = S_0 \times P_{US}$$

This tells us that the British price for something is equal to the U.S. price for that same something multiplied by the exchange rate.

The rationale behind PPP is similar to that behind triangle arbitrage. If PPP did not hold, arbitrage would be possible (in principle) if apples were moved from one country to another. For example, suppose apples are selling in New York for $4 per bushel, whereas in London the price is £2.40 per bushel. Absolute PPP implies that:

$$P_{UK} = S_0 \times P_{US}$$
$$£2.40 = S_0 \times \$4$$
$$S_0 = £2.40/\$4 = £.60$$

That is, the implied spot exchange rate is £.60 per dollar. Equivalently, a pound is worth $1/£.60 = $1.67.

Suppose that, instead, the actual exchange rate is £.50. Starting with $4, a trader could buy a bushel of apples in New York, ship it to London, and sell it there for £2.40. Our trader could then convert the £2.40 into dollars at the prevailing exchange rate, $S_0 = £.50$, yielding a total of £2.40/.50 = $4.80. The round-trip gain would be 80 cents.

Because of this profit potential, forces are set in motion to change the exchange rate and/or the price of apples. In our example, apples would begin moving from New York to London. The reduced supply of apples in New York would raise the price of apples there, and the increased supply in Britain would lower the price of apples in London.

In addition to moving apples around, apple traders would be busily converting pounds back into dollars to buy more apples. This activity would increase the supply of pounds and simultaneously increase the demand for dollars. We would expect the value of a pound to fall. This means that the dollar would be getting more valuable, so it would take more pounds to buy one dollar. Because the exchange rate is quoted as pounds per dollar, we would expect the exchange rate to rise from £.50.

For absolute PPP to hold absolutely, several things must be true:

1. The transaction costs of trading apples—shipping, insurance, spoilage, and so on—must be zero.

2. There must be no barriers to trading apples—no tariffs, taxes, or other political barriers.

3. Finally, an apple in New York must be identical to an apple in London. It won't do for you to send red apples to London if the English eat only green apples.

Given the fact that the transaction costs are not zero and that the other conditions are rarely met exactly, it is not surprising that absolute PPP is really applicable only to traded goods, and then only to very uniform ones.

For this reason, absolute PPP does not imply that a Mercedes costs the same as a Ford or that a nuclear power plant in France costs the same as one in New York. In the case of

McPRICING

As we discussed in the chapter, the idea of absolute purchasing power parity (PPP) does not seem to hold in practice. One of the more famous violations of absolute PPP is the Big Mac index constructed by *The Economist*. To construct the index, prices for a Big Mac in different countries are gathered from McDonald's. We went to www.economist.com to find the January 2019 Big Mac index (we will leave it to you to find the most recent index or check our blog for updates).

According to the index on that day, absolute PPP does not seem to hold, at least for the Big Mac. In fact, in only 3 of the 50 currencies surveyed by *The Economist* is the exchange rate within 10 percent of that predicted by absolute PPP. The largest disparity was in Russia, where the ruble was apparently undervalued by 70 percent. And 31 of the 50 currencies were "incorrectly" priced by more than 40 percent. Why?

There are several reasons. First, a Big Mac is not really transportable. Yes, you can load a ship with Big Macs and send it to a country where the currency is supposedly overvalued. But do you really think people would buy your Big Macs? Probably not. Even though it is relatively easy to transport a Big Mac, it would be relatively expensive, and the hamburger would suffer in quality along the way.

Also, if you look, the price of the Big Mac is the average of the prices from five cities. The reason is that the Big Mac does not sell for the same price in different areas of the United States, where presumably they are all purchased with the dollar. The cost of living and competition are only a few of the factors that affect the price of a Big Mac in the United States. Because Big Macs are not priced the same in the same country and currency, would we expect absolute PPP to hold across currencies?

Finally, differing tastes can also account for the apparent discrepancy. In the United States, hamburgers and fast food have become staples of the American diet. In other countries, hamburgers have not become as entrenched. We would expect the price of the Big Mac to be lower in the United States because there is much more competition.

Having examined Big Mac prices, we should say that absolute PPP should hold more closely for more readily transportable items. For instance, there are many companies with stock listed on both the NYSE and the stock exchange of another country. If you examine the share prices on the two exchanges, you will find that the price of the stock is almost exactly what absolute PPP would predict. The reason is that a share of stock in a particular company is (usually) the same wherever you buy it and whatever currency is used.

the cars, they are not identical. In the case of the power plants, even if they were identical, they are expensive and would be very difficult to ship. On the other hand, we would be very surprised to see a significant violation of absolute PPP for gold. Our nearby *Finance Matters* box explores a famous example of PPP violations.

Relative Purchasing Power Parity

As a practical matter, a relative version of purchasing power parity has evolved. *Relative purchasing power parity* does not tell us what determines the absolute level of the exchange rate. Instead, it tells us what determines the change in the exchange rate over time.

THE BASIC IDEA Suppose the British pound-U.S. dollar exchange rate is currently $S_0 = £.50$. Further suppose that the inflation rate in Britain is predicted to be 10 percent over the coming year, and (for the moment) the inflation rate in the United States is predicted to be zero. What do you think the exchange rate will be in a year?

If you think about it, you see that a dollar currently costs .50 pound in Britain. With 10 percent inflation, we expect prices in Britain to generally rise by 10 percent. So we expect that the price of a dollar will go up by 10 percent, and the exchange rate should rise to $£.50 \times 1.1 = £.55$.

If the inflation rate in the United States is not zero, then we need to worry about the *relative* inflation rates in the two countries. Suppose the U.S. inflation rate is predicted to be 4 percent. Relative to prices in the United States, prices in Britain are rising at a rate of 10 percent − 4 percent = 6 percent per year. So we expect the price of the dollar to rise by 6 percent, and the predicted exchange rate is £.50 × 1.06 = £.53.

THE RESULT   In general, relative PPP says that the change in the exchange rate is determined by the difference in the inflation rates of the two countries. To be more specific, we will use the following notation:

S_0 = Current (Time 0) spot exchange rate (foreign currency per dollar)

$E(S_t)$ = Expected exchange rate in t periods

h_{US} = Inflation rate in the United States

h_{FC} = Foreign country inflation rate

Based on our discussion just preceding, relative PPP says that the expected percentage change in the exchange rate over the next year, $[E(S_1) − S_0]/S_0$, is:

$$[E(S_1) − S_0]/S_0 \cong h_{FC} − h_{US} \qquad [20.1]$$

In words, relative PPP says that the expected percentage change in the exchange rate is equal to the difference in inflation rates.[2] If we rearrange this slightly, we get:

$$E(S_1) \cong S_0 × [1 + (h_{FC} − h_{US})] \qquad [20.2]$$

This result makes a certain amount of sense, but care must be used in quoting the exchange rate.

In our example involving Britain and the United States, relative PPP tells us that the exchange rate will rise by $h_{FC} − h_{US}$ = 10 percent − 4 percent = 6 percent per year. Assuming the difference in inflation rates doesn't change, the expected exchange rate in two years, $E(S_2)$, will therefore be:

$$\begin{aligned} E(S_2) &= E(S_1) × (1 + .06) \\ &= .53 × 1.06 \\ &= .562 \end{aligned}$$

Notice that we could have written this as:

$$\begin{aligned} E(S_2) &= .53 × 1.06 \\ &= .50 × (1.06 × 1.06) \\ &= .50 × 1.06^2 \end{aligned}$$

In general, relative PPP says that the expected exchange rate at some time in the future, $E(S_t)$, is:

$$E(S_t) \cong S_0 × [1 + (h_{FC} − h_{US})]^t \qquad [20.3]$$

As we will see, this is a very useful relationship.

---

[2] Equation 20.1 is actually an approximation; the relative PPP predicts that:

$$\frac{E(S_1)}{S_0} = \frac{1 + h_{FC}}{1 + h_{US}} \text{ and } \frac{E(S_1) − S_0}{S_0} = \frac{E(S_1)}{S_0} − 1$$

will hold precisely. So, in our example, the change in the value of a UK pound per dollar would be:

$$1.058 = \frac{1 + .10}{1 + .04}$$

or 5.8 percent instead of 6 percent. This is a widely used approximation, and we use it from time to time for ease of exposition.

Because we don't really expect absolute PPP to hold for most goods, we will focus on relative PPP in our following discussion. Henceforth, when we refer to PPP without further qualification, we mean relative PPP.

CURRENCY APPRECIATION AND DEPRECIATION   We frequently hear things like "the dollar strengthened (or weakened) in financial markets today" or "the dollar is expected to appreciate (or depreciate) relative to the pound." When we say that the dollar strengthens or appreciates, we mean that the value of a dollar rises, so it takes more foreign currency to buy a dollar.

What happens to the exchange rates as currencies fluctuate in value depends on how exchange rates are quoted. Because we are quoting them as units of foreign currency per dollar, the exchange rate moves in the same direction as the value of the dollar: It rises as the dollar strengthens, and it falls as the dollar weakens.

Relative PPP tells us that the exchange rate will rise if the U.S. inflation rate is lower than the foreign country's. This happens because the foreign currency depreciates in value and therefore weakens relative to the dollar.

20.4 INTEREST RATE PARITY, UNBIASED FORWARD RATES, AND THE INTERNATIONAL FISHER EFFECT

The next issue we need to address is the relationship between spot exchange rates, forward exchange rates, and interest rates. To get started, we need some additional notation:

> F_t = Forward exchange rate for settlement at Time t
> R_{US} = U.S. nominal risk-free interest rate
> R_{FC} = Foreign country nominal risk-free interest rate

As before, we will use S_0 to stand for the spot exchange rate. You can take the U.S. nominal risk-free rate, R_{US}, to be the T-bill rate.

Covered Interest Arbitrage

Suppose we observe the following information about U.S. and Swiss currencies in the market:

> S_0 = Fr 2.00
> F_1 = Fr 1.90
> R_{US} = 10%
> R_S = 5%

where R_S is the nominal risk-free rate in Switzerland. The period is one year, so F_1 is the 360-day forward rate.

Do you see an arbitrage opportunity here? There is one. Suppose you have $1 to invest, and you want a riskless investment. One option you have is to invest the $1 in a riskless U.S. investment such as a 360-day T-bill. If you do this, then in one period your $1 will be worth:

For exchange rates and even pictures of non-U.S. currencies, see www .travlang.com/money.

$$\text{\$ value in 1 period} = \$1 \times (1 + R_{US})$$
$$= \$1.10$$

Alternatively, you can invest in the Swiss risk-free investment. To do this, you need to convert your $1 to Swiss francs and simultaneously execute a forward trade to convert francs back to dollars in one year. The necessary steps would be as follows:

1. Convert your $1 to $1 \times S_0 = $ Fr 2.00.
2. At the same time, enter into a forward agreement to convert Swiss francs back to dollars in one year. Because the forward rate is Fr 1.90, you will get $1 for every Fr 1.90 that you have in one year.
3. Invest your Fr 2.00 in Switzerland at R_S. In one year, you will have:

$$\text{Fr value in 1 year} = \text{Fr } 2.00 \times (1 + R_S)$$
$$= \text{Fr } 2.00 \times 1.05$$
$$= \text{Fr } 2.10$$

4. Convert your Fr 2.10 back to dollars at the agreed-upon rate of Fr 1.90 = $1. You end up with:

$$\text{\$ value in 1 year} = \text{Fr } 2.10/1.90$$
$$= \$1.1053$$

Notice that the value in one year resulting from this strategy can be written as:

$$\text{\$ value in 1 year} = \$1 \times S_0 \times (1 + R_S)/F_1$$
$$= \$1 \times 2 \times 1.05/1.90$$
$$= \$1.1053$$

The return on this investment is apparently 10.53 percent. This is higher than the 10 percent we get from investing in the United States. Because both investments are risk-free, there is an arbitrage opportunity.

To exploit the difference in interest rates, you need to borrow, say, $5 million at the lower U.S. rate and invest it at the higher Swiss rate. What is the round-trip profit from doing this? To find out, we can work through the steps outlined previously:

1. Convert the $5 million at Fr 2 = $1 to get Fr 10 million.
2. Agree to exchange Swiss francs for dollars in one year at Fr 1.90 to the dollar.
3. Invest the Fr 10 million for one year at $R_S = 5$ percent. You end up with Fr 10.5 million.
4. Convert the Fr 10.5 million back to dollars to fulfill the forward contract. You receive Fr 10.5 million/1.90 = $5,526,316.
5. Repay the loan with interest. You owe $5 million plus 10 percent interest, for a total of $5.5 million. You have $5,526,316, so your round-trip profit is a risk-free $26,316.

The activity that we have illustrated here goes by the name of *covered interest arbitrage*. The term *covered* refers to the fact that we are covered in the event of a change in the exchange rate because we lock in the forward exchange rate today.

Interest Rate Parity

If we assume that significant covered interest arbitrage opportunities do not exist, then there must be some relationship between spot exchange rates, forward exchange rates, and relative interest rates. To see what this relationship is, note that, in general, Strategy 1 from the preceding discussion, investing in a riskless U.S. investment, gives us $1 + R_{US}$ for every dollar we invest. Strategy 2, investing in a foreign risk-free investment, gives us $S_0 \times (1 + R_{FC})/F_1$ for every dollar we invest. Because these have to be equal to prevent arbitrage, it must be the case that:

$$1 + R_{US} = S_0 \times (1 + R_{FC})/F_1$$

Rearranging this a bit gets us the famous interest rate parity (IRP) condition:

$$F_1/S_0 = (1 + R_{FC})/(1 + R_{US}) \qquad [20.4]$$

There is a very useful approximation for IRP that illustrates very clearly what is going on and is not difficult to remember.[3] If we define the percentage forward premium or discount as $(F_1 - S_0)/S_0$, then IRP says that this percentage premium or discount is approximately equal to the difference in interest rates:

$$(F_1 - S_0)/S_0 \cong R_{FC} - R_{US} \qquad [20.5]$$

Very loosely, what IRP says is that any difference in interest rates between two countries for some period is offset by the change in the relative value of the currencies, thereby eliminating any arbitrage possibilities. Notice that we could also write:

$$F_1 \cong S_0 \times [1 + (R_{FC} - R_{US})] \qquad [20.6]$$

In general, if we have t periods instead of one, the IRP approximation is written as:

$$F_t \cong S_0 \times [1 + (R_{FC} - R_{US})]^t \qquad [20.7]$$

EXAMPLE 20.5

Parity Check

Suppose the exchange rate for Japanese yen, S_0, is currently ¥120 = \$1. If the interest rate in the United States is $R_{US} = 10$ percent and the interest rate in Japan is $R_J = 5$ percent, then what must the forward rate be to prevent covered interest arbitrage?

From IRP, we have:

$$\begin{aligned} F_1 &\cong S_0 \times [1 + (R_J - R_{US})] \\ &\cong ¥120 \times [1 + (.05 - .10)] \\ &\cong ¥120 \times .95 \\ &\cong ¥114 \end{aligned}$$

Notice that the yen will sell at a premium relative to the dollar. (Why?)

Forward Rates and Future Spot Rates

In addition to PPP and IRP, there is one more basic relationship we need to discuss. What is the connection between the forward rate and the expected future spot rate? The unbiased forward rate (UFR) condition says that the forward rate, F_1, is equal to the *expected* future spot rate, $E(S_1)$:

$$F_1 = E(S_1)$$

---

[3] Here we note that $F_1/S_0 - 1 = (F_1 - S_0)/S_0$ and $(1 + R_{FC})/(1 + R_{US})$ is approximately equal to $R_{FC} - R_{US}$.

With t periods, UFR would be written as:

$$F_t = E(S_t)$$

Loosely, the UFR condition says that, on average, the forward exchange rate is equal to the future spot exchange rate.

If we ignore risk, then the UFR condition should hold. Suppose the forward rate for the Japanese yen is consistently lower than the future spot rate by, say, 10 yen. This means that anyone who wanted to convert dollars to yen in the future would consistently get more yen by not agreeing to a forward exchange. The forward rate would have to rise to get anyone interested in a forward exchange.

Similarly, if the forward rate were consistently higher than the future spot rate, then anyone who wanted to convert yen to dollars would get more dollars per yen by not agreeing to a forward trade. The forward exchange rate would have to fall to attract such traders.

For these reasons, the forward and actual future spot rates should be equal to each other, on average. What the future spot rate will actually be is uncertain, of course. The UFR condition may not hold if traders are willing to pay a premium to avoid this uncertainty. If the condition does hold, then the 180-day forward rate that we see today should be an unbiased predictor of what the exchange rate will actually be in 180 days.

How are the international markets doing? Find out at www.marketwatch .com.

Putting It All Together

We have developed three relationships, PPP, IRP, and UFR, that describe the interaction between key financial variables such as interest rates, exchange rates, and inflation rates. We now explore the implications of these relationships as a group.

UNCOVERED INTEREST PARITY To start, it is useful to collect our international financial market relationships in one place:

$$\text{PPP: } E(S_1) \cong S_0 \times [1 + (h_{FC} - h_{US})]$$
$$\text{IRP: } \quad F_1 \cong S_0 \times [1 + (R_{FC} - R_{US})]$$
$$\text{UFR: } \quad F_1 = E(S_1)$$

We begin by combining UFR and IRP. Because we know that $F_1 = E(S_1)$ from the UFR condition, we can substitute $E(S_1)$ for F_1 in IRP.[4] The result is:

$$\text{UIP: } E(S_1) = S_0 \times [1 + (R_{FC} - R_{US})] \tag{20.8}$$

This important relationship is called *uncovered interest parity (UIP)*, and it will play a key role in our international capital budgeting discussion that follows. With t periods, UIP becomes:

$$E(S_t) = S_0 \times [1 + (R_{FC} - R_{US})]^t \tag{20.9}$$

THE INTERNATIONAL FISHER EFFECT Next, we compare PPP and UIP. Both of them have $E(S_1)$ on the left-hand side, so their right-hand sides must be equal. We thus have that:

$$S_0 \times [1 + (h_{FC} - h_{US})] = S_0 \times [1 + (R_{FC} - R_{US})]$$
$$h_{FC} - h_{US} = R_{FC} - R_{US}$$

[4] Here again, we are dealing in an approximation for ease of exposition. The exact equations are:

$$\text{PPP: } E(S_1) = S_0 \times \left[\frac{(1 + h_{FC})}{(1 + h_{US})}\right]$$
$$\text{IRP: } \quad F_1 = S_0 \times \left[\frac{(1 + R_{FC})}{1 + R_{US}}\right]$$

This tells us that the difference in returns between the United States and a foreign country is equal to the difference in inflation rates. Rearranging this slightly gives us the international Fisher effect (IFE):

$$\text{IFE: } R_{US} - h_{US} = R_{FC} - h_{FC} \qquad [20.10]$$

The IFE says that *real* rates are equal across countries.[5]

The conclusion that real returns are equal across countries is really basic economics. If real returns were higher in, say, Brazil than in the United States, money would flow out of U.S. financial markets and into Brazilian markets. Asset prices in Brazil would rise and their returns would fall. At the same time, asset prices in the United States would fall and their returns would rise. This process acts to equalize real returns.

Having said all this, we need to note a couple of things. First of all, we really haven't explicitly dealt with risk in our discussion. We might reach a different conclusion about real returns once we do, particularly if people in different countries have different tastes and attitudes toward risk. Second, there are many barriers to the movement of money and capital around the world. Real returns might be different in two countries for long periods of time if money can't move freely between them.

Despite these problems, we expect that capital markets will become increasingly internationalized. As this occurs, any differences in real rates that do exist will probably diminish. The laws of economics have very little respect for national boundaries.

20.5 INTERNATIONAL CAPITAL BUDGETING

Kihlstrom Equipment, a U.S.-based international company, is evaluating an overseas investment. Kihlstrom's exports of drill bits have increased to such a degree that it is considering building a distribution center in France. The project will cost €2 million to launch. The cash flows are expected to be €.9 million a year for the next three years.

The current spot exchange rate for euros is €.5. Recall that this is euros per dollar, so a euro is worth $1/.5 = $2. The risk-free rate in the United States is 5 percent, and the risk-free rate in "euroland" is 7 percent. Note that the exchange rate and the two interest rates are observed in financial markets, not estimated.[6] Kihlstrom's required return on dollar investments of this sort is 10 percent.[7]

Should Kihlstrom take this investment? As always, the answer depends on the NPV, but how do we calculate the net present value of this project in U.S. dollars? There are two basic ways to go about doing this:

1. *The Home Currency Approach.* Convert all the euro cash flows into dollars, and then discount at 10 percent to find the NPV in dollars. Notice that for this approach, we have to come up with the future exchange rates to convert the future projected euro cash flows into dollars.

---

[5] Notice that our result here is in terms of the approximate real rate, $R - h$ (see Chapter 5), because we used approximations for PPP and IRP. For the exact result, see Problem 18 at the end of the chapter.

[6] For example, the interest rates might be the short-term Eurodollar and euro deposit rates offered by large money center banks.

[7] Kihlstrom's WACC is determined in the usual way. Suppose that the market values of debt and equity and associated capital costs are:

Debt	$500	5%
Equity	$500	16%
	$1,000	

with the corporate tax rate equal to 20 percent. It follows that:

$$\text{WACC} = \frac{B}{B + S} R_B (1 - T_c) + \frac{S}{B + S} R_S$$

$$= \left(\frac{1}{2}\right)(5\%)(1 - .20) + \left(\frac{1}{2}\right)16\%$$

$$= 10\%$$

2. *The Foreign Currency Approach.* Determine the required return on euro investments, and then discount the euro cash flows to find the NPV in euros. Then convert this euro NPV to a dollar NPV. This approach requires us to somehow convert the 10 percent dollar required return to the equivalent euro required return.

The difference between these two approaches is primarily a matter of when we convert from euros to dollars. In the first case, we convert before estimating the NPV. In the second case, we convert after estimating NPV.

It might appear that the second approach is superior because it only requires us to come up with one number, the euro discount rate. Furthermore, because the first approach requires us to forecast future exchange rates, it probably seems that there is greater room for error with this approach. As we illustrate next, however, based on our previous results, the two approaches are really the same.

Method 1: The Home Currency Approach

To convert the projected future cash flows into dollars, we will invoke the uncovered interest parity, or UIP, relation to come up with the projected exchange rates. Based on our earlier discussion, the expected exchange rate at Time t, $E(S_t)$, is:

$$E(S_t) = S_0 \times [1 + (R_{\euro} - R_{US})]^t$$

where $R_{\euro}$ stands for the nominal risk-free rate in euroland. Because $R_{\euro}$ is 7 percent, R_{US} is 5 percent, and the current exchange rate (S_0) is €.5:

$$E(S_t) = .5 \times [1 + (.07 - .05)]^t$$
$$= .5 \times 1.02^t$$

The projected exchange rates for the drill bit project are thus:

Year	Expected Exchange Rate
1	€.5 × 1.02^1 = €.5100
2	€.5 × 1.02^2 = €.5202
3	€.5 × 1.02^3 = €.5306

Using these exchange rates, along with the current exchange rate, we can convert all of the euro cash flows to dollars (note that all of the cash flows in this example are in millions):

Year	(1) Cash Flow in €mil	(2) Expected Exchange Rate	(3) Cash Flow in $mil (1)/(2)
0	−€2.0	€.5000	−$4.00
1	.9	.5100	1.76
2	.9	.5202	1.73
3	.9	.5306	1.70

To finish off, we calculate the NPV in the ordinary way:

$$NPV_\$ = -\$4 + \$1.76/1.10 + \$1.73/1.10^2 + \$1.70/1.10^3$$
$$= \$.31 \text{ million}$$

So the project appears to be profitable.

Method 2: The Foreign Currency Approach

Kihlstrom requires a nominal return of 10 percent on the dollar-denominated cash flows. We need to convert this to a rate suitable for euro-denominated cash flows. Based on the international Fisher effect, we know that the difference in the nominal rates is:

$$R_\math{\euro} - R_{US} = h_\math{\euro} - h_{US}$$
$$= 7\% - 5\% = 2\%$$

The appropriate discount rate for estimating the euro cash flows from the drill bit project is approximately equal to 10 percent plus an extra 2 percent to compensate for the greater euro inflation rate.

If we calculate the NPV of the euro cash flows at this rate, we get:

$$NPV_\math{\euro} = -\math{\euro}2 + \math{\euro}.9/1.12 + \math{\euro}.9/1.12^2 + \math{\euro}.9/1.12^3$$
$$= \math{\euro}.16 \text{ million}$$

The NPV of this project is €.16 million. Taking this project makes us €.16 million richer today. What is this in dollars? Because the exchange rate today is €.5, the dollar NPV of the project is:

$$NPV_\$ = NPV_\math{\euro}/S_0 = \math{\euro}.16/.5 = \$.31 \text{ million}$$

This is the same dollar NPV that we previously calculated.[8]

The important thing to recognize from our example is that the two capital budgeting procedures are actually the same and will always give the same answer. In this second approach, the fact that we are implicitly forecasting exchange rates is hidden. Even so, the foreign currency approach is computationally a little easier.

Unremitted Cash Flows

The previous example assumed that all aftertax cash flows from the foreign investment could be remitted to (paid out to) the parent firm. Actually, substantial differences can exist between the cash flows generated by a foreign project and the amount that can actually be remitted, or "repatriated," to the parent firm.

A foreign subsidiary can remit funds to a parent in many forms, including the following:

1. Dividends.
2. Management fees for central services.
3. Royalties on the use of trade names and patents.

However cash flows are repatriated, international firms must pay special attention to remittances because there may be current and future controls on remittances. Many governments are sensitive to the charge of being exploited by foreign national firms. In such cases, governments are tempted to limit the ability of international firms to remit cash flows. Funds that cannot currently be remitted are sometimes said to be *blocked*.

20.6 EXCHANGE RATE RISK

Exchange rate risk is the natural consequence of international operations in a world where relative currency values move up and down. Managing exchange rate risk is an important part of international finance. For example, Toyota estimates that it loses about ¥40 billion ($374 million) in operating profit for every yen that the dollar falls. As we discuss next,

---

[8] Actually, there will be a slight difference because we are using the approximate relationships. If we calculate the required return as $1.10 \times (1 + .02) - 1 = .122$, or 12.2 percent, then we get exactly the same NPV. See Problem 18 for more detail.

there are three different types of exchange rate risk, or exposure: short-run exposure, long-run exposure, and translation exposure.

Short-Run Exposure

The day-to-day fluctuations in exchange rates create short-run risks for international firms. Most such firms have contractual agreements to buy and sell goods in the near future at set prices. When different currencies are involved, such transactions have an extra element of risk.

Imagine that you are importing imitation pasta from Italy and reselling it in the United States under the Impasta brand name. Your largest customer has ordered 10,000 cases of Impasta. You place the order with your supplier today, but you won't pay until the goods arrive in 60 days. Your selling price is $6 per case. Your cost is 8.4 euros per case, and the exchange rate is currently €1.50, so it takes 1.50 euros to buy $1.

At the current exchange rate, your cost in dollars of filling the order is €8.4/1.5 = $5.60 per case, so your pretax profit on the order is 10,000 × ($6 − 5.60) = $4,000. However, the exchange rate in 60 days will probably be different, so your profit will depend on what the future exchange rate turns out to be.

For example, if the rate goes to €1.6, your cost is €8.4/1.6 = $5.25 per case. Your profit goes to $7,500. If the exchange rate goes to, say, €1.4, then your cost is €8.4/1.4 = $6, and your profit is zero.

The short-run exposure in our example can be reduced or eliminated in several ways. The most obvious way is by entering into a forward exchange agreement to lock in an exchange rate. Suppose the 60-day forward rate is €1.58. What will be your profit if you hedge? What profit should you expect if you don't?

If you hedge, you lock in an exchange rate of €1.58. Your cost in dollars will thus be €8.4/1.58 = $5.32 per case, so your profit will be 10,000 × ($6 − 5.32) = $6,835. If you don't hedge, then, assuming that the forward rate is an unbiased predictor (in other words, assuming the UFR condition holds), you should expect that the exchange rate will actually be €1.58 in 60 days. You should expect to make $6,835.

Alternatively, if this strategy is not feasible, you could borrow the dollars today, convert them into euros, and invest the euros for 60 days to earn some interest. Based on IRP, this amounts to entering into a forward contract.

Long-Run Exposure

In the long run, the value of a foreign operation can fluctuate because of unanticipated changes in relative economic conditions. For example, imagine that we own a labor-intensive assembly operation located in another country to take advantage of lower wages. Through time, unexpected changes in economic conditions can raise the foreign wage levels to the point where the cost advantage is eliminated or even becomes negative.

The impact of changes in exchange rate levels can be substantial. For example, in 2018, Microsoft reported a currency loss of $178 million, which erased the company's gain of $167 million during 2017.

Hedging long-run exposure is more difficult than hedging short-term risks. For one thing, organized forward markets don't exist for such long-term needs. Instead, the primary option that firms have is to try to match up foreign currency inflows and outflows. The same thing goes for matching foreign currency-denominated assets and liabilities. For example, a firm that sells in a foreign country might try to concentrate its raw material purchases and labor expense in that country. That way, the dollar values of its revenues and costs will move up and down together. Probably the best examples of this type of hedging are the so-called transplant auto manufacturers such as BMW, Honda, Mercedes, and Toyota, which now build a substantial portion of the cars they sell in and outside the United States at plants located in the United States, thereby obtaining some degree of immunization against exchange rate movements.

For example, BMW produces 400,000 cars in South Carolina and exports about 280,000 of them. The costs of manufacturing the cars are paid mostly in dollars, and when BMW exports the cars to Europe, it receives euros. When the dollar weakens, these vehicles become more profitable for BMW. At the same time, BMW imports about 200,000 cars to the United States each year. The costs of manufacturing these imported cars are mostly in euros, so they become less profitable when the dollar weakens. Taken together, these gains and losses tend to offset each other and provide BMW with a natural hedge.

Similarly, a firm can reduce its long-run exchange rate risk by borrowing in the foreign country. Fluctuations in the value of the foreign subsidiary's assets will then be at least partially offset by changes in the value of the liabilities.

Translation Exposure

When a U.S. company calculates its accounting net income and EPS for some period, it must "translate" everything into dollars. This can create some problems for the accountants when there are significant foreign operations. In particular, two issues arise:

1. What is the appropriate exchange rate to use for translating each balance sheet account?

2. How should balance sheet accounting gains and losses from foreign currency translation be handled?

To illustrate the accounting problem, suppose we started a small foreign subsidiary in Lilliputia a year ago. The local currency is the gulliver, abbreviated GL. At the beginning of the year, the exchange rate was GL 2 = $1, and the balance sheet in gullivers looked like this:

Assets	GL 1,000	Liabilities	GL 500
		Equity	500

At 2 gullivers to the dollar, the beginning balance sheet in dollars was as follows:

Assets	$500	Liabilities	$250
		Equity	250

Lilliputia is a quiet place, and nothing at all actually happened during the year. As a result, net income was zero (before consideration of exchange rate changes). However, the exchange rate did change to 4 gullivers = $1 purely because the Lilliputian inflation rate is much higher than the U.S. inflation rate.

Because nothing happened, the accounting ending balance sheet in gullivers is the same as the beginning one. However, if we convert it to dollars at the new exchange rate, we get:

Assets	$250	Liabilities	$125
		Equity	125

Notice that the value of the equity has gone down by $125, even though net income was exactly zero. Despite the fact that absolutely nothing really happened, there is a $125 accounting loss. How to handle this $125 loss has been a controversial accounting question.

One obvious and consistent way to handle this loss is to report the loss on the parent's income statement. During periods of volatile exchange rates, this kind of treatment can dramatically impact an international company's reported EPS. This is a purely accounting phenomenon, but even so, such fluctuations are disliked by some financial managers.

The current approach to handling translation gains and losses is based on rules set out in the Financial Accounting Standards Board (FASB) *Statement of Financial Accounting Standards No. 52* (FASB 52), issued in December 1981. For the most part, FASB 52 requires that all assets and liabilities be translated from the subsidiary's currency into the parent's currency using the exchange rate that currently prevails.

Any translation gains and losses that occur are accumulated in a special account within the shareholders' equity section of the balance sheet. This account might be labeled something like "unrealized foreign exchange gains (losses)." The amounts involved can be substantial, at least from an accounting standpoint. For example, Apple's December 29, 2018, 10-Q showed a loss of $1.1 billion. These gains and losses are not reported on the income statement. As a result, the impact of translation gains and losses will not be recognized explicitly in net income until the underlying assets and liabilities are sold or otherwise liquidated.

Managing Exchange Rate Risk

For a large multinational firm, the management of exchange rate risk is complicated by the fact that there can be many different currencies involved in many different subsidiaries. It is very likely that a change in some exchange rate will benefit some subsidiaries and hurt others. The net effect on the overall firm depends on its net exposure.

Suppose a firm has two divisions. Division A buys goods in the United States for dollars and sells them in Britain for pounds. Division B buys goods in Britain for pounds and sells them in the United States for dollars. If these two divisions are of roughly equal size in terms of their inflows and outflows, then the overall firm obviously has little exchange rate risk.

In our example, the firm's net position in pounds (the amount coming in less the amount going out) is small, so the exchange rate risk is small. However, if one division, acting on its own, were to start hedging its exchange rate risk, then the overall firm's exchange rate risk would go up. The moral of the story is that multinational firms have to be conscious of the overall position that the firm has in a foreign currency. For this reason, management of exchange rate risk is probably best handled on a centralized basis.

20.7 POLITICAL RISK

One final element of risk in international investing is political risk. Political risk refers to changes in value that arise as a consequence of political actions. This is not a problem faced exclusively by international firms. For example, in June 2016, British voters shocked the rest of Europe when they voted in favor of "Brexit," the U.K. exit from the European Union. Although the treaty that tied the U.K. to the rest of Europe required a two-year process to complete the withdrawal, financial markets didn't take that long to react. The British pound dropped 11 percent against the U.S. dollar on the day, and London's FTSE and Stoxx Europe 600 stock market indexes dropped about 8 percent. Preeminent British banks Barclays and Lloyds Banking Group were both hit even harder, as they saw stock price drops of more than 30 percent on the day. Unfortunately (or fortunately, depending on your view), the drop in the British pound wasn't finished. It continued to fall against the U.S. dollar, reaching its lowest level since 1985.

The Tax Cuts and Jobs Act of 2017

In our chapter opener, we described the large cash balances held overseas by U.S. corporations. As we noted, the reason Apple and other large U.S. corporations held such large balances overseas has to do with U.S. tax law. Tax laws are a form of political risk faced by multinational firms.

Specifically, before the signing of the Tax Cuts and Jobs Act of 2017, the U.S. had corporate tax rates that were among the highest in the developed world. At the same time, the U.S. was somewhat unique in that it taxed corporate profits wherever they were earned, but only after the profits were brought back, or "repatriated," to the U.S. But what does this mean, exactly?

To answer, let's go back to Lilliputia, which has a 20 percent corporate tax rate, compared to what would have been 35 percent in the United States. If we earned a profit in our Lilliputian subsidiary, that subsidiary would pay taxes to Lilliputia at the 20 percent rate. If we had left the profits in Lilliputia, then no additional taxes were owed. But, if we had brought the profits back to the United States, we would have owed additional taxes of 15 percent, the difference between the United States and Lilliputian tax rates. Avoiding this extra tax gave U.S. companies a strong incentive not to repatriate profits.

Here is where it gets confusing. In the media, companies like Apple are depicted as having huge piles of cash sitting outside the borders of the United States, but that's not what is really going on. Apple's cash is actually mostly in dollars, and it is mostly invested in various U.S. financial assets. So, the money isn't really "outside" the United States.

Instead, because Apple has chosen not to pay the extra tax on its overseas profits, it is prohibited from using that cash inside the U.S. to do things like pay dividends or build new facilities. Note that Apple can easily get around this limitation by, for example, borrowing against its cash and securities portfolio, if it chooses to do so.

The Tax Cuts and Jobs Act of 2017 changed things in a number of ways. First, the new flat 21 percent tax rate (down from a maximum of 35 percent) reduced the incentive to leave cash overseas. Second, the law imposed a one-time tax of 15.5 percent on cash, securities, and receivables, and a one-time tax of 8 percent on other, less liquid assets (e.g., plant, property, and equipment) purchased with untaxed overseas dollars. Finally, broadly speaking, new repatriated earnings are no longer subject to additional U.S. taxes, thereby eliminating the repatriation issue.

Managing Political Risk

Some countries have more political risk than others. When firms have operations in these riskier countries, the extra political risk may lead the firms to require higher returns on overseas investments to compensate for the possibility that funds may be blocked, critical operations interrupted, and contracts abrogated. In the most extreme case, the possibility of outright confiscation may be a concern in countries with relatively unstable political environments.

A great site for evaluating the political risk of a country is www.cia.gov.

Political risk also depends on the nature of the business; some businesses are less likely to be confiscated because they are not particularly valuable in the hands of a different owner. An assembly operation supplying subcomponents that only the parent company uses would not be an attractive "takeover" target, for example. Similarly, a manufacturing operation that requires the use of specialized components from the parent is of little value without the parent company's cooperation.

Natural resource developments, such as copper mining or oil drilling, are just the opposite. Once the operation is in place, much of the value is in the commodity. The political risk for such investments is much higher for this reason. Also, the issue of exploitation is more pronounced with such investments, again increasing the political risk.

Political risk can be hedged in several ways, particularly when confiscation or nationalization is a concern. The use of local financing, perhaps from the government of the foreign country in question, reduces the possible loss because the company can refuse to pay on the debt in the event of unfavorable political activities. Based on our discussion in this section, structuring the operation in such a way that it requires significant parent company involvement to function is another way to reduce political risk.

SUMMARY AND CONCLUSIONS

The international firm has a more complicated life than the purely domestic firm. Management must understand the connection between interest rates, foreign currency exchange rates, and inflation, and it must become aware of a large number of different financial market regulations and tax systems. This chapter is intended to be a concise introduction to some of the financial issues that come up in international investing.

Our coverage has been necessarily brief. The main topics we discussed are the following:

1. Some basic vocabulary. We briefly defined some exotic terms such as *LIBOR* and *Eurocurrency*.

2. The basic mechanics of exchange rate quotations. We discussed the spot and forward markets and how exchange rates are interpreted.

3. The fundamental relationships between international financial variables:

   a. Absolute and relative purchasing power parity, PPP. Absolute purchasing power parity states that $1 should have the same purchasing power in each country. This means that an orange costs the same whether you buy it in New York or in Tokyo. Relative purchasing power parity means that the expected percentage change in exchange rates between the currencies of two countries is equal to the difference in their inflation rates.

   b. Interest rate parity, IRP. Interest rate parity implies that the percentage difference between the forward exchange rate and the spot exchange rate is equal to the interest rate differential. We showed how covered interest arbitrage forces this relationship to hold.

   c. Unbiased forward rates, UFR. The unbiased forward rates condition indicates that the current forward rate is a good predictor of the future spot exchange rate.

4. International capital budgeting. We showed that the basic foreign exchange relationships imply two other conditions:

   a. Uncovered interest parity.

   b. The international Fisher effect.

   By invoking these two conditions, we learned how to estimate NPVs in foreign currencies and how to convert foreign currencies into dollars to estimate NPV in the usual way.

5. Exchange rate and political risk. We described the various types of exchange rate risk and discussed some commonly used approaches to managing the effect of fluctuating exchange rates on the cash flows and value of the international firm. We also discussed political risk and some ways of managing exposure to it.

CONCEPT QUESTIONS

1. **Spot and Forward Rates**   Suppose the exchange rate for the Swiss franc is quoted as Fr 1.50 in the spot market and Fr 1.53 in the 90-day forward market.
   a. Is the dollar selling at a premium or a discount relative to the franc?
   b. Does the financial market expect the franc to strengthen relative to the dollar? Explain.
   c. What do you suspect is true about relative economic conditions in the United States and Switzerland?

2. **Purchasing Power Parity**   Suppose the rate of inflation in Mexico will run about 3 percent higher than the U.S. inflation rate over the next several years. All other things being the same, what will happen to the Mexican peso-dollar exchange rate? What relationship are you relying on in answering?

3. **Exchange Rates**   The exchange rate for the Australian dollar is currently A$1.15. This exchange rate is expected to rise by 10 percent over the next year.
   a. Is the Australian dollar expected to get stronger or weaker?
   b. What do you think about the relative inflation rates in the United States and Australia?
   c. What do you think about the relative nominal interest rates in the United States and Australia? Relative real rates?

4. **Yankee Bonds**   Which of the following most accurately describes a Yankee bond?
   a. A bond issued by General Motors in Japan with the interest payable in U.S. dollars.
   b. A bond issued by General Motors in Japan with the interest payable in yen.

   c. A bond issued by Toyota in the United States with the interest payable in yen.

   d. A bond issued by Toyota in the United States with the interest payable in dollars.

   e. A bond issued by Toyota worldwide with the interest payable in dollars.

5. **Exchange Rates**   Are exchange rate changes necessarily good or bad for a particular company?

6. **International Risks**   At one point, Duracell International confirmed that it was planning to open battery manufacturing plants in China and India. Manufacturing in these countries allows Duracell to avoid import duties of between 30 and 35 percent that have made alkaline batteries prohibitively expensive for some consumers. What additional advantages might Duracell see in this proposal? What are some of the risks to Duracell?

7. **Multinational Corporations**   Given that many multinationals based in many countries have much greater sales outside their domestic markets than within them, what is the particular relevance of their domestic currency?

8. **Exchange Rate Movements**   Are the following statements true or false? Explain why.

   a. If the general price index in Great Britain were to rise faster than that in the United States, we would expect the pound to appreciate relative to the dollar.

   b. Suppose you are a German machine tool exporter, and you invoice all of your sales in foreign currency. Further suppose that the euroland monetary authorities begin to undertake an expansionary monetary policy. If it is certain that the easy money policy will result in higher inflation rates in euroland relative to those in other countries, then you should use the forward markets to protect yourself against future losses resulting from the deterioration in the value of the euro.

   c. If you could accurately estimate differences in the relative inflation rates of two countries over a long period of time, while other market participants were unable to do so, you could successfully speculate in spot currency markets.

9. **Exchange Rate Movements**   Some countries encourage movements in their exchange rate relative to those of some other country as a short-term means of addressing foreign trade imbalances. For each of the following scenarios, evaluate the impact the announcement would have on an American importer and an American exporter doing business with the foreign country.

   a. Officials in the administration of the U.S. government announce that they are comfortable with a rising euro relative to the dollar.

   b. British monetary authorities announce that they feel the pound has been driven too low by currency speculators relative to the dollar.

   c. The Brazilian government announces that it will print billions of new reais and inject them into the economy in an effort to reduce the country's unemployment rate.

10. **International Capital Market Relationships**   We discussed five international capital market relationships: relative PPP, IRP, UFR, UIP, and the international Fisher effect. Which of these would you expect to hold most closely? Which do you think would be most likely to be violated?

11. **Exchange Rate Risk**   If you are an exporter who must make payments in foreign currency three months after receiving each shipment and you predict that the domestic currency will appreciate in value over this period, is there any value in hedging your currency exposure?

12. **International Capital Budgeting**   Suppose it is your task to evaluate two different investments in new subsidiaries for your company, one in your own country and the other in a foreign country. You calculate the cash flows of both projects to be identical after exchange rate differences. Under what circumstances might you choose to invest in the foreign subsidiary? Give an example of a country where certain factors might influence you to alter this decision and invest at home.

13. **International Capital Budgeting**   An investment in a foreign subsidiary is estimated to have a positive NPV after the discount rate used in the calculations is adjusted for political risk and any advantages from diversification. Does this mean the project is acceptable? Why or why not?

14. **International Borrowing**   If a U.S. firm raises funds for a foreign subsidiary, what are the disadvantages to borrowing in the United States? How would you overcome them?

15. **International Investment**   If financial markets are perfectly competitive and the Eurodollar rate is above that offered in the U.S. loan market, you would immediately want to borrow money in the United States and invest it in Eurodollars. True or false? Explain.

16. **Eurobonds**   What distinguishes a Eurobond from a foreign bond? Which particular feature makes the Eurobond more popular than the foreign bond?

QUESTIONS AND PROBLEMS

1. **Using Exchange Rates**   Take a look back at Figure 20.1 to answer the following questions:

   a. If you have $100, how many euros can you get?

   b. How much is one euro worth?

   c. If you have five million euros, how many dollars do you have?

   d. Which is worth more, a New Zealand dollar or a Singapore dollar?

   e. Which is worth more, a Mexican peso or a Chilean peso?

   f. How many Mexican pesos can you get for a euro? What do you call this rate?

   g. Per unit, what is the most valuable currency of those listed? The least valuable?

Basic
(Questions 1–13)

 2. **Using the Cross-Rate**   Use the information in Figure 20.1 to answer the following questions:

   a. Which would you rather have, $100 or £100? Why?

   b. Which would you rather have, 100 Swiss francs (Fr) or £100? Why?

   c. What is the cross-rate for Swiss francs in terms of British pounds? For British pounds in terms of Swiss francs?

 3. **Forward Exchange Rates**   Use the information in Figure 20.1 to answer the following questions:

   a. What is the six-month forward rate for the Japanese yen in yen per U.S. dollar? Is the yen selling at a premium or a discount? Explain.

   b. What is the three-month forward rate for British pounds in U.S. dollars per pound? Is the dollar selling at a premium or a discount? Explain.

   c. What do you think will happen to the value of the dollar relative to the yen and the pound, based on the information in the figure? Explain.

4. **Using Spot and Forward Exchange Rates**   Suppose the spot exchange rate for the Canadian dollar is Can$1.29 and the six-month forward rate is Can$1.34.

   a. Which is worth more, a U.S. dollar or a Canadian dollar?

   b. Assuming absolute PPP holds, what is the cost in the United States of an Elkhead beer if the price in Canada is Can$2.49? Why might the beer actually sell at a different price in the United States?

   c. Is the U.S. dollar selling at a premium or a discount relative to the Canadian dollar?

   d. Which currency is expected to appreciate in value?

   e. Which country do you think has higher interest rates—the United States or Canada? Explain.

5. **Cross-Rates and Arbitrage**   Suppose the Japanese yen exchange rate is ¥105 = $1, and the British pound exchange rate is £1 = $1.34.

   a. What is the cross-rate in terms of yen per pound?

   b. Suppose the cross-rate is ¥136 = £1. Is there an arbitrage opportunity here? If there is, explain how to take advantage of the mispricing.

6. **Interest Rate Parity**   Use Figure 20.1 to answer the following questions. Suppose interest rate parity holds, and the current six-month risk-free rate in the United States is 1.9 percent. What must the six-month risk-free rate be in Great Britain? In Japan? In Switzerland?

7. **Interest Rates and Arbitrage**   The treasurer of a major U.S. firm has $30 million to invest for three months. The interest rate in the United States is .39 percent per month. The interest rate in Great Britain is .41 percent per month. The spot exchange rate is £.7347, and the three-month forward rate is £.7358. Ignoring transaction costs, in which country would the treasurer want to invest the company's funds? Why?

8. **Inflation and Exchange Rates**   Suppose the current exchange rate for the Polish złoty is zł 3.74. The expected exchange rate in three years is zł 3.93. What is the difference in the annual inflation rates for the United States and Poland over this period? Assume that the anticipated rate is constant for both countries. What relationship are you relying on in answering?

 9. **Exchange Rate Risk**   Suppose your company imports computer motherboards from Singapore. The exchange rate is given in Figure 20.1. You have just placed an order for 30,000 motherboards at a cost to you of 124.60 Singapore dollars each. You will pay for the shipment when it arrives in 90 days. You can sell the motherboards for $98 each. Calculate your profit if the exchange rate goes up or down by 10 percent over the next 90 days. What is the break-even exchange rate? What percentage rise or fall does this represent in terms of the Singapore dollar versus the U.S. dollar?

10. **Exchange Rates and Arbitrage**   Suppose the spot and six-month forward rates on the Norwegian krone are Kr 8.53 and Kr 8.61, respectively. The annual risk-free rate in the United States is 3.2 percent, and the annual risk-free rate in Norway is 4.4 percent.
    a. Is there an arbitrage opportunity here? If so, how would you exploit it?
    b. What must the six-month forward rate be to prevent arbitrage?

11. **The International Fisher Effect**   You observe that the inflation rate in the United States is 2.2 percent per year and that T-bills currently yield 3.4 percent annually. What do you estimate the inflation rate to be in:
    a. Australia, if short-term Australian government securities yield 2.7 percent per year?
    b. Canada, if short-term Canadian government securities yield 4.1 percent per year?
    c. Taiwan, if short-term Taiwanese government securities yield 5.7 percent per year?

12. **Spot versus Forward Rates**   Suppose the spot and three-month forward rates for the yen are ¥114.61 and ¥114.18, respectively.
    a. Is the yen expected to get stronger or weaker?
    b. Estimate the difference between the inflation rates of the United States and Japan.

13. **Expected Spot Rates**   Suppose the spot exchange rate for the Hungarian forint is HUF 268. Interest rates in the United States are 1.63 percent per year. They are 2.19 percent in Hungary. What do you predict the exchange rate will be in one year? In two years? In five years? What relationship are you using?

Intermediate
(Questions 14–16)

14. **Capital Budgeting**   Lakonishok Equipment has an investment opportunity in Europe. The project costs €10.9 million and is expected to produce cash flows of €2.8 million in Year 1, €2.8 million in Year 2, and €3.1 million in Year 3. The current spot exchange rate is $.81/€ and the current risk-free rate in the United States is 2.3 percent, compared to that in euroland of 3.1 percent. The appropriate discount rate for the project is estimated to be 13 percent, the U.S. cost of capital for the company. In addition, the subsidiary can be sold at the end of three years for an estimated €8.9 million. What is the NPV of the project?

 15. **Capital Budgeting**   You are evaluating a proposed expansion of an existing subsidiary located in Switzerland. The cost of the expansion would be Fr 19.6 million. The cash flows from the project would be Fr 6.1 million per year for the next five years. The dollar required return is 12 percent per year, and the current exchange rate is Fr .97. The going rate on Eurodollars is 5 percent per year. It is 6 percent per year on Swiss francs.
    a. What do you project will happen to exchange rates over the next four years?

b. Based on your answer in (a), convert the projected franc flows into dollar flows and calculate the NPV.

c. What is the required return on franc flows? Based on your answer, calculate the NPV in francs and then convert to dollars.

16. Translation Exposure   Herbert International has operations in Arrakis. The balance sheet for this division in Arrakeen solaris shows assets of 48,000 solaris, debt in the amount of 15,000 solaris, and equity of 33,000 solaris.

a. If the current exchange ratio is 1.20 solaris per dollar, what does the balance sheet look like in dollars?

b. Assume that one year from now the balance sheet in solaris is exactly the same as at the beginning of the year. If the exchange rate is 1.40 solaris per dollar, what does the balance sheet look like in dollars now?

c. Rework part (b) assuming the exchange rate is 1.15 solaris per dollar.

17. Translation Exposure   In the previous problem, assume the equity increases by 2,100 solaris due to retained earnings. If the exchange rate at the end of the year is 1.24 solaris per dollar, what does the balance sheet look like?

Challenge
(Questions 17–18)

18. Using the Exact International Fisher Effect   From our discussion of the Fisher effect in Chapter 5, we know that the actual relationship between a nominal rate, R; a real rate, r; and an inflation rate, h, can be written as:

$$1 + r = (1 + R)/(1 + h)$$

This is the domestic Fisher effect.

a. What is the nonapproximate form of the international Fisher effect?

b. Based on your answer in (a), what is the exact form for UIP? (*Hint:* Recall the exact form of IRP and use UFR.)

c. What is the exact form for relative PPP? (*Hint:* Combine your previous two answers.)

d. Recalculate the NPV for the Kihlstrom drill bit project (discussed in Section 20.5) using the exact forms for the UIP and the international Fisher effect. Verify that you get precisely the same answer either way.

WHAT'S ON THE WEB?

1. Purchasing Power Parity   One of the more famous examples of a violation of absolute purchasing power parity is the Big Mac index calculated by *The Economist*. This index calculates the dollar price of a McDonald's Big Mac in different countries. You can find the Big Mac index by going to www.economist .com. Using the most recent index, which country has the most expensive Big Macs? Which country has the cheapest Big Macs? Why is the price of a Big Mac not the same in every country?

2. Inflation and Exchange Rates   Go to www.marketvector.com and follow the "Exchange Rate Forecasts" link. Select the "Australian Dollar" link. Is the U.S. dollar expected to appreciate or depreciate compared to the Australian dollar over the next six months? What is the difference in the annual inflation rates for the United States and Australia over this period? Assume that the anticipated rate is constant for both countries. What relationship are you relying on in answering?

3. Interest Rate Parity   Go to the *Financial Times* site at www.ft.com. Find the current exchange rate between the U.S. dollar and the euro. Find the U.S. dollar LIBOR and the euro LIBOR interest rates. What must the one-year forward rate be to prevent arbitrage? What principle are you relying on in your answer?

EXCEL MASTER IT! PROBLEM

The Federal Reserve Bank of St. Louis has historical exchange rates on its website, www.stlouisfed.org. On the website, look for the FRED data. Download the exchange rate with U.S. dollars over the past five years for the following currencies: Brazilian reais, Canadian dollars, Hong Kong dollars, Japanese yen, Mexican new pesos, South Korean won, Indian rupees, Swiss francs, Australian dollars, and euros. Graph the exchange rate for each of these currencies in a dashboard that can be printed on one page.

CLOSING CASE

EAST COAST YACHTS GOES INTERNATIONAL

Larissa Warren, the owner of East Coast Yachts, has been in discussions with a yacht dealer in Monaco about selling the company's yachts in Europe. Jarek Jachowicz, the dealer, wants to add East Coast Yachts to his current retail line. Jarek has told Larissa that he feels the retail sales will be approximately €4.5 million per month. All sales will be made in euros, and Jarek will retain 5 percent of the retail sales as commission, which will be paid in euros. Because the yachts will be customized to order, the first sales will take place in one month. Jarek will pay East Coast Yachts for the order 90 days after it is filled. This payment schedule will continue for the length of the contract between the two companies.

Larissa is confident the company can handle the extra volume with its existing facilities, but she is unsure about any potential financial risks of selling its yachts in Europe. In her discussion with Jarek, she found that the current exchange rate is $.86/€. At this exchange rate, the company would spend 70 percent of the sales income on production costs. This number does not reflect the sales commission to be paid to Jarek.

Larissa has decided to ask Dan Ervin, the company's financial analyst, to prepare an analysis of the proposed international sales. Specifically, she asks Dan to answer the following questions:

1. What are the pros and cons of the international sales plan? What additional risks will the company face?

2. What happens to the company's profits if the dollar strengthens? What if the dollar weakens?

3. Ignoring taxes, what are East Coast Yachts's projected gains or losses from this proposed arrangement at the current exchange rate of $.86/€? What happens to profits if the exchange rate changes to $.89/€? At what exchange rate will the company break even?

4. How could the company hedge its exchange rate risk? What are the implications for this approach?

5. Taking all factors into account, should the company pursue international sales further? Why or why not?

Mathematical Tables

Table A.1
Present Value of \$1 to Be Received after t Periods = $1/(1 + r)^t$

Table A.2
Present Value of an Annuity of \$1 per Period for t Periods = $[1 - 1/(1 + r)^t]/r$

Table A.3
Future Value of \$1 at the End of t Periods = $1/(1 + r)^t$

Table A.4
Future Value of an Annuity of \$1 per Period for t Periods = $[(1 + r)^t - 1]/r$

Table A.5
Future Value of \$1 with a Continuously Compounded Rate r for t Periods:
Values of e^{rt}

Table A.6
Present Value of \$1 with a Continuous Discount Rate r for t Periods:
Values of e^{-rt}

TABLE A.1 Present Value of $1 to Be Received after t Periods $= 1/(1 + r)^t$

	Interest Rate								
Period	1%	2%	3%	4%	5%	6%	7%	8%	9%
1	.9901	.9804	.9709	.9615	.9524	.9434	.9346	.9259	.9174
2	.9803	.9612	.9426	.9246	.9070	.8900	.8734	.8573	.8417
3	.9706	.9423	.9151	.8890	.8638	.8396	.8163	.7938	.7722
4	.9610	.9238	.8885	.8548	.8227	.7921	.7629	.7350	.7084
5	.9515	.9057	.8626	.8219	.7835	.7473	.7130	.6806	.6499
6	.9420	.8880	.8375	.7903	.7462	.7050	.6663	.6302	.5963
7	.9327	.8706	.8131	.7599	.7107	.6651	.6227	.5835	.5470
8	.9235	.8535	.7894	.7307	.6768	.6274	.5820	.5403	.5019
9	.9143	.8368	.7664	.7026	.6446	.5919	.5439	.5002	.4604
10	.9053	.8203	.7441	.6756	.6139	.5584	.5083	.4632	.4224
11	.8963	.8043	.7224	.6496	.5847	.5268	.4751	.4289	.3875
12	.8874	.7885	.7014	.6246	.5568	.4970	.4440	.3971	.3555
13	.8787	.7730	.6810	.6006	.5303	.4688	.4150	.3677	.3262
14	.8700	.7579	.6611	.5775	.5051	.4423	.3878	.3405	.2992
15	.8613	.7430	.6419	.5553	.4810	.4173	.3624	.3152	.2745
16	.8528	.7284	.6232	.5339	.4581	.3936	.3387	.2919	.2519
17	.8444	.7142	.6050	.5134	.4363	.3714	.3166	.2703	.2311
18	.8360	.7002	.5874	.4936	.4155	.3503	.2959	.2502	.2120
19	.8277	.6864	.5703	.4746	.3957	.3305	.2765	.2317	.1945
20	.8195	.6730	.5537	.4564	.3769	.3118	.2584	.2145	.1784
21	.8114	.6598	.5375	.4388	.3589	.2942	.2415	.1987	.1637
22	.8034	.6468	.5219	.4220	.3418	.2775	.2257	.1839	.1502
23	.7954	.6342	.5067	.4057	.3256	.2618	.2109	.1703	.1378
24	.7876	.6217	.4919	.3901	.3101	.2470	.1971	.1577	.1264
25	.7798	.6095	.4776	.3751	.2953	.2330	.1842	.1460	.1160
30	.7419	.5521	.4120	.3083	.2314	.1741	.1314	.0994	.0754
40	.6717	.4529	.3066	.2083	.1420	.0972	.0668	.0460	.0318
50	.6080	.3715	.2281	.1407	.0872	.0543	.0339	.0213	.0134

	INTEREST RATE									
Period	10%	12%	14%	15%	16%	18%	20%	24%	28%	32%	36%
1	.9091	.8929	.8772	.8696	.8621	.8475	.8333	.8065	.7813	.7576	.7353
2	.8264	.7972	.7695	.7561	.7432	.7182	.6944	.6504	.6104	.5739	.5407
3	.7513	.7118	.6750	.6575	.6407	.6086	.5787	.5245	.4768	.4348	.3975
4	.6830	.6355	.5921	.5718	.5523	.5158	.4823	.4230	.3725	.3294	.2923
5	.6209	.5674	.5194	.4972	.4761	.4371	.4019	.3411	.2910	.2495	.2149
6	.5645	.5066	.4556	.4323	.4104	.3704	.3349	.2751	.2274	.1890	.1580
7	.5132	.4523	.3996	.3759	.3538	.3139	.2791	.2218	.1776	.1432	.1162
8	.4665	.4039	.3506	.3269	.3050	.2660	.2326	.1789	.1388	.1085	.0854
9	.4241	.3606	.3075	.2843	.2630	.2255	.1938	.1443	.1084	.0822	.0628
10	.3855	.3220	.2697	.2472	.2267	.1911	.1615	.1164	.0847	.0623	.0462
11	.3505	.2875	.2366	.2149	.1954	.1619	.1346	.0938	.0662	.0472	.0340
12	.3186	.2567	.2076	.1869	.1685	.1372	.1122	.0757	.0517	.0357	.0250
13	.2897	.2292	.1821	.1625	.1452	.1163	.0935	.0610	.0404	.0271	.0184
14	.2633	.2046	.1597	.1413	.1252	.0985	.0779	.0492	.0316	.0205	.0135
15	.2394	.1827	.1401	.1229	.1079	.0835	.0649	.0397	.0247	.0155	.0099
16	.2176	.1631	.1229	.1069	.0930	.0708	.0541	.0320	.0193	.0118	.0073
17	.1978	.1456	.1078	.0929	.0802	.0600	.0451	.0258	.0150	.0089	.0054
18	.1799	.1300	.0946	.0808	.0691	.0508	.0376	.0208	.0118	.0068	.0039
19	.1635	.1161	.0829	.0703	.0596	.0431	.0313	.0168	.0092	.0051	.0029
20	.1486	.1037	.0728	.0611	.0514	.0365	.0261	.0135	.0072	.0039	.0021
21	.1351	.0926	.0638	.0531	.0443	.0309	.0217	.0109	.0056	.0029	.0016
22	.1228	.0826	.0560	.0462	.0382	.0262	.0181	.0088	.0044	.0022	.0012
23	.1117	.0738	.0491	.0402	.0329	.0222	.0151	.0071	.0034	.0017	.0008
24	.1015	.0659	.0431	.0349	.0284	.0188	.0126	.0057	.0027	.0013	.0006
25	.0923	.0588	.0378	.0304	.0245	.0160	.0105	.0046	.0021	.0010	.0005
30	.0573	.0334	.0196	.0151	.0116	.0070	.0042	.0016	.0006	.0002	.0001
40	.0221	.0107	.0053	.0037	.0026	.0013	.0007	.0002	.0001	*	*
50	.0085	.0035	.0014	.0009	.0006	.0003	.0001	*	*	*	*

* The factor is zero to four decimal places.

TABLE A.2

Present Value of an Annuity of $1 per Period for t Periods $= [1 - 1/(1 + r)^t]/r$

Number of Periods	Interest Rate								
	1%	2%	3%	4%	5%	6%	7%	8%	9%
1	.9901	.9804	.9709	.9615	.9524	.9434	.9346	.9259	.9174
2	1.9704	1.9416	1.9135	1.8861	1.8594	1.8334	1.8080	1.7833	1.7591
3	2.9410	2.8839	2.8286	2.7751	2.7232	2.6730	2.6243	2.5771	2.5313
4	3.9020	3.8077	3.7171	3.6299	3.5460	3.4651	3.3872	3.3121	3.2397
5	4.8534	4.7135	4.5797	4.4518	4.3295	4.2124	4.1002	3.9927	3.8897
6	5.7955	5.6014	5.4172	5.2421	5.0757	4.9173	4.7665	4.6229	4.4859
7	6.7282	6.4720	6.2303	6.0021	5.7864	5.5824	5.3893	5.2064	5.0330
8	7.6517	7.3255	7.0197	6.7327	6.4632	6.2098	5.9713	5.7466	5.5348
9	8.5660	8.1622	7.7861	7.4353	7.1078	6.8017	6.5152	6.2469	5.9952
10	9.4713	8.9826	8.5302	8.1109	7.7217	7.3601	7.0236	6.7101	6.4177
11	10.3676	9.7868	9.2526	8.7605	8.3064	7.8869	7.4987	7.1390	6.8052
12	11.2551	10.5753	9.9540	9.3851	8.8633	8.3838	7.9427	7.5361	7.1607
13	12.1337	11.3484	10.6350	9.9856	9.3936	8.8527	8.3577	7.9038	7.4869
14	13.0037	12.1062	11.2961	10.5631	9.8986	9.2950	8.7455	8.2442	7.7862
15	13.8651	12.8493	11.9379	11.1184	10.3797	9.7122	9.1079	8.5595	8.0607
16	14.7179	13.5777	12.5611	11.6523	10.8378	10.1059	9.4466	8.8514	8.3126
17	15.5623	14.2919	13.1661	12.1657	11.2741	10.4773	9.7632	9.1216	8.5436
18	16.3983	14.9920	13.7535	12.6593	11.6896	10.8276	10.0591	9.3719	8.7556
19	17.2260	15.6785	14.3238	13.1339	12.0853	11.1581	10.3356	9.6036	8.9501
20	18.0456	16.3514	14.8775	13.5903	12.4622	11.4699	10.5940	9.8181	9.1285
21	18.8570	17.0112	15.4150	14.0292	12.8212	11.7641	10.8355	10.0168	9.2922
22	19.6604	17.6580	15.9369	14.4511	13.1630	12.0416	11.0612	10.2007	9.4424
23	20.4558	18.2922	16.4436	14.8568	13.4886	12.3034	11.2722	10.3741	9.5802
24	21.2434	18.9139	16.9355	15.2470	13.7986	12.5504	11.4693	10.5288	9.7066
25	22.0232	19.5235	17.4131	15.6221	14.0939	12.7834	11.6536	10.6748	9.8226
30	25.8077	22.3965	19.6004	17.2920	15.3725	13.7648	12.4090	11.2578	10.2737
40	32.8347	27.3555	23.1148	19.7928	17.1591	15.0463	13.3317	11.9246	10.7574
50	39.1961	31.4236	25.7298	21.4822	18.2559	15.7619	13.8007	12.2335	10.9617

Number of Periods	Interest Rate									
	10%	12%	14%	15%	16%	18%	20%	24%	28%	32%
1	.9091	.8929	.8772	.8696	.8621	.8475	.8333	.8065	.7813	.7576
2	1.7355	1.6901	1.6467	1.6257	1.6052	1.5656	1.5278	1.4568	1.3916	1.3315
3	2.4869	2.4018	2.3216	2.2832	2.2459	2.1743	2.1065	1.9813	1.8684	1.7663
4	3.1699	3.0373	2.9137	2.8550	2.7982	2.6901	2.5887	2.4043	2.2410	2.0957
5	3.7908	3.6048	3.4331	3.3522	3.2743	3.1272	2.9906	2.7454	2.5320	2.3452
6	4.3553	4.1114	3.8887	3.7845	3.6847	3.4976	3.3255	3.0205	2.7594	2.5342
7	4.8684	4.5638	4.2883	4.1604	4.0386	3.8115	3.6046	3.2423	2.9370	2.6775
8	5.3349	4.9676	4.6389	4.4873	4.3436	4.0776	3.8372	3.4212	3.0758	2.7860
9	5.7590	5.3282	4.9464	4.7716	4.6065	4.3030	4.0310	3.5655	3.1842	2.8681
10	6.1446	5.6502	5.2161	5.0188	4.8332	4.4941	4.1925	3.6819	3.2689	2.9304
11	6.4951	5.9377	5.4527	5.2337	5.0286	4.6560	4.3271	3.7757	3.3351	2.9776
12	6.8137	6.1944	5.6603	5.4206	5.1971	4.7932	4.4392	3.8514	3.3868	3.0133
13	7.1034	6.4235	5.8424	5.5831	5.3423	4.9095	4.5327	3.9124	3.4272	3.0404
14	7.3667	6.6282	6.0021	5.7245	5.4675	5.0081	4.6106	3.9616	3.4587	3.0609
15	7.6061	6.8109	6.1422	5.8474	5.5755	5.0916	4.6755	4.0013	3.4834	3.0764
16	7.8237	6.9740	6.2651	5.9542	5.6685	5.1624	4.7296	4.0333	3.5026	3.0882
17	8.0216	7.1196	6.3729	6.0472	5.7487	5.2223	4.7746	4.0591	3.5177	3.0971
18	8.2014	7.2497	6.4674	6.1280	5.8178	5.2732	4.8122	4.0799	3.5294	3.1039
19	8.3649	7.3658	6.5504	6.1982	5.8775	5.3162	4.8435	4.0967	3.5386	3.1090
20	8.5136	7.4694	6.6231	6.2593	5.9288	5.3527	4.8696	4.1103	3.5458	3.1129
21	8.6487	7.5620	6.6870	6.3125	5.9731	5.3837	4.8913	4.1212	3.5514	3.1158
22	8.7715	7.6446	6.7429	6.3587	6.0113	5.4099	4.9094	4.1300	3.5558	3.1180
23	8.8832	7.7184	6.7921	6.3988	6.0442	5.4321	4.9245	4.1371	3.5592	3.1197
24	8.9847	7.7843	6.8351	6.4338	6.0726	5.4509	4.9371	4.1428	3.5619	3.1210
25	9.0770	7.8431	6.8729	6.4641	6.0971	5.4669	4.9476	4.1474	3.5640	3.1220
30	9.4269	8.0552	7.0027	6.5660	6.1772	5.5168	4.9789	4.1601	3.5693	3.1242
40	9.7791	8.2438	7.1050	6.6418	6.2335	5.5482	4.9966	4.1659	3.5712	3.1250
50	9.9148	8.3045	7.1327	6.6605	6.2463	5.5541	4.9995	4.1666	3.5714	3.1250

Future Value of $1 at the End of t Periods $= 1/(1 + r)^t$

Interest Rate

Period	1%	2%	3%	4%	5%	6%	7%	8%	9%
1	1.0100	1.0200	1.0300	1.0400	1.0500	1.0600	1.0700	1.0800	1.0900
2	1.0201	1.0404	1.0609	1.0816	1.1025	1.1236	1.1449	1.1664	1.1881
3	1.0303	1.0612	1.0927	1.1249	1.1576	1.1910	1.2250	1.2597	1.2950
4	1.0406	1.0824	1.1255	1.1699	1.2155	1.2625	1.3108	1.3605	1.4116
5	1.0510	1.1041	1.1593	1.2167	1.2763	1.3382	1.4026	1.4693	1.5386
6	1.0615	1.1262	1.1941	1.2653	1.3401	1.4185	1.5007	1.5869	1.6771
7	1.0721	1.1487	1.2299	1.3159	1.4071	1.5036	1.6058	1.7138	1.8280
8	1.0829	1.1717	1.2668	1.3686	1.4775	1.5938	1.7182	1.8509	1.9926
9	1.0937	1.1951	1.3048	1.4233	1.5513	1.6895	1.8385	1.9990	2.1719
10	1.1046	1.2190	1.3439	1.4802	1.6289	1.7908	1.9672	2.1589	2.3674
11	1.1157	1.2434	1.3842	1.5395	1.7103	1.8983	2.1049	2.3316	2.5804
12	1.1268	1.2682	1.4258	1.6010	1.7959	2.0122	2.2522	2.5182	2.8127
13	1.1381	1.2936	1.4685	1.6651	1.8856	2.1329	2.4098	2.7196	3.0658
14	1.1495	1.3195	1.5126	1.7317	1.9799	2.2609	2.5785	2.9372	3.3417
15	1.1610	1.3459	1.5580	1.8009	2.0789	2.3966	2.7590	3.1722	3.6425
16	1.1726	1.3728	1.6047	1.8730	2.1829	2.5404	2.9522	3.4259	3.9703
17	1.1843	1.4002	1.6528	1.9479	2.2920	2.6928	3.1588	3.7000	4.3276
18	1.1961	1.4282	1.7024	2.0258	2.4066	2.8543	3.3799	3.9960	4.7171
19	1.2081	1.4568	1.7535	2.1068	2.5270	3.0256	3.6165	4.3157	5.1417
20	1.2202	1.4859	1.8061	2.1911	2.6533	3.2071	3.8697	4.6610	5.6044
21	1.2324	1.5157	1.8603	2.2788	2.7860	3.3996	4.1406	5.0338	6.1088
22	1.2447	1.5460	1.9161	2.3699	2.9253	3.6035	4.4304	5.4365	6.6586
23	1.2572	1.5769	1.9736	2.4647	3.0715	3.8197	4.7405	5.8715	7.2579
24	1.2697	1.6084	2.0328	2.5633	3.2251	4.0489	5.0724	6.3412	7.9111
25	1.2824	1.6406	2.0938	2.6658	3.3864	4.2919	5.4274	6.8485	8.6231
30	1.3478	1.8114	2.4273	3.2434	4.3219	5.7435	7.6123	10.063	13.268
40	1.4889	2.2080	3.2620	4.8010	7.0400	10.286	14.974	21.725	31.409
50	1.6446	2.6916	4.3839	7.1067	11.467	18.420	29.457	46.902	74.358
60	1.8167	3.2810	5.8916	10.520	18.679	32.988	57.946	101.26	176.03

Interest Rate

Period	10%	12%	14%	15%	16%	18%	20%	24%	28%	32%	36%
1	1.1000	1.1200	1.1400	1.1500	1.1600	1.1800	1.2000	1.2400	1.2800	1.3200	1.3600
2	1.2100	1.2544	1.2996	1.3225	1.3456	1.3924	1.4400	1.5376	1.6384	1.7424	1.8496
3	1.3310	1.4049	1.4815	1.5209	1.5609	1.6430	1.7280	1.9066	2.0972	2.3000	2.5155
4	1.4641	1.5735	1.6890	1.7490	1.8106	1.9388	2.0736	2.3642	2.6844	3.0360	3.4210
5	1.6105	1.7623	1.9254	2.0114	2.1003	2.2878	2.4883	2.9316	3.4360	4.0075	4.6526
6	1.7716	1.9738	2.1950	2.3131	2.4364	2.6996	2.9860	3.6352	4.3980	5.2899	6.3275
7	1.9487	2.2107	2.5023	2.6600	2.8262	3.1855	3.5832	4.5077	5.6295	6.9826	8.6054
8	2.1436	2.4760	2.8526	3.0590	3.2784	3.7589	4.2998	5.5895	7.2058	9.2170	11.703
9	2.3579	2.7731	3.2519	3.5179	3.8030	4.4355	5.1598	6.9310	9.2234	12.166	15.917
10	2.5937	3.1058	3.7072	4.0456	4.4114	5.2338	6.1917	8.5944	11.806	16.060	21.647
11	2.8531	3.4785	4.2262	4.6524	5.1173	6.1759	7.4301	10.657	15.112	21.199	29.439
12	3.1384	3.8960	4.8179	5.3503	5.9360	7.2876	8.9161	13.215	19.343	27.983	40.037
13	3.4523	4.3635	5.4924	6.1528	6.8858	8.5994	10.699	16.386	24.759	36.937	54.451
14	3.7975	4.8871	6.2613	7.0757	7.9875	10.147	12.839	20.319	31.691	48.757	74.053
15	4.1772	5.4736	7.1379	8.1371	9.2655	11.974	15.407	25.196	40.565	64.359	100.71
16	4.5950	6.1304	8.1372	9.3576	10.748	14.129	18.488	31.243	51.923	84.954	136.97
17	5.0545	6.8660	9.2765	10.761	12.468	16.672	22.186	38.741	66.461	112.14	186.28
18	5.5599	7.6900	10.575	12.375	14.463	19.673	26.623	48.039	86.071	148.02	253.34
19	6.1159	8.6128	12.056	14.232	16.777	23.214	31.948	59.568	108.89	195.39	344.54
20	6.7275	9.6463	13.743	16.367	19.461	27.393	38.338	73.864	139.38	257.92	468.57
21	7.4002	10.804	15.668	18.822	22.574	32.324	46.005	91.592	178.41	340.45	637.26
22	8.1403	12.100	17.861	21.645	26.186	38.142	55.206	113.57	228.36	449.39	866.67
23	8.9543	13.552	20.362	24.891	30.376	45.008	66.247	140.83	292.30	593.20	1178.7
24	9.8497	15.179	23.212	28.625	35.236	53.109	79.497	174.63	374.14	783.02	1603.0
25	10.835	17.000	26.462	32.919	40.874	62.669	95.396	216.54	478.90	1033.6	2180.1
30	17.449	29.960	50.950	66.212	85.850	143.37	237.38	634.82	1645.5	4142.1	10143.
40	45.259	93.051	188.88	267.86	378.72	750.38	1469.8	5455.9	19427.	66521.	*
50	117.39	289.00	700.23	1083.7	1670.7	3927.4	9100.4	46890.	*	*	*
60	304.48	897.60	2595.9	4384.0	7370.2	20555.	56348.	*	*	*	*

* The factor is greater than 99,999.

Number of Periods	Interest Rate								
	1%	2%	3%	4%	5%	6%	7%	8%	9%
1	1.0000	1.0000	1.0000	1.0000	1.0000	1.0000	1.0000	1.0000	1.0000
2	2.0100	2.0200	2.0300	2.0400	2.0500	2.0600	2.0700	2.0800	2.0900
3	3.0301	3.0604	3.0909	3.1216	3.1525	3.1836	3.2149	3.2464	3.2781
4	4.0604	4.1216	4.1836	4.2465	4.3101	4.3746	4.4399	4.5061	4.5731
5	5.1010	5.2040	5.3091	5.4163	5.5256	5.6371	5.7507	5.8666	5.9847
6	6.1520	6.3081	6.4684	6.6330	6.8019	6.9753	7.1533	7.3359	7.5233
7	7.2135	7.4343	7.6625	7.8983	8.1420	8.3938	8.6540	8.9228	9.2004
8	8.2857	8.5830	8.8932	9.2142	9.5491	9.8975	10.260	10.637	11.028
9	9.3685	9.7546	10.159	10.583	11.027	11.491	11.978	12.488	13.021
10	10.462	10.950	11.464	12.006	12.578	13.181	13.816	14.487	15.193
11	11.567	12.169	12.808	13.486	14.207	14.972	15.784	16.645	17.560
12	12.683	13.412	14.192	15.026	15.917	16.870	17.888	18.977	20.141
13	13.809	14.680	15.618	16.627	17.713	18.882	20.141	21.495	22.953
14	14.947	15.974	17.086	18.292	19.599	21.015	22.550	24.215	26.019
15	16.097	17.293	18.599	20.024	21.579	23.276	25.129	27.152	29.361
16	17.258	18.639	20.157	21.825	23.657	25.673	27.888	30.324	33.003
17	18.430	20.012	21.762	23.698	25.840	28.213	30.840	33.750	36.974
18	19.615	21.412	23.414	25.645	28.132	30.906	33.999	37.450	41.301
19	20.811	22.841	25.117	27.671	30.539	33.760	37.379	41.446	46.018
20	22.019	24.297	26.870	29.778	33.066	36.786	40.995	45.762	51.160
21	23.239	25.783	28.676	31.969	35.719	39.993	44.865	50.423	56.765
22	24.472	27.299	30.537	34.248	38.505	43.392	49.006	55.457	62.873
23	25.716	28.845	32.453	36.618	41.430	46.996	53.436	60.893	69.532
24	26.973	30.422	34.426	39.083	44.502	50.816	58.177	66.765	76.790
25	28.243	32.030	36.459	41.646	47.727	54.865	63.249	73.106	84.701
30	34.785	40.568	47.575	56.085	66.439	79.058	94.461	113.28	136.31
40	48.886	60.402	75.401	95.026	120.80	154.76	199.64	259.06	337.88
50	64.463	84.579	112.80	152.67	209.35	290.34	406.53	573.77	815.08
60	81.670	114.05	163.05	237.99	353.58	533.13	813.52	1253.2	1944.8

Number of Periods	Interest Rate										
	10%	12%	14%	15%	16%	18%	20%	24%	28%	32%	36%
1	1.0000	1.0000	1.0000	1.0000	1.0000	1.0000	1.0000	1.0000	1.0000	1.0000	1.0000
2	2.1000	2.1200	2.1400	2.1500	2.1600	2.1800	2.2000	2.2400	2.2800	2.3200	2.3600
3	3.3100	3.3744	3.4396	3.4725	3.5056	3.5724	3.6400	3.7776	3.9184	4.0624	4.2096
4	3.6410	4.7793	4.9211	4.9934	5.0665	5.2154	5.3680	5.6842	6.0156	6.3624	6.7251
5	6.1051	6.3528	6.6101	6.7424	6.8771	7.1542	7.4416	8.0484	8.6999	9.3983	10.146
6	7.7156	8.1152	8.5355	8.7537	8.9775	9.4420	9.9299	10.980	12.136	13.406	14.799
7	9.4872	10.089	10.730	11.067	11.414	12.142	12.916	14.615	16.534	18.696	21.126
8	11.436	12.300	13.233	13.727	14.240	15.327	16.499	19.123	22.163	25.678	29.732
9	13.579	14.776	16.085	16.786	17.519	19.086	20.799	24.712	29.369	34.895	41.435
10	15.937	17.549	19.337	20.304	21.321	23.521	25.959	31.643	38.593	47.062	57.352
11	18.531	20.655	23.045	24.349	25.733	28.755	32.150	40.238	50.398	63.122	78.998
12	21.384	24.133	27.271	29.002	30.850	34.931	39.581	50.895	65.510	84.320	108.44
13	24.523	28.029	32.089	34.352	36.786	42.219	48.497	64.110	84.853	112.30	148.47
14	27.975	32.393	37.581	40.505	43.672	50.818	59.196	80.496	109.61	149.24	202.93
15	31.772	37.280	43.842	47.580	51.660	60.965	72.035	100.82	141.30	198.00	276.98
16	35.950	42.753	50.980	55.717	60.925	72.939	87.442	126.01	181.87	262.36	377.69
17	40.545	48.884	59.118	65.075	71.673	87.068	105.93	157.25	233.79	347.31	514.66
18	45.599	55.750	68.394	75.836	84.141	103.74	128.12	195.99	300.25	459.45	700.94
19	51.159	64.440	78.969	88.212	98.603	123.41	154.74	244.03	385.32	607.47	954.28
20	57.275	72.052	91.025	102.44	115.38	146.63	186.69	303.60	494.21	802.86	1298.8
21	64.002	81.699	104.77	118.81	134.84	174.02	225.03	377.46	633.59	1060.8	1767.4
22	71.403	92.503	120.44	137.63	157.41	206.34	271.03	469.06	812.00	1401.2	2404.7
23	79.543	104.60	138.30	159.28	183.60	244.49	326.24	582.63	1040.4	1850.6	3271.3
24	88.497	118.16	158.66	184.17	213.98	289.49	392.48	723.46	1332.7	2443.8	4450.0
25	98.347	133.33	181.87	212.79	249.21	342.60	471.98	898.09	1706.8	3226.8	6053.0
30	164.49	241.33	356.79	434.75	530.31	790.95	1181.9	2640.9	5873.2	12941.	28172.3
40	442.59	767.09	1342.0	1779.1	2360.8	4163.2	7343.9	22729.	69377.	*	*
50	1163.9	2400.0	4994.5	7217.7	10436.	21813.	45497.	*	*	*	*
60	3034.8	7471.6	18535.	29220.	46058.	*	*	*	*	*	*

* The factor is greater than 99,999.

TABLE A.5 Future Value of $1 with a Continuously Compounded Rate r for t Periods: Values of e^{rt}

Period (t)								Continuously Compounded Rate (r)						
	1%	2%	3%	4%	5%	6%	7%	8%	9%	10%	11%	12%	13%	14%
1	1.0101	1.0202	1.0305	1.0408	1.0513	1.0618	1.0725	1.0833	1.0942	1.1052	1.1163	1.1275	1.1388	1.1503
2	1.0202	1.0408	1.0618	1.0833	1.1052	1.1275	1.1503	1.1735	1.1972	1.2214	1.2461	1.2712	1.2969	1.3231
3	1.0305	1.0618	1.0942	1.1275	1.1618	1.1972	1.2337	1.2712	1.3100	1.3499	1.3910	1.4333	1.4770	1.5220
4	1.0408	1.0833	1.1275	1.1735	1.2214	1.2712	1.3231	1.3771	1.4333	1.4918	1.5527	1.6161	1.6820	1.7507
5	1.0513	1.1052	1.1618	1.2214	1.2840	1.3499	1.4191	1.4918	1.5683	1.6487	1.7333	1.8221	1.9155	2.0138
6	1.0618	1.1275	1.1972	1.2712	1.3499	1.4333	1.5220	1.6161	1.7160	1.8221	1.9348	2.0544	2.1815	2.3164
7	1.0725	1.1503	1.2337	1.3231	1.4191	1.5220	1.6323	1.7507	1.8776	2.0138	2.1598	2.3164	2.4843	2.6645
8	1.0833	1.1735	1.2712	1.3771	1.4918	1.6161	1.7507	1.8965	2.0544	2.2255	2.4109	2.6117	2.8292	3.0649
9	1.0942	1.1972	1.3100	1.4333	1.5683	1.7160	1.8776	2.0544	2.2479	2.4596	2.6912	2.9447	3.2220	3.5254
10	1.1052	1.2214	1.3499	1.4918	1.6487	1.8221	2.0138	2.2255	2.4596	2.7183	3.0042	3.3201	3.6693	4.0552
11	1.1163	1.2461	1.3910	1.5527	1.7333	1.9348	2.1598	2.4109	2.6912	3.0042	3.3535	3.7434	4.1787	4.6646
12	1.1275	1.2712	1.4333	1.6161	1.8221	2.0544	2.3164	2.6117	2.9447	3.3201	3.7434	4.2207	4.7588	5.3656
13	1.1388	1.2969	1.4770	1.6820	1.9155	2.1815	2.4843	2.8292	3.2220	3.6693	4.1787	4.7588	5.4195	6.1719
14	1.1503	1.3231	1.5220	1.7507	2.0138	2.3164	2.6645	3.0649	3.5254	4.0552	4.6646	5.3656	6.1719	7.0993
15	1.1618	1.3499	1.5683	1.8221	2.1170	2.4596	2.8577	3.3201	3.8574	4.4817	5.2070	6.0496	7.0287	8.1662
16	1.1735	1.3771	1.6161	1.8965	2.2255	2.6117	3.0649	3.5966	4.2207	4.9530	5.8124	6.8210	8.0045	9.3933
17	1.1853	1.4049	1.6653	1.9739	2.3396	2.7732	3.2871	3.8962	4.6182	5.4739	6.4883	7.6906	9.1157	10.8049
18	1.1972	1.4333	1.7160	2.0544	2.4596	2.9447	3.5254	4.2207	5.0531	6.0496	7.2427	8.6711	10.3812	12.4286
19	1.2092	1.4623	1.7683	2.1383	2.5857	3.1268	3.7810	4.5722	5.5290	6.6859	8.0849	9.7767	11.8224	14.2963
20	1.2214	1.4918	1.8221	2.2255	2.7183	3.3201	4.0552	4.9530	6.0496	7.3891	9.0250	11.0232	13.4637	16.4446
21	1.2337	1.5220	1.8776	2.3164	2.8577	3.5254	4.3492	5.3656	6.6194	8.1662	10.0744	12.4286	15.3329	18.9158
22	1.2461	1.5527	1.9348	2.4109	3.0042	3.7434	4.6646	5.8124	7.2427	9.0250	11.2459	14.0132	17.4615	21.7584
23	1.2586	1.5841	1.9937	2.5093	3.1582	3.9749	5.0028	6.2965	7.9248	9.9742	12.5535	15.7998	19.8857	25.0281
24	1.2712	1.6161	2.0544	2.6117	3.3201	4.2207	5.3656	6.8210	8.6711	11.0232	14.0132	17.8143	22.6464	28.7892
25	1.2840	1.6487	2.1170	2.7183	3.4903	4.4817	5.7546	7.3891	9.4877	12.1825	15.6426	20.0855	25.7903	33.1155
30	1.3499	1.8221	2.4596	3.3204	4.4817	6.0496	8.1662	11.0232	14.8797	20.0855	27.1126	36.5982	49.4024	66.6863
35	1.4191	2.0138	2.8577	4.0552	5.7546	8.1662	11.5883	16.4446	23.3361	33.1155	46.9931	66.6863	94.6324	134.2898
40	1.4918	2.2255	3.3201	4.9530	7.3891	11.0232	16.4446	24.5235	36.5982	54.5982	81.4509	121.5104	181.2722	270.4264
45	1.5683	2.4596	3.8574	6.0496	9.4877	14.8797	23.3361	36.5982	57.3975	90.0171	141.1750	221.4064	347.2344	544.5719
50	1.6487	2.7183	4.4817	7.3891	12.1825	20.0855	33.1155	54.5982	90.0171	148.4132	244.6919	403.4288	665.1416	1096.633
55	1.7333	3.0042	5.2070	9.0250	15.6426	27.1126	46.9931	81.4509	141.1750	244.6919	424.1130	735.0952	1274.106	2208.348
60	1.8221	3.3201	6.0496	11.0232	20.0855	36.5982	66.6863	121.5104	221.4064	403.4288	735.0952	1339.431	2440.602	4447.067

Period (t)	15%	16%	17%	18%	19%	20%	21%	22%	23%	24%	25%	26%	27%	28%
1	1.1618	1.1735	1.1853	1.1972	1.2092	1.2214	1.2337	1.2461	1.2586	1.2712	1.2840	1.2969	1.3100	1.3231
2	1.3499	1.3771	1.4049	1.4333	1.4623	1.4918	1.5220	1.5527	1.5841	1.6161	1.6487	1.6820	1.7160	1.7507
3	1.5683	1.6161	1.6653	1.7160	1.7683	1.8221	1.8776	1.9348	1.9937	2.0544	2.1170	2.1815	2.2479	2.3164
4	1.8221	1.8965	1.9739	2.0544	2.1383	2.2255	2.3164	2.4109	2.5093	2.6117	2.7183	2.8292	2.9447	3.0649
5	2.1170	2.2255	2.3396	2.4596	2.5857	2.7183	2.8577	3.0042	3.1582	3.3201	3.4903	3.6693	3.8574	4.0552
6	2.4596	2.6117	2.7732	2.9447	3.1268	3.3201	3.5254	3.7434	3.9749	4.2207	4.4817	4.7588	5.0351	5.3656
7	2.8577	3.0649	3.2871	3.5254	3.7810	4.0552	4.3492	4.6646	5.0028	5.3656	5.7546	6.1719	6.6194	7.0993
8	3.3201	3.5966	3.8962	4.2207	4.5722	4.9530	5.3656	5.8124	6.2965	6.8210	7.3891	8.0045	8.6711	9.3933
9	3.8574	4.2207	4.6182	5.0531	5.5290	6.0496	6.6194	7.2427	7.9248	8.6711	9.4877	10.3812	11.3589	12.4286
10	4.4817	4.9530	5.4739	6.0496	6.6859	7.3891	8.1662	9.0250	9.9742	11.0232	12.1825	13.4637	14.8797	16.4446
11	5.2070	5.8124	6.4883	7.2427	8.0849	9.0250	10.0744	11.2459	12.5535	14.0132	15.6426	17.4615	19.4919	21.7584
12	6.0496	6.8210	7.6906	8.6711	9.7767	11.0232	12.4286	14.0132	15.7998	17.8143	20.0855	22.6464	25.5337	28.7892
13	7.0287	8.0045	9.1157	10.3812	11.8224	13.4637	15.3329	17.4615	19.8857	22.6464	25.7903	29.3708	33.4483	38.0918
14	8.1662	9.3933	10.8049	12.4286	14.2963	16.4446	18.9158	21.7584	25.0281	28.7892	33.1155	38.0918	43.8160	50.4004
15	9.4877	11.0232	12.8071	14.8797	17.2878	20.0855	23.3361	27.1126	31.5004	36.5982	42.5211	49.4024	57.3975	66.6863
16	11.0232	12.9358	15.1803	17.8143	20.9052	24.5325	28.7892	33.7844	39.6464	46.5255	54.5982	64.0715	75.1886	88.2347
17	12.8071	15.1803	17.9933	21.3276	25.2797	29.9641	35.5166	42.0980	49.8990	59.1455	70.1054	83.0963	98.4944	116.7459
18	14.8797	17.8143	21.3276	25.5337	30.5694	36.5982	43.8160	52.4573	62.8028	75.1886	90.0171	107.7701	129.0242	154.4700
19	17.2878	20.9052	25.2797	30.5694	36.9661	44.7012	54.0549	65.3659	79.0436	95.5835	115.5843	139.7702	169.0171	204.3839
20	20.0855	24.5325	29.9641	36.5982	44.7012	54.5982	66.6863	81.4509	99.4843	121.5104	148.4132	181.2722	221.4064	270.4264
21	23.3361	28.7892	35.5166	43.8160	54.0549	66.6863	82.2695	101.4940	125.2110	154.4700	190.5663	235.0974	290.0345	357.8092
22	27.1126	33.7844	42.0980	52.4573	65.3659	81.4509	101.4940	126.4694	157.5905	196.3699	244.6919	304.9049	379.9349	473.4281
23	31.5004	39.6464	49.8990	62.8028	79.0436	99.4843	125.2110	157.5905	198.3434	249.6350	314.1907	395.4404	497.7013	626.4068
24	36.5982	46.5255	59.1455	75.1886	95.5835	121.5104	154.4700	196.3699	249.6350	317.3483	403.4288	512.8585	651.9709	828.8175
25	42.5211	54.5982	70.1054	90.0171	115.5843	148.4132	193.5663	244.6919	314.1907	403.4288	518.0128	665.1416	854.0588	1096.633
30	90.0171	121.5104	164.0219	221.4064	298.8674	403.4288	544.5719	735.0952	992.2747	1339.431	1808.042	2440.602	3294.468	4447.067
35	190.5663	270.4264	383.7533	544.5719	772.7843	1096.633	1556.197	2208.348	3133.795	4447.067	6310.688	8955.293	12708.17	18033.74
40	403.4288	601.8450	897.8473	1339.431	1998.196	2980.958	4447.067	6634.244	9897.129	14764.78	22026.47	32859.63	49020.80	73130.44
45	854.0588	1339.431	2100.646	3294.468	5166.754	8103.084	12708.17	19930.37	31257.04	49020.80	76879.92	120571.7	189094.1	296558.6
50	1808.042	2980.958	4914.769	8103.084	13359.73	22026.47	36315.50	59874.14	98715.77	162754.8	268337.3	442413.4	729416.4	1202604.
55	3827.626	6634.244	11498.82	19930.37	34544.37	59874.14	103777.0	179871.9	311763.4	540364.9	936589.2	1623346.	2813669.	4876801.
60	8103.084	14764.78	26903.19	49020.80	89321.72	162754.8	296558.6	540364.9	984609.1	1794075.	3269017.	5956538.	10853520.	19776403.

TABLE A.6 Present Value of $1 with a Continuous Discount Rate r for t Periods: Values of e^{-rt}

Period (t)	Continuous Discount Rate (r)																
	1%	2%	3%	4%	5%	6%	7%	8%	9%	10%	11%	12%	13%	14%	15%	16%	17%
1	.9900	.9802	.9704	.9608	.9512	.9418	.9324	.9231	.9139	.9048	.8958	.8869	.8781	.8694	.8607	.8521	.8437
2	.9802	.9608	.9418	.9231	.9048	.8869	.8694	.8521	.8353	.8187	.8025	.7866	.7711	.7558	.7408	.7261	.7118
3	.9704	.9418	.9139	.8869	.8607	.8353	.8106	.7866	.7634	.7408	.7189	.6977	.6771	.6570	.6376	.6188	.6005
4	.9608	.9231	.8869	.8521	.8187	.7866	.7558	.7261	.6977	.6703	.6440	.6188	.5945	.5712	.5488	.5273	.5066
5	.9512	.9048	.8607	.8187	.7788	.7408	.7047	.6703	.6376	.6065	.5769	.5488	.5220	.4966	.4724	.4493	.4274
6	.9418	.8869	.8353	.7866	.7408	.6977	.6570	.6188	.5827	.5488	.5169	.4868	.4584	.4317	.4066	.3829	.3606
7	.9324	.8694	.8106	.7558	.7047	.6570	.6126	.5712	.5326	.4966	.4630	.4317	.4025	.3753	.3499	.3263	.3042
8	.9231	.8521	.7866	.7261	.6703	.6188	.5712	.5273	.4868	.4493	.4148	.3829	.3535	.3263	.3012	.2780	.2576
9	.9139	.8353	.7634	.6977	.6376	.5827	.5326	.4868	.4449	.4066	.3716	.3396	.3104	.2837	.2592	.2369	.2165
10	.9048	.8187	.7408	.6703	.6065	.5488	.4966	.4493	.4066	.3679	.3329	.3012	.2725	.2466	.2231	.2019	.1827
11	.8958	.8025	.7189	.6440	.5769	.5169	.4630	.4148	.3716	.3329	.2982	.2671	.2393	.2144	.1920	.1720	.1541
12	.8869	.7866	.6977	.6188	.5488	.4868	.4317	.3829	.3396	.3012	.2671	.2369	.2101	.1864	.1653	.1466	.1300
13	.8781	.7711	.6771	.5945	.5220	.4584	.4025	.3535	.3104	.2725	.2393	.2101	.1845	.1620	.1423	.1249	.1097
14	.8694	.7558	.6570	.5712	.4966	.4317	.3753	.3263	.2837	.2466	.2144	.1864	.1620	.1409	.1225	.1065	.0926
15	.8607	.7408	.6376	.5488	.4724	.4066	.3499	.3012	.2592	.2231	.1920	.1653	.1423	.1225	.1054	.0907	.0781
16	.8521	.7261	.6188	.5273	.4493	.3829	.3263	.2780	.2369	.2019	.1720	.1466	.1249	.1065	.0907	.0773	.0659
17	.8437	.7118	.6005	.5066	.4274	.3606	.3042	.2567	.2165	.1827	.1541	.1300	.1097	.0926	.0781	.0659	.0556
18	.8353	.6977	.5827	.4868	.4066	.3396	.2837	.2369	.1979	.1653	.1381	.1153	.0963	.0805	.0672	.0561	.0469
19	.8270	.6839	.5655	.4677	.3867	.3198	.2645	.2187	.1809	.1496	.1237	.1023	.0846	.0699	.0578	.0478	.0396
20	.8187	.6703	.5488	.4493	.3679	.3012	.2466	.2019	.1653	.1353	.1108	.0907	.0743	.0608	.0498	.0408	.0334
21	.8106	.6570	.5326	.4317	.3499	.2837	.2299	.1864	.1511	.1225	.0993	.0805	.0652	.0529	.0429	.0347	.0282
22	.8025	.6440	.5169	.4148	.3329	.2671	.2144	.1720	.1381	.1108	.0889	.0714	.0573	.0460	.0369	.0296	.0238
23	.7945	.6313	.5016	.3985	.3166	.2516	.1999	.1588	.1262	.1003	.0797	.0633	.0503	.0400	.0317	.0252	.0200
24	.7866	.6188	.4868	.3829	.3012	.2369	.1864	.1466	.1153	.0907	.0714	.0561	.0442	.0347	.0273	.0215	.0169
25	.7788	.6065	.4724	.3679	.2865	.2231	.1738	.1353	.1054	.0821	.0639	.0498	.0388	.0302	.0235	.0183	.0143
30	.7408	.5488	.4066	.3012	.2231	.1653	.1225	.0907	.0672	.0498	.0369	.0273	.0202	.0150	.0111	.0082	.0061
35	.7047	.4966	.3499	.2466	.1738	.1225	.0863	.0608	.0429	.0302	.0213	.0150	.0106	.0074	.0052	.0037	.0026
40	.6703	.4493	.3012	.2019	.1353	.0907	.0608	.0408	.0273	.0183	.0123	.0082	.0055	.0037	.0025	.0017	.0011
45	.6376	.4066	.2592	.1653	.1054	.0672	.0429	.0273	.0174	.0111	.0071	.0045	.0029	.0018	.0012	.0007	.0005
50	.6065	.3679	.2231	.1353	.0821	.0498	.0302	.0183	.0111	.0067	.0041	.0025	.0015	.0009	.0006	.0003	.0002
55	.5769	.3329	.1920	.1108	.0639	.0369	.0213	.0123	.0071	.0041	.0024	.0014	.0008	.0005	.0003	.0002	.0001
60	.5488	.3012	.1653	.0907	.0498	.0273	.0150	.0082	.0045	.0025	.0014	.0007	.0004	.0002	.0001	.0001	.0000

Continuous Discount Rate (r)

Period (t)	18%	19%	20%	21%	22%	23%	24%	25%	26%	27%	28%	29%	30%	31%	32%	33%	34%	35%
1	.8353	.8270	.8187	.8106	.8025	.7945	.7866	.7788	.7711	.7634	.7558	.7483	.7408	.7334	.7261	.7189	.7118	.7047
2	.6977	.6839	.6703	.6570	.6440	.6313	.6188	.6065	.5945	.5827	.5712	.5599	.5488	.5379	.5273	.5169	.5066	.4966
3	.5827	.5655	.5488	.5326	.5169	.5016	.4868	.4724	.4584	.4449	.4317	.4190	.4066	.3946	.3829	.3716	.3606	.3499
4	.4868	.4677	.4493	.4317	.4148	.3985	.3829	.3679	.3535	.3396	.3263	.3135	.3012	.2894	.2780	.2671	.2567	.2466
5	.4066	.3867	.3679	.3499	.3329	.3166	.3012	.2865	.2725	.2592	.2466	.2346	.2231	.2122	.2019	.1920	.1827	.1738
6	.3396	.3198	.3012	.2837	.2671	.2516	.2369	.2231	.2101	.1979	.1864	.1755	.1653	.1557	.1466	.1381	.1300	.1225
7	.2837	.2645	.2466	.2299	.2144	.1999	.1864	.1738	.1620	.1511	.1409	.1313	.1225	.1142	.1065	.0993	.0926	.0863
8	.2369	.2187	.2019	.1864	.1720	.1588	.1466	.1353	.1249	.1153	.1065	.0983	.0907	.0837	.0773	.0714	.0659	.0608
9	.1979	.1809	.1653	.1511	.1381	.1262	.1153	.1054	.0963	.0880	.0805	.0735	.0672	.0614	.0561	.0513	.0469	.0429
10	.1653	.1496	.1353	.1225	.1108	.1003	.0907	.0821	.0743	.0672	.0608	.0550	.0498	.0450	.0408	.0369	.0334	.0302
11	.1381	.1237	.1108	.0993	.0889	.0797	.0714	.0639	.0573	.0513	.0460	.0412	.0369	.0330	.0296	.0265	.0238	.0213
12	.1154	.1023	.0907	.0805	.0714	.0633	.0561	.0498	.0442	.0392	.0347	.0308	.0273	.0242	.0215	.0191	.0169	.0150
13	.0963	.0846	.0743	.0652	.0573	.0503	.0442	.0388	.0340	.0299	.0263	.0231	.0202	.0178	.0156	.0137	.0120	.0106
14	.0805	.0699	.0608	.0529	.0460	.0400	.0347	.0302	.0263	.0228	.0198	.0172	.0150	.0130	.0113	.0099	.0086	.0074
15	.0672	.0578	.0498	.0429	.0369	.0317	.0273	.0235	.0202	.0174	.0150	.0129	.0111	.0096	.0082	.0071	.0061	.0052
16	.0561	.0478	.0408	.0347	.0296	.0252	.0215	.0183	.0156	.0133	.0113	.0097	.0082	.0070	.0060	.0051	.0043	.0037
17	.0469	.0396	.0334	.0282	.0238	.0200	.0169	.0143	.0120	.0102	.0086	.0072	.0061	.0051	.0043	.0037	.0031	.0026
18	.0392	.0327	.0273	.0228	.0191	.0159	.0133	.0111	.0093	.0078	.0065	.0054	.0045	.0038	.0032	.0026	.0022	.0018
19	.0327	.0271	.0224	.0185	.0153	.0127	.0105	.0087	.0072	.0059	.0049	.0040	.0033	.0028	.0023	.0019	.0016	.0013
20	.0273	.0224	.0183	.0150	.0123	.0101	.0082	.0067	.0055	.0045	.0037	.0030	.0025	.0020	.0017	.0014	.0011	.0009
21	.0228	.0185	.0150	.0122	.0099	.0080	.0065	.0052	.0043	.0034	.0028	.0023	.0018	.0015	.0012	.0010	.0008	.0006
22	.0191	.0153	.0123	.0099	.0079	.0063	.0051	.0041	.0033	.0026	.0021	.0017	.0014	.0011	.0009	.0007	.0006	.0005
23	.0159	.0127	.0101	.0080	.0063	.0050	.0040	.0032	.0025	.0020	.0016	.0013	.0010	.0008	.0006	.0005	.0004	.0003
24	.0133	.0105	.0082	.0065	.0051	.0040	.0032	.0025	.0019	.0015	.0012	.0009	.0007	.0006	.0005	.0004	.0003	.0002
25	.0111	.0087	.0067	.0052	.0041	.0032	.0025	.0019	.0015	.0012	.0009	.0007	.0006	.0004	.0003	.0002	.0002	.0002
30	.0045	.0033	.0025	.0018	.0014	.0010	.0007	.0006	.0004	.0003	.0002	.0002	.0001	.0001	.0001	.0001	.0000	.0000
35	.0018	.0013	.0009	.0006	.0005	.0003	.0002	.0002	.0001	.0001	.0001	.0000	.0000	.0000	.0000	.0000	.0000	.0000
40	.0007	.0005	.0003	.0002	.0002	.0001	.0001	.0000	.0000	.0000	.0000	.0000	.0000	.0000	.0000	.0000	.0000	.0000
45	.0003	.0002	.0001	.0001	.0001	.0000	.0000	.0000	.0000	.0000	.0000	.0000	.0000	.0000	.0000	.0000	.0000	.0000
50	.0001	.0001	.0000	.0000	.0000	.0000	.0000	.0000	.0000	.0000	.0000	.0000	.0000	.0000	.0000	.0000	.0000	.0000
55	.0001	.0000	.0000	.0000	.0000	.0000	.0000	.0000	.0000	.0000	.0000	.0000	.0000	.0000	.0000	.0000	.0000	.0000
60	.0000	.0000	.0000	.0000	.0000	.0000	.0000	.0000	.0000	.0000	.0000	.0000	.0000	.0000	.0000	.0000	.0000	.0000

Solutions to Selected End-of-Chapter Problems

CHAPTER 2

2. Net income = $125,136
   Addition to RE = $98,136
4. $41,796.50
   Average tax rate = 22.11%
   Marginal tax rate = 32%
6. $1,215,000
8. $48,000
10. $239,000
14. Net income = $124,032
   OCF = $213,732
16. $12,877
18. a. $1,400
   b. $0
20. $34,000
22. a. $3,184; $3,310
   b. $40
   c. Fixed assets sold = $1,261;
      CFA = $7,803
   d. Debt retired = $466;
      CFC = $387

CHAPTER 3

2. Equity multiplier = 1.90
   ROE = 14.63%
   Net income = $128,744
4. $13,424.48
6. 12.41%
8. $758.40
10. 9.30%
12. −12.73%; −$27,314.23
14. 24.67 days
16. 6.84 times
20. $21,450

CHAPTER 4

2. a. $7,834.96
   b. $9,445.30
   c. $14,031.22
4. 9.38%; 11.21%; 9.45%;
   11.44%
6. 14.69 years; 29.39 years
8. −13.17%
10. $4,893.42; $2,909.24;
   $5,408.06; $4,992.27
12. @5%: $26,441.10; $24,851.20
   @21%: $14,528.22; $16,795.15
14. $348,837.21; 3.37%
16. 9.67%; 10.84%; 14.43%;
   15.10%
18. APR = 102.77%;
   EAR = 176.68%
20. APR = 1,733.33%;
   EAR = 313,916,515.69%
22. 5.32%
24. 31.61%
26. $1,552,430.18
28. $68,021.10
30. $611,832.40
32. 13.06%
34. $2,952,092.51
36. 76.56
38. $322,363.44
40. $14,577,923.31
42. $4,398.92; 12.84%
44. $155,716.92
46. $27,972.34
50. $1,427.59
52. $1,710; $10,260

54. $14,113.20
56. a. $4,629,503.60
   b. $4,553,471.68
58. $25,713.43

CHAPTER 5

2. a. $1,000
   b. $823.34
   c. $1,235.56
4. 7.57%
6. 5.30%
8. 5.88%
10. 6.84%
12. $2,162.94
14. $1,018.204
20. 4.86%
22. $1,041.83
24. 5.71%; 5.60%
28. a. $19,454.97
   b. $7,025.41
32. $5,358.64

CHAPTER 6

2. 9.81%
4. $54.33
6. $3.89
8. 3.65%
10. $102.67; $51.33; $34.22
12. $4,370,046
14. $47.18
16. $78.98
18. $74.14
20. $107.78

22. $118.92

24. 1,157.87

26. $4.57

28. $4.40

CHAPTER 7

2. 3.20 years; 5.16 years; Never

4. 3.52 years; 4.19 years; Never

6. 15.96%

8. 14.55%; 15.74%

10. 1.20; 1.48

12. a. 12.02%

    d. −$656.18; $2,212.11

14. a. 1.29; 1.42

    b. $21,987.23; $17,684.45

16. a. 1.53 years; 1.72 years

    b. $102,208.87; $151,904.58

    c. 27.97%; 25.05%

    d. 21.23%

18. a. 1.96 years; 2.03 years

    b. $80,108.94; $148,001.50

    c. 19.19%; 20.41%

20. a. 2.47 years; 1.86 years

    b. $306,175.81; $229,511.65

    c. 16.89%; 22.71%

    d. 12.87%

22. a. $300,751.31; $359,231.80

    b. 28.78%; 22.82%

    c. 17.36%

    d. 1.292; 1.208

CHAPTER 8

2. $2,320.89

4. NPV = $196,971.45

6. NPV = $260,081.89

8. $96,260.54

10. $1,860,774

12. −$230,402.91; −$222,102.73

14. $82,697.62

16. −$243,859.70; −$227,573.38

18. −$4,454,533; −$4,410,005

20. $72,407,889

22. $6,836,364

28. $232,510.91

30. $1,490,790

32. −$7,950.33; −$7,724.69

34. $387,585.31

36. $170,065.92

CHAPTER 9

2. $3,996,187; −$2,269,926

4. 20,664.16

6. Go to market = $16,125,000

    Test market = $15,880,180

8. Go to market = $19,680,000

    Consumer research = $20,041,964

10. 9,861.46

12. $7.02

14. 2.65 years; $11,055,509; 33.16%

16. $\Delta NPV / \Delta P = \$152,449.24$

    $\Delta NPV / \Delta Q = \$1,372.04$

18. a. $678,400.81

    b. $197,669.88

20. a. 1,034.48

    b. 1,298.09

22. $35.37

24. a. −$518,636.17

    b. $853,045.25

CHAPTER 10

2. $R_D = 1.72\%$; $R_{CG} = 14.47\%$

4. a. $69

    b. 6.80%

    c. 3.49%

6. $R_G = 2.82\%$; $R_C = 3.20\%$

8. a. 3.24%; 6.35%

    b. 24.11%; 1.20%

    c. −3.12%; 24.87%

10. a. 6.82%

    b. 6.35%

12. 56.66%

14. 5.14%

16. 7.47%

18. −7.9% to 31.7%; −27.7% to 51.5%

20. $R_A = 10.17\%$; $R_G = 8.24\%$

22. T-bills: 7.47%; 2.31%

    Inflation: 9.29%; 3.08%

    Real return: −1.65%

CHAPTER 11

2. 10.75%
4. X = $2,727.27; Y = $7,272.73
6. Stock A: 9.40%; 3.32%
   Stock B: 15.80%; 16.42%
8. 10.75%
10. 1.21
12. 11.56%
14. 10.54%
18. $E(R_Y) = 12.01\%$; $E(R_Z) = 9.86\%$
20. a. 7.20%
    b. $X_S = .4425$
    c. .9089
    d. $X_f = -100\%$
22. a. 12.30%; .04757; 21.81%
    b. 8.20%
    c. 8.80%; 8.50%; 4.70%; 4.54%
24. −$36,363.64; 1.26
26. Stock J: 12.28%; 14.53%
    Stock K: 6.97%; 3.36%
    Covariance = −.000417; Correlation = −.0855
28. a. 11.80%; 45.85%
    b. 11.80%; 30.68%
30. a. 12.67%
    b. 29.89%
32. 9.71%
34. 2.13%; 10.55%

CHAPTER 12

2. 6.45%; 5.09%
4. BV = $115,000,000
   MV = $96,550,000
   4.04%
6. 9.12%
8. a. .2049; .7951
   b. .7553; .2447
10. a. 4.28%
    b. 11.36%
12. a. .3196; .6804
    b. 8.60%
14. a. 5.76%
    b. $47,749,726
16. $49,474,504
18. .8729
20. $66.53

CHAPTER 14

2. a. $3.43; $4.90; $6.12
   b. $3.59; $5.77; $7.57
4. a. $2.00; $1.85
   b. $2.80; $2.96
   c. $299,250
6. a. Plan I = $1.55; Plan II = $1.50;
      All-equity = $1.58
   b. $10,870; $10,870
   c. $10,870
   d. Plan I = $1.23; Plan II = $1.19;
      All-equity = $1.25; Break-even = $10,870
8. a. $507.04
   b. $543.14
   c. Sell 35 shares
10. $4,254,200
12. a. 14.17%
    b. 9.65%
    c. 16.11%; 12.88%; 9.65%
14. a. $515,914.29
    b. $552,214.29
18. a. $172,347.66
    b. $192,167.64; $211,987.62
    c. $194,743.11; $223,828.13
20. a. $483,000
    b. $483,000
    c. $393,000
    d. $96,600; $78,600
    e. $15,200; $13,940

CHAPTER 15

2. a. Debt issue = $287,000; $432,000
      Equity issue = $267,444; $360,889
4. $536,500
6. a. Steinberg: $1,415,179; $571,429
      Dietrich: $1,071,429; $915,179
8. a. $31,000,000
   b. 14.71%
   c. 5.29%

CHAPTER 16

2. a. 2,200 new shares
   b. 5,500 new shares
4. a. $52.20
   b. $75.65

c. $61.05

d. $152.25

e. 608,333; 419,750; 520,125; 208,571

6. 6,090 shares; $39.22

8. New capital surplus = $1,949,100

10. a. $78

b. $87

c. 20,690

12. $76,439.60

14. a. $2,319,189

b. $72.97

c. $2,319,189; Sell 445.02 shares

16. a. $2.55

b. $2.77

CHAPTER 17

2. a. $2,850

b. $6,000; $17,000

c. $80,880; $7,000; −$2,120

d. $7,120; $9,120; $80.88

4. $1.21

6. 1.96%

8. $C = \$5.82$; $P = \$8.40$

10. $60,347.73

12. a. $0; $2

b. $10.04; $8.65

14. $9.17

16. $5.39

18. Equity = $3,142.19; Debt = $10,657.81

20. Equity = $4,544.53;
Debt = $17,355.47; R_D = 14.18%

22. a. $10.43

b. Buy .5769 share; Borrow $32.26

c. $10.43

24. a. $57.46

b. Buy .2857 ounce of gold;
Borrow $322.54

c. $57.46

26. a. Equity = $7,686.72; Debt = $28,013.28

b. Equity = $5,953.13; Debt = $29,746.87

c. Equity = −$1,733.58; Debt = $1,733.58

CHAPTER 18

2. $1,445; $6,760

6. 41.37 days; 16.34 days

8. a. $411.00; $372.00; $453.00; $434.70

b. $378.00; $411.00; $372:00; $453.00

c. $389.00; $398.00; $399.00; $446.90

10. a. $433,333.33

b. $408,571.43

c. $365,764.29; $387,385.71;
$410,300.00

14. 20.13%

a. 74.35%

b. 11.05%

c. 27.71%

16. $1,170,147; 10.7353 times

18. a. 3.28%

b. 7.09%

c. 7.02%

CHAPTER 19

2. a. $37

b. 1,562,500; $1.73

c. $35.17; $1.83

d. $37,000; $37,000

4. $3,000; −$500

6. 2,272,896

8. $0; −$.64; −$1.49

10. EPS = $14.79; P = $73.58;
BVPS = $80; NPV = −$120,283

12. a. $52.50

b. $15.50

14. $26.21

CHAPTER 20

2. a. £100

b. £100

c. Fr 1.3164/£; £.7596/Fr

4. b. $1.93

6. Great Britain = 2.82%; Japan = 2.04%;
Switzerland = .19%

8. Poland 1.67% higher

10. Kr 8.5810

12. b. −1.49%

14. $1,485,957

16. a. Equity = $27,500

b. Equity = $23,571.43

c. Equity = $28,695.65

CHAPTER 21

2. $580,000

4. **a.** Cash = $42,000,000

  Equity = $41,300,000

 b. NPV$_{Cash}$ = $3,000,000

  NPV$_{Equity}$ = $3,700,000

8. .4043

12. **a.** £23.71

 b. .8168

14. **a.** $9,856,863

 b. $3,370,863

 c. $2,446,863

 d. $50.55

 e. $634,179.44

 g. Cash = $429,049.53

  Equity = −$1,125,907

Using the HP 10B and TI BA II Plus Financial Calculators

This appendix is intended to help you use your Hewlett-Packard HP 10B or Texas Instruments TI BA II Plus financial calculator to solve problems encountered in an introductory finance course. It describes the various calculator settings and provides keystroke solutions for nine selected problems from this book. Please see your owner's manual for more complete instructions. For more examples and problem-solving techniques, please see *Financial Analysis with an Electronic Calculator*, 6th edition, by Mark A. White (New York: McGraw-Hill, 2007).

CALCULATOR SETTINGS

Most calculator errors in introductory finance courses are the result of inappropriate settings. Before beginning a calculation, you should ask yourself the following questions:

1. Did I clear the financial registers?
2. Is the compounding frequency set to once per period?
3. Is the calculator in END mode?
4. Did I enter negative numbers using the +/− key?

CLEARING THE REGISTERS

All calculators have areas of memory, called registers, where variables and intermediate results are stored. There are two sets of financial registers, the time value of money (TVM) registers and the cash flow (CF) registers. These must be cleared before beginning a new calculation. On the Hewlett-Packard HP 10B, pressing █ {CLEAR ALL} clears both the TVM and the CF registers.[1] To clear the TVM registers on the TI BA II Plus, press **2nd** {CLR TVM}. Press **2nd** {CLR Work} from within the cash flow worksheet to clear the CF registers.

COMPOUNDING FREQUENCY

Both the HP 10B and the TI BA II Plus are hardwired to assume monthly compounding, that is, compounding 12 times per period. Because very few problems in introductory finance courses make this assumption, you should change this default setting to once per period. On the HP 10B, press 1 █ {P/YR}. To verify that the default has been changed, press the █ key, then press and briefly hold the **INPUT** key.[2] The display should read "1P_Yr". On the TI BA II Plus, you can specify both payment frequency and compounding frequency, although they should normally be set to the same number. To set both to once per period, press the key sequence **2nd** {P/Y} 1 **ENTER**, then press ↓ 1 **ENTER**. Pressing **2nd** {QUIT} returns you to standard calculator mode.

END MODE AND ANNUITIES DUE

In most problems, payment is made at the end of a period, and this is the default setting (end mode) for both the HP 10B and the TI BA II Plus. *Annuities due* assume payments are made at the *beginning* of each period (begin mode). On the HP 10B, pressing █ {BEG/END} toggles between begin and end mode. Press the key sequence **2nd** {BGN} **2nd** [SET] **2nd** {QUIT} to accomplish the same task on the TI BA II Plus. Both calculators will indicate on the display that your calculator is set for begin mode.

SIGN CHANGES

Sign changes are used to identify the direction of cash inflows and outflows. Generally, cash inflows are entered as positive numbers and cash outflows are entered as negative numbers. To enter a negative number on either the HP 10B or the TI BA II Plus, first press the appropriate digit keys and then press the change sign key, +/−. Do *not* use the minus sign key, − , as its effects are quite unpredictable.

SAMPLE PROBLEMS

This section provides keystroke solutions for selected problems from the text illustrating the nine basic financial calculator skills.

---

[1] The █ key is colored orange and serves as a Shift key for the functions in curly brackets.

[2] This is the same keystroke used to clear all registers; pretty handy, eh?

1. FUTURE VALUE OR PRESENT VALUE OF A SINGLE SUM

Compute the future value of $2,250 at a 17 percent annual rate for 30 years.

HP 10B		TI BA II PLUS	
-2,250.00	PV	-2,250.00	PV
30.00	N	30.00	N
17.00	I/YR	17.00	I/Y
FV	249,895.46	CPT FV	249,895.46

The future value is $249,895.46.

2. PRESENT VALUE OR FUTURE VALUE OF AN ORDINARY ANNUITY

Betty's Bank offers you a $20,000, seven-year term loan at 11 percent annual interest. What will your annual loan payment be?

HP 10B		TI BA II PLUS	
-20,000.00	PV	-20,000.00	PV
7.00	N	7.00	N
11.00	I/YR	11.00	I/Y
PMT	4,244.31	CPT PMT	4,244.31

Your annual loan payment will be $4,244.31.

3. FINDING AN UNKNOWN INTEREST RATE

Assume that the total cost of a college education will be $75,000 when your child enters college in 18 years. You presently have $7,000 to invest. What rate of interest must you earn on your investment to cover the cost of your child's college education?

HP 10B		TI BA II PLUS	
-7,000.00	PV	-7,000.00	PV
18.00	N	18.00	N
75,000.00	FV	75,000.00	FV
I/YR	14.08	CPT I/Y	14.08

You must earn an annual interest rate of at least 14.08 percent to cover the expected future cost of your child's education.

4. FINDING AN UNKNOWN NUMBER OF PERIODS

One of your customers is delinquent on his accounts payable balance. You've mutually agreed to a repayment schedule of $374 per month. You will charge 1.4 percent per month interest on the overdue balance. If the current balance is $12,000, how long will it take for the account to be paid off?

HP 10B		TI BA II PLUS	
-12,000.00	PV	-12,000.00	PV
1.40	I/YR	1.40	I/Y
374.00	PMT	374.00	PMT
N	42.90	CPT N	42.90

The loan will be paid off in 42.90 months.

5. SIMPLE BOND PRICING

Mullineaux Co. issued 11-year bonds one year ago at a coupon rate of 8.25 percent. The bonds make semiannual payments. If the YTM on these bonds is 7.10 percent, what is the current bond price?

HP 10B		TI BA II PLUS	
41.25	PMT	41.25	PMT
1,000.00	FV	1,000.00	FV
20.00	N	20.00	N
3.55	I/YR	3.55	I/Y
PV	1,081.35	CPT PV	1,081.35

Because the bonds make semiannual payments, we must halve the coupon payment (8.25/2 = 4.125 ==> $41.25), halve the YTM (7.10/2 = 3.55), and double the number of periods (10 years remaining × 2 = 20 periods). Then, the current bond price is $1,081.35.

6. SIMPLE BOND YIELDS TO MATURITY

Vasicek Co. has 12.5 percent coupon bonds on the market with eight years left to maturity. The bonds make annual payments. If one of these bonds currently sells for $1,145.68, what is its YTM?

HP 10B		TI BA II PLUS	
-1,145.68	PV	-1,145.68	PV
125.00	PMT	125.00	PMT
1,000.00	FV	1,000.00	FV
8.00	N	8.00	N
I/YR	9.79	CPT I/Y	9.79

The bond has a yield to maturity of 9.79 percent.

7. CASH FLOW ANALYSIS

What are the IRR and NPV of the following set of cash flows? Assume a discount rate of 10 percent.

YEAR	CASH FLOW
0	−$1,300
1	400
2	300
3	1,200

HP 10B		TI BA II PLUS	
-1,300.00	**CFj**	**CF**	
400.00	**CFj**	**2nd** {CLR Work}	
1.00	{Nj}	-1,300.00	**ENTER ↓**
300.00	**CFj**	400.00	**ENTER ↓**
1.00	{Nj}	1.00	**ENTER ↓**
1,200.00	**CFj**	300.00	**ENTER ↓**
1.00	{Nj}	1.00	**ENTER ↓**

HP 10B		TI BA II PLUS	
{IRR/YR} 17.40		1,200.00	**ENTER ↓**
10.00	**I/YR**	1.00	**ENTER ↓**
{NPV} 213.15		**IRR** **CPT** 17.40	
		NPV	
		10.00	**ENTER**
		↓ **CPT** 213.15	

The project has an IRR of 17.40 percent and an NPV of $213.15.

8. LOAN AMORTIZATION

Prepare an amortization schedule for a three-year loan of $24,000. The interest rate is 16 percent per year, and the loan calls for equal annual payments. How much interest is paid in the third year? How much total interest is paid over the life of the loan?

To prepare a complete amortization schedule, you must amortize each payment one at a time:

HP 10B						TI BA II PLUS				
		-24,000.00	**PV**					-24,000.00	**PV**	
		16.00	**I/YR**					16.00	**I/Y**	
		3.00	**N**					3.00	**N**	
		PMT	10,686.19					**CPT** **PMT**	10,686.19	
1.00	**INPUT**	{AMORT}	=	3,840.00	<== Interest	**2nd** {AMORT} **2nd** {CLR Work}				
			=	6,846.19	<== Principal					
			=	-17,153.81	<== Balance	1.00	**ENTER** ↓			
2.00	**INPUT**	{AMORT}	=	2,744.61	<== Interest	1.00	**ENTER** ↓	-17,153.81	<== Balance	
			=	7,941.58	<== Principal		↓	6,846.19	<== Principal	
			=	-9,212.23	<== Balance		↓	3,840.00	<== Interest	
							↓			
3.00	**INPUT**	{AMORT}	=	1,473.96	<== Interest					
			=	9,212.23	<== Principal	2.00	**ENTER** ↓			
			=	0.00	<== Balance	2.00	**ENTER** ↓	-9,212.23	<== Balance	
							↓	7,941.58	<== Principal	
							↓	2,744.61	<== Interest	
							↓			
						3.00	**ENTER** ↓			
						3.00	**ENTER** ↓	0.00	<== Balance	
								9,212.23	<== Principal	
							↓	1,473.96	<== Interest	
							↓			

Interest of $1,473.96 is paid in the third year.

Enter both a beginning and an ending period to compute the total amount of interest or principal paid over a particular period of time.

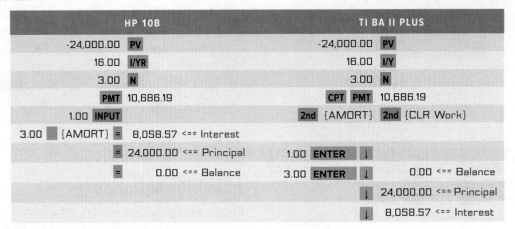

HP 10B		TI BA II PLUS	
-24,000.00 **PV**		-24,000.00 **PV**	
16.00 **I/YR**		16.00 **I/Y**	
3.00 **N**		3.00 **N**	
PMT 10,686.19		**CPT** **PMT** 10,686.19	
1.00 **INPUT**		**2nd** {AMORT} **2nd** {CLR Work}	
3.00 ■ {AMORT} **=** 8,058.57 <== Interest		1.00 **ENTER** ↓	
= 24,000.00 <== Principal		3.00 **ENTER** ↓ 0.00 <== Balance	
= 0.00 <== Balance		↓ 24,000.00 <== Principal	
		↓ 8,058.57 <== Interest	

Total interest of $8,058.57 is paid over the life of the loan.

9. INTEREST RATE CONVERSIONS

Find the effective annual rate, EAR, corresponding to a 7 percent annual percentage rate, APR, compounded quarterly.

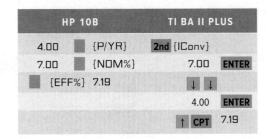

HP 10B		TI BA II PLUS	
4.00 ■ {P/YR}		**2nd** {IConv}	
7.00 ■ {NOM%}		7.00 **ENTER**	
■ {EFF%} 7.19		↓ ↓	
		4.00 **ENTER**	
		↑ **CPT** 7.19	

The effective annual rate equals 7.19 percent.

Key Equations

CHAPTER 2

1. Assets $\equiv$ Liabilities + Stockholders' equity

2. Assets $-$ Liabilities $\equiv$ Stockholders' equity

3. Revenue $-$ Expenses $\equiv$ Income

4. $CF(A) = CF(B) + CF(S)$

5. Capital spending = Ending net fixed assets
  $-$ Beginning net fixed assets
  $+$ Depreciation

6. Cash flow paid to creditors
  = Interest paid $-$ Net new borrowing
  = Interest paid $-$ (Ending long-term debt
  $-$ Beginning long-term debt)

7. Cash flow to stockholders
  = Dividends paid $-$ Net new equity raised
  = Dividends paid $-$ (Stock sold
  $-$ Stock repurchased)

CHAPTER 3

1. Current ratio $= \dfrac{\text{Current assets}}{\text{Current liabilities}}$

2. Quick ratio $= \dfrac{\text{Current assets} - \text{Inventory}}{\text{Current liabilities}}$

3. Cash ratio $= \dfrac{\text{Cash}}{\text{Current liabilities}}$

4. Total debt ratio $= \dfrac{\text{Total assets} - \text{Total equity}}{\text{Total assets}}$

5. Debt-equity ratio = Total debt/Total equity

6. Equity multiplier = Total assets/Total equity

7. Times interest earned ratio $= \dfrac{\text{EBIT}}{\text{Interest}}$

8. Cash coverage ratio
  $= \dfrac{\text{EBIT} + (\text{Depreciation and amortization})}{\text{Interest}}$

9. Inventory turnover $= \dfrac{\text{Cost of goods sold}}{\text{Inventory}}$

10. Days' sales in inventory $= \dfrac{365 \text{ days}}{\text{Inventory turnover}}$

11. Receivables turnover $= \dfrac{\text{Sales}}{\text{Accounts receivable}}$

12. Days' sales in receivables $= \dfrac{365 \text{ days}}{\text{Receivables turnover}}$

13. Total asset turnover $= \dfrac{\text{Sales}}{\text{Total assets}}$

14. Profit margin $= \dfrac{\text{Net income}}{\text{Sales}}$

15. Return on assets $= \dfrac{\text{Net income}}{\text{Total assets}}$

16. Return on equity $= \dfrac{\text{Net income}}{\text{Total equity}}$

17. EPS $= \dfrac{\text{Net income}}{\text{Shares outstanding}}$

18. PE ratio $= \dfrac{\text{Price per share}}{\text{Earnings per share}}$

19. Market-to-book ratio $= \dfrac{\text{Market value per share}}{\text{Book value per share}}$

20. EV = Market capitalization + Market value of interest bearing debt $-$ Cash

21. EV multiple $= \dfrac{\text{EV}}{\text{EBITDA}}$

22. ROE $= \underbrace{\dfrac{\text{Net income}}{\text{Sales}} \times \dfrac{\text{Sales}}{\text{Assets}}}_{\text{Return on assets}} \times \dfrac{\text{Assets}}{\text{Total equity}}$

  $-$ Profit margin $\times$ Total asset turnover
  $\times$ Equity multiplier

23. Dividend payout ratio
  = Cash dividends/Net income

24. EFN $= \dfrac{\text{Assets}}{\text{Sales}} \times \Delta \text{Sales}$
  $- \dfrac{\text{Spontaneous liabilities}}{\text{Sales}} \times \Delta \text{Sales}$
  $- PM \times$ Projected sales $\times (1 - d)$

25. Internal growth rate $= \dfrac{\text{ROA} \times b}{1 - \text{ROA} \times b}$

26. Sustainable growth rate $= \dfrac{\text{ROE} \times b}{1 - \text{ROE} \times b}$

CHAPTER 4

1. Present Value of Investment: $PV = \dfrac{C_1}{1 + r}$

2. $NPV = -\text{Cost} + PV$

3. Future Value of an Investment:
  $FV = C_0 \times (1 + r)^t$

4. Present Value of Investment: $PV = \dfrac{C_t}{(1 + r)^t}$

5. $NPV = -C_0 + \dfrac{C_1}{1 + r} + \dfrac{C_2}{(1 + r)^2} + \cdots + \dfrac{C_T}{(1 + r)^T}$
  $= -C_0 + \sum_{t=1}^{T} \dfrac{C_i}{(1 + r)^t}$

6. Future value with periodic compounding $= C_0 \left(1 + \dfrac{r}{m} \right)^m$

7. Effective Annual Rate: $\left(1 + \dfrac{r}{m}\right)^m - 1$

8. Future Value with Compounding:

$$FV = C_0\left(1 + \dfrac{r}{m}\right)^{mt}$$

9. Value of an Investment, with Continuous Compounding, at t years: $C_0 \times e^{rt}$

10. $PV = \dfrac{C}{r}$

11. Formula for Present Value of Perpetuity:

$$PV = \dfrac{C}{1+r} + \dfrac{C}{(1+r)^2} + \dfrac{C}{(1+r)^3} + \cdots = \dfrac{C}{r}$$

12. Formula for Present Value of Growing Perpetuity:

$$PV = \dfrac{C}{r-g}$$

13. $PV = \dfrac{C}{r}$

14. $PV = \dfrac{C}{r}\left[\dfrac{1}{(1+r)^t}\right]$

15. Formula for Present Value of Annuity:

$$PV = C\left[\dfrac{1}{r} - \dfrac{1}{r(1+r)^t}\right]$$

16. Formula for Future Value of Annuity:

$$FV = C\left[\dfrac{(1+r)^t}{r} - \dfrac{1}{r}\right]$$

$$= C\left[\dfrac{(1+r)^t - 1}{r}\right]$$

17. Formula for Present Value of Growing Annuity:

$$PV = C\left[\dfrac{1}{r-g} - \dfrac{1}{r-g} \times \left(\dfrac{1+g}{1+r}\right)^t\right]$$

$$= C\left[\dfrac{1 - \left(\dfrac{1+g}{1+r}\right)^t}{r-g}\right]$$

CHAPTER 5

1. Bond value $= C \times [1 - 1/1 + r)^t]/r$
$\qquad + F/(1+r)^t$

Bond value $= C \times$ Present value of the coupons
$\qquad +$ Present value of the face
$\qquad$ amount

2. $1 + R = (1 + r) \times (1 + h)$

3. $R = r + h + r \times h$

4. $R \approx r + h$

CHAPTER 6

1. $P_0 = \dfrac{D_1}{1+R} + \dfrac{P_1}{1+R}$

2. $P_1 = \dfrac{D_2}{1+R} + \dfrac{P_2}{1+R}$

3. $P_0 = \dfrac{1}{1+R}\left[D_1 + \left(\dfrac{D_2 + P_2}{1+R}\right)\right]$

$\qquad = \dfrac{D_1}{1+R} + \dfrac{D_2}{(1+R)^2} + \dfrac{P_2}{(1+R)^2}$

4. $P_0 = \dfrac{D_1}{1+R} + \dfrac{D_2}{(1+R)^2} + \dfrac{D_3}{(1+R)^3} + \cdots$

$\qquad = \sum\limits_{t=1}^{\infty} \dfrac{D_t}{(1+R)^t}$

5.

| Earnings next year | = | Earnings this year | + | Retained earnings this year | × | Return on retained earnings |

$$\text{Increase in earnings}$$

6. $\dfrac{\text{Earnings next year}}{\text{Earnings this year}} = \dfrac{\text{Earnings this year}}{\text{Earnings this year}} + \dfrac{\text{Retained earnings this year}}{\text{Earnings this year}}$
$\qquad\qquad\qquad\qquad \times$ Return on retained earnings

7. $1 + g = 1 +$ Retention ratio
$\qquad\qquad \times$ Return on retained earnings

8. Formula for Firm's Growth Rate:

$\qquad g =$ Retention ratio
$\qquad\qquad \times$ Return on retained earnings (ROE)

9. $R - g = D_1/P_0$
$\qquad R = D_1/P_0 + g$

CHAPTER 7

1. Profitability index (PI)

$$= \dfrac{\text{PV of cash flows } subsequent \text{ to initial investment}}{\text{Initial investment}}$$

CHAPTER 8

1. OCF $=$ Net income $+$ Depreciation

2. OCF $=$ Sales $-$ Costs $-$ Taxes

3. OCF $=$ (Sales $-$ Costs) $\times (1 - T_c)$
$\qquad\qquad + $ Depreciation $\times T_c$

CHAPTER 10

1. Total dollar return $=$ Dividend income
$\qquad\qquad\qquad + $ Capital gain (or loss)

2. Dividend yield $= D_{t+1}/P_t$

3. Capital gain $= (P_{t+1} - P_t)/P_t$

4. $R_{t+1} = \dfrac{D_{t+1}}{P_t} + \dfrac{(P_{t+1} - P_t)}{P_t}$

5. Mean $= \bar{R} = \dfrac{R_1 + \ldots + R_T}{T}$

6. Var $= \dfrac{1}{T-1}\left[(R_1 - \bar{R})^2 + (R_2 - \bar{R})^2 + \cdots + (R_T - \bar{R})^2\right]$

7. SE $=$ SD $(\bar{R})$

$\qquad = \dfrac{\text{SD } (R)}{\sqrt{\text{The number of observations}}}$

8. Geometric average return
$$= [(1 + R_1) \times (1 + R_2) \times \cdots \times (1 + R_T)]^{1/T} - 1$$

CHAPTER 11

1. $[R_A - E(R_A)] \times [R_B - E(R_B)]$

2. $\rho_{A,B} = \text{Corr}(R_A, R_B) = \dfrac{\text{Cov}(R_A, R_B)}{\sigma_A \times \sigma_B}$

3. Expected return on portfolio
$$= X_A E(R_A) + X_B E(R_B) = E(R_P)$$

4. The Variance of the Portfolio:
$$\text{Var (portfolio)} = X_A^2 \sigma_A^2 + 2 X_A X_B \sigma_{A,B} + X_B^2 \sigma_B^2$$

5. $\sigma_P = \text{SD(portfolio)}$
$$= \sqrt{\text{Var (portfolio)}}$$

6. Weighted average of standard deviations
$$= X_{\text{Super}} \sigma_{\text{Super}} + X_{\text{Slow}} \sigma_{\text{Slow}}$$

7. $\sigma_{\text{Super, Slow}} = \rho_{\text{Super, Slow}} \sigma_{\text{Super}} \sigma_{\text{Slow}}$

8. Variance of the portfolio's return
$$= X_{\text{Super}}^2 \sigma_{\text{Super}}^2 + 2 X_{\text{Super}} X_{\text{Slow}} \rho_{\text{Super, Slow}} \sigma_{\text{Super}} \sigma_{\text{Slow}} + X_{\text{Slow}}^2 \sigma_{\text{Slow}}^2$$

9. Variance of portfolio composed of one riskless and one risky asset $= X^2 \sigma^2$

10. Standard deviation of portfolio composed of one riskless and one risky asset $= X\sigma$

11. Total return = Expected return + Unexpected return
$$R = E(R) + U$$

12. Announcement = Expected part + Surprise

13. $R = E(R) + \text{Systematic portion} + \text{Unsystematic portion}$

14. Total risk = Systematic risk + Unsystematic risk

15. $\beta_i = \dfrac{\text{Cov}(R_i, R_M)}{\sigma^2(R_M)}$

16. $\displaystyle\sum_{i=1}^{N} X_i \beta_i = 1$

17. Capital Asset Pricing Model:

$E(R)$	$=$	R_F	$+$	β	$\times$	$E(R_M) - R_F$
Expected return on a security		Risk-free rate	$+$	Beta of the security	$\times$	Difference between expected return on market and risk-free rate, or the market risk premium

CHAPTER 12

1. $R_S = R_f + \beta \times (R_M - R_F)$

2. Beta of Security $i = \dfrac{\text{Cov}(R_i, R_M)}{\text{Var}(R_M)} = \dfrac{\sigma_{i,M}}{\sigma_M^2}$

3. $\beta_{\text{Portfolio}} = \beta_{\text{Asset}}$
$$= \dfrac{S}{B + S} \times \beta_{\text{Equity}} + \dfrac{B}{B + S} \times \beta_{\text{Debt}}$$

4. $\beta_{\text{Asset}} = \dfrac{S}{B + S} \times \beta_{\text{Equity}}$

5. Average cost of capital
$$= \left(\dfrac{S}{S + B}\right) \times R_S + \left(\dfrac{B}{S + B}\right) \times R_B \times (1 - T_c)$$

6. $f_0 = (S/V) \times f_S + (B/V) \times f_B$

CHAPTER 14

1. $V = B + S$

2. $\text{WACC} = \dfrac{S}{B + S} \times R_S + \dfrac{B}{B + S} \times R_B$

3. MM Proposition II (no taxes):
$$R_S = R_0 + (R_0 - R_B) \dfrac{B}{S}$$

4. Reduction in corporate taxes
$$= \underbrace{T_C}_{\text{Corporate tax rate}} \times \underbrace{R_B \times B}_{\text{Dollar amount of interest}}$$

5. MM Proposition I with corporate taxes:
$$V_L = \dfrac{\text{EBIT} \times (1 - T_C)}{R_0} + \dfrac{T_C R_B B}{R_B} = V_U + T_C B$$

6. MM Proposition II with corporate taxes:
$$R_S = R_0 + \dfrac{B}{S} \times (1 - T_C) \times (R_0 - R_B)$$

CHAPTER 16

1. $V_0 = D_0 + \dfrac{D_1}{1 + R_S}$

2. Dividend change $\equiv D_1 - D_0$
$$= s \times (t\text{EPS}_1 - D_0)$$

CHAPTER 17

1.

Price of underlying stock	$+$	Price of put	$=$	Price of call	$+$	Present value of exercise price
Cost of first strategy			$=$	Cost of second strategy		

2. Value of call = Stock price $\times$ Delta $-$ Amount borrowed

3. Black-Scholes Model:
$$C = SN(d_1) - Ee^{-Rt} N(d_2)$$

4. Value of risky bond + Put option = Value of risk-free bond

5. Value of risky bond = Value of risk-free bond $-$ Put option
$$= E \times e^{-Rt} - P$$

6. Value of assets (S) = Value of stock $(C) + (E \times e^{-Rt} - P)$

7. Value of assets (S) = Value of stock (C) + Value of bonds $(E \times e^{-Rt} - P)$

CHAPTER 18

1. Net working capital + Fixed assets
= Long-term debt + Equity

2. Net working capital
= Cash + Other current assets
$-$ Current liabilities

3. Cash = Long-term debt + Equity
  + Current liabilities
  − Current assets other than cash
  − Fixed assets

4. Operating cycle = Inventory period
  + Accounts receivable period

5. Cash cycle = Operating cycle
  − Accounts payable period

6. Cash collection = Beginning accounts receivables
  + 1/2 × Sales

CHAPTER 20

1. $[E(S_1) - S_0]/S_0 \cong h_{FC} - h_{US}$

2. $E(S_1) \cong S_0 \times [1 + (h_{FC} - h_{US})]$

3. $E(S_t) \cong S_0 \times [1 + (h_{FC} - h_{US})]^t$

4. $F_1/S_0 = (1 + R_{FC})/(1 + R_{US})$

5. $(F_1 - S_0)/S_0 \cong R_{FC} - R_{US}$

6. $F_1 \cong S_0 \times [1 + (R_{FC} - R_{US})]$

7. $F_t \cong S_0 \times [1 + (R_{FC} - R_{US})]^t$

8. UIP: $E(S_1) = S_0 \times [1 + (R_{FC} - R_{US})]$

9. $E(S_t) = S_0 \times [1 + (R_{FC} - R_{US})]^t$

10. IFE: $R_{US} - h_{US} = R_{FC} - h_{FC}$

CHAPTER 21 (Online Only)

1. NPV $= V_B^* -$ Cost to Firm A of the acquisition

NAME INDEX

A

Agrawal, Anup, 468n
Ang, James S., 498, 498n
Austin, Steve, 599

B

Banz, Rolf W., 404n
Becher, David A., 413–414
Benioff, Marc, 594
Berra, Yogi, 72
Bessler, Wolfgang, 468, 468n
Black, Fischer, 528–535
Blume, Marshall, 309n
Bosanek, Debbie, 26
Bowie, David, 146
Boyle, Barbara, 218
Brau, James C., 602n
Brav, Alon, 501n
Briloff, Abraham, 59
Brin, Sergey, 594
Brown, James, 146
Bruno, Albert V., 585n
Buffett, Warren, 26, 145, 506
Bush, George W., 490

C

Camp, Garrett, 1
Chan, Louis K. C., 404, 404n, 406n
Clooney, George, 13
Collins, Christopher, 16
Corbin, Patrick, 82, 93–94
Cornelli, Francesca, 600n
Cutler, David M., 452–453

D

De Angelo, Harry, 470n, 471n,
    498–499, 501n
DeAngelo, Linda, 470n,
    498–499, 501n
DiMaggio, Joe, 161
Dimson, Elroy, 303–305
Dirksen, Everett, 455n

Disney, Walt, 370
Drobetz, Wolfgang, 468, 468n

E

Ebbers, Bernie, 15
Elizabeth I, Queen, 458
Elton, Edwin J., 337n, 512n
Eovaldi, Nathan, 82

F

Fama, Eugene F., 404–407, 407n, 409,
    409n, 498, 498n
Fan, Joseph P. H., 467n
Fawcett, Stanley E., 602n
Fisher, Irving, 152–153
Flynn, Errol, 455
Franklin, Benjamin, 86, 88n
French, Kenneth R., 404–407, 407n,
    498, 498n
Frohman, Clay, 218

G

Gaye, Marvin, 146
Goldreich, David, 600n
Graham, John R., 217n, 267, 267n,
    274n, 359n, 368n, 468n, 469–470,
    497, 497n, 501n
Gruber, Martin J., 337n, 512n

H

Hadden, M. Shane, 583n
Hall, Brian J., 414, 414n
Haller, Rebekka, 468, 468n
Harvey, Campbell R., 217n, 267, 267n,
    274n, 359n, 368n, 469–470, 501n
Hoberg, Gerard, 600n

I

Ibbotson, Roger G., 291, 291n, 595n,
    596n
Ikenberry, David, 411–412,
    412n

Inmoo, Lee, 604n, 605n, 607n
Iron Maiden, 146

J

Jagannathan, Ravi, 362n
Jamail, Joe, 452
Jegadeesh, Narasimhan, 404, 404n,
    406n
Jensen, Michael C., 461n
Julius Caesar, 89

K

Kalanick, Travis, 1
Keim, Donald B., 404, 404n
Keynes, John Maynard, 88n, 404, 458
Kothari, S. P., 407n
Kumar, Alok, 497, 497n

L

Lakonishok, Josef, 404, 404n, 406n,
    411–412, 412n
Lang, Larry H. P., 463n
La Porta, Rafael, 12n
Liebman, Jeffrey B., 414, 414n
Lintner, John, 499–500
Litwak, Mark, 218
Ljungqvist, Alexander, 600n
Lochhead, Scott, 604n, 605n, 607n
Lopez-de-Silanes, Florencio, 12n
Loughran, Tim, 406n

M

Malkiel, Burton G., 395n
Mankiw, N. Gregory, 26
Marsh, Paul, 303–305
Mayweather, Floyd, 13
McGrattan, Ellen R., 362n
Meckling, William H., 461n
Mehra, Rajnish, 303n, 305
Meier, Iwan, 468, 468n
Metrick, Andrew, 584, 584n
Michaely, Roni, 501n

COMPANY INDEX

Eventbrite, 615
Exploding Kittens, 587
ExxonMobil, 24, 378, 492

F

Facebook, 172, 265, 594
Fannie Mae Corporation, 341–342
Fastenal, 341, 397
Federal Express, 454
Federal-Mogul, 475
Federal Reserve Bank of New York, 452
Federal Reserve Bank of St. Louis, 161,
    313, 355, 646
Fiat SpA, 7
Fidelity Magellan Fund, 301
Fiserv, Inc., 364, 365
Fitch Ratings, 14n
Ford Motor Company, 42, 179, 180,
    324, 396, 551
Formosa Chemical, 194
Fujifilm, 219

G

GE Capital, 148
General Dynamics, 38
General Electric (GE), 58, 186, 287, 324,
    331–333, 462
General Motors (GM), 42–43, 145, 146,
    148, 341, 393, 396, 452,
    458–459, 470, 471, 474
Getty Oil, 452–453
Gillette, 492
Global Crossing, 410
GlyEco, 506
GoDaddy, 59
Goldman, Sachs & Co., 6, 338, 520–521,
    551, 591, 615
Google, 180, 265, 343, 594, 595.
    See also Alphabet (formerly
    Google)
Grace, W. R., 474–475
Gulf & Western, Inc., 418

H

Hackett Group, The, 556
Halliburton, 475
Helios and Matheson, 614
Hess Corporation, 378, 492
Hewlett-Packard (HP), 13, 174,
    175, 405
Hilton Worldwide Holdings, 79

Home Depot, 73, 354
Honda, 50, 637
Honeywell, 354
HP, 13, 174, 175, 405
Huawei Technologies, 592

I

IBM, 331–333, 370, 397, 455, 470,
    471, 513, 516–517
Intel, 186, 229, 277
Intercontinental Exchange (ICE),
    182–183
International Paper Co., 146, 354
ISDEX, 390

J

Johns-Manville, 474
Johnson & Johnson, 59, 143, 192, 324,
    341, 469
JP Morgan, 615

K

Kellogg Company, 341
KeyBanc Capital Markets, 605
Kickstarter, 587
Kroger, 52

L

Lehman Brothers, 452
Limitless Venture Group (LGVI),
    185, 186
Lindt, 506
Lloyd's Banking Group, 639
London Stock Exchange, 15
Lonza, 219
Lumber Liquidators, 421

M

Manpower Group, Inc., 48
Manville, 474
Marathon Petroleum, 164, 378
Marillion, 587
Martha Stewart Omnimedia,
    599
Mattress Firm, 451
Mazda, 219
McDonald's, 73, 205, 402–403, 628,
    645
Mega Millions Lottery, 95
Mercedes-Benz USA, 50, 250, 637
Merck, 338

Merrill Lynch, 183
Microsoft Corporation, 68, 143, 173,
    174, 176, 186, 324, 343,
    363–365, 370, 397, 480, 492,
    505, 551, 620, 637
Mitsubishi America, 50
Molson Brewing, 179, 556
Monster Beverage, 556
Moody's, 14n, 142–143, 146, 161
Morgan Stanley, 594
Morningstar, 148, 161, 185, 301,
    379, 389
Motley Fool, 513
Murphy, 378

N

NASDAQ, 18, 184–187, 390
Nauticol Energy, 194
Nestlé, 129
Netflix, 316, 334–335
New York Mets, 82
New York Stock Exchange (NYSE), 15,
    18, 147, 180, 182–184, 583
NextEra Energy, 363
Nine West, 451
Noble, 378
NYSE Euronext, 182–183

O

Oasis Films, 262
Occidental, 378
Okta, 287
Omnicell, 164
Ontario Lottery, 95
Oracle Corp., 365, 370
OTC Markets (formerly Pink Sheets),
    185–186
Over-the-Counter Bulletin Board
    (OTCBB), 185–186

P

Palm, 405
Paramount, 370
Paramount Pictures, 262
Paychex, Inc., 365
Peach Holdings, 15
Pennzoil, 452–453
Pepsico, 95, 556
Petroleos Mexicanos, 148
Peugeot SA, 7
Pfizer, 42, 324, 338, 363

SUBJECT INDEX

Note: **Bold** type indicates key terms.

A

Abandonment option, 275–277

Abnormal returns (ARs), 398–401, 603

Absolute priority rule (APR), 472–**473**

Absolute purchasing power parity, 627–628

Accelerated depreciation, 23n, 234–235, 237–238

Accounting choices
 for depreciation, 234–235, 237–238, 410
 for inventory, 410

Accounting insolvency, 472

Accounting liquidity, 20–21.
  See also Liquidity measures

Accounting profit
 in break-even analysis, 268–269
 cash flows vs., 8
 as goal of financial management, 10–11

Accounts payable, 27n
 payables period, 554, 555, 556, 558, 559
 payables turnover, 51, 558, 559
 payment of, 567

Accounts payable period, 554, 555, 556, 558, 559

Accounts receivable
 average collection period (ACP), 50
 cash budget and, 566
 days' sales in receivables, 50, 54
 defined, 20
 receivables period, 554, 556, 558
 receivables turnover, 50, 54, 558

Accounts receivable financing, 570

Accounts receivable period, 554, 556, 558

Acid-test (quick) ratio, 47–48, 54

Acquisitions. *See* Mergers and acquisitions

ADRs (American Depository Receipts), 621

Aftermarket, 593–594

Agency costs, 453–455
 of debt, 453–455
 of dividend payments, 495
 of equity, 461–464
 nature of, 12–13
 selfish strategies and, 453–455

Agency problem, 11–14
 agency relationships and, 12
 defined, **12**
 management goals and, 12–13
 managers acting in stockholders' interests, 13–14

Allocated costs, 231

American Depository Receipts (ADRs), 621

American options, 515, 524

American quotes, 623

Amortization schedule, 111

Amortized loans, 111–114

Angel investors/angels, 584, 586

Announcements, impact of, 334–335, 414, 602–603

Annual compounding, 97, 100

Annual percentage rate (APR), 96–98

Annual reports, 15, 16, 379

Annuity, 103–109
 annuity due, 106–107
 delayed, 105–106
 equating present value of two annuities, 107–108
 future value of, 651 (table)
 growing, 108–109
 infrequent, 107
 present value of, 103–109, 130–133, 649 (table)

Annuity due, 106–107

Annuity factor, 104–105

Annuity in arrears, 106–107

Annuity present value, 103–109, 130–133

Anomalies, 403–408

Appreciation. *See also* Capital gains
 currency, 630

APR (annual percentage rate), 96–98

Arbitrage
 covered interest, 630–631
 defined, 393
 efficient capital markets and, 393, 402–403
 limits to, 403–404
 triangle, 623–625

Arithmetic average return, 307–309
 calculating, 306–307
 geometric average return vs., 306–307, 308–309

Arrearage, dividend, 181

Articles of incorporation, 5

Ask/asked price, 149, 182

Asset-backed bonds, 146

Asset beta, 366–367

Assets, 1–2, 19, 20–21. *See also*
  Balance sheet; Current assets

Asset-specific risk. *See* Unsystematic risk

Asset utilization ratios, 49–51
 capital intensity, 54, 62, 65
 days' sales in inventory, 50, 54
 days' sales in receivables, 50, 54
 inventory turnover, 49–50, 54, 554, 555, 557
 receivables turnover, 50, 54, 558
 total asset turnover, 51, 54, 70

Assigning receivables, 570

Asymmetric information, 464

At-the-market offerings, 614

Auction markets
 in bankruptcy, 472–473, 474
 listings and, 15

Average (mean), 297–298

Bounding value, call option, 524, 525

Bowie bonds, 146

Brackets, 589

Break-even analysis, 268–270, 427
  accounting profit, 268–269
  financial break-even, 270

"Brexit," 639

Bridge financing, 586

Brokers, 182, 183

Bubble theory, 390, **407**–408, 599

Budgets and budgeting
  capital budget. *See* Capital budgeting
  cash budget. *See* Cash budget

Business cash advances, 570

Business failure, 472

Business organization forms, 3–7

Buybacks, 487–490, 492–493, 502–503

Bylaws, corporate, 5

C

Calculators
  online
    adjusting return for taxes, 127
    future value, 127
    options, 549
  tips for HP 10B and TI BA II financial calculators, 661–664

Callable preferred stock, 181

Call option(s), 516–517
  buying, 521–523
  collars, 546–547
  firm value expressed in terms of, 439–441, 536–538
  put-call parity and, 522–523
  selling/writing, 519–520, 523
  valuation of
    bounding value of, 524, 525
    at expiration, 516–517, 519
    factors determining value, 524–527, 528
    variability of underlying asset, 526–527

Call premium, 141

Call protected, 141

Call provision, 141

Capital asset pricing model (CAPM), 344–346
  additional points, 345–346
  characteristics of, 345–346

comparison with dividend discount model (DDM), 368
  estimating cost of equity capital, 358–362
  expected return on individual security, 344–346
  formula for, 344–345
  market model variation, 354–355
  relationship between risk and expected return, 344–346
  security market line and, 345–346, 396

Capital budgeting, 2. *See also* Capital investment decisions
  average accounting return method in, 200–202
  Baldwin Company example, 231–238
  beta and, 362–367
  bid price setting, 243–245
  break-even analysis in, 268–270, 427
  cost of equity capital and, 357–358
  decision trees in, 262–264
  discounted payback period method in, 199–200
  discount rate, 357–358, 369–370
  dividend payments vs., 491
  firm vs. project and, 369–370
  incremental cash flows and, 229–231
  industry variations, 216–218, 262, 276–277
  inflation and, 238–241
  internal rate of return in, 202–214
  international, 634–636
  investments of unequal lives, 245–247
  Monte Carlo simulation in, 271–274
  net present value in, 194–196, 197–198, 206, 264, 528, 540–541
  options and, 540–541
  payback period method, 196–200
  practice of, 216–218
  profitability index (PI) and, 214–216
  real options vs., 274–278, 540–541
  for replacement decisions, 247–249
  scenario analysis in, 267–268
  sensitivity analysis in, 264–268
  unremitted cash flows, 636

Capital expenditures, 567

Capital gains, 287–291

calculating, 290–291
  in common stock valuation, 164–165
  defined, **290**
  percentage returns, 289–291

Capital gains yield, 170–171

Capital intensity, 51

Capital intensity ratio, 54, 62, 65

Capital investment decisions, 229–249.
    See also Capital budgeting
  alternative definitions of operating cash flow, 241–243
  Baldwin Company example, 231–238
  equivalent annual cost (EAC) method, 245–247, 270
  financing decisions vs., 206–207
  incremental cash flows, 229–231
  inflation and capital budgeting, 238–241
  special cases, 243–249

Capital losses, 287–289, **290**–291
  calculating, 290–291
  as negative capital gains, 288

Capital market line (CML), 346

Capital rationing, 215–216

Capital spending, 28

Capital structure, 2, 423–444
  components of, 1–2
  debt vs. equity in, 138, 428–444, 466–471
  establishment of, 466–471
  free cash flow hypothesis and, 463–464
  impact of restructuring, 424–425
  industry variations, 468–469, 470–471
  in international corporate finance, 467, 468
  limits to use of debt, 451–475
    agency cost of equity, 461–464
    financial distress costs, 451–455, 457–459, 472–475
    integrating tax effects and financial distress costs, 457–459
    methods of establishing capital structure, 466–471
    pecking-order theory, 464–466
    reducing costs of debt, 455–456
    signaling, 459–461
  MM Propositions in, 428–444
  organization charts, 3, 555
  pie model of, 423–424, 437–438, 458–459